EXPLORING MICROSOFT® OFFICE 97 PROFESSIONAL

Volume I

Robert T. Grauer / Maryann Barber

University of Miami

Prentice Hall, Upper Saddle River, New Jersey 07458

Acquisitions Editor: Carolyn Henderson
Assistant Editor: Audrey Regan
Editorial Assistant: Lori Cardillo
Executive Marketing Manager: Nancy Evans
Editorial/Production Supervisor: Greg Hubit
Project Manager: Lynne Breitfeller
Senior Manufacturing Supervisor: Paul Smolenski
Manufacturing Coordinator: Lisa DiMaulo
Manufacturing Manager: Vincent Scelta
Senior Designer/Interior and Cover Design: Suzanne Behnke
Design Director: Patricia Wosczyk
Composition: GTS Graphics

A Simon & Schuster Company
Upper Saddle River, New Jersey 07458

ISBN 0-13-754243-7

Prentice-Hall International (UK) Limited, London
Prentice-Hall of Australia Pty. Limited, Sydney
Prentice-Hall Canada Inc., Toronto
Prentice-Hall Hispanoamericana, S.A., Mexico
Prentice-Hall of India Private Limited, New Delhi
Prentice-Hall of Japan, Inc., Tokyo
Simon & Schuster Asia Pte. Ltd., Singapore
Editora Prentice-Hall do Brasil, Ltda., Rio de Janeiro

Printed in the United States of America

10 9 8 7 6 5 4 3 2 1

Contents

3

Enhancing a Document: The Web and Other Resources 105

Exploring Microsoft® Excel 97

1

Introduction to Microsoft® Excel: What Is a Spreadsheet? 1

2

Gaining Proficiency: Copying, Formatting, and Isolating Assumptions 39

3

Spreadsheets in Decision Making: What If? 81

4

Graphs and Charts: Delivering a Message 133

Exploring Microsoft® Access 97

Exploring Microsoft® PowerPoint 97

1

Introduction to PowerPoint: Presentations Made Easy 1

2

Creating a Presentation: Content, Formatting, and Animation 49

APPENDIX A: TOOLBARS 91

The Internet Explorer

1

Welcome to Cyberspace: The Internet and World Wide Web 1

2

Search Engines: Finding Information on the Web 35

Prerequisites: Essentials of Windows 95

A PC Buying Guide

INDEX

To Marion, Benjy, Jessica, and Ellie

—Robert Grauer

To Frank, Jessica, and My Parents

—Maryann Barber

PREFACE

We are proud to announce the third edition of the *Exploring Windows* series in conjunction with the release of Microsoft Office 97. There is a separate book for each major application—Word 97, Excel 97, Access 97, and PowerPoint 97—as well as a book on Windows 95, and eventually, Windows 97. There are also two combined texts, *Exploring Microsoft Office 97, Volumes I* and *II. Volume I* contains the introductory chapters for each application, as well as supplementary modules on Internet Explorer and Windows 95. It is designed for the instructor who seeks to cover the basics of all Office applications in a single course, but who does not need the extensive coverage that is provided in the individual books. *Volume II* consists of the advanced chapters for each application and was developed for the rapidly emerging second course in PC applications. The complete set of titles appears on the back cover.

Each book in the *Exploring Windows* series is accompanied by an Instructor's Resource Manual with solutions to all exercises, PowerPoint lectures, and the printed version of our test bank. (The Instructor's Resource Manual is also available on a CD-ROM, which contains a Windows-based testing program.) Instructors can also use the Prentice Hall Computerized Online Testing System to prepare customized tests for their courses and may obtain Interactive Multimedia courseware as a further supplement.

The *Exploring Windows* series is part of the Prentice Hall custom binding program, enabling you to create your own text by selecting any module(s) in *Office Volume I* to suit the needs of a specific course. You could, for example, create a custom text consisting of the introductory (essential) chapters in Word, Excel, and Internet Explorer. You get exactly the material you need, and students realize a cost saving. You can also take advantage of our ValuePack program to shrink-wrap multiple books together. If, for example, you are teaching a course that covers Excel and Access, and you want substantial coverage of both applications, a ValuePack results in significant savings for the student.

Essentials of Microsoft Office 97 Volume I is a revision of our existing book, *Microsoft Office for Windows 95.* In addition to modifying the text to accommodate the new release, we have revised the end-of-chapter material to include a greater number of practice exercises and case studies. The many exercises provide substantial opportunity for students to master the material, while simultaneously giving instructors considerable flexibility in student assignments.

EXPLORING WWW

Our most significant change, however, is the incorporation of the Internet and World Wide Web throughout the text. Students learn Microsoft Word as before, but in addition they are sent to the Web as appropriate for supplementary exercises. The section on Object Linking and Embedding, for example, not only draws on resources within Microsoft Office (e.g., the Clip Gallery), but on the Web as well. Students learn how to download (and cite) photographs and other resources for inclusion in Word documents. Note, too, that the *Exploring Windows* home page (www.prenhall.com/grauer) contains additional practice exercises and case studies, which can be downloaded to supplement the text. The icon at the left of this paragraph appears throughout the text whenever there is a Web reference.

FEATURES AND BENEFITS

Exploring Microsoft Office 97 is written for the computer novice and assumes no previous knowledge of Windows 95. A 48-page appendix introduces the reader to the operating system and emphasizes the file operations he or she will need.

An introductory section on Microsoft Office emphasizes the benefits of the common user interface, which pertains to all six applications in Office 97. Individuals familiar with one Office application are encouraged to leverage what they already know to learn a new application more quickly.

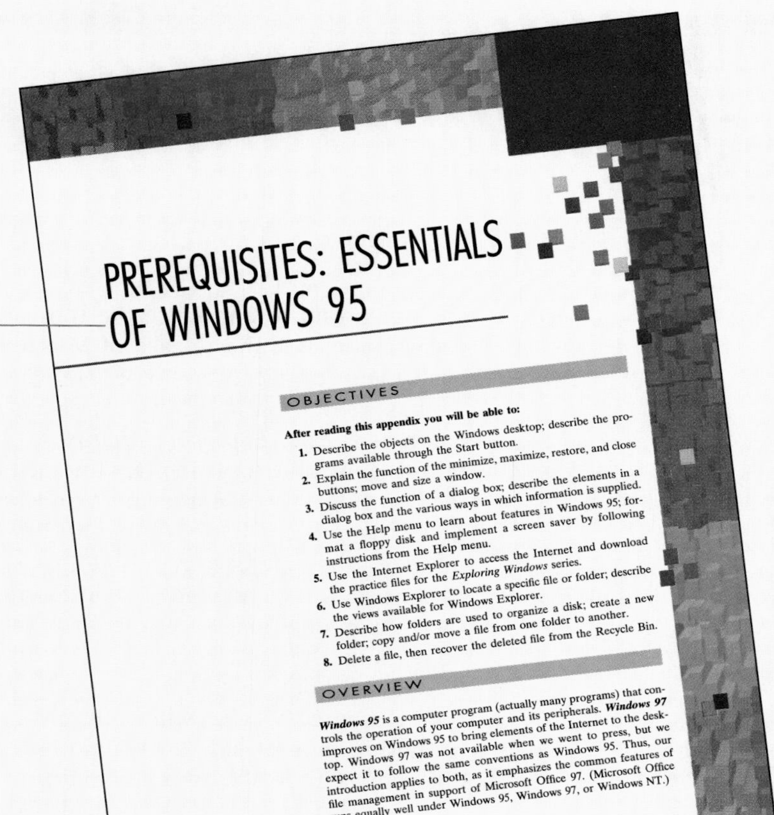

PREREQUISITES: ESSENTIALS OF WINDOWS 95

OBJECTIVES

After reading this appendix you will be able to:

1. Describe the objects on the Windows desktop; describe the programs available through the Start button.
2. Explain the function of the minimize, maximize, restore, and close buttons; move and size a window.
3. Discuss the function of a dialog box; describe the elements in a dialog box and the various ways in which information is supplied.
4. Use the Help menu to learn about features in Windows 95; format a floppy disk and implement a screen saver by following instructions from the Help menu.
5. Use the Internet Explorer to access the Internet and download the practice files for the *Exploring Windows* series.
6. Use Windows Explorer to locate a specific file or folder; describe the views available for Windows Explorer.
7. Describe how folders are used to organize a disk; create a new folder; copy and/or move a file from one folder to another.
8. Delete a file, then recover the deleted file from the Recycle Bin.

OVERVIEW

Windows 95 is a computer program (actually many programs) that controls the operation of your computer and its peripherals. ***Windows 97*** improves on Windows 95 to bring elements of the Internet to the desktop. Windows 97 was not available when we went to press, but we expect it to follow the same conventions as Windows 95. Thus, our introduction applies to both, as it emphasizes the common features of file management in support of Microsoft Office 97. (Microsoft Office runs equally well under Windows 95, Windows 97, or Windows NT.)

1

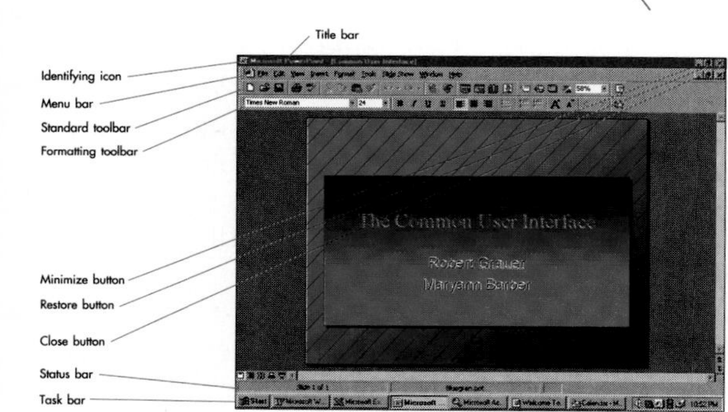

(c) Microsoft PowerPoint

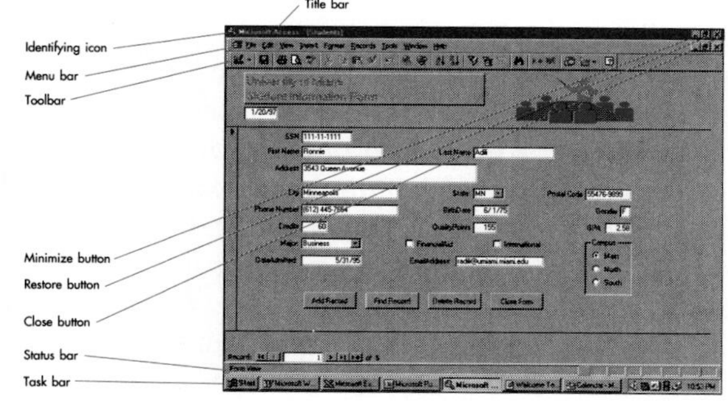

(d) Microsoft Access

FIGURE 1 The Common User Interface (continued)

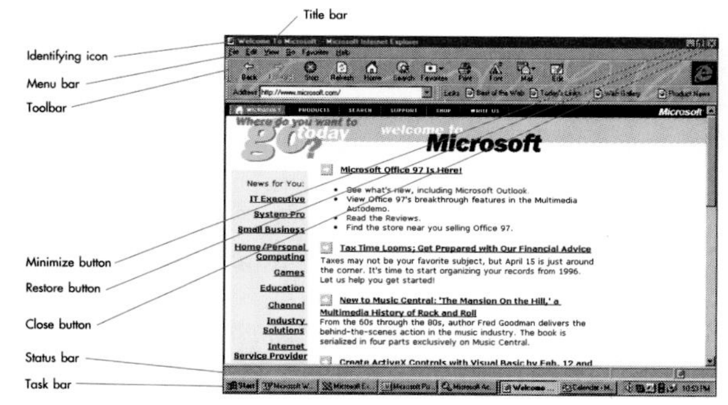

(e) Internet Explorer

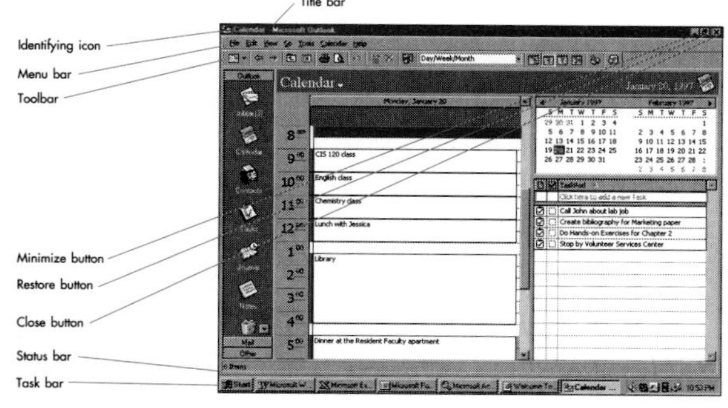

(f) Microsoft Outlook

FIGURE 1 The Common User Interface (continued)

xx MICROSOFT OFFICE 97

MICROSOFT OFFICE 97: SIX APPLICATIONS IN ONE xxi

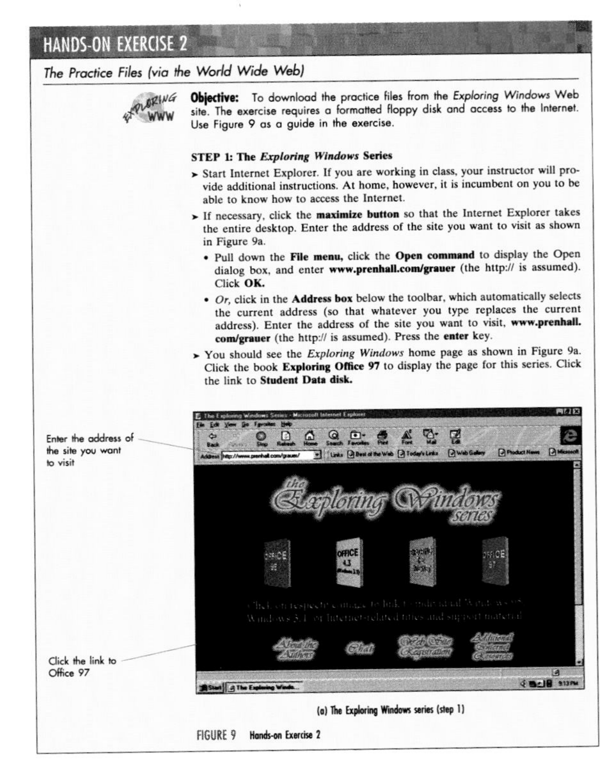

HANDS-ON EXERCISE 2

The Practice Files (via the World Wide Web)

Objective: To download the practice files from the *Exploring Windows* Web site. The exercise requires a formatted floppy disk and access to the Internet. Use Figure 9 as a guide in the exercise.

STEP 1: The *Exploring Windows* Series

- Start Internet Explorer. If you are working in class, your instructor will provide additional instructions. At home, however, it is incumbent on you to be able to know how to access the Internet.
- If necessary, click the **maximize button** so that the Internet Explorer takes the entire desktop. Enter the address of the site you want to visit as shown in Figure 9a.
  - Pull down the **File menu,** click the **Open command** to display the Open dialog box, and enter **www.prenhall.com/grauer** (the http:// is assumed). Click **OK.**
  - *Or,* click in the **Address box** below the toolbar, which automatically selects the current address (so that whatever you type replaces the current address). Enter the address of the site you want to visit, **www.prenhall.com/grauer** (the http:// is assumed). Press the **enter** key.
- You should see the *Exploring Windows* home page as shown in Figure 9a. Click the book **Exploring Office 97** to display the page for this series. Click the link to **Student Data disk.**

(a) The Exploring Windows series (step 1)

FIGURE 9 Hands-on Exercise 2

24 ESSENTIALS OF WINDOWS 95

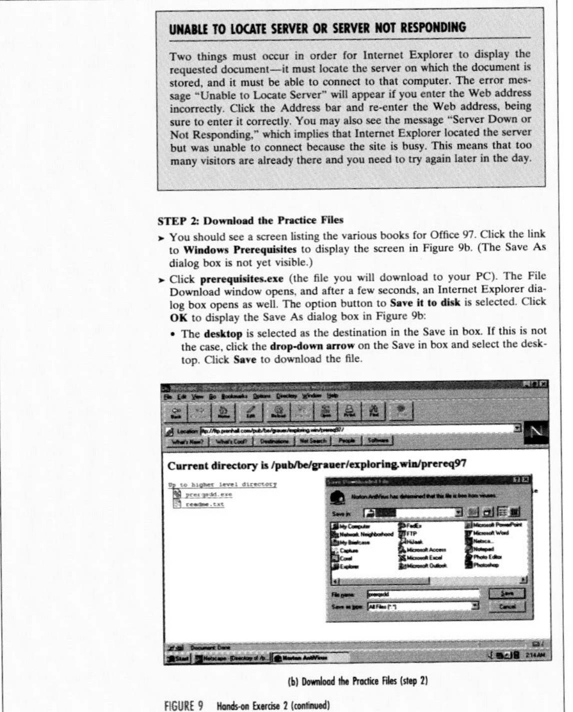

UNABLE TO LOCATE SERVER OR SERVER NOT RESPONDING

Two things must occur in order for Internet Explorer to display the requested document—it must locate the server on which the document is stored, and it must be able to connect to that computer. The error message "Unable to Locate Server" will appear if you enter the Web address incorrectly. Click the Address bar and re-enter the Web address, being sure to enter it correctly. You may also see the message "Server Down or Not Responding," which implies that Internet Explorer located the server but was unable to connect because the site is busy. This means that too many visitors are already there and you need to try again later in the day.

STEP 2: Download the Practice Files

- You should see a screen listing the various books for Office 97. Click the link to **Windows Prerequisites** to display the screen in Figure 9b. (The Save As dialog box is not yet visible.)
- Click **prerequisites.exe** (the file you will download to your PC). The File Download window opens, and after a few seconds, an Internet Explorer dialog box opens as well. The option button to **Save it to disk** is selected. Click **OK** to display the Save As dialog box in Figure 9b:
  - The **desktop** is selected as the destination in the Save in box. If this is not the case, click the **drop-down arrow** on the Save in box and select the desktop. Click **Save** to download the file.

(b) Download the Practice Files (step 2)

FIGURE 9 Hands-on Exercise 2 (continued)

PREREQUISITES: ESSENTIALS OF WINDOWS 95 25

A total of 41 in-depth tutorials (hands-on exercises) guide the reader at the computer and are illustrated with large, full-color, screen captures that are clear and easy to read. This exercise shows the reader how to download the practice files used in the text from the Exploring Windows home page.

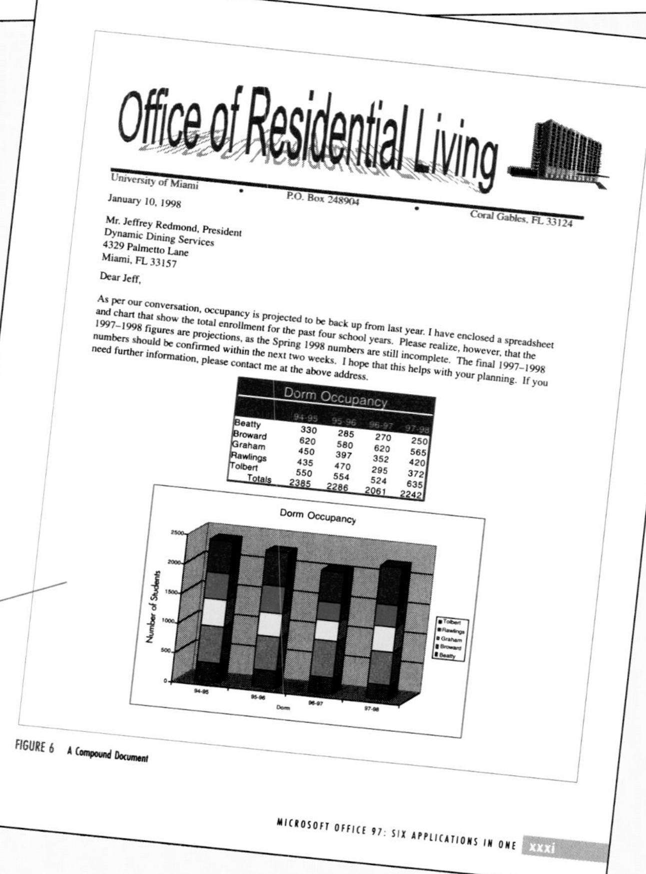

Office of Residential Living

University of Miami • P.O. Box 248904 • Coral Gables, FL 33124

January 10, 1998

Mr. Jeffrey Redmond, President
Dynamic Dining Services
4329 Palmetto Lane
Miami, FL 33157

Dear Jeff,

As per our conversation, occupancy is projected to be back up from last year. I have enclosed a spreadsheet and chart that show the total enrollment for the past four school years. Please realize, however, that the 1997–1998 figures are projections, as the Spring 1998 numbers are still incomplete. The final 1997–1998 numbers should be confirmed within the next two weeks. I hope that this helps with your planning. If you need further information, please contact me at the above address.

Dorm Occupancy	94-95	95-96	96-97	97-98
Beatty	330	285	270	250
Broward	620	580	620	565
Graham	450	397	352	420
Rawlings	435	470	295	372
Tolbert	550	554	524	635
Totals	2385	2286	2061	2242

FIGURE 6 A Compound Document

MICROSOFT OFFICE 97: SIX APPLICATIONS IN ONE xxxi

Object Linking and Embedding is stressed throughout the series, beginning in the introductory section on Microsoft Office where the reader is shown the power of this all-important technology. Appendix A in Word, on pages 151–168, provides additional information.

Practice with Microsoft Access 97

1. Use the Our Students database as the basis for the following queries and reports:
   a. Create a select query for students on the Dean's List (GPA >= 3.50). Include the student's name, major, quality points, credits, and GPA. List the students alphabetically.
   b. Use the Report Wizard to prepare a tabular report based on the query in part a. Include your name in the report header as the academic advisor.
   c. Create a select query for students on academic probation (GPA < 2.00). Include the same fields as the query in part a. List the students in alphabetical order.
   d. Use the Report Wizard to prepare a tabular report similar to the report in part b.
   e. Print both reports and submit them to your instructor as proof that you did this exercise.
2. Use the Employee database in the Exploring Access folder to create the reports listed below. (This is the same database that was used earlier in Chapters 1 and 2.)
   a. A report containing all employees in sequence by location and alphabetically within location. Show the employee's last name, first name, location, title, and salary. Include summary statistics to display the total salaries in each location as well as for the company as a whole.
   b. A report containing all employees in sequence by title and alphabetically within title. Show the employee's last name, first name, location, title, and salary. Include summary statistics to show the average salary for each title as well as the average salary in the company.
   c. Add your name to the report header in the report so that your instructor will know the reports came from you. Print both reports and submit them to your instructor.

3. Use the United States database in the Exploring Access folder to create the report shown in Figure 3.11. (This is the same database that was used in Chapters 1 and 2.) The report lists states by geographic region, and alphabetically within region. It includes a calculated field, Population Density, which is computed by dividing a state's population by its area. Summary statistics are also required as shown in the report.

   Note that the report header contains a map of the United States that was taken from the Microsoft Clip Gallery. The instructions for inserting an object can be found on page 81 in conjunction with an earlier problem. Be sure to include your name in the report footer so that your instructor will know that the report comes from you.

4. Use the Bookstore database in the Exploring Access folder to create the report shown in Figure 3.12. (This is the same database that was used in the hands-on exercises in Chapter 1.)

   The report header in Figure 3.12 contains a graphic object that was taken from the Microsoft Clip Gallery. You are not required to use this specific image, but you are required to insert a graphic. The instructions for inserting an object can be found on page 81 in conjunction with an earlier problem. Be sure to include your name in the report header so that your instructor will know that the report comes from you.

130 MICROSOFT ACCESS 97

United States By Region

Region	Name	Capital	Population	Area	Population Density
Middle Atlantic					
	Delaware	Dover	666,168	2,057	323.85
	Maryland	Annapolis	4,781,468	10,577	452.06
	New Jersey	Trenton	7,730,188	7,836	986.50
	New York	Albany	17,990,455	49,576	362.89
	Pennsylvania	Harrisburg	11,881,643	45,333	262.10
		Total for Region:	43,049,922	115,379	
		Average for Region:	8,609,984.40	23,075.80	477.48
Mountain					
	Arizona	Phoenix	3,665,228	113,909	32.18
	Colorado	Denver	3,294,394	104,247	31.60
	Idaho	Boise	1,006,749	83,557	12.05
	Montana	Helena	799,065	147,138	5.43
	Nevada	Carson City	1,201,833	110,540	10.87
	New Mexico	Santa Fe	1,515,069	121,666	12.45
	Utah	Salt Lake City	1,722,850	84,916	20.29
	Wyoming	Cheyenne	453,588	97,914	4.63
		Total for Region:	13,658,776	863,887	
		Average for Region:	1,707,347.00	107,985.88	16.19
New England					
	Connecticut	Hartford	3,287,116	5,009	656.24
	Maine	Augusta	1,227,928	33,215	36.97
	Massachusetts	Boston	6,016,425	8,257	728.65
	New	Concord	1,109,252	9,304	119.22
	Rhode Island	Providence	1,003,464	1,214	826.58
	Vermont	Montpelier	562,758	9,609	58.57
		Total for Region:	13,206,943	66,608	
		Average for Region:	2,201,157.17	11,101.33	404.37

Saturday, January 11, 1997 Page 1 of 3

FIGURE 3.11 Screen for Practice Exercise 3

FROM THE DATABASE 131

Every chapter contains a large number of practice exercises, to avoid repetition from one semester to the next. The practice exercises review and extend the material in the chapter so that the student is exposed to a wide range of documents.

The Federal Budget

The National debt is staggering—in excess of $5 trillion, more than $1 trillion of which has been added under President Clinton. The per capita share is almost $20,000 for every man, woman, and child in the United States. The annual budget is approximately $1.5 trillion, with the deficit in the neighborhood of $150 billion. Medicare, defense, and interest on the debt itself are the largest expenditures and consume approximately 35%, 24%, and 14%, respectively. Personal income taxes and Social Security (including Medicare) taxes account for approximately 36% and 31% of the government's income.

Use the Internet to obtain exact figures for the current year, then create the appropriate charts to reflect the government's distribution of income and expenditures. Do some additional research and obtain data on the budget, the deficit, and the national debt for the years 1945, 1967, and 1980. The numbers may surprise you. For example, how does the interest expense for the current year compare to the total budget in 1967 (at the height of the Viet Nam War)? To the total budget in 1945 (at the end of World War II)?

The Annual Report

Corporate America spends a small fortune to produce its annual reports, which are readily available to the public at large. Choose any company and obtain a copy of its most recent annual report. Consolidate the information in the company's report to produce a two-page document of your own. Your report should include a description of the company's progress in the last year, a worksheet with any data you deem relevant, and at least two charts in support of the worksheet or written material. Use Microsoft Word in addition to the worksheet to present the information in an attractive manner.

Every chapter also contains a number of less structured case studies to challenge the student. The Web icon appears throughout the text whenever the student is directed to the World Wide Web as a source of additional material.

Computer Mapping

Your boss has asked you to look into computer mapping in an effort to better analyze sales data for your organization. She suggested you use the online help facility to explore the Data Map feature within Excel, which enables you to create color-coded maps from columns of numerical data. You mentioned this assignment to a colleague who suggested that you open the *Mapstats workbook* that is installed with Excel to see the sample maps and demographic data included with Excel. You have two days to learn the potential for computer mapping. Your boss expects at least a three-page written report with real examples.

The Census Bureau

Use your favorite search engine to locate the home page of the United States Census Bureau, then download one or more series of population statistics of interest to you. Use the data to plot one or more charts that describe the population growth of the United States. There is an abundance of information available and you are free to choose any statistics you deem relevant.

186 MICROSOFT EXCEL 97

The *Exploring Windows* series is a unique combination of concepts as well as hands-on exercises. Chapter 1 in each section starts with the basics of the application and assumes no previous knowledge on the part of the reader.

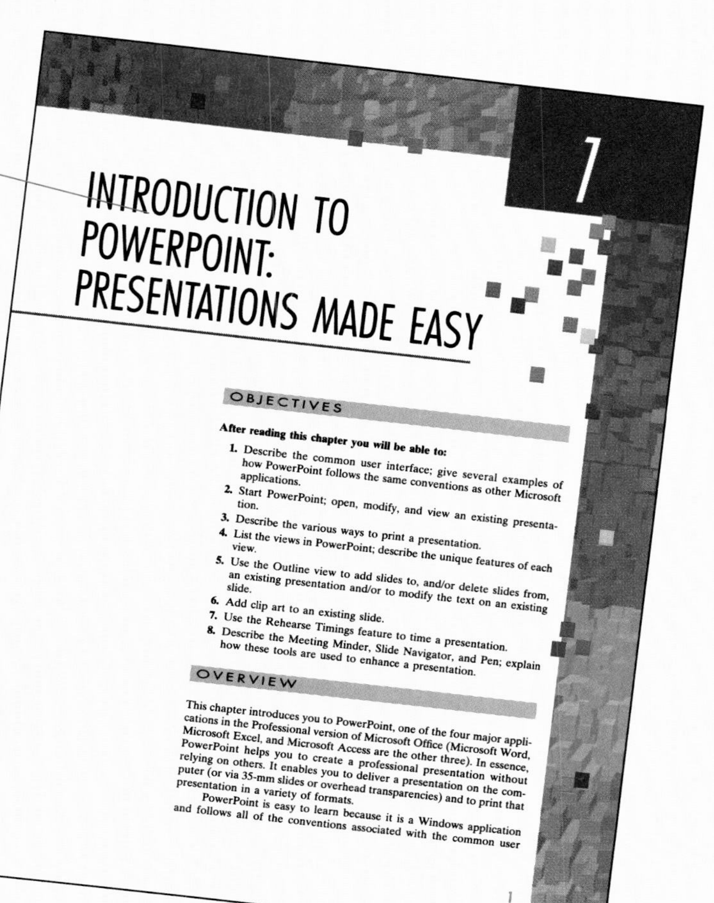

1

INTRODUCTION TO POWERPOINT: PRESENTATIONS MADE EASY

OBJECTIVES

After reading this chapter you will be able to:

1. Describe the common user interface; give several examples of how PowerPoint follows the same conventions as other Microsoft applications.
2. Start PowerPoint; open, modify, and view an existing presentation.
3. Describe the various ways to print a presentation.
4. List the views in PowerPoint; describe the unique features of each view.
5. Use the Outline view to add slides to, and/or delete slides from, an existing presentation and/or to modify the text on an existing slide.
6. Add clip art to an existing slide.
7. Use the Rehearse Timings feature to time a presentation.
8. Describe the Meeting Minder, Slide Navigator, and Pen; explain how these tools are used to enhance a presentation.

OVERVIEW

This chapter introduces you to PowerPoint, one of the four major applications in the Professional version of Microsoft Office (Microsoft Word, Microsoft Excel, and Microsoft Access are the other three). In essence, PowerPoint helps you to create a professional presentation without relying on others. It enables you to deliver a presentation on the computer (or via 35-mm slides or overhead transparencies) and to print that presentation in a variety of formats.

PowerPoint is easy to learn because it is a Windows application and follows all of the conventions associated with the common user

1

Knowledge of search engines is essential in order to use the Internet effectively. This example from Chapter 2 of *Internet Explorer* shows the importance of using multiple engines for the same query.

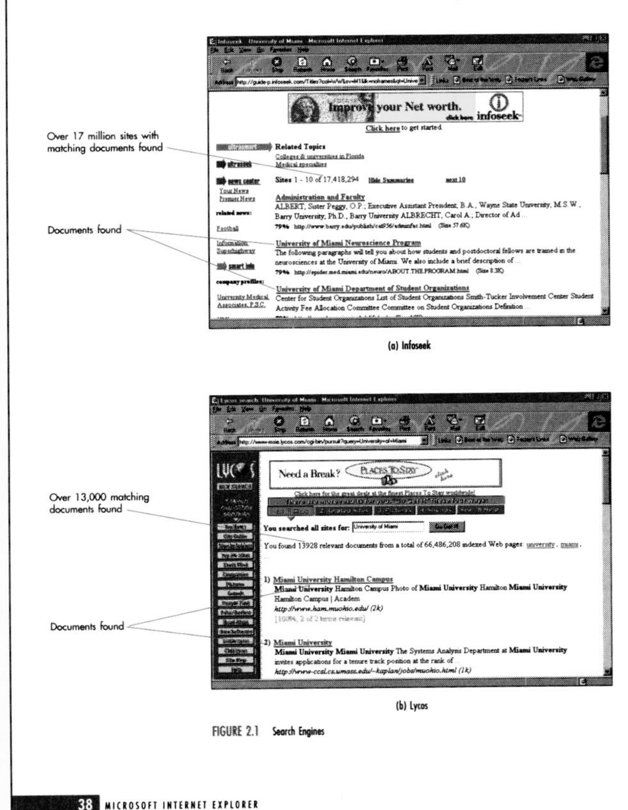

(a) Infoseek

(b) Lycos

FIGURE 2.1 Search Engines

38 MICROSOFT INTERNET EXPLORER

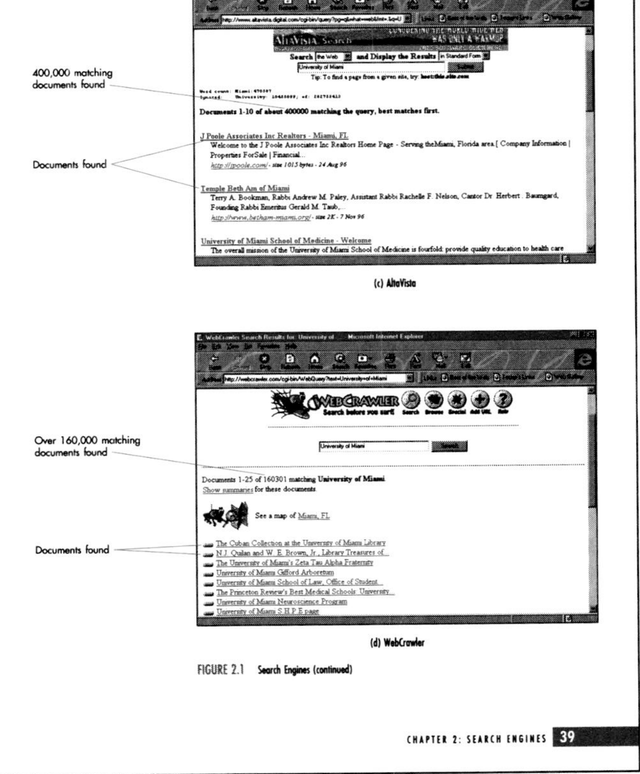

(c) AltaVista

(d) WebCrawler

FIGURE 2.1 Search Engines (continued)

CHAPTER 2: SEARCH ENGINES 39

Acknowledgments

We want to thank the many individuals who helped bring this project to fruition. We are especially grateful to our editor at Prentice Hall, Carolyn Henderson, without whom the series would not have been possible. Cecil Yarbrough and Susan Hoffman did an outstanding job in checking the manuscript and proofs for technical accuracy. Suzanne Behnke developed the innovative and attractive design. John DeLara and David Nusspickle were responsible for our Web site. Carlotta Eaton of Radford University and Karen Vignare wrote the Instructor Manuals, and Dave Moles produced the CD. Paul Smolenski was senior manufacturing supervisor. Lynne Breitfeller was project manager. Greg Hubit was in charge of production and kept the project on target from beginning to end. Nancy Evans, our marketing manager at Prentice Hall, developed the innovative campaigns that made the series a success. Lori Cardillo, editorial assistant at Prentice Hall, helped in ways too numerous to mention. We also want to acknowledge our reviewers who, through their comments and constructive criticism, greatly improved the *Exploring Windows* series.

Lynne Band, Middlesex Community College
Stuart P. Brian, Holy Family College
Carl M. Briggs, Indiana University School of Business
Kimberly Chambers, Scottsdale Community College
Alok Charturvedi, Purdue University
Jerry Chin, Southwest Missouri State University
Dean Combellick, Scottsdale Community College
Cody Copeland, Johnson County Community College
Larry S. Corman, Fort Lewis College
Janis Cox, Tri-County Technical College
Martin Crossland, Southwest Missouri State University
Paul E. Daurelle, Western Piedmont Community College
David Douglas, University of Arkansas
Carlotta Eaton, Radford University
Raymond Frost, Central Connecticut State University
James Gips, Boston College
Vernon Griffin, Austin Community College
Michael Hassett, Fort Hays State University
Wanda D. Heller, Seminole Community College
Bonnie Homan, San Francisco State University
Ernie Ivey, Polk Community College
Mike Kelly, Community College of Rhode Island
Jane King, Everett Community College
John Lesson, University of Central Florida
David B. Meinert, Southwest Missouri State University
Bill Morse, DeVry Institute of Technology
Alan Moltz, Naugatuck Valley Technical Community College
Kim Montney, Kellogg Community College
Kevin Pauli, University of Nebraska
Mary McKenry Percival, University of Miami
Delores Pusins, Hillsborough Community College
Gale E. Rand, College Misericordia
Judith Rice, Santa Fe Community College
David Rinehard, Lansing Community College
Marilyn Salas, Scottsdale Community College
John Shepherd, Duquesne University
Helen Stoloff, Hudson Valley Community College
Margaret Thomas, Ohio University
Mike Thomas, Indiana University School of Business
Suzanne Tomlinson, Iowa State University
Karen Tracey, Central Connecticut State University
Sally Visci, Lorain County Community College
David Weiner, University of San Francisco
Connie Wells, Georgia State University
Wallace John Whistance-Smith, Ryerson Polytechnic University
Jack Zeller, Kirkwood Community College

A final word of thanks to the unnamed students at the University of Miami, who make it all worthwhile. And most of all, thanks to you, our readers, for choosing this book. Please feel free to contact us with any comments and suggestions.

Robert T. Grauer
rgrauer@umiami.miami.edu
www.bus.miami.edu/~rgrauer
www.prenhall.com/grauer

Maryann Barber
mbarber@homer.bus.miami.edu
www.bus.miami.edu/~mbarber

MICROSOFT OFFICE 97: SIX APPLICATIONS IN ONE

OVERVIEW

Word processing, spreadsheets, and data management have always been significant microcomputer applications. The early days of the PC saw these applications emerge from different vendors with radically different user interfaces. WordPerfect, Lotus, and dBASE, for example, were dominant applications in their respective areas, and each was developed by a different company. The applications were totally dissimilar, and knowledge of one did not help in learning another.

The widespread acceptance of Windows 3.1 promoted the concept of a common user interface, which required all applications to follow a consistent set of conventions. This meant that all applications worked essentially the same way, and it provided a sense of familiarity when you learned a new application, since every application presented the same user interface. The development of a suite of applications from a single vendor extended this concept by imposing additional similarities on all applications within the suite.

This introduction will acquaint you with ***Microsoft Office 97*** and its four major applications—***Word, Excel, PowerPoint,*** and ***Access.*** The single biggest difference between Office 97 and its predecessor, Office 95, is that the Internet has become an integral part of the Office suite. Thus, we also discuss ***Internet Explorer,*** the Web browser included in Office 97, and ***Microsoft Outlook,*** the e-mail and scheduling program that is built into Office 97. The icon at the left of this paragraph appears throughout the text to highlight references to the Internet and enhance your use of Microsoft Office. Our introduction also includes the Clip Gallery, WordArt, and Office Art, three tools built into Microsoft Office that help you to add interest to your documents. And finally, we discuss Object Linking and Embedding, which enables you to combine data from multiple applications into a single document.

Our primary purpose in this introduction is to emphasize the similarities between the applications in Office 97 and to help you transfer your knowledge from one application to the next. You will find the same commands in the same menus. You will also recognize familiar toolbars and will be able to take advantage of similar keyboard shortcuts. You will learn that help can be obtained in a variety of ways, and that it is consistent in every application. Our goal is to show you how much you already know and to get you up and running as quickly as possible.

TRY THE COLLEGE BOOKSTORE

Any machine you buy will come with Windows 95 (or Windows 97), but that is only the beginning since you must also obtain the application software you intend to run. Some hardware vendors will bundle (at no additional cost) Microsoft Office as an inducement to buy from them. If you have already purchased your system and you need software, the best place to buy Microsoft Office is the college bookstore, where it can be obtained at a substantial educational discount.

MICROSOFT OFFICE 97

All Office applications share the ***common Windows interface*** with which you may already be familiar. (If you are new to Windows 95, then read the appendix on the "Essentials of Windows.") Microsoft Office 97 runs equally well under Windows 95, Windows 97, or Windows NT.

Figure 1 displays a screen from each major application in Microsoft Office—Word, Excel, PowerPoint, and Access. Our figure also includes screens from Internet Explorer and Mircosoft Outlook, both of which are part of Office 97. Look closely at Figure 1, and realize that each screen contains both an application window and a document window, and that each document window has been maximized within the application window. The title bars of the application and document windows have been merged into a single title bar that appears at the top of the application window. The title bar displays the application (e.g., Microsoft Word in Figure 1a) as well as the name of the document (Web Enabled in Figure 1a) on which you are working.

All six screens in Figure 1 are similar in appearance even though the applications accomplish very different tasks. Each application window has an identifying icon, a menu bar, a title bar, and a minimize, maximize or restore, and a close button. Each document window has its own identifying icon, and its own minimize, maximize or restore, and close button. The Windows taskbar appears at the bottom of each application window and shows the open applications. The status bar appears above the taskbar and displays information relevant to the window or selected object.

Each major application in Microsoft Office uses a consistent command structure in which the same basic menus are found in all applications. The File, Edit, View, Insert, Tools, Window, and Help menus are present in all six applications. The same commands are found in the same menus. The Save, Open, Print, and Exit commands, for example, are contained in the File menu. The Cut, Copy, Paste, and Undo commands are found in the Edit menu.

The means for accessing the pull-down menus are consistent from one application to the next. Click the menu name on the menu bar, or press the Alt key plus the underlined letter of the menu name; for example, press Alt+F to pull down the File menu. If you already know some keyboard shortcuts in one application, there is a good chance that the shortcuts will work in another application. Ctrl+Home and Ctrl+End, for example, move to the beginning and end of a document, respectively. Ctrl+B, Ctrl+I, and Ctrl+U boldface, italicize, and underline text. Ctrl+X (the "X" is supposed to remind you of a pair of scissors), Ctrl+C, and Ctrl+V will cut, copy, and paste, respectively.

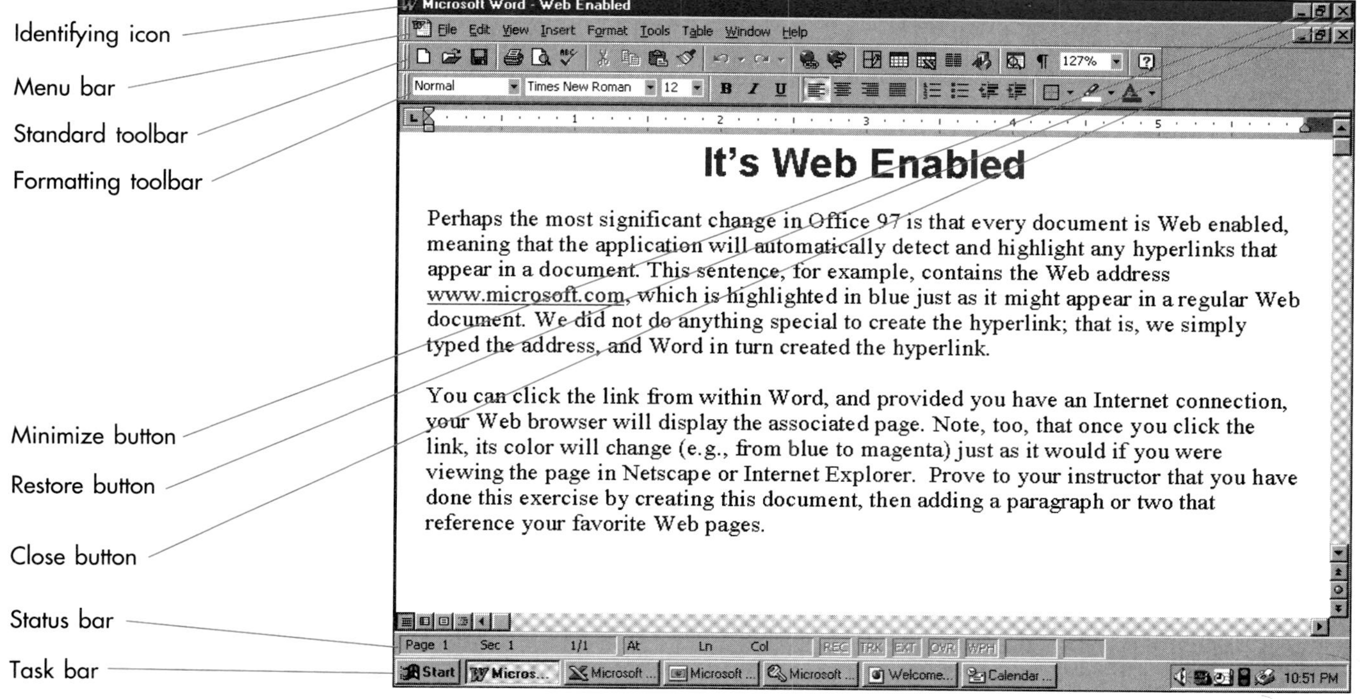

(a) Microsoft Word

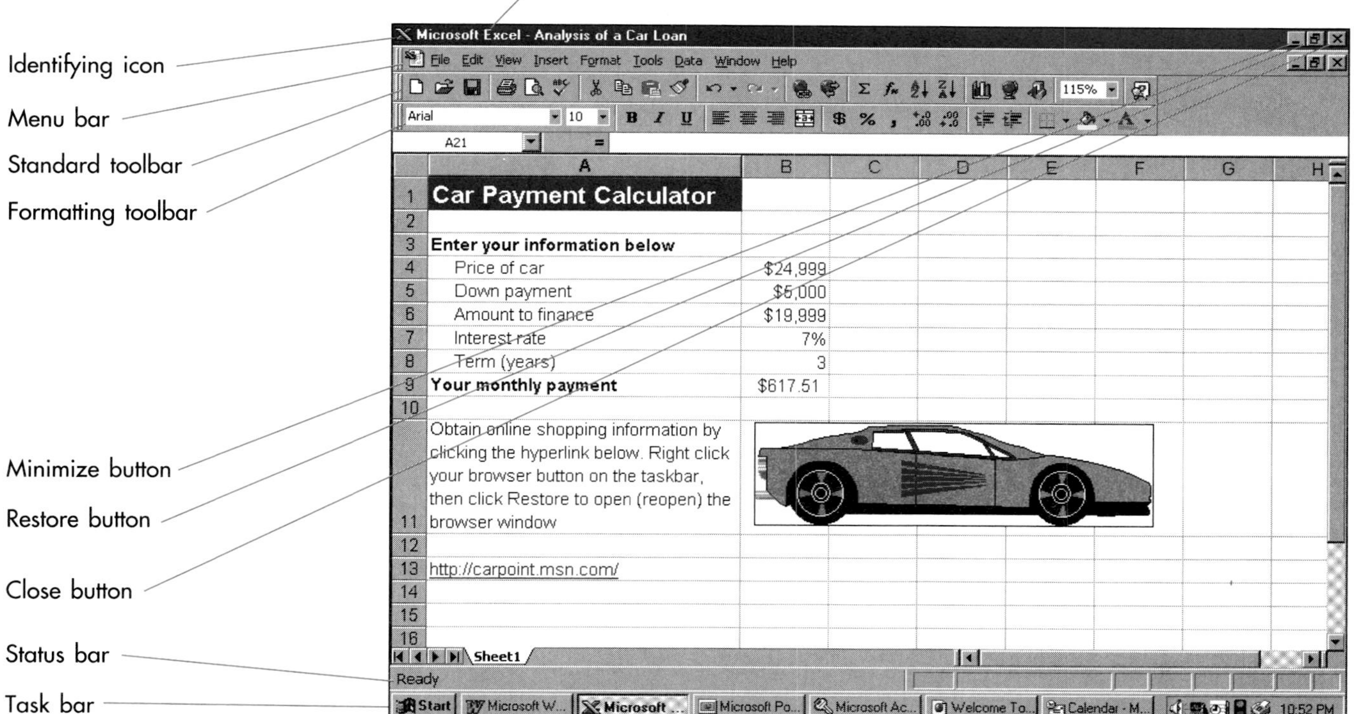

(b) Microsoft Excel

FIGURE 1 The Common User Interface

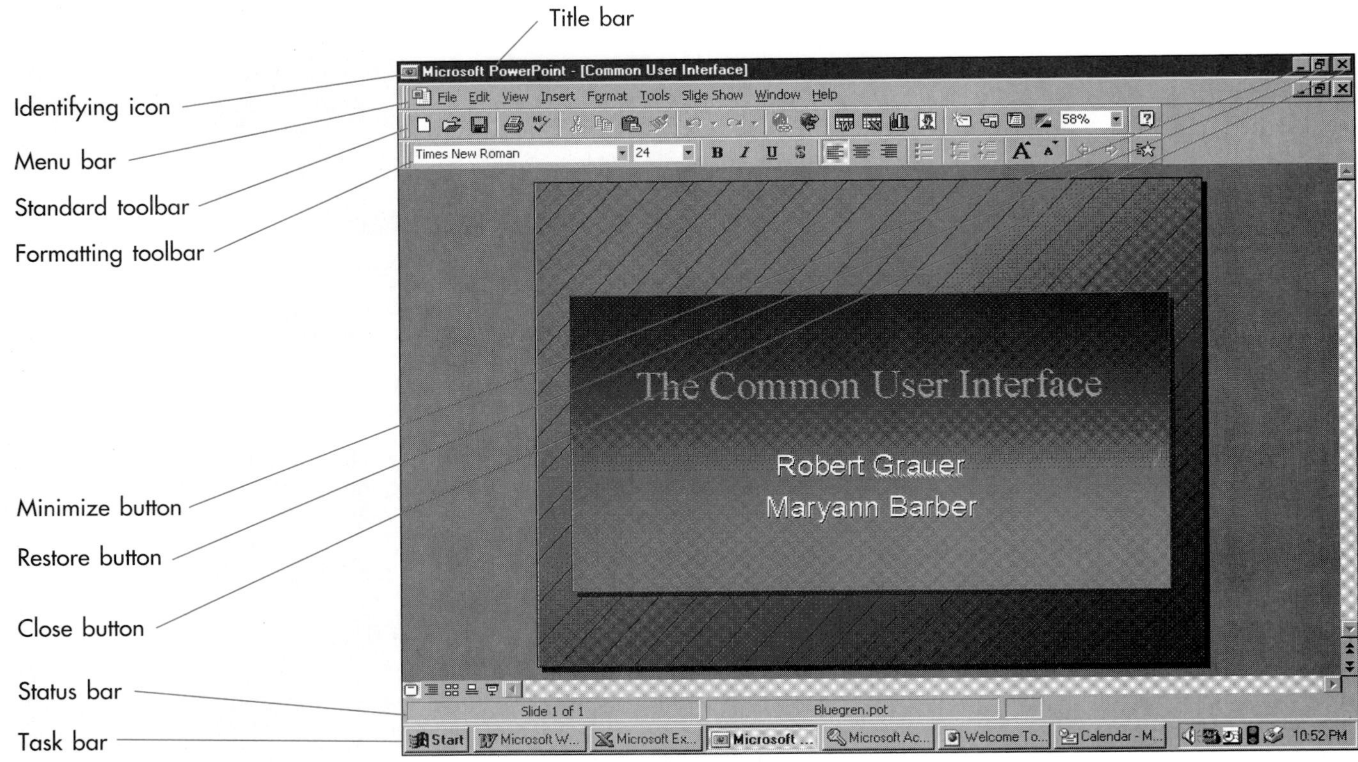

(c) Microsoft PowerPoint

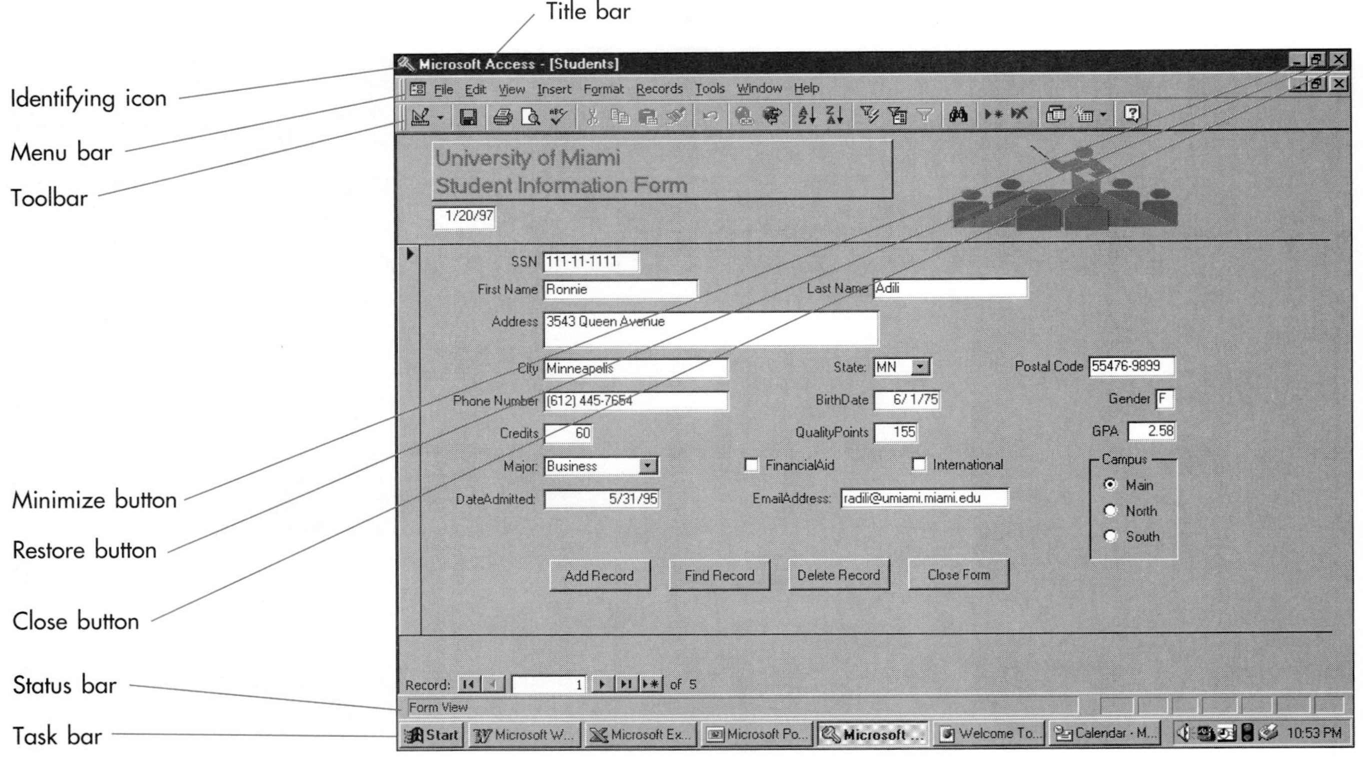

(d) Microsoft Access

FIGURE 1 The Common User Interface (continued)

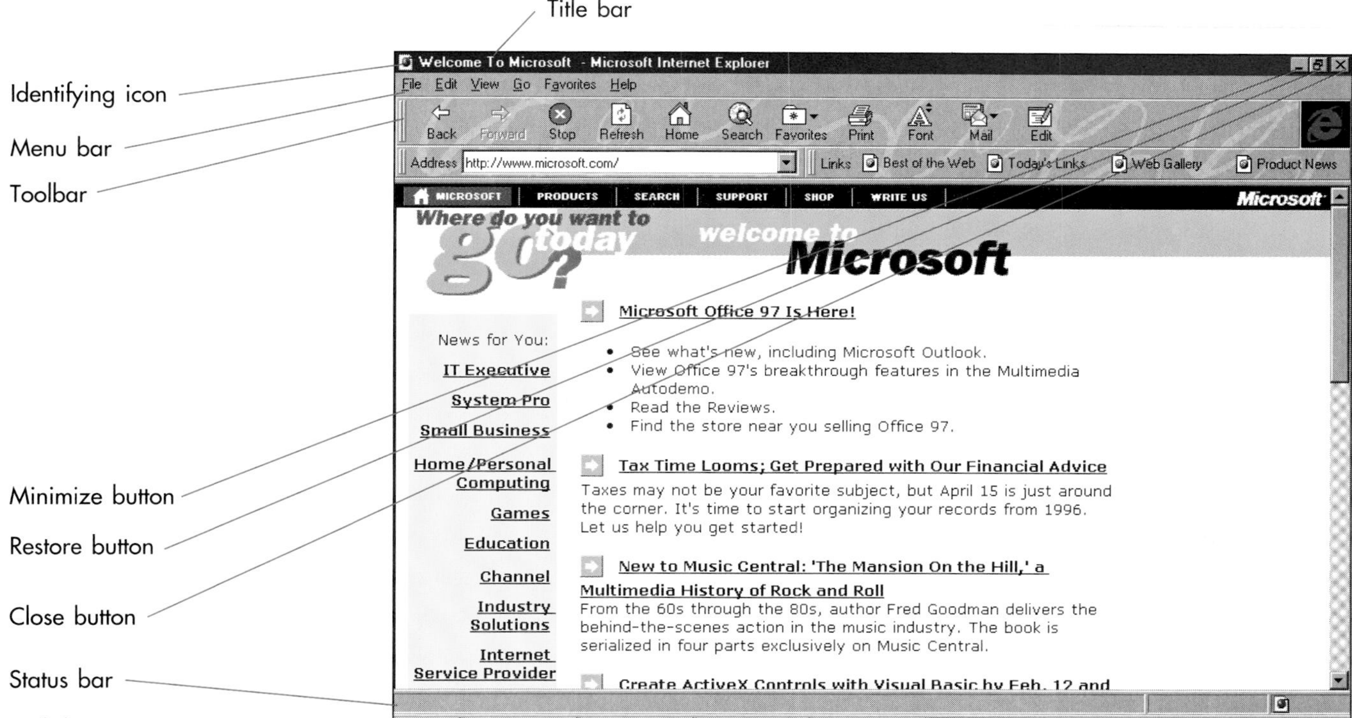

(e) Internet Explorer

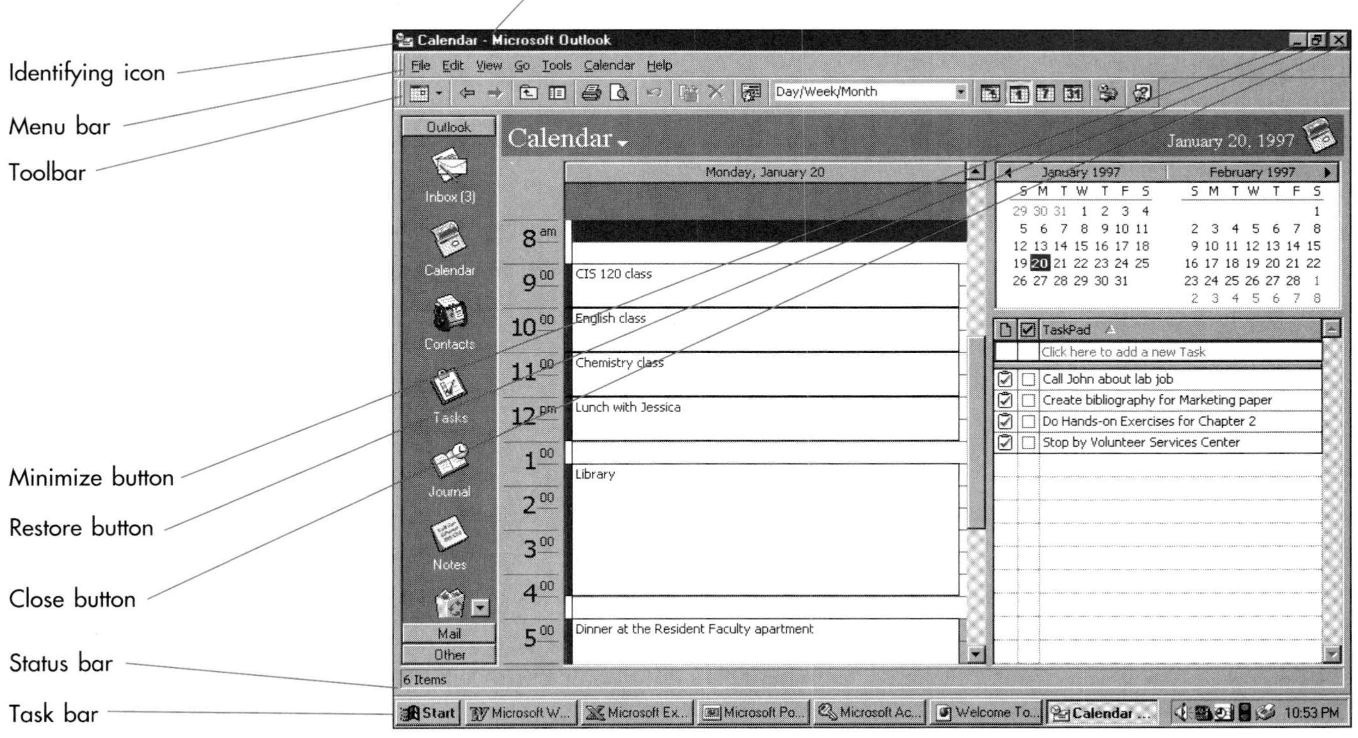

(f) Microsoft Outlook

FIGURE 1 The Common User Interface (continued)

The four major applications use consistent (and often identical) dialog boxes. The dialog boxes to open and close a file, for example, are identical in every application. All four applications also share a common dictionary. The AutoCorrect feature (to correct common spelling mistakes) works identically in all four applications. The help feature also functions identically.

There are, of course, differences between the applications. Each application has unique menus and toolbars. Nevertheless, the Standard and Formatting toolbars in the major applications contain many of the same tools (especially the first several tools on the left of each toolbar). The ***Standard toolbar*** contains buttons for basic commands such as Open, Save, or Print. It also contains buttons to cut, copy, and paste, and these buttons are identical in all four applications. The ***Formatting toolbar*** provides access to common operations such as boldface or italics, or changing the font or point size; again, these buttons are identical in all four applications. ScreenTips are present in all applications.

STANDARD OFFICE VERSUS OFFICE PROFESSIONAL

Microsoft distributes both a Standard and a Professional edition of Office 97. Both versions include Word, Excel, PowerPoint, Internet Explorer, and Outlook. Office Professional also has Microsoft Access. The difference is important when you are shopping and you are comparing prices from different sources. Be sure to purchase the version that is appropriate for your needs.

Help for Office 97

Several types of help are available in Office 97. The most basic is accessed by pulling down the Help menu and clicking the Contents and Index command to display the Help Contents window as shown in Figures 2a and 2b. (The Help screens are from Microsoft Word, but similar screens are available for each of the other applications.) The ***Contents tab*** in Figure 2a is analogous to the table of contents in an ordinary book. It displays the major topics in the application as a series of books that are open or closed. You can click any closed book to open it, which in turn displays additional books and/or help topics. Conversely, you can click any open book to close it and gain additional space on the screen.

The ***Index tab*** in Figure 2b is similar to the index of an ordinary book. Enter the first several letters of the topic to look up, such as "we" in Figure 2b. Help then returns all of the topics beginning with the letters you entered. Select the topic you want, then display the topic for immediate viewing, or print it for later reference. (The Find tab, not shown in Figure 2, contains a more extensive listing of entries than does the Index tab. It lets you enter a specific word, then it returns every topic that contains that word.)

The ***Office Assistant*** in Figure 2c is new to Office 97 and is activated by clicking the Office Assistant button on the Standard toolbar or by pressing the F1 function key. The Assistant enables you to ask a question in English, then it returns a series of topics that attempt to answer your question.

Additional help can be obtained from the Microsoft Web site as shown in Figure 2d, provided you have access to the Internet. The easiest way to access the site is to pull down the Help menu from any Office application, click Microsoft on the Web, then click Online Support. This, in turn, will start the Internet Explorer and take you to the appropriate page on the Web, where you will find the most current information available as well as the most detailed support. You can, for example, access the same knowledge base as that used by Microsoft support engineers when you call for technical assistance.

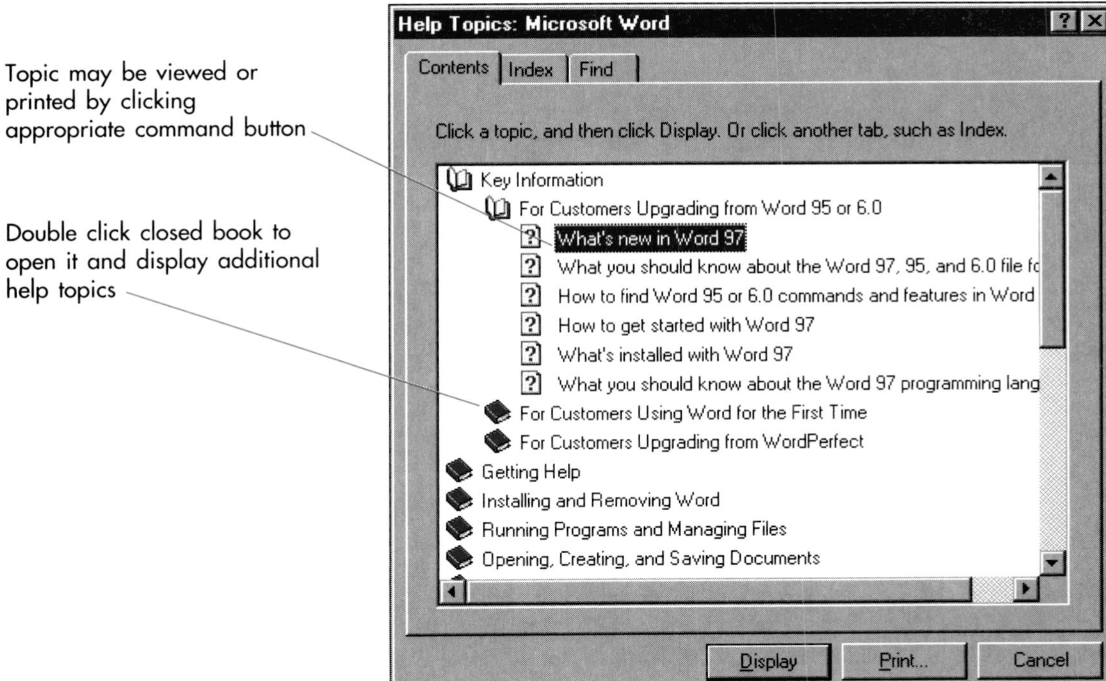

(a) Contents Tab

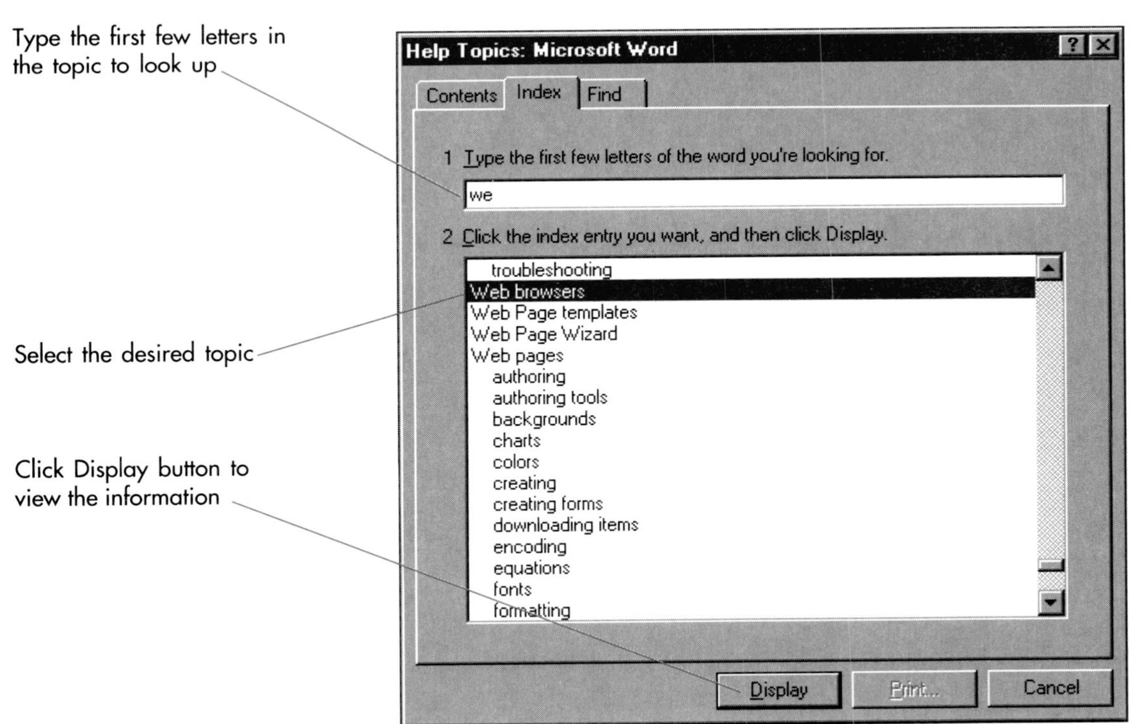

(b) Index Tab

FIGURE 2 Help with Microsoft Office

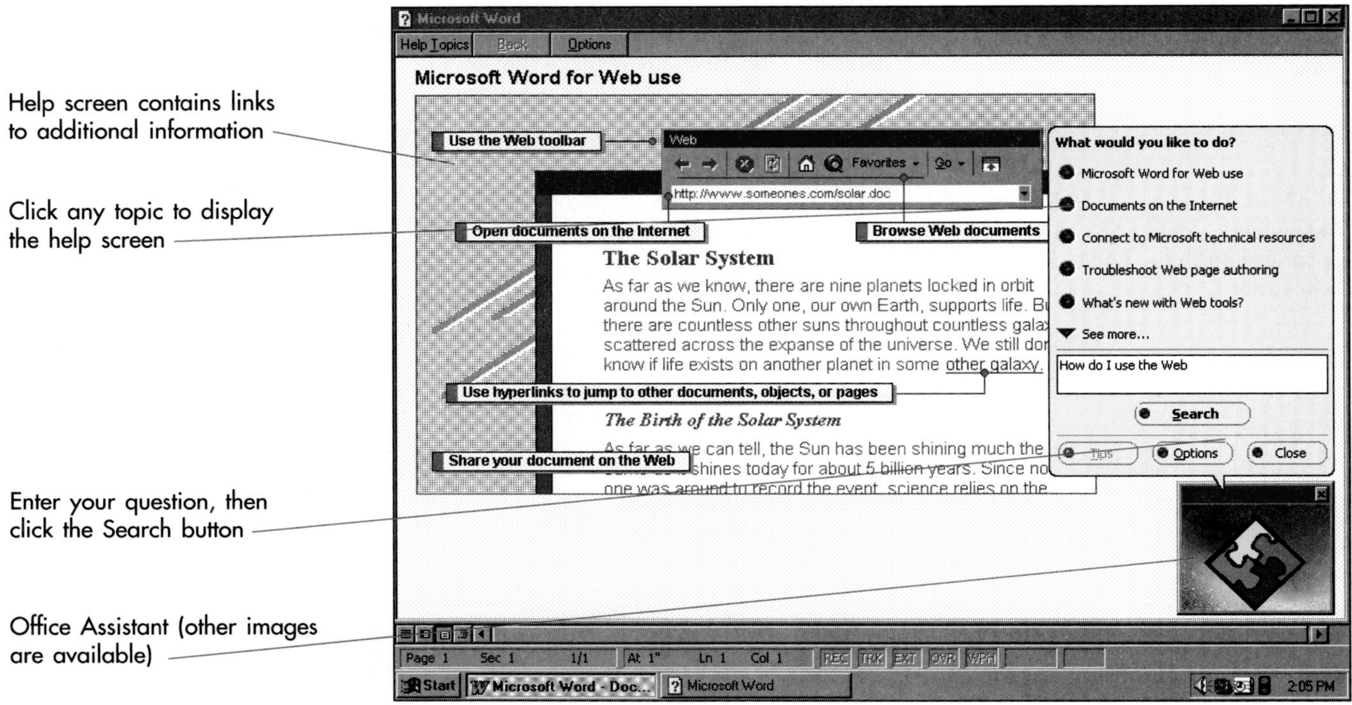

(c) The Office Assistant

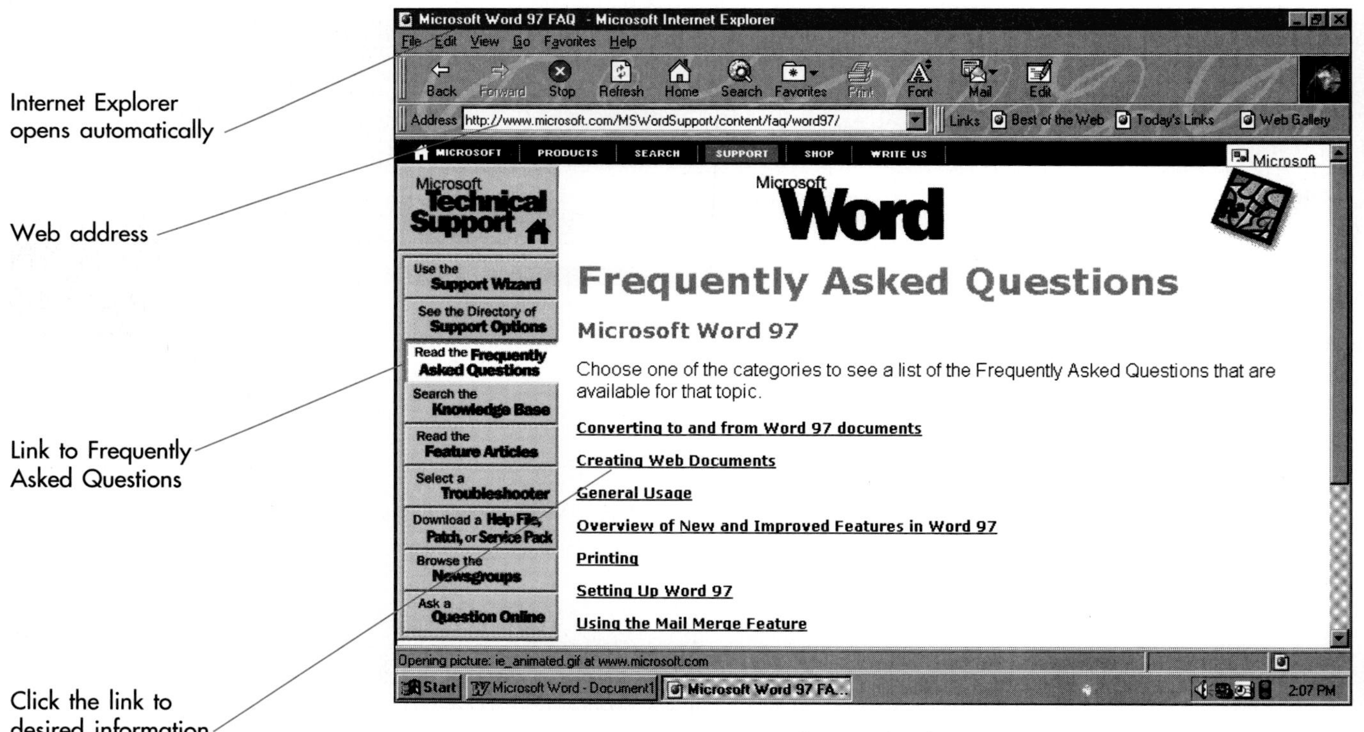

(d) Microsoft Online

FIGURE 2 Help with Microsoft Office (continued)

Office Shortcut Bar

The ***Microsoft Office Shortcut Bar*** provides immediate access to each application within Microsoft Office. It consists of a row of buttons and can be placed anywhere on the screen. The Shortcut Bar is anchored by default on the right side of the desktop, but you can position it along any edge, or have it "float" in the middle of the desktop. You can even hide it from view when it is not in use.

Figure 3a displays the Shortcut Bar as it appears on our desktop. The buttons that are displayed (and the order in which they appear) are established through the Customize dialog box in Figure 3b. Our Shortcut Bar contains a button for each Office application, a button for the Windows Explorer, and a button for Bookshelf Basics.

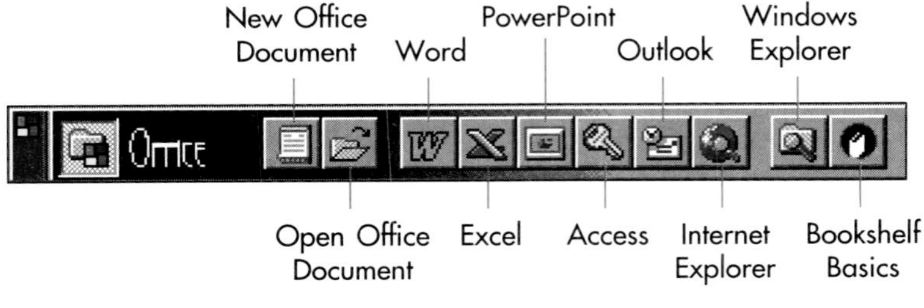

(a) Office Shortcut Bar

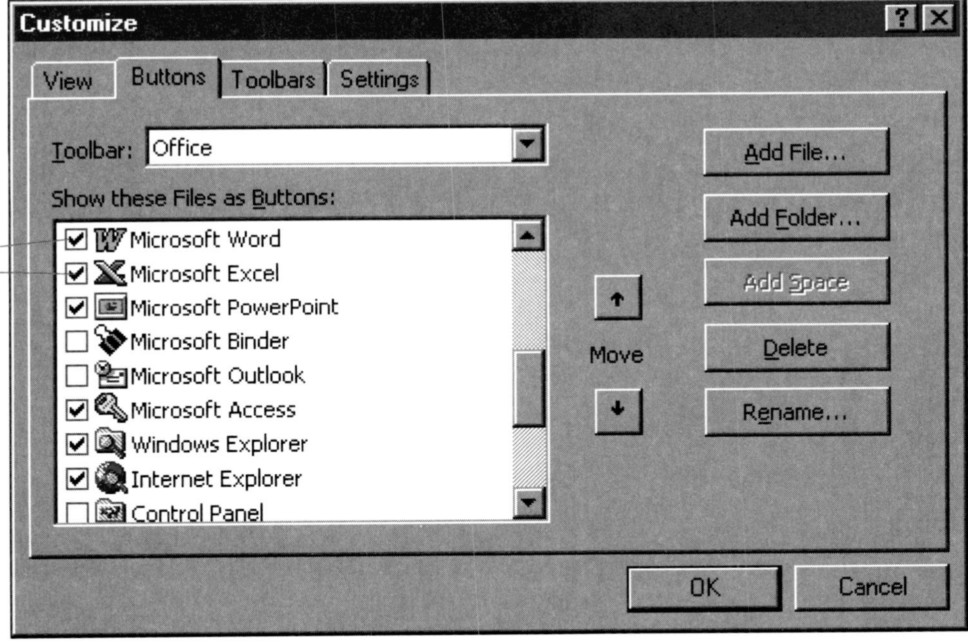

(b) Customize Dialog Box

FIGURE 3 Microsoft Office Shortcut Bar

Docucentric Orientation

Our Shortcut Bar contains two additional buttons: to open an existing document and to start a new document. These buttons are very useful and take advantage of the "docucentric" orientation of Microsoft Office, which lets you think in terms

(a) Open an Existing Document

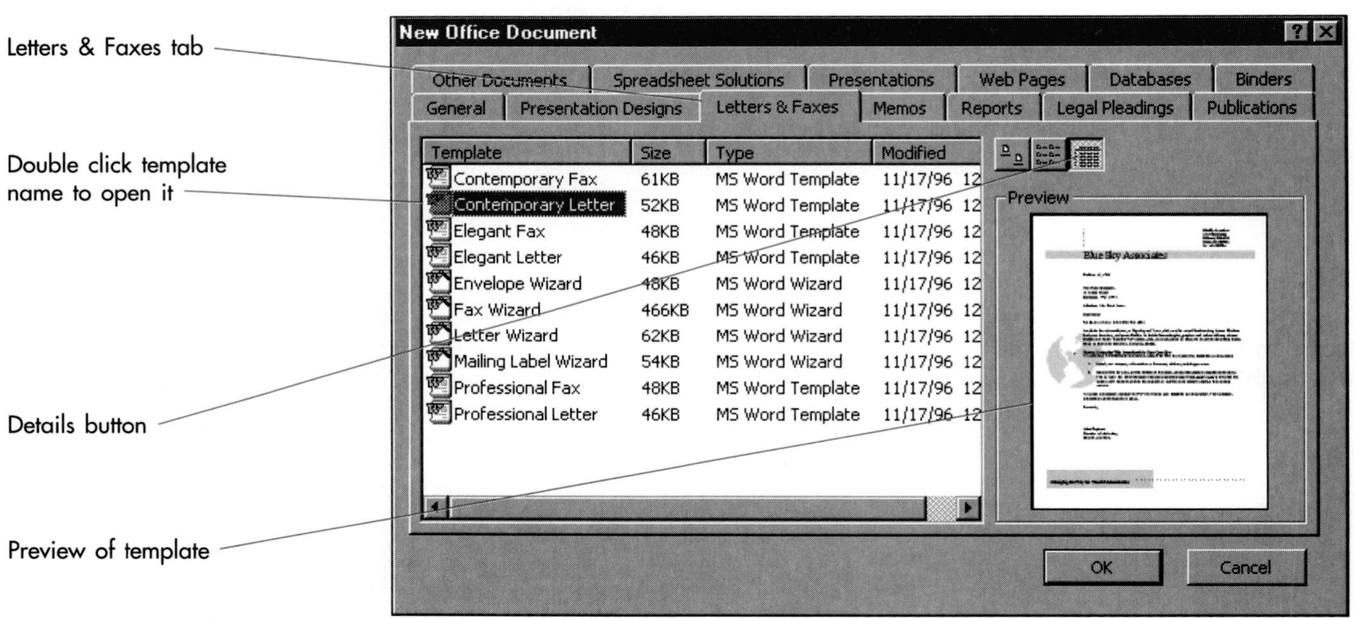

(b) Start a New Document

FIGURE 4 Document Orientation

of a document rather than the associated application. You can still open a document in traditional fashion, by starting the application (e.g., clicking its button on the Shortcut Bar), then using the File Open command to open the document. It's easier, however, to locate the document, then double click its icon, which automatically loads the associated program.

Consider, for example, the Open dialog box in Figure 4a, which is displayed by clicking the Open a Document button on the Shortcut Bar. The Open dialog box is common to the major Office applications, and it works identically in each application. The My Documents folder is selected in Figure 4a, and it contains four documents of various file types. The documents are displayed in the Details view, which shows the document name, size, file type, and date and time the document was last modified. To open any document—for example, "Analysis of a Car Loan"—just double click its name or icon. The associated application (Microsoft Excel in this example) will be started automatically; and it, in turn, will open the selected workbook.

The "docucentric" orientation also applies to new documents. Click the Start a New Document button on the Office Shortcut Bar, and you display the New dialog box in Figure 4b. Click the tab corresponding to the type of document you want to create, such as Letters & Faxes in Figure 4b. Change to the Details view, then click (select) various templates so that you can choose the one most appropriate for your purpose. Double click the desired template to start the application, which opens the template and enables you to create the document.

CHANGE THE VIEW

The toolbar in the Open dialog box contains buttons to display the documents within the selected folder in one of several views. Click the Details button to switch to the Details view and see the date and time the file was last modified, as well as its size and type. Click the List button to display an icon representing the associated application, enabling you to see many more files than in the Details view. The Preview button lets you see a document before you open it. The Properties button displays information about the document, including the number of revisions.

SHARED APPLICATIONS AND UTILITIES

Microsoft Office includes additional applications and shared utilities, several of which are illustrated in Figure 5. The ***Microsoft Clip Gallery*** in Figure 5a has more than 3,000 clip art images and almost 150 photographs, each in a variety of categories. It also contains a lesser number of sound files and video clips. The Clip Gallery can be accessed from every Office application, most easily through the Insert Picture command, which displays the Clip Gallery dialog box.

The ***Microsoft WordArt*** utility adds decorative text to a document, and is accessed through the Insert Picture command from Word, Excel, or PowerPoint. WordArt is intuitive and easy to use. In essence, you choose a style for the text from among the selections in the dialog box of Figure 5b, then you enter the specific text in a second dialog box (which is not shown in Figure 5). It's fun, it's easy, and you can create some truly dynamite documents that will add interest to a document.

Office Art consists of a set of drawing tools that is found on the Drawing toolbar in Word, Excel, or PowerPoint. You don't have to be an artist—all it takes is a little imagination and an appreciation for what the individual tools can do. In Figure 5c, for example, we began with a single clip art image, copied it several times within the PowerPoint slide, then rotated and colored the students as shown. We also used the AutoShapes tool to add a callout for our student.

Microsoft Bookshelf Basics contains three of the nine books available in the complete version of Microsoft Bookshelf (which is an additional cost item). The *American Heritage Dictionary,* the *Original Roget's Thesaurus,* and the *Columbia Dictionary of Quotations* are provided at no charge. An excerpt from the *American Heritage Dictionary* is illustrated in Figure 5d. Enter the word you are looking for in the text box on the left, then read the definition on the right. You can click the sound icon and hear the pronunciation of the word.

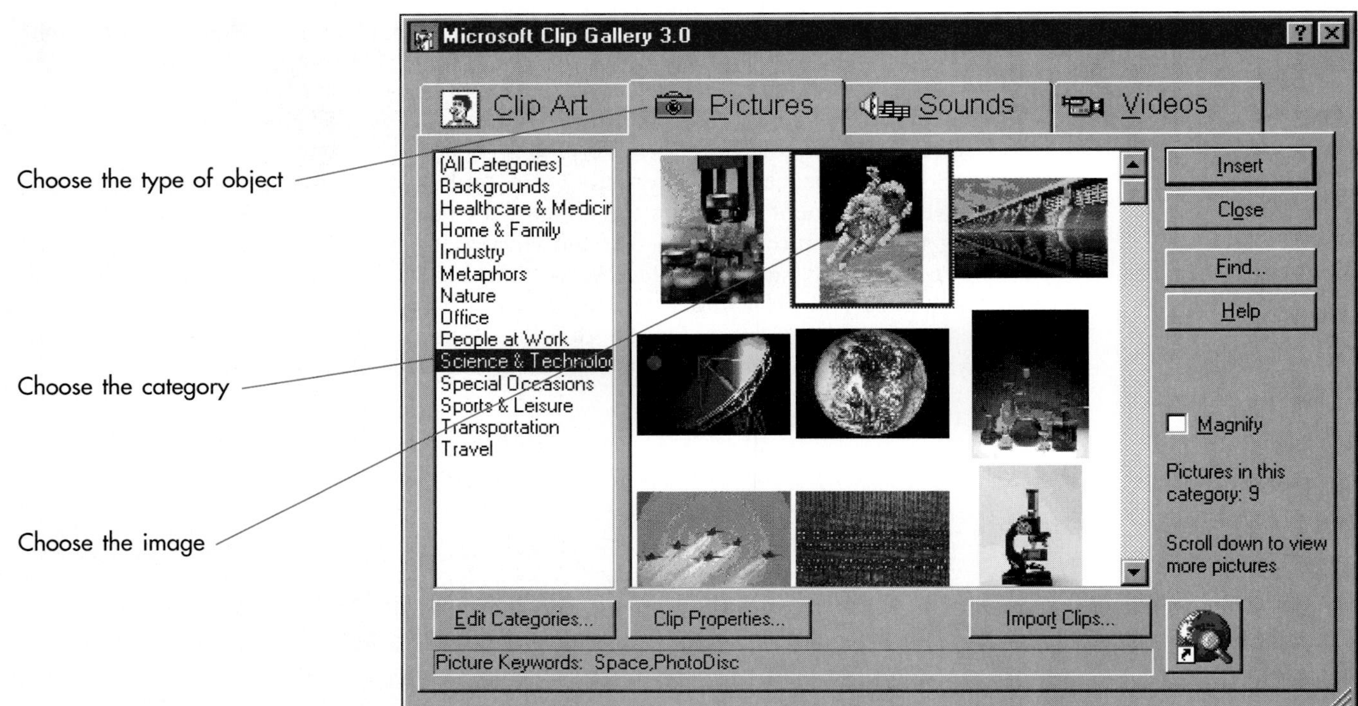

(a) Microsoft Clip Gallery

WordArt Gallery

Select a WordArt style:

OK

Cancel

Select the style to display a second dialog box in which you enter your text

(b) WordArt

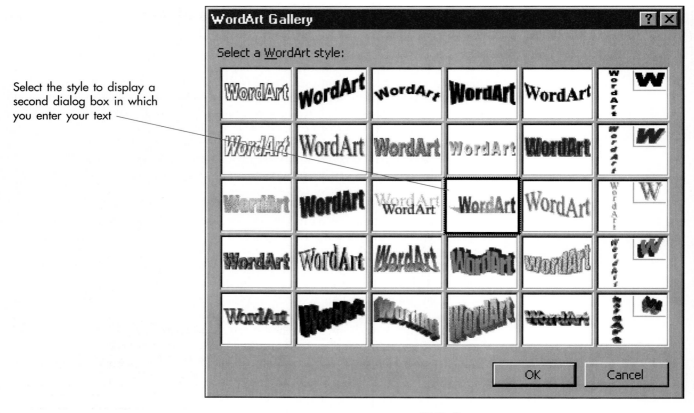

FIGURE 5 Shared Applications

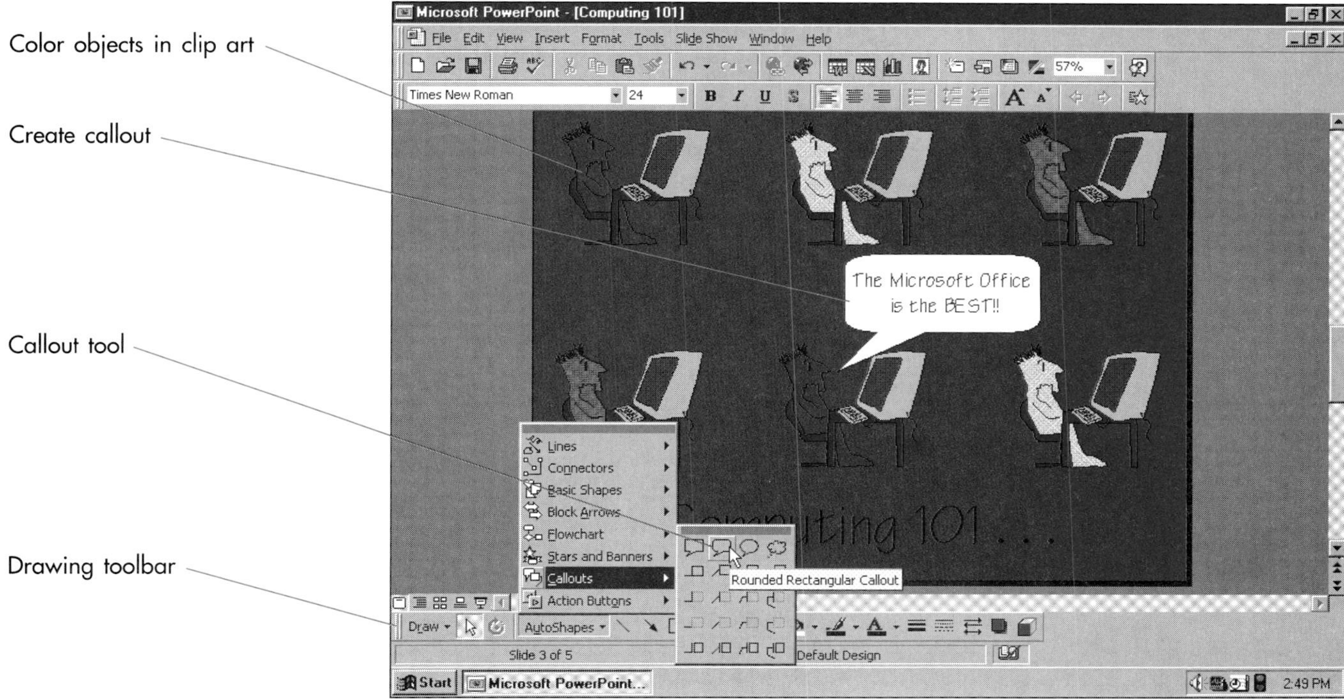

(c) Office Art

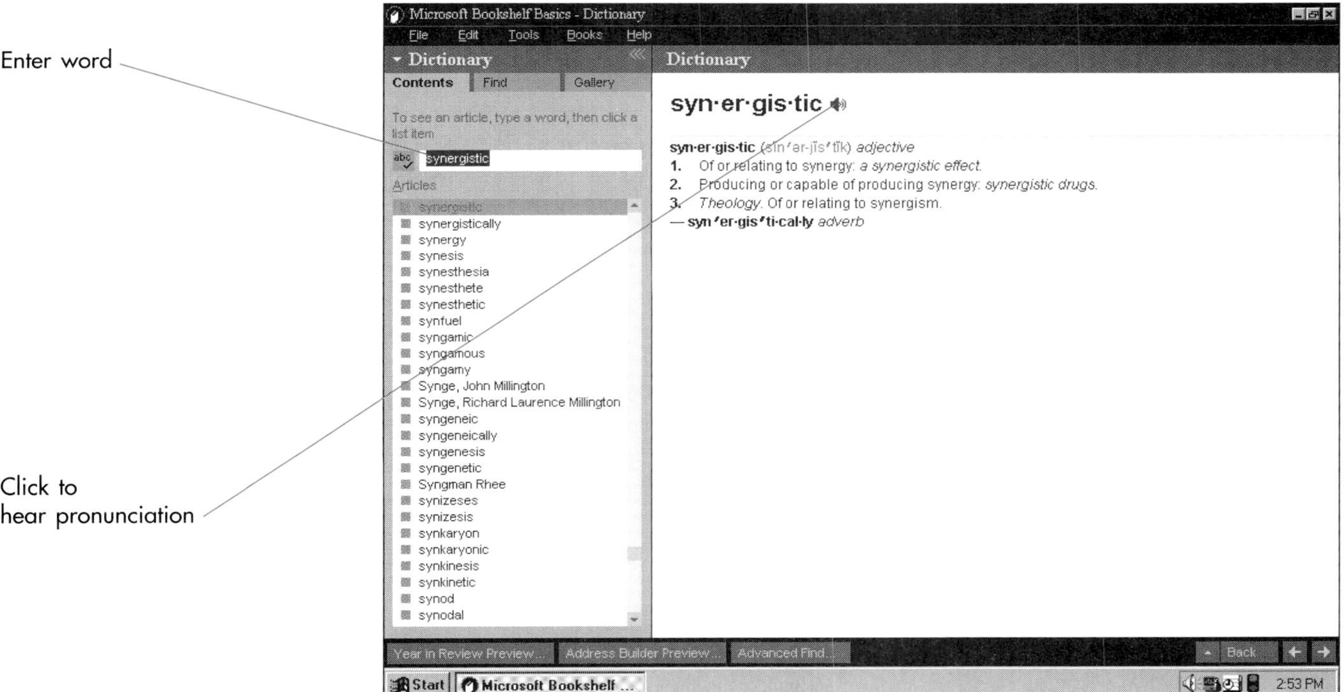

(d) Bookshelf Basics

FIGURE 5 Shared Applications (continued)

THE OTHER SHARED APPLICATIONS

Microsoft Office includes several additional applications whose functions can be inferred from their names. The Equation Editor, Organization Chart, Data Map, and Graph utilities are accessed through the Insert Object command. All of these applications are straightforward and easy to use as they follow the common user interface and provide online help.

OBJECT LINKING AND EMBEDDING

The applications in Microsoft Office are thoroughly integrated with one another. They look alike and they work in consistent fashion. Equally important, they share information through a technology known as ***Object Linking and Embedding (OLE),*** which enables you to create a ***compound document*** containing data (objects) from multiple applications.

The compound document in Figure 6 was created in Word, and it contains objects (a worksheet and a chart) that were created in Excel. The letterhead uses a logo that was taken from the Clip Gallery, while the name and address of the recipient were drawn from an Access database. The various objects were inserted into the compound document through linking or embedding, which are actually two very different techniques. Both operations, however, are much more sophisticated than simply pasting an object, because with either linking or embedding, you can edit the object by using the tools of the original application.

The difference between linking and embedding depends on whether the object is stored within the compound document (***embedding***) or in its own file (***linking***). An *embedded object* is stored in the compound document, which in turn becomes the only user (client) of that object. A *linked object* is stored in its own file, and the compound document is one of many potential clients of that object. The compound document does not contain the linked object per se, but only a representation of the object as well as a pointer (link) to the file containing the object. The advantage of linking is that the document is updated automatically if the object changes.

The choice between linking and embedding depends on how the object will be used. Linking is preferable if the object is likely to change and the compound document requires the latest version. Linking should also be used when the same object is placed in many documents so that any change to the object has to be made in only one place. Embedding should be used if you need to take the object with you (to a different computer) and/or if there is only a single destination document for the object.

OBJECT LINKING AND EMBEDDING

Object Linking and Embedding (OLE) enables you to create a compound document containing objects (data) from multiple Windows applications. OLE is one of the major benefits of working in the Windows environment, but it would be impossible to illustrate all of the techniques in a single discussion. Accordingly, we have created the icon at the left to help you identify the many examples of object linking and embedding that appear throughout the Exploring Windows series.

Office of Residential Living

University of Miami • P.O. Box 248904 • Coral Gables, FL 33124

January 10, 1998

Mr. Jeffrey Redmond, President
Dynamic Dining Services
4329 Palmetto Lane
Miami, FL 33157

Dear Jeff,

As per our conversation, occupancy is projected to be back up from last year. I have enclosed a spreadsheet and chart that show the total enrollment for the past four school years. Please realize, however, that the 1997–1998 figures are projections, as the Spring 1998 numbers are still incomplete. The final 1997–1998 numbers should be confirmed within the next two weeks. I hope that this helps with your planning. If you need further information, please contact me at the above address.

Dorm Occupancy

	94-95	95-96	96-97	97-98
Beatty	330	285	270	250
Broward	620	580	620	565
Graham	450	397	352	420
Rawlings	435	470	295	372
Tolbert	550	554	524	635
Totals	2385	2286	2061	2242

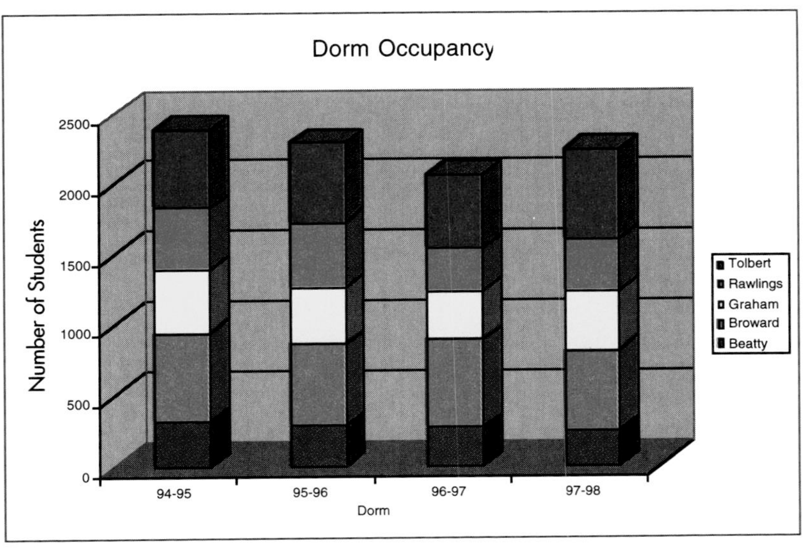

FIGURE 6 A Compound Document

SUMMARY

The common user interface requires every Windows application to follow a consistent set of conventions and ensures that all applications work basically the same way. The development of a suite of applications from a single vendor extends this concept by imposing additional similarities on all applications within the suite.

Microsoft distributes both a Standard and a Professional edition of Office 97. Both versions include Word, Excel, PowerPoint, Internet Explorer, and Outlook. Office Professional also has Microsoft Access. The single biggest difference between Office 97 and its predecessor, Office 95, is that the Internet has become an integral part of the Office suite.

Help for all Office applications is available in a variety of formats. The Help Contents window provides access to a Contents and Index tab in which you look up specific topics. The Office Assistant enables you to ask a question in English. Still additional help is available from the Microsoft Web site, provided you have access to the Internet.

Microsoft Office includes several additional applications and shared utilities that can be used to add interest to a document. The Clip Gallery has more than 3,000 clip art images, 150 photographs, and a lesser number of sound files and video clips. WordArt enables you to create decorative text, while Office Art consists of a powerful set of drawing tools.

The Microsoft Office Shortcut Bar provides immediate access to each application in Microsoft Office. The Shortcut Bar is fully customizable with respect to the buttons it displays, its appearance, and its position on the desktop. The Open a Document and Start a New Document buttons enable you to think in terms of a document rather than the associated application.

Object Linking and Embedding (OLE) enables you to create a compound document containing data (objects) from multiple applications. Linking and embedding are different operations. The difference between the two depends on whether the object is stored within the compound document (embedding) or in its own file (linking).

KEY WORDS AND CONCEPTS

- Common Windows interface
- Compound document
- Contents tab
- Docucentric orientation
- Embedding
- Formatting toolbar
- Index tab
- Internet Explorer
- Linking
- Microsoft Access
- Microsoft Bookshelf Basics
- Microsoft Clip Gallery
- Microsoft Excel
- Microsoft Office Professional
- Microsoft Office Shortcut Bar
- Microsoft Outlook
- Microsoft PowerPoint
- Microsoft Standard Office
- Microsoft Word
- Microsoft WordArt
- Object Linking and Embedding (OLE)
- Office Art
- Office Assistant
- Online help
- Shared applications
- Standard toolbar

1

MICROSOFT® WORD 97: WHAT WILL WORD PROCESSING DO FOR ME?

OBJECTIVES

After reading this chapter you will be able to:

1. Define word wrap; differentiate between a hard and a soft return.
2. Distinguish between the insert and overtype modes.
3. Describe the elements on the Microsoft Word screen.
4. Create, save, retrieve, edit, and print a simple document.
5. Check a document for spelling; describe the function of the custom dictionary.
6. Describe the AutoCorrect feature; explain how it can be used to create your own shorthand.
7. Use the thesaurus to look up synonyms and antonyms.
8. Explain the objectives and limitations of the grammar check; customize the grammar check for business or casual writing.
9. Differentiate between the Save and Save As commands; describe various backup options that can be selected.

OVERVIEW

Have you ever produced what you thought was the perfect term paper only to discover that you omitted a sentence or misspelled a word, or that the paper was three pages too short or one page too long? Wouldn't it be nice to make the necessary changes, and then be able to reprint the entire paper with the touch of a key? Welcome to the world of word processing, where you are no longer stuck with having to retype anything. Instead, you retrieve your work from disk, display it on the monitor and revise it as necessary, then print it at any time, in draft or final form.

This chapter provides a broad-based introduction to word processing in general and Microsoft Word in particular. We begin by presenting (or perhaps reviewing) the essential concepts of a word processor, then show you how these concepts are implemented in Word. We show you how to create a document, how to save it on disk, then retrieve the document you just created. We introduce you to the spell check and thesaurus, two essential tools in any word processor. We also present the grammar check as a convenient way of finding a variety of errors but remind you there is no substitute for carefully proofreading the final document.

THE BASICS OF WORD PROCESSING

All word processors adhere to certain basic concepts that must be understood if you are to use the programs effectively. The next several pages introduce ideas that are applicable to any word processor (and which you may already know). We follow the conceptual material with a hands-on exercise that enables you to apply what you have learned.

The Insertion Point

The ***insertion point*** is a flashing vertical line that marks the place where text will be entered. The insertion point is always at the beginning of a new document, but it can be moved anywhere within an existing document. If, for example, you wanted to add text to the end of a document, you would move the insertion point to the end of the document, then begin typing.

Word Wrap

A newcomer to word processing has one major transition to make from a typewriter, and it is an absolutely critical adjustment. Whereas a typist returns the carriage at the end of every line, just the opposite is true of a word processor. One types continually *without* pressing the enter key at the end of a line because the word processor automatically wraps text from one line to the next. This concept is known as ***word wrap*** and is illustrated in Figure 1.1.

The word *primitive* does not fit on the current line in Figure 1.1a, and is automatically shifted to the next line, *without* the user having to press the enter key. The user continues to enter the document, with additional words being wrapped to subsequent lines as necessary. The only time you use the enter key is at the end of a paragraph, or when you want the insertion point to move to the next line and the end of the current line doesn't reach the right margin.

Word wrap is closely associated with another concept, that of hard and soft returns. A ***hard return*** is created by the user when he or she presses the enter key at the end of a paragraph; a ***soft return*** is created by the word processor as it wraps text from one line to the next. The locations of the soft returns change automatically as a document is edited (e.g., as text is inserted or deleted, or as margins or fonts are changed). The locations of the hard returns can be changed only by the user, who must intentionally insert or delete each hard return.

There are two hard returns in Figure 1.1b, one at the end of each paragraph. There are also six soft returns in the first paragraph (one at the end of every line except the last) and three soft returns in the second paragraph. Now suppose the margins in the document are made smaller (that is, the line is made longer) as shown in Figure 1.1c. The number of soft returns drops to four and two (in the first and second paragraphs, respectively) as more text fits on a line and fewer lines are needed. The revised document still contains the two original hard returns, one at the end of each paragraph.

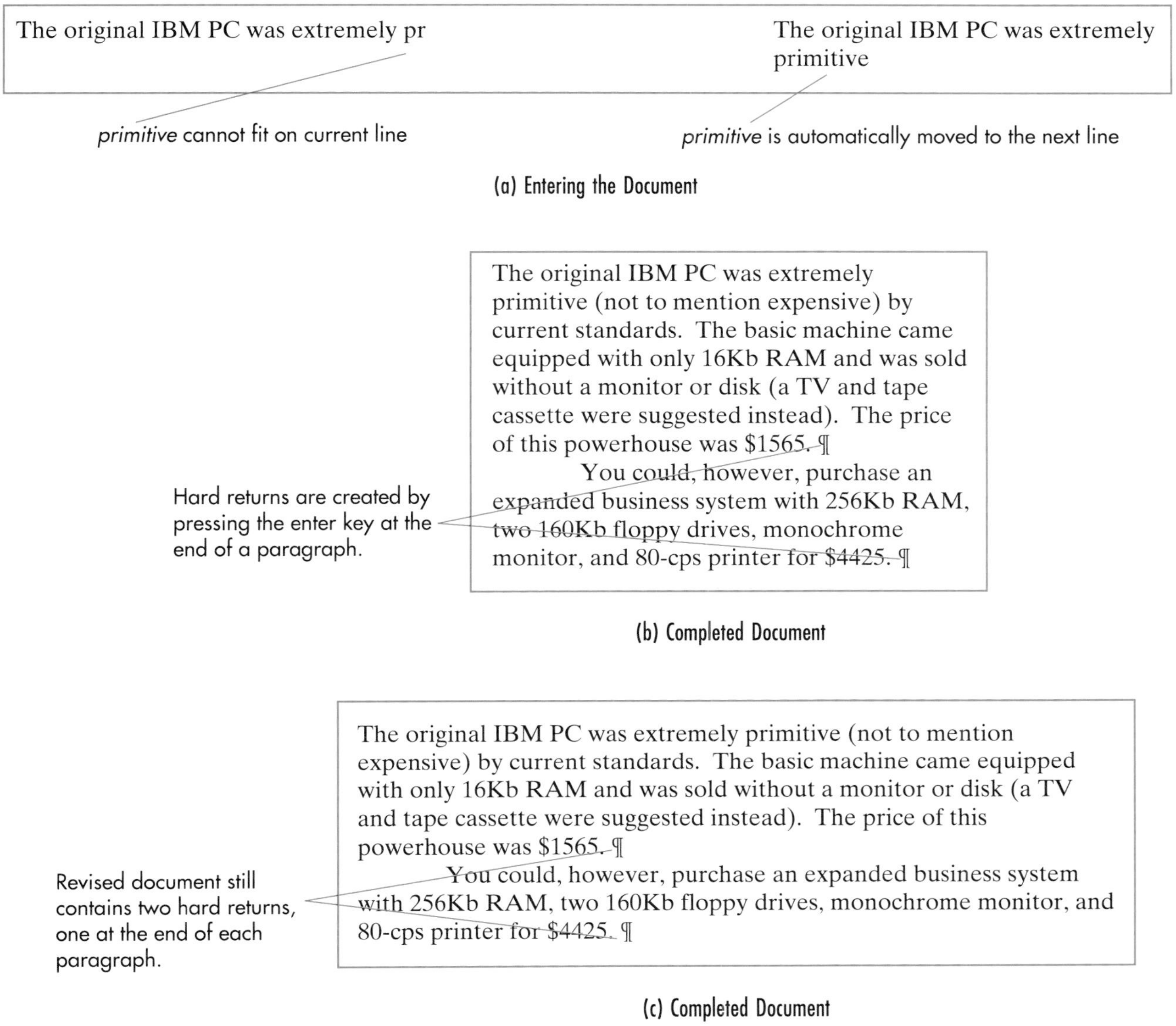

The original IBM PC was extremely pr

The original IBM PC was extremely primitive

primitive cannot fit on current line

primitive is automatically moved to the next line

(a) Entering the Document

The original IBM PC was extremely primitive (not to mention expensive) by current standards. The basic machine came equipped with only 16Kb RAM and was sold without a monitor or disk (a TV and tape cassette were suggested instead). The price of this powerhouse was $1565. ¶

You could, however, purchase an expanded business system with 256Kb RAM, two 160Kb floppy drives, monochrome monitor, and 80-cps printer for $4425. ¶

Hard returns are created by pressing the enter key at the end of a paragraph.

(b) Completed Document

The original IBM PC was extremely primitive (not to mention expensive) by current standards. The basic machine came equipped with only 16Kb RAM and was sold without a monitor or disk (a TV and tape cassette were suggested instead). The price of this powerhouse was $1565. ¶

You could, however, purchase an expanded business system with 256Kb RAM, two 160Kb floppy drives, monochrome monitor, and 80-cps printer for $4425. ¶

Revised document still contains two hard returns, one at the end of each paragraph.

(c) Completed Document

FIGURE 1.1 Word Wrap

Toggle Switches

Suppose you sat down at the keyboard and typed an entire sentence without pressing the Shift key; the sentence would be in all lowercase letters. Then you pressed the Caps Lock key and retyped the sentence, again without pressing the Shift key. This time the sentence would be in all uppercase letters. You could repeat the process as often as you like. Each time you pressed the Caps Lock key, the sentence would switch from lowercase to uppercase and vice versa.

The point of this exercise is to introduce the concept of a ***toggle switch,*** a device that causes the computer to alternate between two states. The Caps Lock key is an example of a toggle switch. Each time you press it, newly typed text will change from uppercase to lowercase and back again. We will see several other examples of toggle switches as we proceed in our discussion of word processing.

Insert versus Overtype

Microsoft Word is always in one of two modes, ***insert*** or ***overtype.*** (The insert mode is the default and the one you will be in most of the time.) Text that is entered into a document during the insert mode moves existing text to the right to accommodate the characters being added. Text entered from the overtype mode replaces (overtypes) existing text. Regardless of which mode you are in, text is always entered or replaced immediately to the right of the insertion point.

The insert mode is best when you enter text for the first time, but either mode can be used to make corrections. The insert mode is the better choice when the correction requires you to add new text; the overtype mode is easier when you are substituting one or more character(s) for another. The difference is illustrated in Figure 1.2.

Figure 1.2a displays the text as it was originally entered, with two misspellings. The letters *se* have been omitted from the word *insert,* and an *x* has been erroneously typed instead of an *r* in the word *overtype.* The insert mode is used in Figure 1.2b to add the missing letters, which in turn moves the rest of the line to the right. The overtype mode is used in Figure 1.2c to replace the *x* with an *r.*

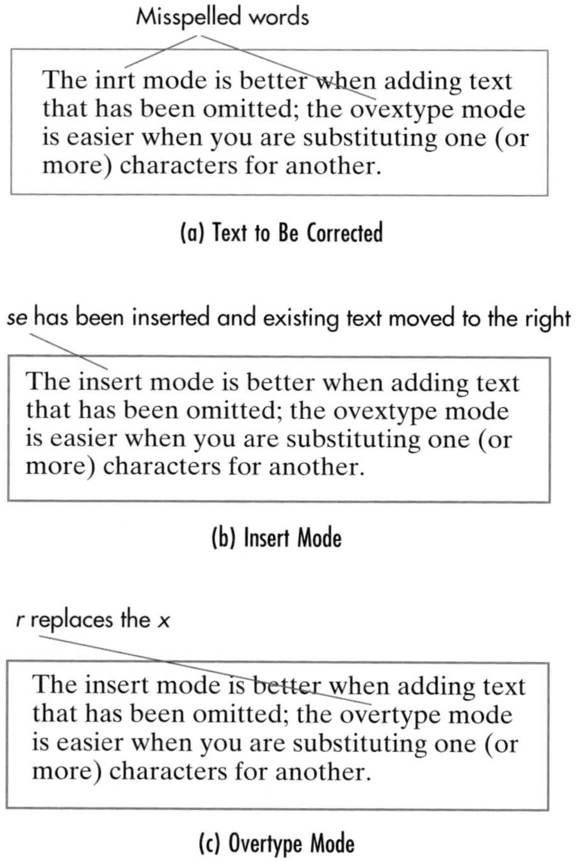

Misspelled words
The inrt mode is better when adding text that has been omitted; the ovextype mode is easier when you are substituting one (or more) characters for another.

(a) Text to Be Corrected

se has been inserted and existing text moved to the right
The insert mode is better when adding text that has been omitted; the ovextype mode is easier when you are substituting one (or more) characters for another.

(b) Insert Mode

r replaces the *x*
The insert mode is better when adding text that has been omitted; the overtype mode is easier when you are substituting one (or more) characters for another.

(c) Overtype Mode

FIGURE 1.2 Insert and Overtype Modes

Deleting Text

The backspace and Del keys delete one character immediately to the left or right of the insertion point, respectively. The choice between them depends on when you need to erase a character(s). The backspace key is easier if you want to delete a character immediately after typing it. The Del key is preferable during subsequent editing.

You can delete several characters at one time by selecting (dragging the mouse over) the characters to be deleted, then pressing the Del key. And finally, you can delete and replace text in one operation by selecting the text to be replaced and then typing the new text in its place.

LEARN TO TYPE

The ultimate limitation of any word processor is the speed at which you enter data; hence the ability to type quickly is invaluable. Learning how to type is easy, especially with the availability of computer-based typing programs. As little as a half hour a day for a couple of weeks will have you up to speed, and if you do any significant amount of writing at all, the investment will pay off many times.

INTRODUCTION TO MICROSOFT WORD

We used Microsoft Word to write this book, as can be inferred from the screen in Figure 1.3. Your screen will be different from ours in many ways. You will not have the same document nor is it likely that you will customize Word in exactly the same way. You should, however, be able to recognize the basic elements that are found in the Microsoft Word window that is open on the desktop.

There are actually two open windows in Figure 1.3—an application window for Microsoft Word and a document window for the specific document on which you are working. Each window has its own Minimize, Maximize (or Restore), and Close buttons. Both windows have been maximized, and thus the title bars have been merged into a single title bar that appears at the top of the application window and reflects the application (Microsoft Word) as well as the document name (Word Chapter 1). A menu bar appears immediately below the title bar. Vertical and horizontal scroll bars appear at the right and bottom of the document window. The Windows taskbar appears at the bottom of the screen and shows the open applications.

Microsoft Word is also part of the Microsoft Office suite of applications, and thus shares additional features with Excel, Access, and PowerPoint, that are also part of the Office suite. ***Toolbars*** provide immediate access to common commands and appear immediately below the menu bar. The toolbars can be displayed or hidden using the Toolbars command in the View menu.

The ***Standard toolbar*** contains buttons corresponding to the most basic commands in Word—for example, opening a file or printing a document. The icon on the button is intended to be indicative of its function (e.g., a printer to indicate the Print command). You can also point to the button to display a ***ScreenTip*** showing the name of the button. The ***Formatting toolbar*** appears under the Standard toolbar and provides access to common formatting operations such as boldface, italics, or underlining.

The toolbars may appear overwhelming at first, but there is absolutely no need to memorize what the individual buttons do. That will come with time. We

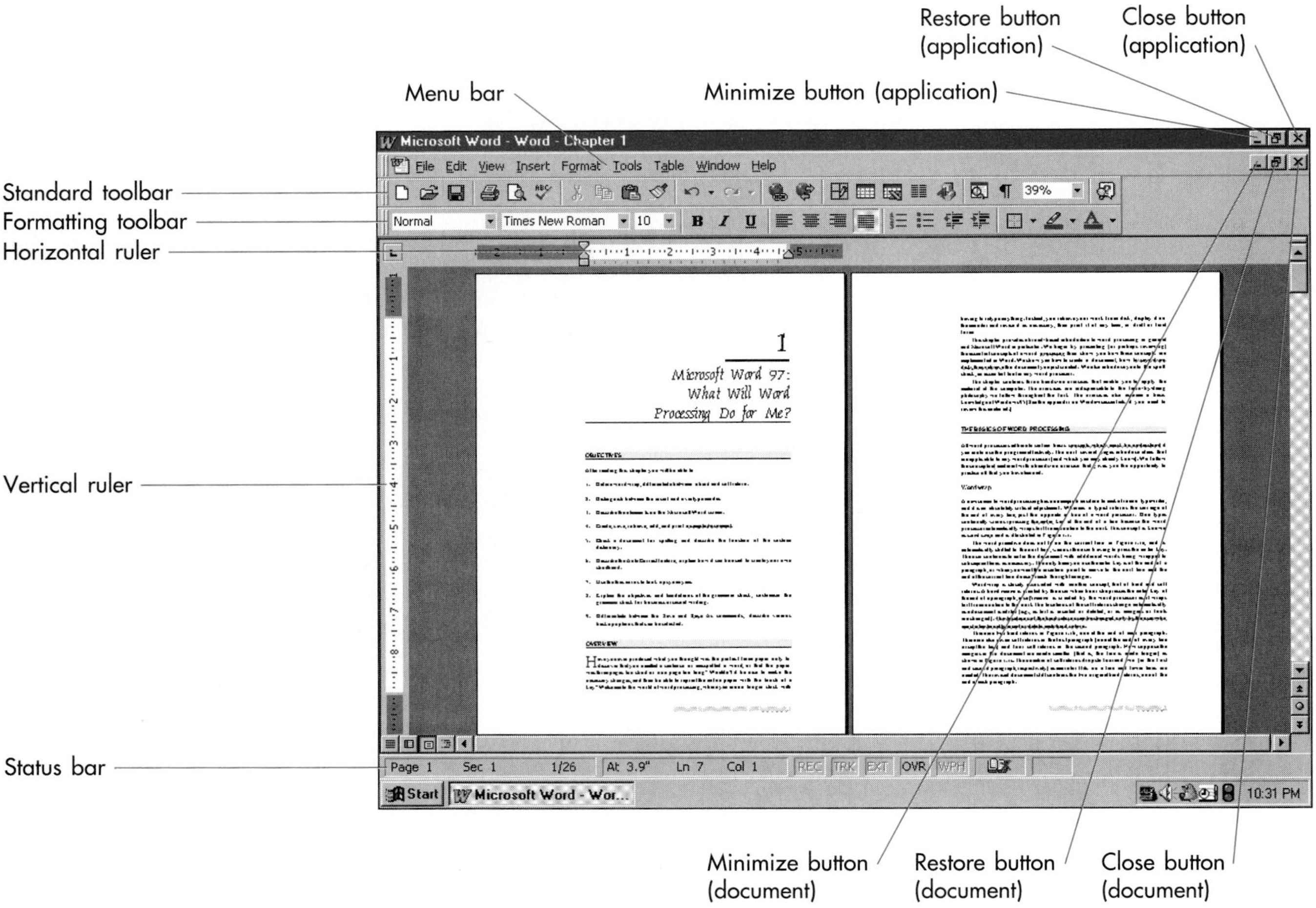

Restore button (application)
Close button (application)
Menu bar
Minimize button (application)
Standard toolbar
Formatting toolbar
Horizontal ruler
Vertical ruler
Status bar
Minimize button (document)
Restore button (document)
Close button (document)

FIGURE 1.3 Microsoft Word

suggest, however, that you will have a better appreciation for the various buttons if you consider them in groups, according to their general function, as shown in Figure 1.4a.

The ***horizontal ruler*** is displayed underneath the toolbars and enables you to change margins, tabs, and/or indents for all or part of a document. A ***vertical ruler*** shows the vertical position of text on the page and can be used to change the top or bottom margins.

The ***status bar*** at the bottom of the document window displays the location of the insertion point (or information about the command being executed.) The status bar also shows the status (settings) of various indicators—for example, OVR to show that Word is in the overtype, as opposed to the insert, mode.

HELP FOR MICROSOFT WORD

Office 97 offers help from a variety of sources. You can pull down the Help menu as you can with any Windows application and/or you can click the Office Assistant button on the Standard toolbar. You can also go to the Microsoft Web site to obtain more recent, and often more detailed, information. You will find the answer to frequently asked questions, and you can access the same Knowledge Base used by Microsoft support engineers.

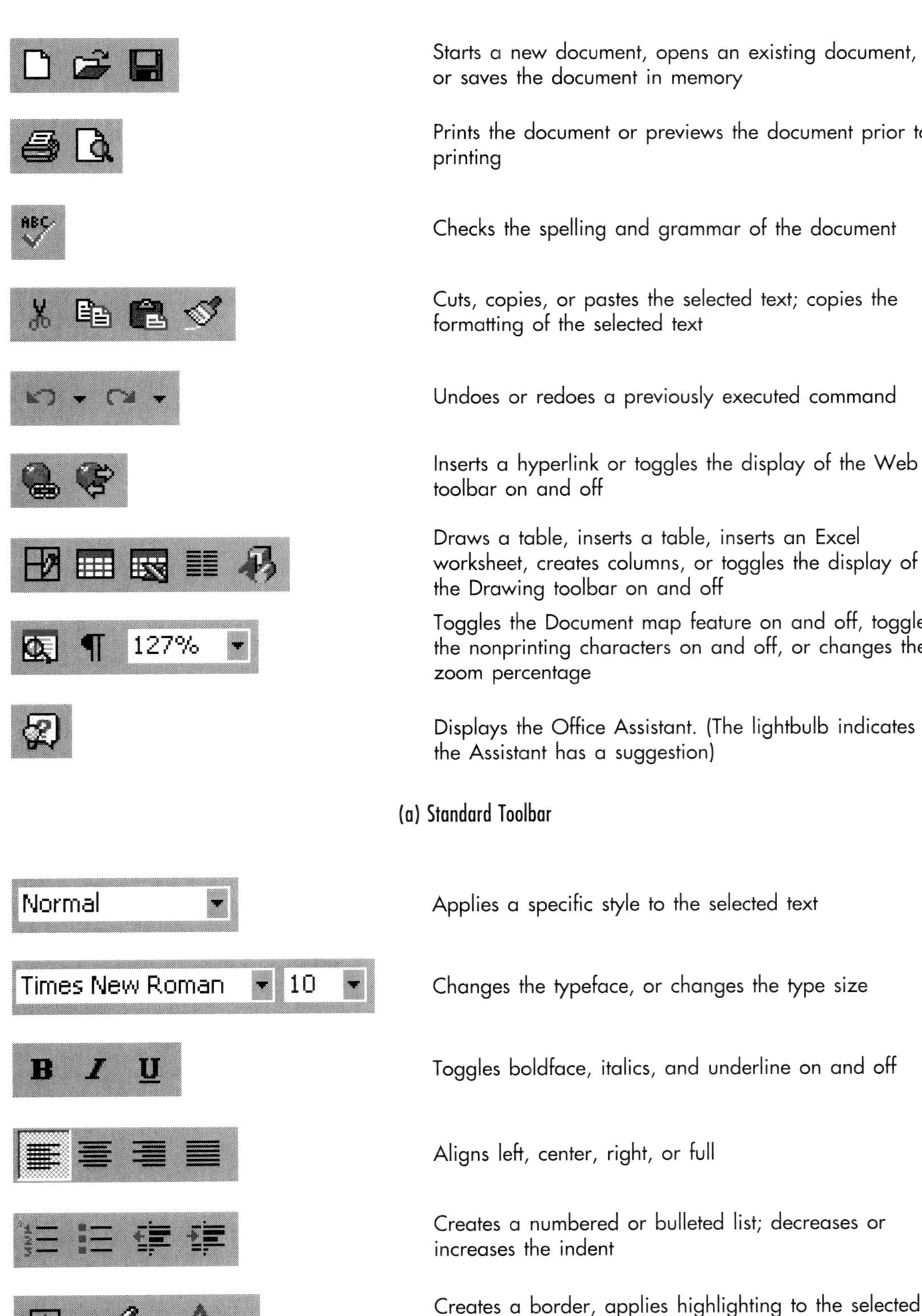
Starts a new document, opens an existing document, or saves the document in memory
Prints the document or previews the document prior to printing
ABC
Checks the spelling and grammar of the document
Cuts, copies, or pastes the selected text; copies the formatting of the selected text
Undoes or redoes a previously executed command
Inserts a hyperlink or toggles the display of the Web toolbar on and off
Draws a table, inserts a table, inserts an Excel worksheet, creates columns, or toggles the display of the Drawing toolbar on and off
127%
Toggles the Document map feature on and off, toggles the nonprinting characters on and off, or changes the zoom percentage
Displays the Office Assistant. (The lightbulb indicates the Assistant has a suggestion)
(a) Standard Toolbar
Normal
Applies a specific style to the selected text
Times New Roman
10
Changes the typeface, or changes the type size
B I U
Toggles boldface, italics, and underline on and off
Aligns left, center, right, or full
Creates a numbered or bulleted list; decreases or increases the indent
Creates a border, applies highlighting to the selected text, or applies color to the selected text
(b) Formatting Toolbar

FIGURE 1.4 Toolbars

The ***File menu*** is a critically important menu in virtually every Windows application. It contains the Save and Open commands to save a document on disk, then subsequently retrieve (open) that document at a later time. The File menu also contains the Print command to print a document, the Close command to close the current document but continue working in the application, and the Exit command to quit the application altogether.

The ***Save command*** copies the document that is being edited (the document in memory) to disk. The Save As dialog box appears the first time that the document is saved so that you can specify the file name and other required information. All subsequent executions of the Save command save the document under the assigned name, replacing the previously saved version with the new version.

The Save As dialog box requires a file name (e.g., My First Document in Figure 1.5a), which can be up to 255 characters in length. The file name may contain spaces and commas. (Periods are permitted, but discouraged, since they are too easily confused with DOS extensions.)

The dialog box also requires the specification of the drive and folder in which the file is to be saved as well as the file type that determines which application the file is associated with. (Long-time DOS users will remember the three-character extension at the end of a file name—for example, DOC—to indicate the associated application. The extension may be hidden in Windows 95 according to options set through the View menu in My Computer or the Windows Explorer.

The ***Open command*** brings a copy of a previously saved document into memory enabling you to work with that document. The Open command displays the Open dialog box in which you specify the file to retrieve. You indicate the drive (and optionally the folder) that contains the file, as well as the type of file you want to retrieve. Word will then list all files of that type on the designated drive (and folder), enabling you to open the file you want.

The Save and Open commands work in conjunction with one another. The Save As dialog box in Figure 1.5a, for example, saves the file *My First Document* onto the disk in drive A. The Open dialog box in Figure 1.5b brings that file back into memory so that you can work with the file, after which you can save the revised file for use at a later time.

The toolbars in the Save As dialog and Open dialog boxes have several buttons in common that enable you to list the files in different ways. The Details view is selected in both dialog boxes and shows the file size as well as the date and time a file was last modified. The List button displays only the file names, and hence more files are visible at one time. The Preview button lets you see a document before you open it. The Properties button displays information about the document including the number of revisions.

SEARCH THE WEB

Microsoft Office 97 enables you to open and/or search for a Web document without having to exit from the application. Pull down the File menu and click the Open command to display the Open dialog box, from where you can click the Search the Web button. Your Web browser will open automatically and connect you to a search page in which you enter keywords, provided you have an Internet connection.

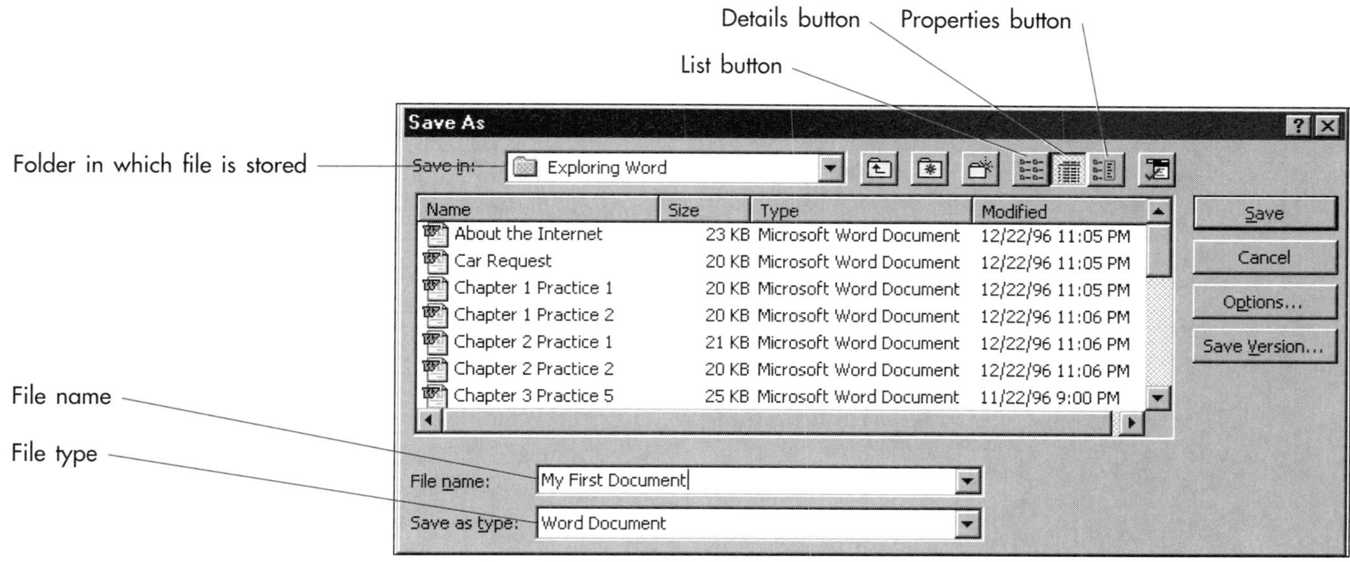

(a) Save As Dialog Box

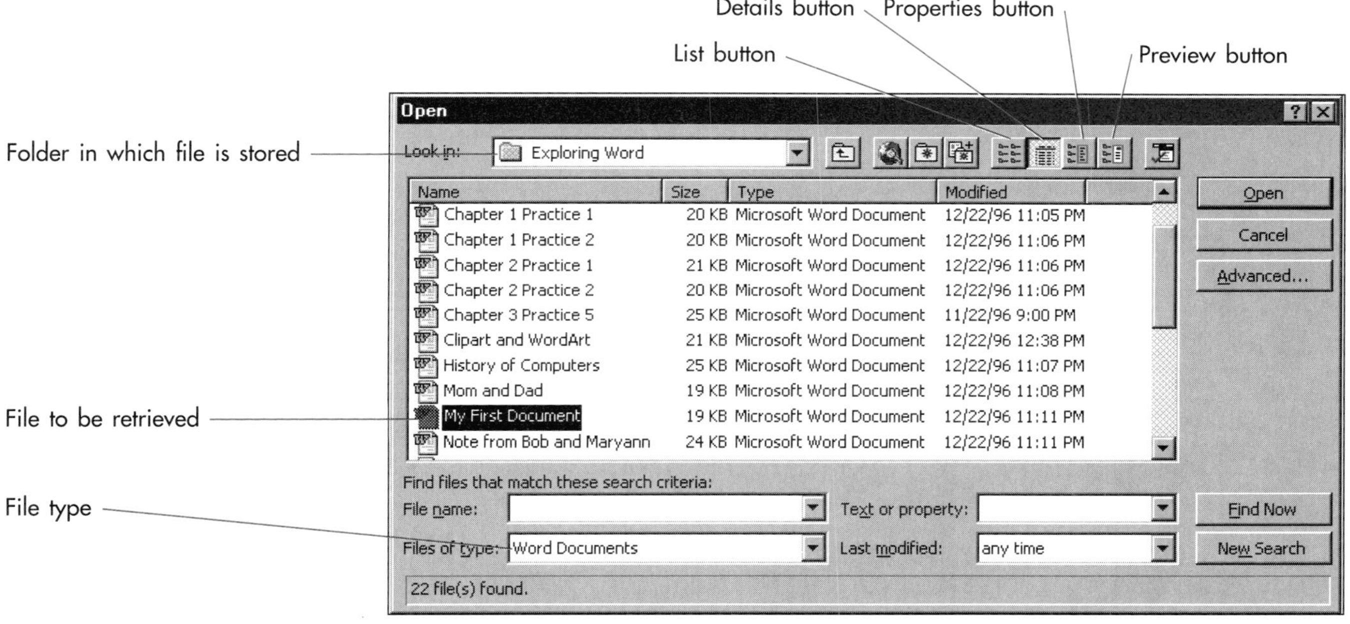

(b) Open Dialog Box

FIGURE 1.5 The Save and Open Commands

LEARNING BY DOING

Every chapter contains a series of hands-on exercises that enable you to apply what you learn at the computer. The exercises in this chapter are linked to one another in that you create a simple document in exercise one, then open and edit that document in exercise two. The ability to save and open a document is critical, and you do not want to spend an inordinate amount of time entering text unless you are confident in your ability to retrieve it later.

HANDS-ON EXERCISE 1

My First Document

Objective: To start Microsoft Word in order to create, save, and print a simple document. To execute commands via the toolbar or from pull-down menus. Use Figure 1.6 as a guide in doing the exercise.

STEP 1: Welcome to Windows

➤ Turn on the computer and all of its peripherals. The floppy drive should be empty prior to starting your machine. This ensures that the system starts from the hard disk, which contains the Windows files, as opposed to a floppy disk, which does not.

➤ Your system will take a minute or so to get started, after which you should see the Windows desktop in Figure 1.6a. Do not be concerned if the appearance of your desktop is different from ours.

➤ You may see additional objects on the desktop in Windows 95 and/or the active desktop content in Windows 97. It doesn't matter which operating system you are using because Office 97 runs equally well under both Windows 95 and Windows 97 (as well as Windows NT).

➤ You may see a Welcome to Windows 95/Windows 97 dialog box with command buttons to take a tour of the operating system. If so, click the appropriate button(s) or close the dialog box.

(a) The Windows Desktop (step 1)

FIGURE 1.6 Hands-on Exercise 1

TAKE THE WINDOWS TOUR

Windows 95 greets you with a Welcome window that contains a command button to take you on a 10-minute tour. Click the command button and enjoy the show. If you do not see the Welcome window when you start Windows 95, click the Start button, click Run, type C:\WELCOME in the Open ***text box,*** and press the enter key. Windows 97 was not available when we went to press, but we expect it to have a similar option.

STEP 2: Obtain the Practice Files

- We have created a series of practice files (commonly called a "data disk") for you to use throughout the text. Your instructor will make these files available to you in a variety of ways:
  - You can download the files from our Web site if you have access to the Internet and World Wide Web (see boxed tip).
  - The files may be on a network drive, in which case you can use the Windows Explorer to copy the files from the network to a floppy disk.
  - There may be an actual "data disk" that you are to check out from the lab in order to use the Copy Disk command to duplicate the disk.
- Check with your instructor for additional information.

DOWNLOAD THE PRACTICE FILES

You can download the practice files for any book in the *Exploring Windows* series from Bob Grauer's home page (www.bus.miami.edu/~rgrauer). Use any Web browser to get to Bob's page, then click the link to the *Exploring Windows* series, where you choose the appropriate book and download the file. Be sure to read the associated "read me" file, which provides additional information about downloading the file.

STEP 3: Start Microsoft Word

- Click the **Start button** to display the Start menu. Click (or point to) the **Programs menu,** then click **Microsoft Word** to start the program.
- Close the Office Assistant if it appears. (The Office Assistant is illustrated in step 6 of this exercise.)
- If necessary, click the **Maximize button** in the application window so that Word takes the entire desktop as shown in Figure 1.6b. Click the **Maximize button** in the document window (if necessary) so that the document window is as large as possible.
- Do not be concerned if your screen is different from ours as we include a troubleshooting section immediately following this exercise.

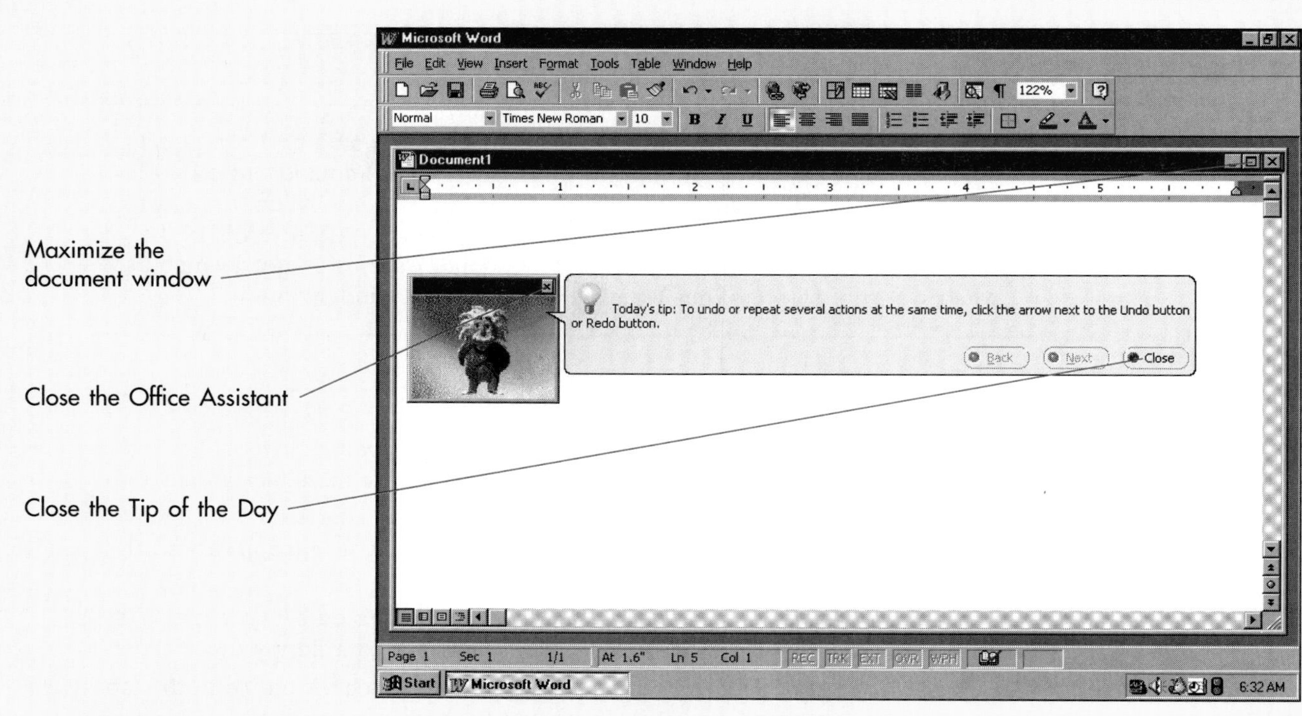

(b) Start Word (step 3)

FIGURE 1.6 Hands-on Exercise 1 (continued)

CHOOSE YOUR OWN ASSISTANT

You can choose your own personal assistant from one of several available images. Click the Office Assistant button on the Standard toolbar to display the Assistant, click the Options button to display the Office Assistant dialog box, click the Gallery tab, then click the Next button repeatedly to cycle through the available images. Click OK to select the image and close the dialog box. (The Office 97 CD is required for certain characters.)

STEP 4: Create the Document

- Create the document in Figure 1.6c. Type just as you would on a typewriter with one exception; do *not* press the enter key at the end of a line because Word will automatically wrap text from one line to the next.
- Press the **enter key** at the end of the paragraph.
- You may see a red or green wavy line to indicate spelling or grammatical errors respectively. Both features are discussed later in the chapter.
- Point to the red wavy line (if any), click the **right mouse button** to display a list of suggested corrections, then click (select) the appropriate substitution.
- Ignore the green wavy line (if any).

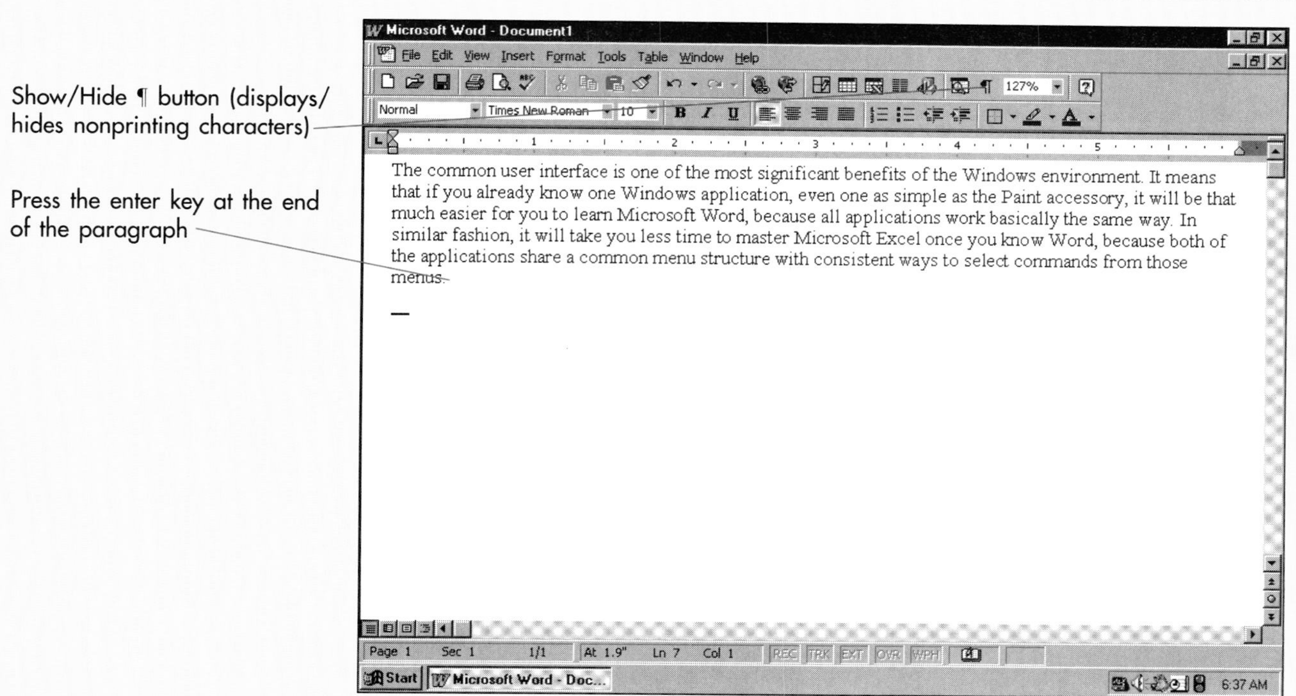

(c) Create the Document (step 4)

FIGURE 1.6 Hands-on Exercise 1 (continued)

WHAT HAPPENED TO THE INS KEY?

Every previous version of Word has used the Ins key to toggle between the Insert and Overtype modes. Unfortunately this simple technique no longer works in Word 97, as the key has been disabled. Instead, Microsoft directs you to pull down the Tools menu, click the Options command, select the Edit tab, then check (clear) the box for Overtype (Insert) mode. Fortunately, we found our own toggle switch—double click the OVR indicator on the status bar to switch back and forth between the two modes.

STEP 5: Save the Document

- Pull down the **File menu** and click **Save** (or click the **Save button** on the Standard toolbar). You should see the Save As dialog box in Figure 1.6d. If necessary, click the **Details button** so that the display on your monitor more closely matches our figure.
- To save the file:
  - Click the **drop-down arrow** on the Save In list box.
  - Click the appropriate drive, drive C or drive A, depending on whether or not you installed the data disk on your hard drive.
  - Double click the **Exploring Word folder,** to make it the active folder (the folder in which you will save the document).

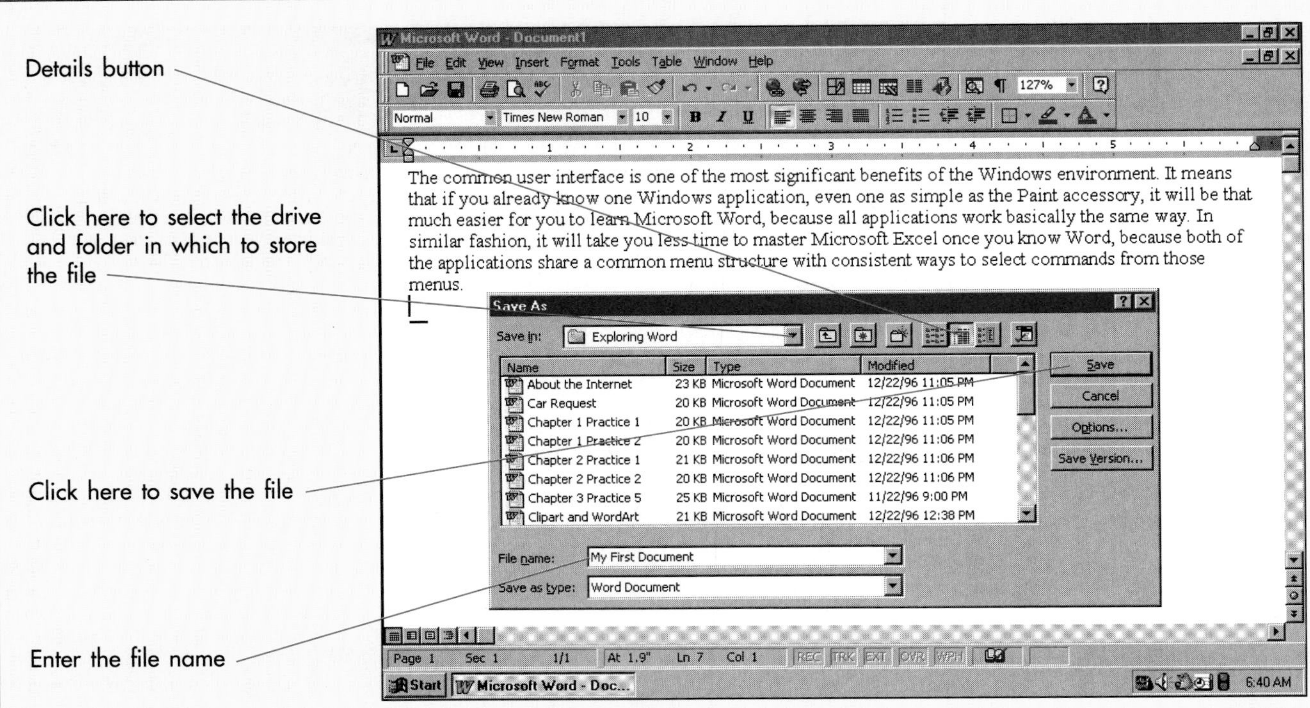

(d) Save the Document (step 5)

FIGURE 1.6 Hands-on Exercise 1 (continued)

- Click and drag over the default entry in the File name text box. Type **My First Document** as the name of your document. (A DOC extension will be added automatically when the file is saved to indicate that this is a Word document.)
- Click **Save** or press the **enter key.** The title bar changes to reflect the document name.

➤ Add your name at the end of the document, then click the **Save button** on the Standard toolbar to save the document with the revision. This time the Save As dialog box does not appear, since Word already knows the name of the document.

CHANGE THE DEFAULT FOLDER

The default folder is the folder where Word opens (saves) documents unless it is otherwise instructed. To change the default folder, pull down the Tools menu, click Options, click the File Locations tab, click Documents, and click the Modify command button. Enter the name of the new folder (for example, C:\Exploring Word), click OK, then click the Close button. The next time you access the File menu, the default folder will reflect these changes.

STEP 6: The Office Assistant

- Click the **Office Assistant button** on the Standard toolbar to display the Office Assistant. (You may see a different character than the one we have selected.)
- Enter your question—for example, **How do I print a document?**—as shown in Figure 1.6e, then click the **Search button** to look for the answer.
- The size of the dialog box expands as the Assistant suggests several topics that may be appropriate to answer your question.
- Click the first topic, **Print a document,** which in turn displays a help screen with detailed information. Read the help screen, then close the Help window.

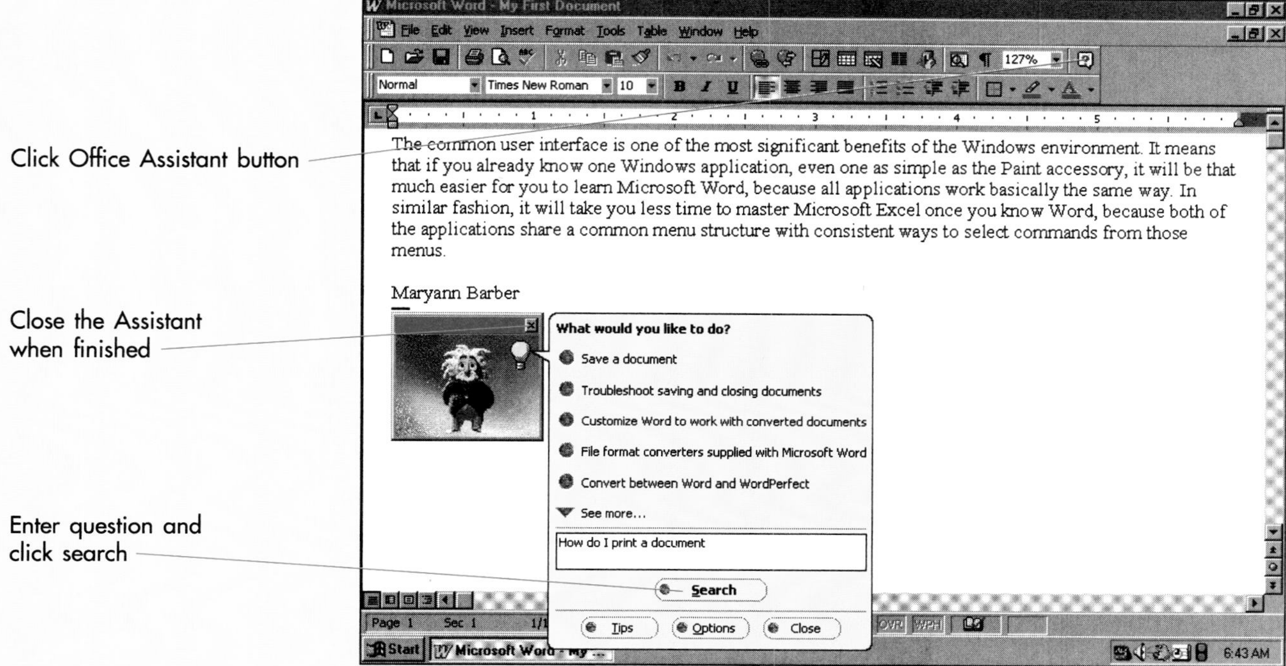

(e) The Office Assistant (step 6)

FIGURE 1.6 Hands-on Exercise 1 (continued)

TIP OF THE DAY

You can set the Office Assistant to greet you with a "Tip of the Day" whenever you start Word. If the Office Assistant is not visible, click the Office Assistant button on the Standard toolbar to start the Assistant, then click the Options button to display the Office Assistant dialog box. Check the Show the Tip of the Day at the startup box, then click OK. The next time you start Word, you will be greeted by the Assistant, who will offer you a tip of the day.

STEP 7: Print the Document

➤ You can print the document in one of two ways:

- Pull down the **File menu.** Click **Print** to display the dialog box of Figure 1.6f. Click the **OK command button** to print the document.
- Click the **Print button** on the Standard toolbar to print the document immediately without displaying the Print dialog box.

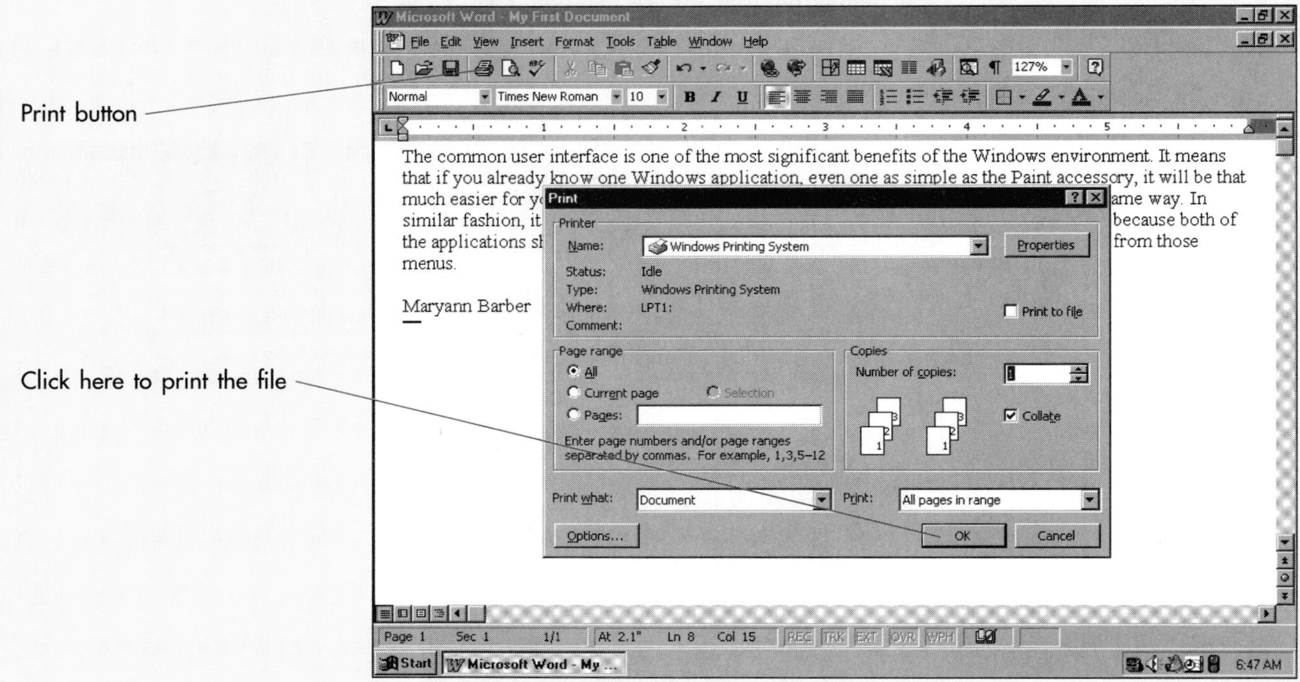

(f) The Print Command (step 7)

FIGURE 1.6 Hands-on Exercise 1 (continued)

> **ABOUT MICROSOFT WORD**
>
> Pull down the Help menu and click About Microsoft Word to display the specific release number and other licensing information, including the product serial number. This help screen also contains two very useful command buttons, System Information and Technical Support. The first button displays information about the hardware installed on your system, including the amount of memory and available space on the hard drive. The Technical Support button provides telephone numbers for technical assistance.

STEP 8: Close the Document

➤ Pull down the **File menu.** Click **Close** to close this document but remain in Word. (Click **Yes** if prompted to save the document.) The document disappears from the screen, but Word is still open.

➤ Pull down the **File menu** a second time. Click **Exit** to close Word if you do not want to continue with the next exercise at this time.

We trust that you completed the hands-on exercise without difficulty, and that you were able to create, save, and print the document in Figure 1.6. There is, however, one area of potential confusion in that Word offers different views of the same document, depending on the preferences of the individual user. It also gives you the option to display (hide) its various toolbars. Thus your screen will not match ours exactly, and, indeed, there is no requirement that it should. The *contents* of the document, however, should be identical to ours.

Figure 1.6 displayed the document in the ***Normal view.*** Figure 1.7 displays an entirely different view called the ***Page Layout view.*** Each view has its advantages. The Normal view is generally faster, but the Page Layout view more closely resembles the printed page as it displays top and bottom margins, headers and footers, graphic elements in their exact position, a vertical ruler, and other elements not seen in the Normal view. The Normal view is preferable only when entering text and editing. The Page Layout view is used to apply the finishing touches and check a document prior to printing. Note, too, that each view can be displayed at different magnifications.

Your screen may or may not match either figure, and you will undoubtedly develop preferences of your own. The following suggestions will help you match the screens of Figure 1.6:

- If the application window for Word does not take the entire screen, and/or the document does not take the entire window within Word, click the Maximize button in the application and/or the document window.

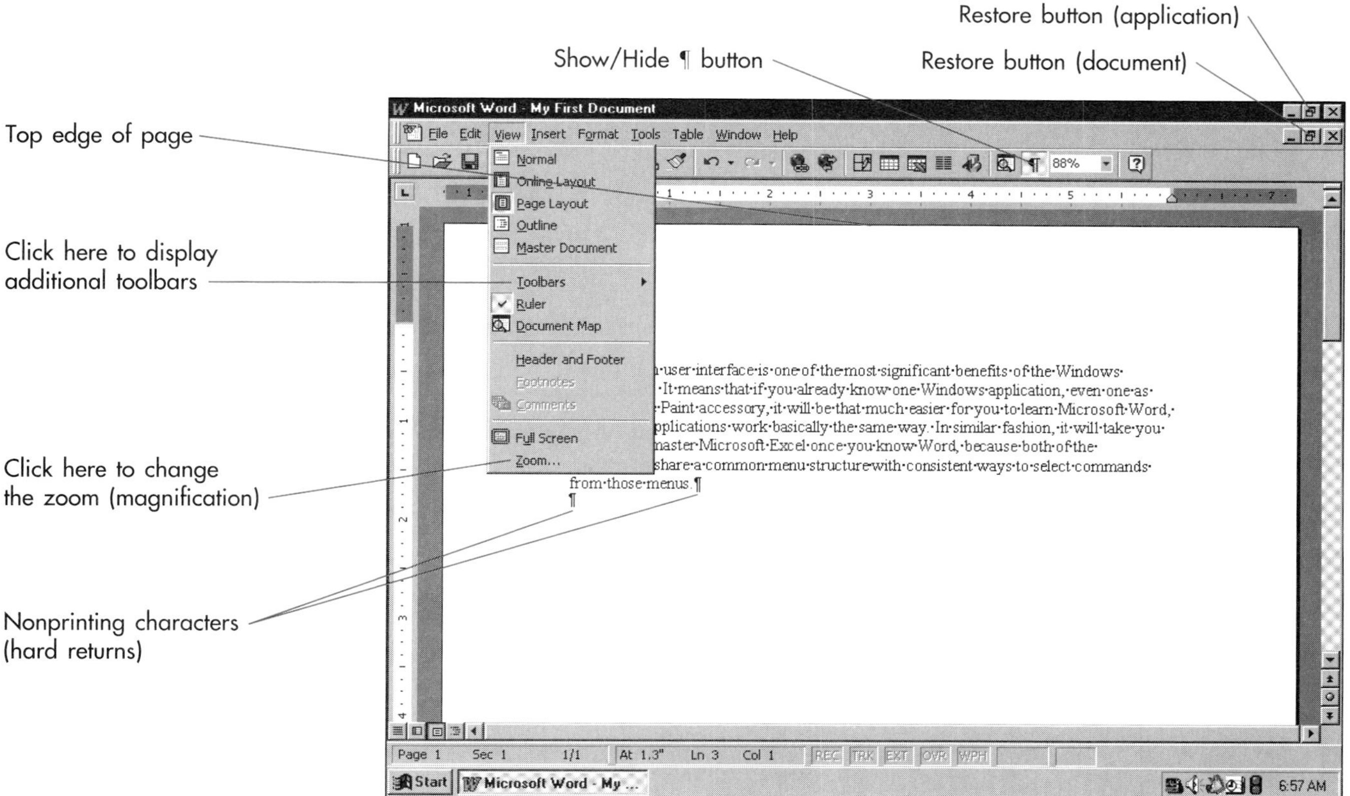

FIGURE 1.7 Troubleshooting

- If the text does not come up to the top of the screen—that is, you see the top edge of the page (as in Figure 1.7)—it means that you are in the Page Layout view instead of the Normal view. Pull down the View menu and click Normal to match the document in Figure 1.6c.
- If the text seems unusually large or small, it means that you or a previous user elected to zoom in or out to get a different perspective on the document. Pull down the View menu, click Zoom, then click Page Width so that the text takes the entire line.
- If you see the ¶ and other nonprinting symbols, it means that you or a previous user elected to display these characters. Click the Show/Hide ¶ button on the Standard toolbar to make the symbols disappear.
- If the Standard or Formatting toolbar is missing and/or a different toolbar is displayed, pull down the View menu, click Toolbars, then click the appropriate toolbars on or off. If the ruler is missing, pull down the View menu and click Ruler.
- The automatic spell check may (or may not) be implemented as indicated by the appearance (absence) of the open book icon on the status bar. If you do not see the icon, pull down the Tools menu, click Options, click the Spelling and Grammar tab, then check the box for Check Spelling as you type.

THE WRONG KEYBOARD

Microsoft Word facilitates conversion from WordPerfect by providing an alternative (software-controlled) keyboard that implements WordPerfect conventions. If you are sharing your machine with others, and if various keyboard shortcuts do not work as expected, it could be because someone else has implemented the WordPerfect keyboard. Pull down the Tools menu, click Options, then click the General tab in the dialog box. Clear the check box next to Navigation keys for WordPerfect users to return to the normal Word keyboard.

HANDS-ON EXERCISE 2

Modifying an Existing Document

Objective: To open an existing document, revise it, and save the revision. To demonstrate the Undo command and online help. Use Figure 1.8 as a guide in doing the exercise.

STEP 1: Open an Existing Document

- Click the **Start menu.** Click (or point to) the **Program menu,** then click **Microsoft Word** to start the program. Close the Office Assisant if it appears.
- Maximize the application window (if necessary). Maximize the document window as well.
- Pull down the **File menu** and click **Open** (or click the **Open button** on the Standard toolbar). You should see a dialog box similar to the one in Figure 1.8a. (The Exploring Word folder is not yet selected.)

➤ To open a file:

- Click the **Details button** to change to the Details view. Click and drag the vertical border between columns to increase (or decrease) the size of a column.
- Click the **drop-down arrow** on the Look In list box.
- Click the appropriate drive, drive C or drive A, depending on the location of your data.
- Double click the **Exploring Word folder** to make it the active folder (the folder in which you will save the document).
- Click the **down arrow** in the Name list box, then scroll until you can select **My First Document** from the first exercise. Click the **Open command button** to open the file.

➤ Your document should appear on the screen.

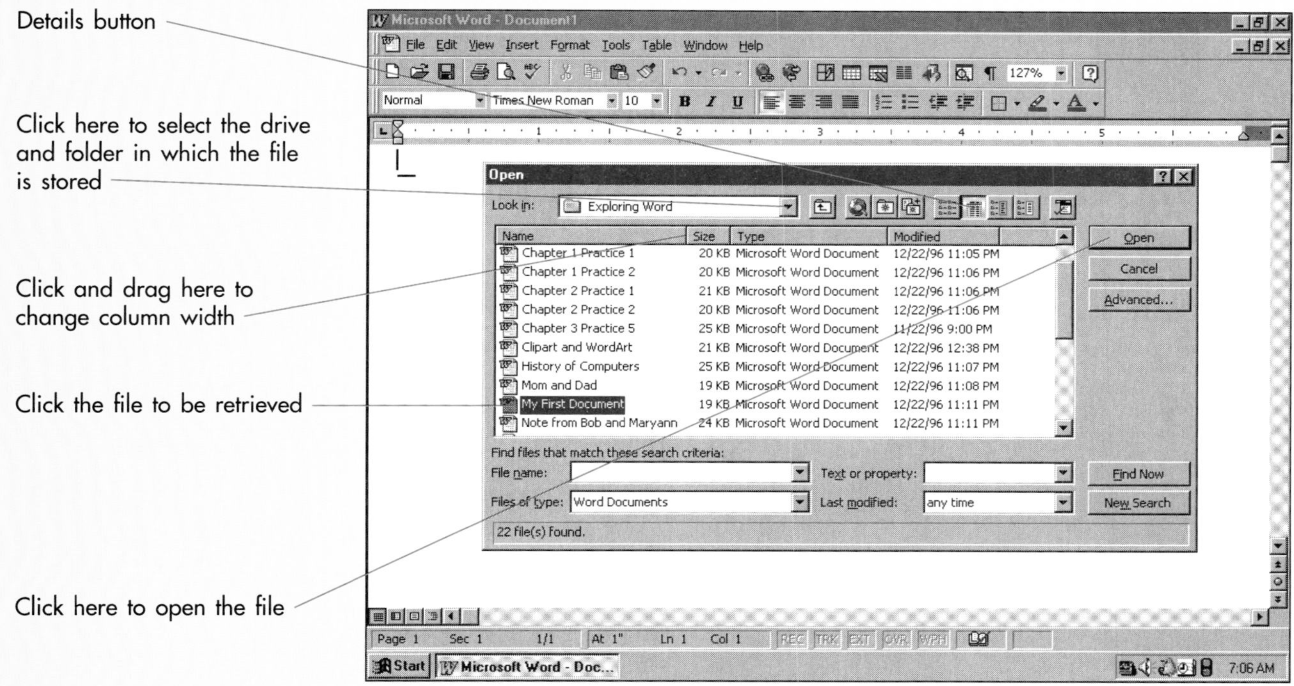

(a) The Open Command (step 1)

FIGURE 1.8 Hands-on Exercise 2

THE MOST RECENTLY OPENED FILE LIST

The easiest way to open a recently used document is to select the document directly from the File menu. Pull down the File menu, but instead of clicking the Open command, check to see if the document appears on the list of the most recently opened documents at the bottom of the menu. If so, you can click the document name rather than having to make the appropriate selections through the Open dialog box.

STEP 2: The View Menu (Troubleshooting)

➤ Modify the settings within Word so that the appearance of your document matches Figure 1.8b.

- To change to the Normal view, pull down the **View menu** and click **Normal** (or click the **Normal View** button at the bottom of the window).
- To change the amount of text that is visible on the screen, click the **drop-down arrow** on the Zoom Control box on the Standard toolbar and select **Page Width.**
- To display (hide) the ruler, pull down the **View menu** and toggle the **Ruler command** on or off. End with the ruler on.

➤ There may still be subtle differences between your screen and ours, depending on the resolution of your monitor. These variations, if any, need not concern you at all as long as you are able to complete the exercise.

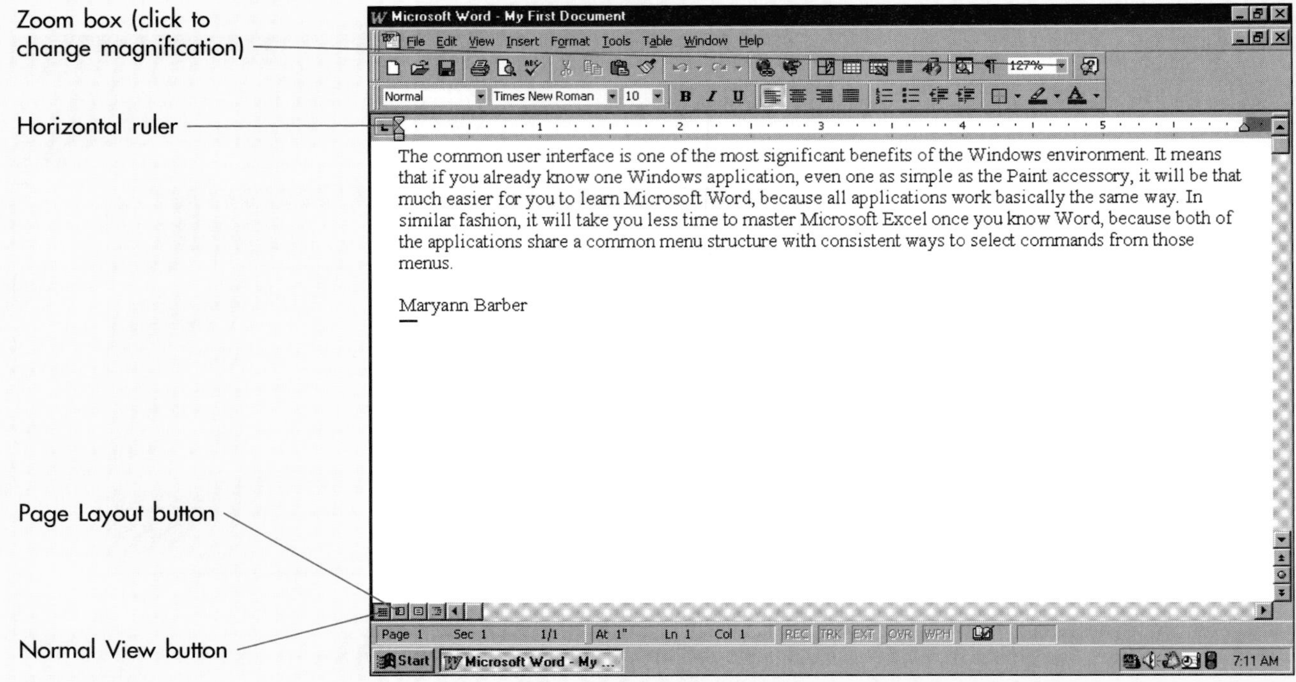

(b) The View Menu (step 2)

FIGURE 1.8 Hands-on Exercise 2 (continued)

DISPLAY (HIDE) TOOLBARS WITH THE RIGHT MOUSE BUTTON

Point to any visible toolbar, then click the right mouse button to display a shortcut menu listing the available toolbars. Click the individual toolbars on or off as appropriate. If no toolbars are visible, pull down the View menu, click Toolbars, then display or hide the desired toolbars.

STEP 3: Display the Hard Returns

- The **Show/Hide ¶** button on the Standard toolbar functions as a toggle switch to display (hide) the hard returns (and other nonprinting characters) in a document.
- Click the **Show/Hide ¶ button** to display the hard returns as in Figure 1.8c. Click the **Show/Hide ¶ button** a second time to hide the nonprinting characters. Display or hide the paragraph markers as you see fit.

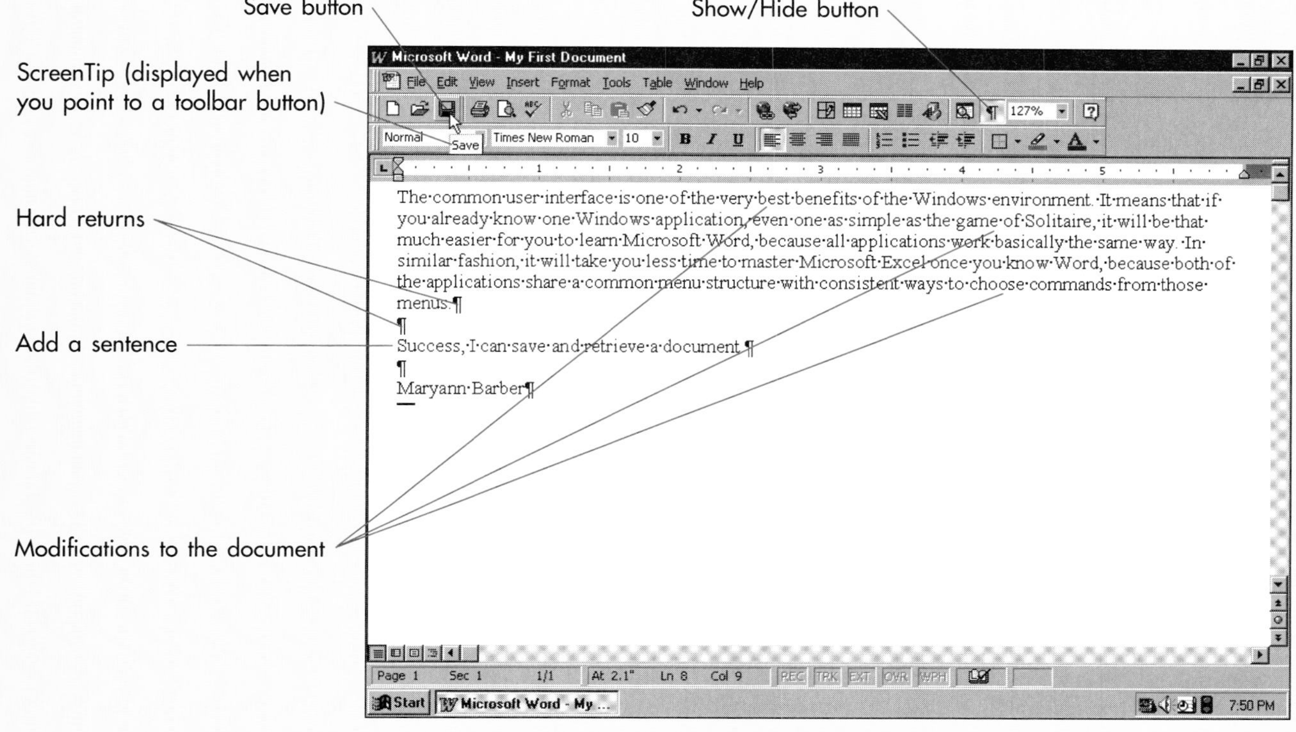

(c) Modify the Document (steps 3 and 4)

FIGURE 1.8 Hands-on Exercise 2 (continued)

SCREENTIPS

Point to any button on any toolbar and Word displays a ScreenTip containing the name of the button to indicate its function. If pointing to a button has no effect, pull down the View menu, click Toolbars, then click Customize to display the Customize dialog box. Click the Options tab, check the box to Show ScreenTips on Toolbars, then close the dialog box.

STEP 4: Modify the Document

- Press **Ctrl+End** to move to the end of the document. Press the **up arrow key** once or twice until the insertion point is on a blank line above your name. If necessary, press the **enter key** once (or twice) to add blank line(s).
- Add the sentence, **Success, I can save and retrieve a document!,** as shown in Figure 1.8c.

- Make the following additional modifications to practice editing:
  - Change the phrase *most significant* to **very best.**
  - Change *Paint accessory* to **game of Solitaire.**
  - Change the word *select* to **choose.**
- Switch between the insert and overtype modes as necessary. Double click the **OVR indicator** on the status bar to toggle between the insert and overtype modes.

MOVING WITHIN A DOCUMENT

Press Ctrl+Home and Ctrl+End to move to the beginning and end of a document, respectively. These shortcuts work not just in Word, but in any other Windows application, and are worth remembering as they allow your hands to remain on the keyboard as you type.

STEP 5: Save the Changes

- It is very, very important to save your work repeatedly during a session so that you do not lose it all in the event of a power failure or other unforeseen event.
- Pull down the **File menu** and click **Save,** or click the **Save button** on the Standard toolbar. You will not see the Save As dialog box because the document is saved automatically under the existing name (My First Document).

KEEP DUPLICATE COPIES OF IMPORTANT FILES

It is absolutely critical to maintain duplicate copies of important files on a separate disk stored away from the computer. In addition, you should print each new document at the end of every session, saving it before printing (power failures happen when least expected—for example, during the print operation). Hard copy is not as good as a duplicate disk, but it is better than nothing.

STEP 6: Selecting Text

- Point to the first letter in the first sentence. Press and hold the left mouse button as you drag the mouse over the first sentence. Release the mouse.
- The sentence should remain selected as shown in Figure 1.8d. The selected text is the text that will be affected by the next command. Click anywhere else in the document to deselect the text.
- Point to any word in the first sentence, then press and hold the **Ctrl key** as you click the mouse, to select the entire sentence. Press the **Del key** to delete the selected text (the first sentence) from the document.

Click and drag over the first sentence to select it

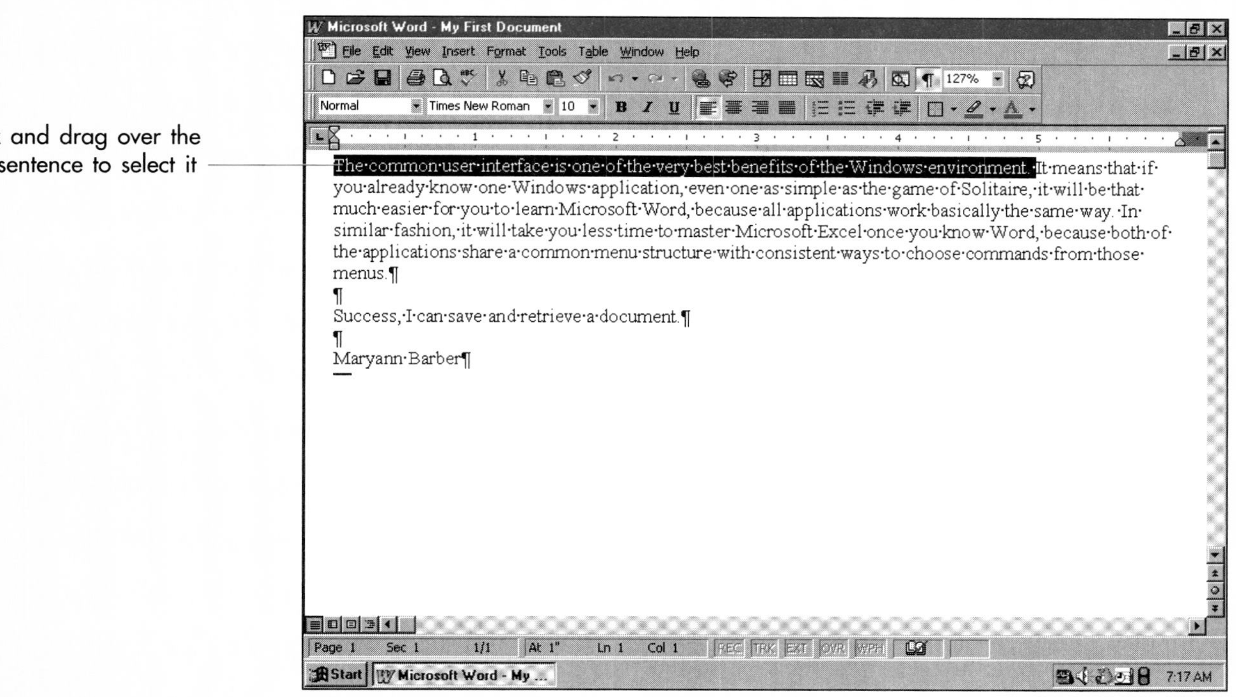

(d) Selecting Text (step 6)

FIGURE 1.8 Hands-on Exercise 2 (continued)

PICK UP THE MOUSE

It seems that you always run out of room on your real desk, just when you need to move the mouse a little further. The solution is to pick up the mouse and move it closer to you—the pointer will stay in its present position on the screen, but when you put the mouse down, you will have more room on your desk in which to work.

STEP 7: The Undo Command

➤ Pull down the **Edit menu** as shown in Figure 1.8e. Click **Undo** to reverse (undo) the last command.

100 LEVELS OF UNDO

The ***Undo command*** is present in Word as it is in every Windows application. Incredible as it sounds, however, Word enables you to undo the last 100 changes to a document. Click the drop-down arrow next to the Undo button to produce a list of your previous actions. (The most recent command is listed first.) Click the action you want to undo, which also undoes all of the preceding commands. Undoing the fifth command in the list, for example, will also undo the preceding four commands.

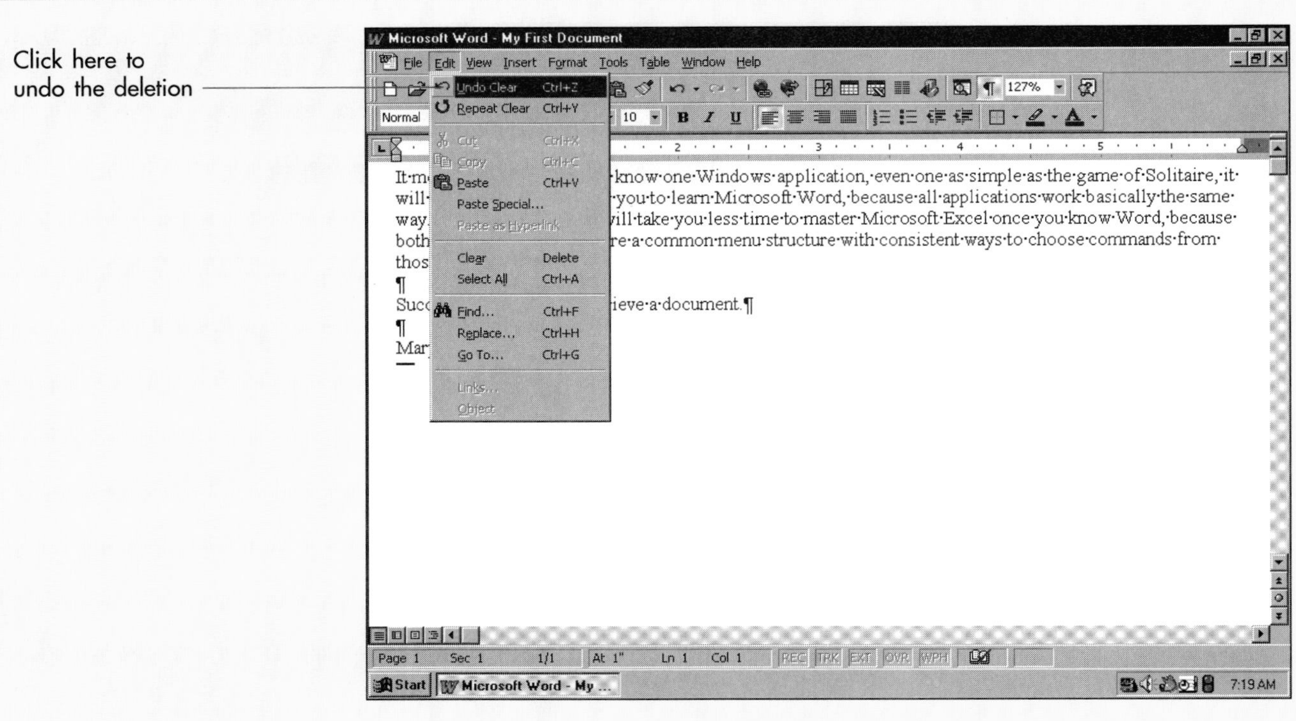

(e) The Undo Command (step 7)

FIGURE 1.8 Hands-on Exercise 2 (continued)

- The deleted text should be returned to your document. The Undo command is a tremendous safety net and can be used at almost any time.
- Click anywhere outside the selected text to deselect the sentence.

STEP 8: The Help Menu

- Pull down the **Help menu.** Click **Contents and Index** to display the Help topics window in Figure 1.8f.
- Click the **Index tab.** Type **Undo** (the topic you wish to look up). The Undo topic is automatically selected.
- Click **Display** to show a second help screen with detailed information.
- Click the **Close button** to close the Help window.

TIPS FROM THE OFFICE ASSISTANT

The Office Assistant indicates it has a suggestion by displaying a lightbulb. Click the lightbulb to display the tip, then click the Back or Next button as appropriate to view additional tips. The Assistant will not, however, repeat a tip from an earlier session unless you reset it at the start of a new session. This is especially important to remember in a laboratory situation where you are sharing a computer with other students. To reset the tips, click the Assistant to display a balloon asking what you want to do, click the Options button in the balloon, click Options, then click the button to Reset My Tips.

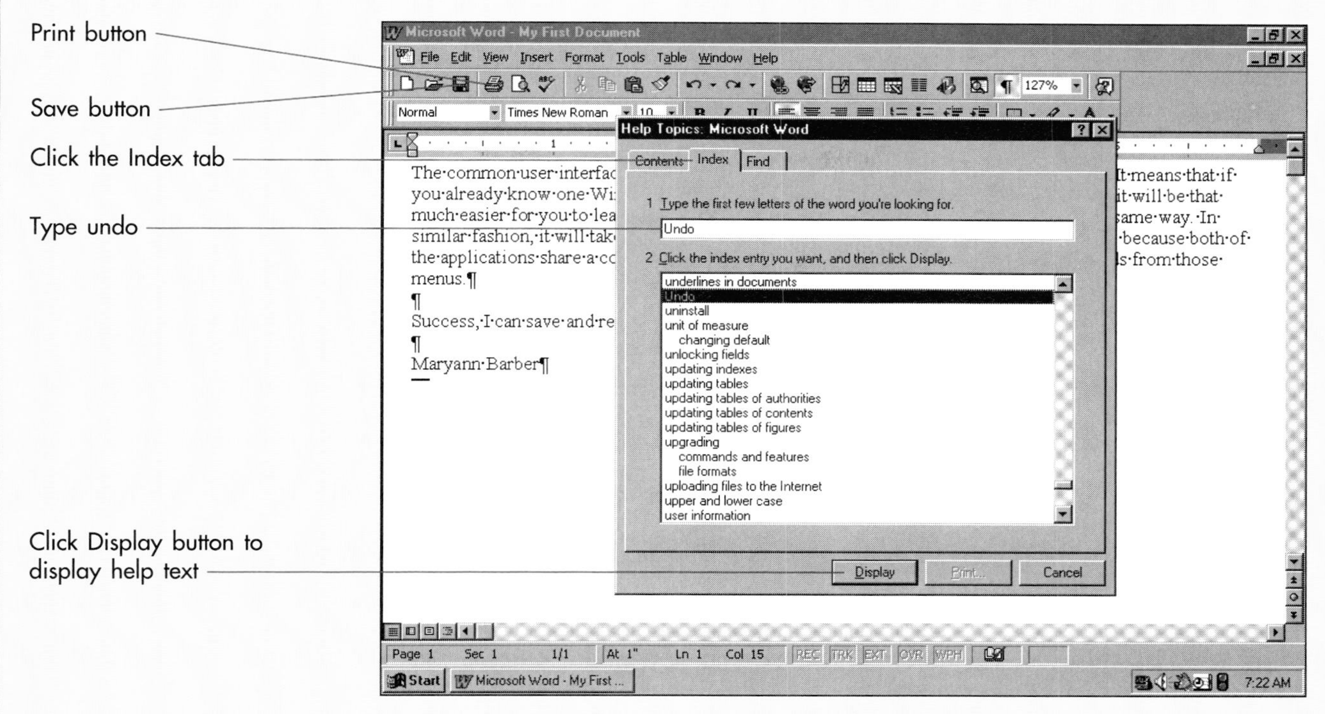

(f) The Help Menu (step 8)

FIGURE 1.8 Hands-on Exercise 2 (continued)

STEP 9: Print the Revised Document

- Click the **Save button** on the Standard toolbar to save the revised document a final time.
- Click the **Print button** to print the document. Submit the printed document to your instructor as proof you did Hands-on Exercises 1 and 2.
- Pull down the **File menu.** Click **Close** to close the document and remain in Word. Click **Exit** if you do not want to continue with the next exercise at this time.

DOCUMENT PROPERTIES

Prove to your instructor how hard you've worked by printing various statistics about your document, including the number of revisions and the total editing time. Pull down the File menu, click the Print command to display the Print dialog box, click the drop down arrow in the Print What list box, select Document properties, then click OK. You can view the information (without printing) by pulling down the File menu, clicking the Properties command, then selecting the Statistics tab from the resulting dialog box.

There is simply no excuse to misspell a word, since the ***spell check*** is an integral part of Microsoft Word. (The spell check is also available for every other application in the Microsoft Office.) Spelling errors make your work look sloppy and discourage the reader before he or she has read what you had to say. They can cost you a job, a grade, a lucrative contract, or an award you deserve.

The spell check can be set to automatically check a document as text is entered, or it can be called explicitly by clicking the Spelling and Grammar button on the Standard toolbar. The spell check compares each word in a document to the entries in a built-in dictionary, then flags any word that is in the document, but not in the built-in dictionary, as an error.

The dictionary included with Microsoft Office is limited to standard English and does not include many proper names, acronyms, abbreviations, or specialized terms, and hence, the use of any such item is considered a misspelling. You can, however, add such words to a ***custom dictionary*** so that they will not be flagged in the future. The spell check will inform you of repeated words and irregular capitalization. It cannot, however, flag properly spelled words that are used improperly, and thus cannot tell you that *Two bee or knot too be* is not the answer.

The capabilities of the spell check are illustrated in conjunction with Figure 1.9a. The spell check goes through the document and returns the errors one at a time, offering several options for each mistake. You can change the misspelled word to one of the alternatives suggested by Word, leave the word as is, or add the word to a custom dictionary.

The first error is the word *embarassing,* with Word's suggestion(s) for correction displayed in the list box in Figure 1.9b. To accept the highlighted suggestion, click the Change command button and the substitution will be made automatically in the document. To accept an alternative suggestion, click the desired word, then click the Change command button. Alternatively, you can click the AutoCorrect button to correct the mistake in the current document, and, in addition, automatically correct the same mistake in any future document.

The spell check detects both irregular capitalization and duplicated words, as shown in Figures 1.9c and 1.9d, respectively. The error in Figure 1.9e, *Grauer,* is not a misspelling per se, but a proper noun not found in the standard dictionary. No correction is required and the appropriate action is to ignore the word (taking no further action)—or better yet, add it to the custom dictionary so that it will not be flagged in future sessions. And finally, we could not resist including the example in Figure 1.9f, which shows another use of the spell check. (It's included for devotees of crossword puzzles who need a five-letter word beginning with *s* and ending with *n.*)

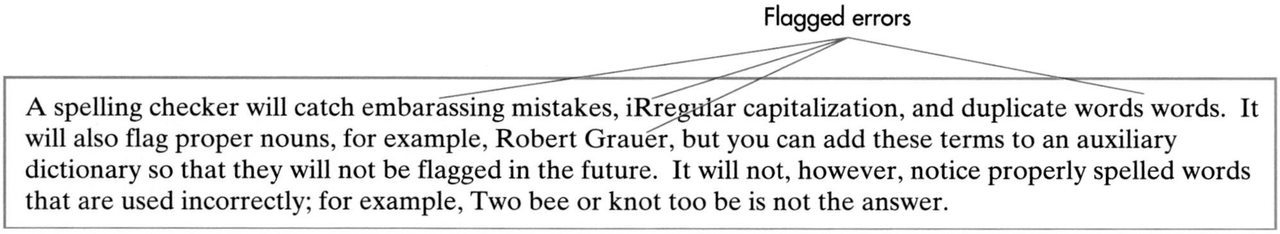

Flagged errors
A spelling checker will catch embarassing mistakes, iRregular capitalization, and duplicate words words. It will also flag proper nouns, for example, Robert Grauer, but you can add these terms to an auxiliary dictionary so that they will not be flagged in the future. It will not, however, notice properly spelled words that are used incorrectly; for example, Two bee or knot too be is not the answer.

(a) The Text

FIGURE 1.9 The Spell Check

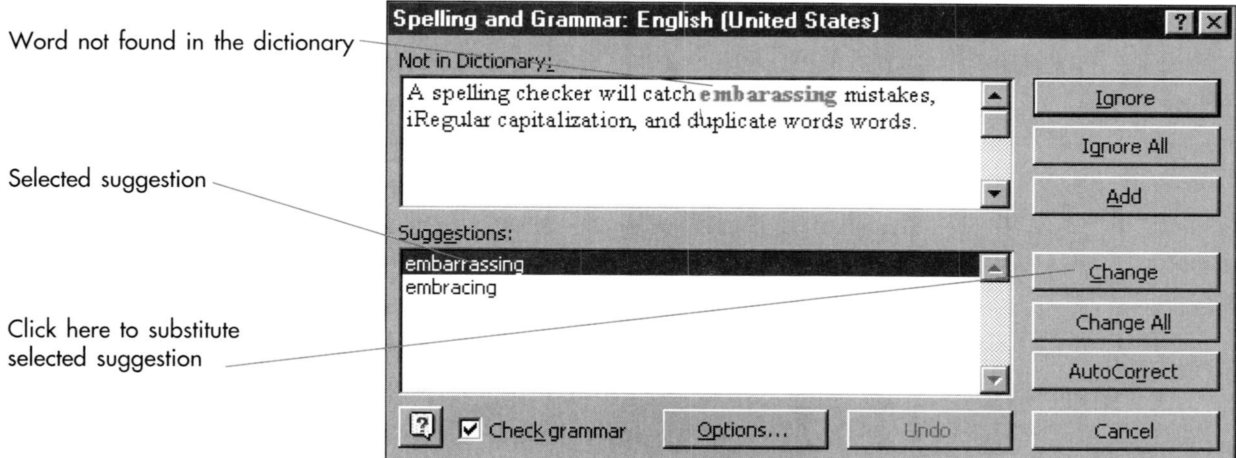

(b) Ordinary Misspelling

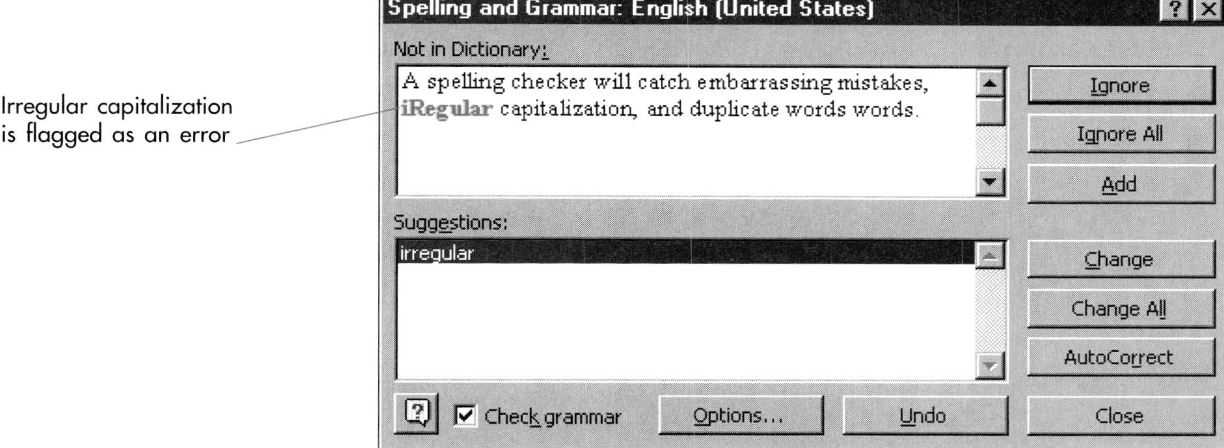

(c) Irregular Capitalization

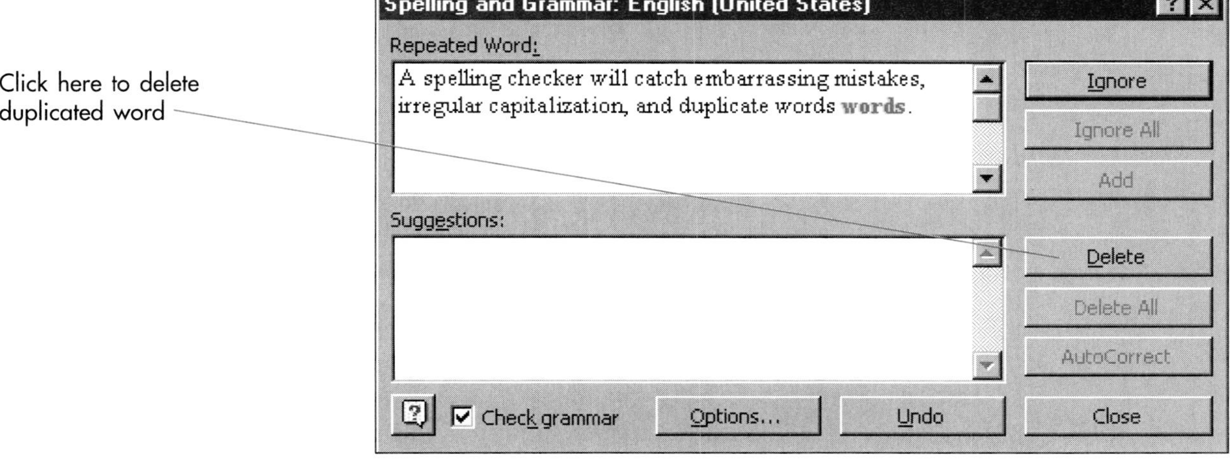

(d) Duplicated Word

FIGURE 1.9 The Spell Check (continued)

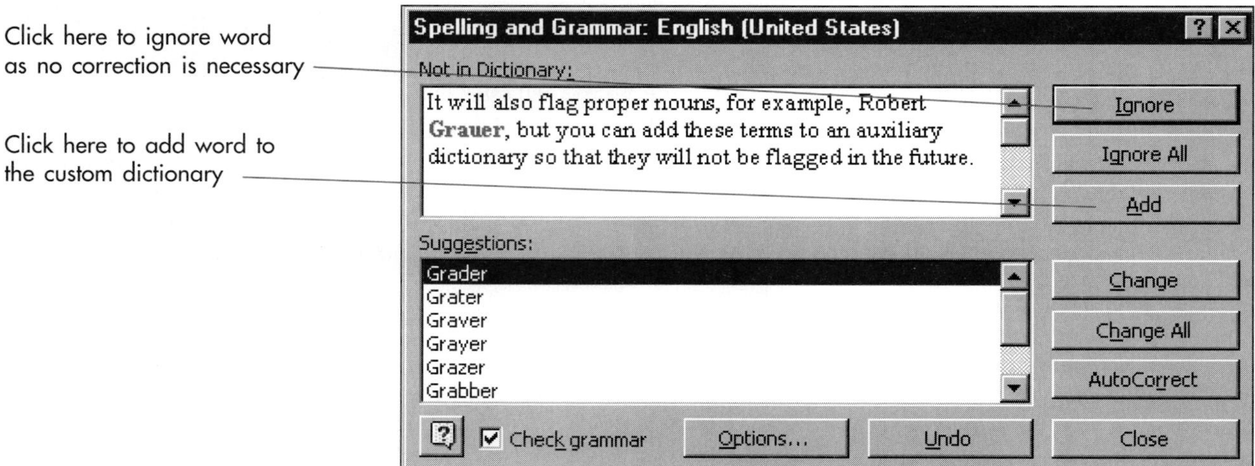

(e) Proper Noun

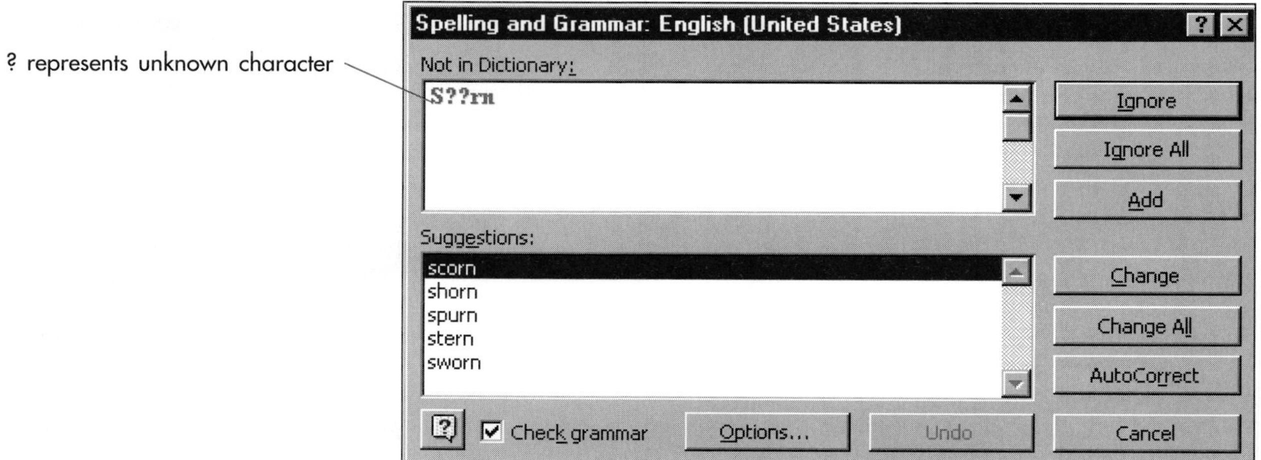

(f) Help with Crosswords

FIGURE 1.9 The Spell Check (continued)

AutoCorrect

The ***AutoCorrect*** feature corrects mistakes as they are made without any effort on your part. It makes you a better typist. If, for example, you typed *teh* instead of *the,* Word would change the spelling without even telling you. Word will also change *adn* to *and, i* to *I,* and occu*r*ence to occu*rr*ence.

Microsoft Word includes a predefined table of common mistakes and uses that table to make substitutions whenever it encounters an error it recognizes. You can add additional items to the table to include the frequent errors you make. You can also use the feature to define your own shorthand—for example, cis for Computer Information Systems as shown in Figure 1.10.

The AutoCorrect will also correct mistakes in capitalization; for example, it will capitalize the first letter in a sentence, recognize that MIami should be Miami, and capitalize the days of the week. It's even smart enough to correct the accidental use of the Caps Lock key, and it will toggle the key off!

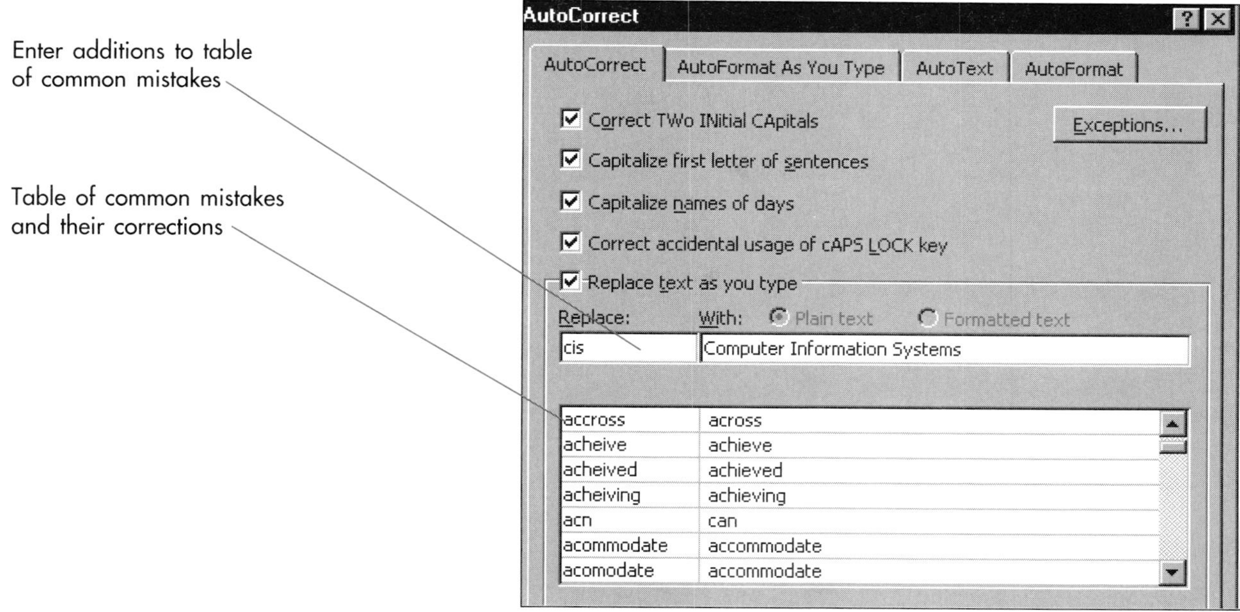

FIGURE 1.10 AutoCorrect

THESAURUS

Mark Twain said the difference between the right word and almost the right word is the difference between a lightning bug and lightning. The ***thesaurus*** is an important tool in any word processor and is both fun and educational. It helps you to avoid repetition, and it will polish your writing.

The thesaurus is called from the Language command in the Tools menu. You position the cursor at the appropriate word within the document, then invoke the thesaurus and follow your instincts. The thesaurus recognizes multiple meanings and forms of a word (for example, adjective, noun, and verb) as in Figure 1.11a, and (by double clicking) allows you to look up any listed meaning to produce additional choices as in Figure 1.11b. You can explore further alternatives by selecting a synonym and clicking the Look Up button. The thesaurus also provides a list of antonyms for most entries, as in Figure 1.11c.

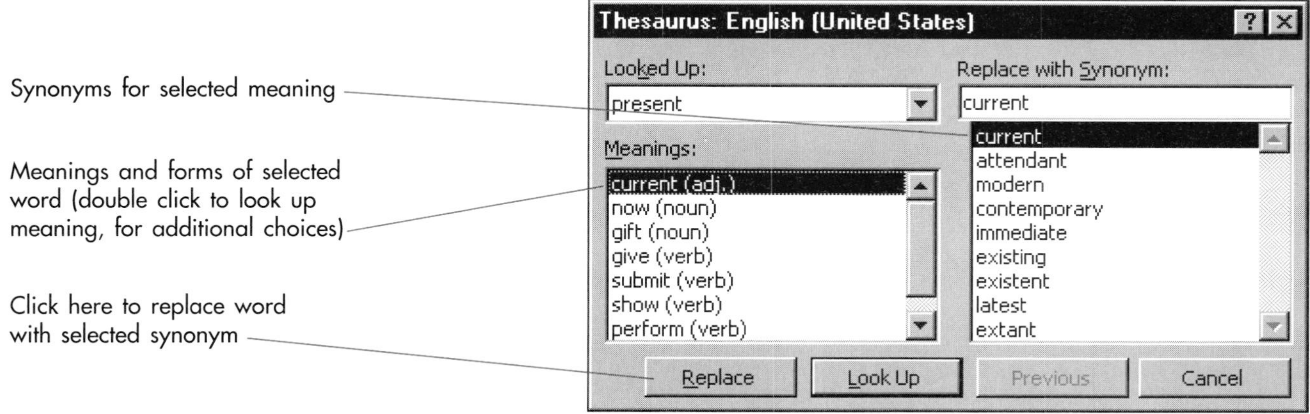

(a) Initial Word

FIGURE 1.11 The Thesaurus

Additional choices produced by double clicking selected meaning

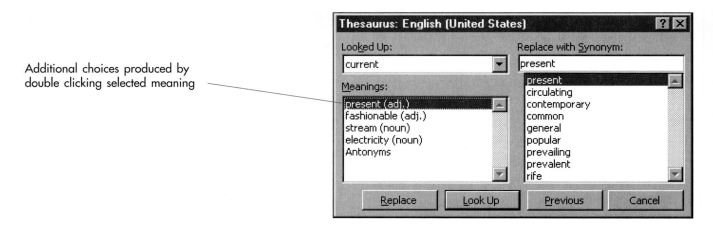

(b) Additional Choices

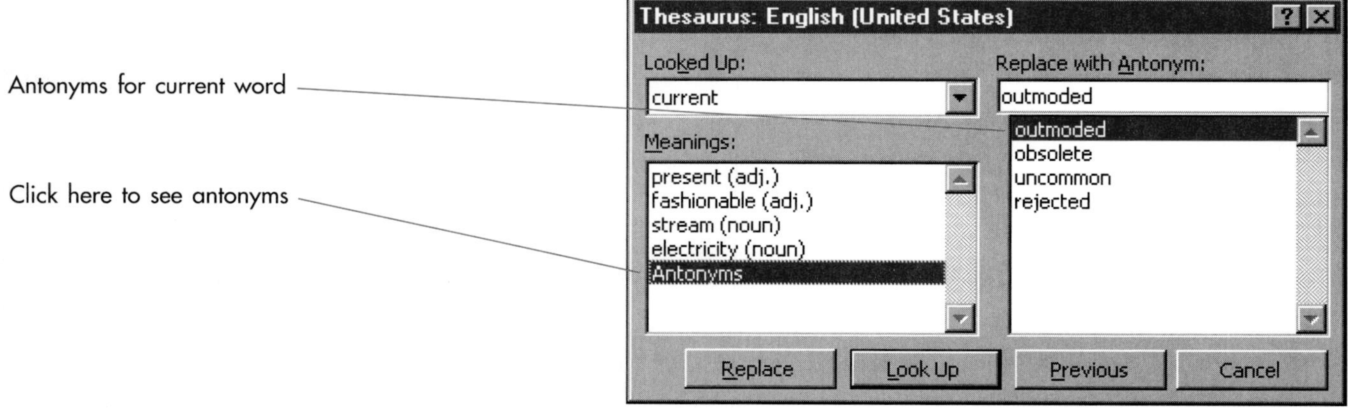

(c) Antonyms

FIGURE 1.11 The Thesaurus (continued)

GRAMMAR CHECK

The ***grammar check*** attempts to catch mistakes in punctuation, writing style, and word usage by comparing strings of text within a document to a series of predefined rules. As with the spell check, errors are brought to the screen where you can accept the suggested correction and make the replacement automatically, or more often, edit the selected text and make your own changes.

You can also ask the grammar check to explain the rule it is attempting to enforce. Unlike the spell check, the grammar check is subjective, and what seems appropriate to you may be objectionable to someone else. Indeed, the grammar check is quite flexible, and can be set to check for different writing styles; that is, you can implement one set of rules to check a business letter and a different set of rules for casual writing. Many times, however, you will find that the English language is just too complex for the grammar check to detect every error, although it will find many errors.

The grammar check caught the inconsistency between subject and verb in Figure 1.12a and suggested the appropriate correction (am instead of are). In Figure 1.12b, it suggested the elimination of the superfluous comma. These examples show the grammar check at its best, but it is often more subjective and less capable. It detected the error in Figure 1.12c, for example, but suggested an inappropriate correction, “to complicate” as opposed to “too complicated”. Suffice it to say, that there is no substitute for carefully proofreading every document.

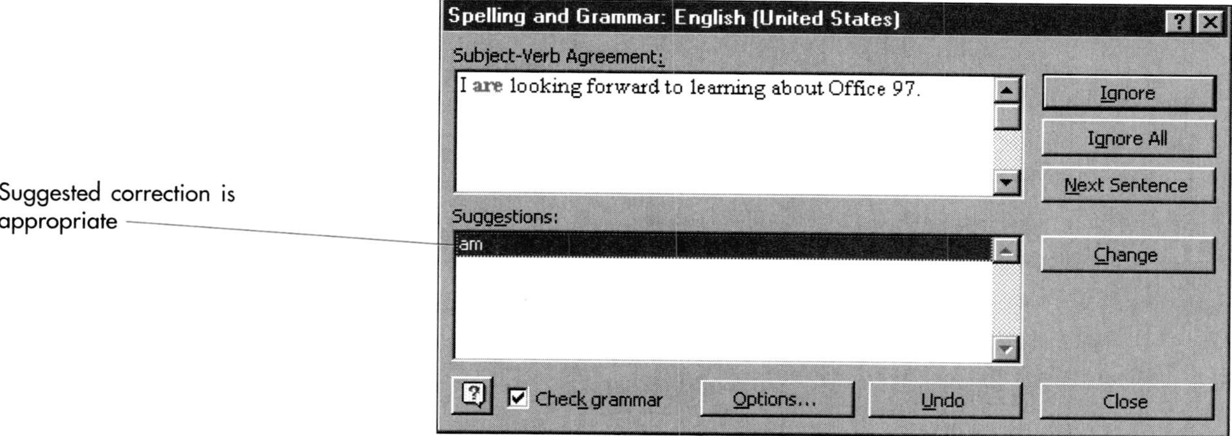

(a) Inconsistent Verb

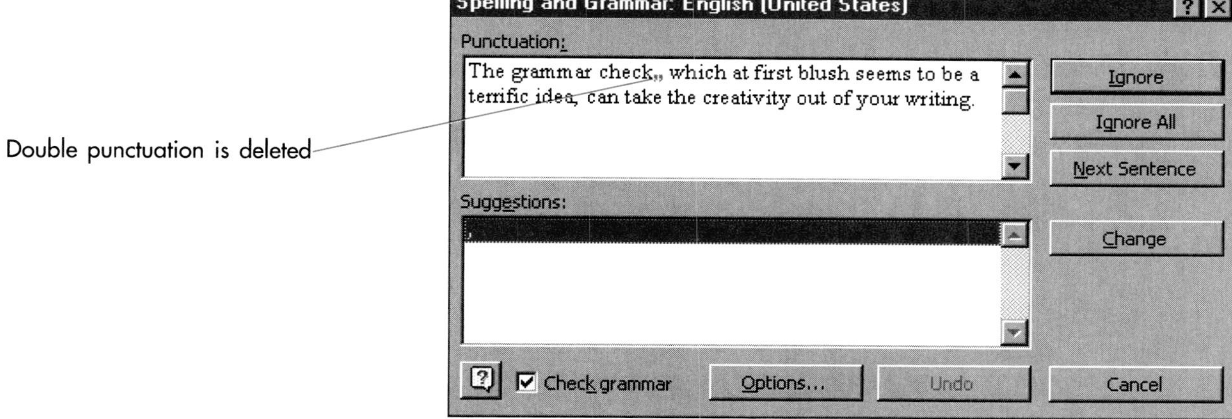

(b) Doubled Punctuation

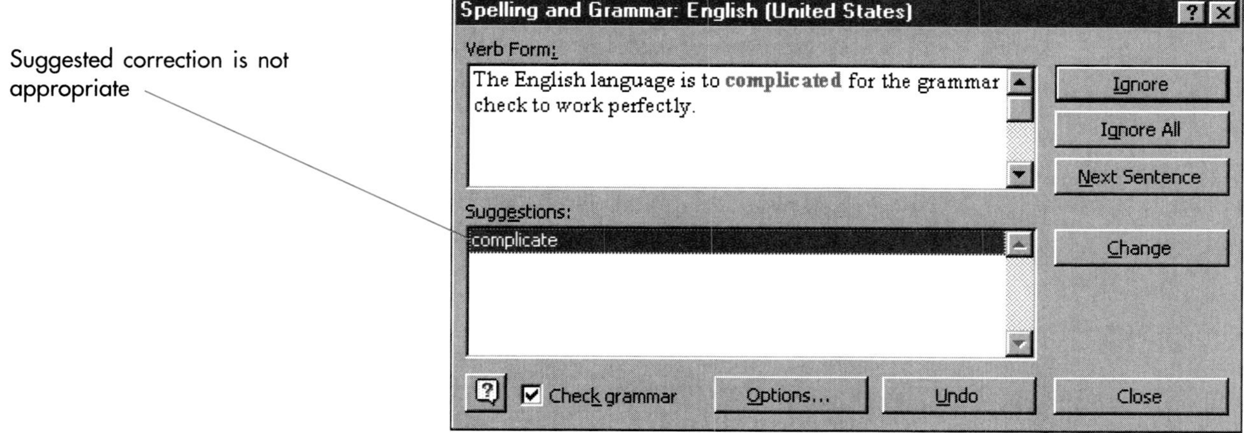

(c) Limitations

FIGURE 1.12 The Grammar Check

The Save command was used in the first two exercises. The Save As command will be introduced in the next exercise as a very useful alternative. We also introduce you to different backup options. We believe that now, when you are first starting to learn about word processing, is the time to develop good working habits.

You already know that the Save command copies the document currently being edited (the document in memory) to disk. The initial execution of the command requires you to assign a file name and to specify the drive and folder in which the file is to be stored. All subsequent executions of the Save command save the document under the original name, replacing the previously saved version with the new one.

The ***Save As command*** saves another copy of a document under a different name (and/or a different file type), and is useful when you want to retain a copy of the original document. The Save As command provides you with two copies of a document. The original document is kept on disk under its original name. A copy of the document is saved on disk under a new name and remains in memory. All subsequent editing is done on the new document.

We cannot overemphasize the importance of periodically saving a document, so that if something does go wrong, you won't lose all of your work. Nothing is more frustrating than to lose two hours of effort, due to an unexpected program crash or to a temporary loss of power. Save your work frequently, at least once every 15 minutes. Pull down the File menu and click Save, or click the Save button on the Standard toolbar. Do it!

QUIT WITHOUT SAVING

There will be times when you do not want to save the changes to a document, such as when you have edited it beyond recognition and wish you had never started. Pull down the File menu and click the Close command, then click No in response to the message asking whether you want to save the changes to the document. Pull down the File menu and reopen the file (it should be the first file in the list of most recently edited documents), then start over from the beginning.

Backup Options

Microsoft Word offers several different ***backup*** options. We believe the two most important options are to create a backup copy in conjunction with every save command, and to periodically (and automatically) save a document. Both options are implemented in step 3 in the next hands-on exercise.

Figure 1.13 illustrates the option to create a backup copy of the document every time a Save command is executed. Assume, for example, that you have created the simple document, *The fox jumped over the fence* and saved it under the name "Fox". Assume further that you edit the document to read, *The quick brown fox jumped over the fence,* and that you saved it a second time. The second save command changes the name of the original document from "Fox" to "Backup of Fox", then saves the current contents of memory as "Fox". In other words, the disk now contains two versions of the document: the current version "Fox" and the most recent previous version "Backup of Fox".

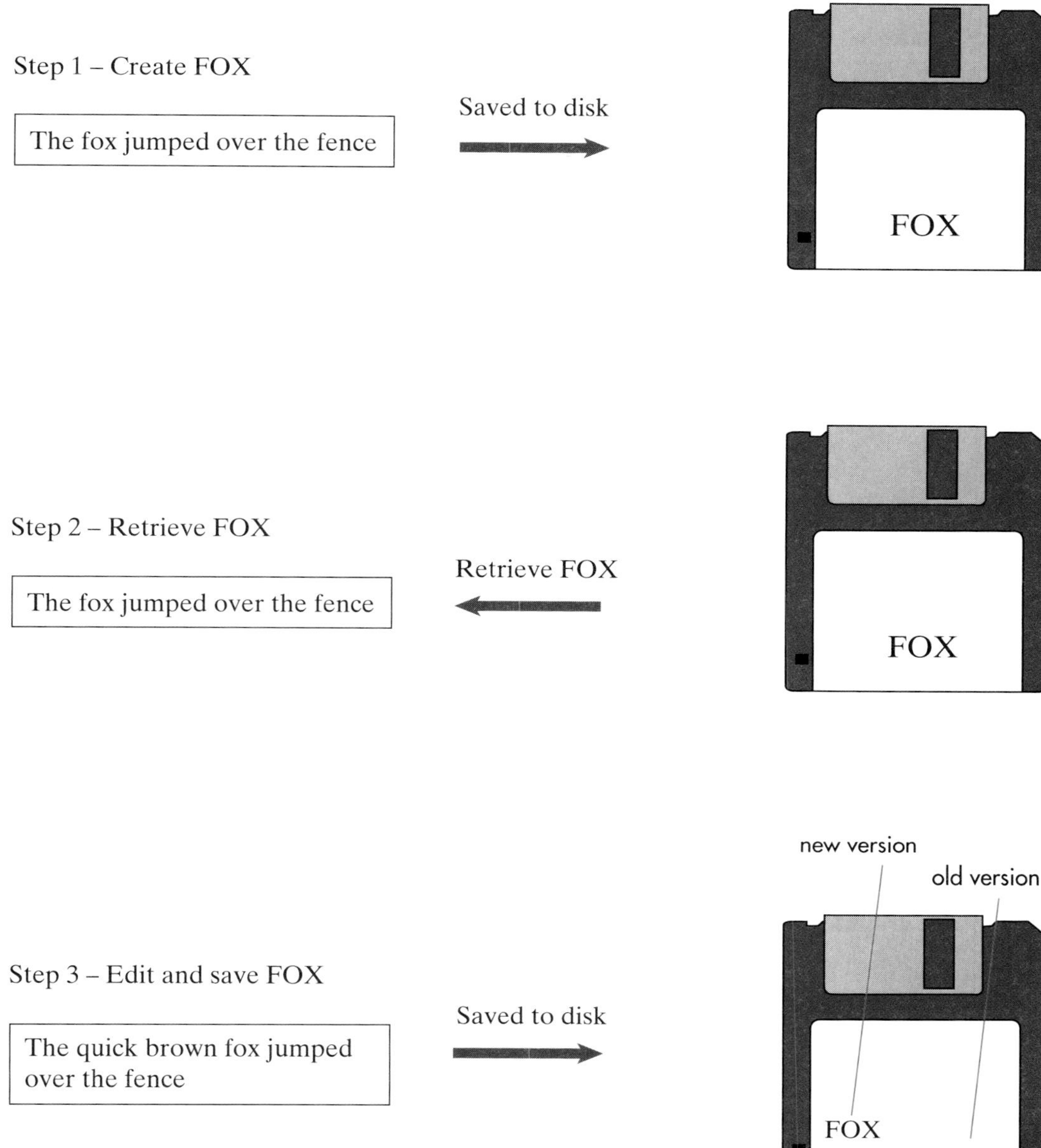

FIGURE 1.13 Backup Procedures

The cycle goes on indefinitely, with "Fox" always containing the current version, and "Backup of Fox" the most recent previous version. Thus if you revise and save the document a third time, "Fox" will contain the latest revision while "Backup of Fox" would contain the previous version alluding to the quick brown fox. The original (first) version of the document disappears entirely since only two versions are kept.

The contents of "Fox" and "Backup of Fox" are different, but the existence of the latter enables you to retrieve the previous version if you inadvertently edit beyond repair or accidentally erase the current "Fox" version. Should this occur (and it will), you can always retrieve its predecessor and at least salvage your work prior to the last save operation.

HANDS-ON EXERCISE 3

The Spell Check

Objective: To open an existing document, check it for spelling, then use the Save As command to save the document under a different file name. Use Figure 1.14 as a guide in the exercise.

STEP 1: Preview a Document

- Start Microsoft Word. Pull down the **File menu** and click **Open** (or click the **Open button** on the Standard toolbar). You should see a dialog box similar to the one in Figure 1.14a.
- Select the appropriate drive, drive C or drive A, depending on the location of your data. Double click the **Exploring Word folder** to make it the active folder (the folder in which you will save the document).
- Scroll in the Name list box until you can select (click) the **Try the Spell Check** document. Click the **Preview button** on the toolbar to preview the document as shown in Figure 1.14a.
- Click the **Open command button** to open the file. Your document should appear on the screen.

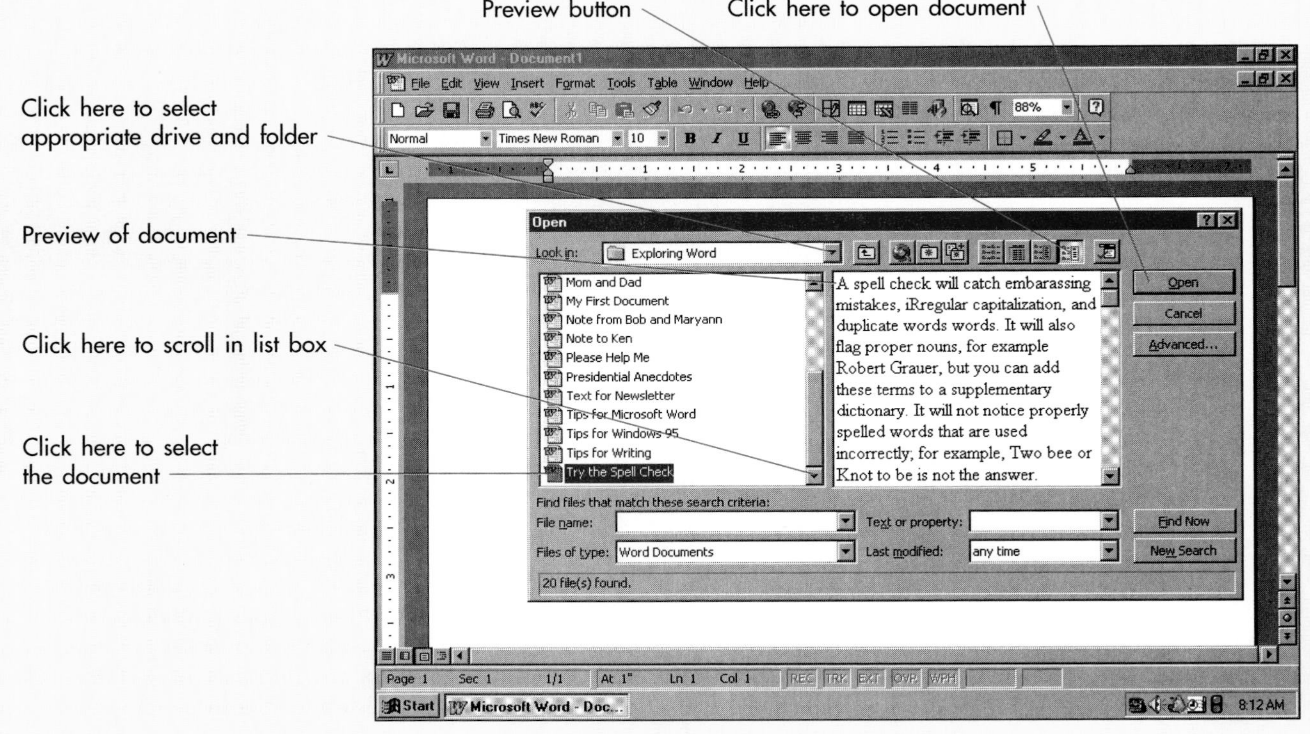

(a) Preview a Document (step 1)

FIGURE 1.14 Hands-on Exercise 3

STEP 2: The Save As Command

- Pull down the **File menu.** Click **Save As** to produce a dialog box in Figure 1.14b.
- Enter **Modified Spell Check** as the name of the new document. (A file name may contain up to 255 characters, and blanks are permitted.) Click the **Save command button.**
- There are now two identical copies of the file on disk: Try the Spell Check, which we supplied, and Modified Spell Check, which you just created. The title bar of the document window shows the latter name.

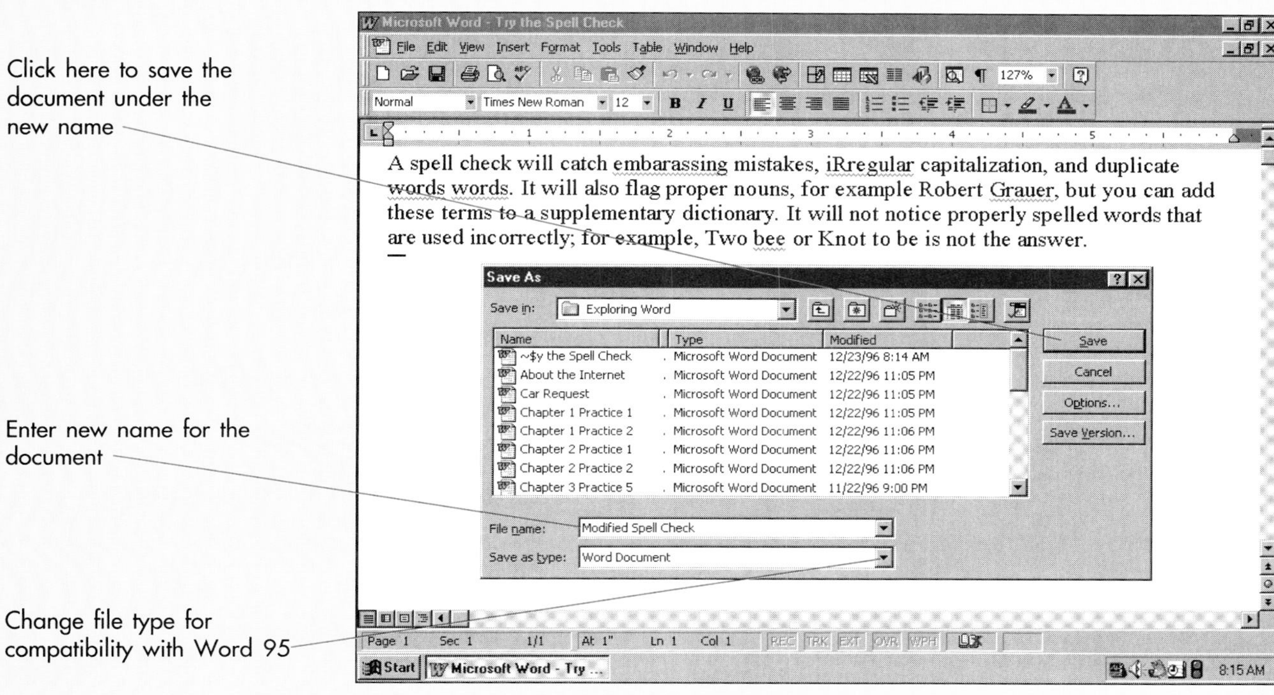

(b) The Save As Command (step 2)

FIGURE 1.14 Hands-on Exercise 3 (continued)

DIFFERENT FILE TYPES

The file format for Word 97 is incompatible with the format for Word 95. The newer release (Word 97) can open a document created in its predecessor (Word 95), but the reverse is not possible; that is, you cannot open a document created in Word 97 in Word 95. You can, however, use the Save As command in Word 97 to specify the Word 6.0/95 file type, enabling you to create a document in the new release and read it in the old (although you will lose any formatting unique to Word 97).

STEP 3: Establish Automatic Backup

- Pull down the **Tools menu.** Click **Options.** Click the **Save tab** to display the dialog box of Figure 1.14c.
- Click the first check box to choose **Always Create Backup Copy.**
- Set the other options as you see fit; for example, you can specify that the document be saved automatically every 10–15 minutes. Click **OK.**

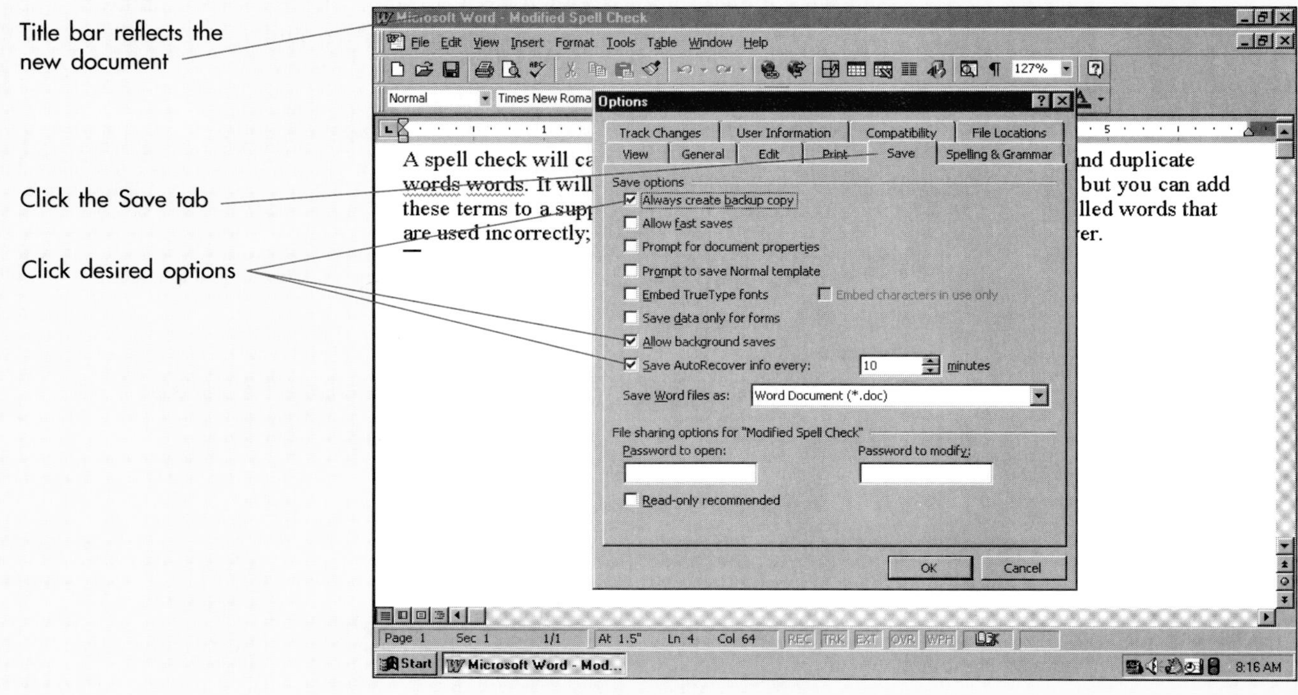

(c) Create a Backup (step 3)

FIGURE 1.14 Hands-on Exercise 3 (continued)

STEP 4: The Spell Check

- If necessary, press **Ctrl+Home** to move to the beginning of the document. Click the **Spelling and Grammar button** on the Standard toolbar to check the document.
- "Embarassing" is flagged as the first misspelling as shown in Figure 1.14d. Click the **Change button** to accept the suggested spelling.
- "iRregular" is flagged as an example of irregular capitalization. Click the **Change button** to accept the suggested correction.
- Continue checking the document, which displays misspellings and other irregularities one at a time. Click the appropriate command button as each mistake is found.
  - Click the **Delete button** to remove the duplicated word.
  - Click the **Ignore button** to accept Grauer (or click the **Add button** to add Grauer to the custom dictionary).
- The grammar check is illustrated in step 5.

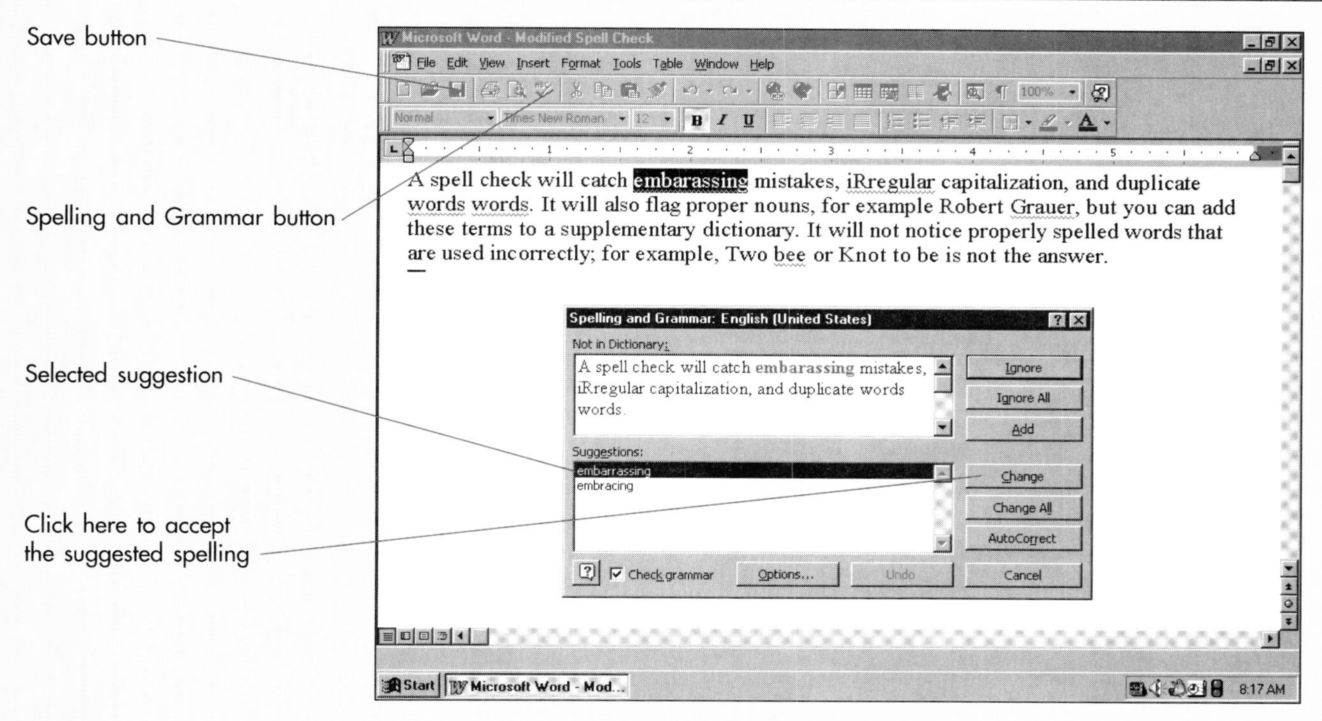
Save button
Spelling and Grammar button
Selected suggestion
Click here to accept the suggested spelling
Microsoft Word - Modified Spell Check
A spell check will catch embarassing mistakes, iRregular capitalization, and duplicate words words. It will also flag proper nouns, for example Robert Grauer, but you can add these terms to a supplementary dictionary. It will not notice properly spelled words that are used incorrectly; for example, Two bee or Knot to be is not the answer.
Spelling and Grammar: English (United States)
Not in Dictionary:
A spell check will catch embarassing mistakes, iRregular capitalization, and duplicate words words.
Suggestions:
embarrassing
embracing
Ignore
Ignore All
Add
Change
Change All
AutoCorrect
Check grammar
Options...
Undo
Cancel
Start
Microsoft Word - Mod...
8:17 AM

(d) The Spell Check (step 4)

FIGURE 1.14 Hands-on Exercise 3 (continued)

> **AUTOMATIC SPELLING AND GRAMMAR CHECKING**
>
> Red and green wavy lines may appear throughout a document to indicate spelling and grammatical errors, respectively. Point to any underlined word, then click the right mouse button to display a context-sensitive help menu with suggested corrections. To enable (disable) these options, pull down the Tools menu, click the Options command, click the Spelling and Grammar tab, and check (clear) the options to check spelling (or grammar) as you type.

STEP 5: The Grammar Check

- The last sentence, "Two bee or knot to be is not the answer", should be flagged as an error, as shown in Figure 1.14e. If this is not the case:
  - Pull down the **Tools menu,** click **Options,** then click the **Spelling and Grammar tab.**
  - Check the box to **Check Grammar with Spelling,** then click the button to **Recheck document.** Click **Yes** when told that the spelling and grammar check will be reset, then click **OK** to close the Options dialog box.
  - Press **Ctrl+Home** to return to the beginning of the document, then click the **Spelling and Grammar button** to recheck the document.
- Click the **Assistant button** in the Spelling and Grammar dialog box for an explanation of the error. The Office Assistant will appear, indicating that

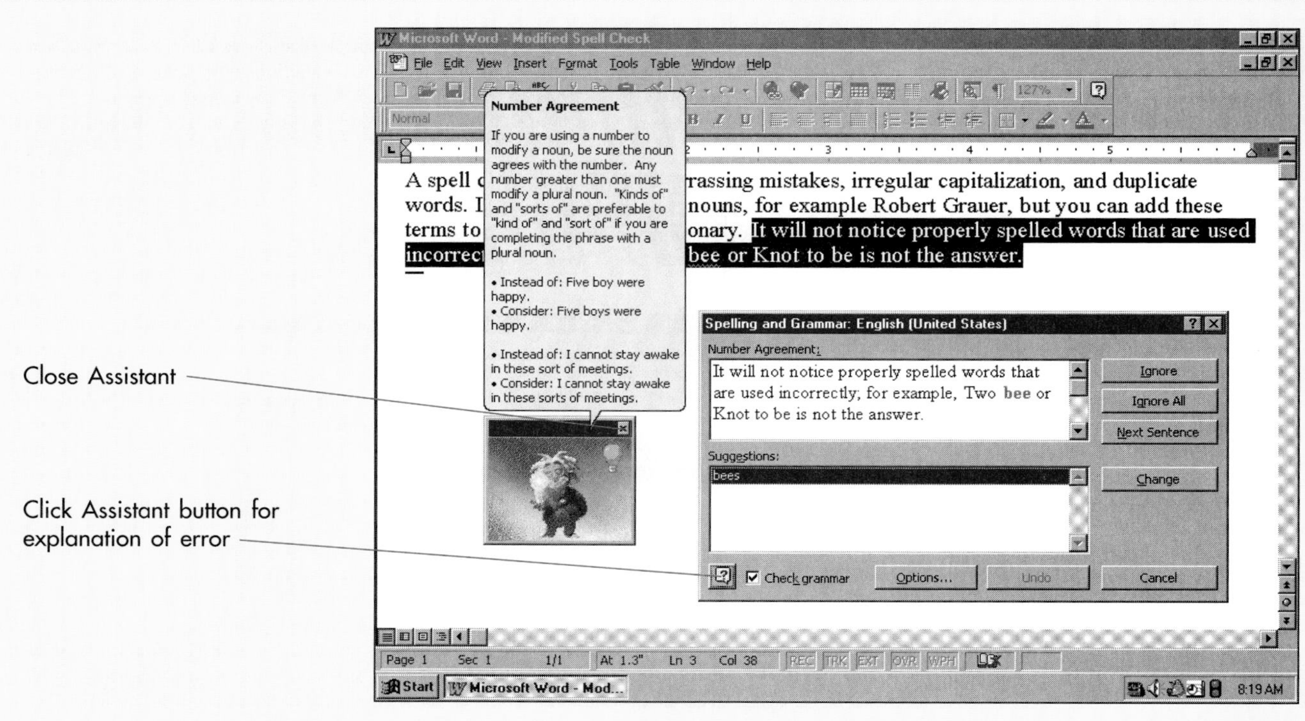

(e) The Grammar Check (step 5)

FIGURE 1.14 Hands-on Exercise 3 (continued)

there needs to be number agreement between subject and verb. Close the Office Assistant after you have read the explanation.

- Click **Ignore** to reject the suggestion. Click **OK** when you see the dialog box, indicating the spelling and grammar check is complete.

CHECK SPELLING ONLY

The grammar check is invoked by default in conjunction with the spell check. You can, however, check the spelling of a document without checking its grammar. Pull down the Tools menu, click Options to display the Options dialog box, then click the Spelling and Grammar tab. Clear the box to check grammar with spelling, then click OK to accept the change and close the dialog box.

STEP 6: The Thesaurus

- Select (click) the word *incorrectly,* which appears on the last line of your document as shown in Figure 1.14f.
- Pull down the **Tools menu,** click **Language,** then click **Thesaurus** to display synonyms for the word you selected.
- Select (click) *inaccurately,* the synonym you will use in place of the original word. Click the **Replace button** to make the change automatically.

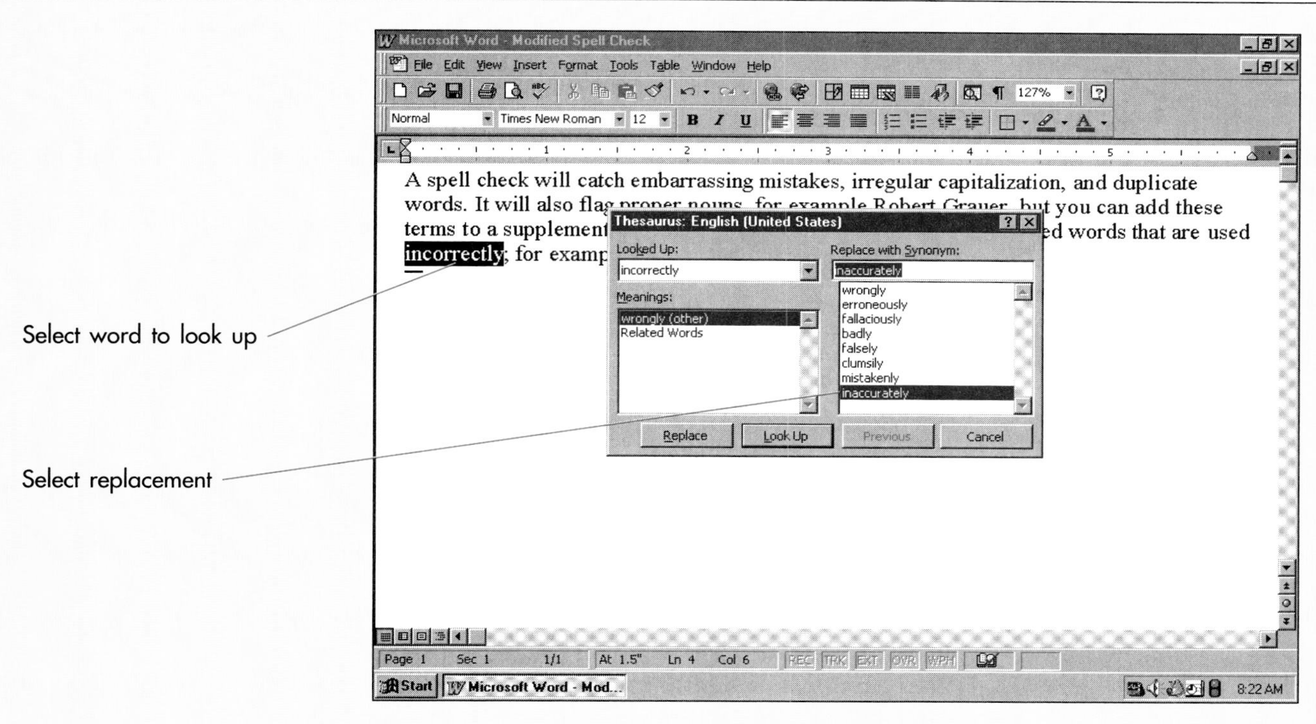

(f) The Thesaurus (step 6)

FIGURE 1.14 Hands-on Exercise 3 (continued)

STEP 7: AutoCorrect

- Press **Ctrl+Home** to move to the beginning of the document.
- Type the *misspelled* phrase **Teh Spell Check was used to check this document.** Try to look at the monitor as you type to see the AutoCorrect feature in action; Word will correct the misspelling and change *Teh* to *The.*
- If you did not see the correction being made, click the arrow next to the Undo command on the Standard toolbar and undo the last several actions. Click the arrow next to the Redo command and redo the corrections.
- Save the document.

CREATE YOUR OWN SHORTHAND

Use AutoCorrect to expand abbreviations such as "usa" for United States of America. Pull down the Tools menu, click AutoCorrect, type the abbreviation in the Replace text box and the expanded entry in the With text box. Click the Add command button, then click OK to exit the dialog box and return to the document. The next time you type usa in a document, it will automatically be expanded to United States of America.

STEP 8: Exit Word

- Pull down the **File menu.** Click **Exit** to exit Word.

SUMMARY

The chapter provided a broad-based introduction to word processing in general and to Microsoft Word in particular. Help is available from many sources. You can use the Help menu or the Office Assistant as you can in any Office application. You can also go to the Microsoft Web site to obtain more recent, and often more detailed, information.

Microsoft Word is always in one of two modes, insert or overtype; the choice between the two depends on the desired editing. The insertion point marks the place within a document where text is added or replaced.

The enter key is pressed at the end of a paragraph, but not at the end of a line because Word automatically wraps text from one line to the next. A hard return is created by the user when he or she presses the enter key; a soft return is created by Word as it wraps text and begins a new line.

The Save and Open commands work in conjunction with one another. The Save command copies the document in memory to disk under its existing name. The Open command retrieves a previously saved document. The Save As command saves the document under a different name and is useful when you want to retain a copy of the current document prior to all changes.

A spell check compares the words in a document to those in a standard and/or custom dictionary and offers suggestions to correct the mistakes it finds. It will detect misspellings, duplicated phrases, and/or irregular capitalization, but will not flag properly spelled words that are used incorrectly.

The AutoCorrect feature corrects predefined spelling errors and/or mistakes in capitalization, automatically, as the words are entered. The feature can also be used to create a personal shorthand as it will expand abbreviations as they are typed.

The thesaurus suggests synonyms and/or antonyms. It can also recognize multiple forms of a word (noun, verb, and adjective) and offer suggestions for each. The grammar check searches for mistakes in punctuation, writing style, and word usage by comparing strings of text within a document to a series of predefined rules.

KEY WORDS AND CONCEPTS

AutoCorrect
Backup
Custom dictionary
File menu
Formatting toolbar
Grammar check
Hard return
Horizontal ruler
Insert mode
Insertion point
Normal view
Office Assistant
Open command
Overtype mode
Page Layout view
Save As command
Save command
ScreenTip
Show/Hide ¶ button
Soft return
Spell check
Standard toolbar
Status bar
Text box
Thesaurus
Toggle switch
Toolbar
Undo command
Vertical ruler
View menu
Word wrap

Multiple Choice

1. When entering text within a document, the enter key is normally pressed at the end of every:
   (a) Line
   (b) Sentence
   (c) Paragraph
   (d) All of the above

2. Which menu contains the commands to save the current document, or to open a previously saved document?
   (a) The Tools menu
   (b) The File menu
   (c) The View menu
   (d) The Edit menu

3. How do you execute the Print command?
   (a) Click the Print button on the standard toolbar
   (b) Pull down the File menu, then click the Print command
   (c) Use the appropriate keyboard shortcut
   (d) All of the above

4. The Open command:
   (a) Brings a document from disk into memory
   (b) Brings a document from disk into memory, then erases the document on disk
   (c) Stores the document in memory on disk
   (d) Stores the document in memory on disk, then erases the document from memory

5. The Save command:
   (a) Brings a document from disk into memory
   (b) Brings a document from disk into memory, then erases the document on disk
   (c) Stores the document in memory on disk
   (d) Stores the document in memory on disk, then erases the document from memory

6. What is the easiest way to change the phrase, *revenues, profits, gross margin,* to read *revenues, profits, and gross margin?*
   (a) Use the insert mode, position the cursor before the *g* in *gross,* then type the word *and* followed by a space
   (b) Use the insert mode, position the cursor after the *g* in *gross,* then type the word *and* followed by a space
   (c) Use the overtype mode, position the cursor before the *g* in *gross,* then type the word *and* followed by a space
   (d) Use the overtype mode, position the cursor after the *g* in *gross,* then type the word *and* followed by a space

7. A document has been entered into Word with a given set of margins, which are subsequently changed. What can you say about the number of hard and soft returns before and after the change in margins?
   (a) The number of hard returns is the same, but the number and/or position of the soft returns is different
   (b) The number of soft returns is the same, but the number and/or position of the hard returns is different
   (c) The number and position of both hard and soft returns is unchanged
   (d) The number and position of both hard and soft returns is different

8. Which of the following will be detected by the spell check?
   (a) Duplicate words
   (b) Irregular capitalization
   (c) Both (a) and (b)
   (d) Neither (a) nor (b)

9. Which of the following is likely to be found in a custom dictionary?
   (a) Proper names
   (b) Words related to the user's particular application
   (c) Acronyms created by the user for his or her application
   (d) All of the above

10. Ted and Sally both use Word but on different computers. Both have written a letter to Dr. Joel Stutz and have run a spell check on their respective documents. Ted's program flags *Stutz* as a misspelling, whereas Sally's accepts it as written. Why?
    (a) The situation is impossible; that is, if they use identical word processing programs they should get identical results
    (b) Ted has added *Stutz* to his custom dictionary
    (c) Sally has added *Stutz* to her custom dictionary
    (d) All of the above reasons are equally likely as a cause of the problem

11. The spell check will do all of the following *except:*
    (a) Flag properly spelled words used incorrectly
    (b) Identify misspelled words
    (c) Accept (as correctly spelled) words found in the custom dictionary
    (d) Suggest alternatives to misspellings it identifies

12. The AutoCorrect feature will:
    (a) Correct errors in capitalization as they occur during typing
    (b) Expand user-defined abbreviations as the entries are typed
    (c) Both (a) and (b)
    (d) Neither (a) nor (b)

13. When does the Save As dialog box appear?
    (a) The first time a file is saved using either the Save or Save As commands
    (b) Every time a file is saved by clicking the Save button on the Standard toolbar
    (c) Both (a) and (b)
    (d) Neither (a) nor (b)

14. Which of the following is true about the thesaurus?
    (a) It recognizes different forms of a word; for example, a noun and a verb
    (b) It provides antonyms as well as synonyms
    (c) Both (a) and (b)
    (d) Neither (a) nor (b)

15. The grammar check:
    (a) Implements different rules for casual and business writing
    (b) Will detect all subtleties in the English language
    (c) Is always run in conjunction with a spell check
    (d) All of the above

ANSWERS

1. c	**6.** a	**11.** a
2. b	**7.** a	**12.** c
3. d	**8.** c	**13.** a
4. a	**9.** d	**14.** c
5. c	**10.** c	**15.** a

PRACTICE WITH MICROSOFT WORD

1. Retrieve the *Chapter1 Practice 1* document shown in Figure 1.15 from the Exploring Word folder, then make the following changes:
   a. Select the text *Your name* and replace it with your name.
   b. Replace *May 31, 1995* with the current date.
   c. Insert the phrase *one or* in line 2 so that the text reads . . . *one or more characters than currently exist.*
   d. Delete the word *And* from sentence four in line 5, then change the w in *when* to a capital letter to begin the sentence.
   e. Change the phrase *most efficient* to *best.*
   f. Place the insertion point at the end of sentence 2, make sure you are in the insert mode, then add the following sentence: *The insert mode adds characters at the insertion point while moving existing text to the right in order to make room for the new text.*
   g. Place the insertion point at the end of the last sentence, press the enter key twice in a row, then enter the following text: *There are several keys that function as toggle switches of which you should be aware. The Caps Lock key toggles between upper- and lowercase letters, and the Num Lock key alternates between typing numbers and using the arrow keys.*
   h. Save the revised document, then print it and submit it to your instructor.

2. Select-then-do: Formatting is not covered until Chapter 2, but we think you are ready to try your hand at basic formatting now. Most formatting operations are done in the context of select-then-do as described in the document in Figure 1.16. You select the text you want to format, then you execute the appropriate formatting command, most easily by clicking the appropriate button on the Formatting toolbar. The function of each button should be apparent from its icon, but you can simply point to a button to display a ScreenTip that is indicative of the button's function.

To: Your Name

From: Robert Grauer and Maryann Barber

Subject: Microsoft Word for Windows

Date: May 31, 1997

This is just a short note to help you get acquainted with the insertion and replacement modes in Word for Windows. When the editing to be done results in more characters than currently exist, you want to be in the insertion mode when making the change. On the other hand, when the editing to be done contains the same or fewer characters, the replacement mode is best. And when replacing characters, it is most efficient to use the mouse to select the characters to be deleted and then just type the new characters; the selected characters are automatically deleted and the new characters typed take their place.

FIGURE 1.15 Document for Practice Exercise 1

An unformatted version of the document in Figure 1.16 exists on the data disk as *Chapter1 Practice 2.* Open the document, then format it to match the completed version in Figure 1.16. Just select the text to format, then click the appropriate button. We changed type size in the original document to 24 points for the title and 12 points for text in the document itself. Be sure to add your name and date as shown in the figure, then submit the completed document to your instructor.

3. Your background: Write a short description of your computer background similar to the document in Figure 1.17. The document should be in the form of a note from student to instructor that describes your background and should mention any previous knowledge of computers you have, prior computer courses you have taken, your objectives for this course, and so on. Indicate whether you own a PC, whether you have access to one at work, and/or whether you are considering purchase. Include any other information about yourself and/or your computer-related background.

   Place your name somewhere in the document in boldface italics. We would also like you to use boldface and italics to emphasize the components of any computer system you describe. Use any font or point size you like. Note, too, the last paragraph, which asks you to print the summary statistics for the document when you submit the assignment to your instructor. (Use the tip on Document Properties on page 25 to print the total editing time and other information about your document.)

4. The cover page: Create a cover page that you can use for your assignments this semester. Your cover page should be similar to the one in Figure 1.18 with respect to content and should include the title of the assignment, your name, course information, and date. The formatting is up to you. Print the completed cover page and submit it to your instructor for inclusion in a class contest to judge the most innovative design.

Select-Then-Do

Many operations in Word are executed as select-then-do operations. You first select a block of text, then you issue a command that will affect the selected text. You may select the text in many different ways, the most basic of which is to click and drag over the desired characters. You may also take one of many shortcuts, which include double clicking on a word, pressing Ctrl as you click a sentence, and triple clicking on a paragraph.

Once text is selected, you may then delete it, **boldface** or *italicize* it, or even change its color. You may move it or copy it to another location, in the same or a different document. You can highlight it, underline, or even check its spelling. Then, depending on whether or not you like what you have done, you may undo it, redo it, and/or repeat it on subsequently selected text.

Jessica Kinzer
September 1, 1997

FIGURE 1.16 Document for Practice Exercise 2

The Computer and Me

My name is Jessica Kinzer and I am a complete novice when it comes to computers. I did not take a computer course in high school and this is my first semester at the University of Miami. My family does not own a computer, nor have I had the opportunity to use one at work. So when it comes to beginners, I am a beginner's beginner. I am looking forward to taking this course, as I have heard that it will truly make me computer literate. I know that I desperately need computer skills not only when I enter the job market, but to survive my four years here as well. I am looking forward to learning Word, Excel, and PowerPoint and I hope that I can pick up some Internet skills as well.

I did not buy a computer before I came to school as I wanted to see what type of system I would be using for my classes. After my first few weeks in class, I think that I would like to buy a ***200 Mz Pentium*** machine with ***32Mb RAM*** and a ***3 Gb hard drive.*** I would like a ***12X speed CD-ROM*** and a ***sound card*** (with ***speakers,*** of course). I also would like to get a ***laser printer.*** Now, if only I had the money.

This document did not take long at all to create as you can see by the summary statistics that are printed on the next page. I think I will really enjoy this class.

Jessica Kinzer
March 2, 1997

FIGURE 1.17 Document for Practice Exercise 3

Exploring Word Assignment

Jessica Kinzer
CIS 120
September 1, 1997

FIGURE 1.18 Document for Practice Exercise 4

5. Figure 1.19 contains the draft version of the *Chapter 1 Practice 5* document contained on the data disk.
   a. Proofread the document and circle any mistakes in spelling, grammar, capitalization, or punctuation.
   b. Open the document in Word and run the spell check. Did Word catch any mistakes you missed? Did you find any errors that were missed by the program?
   c. Use the thesaurus to come up with alternative words for *document,* which appears entirely too often within the paragraph.
   d. Run the grammar check on the revised document. Did the program catch any grammatical errors you missed? Did you find any mistakes that were missed by the program?
   e. Add your name to the revised document, save it, print it, and submit the completed document to your instructor.

6. The document in Figure 1.20 illustrates a new feature in Office 97 in which all applications automatically detect any hyperlinks that are embedded in a document. All you need to do is enter the link, and the application automatically converts it to a hyperlink. You can then click on the link to open Internet Explorer and display the associated Web page, provided you have an Internet connection. See for yourself by creating the document in Figure 1.20 and submitting it to your instructor.

   As indicated, Word will, by default, convert any Internet path (e.g., any text beginning with http:// or www) to a hyperlink. If this is not the case, pull down the Tools menu, click AutoCorrect, then click the AutoFormat-as-you-Type tab. Check the box in the Replace-as-you-Type area for Internet and Network paths. Click OK. The next time you enter a Web or e-mail address, it will be converted automatically to a hyperlink.

The Grammar Check

All documents should be thoroughly proofed before they be printed and distributed. This means that documents, at a minimum should be spell cheked,, grammar cheked, and proof read by the author. A documents that has spelling errors and/or grammatical errors makes the Author look unprofessional and illiterate and their is nothing worse than allowing a first impression too be won that makes you appear slopy and disinterested, and a document full or of misteakes will do exactly that. Alot of people do not not realize how damaging a bad first impression could be, and documents full of misteakes has cost people oppurtunities that they trained and prepared many years for.

Microsoft Word includes an automated grammar check that will detect many, but certainly not all, errors as the previous paragraph demonstrates. Unlike the spell check, the grammar check is subjective, and what seems appropriate to you may be objectionable to someone else. The English language is just to complicated for the grammar check to detect every error, or even most errors. Hence there is no substitute for carefully proof reading a document your self. Hence there is no substitute for carefully proof reading a document your self.

FIGURE 1.19 Document for Practice Exercise 5

It's Web-Enabled

Perhaps the most significant change in Office 97 is that every document is Web-enabled, meaning that the application will automatically detect and highlight any hyperlinks that appear in a document. This sentence, for example, contains the Web address, www.microsoft.com, which is highlighted in blue just as it might appear in a regular Web document. We did not do anything special to create the hyperlink; that is, we simply typed the address, and Word in turn created the hyperlink.

You can click the link from within Word, and provided you have an Internet connection, your Web browser will display the associated page. Note, too, that once you click the link, its color will change (e.g., from blue to magenta) just as it would if you were viewing the page in Netscape or the Internet Explorer. Prove to your instructor that you have done this exercise by creating this document, then adding a paragraph or two that reference your favorite Web pages.

FIGURE 1.20 Document for Practice Exercise 6

7. Webster Online: Figure 1.21 shows our favorite online dictionary, which is accessed most easily by clicking the Search button in Internet Explorer, then clicking the link to Definitions and Quotes. Enter the word you want to look up (*oxymoron,* for example), then press the Look Up Word button to display the definition in Figure 1.21. This is truly an interactive dictionary because most words in it are created as hyperlinks, which in turn will lead you to other definitions. Use the dictionary to look up the meaning of the word *palindrome.* How many examples of oxymorons and palindromes can you think of?

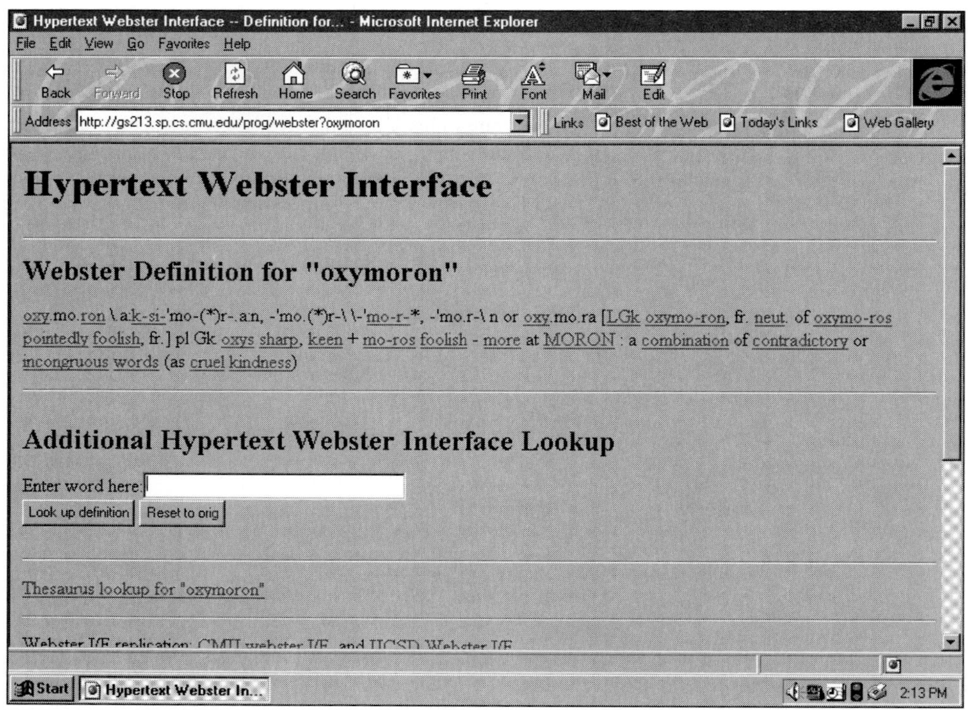

FIGURE 1.21 Screen for Practice Exercise 7

CASE STUDIES

It's a Mess

Newcomers to word processing quickly learn the concept of word wrap and the distinction between hard and soft returns. This lesson was lost, however, on your friend who created the *Please Help Me* document on the data disk. The first several sentences were entered without any hard returns at all, whereas the opposite problem exists toward the end of the document. This is a good friend, and her paper is due in one hour. Please help.

Planning for Disaster

Do you have a backup strategy? Do you even know what a backup strategy is? You should learn, because sooner or later you will wish you had one. You will erase a file, be unable to read from a floppy disk, or worse yet suffer a hardware failure in which you are unable to access the hard drive. The problem always seems to occur the night before an assignment is due. The ultimate disaster is the disappearance of your computer, by theft or natural disaster (e.g., Hurricane Andrew). Describe in 250 words or less the backup strategy you plan to implement in conjunction with your work in this class.

A Letter Home

You really like this course and want very much to have your own computer, but you're strapped for cash and have decided to ask your parents for help. Write a one-page letter describing the advantages of having your own system and how it will help you in school. Tell your parents what the system will cost, and that you can save money by buying through the mail. Describe the configuration you intend to buy (don't forget to include the price of software) and then provide prices from at least three different companies. Cut out the advertisements and include them in your letter. Bring your material to class and compare your research with that of your classmates.

Computer Magazines

A subscription to a computer magazine should be given serious consideration if you intend to stay abreast in a rapidly changing field. The reviews on new products are especially helpful and you will appreciate the advertisements should you need to buy. Go to the library or a newsstand and obtain a magazine that appeals to you, then write a brief review of the magazine for class. Devote at least one paragraph to an article or other item you found useful.

A Junior Year Abroad

How lucky can you get? You are spending the second half of your junior year in Paris. The problem is you will have to submit your work in French, and the English version of Microsoft Word won't do. Is there a foreign-language version available? What about the dictionary and thesaurus? How do you enter the accented characters, which occur so frequently? You are leaving in two months, so you'd better get busy. What are your options? *Bon voyage!*

The Writer's Reference

The chapter discussed the use of a spell check, thesaurus, and grammar check, but many other resources are available. The Web contains a host of sites with additional resources that are invaluable to the writer. You can find Shakespeare online, as well as Bartlett's quotations. You can also find Webster's dictionary as well as a dictionary of acronyms. One way to find these resources is to click the Search button in Internet Explorer, then scroll down the page to the Writer's Reference section. You can also go to the address directly (home.microsoft.com/access.allinone.asp). Explore one or more of these resources, then write a short note to your instructor to summarize your findings.

Microsoft Online

Help for Microsoft Word is available from a variety of sources. You can consult the Office Assistant, or you can pull down the Help menu to display the Help Contents and Index. Both techniques were illustrated in the chapter. In addition, you can go to the Microsoft Web site to obtain more recent, and often more detailed, information. You will find the answers to the most frequently asked questions and you can access the same knowledge base used by Microsoft support engineers. Experiment with various sources of help, then submit a summary of your findings to your instructor. Try to differentiate among the various techniques and suggest the most appropriate use for each.

Microsoft Bookshelf

Bookshelf Basics is contained on the CD-ROM version of Microsoft Office and provides access to three frequently used reference books: *The American Heritage Dictionary, The Original Roget's Thesaurus,* and *The Columbia Dictionary of Quotations.* Examine each of these references and determine how useful they are to you as a student. Bookshelf Basics is free with Office 97, but the rest of Microsoft Bookshelf is not. What additional books are found in the complete version of Microsoft Bookshelf? How much does it cost? Is it worth the price, or can you find the equivalent information for free on the Web? Summarize your findings in a short note to your instructor.

2

GAINING PROFICIENCY: EDITING AND FORMATTING

OBJECTIVES

After reading this chapter you will be able to:

1. Define the select-then-do methodology; describe several shortcuts with the mouse and/or the keyboard to select text.
2. Use the clipboard and/or the drag-and-drop capability to move and copy text within a document.
3. Use the Find, Replace, and Go To commands to substitute one character string for another.
4. Define scrolling; scroll to the beginning and end of a document.
5. Distinguish between the Normal and Page Layout views; state how to change the view and/or magnification of a document.
6. Define typography; distinguish between a serif and a sans serif typeface; use the Format Font command to change the font and/or type size.
7. Use the Format Paragraph command to change line spacing, alignment, tabs, and indents, and to control pagination.
8. Use the Borders and Shading command to box and shade text.
9. Describe the Undo and Redo commands and how they are related to one another.
10. Use the Page Setup command to change the margins and/or orientation; differentiate between a soft and a hard page break.

OVERVIEW

The previous chapter taught you the basics of Microsoft Word and enabled you to create and print a simple document. The present chapter significantly extends your capabilities, by presenting a variety of commands to change the contents and appearance of a document. These operations are known as editing and formatting, respectively.

You will learn how to move and copy text within a document and how to find and replace one character string with another. You will also learn the basics of typography and be able to switch between the different fonts included within Windows. You will be able to change alignment, indentation, line spacing, margins, and page orientation. All of these commands are used in three hands-on exercises, which require your participation at the computer, and which are the very essence of the chapter.

As you read the chapter, realize that there are many different ways to accomplish the same task and that it would be impossible to cover them all. Our approach is to present the overall concepts and suggest the ways we think are most appropriate at the time we introduce the material. We also offer numerous shortcuts in the form of boxed tips that appear throughout the chapter and urge you to explore further on your own. It is not necessary for you to memorize anything as online help is always available. Be flexible and willing to experiment.

WRITE NOW, EDIT LATER

You write a sentence, then change it, and change it again, and one hour later you've produced a single paragraph. It happens to every writer—you stare at a blank screen and flashing cursor and are unable to write. The best solution is to brainstorm and write down anything that pops into your head, and to keep on writing. Don't worry about typos or spelling errors because you can fix them later. Above all, resist the temptation to continually edit the few words you've written because overediting will drain the life out of what you are writing. The important thing is to get your ideas on paper.

SELECT-THEN-DO

Many operations in Word take place within the context of a ***select-then-do*** methodology; that is, you select a block of text, then you execute the command to operate on that text. The most basic way to select text is by dragging the mouse; that is, click at the beginning of the selection, press and hold the left mouse button as you move to the end of the selection, then release the mouse.

There are, however, a variety of shortcuts to facilitate the process; for example, double click anywhere within a word to select the word, or press the Ctrl key and click the mouse anywhere within a sentence to select the sentence. Additional shortcuts are presented in each of the hands-on exercises, at which point you will have many opportunities to practice selecting text.

Selected text is affected by any subsequent operation; for example, clicking the Bold or Italic button changes the selected text to boldface or italics, respectively. You can also drag the selected text to a new location, press the Del key to erase the selected text, or execute any other editing or formatting command. The text continues to be selected until you click elsewhere in the document.

THE RIGHT MOUSE BUTTON

Point anywhere within a document, then click the right mouse button to display a shortcut menu. Shortcut menus contain commands appropriate to the item you have selected. Click in the menu to execute a command, or click outside the menu to close the menu without executing a command.

MOVING AND COPYING TEXT

The ability to move and/or copy text is essential in order to develop any degree of proficiency in editing. A move operation removes the text from its current location and places it elsewhere in the same (or even a different) document; a copy operation retains the text in its present location and places a duplicate elsewhere. Either operation can be accomplished using the Windows clipboard and a combination of the ***Cut, Copy,*** and ***Paste commands.*** (A shortcut, using the mouse to ***drag-and-drop*** text from one location to another, is described in step 8 in the first hands-on exercise.)

The ***clipboard*** is a temporary storage area available to any Windows application. Selected text is cut or copied from a document and placed onto the clipboard from where it can be pasted to a new location(s). A move requires that you select the text and execute a Cut command to remove the text from the document and place it on the clipboard. You then move the insertion point to the new location and paste the text from the clipboard into that location. A copy operation necessitates the same steps except that a Copy command is executed rather than a cut, leaving the selected text in its original location as well as placing a copy on the clipboard.

The Cut, Copy, and Paste commands are found in the Edit menu, or alternatively, can be executed by clicking the appropriate buttons on the Standard toolbar. The contents of the clipboard are replaced by each subsequent Cut or Copy command, but are unaffected by the Paste command; that is, the contents of the clipboard can be pasted into multiple locations in the same or different documents.

DELETE WITH CAUTION

You work too hard developing your thoughts to see them disappear in a flash. Hence, instead of deleting large blocks of text, try moving them to the end of your document (or even a new document) from where they can be recalled later if you change your mind. A related practice is to remain in the insert mode (as opposed to overtype) to prevent the inadvertent deletion of existing text as new ideas are added.

UNDO AND REDO COMMANDS

The ***Undo command*** was introduced in Chapter 1, but it is repeated here because it is so valuable. The command is executed from the Edit menu or by clicking the Undo button on the Standard toolbar. Word enables you to undo up to the last 100 changes to a document. You just click the arrow next to the Undo button on the Standard toolbar to display a reverse-order list of your previous commands, then you click the command you want to undo, which also undoes all of the preceding commands. Undoing the fifth command in the list, for example, will also undo the preceding four commands.

The ***Redo command*** redoes (reverses) the last command that was undone. As with the Undo command, the Redo command redoes all of the previous commands prior to the command you select. Redoing the fifth command in the list, for example, will also redo the preceding four commands. The Undo and Redo commands work in conjunction with one another; that is, every time a command is undone it can be redone at a later time.

FIND, REPLACE, AND GO TO COMMANDS

The Find, Replace, and Go To commands share a common dialog box with different tabs for each command as shown in Figure 2.1. The ***Find command*** locates one or more occurrences of specific text (e.g., a word or phrase). The ***Replace command*** goes one step further in that it locates the text, and then enables you to optionally replace (one or more occurrences of) that text with different text. The ***Go To command*** goes directly to a specific place (e.g., a specific page) in the document.

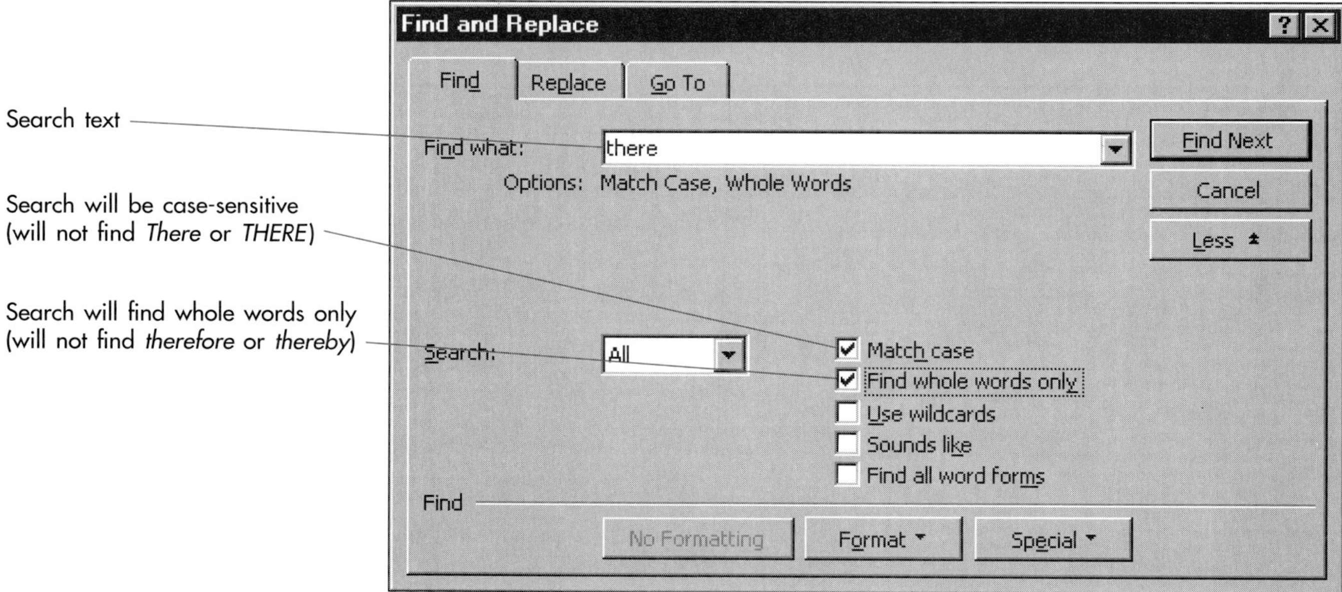

(a) Find Command

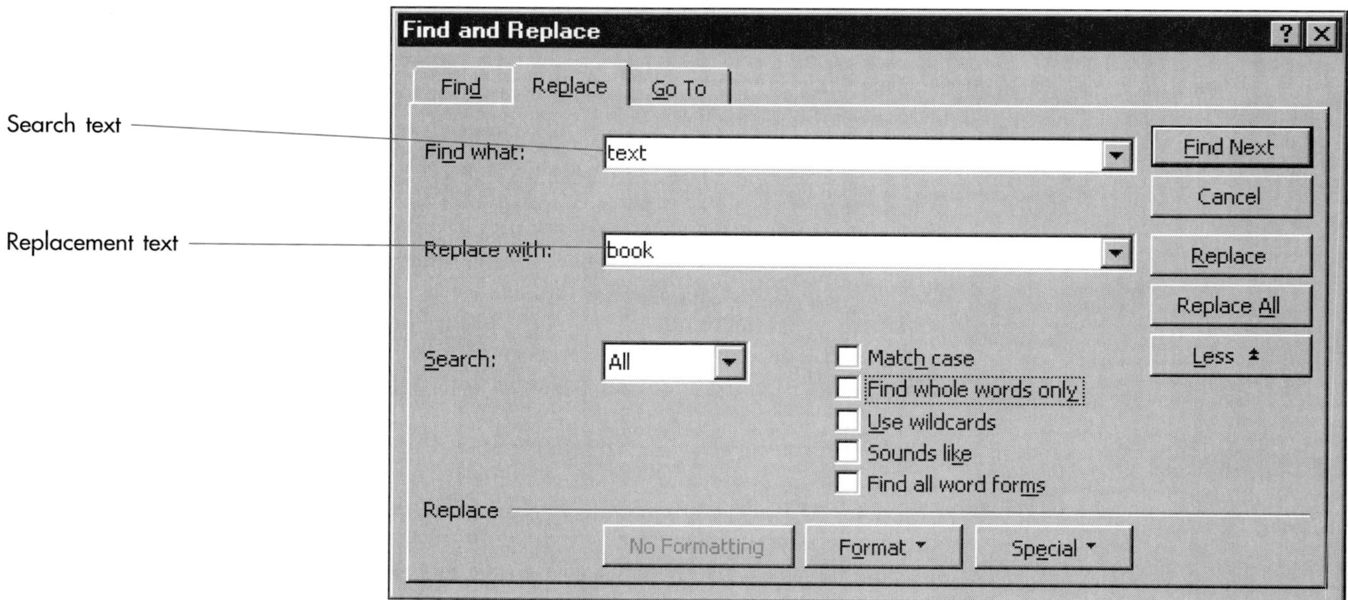

(b) Replace Command

FIGURE 2.1 The Find, Replace, and Go To Commands

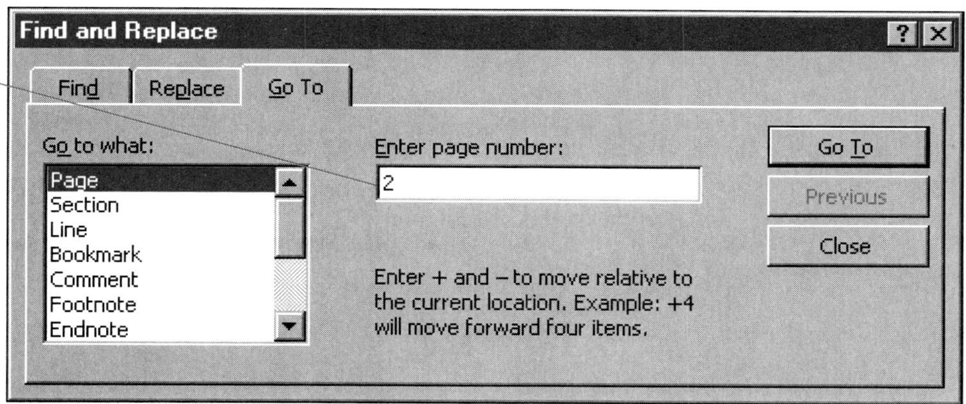

(c) Go To Command

FIGURE 2.1 The Find, Replace, and Go To Commands (continued)

The search in both the Find and Replace commands is case-sensitive or case-insensitive. A ***case-sensitive search*** (where Match Case is selected as in Figure 2.1a) matches not only the text, but also the use of upper- and lowercase letters. Thus, *There* is different from *there,* and a search on one will not identify the other. A ***case-sensitive search*** (where Match Case is *not* as selected in Figure 2.1b) is just the opposite and finds both *There* and *there.* A search may also specify ***whole words only*** to identify *there,* but not *therefore* or *thereby.* And finally, the search and replacement text can also specify different numbers of characters; for example, you could replace *16* with *sixteen.*

The Replace command in Figure 2.1b implements either ***selective replacement,*** which lets you examine each occurrence of the character string in context and decide whether to replace it, or ***automatic replacement,*** where the substitution is made automatically. Selective replacement is implemented by clicking the Find Next command button, then clicking (or not clicking) the Replace button to make the substitution. Automatic replacement (through the entire document) is implemented by clicking the Replace All button. This often produces unintended consequences and is not recommended; for example, if you substitute the word *text* for *book,* the phrase *text book* would become *text text,* which is not what you had in mind.

The Find and Replace commands can include formatting and/or special characters. You can, for example, change all italicized text to boldface, or you can change five consecutive spaces to a tab character. You can also use ***wild cards*** in the character string. For example, to find all four-letter words that begin with "f" and end with "l" (such as *fall, fill,* or *fail*), search for f??l. (The question mark stands for any character, just like a wild card in a card game.) You can also search for all forms of a word; for example, if you specify *am,* it will also find *is* and *are.* You can even search for a word based on how it sounds. When searching for *Marion,* for example, check the Sounds Like check box, and the search will find both *Marion* and *Marian.*

SCROLLING

Scrolling occurs when a document is too large to be seen in its entirety. Figure 2.2a displays a large printed document, only part of which is visible on the screen as illustrated in Figure 2.2b. In order to see a different portion of the document, you need to scroll, whereby new lines will be brought into view as the old lines disappear.

To: Our Students
From: Robert Grauer and Maryann Barber

Welcome to the wonderful world of word processing. Over the next several chapters we will build a foundation in the basics of Microsoft Word, then teach you to format specialized documents, create professional looking tables and charts, and produce well-designed newsletters. Before you know it, you will be a word processing and desktop publishing wizard!

The first chapter presented the basics of word processing and showed you how to create a simple document. You learned how to insert, replace, and/or delete text. This chapter will teach you about fonts and special effects (such as boldfacing and italicizing) and how to use them effectively — how too little is better than too much.

You will go on to experiment with margins, tab stops, line spacing, and justification, learning first to format simple documents and then going on to longer, more complex ones. It is with the latter that we explore headers and footers, page numbering, widows and orphans (yes, we really did mean widows and orphans). It is here that we bring in graphics, working with newspaper-type columns, and the elements of a good page design. And without question, we will introduce the tools that make life so much easier (and your writing so much more impressive) — the Speller, Grammar Checker, Thesaurus, Glossaries, and Styles.

If you are wondering what all these things are, read on in the text and proceed with the hands-on exercises. Create a simple newsletter, then really knock their socks off by adding graphics, fonts, and WordArt. Create a simple calendar and then create more intricate forms that no one will believe were done by little old you. Create a resume with your beginner's skills, and then make it look like so much more with your intermediate (even advanced) skills. Last, but not least, run a mail merge to produce the cover letters that will accompany your resume as it is mailed to companies across the United States (and even the world).

It is up to you to practice, for it is only through working at the computer that you will learn what you need to know. Experiment and don't be afraid to make mistakes. Practice and practice some more.

Our goal is for you to learn and to enjoy what you are learning. We have great confidence in you, and in our ability to help you discover what you can do. You can visit the home page for the *Exploring Windows* series at www.prenhall.com/grauer. You can also send us e-mail. Bob's address is rgrauer@umiami.miami.edu. Maryann's address is mbarber@homer.bus.miami.edu. As you read the last sentence, notice that Word 97 is Web-enabled and that the Internet and e-mail references appear as hyperlinks in this document. You can click the address of our home page from within Word and your browser will display the page, provided you have an Internet connection. You can also click the e-mail address to open your mail program, provided it has been configured correctly.

We look forward to hearing from you and hope that you will like our textbook. You are about to embark on a wonderful journey toward computer literacy. Be patient and inquisitive.

(a) Printed Document

FIGURE 2.2 Scrolling

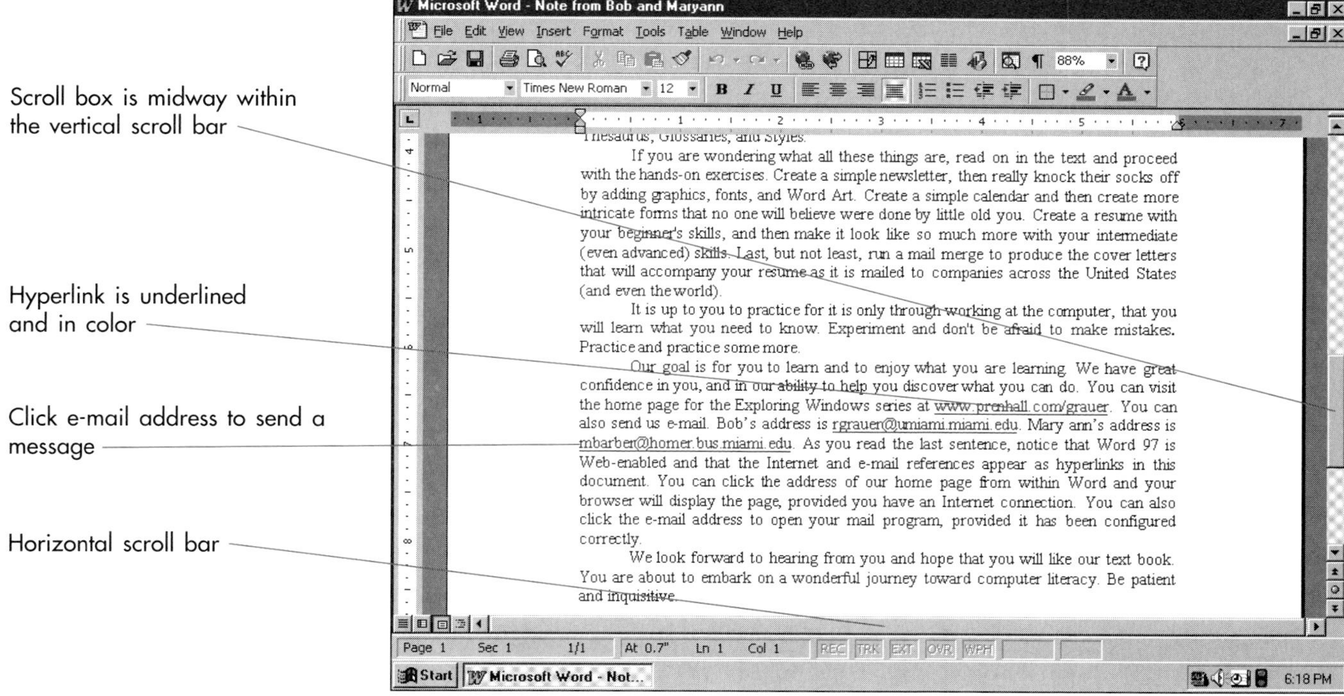

(b) Screen Display

FIGURE 2.2 Scrolling (continued)

Scrolling comes about automatically as you reach the bottom of the screen. Entering a new line of text, clicking on the down arrow within the scroll bar, or pressing the down arrow key brings a new line into view at the bottom of the screen and simultaneously removes a line at the top. (The process is reversed at the top of the screen.)

Scrolling can be done with either the mouse or the keyboard. Scrolling with the mouse (e.g., clicking the down arrow in the scroll bar) changes what is displayed on the screen, but does not move the insertion point, so that you must click the mouse after scrolling prior to entering the text at the new location. Scrolling with the keyboard, however (e.g., pressing Ctrl+Home or Ctrl+End to move to the beginning or end of a document, respectively), changes what is displayed on the screen as well as the location of the insertion point, and you can begin typing immediately.

Scrolling occurs most often in a vertical direction as shown in Figure 2.2. It can also occur horizontally, when the length of a line in a document exceeds the number of characters that can be displayed horizontally on the screen.

IT'S WEB ENABLED

Every document in Office 97 is Web-enabled, which means that Internet and e-mail references appear as hyperlinks within a document. Thus you can click the address of any Web page from within Word and your browser will display the page, provided you have an Internet connection. You can also click the e-mail address to open your mail program, provided it has been configured correctly.

VIEW MENU

The ***View menu*** provides different views of a document. Each view can be displayed at different magnifications, which in turn determine the amount of scrolling necessary to see remote parts of a document.

The ***Normal view*** is the default view and it provides the fastest way to enter text. The ***Page Layout*** view more closely resembles the printed document and displays the top and bottom margins, headers and footers, page numbers, graphics, and other features that do not appear in the Normal view. The Normal view tends to be faster because Word spends less time formatting the display.

The ***Zoom command*** displays the document on the screen at different magnifications; for example, 75%, 100%, or 200%. (The Zoom command does not affect the size of the text on the printed page.) A Zoom percentage (magnification) of 100% displays the document in the approximate size of the text on the printed page. You can increase the percentage to 200% to make the characters appear larger. You can also decrease the magnification to 75% to see more of the document at one time.

Word will automatically determine the magnification if you select one of three additional Zoom options—Page Width, Whole Page, or Many Pages (Whole Page and Many Pages are available only in the Page Layout view). Figure 2.3a, for example, displays a two-page document in Page Layout view. Figure 2.3b shows the corresponding settings in the Zoom command. (The 37% magnification is determined automatically once you specify the number of pages as shown in the figure.)

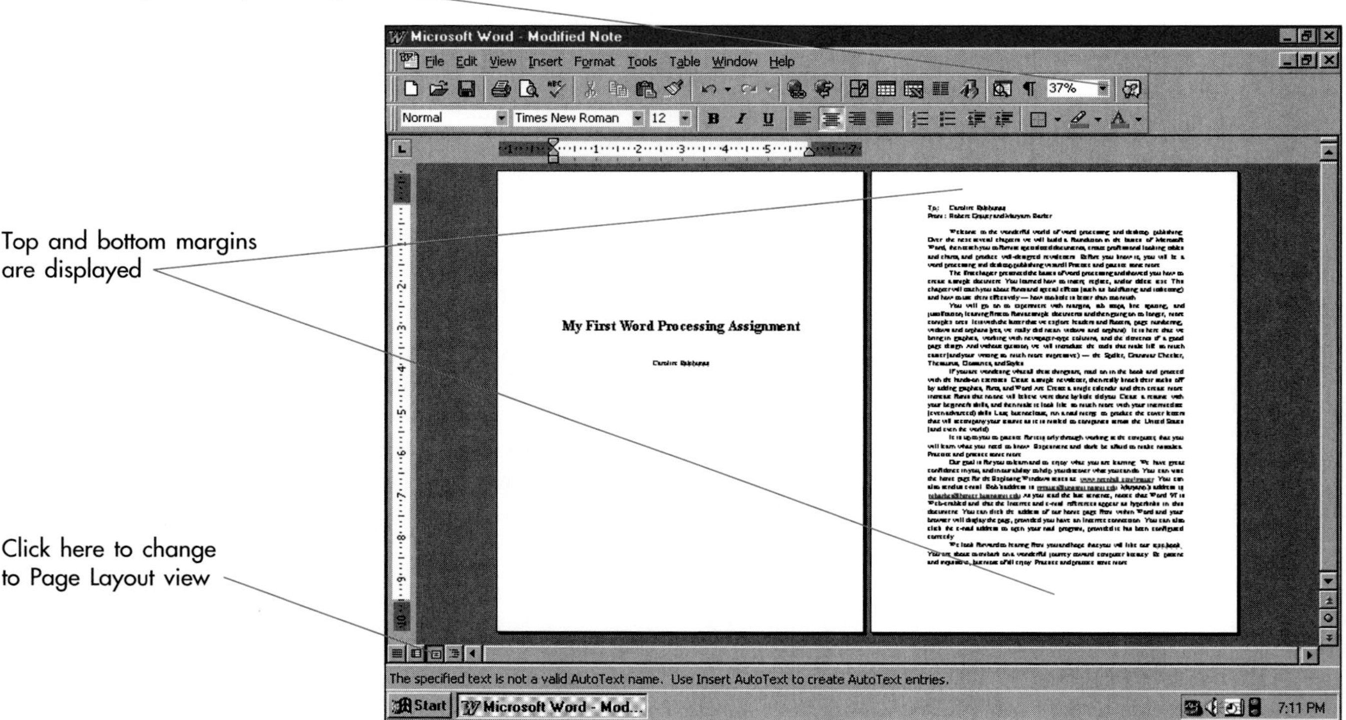

(a) Page Layout View

FIGURE 2.3 View Menu and Zoom Command

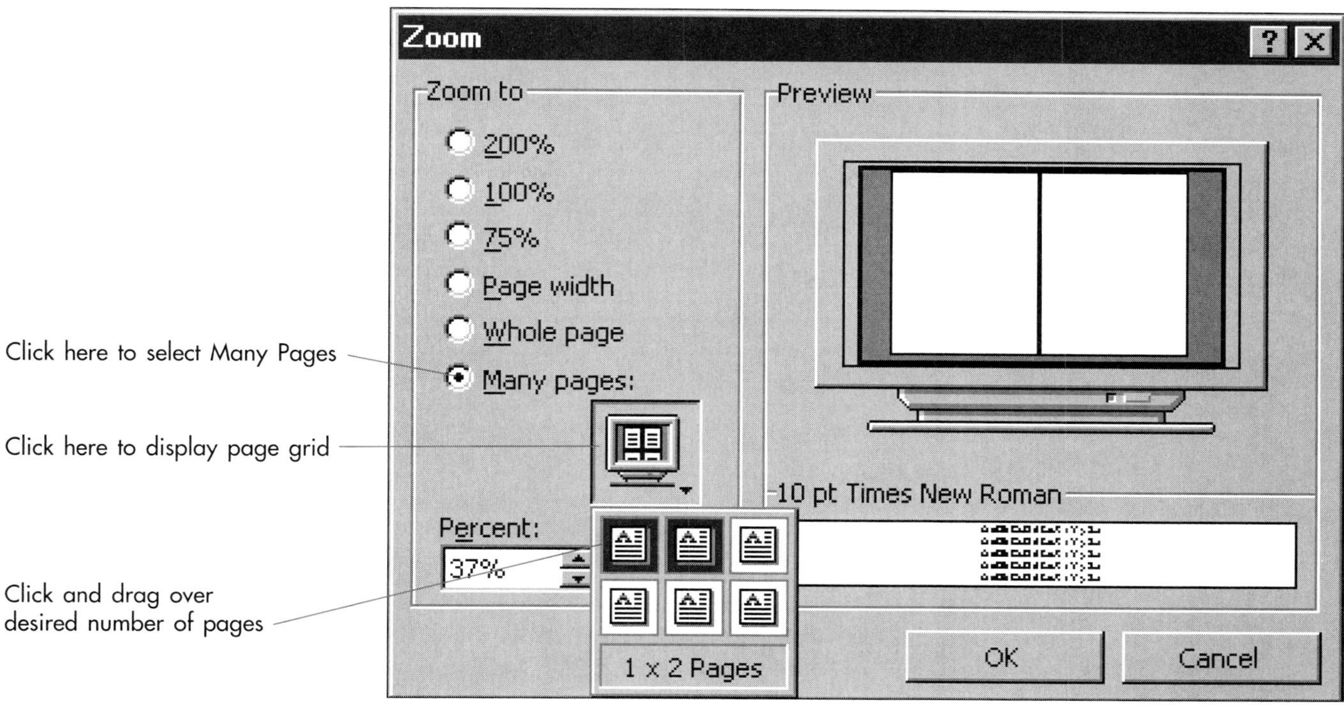

(b) Zoom Command

FIGURE 2.3 View Menu and Zoom Command (continued)

HANDS-ON EXERCISE 1

Editing a Document

Objective: To edit an existing document; to change the view and magnification of a document; to scroll through a document. To use the Find and Replace commands; to move and copy text using the clipboard and the drag-and-drop facility. Use Figure 2.4 as a guide in the exercise.

STEP 1: View Menu and Zoom Command

- Start Word as described in the hands-on exercises from Chapter 1. Pull down the **File menu** and click **Open** (or click the **Open button** on the toolbar).
  - Click the **drop-down arrow** on the Look In list box. Click the appropriate drive, drive C or drive A, depending on the location of your data.
  - Double click the **Exploring Word folder** to make it the active folder (the folder in which you will save the document).
  - Scroll in the Name list box (if necessary) until you can click the **Note from Bob and Maryann** to select this document. Double click the **document icon** or click the **Open command button** to open the file.
- The document should appear on the screen as shown in Figure 2.4a.
- Change to the Page Layout view at Page Width magnification:
  - Pull down the **View menu** and click **Page Layout** (or click the **Page Layout button** above the status bar) as shown in Figure 2.4a.
  - Click the **down arrow** in the Zoom box to change to **Page Width.**

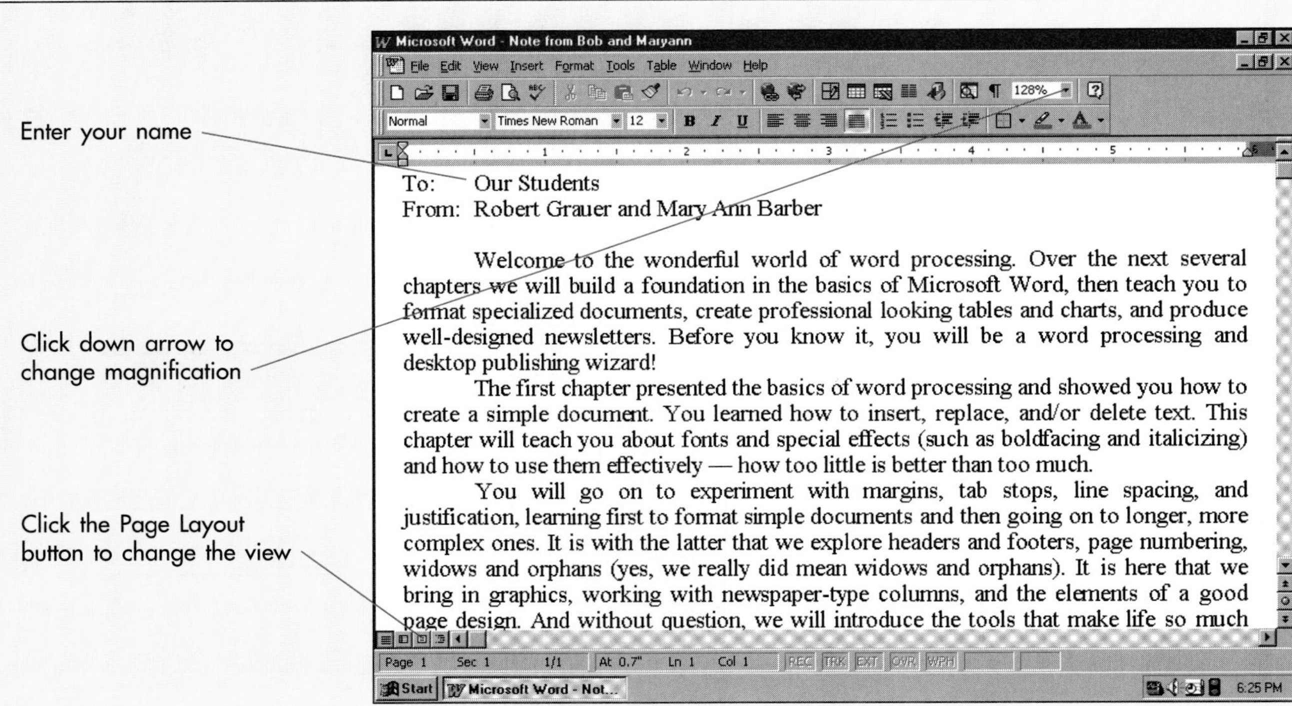

(a) The View Menu and Zoom Command (step 1)

FIGURE 2.4 Hands-on Exercise 1

- Click and drag the mouse to select the phrase **Our Students,** which appears at the beginning of the document. Type your name to replace the selected text.
- Pull down the **File menu,** click the **Save As** command, then save the document as **Modified Note.** (This creates a second copy of the document and leaves the original unchanged.)

CREATE A BACKUP COPY

The Options button in the Save As dialog box enables you to specify the backup options in effect. Click the Options command button, then check the box to Always Create Backup Copy. The next time you save the document, the previous version on disk becomes a backup copy while the document in memory becomes the current version on disk.

STEP 2: Scrolling

- Click and drag the **scroll box** within the vertical scroll bar to scroll to the end of the document as shown in Figure 2.4b. Click immediately before the period at the end of the last sentence.
- Type a **comma,** then insert the phrase **but most of all, enjoy.**
- Drag the **scroll box** to the top of the scroll bar to get back to the beginning of the document. Click immediately before the period ending the first sentence, press the **space bar,** then add the phrase **and desktop publishing.**
- Save the document.

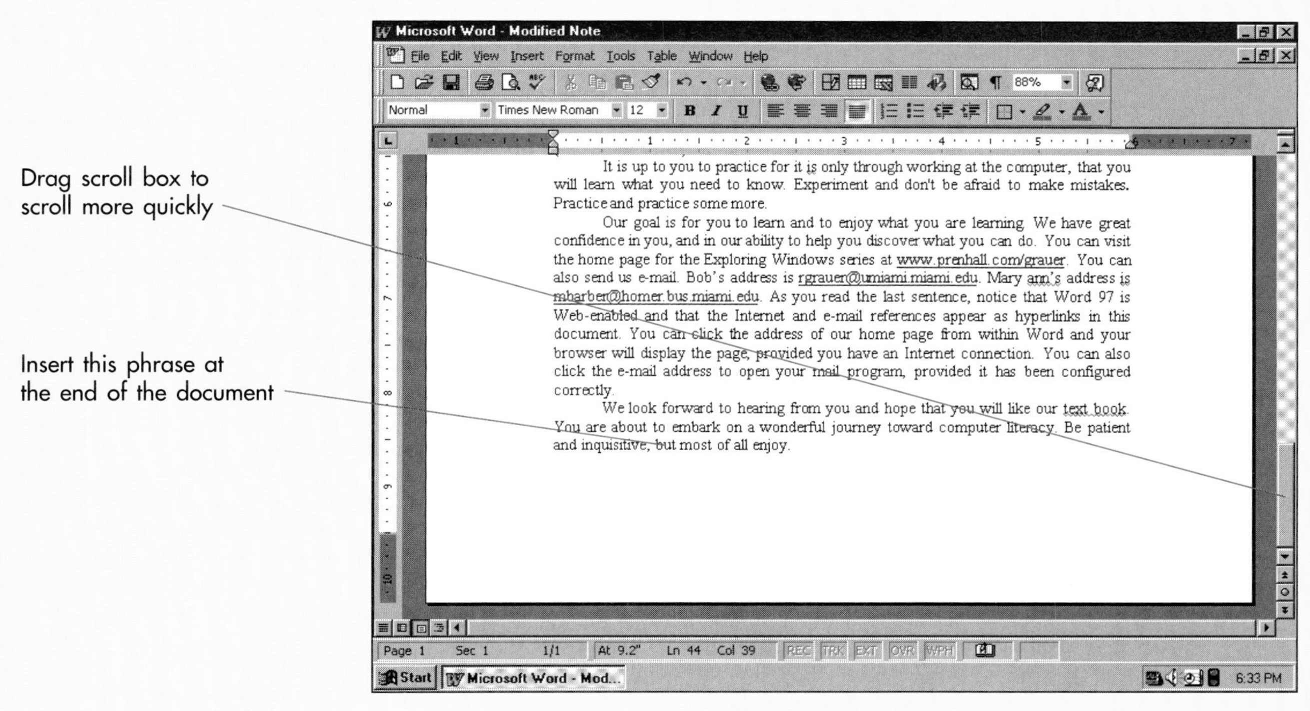

(b) Scrolling (step 2)

FIGURE 2.4 Hands-on Exercise 1 (continued)

THE MOUSE AND THE SCROLL BAR

Scroll quickly through a document by clicking above or below the scroll box to scroll up or down an entire screen. Move to the top, bottom, or an approximate position within a document by dragging the scroll box to the corresponding position in the scroll bar; for example, dragging the scroll box to the middle of the bar moves the mouse pointer to the middle of the document. Scrolling with the mouse does not change the location of the insertion point, however, and thus you must click the mouse at the new location prior to entering text at that location.

STEP 3: The Replace Command

- Press **Ctrl+Home** to move to the beginning of the document. Pull down the **Edit menu.** Click **Replace** to produce the dialog box of Figure 2.4c. Click the **More button** to display the available options.
  - Type **text** in the Find what text box.
  - Press the **Tab key.** Type **book** in the Replace with text box.
- Click the **Find Next button** to find the first occurrence of the word *text.* The dialog box remains on the screen and the first occurrence of *text* is selected. This is *not* an appropriate substitution; that is, you should not substitute *book* for *text* at this point.
- Click the **Find Next button** to move to the next occurrence without making the replacement. This time the substitution is appropriate.

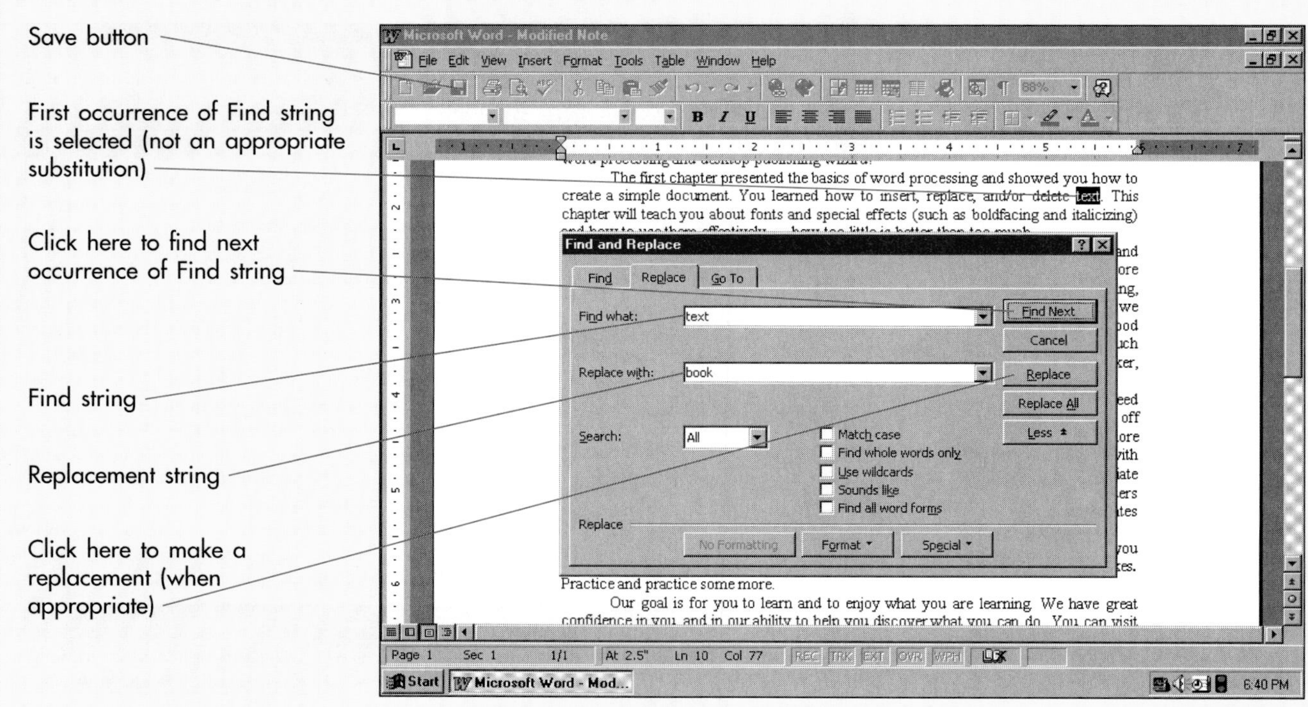

(c) Replace Command (step 3)

FIGURE 2.4 Hands-on Exercise 1 (continued)

- Click **Replace** to make the change and automatically move to the next occurrence where the substitution is again inappropriate. Click **Find Next** a final time. Word will indicate that it has finished searching the document. Click **OK.**
- Change the Find and Replace strings to **Mary Ann** and **Maryann,** respectively. Click the **Replace All** button to make the substitution globally without confirmation. Word will indicate that it has finished searching and that two replacements were made. Click **OK.**
- Click the **Close command button** to close the dialog box. Click the **Save button** to save the document. Scroll through the document to review your changes.

SCROLLING WITH THE KEYBOARD

Press Ctrl+Home and Ctrl+End to move to the beginning and end of a document, respectively. Press Home and End to move to the beginning and end of a line. Press PgUp or PgDn to scroll one screen in the indicated direction. The advantage of scrolling via the keyboard (instead of the mouse) is that the location of the insertion point changes automatically and you can begin typing immediately.

STEP 4: The Clipboard

- Press **PgDn** to scroll toward the end of the document until you come to the paragraph beginning **It is up to you.** Select the sentence **Practice and practice some more** by dragging the mouse over the sentence. (Be sure to include the period.) The sentence will be selected as shown in Figure 2.4d.
- Pull down the **Edit menu** and click the **Copy command** or click the **Copy button** on the Standard toolbar.
- Press **Ctrl+End** to scroll to the end of the document. Press the **space bar.** Pull down the **Edit menu** and click the **Paste command** (or click the **Paste button** on the Standard toolbar).
- Move the insertion point to the end of the first paragraph (following the exclamation point after the word *Wizard*). Press the **space bar.** Click the **Paste button** on the Standard toolbar to paste the sentence a second time.

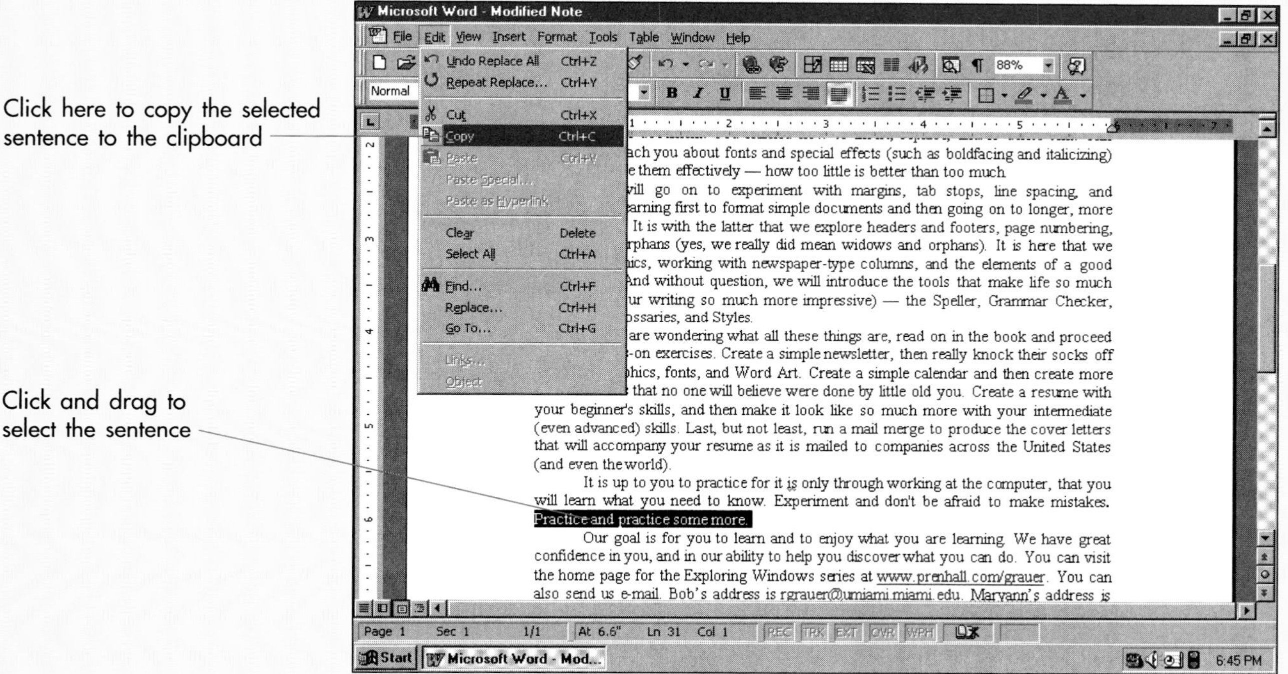

(d) Copy Command (step 4)

FIGURE 2.4 Hands-on Exercise 1 (continued)

CUT, COPY, AND PASTE

Ctrl+X, Ctrl+C, and **Ctrl+V** are keyboard shortcuts to cut, copy, and paste, respectively. (The shortcuts are easier to remember when you realize that the operative letters X, C, and V are next to each other at the bottom left side of the keyboard.) You can also use the Cut, Copy, and Paste buttons on the Standard toolbar.

STEP 5: Undo and Redo Commands

- Click the **drop-down arrow** next to the Undo button to display the previously executed actions as in Figure 2.4e. The list of actions corresponds to the editing commands you have issued since the start of the exercise. (Your list will be different from ours if you deviated from any instructions in the hands-on exercise.)
- Click **Paste** (the first command on the list) to undo the last editing command; the sentence, Practice and practice some more, disappears from the end of the first paragraph.
- Click the remaining steps on the undo list to retrace your steps through the exercise one command at a time. Alternatively, you can scroll to the bottom of the list and click the last command, which automatically undoes all of the preceding commands.
- Either way, when the undo list is empty, you will have the document as it existed at the start of the exercise.
- Click the **drop-down arrow** for the Redo command to display the list of commands you have undone; click each command in sequence (or click the command at the bottom of the list) and you will restore the document.
- Save the document.

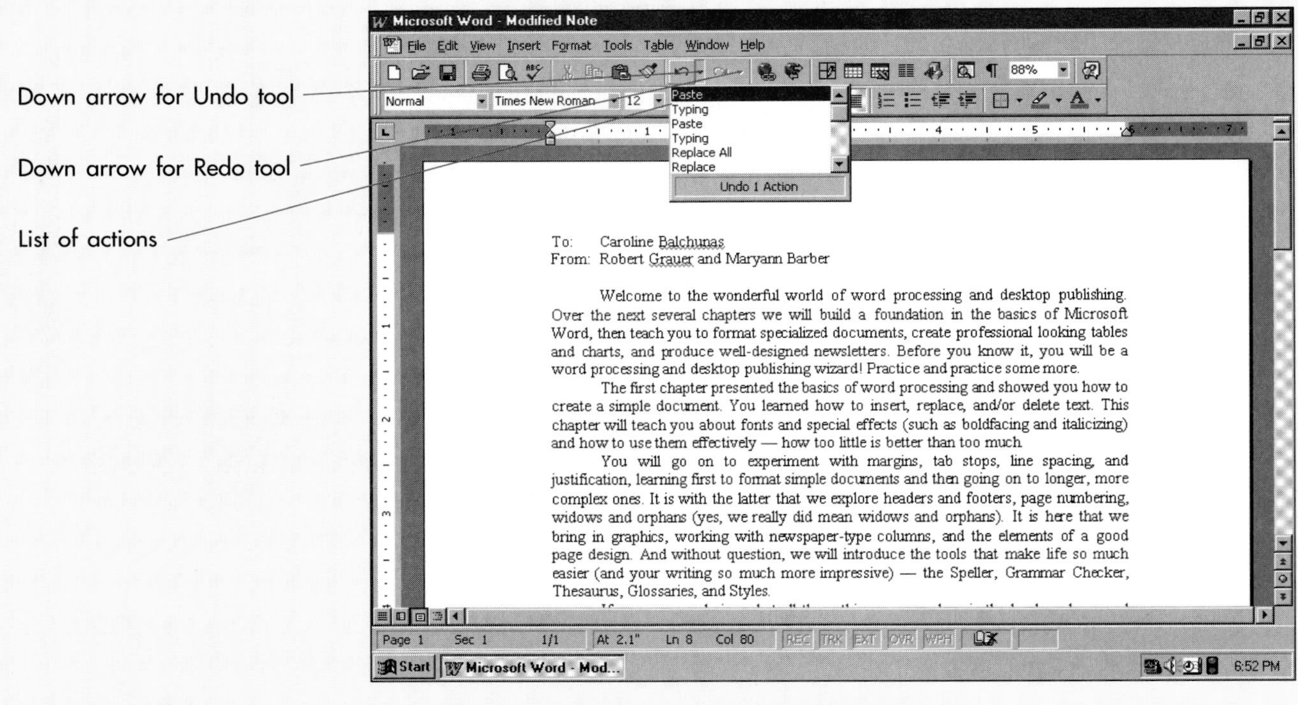

(e) Undo and Redo Commands (step 5)

FIGURE 2.4 Hands-on Exercise 1 (continued)

STEP 6: Drag and Drop

- Click and drag to select the phrase **format specialized documents** (including the comma and space) as shown in Figure 2.4f, then drag the phrase to its new location immediately before the word *and*. (A dotted vertical bar appears as you drag the text, to indicate its new location.)
- Release the mouse button to complete the move.
- Click the **drop-down arrow** for the Undo command; click **Move** to undo the move.
- To copy the selected text to the same location (instead of moving it), press and hold the **Ctrl key** as you drag the text to its new location. (A plus sign appears as you drag the text, to indicate it is being copied rather than moved.)
- Practice the drag-and-drop procedure several times until you are confident you can move and copy with precision.
- Click anywhere in the document to deselect the text. Save the document.

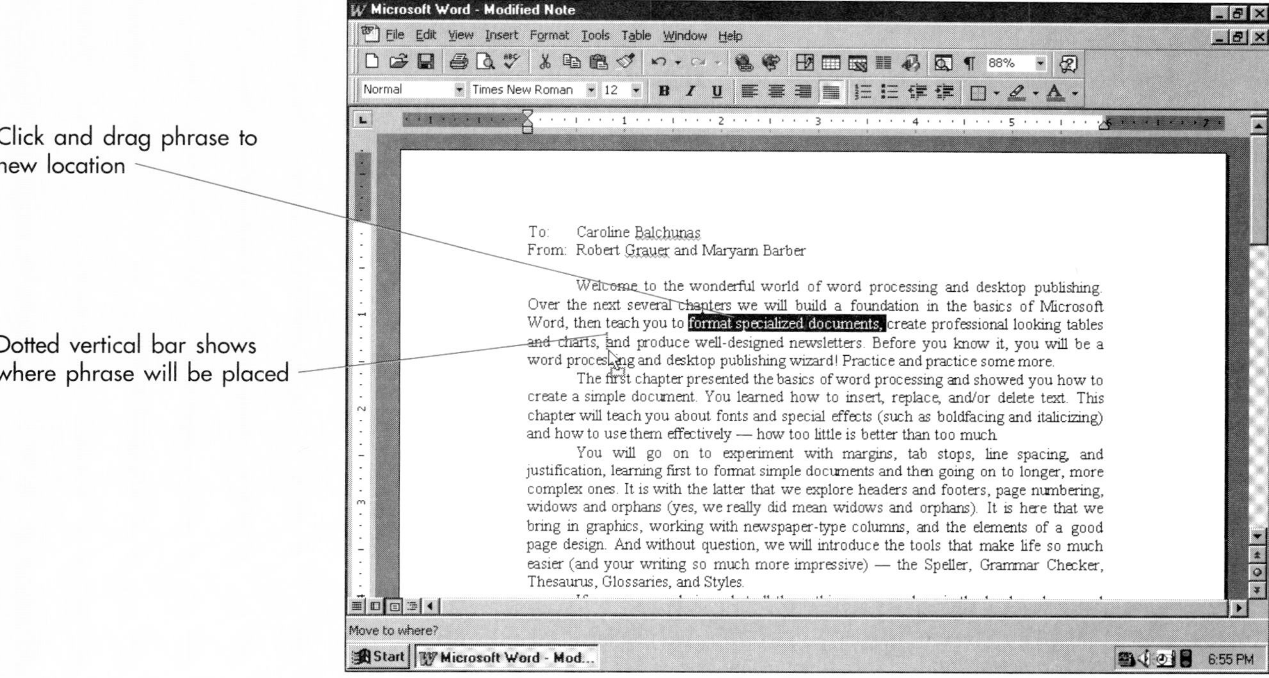

(f) Drag and Drop (step 6)

FIGURE 2.4 Hands-on Exercise 1 (continued)

STEP 7: The Print Preview Command

- Pull down the **File menu** and click **Print Preview** (or clock the **Print Preview button** on the Standard toolbar). You should see your entire document as shown in Figure 2.4g.
- Check that the entire document fits on one page—that is, check that you can see all three lines in the last paragraph. If not, click the **Shrink to Fit button** on the toolbar to automatically change the font sizes in the document to force it on one page.

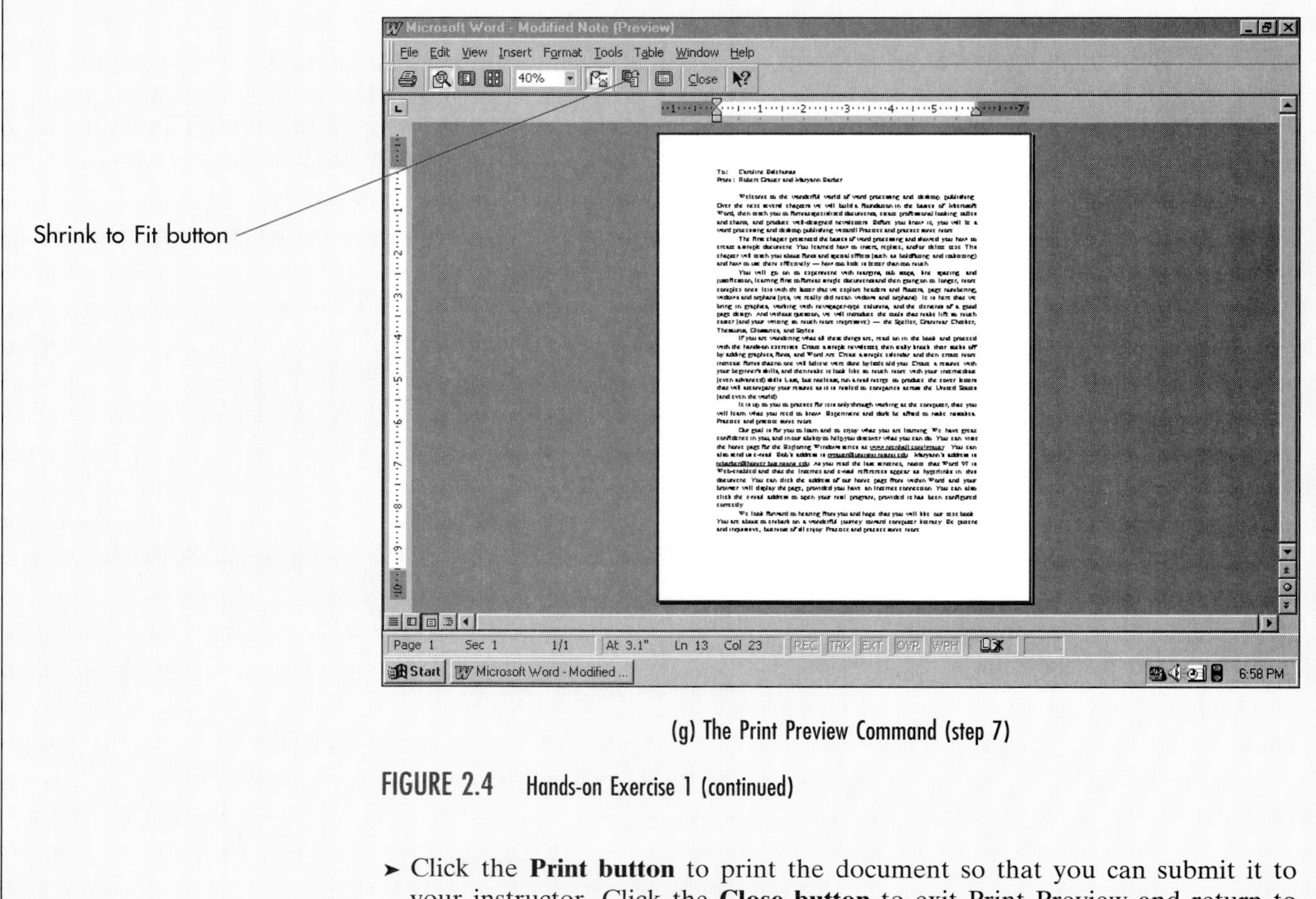

(g) The Print Preview Command (step 7)

FIGURE 2.4 Hands-on Exercise 1 (continued)

- ➤ Click the **Print button** to print the document so that you can submit it to your instructor. Click the **Close button** to exit Print Preview and return to your document.
- ➤ Close the document. Exit Word if you do not want to continue with the next exercise at this time.

TYPOGRAPHY

Typography is the process of selecting typefaces, type styles, and type sizes. The importance of these decisions is obvious, for the ultimate success of any document depends greatly on its appearance. Type should reinforce the message without calling attention to itself and should be consistent with the information you want to convey.

Typeface

A ***typeface*** is a complete set of characters (upper- and lowercase letters, numbers, punctuation marks, and special symbols). Figure 2.5 illustrates three typefaces—***Times New Roman, Arial,*** and ***Courier New***—that are supplied with Windows, and which in turn are accessible from any Windows application.

One definitive characteristic of any typeface is the presence or absence of tiny cross lines that end the main strokes of each letter. A ***serif*** typeface has these lines. A ***sans serif*** typeface (*sans* from the French for *without*) does not. Times New Roman and Courier New are examples of a serif typeface. Arial is a sans serif typeface.

Typography is the process of selecting typefaces, type styles, and type sizes. A serif typeface has tiny cross strokes that end the main strokes of each letter. A sans serif typeface does not have these strokes. Serif typefaces are typically used with large amounts of text. Sans serif typefaces are used for headings and limited amounts of text. A proportional typeface allocates space in accordance with the width of each character and is what you are used to seeing. A monospaced typeface uses the same amount of space for every character. A well-designed document will limit the number of typefaces so as not to overwhelm the reader.

(a) Times New Roman (serif and proportional)

Typography is the process of selecting typefaces, type styles, and type sizes. A serif typeface has tiny cross strokes that end the main strokes of each letter. A sans serif typeface does not have these strokes. Serif typefaces are typically used with large amounts of text. Sans serif typefaces are used for headings and limited amounts of text. A proportional typeface allocates space in accordance with the width of each character and is what you are used to seeing. A monospaced typeface uses the same amount of space for every character. A well-designed document will limit the number of typefaces so as not to overwhelm the reader.

(b) Arial (sans serif and proportional)

Typography is the process of selecting typefaces, type styles, and type sizes. A serif typeface has tiny cross strokes that end the main strokes of each letter. A sans serif typeface does not have these strokes. Serif typefaces are typically used with large amounts of text. Sans serif typefaces are used for headings and limited amounts of text. A proportional typeface allocates space in accordance with the width of each character and is what you are used to seeing. A monospaced typeface uses the same amount of space for every character. A well-designed document will limit the number of typefaces so as not to overwhelm the reader.

(c) Courier New (serif and monospaced)

FIGURE 2.5 Typefaces

Serifs help the eye to connect one letter with the next and are generally used with large amounts of text. This book, for example, is set in a serif typeface. A sans serif typeface is more effective with smaller amounts of text and appears in headlines, corporate logos, airport signs, and so on.

A second characteristic of a typeface is whether it is monospaced or proportional. A ***monospaced typeface*** (e.g., Courier New) uses the same amount of space for every character regardless of its width. A ***proportional typeface*** (e.g., Times New Roman or Arial) allocates space according to the width of the character. Monospaced fonts are used in tables and financial projections where text must be precisely lined up, one character underneath the other. Proportional typefaces create a more professional appearance and are appropriate for most documents.

Any typeface can be set in different ***type styles*** (e.g., regular, **bold,** or *italic*). A ***font*** (as the term is used in Windows) is a specific typeface in a specific style; for example, *Times New Roman Italic,* Arial Bold, or ***Courier New Bold Italic.***

TYPOGRAPHY TIP—USE RESTRAINT

More is not better, especially in the case of too many typefaces and styles, which produce cluttered documents that impress no one. Try to limit yourself to a maximum of two typefaces per document, but choose multiple sizes and/or styles within those typefaces. Use boldface or italics for emphasis; but do so in moderation, because if you emphasize too many elements, the effect is lost.

Type Size

Type size is a vertical measurement and is specified in points, where one ***point*** is equal to 1/72 of an inch; that is, there are 72 points to the inch. The measurement is made from the top of the tallest letter in a character set (for example, an uppercase T) to the bottom of the lowest letter (for example, a lowercase y). Most documents are set in 10 or 12 point type. Newspaper columns may be set as small as 8 point type. Type sizes of 14 points or higher are ineffective for large amounts of text. Figure 2.6 shows the same phrase set in varying type sizes.

Some typefaces appear larger (smaller) than others even though they may be set in the same point size. The type in Figure 2.6a, for example, looks smaller than the corresponding type in Figure 2.6b even though both are set in the same point size.

Format Font Command

The ***Format Font command*** gives you complete control over the typeface, size, and style of the text in a document. Executing the command before entering text will set the format of the text you type from that point on. You can also use the command to change the font of existing text by selecting the text, then executing the command. Either way, you will see the dialog box in Figure 2.7, in which you specify the font (typeface), style, and point size.

You can choose any of the special effects (e.g., ~~strikethrough~~ or SMALL CAPS) and/or change the underline options (whether or not spaces are to be underlined). You can even change the color of the text on the monitor, but you need a color printer for the printed document. (The Character Spacing and Animation tabs produce different sets of options in which you control the spacing and appearance of the characters and are beyond the scope of our discussion.)

This is Arial 8 point type

This is Arial 10 point type

This is Arial 12 point type

This is Arial 18 point type

This is Arial 24 point type

This is Arial 30 point type

(a) Sans Serif Typeface

This is Times New Roman 8 point type

This is Times New Roman 10 point type

This is Times New Roman 12 point type

This is Times New Roman 18 point type

This is Times New Roman 24 point type

This is Times New Roman 30 point

(b) Serif Typeface

FIGURE 2.6 Type Size

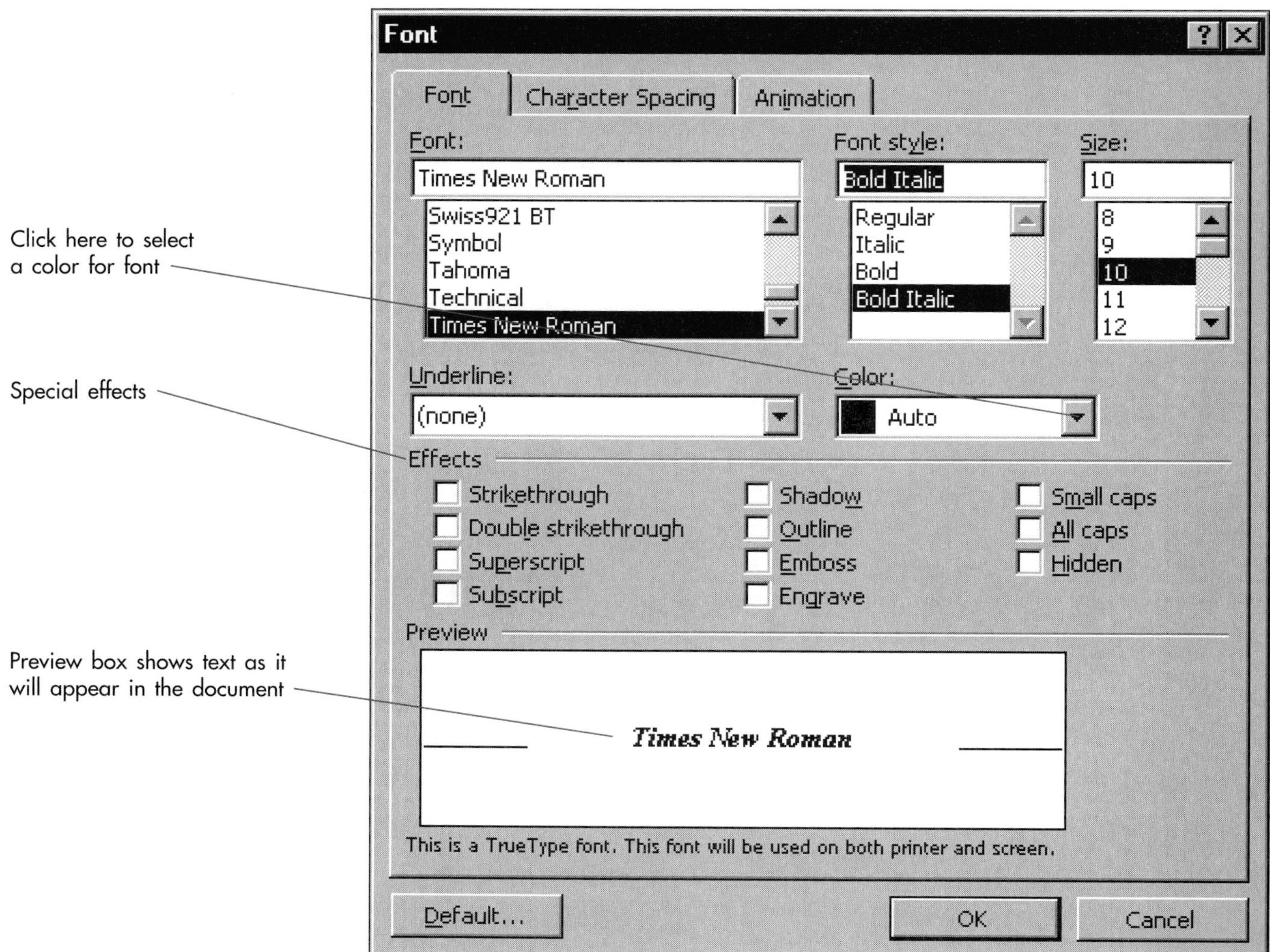

FIGURE 2.7 Format Font Command

The Preview box shows the text as it will appear in the document. The message at the bottom of the dialog box indicates that Times New Roman is a TrueType font and that the same font will be used on both the screen and the monitor. TrueType fonts ensure that your document is truly WYSIWYG (What You See Is What You Get) because the fonts you see on the monitor will be identical to those in the printed document.

PAGE SETUP COMMAND

The ***Page Setup command*** in the File menu lets you change margins, paper size, orientation, paper source, and/or layout. All parameters are accessed from the dialog box in Figure 2.8 by clicking the appropriate tab within the dialog box.

The default margins are indicated in Figure 2.8a and are one inch on the top and bottom of the page, and one and a quarter inches on the left and right. You can change any (or all) of these settings by entering a new value in the appropriate text box, either by typing it explicitly or clicking the up/down arrow. All of the settings in the Page Setup command apply to the whole document regardless of the position of the insertion point. (Different settings can be established for different parts of a document by creating sections, which is beyond the scope of our present discussion.)

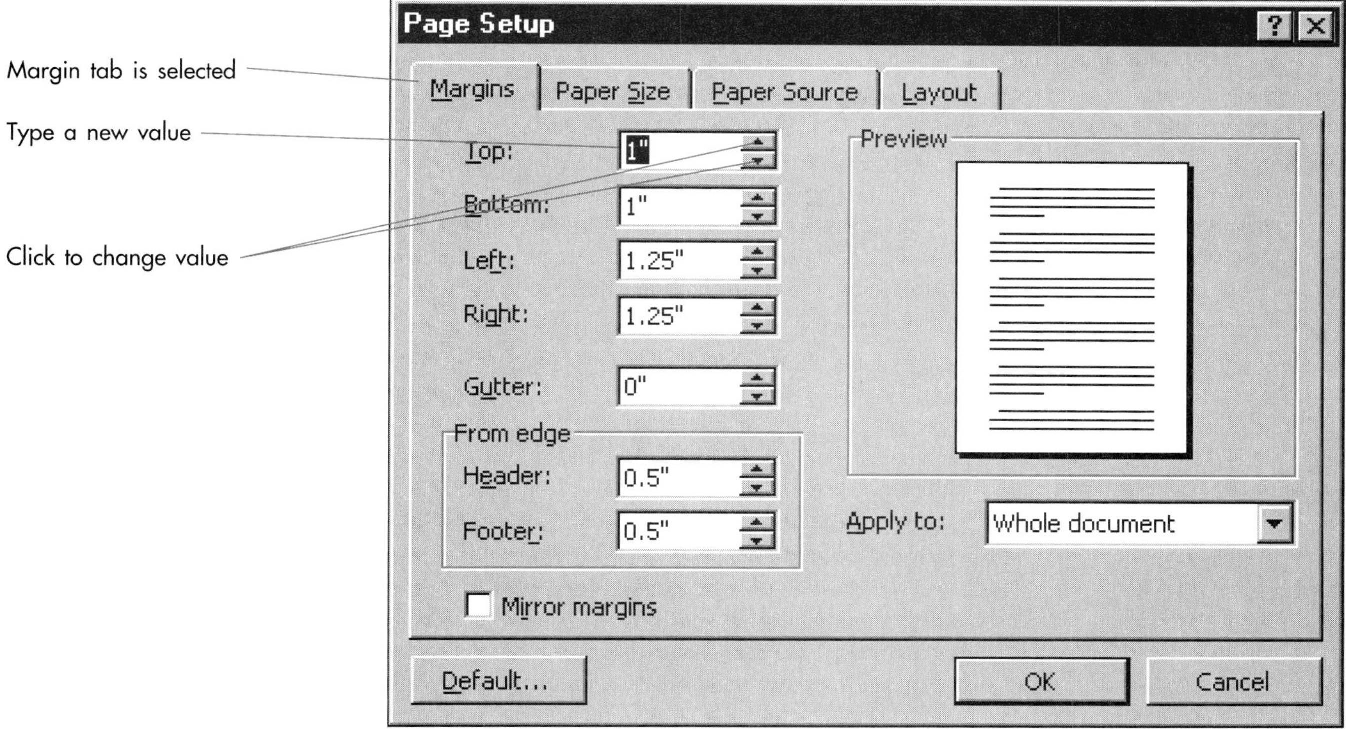

(a) Margins

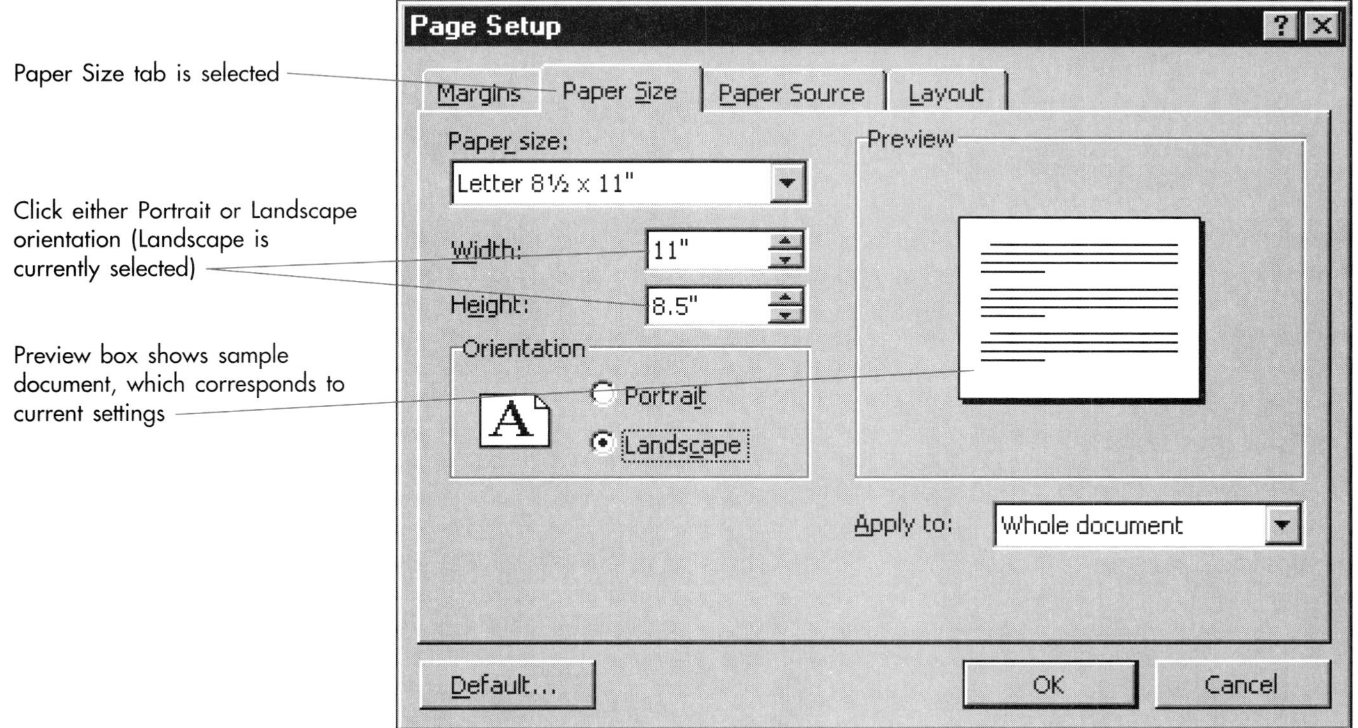

(b) Size and Orientation

FIGURE 2.8 Page Setup Command

The Paper Size tab within the Page Setup command enables you to change the orientation of a page as shown in Figure 2.8b. ***Portrait orientation*** is the default. ***Landscape orientation*** flips the page 90 degrees so that its dimensions are 11 × 8½ rather than the other way around. Note, too, the Preview area in both Figures 2.8a and 2.8b, which shows how the document will appear with the selected parameters.

The Paper Source tab is used to specify which tray should be used on printers with multiple trays, and is helpful when you want to load different types of paper simultaneously. The Layout tab is used to specify options for headers and footers (text that appears at the top or bottom of each page in a document).

Page Breaks

One of the first concepts you learned was that of word wrap, whereby Word inserts a soft return at the end of a line in order to begin a new line. The number and/or location of the soft returns change automatically as you add or delete text within a document. Soft returns are very different from the hard returns inserted by the user, whose number and location remain constant.

In much the same way, Word creates a ***soft page break*** to go to the top of a new page when text no longer fits on the current page. And just as you can insert a hard return to start a new paragraph, you can insert a ***hard page break*** to force any part of a document to begin on a new page. A hard page break is inserted into a document using the Break command in the Insert menu or through the Ctrl+enter keyboard shortcut. (You can prevent the occurrence of awkward page breaks through the Format Paragraph command as described later in the chapter.

AN EXERCISE IN DESIGN

The following exercise has you retrieve an existing document from the set of practice files, then experiment with various typefaces, type styles, and point sizes. The original document uses a monospaced (typewriter style) font, without boldface or italics, and you are asked to improve its appearance. The first step directs you to save the document under a new name so that you can always return to the original if necessary.

There is no right and wrong with respect to design, and you are free to choose any combination of fonts that appeals to you. The exercise takes you through various formatting options but lets you make the final decision. It does, however, ask you to print the final document and submit it to your instructor.

IMPOSE A TIME LIMIT

A word processor is supposed to save time and make you more productive. It will do exactly that, provided you use the word processor for its primary purpose—writing and editing. It is all too easy, however, to lose sight of that objective and spend too much time formatting the document. Concentrate on the content of your document rather than its appearance. Impose a time limit on the amount of time you will spend on formatting. End the session when the limit is reached.

HANDS-ON EXERCISE 2

Character Formatting

Objective: To experiment with character formatting; to change fonts and to use boldface and italics; to copy formatting with the format painter; to insert a page break and see different views of a document. Use Figure 2.9 as a guide in the exercise.

STEP 1: Open the Existing Document

- Start Word. Pull down the **File menu** and click **Open** (or click the **Open button** on the toolbar). To open a file:
  - Click the **drop-down arrow** on the Look In list box. Click the appropriate drive, drive C or drive A, depending on the location of your data.
  - Double click the **Exploring Word folder** to make it the active folder (the folder in which you will open and save the document).
  - Scroll in the **Open list box** (if necessary) until you can click **Tips for Writing** to select this document. Double click the **document icon** or click the **Open command button** to open the file.
- Pull down the **File menu.** Click the **Save As command** to save the document as **Modified Tips.**
- Pull down the **View menu** and click **Normal** (or click the **Normal View button** above the status bar).
- Set the magnification (zoom) to **Page Width.**

SELECTING TEXT

The ***selection bar,*** a blank column at the far left of the document window, makes it easy to select a line, paragraph, or the entire document. To select a line, move the mouse pointer to the selection bar, point to the line and click the left mouse button. To select a paragraph, move the mouse pointer to the selection bar, point to any line in the paragraph, and double click the mouse. To select the entire document, move the mouse pointer to the selection bar and press the Ctrl key while you click the mouse.

STEP 2: The Right Mouse Button

- Select the first tip as shown in Figure 2.9a. Point to the selected text and click the **right mouse button** to display the shortcut menu.
- Click outside the menu to close the menu without executing a command.
- Press the **Ctrl key** as you click the selection bar to select the entire document, then click the **right mouse button** to display the shortcut menu.
- Click **Font** to execute the Format Font command.

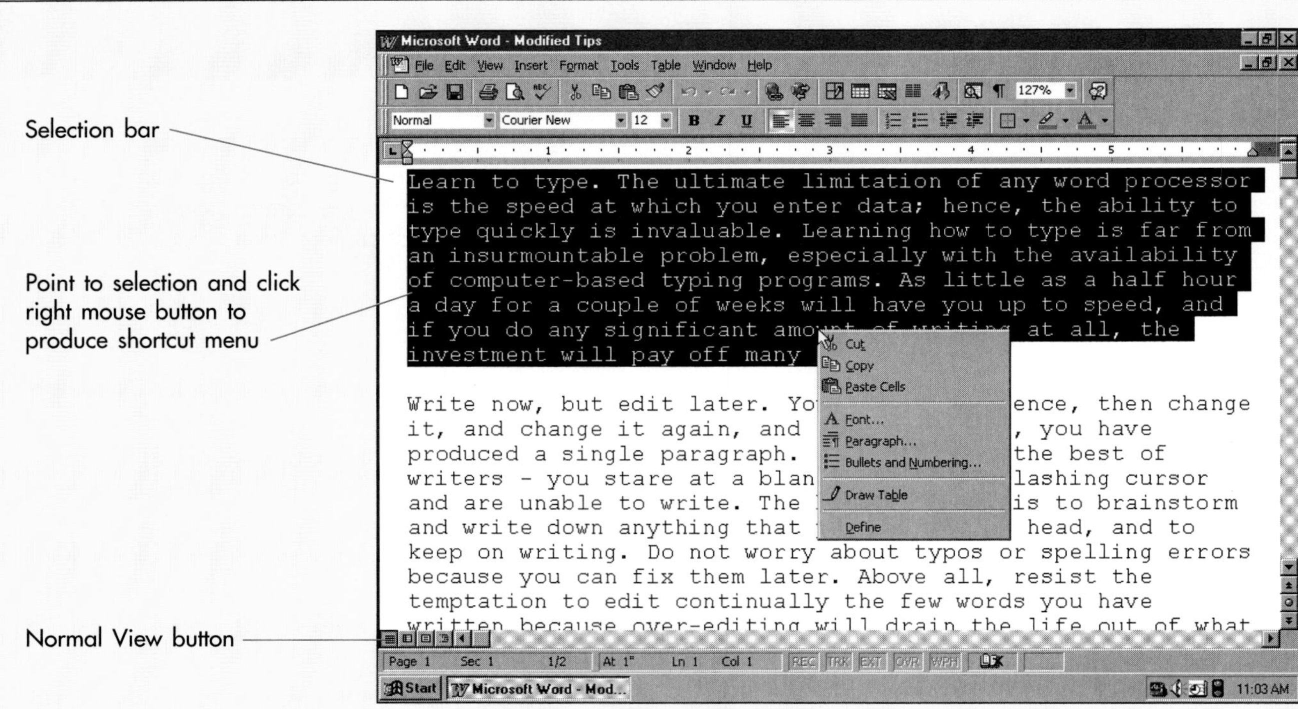

(a) Shortcut Menu (step 2)

FIGURE 2.9 Hands-on Exercise 2

STEP 3: Changing Fonts

- Click the **down arrow** on the Font list box of Figure 2.9b to scroll through the available fonts. Select a different font, such as Times New Roman.
- Click the **down arrow** in the Font Size list box to choose a point size.
- Click **OK** to change the font and point size for the selected text.
- Pull down the **Edit menu** and click **Undo** (or click the **Undo button** on the Standard toolbar) to return to the original font.
- Experiment with different fonts and/or different point sizes until you are satisfied with the selection. We chose 12 point Times New Roman.

FIND AND REPLACE FORMATTING

The Replace command enables you to replace formatting as well as text. To replace any text set in bold with the same text in italics, pull down the Edit menu, and click the Replace command. Click the Find what text box, but do *not* enter any text. Click the More button to expand the dialog box. Click the Format command button, click Font, click Bold in the Font Style list, and click OK. Click the Replace with text box and again do *not* enter any text. Click the Format command button, click Font, click Italic in the Font Style list, and click OK. Click the Find Next or Replace All command button to do selective or automatic replacement. Use a similar technique to replace one font with another.

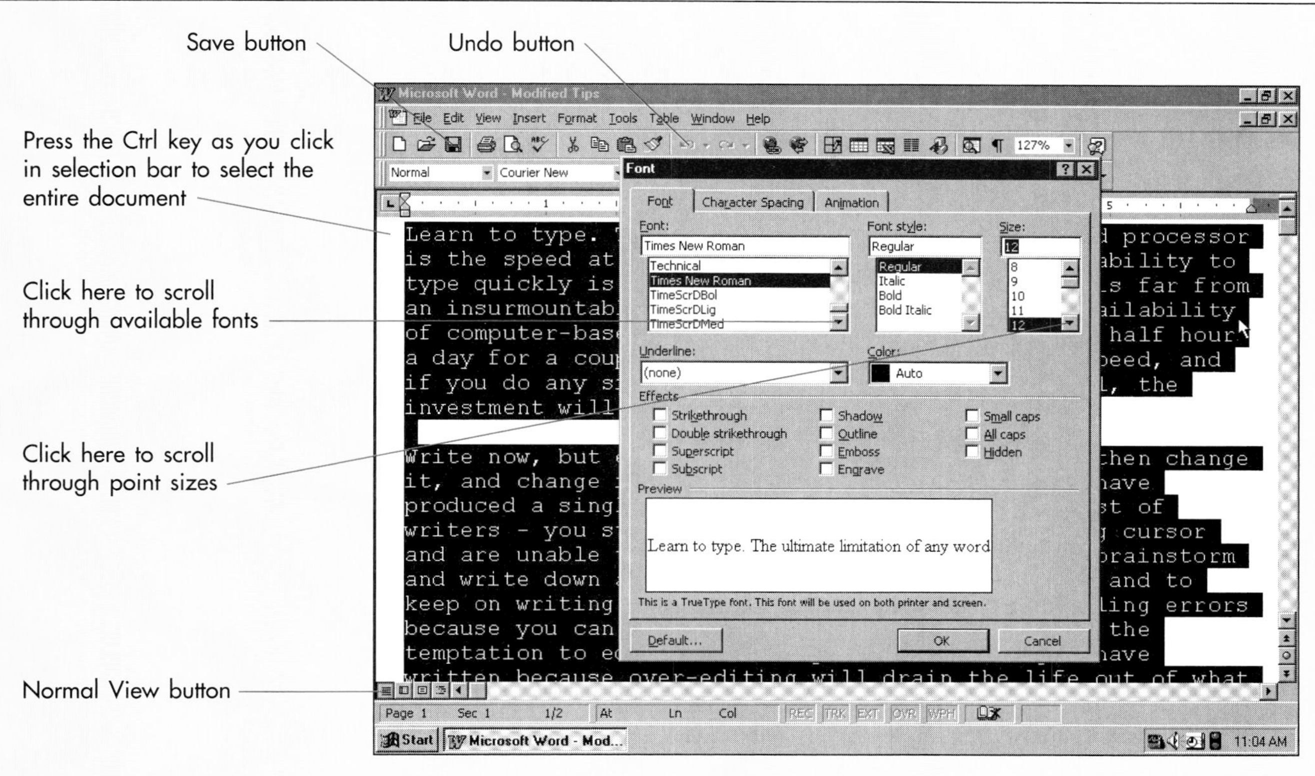

(b) Format Font Command (step 3)

FIGURE 2.9 Hands-on Exercise 2 (continued)

STEP 4: Boldface and Italics

- Drag the mouse over the sentence **Learn to type** at the beginning of the document.
- Click the **Italic button** on the Formatting toolbar to italicize the selected phrase, which will remain selected after the italics take effect.
- Click the **Bold button** to boldface the selected text. The text is now in bold italic.
- Experiment with different styles (bold, italics, underlining, or bold italic) until you are satisfied. The Italic, Bold, and Underline buttons function as toggle switches; that is, clicking the Italic button when text is already italicized returns the text to normal.
- Save the document

THE "WHAT'S THIS" BUTTON

Pull down the Help menu and click the What's This button command (or press Shift+F1). Point to any button on any toolbar (the mouse pointer changes to an arrow with a question mark), then click the button to display a Help balloon to explain the function of that button. Press the Esc key to close the balloon and return the mouse pointer to normal.

STEP 5: The Format Painter

- Click anywhere within the sentence Learn to Type. **Double click** the **Format Painter button** on the Standard toolbar. The mouse pointer changes to a paintbrush as shown in Figure 2.9c.
- Drag the mouse pointer over the next title, **Write now, edit later,** and release the mouse. The formatting from the original sentence (bold italic as shown in Figure 2.9c) has been applied to this sentence as well.
- Drag the mouse pointer (in the shape of a paintbrush) over the remaining titles (the first sentence in each paragraph) to copy the formatting.
- Click the **Format Painter button** after you have painted the title of the last tip to turn the feature off.

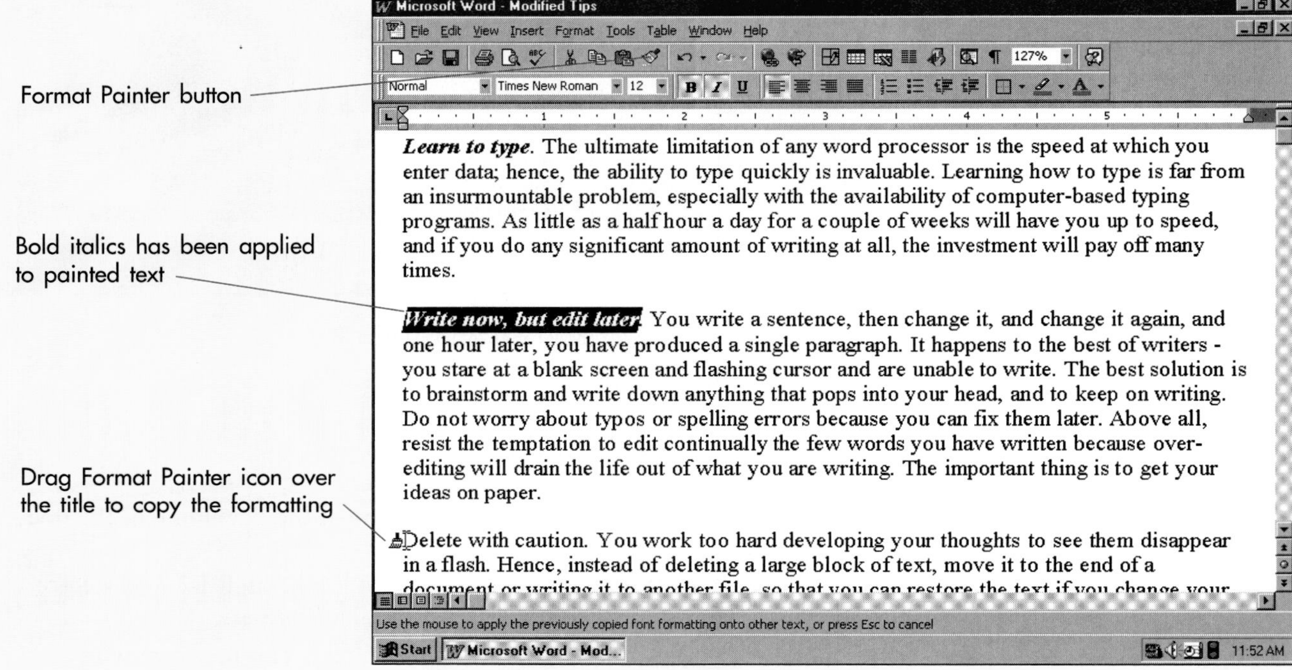

(c) Format Painter (step 5)

FIGURE 2.9 Hands-on Exercise 2 (continued)

> **THE FORMAT PAINTER**
>
> The ***Format Painter*** copies the formatting of the selected text to other places in a document. Select the text with the formatting you want to copy, then click or double click the Format Painter button on the Standard toolbar. Clicking the button will paint only one selection. Double clicking the button will paint multiple selections until the feature is turned off by again clicking the Format Painter button. Either way, the mouse pointer changes to a paintbrush, which you can drag over text to give it the identical formatting characteristics as the original selection.

STEP 6: Change Margins

➤ Press **Ctrl+End** to move to the end of the document as shown in Figure 2.9d. You will see a dotted line indicating a soft page break. (If you do not see the page break, it means that your document fits on one page because you used a different font and/or a smaller point size. We used 12 point Times New Roman.)

➤ Pull down the **File menu.** Click **Page Setup.** Click the **Margins tab** if necessary. Change the bottom margin to **.75** inch. Check that these settings apply to the **Whole Document.** Click **OK.** The page break disappears because more text fits on the page.

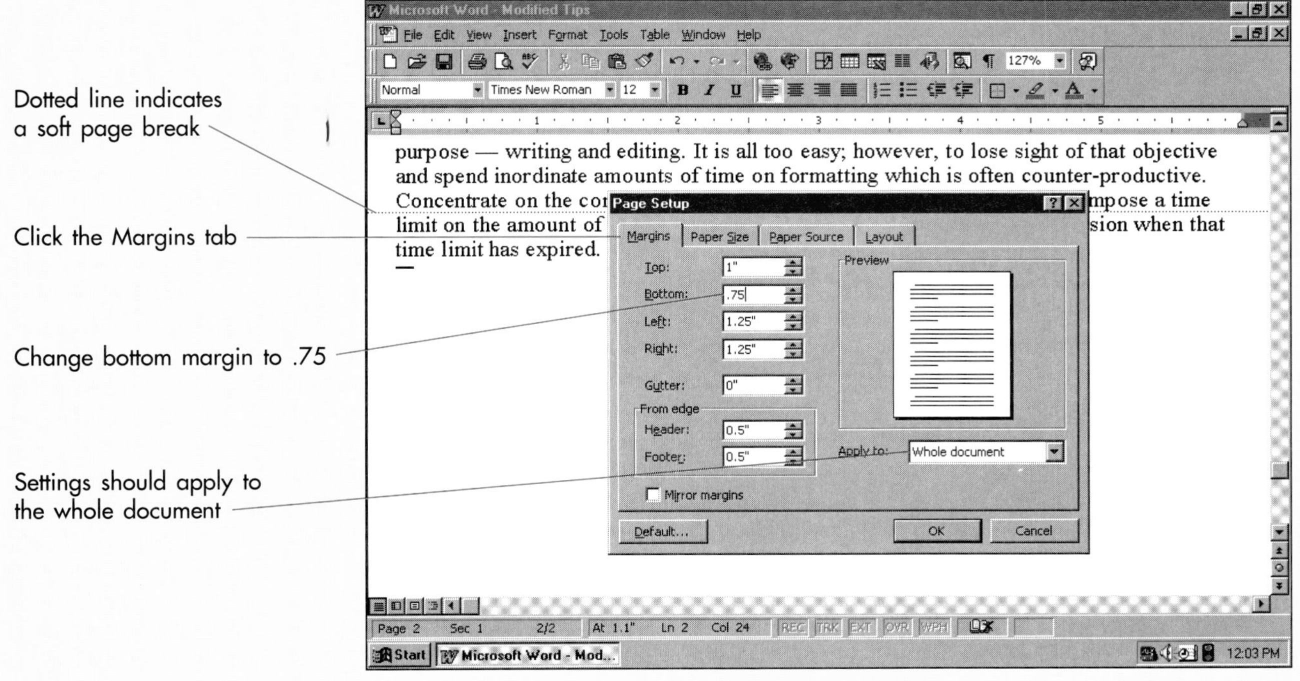

(d) Change Margins (step 6)

FIGURE 2.9 Hands-on Exercise 2 (continued)

DIALOG BOX SHORTCUTS

You can use keyboard shortcuts to select options in a dialog box. Press Tab (Shift+Tab) to move forward (backward) from one field or command button to the next. Press Alt plus the underlined letter to move directly to a field or command button. Press enter to activate the selected command button. Press Esc to exit the dialog box without taking action. Press the space bar to toggle check boxes on or off. Press the down arrow to open a drop-down list box once the list has been accessed, then press the up or down arrow to move between options in a list box.

STEP 7: Create a Title Page

- Press **Ctrl+Home** to move to the beginning of the document. Press **enter** three or four times to add a few blank lines.
- Press **Ctrl+enter** to insert a hard page break. You will see the words "Page Break" in the middle of a dotted line as shown in Figure 2.9e.
- Press the **up arrow key** three times. Enter the title **Tips for Writing.** Select the title, and format it in a larger point size, such as 24 points.
- Enter your name on the next line and format it in a different point size, such as 14 points. Select both the title and your name as shown in the figure. Click the **Center button** on the Formatting toolbar. Save the document.

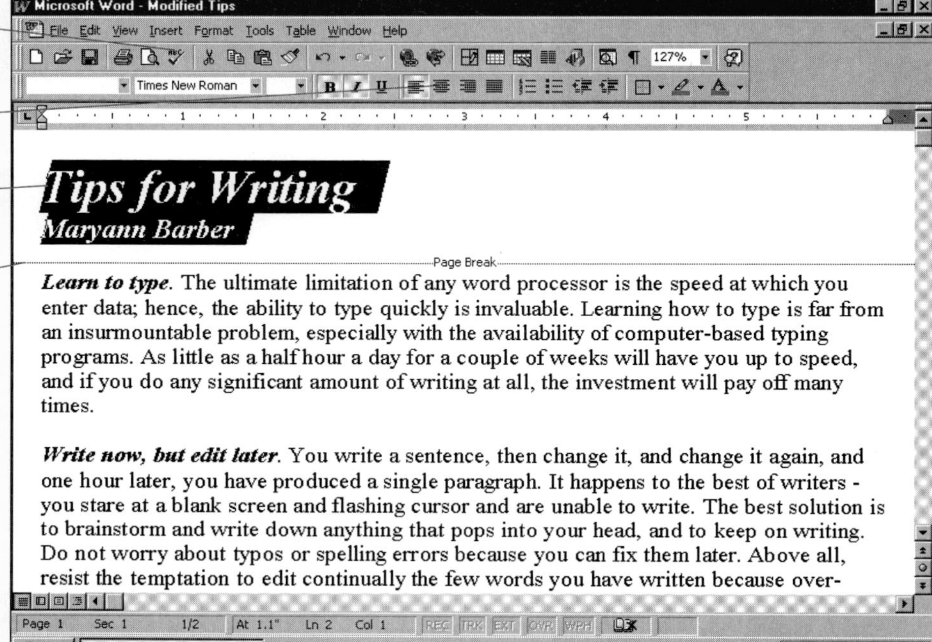

(e) Create the Title Page (step 7)

FIGURE 2.9 Hands-on Exercise 2 (continued)

THE SPELL CHECK

Use the spell check prior to saving a document for the last time, even if the document is just a sentence or two. Spelling errors make your work look sloppy and discourage the reader before he or she has read what you had to say. Spelling errors can cost you a job, a grade, or a lucrative contract. The spell check requires but a single click, so why not use it?

STEP 8: The Completed Document

- Pull down the **View menu** and click **Page Layout** (or click the **Page Layout button** above the status bar).
- Click the **Zoom Control arrow** on the Standard toolbar and select **Two Pages.** Release the mouse to view the completed document in Figure 2.9f. You may want to add additional blank lines at the top of the title page to move the title further down on the page.
- Save the document a final time. Exit Word if you do not want to continue with the next exercise at this time.

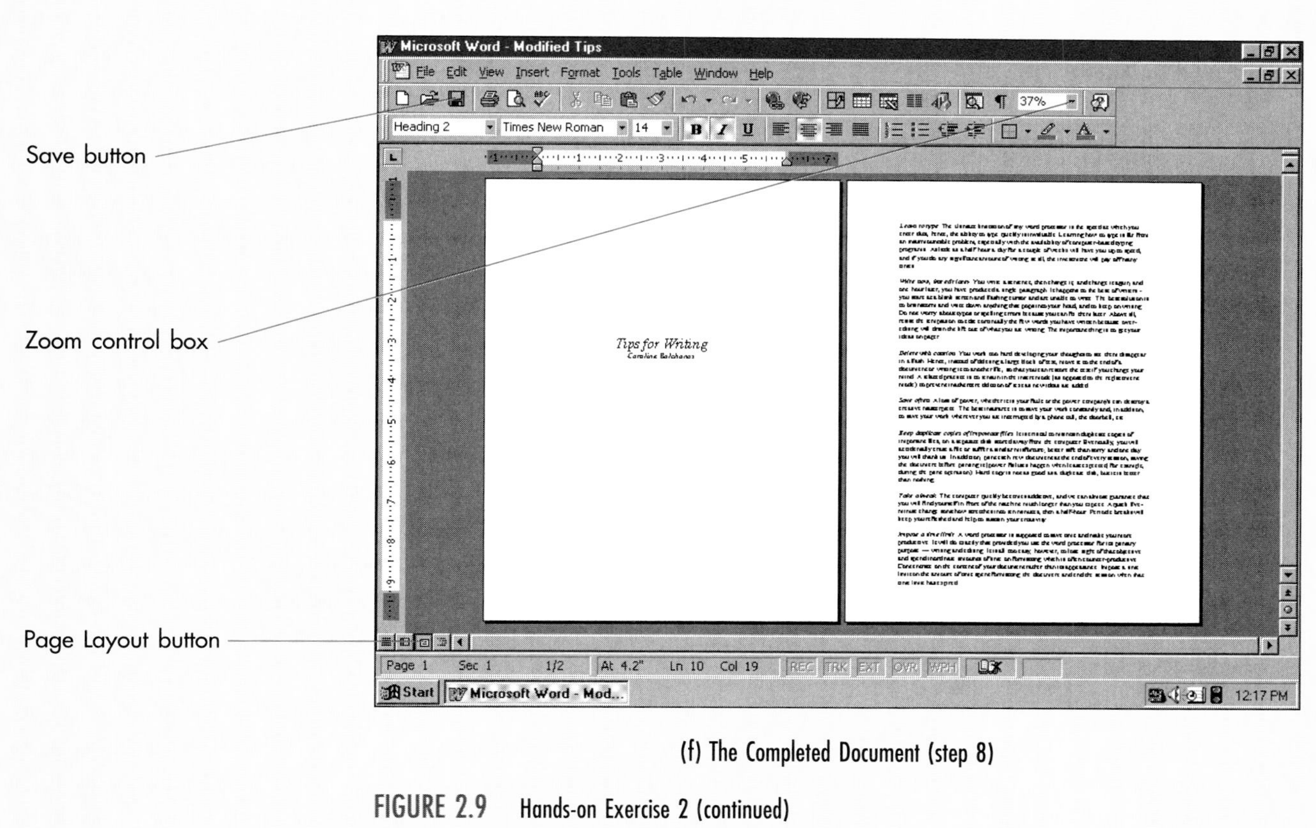

(f) The Completed Document (step 8)

FIGURE 2.9 Hands-on Exercise 2 (continued)

PARAGRAPH FORMATTING

A change in typography is only one way to alter the appearance of a document. You can also change the alignment, indentation, tab stops, or line spacing for any paragraph(s) within the document. You can control the pagination and prevent the occurrence of awkward page breaks by specifying that an entire paragraph has to appear on the same page, or that a one-line paragraph (e.g., a heading) should appear on the same page as the next paragraph. You can include borders or shading for added emphasis around selected paragraphs.

All of these features are implemented at the paragraph level and affect all selected paragraphs. If no paragraphs are selected, the commands affect the entire current paragraph (the paragraph containing the insertion point), regardless of the position of the insertion point when the command is executed.

Alignment

Text can be aligned in four different ways as shown in Figure 2.10. It may be justified (flush left/flush right), left aligned (flush left with a ragged right margin), right aligned (flush right with a ragged left margin), or centered within the margins (ragged left and right).

Left aligned text is perhaps the easiest to read. The first letters of each line align with each other, helping the eye to find the beginning of each line. The lines themselves are of irregular length. There is uniform spacing between words, and the ragged margin on the right adds white space to the text, giving it a lighter and more informal look.

Justified text produces lines of equal length, with the spacing between words adjusted to align at the margins. It may be more difficult to read than text that is left aligned because of the uneven (sometimes excessive) word spacing and/or the greater number of hyphenated words needed to justify the lines.

Type that is centered or right aligned is restricted to limited amounts of text where the effect is more important than the ease of reading. Centered text, for example, appears frequently on wedding invitations, poems, or formal announcements. Right aligned text is used with figure captions and short headlines.

Indents

Individual paragraphs can be indented so that they appear to have different margins from the rest of a document. Indentation is established at the paragraph level; thus different indentation can be in effect for different paragraphs. One paragraph may be indented from the left margin only, another from the right margin only, and a third from both the left and right margins. The first line of any paragraph may be indented differently from the rest of the paragraph. And finally, a paragraph may be set with no indentation at all, so that it aligns on the left and right margins.

The indentation of a paragraph is determined by three settings: the ***left indent,*** the ***right indent,*** and a ***special indent*** (if any). There are two types of special indentation, first line and hanging, as will be explained shortly. The left and right indents are set to zero by default, as is the special indent, and produce a paragraph with no indentation at all as shown in Figure 2.11a. Positive values for the left and right indents offset the paragraph from both margins as shown in Figure 2.11b.

The ***first line indent*** (Figure 2.11c) affects only the first line in the paragraph and is implemented by pressing the Tab key at the beginning of the paragraph. A ***hanging indent*** (Figure 2.11d) sets the first line of a paragraph at the left indent and indents the remaining lines according to the amount specified. Hanging indents are often used with bulleted or numbered lists.

INDENTS VERSUS MARGINS

Indents measure the distance between the text and the margins. ***Margins*** mark the distance from the text to the edge of the page. Indents are determined at the paragraph level, whereas margins are established at the section (document) level. The left and right margins are set (by default) to 1.25 inches each; the left and right indents default to zero. The first line indent is measured from the setting of the left indent.

We, the people of the United States, in order to form a more perfect Union, establish justice, insure domestic tranquillity, provide for the common defense, promote the general welfare, and secure the blessings of liberty to ourselves and our posterity, do ordain and establish this Constitution for the United States of America.

(a) Justified (flush left/flush right)

We, the people of the United States, in order to form a more perfect Union, establish
justice, insure domestic tranquillity, provide for the common defense, promote the general
welfare, and secure the blessings of liberty to ourselves and our posterity, do ordain and
establish this Constitution for the United States of America.

(b) Left Aligned (flush left/ragged right)

We, the people of the United States, in order to form a more perfect Union, establish
justice, insure domestic tranquillity, provide for the common defense, promote the general
welfare, and secure the blessings of liberty to ourselves and our posterity, do ordain and
establish this Constitution for the United States of America.

(c) Right Aligned (ragged left/flush right)

We, the people of the United States, in order to form a more perfect Union, establish
justice, insure domestic tranquillity, provide for the common defense, promote the general
welfare, and secure the blessings of liberty to ourselves and our posterity, do ordain and
establish this Constitution for the United States of America.

(d) Centered (ragged left/ragged right)

FIGURE 2.10 Alignment

The left and right indents are defined as the distance between the text and the left and right margins, respectively. Both parameters are set to zero in this paragraph and so the text aligns on both margins. Different indentation can be applied to different paragraphs in the same document.

(a) No Indents

Positive values for the left and right indents offset a paragraph from the rest of a document and are often used for long quotations. This paragraph has left and right indents of one-half inch each. Different indentation can be applied to different paragraphs in the same document.

(b) Left and Right Indents

A first line indent affects only the first line in the paragraph and is implemented by pressing the Tab key at the beginning of the paragraph. The remainder of the paragraph is aligned at the left margin (or the left indent if it differs from the left margin) as can be seen from this example. Different indentation can be applied to different paragraphs in the same document.

(c) First Line Indent

A hanging indent sets the first line of a paragraph at the left indent and indents the remaining lines according to the amount specified. Hanging indents are often used with bulleted or numbered lists. Different indentation can be applied to different paragraphs in the same document.

(d) Hanging (Special) Indent

FIGURE 2.11 Indents

Tabs

Anyone who has used a typewriter is familiar with the function of the Tab key; that is, press Tab and the insertion point moves to the next ***tab stop*** (a measured position to align text at a specific place). The Tab key is much more powerful in Word as you can choose from four different types of tab stops (left, center, right, and decimal). You can also specify a ***leader character,*** typically dots or hyphens, to draw the reader's eye across the page. Tabs are often used to create tables within a document.

The default tab stops are set every ½ inch and are left aligned, but you can change the ***alignment*** and/or position with the Format Tabs command. Figure 2.12 illustrates a dot leader in combination with a right tab to produce a Table of Contents. The default tab stops have been cleared in Figure 2.12a, in favor of a single right tab at 5.5 inches. The option button for a dot leader has also been checked. The resulting document is shown in Figure 2.12b.

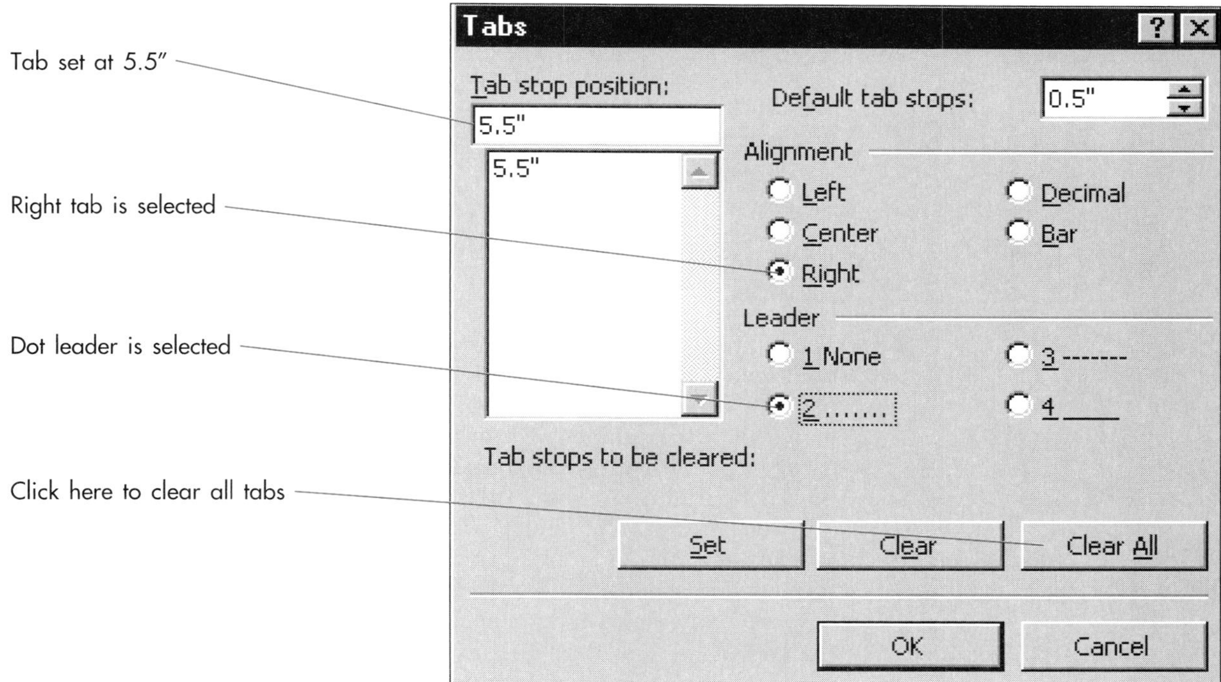

(a) Tab Stops

Right tab with dot leader

Chapter 1: Introduction 3
Chapter 2: Gaining Proficiency 32
Chapter 3: The Tools 61
Chapter 4: The Professional Document 99
Chapter 5: Desktop Publishing 124

(b) Table of Contents

FIGURE 2.12 Tabs

The Format Tabs command is quite powerful, so it is useful to repeat the different alignments:

- Left alignment, where the text *begins* at the tab stop, corresponds to the Tab key on a typewriter.
- Right alignment, where the text *ends* at the tab stop, is used to align page numbers in a table of contents or to align text at the right margin.
- Center alignment, where text centers over the tab stop, is used infrequently for special effect.
- Decimal alignment, which lines up numeric values in a column on the decimal point, is helpful with statistical text.

Line Spacing

Line spacing determines the space between the lines in a paragraph. Word provides complete flexibility and enables you to select any multiple of line spacing (single, double, line and a half, and so on). You can also specify line spacing in terms of points (there are 72 points per inch).

Line spacing is set at the paragraph level through the Format Paragraph command, which sets the spacing within a paragraph. The command also enables you to add extra spacing before the first line in a paragraph or after the last line. (Either technique is preferable to the common practice of single spacing the paragraphs within a document, then adding a blank line between paragraphs.)

FORMAT PARAGRAPH COMMAND

The ***Format Paragraph command*** is where you specify the alignment, indentation, line spacing, and pagination for the selected paragraph(s). As indicated, all of these features are implemented at the paragraph level and affect all selected paragraphs. If no paragraphs are selected, the command affects the entire current paragraph (the paragraph containing the insertion point), regardless of the position of the insertion point when the command is executed.

The Format Paragraph command is illustrated in Figure 2.13. The Indents and Spacing tab in Figure 2.13a calls for a hanging indent, line spacing of 1.5 lines, and justified alignment. The preview area within the dialog box enables you to see how the paragraph will appear within the document.

The Line and Page Breaks tab in Figure 2.13b illustrates an entirely different set of parameters in which you control the pagination within a document. You are already familiar with the concept of page breaks, and the distinction between soft page breaks (inserted by Word) versus hard page breaks (inserted by the user). The check boxes in Figure 2.13b enable you to prevent the occurrence of awkward soft page breaks that detract from the appearance of a document.

You might, for example, want to prevent widows and orphans, terms used to describe isolated lines that seem out of place. A ***widow*** refers to the last line of a paragraph appearing by itself at the top of a page. An ***orphan*** is the first line of a paragraph appearing by itself at the bottom of a page.

You can also impose additional controls by clicking one or more check boxes. Use the Keep Lines Together option to prevent a soft page break from occurring within a paragraph and ensure that the entire paragraph appears on the same page. (The paragraph is moved to the top of the next page if it doesn't fit on the bottom of the current page.) Use the Keep with Next option to prevent a soft page break between the two paragraphs. This option is typically used to keep a heading (a one-line paragraph) with its associated text in the next paragraph.

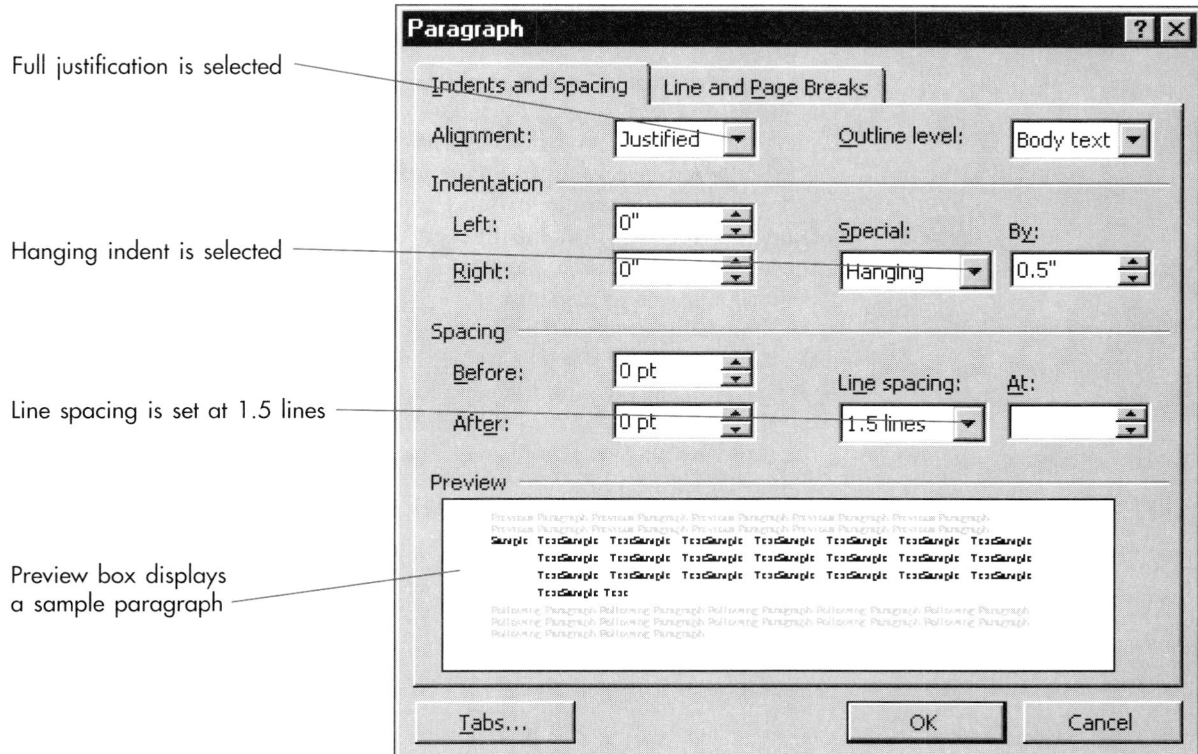

(a) Indents and Spacing

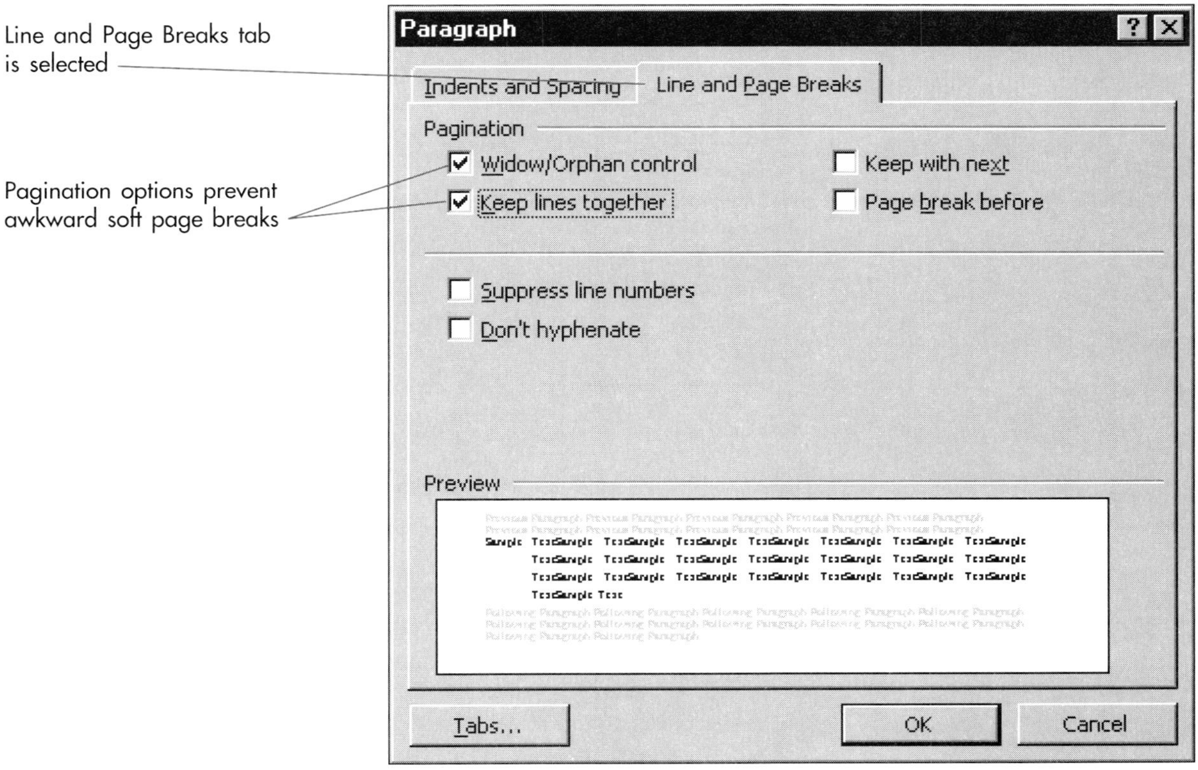

(b) Line and Page Breaks

FIGURE 2.13 Format Paragraph Command

Borders and Shading

The ***Borders and Shading command*** puts the finishing touches on a document and is illustrated in Figure 2.14. It lets you create boxed and/or shaded text as well as place horizontal or vertical lines around a paragraph. You can choose from several different line styles in any color (assuming you have a color printer). You can place a uniform border around a paragraph (choose Box), or you can choose a shadow effect with thicker lines at the right and bottom. You can also apply lines to selected sides of a paragraph(s) by selecting a line style, then clicking the desired sides as apprpriate.

Shading is implemented independently of the border. Clear (no shading) is the default. Solid (100%) shading creates a solid box where the text is turned white so you can read it. Shading of 10 or 20 percent is generally most effective to add emphasis to the selected paragraph. The Borders and Shading command is implemented on the paragraph level and affects the entire paragraph—either the current or selected paragraph(s).

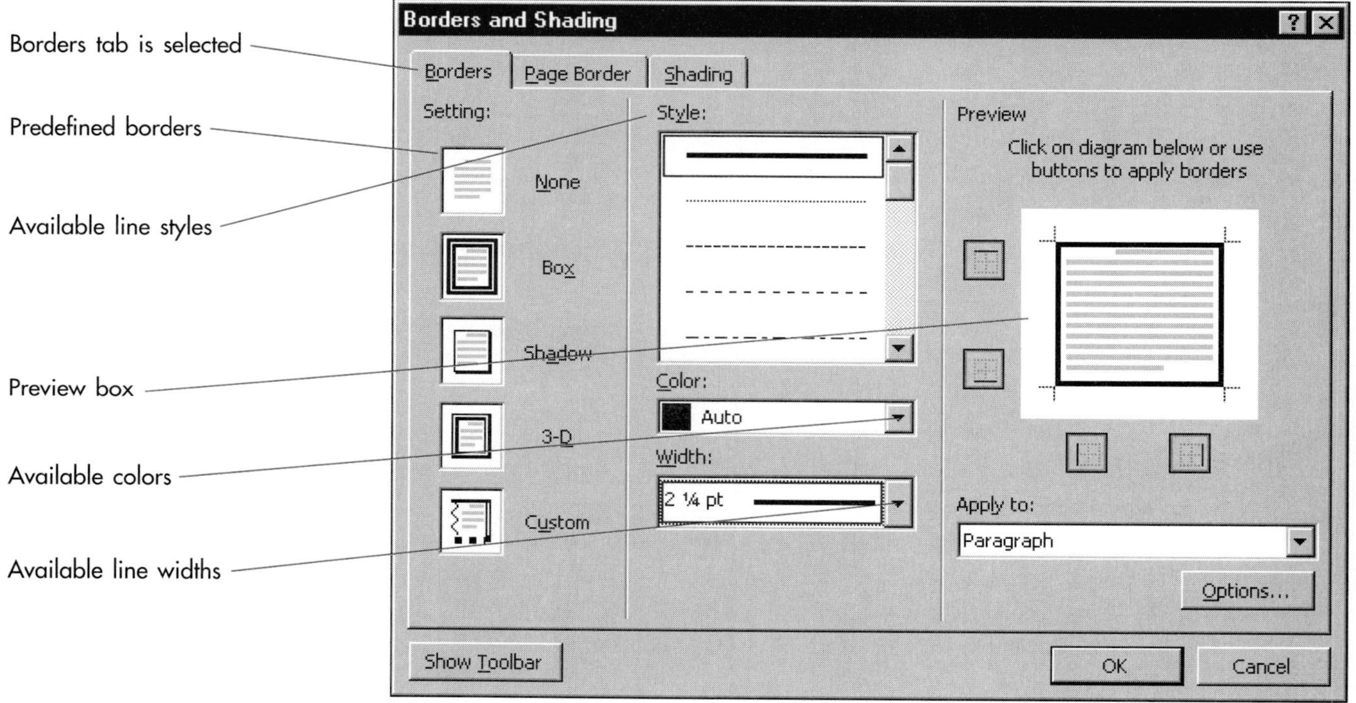

(a) Borders

FIGURE 2.14 Paragraph Borders and Shading

FORMATTING AND THE PARAGRAPH MARK

The paragraph mark ¶ at the end of a paragraph does more than just indicate the presence of a hard return. It also stores all of the formatting in effect for the paragraph. Hence in order to preserve the formatting when you move or copy a paragraph, you must include the paragraph mark in the selected text. Click the Show/Hide ¶ button on the toolbar to display the paragraph mark and make sure it has been selected.

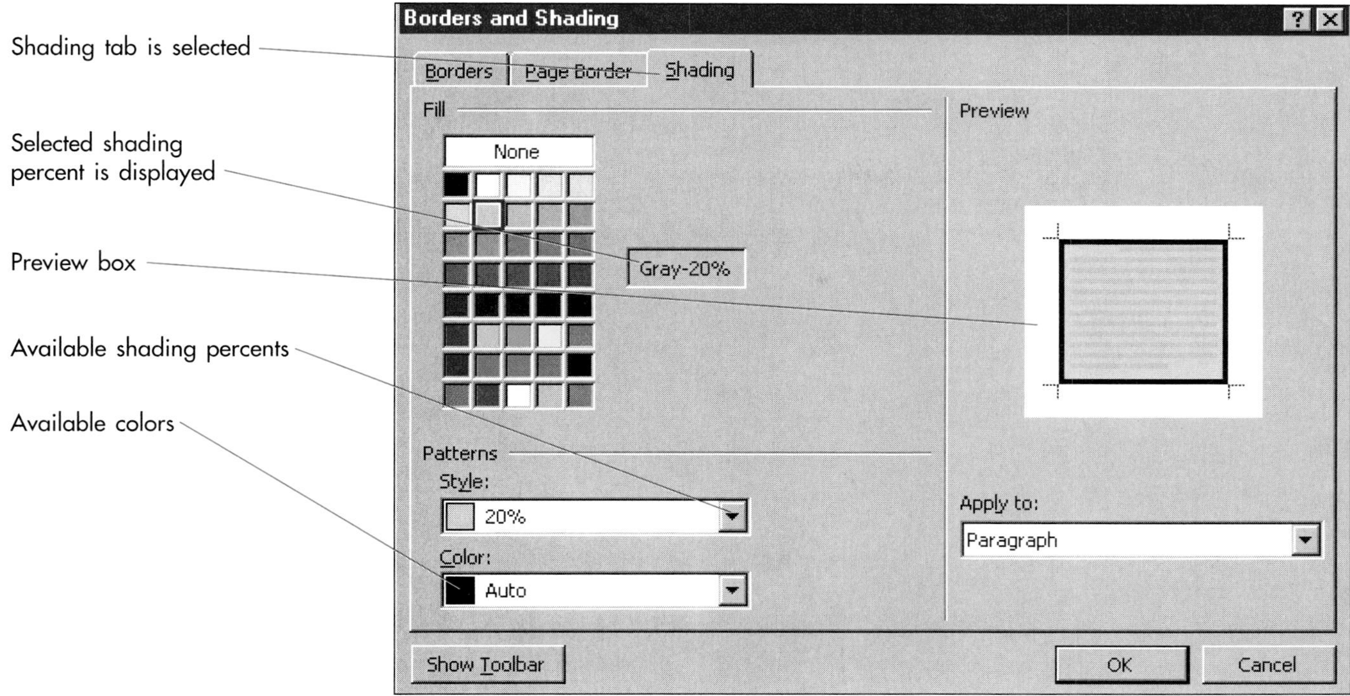

(b) Shading

FIGURE 2.14 Paragraph Borders and Shading (continued)

PARAGRAPH FORMATTING AND THE INSERTION POINT

Indents, tab stops, line spacing, alignment, pagination, borders, and shading are all set at the paragraph level and affect all selected paragraphs and/or the current paragraph (the paragraph containing the insertion point). The position of the insertion point within the paragraph does not matter as the insertion point can be anywhere within the paragraph when the Format Paragraph command is executed. Keep the concept of paragraph formatting in mind as you do the following hands-on exercise.

HANDS-ON EXERCISE 3

Paragraph Formatting

Objective: To implement line spacing, alignment, and indents; to implement widow and orphan protection; to box and shade a selected paragraph.

STEP 1: Load the Practice Document

- Open the **Modified Tips** document from the previous exercise. If necessary, change to the Page Layout view. Click the **Zoom drop-down arrow** and click **Two Pages** to match the view in Figure 2.15a.
- Select the entire second page as shown in the figure. Click the **right mouse button** to produce the shortcut menu. Click **Paragraph.**

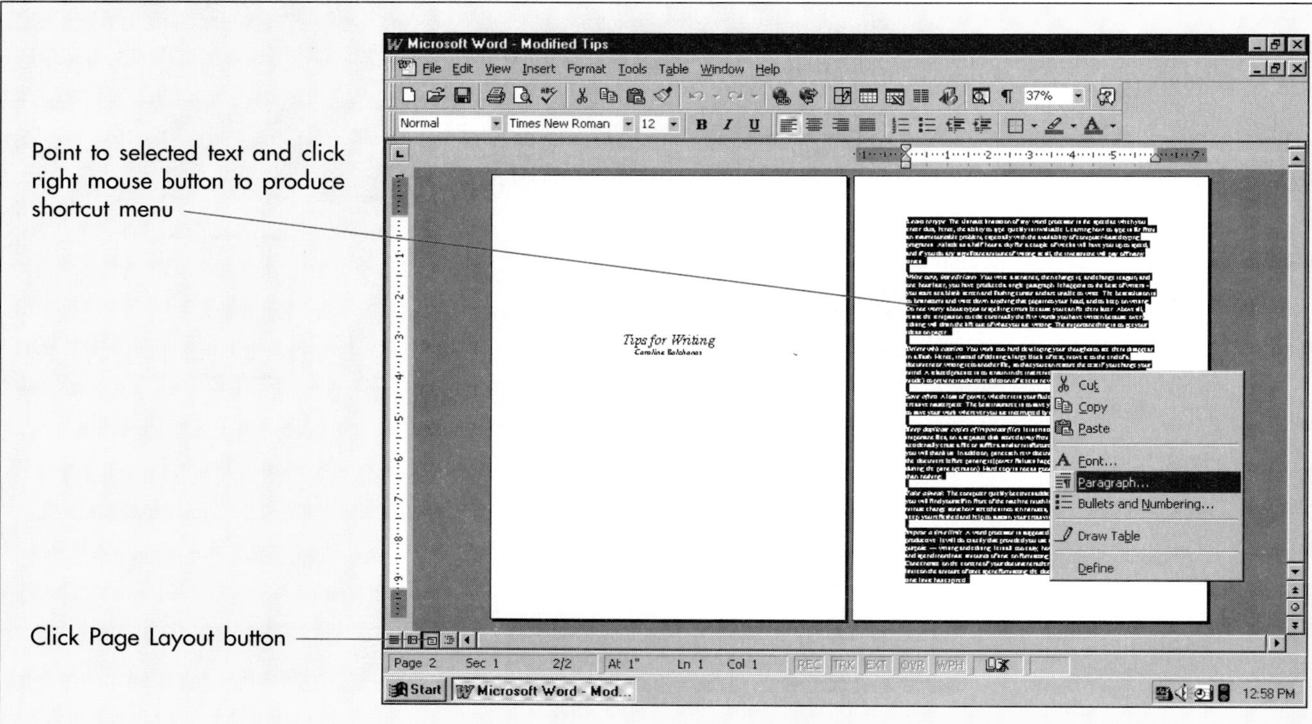

(a) Select-then-do (step 1)

FIGURE 2.15 Hands-on Exercise 3

> **SELECT TEXT WITH THE F8 EXTEND KEY**
>
> Move to the beginning of the text you want to select, then press the F8 (extend) key. The letters EXT will appear in the status bar. Use the arrow keys to extend the selection in the indicated direction; for example, press the down arrow key to select the line. You can also press any character—for example, a letter, space, or period—to extend the selection to the first occurrence of that character. Press Esc to cancel the selection mode.

STEP 2: Line Spacing, Justification, and Pagination

- If necessary, click the **Indents and Spacing tab** to view the options in Figure 2.15b.
  - Click the **down arrow** on the list box for Line Spacing and select **1.5 Lines.**
  - Click the **down arrow** on the Alignment list box and select **Justified** as shown in Figure 2.15b.
  - The Preview area shows the effect of these settings.
- Click the tab for **Line and Page Breaks.**
  - Check the box for **Keep Lines Together.** If necessary, check the box for **Widow/Orphan Control.**
- Click **OK** to accept all of the settings in the dialog box.

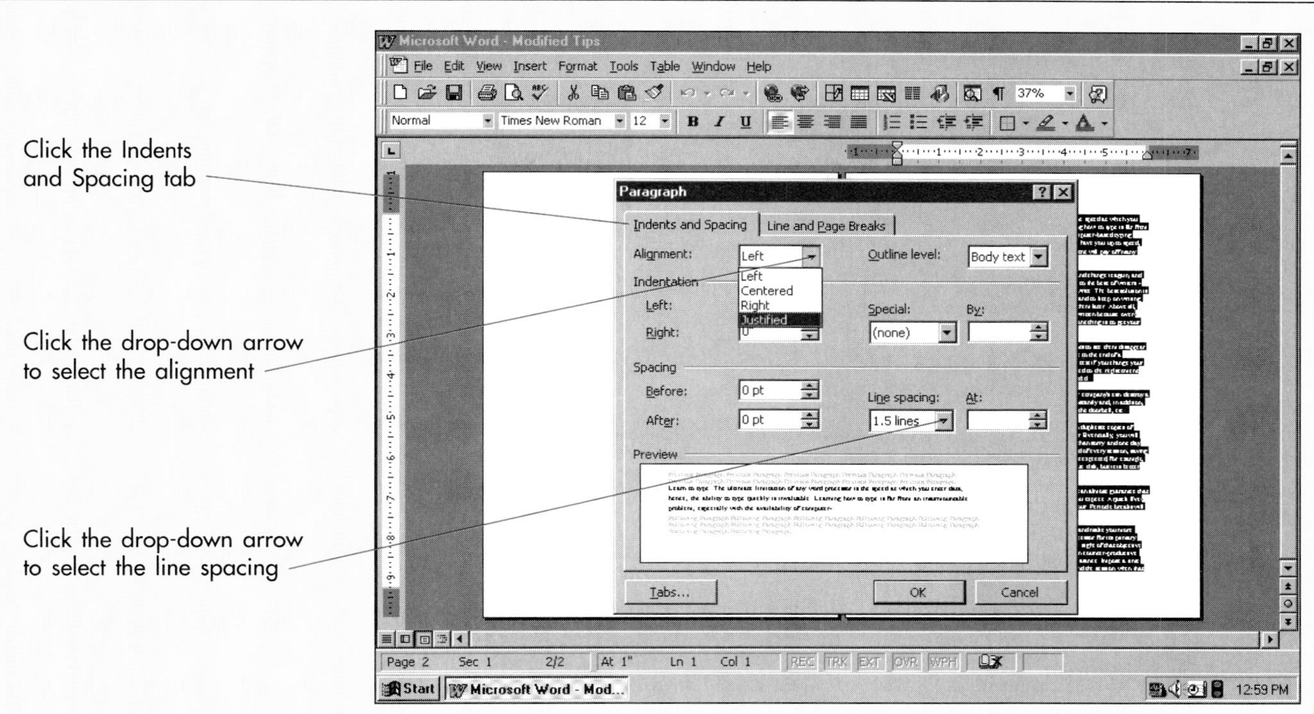

(b) Format Paragraph Command (step 2)

FIGURE 2.15 Hands-on Exercise 3 (continued)

➤ Click anywhere in the document to deselect the text and see the effects of the formatting changes:

- The document is fully justified and the line spacing has increased.
- The document now extends to three pages, with all of the fifth paragraph appearing on the last page.
- There is a large bottom margin on the second page as a consequence of keeping the lines together in paragraph five.

➤ Save the document.

CUSTOMIZE THE TOOLBAR

Customize the Formatting toolbar to display the buttons for line spacing. Point to any toolbar, click the right mouse button to display a shortcut menu, and click Customize to display the Customize dialog box. Click the Commands tab, select Format from the Categories list box, then scroll in the Commands list box until you click and drag the line spacing buttons to the end of the Formatting toolbar. You must drag the button within the Formatting toolbar (the mouse pointer will change to a + from an ×, indicating that you can copy the button). Close the Customize dialog box. The next time you want to change line spacing, just click the appropriate button on the Formatting toolbar.

STEP 3: Indents

- Select the second paragraph as shown in Figure 2.15c. (The second paragraph will not yet be indented.)
- Pull down the **Format menu** and click **Paragraph** (or press the **right mouse button** to produce the shortcut menu and click **Paragraph**).
- If necessary, click the **Indents and Spacing tab** in the Paragraph dialog box. Click the **up arrow** on the Left Indentation text box to set the **Left Indent** to **.5** inch. Set the **Right indent** to **.5** inch. Click **OK.** Your document should match Figure 2.15c.
- Save the document.

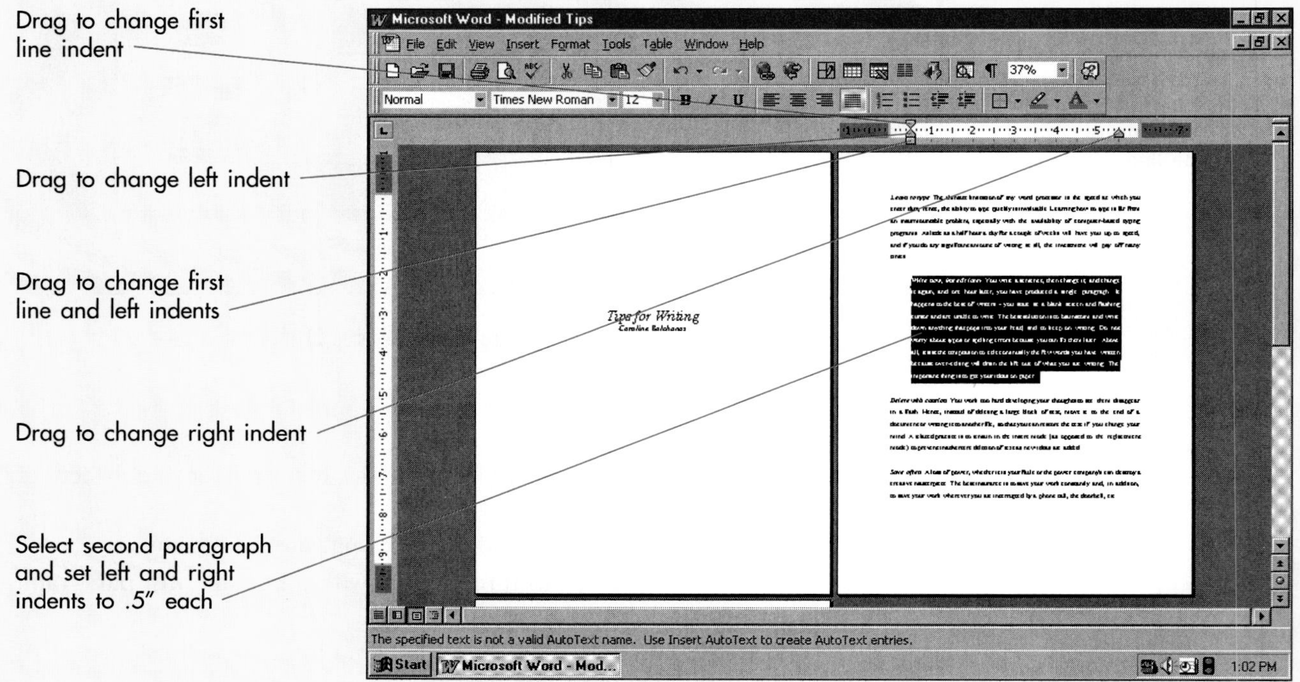

(c) Indents and the Ruler (step 3)

FIGURE 2.15 Hands-on Exercise 3 (continued)

INDENTS AND THE RULER

Use the ruler to change the special, left, and/or right indents. Select the paragraph (or paragraphs) in which you want to change indents, then drag the appropriate indent markers to the new location(s). If you get a hanging indent when you wanted to change the left indent, it means you dragged the bottom triangle instead of the box. Click the Undo button and try again. (You can always use the Format Paragraph command rather than the ruler if you continue to have difficulty.)

STEP 4: Borders and Shading

➤ Pull down the **Format menu.** Click **Borders and Shading** to produce the dialog box in Figure 2.15d.

➤ If necessary, click the **Borders tab.** Select a style and width for the line around the box. Click the rectangle labeled **Box** under Settings.

➤ Click the **Shading Tab.** Click the **down arrow** on the Style list box. Click **10%.**

➤ Click **OK** to accept the settings for both Borders and Shading.

➤ Save the document.

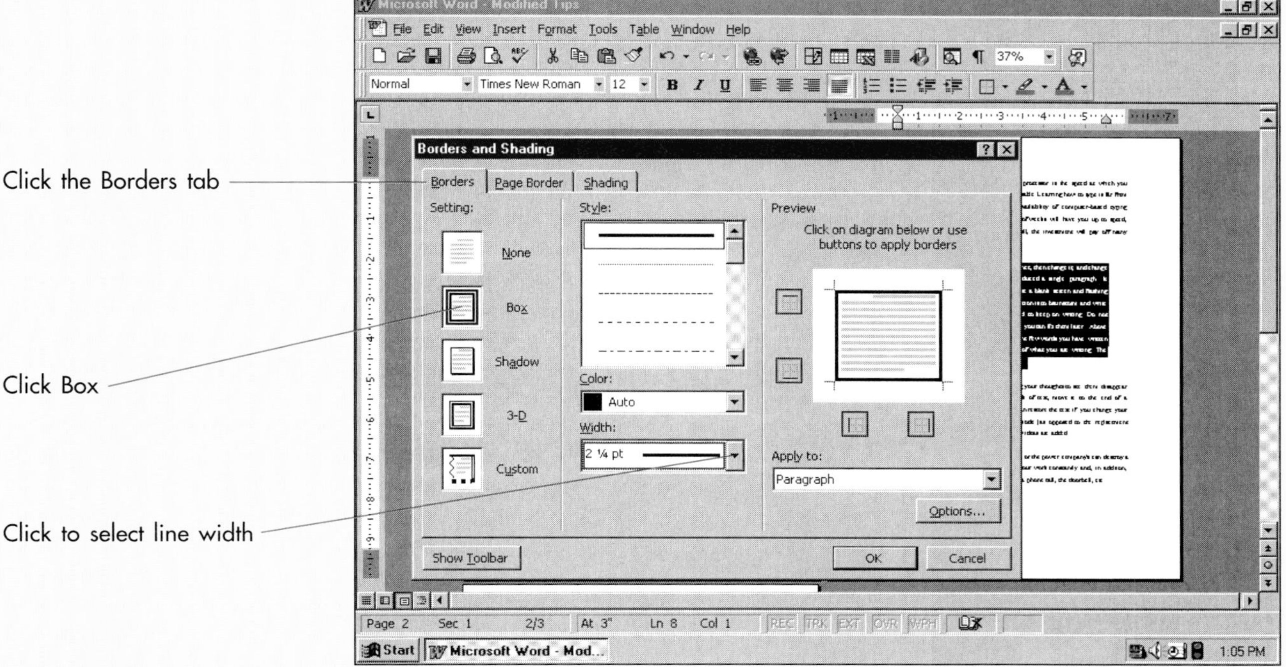

(d) Borders and Shading Command (step 4)

FIGURE 2.15 Hands-on Exercise 3 (continued)

THE PAGE BORDER COMMAND

You can apply a border to the title page of your document, to every page except the title page, or to every page including the title page. Pull down the Format menu, click Borders and Shading, and click the Page Borders tab. First design the border by selecting a style, color, width, and art (if any). Then choose the page(s) to which you want to apply the border by clicking the drop-down arrow in the Apply to list box. Close the Borders and Shading dialog box. See practice exercise 5 at the end of the chapter.

STEP 5: Help with Formatting

- Pull down the **Help menu** and click the **What's This command** (or press **Shift+F1**). The mouse pointer changes to an arrow with a question mark.
- Click anywhere inside the boxed paragraph to display the formatting information shown in Figure 2.15e.
- Click in a different paragraph to see its formatting. Press the **Esc key** to return the pointer to normal.

DISPLAY THE HARD RETURNS

Many formattting commands are implemented at the paragraph level, and thus it helps to know where a paragraph ends. Click the Show/Hide ¶ button on the Standard toolbar to display the hard returns (paragraph marks) and other nonprinting characters (such as tab characters or blank spaces) contained within a document. The Show/Hide ¶ functions as a toggle switch; the first time you click it the hard returns are displayed, the second time you press it the returns are hidden, and so on.

STEP 6: The Zoom Command

- Pull down the **View menu.** Click **Zoom** to produce the dialog box in Figure 2.15f.
- Click the **Many Pages** option button. Click the **monitor icon** to display a sample selection box, then click and drag to display three pages across as shown in the figure. Release the mouse. Click **OK.**

STEP 7: Advice from the Office Assistant

- Click the **Office Assistant button** on the Standard toolbar or press the **F1 key** to display the Assistant. Click the lightbulb (assuming the Assistant has a suggestion) to display the tip. Click the **Back** or **Next** buttons as appropriate to view additional tips.
- The Assistant will not, however, repeat a tip from an earlier session unless you reset it at the start of a new session. To reset the tips, click the Assistant to display a balloon asking what you want to do, click the **Options button** in the balloon, click **Options,** then click the button to **Reset My Tips.**

HELP FOR MICROSOFT WORD

Microsoft Word offers help from a variety of sources. You can pull down the Help menu as you can with any Windows application and/or you can click the Office Assisant button on the Standard toolbar. You can also go to the Microsoft Web site to obtain more recent, and often more detailed, information. Pull down the Help menu, click Microsoft on the Web, then click Online Support to go to the Microsoft Web site, provided you have an Internet connection.

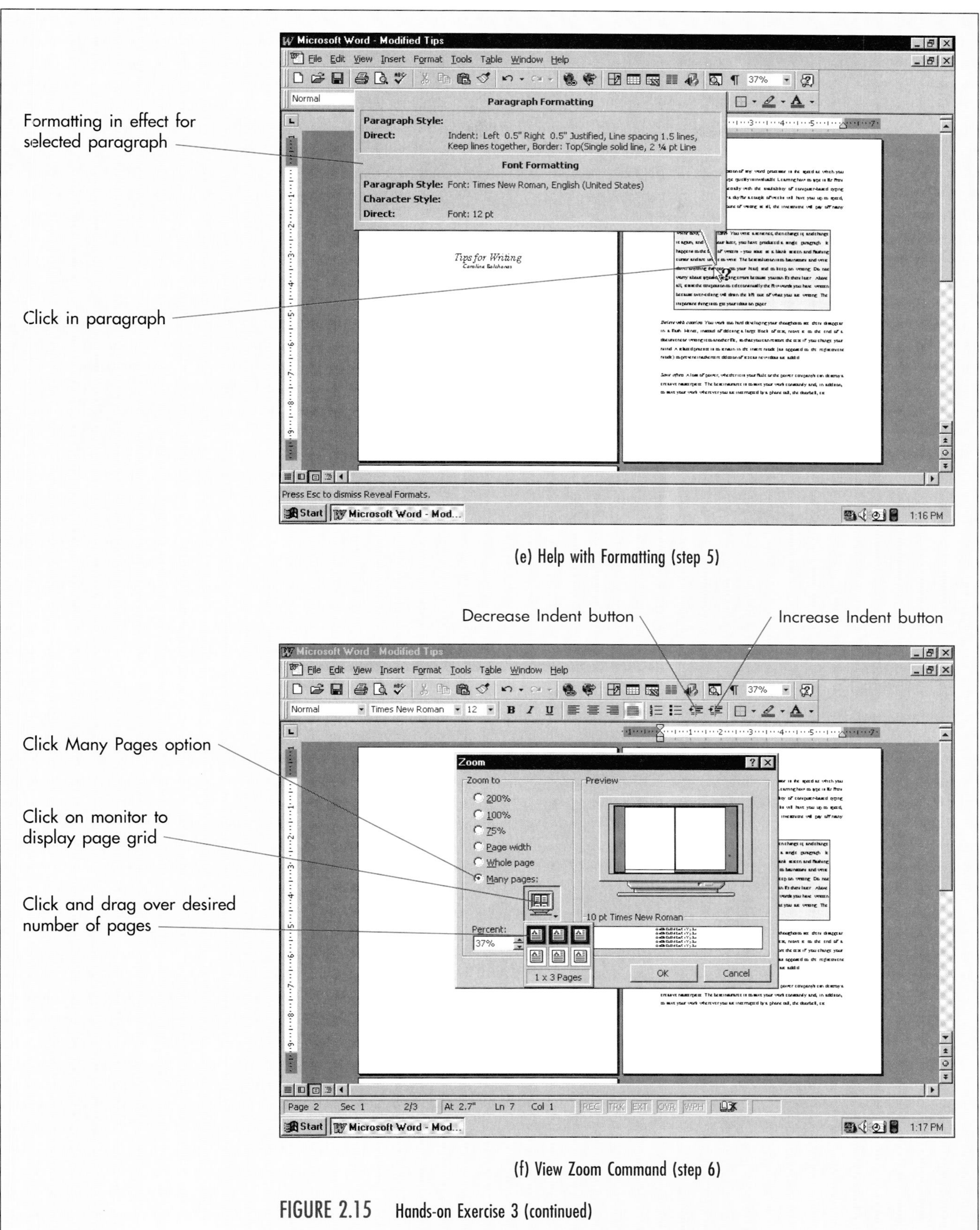

(e) Help with Formatting (step 5)

(f) View Zoom Command (step 6)

FIGURE 2.15 Hands-on Exercise 3 (continued)

STEP 8: The Completed Document

- Your screen should match the one in Figure 2.15g, which displays all three pages of the document.
- The Page Layout view displays both a vertical and a horizontal ruler. The boxed and indented paragraph is clearly shown in the second page.
- The soft page break between pages two and three occurs between tips rather than within a tip; that is, the text of each tip is kept together on the same page.
- Save the document a final time. Print the completed document and submit it to your instructor. Exit Word.

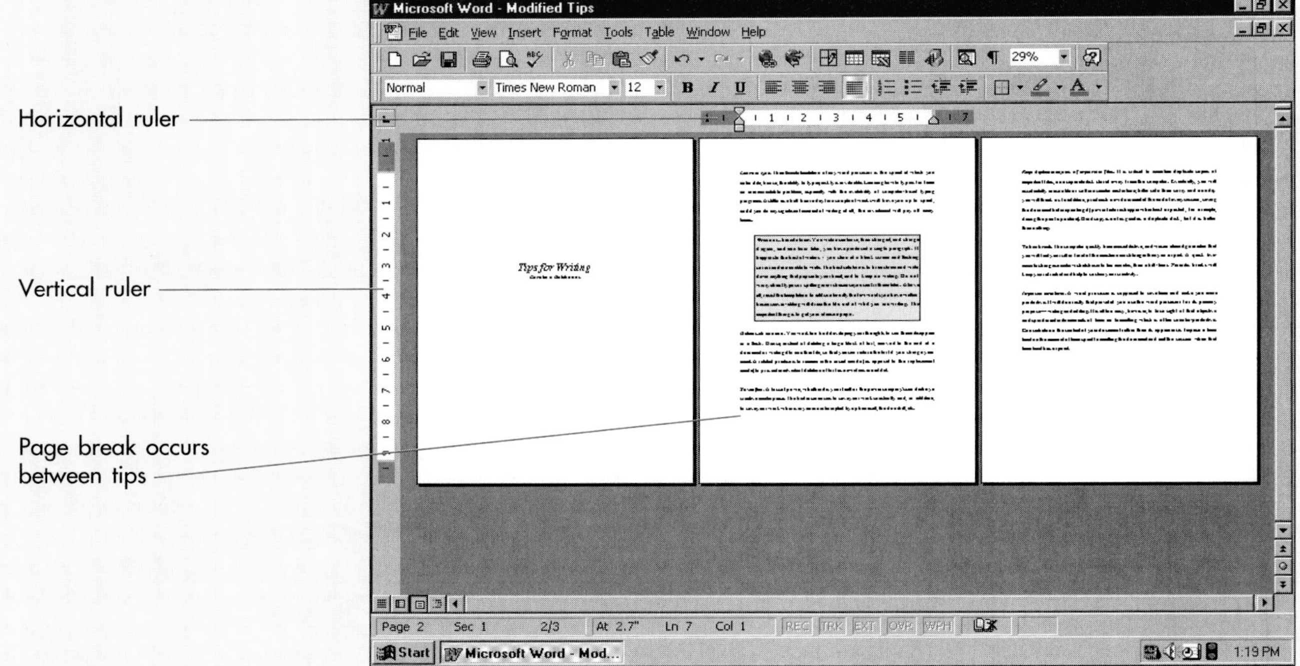

(g) The Completed Document (step 8)

FIGURE 2.15 Hands-on Exercise 3 (continued)

> **PRINT SELECTED PAGES**
>
> Why print an entire document if you want only a few pages? Pull down the File menu and click Print as you usually do to initiate the printing process. Click the Pages option button, then enter the page numbers and/or page ranges you want; for example, 3, 6–8 will print page three and pages six through eight.

SUMMARY

Many operations in Word are done within the context of select-then-do; that is, select the text, then execute the necessary command. Text may be selected by dragging the mouse, by using the selection bar to the left of the document, or by using the keyboard. Text is deselected by clicking anywhere within the document.

The Find and Replace commands locate a designated character string and optionally replace one or more occurrences of that string with a different character string. The search may be case-sensitive and/or restricted to whole words as necessary.

Text is moved or copied through a combination of the Cut, Copy, and Paste commands and/or the drag-and-drop facility. The contents of the clipboard are replaced by any subsequent Cut or Copy command, but are unaffected by the Paste command; that is, the same text can be pasted into multiple locations.

The Undo command reverses the effect of previous commands. The Undo and Redo commands work in conjunction with one another; that is, every command that is undone can be redone at a later time.

Scrolling occurs when a document is too large to be seen in its entirety. Scrolling with the mouse changes what is displayed on the screen, but does not move the insertion point; that is, you must click the mouse to move the insertion point. Scrolling via the keyboard (for example, PgUp and PgDn) changes what is seen on the screen as well as the location of the insertion point.

The Page Layout view displays top and bottom margins, headers and footers, and other elements not seen in the Normal view. The Normal view is faster because Word spends less time formatting the display. Both views can be seen at different magnifications.

TrueType fonts are scaleable and accessible from any Windows application. The Format Font command enables you to choose the typeface (e.g., Times New Roman or Arial), style (e.g., bold or italic), point size, and color of text.

The Format Paragraph command determines the line spacing, alignment, indents, and text flow, all of which are set at the paragraph level. Borders and shading are also set at the paragraph level. Margins, page size, and orientation, are set in the Page Setup command and affect the entire document (or section).

KEY WORDS AND CONCEPTS

Alignment
Arial
Automatic replacement
Borders and Shading command
Case-insensitive replacement
Case-sensitive replacement
Clipboard
Copy command
Courier New
Cut command
Drag and drop
Find command
First line indent
Font
Format Font command
Format Painter
Format Paragraph command
Go To command
Hanging indent
Hard page break
Indents
Landscape orientation
Leader character
Left indent
Line spacing
Margins
Monospaced typeface
Normal view
Page break
Page Layout view
Page Setup command
Paste command
Point size
Portrait orientation
Proportional typeface
Redo command
Replace command
Right indent
Sans serif typeface
Scrolling
Select-then-do

Selection bar
Selective replacement
Serif typeface
Shortcut menu
Soft page break
Special indent
Tab stop
Times New Roman
Typeface
Type size
Type style
Typography
Undo command
View menu
Whole word replacement
Widows and orphans
Wild card
Zoom command

MULTIPLE CHOICE

1. Which of the following commands does *not* place data onto the clipboard?
   (a) Cut
   (b) Copy
   (c) Paste
   (d) All of the above
2. What happens if you select a block of text, copy it, move to the beginning of the document, paste it, move to the end of the document, and paste the text again?
   (a) The selected text will appear in three places: at the original location, and at the beginning and end of the document
   (b) The selected text will appear in two places: at the beginning and end of the document
   (c) The selected text will appear in just the original location
   (d) The situation is not possible; that is, you cannot paste twice in a row without an intervening cut or copy operation
3. What happens if you select a block of text, cut it, move to the beginning of the document, paste it, move to the end of the document, and paste the text again?
   (a) The selected text will appear in three places: at the original location and at the beginning and end of the document
   (b) The selected text will appear in two places: at the beginning and end of the document
   (c) The selected text will appear in just the original location
   (d) The situation is not possible; that is, you cannot paste twice in a row without an intervening cut or copy operation
4. Which of the following are set at the paragraph level?
   (a) Alignment
   (b) Tabs and indents
   (c) Line spacing
   (d) All of the above
5. How do you change the font for *existing* text within a document?
   (a) Select the text, then choose the new font
   (b) Choose the new font, then select the text
   (c) Either (a) or (b)
   (d) Neither (a) nor (b)

6. The Page Setup command can be used to change:
   (a) The margins in a document
   (b) The orientation of a document
   (c) Both (a) and (b)
   (d) Neither (a) nor (b)

7. Which of the following is a true statement regarding indents?
   (a) Indents are measured from the edge of the page rather than from the margin
   (b) The left, right, and first line indents must be set to the same value
   (c) The insertion point can be anywhere in the paragraph when indents are set
   (d) Indents must be set with the Format Paragraph command

8. The spacing in an existing multipage document is changed from single spacing to double spacing throughout the document. What can you say about the number of hard and soft page breaks before and after the formatting change?
   (a) The number of soft page breaks is the same, but the number and/or position of the hard page breaks is different
   (b) The number of hard page breaks is the same, but the number and/or position of the soft page breaks is different
   (c) The number and position of both hard and soft page breaks is the same
   (d) The number and position of both hard and soft page breaks is different

9. The default tab stops are set to:
   (a) Left indents every ½ inch
   (b) Left indents every ¼ inch
   (c) Right indents every ½ inch
   (d) Right indents every ¼ inch

10. Which of the following describes the Arial and Times New Roman fonts?
    (a) Arial is a sans serif font, Times New Roman is a serif font
    (b) Arial is a serif font, Times New Roman is a sans serif font
    (c) Both are serif fonts
    (d) Both are sans serif fonts

11. The find and replacement strings must be
    (a) The same length
    (b) The same case, either upper or lower
    (c) The same length and the same case
    (d) None of the above

12. Assume that you are in the middle of a multipage document. How do you scroll to the beginning of the document and simultaneously change the insertion point?
    (a) Press Ctrl+Home
    (b) Drag the scroll bar to the top of the scroll box
    (c) Both (a) and (b)
    (d) Neither (a) nor (b)

13. Which of the following substitutions can be accomplished by the Find and Replace command?
    (a) All occurrences of the words "Times New Roman" can be replaced with the word "Arial"
    (b) All text set in the Times New Roman font can be replaced by the Arial font
    (c) Both (a) and (b)
    (d) Neither (a) nor (b)

14. Which of the following deselects a selected block of text?
    (a) Clicking anywhere outside the selected text
    (b) Clicking any alignment button on the toolbar
    (c) Clicking the Bold, Italic, or Underline button
    (d) All of the above

15. Which view, and which magnification, lets you see the whole page, including top and bottom margins?
    (a) Page Layout view at 100% magnification
    (b) Page Layout view at Whole Page magnification
    (c) Normal view at 100% magnification
    (d) Normal view at Whole Page magnification

ANSWERS

1. c	**6.** c	**11.** d
2. a	**7.** c	**12.** a
3. b	**8.** b	**13.** c
4. d	**9.** a	**14.** a
5. a	**10.** a	**15.** b

PRACTICE WITH MICROSOFT WORD

1. Open the *Chapter 2 Practice 1* document that is displayed in Figure 2.16 and make the following changes.
   a. Copy the sentence *Discretion is the better part of valor* to the beginning of the first paragraph.
   b. Move the second paragraph to the end of the document.
   c. Change the typeface of the entire document to 12 point Arial.
   d. Change all whole word occurrences of *feel* to *think.*
   e. Change the spacing of the entire document from single spacing to 1.5. Change the alignment of the entire document to justified.
   f. Set the phrases *Format Font command* and *Format Paragraph command* in italics.
   g. Indent the second paragraph .25 inch on both the left and right.
   h. Box and shade the last paragraph.
   i. Create a title page that precedes the document. Set the title, *Discretion in Design,* in 24 point Arial bold and center it approximately two inches from the top of the page. Right align your name toward the bottom of the title page in 12 point Arial regular.
   j. Print the revised document and submit it to your instructor.

It is not difficult, especially with practice, to learn to format a document. It is not long before the mouse goes automatically to the Format Font command to change the selected text to a sans-serif font, to increase the font size, or to apply a boldface or italic style. Nor is it long before you go directly to the Format Paragraph command to change the alignment or line spacing for selected paragraphs.

What is not easy, however, is to teach discretion in applying formats. Too many different formats on one page can be distracting, and in almost all cases, less is better. Be conservative and never feel that you have to demonstrate everything you know how to do in each and every document that you create. Discretion is the better part of valor. No more than two different typefaces should be used in a single document, although each can be used in a variety of different styles and sizes.

It is always a good idea to stay on the lookout for what you feel are good designs and then determine exactly what you like and don't like about each. In that way, you are constantly building ideas for your own future designs.

FIGURE 2.16 Document for Practice Exercise 1

2. Figure 2.17 displays a completed version of the *Chapter 2 Practice 2* document that exists on the data disk. We want you to retrieve the original document from the data disk, then change the document so that it matches Figure 2.17. No editing is required as the text in the original document is identical to the finished document.

   The only changes are in formatting, but you will have to compare the documents in order to determine the nature of the changes. Color is a nice touch (which depends on the availability of a color printer) and is not required. Add your name somewhere in the document, then print the revised document and submit it to your instructor.

3. Create a simple document containing the text of the Preamble to the Constitution as shown in Figure 2.18.
   a. Set the Preamble in 12 point Times New Roman.
   b. Use single spacing and left alignment.
   c. Copy the Preamble to a new page, then change to a larger point size and more interesting typeface.
   d. Create a title page for your assignment, containing your name, course name, and appropriate title.
   e. Use a different typeface for the title page than in the rest of the document, and set the title in at least 24 points.
   f. Submit all three pages (the title page and both versions of the Preamble) to your instructor.

TYPOGRAPHY

The art of formatting a document is more than just knowing definitions, but knowing the definitions is definitely a starting point. A ***typeface*** is a complete set of characters with the same general appearance, and can be *serif* (cross lines at the end of the main strokes of each letter) or *sans serif* (without the cross lines). A ***type size*** is a vertical measurement, made from the top of the tallest letter in the character set to the bottom of the lowest letter in the character set. ***Type style*** refers to variations in the typeface, such as boldface and italics.

Several typefaces are shipped with Windows, including ***Times New Roman,*** a serif typeface, and ***Arial***, a sans serif typeface. Times New Roman should be used for large amounts of text, whereas Arial is best used for titles and subtitles. It is best not to use too many different typefaces in the same document, but rather to use only one or two and then make the document interesting by varying their size and style.

FIGURE 2.17 Document for Practice Exercise 2

We, the people of the United States, in order to form a more perfect Union, establish justice, insure domestic tranquillity, provide for the common defense, promote the general welfare, and secure the blessings of liberty to ourselves and our posterity, do ordain and establish this Constitution for the United States of America.

FIGURE 2.18 Document for Practice Exercise 3

4. As indicated in the chapter, anyone who has used a typewriter is familiar with the function of the Tab key; that is, press Tab and the insertion point moves to the next tab stop (a measured position to align text at a specific place). The Tab key is more powerful in Word because you can choose from four different types of tab stops (left, center, right, and decimal). You can also specify a leader character, typically dots or hyphens, to draw the reader's eye across the page.

   Create the document in Figure 2.19 and add your name in the indicated position. (Use the Help facility to discover how to work with tab stops.) Submit the completed document to your instructor as proof that you have mastered the Tab key.

EXAMPLES OF TAB STOPS

Example 1 - Right tab at 6":

CIS 120	**Maryann Barber**
FALL 1997	**September 21, 1997**

Example 2 - Right tab with a dot leader at 6":

Chapter 1 1
Chapter 2 31
Chapter 3 56

Example 3 - Right tab at 1" and left tab at 1.25":

To:	Maryann Barber
From:	Joel Stutz
Department:	Computer Information Systems
Subject:	Exams

Example 4 - Left tab at 2" and a decimal tab at 3.5":

Rent	$375.38
Utilities	$125.59
Phone	$56.92
Cable	$42.45

FIGURE 2.19 Document for Practice Exercise 4

5. The Page Borders Command: Figure 2.20 illustrates a hypothetical title page for a paper describing the capabilities of borders and shading. The Borders and Shading command is applied at the paragraph level as indicated in the chapter. You can, however, select the Page Border tab within the Borders and Shading dialog box to create an unusual and attractive document. Experiment with the command to create a title page similar to Figure 2.20. Submit the document to your instructor as proof you did the exercise.

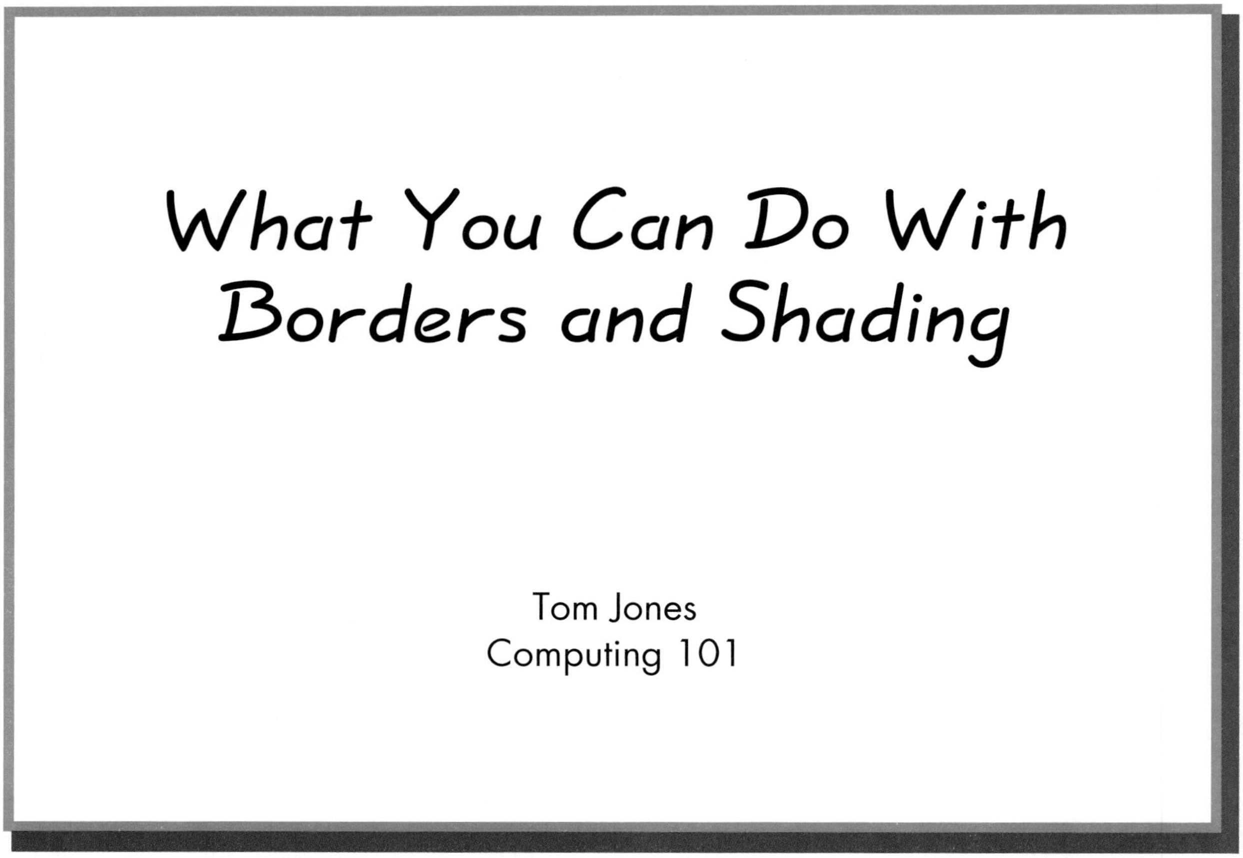

What You Can Do With Borders and Shading

Tom Jones
Computing 101

FIGURE 2.20 Document for Practice Exercise 5

6. Exploring Fonts: The Font Folder within the Control Panel displays the names of the fonts available on a system and enables you to obtain a printed sample of any specific font. Click the Start button, click (or point to) the Settings command, click (or point to) Control Panel, then click the Fonts command to open the font folder and display the fonts on your system.
   a. Double click a font you want to view (e.g., Contemporary Brush in Figure 2.21), then click the Print button to print a sample of the selected font.
   b. Click the Fonts button on the Taskbar to return to the Fonts window and open a different font. Print a sample page of this font as well.
   c. Start Word. Create a title page containing your name, class, date, and the title of this assignment (My Favorite Fonts). Center the title. Use boldface or italics as you see fit. Be sure to use appropriate type sizes.
   d. Staple the three pages together (the title page and two font samples), then submit them to your instructor.

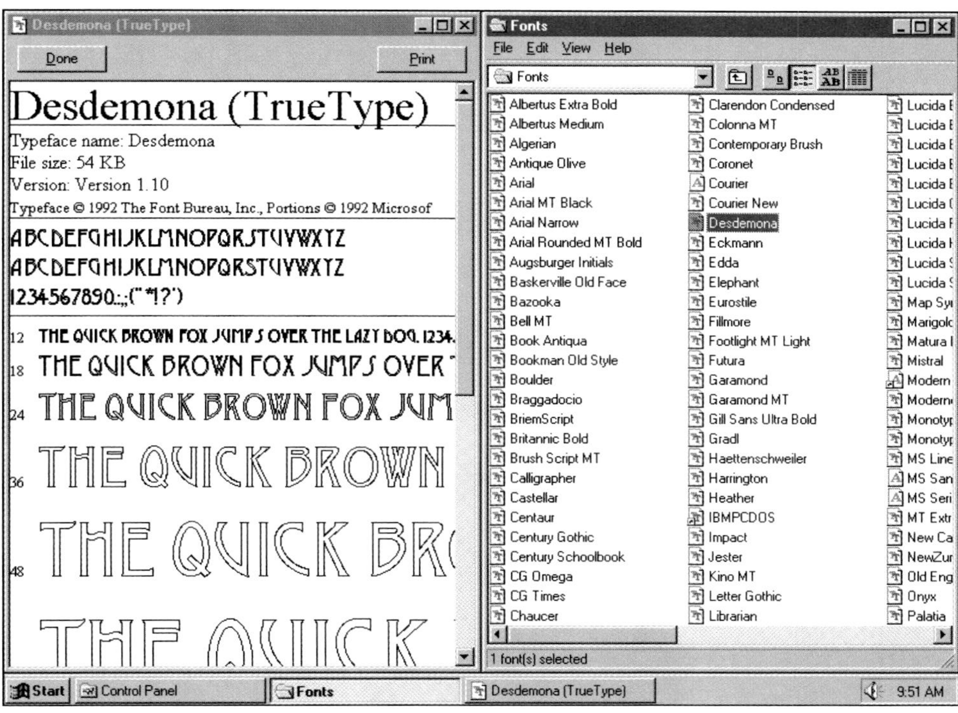

FIGURE 2.21 Screen for Practice Exercise 6

CASE STUDIES

Computers Past and Present

The ENIAC was the scientific marvel of its day and the world's first operational electronic computer. It could perform 5,000 additions per second, weighed 30 tons, and took 1,500 square feet of floor space. The price was a modest $486,000 in 1946 dollars. The story of the ENIAC and other influential computers of the author's choosing is found in the file *History of Computers,* which we forgot to format, so we are asking you to do it for us.

Be sure to use appropriate emphasis for the names of the various computers. Create a title page in front of the document, then submit the completed assignment to your instructor. If you are ambitious, you can enhance this assignment by using your favorite search engine to look for computer museums on the Web. Visit one or two sites, and include this information on a separate page at the end of the document. One last task, and that is to update the description of Today's PC (the last computer in the document).

Your First Consultant's Job

Go to a real installation, such as a doctor's or an attorney's office, the company where you work, or the computer lab at school. Determine the backup procedures that are in effect, then write a one-page report indicating whether the policy is adequate and, if necessary, offering suggestions for improvement. Your report should be addressed to the individual in charge of the business, and it should cover all aspects of the backup strategy—that is, which files are backed up and how often, and what software is used for the backup operation. Use appropriate emphasis (for example, bold italics) to identify any potential problems. This is a professional document (it is your first consultant's job), and its appearance must be perfect in every way.

Paper Makes a Difference

Most of us take paper for granted, but the right paper can make a significant difference in the effectiveness of the document. Reports and formal correspondence are usually printed on white paper, but you would be surprised how many different shades of white there are. Other types of documents lend themselves to colored paper for additional impact. In short, which paper you use is far from an automatic decision. Walk into a local copy store and see if they have any specialty papers available. Our favorite source for paper is a company called *Paper Direct* (1-800-APAPERS). Ask for a catalog, then consider the use of a specialty paper the next time you have an important project.

The Invitation

Choose an event and produce the perfect invitation. The possibilities are endless and limited only by your imagination. You can invite people to your wedding or to a fraternity party. Your laser printer and abundance of fancy fonts enable you to do anything a professional printer can do. Clip art and/or special paper will add the finishing touch. Go to it—this assignment is a lot of fun.

One Space After a Period

Touch typing classes typically teach the student to place two spaces after a period. The technique worked well in the days of the typewriter and monospaced fonts, but it creates an artificially large space when used with proportional fonts and a word processor. Select any document that is at least several paragraphs in length and print the document with the current spacing. Use the Find and Replace commands to change to the alternate spacing, then print the document a second time. Which spacing looks better to you? Submit both versions of the document to your instructor with a brief note summarizing your findings.

The Contest

Almost everyone enjoys some form of competition. Ask your instructor to choose a specific type of document, such as a flyer or résumé, and declare a contest in the class to produce the "best" document. Submit your entry, but write your name on the back of the document so that it can be judged anonymously. Your instructor may want to select a set of semifinalists and then distribute copies of those documents so that the class can vote on the winner.

3

ENHANCING A DOCUMENT: THE WEB AND OTHER RESOURCES

OBJECTIVES

After reading this chapter you will be able to:

1. Describe object linking and embedding; explain how it is used to create a compound document.
2. Describe the resources in the Microsoft Clip Gallery; insert clip art and/or a photograph into a document.
3. Use the Format Picture command to wrap text around a clip art image; describe various tools on the Picture toolbar.
4. Use WordArt to insert decorative text into a document.
5. Describe the Internet and World Wide Web; explain how to display the Web toolbar within Microsoft Word.
6. Define a Web-enabled document; download resources from the Web for inclusion in a Word document.
7. Insert a footnote or endnote into a document to cite a reference.
8. Use wizards and templates to create a document; list several wizards provided with Microsoft Word.

OVERVIEW

This chapter describes how to enhance a document using resources within Microsoft Office as well as resources on the Internet and World Wide Web. We begin with the Microsoft Clip Gallery, a collection of clip art, photographs, sounds, and video clips that can be inserted into any Office document. We also introduce Microsoft WordArt to create special effects with text.

The clip art and photographs included within the Microsoft Clip Gallery pale in comparison to the resources on the Internet. Accordingly, we present a brief introduction to the Internet, then show you how to download a picture from the Web and insert it into a document. We also show you how to add footnotes to give appropriate credit to your sources.

The chapter also describes the various wizards and templates that are built into Microsoft Word to help you create professionally formatted documents. We believe this to be a very enjoyable chapter that will add significantly to your capability in Microsoft Word. As always, learning is best accomplished by doing, and the hands-on exercises are essential to master the material.

A COMPOUND DOCUMENT

The applications in Microsoft Office are thoroughly integrated with one another. Equally important, they share information through a technology known as ***Object Linking and Embedding (OLE),*** which enables you to create a ***compound document*** containing data (objects) from multiple applications.

Consider, for example, the compound document in Figure 3.1, which was created in Microsoft Word but contains objects (data) from other applications. The ***clip art*** (a graphic as opposed to a photograph) was taken from the Microsoft Clip Gallery. The title of the document was created using Microsoft WordArt. The document also illustrates the Insert Symbol command to insert special characters such as the Windows logo.

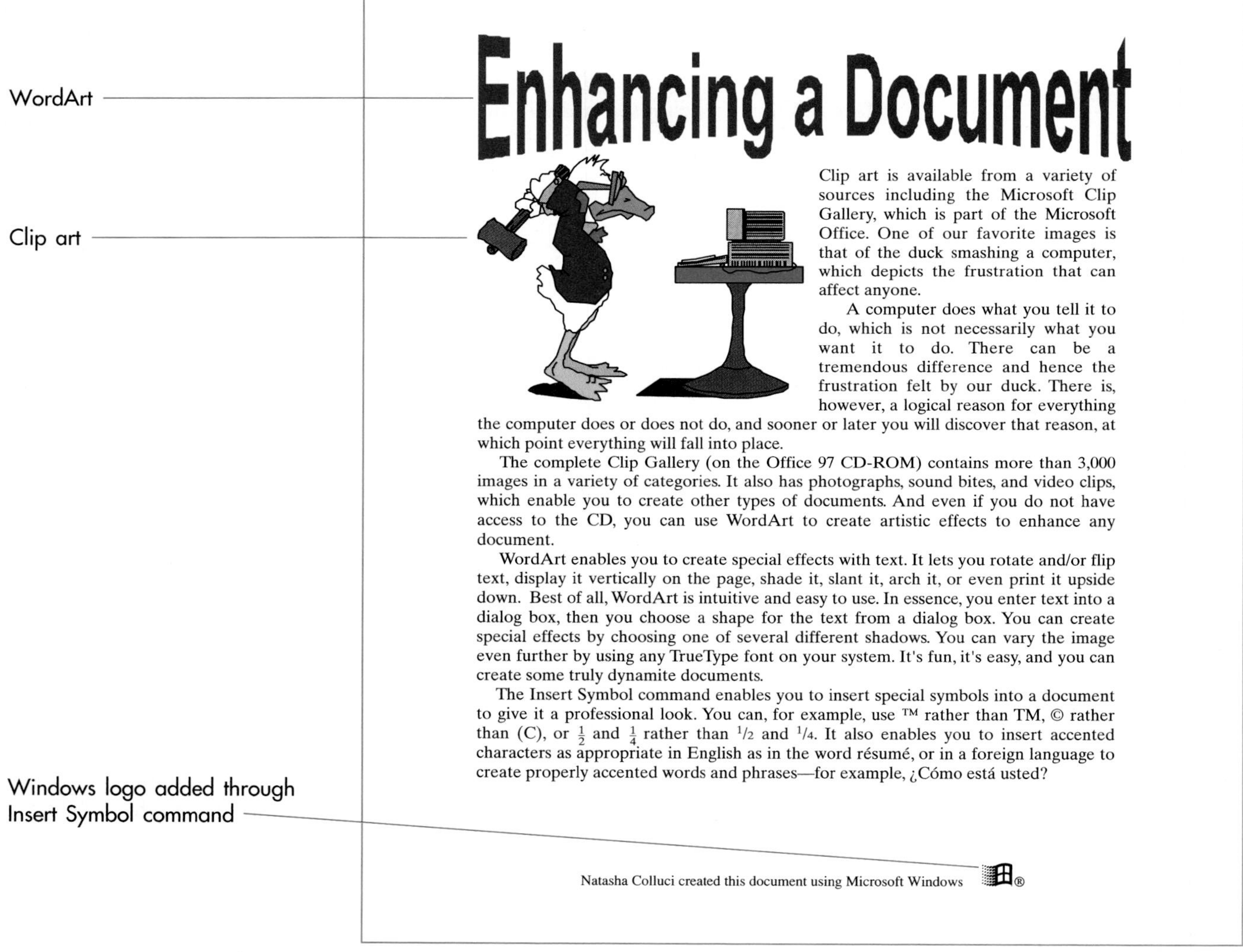
WordArt

Clip art

Windows logo added through Insert Symbol command

Enhancing a Document

Clip art is available from a variety of sources including the Microsoft Clip Gallery, which is part of the Microsoft Office. One of our favorite images is that of the duck smashing a computer, which depicts the frustration that can affect anyone.

A computer does what you tell it to do, which is not necessarily what you want it to do. There can be a tremendous difference and hence the frustration felt by our duck. There is, however, a logical reason for everything the computer does or does not do, and sooner or later you will discover that reason, at which point everything will fall into place.

The complete Clip Gallery (on the Office 97 CD-ROM) contains more than 3,000 images in a variety of categories. It also has photographs, sound bites, and video clips, which enable you to create other types of documents. And even if you do not have access to the CD, you can use WordArt to create artistic effects to enhance any document.

WordArt enables you to create special effects with text. It lets you rotate and/or flip text, display it vertically on the page, shade it, slant it, arch it, or even print it upside down. Best of all, WordArt is intuitive and easy to use. In essence, you enter text into a dialog box, then you choose a shape for the text from a dialog box. You can create special effects by choosing one of several different shadows. You can vary the image even further by using any TrueType font on your system. It's fun, it's easy, and you can create some truly dynamite documents.

The Insert Symbol command enables you to insert special symbols into a document to give it a professional look. You can, for example, use ™ rather than TM, © rather than (C), or ½ and ¼ rather than 1/2 and 1/4. It also enables you to insert accented characters as appropriate in English as in the word résumé, or in a foreign language to create properly accented words and phrases—for example, ¿Cómo está usted?

Natasha Colluci created this document using Microsoft Windows ®

FIGURE 3.1 **A Compound Document**

Microsoft Clip Gallery

The ***Microsoft Clip Gallery*** contains more than 3,000 clip art images and almost 150 photographs. It also contains sound files and video clips, although these objects are more common in PowerPoint presentations than in Word documents. The Clip Gallery can be accessed in a variety of ways, most easily through the ***Insert Picture command,*** which is available in every Office application.

To use the Clip Gallery, you choose the type of object by clicking the appropriate tab—for example, clip art in Figure 3.2a. Next you select the category, such as Science and Technology in Figure 3.2b, and an image within that category, such as the astronaut walking in space. And finally, you click the Insert button to insert the object (the clip art or photograph) into the document.

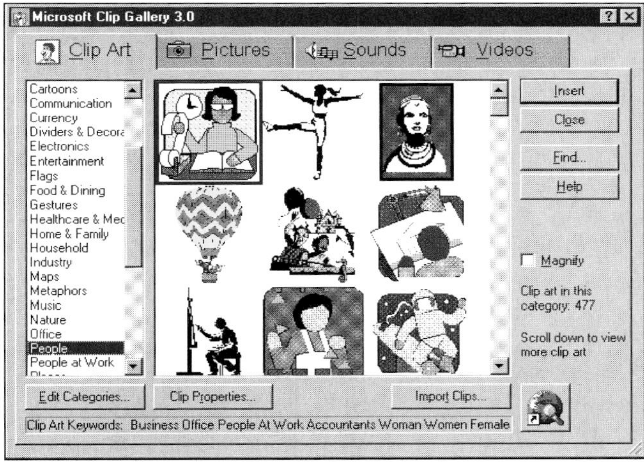

(a) Clip Art

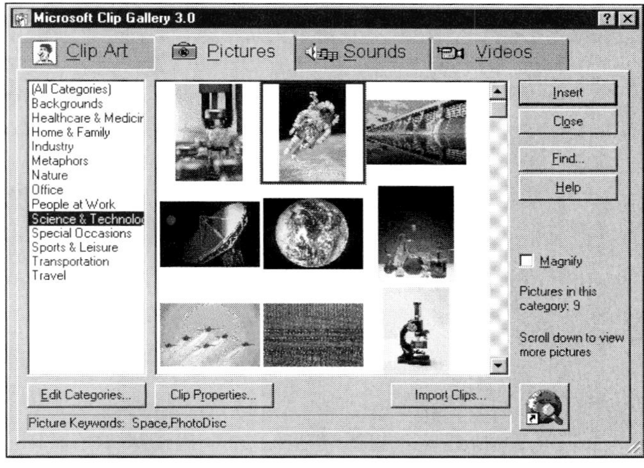

(b) Photographs

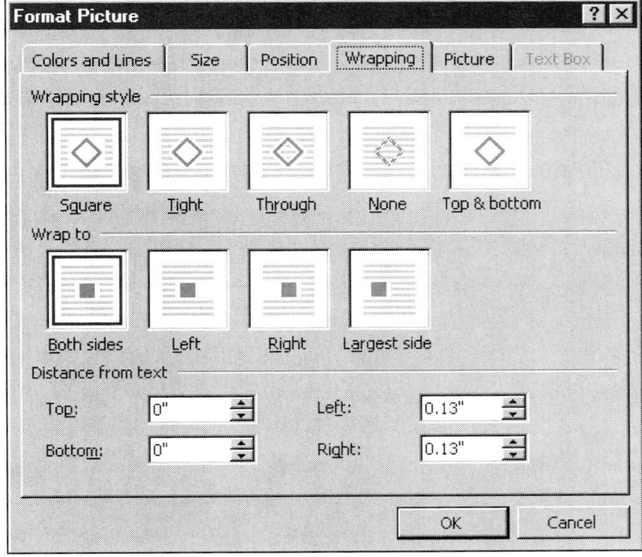

(c) Format Picture Command

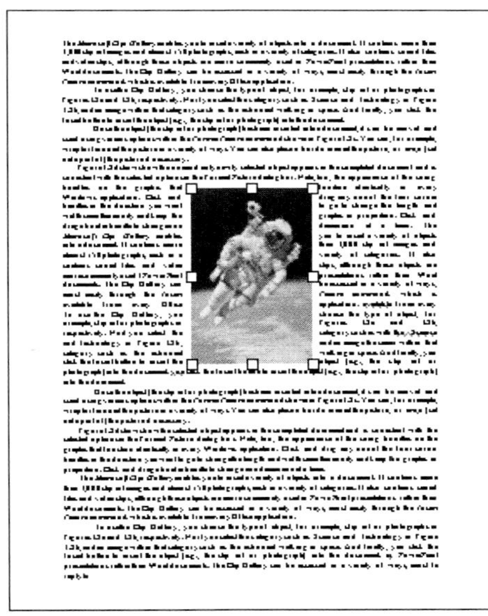

(d) Compound Document

FIGURE 3.2 Microsoft Clip Gallery

Once the object has been inserted into a document, it can be moved and sized using various options within the ***Format Picture command*** shown in Figure 3.2c. You can, for example, wrap text around the picture, place a border around the picture, or even ***crop*** (cut out a part of) the picture if necessary. Figure 3.2d shows how the selected object appears in the completed document and is consistent with the selected options in the Format Picture dialog box. Note, too, the ***sizing handles*** on the graphic, which enable you to move and size the figure within the document.

The Insert Symbol Command

One characteristic of a professional document is the use of typographic symbols in place of ordinary typing—for example, ® rather than (R), © rather than (C), or ½ and ¼ rather than 1/2 and 1/4. Much of this formatting is implemented automatically by Word through substitutions built into the ***AutoCorrect command.*** Other characters, especially accented characters such as the "é" in résumé, or those in a foreign language (e.g., ¿Cómo está usted?), have to be inserted manually into a document.

Look carefully at the last line of Figure 3.1, and notice the Windows 95 logo at the end of the sentence. The latter was created through the ***Insert Symbol command,*** as shown in Figure 3.3. You select the font containing the desired character (e.g., Wingdings in Figure 3.3), then you select the character, and finally you click the Insert command button to place the character in the document.

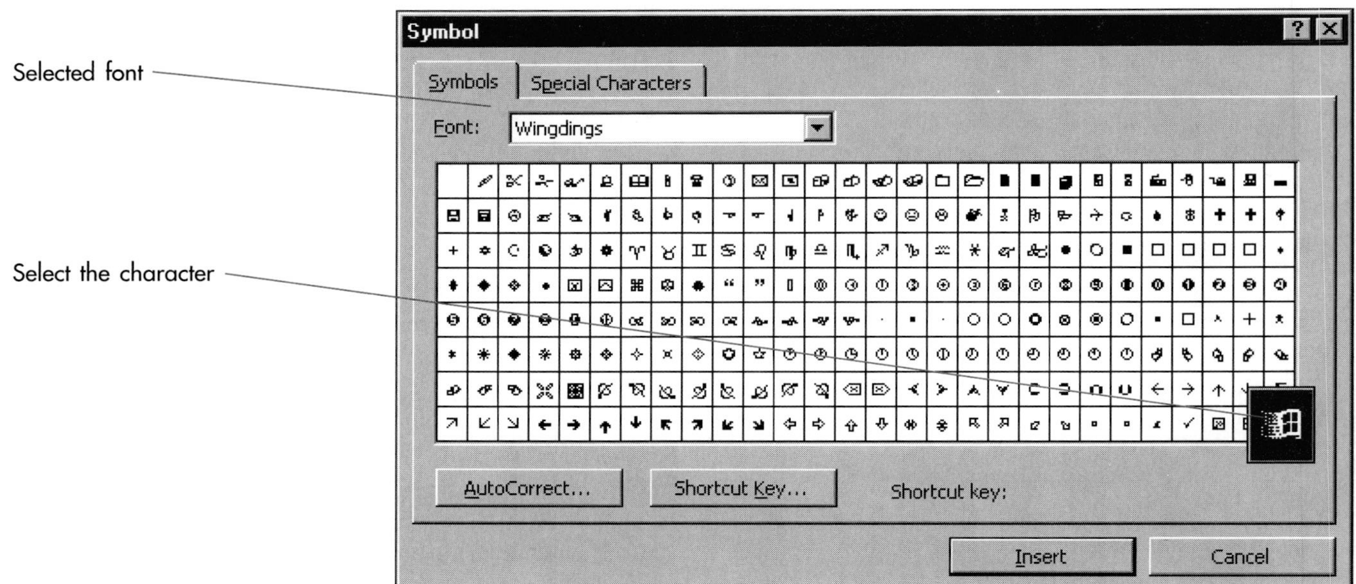

FIGURE 3.3 The Insert Symbol Command

THE WINGDINGS AND SYMBOLS FONTS

The Wingdings and Symbols fonts are two of the best-kept secrets in Windows 95. Both fonts contain a variety of special characters that can be inserted into a document through the Insert Symbol command. These fonts are scaleable to any point size, enabling you to create some truly unusual documents. (See practice exercise 3 at the end of the chapter.)

Microsoft WordArt

Microsoft WordArt is an application within Microsoft Office that creates decorative text to add interest to a document. You can use WordArt in addition to clip art, as was done in Figure 3.1, or in place of clip art if the right image is not available. You're limited only by your imagination, as you can rotate text in any direction, add three-dimensional effects, display the text vertically down the page, shade it, slant it, arch it, or even print it upside down.

WordArt is intuitive and easy to use. In essence, you choose a style for the text from among the selections in the dialog box of Figure 3.4a, then you enter your specific text as shown in Figure 3.4b. You can modify the style through various special effects, you can use any TrueType font on your system, and you can change the color or shading. Figure 3.4c shows the completed WordArt object. It's fun, it's easy, and you can create some truly dynamite documents.

Select WordArt style

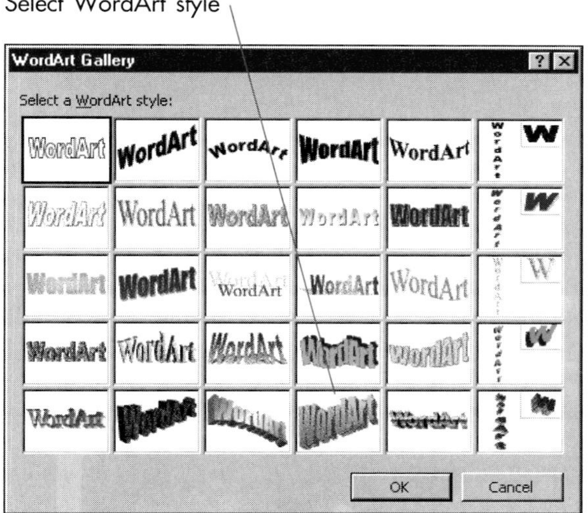

(a) Choose the Style

Enter text

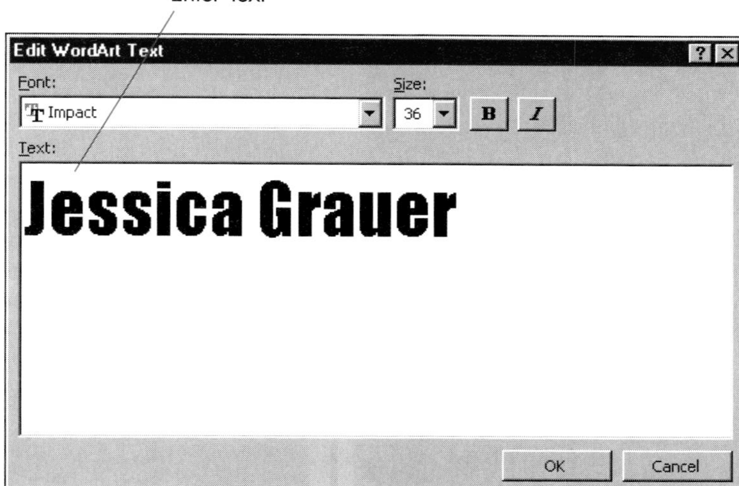

(b) Enter the Text

(c) Completed WordArt

FIGURE 3.4 Microsoft WordArt

HANDS-ON EXERCISE 1

Object Linking and Embedding

Objective: To create a compound document containing clip art and WordArt. To illustrate the Insert Symbol command to place typographical symbols into a document. Use Figure 3.5 as a guide in the exercise.

STEP 1: The Microsoft Clip Gallery

- Start Word. Open the **Clipart and WordArt** document in the Exploring Word folder. Save the document as **Modified Clip Art and WordArt.**
- Check that the insertion point is at the beginning of the document. Pull down the **Insert menu,** click **Picture,** then click **ClipArt** to display the Microsoft Clip Gallery as shown in Figure 3.5a. Click **OK** if you see a dialog box reminding you that additional clip art is available on a CD-ROM.
- If necessary, click the **ClipArt tab** and select (click) the **Cartoons category.** Select the **Duck and Computer** (or a different image if you prefer), then click the **Insert button** to place the clip art into your document.
- The Microsoft Clip Gallery dialog box will close and the picture will be inserted into your document, where it can be moved and sized as described in the next several steps.

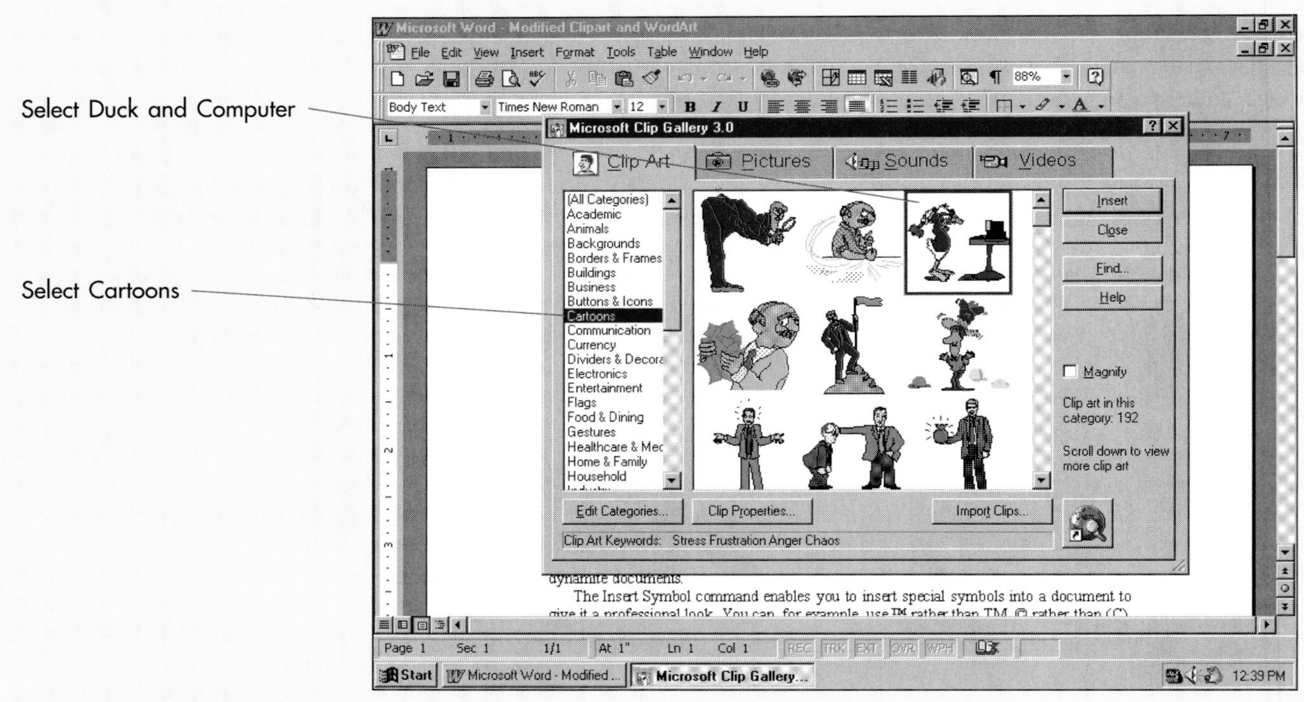

(a) The Clip Gallery (step 1)

FIGURE 3.5 Hands-on Exercise 1

ADDITIONAL CLIP IMAGES

The Microsoft Clip Gallery contains over 100MB of data consisting of more than 3,000 clip art images, 144 photographs, 28 sounds, and 20 video clips. Only a fraction of these are installed with Microsoft Office, but you can access the additional objects from the Office CD at any time. You can also install some or all of the objects on your hard disk, provided you have sufficient space. Start the Windows Explorer, then open the ClipArt folder on the Office CD. Double click the Setup icon to start the Setup Wizard, then follow the on-screen instructions to install the additional components you want.

STEP 2: Move and Size the Picture

- ➤ Word automatically selects the duck and changes to the Page Layout view in Figure 3.5b. Move and size the duck as described below.
- ➤ To move an object:
  - Click the object (e.g., the duck) to display the sizing handles.
  - Point to any part of the duck except a sizing handle (the mouse pointer changes to a four-sided arrow), then click and drag to move the duck elsewhere in the document. You can position the duck anywhere in the document, but you cannot wrap text around the duck until you execute the Format Picture command in step 3.

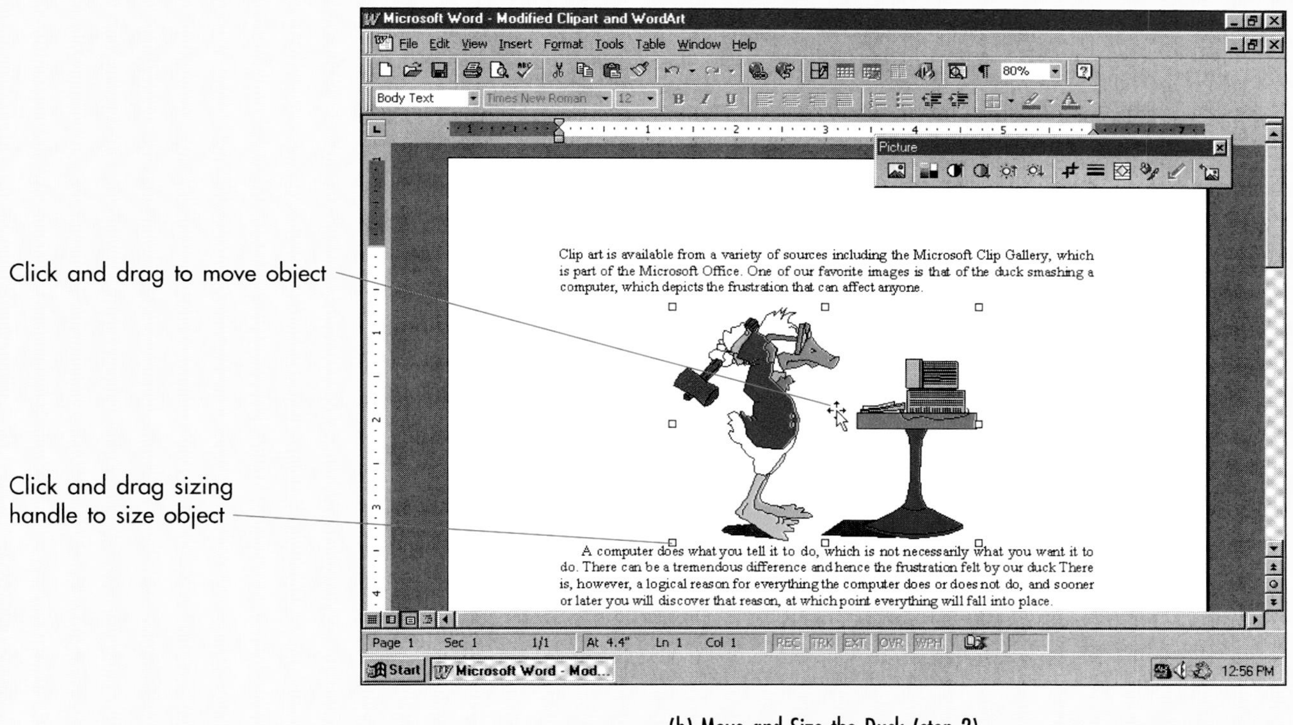

(b) Move and Size the Duck (step 2)

FIGURE 3.5 Hands-on Exercise 1 (continued)

- To size an object:
  - Click the object (e.g., the duck) to display the sizing handles.
  - Drag a corner handle (the mouse pointer changes to a double arrow) to change the length and width of the picture simultaneously; this keeps the graphic in proportion as it sizes it.
  - Drag a handle on the horizontal or vertical border to change one dimension only; this distorts the picture.
- Save the document.

> **TO CLICK OR DOUBLE CLICK**
>
> Clicking an object selects the object and displays the sizing handles, allowing you to move and/or size the object. Double clicking an object starts the application that created it and enables you to modify the object using that application. Double click the duck, for example, and you display the Microsoft Clip Gallery dialog box, in which you can select a different picture and insert it into the document in place of the original.

STEP 3: Format the Picture

- Be sure the duck is still selected, then pull down the **Format menu** and select the **Picture command** to display the Format Picture dialog box in Figure 3.5c.

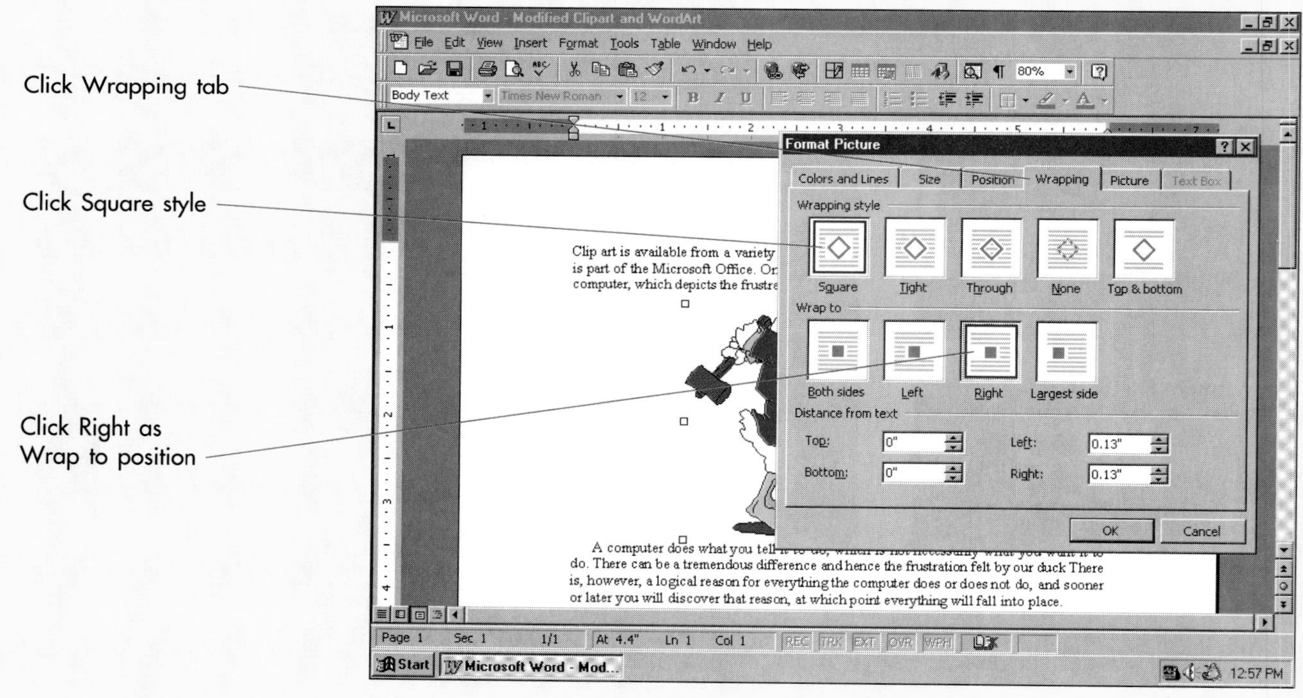

(c) Format the Picture (step 3)

FIGURE 3.5 Hands-on Exercise 1 (continued)

- Click the **Wrapping tab,** select **Square** as the Wrapping style, and click **right** as the Wrap to position. Click **OK** to close the Format Picture dialog box and implement these selections.
- The text should be wrapped to the right of the duck. Move and size the duck until you are satisfied with its position. Note, however, that the duck will always be positioned (wrapped) according to the settings in the Format Picture command.
- Save the document.

THE PICTURE TOOLBAR

The Picture toolbar offers the easiest way to execute various commands associated with a picture or clip art image. It is displayed automatically when a picture is selected; otherwise it is suppressed. As with any toolbar, you can point to a button to display a ScreenTip containing the name of the button, which indicates its function. You will find buttons for wrapping and formatting a picture, a Line Styles button to place a border around a picture, and a cropping button to crop (erase) part of a picture.

STEP 4: WordArt

- Press **Ctrl+Home** to move to the beginning of the document. Pull down the **Insert menu,** click **Picture,** then click **WordArt** to display the WordArt Gallery dialog box.
- Select the WordArt style you like (you can change it later). Click **OK.** You will see a second dialog box in which you enter the text. Enter **Enhancing a Document.** Click **OK.**
- The WordArt object appears in your document in the style you selected. Point to the WordArt object and click the **right mouse button** to display the shortcut menu in Figure 3.5d. Click **Format WordArt** to display the Format WordArt dialog box.
- Click the **Wrapping tab,** then select **Top & Bottom** as the Wrapping style. Click **OK.** It is important to select this wrapping option to facilitate placing the WordArt at the top of the document. Save the document.

FORMATTING WORDART

The WordArt toolbar offers the easiest way to execute various commands associated with a WordArt object. It is displayed automatically when a WordArt object is selected; otherwise it is suppressed. As with any toolbar, you can point to a button to display a ScreenTip containing the name of the button, which indicates its function. You will find buttons to display the text vertically, change the style or shape, and/or edit the text.

WordArt toolbar appears when WordArt object is selected

Click the right mouse button to display the shortcut menu

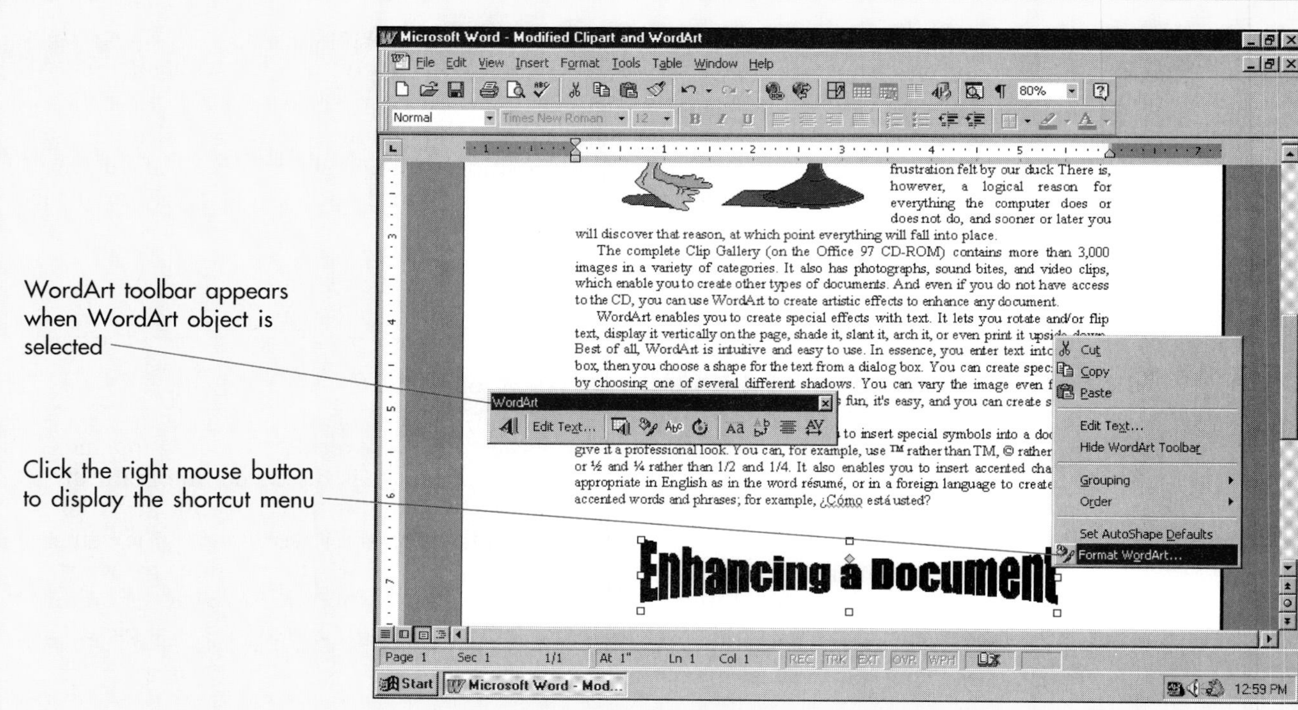

(d) WordArt (step 4)

FIGURE 3.5 Hands-on Exercise 1 (continued)

STEP 5: WordArt (continued)

- Click and drag the WordArt object to move it to the top of the document, as shown in Figure 3.5e. (The Format WordArt dialog box is not yet visible.)
- Point to the WordArt object, click the **right mouse button** to display a shortcut menu, then click **Format WordArt** to display the Format WordArt dialog box.
- Click the **Colors and Lines tab,** then click the **Fill Color drop-down arrow** to display the available colors. Select a different color (e.g., blue).
- Move and/or size the WordArt object as necessary. Save the document.

THE THIRD DIMENSION

You can make your WordArt images even more dramatic by adding 3-D effects. You can tilt the text up or down, right or left, increase or decrease the depth, and change the shading. Pull down the View menu, click Toolbars, click Customize to display the complete list of available toolbars, then check the box to display the 3-D Settings toolbar. Select the WordArt object, then experiment with various tools and special effects. The results are even better if you have a color printer.

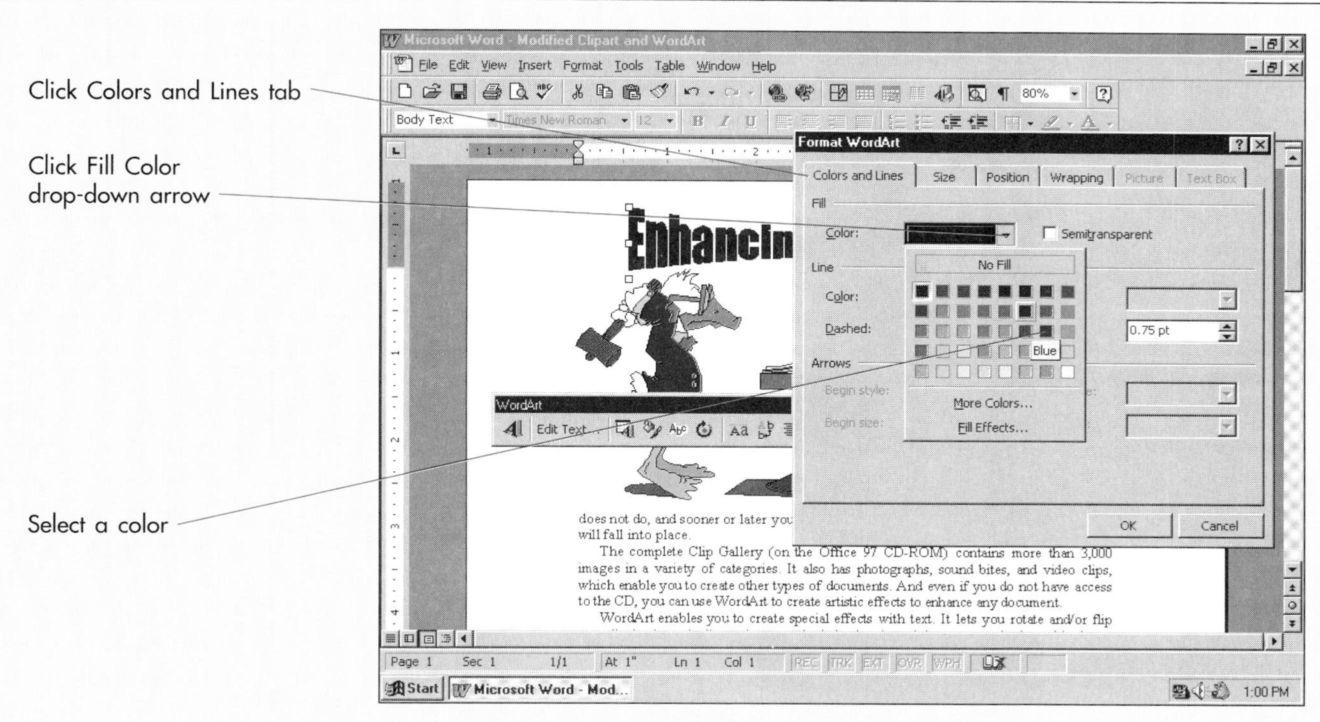

(e) WordArt Continued (step 5)

FIGURE 3.5 Hands-on Exercise 1 (continued)

STEP 6: The Insert Symbol Command

- Press **Ctrl+End** to move to the end of the document, as shown in Figure 3.5f. (The Symbol dialog box is not yet visible.) Press the **enter key** to insert a blank line at the end of the document.
- Type the sentence, **John Smith created this document using Microsoft Windows,** substituting your name for John Smith. Click the **Center button** on the Formatting toolbar to center the sentence.
- Pull down the **Insert menu,** click **Symbol,** then choose **Wingdings** from the Font list box. Click the **Windows logo** (the last character in the last line), click **Insert,** then close the Symbol dialog box.
- Click and drag to select the newly inserted symbol, click the **drop-down arrow** on the **Font Size box,** then change the font to **24** points. Press the **right arrow key** to deselect the symbol.
- Click the **drop-down arrow** on the **Font Size box** and change to **10 point type** so that subsequent text is entered in this size.
- Type **(r)** after the Windows logo and try to watch the monitor as you enter the text. The (r) will be converted automatically to ® because of the AutoFormat command, as described in the boxed tip on page 116.
- Save the document.

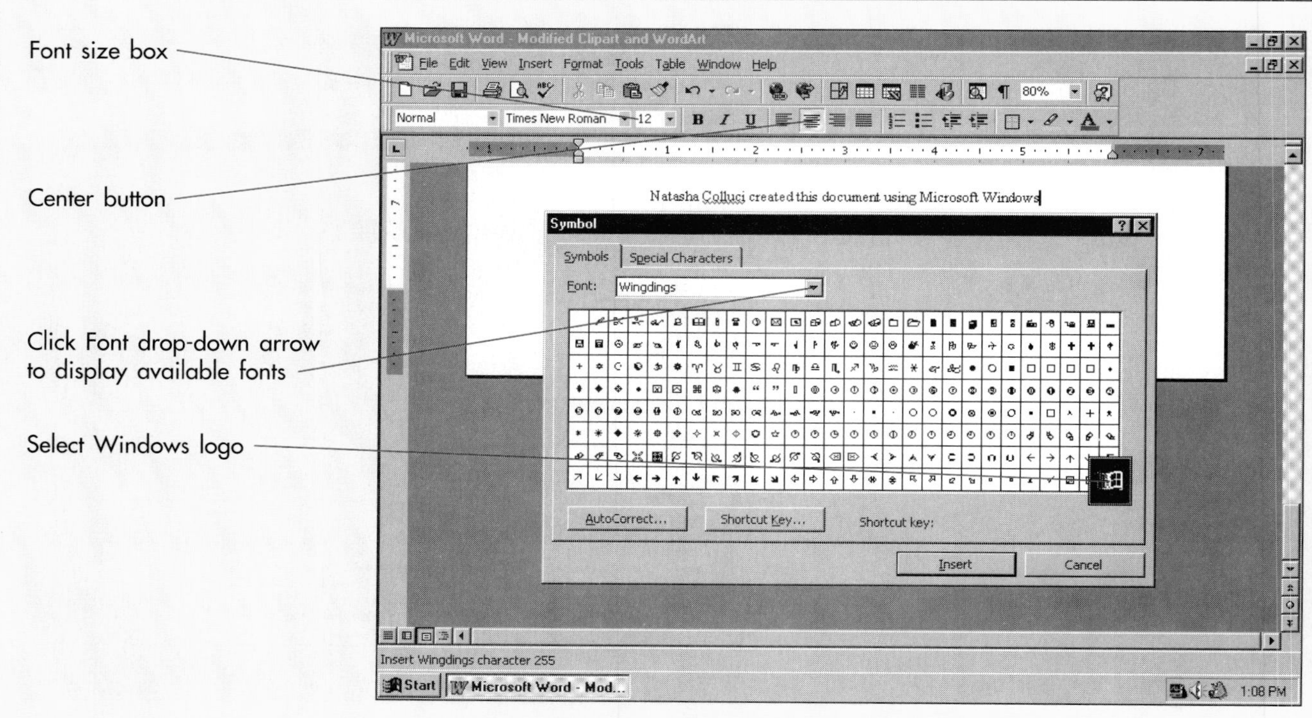

(f) Insert Symbol Command (step 6)

FIGURE 3.5 Hands-on Exercise 1 (continued)

AUTOCORRECT AND AUTOFORMAT

The AutoCorrect feature not only corrects mistakes as you type by substituting one character string for another (e.g., *the* for *teh*), but it will also substitute symbols for typewritten equivalents such as © for (c), provided the entries are included in the table of substitutions. The AutoFormat feature is similar in concept and replaces common fractions such as 1/2 or 1/4 with ½ or ¼. It also converts ordinal numbers such as 1st or 2nd to 1st or 2nd. See practice exercise 3 for additional examples. If either feature is not working, pull down the Tools menu, click the AutoCorrect command, then choose the appropriate settings within the AutoCorrect dialog box.

STEP 7: The Completed Document

- Click the **drop-down arrow** on the Zoom box and select **Whole Page** to preview the completed document as shown in Figure 3.5g.
- Print the document and submit it to your instructor as proof that you did the exercise. Close the document. Exit Word if you do not want to continue with the next exercise at this time.

Print icon

Zoom box

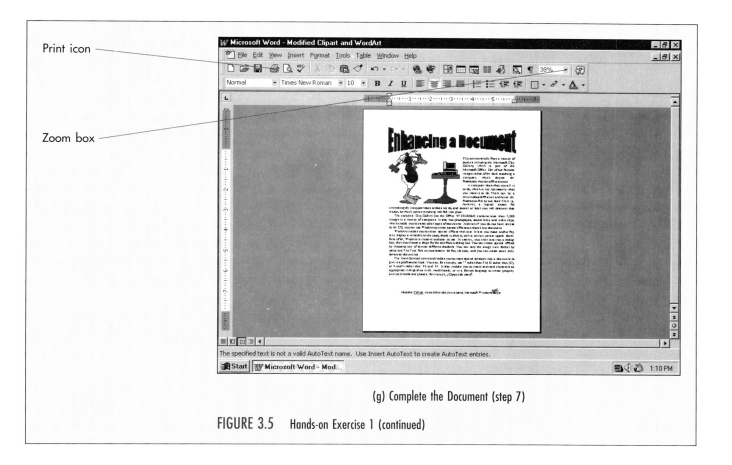

(g) Complete the Document (step 7)

FIGURE 3.5 Hands-on Exercise 1 (continued)

RESOURCES FROM THE INTERNET AND WORLD WIDE WEB

The resources in the Microsoft Clip Gallery in Office 97 are impressive when compared to previous versions of Microsoft Office, but pale in comparison to what is available on the Internet and World Wide Web. Hence, any discussion of enhancing a document through clip art and/or photographs must also include the Internet. We begin with a brief description of the Internet and World Wide Web and then describe how to incorporate these resources into a Word document.

The ***Internet*** is a network of networks that connects computers across the country and around the world. It grew out of a U.S. Department of Defense (DOD) experimental project begun in 1969 to test the feasibility of a wide area (long distance) computer network over which scientists and military personnel could share messages and data.

The ***World Wide Web*** (***WWW,*** or simply, the Web) is a very large subset of the Internet, consisting of those computers containing hypertext and/or hypermedia documents. A ***hypertext document*** is a document that contains a link (reference) to another document, which may be on the same computer, or even on a different computer, with the latter located anywhere in the world. ***Hypermedia*** is similar in concept, except that it provides links to graphic, sound, and video files in addition to text files.

Either type of document enables you to move effortlessly from one document (or computer) to another. And therein lies the fascination of the Web: By simply clicking link after link you move smoothly from one document to the next.

You can start your journey at your professor's home page in New York, for example, which may contain a reference to the Library of Congress, which in turn may take you to a different document, and on. So, off you go to Washington D.C., and from there to a different document on a computer across the country or perhaps around the world.

Every document in Office 97 is ***Web-enabled,*** meaning that the application (e.g., Microsoft Word) will automatically detect and highlight any ***hyperlinks*** that are entered into a document. The Word document in Figure 3.6, for example, displays the Web address www.microsoft.com in underlined blue text just as it would appear in a regular Web (hypertext) document. This is not merely a change in formatting, but an actual hyperlink to a document on the Web (or corporate intranet).

You can click the link from within Word and, provided you have an Internet connection, your Web browser will display the associated page. Note, too, that once you click the link, its color will change (e.g., from blue to magenta) just as it would if you were viewing the page in Netscape or the Internet Explorer. We did not do anything special to create the hyperlink; we simply typed the address as we were creating the document, and Word in turn created the hyperlink.

Look carefully at the screen in Figure 3.6, noting the presence of the ***Web toolbar,*** which appears immediately under the Formatting toolbar. (The Web toolbar is displayed by executing the Toolbars command from the View menu.) The Web toolbar contains buttons similar to those on the toolbar in Internet Explorer. You can, for example, enter the address (URL) of a Web page (or a local document) to activate your browser and access the page. You can use the Favorites button to add a page to your list of favorites and/or open a previously added page. You can click the Back and Forward buttons to move between previously displayed pages. And, as with any toolbar, ScreenTips are displayed when you point to a button whose name indicates its function.

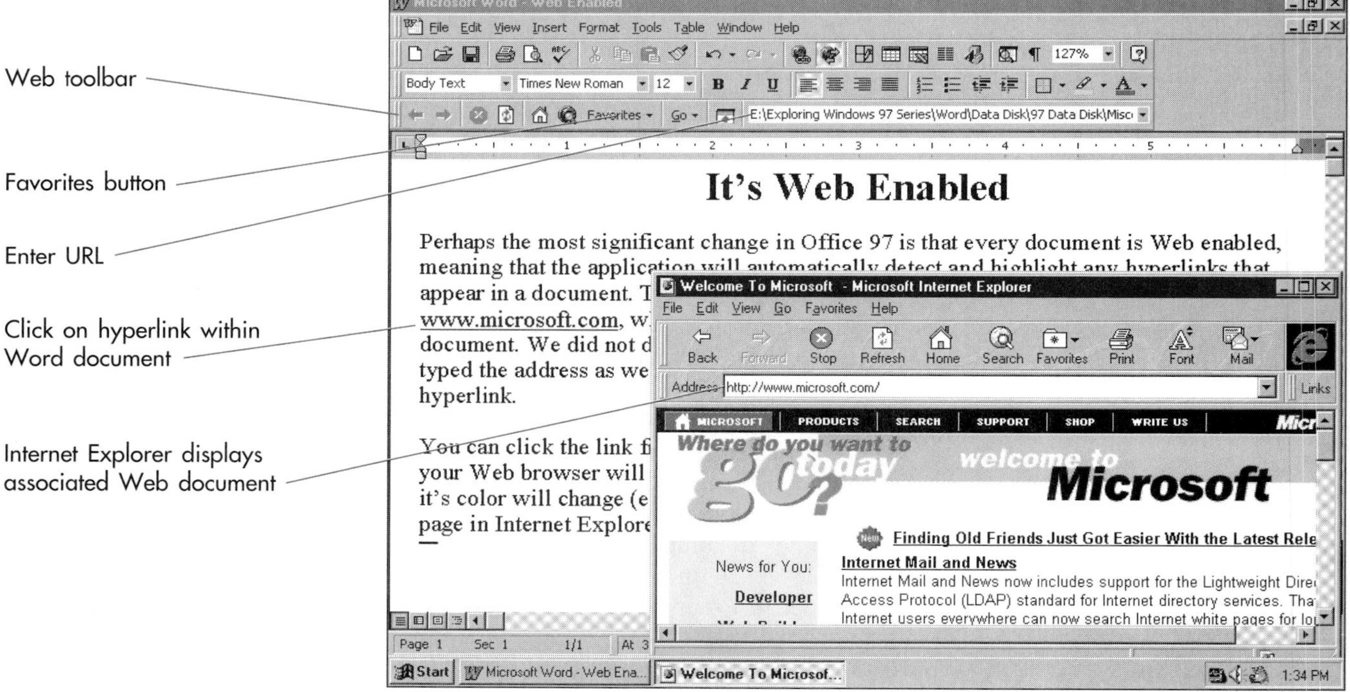

FIGURE 3.6 Internet Enhancements

Copyright Protection

A ***copyright*** provides legal protection for a written or artistic work, giving the author exclusive rights to its use and reproduction, except as governed under the fair use exclusion as explained below. Anything on the Internet or World Wide Web should be considered copyrighted unless the document specifically says it is in the ***public domain,*** in which case the author is giving everyone the right to freely reproduce and distribute the material.

Does copyright protection mean you cannot quote in your term papers statistics and other facts you find while browsing the Web? Does it mean you cannot download an image to include in your report? The answer to both questions depends on the amount of the material and on your intended use of the information. It is considered ***fair use,*** and thus not an infringement of copyright, to use a portion of the work for educational, nonprofit purposes, or for the purpose of critical review or commentary. In other words, you can use a quote, downloaded image, or other information from the Web *if* you cite the original work in your footnotes and/or bibliography. Facts themselves are not covered by copyright, so you can use statistical and other data without fear of infringement. You should, however, cite the original source in your document.

Footnotes and Endnotes

A ***footnote*** provides additional information about an item, such as its source, and appears at the bottom of the page where the reference occurs. An ***endnote*** is similar in concept but appears at the end of a document. A horizontal line separates the notes from the rest of the document.

The ***Insert Footnote command*** inserts a note into a document, and automatically assigns the next sequential number to that note. To create a note, position the insertion point where you want the reference, pull down the Insert menu, click Footnote to display the dialog box in Figure 3.7a, then choose either the

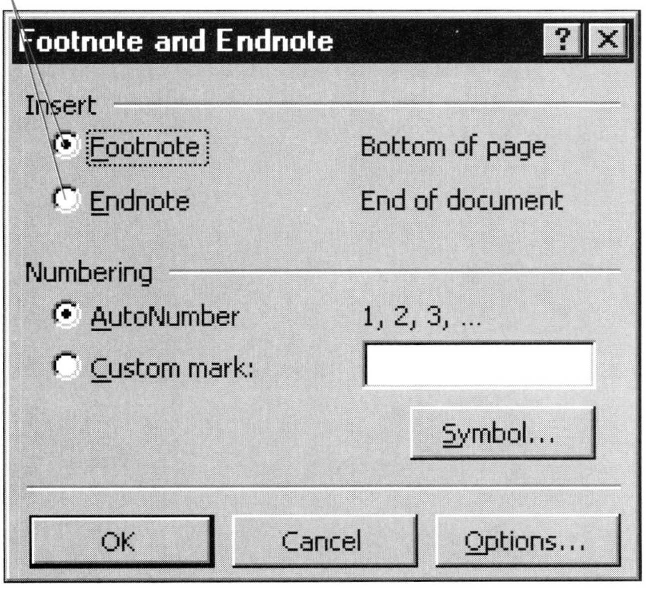

(a) Footnotes and Endnotes

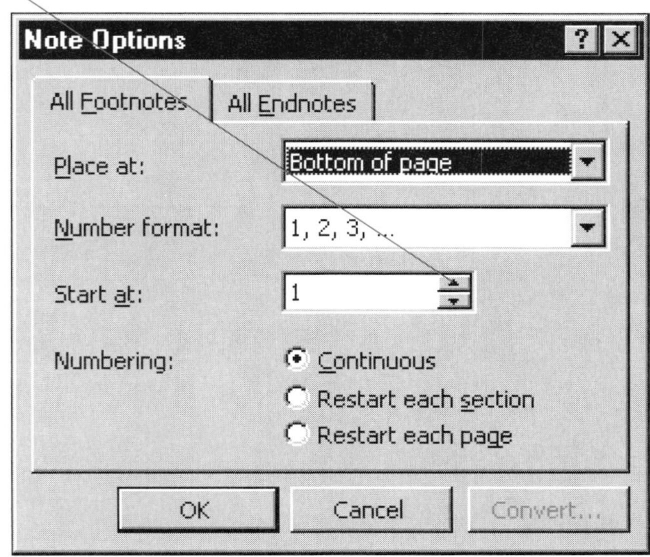

(b) Options

FIGURE 3.7 Footnotes and Endnotes

Footnote or Endnote option button. A superscript reference is inserted into the document, and you will be positioned at the bottom of the page (a footnote) or at the end of the document (an endnote) where you enter the text of the note.

The Options command button in the Footnote and Endnote dialog box enables you to modify the formatting of either type of note as shown in Figure 3.7b. You can change the numbering format (e.g., to Roman numerals) and/or start numbering from a number other than 1. You can also convert footnotes to endnotes or vice versa.

The Insert Footnote command adjusts for last-minute changes, either in your writing or in your professor's requirements. It will, for example, renumber all existing notes to accommodate the addition or deletion of a footnote or endnote. Existing notes are moved (or deleted) within a document by moving (deleting) the reference mark rather than the text of the footnote.

HANDS-ON EXERCISE 2

The Internet as a Resource

Objective: To download a picture from the Internet and use it in a Word document. Use Figure 3.8 as a guide in the exercise. The exercise requires that you have an Internet connection.

STEP 1: The Web Toolbar

- Start Word. Point to any toolbar, then click the **right mouse button** to display a context-sensitive menu, which lists the available toolbars in Word.
- Click **Web** to display the Web toolbar, as shown in Figure 3.8a. Do not be concerned if the position of your toolbars is different from ours.
- Click the **Address box.** Enter **www.whitehouse.gov** (the http:// is assumed), then press the **enter key** to connect to this site. Your Web browser (e.g., Internet Explorer) will open automatically and connect you to the White House home page.
- If the Internet Explorer window does not open on your desktop, point to its button on the Windows 95 taskbar, click the **right mouse button** to display a context-sensitive menu, then click the **Restore command** to display the window. Click the **Maximize button** so that your browser takes up the entire screen.

DOCKED VERSUS FLOATING TOOLBARS

A toolbar is either docked along an edge of a window or floating within the window. To move a docked toolbar, click and drag the move handle (the parallel lines that appear at the left of the toolbar) to a new position. To move a floating toolbar, click and drag its title bar—if you drag a floating toolbar to the edge of the window, it becomes a docked toolbar and vice versa. You can also change the shape of a floating toolbar by dragging any border in the direction you want to go. And finally, you can double click the background of any toolbar to toggle between a floating toolbar and a docked (fixed) toolbar.

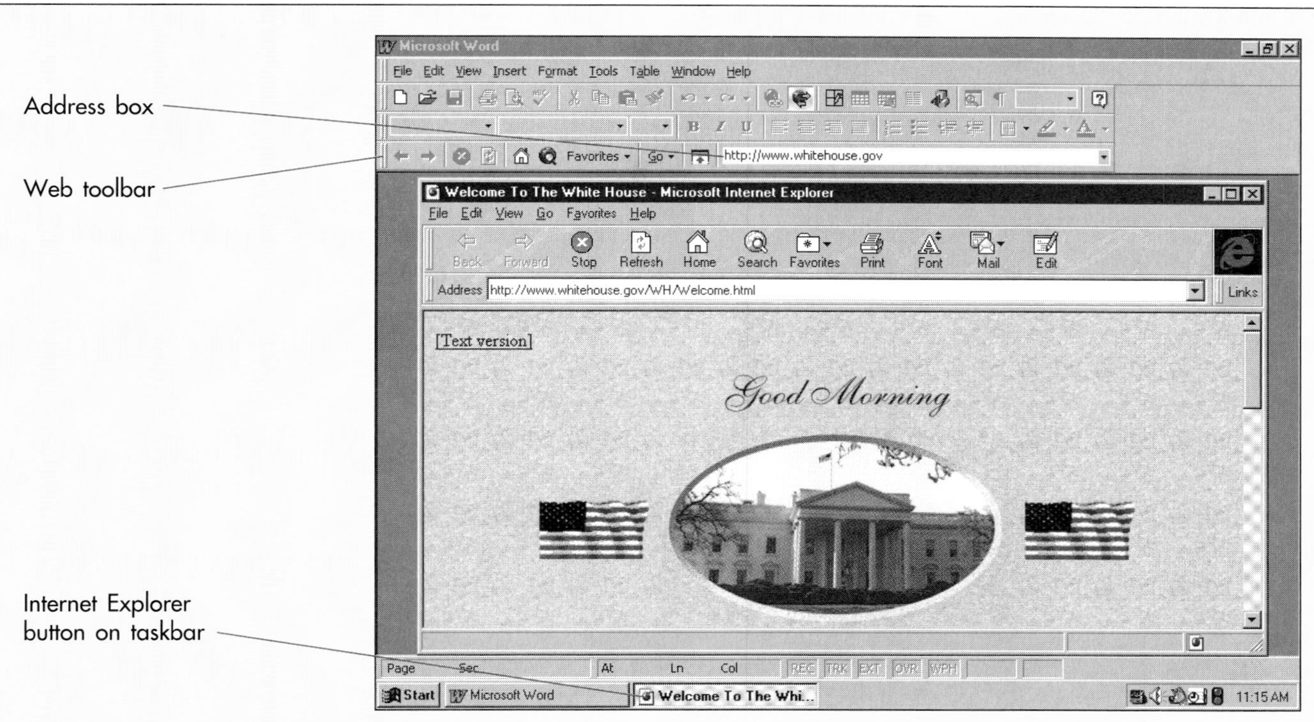

(a) The Web Toolbar (step 1)

FIGURE 3.8 Hands-on Exercise 2

STEP 2: Save the Picture

- You should be connected to the White House Web site. Click the **down arrow** on the vertical scroll bar until you can click the link to **White House History and Tours.**
- Click the link to **The Presidents of the United States** (or a similar link if the site has changed since our last visit), then click the link to your favorite president, e.g., **John F. Kennedy.** You should see the screen in Figure 3.8b (the Save As dialog box is not yet visible).
- Point to the picture of President Kennedy, click the **right mouse button** to display a shortcut menu, then click the **Save Picture as command** to display the Save As dialog box.
    - Click the **drop-down arrow** in the Save in list box to specify the drive and folder in which you want to save the graphic (e.g., the Exploring Word folder on drive C).
    - The file name and file type are entered automatically by Internet Explorer. (You may change the name, but don't change the file type.) Click the **Save button** to download the image. Remember the file name and location because you will need to access the file in the next step.
- The Save As dialog box will close automatically as soon as the picture has been downloaded to your PC. Click the link to the **Inaugural Address** after the dialog box closes.

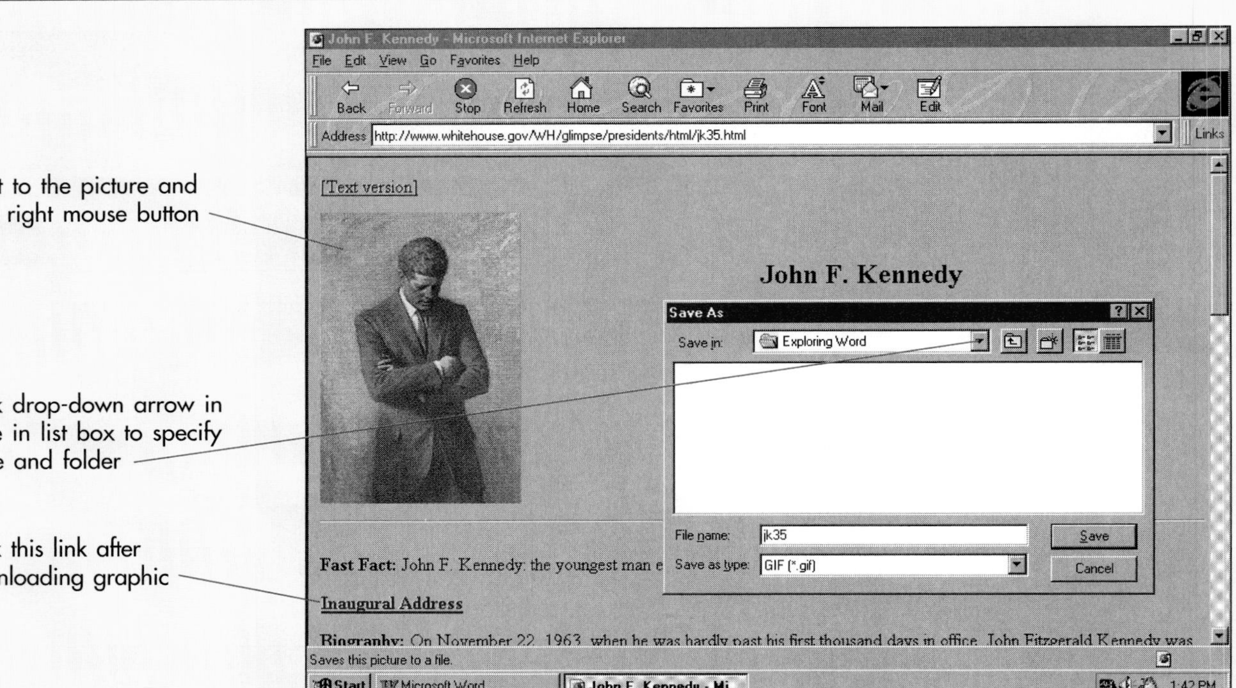

(b) Save the Picture (step 2)

FIGURE 3.8 Hands-on Exercise 2 (continued)

MULTITASKING

Multitasking—the ability to run multiple applications at the same time—is one of the primary advantages of the Windows environment. Minimizing an application is different from closing it, and you want to minimize, rather than close, an application to take advantage of multitasking. Closing an application removes it from memory so that you have to restart the application if you want to return to it later in the session. Minimizing, however, leaves the application open in memory, but shrinks its window to a button on the Windows 95 taskbar.

STEP 3: Copy the Quotation

- You should see the text of President Kennedy's address as shown in Figure 3.8c. Scroll down in the document until you can select the sentence beginning with **"And so, my fellow Americans . . ."**
- Point to the selected sentence, then click the **right mouse button** to display the shortcut menu. Click **Copy** to copy the selected text to the clipboard.
- Click the button for Microsoft Word on the taskbar, then open a new document. Pull down the **Edit menu** and click the **Paste command** (or click the **Paste button** on the Standard toolbar) to paste the contents of the clipboard (the quotation from President Kennedy) into the Word document.
- Save the document as **President Kennedy.** Close the Internet Explorer.

Point to selected text and click right mouse button to display shortcut menu

Click the Microsoft Word button on taskbar

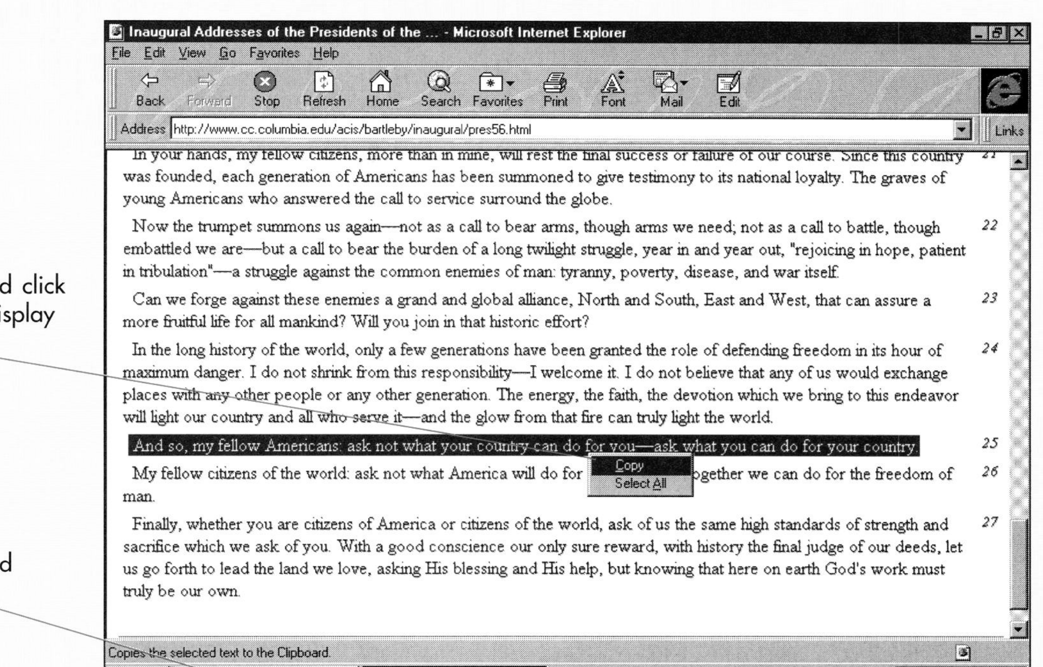

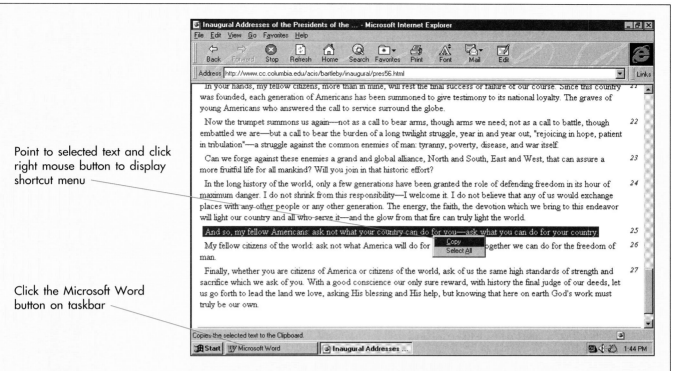

(c) Copy the Quotation (step 3)

FIGURE 3.8 Hands-on Exercise 2 (continued)

THE CLIPBOARD

The clipboard is a temporary storage area that is available to all Windows applications. Selected text is cut or copied from a document and placed on the clipboard from where it can be pasted to a new location(s). You can use the clipboard (with the appropriate combination of Cut, Copy, and Paste commands) to move and copy text within a document. You can also use it to move and copy text from one document to another or from one application to another, e.g., from Internet Explorer to Microsoft Word.

STEP 4: Insert a Footnote

- Add quotation marks as shown in Figure 3.8d. Change the font to **28 point Times New Roman.** Click at the end of the quotation.
- Pull down the **Insert menu.** Click **Footnote** to display the Footnote and Endnote dialog box. Check that the option buttons for **Footnote** and **AutoNumber** are selected, then click **OK.**
- The insertion point moves to the bottom of the page, where you can add the text of the footnote. Enter **Inaugural Address, John F. Kennedy, January 20, 1961.** Click the **Close button** on the Footnote toolbar.
- Save the document.

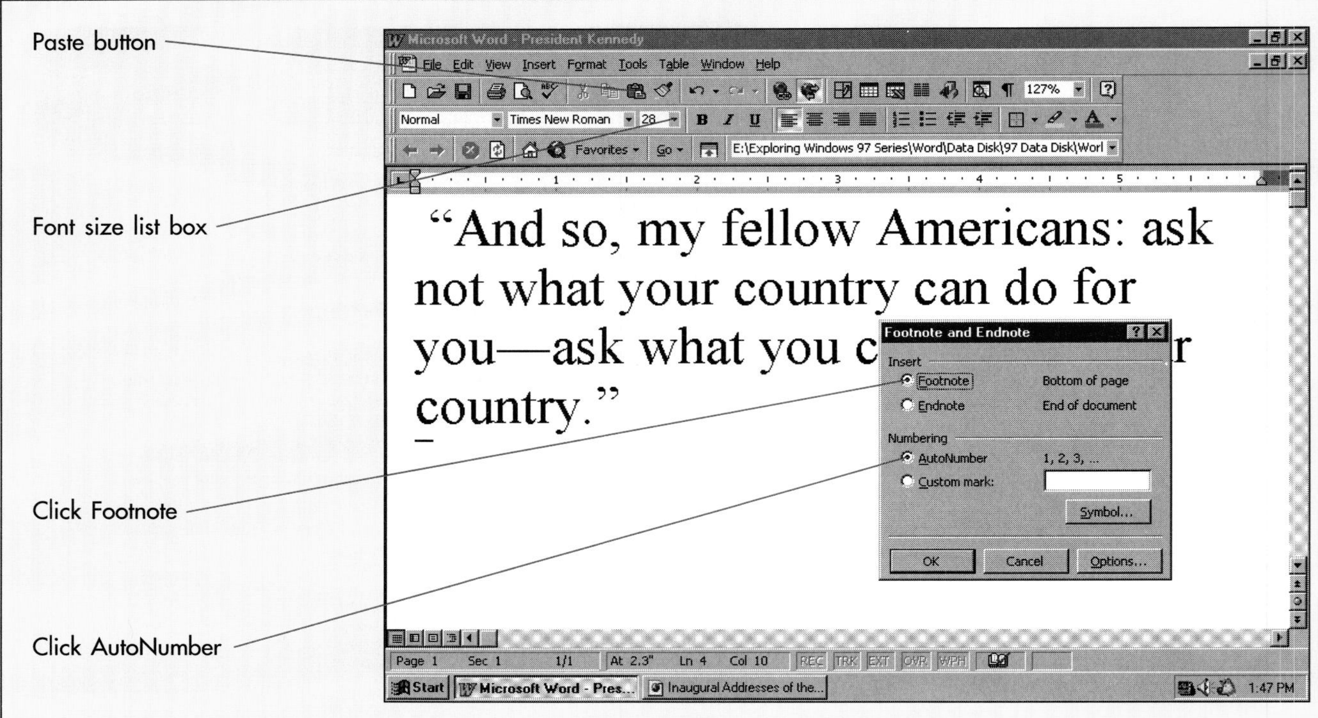

(d) Add a Footnote (step 4)

FIGURE 3.8 Hands-on Exercise 2 (continued)

STEP 5: Insert the Picture

- Press **Ctrl+Home** to move to the beginning of the document. Pull down the **Insert menu,** point to (or click) **Picture,** then click **From File** to display the Insert Picture dialog box shown in Figure 3.8e.
- Click the **drop-down arrow** on the Look in text box to select the drive and folder where you previously saved the picture (e.g., the Exploring Word folder on drive C).
- Select (click) **jk35,** which is the file containing the picture of President Kennedy. Click the **Preview button** (if necessary) to display the picture before inserting it into the document.
- Click **Insert,** and the picture of President Kennedy will appear in your document. Do not worry about its size or position at this time.

CROPPING A PICTURE

Select (click) a picture and Word automatically displays the Picture toolbar, which lets you modify the picture in subtle ways. The Crop tool is one of the most useful as it enables you to eliminate (crop) part of a picture. Select the picture to display the Picture toolbar and display the sizing handles. Click the Crop tool (the ScreenTip will display the name of the tool), then click and drag a sizing handle to crop the part of the picture you want to eliminate.

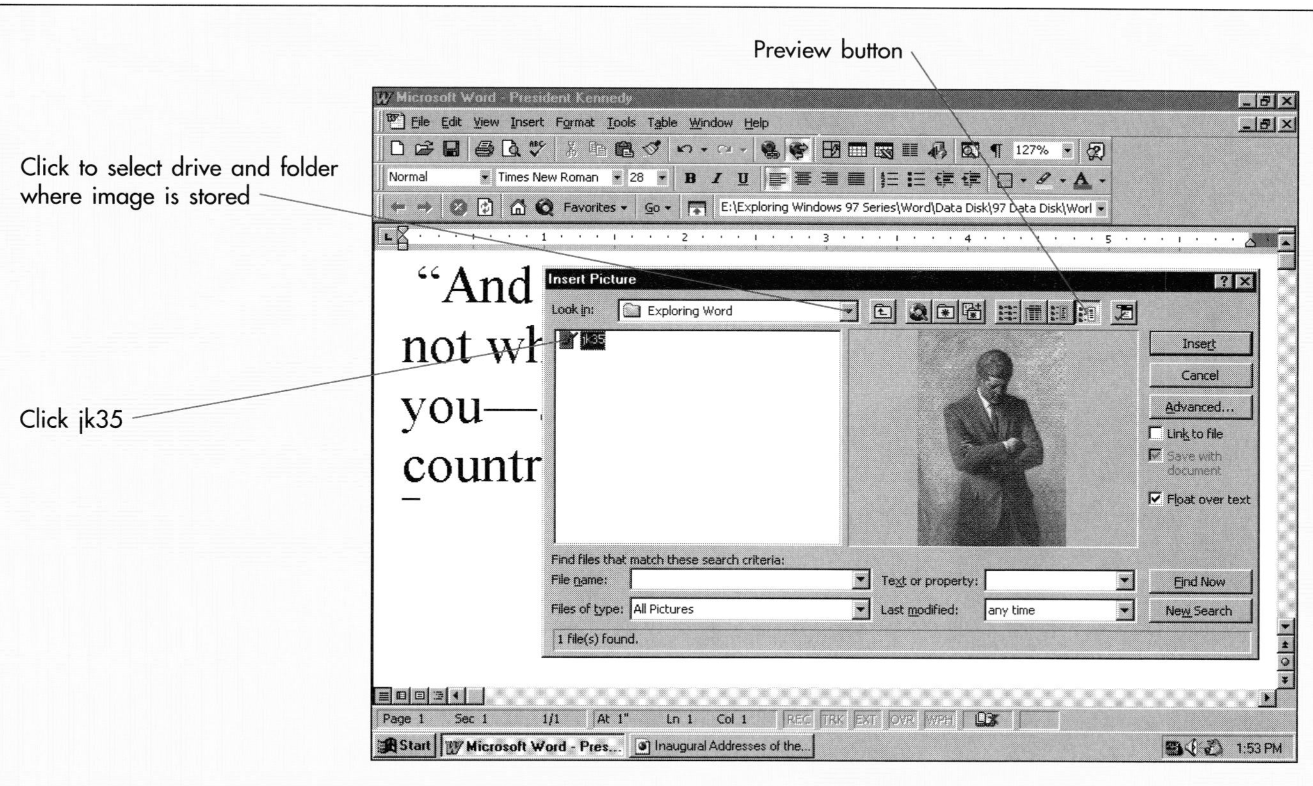

(e) Insert the Picture (step 5)

FIGURE 3.8 Hands-on Exercise 2 (continued)

STEP 6: Move and Size the Picture

- Word automatically changes to the Page Layout View when you insert a picture. Zoom to **Whole Page** to view the document as shown in Figure 3.8f (the line styles are not yet visible).
- Move and size the picture until it is positioned as shown. Alternatively, you can experiment with a different layout for your document.
- Check that the picture is still selected. Click the **Line Styles button** on the Picture toolbar to display the styles in Figure 3.8f. Click the **1 pt line** to place a 1 point border around the picture.
- Center the quotation as a finishing touch. Save the document.

MISSING HYPERLINK

Word will, by default, convert any Internet path (e.g., any text beginning with http:// or www) to a hyperlink. If this is not the case, pull down the Tools menu, click AutoCorrect, then click the AutoFormat As You Type tab. Check the box in the Replace as you type area for Internet and Network paths. Click OK. The next time you enter a Web or e-mail address, it will be converted automatically to a hyperlink.

STEP 7: Insert a Second Footnote

- Click the **drop-down arrow** on the Zoom box to return to **Page Width.** Click below the picture. Press **enter** to add a blank line.
- Select the blank line and change the point size to 12, then add the text **Photograph is from the White House Web page** as shown in Figure 3.8g. Do not press the enter key.
- The insertion point should be immediately after the sentence you just entered. Pull down the **Insert menu,** click **Footnote** to display the Footnote and Endnote dialog box, then check that the option buttons for **Footnote** and **AutoNumber** are selected. Click **OK.**
- Word inserts a new footnote and simultaneously positions you at the bottom of the page to add the actual note. (If both footnotes do not fit on the bottom of the page, zoom back to the Whole Page and resize the picture.) The existing footnote has been changed to note number 2 (since it comes after the new footnote).
- Enter the complete reference **www.whitehouse.gov/WH/glimpse/presidents/html/jk35.html** as well as today's date. Word recognizes the Web address and automatically converts it to a hyperlink, enabling you to click on the link and return to the Web page from where you obtained the picture.
- Save the document, then print the document to submit to your instructor as proof you did the exercise.
- Exit Word if you do not want to continue with the next exercise at this time.

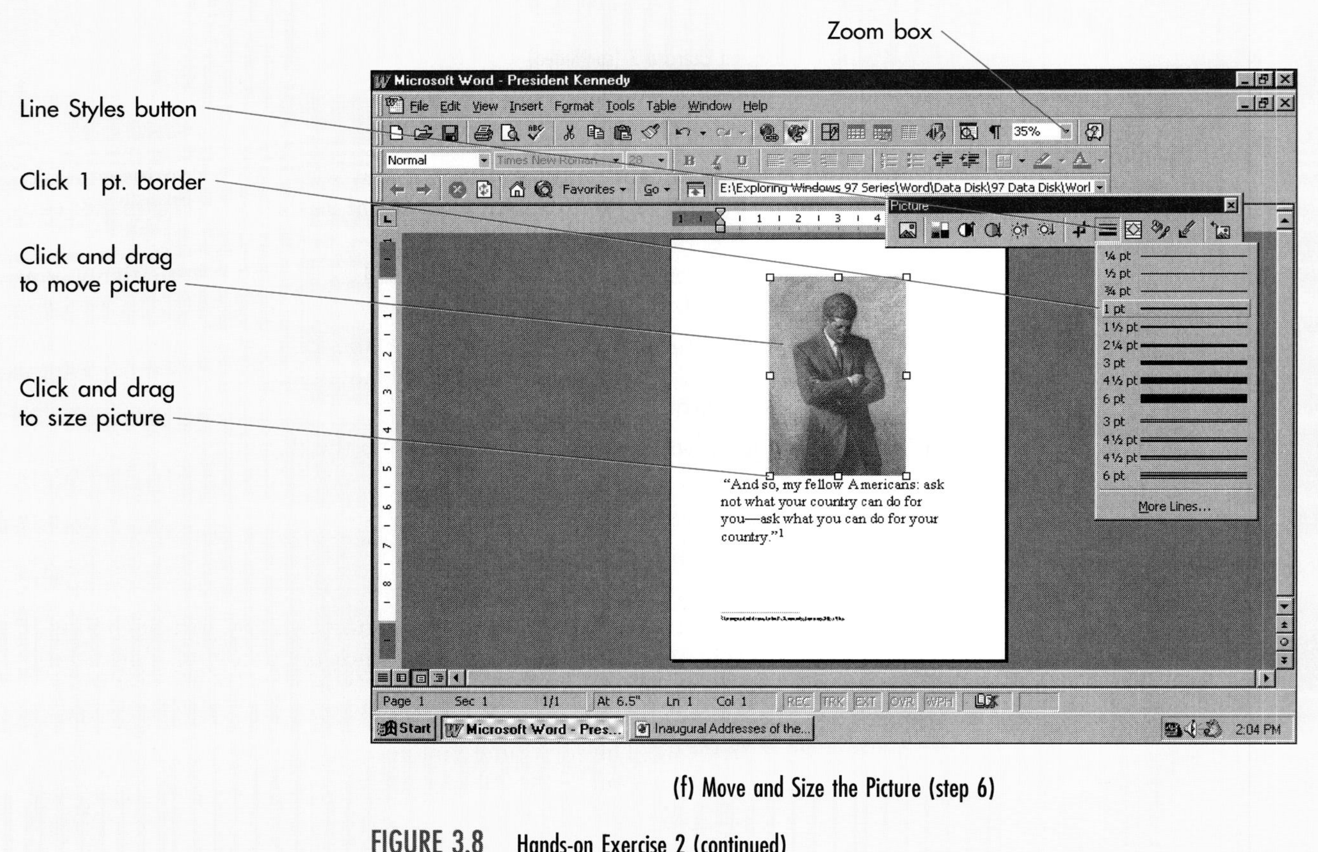

(f) Move and Size the Picture (step 6)

FIGURE 3.8 Hands-on Exercise 2 (continued)

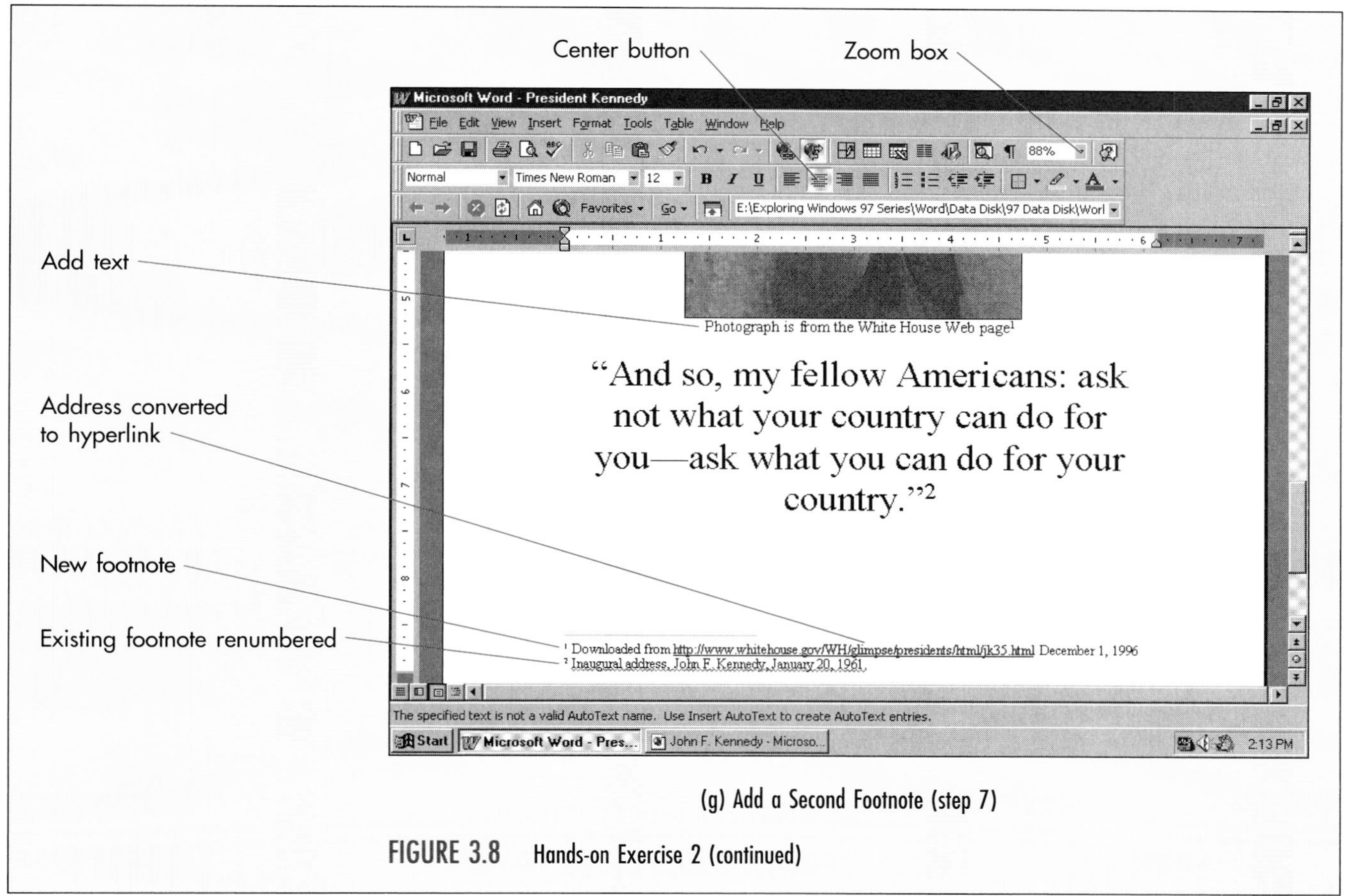
Center button
Zoom box
Add text
Address converted to hyperlink
New footnote
Existing footnote renumbered
Microsoft Word - President Kennedy
Photograph is from the White House Web page1
"And so, my fellow Americans: ask not what your country can do for you—ask what you can do for your country."2
1 Downloaded from http://www.whitehouse.gov/WH/glimpse/presidents/html/jk35.html December 1, 1996
2 Inaugural address, John F. Kennedy, January 20, 1961.
The specified text is not a valid AutoText name. Use Insert AutoText to create AutoText entries.

(g) Add a Second Footnote (step 7)

FIGURE 3.8 Hands-on Exercise 2 (continued)

WIZARDS AND TEMPLATES

We have created some very interesting documents throughout the text, but in every instance we have formatted the document entirely on our own. It is time now to see what is available to "jump start" the process by borrowing professional designs from others. Accordingly, we discuss the wizards and templates that are built into Microsoft Word.

A ***template*** is a partially completed document that contains formatting, text, and/or graphics. It may be as simple as a memo or as complex as a résumé or newsletter. Microsoft Word provides a variety of templates for common documents including a résumé, agenda, and fax cover sheet. You simply open the template, then modify the existing text as necessary, while retaining the formatting in the template. A ***wizard*** makes the process even easier by asking a series of questions, then creating a customized template based on your answers.

Figure 3.9 illustrates the use of wizards and templates in conjunction with a résumé. You can choose from one of three existing templates (contemporary, elegant, and professional) to which you add personal information. Alternatively, you can select the ***Résumé Wizard*** to create a customized template, as was done in Figure 3.9a.

After the Résumé Wizard is selected, it prompts you for the information it needs to create a basic résumé. You specify the style in Figure 3.9b, enter the requested information in Figure 3.9c, and choose the categories in Figure 3.9d. The wizard continues to ask additional questions (not shown in Figure 3.9), after which it displays the (partially) completed résumé based on your responses. You then complete the résumé by entering the specifics of your employment and/or

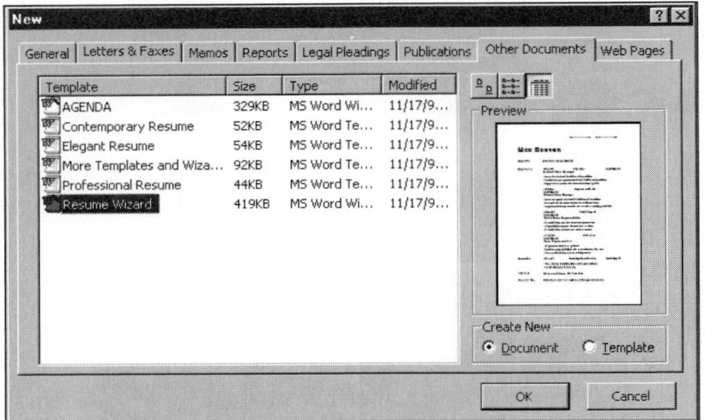

(a) Résumé Wizard

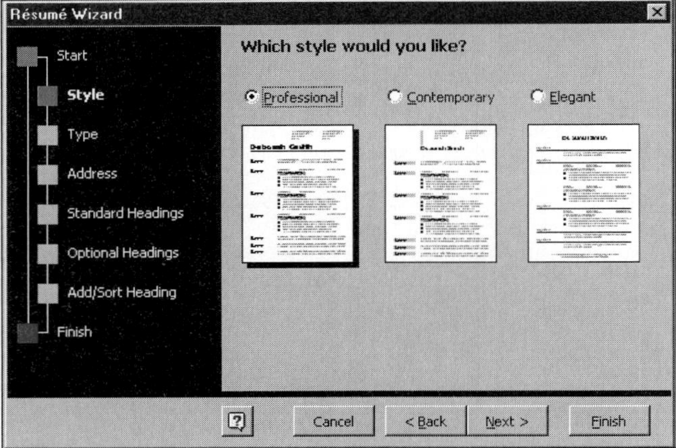

(b) Choose the Style

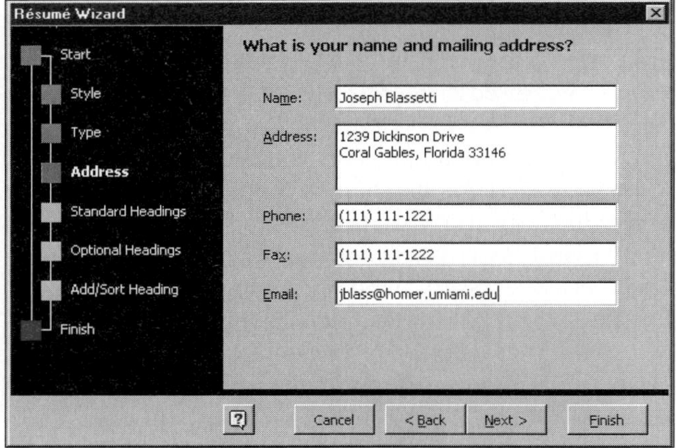

(c) Supply the Information

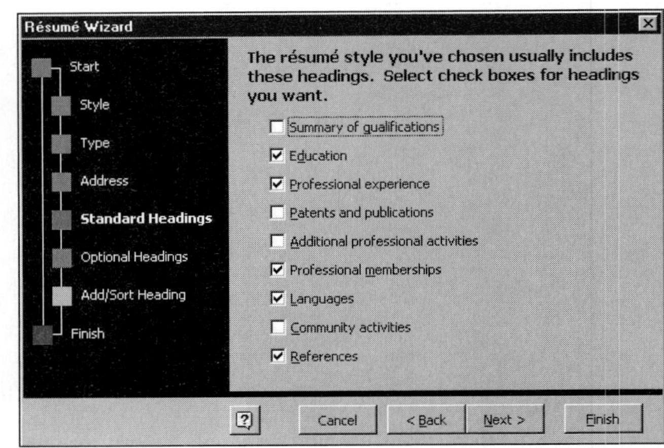

(d) Choose the Headings

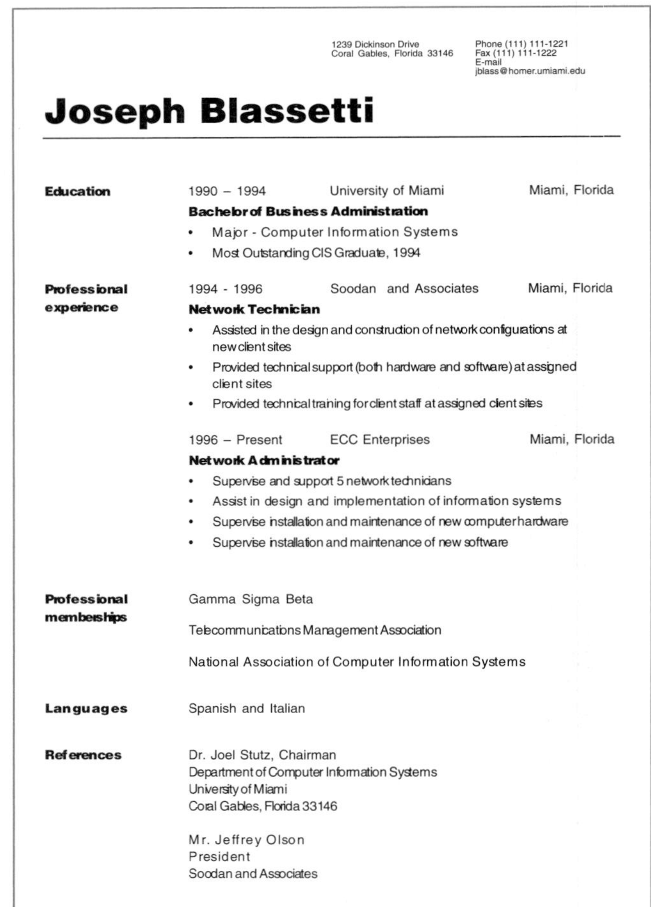

1239 Dickinson Drive
Coral Gables, Florida 33146

Phone (111) 111-1221
Fax (111) 111-1222
E-mail
jblass@homer.umiami.edu

Joseph Blassetti

Education

1990 – 1994 University of Miami Miami, Florida

Bachelor of Business Administration

- Major - Computer Information Systems
- Most Outstanding CIS Graduate, 1994

Professional experience

1994 - 1996 Soodan and Associates Miami, Florida

Network Technician

- Assisted in the design and construction of network configurations at new client sites
- Provided technical support (both hardware and software) at assigned client sites
- Provided technical training for client staff at assigned client sites

1996 – Present ECC Enterprises Miami, Florida

Network Administrator

- Supervise and support 5 network technicians
- Assist in design and implementation of information systems
- Supervise installation and maintenance of new computer hardware
- Supervise installation and maintenance of new software

Professional memberships

Gamma Sigma Beta

Telecommunications Management Association

National Association of Computer Information Systems

Languages

Spanish and Italian

References

Dr. Joel Stutz, Chairman
Department of Computer Information Systems
University of Miami
Coral Gables, Florida 33146

Mr. Jeffrey Olson
President
Soodan and Associates

(e) The Completed Résumé

FIGURE 3.9 Creating a Résumé

additional information. As you edit the document, you can copy and paste information within the résumé, just as you would with a regular document. It takes a little practice, but the end result is a professionally formatted résumé in a minimum of time.

Microsoft Word contains templates and wizards for a variety of other documents. (Look carefully at the tabs within the dialog box of Figure 3.9a and you can infer that Word will help you to create letters, faxes, memos, reports, legal pleadings, publications, and even Web pages.) Consider, too, Figure 3.10, which displays four attractive documents that were created using the respective wizards. Realize, however, that while wizards and templates will help you to create professionally designed documents, they are only a beginning. *The content is still up to you.*

THIRTY SECONDS IS ALL YOU HAVE

Thirty seconds is the average amount of time a personnel manager spends skimming your résumé and deciding whether or not to call you for an interview. It doesn't matter how much training you have had or how good you are if your résumé and cover letter fail to project a professional image. Know your audience and use the vocabulary of your targeted field. Be positive and describe your experience from an accomplishment point of view. Maintain a separate list of references and have it available on request. Be sure that all information is accurate. Be conscientious about the design of your résumé, and proofread the final documents very carefully.

June 1997

Sun	Mon	Tue	Wed	Thu	Fri	Sat
1	2	3	4	5	6	7
8	9	10	11	12	13	14
15	16	17	18	19	20	21
22	23	24	25	26	27	28
29	30					

(a) Calendar

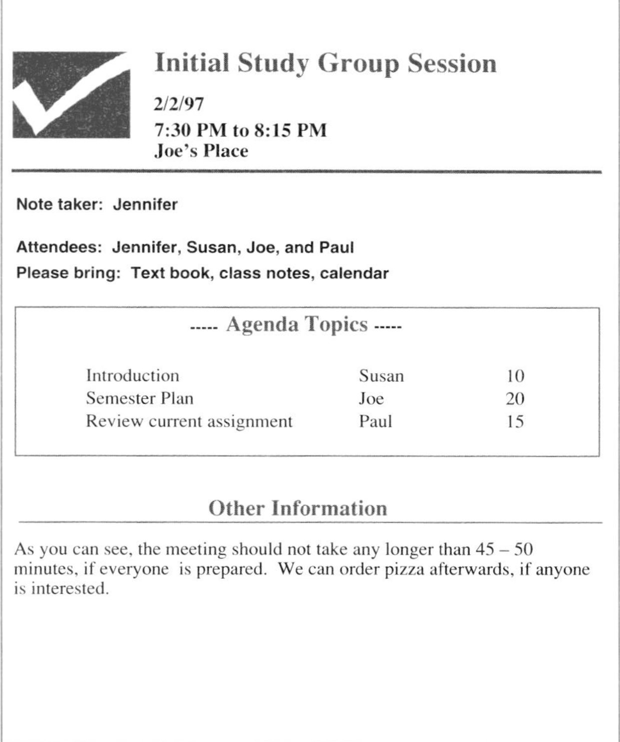

Initial Study Group Session

2/2/97

7:30 PM to 8:15 PM

Joe's Place

Note taker: Jennifer

Attendees: Jennifer, Susan, Joe, and Paul

Please bring: Text book, class notes, calendar

----- Agenda Topics -----

Introduction	Susan	10
Semester Plan	Joe	20
Review current assignment	Paul	15

Other Information

As you can see, the meeting should not take any longer than 45 – 50 minutes, if everyone is prepared. We can order pizza afterwards, if anyone is interested.

(b) Agenda

FIGURE 3.10 What You Can Do with Wizards

277 Rivera Drive
Coral Gables, FL 33146
Phone (111) 111-8897
Fax: (111) 111-9822

Fax

To: Jennifer	**From:** Susan Peterson
Fax: (305) 222-8977	**Date:** January 27, 1997
Phone: (305) 222-3009	**Pages:** 2
Re: Initial Study Group Session	**CC:**

☐**Urgent** ☐**For Review** ☐**Please Comment** ☐**Please Reply** ☐**Please Recycle**

Comments: Attached you should find the agenda for our initial study group session. Please let me know if you have any questions. I look forward to seeing you on Friday 2 nd .

(c) Fax Cover Sheet

Interoffice Memo

Date: 12/22/96

To: Dr. Robert Plant
Dr. John Stewart

From: Maryann M. Barber

RE: CIS 120 Final Exam

The meeting to prepare the final exam for CIS 120 will be on Friday, April 18, 1997 at 3:00 PM in my office. I have attached a copy of last semester's final, which I would like for you to review prior to the meeting. In addition, if you could take a few minutes and create approxiumately 20 new questions for this semester's test, it would make our job at the meeitng a lot easier. The meeting should last no longer than an hour, provided that we all do our homework before the meeting. If you have any questions before that time, please let me know.

Attachments

12/22/96 Confidential 1

(d) Memo

FIGURE 3.10 What You Can Do with Wizards (continued)

The following exercise introduces you to the Agenda and Fax wizards. We ask you to create an agenda, then optionally fax the agenda to a classmate. As you do the exercise you will notice that the two wizards have several features in common, and that once you master one wizard, you intuitively know how to use the others. Note, too, that you can use the ***Fax Wizard*** to create a cover sheet, even if you do not send an actual fax.

Our next exercise directs you in the use of the ***Agenda Wizard*** to create an agenda for a hypothetical meeting. To add realism to the exercise, we suggest that you form a study group consisting of three or four members of this class, then create an agenda for the first meeting of your group. Not only will it help you in this exercise, but you will have a study group for the semester.

MISSING WIZARDS

The Agenda Wizard is not installed in a typical setup and hence you may not see it initially. To install the Wizard, just copy the file from the ValuePack\Template\Word folder on the Office 97 CD-ROM to the Program Files\Microsoft Office\Templates\Other Documents folder on your hard drive. Alternatively, you can download the Agenda Wizard from the Microsoft Web site. Pull down the Help menu, click Microsoft on the Web, then click Free Stuff to connect to the site. Follow the directions on the Web page to download the Wizard.

HANDS-ON EXERCISE 3

Wizards and Templates

Objective: To use the Agenda Wizard to create an agenda for a study group, then use the Fax Wizard to fax the agenda to your group. You can do the exercise even if you do not send an actual fax. Use Figure 3.11 as a guide in the exercise.

STEP 1: The File New Command

- Start Word. Pull down the **File menu.** Click **New** to display the New dialog box shown in Figure 3.11a. Click the **Other Documents tab** to display the documents shown in Figure 3.11a.
- Click the **Details button** to switch to the Details view to see the file name, type, size, and date of last modification. Click and drag the vertical line between the Template and Size columns, to increase the size of the Template column, so that you can see the complete document name.
- Select (click) **Agenda.** (See boxed tip on page 130 if you cannot find the Agenda Wizard.) If necessary, click the option button to **Create New Document** (as opposed to a template). Click **OK** to start the **Agenda Wizard.**

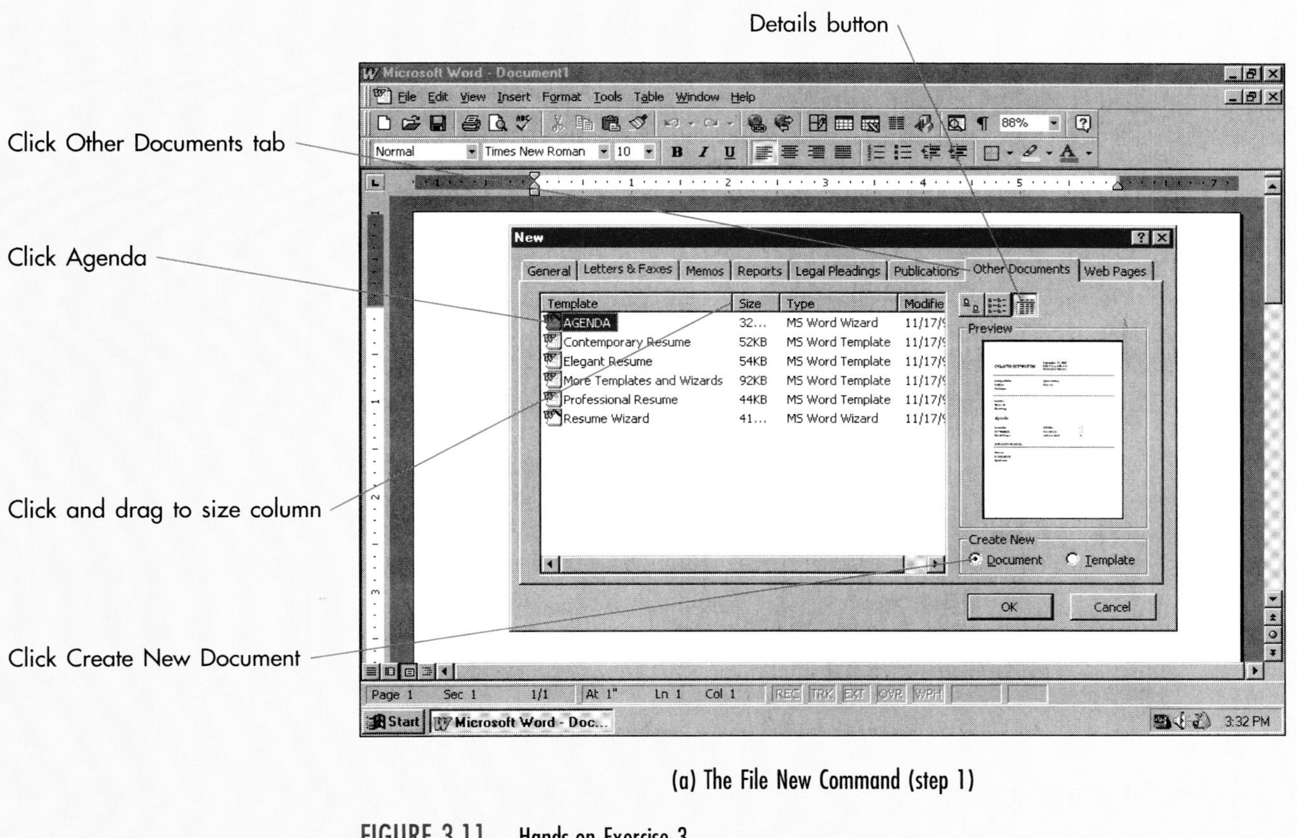

(a) The File New Command (step 1)

FIGURE 3.11 Hands-on Exercise 3

STEP 2: The Agenda Wizard

➤ You should see the main screen of the Agenda Wizard as shown in Figure 3.11b. Click **Next** to begin. The Wizard will take you through a series of questions, from start to finish. To create the desired agenda:

- Click **Boxes** as the style of the agenda. Click **Next.**
- Enter the date and time of your meeting. Enter **Initial Study Group Session** as the title. Enter **Joe's Place** as the location. Click **Next.**
- The Wizard asks which headings you want and supplies a check box next to each heading. The check boxes function as toggle switches to select (deselect) each heading. We suggest you clear all entries except **Please bring.** Click **Next.**
- The Wizard asks which names you want in the agenda. Clear all headings except **Note Taker** and **Attendees.** Click **Next.**
- Enter at least three topics for the agenda. Press the **Tab key** to move from one text box to the next (e.g., from Agenda topic, to Person, to Minutes). Click the **Add** button when you have completed the information for one topic.
- If necessary, reorder the topics by clicking the desired topic, then clicking the **Move Up** or **Move Down** command button. Click **Next** when you are satisfied with the agenda.
- Click **No** when asked whether you want a form to record the minutes of the meeting. Click **Next.**

➤ The final screen of the Agenda Wizard indicates that the Wizard has all the information it needs. Click the **Finish button.**

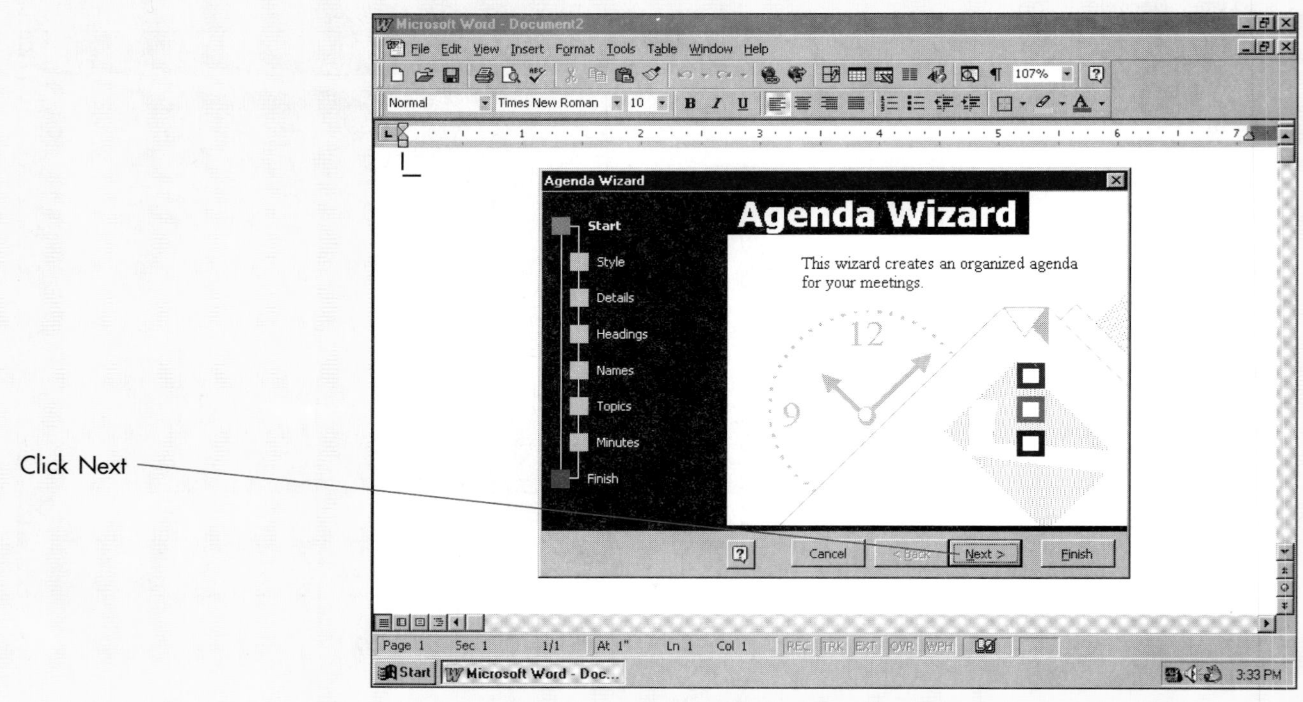

(b) The Agenda Wizard (step 2)

FIGURE 3.11 Hands-on Exercise 3 (continued)

RETRACE YOUR STEPS

The Agenda Wizard guides you every step of the way, but what if you make a mistake or change your mind? Click the Back command button at any time to return to a previous screen in order to enter different information, then continue working with the Wizard.

STEP 3: Complete the Agenda

- You should see an initial agenda similar to the document in Figure 3.11c. Close the Office Assistant if it appears (or you can leave it open and request help as necessary).
- Save the agenda as **Initial Study Group Session** in the **Exploring Word** folder. If necessary, change to the **Normal view** and zoom to **Page Width** so that your document more closely matches ours.
- Complete the Agenda by entering the additional information, such as the names of the note taker and attendees as well as the specifics of what to read or bring, as shown in the figure. Click at the indicated position on the figure prior to entering the text, so that your entries align properly.
- Click the **Spelling and Grammar button** to check the agenda for spelling.
- Save the document but do not close it.
- Click the **Print button** on the Standard toolbar to print the completed document and submit it to your instructor.

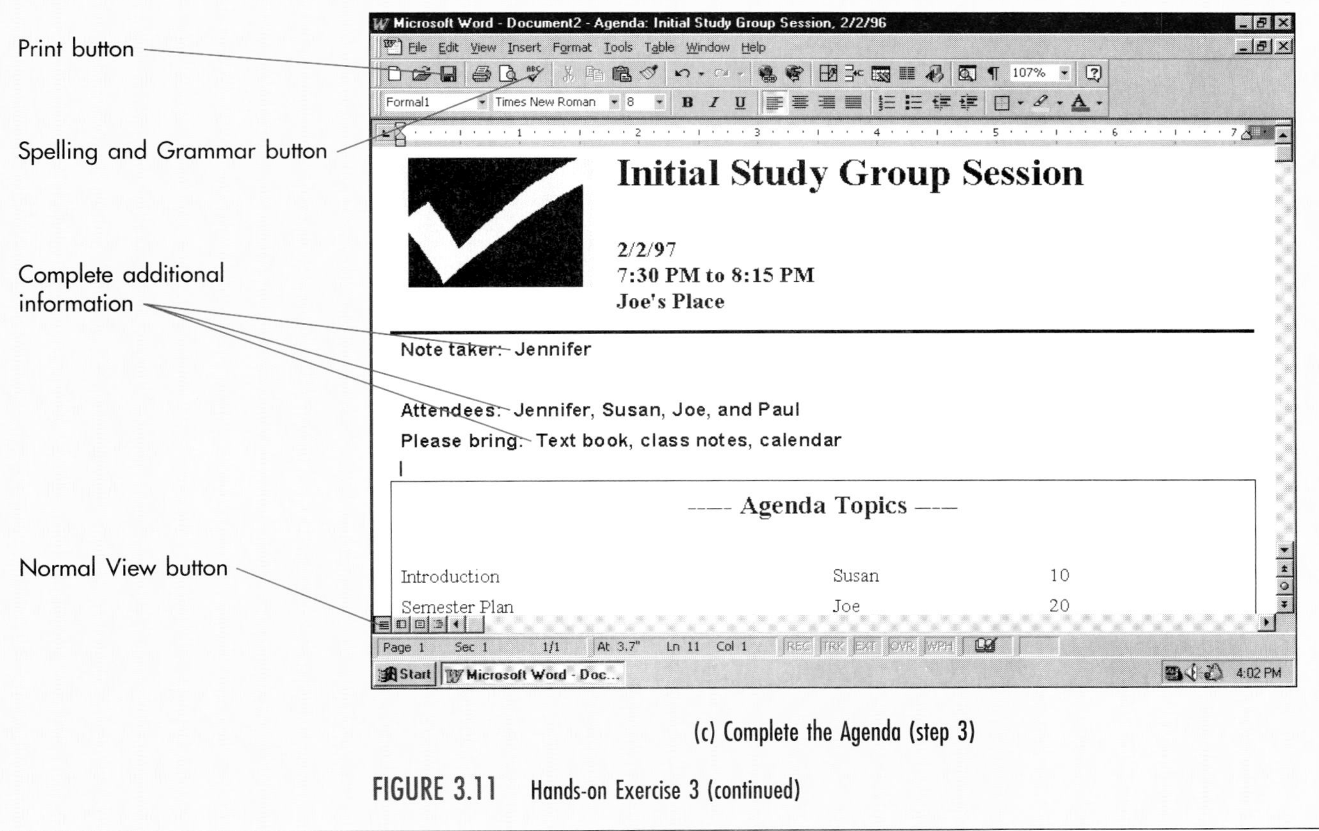

(c) Complete the Agenda (step 3)

FIGURE 3.11 Hands-on Exercise 3 (continued)

CHANGING THE VIEW

Word provides different views of a document and different magnifications of each view. The choice depends on your preference and need. (We switch all the time.) The Normal view suppresses the margins, giving you more room in which to work. The Page Layout view, on the other hand, displays the margins, so that what you see on the monitor more closely resembles the printed page. The easiest way to change from one view to the other is by clicking the appropriate icon above the status bar. The easiest way to change the magnification is to click the drop-down arrow in the Zoom box on the Standard toolbar.

STEP 4: The Fax Wizard

- Pull down the **File menu** and click **New** to display the New dialog box. Click the **Letters & Faxes tab** to display the indicated wizards and templates. Check that the **Document option button** is selected. Double click the **Fax Wizard** to start it.
- You should see the main screen of the Fax Wizard. Click **Next** to begin. The Wizard will take you through a series of questions, from start to finish, as shown in Figure 3.11d:

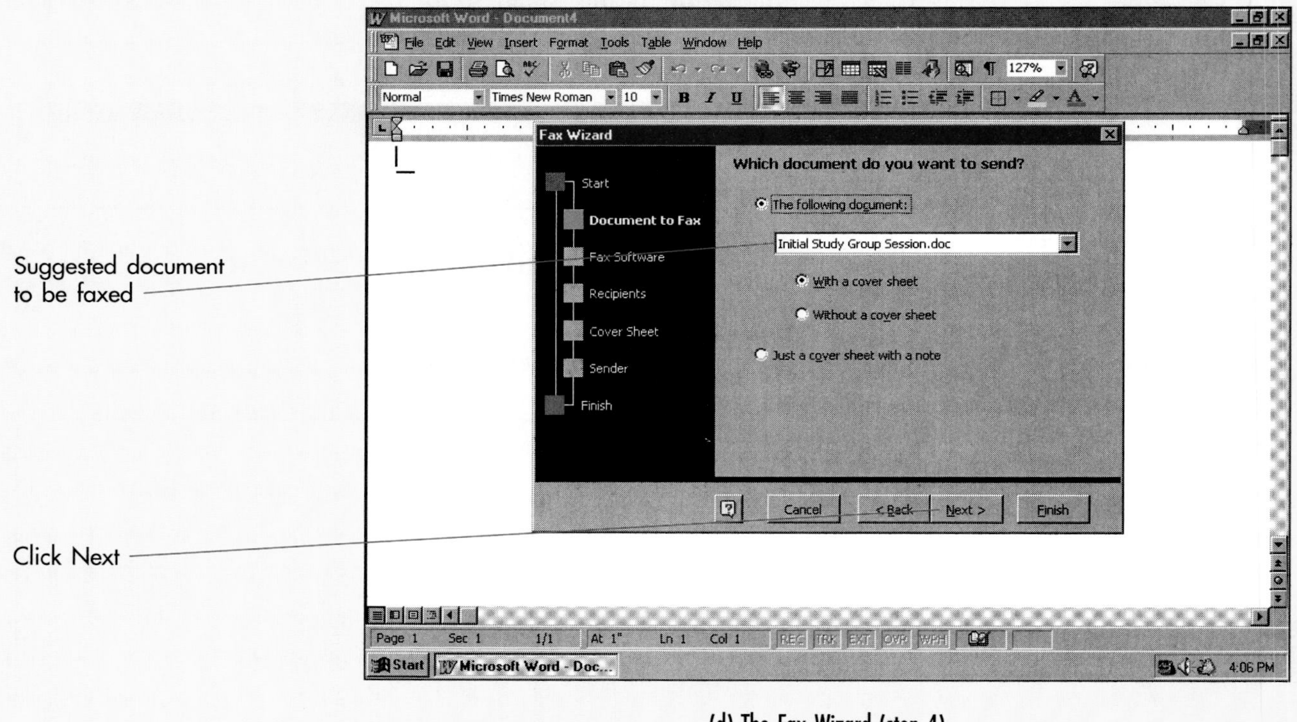

(d) The Fax Wizard (step 4)

FIGURE 3.11 Hands-on Exercise 3 (continued)

- The Fax Wizard suggests Initial Study Group as the name of the document you want to fax (because the document is still open). The option button **With a Cover Sheet** is selected. Click **Next.**
- **Microsoft Fax** is selected as the software to use. Click **Next.**
- Enter the name and fax number of one person in your group. Complete this entry even if you do not intend to send an actual fax. Click **Next.**
- Choose the style of the cover sheet. We selected **Professional.** Click **Next.**
- If necessary, complete and/or modify the information about the sender so that it reflects your name and telephone number. Click **Next.**
- Read the last screen reminding you about how to list phone numbers correctly. Click **Finish.**

STEP 5: Complete the Fax

- ➤ You should see a fax cover sheet similar to the document in Figure 3.11e. Close the Office Assistant if it appears, or request help as you see fit. Do *not* click the button to Send Fax Now.
- ➤ Save the cover sheet as **Fax Cover Sheet** in the **Exploring Word** folder. If necessary, change to the **Normal view** and zoom to **Page Width** so that your document more closely matches ours.
- ➤ Complete the cover sheet by entering the additional information as appropriate. Click at the indicated position in Figure 3.11e prior to entering the text, so that your entries align properly.

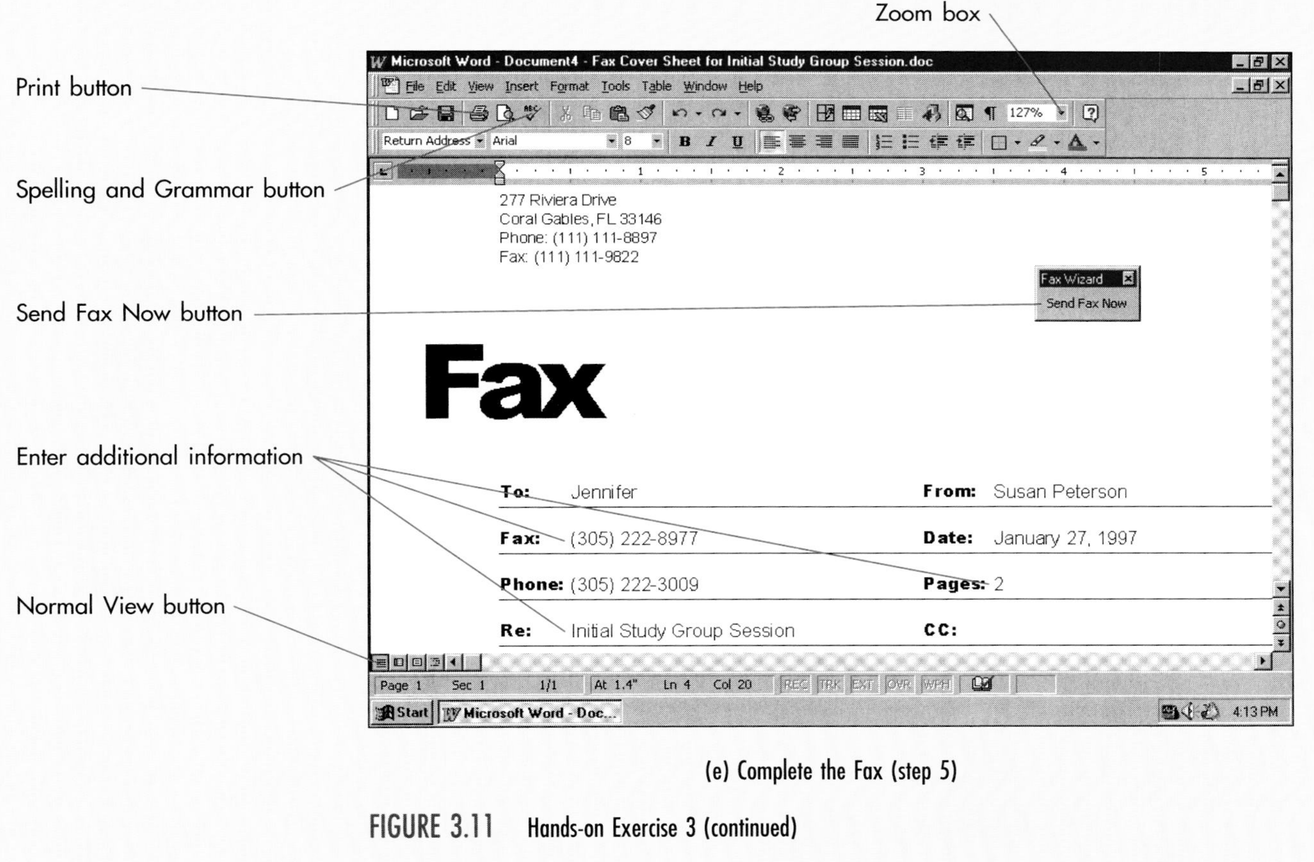

(e) Complete the Fax (step 5)

FIGURE 3.11 Hands-on Exercise 3 (continued)

- Click the **Spelling and Grammar button** to check the agenda for spelling. Save the document.
- Save the document a final time. Click the **Print button** on the Standard toolbar to print the completed document, and submit it to your instructor as proof that you did the exercise.

STEP 6: Send the Fax

- Do this step only if you want to send the fax. You cannot do this from your lab at school! Click the **Send Fax Now** button to begin sending the fax.
- Just sit back and relax and watch the Fax Wizard as it goes through the steps of sending the fax as shown in Figure 3.11f. Check with the recipient to be sure he or she received the fax. Click **OK** to return to the document.
- Exit Word. Congratulations on a job well done.

TROUBLESHOOTING

If you're having difficulty sending a fax it could be because the dialing properties of your modem are set improperly. Click the Start menu, click Settings, click Control Panel, then double click the Modems icon to display the Modems Properties dialog box. If necessary, click the General tab, click the Dialing Properties button, verify that your settings are correct, then click OK to close the Dialing Properties dialog box.

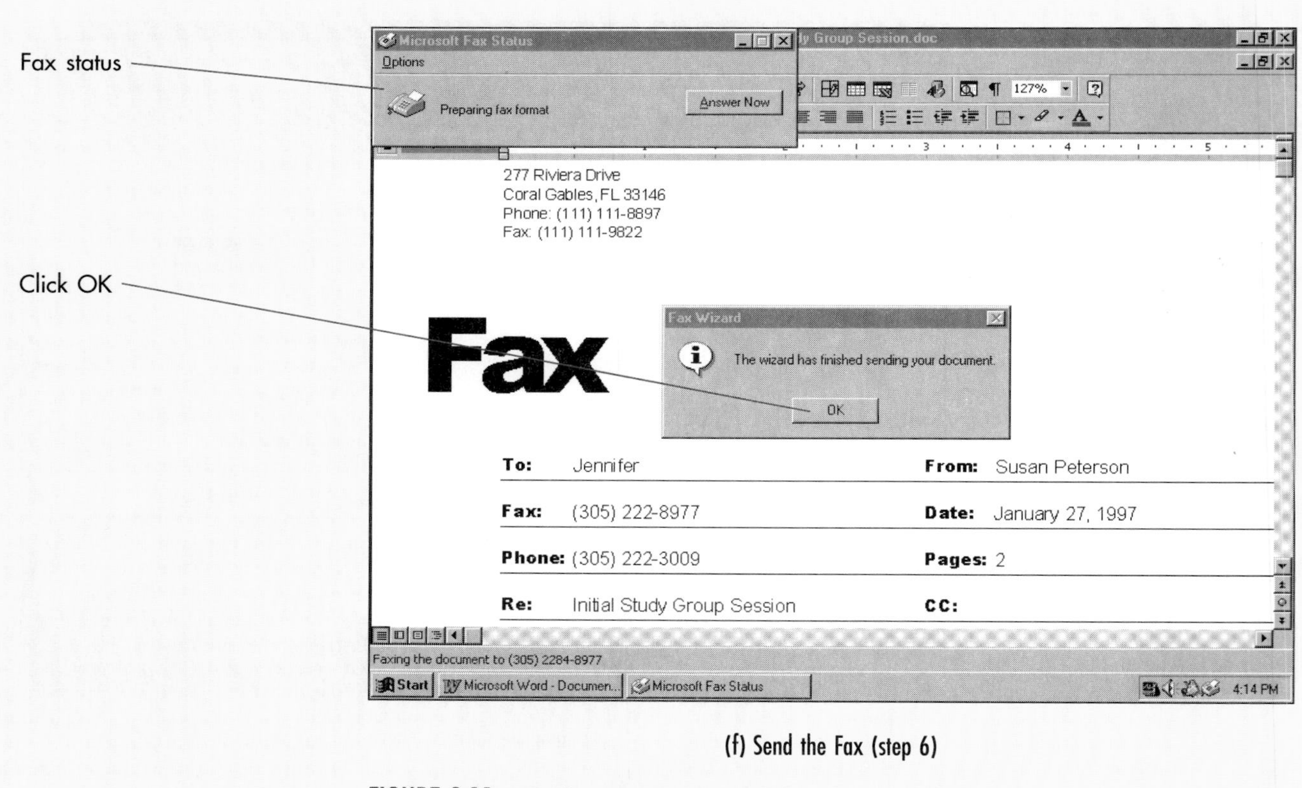

(f) Send the Fax (step 6)

FIGURE 3.11 Hands-on Exercise 3 (continued)

SUMMARY

The applications in Microsoft Office are thoroughly integrated with one another. They look alike and work alike. Equally important, they share information through a technology known as Object Linking and Embedding (OLE), which enables you to create a compound document containing data (objects) from multiple applications.

The Microsoft Clip Gallery contains more than 3,000 clip art images and almost 150 photographs, each in a variety of categories. It also contains sound files and video clips, although these objects are more commonly used in PowerPoint presentations than in Word documents. Microsoft WordArt is an application within Microsoft Office that creates decorative text, which can be used to add interest to a document.

The Insert Symbol command provides access to special characters, making it easy to place typographic characters into a document. The symbols can be taken from any TrueType font and can be displayed in any point size.

The Internet is a network of networks. The World Wide Web (WWW, or simply the Web) is a very large subset of the Internet, consisting of those computers containing hypertext and/or hypermedia documents. Resources (e.g., clip art or photographs) can be downloaded from the Web for inclusion in a Word document.

Every document in Office 97 is Web-enabled, meaning that the application will automatically detect and highlight any hyperlinks that are entered in a document. You can click a hyperlink from within Word and, provided you have an Internet connection, your Web browser will display the associated page. Each Office application also contains a Web toolbar with icons similar to those found on the toolbar in Internet Explorer.

A copyright provides legal protection to a written or artistic work, giving the author exclusive rights to its use and reproduction except as governed under the fair use exclusion. Anything on the Internet or World Wide Web should be considered copyrighted unless the document specifically says it is in the public domain. The fair use exclusion enables you to use a portion of the work for educational, nonprofit purposes, or for the purpose of critical review or commentary.

A footnote provides additional information about an item, such as its source, and appears at the bottom of the page where the reference occurs. The Insert Footnote command inserts a footnote into a document and automatically assigns the next sequential number to that note.

Wizards and templates help create professionally designed documents with a minimum of time and effort. A template is a partially completed document that contains formatting and other information. A wizard is an interactive program that creates a customized template based on the answers you supply.

OBJECT LINKING AND EMBEDDING

Object Linking and Embedding (OLE) enables you to create a compound document containing objects (data) from multiple Windows applications. Each of the techniques, linking and embedding, can be implemented in various ways. Althogh OLE is one of the major benefits of working in the Windows environment, it would be impossible to illustrate all of the techniques in a single exercise. Accordingly, we have created the icon at the left to help you identify the many OLE examples that appear throughout the *Exploring Windows* series.

KEY WORDS AND CONCEPTS

Agenda Wizard
AutoCorrect
AutoFormat
Clip art
Clipboard
Compound document
Copyright
Crop
Endnote
Fair use exclusion
Fax Wizard
Footnote
Format Picture command
Hyperlink
Hypermedia
Hypertext
Insert Footnote command
Insert Picture command
Insert Symbol command
Internet
Microsoft Clip Gallery
Microsoft WordArt
Object Linking and Embedding (OLE)
Picture toolbar
Public domain
Résumé Wizard
Sizing handle
Template
Web-enabled
Web toolbar
Wizard
WordArt
WordArt toolbar
World Wide Web

MULTIPLE CHOICE

1. How do you change the size of a selected object so that the height and width change in proportion to one another?
   (a) Click and drag any of the four corner handles in the direction you want to go
   (b) Click and drag the sizing handle on the top border, then click and drag the sizing handle on the left side
   (c) Click and drag the sizing handle on the bottom border, then click and drag the sizing handle on the right side
   (d) All of the above

2. The Microsoft Clip Galley:
   (a) Is accessed through the Insert Picture command
   (b) Is available to every application in the Microsoft Office
   (c) Enables you to search for a specific piece of clip art by specifying a key word in the description of the clip art
   (d) All of the above

3. Which view, and which magnification, offers the most convenient way to position a graphic within a document?
   (a) Page Width in the Page Layout view
   (b) Full Page in the Page Layout view
   (c) Page Width in the Normal view
   (d) Full Page in the Normal view

4. Which of the following objects can be inserted from the Microsoft Clip Gallery?
   (a) Clip art
   (b) Photographs
   (c) Sound and video files
   (d) All of the above

5. Which of the following is the most likely explanation of why photographs do not appear in the Microsoft Clip Gallery dialog box?
   (a) The user executed the Insert Picture Clip Art command, rather than the Insert Picture Photograph command
   (b) Photographs are not accessible through the Clip Gallery regardless of which command is executed
   (c) The photographs are not included in the default installation of Office and hence are available only with the Office CD-ROM
   (d) None of the above
6. What is the difference between clicking and double clicking an object within a compound document?
   (a) Clicking selects the object; double clicking opens the application that created the object
   (b) Double clicking selects the object; clicking opens the application that created the object
   (c) Clicking changes to Normal view; double clicking changes to Page Layout view
   (d) Double clicking changes to Normal view; clicking changes to Page Layout view
7. Which of the following is true about footnotes or endnotes?
   (a) The addition of a footnote or endnote automatically renumbers the notes that follow
   (b) The deletion of a footnote or endnote automatically renumbers the notes that follow
   (c) Both (a) and (b)
   (d) Neither (a) nor (b)
8. Which of the following is true about the Insert Symbol command?
   (a) It can insert a symbol in different type sizes
   (b) It can access any TrueType font installed on the system
   (c) Both (a) and (b)
   (d) Neither (a) nor (b)
9. Which of the following is true regarding objects and the associated toolbars?
   (a) Clicking on a WordArt object displays the WordArt toolbar
   (b) Clicking on a Picture displays the Picture Toolbar
   (c) Both (a) and (b)
   (d) Neither (a) nor (b)
10. Which of the following objects can be downloaded from the Web for inclusion in a Word document?
    (a) Clip art
    (b) Photographs
    (c) Sound and video files
    (d) All of the above
11. Which of the following is true regarding the Web toolbar?
    (a) It enables you to enter the address of a Web page from within a Word document
    (b) It enables you to add a Web page to a list of favorite pages
    (c) It contains a button to return to previous Web pages
    (d) All of the above

12. What happens if you enter the text *www.intel.com* into a document?
    (a) The entry is converted to a hyperlink, and the text will be underlined and displayed in a different color
    (b) The associated page will be opened, provided your computer has access to the Internet
    (c) Both (a) and (b)
    (d) Neither (a) nor (b)

13. Which of the following is a true statement about wizards?
    (a) They are accessed through the New command in the File menu
    (b) They always produce a finished document
    (c) Both (a) and (b)
    (d) Neither (a) nor (b)

14. How do you access the wizards built into Microsoft Word?
    (a) Pull down the Wizards and Templates menu
    (b) Pull down the Insert menu and choose the Wizards and Templates command
    (c) Pull down the File menu and choose the New command
    (d) None of the above

15. Which of the following is true regarding wizards and templates?
    (a) A wizard may create a template
    (b) A template may create a wizard
    (c) Both (a) and (b)
    (d) Neither (a) nor (b)

ANSWERS

1. a	**6.** a	**11.** d
2. d	**7.** c	**12.** a
3. b	**8.** c	**13.** a
4. d	**9.** c	**14.** c
5. c	**10.** d	**15.** a

PRACTICE WITH MICROSOFT WORD

1. Inserting Objects: Figure 3.12 illustrates a flyer that we created for a hypothetical computer sale. We embedded clip art and WordArt and created what we believe is an attractive flyer. Try to duplicate our advertisement, or better yet, create your own. Include your name somewhere in the document as a sales associate. Be sure to spell check your ad, then print the completed flyer and submit it to your instructor.

2. Exploring TrueType: Installing Windows 95 also installs several TrueType fonts, which in turn are accessible from any application. Two of the fonts, Symbols and Wingdings, contain a variety of special characters that can be used to create some unusual documents. Use the Insert Symbol command, your imagination, and the fact that TrueType fonts are scaleable to any point size to re-create the documents in Figure 3.13. Better yet, use your imagination to create your own documents.

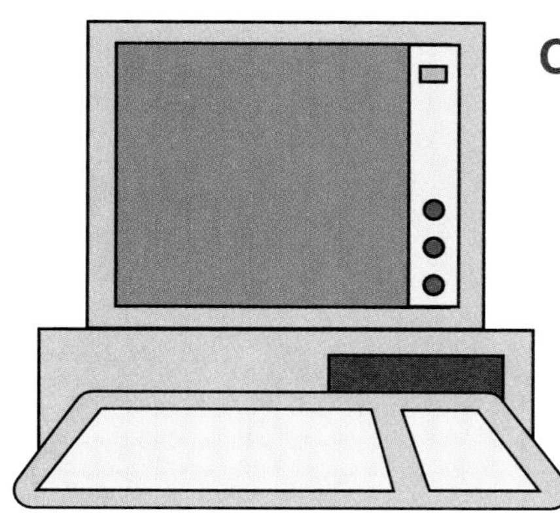

Computer World's Annual Pre-Inventory Sale

When: **Saturday, June 21, 1997**
8:00AM - 10:00PM

Where: **13640 South Dixie Highway**

Computer World

Computers
Printers
Fax/Modems
CD-ROM drives
Sound Systems
Software
Etc.

Pre-Inventory Sale

Sales Associate: Bianca Costo

FIGURE 3.12 Document for Practice Exercise 1

Valentine's Day
We'll serenade your sweetheart
Call 284-LOVE

STUDENT COMPUTER LAB
Fall Semester Hours

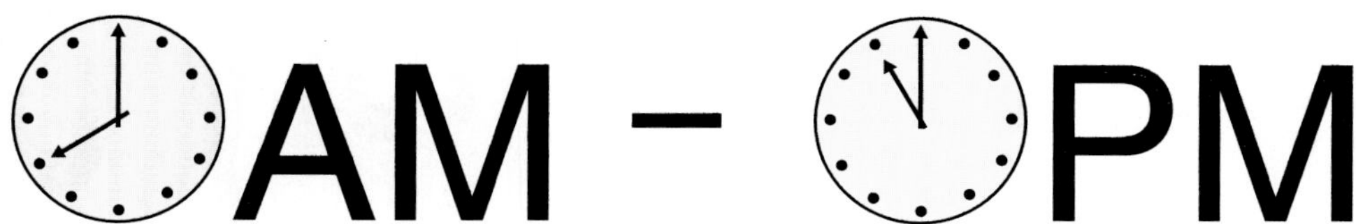

FIGURE 3.13 Documents for Practice Exercise 2

3. It's Easier Than It Looks: The document in Figure 3.14 was created to illustrate the automatic formatting and correction facilities that are built into Microsoft Word. We want you to create the document, include your name at the bottom, then submit the completed document to your instructor as proof that you did the exercise. All you have to do is follow the instructions within the document and let Word do the formatting and correcting for you.

The only potential difficulty is that the options on your system may be set to negate some of the features to which we refer. Accordingly, you need to pull down the Tools menu, click the AutoCorrect command, and click the AutoFormat As You Type tab. Verify that the options referenced in the document are in effect. You also need to review the table of predefined substitutions on the AutoCorrect tab to learn the typewritten characters that will trigger the smiley faces, copyright, and registered trademark substitutions.

It's Easier Than It Looks

This document was created to demonstrate the AutoCorrect and AutoFormat features that are built into Microsoft Word. In essence, you type as you always did and enter traditional characters, then let Word perform its "magic" by substituting symbols and other formatting for you. Among the many features included in these powerful commands are the:

1. Automatic creation of numbered lists by typing a number followed by a period, tab, or right parenthesis. Just remember to press the return key twice to turn off this feature.
2. Symbols for common fractions such as ½ or ¼.
3. Ordinal numbers with superscripts created automatically such as 1st, 2nd, or 3rd.
4. Copyright © and Registered trademark ® symbols.

AutoFormat will even add a border to a paragraph any time you type three or more hyphens, equal signs, or underscores on a line by itself.

===

And finally, the AutoCorrect feature has built-in substitution for smiley faces that look best when set in a larger point size such as 72 points.

FIGURE 3.14 Document for Practice Exercise 3

4. What You Can Do with Clip Art: We are not artistic by nature, and there is no way that we could have created the original clip art image of the duck smashing the computer. We did, however, create the variation shown in Figure 3.15 by using various tools on the Drawing toolbar. All it took was a little imagination and a sense of what can be done.

   Start by inserting the clip art image into a new document and displaying the Drawing toolbar. Select the clip art image, click the drop-down arrow on the Draw button on the Drawing toolbar, and click the Ungroup command. The duck and the computer are now separate objects, each of which can be selected and manipulated separately.

   Click anywhere in the document to deselect both the duck and the computer, then select just the duck. Click the Copy button to copy the duck to the clipboard, then click the Paste button to duplicate the duck. Click and drag the second duck to the right side of the document. Click the drop-down arrow on the Draw button on the Drawing toolbar, click the Rotate or Flip command, then click Flip Horizontal to turn the duck around. To change the color and design of the duck's jacket, you need to ungroup the duck itself, then select the jacket and execute the appropriate command(s).

   The rest is up to you. Use the ScreenTips and online help to learn about the different tools. Create one or more variations of the duck or any other clip art image and submit them to your instructor.

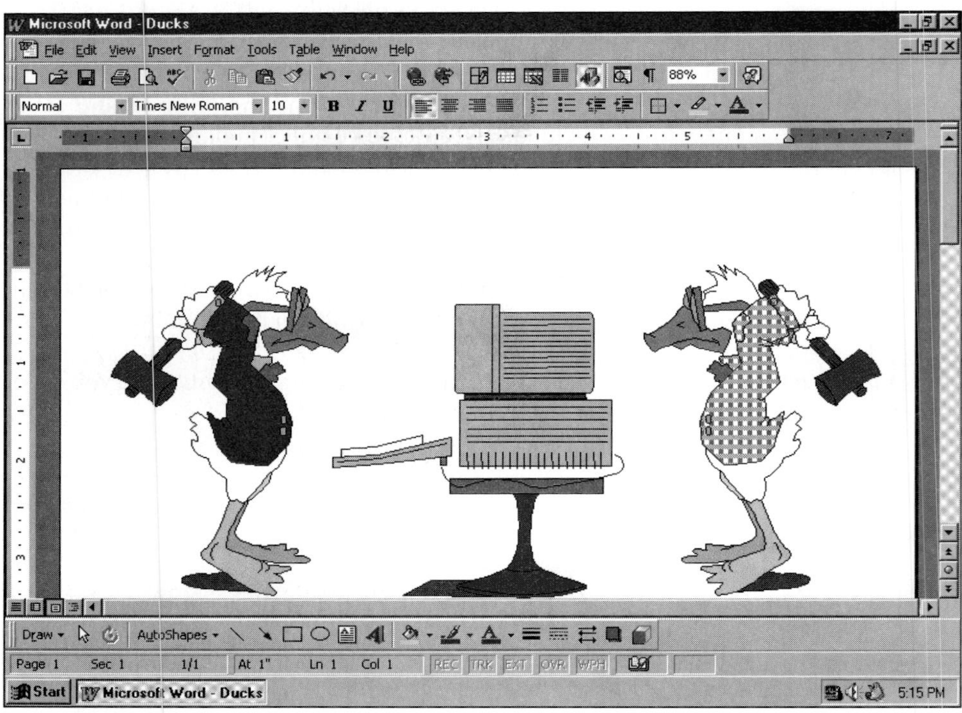

FIGURE 3.15 Screen for Practice Exercise 4

5. Presidential Anecdotes: Figure 3.16 displays the finished version of a document containing 10 presidential anecdotes. The anecdotes were taken from the book *Presidential Anecdotes,* by Paul F. Boller, Jr., published by Penguin Books (New York, NY, 1981). Open the *Chapter 3 Practice 5* document that is found on the data disk, then make the following changes:

   a. Add a footnote after Mr. Boller's name, which appears at the end of the second sentence, citing the information about the book. This, in turn, renumbers all existing footnotes in the document.

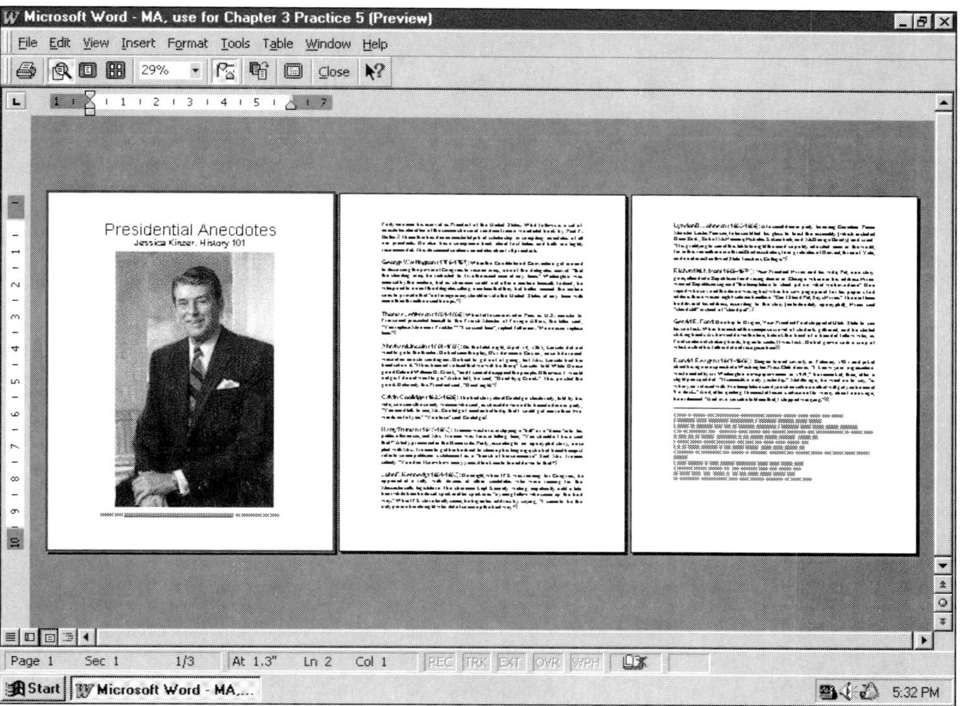

FIGURE 3.16 Screen for Practice Exercise 5

b. Switch the order of the anecdotes for Lincoln and Jefferson so that the presidents appear in order. The footnotes for these references are changed automatically.

c. Convert all of the footnotes to endnotes, as shown in the figure.

d. Go to the White House Web site and download a picture of any of the 10 presidents, then incorporate that picture into a cover page. Remember to cite the reference with an appropriate footnote.

e. Submit the completed document to your instructor.

6. Photographs Online: The Smithsonian Institution is a priceless resource for all Americans. Go to the home page of the Smithsonian (*www.si.edu*) and click the link to Resources, which in turn takes you to the Photographs online page (*photo2.si.edu*) shown in Figure 3.17. Click the link to search the photo database, then choose one or two photographs on any subject that you find especially interesting.

Use the technique described in the chapter to download those photographs to your PC, then use the Insert Picture command to incorporate those pictures into a Word document. Write a short paper (250 to 500 words) describing those photographs and submit the paper to your professor as proof you did this exercise. Be sure to include an appropriate footnote to cite the source of the photographs.

7. Music on the Web: The World Wide Web is a source of infinite variety, including music from your favorite rock group. You can find biographical information and/or photographs such as the one in Figure 3.18. You can even find music, which you can download and play, provided you have the necessary hardware. It's fun, it's easy, so go to it. Use any search engine to find documents about your favorite rock group. Try to find biographical information as well as a picture, then incorporate the results of your research into a short paper to submit to your instructor.

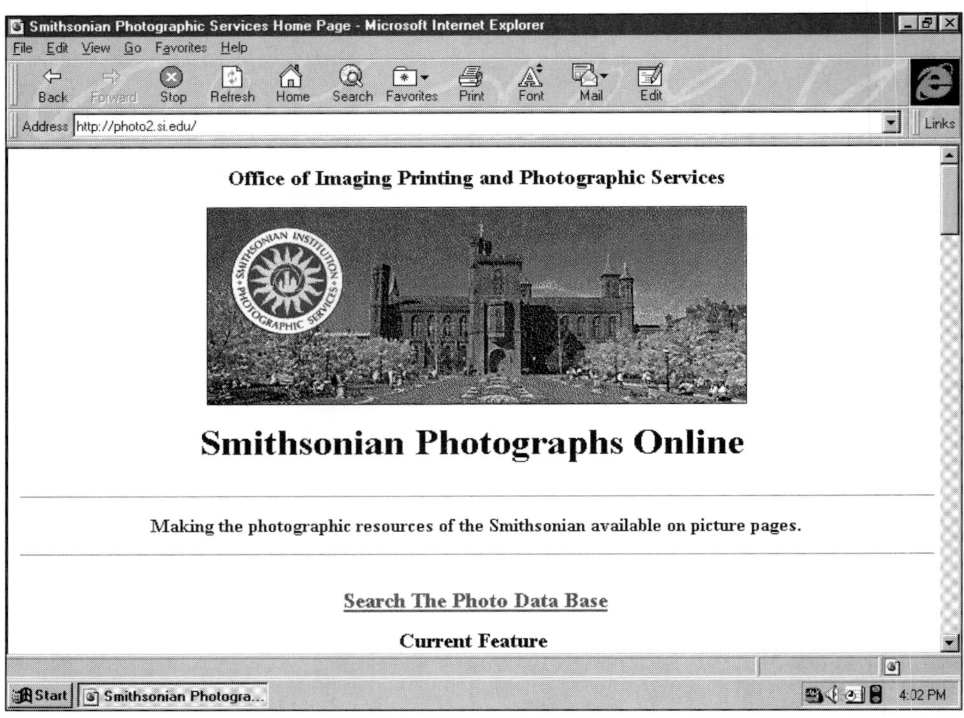

FIGURE 3.17 Screen for Practice Exercise 6

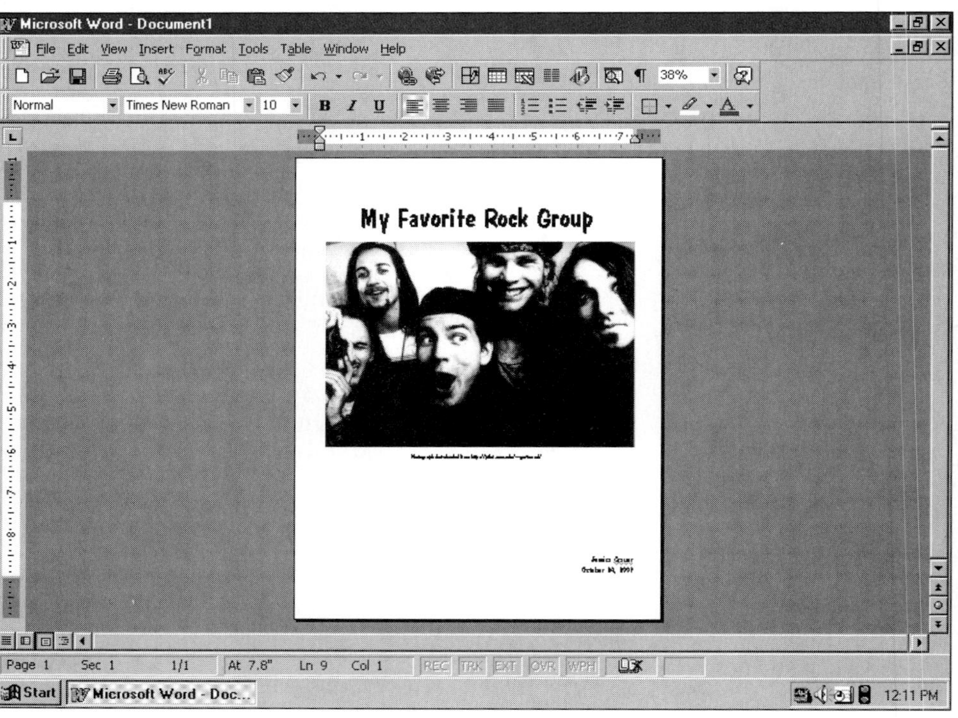

FIGURE 3.18 Screen for Practice Exercise 7

8. The iCOMP index was developed by Intel to compare the speeds of various microprocessors. We want you to search the Web and find a chart showing values in the current iCOMP index. (The chart you find need not be the same as the one in Figure 3.19.) Once you find the chart, download the graphic and incorporate it into a memo to your instructor. Add a paragraph or two describing the purpose of the index as shown in Figure 3.19.

A Comparison of Microcomputers

John Doe, CIS 120

(http://pentium.intel.com/procs/perf/icomp/index.htm)

The capability of a PC depends on the microprocessor on which it is based. Intel microprocessors are currently in their sixth generation, with each generation giving rise to increasingly powerful personal computers. All generations are upward compatible; that is, software written for one generation will automatically run on the next. This upward compatibility is crucial because it protects your investment in software when you upgrade to a faster computer.

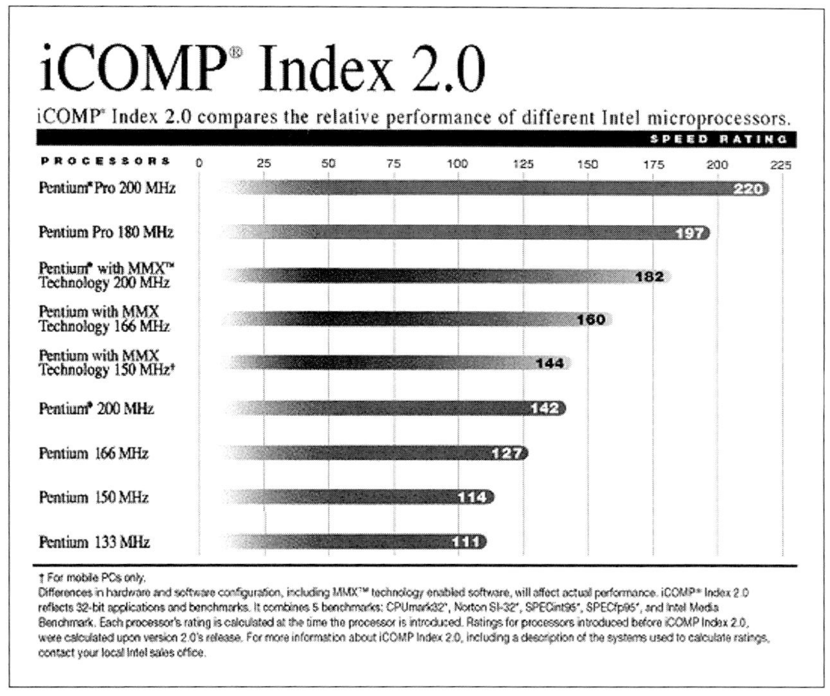

Each generation has multiple microprocessors that are differentiated by *clock speed*, an indication of how fast instructions are executed. Clock speed is measured in *megahertz* (MHz). The higher the clock speed, the faster the machine. Thus, all Pentiums are not created equal, because they operate at different clock speeds. The *Intel CPU Performance Index* (see chart) was created to compare the performance of one microprocessor to another. The index consists of a single number to indicate the relative performance of the microprocessor; the higher the number, the faster the processor.

FIGURE 3.19 Document for Practice Exercise 8

CASE STUDIES

The Letterhead

A well-designed letterhead adds impact to your correspondence. Collect samples of professional stationery, then design your own letterhead, which includes your name, address, phone, and any other information you deem relevant. Include a fax number and/or e-mail address as appropriate. Using your imagination, design the letterhead for your planned career. Try different fonts and/or the Format Border command to add horizontal line(s) under the text. Consider a graphic logo, but keep it simple. You might also want to decrease the top margin so that the letterhead prints closer to the top of the page.

An Ad for Travel

The Clip Gallery includes the maps and flags of many foreign countries. It also has maps of all 50 states as well as pictures of many landmarks. Design a one-page flyer for a place you want to visit, either in the United States or abroad. Collect the assignments, then ask your instructor to hold a contest to decide the most appealing document. It's fun, it's easy, and it's educational. Bon voyage!

The Cover Page

Use WordArt and/or the Clip Gallery to create a truly original cover page that you can use with all of your assignments. The cover page should include the title of the assignment, your name, course information, and date. (Use the Insert Date and Time command to insert the date as a field so that it will be updated automatically every time you retrieve the document.) The formatting is up to you. Print the completed cover page and submit it to your instructor, then use the cover page for all future assignments.

The Résumé

Use your imagination to create a résumé for Benjamin Franklin or Leonardo da Vinci, two acknowledged geniuses. The résumé is limited to one page and will be judged for content (yes, you have to do a little research on the Web) as well as appearance. You can intersperse fact and fiction as appropriate; for example, you may want to leave space for a telephone and/or a fax number, but could indicate that these devices have not yet been invented. You can choose a format for the résumé using the Résumé Wizard, or better yet, design your own.

File Compression

Photographs add significantly to the appearance of a document, but they also add to its size. Accordingly, you might want to consider acquiring a file compression program to facilitate copying large documents to a floppy disk in order to transport your documents to and from school, home, or work. You can download an evaluation copy of the popular WinZip program at *www.winzip.com.* Investigate the subject of file compression, then submit a summary of your findings to your instructor.

Copyright Infringement

It's fun to download images from the Web for inclusion in a document, but is it legal? Copyright protection (infringement) is one of the most pressing legal issues on the Web. Search the Web for sites that provide information on current copyright law. One excellent site is the copyright page at the Institute for Learning Technologies at *www.ilt.columbia.edu/projects/copyright.* Another excellent reference is the page at *www.benedict.com.* Research these and other sites, then summarize your findings in a short note to your instructor.

Macros

The Insert Symbol command can be used to insert foreign characters into a document, but this technique is too slow if you use these characters with any frequency. It is much more efficient to develop a series of macros (keyboard shortcuts) that will insert the characters for you. You could, for example, create a macro to insert an accented *e,* then invoke that macro through the Ctrl+e keyboard shortcut. Parallel macros could be developed for the other vowels or special characters that you use frequently. Use the Help menu to learn about macros, then summarize your findings in a short note to your instructor.

A

APPENDIX A: OBJECT LINKING AND EMBEDDING

OVERVIEW

OLE

The ability to create a document containing data (objects) from multiple applications is one of the primary advantages of the Windows environment. The memo in Figure A.1, for example, was created in Microsoft Word, and it contains a worksheet from Microsoft Excel. ***Object Linking and Embedding*** (abbreviated OLE and pronounced "OH-lay") is the means by which you insert an object from a source file (e.g., an Excel workbook) into a destination file (e.g., a Word document).

The essential difference between linking and embedding is whether the object in the destination file maintains a connection to the source file. A ***linked*** object maintains the connection. An ***embedded object*** does not. A linked object can be associated with many different destination files that do not contain the object per se, but only a representation of the object as well as a pointer (link) to the source file containing the object. Any change to the object in the source file is reflected automatically in every destination file that is linked to that object. An embedded object, however, is contained entirely within the destination file. Changes to the object in the destination file are *not* reflected in the source file.

The choice between linking and embedding depends on how the object will be used. Linking is preferable if the object is likely to change and the destination file requires the latest version. Linking should also be used when the same object is placed in many documents, so that any change to the object has to be made in only one place. Embedding is preferable if you intend to edit the destination file on a computer other than the one on which it was created.

The exercise that follows shows you how to create the compound document in Figure A.1. The exercise uses the ***Insert Object command*** to embed a copy of the Excel worksheet into a Word document. Once an object has been embedded into a document, it can be modified

Lionel Douglas

402 Mahoney Hall • Coral Gables, Florida 33124

June 25, 1997

Dear Folks,

I heard from Mr. Black, the manager at University Commons, and the apartment is a definite for the Fall. Ken and I are very excited, and can't wait to get out of the dorm. The food is poison, not that either of us are cooks, but anything will be better than this! I have been checking into car prices (we are definitely too far away from campus to walk!), and have done some estimating on what it will cost. The figures below are for a Jeep Wrangler, the car of my dreams:

Price of car	$11,995			
Manufacturer's rebate	$1,000			
Down payment	$3,000		**My assumptions**	
Amount to be financed	$7,995		Interest rate	7.90%
Monthly payment	$195		Term (years)	4
Gas	$40			
Maintenance	$50			
Insurance	$100			
Total per month	$385			

My initial estimate was $471 based on a $2,000 down payment and a three year loan at 7.9%. I know this is too much so I plan on earning an additional $1,000 and extending the loan to four years. That will bring the total cost down to a more manageable level (see the above calculations). If that won't do it, I'll look at other cars.

Lionel

FIGURE A.1 A Compound Document

through ***in-place editing.*** In-place editing enables you to double click an embedded object (the worksheet) and change it, using the tools of the source application (Excel). In other words, you remain in Microsoft Word, but you have access to the Excel toolbar and pull-down menus. In-place editing modifies the copy of the embedded object in the destination file. It does *not* change the original object because there is no connection (or link) between the source file (if indeed there is a source file) and the destination file.

HANDS-ON EXERCISE 1

Embedding

Objective: To embed an Excel worksheet into a Word document; to use in-place editing to modify the worksheet within Word. Use Figure A.2 as a guide in the exercise.

STEP 1: Open the Word Document

- Start Word. Open the **Car Request document** in the **Exploring Word folder.** Zoom to **Page Width** so that the display on your monitor matches ours.
- Save the document as **Modified Car Request** so that you can return to the original document if you edit the duplicated file beyond redemption.
- Point to the date field, click the **right mouse button** to display the shortcut menu in Figure A.2a, then click the **Update Field command.**

> **THE DATE FIELD**
>
> The Insert Date and Time command enables you to insert the date as a specific value (the date on which a document is created) or as a field. The latter will be updated automatically whenever the document is printed or when the document is opened in Page Layout view. Opening the document in the Normal view requires the date field to be updated manually.

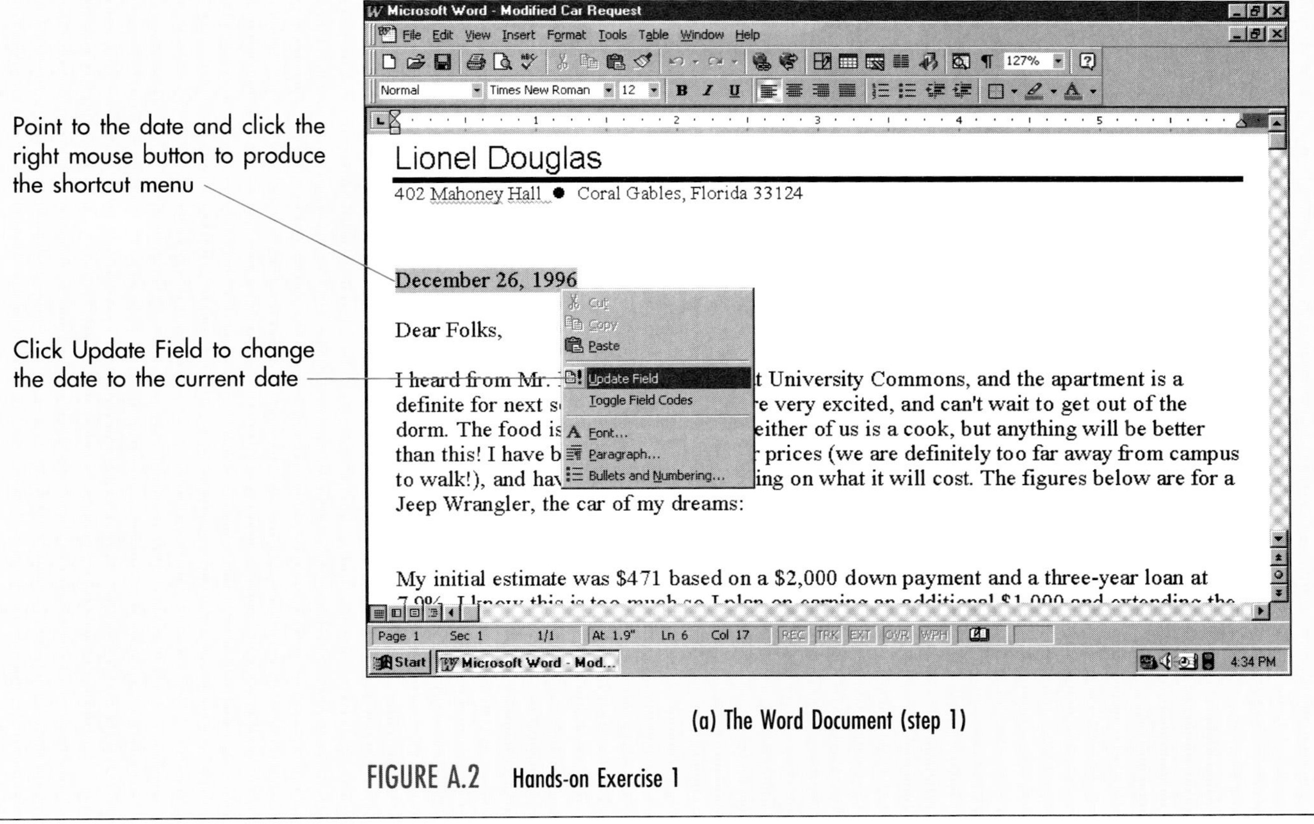

(a) The Word Document (step 1)

FIGURE A.2 Hands-on Exercise 1

STEP 2: Insert an Object

- Click the blank line above paragraph two as shown in Figure A.2b. This is the place in the document where the worksheet is to go.
- Pull down the **Insert menu**, and click the **Object command** to display the Object dialog box in Figure A.2b.
- Click the **Create from File tab,** then click the **Browse command button** in order to open the Browse dialog box and select the object.
- Click (select) the **Car Budget workbook** (note the Excel icon), which is in the Exploring Word folder.
- Click **OK** to select the workbook and close the Browse dialog box.

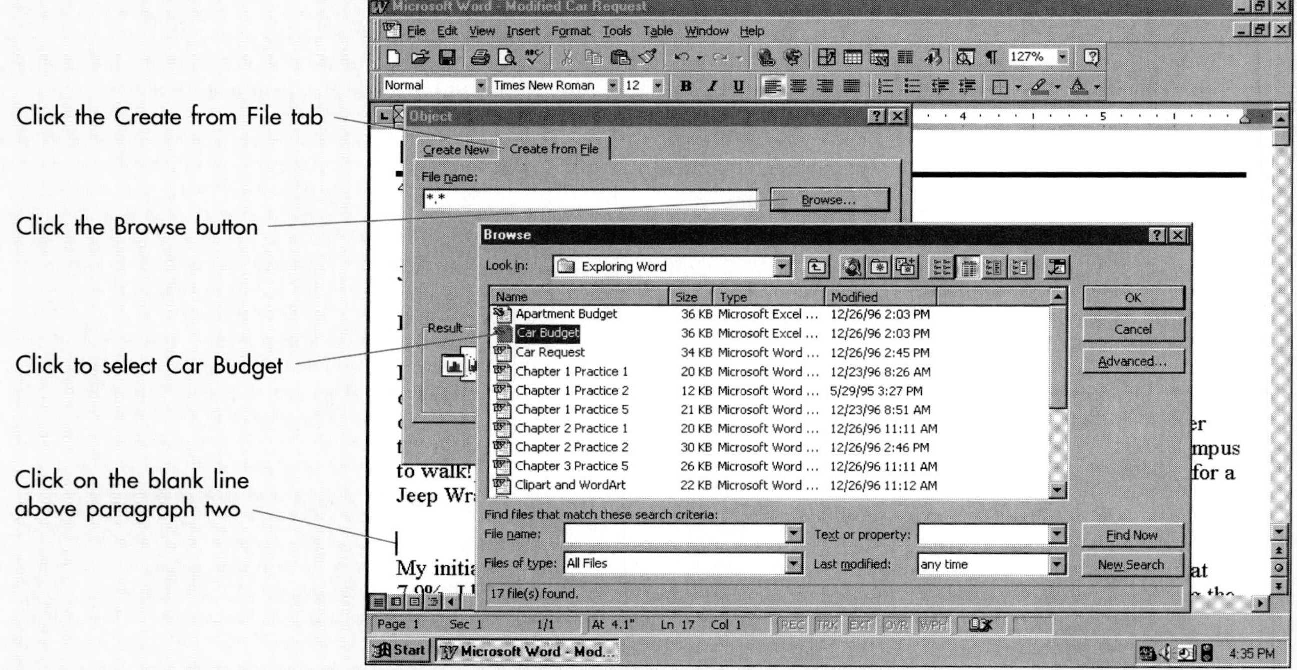

(b) Insert Object Command (step 2)

FIGURE A.2 Hands-on Exercise 1 (continued)

STEP 3: Insert an Object (continued)

- The file name of the object (Car Budget.xls) has been placed into the File Name text box, as shown in Figure A.2c.
- Verify that the Link to File and Display as Icon check boxes are clear and that the Float over text box is checked.
- Note the description at the bottom of the Object dialog box, which indicates that you will be able to edit the object using the application that created the source file.
- Click **OK** to insert the Excel worksheet into the Word document. Save the document.

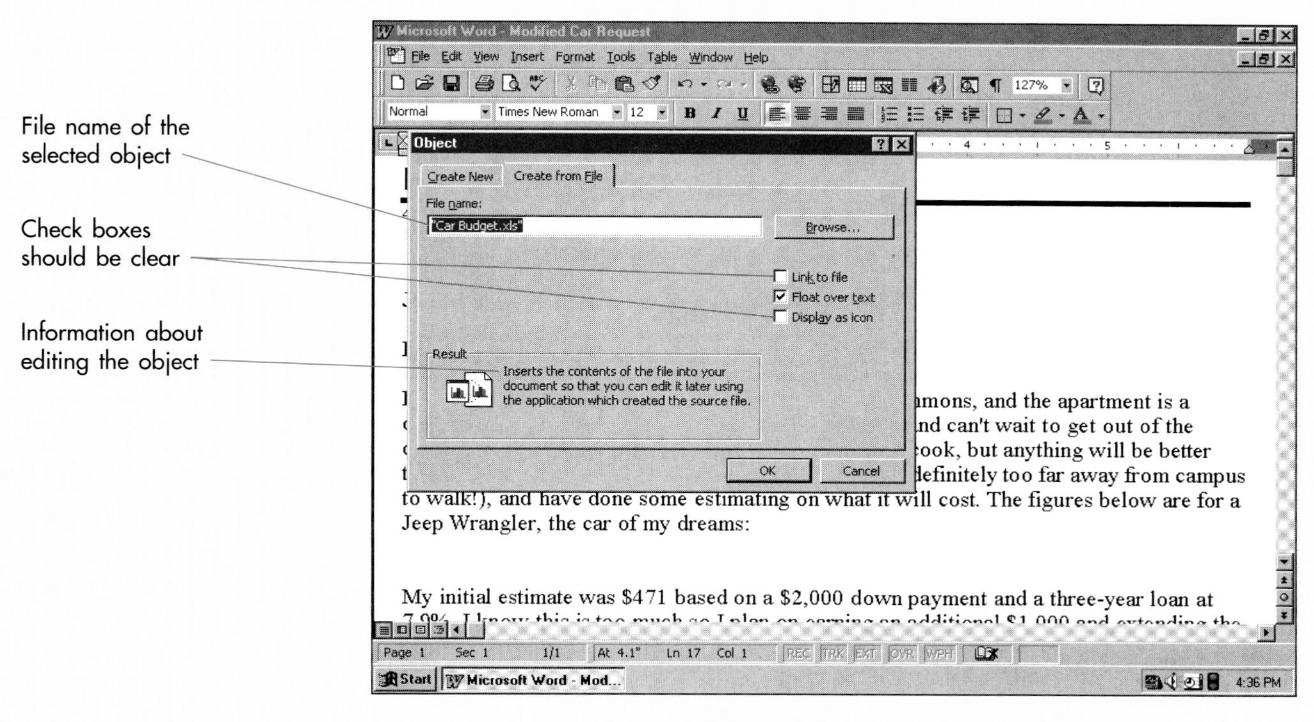

(c) Insert Object Command, continued (step 3)

FIGURE A.2 Hands-on Exercise 1 (continued)

STEP 4: Position the Worksheet

- The worksheet should appear within the Word document. If necessary, click (select) the worksheet to display the sizing handles as shown in Figure A.2d.
- To move the worksheet:
  - Point to any part of the worksheet except a sizing handle (the mouse pointer changes to a four-sided arrow), then click and drag to move the worksheet.
- To size the worksheet:
  - Drag a corner handle (the mouse pointer changes to a double arrow) to change the length and width simultaneously and keep the worksheet in proportion.
  - Drag a handle on the horizontal or vertical border to change one dimension only (which distorts the worksheet).
- Click anywhere in the document, except for the worksheet. The sizing handles disappear and the worksheet is no longer selected.
- If necessary, click above and/or below the worksheet, then press the **enter key** to insert a blank line(s) for better spacing.
- Save the document.

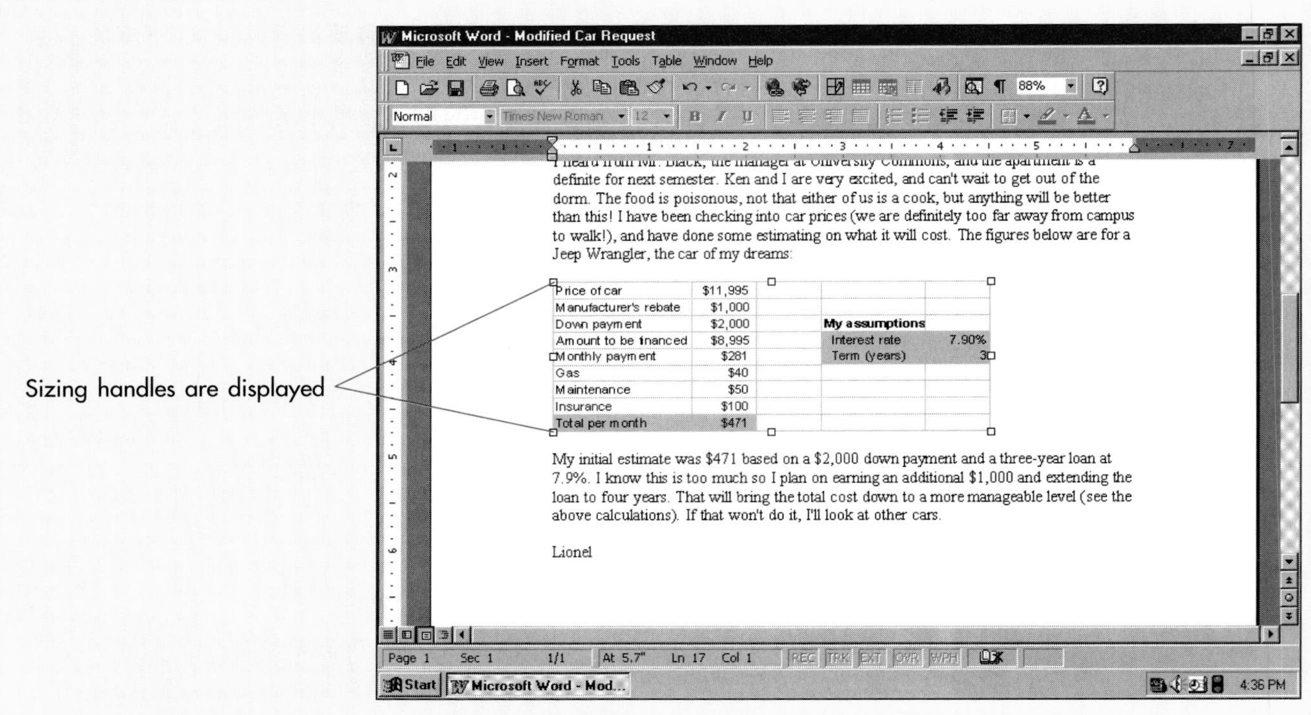

Sizing handles are displayed
Microsoft Word - Modified Car Request
File Edit View Insert Format Tools Table Window Help
Normal
Times New Roman
12
88%
definite for next semester. Ken and I are very excited, and can't wait to get out of the
dorm. The food is poisonous, not that either of us is a cook, but anything will be better
than this! I have been checking into car prices (we are definitely too far away from campus
to walk!), and have done some estimating on what it will cost. The figures below are for a
Jeep Wrangler, the car of my dreams:
Price of car $11,995
Manufacturer's rebate $1,000
Down payment $2,000
Amount to be financed $8,995
Monthly payment $281
Gas $40
Maintenance $50
Insurance $100
Total per month $471
My assumptions
Interest rate 7.90%
Term (years) 3
My initial estimate was $471 based on a $2,000 down payment and a three-year loan at
7.9%. I know this is too much so I plan on earning an additional $1,000 and extending the
loan to four years. That will bring the total cost down to a more manageable level (see the
above calculations). If that won't do it, I'll look at other cars.
Lionel
Page 1 Sec 1 1/1 At 5.7" Ln 17 Col 1
REC TRK EXT OVR WPH
Start
Microsoft Word - Mod...
4:36 PM

(d) Position the Worksheet (step 4)

FIGURE A.2 Hands-on Exercise 1 (continued)

TO CLICK OR DOUBLE CLICK

Clicking an object selects the object and displays the sizing handles, which let you move and/or size the object. Double clicking an object starts the application that created the object and enables you to modify the object using that application. Double click a worksheet, for example, and you start Microsoft Excel from where you can modify the worksheet without exiting from Microsoft Word.

STEP 5: In-place Editing

- We will change the worksheet to reflect Lionel's additional $1,000 for the down payment. Double click the worksheet object to edit the worksheet in place.
- Be patient as this step takes a while, even on a fast machine. The Excel grid, consisting of the row and column labels, will appear around the worksheet, as shown in Figure A.2e.
- You are still in Word, as indicated by the title bar (Microsoft Word - Modified Car Request), but the Excel toolbars are displayed.
- Click in cell **B3,** type the new down payment of **$3,000,** and press **enter.**
- Click in cell **E5,** type **4,** and press **enter.** The Monthly payment (cell B5) and Total per month (cell B9) drop to $195 and $385, respectively.

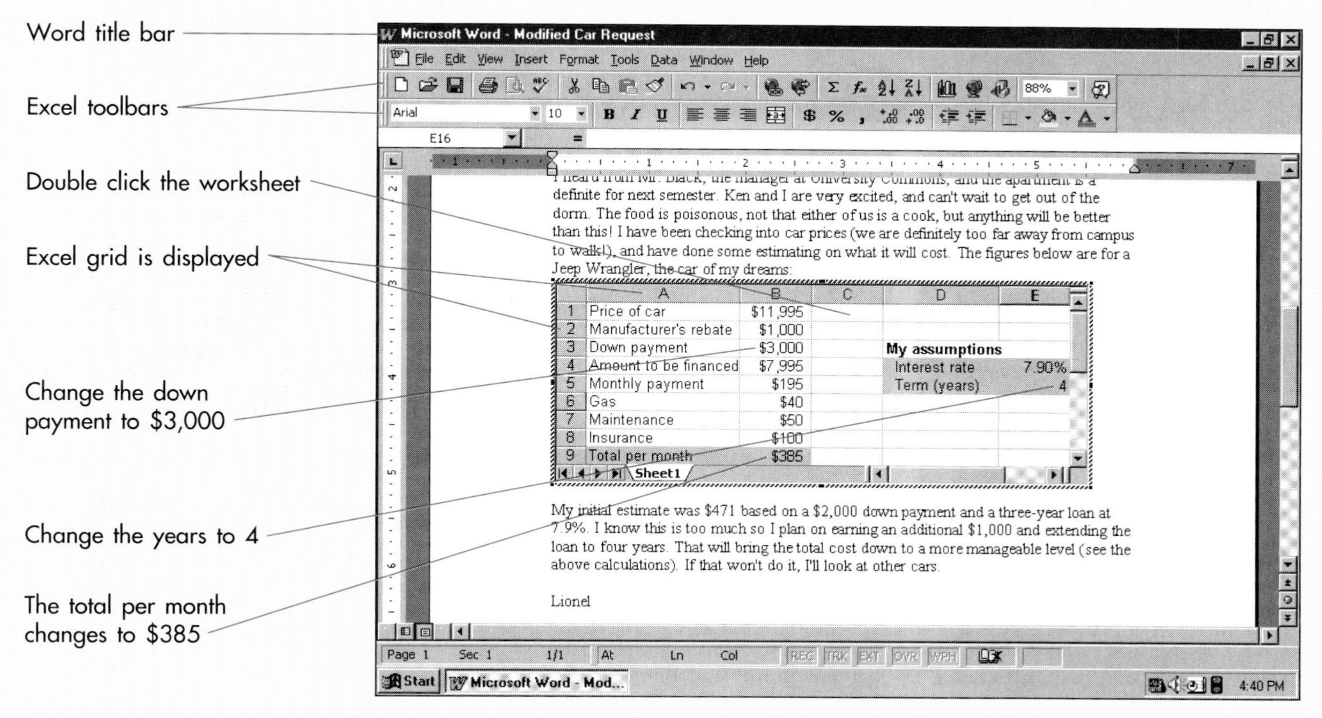

(e) In-place Editing (step 5)

FIGURE A.2 Hands-on Exercise 1 (continued)

IN-PLACE EDITING

In-place editing enables you to edit an embedded object using the toolbar and pull-down menus of the original application. Thus, when editing an Excel worksheet embedded into a Word document, the title bar is that of Microsoft Word, but the toolbars and pull-down menus are from Excel. There are, however, two exceptions; the File and Window menus are from Microsoft Word, so that you can save the compound document and/or arrange multiple documents.

STEP 6: The Completed Document

- Click anywhere outside the worksheet to deselect it. Press **Ctrl+Home** to move to the beginning of the document, then scroll as necessary to view the completed Word document as shown in Figure A.2f.
- Pull down the **File menu** and click **Save** (or click the **Save button** on the Standard toolbar).
- Pull down the **File menu** a second time. Click **Exit** if you do not want to continue with the next hands-on exercise once this exercise is completed. Otherwise click **Close** to remove the document from memory but leave Word open.

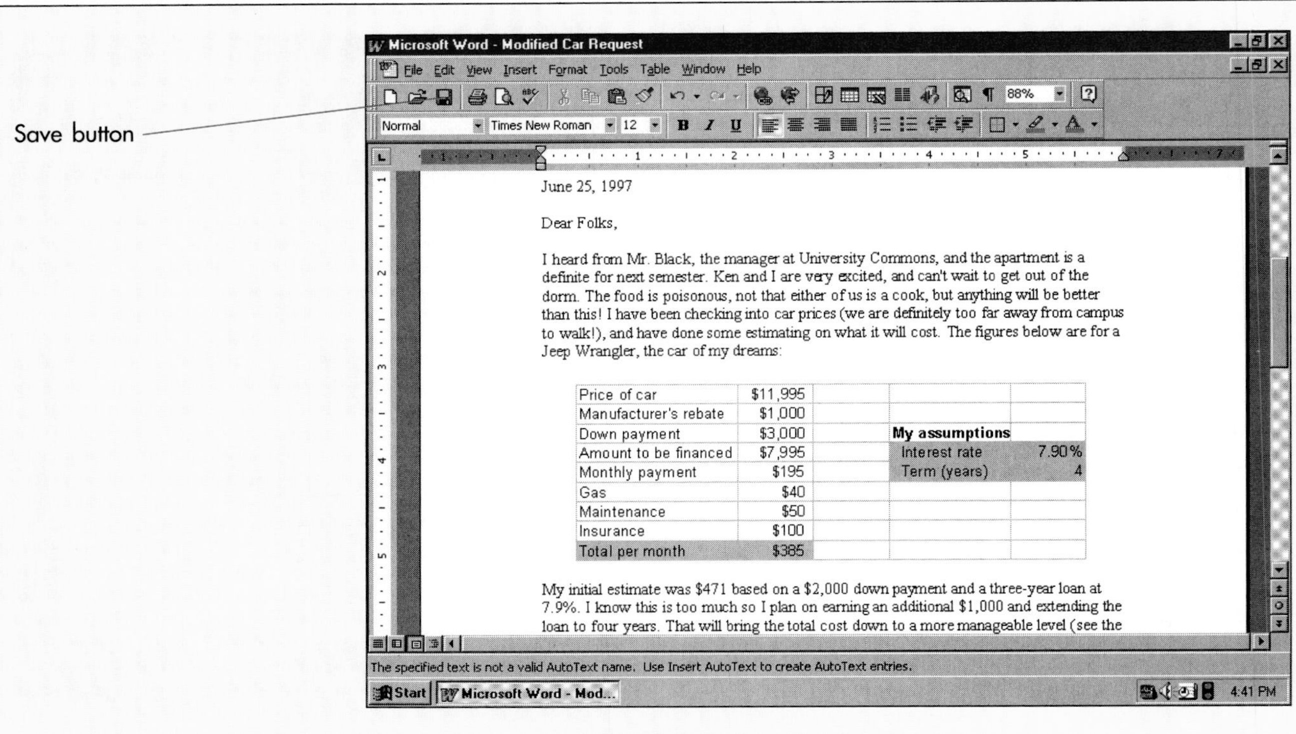

(f) The Completed Word Document (step 6)

FIGURE A.2 Hands-on Exercise 1 (continued)

STEP 7: View the Original Object

- Click the **Start Button,** click (or point to) the **Programs menu,** then click **Microsoft Excel** to open the program.
- If necessary, click the **Maximize button** in the application window so that Excel takes the entire desktop, as shown in Figure A.2g.
- Pull down the **File menu** and click **Open** (or click the **Open button** on the Standard toolbar) to display the Open dialog box.
  - Click the **drop-down arrow** on the Look In list box. Click the appropriate drive, drive C or drive A, depending on the location of your data.
  - Double click the **Exploring Word folder** to make it the active folder.
  - Click (select) **Car Budget** to select the workbook that we have used throughout the exercise.
  - Click the **Open command button** to open the workbook, as shown in Figure A.2g.
  - Click the **Maximize button** in the document window (if necessary) so that the document window is as large as possible.
- You should see the original (unmodified) worksheet, with a down payment of $2,000, a three-year loan, a monthly car payment of $281, and total expenses per month of $471. The changes that were made in step 6 were made to the compound document and are *not* reflected in the source file.
- Pull down the **File menu.** Click **Exit** to exit Microsoft Excel.

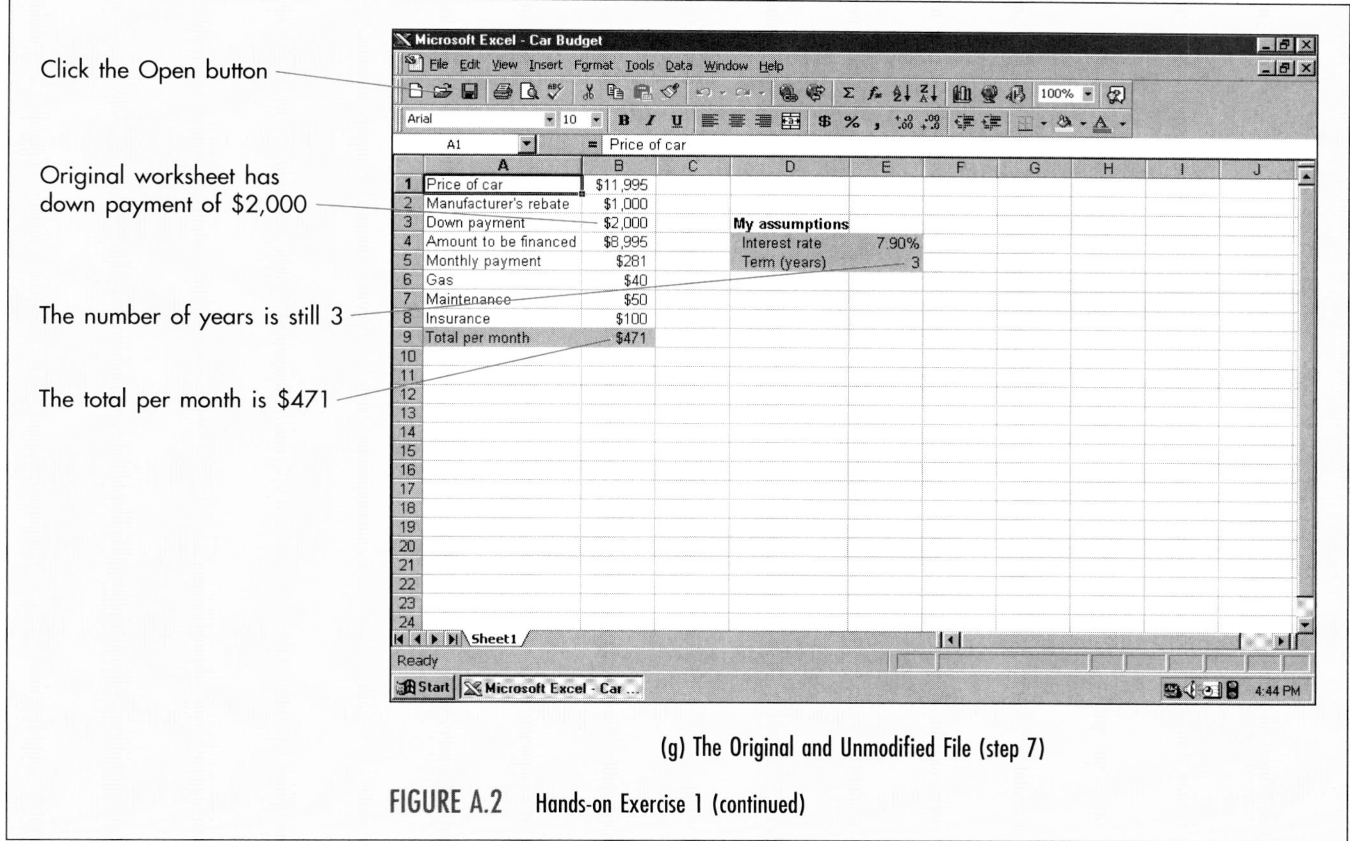

(g) The Original and Unmodified File (step 7)

FIGURE A.2 Hands-on Exercise 1 (continued)

LINKING

The exercise just completed used embedding rather than linking to place a copy of the Excel worksheet into the Word document. The last step in the exercise demonstrated that the original worksheet was unaffected by changes made to the embedded copy within the compound document (destination file).

Linking is very different from embedding as you shall see in the next exercise. Linking maintains a dynamic connection between the source and destination files. Embedding does not. With linking, the object created by the source application (e.g., an Excel worksheet) is tied to the destination file (e.g., a Word document) in such a way that any changes in the Excel worksheet are automatically reflected in the Word document. The Word document does not contain the worksheet per se, but only a representation of the worksheet, as well as a pointer (or link) to the Excel workbook.

Linking requires that an object be saved in its own file because the object does not actually exist within the destination file. Embedding, on the other hand, lets you place the object directly in a destination file without having to save it as a separate file. (The embedded object simply becomes part of the destination file.)

Consider now Figure A.3, in which the same worksheet is linked to two different documents. Both documents contain a pointer to the worksheet, which may be edited by double clicking the object in either document. Alternatively, you may open the source application and edit the object directly. In either case, changes to the Excel workbook are reflected in every destination file that is linked to the workbook.

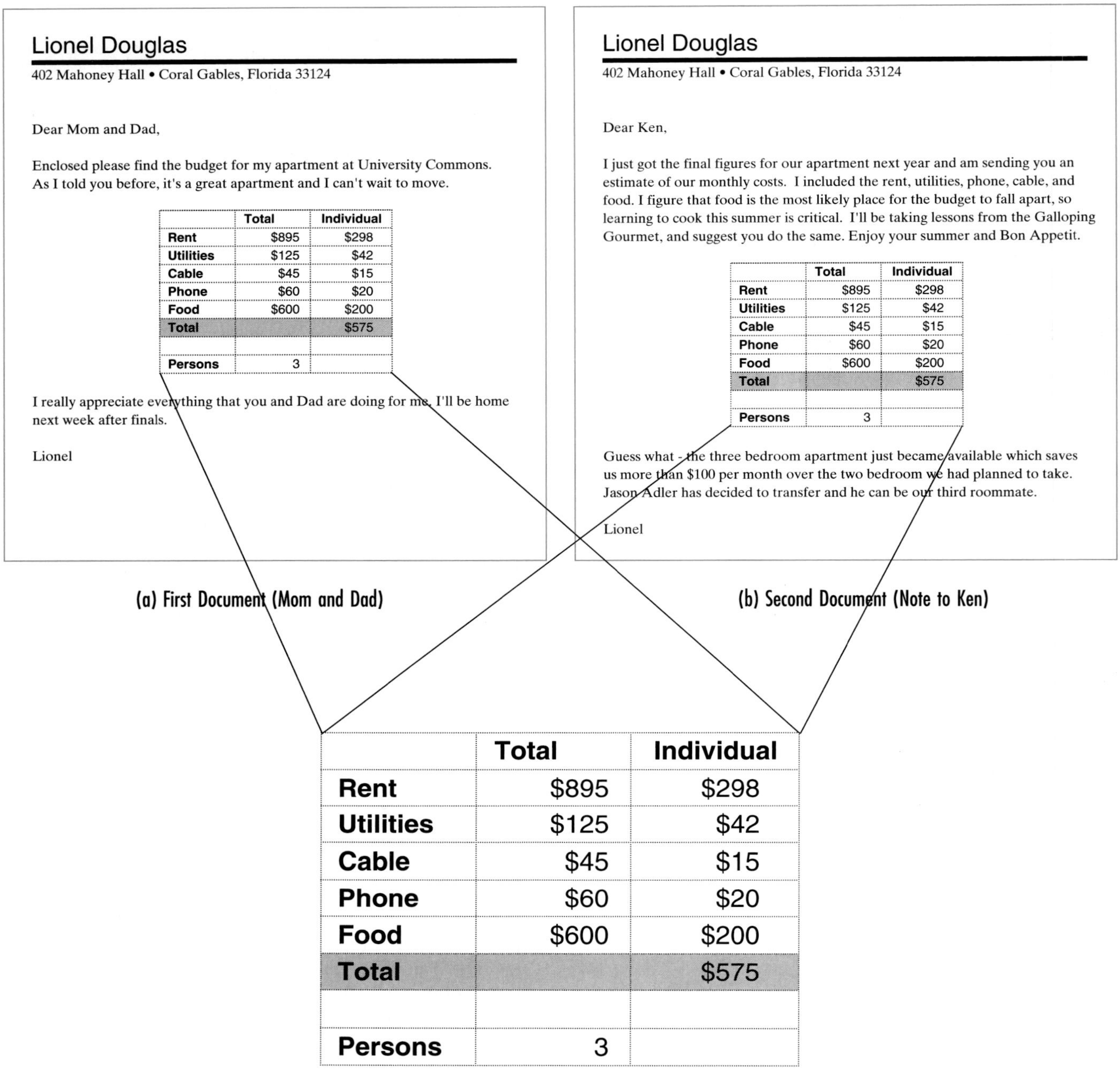

Lionel Douglas

402 Mahoney Hall • Coral Gables, Florida 33124

Dear Mom and Dad,

Enclosed please find the budget for my apartment at University Commons. As I told you before, it's a great apartment and I can't wait to move.

	Total	Individual
Rent	$895	$298
Utilities	$125	$42
Cable	$45	$15
Phone	$60	$20
Food	$600	$200
Total		$575
Persons	3	

I really appreciate everything that you and Dad are doing for me. I'll be home next week after finals.

Lionel

(a) First Document (Mom and Dad)

Lionel Douglas

402 Mahoney Hall • Coral Gables, Florida 33124

Dear Ken,

I just got the final figures for our apartment next year and am sending you an estimate of our monthly costs. I included the rent, utilities, phone, cable, and food. I figure that food is the most likely place for the budget to fall apart, so learning to cook this summer is critical. I'll be taking lessons from the Galloping Gourmet, and suggest you do the same. Enjoy your summer and Bon Appetit.

	Total	Individual
Rent	$895	$298
Utilities	$125	$42
Cable	$45	$15
Phone	$60	$20
Food	$600	$200
Total		$575
Persons	3	

Guess what - the three bedroom apartment just became available which saves us more than $100 per month over the two bedroom we had planned to take. Jason Adler has decided to transfer and he can be our third roommate.

Lionel

(b) Second Document (Note to Ken)

	Total	Individual
Rent	$895	$298
Utilities	$125	$42
Cable	$45	$15
Phone	$60	$20
Food	$600	$200
Total		$575
Persons	3	

(c) Worksheet (Apartment Budget)

FIGURE A.3 Linking

The next exercise links a single Excel worksheet to two different Word documents. During the course of the exercise both applications (Word and Excel) will be explicitly open, and it will be necessary to switch back and forth between the two. Thus, the exercise also demonstrates the multitasking capability within Windows and the use of the taskbar to switch between the open applications.

HANDS-ON EXERCISE 2

Linking

Objective: To demonstrate multitasking and the ability to switch between applications; to link an Excel worksheet to multiple Word documents. Use Figure A.4 as a guide in the exercise.

STEP 1: Open the Word Document

- Check the taskbar to see whether there is a button for Microsoft Word indicating that the application is already active in memory. Start Word if you do not see its button on the taskbar.
- Open the **Mom and Dad document** in the **Exploring Word folder** as shown in Figure A.4a. The document opens in the Normal view (the view in which it was last saved). If necessary, zoom to **Page Width** so that the display on your monitor matches ours.
- Save the document as **Modified Mom and Dad.**

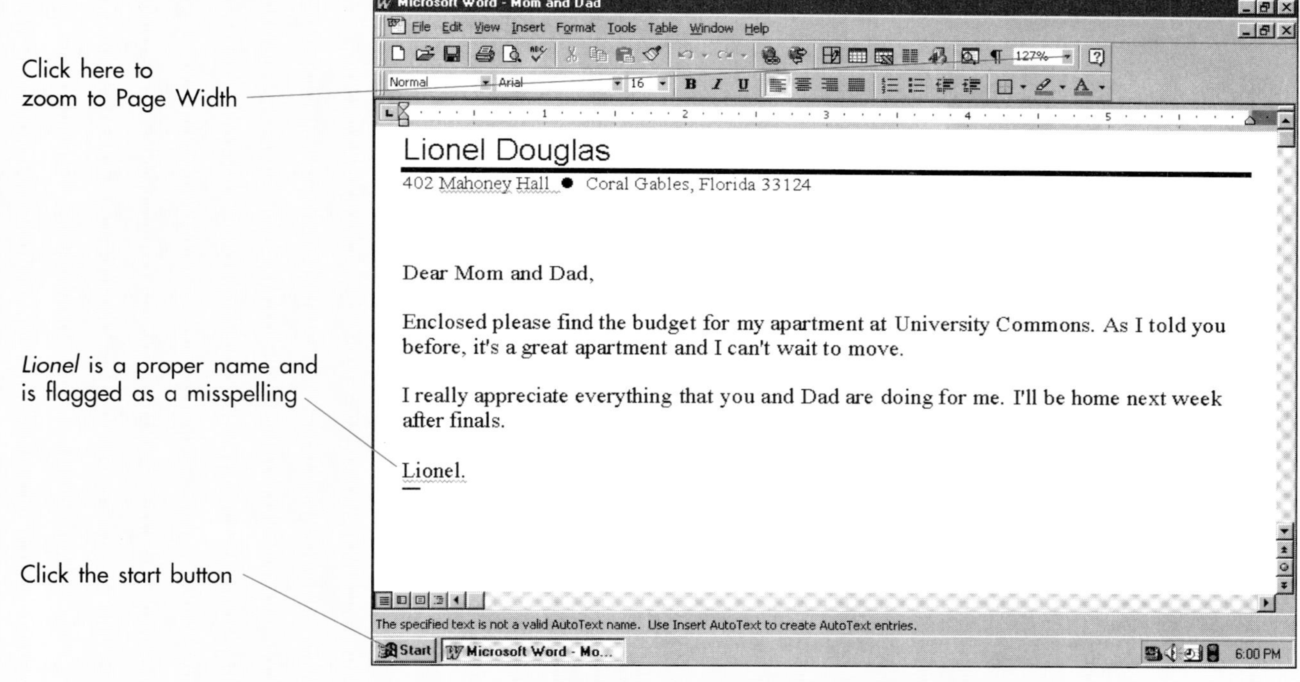

(a) Open the First Word Document (step 1)

FIGURE A.4 Hands-on Exercise 2

STEP 2: Open the Excel Worksheet

- Click the **Start button,** click (or point to) the **Programs menu,** then click **Microsoft Excel** to open the program.
- If necessary, click the **Maximize button** in the application window so that Excel takes the entire desktop. Click the **Maximize button** in the document window (if necessary) so that the document window is as large as possible.

- ➤ The taskbar should now contain buttons for both Microsoft Word and Microsoft Excel. Click either button to move back and forth between the open applications. End by clicking the Microsoft Excel button, since you want to work in that application.
- ➤ Pull down the **File menu** and click **Open** (or click the **Open button** on the Standard toolbar) to display the Open dialog box in Figure A.4b.
- ➤ Click the **drop-down arrow** on the Look In list box. Click the appropriate drive, drive C or drive A, depending on the location of your data. Double click the **Exploring Word folder** to make it the active folder. Double click **Apartment Budget** to open the workbook.

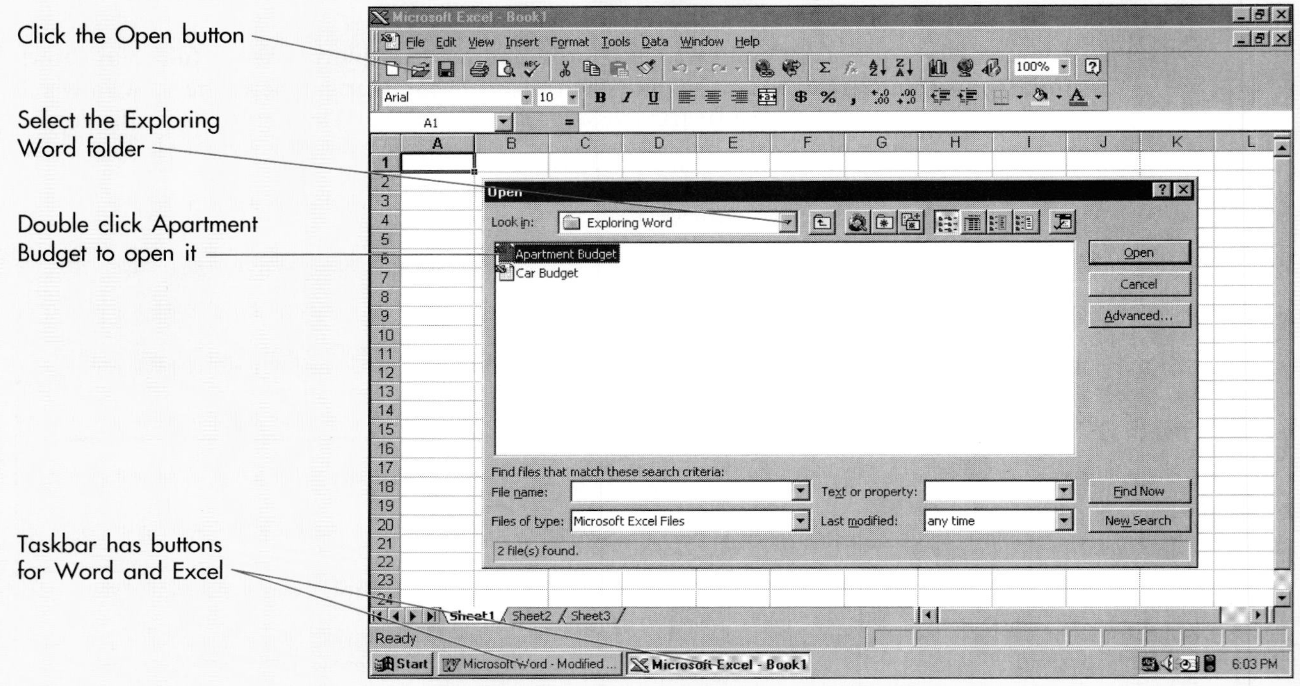

(b) Open the Excel Workbook (step 2)

FIGURE A.4 Hands-on Exercise 2 (continued)

THE COMMON USER INTERFACE

The ***common user interface*** provides a sense of familiarity from one Windows application to the next. Even if you have never used Excel, you will recognize many of the elements present in Word. Both applications share a common menu structure with consistent ways to execute commands from those menus. The Standard and Formatting toolbars are present in both applications. Many keyboard shortcuts are also common—for example Ctrl+Home and Ctrl+End to move to the beginning and end of a document.

STEP 3: Copy the Worksheet to the Clipboard

- Click in cell **A1.** Drag the mouse over cells **A1 through C9** so that the entire worksheet is selected as shown in Figure A.4c.
- Point to the selected cells, then click the **right mouse button** to display the shortcut menu shown in the figure. Click **Copy.** A moving border appears around the selected area in the worksheet, indicating that it has been copied to the clipboard.
- Click the **Microsoft Word button** on the Windows taskbar to return to the Word document.

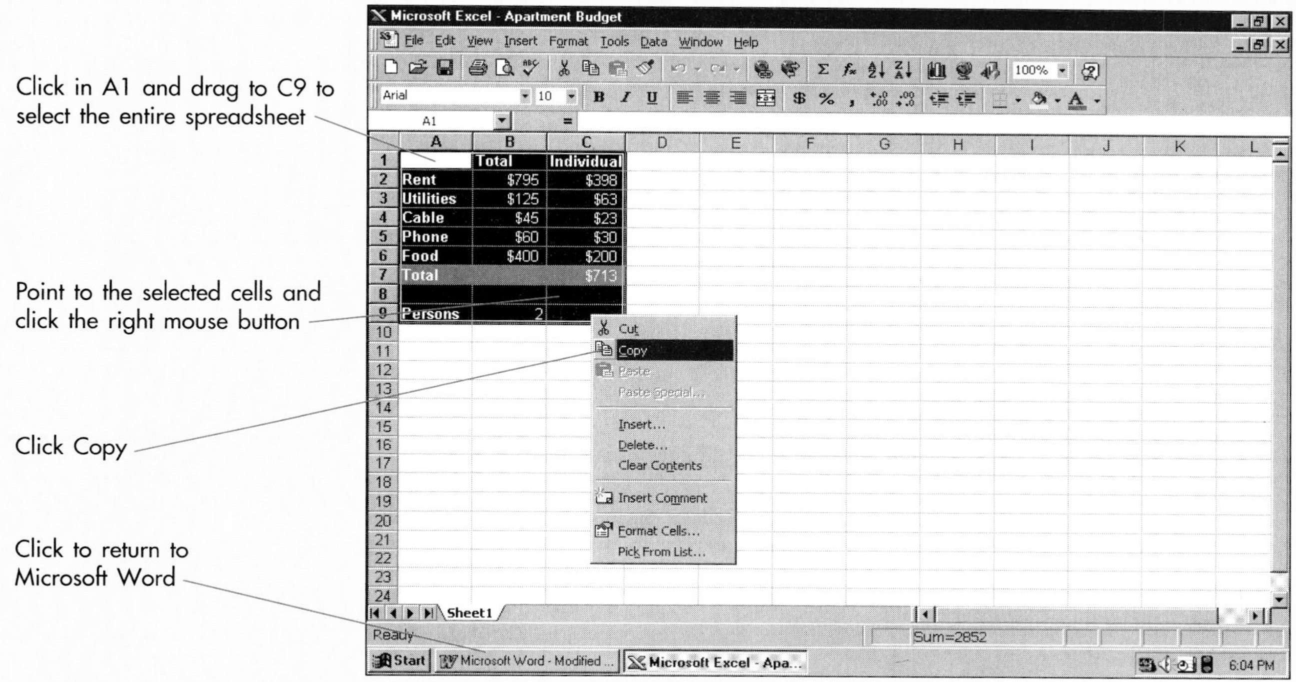

(c) Copy the Worksheet to the Clipboard (step 3)

FIGURE A.4 Hands-on Exercise 2 (continued)

THE WINDOWS TASKBAR

Multitasking, the ability to run multiple applications at the same time, is one of the primary advantages of the Windows environment. Each button on the taskbar appears automatically when its application or folder is opened and disappears upon closing. (The buttons on are resized automatically according to the number of open windows.) You can customize the taskbar by right clicking an empty area to display a shortcut menu, then clicking the Properties command. You can resize the taskbar by pointing to its inside edge, then dragging when you see a double-headed arrow. You can also move the taskbar to the left or right edge of the desktop, or to the top of the desktop, by dragging a blank area of the taskbar to the desired position.

STEP 4: Create the Link

- Click in the document between the two paragraphs. Press **enter** to enter an additional blank line.
- Pull down the **Edit menu.** Click **Paste Special** to produce the dialog box in Figure A.4d.
- Click the **Paste Link option button.** Click **Microsoft Excel Worksheet Object.** Click **OK** to insert the worksheet into the document. You may want to insert a blank line before and/or after the worksheet to make it easier to read.
- Save the document containing the letter to Mom and Dad.

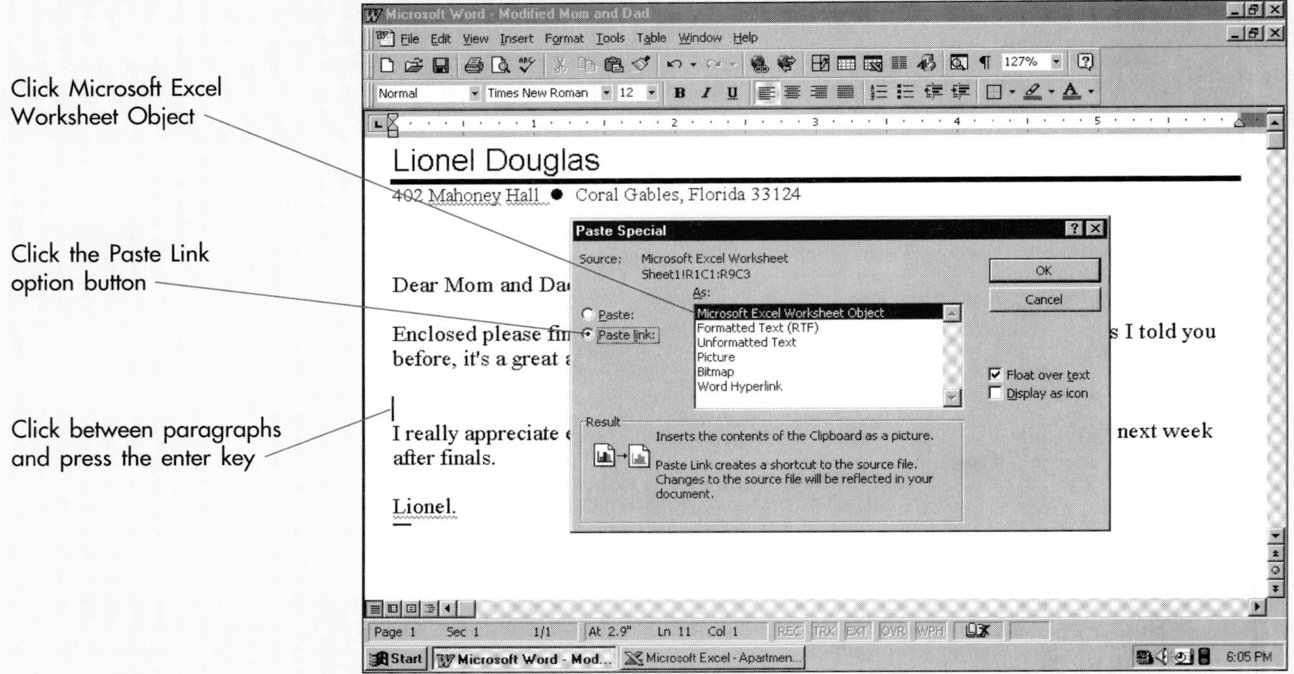

(d) Create the Link (step 4)

FIGURE A.4 Hands-on Exercise 2 (continued)

LINKING VERSUS EMBEDDING

The ***Paste Special command*** will link or embed an object, depending on whether the Paste Link or Paste Option button is checked. Linking stores a pointer to the source file containing the object together with a reference to the source application. Changes to the object are automatically reflected in all destination files that are linked to the object. Embedding stores a copy of the object with a reference to the source application. Changes to the object within the destination file, however, are not reflected in the original object. Linking and embedding both allow you to double click the object in the destination file to edit the object by using the tools of the source application.

STEP 5: Open the Second Word Document

- Open the **Note to Ken document** in the **Exploring Word folder.** Save the document as **Modified Note to Ken** so that you can always return to the original document.
- The Apartment Budget worksheet is still in the clipboard since the contents of the clipboard have not been changed. Click at the end of the first paragraph (after the words Bon Appetit). Press the **enter key** to insert a blank line after the paragraph.
- Pull down the **Edit menu.** Click **Paste Special.** Click the **Paste Link option button.** Click **Microsoft Excel Worksheet Object.** Click **OK** to insert the worksheet into the document, as shown in Figure A.4e.
- If necessary, enter a blank line before or after the object to improve the appearance of the document. Save the document.
- Click anywhere on the worksheet to select the worksheet, as shown in Figure A.4e. The message on the status bar indicates you can double click the worksheet to edit the object.

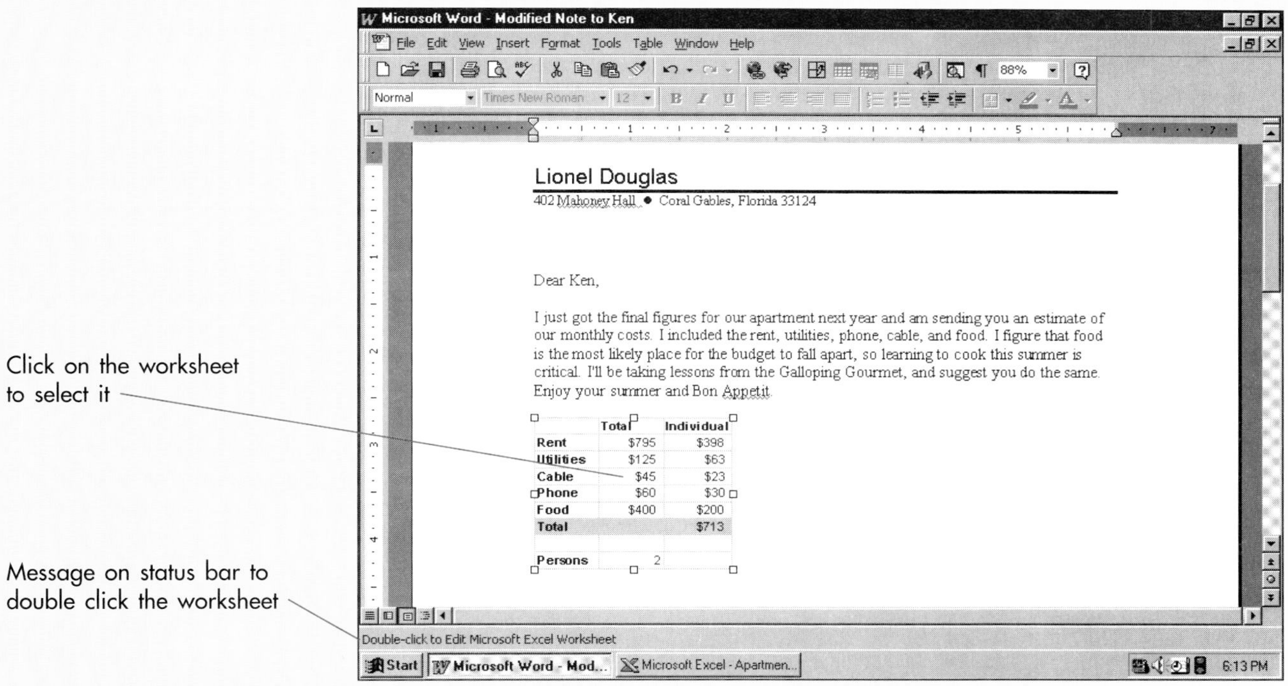

(e) Open the Second Document (step 5)

FIGURE A.4 Hands-on Exercise 2 (continued)

STEP 6: Modify the Worksheet

- The existing spreadsheet indicates the cost of a two-bedroom apartment, but you want to show the cost of a three-bedroom apartment. Double click the worksheet in order to change it.
- The system pauses (the faster your computer, the better) as it switches back to Excel. Maximize the document window.
- Cells **A1 through C9** are still selected from step 3. Click outside the selected range to deselect the worksheet. Press **Esc** to remove the moving border.

- Click in cell **B2.** Type **$895** (the rent for a three-bedroom apartment).
- Click in cell **B6.** Type **$600** (the increased amount for food).
- Click in cell **B9.** Type **3** to change the number of people sharing the apartment. Press **enter.** The total expenses (in cell C9) change to $575, as shown in Figure A.4f.
- Save the worksheet.

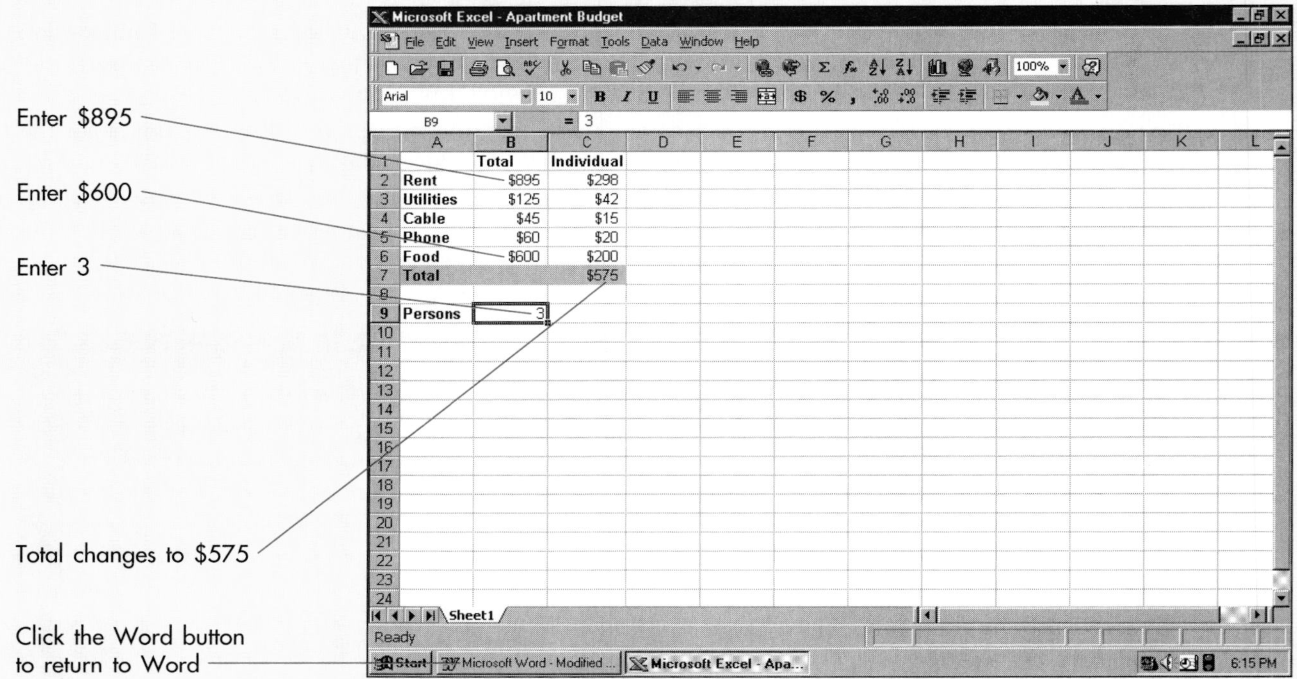

(f) Modify the Worksheet (step 6)

FIGURE A.4 Hands-on Exercise 2 (continued)

STEP 7: View the Modified Document

- Click the **Microsoft Word button** on the taskbar to return to Microsoft Word and the note to Ken, as shown in Figure A.4g.
- The note to Ken displays the modified worksheet because of the link established earlier.
- Click below the worksheet and add the additional text shown in Figure A.4g to let Ken know about the new apartment.
- Save the document.

STEP 8: View the Completed Note to Mom and Dad

- Pull down the **Window menu.** Click **Modified Mom and Dad** to switch to this document as shown in Figure A.4h.
- The note to your parents also contains the updated worksheet (with three roommates) because of the link established earlier.
- Save the completed document.

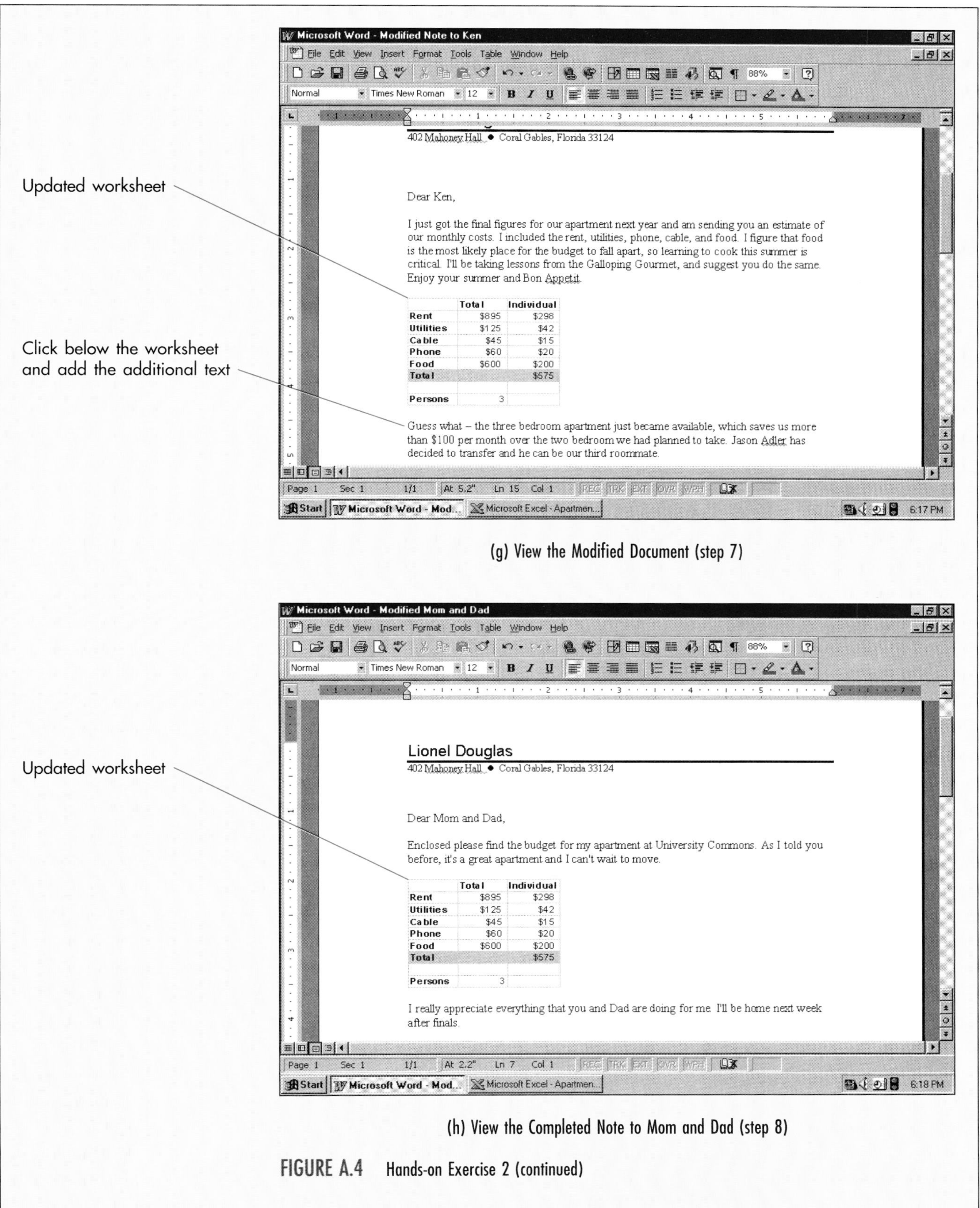

(g) View the Modified Document (step 7)

(h) View the Completed Note to Mom and Dad (step 8)

FIGURE A.4 Hands-on Exercise 2 (continued)

ALT+TAB STILL WORKS

Alt+Tab was a treasured shortcut in Windows 3.1 that enabled users to switch back and forth between open applications. The shortcut also works in Windows 95. Press and hold the Alt key while you press and release the Tab key repeatedly to cycle through the open applications. Note that each time you release the Tab key, the icon of a different application is selected in the small rectangular window that is displayed in the middle of the screen. Release the Alt key when you have selected the icon for the application you want.

STEP 9: Exit

➤ Exit Word. Save the files if you are requested to do so. The button for Microsoft Word disappears from the taskbar.

➤ Exit Excel. Save the files if you are requested to do so. The button for Microsoft Excel disappears from the taskbar.

SUMMARY

The essential difference between linking and embedding is that linking does not place an object into the destination file (compound document), but only a pointer (link) to that object. Embedding, on the other hand, places (a copy of) the object into the destination file. Linking is dynamic whereas embedding is not.

Linking requires that an object be saved in its own (source) file, and further that the link between the source file and the destination file be maintained. Linking is especially useful when the same object is present in multiple documents, because any subsequent change to the object is made in only one place (the source file), but will be automatically reflected in the multiple destination files.

Embedding does not require an object to be saved in its own file because the object is contained entirely within the destination file. Thus, embedding lets you distribute a copy of the destination file, without including a copy of the source file, and indeed, there need not be a separate source file. You would not, however, want to embed the same object into multiple documents because any subsequent change to the object would have to be made in every document.

KEY WORDS AND CONCEPTS

Common user interface
Compound document
Embedding
In-place editing
Insert Object command
Linking
Multitasking
Object linking and embedding (OLE)
Paste Special command

B

APPENDIX B: TOOLBARS

OVERVIEW

Microsoft Word has 16 predefined toolbars that provide access to commonly used commands. The toolbars are displayed in Figure B.1 and are listed here for convenience. They are the Standard, Formatting, AutoText, Control toolbox, Database, Drawing, Forms, Microsoft, Picture, Reviewing, Shadow Settings, Tables and Borders, Visual Basic, Web, WordArt, and 3-D Settings toolbars.

The Standard and Formatting toolbars are displayed by default immediately below the menu bar. The other predefined toolbars are displayed (hidden) at the discretion of the user. Six additional toolbars are displayed automatically when their corresponding features are in use. These toolbars appear (and disappear) automatically and are shown in Figure B.2. They are the Equation Editor, Header/Footer, Macro, Mail Merge, Master Document, and Outlining toolbars.

The buttons on the toolbars are intended to indicate their functions. Clicking the Printer button, for example, executes the Print command. If you are unsure of the purpose of any toolbar button, point to it, and a ScreenTip will appear that displays its name.

You can display multiple toolbars at one time, move them to new locations on the screen, or customize their appearance.

- To display or hide a toolbar, pull down the View menu and click the Toolbars command. Select (deselect) the toolbar(s) that you want to display (hide). The selected toolbar(s) will be displayed in the same position as when last displayed. You may also point to any toolbar and click with the right mouse button to bring up a shortcut menu, after which you can select the toolbar to be displayed (hidden).
- To change the size of the buttons, suppress the display of the ScreenTips or display the associated shortcut key (if available), pull down the View menu, click Toolbars, and click Customize to display the Customize dialog box. If necessary, click the Options tab, then select (deselect) the appropriate check box.

- Toolbars are either docked (along the edge of the window) or floating (in their own window). A toolbar moved to the edge of the window will dock along that edge. A toolbar moved anywhere else in the window will float in its own window. Docked toolbars are one tool wide (high), whereas floating toolbars can be resized by clicking and dragging a border or corner as you would with any window.
  - To move a docked toolbar, click and drag the move handle (the pair of parallel lines) at the left of the toolbar.
  - To move a floating toolbar, drag its title bar to its new location.
- To customize one or more toolbars, display the toolbar(s) on the screen. Then pull down the View menu, click Toolbars, click Customize to display the Customize dialog box, then select the Toolbars tab. Alternatively, you can click on any toolbar with the right mouse button, select Customize from the shortcut menu, and then click the Toolbars tab.
  - To move a button, drag the button to its new location on that toolbar or any other displayed toolbar.
  - To copy a button, press the Ctrl key as you drag the button to its new location on that toolbar or any other displayed toolbar.
  - To delete a button, drag the button off the toolbar and release the mouse button.
  - To add a button, click the Commands tab in the Customize dialog box, select the category from the Categories list box that contains the button you want to add, then drag the button to the desired location on the toolbar. (To see a description of a tool's function before adding it to a toolbar, select the tool, then click the Description command button.)
  - To restore a predefined toolbar to its default appearance, pull down the View menu, click Toolbars, click Customize, click the Toolbars tab, select (highlight) the desired toolbar, and click the Reset command button.
- Buttons can also be moved, copied, or deleted without displaying the Customize dialog box.
  - To move a button, press the Alt key as you drag the button to the new location.
  - To copy a button, press the Alt and Ctrl keys as you drag the button to the new location.
  - To delete a button, press the Alt key as you drag the button off the toolbar.
- To create your own toolbar, pull down the View menu, click Toolbars, click Customize, click the Toolbars tab, then click the New command button. Alternatively, you can click on any toolbar with the right mouse button, select Customize from the shortcut menu, click the Toolbars tab, and then click the New command button.
  - Enter a name for the toolbar in the dialog box that follows. The name can be any length and can contain spaces.
  - The new toolbar will appear on the screen. Initially it will be big enough to hold only one button. Add, move, and delete buttons following the same procedures as outlined above. The toolbar will automatically size itself as new buttons are added and deleted.
  - To delete a custom toolbar, pull down the View menu, click Toolbars, click Customize, and click the Toolbars tab. *Verify that the custom toolbar to be deleted is the only one selected (highlighted).* Click the Delete command button. Click Yes to confirm the deletion. (Note that a predefined toolbar cannot be deleted.)

Standard Toolbar

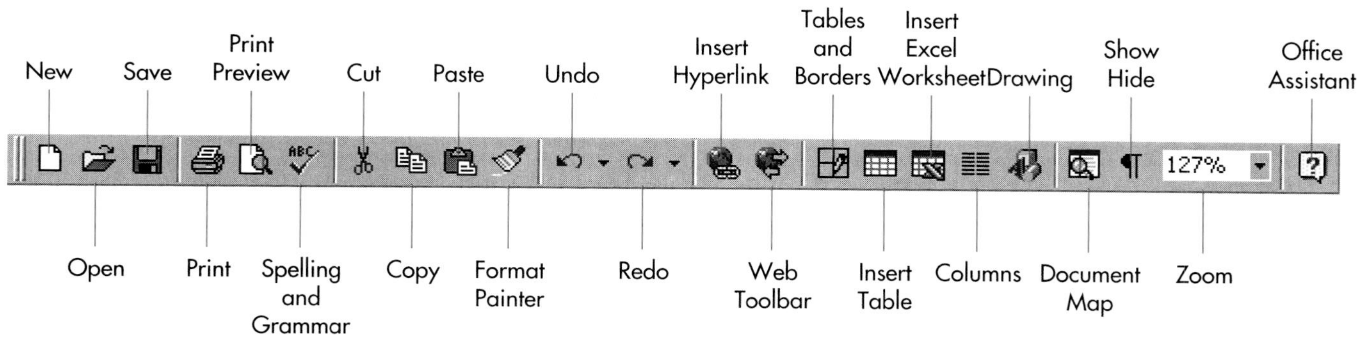

Formatting Toolbar

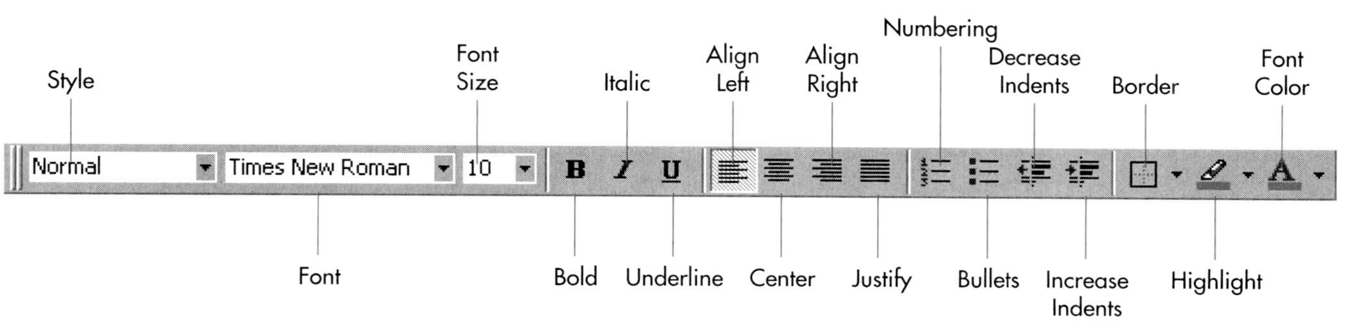

AutoText Toolbar

Database Toolbar

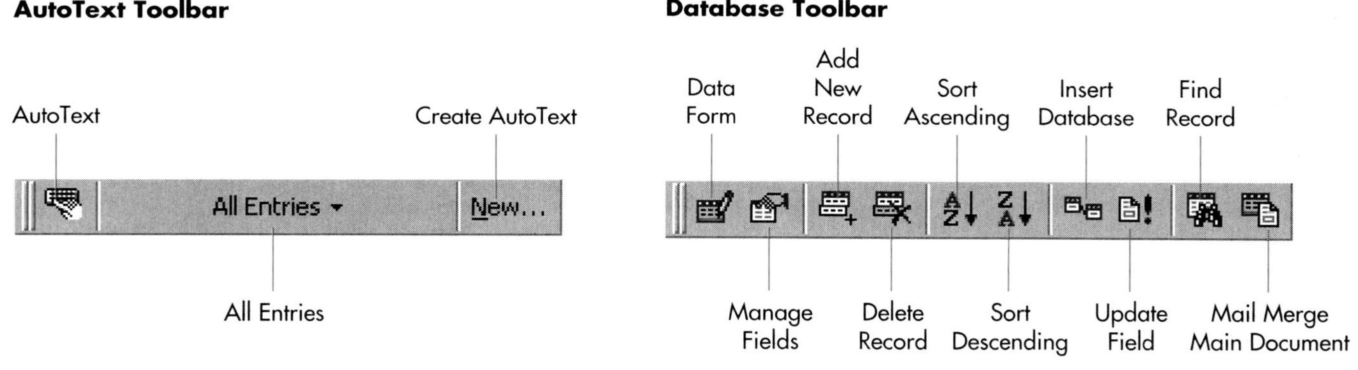

Control Toolbox

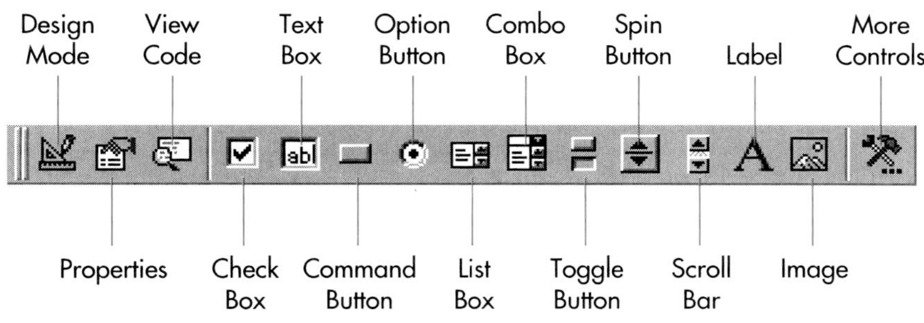

FIGURE B.1

Drawing Toolbar

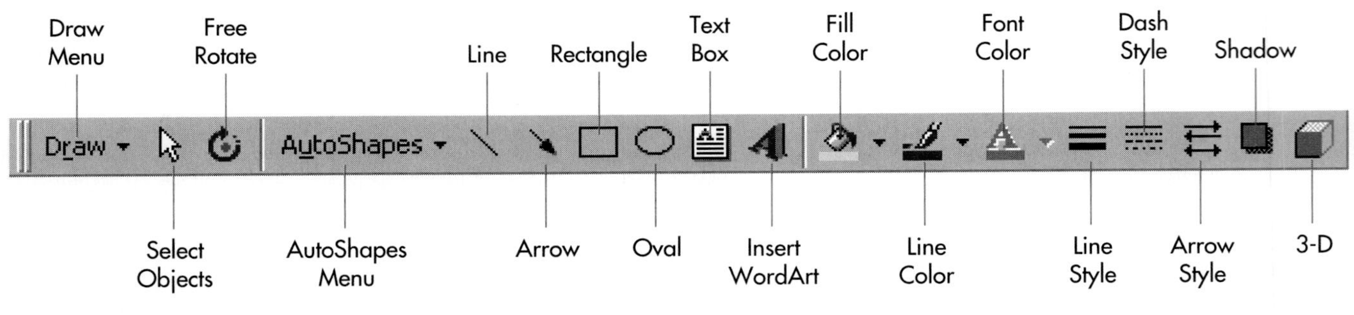

Forms Toolbar

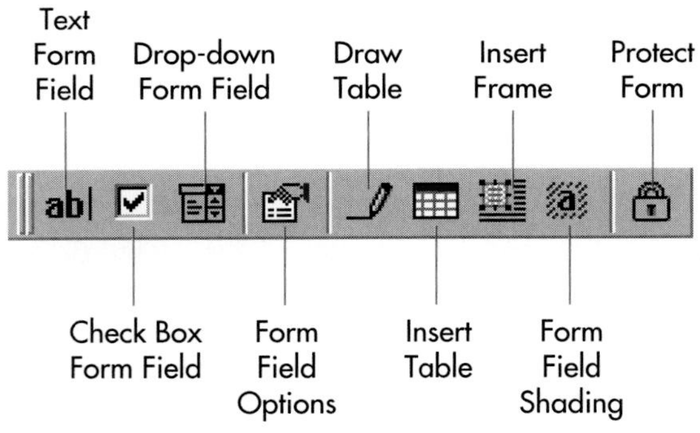

Microsoft Toolbar

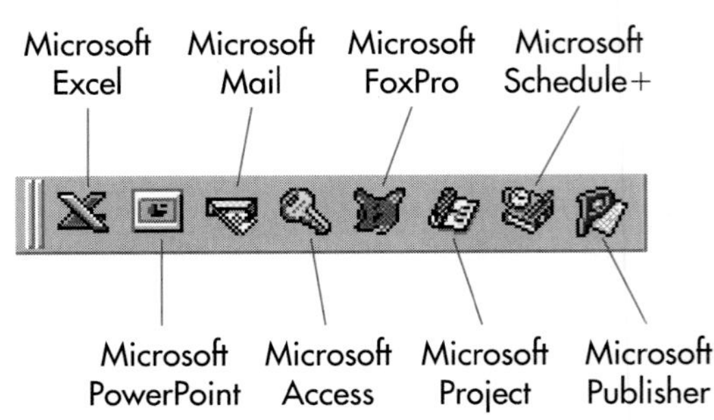

Picture Toolbar

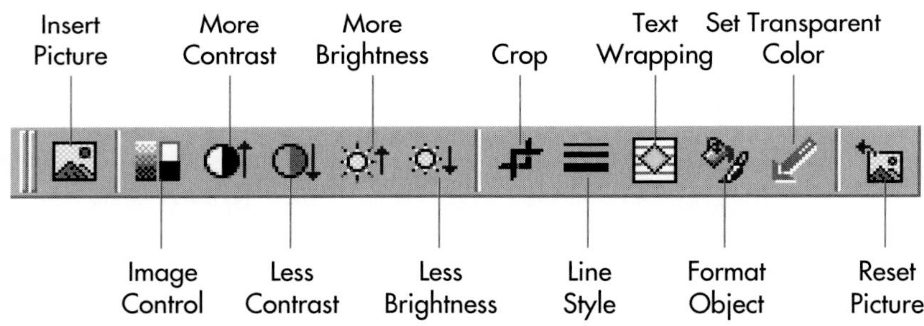

Reviewing Toolbar

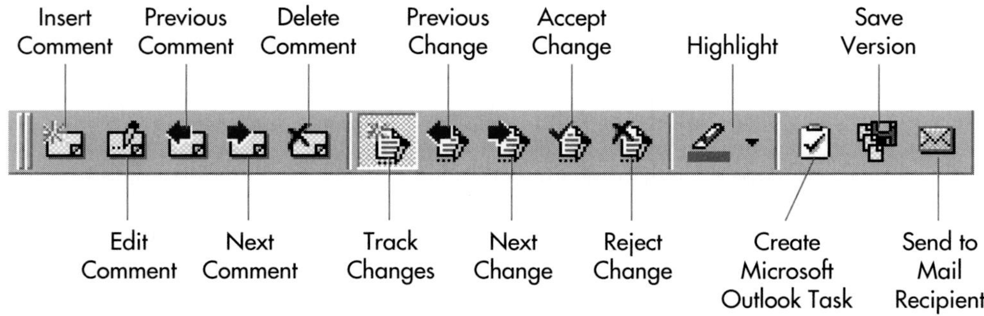

FIGURE B.1 (continued)

Shadow Settings Toolbar

Shadow On/Off
Nudge Shadow Down
Nudge Shadow Right
Nudge Shadow Up
Nudge Shadow Left
Shadow Color

Visual Basic Toolbar

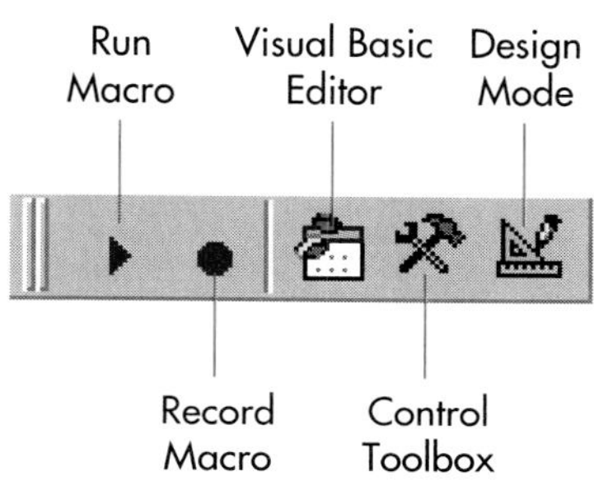

Tables and Borders Toolbar

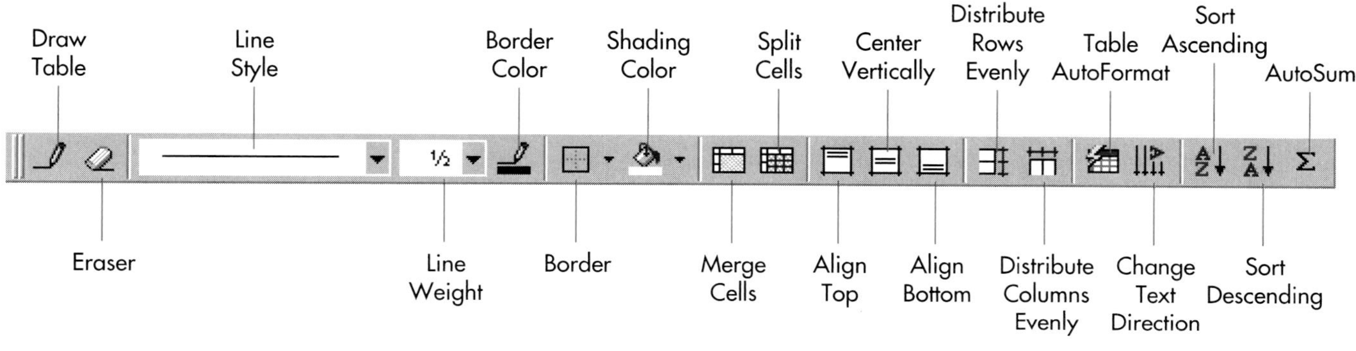

Web Toolbar

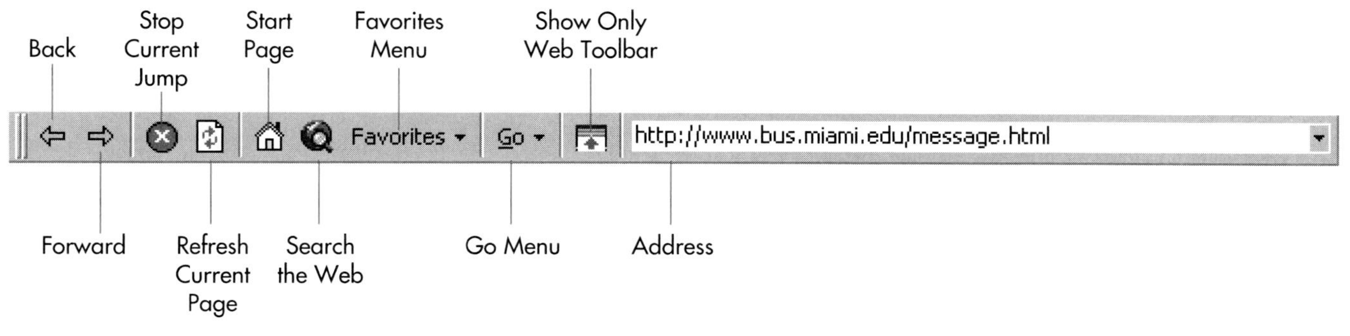

WordArt Toolbar

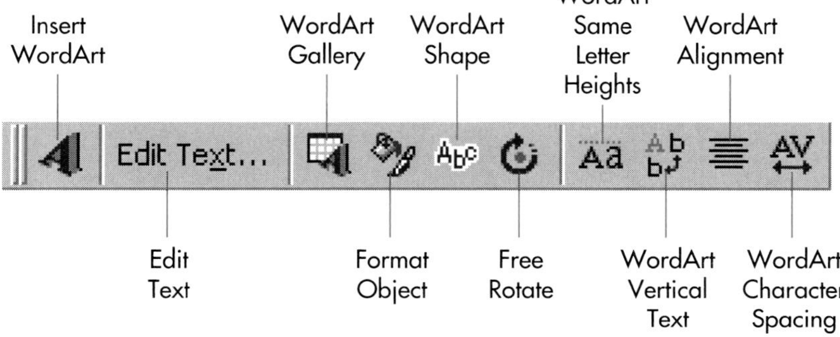

FIGURE B.1 (continued)

3-D Settings Toolbar

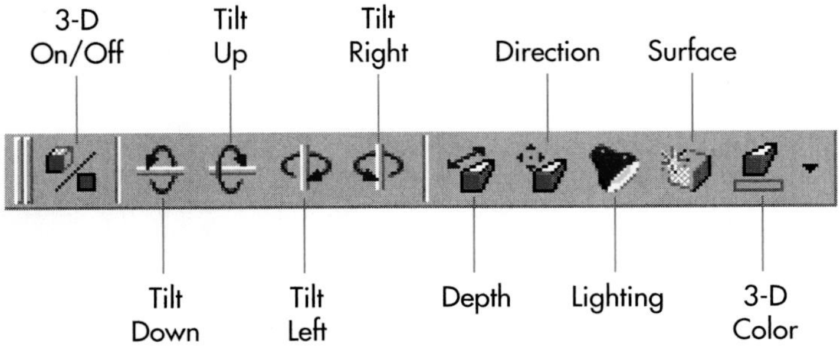

FIGURE B.1 (continued)

Equation Editor Toolbar

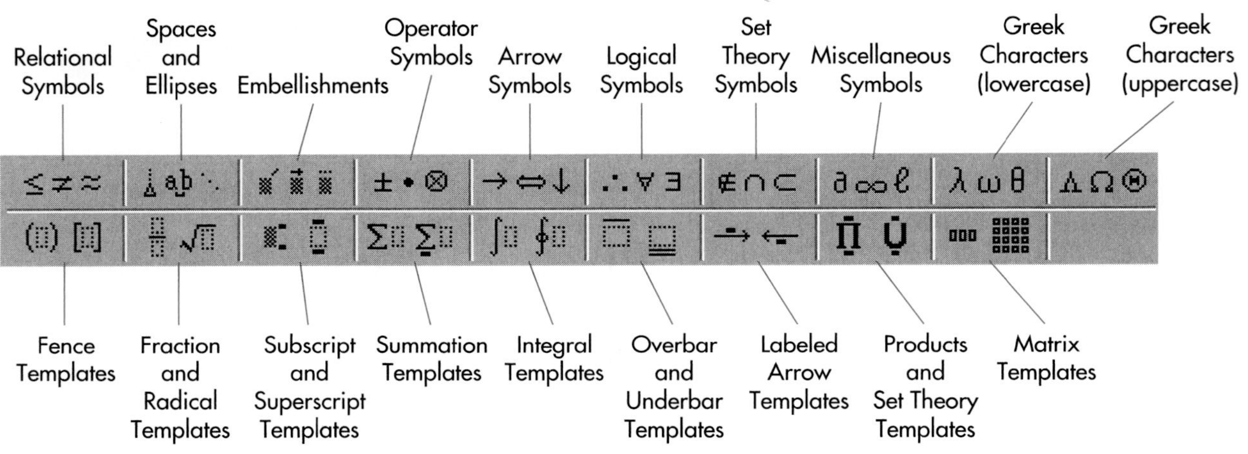

Header/Footer Toolbar

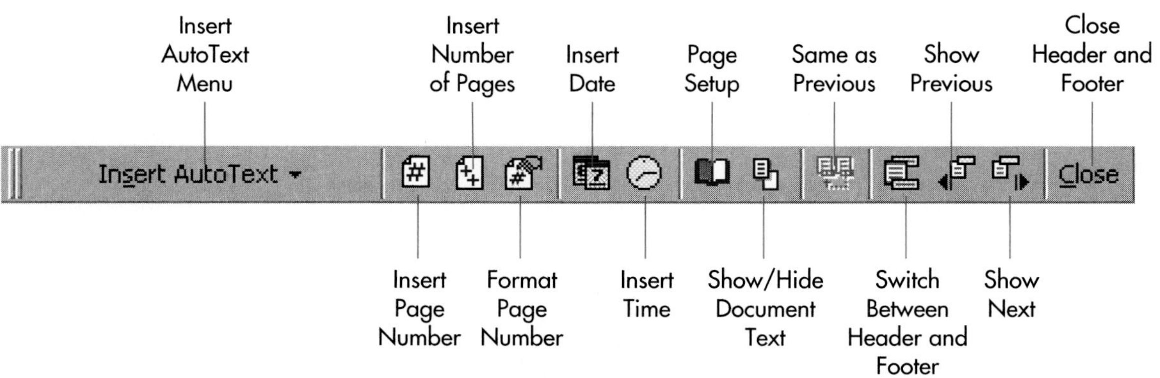

FIGURE B.2

Macro Toolbar

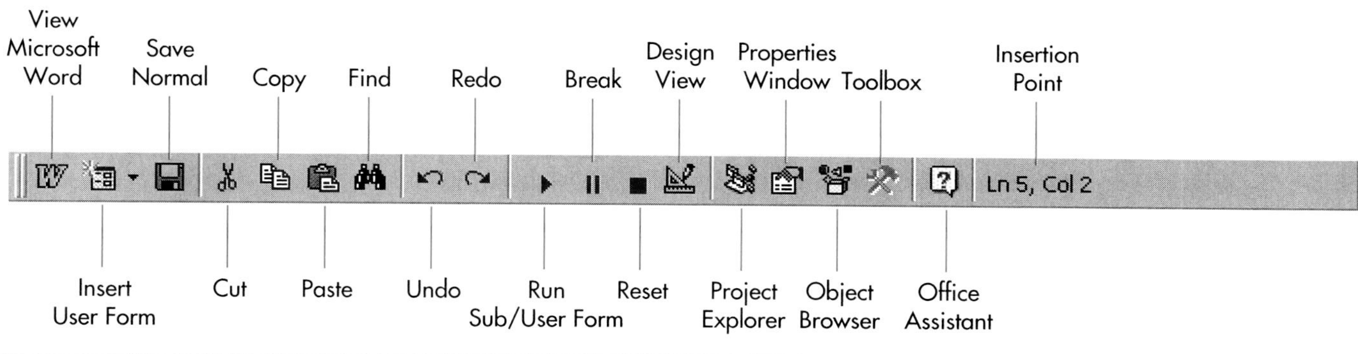

Mail Merge Toolbar

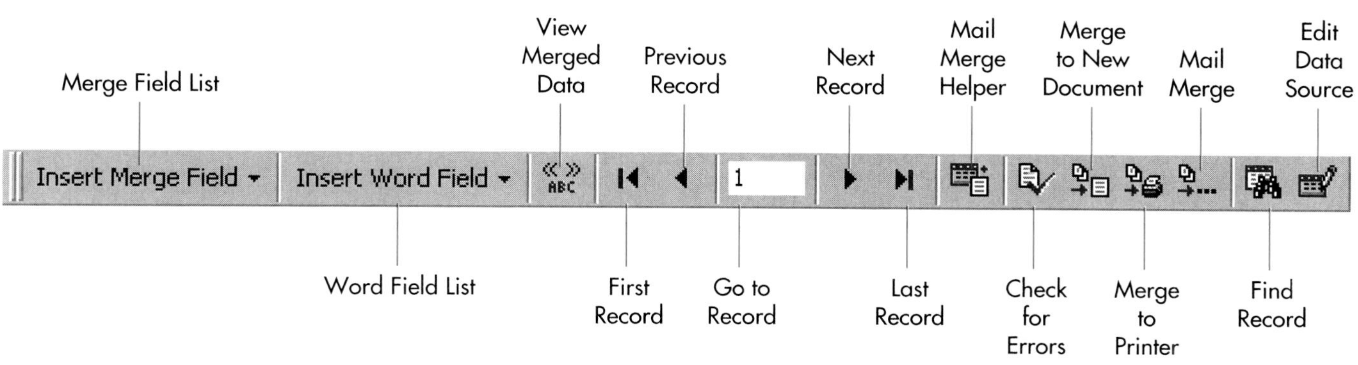

Master Document Toolbar

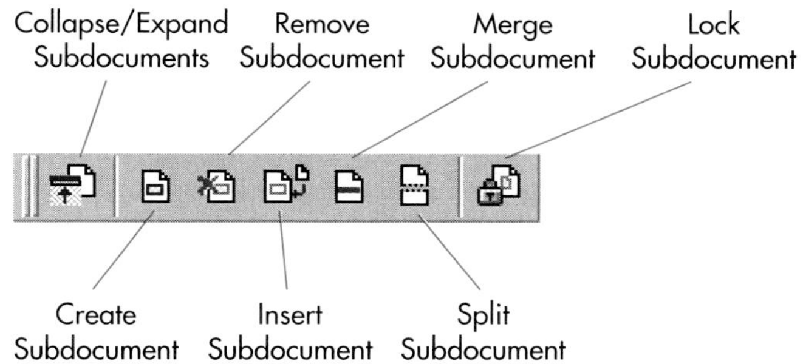

Outlining Toolbar

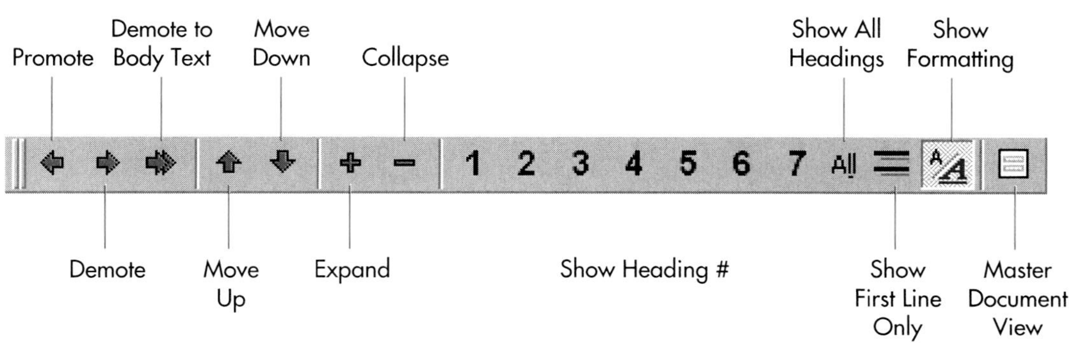

FIGURE B.2 (continued)

7

INTRODUCTION TO MICROSOFT EXCEL: WHAT IS A SPREADSHEET?

OBJECTIVES

After reading this chapter you will be able to:

1. Describe a spreadsheet and suggest several potential applications; explain how the rows and columns of a spreadsheet are identified, and how its cells are labeled.
2. Distinguish between a formula and a constant; explain the use of a predefined function within a formula.
3. Open an Excel workbook; insert and delete rows and columns of a worksheet; save and print the modified worksheet.
4. Distinguish between a pull-down menu, a shortcut menu, and a toolbar.
5. Describe the three-dimensional nature of an Excel workbook; distinguish between a workbook and a worksheet.
6. Print a worksheet two ways: to show the computed values or the cell formulas.
7. Use the Page Setup command to print a worksheet with or without gridlines and/or row and column headings; preview a worksheet before printing.

OVERVIEW

This chapter provides a broad-based introduction to spreadsheets in general, and to Microsoft Excel in particular. The spreadsheet is the microcomputer application that is most widely used by managers and executives. Our intent is to show the wide diversity of business and other uses to which the spreadsheet model can be applied. For one example, we draw an analogy between the spreadsheet and the accountant's ledger. For a second example, we create an instructor's grade book.

The chapter covers the fundamentals of spreadsheets as implemented in Excel, which uses the term worksheet rather than spreadsheet. It discusses how the rows and columns of an Excel worksheet are labeled, the difference between a formula and a constant, and the ability of a worksheet to recalculate itself after a change is made. We also distinguish between a worksheet and a workbook.

The hands-on exercises in the chapter enable you to apply all of the material at the computer, and are indispensable to the learn-by-doing philosophy we follow throughout the text. As you do the exercises, you may recognize many commands from other Windows applications, all of which share a common user interface and consistent command structure. Excel will be even easier to learn if you already know another application in Microsoft Office.

INTRODUCTION TO SPREADSHEETS

A ***spreadsheet*** is the computerized equivalent of an accountant's ledger. As with the ledger, it consists of a grid of rows and columns that enables you to organize data in a readily understandable format. Figures 1.1a and 1.1b show the same information displayed in ledger and spreadsheet format, respectively.

"What is the big deal?" you might ask. The big deal is that after you change an entry (or entries), the spreadsheet will, automatically and almost instantly, recompute all of the formulas. Consider, for example, the profit projection spreadsheet shown in Figure 1.1b. As the spreadsheet is presently constructed, the unit price is $20 and the projected sales are 1,200 units, producing gross sales of $24,000 ($20/unit × 1,200 units). The projected expenses are $19,200, which yields a profit of $4,800 ($24,000 − $19,200). If the unit price is increased to $22 per unit, the spreadsheet recomputes the formulas, adjusting the values of gross sales and net profit. The modified spreadsheet of Figure 1.1c appears automatically.

With a calculator and bottle of correction fluid or a good eraser, the same changes could also be made to the ledger. But imagine a ledger with hundreds of entries and the time that would be required to make the necessary changes to the ledger by hand. The same spreadsheet will be recomputed automatically by the computer. And the computer will not make mistakes. Herein lies the advantage of a spreadsheet—the ability to make changes, and to have the computer carry out the recalculation faster and more accurately than could be accomplished manually.

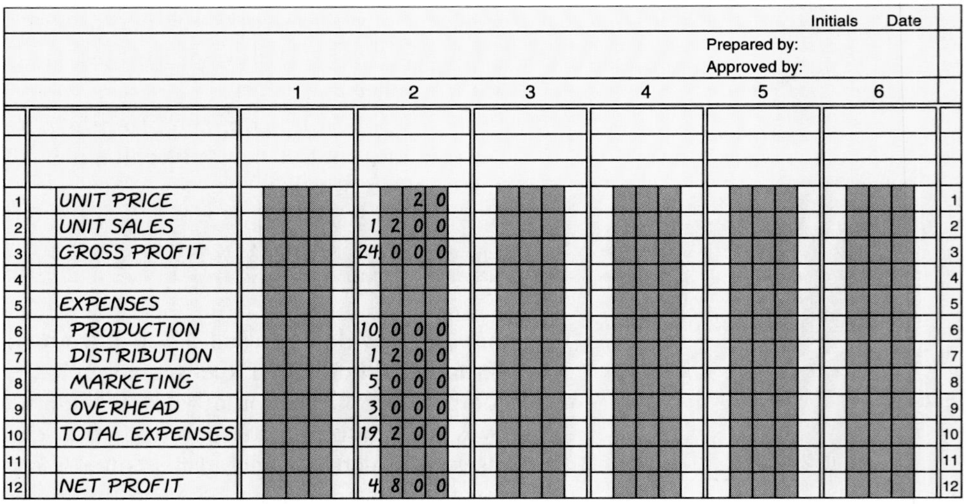

Initials Date

Prepared by:

Approved by:

		1	2	3	4	5	6	
1	UNIT PRICE		20					1
2	UNIT SALES		1200					2
3	GROSS PROFIT		24000					3
4								4
5	EXPENSES							5
6	PRODUCTION		10000					6
7	DISTRIBUTION		1200					7
8	MARKETING		5000					8
9	OVERHEAD		3000					9
10	TOTAL EXPENSES		19200					10
11								11
12	NET PROFIT		4800					12

(a) The Accountant's Ledger

FIGURE 1.1 The Accountant's Ledger

Unit price is increased to $22

Formulas recompute automatically

	A	B
1	Profit Projection	
2		
3	Unit Price	$20
4	Unit Sales	1,200
5	Gross Sales	$24,000
6		
7	Expenses	
8	Production	$10,000
9	Distribution	$1,200
10	Marketing	$5,000
11	Overhead	$3,000
12	Total Expenses	$19,200
13		
14	Net Profit	$4,800

(b) Original Spreadsheet

	A	B
1	Profit Projection	
2		
3	Unit Price	$22
4	Unit Sales	1,200
5	Gross Sales	$26,400
6		
7	Expenses	
8	Production	$10,000
9	Distribution	$1,200
10	Marketing	$5,000
11	Overhead	$3,000
12	Total Expenses	$19,200
13		
14	Net Profit	$7,200

(c) Modified Spreadsheet

FIGURE 1.1 The Accountant's Ledger (continued)

The Professor's Grade Book

A second example of a spreadsheet, one with which you can easily identify, is that of a professor's grade book. The grades are recorded by hand in a notebook, which is nothing more than a different kind of accountant's ledger. Figure 1.2 contains both manual and spreadsheet versions of a grade book.

Figure 1.2a shows a handwritten grade book as it has been done since the days of the little red schoolhouse. For the sake of simplicity, only five students are shown, each with three grades. The professor has computed class averages for each exam, as well as a semester average for every student, in which the final counts *twice* as much as either test; for example, Adams's average is equal to (100+90+81+81)/4 = 88.

Figure 1.2b shows the grade book as it might appear in a spreadsheet, and is essentially unchanged from Figure 1.2a. Walker's grade on the final exam in Figure 1.2b is 90, giving him a semester average of 85 and producing a class average on the final of 75.2 as well. Now consider Figure 1.2c, in which the grade on Walker's final has been changed to 100, causing Walker's semester average to change from 85 to 90, and the class average on the final to go from 75.2 to 77.2. As with the profit projection, a change to any entry within the grade book automatically recalculates all other dependent formulas as well. Hence, when Walker's final exam was regraded, all dependent formulas (the class average for the final as well as Walker's semester average) were recomputed.

As simple as the idea of a spreadsheet may seem, it provided the first major reason for managers to have a personal computer on their desks. Essentially, anything that can be done with a pencil, a pad of paper, and a calculator can be done faster and far more accurately with a spreadsheet. The spreadsheet, like the personal computer, has become an integral part of every type of business. Indeed, it is hard to imagine that these calculations were ever done by hand.

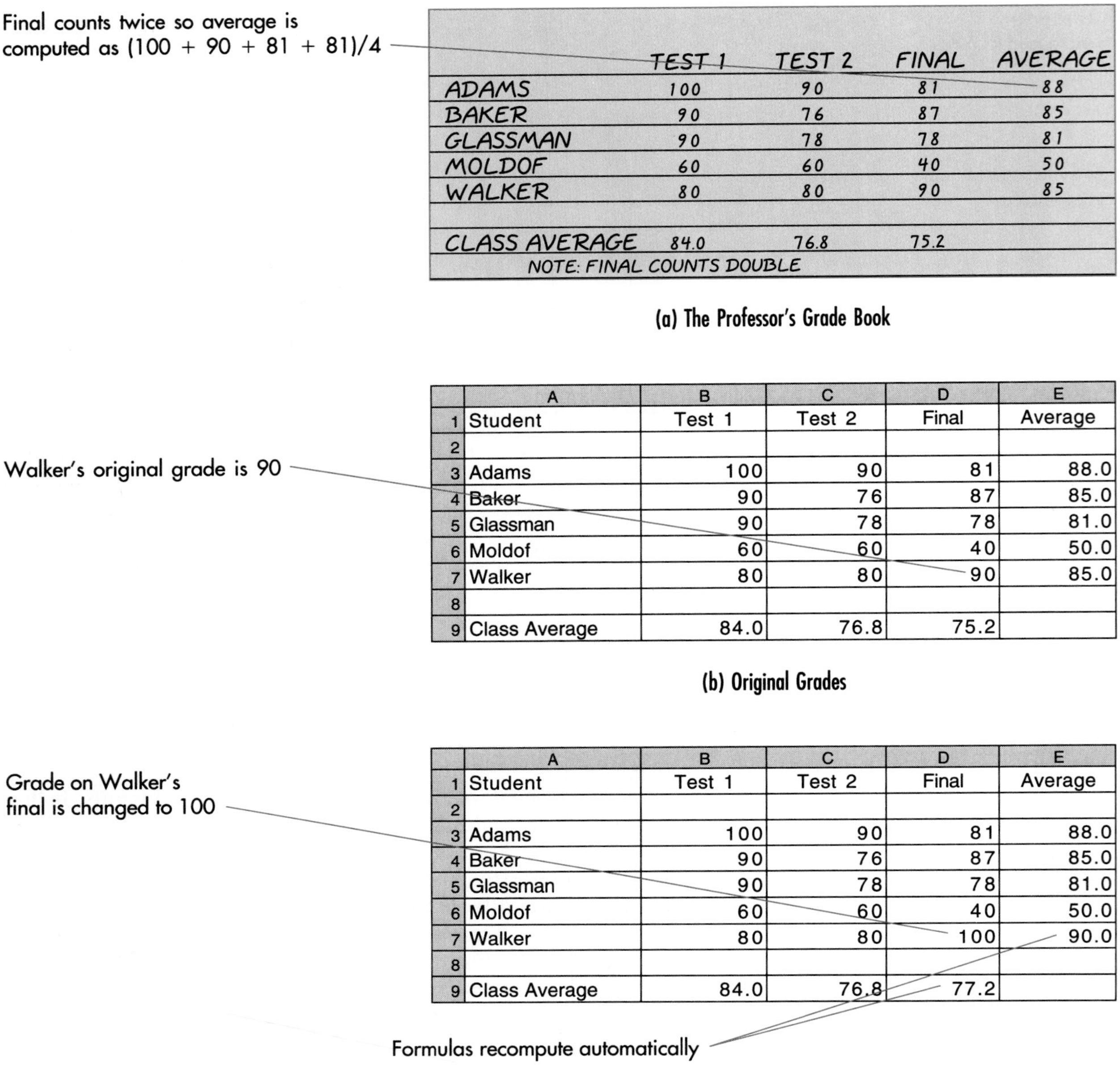

Final counts twice so average is computed as (100 + 90 + 81 + 81)/4

	TEST 1	TEST 2	FINAL	AVERAGE
ADAMS	100	90	81	88
BAKER	90	76	87	85
GLASSMAN	90	78	78	81
MOLDOF	60	60	40	50
WALKER	80	80	90	85
CLASS AVERAGE	84.0	76.8	75.2	
NOTE: FINAL COUNTS DOUBLE				

(a) The Professor's Grade Book

Walker's original grade is 90

	A	B	C	D	E
1	Student	Test 1	Test 2	Final	Average
2					
3	Adams	100	90	81	88.0
4	Baker	90	76	87	85.0
5	Glassman	90	78	78	81.0
6	Moldof	60	60	40	50.0
7	Walker	80	80	90	85.0
8					
9	Class Average	84.0	76.8	75.2	

(b) Original Grades

Grade on Walker's final is changed to 100

	A	B	C	D	E
1	Student	Test 1	Test 2	Final	Average
2					
3	Adams	100	90	81	88.0
4	Baker	90	76	87	85.0
5	Glassman	90	78	78	81.0
6	Moldof	60	60	40	50.0
7	Walker	80	80	100	90.0
8					
9	Class Average	84.0	76.8	77.2	

Formulas recompute automatically

(c) Modified Spreadsheet

FIGURE 1.2 The Professor's Grade Book

Row and Column Headings

A spreadsheet is divided into rows and columns, with each row and column assigned a heading. Rows are given numeric headings ranging from 1 to 16,384 (the maximum number of rows allowed). Columns are assigned alphabetic headings from column A to Z, then continue from AA to AZ and then from BA to BZ and so on, until the last of 256 columns (column IV) is reached.

The intersection of a row and column forms a ***cell,*** with the number of cells in a spreadsheet equal to the number of rows times the number of columns. The professor's grade book in Figure 1.2, for example, has 5 columns labeled A through E, 9 rows numbered from 1 to 9, and a total of 45 cells. Each cell has a unique ***cell reference;*** for example, the cell at the intersection of column A and row 9 is known as cell A9. The column heading always precedes the row heading in the cell reference.

Formulas and Constants

Figure 1.3 shows an alternate view of the spreadsheet for the professor's grade book that displays the ***cell contents*** rather than the computed ***values.*** This figure displays the actual entries (formulas and constants) that were entered into the individual cells, which enable the spreadsheet to recalculate formulas whenever any entry changes.

A ***constant*** is an entry that does not change. It may be a number, such as a student's grade on an exam, or it may be descriptive text (a label), such as a student's name. A ***formula*** is a combination of numeric constants, cell references, arithmetic operators, and/or functions (described below) that displays the result of a calculation. Every cell contains either a formula or a constant.

A formula always begins with an equal sign. Consider, for example, the formula in cell E3, =(B3+C3+2*D3)/4, which computes Adams's semester average. The formula is built in accordance with the professor's rules for computing a student's semester average, which counts the final twice as much as the other tests. Excel uses symbols +, −, *, /, and ^ to indicate addition, subtraction, multiplication, division, and exponentiation, respectively, and follows the normal rules of arithmetic precedence. Any expression in parentheses is evaluated first, then within an expression exponentiation is performed first, followed by multiplication or division in left to right order, then finally addition or subtraction, also in left-to-right order.

The formula in cell E3 takes the grade on the first exam (in cell B3), plus the grade on the second exam (in cell C3), plus two times the grade on the final (in cell D3), and divides the result by four. Thus, should any of the exam grades change, the semester average (a formula whose results depend on the individual exam grades) will also change. This, in essence, is the basic principle behind the spreadsheet and explains why, when one number changes, various other numbers throughout the spreadsheet change as well.

A formula may also include a ***function,*** or predefined computational task, such as the ***AVERAGE function*** in cells B9, C9, and D9. The function in cell B9, for example, =AVERAGE(B3:B7), is interpreted to mean the average of all cells starting at cell B3 and ending at cell B7 and is equivalent to the formula =(B3+B4+B5+B6+B7)/5. You can appreciate that functions are often easier to use than the corresponding formulas, especially with larger spreadsheets (and classes with many students).

Constant (entry that does not change)

Function (predefined computational task)

Formula (displays the result of a calculation)

	A	B	C	D	E
1	Student	Test 1	Test 2	Final	Average
2					
3	Adams	100	90	81	=(B3+C3+2*D3)/4
4	Baker	90	76	87	=(B4+C4+2*D4)/4
5	Glassman	90	78	78	=(B5+C5+2*D5)/4
6	Moldof	60	60	40	=(B6+C6+2*D6)/4
7	Walker	80	80	90	=(B7+C7+2*D7)/4
8					
9	Class Average	=AVERAGE(B3:B7)	=AVERAGE(C3:C7)	=AVERAGE(D3:D7)	

FIGURE 1.3 The Professor's Grade Book (cell formulas)

Figure 1.4 displays the professor's grade book as it is implemented in Microsoft Excel. Microsoft Excel is a Windows application, and thus shares the common user interface with which you are familiar. (It's even easier to learn Excel if you already know another Office application such as Microsoft Word.) You should recognize, therefore, that the desktop in Figure 1.4 has two open windows—an application window for Microsoft Excel and a document window for the workbook, which is currently open.

Each window has its own Minimize, Maximize (or Restore), and Close buttons. Both windows have been maximized and thus the title bars have been merged into a single title bar that appears at the top of the application window. The title bar reflects the application (Microsoft Excel) as well as the name of the workbook (Grade Book) on which you are working. A menu bar appears immediately below the title bar. Two toolbars, which are discussed in depth on page 8, appear below the menu bar. Vertical and horizontal scroll bars appear at the right and bottom of the document window. The Windows 95 taskbar appears at the bottom of the screen and shows the open applications.

The terminology is important, and we distinguish between spreadsheet, worksheet, and workbook. Excel refers to a spreadsheet as a ***worksheet.*** Spreadsheet is a generic term; *workbook* and *worksheet* are unique to Excel. An Excel ***workbook*** contains one or more worksheets. The professor's grades for this class are contained in the CIS120 worksheet within the Grade Book workbook. This workbook also contains additional worksheets (CIS223 and CIS316) as indicated by the worksheet tabs at the bottom of the window. These worksheets contain the professor's grades for other courses that he or she is teaching this semester. (See practice exercise 1 at the end of the chapter.)

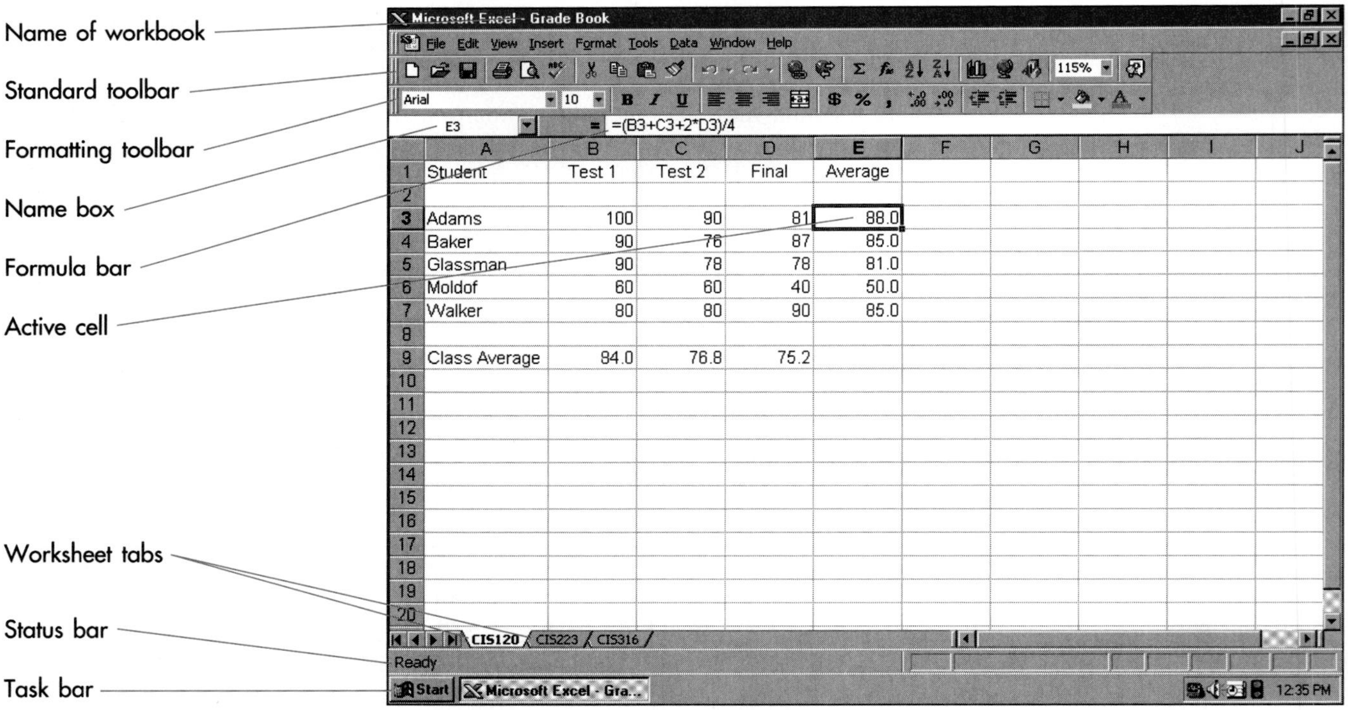

Name of workbook
Standard toolbar
Formatting toolbar
Name box
Formula bar
Active cell
Worksheet tabs
Status bar
Task bar

FIGURE 1.4 Professor's Grade Book

Figure 1.4 resembles the grade book shown earlier, but it includes several other elements that enable you to create and/or edit the worksheet. The heavy border around cell E3 indicates that it (cell E3) is the ***active cell.*** Any entry made at this time is made into the active cell, and any commands that are executed affect the contents of the active cell. The active cell can be changed by clicking a different cell, or by using the arrow keys to move to a different cell.

The displayed value in cell E3 is 88.0, but as indicated earlier, the cell contains a formula to compute the semester average rather than the number itself. The contents of the active cell, =(B3+C3+2*D3)/4, are displayed in the ***formula bar*** near the top of the worksheet. The cell reference for the active cell, cell E3 in Figure 1.4, appears in the ***Name box*** at the left of the formula bar.

The ***status bar*** at the bottom of the worksheet keeps you informed of what is happening as you work within Excel. It displays information about a selected command or an operation in progress.

THE EXCEL WORKBOOK

An Excel workbook is the electronic equivalent of the three-ring binder. A workbook contains one or more worksheets (or chart sheets), each of which is identified by a tab at the bottom of the workbook. The worksheets in a workbook are normally related to one another; for example, each worksheet may contain the sales for a specific division within a company. The advantage of a workbook is that all of its worksheets are stored in a single file, which is accessed as a unit.

Toolbars

Excel provides several different ways to accomplish the same task. Commands may be accessed from a pull-down menu, from a shortcut menu (which is displayed by pointing to an object and clicking the right mouse button), and/or through keyboard equivalents. Commands can also be executed from one of many ***toolbars*** that appear immediately below the menu bar. The Standard and Formatting toolbars are displayed by default. (All toolbars can be displayed or hidden by using the Tools command in the View menu.)

The ***Standard toolbar*** contains buttons corresponding to the most basic commands in Excel—for example, opening and closing a workbook, printing a workbook, and so on. The icon on the button is intended to be indicative of its function (e.g., a printer to indicate the Print command). You can also point to the button to display a ***ScreenTip*** showing the name of the button.

The ***Formatting toolbar*** appears under the Standard toolbar, and provides access to common formatting operations such as boldface, italics, or underlining. It also enables you to change the alignment of entries within a cell and/or change the font or color. The easiest way to master the toolbars is to view the buttons in groups according to their general function, as shown in Figure 1.5.

The toolbars may appear overwhelming at first, but there is absolutely no need to memorize what the individual buttons do. That will come with time. Indeed, if you use another office application such as Microsoft Word, you may already recognize many of the buttons on the Standard and Formatting toolbars. Most individuals start by using the pull-down menus, then look for shortcuts along the way.

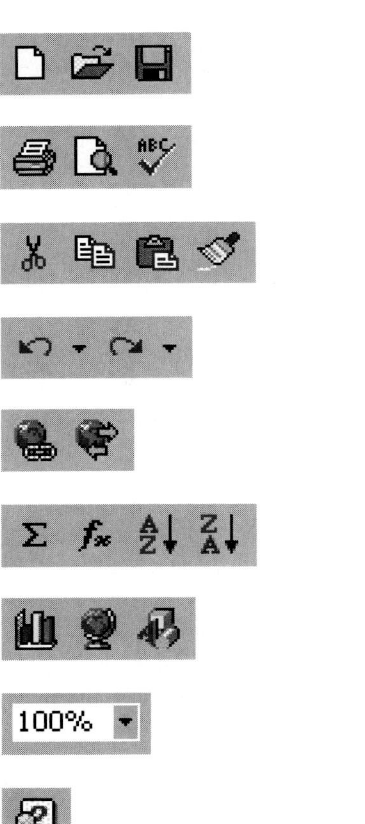

Opens a new workbook; opens an existing workbook; or saves the workbook to disk

Prints the workbook; previews the workbook prior to printing; checks spelling

Cuts or copies the selection to the clipboard; pastes the clipboard contents; copies the formatting of the selected cells

Undoes or redoes a previously executed command

Inserts a hyperlink or displays the Web toolbar

Sums the suggested range; displays the Paste Function dialog box; performs an ascending or descending sort

Starts the Chart Wizard; starts Microsoft Map; displays the Drawing toolbar

Changes the magnification

Displays the Office Assistant. The lightbulb indicates the Assistant has a suggestion.

(a) The Standard Toolbar

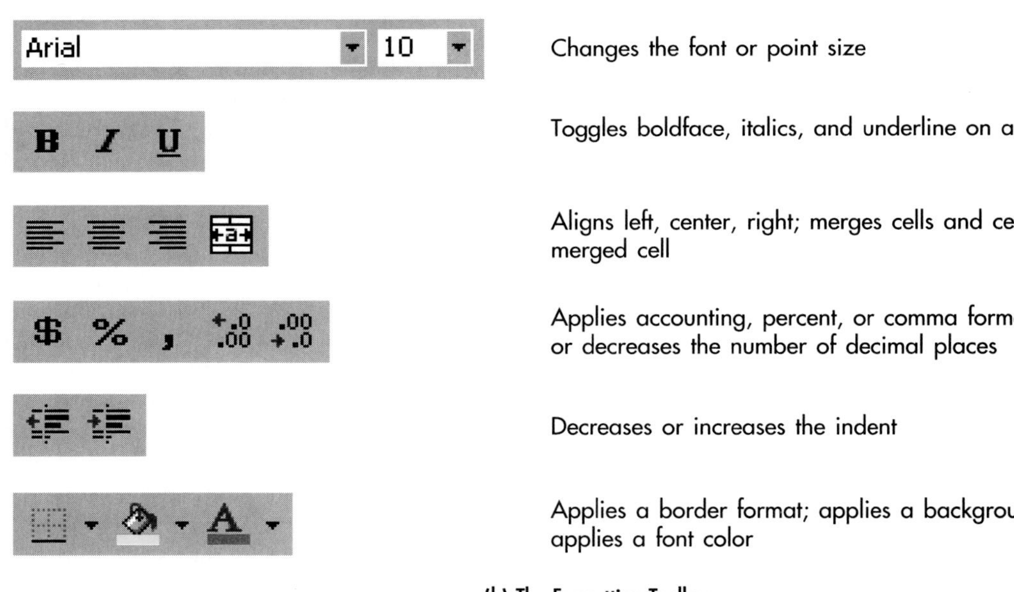

Changes the font or point size

Toggles boldface, italics, and underline on and off

Aligns left, center, right; merges cells and centers text in merged cell

Applies accounting, percent, or comma formatting; increases or decreases the number of decimal places

Decreases or increases the indent

Applies a border format; applies a background color; applies a font color

(b) The Formatting Toolbar

FIGURE 1.5 Toolbars

HELP FOR MICROSOFT EXCEL

Office 97 offers help from a variety of sources. You can pull down the Help menu, as you can with any Windows application, and/or you can click the Office Assistant button on the Standard toolbar. You can also go to the Microsoft Web site (www.microsoft.com) to obtain more recent, and often more detailed, information. You will find the answer to the most frequently asked questions, and you can access the same Knowledge Base used by Microsoft support engineers.

Entering Data

Data is entered into a worksheet by selecting a cell, then typing the constant or formula that is to go into that cell. The entry is displayed in the formula bar at the top of the window as it is being typed. The entry is completed by pressing the enter key, which moves the active cell to the cell immediately below the current cell, or by pressing any of the arrow keys to move to the next cell in the indicated direction. Pressing the right arrow key, for example, completes the entry and moves the active cell to the next cell in the same row. You can also complete the entry by clicking in a new cell, or by clicking the green check that appears to the left of the formula bar as data is entered.

To replace an existing entry, select the cell by clicking in the cell, or by using the keyboard to move to the cell. Type the corrected entry (as though you were entering it for the first time), then complete the entry as described above. To edit an entry, click in the formula bar, make the necessary changes, then press the enter key.

THE FILE MENU

The ***File menu*** is a critically important menu in virtually every Windows application. It contains the ***Save command*** to save a workbook to disk, and the ***Open command*** to subsequently retrieve (open) the workbook at a later time. The File Menu also contains the ***Print command*** to print a workbook, the ***Close command*** to close the current workbook but continue working in Excel, and the ***Exit command*** to quit Excel altogether.

The ***Save command*** copies the workbook that is currently being edited (the workbook in memory) to disk. The Save As dialog box appears the first time a workbook is saved so that you can specify the filename and other required information. All subsequent executions of the Save command save the workbook under the assigned name, replacing the previously saved version with the new version.

The Save As dialog box requires a filename (e.g., My First Spreadsheet in Figure 1.6a), which can be up to 255 characters in length. The filename may contain spaces and commas. The dialog box also requires the drive (and folder) in which the file is to be saved, as well as the file type that determines which application the file is associated with. (Long-time DOS users will remember the three-character extension at the end of a filename such as XLS to indicate an Excel workbook. The extension is generally hidden in Windows 95, according to options that are set through the View menu in My Computer or the Windows Explorer.)

The Open command brings a copy of a previously saved workbook into memory, enabling you to edit the workbook. The Open command displays the Open dialog box in which you specify the file to retrieve. You indicate the drive (and optionally the folder) that contains the file, as well as the type of file you want to retrieve. Excel will then list all files of that type on the designated drive (and folder), enabling you to open the file you want.

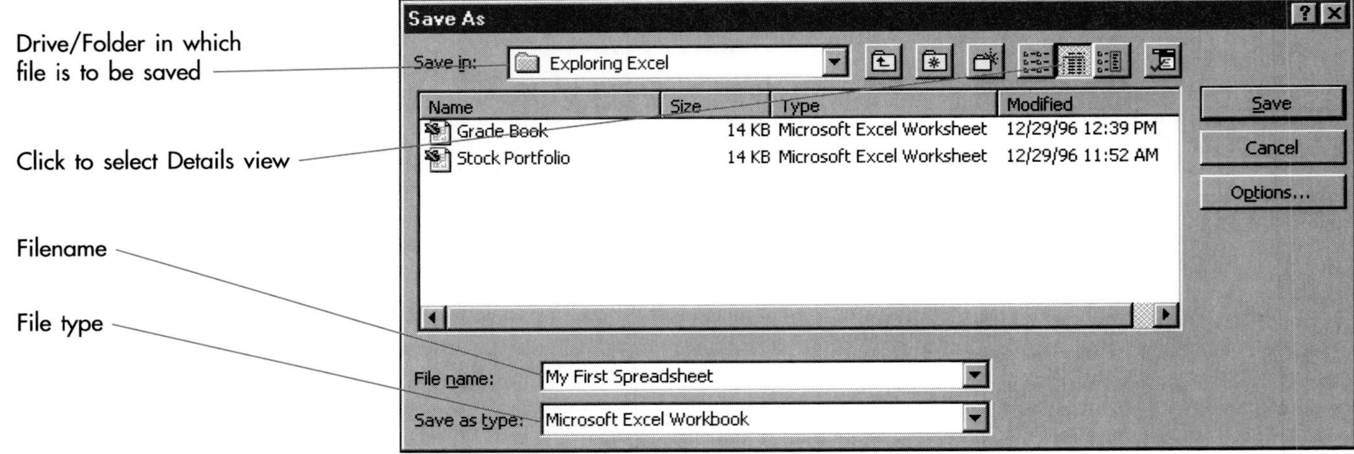

(a) Save As Dialog Box

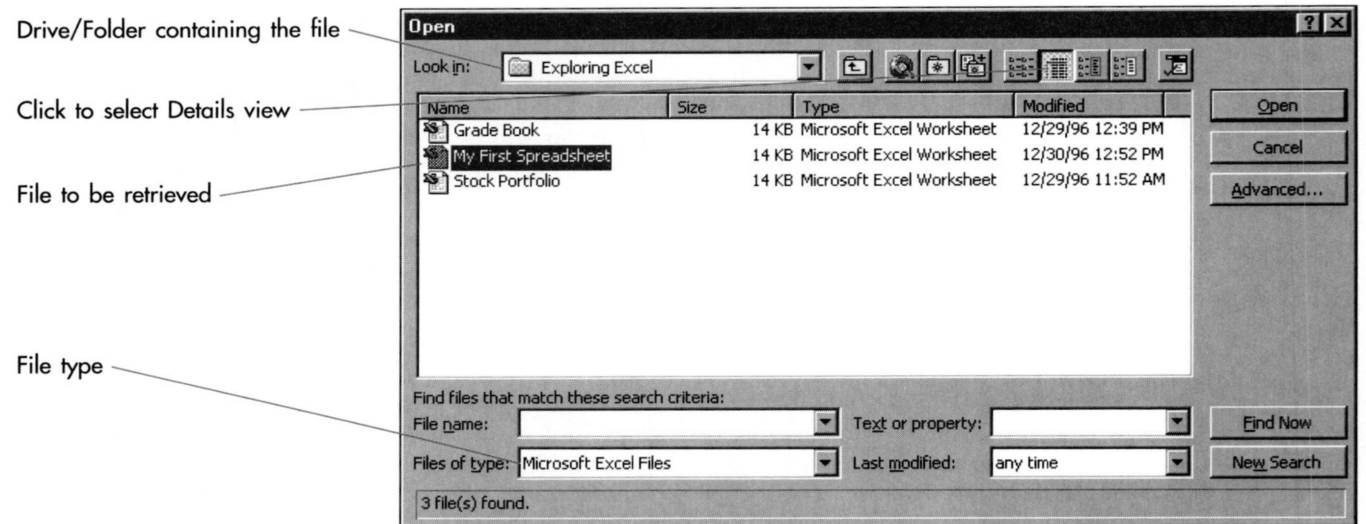

(b) Open Dialog Box

FIGURE 1.6 The Save and Open Commands (continued)

The Save and Open commands work in conjunction with one another. The Save As dialog box in Figure 1.6a, for example, saves the file *My First Spreadsheet* in the Exploring Excel folder. (The drive is not visible in the figure.) The Open dialog box in Figure 1.6b brings that file back into memory so that you can work with the file, after which you can save the revised file for use at a later time.

The toolbars in the Save As dialog and Open dialog boxes have several buttons in common that enable you to list the files in different ways. The Details view is selected in both dialog boxes and shows the file size as well as the date and time a file was last modified. The List button displays only the file names and hence more files are visible at one time. The Preview button lets you see a workbook before you open it. The Properties button displays information about the workbook including the number of revisions.

We come now to the first of two hands-on exercises in this chapter that implement our learn-by-doing philosophy. The exercise shows you how to start Microsoft Excel and open the professor's grade book from the practice files that are referenced throughout the text. You can obtain a copy of the practice files from your instructor, or you can download the files as described in the exercise. The practice files contain a series of Excel workbooks that are used in various exercises throughout the text.

HANDS-ON EXERCISE 1

Introduction to Microsoft Excel

Objectives: To start Microsoft Excel; to open, modify, and print an existing worksheet. Use Figure 1.7 as a guide in the exercise.

STEP 1: Welcome to Windows

- Turn on the computer and all of its peripherals. The floppy drive should be empty prior to starting your machine. This ensures that the system starts by reading from the hard disk, which contains the Windows files, as opposed to a floppy disk, which does not.
- Your system will take a minute or so to get started, after which you should see the desktop in Figure 1.7a. Do not be concerned if the appearance of your desktop is different from ours.
- You may see additional objects on the desktop in Windows 95 and/or the active desktop content in Windows 97. It doesn't matter which operating system you are using because Office 97 runs equally well under both Windows 95 and Windows 97 (as well as Windows NT).
- You may see a Welcome to Windows 95 / Windows 97 dialog box with command buttons to take a tour of the operating system. If so, click the appropriate button(s) or close the dialog box.

TAKE THE WINDOWS TOUR

Windows 95 greets you with a Welcome window that contains a command button to take you on a 10-minute tour of Windows 95. Click the command button and enjoy the show. You might also try the What's New command button for a quick overview of changes from Windows 3.1. If you do not see the Welcome window when you start Windows 95, click the Start button, click Run, type WELCOME in the Open ***text box,*** and press enter. Windows 97 was not available when we went to press, but we expect it to have a similar feature.

Click the Start button

(a) Welcome to Windows (step 1)

FIGURE 1.7 Hands-on Exercise 1

STEP 2: Obtain the Practice Files

➤ We have created a series of practice files for you to use throughout the text. Your instructor will make these files available to you in a variety of ways:

- You can download the files from our Web site if you have access to the Internet and World Wide Web (see boxed tip).
- The files may be on a network drive, in which case you use the Windows Explorer to copy the files from the network to a floppy disk.
- There may be an actual "data disk" that you are to check out from the lab in order to use the Copy Disk command to duplicate the disk.

➤ Check with your instructor for additional information.

DOWNLOAD THE PRACTICE FILES

You can download the practice files for any book in the *Exploring Windows* series from Bob Grauer's home page (www.bus.miami.edu/~rgrauer). Use any Web browser to get to Bob's page, then click the link to the *Exploring Windows* series where you choose the appropriate book and download the file. Be sure to read the associated "read me" file, which provides additional information about downloading the file.

STEP 3: Start Microsoft Excel

- Click the **Start button** to display the Start menu. Click (or point to) the **Programs menu,** then click **Microsoft Excel** to start the program.
- Close the Office Assistant if it appears. (The Office Assistant is illustrated in step 7 of this exercise.)
- If necessary, click the **Maximize button** in the application window so that Excel takes the entire desktop as shown in Figure 1.7b. Click the **Maximize button** in the document window (if necessary) so that the document window is as large as possible.

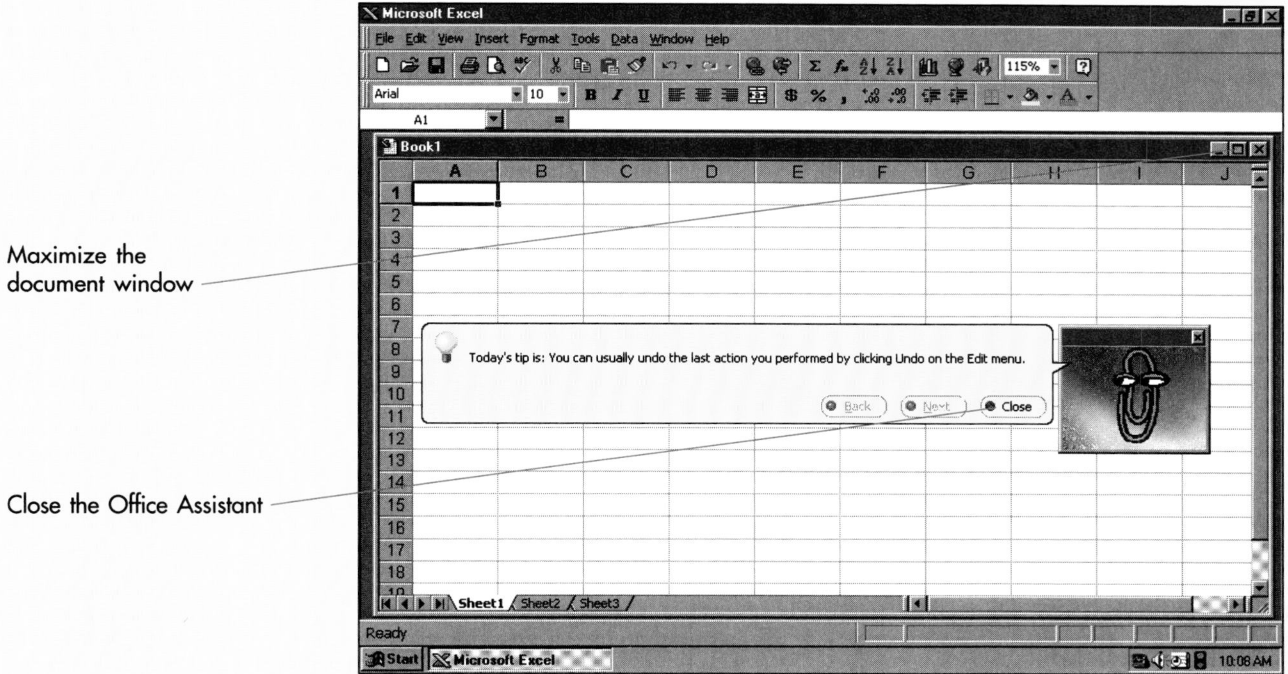

(b) Start Excel (step 3)

FIGURE 1.7 Hands-on Exercise 1 (continued)

CHOOSE YOUR OWN ASSISTANT

You can choose your own personal assistant from one of several available images. Click the Office Assistant button on the Standard toolbar to display the Assistant, click the options button to display the Office Assistant dialog box, click the Gallery tab, then click the Next button repeatedly to cycle through the available images. Click OK to select the image and close the dialog box. (The Office CD is required for some of the characters.)

STEP 4: Open the Workbook

- Pull down the **File menu** and click **Open** (or click the **Open button** on the Standard toolbar). You should see a dialog box similar to the one in Figure 1.7c.
- Click the **Details button** to change to the Details view. Click and drag the vertical border between two columns to increase (or decrease) the size of a column.
- Click the **drop-down arrow** on the Look In list box. Click the appropriate drive, drive C or drive A, depending on the location of your data. Double click the **Exploring Excel folder** to make it the active folder (the folder from which you will retrieve and into which you will save the workbook).
- Click the **down scroll arrow** if necessary in order to click **Grade Book** to select the professor's grade book. Click the **Open command button** to open the workbook and begin the exercise.

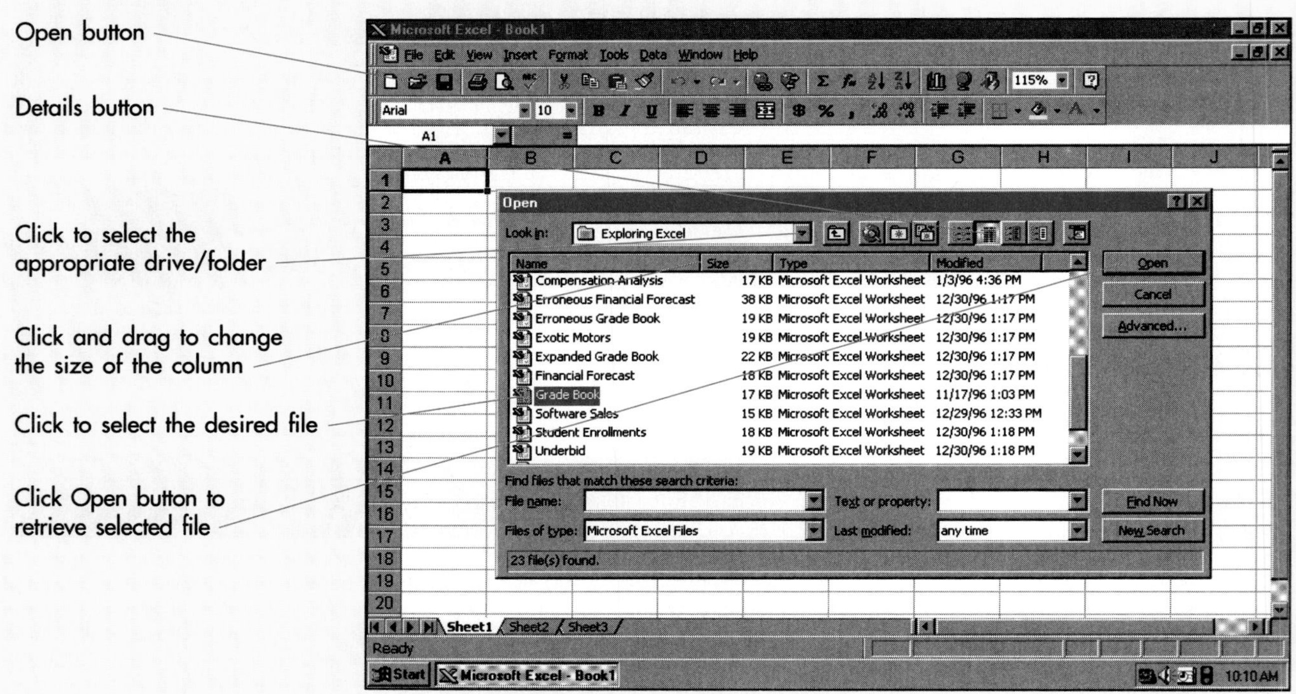

(c) Open the Grade Book (step 4)

FIGURE 1.7 Hands-on Exercise 1 (continued)

MISSING TOOLBARS

The Standard and Formatting toolbars are displayed by default, but either or both can be hidden from view. To display (or hide) a toolbar, point to any toolbar, click the right mouse button to display the Toolbar shortcut menu, then click the individual toolbars on or off as appropriate. If you do not see any toolbars at all, pull down the View menu, click Toolbars to display a dialog box listing the available toolbars, check the toolbars you want displayed, and click OK.

STEP 5: The Active Cell, Formula Bar, and Worksheet Tabs

- You should see the workbook in Figure 1.7d. Click in **cell B3,** the cell containing Adams's grade on the first test. Cell B3 is now the active cell and is surrounded by a heavy border. The Name box indicates that cell B3 is the active cell, and its contents are displayed in the formula bar.
- Click in **cell B4** (or press the **down arrow key**) to make it the active cell. The Name box indicates cell B4 while the formula bar indicates a grade of 90.
- Click in **cell E3,** the cell containing the formula to compute Adams's semester average; the worksheet displays the computed average of 88.0, but the formula bar displays the formula, =(B3+C3+2*D3)/4, to compute that average based on the test grades.
- Click the **CIS223 tab** to view a different worksheet within the same workbook. This worksheet contains the grades for a different class.
- Click the **CIS316 tab** to view this worksheet. Click the **CIS120 tab** to return to this worksheet and continue with the exercise.

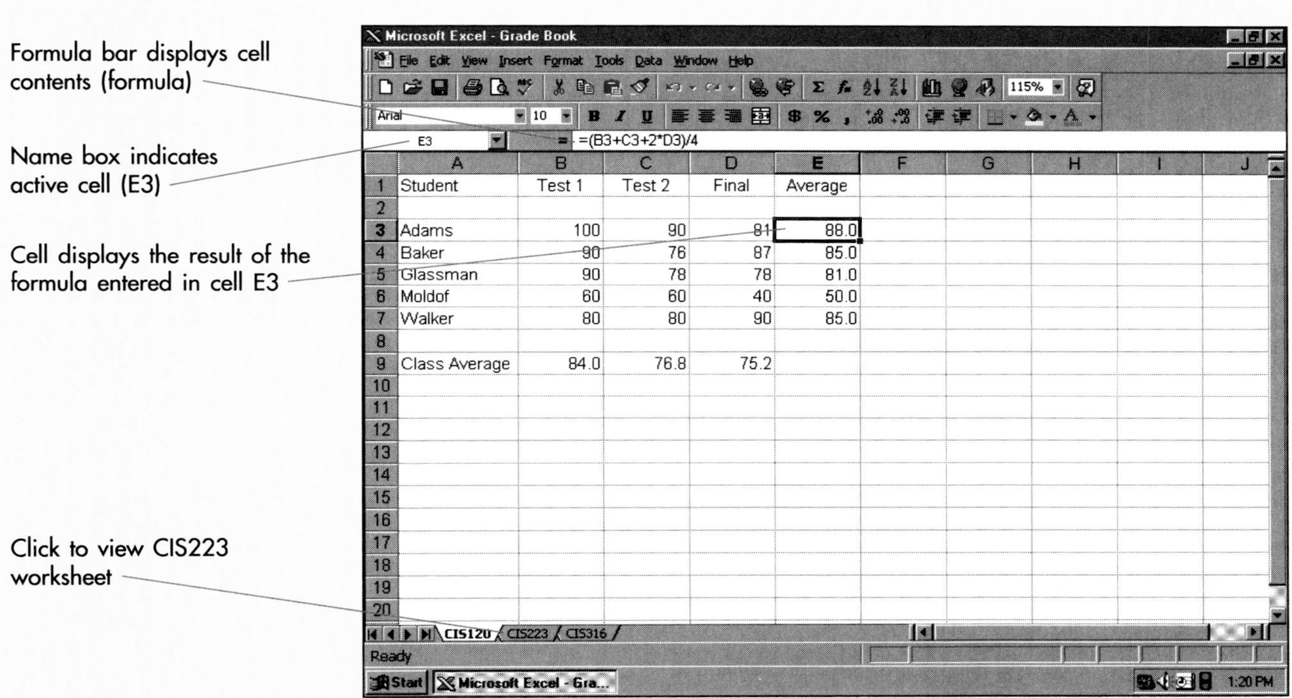

	A	B	C	D	E
1	Student	Test 1	Test 2	Final	Average
2					
3	Adams	100	90	81	88.0
4	Baker	90	76	87	85.0
5	Glassman	90	78	78	81.0
6	Moldof	60	60	40	50.0
7	Walker	80	80	90	85.0
8					
9	Class Average	84.0	76.8	75.2	

(d) The Active Cell, Formula Bar, and Worksheet Tabs (step 5)

FIGURE 1.7 **Hands-on Exercise 1 (continued)**

SCREENTIPS

Point to any button on any toolbar and Excel displays a ScreenTip containing the name of the button. If pointing to a button has no effect, pull down the View menu, click Toolbars, and then click Customize to display the Customize dialog box. Click the Options tab, check the box to Show ScreenTips on Toolbars, then close the dialog box.

STEP 6: Experiment (What If?)

- Click in **cell C4,** the cell containing Baker's grade on the second test. Enter a corrected value of **86** (instead of the previous entry of 76). Press **enter** (or click in another cell).
- The effects of this change ripple through the worksheet, automatically changing the computed value for Baker's average in cell E4 to 87.5. The class average on the second test in cell C9 changes to 78.8.
- Change Walker's grade on the final from 90 to **100.** Press **enter** (or click in another cell). Walker's average in cell E7 changes to 90.0, while the class average in cell D9 changes to 77.2.
- Your worksheet should match Figure 1.7e.

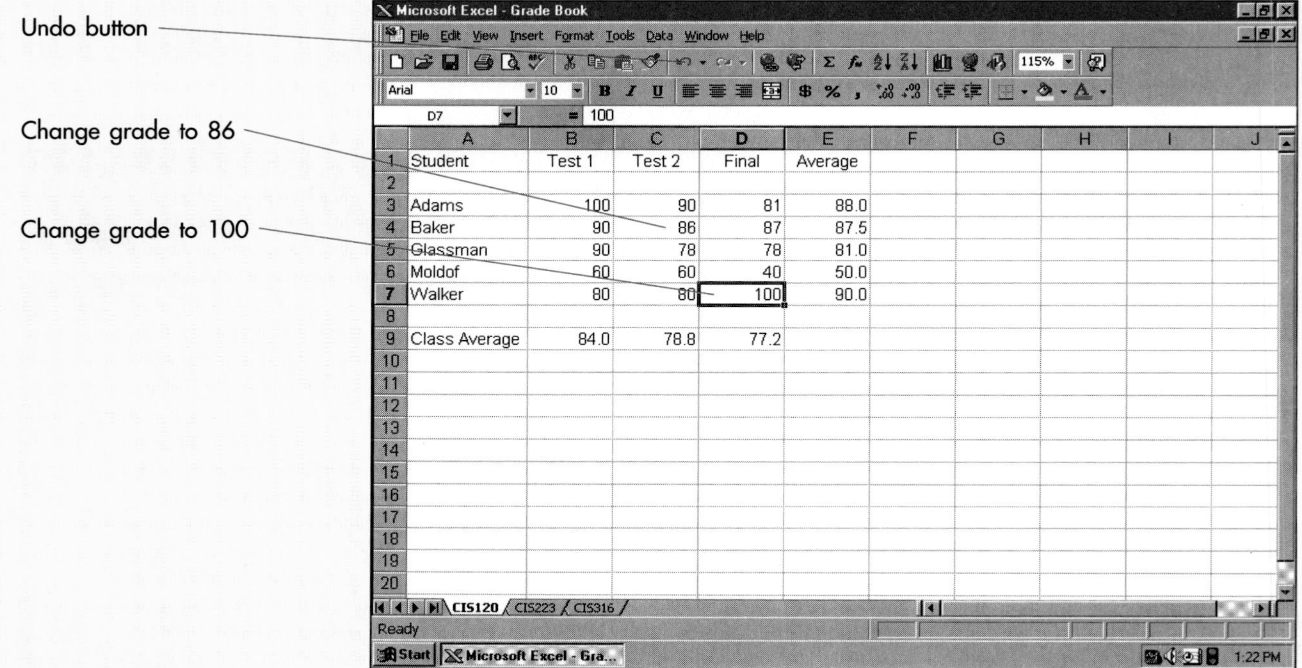

(e) What If (step 6)

FIGURE 1.7 Hands-on Exercise 1 (continued)

ABOUT MICROSOFT EXCEL

Pull down the Help menu and click About Microsoft Excel to display the specific release number as well as other licensing information, including the product serial number. This help screen also contains two very useful command buttons, System Info and Technical Support. The first button displays information about the hardware installed on your system, including the amount of memory and available space on the hard drive. The Technical Support button provides information on obtaining technical assistance.

STEP 7: The Office Assistant

- Click the **Office Assistant button** on the Standard toolbar to display the Office Assistant. (You may see a different character than the one we have selected.)
- Enter your question, for example, **How do I use the Office Assistant?** as shown in Figure 1.7f, then click the **Search button** to look for the answer.
- The size of the dialog box expands as the Assistant suggests several topics that may be appropriate to answer your question.
- Click any of the suggested topics, which in turn displays a help screen with detailed information. Read the help screen(s), close the Help Window, then close the Office Assistant.

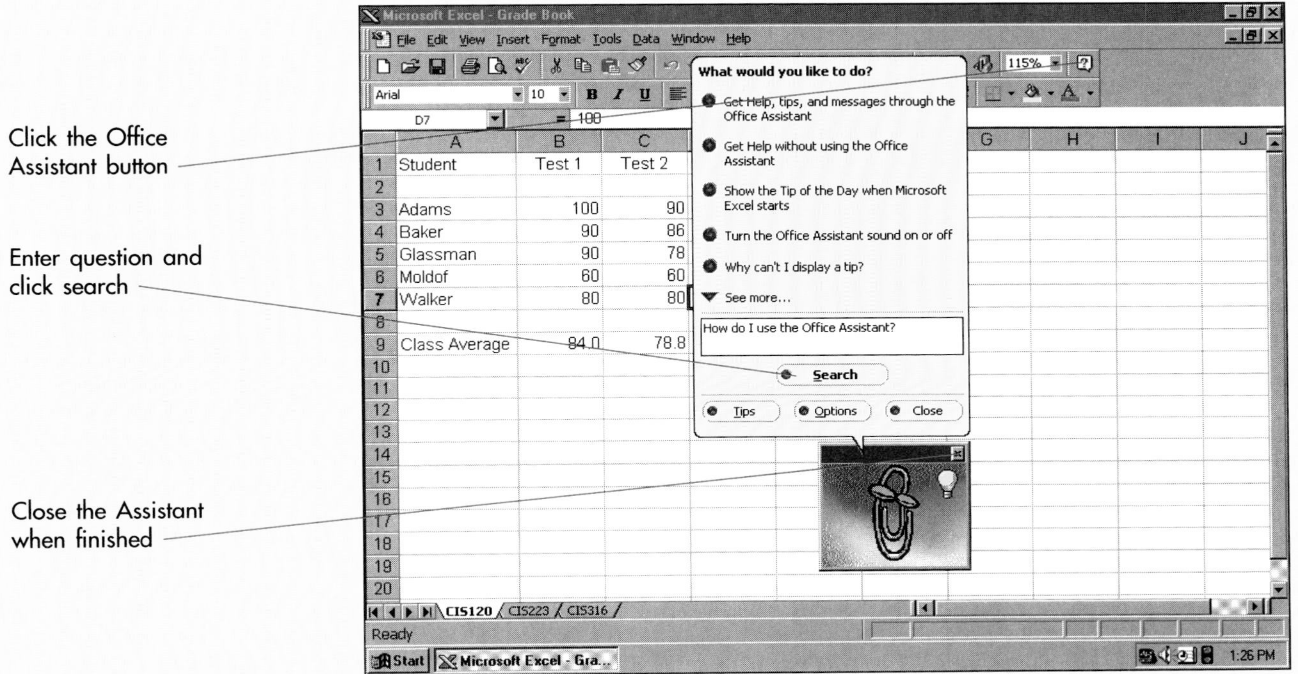

(f) The Office Assistant (step 7)

FIGURE 1.7 Hands-on Exercise 1 (continued)

TIP OF THE DAY

You can set the Office Assistant to greet you with a "Tip of the Day" whenever you start Word. If the Office Assistant is not visible, click the Office Assistant button on the Standard toolbar to start the Assistant, then click the options button to display the Office Assistant dialog box. Check the Show the Tip of the Day at the startup box, then click OK. The next time you start Excel, the Assistant will greet you and offer you a tip of the day.

STEP 8: Print the Worksheet

- Pull down the **File menu** and click **Save** (or click the **Save button** on the Standard toolbar).
- Pull down the **File menu.** Click **Print** to display a dialog box requesting information for the Print command as shown in Figure 1.7g. Click **OK** to accept the default options (you want to print only the selected worksheet).

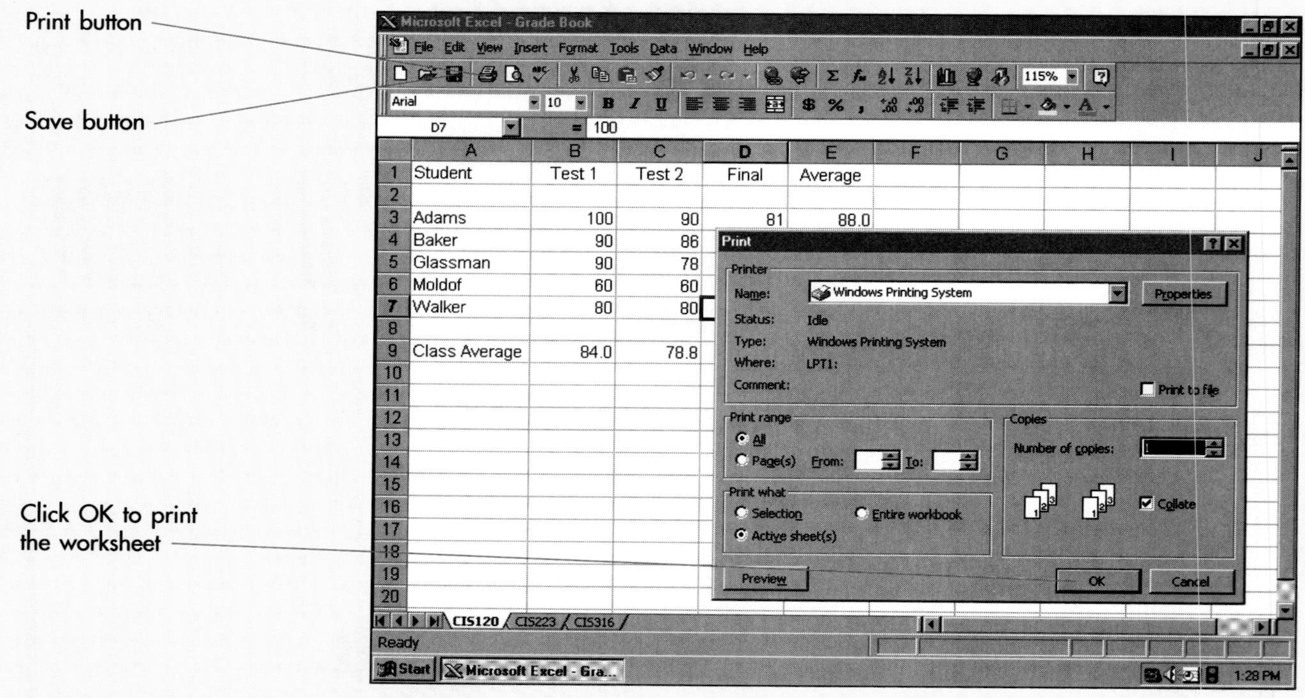

(g) Print the Workbook (step 8)

FIGURE 1.7 Hands-on Exercise 1 (continued)

> **THE PRINT PREVIEW COMMAND**
>
> The ***Print Preview command*** displays the worksheet as it will appear when printed. The command is invaluable and will save you considerable time as you don't have to rely on trial and error to obtain the perfect printout. The Print Preview command can be executed from the File menu, via the Print Preview button on the Standard toolbar, or from the Print Preview command button within the Page Setup command.

STEP 9: Close the Workbook

- Pull down the **File menu.** Click **Close** to close the workbook but leave Excel open.
- Pull down the **File menu** a second time. Click **Exit** if you do not want to continue with the next exercise at this time.

MODIFYING THE WORKSHEET

We trust that you completed the hands-on exercise without difficulty and that you are more confident in your ability than when you first began. The exercise was not complicated, but it did accomplish several objectives and set the stage for a second exercise, which follows shortly.

Consider now Figure 1.8, which contains a modified version of the professor's grade book. Figure 1.8a shows the grade book at the end of the first hands-on exercise and reflects the changes made to the grades for Baker and Walker. Figure 1.8b shows the worksheet as it will appear at the end of the second exercise. Several changes bear mention:

1. One student has dropped the class and two other students have been added. Moldof appeared in the original worksheet in Figure 1.8a, but has somehow managed to withdraw; Coulter and Courier did not appear in the original grade book but have been added to the worksheet in Figure 1.8b.
2. A new column containing the students' majors has been added.

The implementation of these changes is accomplished through a combination of the Insert and Delete commands, which enable you to add or remove rows or columns as necessary.

Insert and Delete Commands

The ***Insert command*** adds row(s) or column(s) to an existing worksheet. The ***Delete command*** removes existing row(s) or column(s). Both commands auto-

Moldof will be dropped from class

	A	B	C	D	E
1	Student	Test 1	Test 2	Final	Average
2					
3	Adams	100	90	81	88.0
4	Baker	90	86	87	87.5
5	Glassman	90	78	78	81.0
6	Moldof	60	60	40	50.0
7	Walker	80	80	100	90.0
8					
9	Class Average	84.0	78.8	77.2	

(a) After Hands-on Exercise 1

A new column has been added (Major)

Two new students have been added

Moldof has been deleted

	A	B	C	D	E	F
1	Student	Major	Test 1	Test 2	Final	Average
2						
3	Adams	CIS	100	90	81	88.0
4	Baker	MKT	90	86	87	87.5
5	Coulter	ACC	85	95	100	95.0
6	Courier	FIN	75	75	85	80.0
7	Glassman	CIS	90	78	78	81.0
8	Walker	CIS	80	80	100	90.0
9						

(b) After Hands-on Exercise 2

FIGURE 1.8 The Modified Grade Book

matically adjust the cell references in existing formulas to account for the insertion or deletion of rows and columns within the worksheet.

Figure 1.9 displays the cell formulas in the professor's grade book and corresponds to the worksheets in Figure 1.8. The "before" and "after" worksheets reflect the insertion of a new column containing the students' majors, the addition of two new students, Coulter and Courier, and the deletion of an existing student, Moldof.

Let us consider the formula to compute Adams's semester average, which is contained in cell E3 of the original grade book, but in cell F3 in the modified grade book. The formula in Figure 1.9a referenced cells B3, C3, and D3 (the grades on test 1, test 2, and the final). The corresponding formula in Figure 1.9b reflects the fact that a new column has been inserted, and references cells C3, D3, and E3. The change in the formula is made automatically by Excel, without any action on the part of the user other than to insert the new column. The formulas for all other students have been adjusted in similar fashion.

Some students (all students below Baker) have had a further adjustment to reflect the addition of the new students through insertion of new rows in the worksheet. Glassman, for example, appeared in row 5 of the original worksheet, but appears in row 7 of the revised worksheet. Hence the formula to compute Glassman's semester average now references the grades in row 7, rather than in row 5 as in the original worksheet.

Finally, the formulas to compute the class averages have also been adjusted. These formulas appeared in row 9 of Figure 1.9a and averaged the grades in rows 3 through 7. The revised worksheet has a net increase of one student, which automatically moves these formulas to row 10, where the formulas are adjusted to average the grades in rows 3 through 8.

Formula references grades in B3, C3, and D3

Function references grades in rows 3–7

	A	B	C	D	E
1	Student	Test1	Test2	Final	Average
2					
3	Adams	100	90	81	=(B3+C3+2*D3)/4
4	Baker	90	86	87	=(B4+C4+2*D4)/4
5	Glassman	90	78	78	=(B5+C5+2*D5)/4
6	Moldof	60	60	40	=(B6+C6+2*D6)/4
7	Walker	80	80	100	=(B7+C7+2*D7)/4
8					
9	Class Average	=AVERAGE(B3:B7)	=AVERAGE(C3:C7)	=AVERAGE(D3:D7)	

(a) Before

	A	B	C	D	E	F
1	Student	Major	Test1	Test2	Final	Average
2						
3	Adams	CIS	100	90	81	=(C3+D3+2*E3)/4
4	Baker	MKT	90	86	87	=(C4+D4+2*E4)/4
5	Coulter	ACC	85	95	100	=(C5+D5+2*E5)/4
6	Courier	FIN	75	75	85	=(C6+D6+2*E6)/4
7	Glassman	CIS	90	78	78	=(C7+D7+2*E7)/4
8	Walker	CIS	80	80	100	=(C8+D8+2*E8)/4
9						
10	Class Average		=AVERAGE(C3:C8)	=AVERAGE(D3:D8)	=AVERAGE(E3:E8)	

Function changes to reference grades in rows 3–8 (due to addition of 2 new students and deletion of 1)

Formula changes to reference grades in C3, D3, and E3 due to addition of new column

(b) After

FIGURE 1.9 The Insert and Delete Commands

THE PAGE SETUP COMMAND

The Print command was used at the end of the first hands-on exercise to print the completed workbook. The ***Page Setup command*** gives you complete control of the printed worksheet as illustrated in Figure 1.10. Many of the options may not appear important now, but you will appreciate them as you develop larger and more complicated worksheets later in the text.

The Page tab in Figure 1.10a determines the orientation and scaling of the printed page. ***Portrait orientation*** (8½ × 11) prints vertically down the page. ***Landscape orientation*** (11 × 8½) prints horizontally across the page and is used

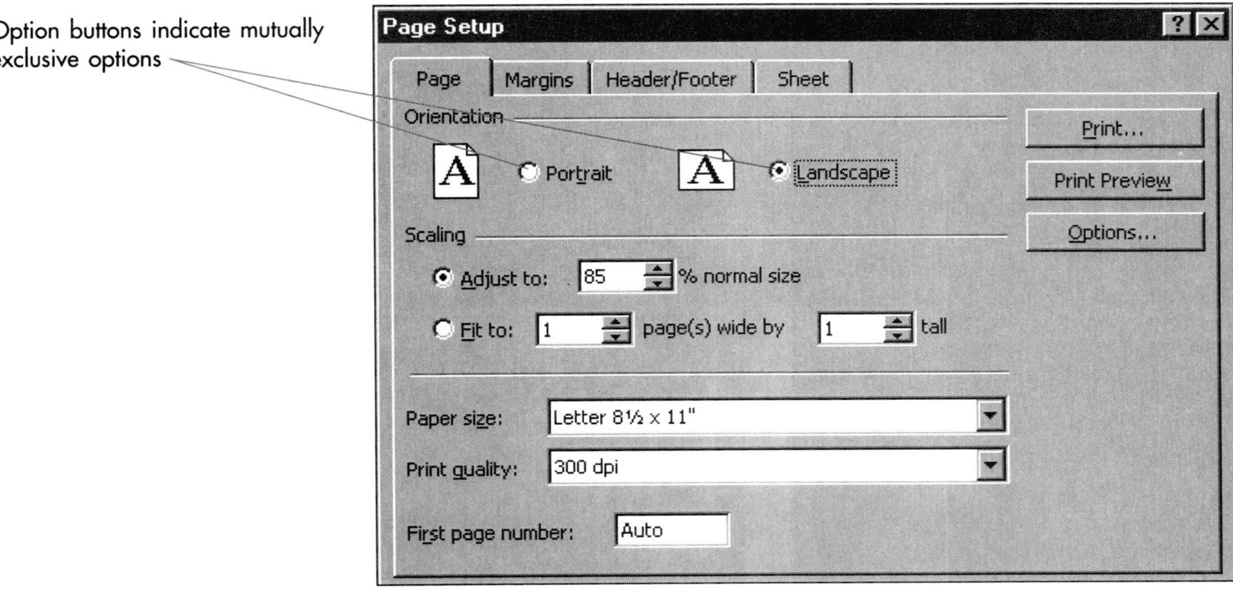

(a) The Page Tab

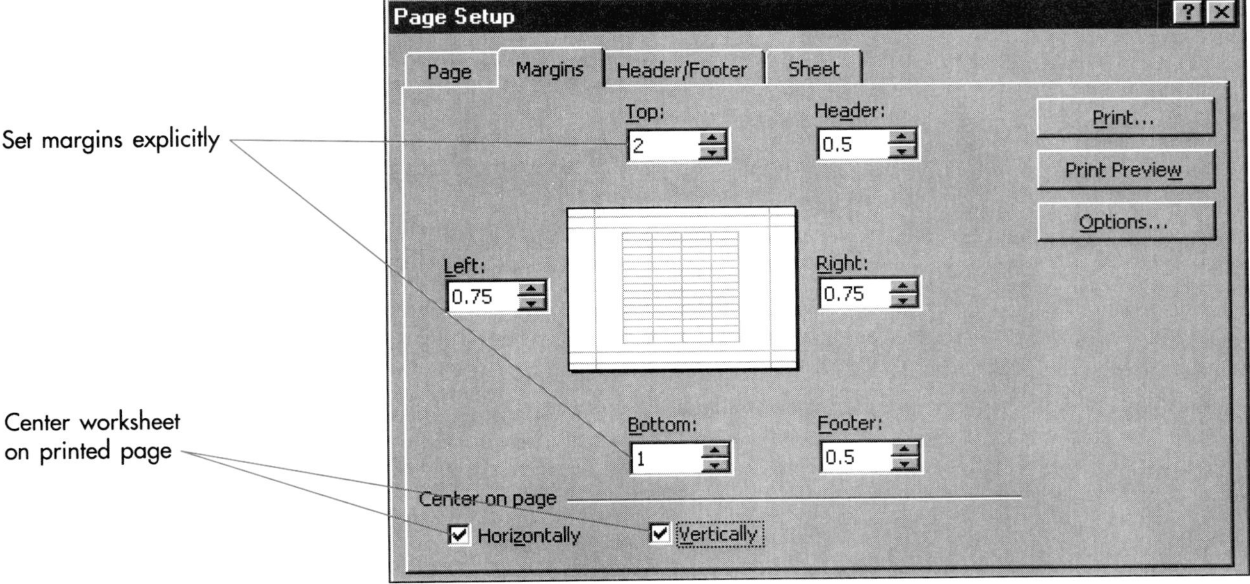

(b) The Margins Tab

FIGURE 1.10 The Page Setup Command

when the worksheet is too wide to fit on a portrait page. The option buttons indicate mutually exclusive items, one of which *must* be selected; that is, a worksheet must be printed in either portrait or landscape orientation. Option buttons are also used to choose the scaling factor. You can reduce (enlarge) the output by a designated scaling factor, or you can force the output to fit on a specified number of pages. The latter option is typically used to force a worksheet to fit on a single page.

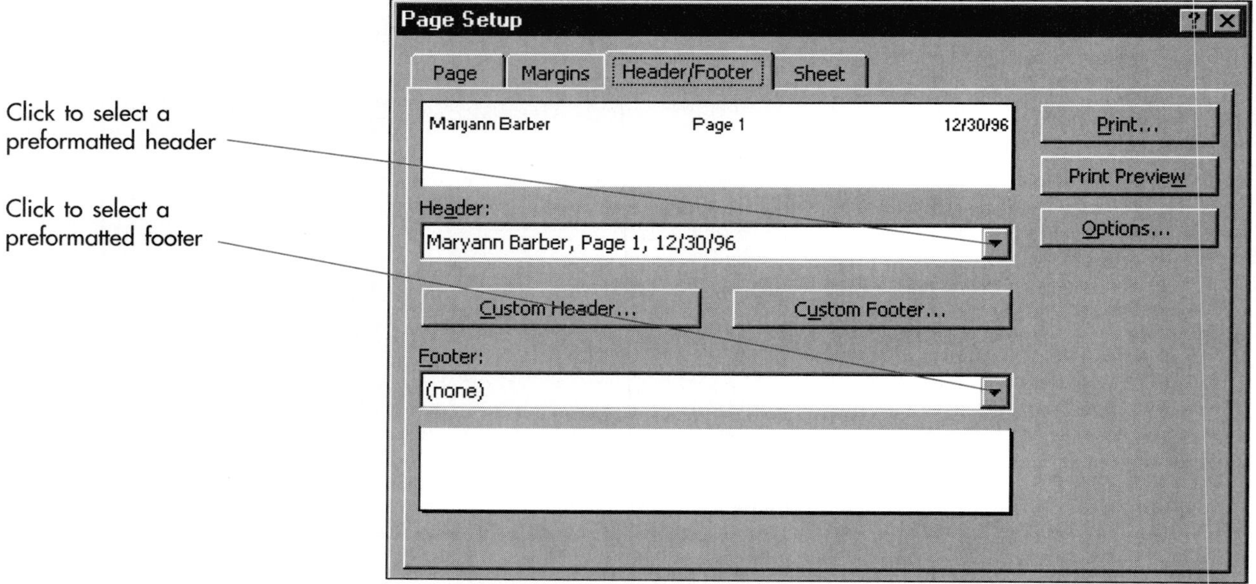

(c) The Header/Footer Tab

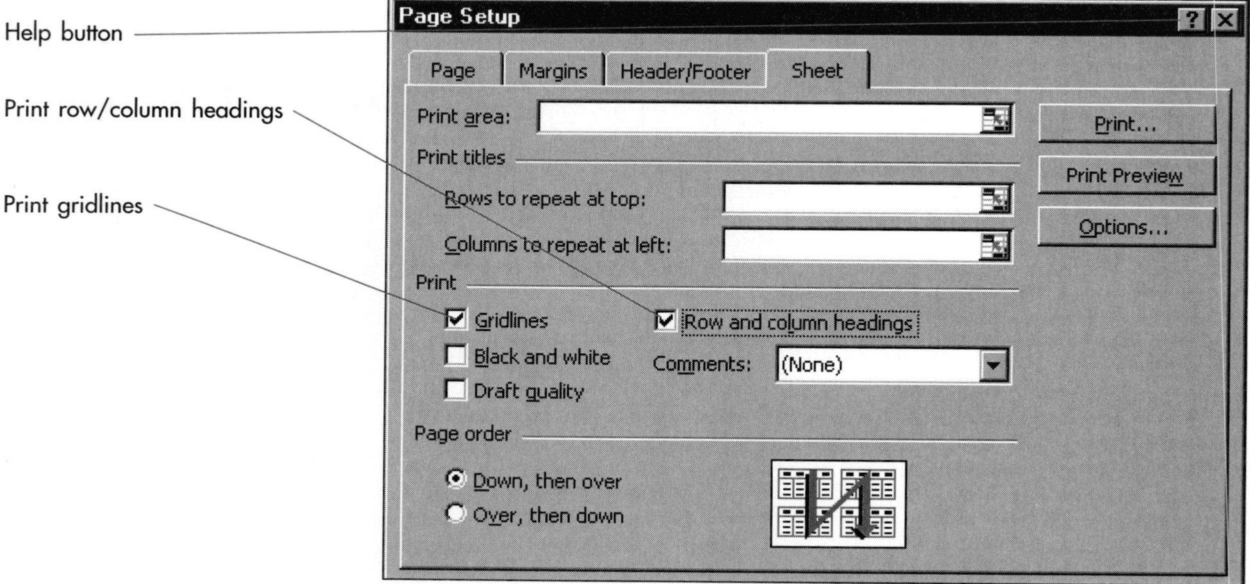

(d) The Sheet Tab

FIGURE 1.10 The Page Setup Command (continued)

The Margins tab in Figure 1.10b not only controls the margins, but will also center the worksheet horizontally and/or vertically. Check boxes are associated with the centering options and indicate that multiple options can be chosen; for example, horizontally and vertically are both selected. The Margins tab also determines the distance of the header and footer from the edge of the page.

The Header/Footer tab in Figure 1.10c lets you create a header (and/or footer) that appears at the top (and/or bottom) of every page. The pull-down list boxes let you choose from several preformatted entries, or alternatively, you can click the appropriate command button to customize either entry.

The Sheet tab in Figure 1.10d offers several additional options. The Gridlines option prints lines to separate the cells within the worksheet. The Row and Column Headings option displays the column letters and row numbers. Both options should be selected for most worksheets. Information about the additional entries can be obtained by clicking the Help button.

HANDS-ON EXERCISE 2

Modifying a Worksheet

Objective: To open an existing workbook; to insert and delete rows and columns in a worksheet; to print cell formulas and displayed values; to use the Page Setup command to modify the appearance of a printed workbook. Use Figure 1.11 as a guide in doing the exercise.

STEP 1: Open the Workbook

- Open the grade book as you did in the previous exercise. Pull down the **File menu** and click **Open** (or click the **Open button** on the Standard toolbar) to display the Open dialog box.
- Click the **drop-down arrow** on the Look In list box. Click the appropriate drive, drive C or drive A, depending on the location of your data. Double click the **Exploring Excel folder** to make it the active folder (the folder in which you will save the workbook).
- Click the **down scroll arrow** until you can select (click) the **Grade Book** workbook. Click the **Open button** to open the workbook and begin the exercise.

THE MOST RECENTLY OPENED FILE LIST

The easiest way to open a recently used workbook is to select the workbook directly from the File menu. Pull down the File menu, but instead of clicking the Open command, check to see if the workbook appears on the list of the most recently opened workbooks located at the bottom of the menu. If it does, you can click the workbook name rather than having to make the appropriate selections through the Open dialog box.

STEP 2: The Save As Command

- Pull down the **File menu.** Click **Save As** to display the dialog box shown in Figure 1.11a.
- Enter **Finished Grade Book** as the name of the new workbook. (A filename may contain up to 255 characters. Spaces and commas are allowed in the filename.)
- Click the **Save button.** Press the **Esc key** or click the **Close button** if you see a Properties dialog box.
- There are now two identical copies of the file on disk: "Grade Book," which is the completed workbook from the previous exercise, and "Finished Grade Book," which you just created. The title bar shows the latter name, which is the workbook currently in memory.

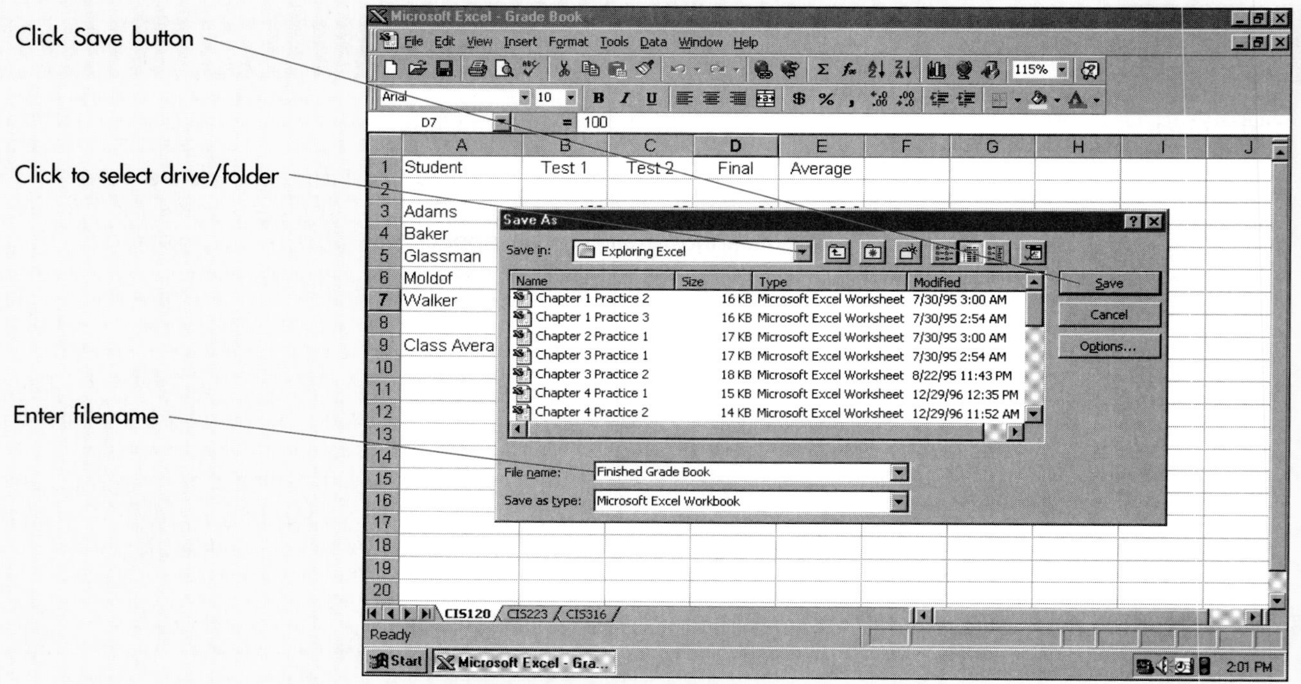

(a) Save As Command (step 2)

FIGURE 1.11 Hands-on Exercise 2

INCOMPATIBLE FILE TYPES

The file format for Excel 97 is incompatible with the format for Excel 95. The newer release (Excel 97) can open a workbook created in its predecessor (Excel 95), but the reverse is not true; that is, you cannot open a workbook created in Excel 97 in Excel 95. You can, however, maintain compatibility with the earlier version by using the Save As command to specify a dual file type (Microsoft Excel 97 & 5.0/95 format). (You will lose formatting features unique to Excel 97.)

STEP 3: Delete a Row

- Click any cell in **row 6** (the row you will delete). Pull down the **Edit menu.** Click **Delete** to display the dialog box in Figure 1.11b. Click **Entire Row.** Click **OK** to delete row 6.
- Moldof has disappeared from the grade book, and the class averages (now in row 8) have been updated automatically to reflect the fact that Moldof is gone.

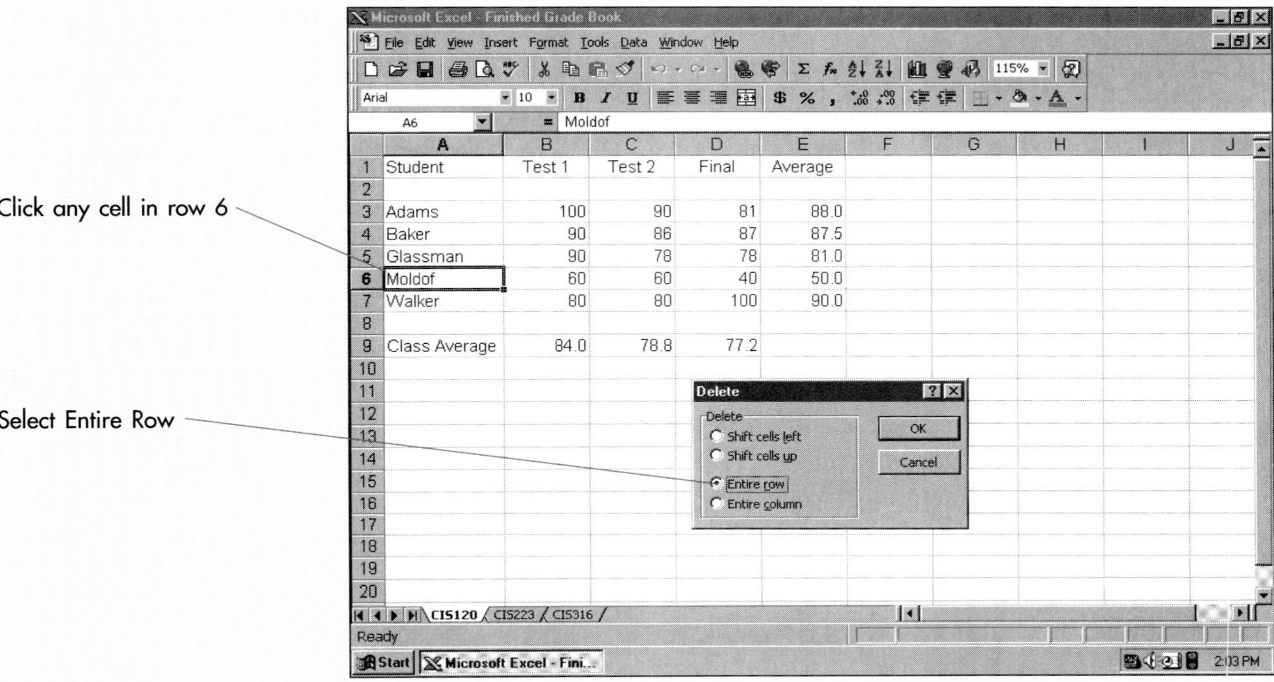

(b) Delete a Row (step 3)

FIGURE 1.11 Hands-on Exercise 2 (continued)

ERASING VERSUS DELETING

The Edit Delete command deletes the selected cell, row, or column from the worksheet. It is very different from the Edit Clear command, which erases the contents (and/or formatting) of the selected cells, but does not delete the cells from the worksheet. The Edit Delete command causes Excel to adjust cell references throughout the worksheet. The Edit Clear command does not adjust cell references as no cells are moved.

THE "WHAT'S THIS" BUTTON

Pull down the Help menu and click the What's This button command (or press the Shift+F1 key). Point to any button on any toolbar (the mouse pointer changes to an arrow with a question mark), then click the button to display a Help balloon to explain the function of that button. Press the Esc key to close the balloon and return the mouse pointer to normal.

STEP 4: The Undo Command

- ➤ Pull down the **Edit menu** and click **Undo Delete** (or click the **Undo button** on the Standard toolbar) to reverse the last command.
- ➤ The row for Moldof has been put back in the worksheet.
- ➤ Click any cell in **row 6,** and this time delete the entire row for good.

16 LEVELS OF UNDO

One of the best enhancements in Excel 97 is the multiple-level Undo command. Excel now enables you to reverse the last 16 changes to a workbook (as opposed to a single change in Excel 95). Click the drop-down arrow next to the Undo button to produce a list of your previous actions, then click the action you want to undo, which also undoes all of the preceding commands. Undoing the fifth command in the list, for example, will also undo the preceding four commands.

STEP 5: Insert a Row

- ➤ Click any cell in **row 5** (the row containing Glassman's grades).
- ➤ Pull down the **Insert menu.** Click **Rows** to add a new row above the current row. Row 5 is now blank (it is the newly inserted row), and Glassman (who was in row 5) is now in row 6.
- ➤ Enter the data for the new student in row 5 as shown in Figure 1.11c:
  - Click in **cell A5.** Type **Coulter.** Press the **right arrow key** or click in **cell B5.**
  - Type **85.** Press the **right arrow key** or click in **cell C5.**
  - Type **95.** Press the **right arrow key** or click in **cell D5.**
  - Type **100.** Press the **right arrow key** or click in **cell E5.**
  - Enter the formula to compute the semester average, **=(B5+C5+2*D5)/4.** Be sure to begin the formula with an equal sign. Press **enter.**
  - Click the **Save button** on the Standard toolbar, or pull down the **File menu** and click **Save** to save the changes made to this point.

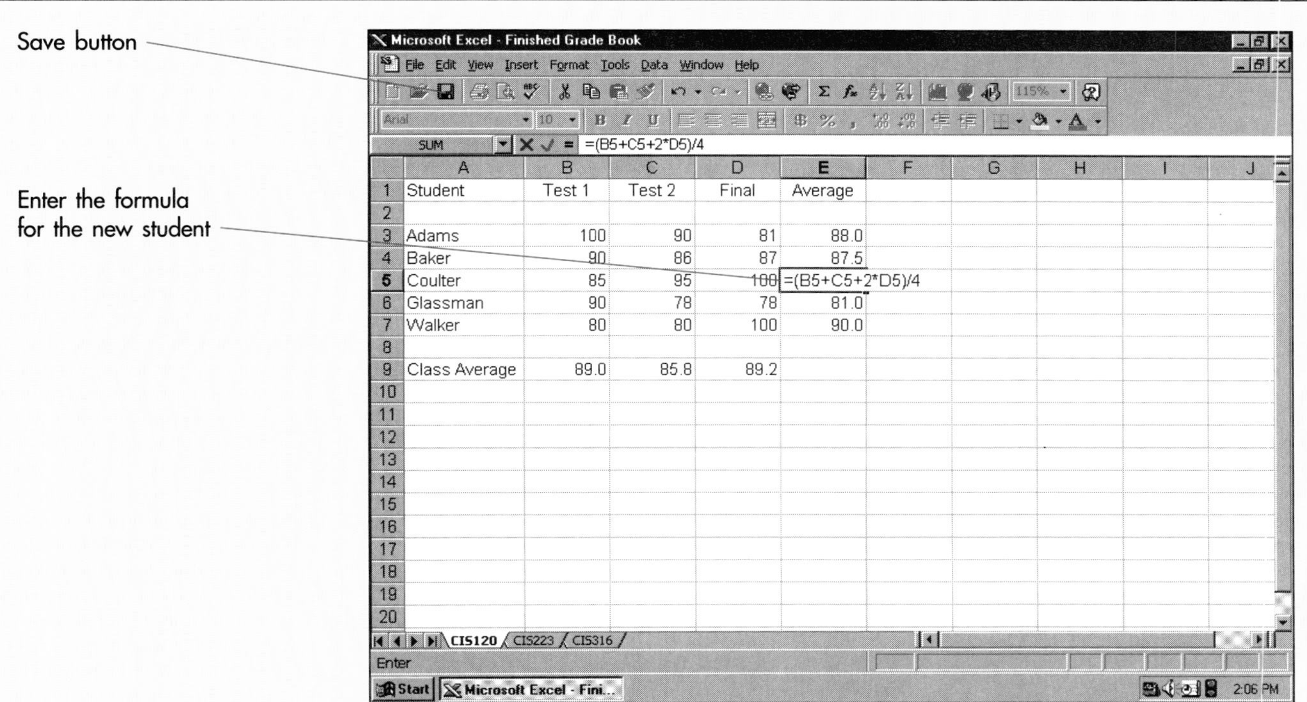

(c) Insert a Row (step 5)

FIGURE 1.11 Hands-on Exercise 2 (continued)

INSERTING (DELETING) ROWS AND COLUMNS

The fastest way to insert or delete a row is to point to the row number, then click the right mouse button to simultaneously select the row and display a shortcut menu. Click Insert to add a row above the selected row, or click Delete to delete the selected row. Use a similar technique to insert or delete a column, by pointing to the column heading, then clicking the right mouse button to display a shortcut menu from which you can select the appropriate command.

STEP 6: Insert a Second Row

- Point to the row heading for **row 6** (which now contains Glassman's grades), then click the **right mouse button** to select the row and display a shortcut menu. Click **Insert** to insert a new row 6, which moves Glassman to row 7.
- Click in **cell A6.** Type **C,** the first letter in "Courier," which also happens to be the first letter in "Coulter," a previous entry in column A. If the AutoComplete feature is on (see boxed tip), Coulter's name will be automatically inserted in cell A6 with "oulter" selected. Type **ourier** (the remaining letters in "Courier," which replace "oulter."
- Enter Courier's grades in the appropriate cells (75, 75, and 85 in cells B6, C6, and D6, respectively).

- ➤ Click in **cell E6.** Enter the formula to compute the semester average, **=(B6+C6+2*D6)/4.** Press **enter.**
- ➤ Save the workbook.

> ## AUTOCOMPLETE
>
> The ***AutoComplete*** feature is Excel's way of trying to speed data entry. As soon as you begin typing a label into a cell, Excel searches for and (automatically) displays any other label in that column that matches the letters you typed. It's handy if you want to repeat a label, but it can be distracting if you want to enter a different label that just happens to begin with the same letter. To turn the feature on (off), pull down the Tools menu, click Options, then click the Edit tab. Check (clear) the box to enable the AutoComplete feature.

STEP 7: Insert a Column

- ➤ Point to the column heading for column B, then click the **right mouse button** to display a shortcut menu as shown in Figure 1.11d.
- ➤ Click **Insert** to insert a new column, which becomes the new column B. All existing columns have been moved to the right.

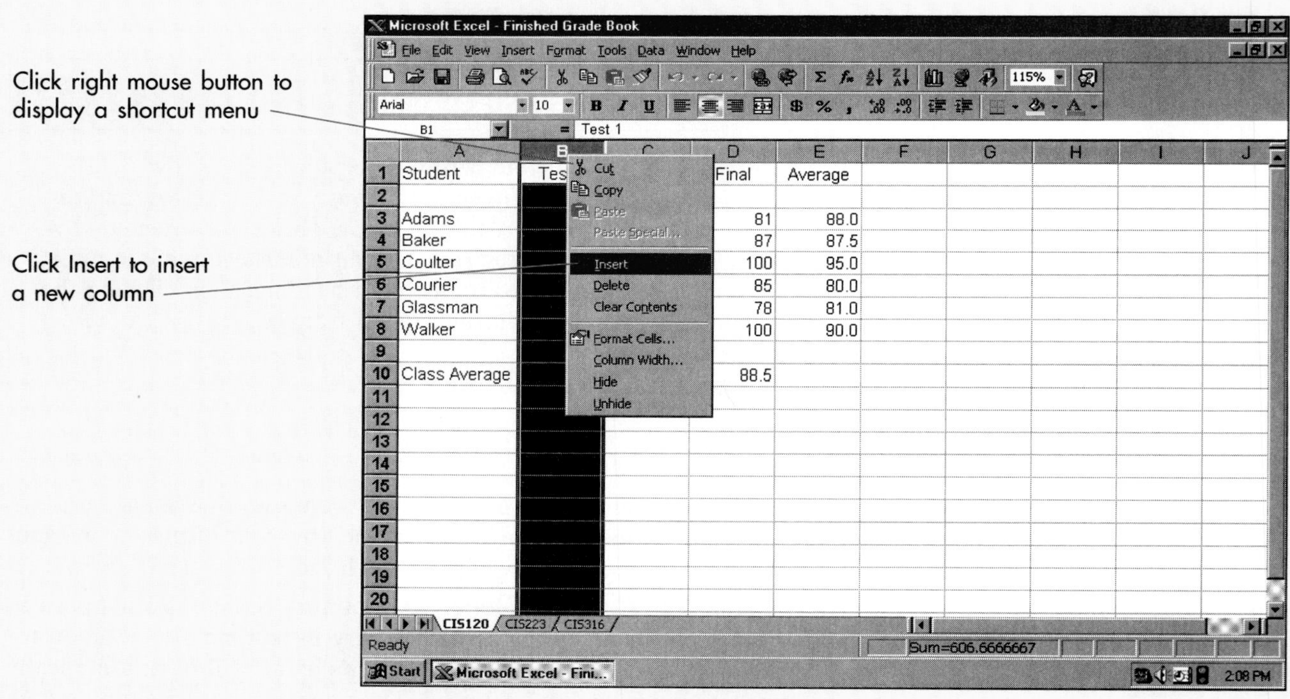

(d) Insert a Column (step 7)

FIGURE 1.11 Hands-on Exercise 2 (continued)

- Click in **cell B1.** Type **Major.**
- Click in **cell B3.** Enter **CIS** as Adams's major. Press the **down arrow** to move automatically to the major for the next student.
- Type **MKT** in cell B4. Press the **down arrow.** Type **ACC** in cell B5. Press the **down arrow.** Type **FIN** in cell B6.
- Press the **down arrow** to move to cell B7. Type **C** (AutoComplete will automatically enter "IS" to complete the entry). Press the **down arrow** to move to cell B8. Type **C** (the AutoComplete feature again enters "IS"), then press **enter** to complete the entry.
- Save the workbook.

THE RIGHT MOUSE BUTTON

Point to any object in a worksheet—a cell, a row or column heading, a worksheet tab, or a toolbar—then click the right mouse button to display a context-sensitive menu with commands appropriate to the object you are pointing to. Click the left mouse button to select a command from the menu, or press the Esc key (or click outside the menu) to close the menu without executing a command.

STEP 8: Display the Cell Formulas

- Pull down the **Tools menu.** Click **Options** to display the Options dialog box. Click the **View tab.** Check the box for **Formulas.** Click **OK.**
- The worksheet should display the cell formulas as shown in Figure 1.11e. If necessary, click the **right scroll arrow** on the horizontal scroll bar until column F, the column containing the formulas to compute the semester averages, comes into view.
- If necessary (i.e., if the formulas are not completely visible), double click the border between the column headings for columns F and G. This increases the width of column F to accommodate the widest entry in that column.

DISPLAY CELL FORMULAS

A worksheet should always be printed twice, once to show the computed results, and once to show the cell formulas. The fastest way to toggle (switch) between cell formulas and displayed values is to use the Ctrl+` keyboard shortcut. (The ` is on the same key as the ~ at the upper left of the keyboard.) Press Ctrl+` to switch from displayed values to cell formulas. Press Ctrl+` a second time and you are back to the displayed values.

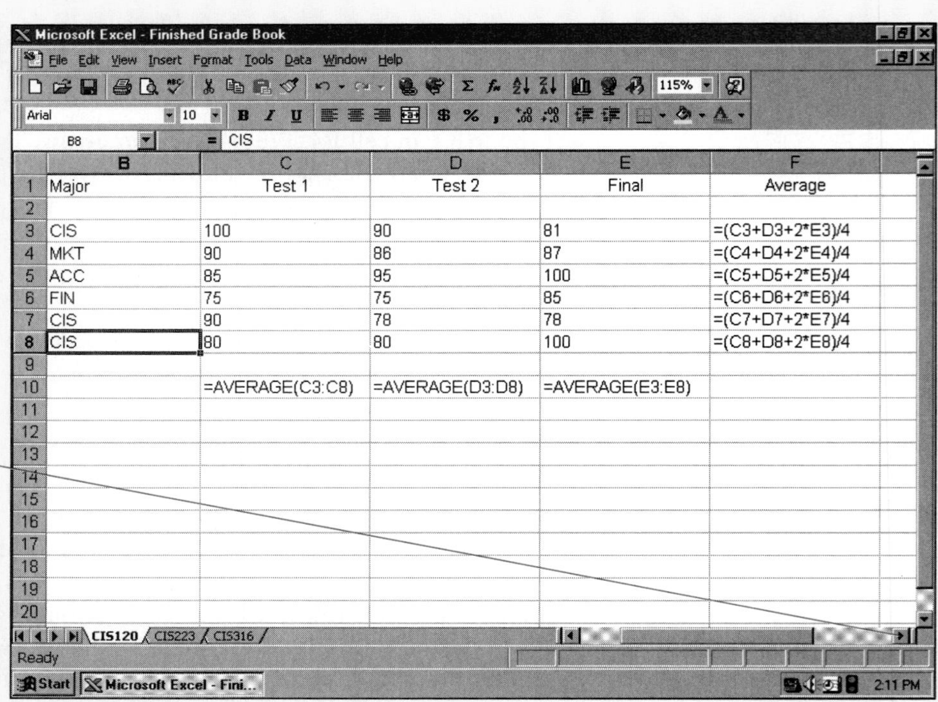

(e) Display the Cell Formulas (step 8)

FIGURE 1.11 Hands-on Exercise 2 (continued)

STEP 9: The Page Setup Command

➤ Pull down the **File menu.** Click the **Page Setup command** to display the Page Setup dialog box as shown in Figure 1.11f.

- Click the **Page tab.** Click the **Landscape option button.** Click the option button to **Fit to 1 page.**
- Click the **Margins tab.** Check the box to center the worksheet horizontally.
- Click the **Header/Footer tab.** Click the **drop-down arrow** on the Footer list box. Scroll to the top of the list and click **(none)** to remove the footer.
- Click the **Sheet tab.** Check the boxes to print Row and Column Headings and Gridlines.

➤ Click **OK** to exit the Page Setup dialog box. Save the workbook.

> **KEYBOARD SHORTCUTS—THE DIALOG BOX**
>
> Press Tab or Shift+Tab to move forward (backward) between fields in a dialog box, or press the Alt key plus the underlined letter to move directly to an option. Use the space bar to toggle check boxes on or off and the up (down) arrow keys to move between options in a list box. Press enter to activate the highlighted command button and Esc to exit the dialog box without accepting the changes.

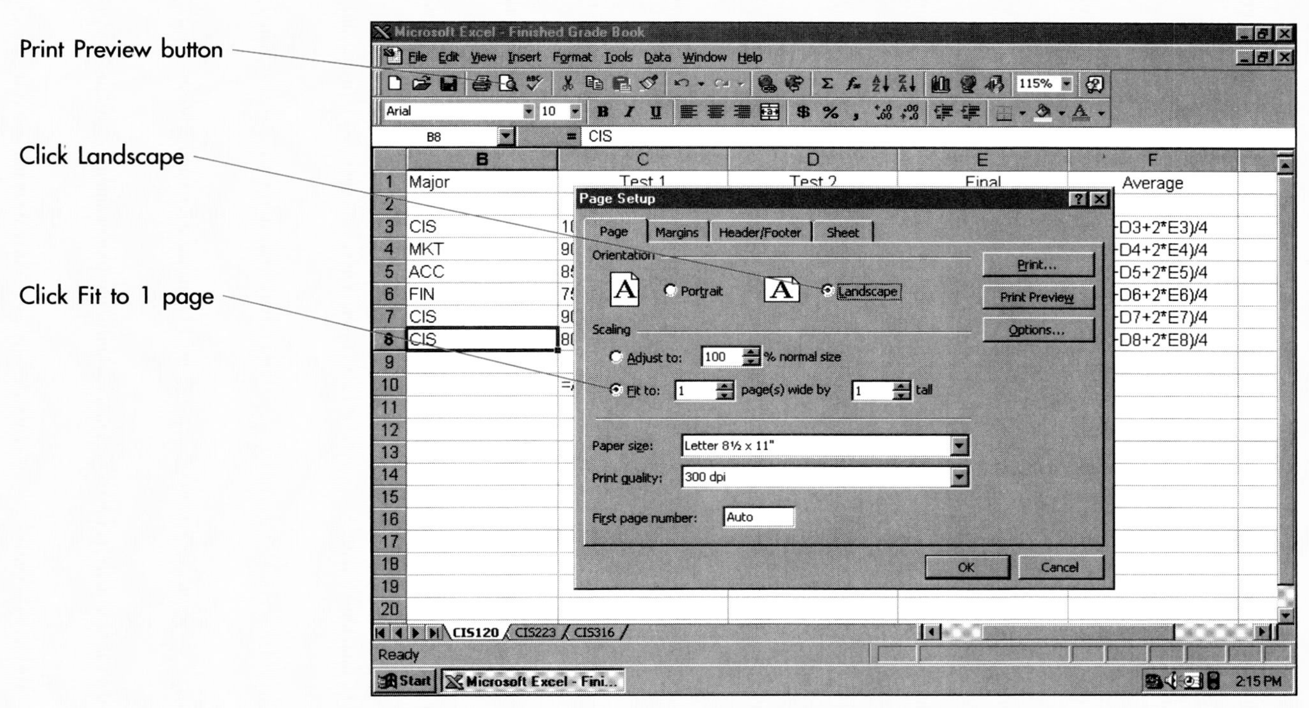

(f) The Page Setup Command (step 9)

FIGURE 1.11 Hands-on Exercise 2 (continued)

STEP 10: The Print Preview Command

- Pull down the **File menu** and click **Print Preview** (or click the **Print Preview button** on the Standard toolbar). Your monitor should match the display in Figure 1.11g.
- Click the **Print command button** to display the Print dialog box, then click **OK** to print the worksheet.
- Press **Ctrl+`** to switch to displayed values rather than cell formulas. Click the **Print button** on the Standard toolbar to print the worksheet without displaying the Print dialog box.
- Pull down the **File menu.** Click **Exit** to leave Excel. Click **Yes** if asked to save the workbook.

TIPS FROM THE OFFICE ASSISTANT

The Office Assistant indicates it has a suggestion by displaying a lightbulb. Click the lightbulb to display the tip, then click the Back or Next buttons as appropriate to view additional tips. The Assistant will not, however, repeat a tip from an earlier session unless you reset it at the start of a new session. This is especially important in a laboratory situation where you are sharing a computer with many students. To reset the tips, click the Assistant to display a balloon asking what you want to do, click the Options button in the balloon, click Options, then click the button to Reset My Tips.

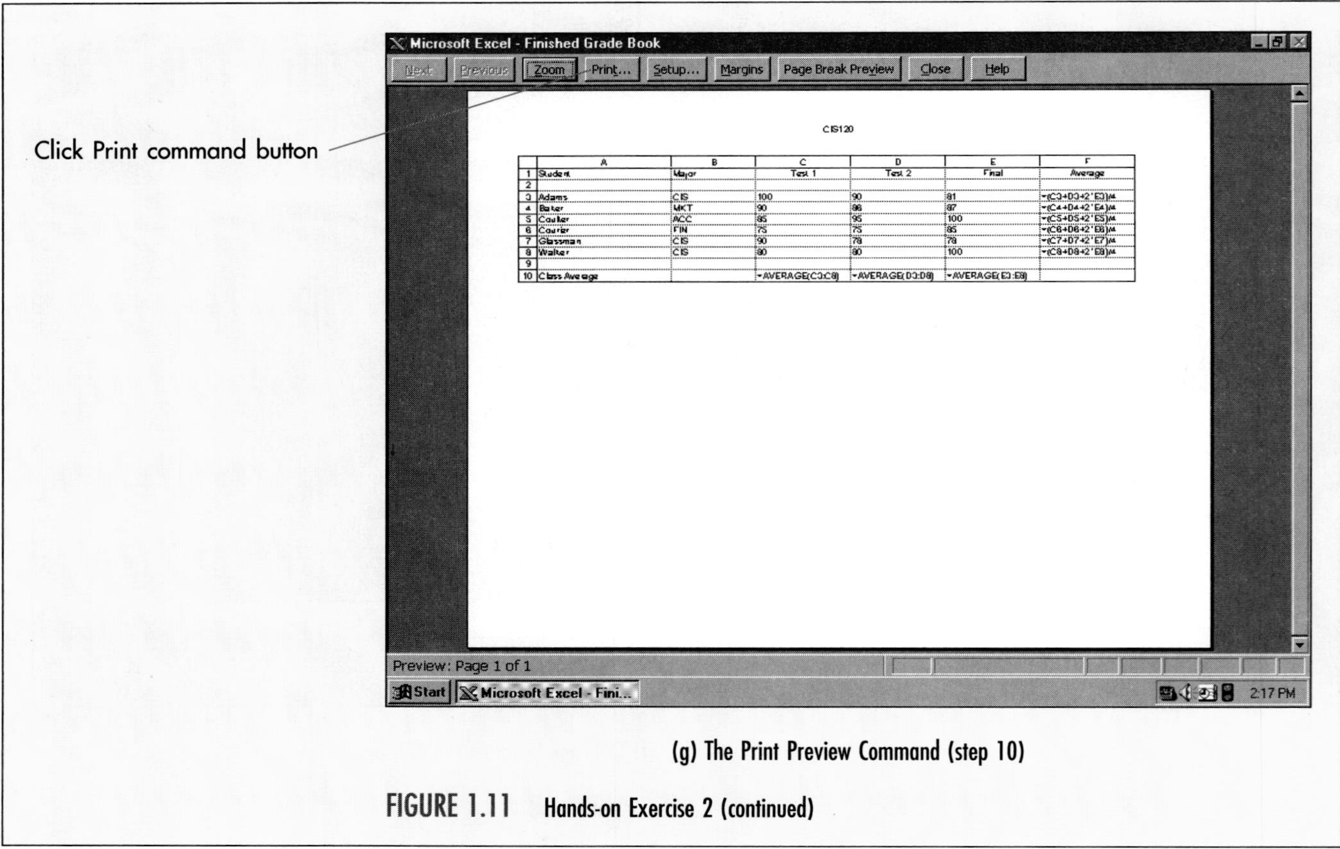

(g) The Print Preview Command (step 10)

FIGURE 1.11 Hands-on Exercise 2 (continued)

SUMMARY

A spreadsheet is the computerized equivalent of an accountant's ledger. It is divided into rows and columns, with each row and column assigned a heading. The intersection of a row and column forms a cell.

Spreadsheet is a generic term. Workbook and worksheet are Excel specific. An Excel workbook contains one or more worksheets.

Every cell in a worksheet (spreadsheet) contains either a formula or a constant. A formula begins with an equal sign; a constant does not. A constant is an entry that does not change and may be numeric or descriptive text. A formula is a combination of numeric constants, cell references, arithmetic operators, and/or functions that produces a new value from existing values.

The Insert and Delete commands add or remove rows or columns from a worksheet. The Open command brings a workbook from disk into memory. The Save command copies the workbook in memory to disk.

The Page Setup command provides complete control over the printed page, enabling you to print a worksheet with or without gridlines or row and column headings. The Page Setup command also controls margins, headers and footers, centering, and orientation. The Print Preview command shows the worksheet as it will print and should be used prior to printing.

A worksheet should always be printed twice, once with displayed values and once with cell formulas. The latter is an important tool in checking the accuracy of a worksheet, which is far more important than its appearance.

KEY WORDS AND CONCEPTS

Active cell
AutoComplete
AVERAGE function
Cell
Cell contents
Cell reference
Close command
Constant
Delete command
Exit command
File menu
Formatting toolbar
Formula
Formula bar
Function
Insert command
Landscape orientation
Name box
Office Assistant
Open command
Page Setup command
Portrait orientation
Print command
Print Preview command
Save command
ScreenTip
Spreadsheet
Standard toolbar
Status bar
Text box
Toolbar
Undo command
Value
Workbook
Worksheet

MULTIPLE CHOICE

1. Which of the following is true?
(a) A worksheet contains one or more workbooks
(b) A workbook contains one or more worksheets
(c) A spreadsheet contains one or more worksheets
(d) A worksheet contains one or more spreadsheets

2. A worksheet is superior to manual calculation because:
(a) The worksheet computes its entries faster
(b) The worksheet computes its results more accurately
(c) The worksheet recalculates its results whenever cell contents are changed
(d) All of the above

3. The cell at the intersection of the second column and third row has the cell reference:
(a) B3
(b) 3B
(c) C2
(d) 2C

4. A right-handed person will normally:
(a) Click the right and left mouse button to access a pull-down menu and shortcut menu, respectively
(b) Click the left and right mouse button to access a pull-down menu and shortcut menu, respectively
(c) Click the left mouse button to access both a pull-down menu and a shortcut menu
(d) Click the right mouse button to access both a pull-down menu and a shortcut menu

5. What is the effect of typing F5+F6 into a cell without a beginning equal sign?
   (a) The entry is equivalent to the formula =F5+F6
   (b) The cell will display the contents of cell F5 plus cell F6
   (c) The entry will be treated as a text entry and display F5+F6 in the cell
   (d) The entry will be rejected by Excel, which will signal an error message
6. The Open command:
   (a) Brings a workbook from disk into memory
   (b) Brings a workbook from disk into memory, then erases the workbook on disk
   (c) Stores the workbook in memory on disk
   (d) Stores the workbook in memory on disk, then erases the workbook from memory
7. The Save command:
   (a) Brings a workbook from disk into memory
   (b) Brings a workbook from disk into memory, then erases the workbook on disk
   (c) Stores the workbook in memory on disk
   (d) Stores the workbook in memory on disk, then erases the workbook from memory
8. How do you open an Excel workbook?
   (a) Pull down the File menu and click the Open command
   (b) Click the Open button on the Standard toolbar
   (c) Either (a) or (b)
   (d) Neither (a) nor (b)
9. In the absence of parentheses, the order of operation is:
   (a) Exponentiation, addition or subtraction, multiplication or division
   (b) Addition or subtraction, multiplication or division, exponentiation
   (c) Multiplication or division, exponentiation, addition or subtraction
   (d) Exponentiation, multiplication or division, addition or subtraction
10. Given that cells A1, A2, and A3 contain the values 10, 20, and 40, respectively, what value will be displayed in a cell containing the cell formula =A1/A2*A3+1?
    (a) 1.125
    (b) 21
    (c) 20.125
    (d) Impossible to determine
11. The entry =AVERAGE(A4:A6):
    (a) Is invalid because the cells are not contiguous
    (b) Computes the average of cells A4 and A6
    (c) Computes the average of cells A4, A5, and A6
    (d) None of the above
12. Which of the following was suggested with respect to printing a workbook?
    (a) Print the displayed values only
    (b) Print the cell formulas only
    (c) Print both the displayed values and cell formulas
    (d) Print neither the displayed values nor the cell formulas

13. Which of the following is true regarding a printed worksheet?
    (a) It may be printed with or without the row and column headings
    (b) It may be printed with or without the gridlines
    (c) Both (a) and (b) above
    (d) Neither (a) nor (b)

14. Which options are mutually exclusive in the Page Setup menu?
    (a) Portrait and landscape orientation
    (b) Cell gridlines and row and column headings
    (c) Headers and footers
    (d) Left and right margins

15. Which of the following is controlled by the Page Setup command?
    (a) Headers and footers
    (b) Margins
    (c) Orientation
    (d) All of the above

ANSWERS

1. b	**6.** a	**11.** c
2. d	**7.** c	**12.** c
3. a	**8.** c	**13.** c
4. b	**9.** d	**14.** a
5. c	**10.** b	**15.** d

PRACTICE WITH EXCEL 97

1. Your professor is very impressed with the way you did the hands-on exercises in the chapter and has hired you as his grading assistant to handle all of his classes this semester. He would like you to take the Finished Grade Book that you used in the chapter, and save it as *Chapter 1 Practice 1 Solution.* Make the following changes in the new workbook:
    a. Click the worksheet tab for CIS120. Add Milgrom as a new student majoring in Finance with grades of 88, 80, and 84, respectively. Delete Baker. Be sure that the class averages adjust automatically for the insertion and deletion of these students.
    b. Click the worksheet tab for CIS223. Enter the formulas to compute the class averages on all tests as well as each student's semester average. All tests count equally.
    c. Click the worksheet tab for CIS316 to move to this worksheet. Insert a new column for the Final, then enter the following grades for the students in this class (Bippen, 90; Freeman, 75; Manni, 84; Peck, 93; Tanney, 87).
    d. Enter the formulas to compute the semester average for each student in the class. (Tests 1, 2, and 3 each count 20%. The final counts 40%.)
    e. Enter the formulas to compute the class average on each test and the final.
    f. Enter the label *Grading Assistant* followed by your name on each worksheet. Print the entire workbook and submit all three pages of the printout to your instructor as proof that you did this exercise.

2. The worksheet in Figure 1.12 displays last week's sales from the Exotic Gardens Nurseries. There are four locations, each of which divides its sales into three general areas.
   a. Open the partially completed *Chapter 1 Practice 2* workbook on the data disk. Save the workbook as *Finished Chapter 1 Practice 2.*
   b. Enter the appropriate formulas in row 5 of the worksheet to compute the total sales for each location. Use the SUM function to compute the total for each location; for example, type =SUM(B2:B4) in cell B5 (as opposed to =B2+B3+B4) to compute the total sales for the Las Olas location.
   c. Insert a new row 4 for a new category of product. Type *Insecticides* in cell A4, and enter $1,000 for each store in this category. The total sales for each store should adjust automatically to include the additional business.
   d. Enter the appropriate formulas in column F of the worksheet to compute the total sales for each category.
   e. Delete column D, the column containing the sales for the Galleria location. Check to be sure that the totals for each product adjust automatically.
   f. Add your name somewhere in the worksheet as the bookkeeper.
   g. Print the completed worksheet two times, to show both displayed values and cell formulas. Submit both pages to your instructor.

	A	B	C		E	F
1		Las Olas	Coral Gables	Galleria	Miracle Mile	Total
2	Indoor Plants	1,500	3,000	4,500	800	
3	Accessories	350	725	1,200	128	
4	Landscaping	3,750	7,300	12,000	1,500	
5	Total					
6						
7						
8						

FIGURE 1.12 Spreadsheet for Practice Exercise 2

3. Formatting is not covered until Chapter 2, but we think you are ready to try your hand at basic formatting now. Most formatting operations are done in the context of select-then-do. You select the cell or cells you want to format, then you execute the appropriate formatting command, most easily by clicking the appropriate button on the Formatting toolbar. The function of each button should be apparent from its icon, but you can simply point to a button to display a ScreenTip that is indicative of the button's function.

   Open the unformatted version of the *Chapter 1 Practice 3* workbook on the data disk, and save it as *Chapter 1 Practice 3 Solution.* Add a new row 6 and enter data for Hume Hall as shown in Figure 1.13. Format the

Residential Colleges						
	Freshmen	***Sophomores***	***Juniors***	***Seniors***	***Graduates***	***Totals***
Broward Hall	176	143	77	29	13	438
Graham Hall	375	112	37	23	7	554
Hume Hall	212	108	45	43	12	420
Jennings Hall	89	54	23	46	23	235
Rawlings Hall	75	167	93	145	43	523
Tolbert Hall	172	102	26	17	22	339
Totals	1099	686	301	303	120	2509

FIGURE 1.13 Spreadsheet for Practice Exercise 3

remainder of the worksheet so that it matches the completed worksheet in Figure 1.13. Add your name in bold italics somewhere in the worksheet as the Residence Hall Coordinator, then print the completed worksheet and submit it to your instructor.

4. Create a worksheet that shows your income and expenses for a typical semester according to the format in Figure 1.14. Enter your budget rather than ours by entering your name in cell A1.
   a. Enter at least five different expenses in consecutive rows, beginning in A6, and enter the corresponding amounts in column B.
   b. Enter the text *Total Expenses* in the row immediately below your last expense item and then enter the formula to compute the total in the corresponding cells in columns B through E.
   c. Skip one blank row and then enter the text *What's Left For Fun* in column A and the formula to compute how much money you have left at the end of the month in columns B through E.
   d. Insert a new row 8. Add an additional expense that you left out, entering the text in A8 and the amount in cells B8 through E8. Do the formulas for total expenses reflect the additional expense? If not, change the formulas so they adjust automatically.
   e. Save the workbook as *Chapter 1 Practice 4 Solution.* Center the worksheet horizontally, then print the worksheet two ways, to show cell formulas and displayed values. Submit both printed pages to your instructor.

	A	B	C	D	E
1	**Maryann Barber's Budget**				
2		**Sept**	**Oct**	**Nov**	**Dec**
3	**Monthly Income**	$1,000	$1,000	$1,000	$1,400
4					
5	**Monthly Expenses**				
6	**Food**	$250	$250	$250	$250
7	**Rent**	$350	$350	$350	$350
8	**Cable**	$40	$40	$40	$40
9	**Utilities**	$100	$100	$125	$140
10	**Phone**	$30	$30	$30	$20
11	**Gas**	$40	$40	$40	$75
12	**Total Expenses**	$810	$810	$835	$875
13					
14	**What's Left for Fun**	$190	$190	$165	$525

FIGURE 1.14 Spreadsheet for Practice Exercise 4

CASE STUDIES

Buying a Computer

You have decided to buy a PC and have settled on a minimum configuration consisting of an entry-level Pentium, with 16MB of RAM, a CD-ROM, a 2GB hard disk, a 15-inch monitor, and a 28,800 bps modem. You also need a printer and Microsoft Office 97. You can spend up to $2,500 and hope that at today's prices, you can find a system that goes beyond your minimum requirements.

Create a spreadsheet based on real data that presents several alternatives. Show different configurations from the same vendor and/or comparable systems from different vendors. Include the vendor's telephone number with its estimate. Bring the spreadsheet to class, together with the supporting documentation in the form of printed advertisements. The best place to obtain current information is the Web. Go to www.bus.miami.edu/~rgrauer and click the link to Buying a Computer.

Portfolio Management

A spreadsheet is an ideal vehicle to track the progress of your investments. You need to maintain the name of the company, the number of shares purchased, the date of the purchase, and the purchase price. You can then enter the current price and see immediately the potential gain or loss on each investment as well as the current value of the portfolio. Retrieve the *Wishful Thinking Portfolio* workbook from the data disk, enter the closing prices of the listed investments, and compute the current value of the portfolio.

There are many sites on the Web where you can obtain the current price of each stock listed in the *Wishful Thinking Portfolio* workbook. Try starting at investor.msn.com or use your favorite search engine to locate a different site.

Accuracy Counts

The *Underbid* workbook on the data disk was the last assignment completed by your predecessor prior to his unfortunate dismissal. The worksheet contains a significant error, which caused your company to underbid a contract and assume a subsequent loss of $100,000. As you look for the error, don't be distracted by the attractive formatting. The shading, lines, and other touches are nice, but accuracy is more important than anything else. Write a memo to your instructor describing the nature of the error. Include suggestions in the memo on how to avoid similar mistakes in the future.

Microsoft Online

Help for Microsoft Excel is available from a variety of sources. You can consult the Office Assistant or you can pull down the Help menu to display the Help Contents and Index. Both techniques were illustrated in the chapter. In addition, you can go to the Microsoft Web site to obtain more recent, and often more detailed, information. You will find answers to the most frequently asked questions and you can access the same Knowledge Base used by Microsoft support engineers. Experiment with various sources of help, then submit a summary of your findings to your instructor. Try to differentiate between the various techniques and suggest the most appropriate use for each.

2

GAINING PROFICIENCY: COPYING, FORMATTING, AND ISOLATING ASSUMPTIONS

OBJECTIVES

After reading this chapter you will be able to:

1. Explain the importance of isolating assumptions within a worksheet.
2. Define a cell range; select and deselect ranges within a worksheet.
3. Copy and/or move cells within a worksheet; differentiate between relative, absolute, and mixed addresses.
4. Format a worksheet to include boldface, italics, shading, and borders; change the font and/or alignment of a selected entry.
5. Change the width of a column; explain what happens if a column is too narrow to display the computed result.
6. Describe in general terms the steps to build a worksheet for a financial forecast.

OVERVIEW

This chapter continues the grade book example of Chapter 1. It is perhaps the most important chapter in the entire text as it describes the basic commands to create a worksheet. We begin with the definition of a cell range and the commands to build a worksheet without regard to its appearance. We focus on the Copy command and the difference between relative and absolute addresses. We stress the importance of isolating the assumptions within a worksheet so that alternative strategies may be easily evaluated.

The second half of the chapter presents formatting commands to improve the appearance of a worksheet after it has been created. You will be pleased with the dramatic impact you can achieve with a few simple commands, but we emphasize that accuracy in a worksheet is much more important than appearance.

The hands-on exercises are absolutely critical if you are to master the material. As you do the exercises, you will realize that there are many different ways to accomplish the same task. Our approach is to present the most basic way first and the shortcuts later. You will like the shortcuts better, but you may not remember them all. Do not be concerned because it is much more important to understand the underlying concepts. You can always find the necessary command from the appropriate menu, and if you don't know which menu, you can always look to online help.

A BETTER GRADE BOOK

Figure 2.1 contains a much improved version of the professor's grade book over the one from the previous chapter. The most obvious difference is in the appearance of the worksheet, as a variety of formatting commands have been used to make it more attractive. The exam scores and semester averages are centered under the appropriate headings. The exam weights are formatted with percentages, and all averages are displayed with exactly one decimal point. Boldface and italics are used for emphasis. Shading and borders are used to highlight various areas of the worksheet. The title has been centered over the worksheet and is set in a larger typeface.

The most *significant* differences, however, are that the weight of each exam is indicated within the worksheet, and that the formulas to compute the students' semester averages reference these cells in their calculations. The professor can change the contents of the cells containing the exam weights and see immediately the effect on the student averages.

The isolation of cells whose values are subject to change is one of the most important concepts in the development of a spreadsheet. This technique lets the professor explore alternative grading strategies. He or she may notice, for example, that the class did significantly better on the final than on either of the first two exams. The professor may then decide to give the class a break and increase the weight of the final relative to the other tests. But before the professor says anything to the class, he or she wants to know the effect of increasing the weight of the final to 60%. What if the final should count 70%? The effect of these and other changes can be seen immediately by entering the new exam weights in the appropriate cells at the bottom of the worksheet.

Title is centered and in a larger typeface

Boldface, italics, shading, and borders are used for emphasis

Exam scores are centered

Exam weights are used to calculate the students' semester averages

	A	B	C	D	E
1		***CIS 120 - Spring 1997***			
2					
3	***Student***	***Test 1***	***Test 2***	***Final***	***Average***
4	Costa, Frank	70	80	90	82.5
5	Ford, Judd	70	85	80	78.8
6	Grauer, Jessica	90	80	98	91.5
7	Howard, Lauren	80	78	98	88.5
8	Krein, Darren	85	70	95	86.3
9	Moldof, Adam	75	75	80	77.5
10					
11	***Class Averages***	***78.3***	***78.0***	***90.2***	
12					
13	***Exam Weights***	***25%***	***25%***	***50%***	

FIGURE 2.1 A Better Grade Book

CELL RANGES

Every command in Excel operates on a rectangular group of cells known as a ***range***. A range may be as small as a single cell or as large as the entire worksheet. It may consist of a row or part of a row, a column or part of a column, or multiple rows and/or columns. The cells within a range are specified by indicating the diagonally opposite corners, typically the upper-left and lower-right corners of the rectangle. Many different ranges could be selected in conjunction with the worksheet of Figure 2.1. The exam weights, for example, are found in the range B13:D13. The students' semester averages are found in the range E4:E9. The student data is contained in the range A4:E9.

The easiest way to select a range is to click and drag—click at the beginning of the range, then press and hold the left mouse button as you drag the mouse to the end of the range where you release the mouse. Once selected, the range is highlighted and its cells will be affected by any subsequent command. The range remains selected until another range is defined or until you click another cell anywhere on the worksheet.

COPY COMMAND

The ***Copy command*** duplicates the contents of a cell, or range of cells, and saves you from having to enter the contents of every cell individually. It is much easier, for example, to enter the formula to compute the class average once (for test 1), then copy it to obtain the average for the remaining tests, rather than explicitly entering the formula for every test.

Figure 2.2 illustrates how the Copy command can be used to duplicate the formula to compute the class average. The cell(s) that you are copying from, cell B11, is called the ***source range.*** The cells that you are copying to, cells C11 and D11, are the ***destination*** (or target) ***range***. The formula is not copied exactly, but is adjusted as it is copied, to compute the average for the pertinent test.

The formula to compute the average on the first test was entered in cell B11 as =AVERAGE(B4:B9). The range in the formula references the cell seven rows above the cell containing the formula (i.e., cell B4 is seven rows above cell B11) as well as the cell two rows above the formula (i.e., cell B9). When the formula in cell B11 is copied to C11, it is adjusted so that the cells referenced in the new formula are in the same relative position as those in the original formula; that is, seven and two rows above the formula itself. Thus, the formula in cell C11

	A	B	C	D	E
1	CIS 120 - Spring 1997				
2					
3	Student	Test 1	Test 2	Final	Average
4	Costa, Frank	70	80	90	=$B$13*B4+$C$13*C4+$D$13*D4
5	Ford, Judd	70	85	80	=$B$13*B5+$C$13*C5+$D$13*D5
6	Grauer, Jessica	90	80	98	=$B$13*B6+$C$13*C6+$D$13*D6
7	Howard, Lauren	80	78	98	=$B$13*B7+$C$13*C7+$D$13*D7
8	Krein, Darren	85	70	95	=$B$13*B8+$C$13*C8+$D$13*D8
9	Moldof, Adam	75	75	80	=$B$13*B9+$C$13*C9+$D$13*D9
10					
11	Class Averages	=AVERAGE(B4:B9)	=AVERAGE(C4:C9)	=AVERAGE(D4:D9)	
12					
13	Exam Weights	25%	25%	50%	

FIGURE 2.2 The Copy Command

becomes =AVERAGE(C4:C9). In similar fashion, the formula in cell D11 becomes =AVERAGE(D4:D9).

Figure 2.2 also illustrates how the Copy command is used to copy the formula for a student's semester average, from cell E4 (the source range) to cells E5 through E9 (the destination range). This is slightly more complicated than the previous example because the formula is based on a student's grades, which vary from one student to the next, and on the exam weights, which do not. The cells referring to the student's grades should adjust as the formula is copied, but the addresses referencing the exam weights should not.

The distinction between cell references that remain constant versus cell addresses that change is made by means of a dollar sign. An ***absolute reference*** remains constant throughout the copy operation and is specified with a dollar sign in front of the column and row designation, for example, $B$13. A ***relative reference***, on the other hand, adjusts during a copy operation and is specified without dollar signs; for example, B4. (A ***mixed reference*** uses a single dollar sign to make the column absolute and the row relative; for example, $A5. Alternatively, you can make the column relative and the row absolute as in A$5.)

Consider, for example, the formula to compute a student's semester average as it appears in cell E4 of Figure 2.2:

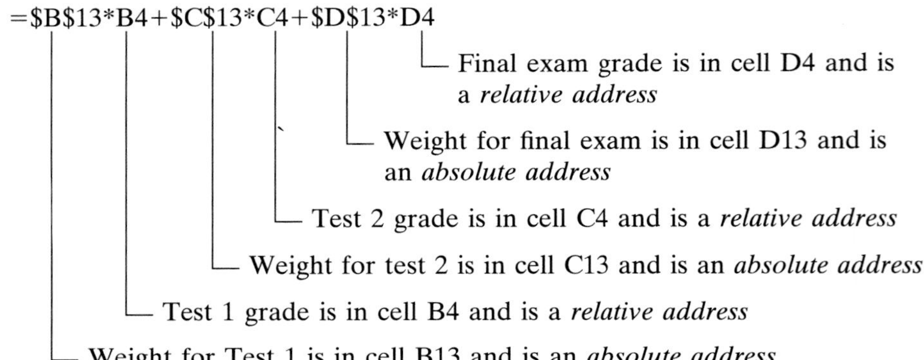
=$B$13*B4+$C$13*C4+$D$13*D4
Final exam grade is in cell D4 and is a relative address
Weight for final exam is in cell D13 and is an absolute address
Test 2 grade is in cell C4 and is a relative address
Weight for test 2 is in cell C13 and is an absolute address
Test 1 grade is in cell B4 and is a relative address
Weight for Test 1 is in cell B13 and is an absolute address

The formula in cell E4 uses a combination of relative and absolute addresses to compute the student's semester average. Relative addresses are used for the exam grades (found in cells B4, C4, and D4) and change automatically when the formula is copied to the other rows. Absolute addresses are used for the exam weights (found in cells B13, C13, and D13) and remain constant from student to student.

The copy operation is implemented by using the Windows ***clipboard*** and a combination of the ***Copy*** and ***Paste commands*** from the Edit menu. The contents of the source range are copied to the clipboard, from where they are pasted to the destination range. The contents of the clipboard are replaced with each subsequent Copy command but are unaffected by the Paste command. Thus, you can execute the Paste command several times in succession to paste the contents of the clipboard to multiple locations.

MIXED REFERENCES

Most spreadsheets can be developed using only absolute or relative references such as $A1$1 or A, respectively. Mixed references, where only the row ($A1) or column (A$1) changes, are more subtle, and thus are typically not used by beginners. Mixed references are necessary in more sophisticated worksheets and add significantly to the power of Excel. See practice exercise 4 at the end of the chapter.

The ***move operation*** is not used in the grade book, but its presentation is essential for the sake of completeness. The move operation transfers the contents of a cell (or range of cells) from one location to another. After the move is completed, the cells where the move originated (that is, the source range) are empty. This is in contrast to the Copy command, where the entries remain in the source range and are duplicated in the destination range.

A simple move operation is depicted in Figure 2.3a, in which the contents of cell A3 are moved to cell C3, with the formula in cell C3 unchanged after the move. In other words, the move operation simply picks up the contents of cell A3 (a formula that adds the values in cells A1 and A2) and puts it down in cell C3. The source range, cell A3, is empty after the move operation has been executed.

Figure 2.3b depicts a situation where the formula itself remains in the same cell, but one of the values it references is moved to a new location; that is, the

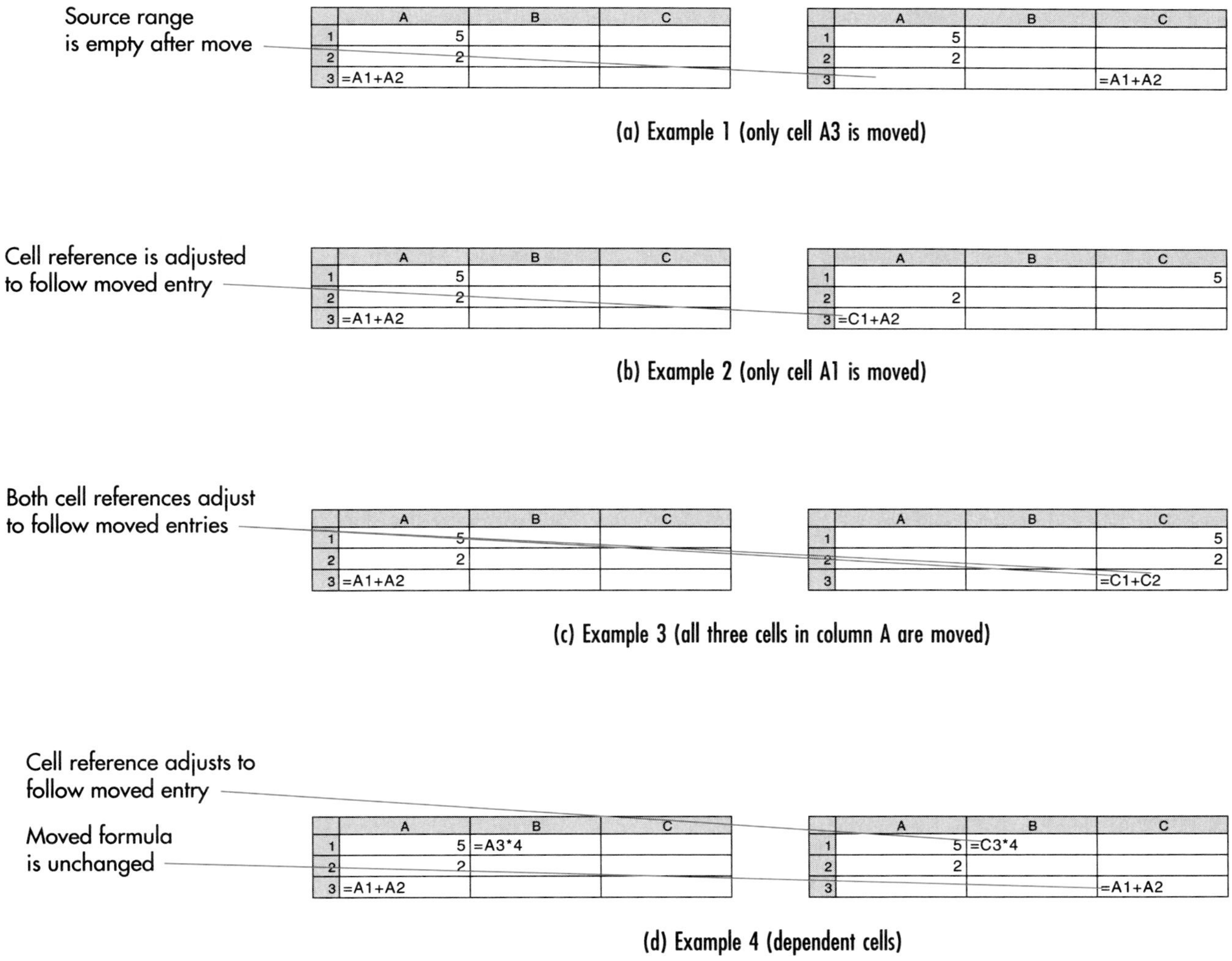

Source range is empty after move

	A	B	C
1	5		
2	2		
3	=A1+A2		

	A	B	C
1	5		
2	2		
3			=A1+A2

(a) Example 1 (only cell A3 is moved)

Cell reference is adjusted to follow moved entry

	A	B	C
1	5		
2	2		
3	=A1+A2		

	A	B	C
1			5
2	2		
3	=C1+A2		

(b) Example 2 (only cell A1 is moved)

Both cell references adjust to follow moved entries

	A	B	C
1	5		
2	2		
3	=A1+A2		

	A	B	C
1			5
2			2
3			=C1+C2

(c) Example 3 (all three cells in column A are moved)

Cell reference adjusts to follow moved entry

Moved formula is unchanged

	A	B	C
1	5	=A3*4	
2	2		
3	=A1+A2		

	A	B	C
1	5	=C3*4	
2	2		
3			=A1+A2

(d) Example 4 (dependent cells)

FIGURE 2.3 The Move Command

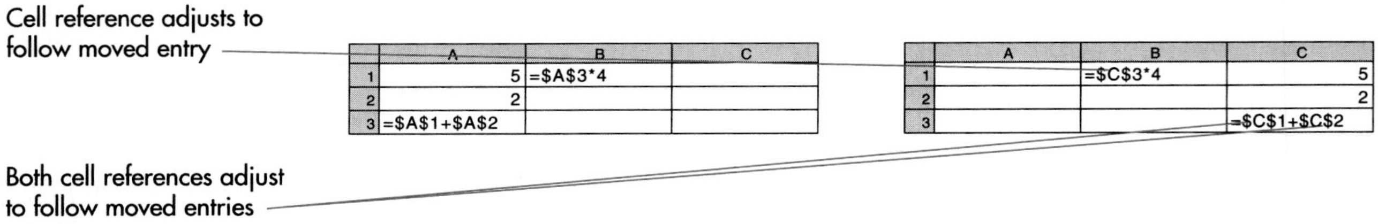

Cell reference adjusts to follow moved entry

	A	B	C
1	5	=$A$3*4	
2	2		
3	=$A$1+$A$2		

	A	B	C
1		=$C$3*4	5
2			2
3			=$C$1+$C$2

Both cell references adjust to follow moved entries

(e) Example 5 (absolute cell addresses)

FIGURE 2.3 The Move Command (continued)

entry in A1 is moved to C1. The formula in cell A3 is adjusted to follow the moved entry to its new location; that is, the formula is now =C1+A2.

The situation is different in Figure 2.3c as the contents of all three cells—A1, A2, and A3—are moved. After the move has taken place, cells C1 and C2 contain the 5 and the 2, respectively, with the formula in cell C3 adjusted to reflect the movement of the contents of cells A1 and A2. Once again the source range (A1:A3) is empty after the move is completed.

Figure 2.3d contains an additional formula in cell B1, which is *dependent* on cell A3, which in turn is moved to cell C3. The formula in cell C3 is unchanged after the move because *only* the formula was moved, *not* the values it referenced. The formula in cell B1 changes because cell B1 refers to an entry (cell A3) that was moved to a new location (cell C3).

Figure 2.3e shows that the specification of an absolute reference has no meaning in a move operation, because the cell addresses are adjusted as necessary to reflect the cells that have been moved. Moving a formula that contains an absolute reference does not adjust the formula. Moving a value that is specified as an absolute reference, however, adjusts the formula to follow the cell to its new location. Thus all of the absolute references in Figure 2.3e are changed to reflect the entries that were moved.

The move operation is a convenient way to improve the appearance of a worksheet after it has been developed. It is subtle in its operation, and we suggest you think twice before moving cell entries because of the complexities involved.

The move operation is implemented by using the Windows clipboard and a combination of the ***Cut*** and ***Paste commands*** from the Edit menu. The contents of the source range are transferred to the clipboard, from which they are pasted to the destination range. (Executing a Paste command after a Cut command empties the clipboard. This is different from pasting after a Copy command, which does not affect the contents of the clipboard.)

LEARNING BY DOING

As we have already indicated, there are many different ways to accomplish the same task. You can execute commands using a pull-down menu, a shortcut menu, a toolbar, or the keyboard. In the exercise that follows we emphasize pull-down menus (the most basic technique) but suggest various shortcuts as appropriate.

Realize, however, that while the shortcuts are interesting, it is far more important to focus on the underlying concepts in the exercise, rather than specific key strokes or mouse clicks. The professor's grade book was developed to emphasize the difference between relative and absolute cell references. The grade book also illustrates the importance of isolating assumptions so that alternative strategies (e.g., different exam weights) can be considered.

HANDS-ON EXERCISE 1

Creating a Workbook

Objective: To create a new workbook; to develop a formula containing relative and absolute references; to use the Copy command within a worksheet. Use Figure 2.4 as a guide.

STEP 1: Create a New Workbook

- Start Microsoft Excel as described in Chapter 1. Close the Office Assistant if it appears.
- Click in **cell A1.** Enter the title of the worksheet, **CIS120 - Spring 1997** as in Figure 2.4a. (The Save As dialog box is not yet visible.)
- Press the **down arrow key** to move to cell A3. Type **Student.**
- Press the **right arrow key** to move to cell B3. Type **Test 1.**
- Press the **right arrow key** to move to cell C3. Type **Test 2.**
- Press the **right arrow key** to move to cell D3. Type **Final.**
- Press the **right arrow key** to move to cell E3. Type **Average.** Press **enter.**

STEP 2: Save the Workbook

- Pull down the **File menu** and click **Save** (or click the **Save button** on the Standard toolbar) to display the Save As dialog box.
- Click the **drop-down arrow** on the Save In list box. Click the appropriate drive, drive C or drive A, depending on where you are saving your Excel workbook.

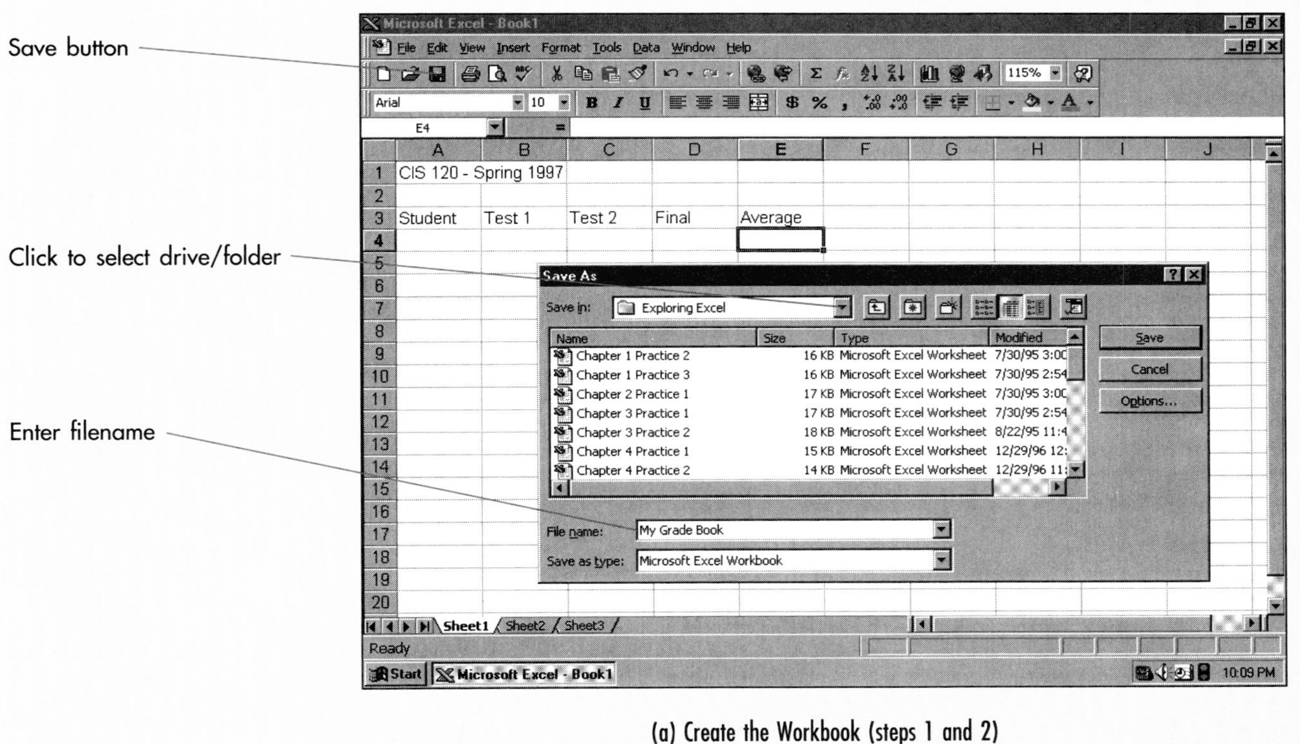

(a) Create the Workbook (steps 1 and 2)

FIGURE 2.4 Hands-on Exercise 1

- ➤ Double click the **Exploring Excel folder** to make it the active folder (the folder in which you will save the document).
- ➤ Click and drag to select **Book1** (the default entry) in the File name text box. Type **My Grade Book** as the name of the workbook. Press the **enter key.**
- ➤ The title bar changes to reflect the name of the workbook.

LONG FILENAMES

Windows 95 allows filenames of up to 255 characters (spaces and commas are permitted). Anyone using Windows 95 for the first time will take descriptive names such as *My Grade Book* for granted, but veterans of MS-DOS and Windows 3.1 will appreciate the improvement over the earlier 8.3 naming convention (an eight-character name followed by a three-letter extension to indicate the file type).

STEP 3: Enter Student Data

- ➤ Click in **cell A4** and type **Costa, Frank.** Move across row 4 and enter Frank's grades on the two tests and the final. Use Figure 2.4b as a guide.
  - Do *not* enter Frank's average in cell E4 as that will be entered as a formula in step 5.
  - Do *not* be concerned that you cannot see Frank's entire name because the default width of column A is not wide enough to display the entire name.
- ➤ Enter the names and grades for the other students in rows 5 through 9. Do *not* enter their averages.
- ➤ Complete the entries in column A by typing **Class Averages** and **Exam Weights** in cells **A11** and **A13,** respectively.
- ➤ Click the **Save button** on the Standard toolbar to save the workbook.

SAVE YOUR WORK

We cannot overemphasize the importance of periodically saving a workbook, so if something goes wrong you won't lose everything. Nothing is more frustrating than to lose two hours of effort due to an unexpected problem in Windows or to a temporary loss of power. Save your work frequently, at least once every 15 minutes. Click the Save button on the Standard toolbar or pull down the File menu and click Save. Do it!

STEP 4: Enter Exam Weights

- ➤ Click in **cell B13** and enter **.25** (the weight for the first exam).
- ➤ Press the **right arrow key** to move to cell C13 and enter **.25** (the weight for the second exam).
- ➤ Press the **right arrow key** to move to cell D13 and enter **.5** (the weight for the final). Press **enter.** Do *not* be concerned that the exam weights do not

Enter exam weights in B13:D13

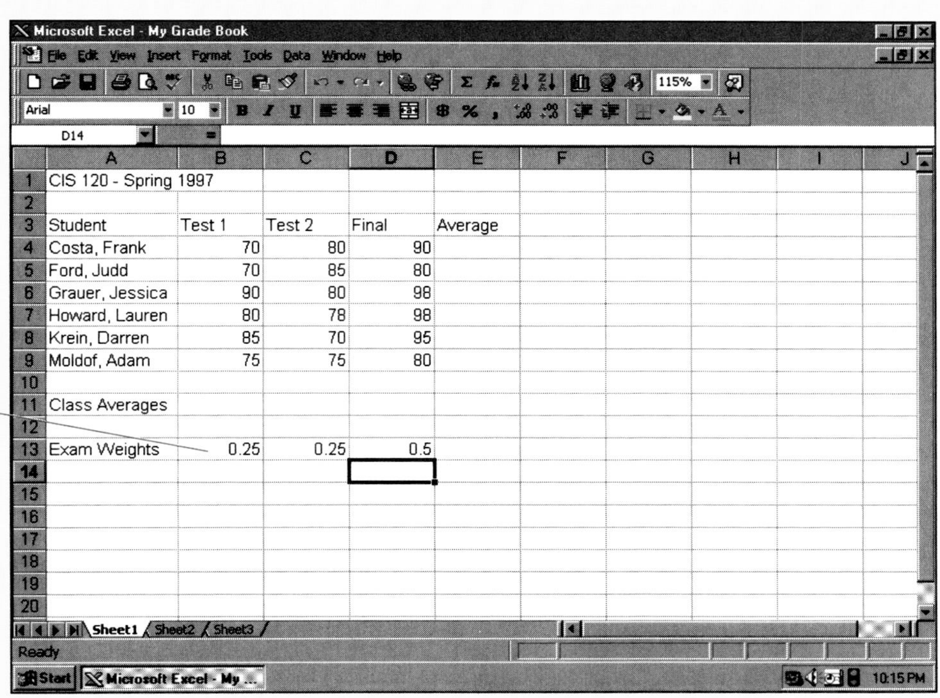

(b) Enter Student Data (steps 3 and 4)

FIGURE 2.4 Hands-on Exercise 1 (continued)

appear as percentages; they will be formatted in the second exercise later in the chapter.

➤ The worksheet should match Figure 2.4b except that column A is too narrow to display the entire name of each student.

STEP 5: Compute the Semester Average

➤ Click in **cell E4** and type the formula **=$B$13*B4+$C$13*C4+$D$13*D4** as shown in Figure 2.4c. Press the **enter key** when you have completed the formula.

➤ Check that the displayed value in cell E4 is 82.5, which indicates you entered the formula correctly. Correct the formula if necessary.

➤ Save the workbook.

CORRECTING MISTAKES

The most basic way to correct an erroneous entry is to click in the cell, then re-enter the cell contents in their entirety. It's faster, however, to edit the cell contents rather than retyping them. Click in the cell whose contents you want to change, then make the necessary changes in the formula bar near the top of the Excel window. Use the mouse or arrow keys to position the insertion point. You can also press the Home and End keys to move to the first and last character in the cell, respectively. Make the necessary correction(s), then press the enter key.

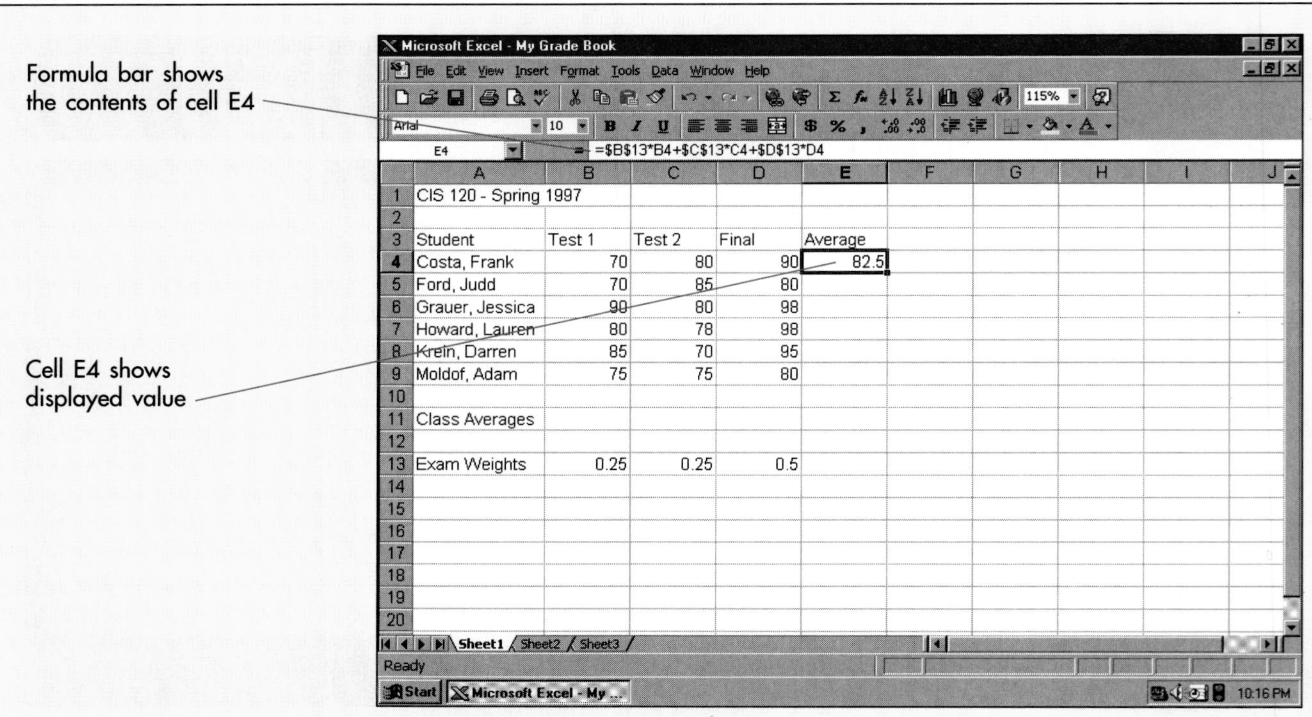

(c) Compute the Semester Average (step 5)

FIGURE 2.4 Hands-on Exercise 1 (continued)

STEP 6: Copy the Semester Average

- Click in **cell E4.** Pull down the **Edit menu** and click **Copy** (or click the **copy button** on the standard toolbar). A moving border will surround cell E4, indicating that its contents have been copied to the clipboard.
- Click **cell E5.** Drag the mouse over cells **E5** through **E9** to select the destination range as in Figure 2.4d.
- Pull down the **Edit menu** and click **Paste** to copy the contents of the clipboard to the destination range. You should see the semester averages for the other students in cells E5 through E9.
- Press **Esc** to remove the moving border around cell E4. Click anywhere in the worksheet to deselect cells E5 through E9.

CUT, COPY AND PASTE

Ctrl+X (the X is supposed to remind you of a pair of scissors), Ctrl+C, and Ctrl+V are keyboard equivalents to cut, copy, and paste, respectively, and apply to Excel, Word, PowerPoint and Access, as well as Windows applications in general. (The keystrokes are easier to remember when you realize that the operative letters, X, C, and V, are next to each other at the bottom-left side of the keyboard.) Alternatively, you can use the Cut, Copy, and Paste buttons on the Standard toolbar, which are also found on the Standard toolbar in the other Office applications.

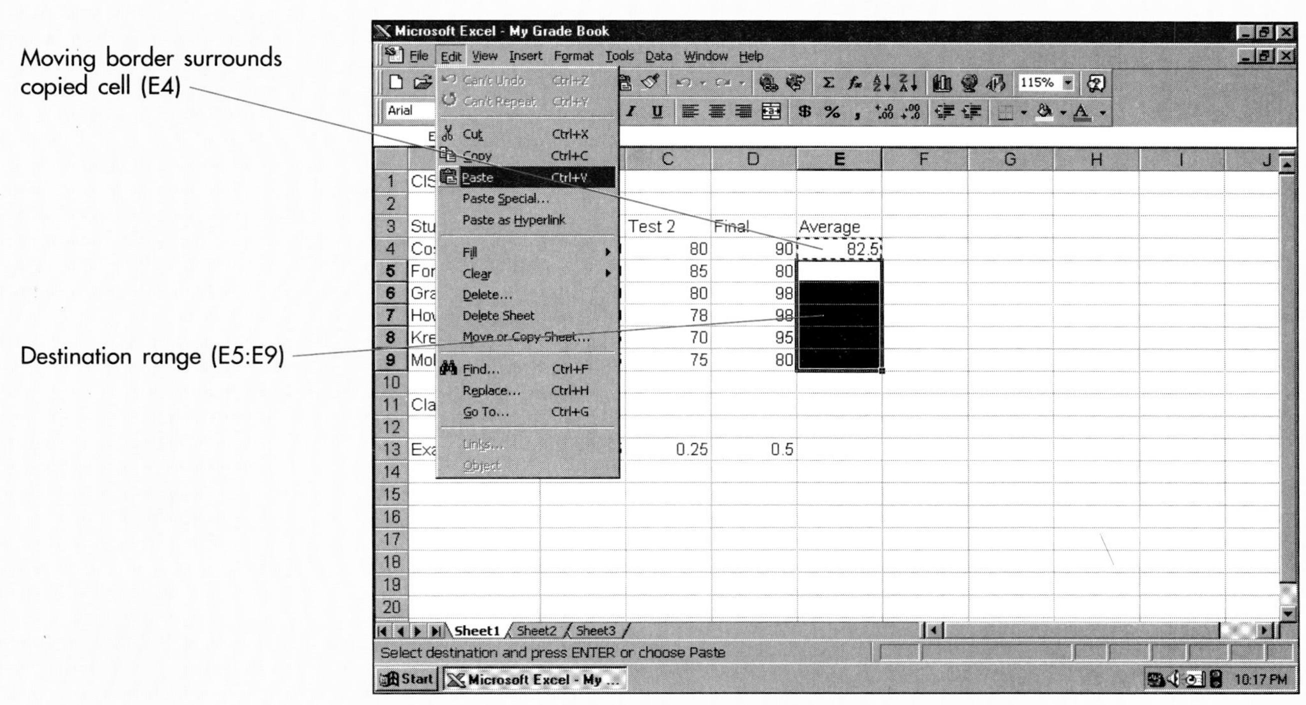

(d) Copy the Semester Average (step 6)

FIGURE 2.4 Hands-on Exercise 1 (continued)

- Click in **cell E5** and look at the formula. The cells that reference the grades have changed to B5, C5, and D5. The cells that reference the exam weights—\$B\$13, \$C\$13, and \$D\$13—are the same as in cell E4.
- Save the workbook.

STEP 7: Compute Class Averages

- Click in **cell B11** and type the formula **=AVERAGE(B4:B9)** to compute the class average on the first test. Press the **enter key** when you have completed the formula.
- Point to **cell B11,** then click the **right mouse button** to display the shortcut menu in Figure 2.4e. Click **Copy,** which produces the moving border around cell B11.
- Click **cell C11.** Drag the mouse over cells **C11** and **D11,** the destination range for the Copy command.

THE RIGHT MOUSE BUTTON

Point to a cell (or cell range), a worksheet tab, or a toolbar, then click the right mouse button to display a context-sensitive menu with commands appropriate to the item you are pointing to. Right clicking a cell, for example, displays a menu with selected commands from the Edit, Insert, and Format menus. Right clicking a toolbar displays a menu that lets you display (hide) additional toolbars. Right clicking a worksheet tab enables you to rename, move, copy, or delete the worksheet.

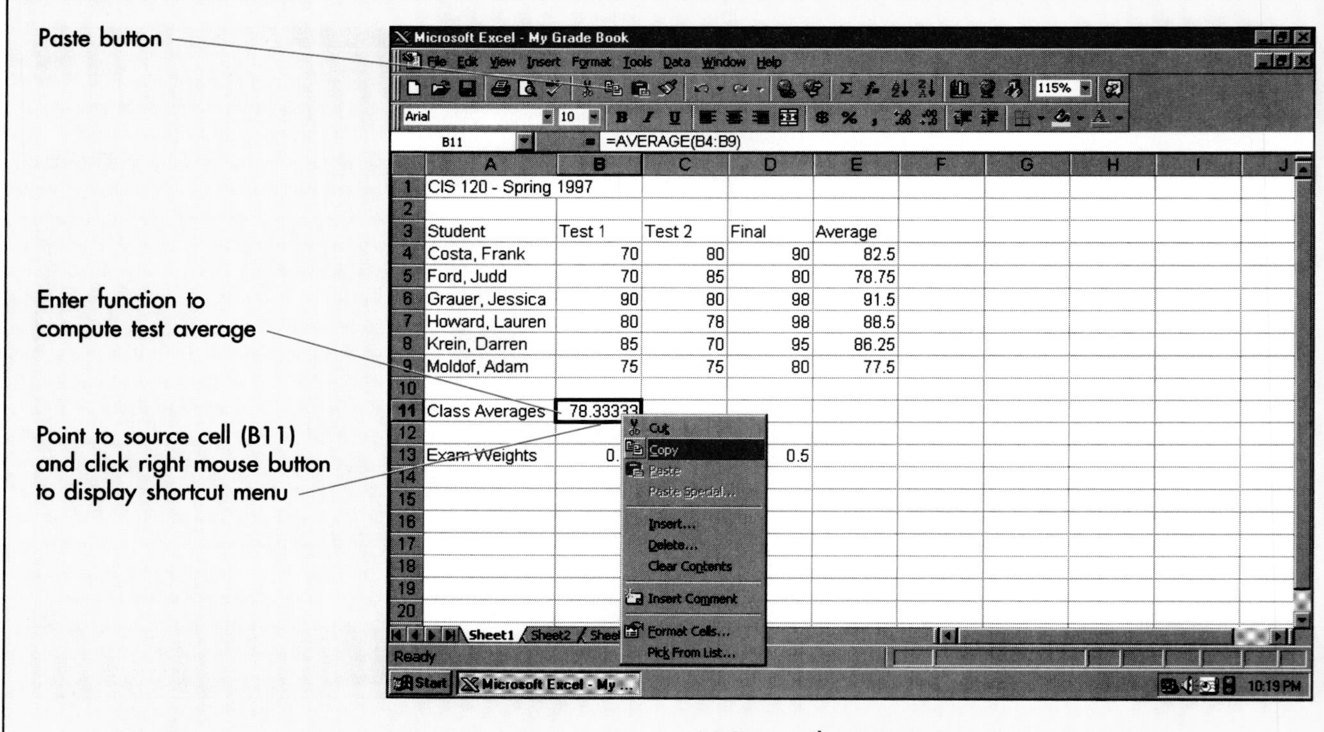

(e) Compute Class Averages (step 7)

FIGURE 2.4 Hands-on Exercise 1 (continued)

➤ Click the **Paste button** on the Standard toolbar (or press Ctrl+V) to paste the contents of the clipboard to the destination range.

➤ Press **Esc** to remove the moving border. Click anywhere in the worksheet to deselect cells C11 through D11.

STEP 8: What If? Change Exam Weights

➤ Change the entries in cells B13 and C13 to **.20** and the entry in cell D13 to **.60.** The semester average for every student changes automatically; for example, Costa and Moldof change to 84 and 78, respectively.

➤ The professor decides this does not make a significant difference and wants to go back to the original weights. Click the **Undo button** three times to reverse the last three actions. You should see .25, .25, and .50 in cells B13, C13, and D13, respectively.

➤ Click the **Save button.** Exit Excel if you are not ready to begin the next exercise at this time.

FORMATTING

In this chapter the professor's grade book is developed in two stages, as shown in Figure 2.5. The exercise just completed created the grade book, but paid no attention to its appearance. It had you enter the data for every student, develop the formulas to compute the semester average for every student based on the exam weights at the bottom of the worksheet, and finally, develop the formulas to compute the class averages for each exam.

Figure 2.5a shows the grade book as it exists at the end of the first hands-on exercise. Figure 2.5b shows the grade book at the end of the second exercise after it has been formatted. The differences between the two are due entirely to formatting. Consider:

- The exam weights are formatted as percentages in Figure 2.5b, as opposed to decimals in Figure 2.5a. The class and semester averages are displayed with a single decimal place in Figure 2.5b.
- Boldface and italics are used for emphasis, as are shading and borders.
- Exam grades and computed averages are centered under their respective headings.
- The worksheet title is centered across all five columns.
- The width of column A has been increased so that the students' names are completely visible.

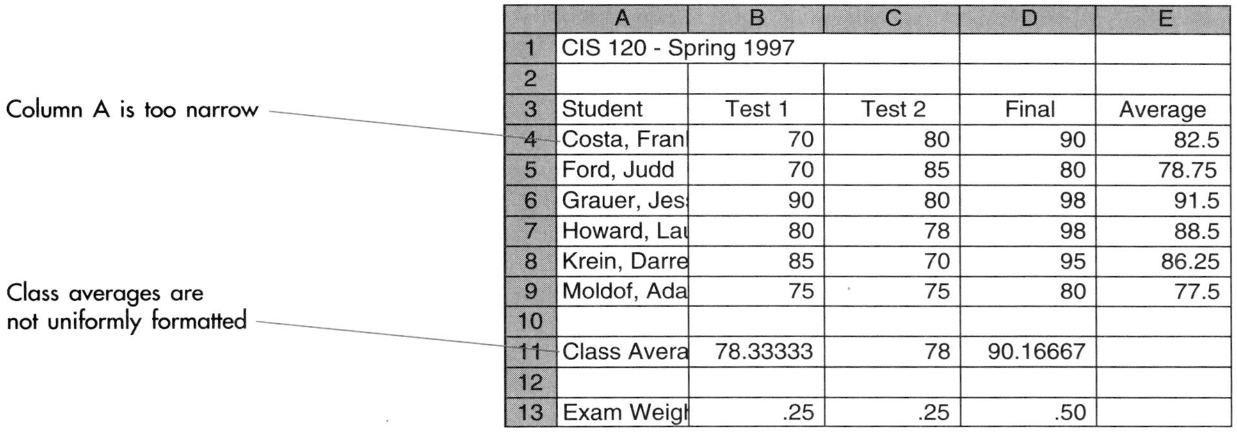

	A	B	C	D	E
1	CIS 120 - Spring 1997				
2					
3	Student	Test 1	Test 2	Final	Average
4	Costa, Fran	70	80	90	82.5
5	Ford, Judd	70	85	80	78.75
6	Grauer, Jes	90	80	98	91.5
7	Howard, La	80	78	98	88.5
8	Krein, Darre	85	70	95	86.25
9	Moldof, Ada	75	75	80	77.5
10					
11	Class Avera	78.33333	78	90.16667	
12					
13	Exam Weig	.25	.25	.50	

Column A is too narrow
Class averages are not uniformly formatted

(a) At the End of Hands-on Exercise 1

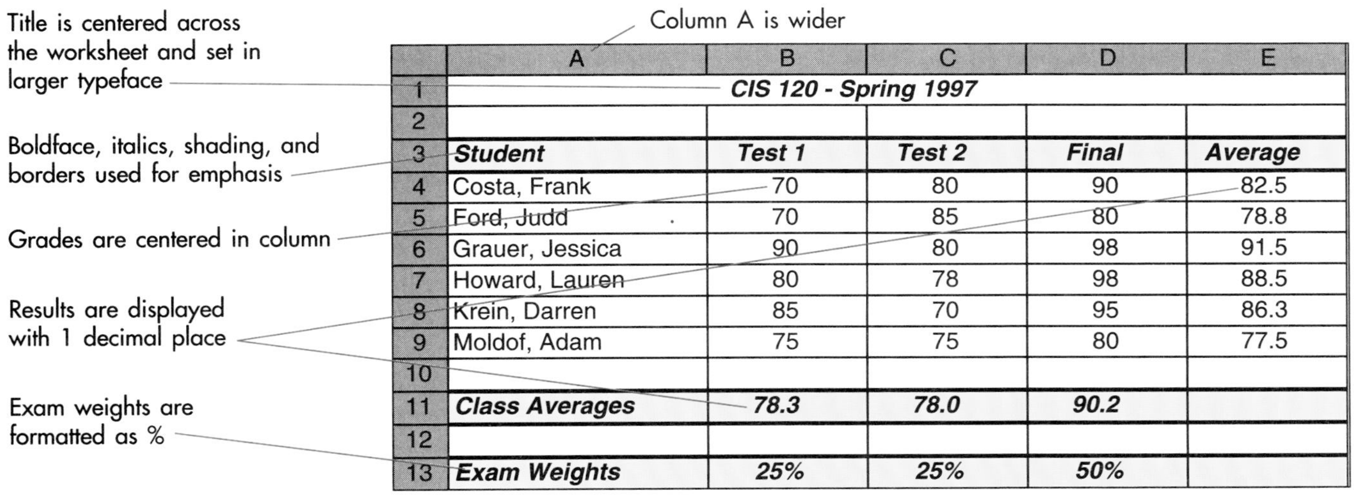

	A	B	C	D	E
1	***CIS 120 - Spring 1997***				
2					
3	***Student***	***Test 1***	***Test 2***	***Final***	***Average***
4	Costa, Frank	70	80	90	82.5
5	Ford, Judd	70	85	80	78.8
6	Grauer, Jessica	90	80	98	91.5
7	Howard, Lauren	80	78	98	88.5
8	Krein, Darren	85	70	95	86.3
9	Moldof, Adam	75	75	80	77.5
10					
11	***Class Averages***	***78.3***	***78.0***	***90.2***	
12					
13	***Exam Weights***	***25%***	***25%***	***50%***	

Column A is wider
Title is centered across the worksheet and set in larger typeface
Boldface, italics, shading, and borders used for emphasis
Grades are centered in column
Results are displayed with 1 decimal place
Exam weights are formatted as %

(b) At the End of Hands-on Exercise 2

FIGURE 2.5 Developing the Grade Book

Column Widths

A column is often too narrow to display the contents of one or more cells in that column. When this happens, the display depends on whether the cell contains a text or numeric entry, and if it is a text entry, on whether or not the adjacent cell is empty.

The student names in Figure 2.5a, for example, are partially hidden because column A is too narrow to display the entire name. Cells A4 through A9 contain the complete names of each student, but because the adjacent cells in column B contain data, the displayed entries in column A are truncated (cut off) at the cell width. The situation is different for the worksheet title in cell A1. This time the adjacent cell (cell B1) is empty, so that the contents of cell A1 overflow into that cell and are completely visible.

Numbers are treated differently from text and do not depend on the contents of the adjacent cell. Excel displays a series of number signs (######) when a cell containing a numeric entry is too narrow to display the entry in its current format. You may be able to correct the problem by changing the format of the number (e.g., display the number with fewer decimal places). Alternatively, you can increase the ***column width*** by using the ***Column command*** in the Format menu.

Row Heights

The ***row height*** changes automatically as the font size is increased. Row 1 in Figure 2.5b, for example, has a greater height than the other rows to accommodate the larger font size in the title of the worksheet. The row height can also be changed manually through the ***Row command*** in the Format menu.

FORMAT CELLS COMMAND

The ***Format Cells command*** controls the formatting for numbers, alignment, fonts, borders, and patterns (color). Execution of the command produces a tabbed dialog box in which you choose the particular formatting category, then enter the desired options. (Many of the formatting options can also be specified from the Formatting toolbar.)

All formatting is done within the context of ***select-then-do.*** You select the cells to which the formatting is to apply, then you execute the Format Cells command or click the appropriate button on the Formatting toolbar.

FORMATS VERSUS VALUES

Changing the format of a number changes the way the number is displayed but does *not* change its value. If, for example, you entered 1.2345 into a cell but displayed the number as 1.23, the actual value (1.2345) would be used in all calculations involving that cell.

Numeric Formats

General format is the default format for numeric entries and displays a number according to the way it was originally entered. Numbers are shown as integers (e.g., 123), decimal fractions (e.g., 1.23), or in scientific notation (e.g., 1.23E+10) if the number exceeds 11 digits. You can also display a number in one of several formats as shown in Figure 2.6a:

- ***Number format,*** which displays a number with or without the 1000 separator (e.g., a comma) and with any number of decimal places. Negative numbers are displayed with parentheses and/or can be shown in red.
- ***Currency format,*** which displays a number with the 1000 separator and an optional dollar sign (which is placed immediately to the left of the number). Negative values are preceded by a minus sign or are shown in red.
- ***Accounting format,*** which displays a number with the 1000 separator, an optional dollar sign (at the left of the cell that vertically aligns the dollar signs within a column), negative values in parentheses, and zero values as hyphens.
- ***Date format,*** which displays the date in different ways, such as March 4, 1994, 3/4/94, or 4-Mar-94.
- ***Time format,*** which displays the time in different formats, such as 10:50 PM or the equivalent 22:50 (24-hour time).
- ***Percentage format,*** whereby the number is multiplied by 100 for display purposes only, a percent sign is included, and any number of decimal places can be specified.
- ***Fraction format,*** which displays a number as a fraction, and is appropriate when there is no exact decimal equivalent, for example, ⅓.
- ***Scientific format,*** which displays a number as a decimal fraction followed by a whole number exponent of 10; for example, the number 12345 would

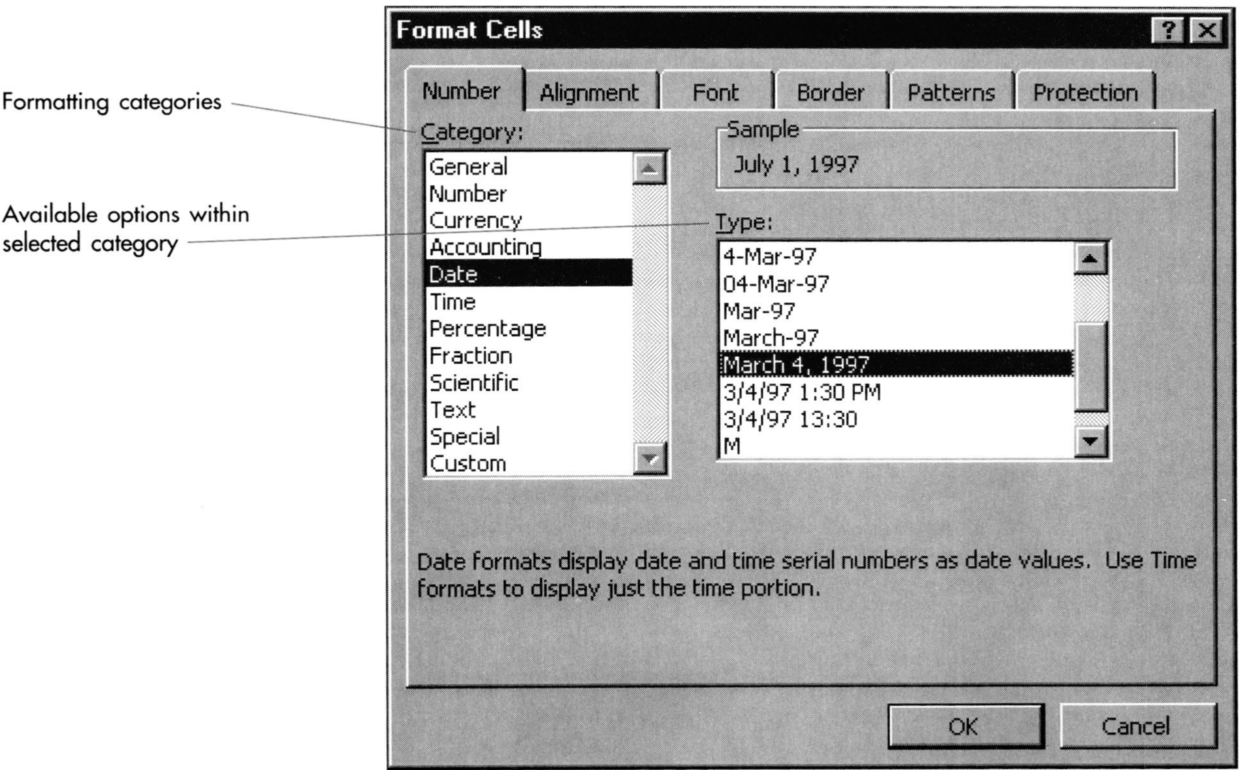

(a) The Number Tab

FIGURE 2.6 The Format Cells Command

appear as 1.2345E+04. The exponent, +04 in the example, is the number of places the decimal point is moved to the left (or right if the exponent is negative). Very small numbers have negative exponents; for example, the entry .0000012 would be displayed as 1.2E−06. Scientific notation is used only with very large or very small numbers.

- ***Text format,*** which left aligns the entry and is useful for numerical values that have leading zeros and should be treated as text, such as ZIP codes.
- ***Special format,*** which displays a number with editing characters, such as hyphens in a social security number or parentheses around the area code of a telephone number.
- ***Custom format,*** which allows you to develop your own formats.

DATES VERSUS FRACTIONS

A fraction may be entered into a cell by preceding the fraction with an equal sign, for example, =1/3. The fraction is converted to its decimal equivalent and displayed in that format in the worksheet. Omission of the equal sign causes Excel to treat the entry as a date; that is, 1/3 will be stored as January 3 (of the current year).

Alignment

The contents of a cell (whether text or numeric) may be aligned horizontally and/or vertically as indicated by the dialog box of Figure 2.6b. The default horizontal alignment is general, which left-aligns text and right-aligns date and numbers. You can also center an entry across a range of selected cells, as in the professor's grade book, which centered the title that was entered in cell A1 across columns A through E. The Fill option duplicates the characters in the cell across the entire width of that cell.

Vertical alignment is important only if the row height is changed and the characters are smaller than the height of the row. Entries may be vertically aligned at the top, center, or bottom (the default) of a cell.

It is also possible to wrap the text within a cell to emulate the word wrap of a word processor. And finally, you can achieve some very interesting effects by rotating text up to 90° in either direction.

Fonts

You can use the same fonts (typefaces) in Excel as you can in any other Windows application. Windows itself includes a limited number of fonts (Arial, Times New Roman, Courier New, Symbol, and Wingdings) to provide variety in creating documents. (Additional fonts are also installed with Microsoft Office.) All fonts are WYSIWYG (What You See Is What You Get), meaning that the worksheet you see on the monitor will match the worksheet produced by the printer.

Any entry in a worksheet may be displayed in any font, style, or point size as indicated by the dialog box of Figure 2.6c. The example shows Arial, Bold Italic, and 14 points, and corresponds to the selection for the worksheet title in the improved grade book. Special effects, such as subscripts or superscripts, are also possible. You can even select a different color, but you will need a color printer to see the effect on the printed page. The Preview box shows the text as it will appear in the worksheet.

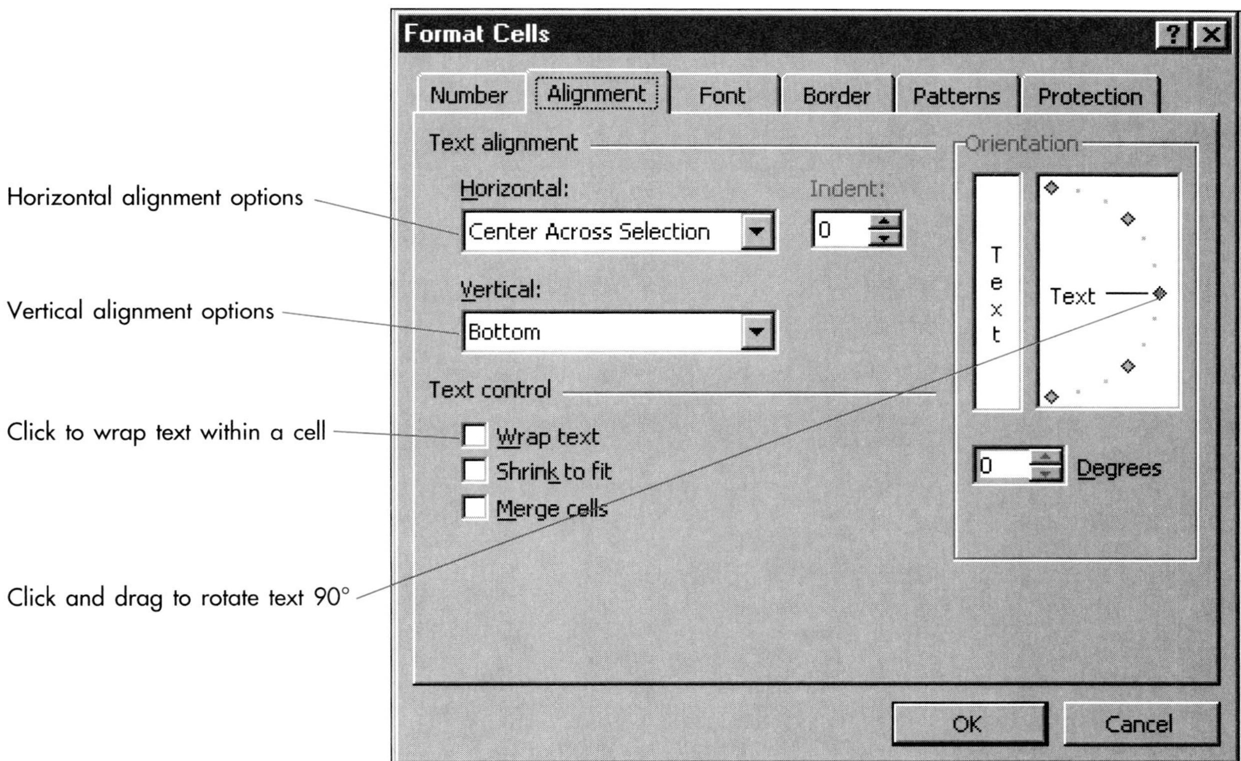

(b) The Alignment Tab

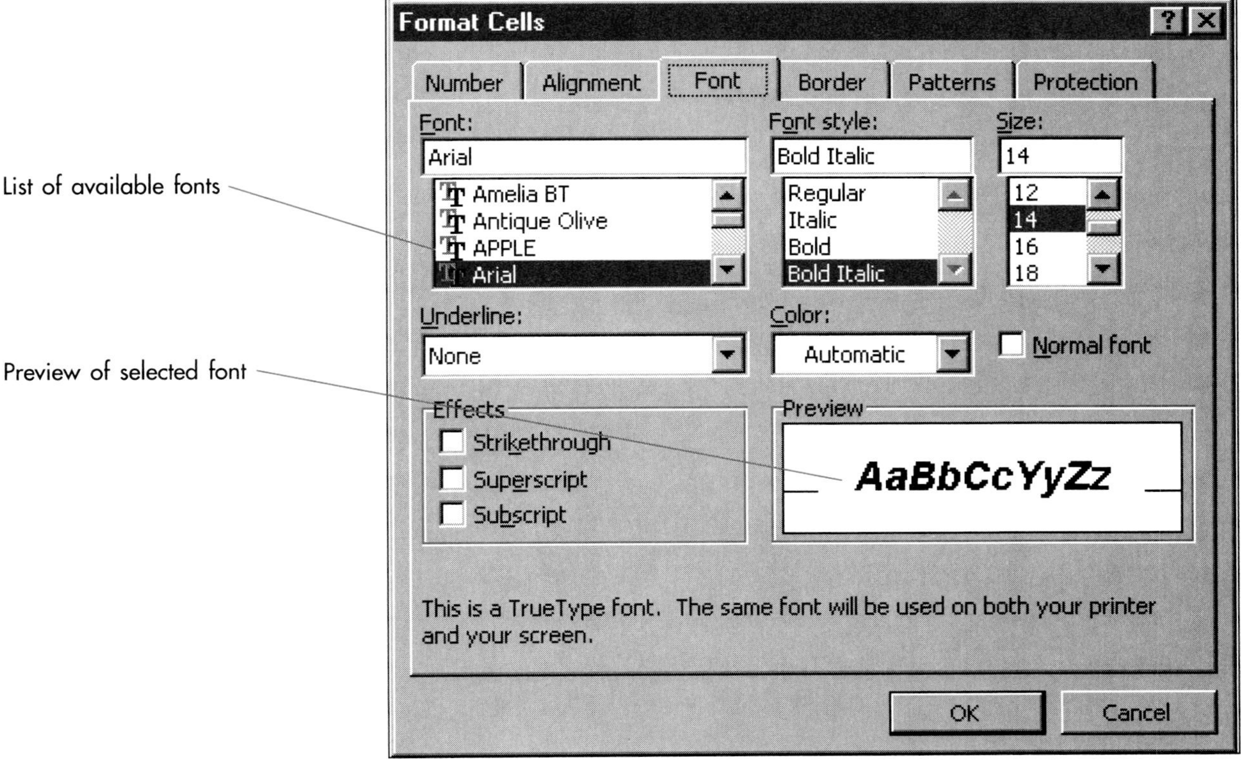

(c) The Font Tab

FIGURE 2.6 The Format Cells Command (continued)

Borders, Patterns, and Shading

The ***Border tab*** in Figure 2.6d enables you to create a border around a cell (or cells) for additional emphasis. You can outline the entire selection, or you can choose the specific side or sides; for example, thicker lines on the bottom and right sides produce a drop shadow, which is very effective. You can also specify a different color for the border, but you will need a color printer to see the effect on the printed output.

The ***Patterns tab*** in Figure 2.6e lets you choose a different color in which to shade the cell and further emphasize its contents. The Pattern drop-down list box lets you select an alternate pattern, such as dots or slanted lines.

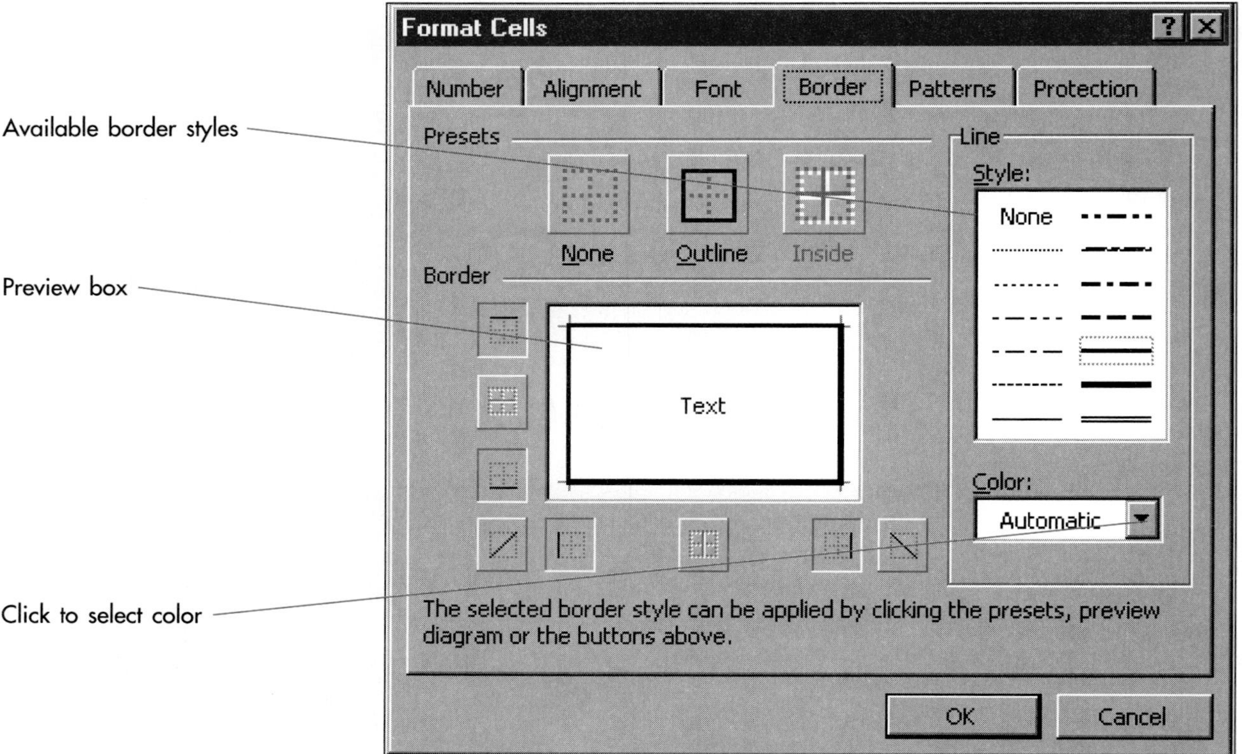

(d) The Border Tab

FIGURE 2.6 The Format Cells Command (continued)

USE RESTRAINT

More is not better, especially in the case of too many typefaces and styles, which produce cluttered worksheets that impress no one. Limit yourself to a maximum of two typefaces per worksheet, but choose multiple sizes and/or styles within those typefaces. Use boldface or italics for emphasis, but do so in moderation, because if you emphasize too many elements, the effect is lost.

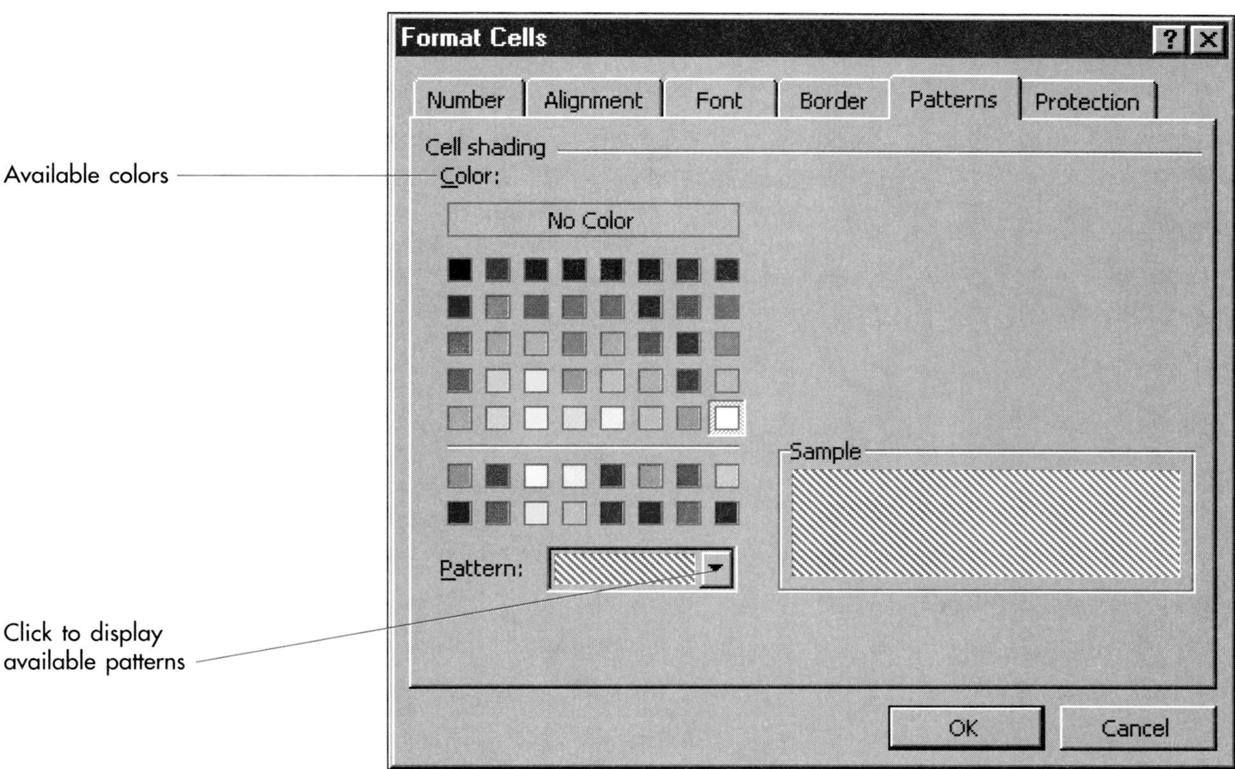

(e) The Patterns Tab

FIGURE 2.6 The Format Cells Command (continued)

HANDS-ON EXERCISE 2

Formatting a Worksheet

Objective: To format a worksheet using both pull-down menus and the Formatting toolbar; to use boldface, italics, shading, and borders; to change the font and/or alignment of a selected entry; to change the width of a column; to print the cell contents as well as the computed values. Use Figure 2.7 as a guide in the exercise.

STEP 1: Center Across Selection

- Open **My Grade Book** from the previous exercise.
- Click in **cell A1** to select the cell containing the title of the worksheet.
- Pull down the **Format menu.** Click **Cells.** If necessary, click the **Font tab.** Click **Arial** in the Font list box, **Bold Italic** in the Font Style box, and then scroll to select **14** from the Size box. Click **OK.**
- Click and drag to select cells **A1** through **E1,** which represents the width of the entire worksheet.
- Pull down the **Format menu** a second time. Click **Cells.** Click the **Alignment tab.** Click the **down arrow** in the Horizontal list box, then click **Center Across**

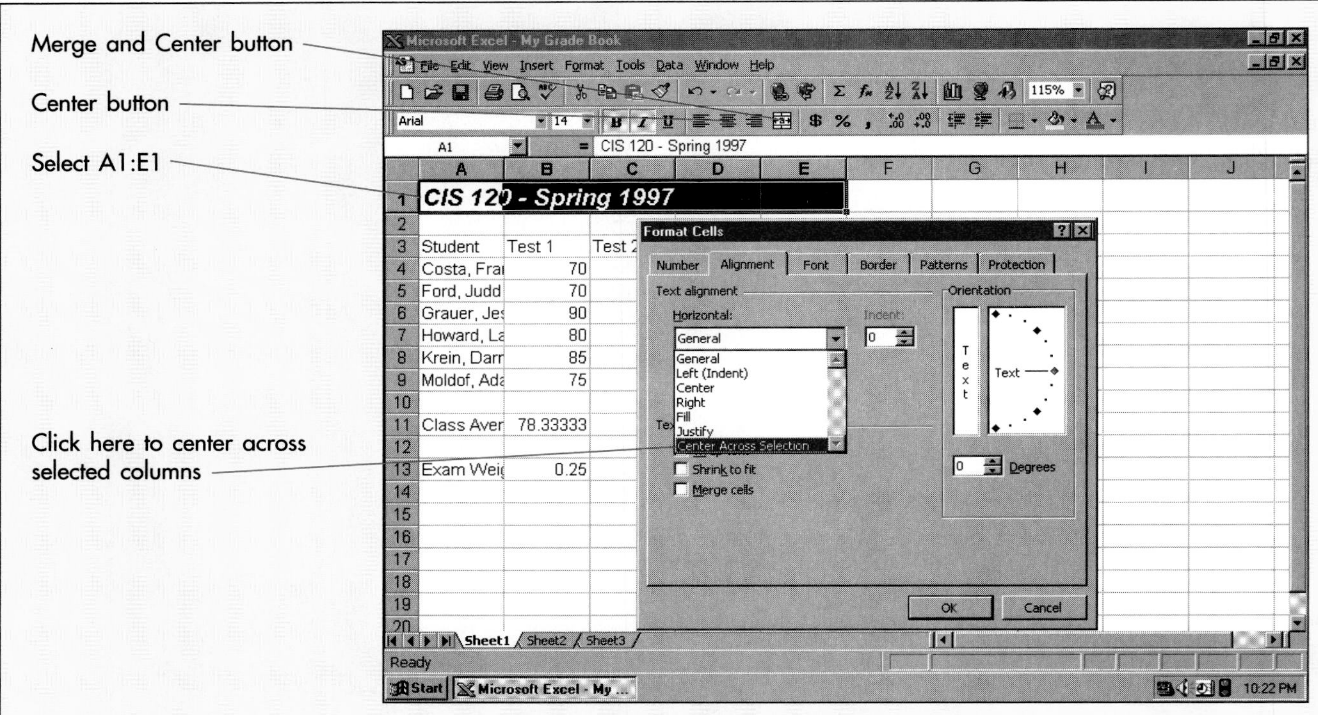

(a) Center across Selection (step 1)

FIGURE 2.7 Hands-on Exercise 2

Selection as in Figure 2.7a. (You can also click the **Merge and Center button** on the Formatting toolbar.) Click **OK**.

➤ Click and drag over cells **B3** through **E13.** Click the **Centering button** on the Formatting toolbar.

CHANGE THE DEFAULT FILE LOCATION

The *default file location* is the folder Excel uses to open (save) a workbook unless it is otherwise instructed. To change the default location, pull down the Tools menu, click Options, and click the General tab. Type the name of the new folder (e.g., C:\Exploring Excel) in the Default File Location text box, then click OK. The next time you access the Open or Save commands from the File menu, the Look In text box will reflect the change.

STEP 2: Increase the Width of Column A

➤ Click in **cell A4.** Drag the mouse over cells **A4** through **A13.**

➤ Pull down the **Format menu,** click **Column,** then click **AutoFit Selection** as shown in Figure 2.7b. The width of the selected cells increases to accommodate the longest entry in the selected range.

➤ Save the workbook.

Select A4:A13

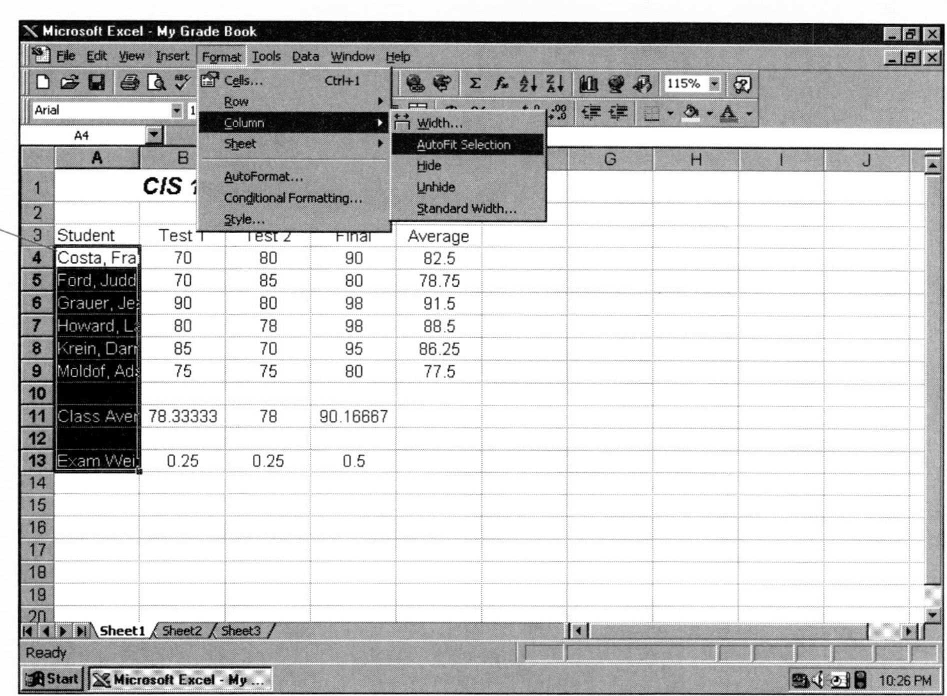

(b) Changing Column Widths (step 2)

FIGURE 2.7 Hands-on Exercise 2 (continued)

COLUMN WIDTHS AND ROW HEIGHTS

Drag the border between column headings to change the column width; for example, to increase (decrease) the width of column A, drag the border between column headings A and B to the right (left). Double click the right boundary of a column heading to change the column width to accommodate the widest entry in that column. Use the same techniques to change the row heights.

STEP 3: Format the Exam Weights

- Click and drag to select cells **B13** through **D13.** Point to the selected cells and click the **right mouse button** to display the shortcut menu in Figure 2.7c. Click **Format Cells** to produce the Format Cells dialog box.
- If necessary, click the **Number tab.** Click **Percentage** in the Category list box. Click the **down arrow** in the Decimal Places box to reduce the number of decimals to zero, then click **OK.** The exam weights are displayed with percent signs and no decimal places.
- Click the **Undo button** on the Standard toolbar to cancel the formatting command.
- Click the **% button** on the Formatting toolbar to reformat the exam weights as percentages. (This is an alternate and faster way to change to the percent format.)

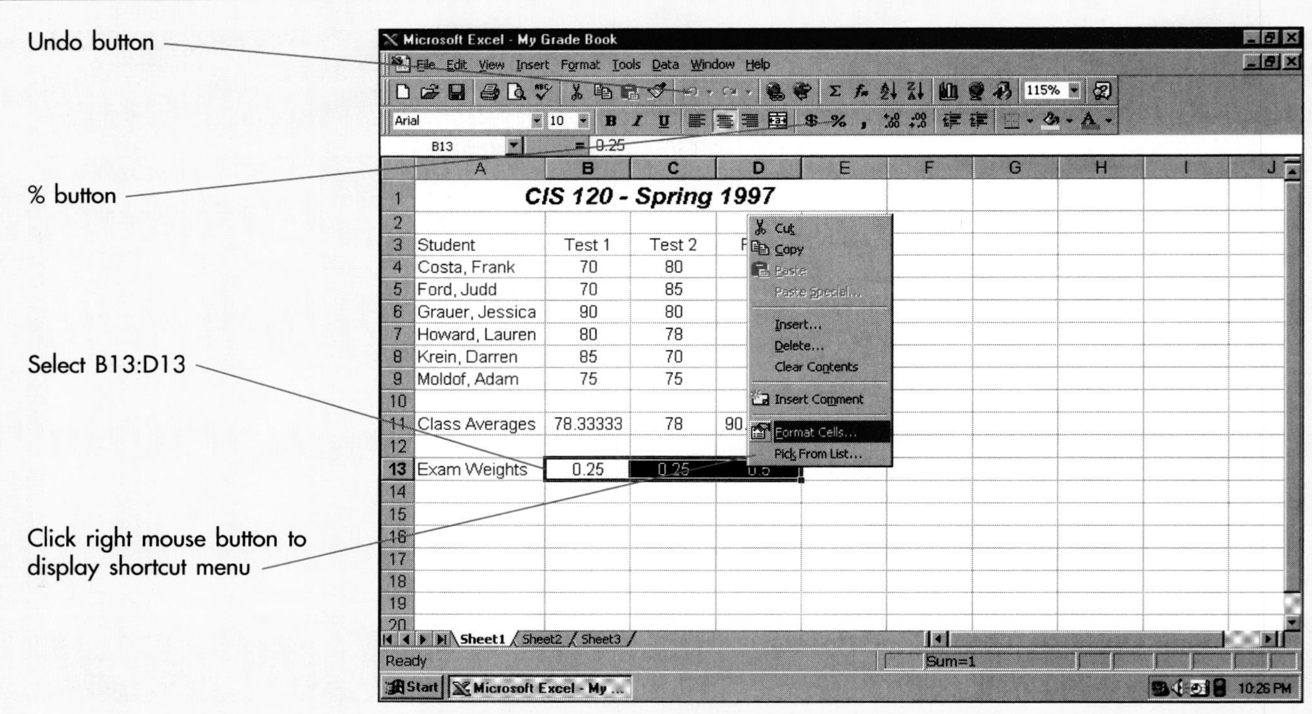

(c) Format Exam Weights (step 3)

FIGURE 2.7 Hands-on Exercise 2 (continued)

> **AUTOMATIC FORMATTING**
>
> Excel converts any number entered with a beginning dollar sign to currency format, and any number entered with an ending percent sign to percentage format. The automatic formatting enables you to save a step by typing $100,000 or 7.5% directly into a cell, rather than entering 100000 or .075 and having to format the number. The formatting is applied to the cell and affects any subsequent numbers in that cell.

STEP 4: Noncontiguous Ranges

- Select cells **B11** through **D11,** the cells that contain the class averages for the three exams.
- Press *and* hold the **Ctrl key** as you click and drag to select cells **E4** through **E9.** Release the **Ctrl key.**
- You will see two noncontiguous (nonadjacent) ranges highlighted, cells B11:D11 and cells E4:E9 as in Figure 2.7d. Format the selected cells using either the Formatting toolbar or the Format menu:
  - To use the Formatting toolbar, click the appropriate button to increase or decrease the number of decimal places to one.
  - To use the Format menu, pull down the **Format menu,** click **Cells,** click the **Number tab,** then click **Number** in the Category list box. Click the **down arrow** in the Decimal Places text box to reduce the decimal places to one. Click **OK.**

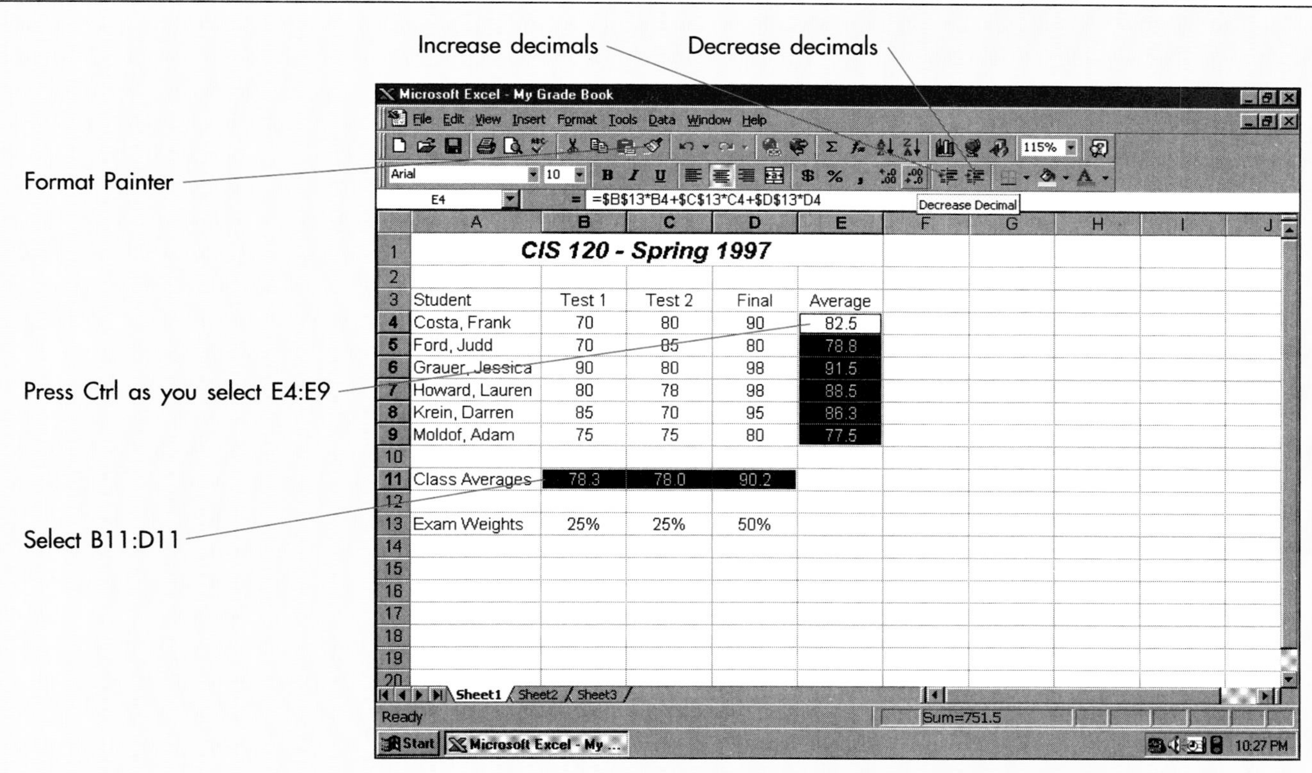

(d) Noncontiguous Ranges (step 4)

FIGURE 2.7 Hands-on Exercise 2 (continued)

THE FORMAT PAINTER

The ***Format Painter*** copies the formatting of the selected cell to other cells in the worksheet. Click the cell whose formatting you want to copy, then double click the Format Painter button on the Standard toolbar. The mouse pointer changes to a paintbrush to indicate that you can copy the current formatting; just click and drag the paintbrush over the additional cells to which you want to apply the formatting. Repeat the painting process as often as necessary, then click the Format Painter button a second time to return to normal editing.

STEP 5: Borders

- Click and drag to select cells **A3** through **E3.** Press *and* hold the **Ctrl key** as you click and drag to select the range **A11:E11.** Continue to press the **Ctrl key** as you click and drag to select cells **A13:E13.**
- Pull down the **Format menu** and click **Cells** (or click the **right mouse button** to produce a shortcut menu, then click **Format Cells**). Click the **Border tab** to access the dialog box in Figure 2.7e.
- Choose a line width from the Style section. Click the **Top** and **Bottom** boxes in the Border section. Click **OK** to exit the dialog box and return to the worksheet.

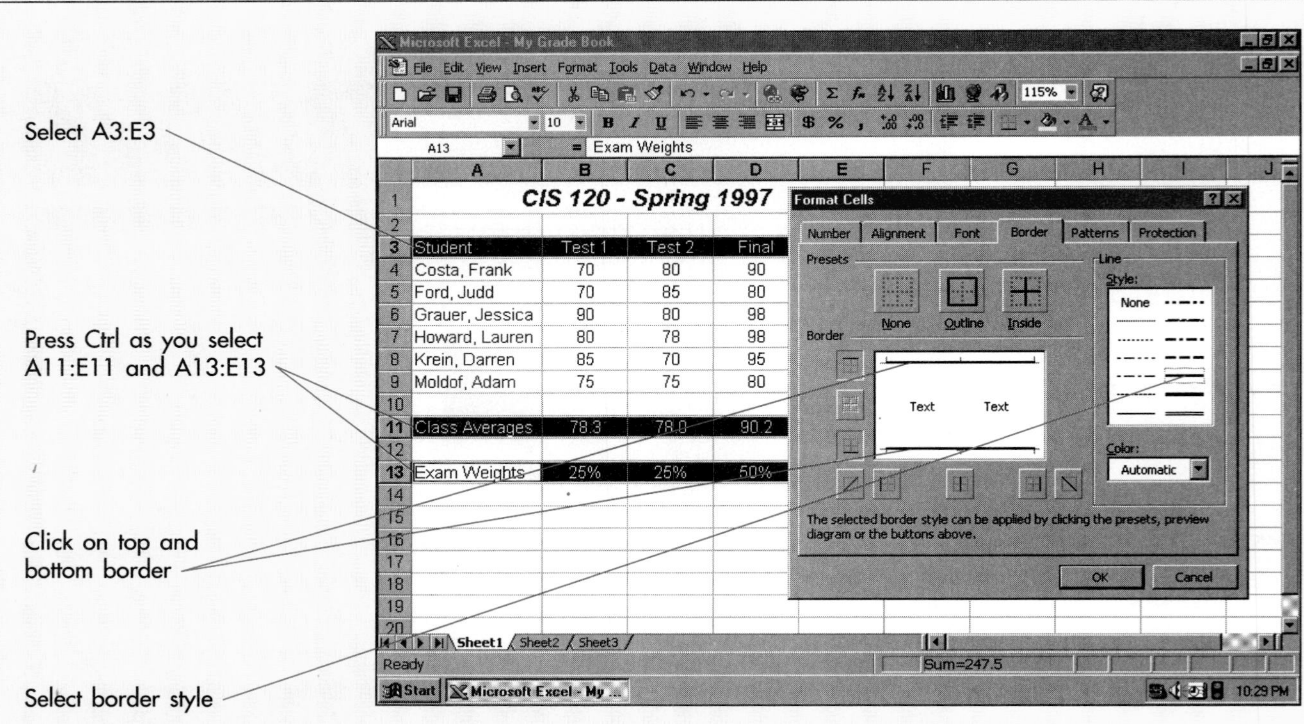

(e) Border Command (step 5)

FIGURE 2.7 Hands-on Exercise 2 (continued)

SELECTING NONCONTIGUOUS RANGES

Dragging the mouse to select a range always produces some type of rectangle; that is, a single cell, a row or column, or a group of rows and columns. You can, however, select ***noncontiguous*** (nonadjacent) ***ranges*** by selecting the first range in the normal fashion, then pressing and holding the Ctrl key as you select the additional range(s). This is especially useful when the same command is to be applied to multiple ranges within a worksheet.

STEP 6: Color

- Check that all three ranges are still selected (A3:E3, A11:E11, *and* A13:E13).
- Click the **down arrow** on the **Fill Color button** on the Formatting toolbar. Click yellow (or whatever color appeals to you) as shown in Figure 2.7f.
- Click the **boldface** and **italics buttons** on the Formatting toolbar. Click outside the selected cells to see the effects of the formatting change.
- Save the workbook.

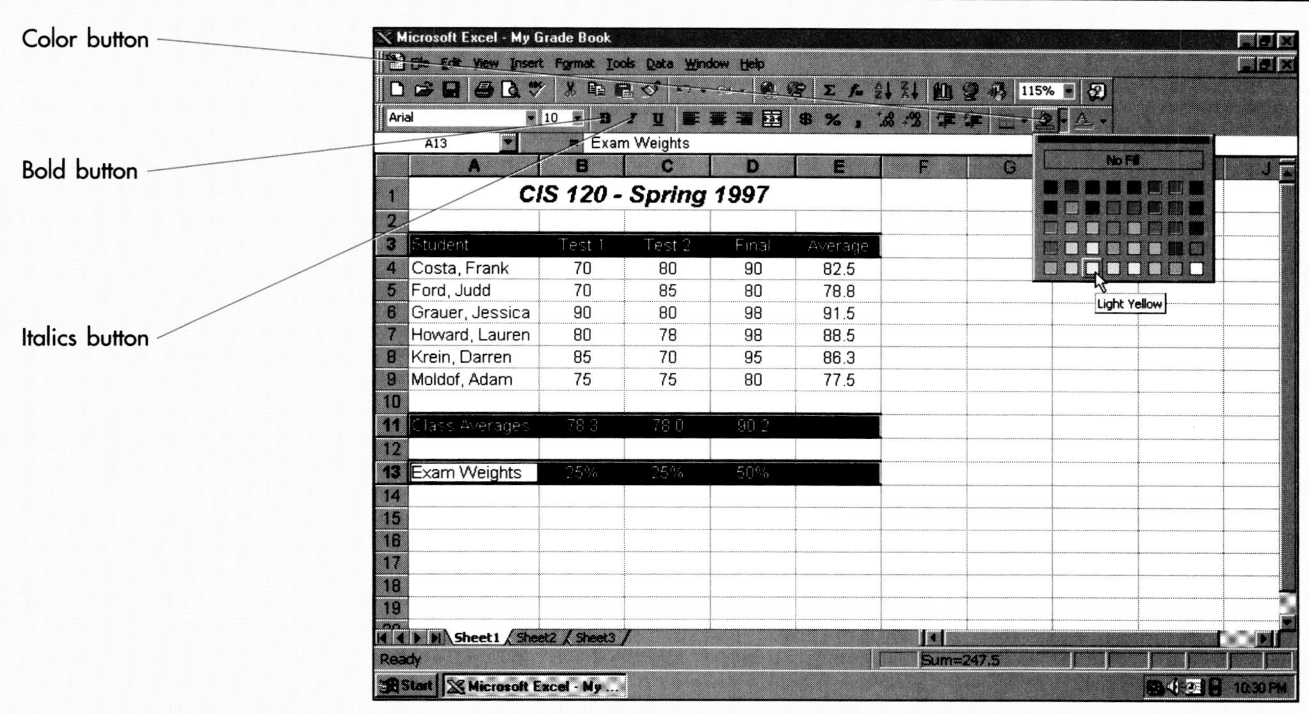

(f) Patterns (step 6)

FIGURE 2.7 Hands-on Exercise 2 (continued)

DESELECTING A RANGE

The effects of a formatting change are often difficult to see when the selected cells are highlighted. Thus, you may need to deselect the range by clicking elsewhere in the worksheet to see the results of a formatting command.

STEP 7: Enter Your Name and Social Security Number

- Click in **cell A15.** Type **Grading Assistant.** Press the **down arrow key.** Type your name, press the **down arrow key,** and enter your social security number *without* the hyphens. Press **enter.**
- Point to **cell A17,** then click the **right mouse button** to display a shortcut menu. Click **Format Cells** to display the dialog box in Figure 2.7g.
- Click the **Number tab,** click **Special** in the Category list box, then click **Social Security Number** in the Type list box. Click **OK.** Hyphens have been inserted into your social security number.

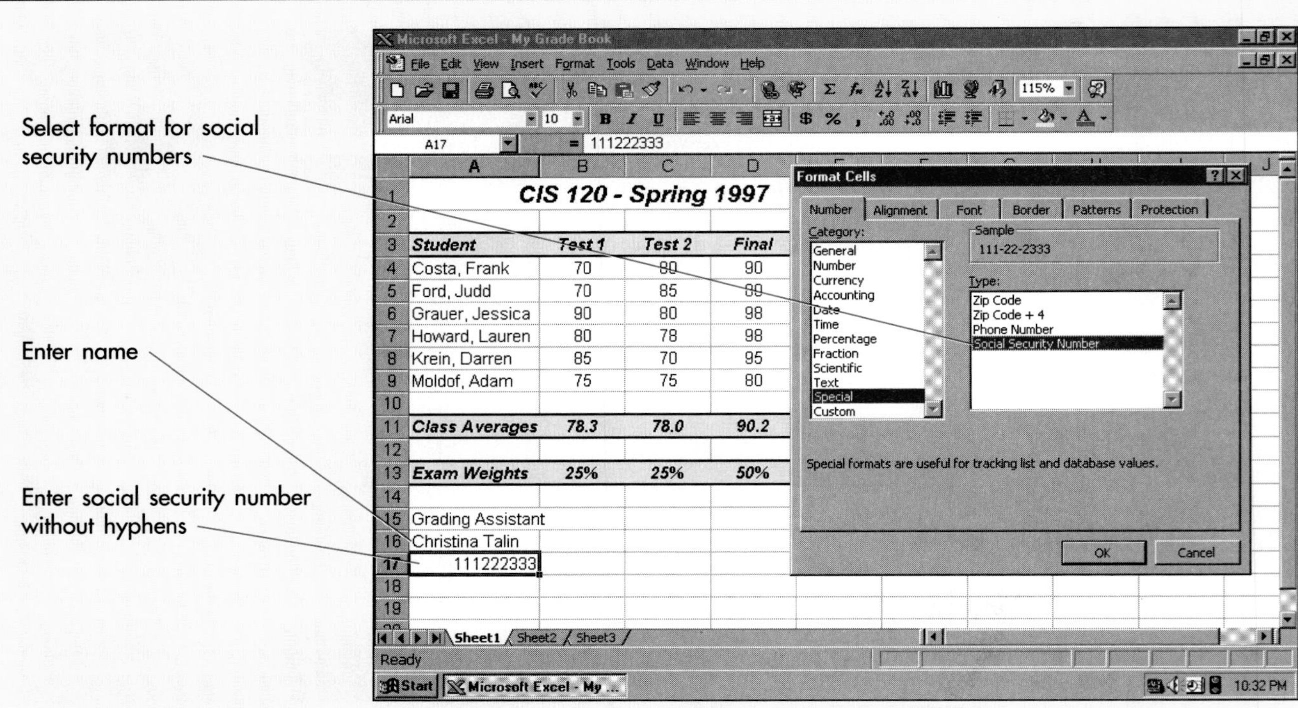

(g) Add Your Name and Social Security Number (step 7)

FIGURE 2.7 Hands-on Exercise 2 (continued)

STEP 8: The Page Setup Command

- Pull down the **File menu.** Click **Page Setup** to display the Page Setup dialog box.
  - Click the **Margins tab.** Check the box to center the worksheet Horizontally.
  - Click the **Sheet tab.** Check the boxes to print Row and Column Headings and Gridlines.
  - Click **OK** to exit the Page Setup dialog box.
- Click the **Print Preview button** to preview the worksheet before printing:
  - If you are satisfied with the appearance of the worksheet, click the **Print button** within the Preview window, then click **OK** to print the worksheet.
  - If you are not satisfied with the appearance of the worksheet, click the **Setup button** within the Preview window to make the necessary changes, after which you can print the worksheet.
- Save the workbook.

THE INSERT COMMENT COMMAND

You can add a comment, which displays a ScreenTip, to any cell in a worksheet. Click in the cell, pull down the Insert menu, and click Comment to display a box in which you enter the comment. Click outside the box when you have completed the entry. Point to the cell (which should have a tiny red triangle) and you will see the ScreenTip you just created. (If you do not see the triangle or the tip, pull down the Tools menu, click Options, click the View tab, then click the options button for Comment Indicator Only in the Comments area.)

STEP 9: Print the Cell Formulas

- Pull down the **Tools menu,** click **Options,** click the **View tab,** check the box for **Formulas,** then click **OK** (or use the keyboard shortcut **Ctrl+`**). The worksheet should display the cell formulas.
- If necessary, click the arrow to the right of the horizontal scroll box so that column E, the column containing the cell formulas, comes into view.
- Double click the border between the column headings for columns E and F to increase the width of column E to accommodate the widest entry in the column.
- Pull down the **File menu.** Click the **Page Setup** command to display the Page Setup dialog box.
  - Click the **Page tab.** Click the **Landscape orientation button.**
  - Click the option button to **Fit to 1 page.** Click **OK** to exit the Page Setup dialog box.
- Click the **Print Preview button** to preview the worksheet before printing. It should match the display in Figure 2.7h:
  - If you are satisfied with the appearance of the worksheet, click the **Print button** within the Preview window, then click **OK** to print the worksheet.
  - If you are not satisfied with the appearance of the worksheet, click the **Setup button** within the Preview window to make the necessary changes, after which you can print the worksheet.
- Pull down the **File menu.** Click **Close.** Click **No** if prompted to save changes.
- Exit Excel if you do not want to continue with the next exercise at this time.

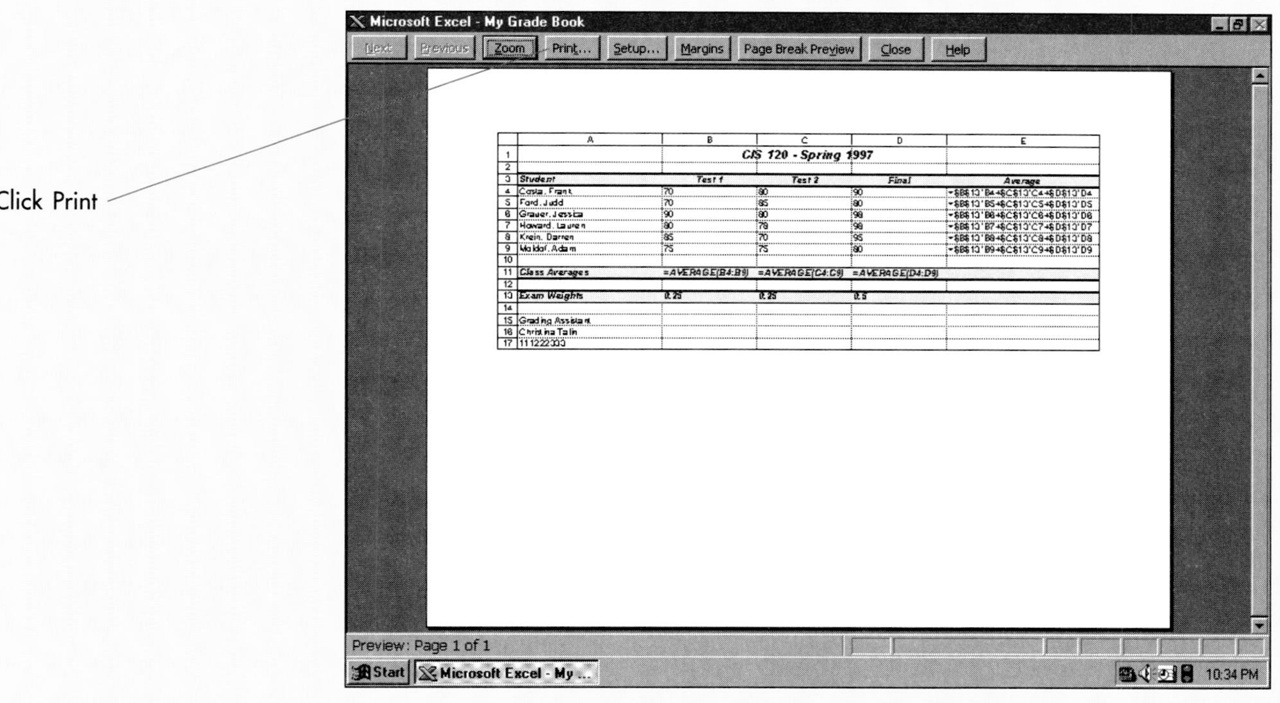

(h) Print Preview Command (step 9)

FIGURE 2.7 Hands-on Exercise 2 (continued)

Financial forecasting is one of the most common business applications of spreadsheets. Figure 2.8 depicts one such illustration, in which the income and expenses of Get Rich Quick Enterprises are projected over a five-year period. The displayed values are shown in Figure 2.8a, and the cell formulas are shown in Figure 2.8b.

Income in any given year is equal to the number of units sold times the unit price. The projected income in 1996, for example, is $300,000 based on sales of 100,000 units at a price of $3.00 per unit. The variable costs for the same year are estimated at $150,000 (100,000 units times $1.50 per unit). The production facility costs an additional $50,000, and administrative expenses add another $25,000. Subtracting the total expenses from the estimated income yields a net income before taxes of $75,000.

100,000 units at $3.00 per unit

100,000 units at $1.50 per unit

Assumptions and initial conditions are isolated and are used in developing formulas

	A	B	C	D	E	F
1	Get Rich Quick Enterprises					
2		1996	1997	1998	1999	2000
3	**Income**					
4	Units Sold	$100,000	$110,000	$121,000	$133,100	$146,410
5	Unit Price	$3.00	$3.15	$3.31	$3.47	$3.65
6	**Gross Revenue**	$300,000	$346,500	$400,208	$462,240	$533,887
7						
8	**Fixed costs**					
9	Production facility	$50,000	$54,000	$58,320	$62,986	$68,024
10	Administration	$25,000	$26,250	$27,563	$28,941	$30,388
11	**Variable cost**					
12	Unit mfg cost	$1.50	$1.65	$1.82	$2.00	$2.20
13	Variable mfg cost	$150,000	$181,500	$219,615	$265,734	$321,538
14						
15	Earnings before taxes	$75,000	$84,750	$94,710	$104,579	$113,936
16						
17	**Initial conditions**			**Annual increase**		
18	First year sales	$100,000		10.0%		
19	Selling price	$3.00		5.0%		
20	Unit mfg cost	$1.50		10.0%		
21	Production facility	$50,000		8.0%		
22	Administration	$25,000		5.0%		
23	First year of forecast	1996				

(a) Displayed Values

	A	B	C	D	E	F
1	Get Rich Quick Enterprises					
2		=B23	=B2+1	=C2+1	=D2+1	=E2+1
3	**Income**					
4	Units Sold	=B18	=B4+B4*$D$18	=C4+C4*$D$18	=D4+D4*$D$18	=E4+E4*$D$18
5	Unit Price	=B19	=B5+B5*$D$19	=C5+C5*$D$19	=D5+D5*$D$19	=E5+E5*$D$19
6	**Gross Revenue**	=B4*B5	=C4*C5	=D4*D5	=E4*E5	=F4*F5
7						
8	**Fixed costs**					
9	Production facility	=B21	=B9+B9*$D$21	=C9+C9*$D$21	=D9+D9*$D$21	=E9+E9*$D$21
10	Administration	=B22	=B10+B10*$D$22	=C10+C10*$D$22	=D10+D10*$D$22	=E10+E10*$D$22
11	**Variable cost**					
12	Unit mfg cost	=B20	=B12+B12*$D$20	=C12+C12*$D$20	=D12+D12*$D$20	=E12+E12*$D$20
13	Variable mfg cost	=B4*B12	=C4*C12	=D4*D12	=E4*E12	=F4*F12
14						
15	Earnings before taxes	=B6-(B9+B10+B13)	=C6-(C9+C10+C13)	=D6-(D9+D10+D13)	=E6-(E9+E10+E13)	=F6-(F9+F10+F13)
16						
17	**Initial conditions**			**Annual increase**		
18	First year sales	$100,000		10.0%		
19	Selling price	$3.00		5.0%		
20	Unit mfg cost	$1.50		10.0%		
21	Production facility	$50,000		8.0%		
22	Administration	$25,000		5.0%		
23	First year of forecast	1996				

(b) Cell Formulas

FIGURE 2.8 The Financial Forecast

The estimated income and expenses for each succeeding year are based on an assumed percentage increase over the previous year. The projected rates of increase as well as the initial conditions are shown at the bottom of the worksheet. We cannot overemphasize the importance of isolating ***assumptions*** and ***initial conditions*** in this manner, and further, that all entries in the body of the spreadsheet be developed as formulas that reference these cells. The entry in cell B4, for example, is *not* the constant 100,000, but rather a reference to cell B18, which contains the value 100,000.

The distinction may seem trivial, but most assuredly it is not, as two important objectives are achieved. The user sees at a glance which factors affect the results of the spreadsheet (i.e., the cost and earnings projections), and further, the user can easily change any of those values to see their effect on the overall forecast. Assume, for example, that the first-year forecast changes to 80,000 units and that this number will increase at 8 percent a year (rather than 10). The only changes in the worksheet are to the entries in cells B18 and D18, because the projected sales are calculated using the values in these cells.

Once you appreciate the necessity of isolating the assumptions and initial conditions, you can design the actual spreadsheet. Ask yourself why you are building the spreadsheet in the first place and what you hope to accomplish. (The financial forecast in this example is intended to answer questions regarding projected rates of growth, and more important, how changes in the assumptions and initial conditions will affect the income, expenses, and earnings in later years.) By clarifying what you hope to accomplish, you facilitate the creation of the spreadsheet, which is done in five general stages:

1. Enter the row and column headings, and the values for the initial conditions and the assumed rates of change.
2. Develop the formulas for the first year of the forecast based on the initial conditions at the bottom of the spreadsheet.
3. Develop the formulas for the second year based on the values in year one and the assumed rates of change.
4. Copy the formulas for year two to the remaining years of the forecast.
5. Format the spreadsheet, then print the completed forecast.

Perhaps the most critical step is the development of the formulas for the second year (1997 in Figure 2.8), which are based on the results of 1996 and the assumptions about how these results will change for the next year. The units sold in 1997, for example, are equal to the sales in 1996 (cell B4) plus the estimated increase (B4*$D$18); that is,

1997 sales = 1996 sales + 1996 sales * percent increase

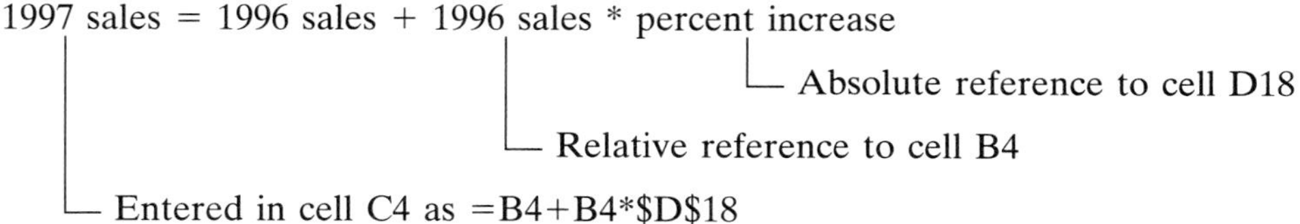

The formula to compute the sales for 1997 uses both absolute and relative references, so that it will be copied properly to the other columns for the remaining years in the forecast. An absolute reference ($D$18) is used for the cell containing the percent increase in sales, because this reference should remain the same when the formula is copied. A relative reference (B4) is used for the sales from the previous year, because this reference should change when the formula is copied. Many of the other formulas in column C are also based on percentage increases from column B, and are developed in similar fashion.

HANDS-ON EXERCISE 3

A Financial Forecast

Objective: To develop a spreadsheet for a financial forecast based on the principles of absolute and relative addresses, and the importance of isolating assumptions and initial conditions. Use Figure 2.9 as a guide in the exercise.

STEP 1: Enter the Formulas for Year One

- Start Excel. Open the **Financial Forecast** workbook in the **Exploring Excel folder** to display the workbook in Figure 2.9a. (Cells B4 through B15 will be empty on your worksheet.)
- Click in **cell B2.** Type **=B23** and press **enter.** This is very different from entering 1996 in cell B2 as described in the boxed tip on isolating assumptions.
- Enter the remaining formulas for year one:
  - Click in **cell B4.** Type =**B18.**
  - Click in **cell B5.** Type =**B19.**
  - Click in **cell B6.** Type =**B4*B5.**
  - Click in **cell B9.** Type =**B21.**
  - Click in **cell B10.** Type =**B22.**
  - Click in **cell B12.** Type =**B20.**
  - Click in **cell B13.** Type =**B4*B12.**
  - Click in **cell B15.** Type =**B6−(B9+B10+B13).**
- Save the workbook as **Finished Financial Forecast.**

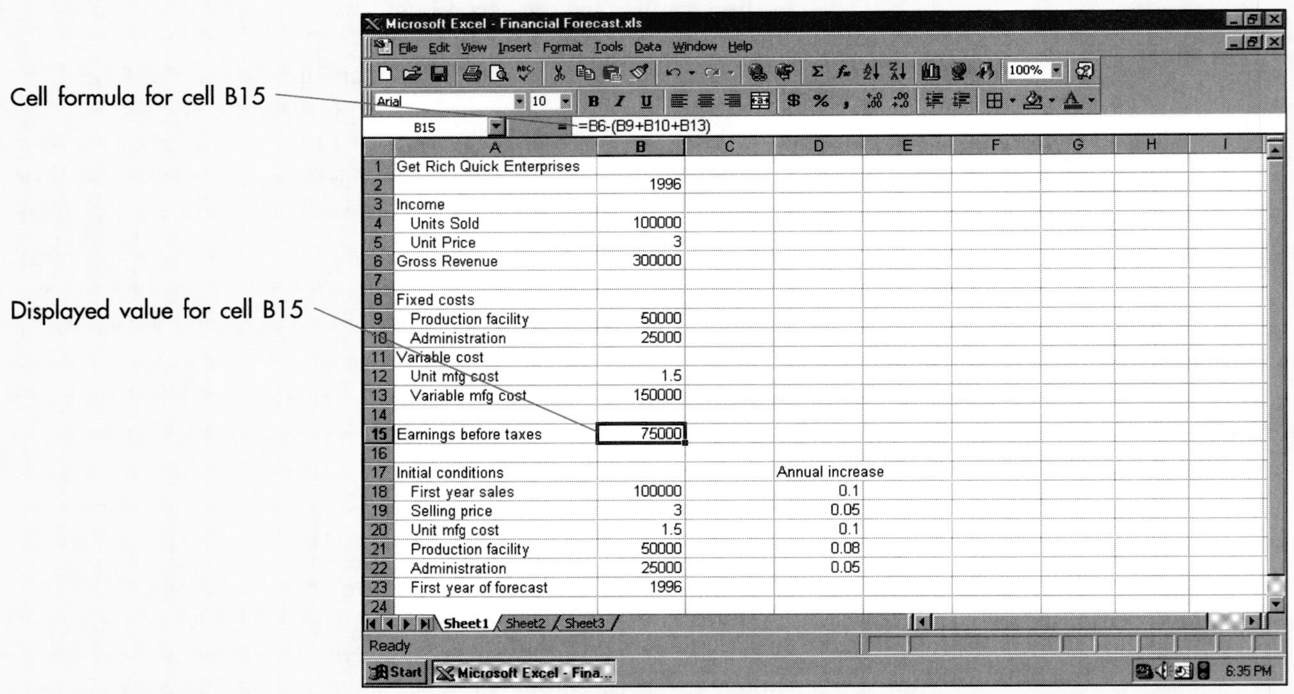

	A	B	C	D
1	Get Rich Quick Enterprises			
2		1996		
3	Income			
4	Units Sold	100000		
5	Unit Price	3		
6	Gross Revenue	300000		
7				
8	Fixed costs			
9	Production facility	50000		
10	Administration	25000		
11	Variable cost			
12	Unit mfg cost	1.5		
13	Variable mfg cost	150000		
14				
15	Earnings before taxes	75000		
16				
17	Initial conditions			Annual increase
18	First year sales	100000		0.1
19	Selling price	3		0.05
20	Unit mfg cost	1.5		0.1
21	Production facility	50000		0.08
22	Administration	25000		0.05
23	First year of forecast	1996		

(a) Enter Formulas for Year One (step 1)

FIGURE 2.9 Hands-on Exercise 3

ISOLATE ASSUMPTIONS

The formulas in a worksheet should be based on cell references rather than specific values; for example, B17 or $B$17 rather than 100,000. The cells containing these values should be clearly labeled and set apart from the rest of the worksheet. You can then vary the inputs (assumptions) to the worksheet and immediately see the effect. The chance for error is also minimized because you are changing the contents of a single cell, rather than changing the multiple formulas that reference the values.

STEP 2: Enter the Formulas for Year Two

- The formulas in column B will be used to develop the formulas for column C.
- Click in **cell C2.** Type **=B2+1,** which is the formula to determine the second year of the forecast.
- Click in **cell C4.** Type **=B4+B4*$D$18.** This formula computes the sales for year two as a function of the sales in year one and the assumed rate of increase.
- Enter the remaining formulas for year two:
  - Click in **cell C5.** Type **=B5+B5*$D$19.**
  - Click in **cell C6.** Type **=C4*C5.**
  - Click in **cell C9.** Type **=B9+B9*$D$21.**
  - Click in **cell C10.** Type **=B10+B10*$D$22.**
  - Click in **cell C12.** Type **=B12+B12*$D$20**
  - Click in **cell C13.** Type **=C4*C12.**
  - Click in **cell C15.** Type **=C6−(C9+C10+C13).**
- The cell contents for the second year (1997) are complete. The displayed values in this column should match the numbers shown in Figure 2.9b.
- Save the workbook.

STEP 3: Copy the Formulas to the Remaining Years

- Click and drag to select cells **C2** through **C15** (the cells containing the formulas for year two). Click the **Copy button** on the Standard toolbar. A moving border will surround these cells to indicate that their contents have been copied to the clipboard.
- Click and drag to select cells **D2** through **F15** (the cells that will contain the formulas for years three to five). Point to the selection and click the **right mouse button** to display the shortcut menu in Figure 2.9c.
- Click **Paste** to paste the contents of the clipboard into the selected cells. The displayed values for the last three years of the forecast should be visible in the worksheet. (You should see earnings before taxes of 113936.384 for the year 2000.)
- Press **Esc** to remove the moving border. Save the workbook.

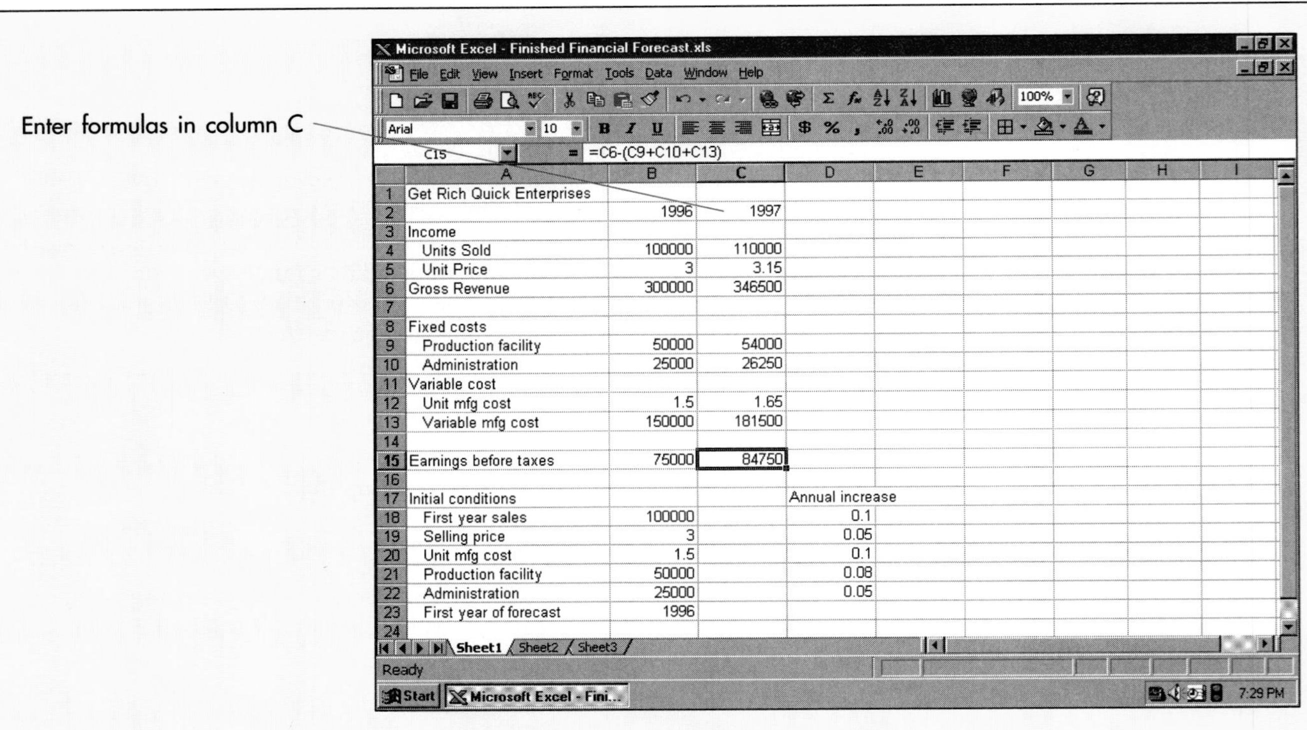

(b) Enter Formulas for Year Two (step 2)

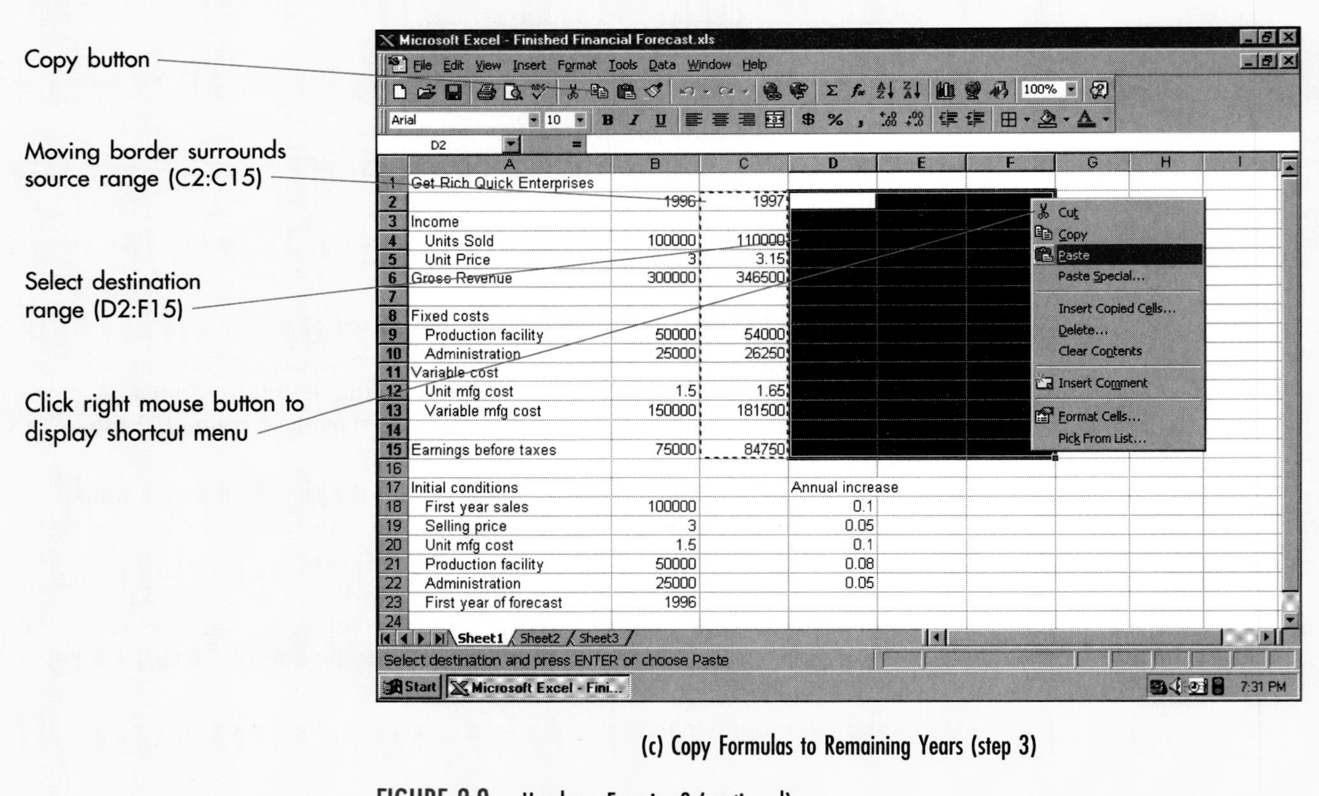

(c) Copy Formulas to Remaining Years (step 3)

FIGURE 2.9 Hands-on Exercise 3 (continued)

THE RANGE FINDER

The fastest way to change the contents of a cell is to double click in the cell, then make the changes directly in the cell rather than on the formula bar. Note, too, that if the cell contains a formula (as opposed to a literal entry), Excel will display each cell reference in the formula in a different color, which corresponds to the border color of the referenced cells elsewhere in the worksheet. This feature, known as the range finder, makes it easy to see which cell or cell range is referenced by the formula.

STEP 4: Format the Spreadsheet

- The hard part is done, and you are ready to format the worksheet. The specifics of the formatting operation are left to you, but Figure 2.9d is provided to guide you to the completed result.
- Formatting is done within the context of select-then-do; that is, you select the cell(s) to which you want the formatting to apply, then you execute the appropriate formatting command.
- Remember to press and hold the Ctrl key if you want to select noncontiguous cells prior to executing a formatting command.

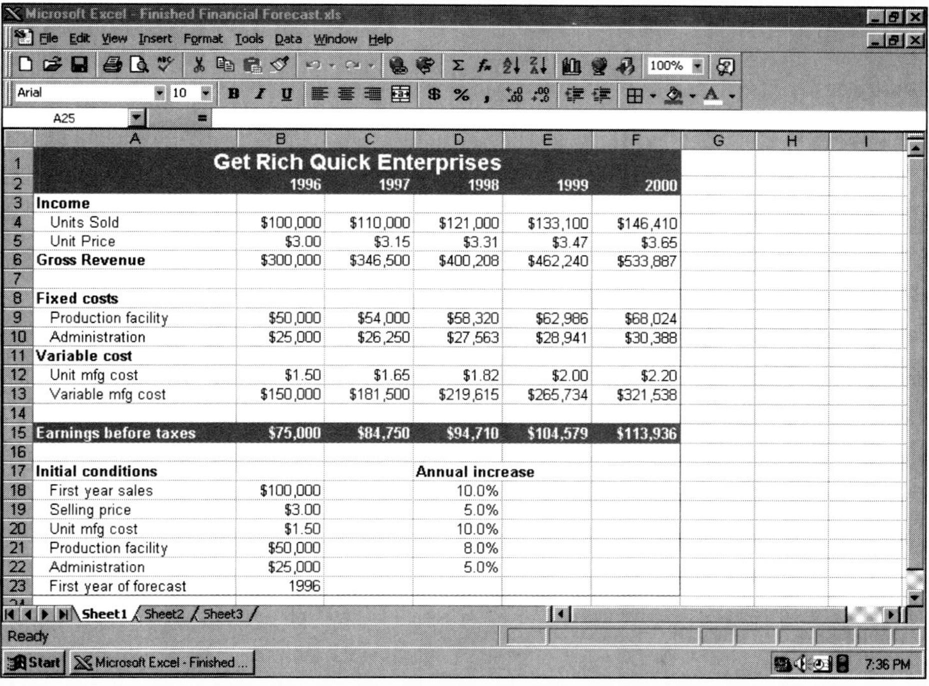

(d) Format the Spreadsheet (step 4)

FIGURE 2.9 Hands-on Exercise 3 (continued)

THE FORMATTING TOOLBAR

The ***Formatting toolbar*** is the fastest way to implement most formatting operations. There are buttons for boldface, italics, and underlining, alignment (including centering across columns), currency, percent, and comma formats, as well as buttons to increase or decrease the number of decimal places. There are also several list boxes, which enable you to choose the font, point size, and font color, as well as the type of border and shading.

STEP 5: Print the Completed Spreadsheet

- Add your name somewhere in the worksheet to prove to your instructor that you did the exercise.
- Print the completed spreadsheet twice, once to show the displayed values and once to show the cell formulas. Submit both printouts to your instructor.
- Congratulations on a job well done! Exit Excel.

CHANGE THE YEAR

A well-designed spreadsheet facilitates change by isolating the assumptions and initial conditions. 1996 has come and gone, but all you have to do to update the forecast is to click in cell B23, and enter 1997 as the initial year. The entries in cells B2 through F2 (containing the years of the forecast) are changed automatically as they contain formulas (rather than specific values) that reference the initial year in cell B23.

SUMMARY

All worksheet commands operate on a cell or group of cells known as a range. A range is selected by dragging the mouse to highlight the range. The range remains selected until another range is defined or you click another cell in the worksheet. Noncontiguous (nonadjacent) ranges may be selected in conjunction with the Ctrl key.

The formulas in a cell or range of cells may be copied or moved anywhere within a worksheet. An absolute reference remains constant throughout a copy operation, whereas a relative address is adjusted for the new location. Absolute and relative references have no meaning in a move operation. The copy and move operations are implemented through the Copy and Paste commands, and the Cut and Paste commands, respectively.

Formatting is done within the context of select-then-do; that is, select the cell or range of cells, then execute the appropriate command. The Format Cells command controls the formatting for Numbers, Alignment, Fonts, Borders, and Patterns (colors). The Formatting toolbar simplifies the formatting process.

A spreadsheet is first and foremost a tool for decision making, and as such, the subject of continual what-if speculation. It is critical, therefore, that the initial conditions and assumptions be isolated and clearly visible, and further that all formulas in the body of the spreadsheet be developed using these cells.

KEY WORDS AND CONCEPTS

Absolute reference
Accounting format
Alignment
Assumptions
Automatic formatting
Border tab
Cell formulas
Clipboard
Column command
Column width
Copy command
Currency format
Custom format
Cut command
Date format
Destination range
Format cells command
Format menu
Format Painter
Formatting toolbar
Fraction format
General format
Horizontal alignment
Initial conditions
Mixed reference
Move operation
Noncontiguous range
Number format
Paste command
Patterns tab
Percentage format
Range
Relative reference
Row command
Row height
Scientific format
Select-then-do
Source range
Special format
Text format
Time format
Vertical alignment

MULTIPLE CHOICE

1. Cell F6 contains the formula =AVERAGE(B6:D6). What will be the contents of cell F7 if the entry in cell F6 is *copied* to cell F7?
(a) =AVERAGE(B6:D6)
(b) =AVERAGE(B7:D7)
(c) =AVERAGE($B$6:$D$6)
(d) =AVERAGE($B$7:$D$7)

2. Cell F6 contains the formula =AVERAGE(B6:D6). What will be the contents of cell F7 if the entry in cell F6 is *moved* to cell F7?
(a) =AVERAGE(B6:D6)
(b) =AVERAGE(B7:D7)
(c) =AVERAGE($B$6:$D$6)
(d) =AVERAGE($B$7:$D$7)

3. A formula containing the entry =$A$4 is copied to a cell one column over and two rows down. How will the entry appear in its new location?
(a) Both the row and column will change
(b) Neither the row nor column will change
(c) The row will change but the column will remain the same
(d) The column will change but the row will remain the same

4. Which commands are necessary to implement a move?
(a) Cut and Paste commands
(b) Move command from the Edit menu
(c) Either (a) or (b)
(d) Neither (a) nor (b)

5. A cell range may consist of:
   (a) A single cell
   (b) A row or set of rows
   (c) A column or set of columns
   (d) All of the above

6. Which command will take a cell, or group of cells, and duplicate them elsewhere in the worksheet, without changing the original cell references?
   (a) Copy command, provided relative addresses were specified
   (b) Copy command, provided absolute addresses were specified
   (c) Move command, provided relative addresses were specified
   (d) Move command, provided absolute addresses were specified

7. The contents of cell B4 consist of the formula =B2*B3, yet the displayed value in cell B4 is a series of pound signs. What is the most likely explanation for this?
   (a) Cells B2 and B3 contain text entries rather than numeric entries and so the formula in cell B4 cannot be evaluated
   (b) Cell B4 is too narrow to display the computed result
   (c) Both (a) and (b)
   (d) Neither (a) nor (b)

8. The Formatting toolbar contains buttons to
   (a) Change to percent format
   (b) Increase or decrease the number of decimal places
   (c) Center an entry across columns
   (d) All of the above

9. Given that the percentage format is in effect, and that the number .056 has been entered into the active cell, how will the contents of the cell appear?
   (a) .056
   (b) 5.6%
   (c) .056%
   (d) 56%

10. Which of the following entries is equivalent to the decimal number .2?
    (a) ⅕
    (b) =1/5
    (c) Both (a) and (b)
    (d) Neither (a) nor (b)

11. What is the effect of two successive Undo commands, one right after the other?
    (a) The situation is not possible because the Undo command is not available in Microsoft Excel
    (b) The situation is not possible because the Undo command cannot be executed twice in a row
    (c) The Undo commands cancel each other out; that is, the worksheet is as it was prior to the first Undo command
    (d) The last two commands prior to the first Undo command are reversed

12. Which of the following fonts are included in Windows?
    (a) Arial and Times New Roman
    (b) Courier New
    (c) Wingdings and Symbol
    (d) All of the above

13. A numerical entry may be
    (a) Displayed in boldface and/or italics
    (b) Left, centered, or right aligned in a cell
    (c) Displayed in any TrueType font in any available point size
    (d) All of the above

14. Which of the following best describes the formula to compute the sales in the second year of the financial forecast?
    (a) It contains a relative reference to the assumed rate of increase and an absolute reference to the sales from the previous year
    (b) It contains an absolute reference to the assumed rate of increase and a relative reference to the sales from the previous year
    (c) It contains absolute references to both the assumed rate of increase and the sales from the previous year
    (d) It contains relative references to both the assumed rate of increase and the sales from the previous year

15. The estimated sales for the first year of a financial forecast are contained in cell B3. The sales for year two are assumed to be 10% higher than the first year, with the rate of increase (10%) stored in cell C23 at the bottom of the spreadsheet. Which of the following is the best way to enter the projected sales for year two, assuming that this formula is to be copied to the remaining years of the forecast?.
    (a) =B3+B3*.10
    (b) =B3+B3*C23
    (c) =B3+B3*$C$23
    (d) All of the above are equivalent entries

ANSWERS

1. b	**6.** b	**11.** c
2. a	**7.** b	**12.** d
3. b	**8.** d	**13.** d
4. a	**9.** b	**14.** b
5. d	**10.** b	**15.** c

PRACTICE WITH EXCEL 97

1. Figure 2.10 contains a worksheet that was used to calculate the difference between the Asking Price and Selling Price on various real estate listings that were sold during June, as well as the commission paid to the real estate agency as a result of selling those listings. Complete the worksheet, following the steps on the next page.

	A	B	C	D	E	F
1	Coaches Realty - Sales for June					
2						
3						
4	Customer	Address	Asking Price	Selling Price	Difference	Commission
5	Landry	122 West 75 Terr.	450000	350000		
6	Spurrier	4567 S.W. 95 Street	750000	648500		
7	Shula	123 Alamo Road	350000	275000		
8	Lombardi	9000 Brickell Place	275000	250000		
9	Johnson	5596 Powerline Road	189000	189000		
10	Erickson	8900 N.W. 89 Street	456000	390000		
11	Bowden	75 Maynada Blvd.	300000	265000		
12						
13		Totals:				
14						
15	Commission %:	0.035				

FIGURE 2.10 Spreadsheet for Practice Exercise 1

a. Open the partially completed *Chapter 2 Practice 1* workbook on the data disk, then save the workbook as *Chapter 2 Practice 1 Solution.*
b. Click cell E5 and enter the formula to calculate the difference between the asking price and the selling price for the property belonging to Mr. Landry.
c. Click cell F5 and enter the formula to calculate the commission paid to the agency as a result of selling the property. (Pay close attention to the difference between relative and absolute cell references.)
d. Select cells E5:F5 and copy the formulas to E6:F11 to calculate the difference and commission for the rest of the properties.
e. Click cell C13 and enter the formula to calculate the total asking price, which is the sum of the asking prices for the individual listings.
f. Copy the formula in C13 to the range D13:F13 to calculate the other totals.
g. Select the range C5:F13 and format the numbers so that they display with dollar signs and commas, and no decimal places (e.g., $450,000).
h. Click cell B15 and format the number as a percentage.
i. Click cell A1 and center the title across the width of the worksheet. With the cell still selected, select cells A2:F4 as well and change the font to 12 point Arial bold italic.
j. Select cells A4:F4 and create a bottom border to separate the headings from the data. Select cells F5:F11 and shade the commissions.
k. Add your name as the realtor in cell B.
l. Print the worksheet and submit it to your instructor.

2. The Sales Invoice: Use Figure 2.11 as the basis for a sales invoice that you will create and submit to your instructor. Your spreadsheet should follow the general format shown in the figure with respect to including a uniform discount for each item. Your spreadsheet should also include the sales tax. The discount percentage and sales tax percentage should be entered in a separate area so that they can be easily modified.

Use your imagination and sell any product at any price. You must, however, include at least four items in your invoice. Formatting is important, but you need not follow our format exactly. See how creative you can be, then submit your completed invoice to your instructor for inclusion in a class contest for the best invoice. Be sure your name appears somewhere on the worksheet as a sales associate. If you are really ambitious, you might include an object from the Microsoft Clip Gallery.

	A	B	C	D	E	F
1	Bargain Basement Shopping					
2						
3	Item	Quantity	List Price	Discount	Your Price	Total
4	US Robotics ISDN V.34 Fax/Modem	2	$293.14	$58.63	$234.51	$469.02
5	NEC 8X CD-ROM	6	$151.71	$30.34	$121.37	$728.21
6	Seagate 2.1 Gb Hard Drive	4	$299.95	$59.99	$239.96	$959.84
7	Iomega Zip Drive	10	$199.95	$39.99	$159.96	$1,599.60
8						
9	Subtotal					$3,756.67
10	Tax					$244.18
11	Amount Due					$3,512.49
12						
13	Discount Percentage	20.0%				
14	Sales Tax Percentage	6.5%				
15	Sales Associate	Conner Smith				

FIGURE 2.11 Spreadsheet for Practice Exercise 2

3. The Probability Expert: How much would you bet *against* two people in your class having the same birthday? Don't be too hasty, for the odds of two classmates sharing the same birthday (month and day) are much higher than you would expect. For example, there is a fifty percent chance (.5063) in a class of 23 students that two people will have been born on the same day, as shown in the spreadsheet in Figure 2.12. The probability jumps to seventy percent (.7053) in a class of 30, and to ninety percent (.9025) in a class of 41. Don't take our word for it, but try the experiment in your class.

   You need a basic knowledge of probability to create the spreadsheet. In essence you calculate the probability of individuals not having the same birthday, then subtract this number from one, to obtain the probability of the event coming true. In a group of two people, for example, the probability of not being born on the same day is 365/366; i.e., the second person can

	A	B	C
1	The Birthday Problem		
2	Number of People	Probability of Different Birthdays	Probability of the Same Birthday
3	2	99.73%	0.27%
4	3	99.18%	0.82%
5	4	98.37%	1.63%
6	5	97.29%	2.71%
7	6	95.96%	4.04%
8	7	94.39%	5.61%
9	8	92.59%	7.41%
10	9	90.56%	9.44%
11	10	88.34%	11.66%
	...	...	...
24	**23**	**49.37%**	**50.63%**
	...	...	...
42	**41**	**9.75%**	**90.25%**
	...	...	...
51	**50**	**2.99%**	**97.01%**

FIGURE 2.12 Spreadsheet for Practice Exercise 3

be born on any of 365 days and still have a different birthday. The probability of two people having the same birthday becomes 1 − 365/366.

The probability for different birthdays in a group of three is (365/366)*(364/366); the probability of not having different birthdays—that is, of two people having the same birthday, is one minus this number. Each row in the spreadsheet is calculated from the previous row. It's not as hard as it looks, and the results are quite interesting! As you can see, there is a 97% probability that two people in a group of 50 will have the same birthday.

4. Help for Your Sibling: Develop the multiplication table for a younger sibling shown in Figure 2.13. Creating the row and column headings is easy in that you can enter the numbers manually, or you can use online help to learn about the AutoFill feature. The hard part is creating the formulas in the body of the worksheet (we don't want you to enter the numbers manually). The trick is to use mixed references for the formula in cell B4, then copy that single cell to the remainder of the table.

Add your name to the worksheet and submit it to your instructor. Remember, this worksheet is for a younger sibling, and so formatting is important. Print the cell formulas as well so that you can see how the mixed reference changes throughout the worksheet. Submit the complete assignment (title page, displayed values, and cell formulas) to your instructor. Using mixed references correctly is challenging, but once you arrive at the correct solution, you will have learned a lot about this very powerful spreadsheet feature.

	A	B	C	D	E	F	G	H	I	J	K	L	M
1	A Multiplication Table for My Younger Sister												
2													
3		1	2	3	4	5	6	7	8	9	10	11	12
4	1	1	2	3	4	5	6	7	8	9	10	11	12
5	2	2	4	6	8	10	12	14	16	18	20	22	24
6	3	3	6	9	12	15	18	21	24	27	30	33	36
7	4	4	8	12	16	20	24	28	32	36	40	44	48
8	5	5	10	15	20	25	30	35	40	45	50	55	60
9	6	6	12	18	24	30	36	42	48	54	60	66	72
10	7	7	14	21	28	35	42	49	56	63	70	77	84
11	8	8	16	24	32	40	48	56	64	72	80	88	96
12	9	9	18	27	36	45	54	63	72	81	90	99	108
13	10	10	20	30	40	50	60	70	80	90	100	110	120
14	11	11	22	33	44	55	66	77	88	99	110	121	132
15	12	12	24	36	48	60	72	84	96	108	120	132	144

FIGURE 2.13 Spreadsheet for Practice Exercise 4

5. Figure 2.14 illustrates how a spreadsheet can be used to compute a payroll for hourly employees. A partially completed version of the worksheet can be found in the file *Chapter 2 Practice 5.* Your job is to complete the worksheet by developing the entries for the first employee, then copying those entries to the remaining rows. (An employee receives time and a half for overtime.)

To receive full credit for this assignment, the formulas for the withholding and Social Security taxes must reference the percentages in cells C12 and C13, respectively. Format the worksheet after it has been completed. Add your name anywhere in the worksheet, then print it two ways, once with displayed values and once with cell contents; then submit both pages to your instructor.

	A	B	C	D	E	F	G	H
1	Employee Name	Hourly Wage	Regular Hours	Overtime Hours	Gross Pay	Withholding Tax	Soc Sec Tax	Net Pay
2								
3	Jones	$8.00	40	10	$440.00	$123.20	$28.60	$288.20
4	Smith	$9.00	35	0	$315.00	$88.20	$20.48	$206.33
5	Baker	$7.20	40	0	$288.00	$80.64	$18.72	$188.64
6	Barnard	$7.20	40	8	$374.40	$104.83	$24.34	$245.23
7	Adams	$10.00	40	4	$460.00	$128.80	$29.90	$301.30
8								
9	Totals				$1,877.40	$525.67	$122.03	$1,229.70
10								
11	Assumptions							
12	Withholding tax		28.0%					
13	FICA		6.5%					

FIGURE 2.14 Spreadsheet for Practice Exercise 5

CASE STUDIES

Establishing a Budget

You want to join a sorority, and you really would like a car. Convince your parents that you can afford both by developing a detailed budget for your four years at school. Your worksheet should include all sources of income (scholarships, loans, summer jobs, work-study, etc.) as well as all expenses (tuition, books, room and board, and entertainment). Make the budget as realistic as possible by building in projected increases over the four-year period.

Be sure to isolate the assumptions and initial conditions so that your spreadsheet is amenable to change. Print the spreadsheet twice, once to show displayed values, and once to show the cell formulas. Submit both pages to your instructor together with a cover page for your assignment.

The Entrepreneur

You have developed the perfect product and are seeking venture capital to go into immediate production. Your investors are asking for a projected income statement for the first four years of operation. The sales of your product are estimated at $200,000 the first year and are projected to grow at 10 percent annually. The cost of goods sold is 60 percent of the sales amount, which is expected to remain constant. You also have to pay a 10 percent sales commission, which is also expected to remain constant.

Develop a financial forecast that will show the projected profits before and after taxes (assuming a tax rate of 36 percent). Your worksheet should be completely flexible and capable of accommodating a change in any of the initial conditions or projected rates of increase, *without* having to edit or recopy any of the formulas.

Break-even Analysis

Widgets of America has developed the perfect product and is ready to go into production, pending a review of a five-year break-even analysis. The manufacturing cost in the first year is $1.00 per unit and is estimated to increase at 5% annually. The projected selling price is $2.00 per unit and can increase at 10% annually. Overhead expenses are fixed at $100,000 per year over the life of the project. The advertising budget is $50,000 in the first year but will decrease 15% a year as the product gains acceptance. How many units have to be sold each year for the company to break even, given the current cost estimates and projected rates of increase?

As in the previous case, your worksheet should be completely flexible and capable of accommodating a change in any of the initial conditions or projected rates of increase or decrease. Be sure to isolate all of the assumptions (i.e., the initial conditions and rates of increase) in one area of the worksheet, and then reference these cells as absolute references when building the formulas.

The Corporate Balance Sheet

A balance sheet is a snapshot of a firm's condition at a given point in time. One part of the balance sheet shows the firm's assets and includes items such as cash on hand, accounts receivable, and inventory. It also includes the value of fixed assets, such as the land and/or buildings owned by the firm. The other part of the balance sheet shows the firm's liabilities and includes accounts payable, accrued wages, and debt. It also includes owner's equity and retained earnings.

The best place to see examples of a real balance sheet is in an annual report, which is easily obtained from any public corporation. Obtain a copy of the annual report, find the balance sheet, then recreate the balance sheet for your instructor. Formatting and accuracy are important so do the best job you can. Include your name somewhere on the balance sheet as the financial auditor.

The Office Assistant

The Office Assistant monitors your work and offers advice throughout a session. You can tell that the Assistant has a suggestion when you see a lightbulb on the Office Assistant button on the Standard toolbar or in the Office Assistant window. You can read the suggestions as they occur and/or review them at the end of a session. Redo one or more of the exercises in this chapter, but this time pay attention to the Assistant. Write a brief note to your instructor describing three tips (shortcuts) offered by the Assistant. (You should, however, reset the Assistant before you begin or else the Assistant will not repeat tips that were offered in a previous session.) Start the Assistant, click the Options button, click the Options tab, then click the button to Reset tips.

The Spreadsheet Audit

The spreadsheet is an invaluable tool in decision making, but what if the spreadsheet contains an error? Unfortunately, it is all too easy to get caught up in the appearance of an attractively formatted spreadsheet without paying attention to its underlying accuracy. The *Erroneous Financial Forecast* is based on the financial forecast in the chapter, but it contains a different set of assumptions, which lead to a different set of profit projections. Open the workbook, and correct the initial error, which displays a series of #VALUE indicators throughout the worksheet. You will then see a projected profit of $24,877 for the final year, but is this number correct? Examine the spreadsheet carefully, make any additional corrections that are necessary, then submit the revised forecast based on the new assumptions to your instructor.

3

SPREADSHEETS IN DECISION MAKING: WHAT IF?

OBJECTIVES

After reading this chapter you will be able to:

1. Describe the use of spreadsheets in decision making; explain how the Goal Seek command and Scenario Manager facilitate the decision making process.
2. List the arguments of the PMT function and describe its use in financial decisions.
3. Use the Paste Function dialog box to select a function, identify the function arguments, then enter the function into a worksheet.
4. Use the fill handle to copy a cell range to a range of adjacent cells; use the AutoFill capability to enter a series into a worksheet.
5. Use pointing to create a formula; explain the advantage of pointing over explicitly typing cell references.
6. Use the AVERAGE, MAX, MIN, and COUNT functions in a worksheet.
7. Use the IF function to implement a decision; explain the VLOOKUP function and how it is used in a worksheet.
8. Describe the additional measures needed to print large worksheets; explain how freezing panes may help in the development of a large worksheet.

OVERVIEW

Excel is a fascinating program, but it is only a means to an end. A spreadsheet is first and foremost a tool for decision making, and the objective of this chapter is to show you just how valuable that tool can be. We begin by presenting two worksheets that we think will be truly useful to you. The first evaluates the purchase of a car and helps you determine just how much car you can afford. The second will be of interest when you are looking for a mortgage to buy a home.

The chapter continues to develop your knowledge of Excel with emphasis on the predefined functions that are built into the program. We consider financial functions such as the PMT function to determine the monthly payment on a loan. We introduce the MAX, MIN, COUNT, and COUNTA statistical functions. We also present the IF and VLOOKUP functions that provide decision making within a worksheet.

The chapter also discusses two important commands that facilitate the decision-making process. The Goal Seek command lets you enter the desired end result (such as the monthly payment on a car loan) and from that, determines the input (e.g., the price of the car) to produce that result. The Scenario Manager enables you to specify multiple sets of assumptions and input conditions (scenarios), then see at a glance the results of any given scenario.

The examples in this chapter review the important concepts of relative and absolute cell references, as well as the need to isolate the assumptions and initial conditions in a worksheet. The hands-on exercises introduce new techniques in the form of powerful shortcuts that will make you more proficient in Excel. We show you how to use the fill handle to copy cells within a worksheet and how to use the AutoFill capability to enter a data series. We also explain how to enter formulas by pointing to cells within a worksheet, as opposed to having to explicitly type the cell references.

ANALYSIS OF A CAR LOAN

Figure 3.1 shows how a worksheet might be applied to the purchase of a car. In essence, you need to know the monthly payment, which depends on the price of the car, the down payment, and the terms of the loan. In other words:

- Can you afford the monthly payment on the car of your choice?
- What if you settle for a less expensive car and receive a manufacturer's rebate?
- What if you work next summer to earn money for a down payment?
- What if you extend the life of the loan and receive a more favorable interest rate?

The answers to these and other questions determine whether you can afford a car, and if so, which car, and how you will pay for it. The decision is made easier by developing the worksheet in Figure 3.1, and then by changing the various parameters as indicated.

Figure 3.1a contains the ***template***, or "empty" worksheet, in which the text entries and formulas have already been entered, the formatting has already been applied, but no specific data has been input. The template requires that you enter the price of the car, the manufacturer's rebate, the down payment, the interest rate, and the length of the loan. The worksheet uses these parameters to compute the monthly payment. (Implicit in this discussion is the existence of a PMT function within the worksheet program, which is explained in the next section.)

The availability of the worksheet lets you consider several alternatives, and therein lies its true value. You quickly realize that the purchase of a $14,999 car as shown in Figure 3.1b is prohibitive because the monthly payment is almost $500. Settling for a less expensive car, coming up with a substantial down payment, and obtaining a manufacturer's rebate in Figure 3.1c help considerably, but the $317 monthly payment is still too steep. Extending the loan to a fourth year at a lower interest rate in Figure 3.1d reduces the monthly payment to (a more affordable) $244.

No specific data has been input

	A	B
1	Price of car	
2	Manufacturer's rebate	
3	Down payment	
4	Amount to finance	=B1-(B2+B3)
5	Interest rate	
6	Term (in years)	
7	Monthly payment	=PMT(B5/12,B6*12,-B4)

(a) The Template

Data entered

	A	B
1	Price of car	$14,999
2	Manufacturer's rebate	
3	Down payment	
4	Amount to finance	$14,999
5	Interest rate	9%
6	Term (in years)	3
7	Monthly payment	$476.96

(b) Initial Parameters

Less expensive car

Rebate

Down payment made

	A	B
1	Price of car	$13,999
2	Manufacturer's rebate	$1,000
3	Down payment	$3,000
4	Amount to finance	$9,999
5	Interest rate	9%
6	Term (in years)	3
7	Monthly payment	$317.97

(c) Less Expensive Car with Down Payment and Rebate

Lower interest rate

Longer term

	A	B
1	Price of car	$13,999
2	Manufacturer's rebate	$1,000
3	Down payment	$3,000
4	Amount to finance	$9,999
5	Interest rate	8%
6	Term (in years)	4
7	Monthly payment	$244.10

(d) Longer Term and Better Interest Rate

FIGURE 3.1 Spreadsheets in Decision Making

EXPLORING WWW

CAR SHOPPING ON THE WEB

Why guess about the price of a car or its features if you can obtain exact information from the Web? You can go to the site of a specific manufacturer, usually by entering an address of the form www.company.com (e.g., www.ford.com). You can also go to a site that provides information about multiple vendors. Our favorite is carpoint.msn.com, which provides detailed information about specifications and current prices. See practice exercise 6 at the end of the chapter.

PMT Function

A ***function*** is a predefined formula that accepts one or more ***arguments*** as input, performs the indicated calculation, then returns another value as output. Excel has more than 100 different functions in various categories. Financial functions, such as the PMT function we are about to study, are especially important in business.

The ***PMT function*** requires three arguments (the interest rate per period, the number of periods, and the amount of the loan) from which it computes the associated payment on a loan. The arguments are placed in parentheses and are separated by commas. Consider, for example, the PMT function as it might apply to Figure 3.1b:

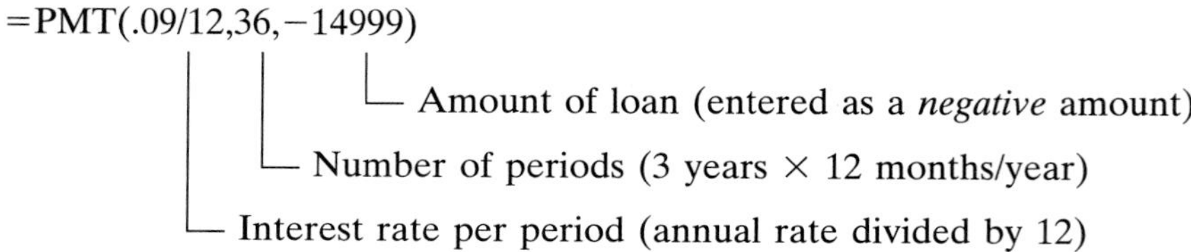

Instead of using specific values, however, the arguments in the PMT function are supplied as cell references, so that the computed payment can be based on values supplied by the user elsewhere in the worksheet. Thus, the PMT function is entered as =PMT(B5/12,B6*12,−B4) to reflect the terms of a specific loan whose arguments are in cells B4, B5, and B6. (The principal is entered as a negative amount because the money is lent to you and represents an outflow of cash from the bank.)

The Goal Seek Command

The analysis in Figure 3.1 enabled us to reduce the projected monthly payment from $476 to a more affordable $244. What if, however, you can afford a payment of only $200, and you want to know the maximum you can borrow in order to keep the payment to the specified amount. The ***Goal Seek command*** is designed to solve this type of problem as it enables you to set an end result (e.g., the monthly payment) in order to determine the input (the price of the car) to produce that result. Only one parameter (e.g., the price of the car *or* the interest rate) can be varied at a time.

Figure 3.2 extends our earlier analysis to illustrate the Goal Seek command. You create the spreadsheet as usual, then you pull down the Tools menu, and select the Goal Seek command to display the dialog box in Figure 3.2a. Enter the address of the cell containing the dependent formula (the monthly payment in cell B7) and the desired value of this cell ($200). Indicate the cell whose contents should be varied (the price of the car in cell B1), then click OK to execute the command. The Goal Seek command then varies the price of the car until the monthly payment returns the desired value of $200. (Not every problem has a solution, in which case Excel returns a message indicating that a solution cannot be found.)

In this example the Goal Seek command is able to find a solution and returns a purchase price of $12,192 as shown in Figure 3.2b. You now have all the information you need. Find a car that sells for $12,192 (or less), hold the other parameters to the values shown in the figure, and your monthly payment will be (at most) $200. The analyses in Figures 3.1 and 3.2 illustrate how a worksheet is used in the decision-making process. An individual defines a problem, then develops a worksheet that includes all of the associated parameters. He or she can then plug in specific numbers, changing one or more of the variables until a decision can be reached.

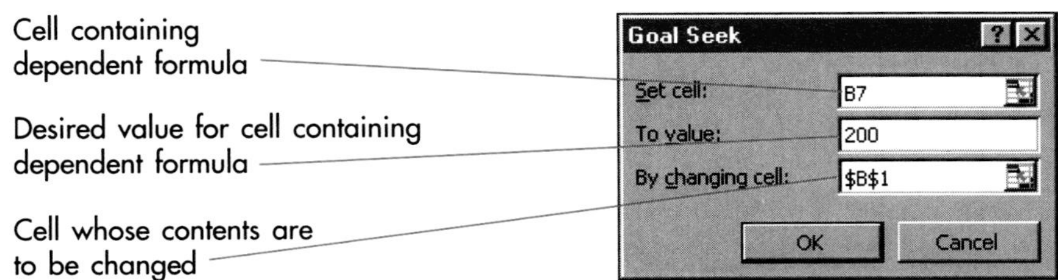

(a) Set the Maximum Payment

Required purchase price for a $200 monthly payment

	A	B
1	Price of car	$12,192
2	Manufacturer's rebate	$1,000
3	Down payment	$3,000
4	Amount to finance	$8,192
5	Interest rate	8%
6	Term (in years)	4
7	Monthly payment	$200.00

(b) Solution

FIGURE 3.2 The Goal Seek Command

LIMITATIONS OF THE GOAL SEEK COMMAND

The Goal Seek command, powerful as it is, is limited to a single variable; that is, you set the desired result but are limited to changing the value of a single input variable. Excel does, however, provide a more powerful tool known as Solver that can vary multiple input variables. This is a much more complex analysis and is beyond the scope of the present discussion.

HANDS-ON EXERCISE 1

Analysis of a Car Loan

Objective: To create a spreadsheet that will analyze a car loan; to illustrate the PMT function and the Goal Seek command. Use Figure 3.3 as a guide.

STEP 1: Enter the Descriptive Labels

- Start Excel. If necessary, click the **New button** on the Standard toolbar to open a new workbook.
- Click in **cell A1,** type the label **Price of car,** then press the **enter key** or **down arrow** to complete the entry and move automatically to cell A2.
- Enter the remaining labels for column A as shown in Figure 3.3a.
- Click and drag the column border between columns A and B to increase the width of column A to accommodate its widest entry.
- Save the workbook as **Analysis of a Car Loan** in the **Exploring Excel folder** as shown in Figure 3.3a.

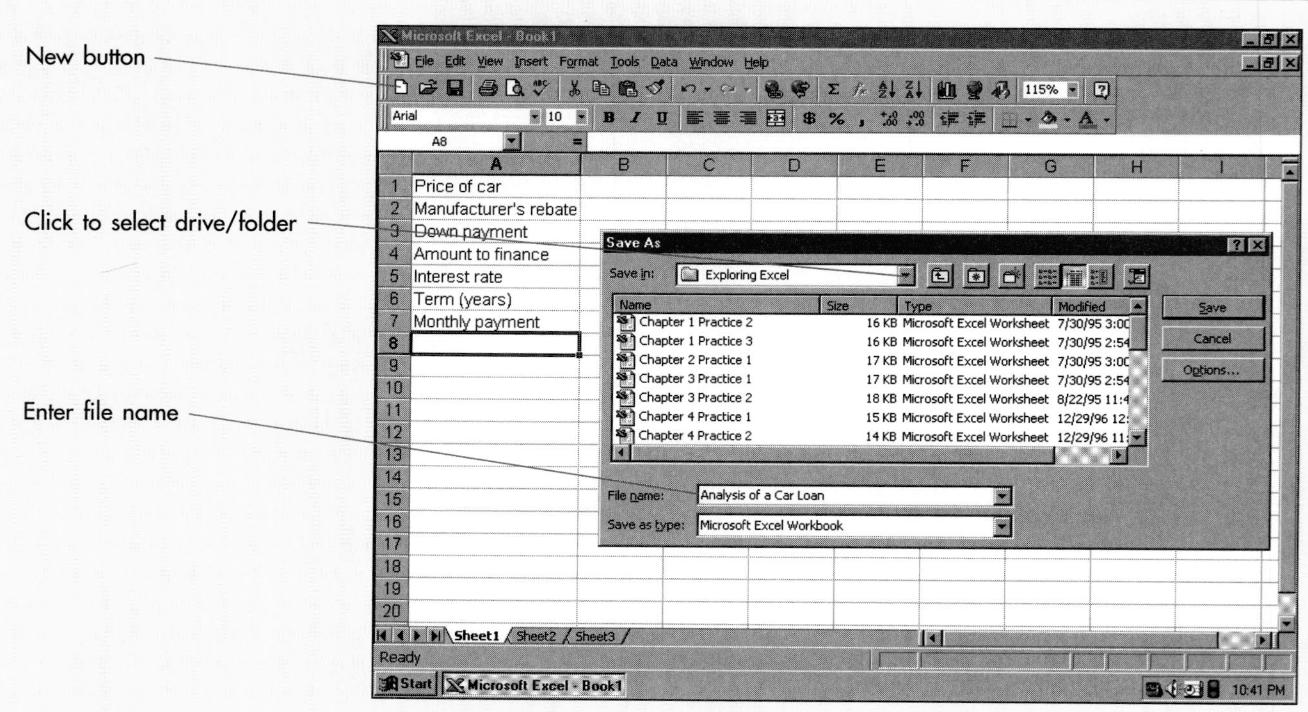

(a) Enter the Descriptive Labels (step 1)

FIGURE 3.3 Hands-on Exercise 1

STEP 2: Enter the PMT Function and Its Parameters

- Enter **$14,999** in cell B1 as shown in Figure 3.3b.
- Click in **cell B4.** Enter **=B1−(B2+B3),** which calculates the amount to finance (i.e., the principal of the loan).
- Enter **9%** and **3** in cells B5 and B6 as shown in Figure 3.3b.
- Click in **cell B7.** Enter **=PMT(B5/12,B6*12,−B4)** as the payment function. The arguments in the PMT function are the interest rate per period, the number of periods, and the principal, and correspond to the parameters of the loan. Save the workbook.

THE FORMATTING IS IN THE CELL

Once a number format has been assigned to a cell, either by including the format as you entered a number or through execution of a formatting command, the formatting remains in the cell. Thus, to change the contents in a formatted cell, all you need to do is enter the new number without the formatting. Entering 5000, for example, in a cell that was previously formatted as currency will display the number as $5,000.

Enter formulas in column B

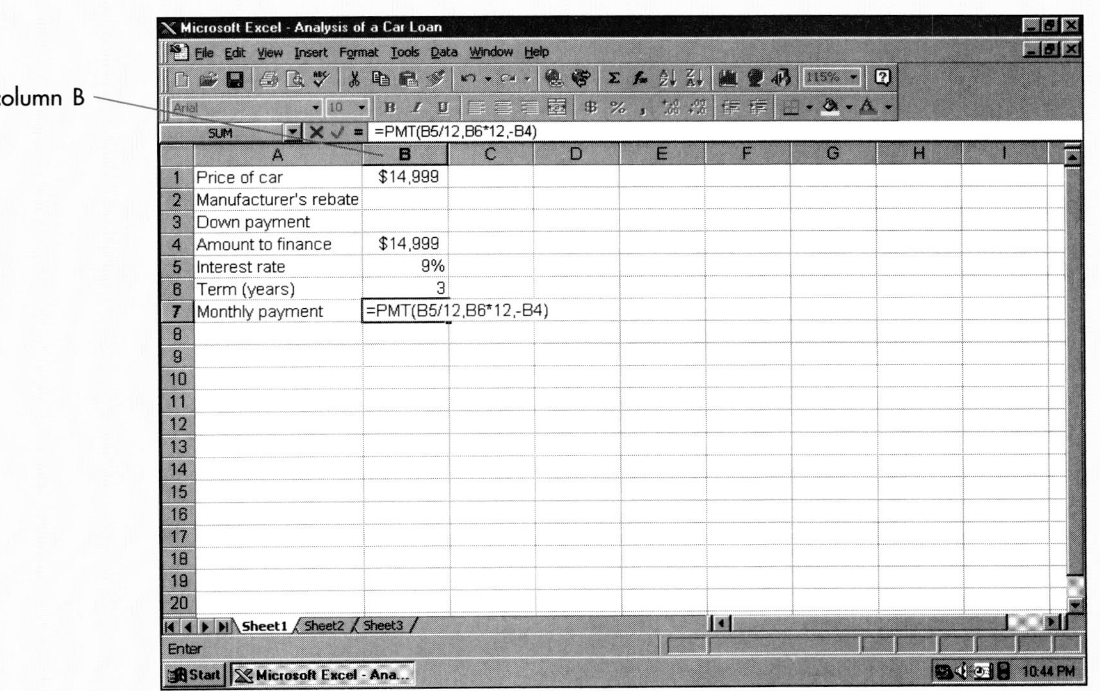

(b) Enter the PMT Function and Its Parameters (step 2)

FIGURE 3.3 Hands-on Exercise 1 (continued)

STEP 3: What If?

- Click in **cell B1** and change the price of the car to **$13,999.** The monthly payment drops to $445.16.
- Click in **cell B2** and enter a manufacturer's rebate of **$1,000.** The monthly payment drops to $413.36.
- Click in **cell B3** and enter a down payment of **$3,000.** The monthly payment drops to $317.97.
- Change the interest rate to **8%** and the term of the loan to **4** years. The payment drops to $244.10.

STEP 4: The Goal Seek Command

- Click in **cell B7,** the cell containing the formula for the monthly payment. This is the cell whose value we want to set to a fixed amount.
- Pull down the **Tools menu.** Click **Goal Seek** to display the dialog box in Figure 3.3c. If necessary, click and drag the title bar of the Goal Seek dialog box so that you can see the cells containing the data for your loan.
- Click in the **To value** text box. Type **200** (the desired value of the monthly payment).
- Click in the **By changing cell** text box. Type **B1,** the cell containing the price of the car. This is the cell whose value will be determined.
- Click **OK.**

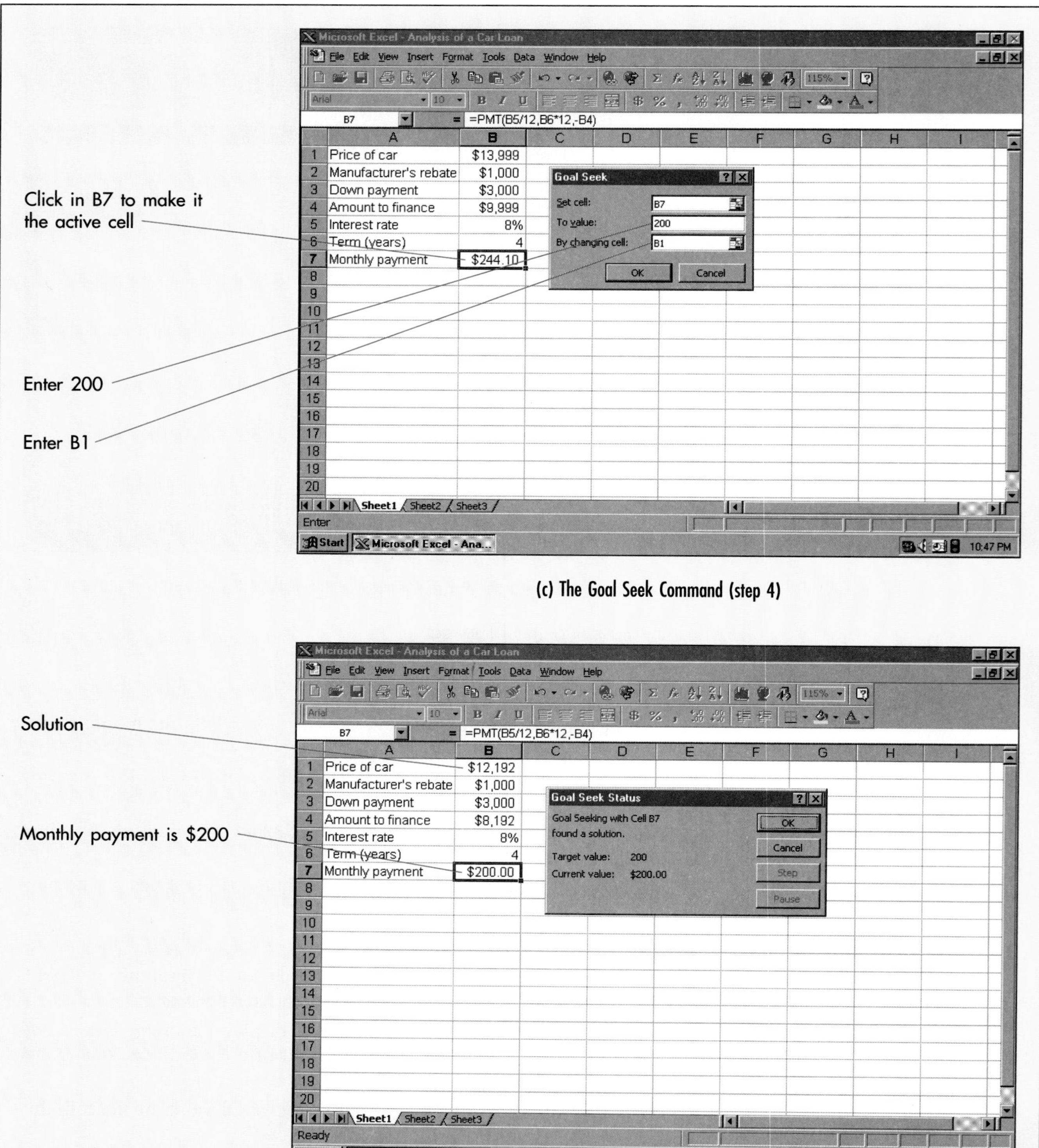

(c) The Goal Seek Command (step 4)

(d) The Completed Worksheet (step 5)

FIGURE 3.3 Hands-on Exercise 1 (continued)

STEP 5: The Goal Seek Command (continued)

- The Goal Seek command returns a successful solution as indicated by the dialog box in Figure 3.3d. The worksheet changes to display $12,192 and $200 in cells B1 and B7, respectively, corresponding to the parameters in the Goal Seek command:
  - Click **OK** to accept the solution and close the Goal Seek dialog box, *or*
  - Click **Cancel** if you don't like the solution and want to return to the original values.
- Save the workbook. Close the workbook. Exit Excel if you do not want to continue with the next exercise at this time.

HOME MORTGAGES

The PMT function is used in our next example in conjunction with the purchase of a home. The example also reviews the concept of relative and absolute addresses from Chapter 2. In addition, it introduces several other techniques to make you more proficient in Excel.

The spreadsheet in Figure 3.4 illustrates a variable rate mortgage, which will be developed over the next several pages. The user enters the amount he or she wishes to borrow and a starting interest rate, and the spreadsheet displays the associated monthly payment. The spreadsheet enables the user to see the monthly payment at varying interest rates, and to contrast the amount of the payment for a 15- and a 30-year mortgage.

Most first-time buyers opt for the longer term, but they would do well to consider a 15-year mortgage. Note, for example, that the difference in monthly payments for a $100,000 mortgage at 7.5% is only $227.80 (the difference between $927.01 for a 15-year mortgage versus $699.21 for the 30-year mortgage). This is a significant amount of money, but when viewed as a percentage of the total cost of a home (property taxes, maintenance, and so on), it becomes less important, especially when you consider the substantial saving in interest over the life of the mortgage.

Figure 3.5 expands the spreadsheet to show the total interest over the life of the loan for both the 15- and the 30-year mortgage. The total interest on a $100,000 loan at 7.5% is $151,717 for a 30-year mortgage, but only $66,862 for a 15-year mortgage. In other words, you will pay back the $100,000 in principal plus another $151,717 in interest if you select the longer term. This is more than twice the interest for the 15-year mortgage.

Difference between a 30-year and a 15-year mortgage at 7.5%

	A	B	C	D
1	Amount Borrowed		$100,000	
2	Starting Interest		7.50%	
3				
4		Monthly Payment		
5	Interest	30 Years	15 Years	Difference
6	7.50%	$699.21	$927.01	$227.80
7	8.50%	$768.91	$984.74	$215.83
8	9.50%	$840.85	$1,044.22	$203.37
9	10.50%	$914.74	$1,105.40	$190.66
10	11.50%	$990.29	$1,168.19	$177.90
11	12.50%	$1,067.26	$1,232.52	$165.26

FIGURE 3.4 Variable Rate Mortgages

Less interest is paid on a 15-year loan ($66,862 vs $151,717 on a 30-year loan)

	A	B	C	D	E
1	Amount Borrowed			$100,000	
2	Starting Interest			7.50%	
3					
4		30 Years		15 Years	
5	Interest	Monthly Payment	Total Interest	Monthly Payment	Total Interest
6	7.50%	$699.21	$151,717	$927.01	$66,862
7	8.50%	$768.91	$176,809	$984.74	$77,253
8	9.50%	$840.85	$202,708	$1,044.22	$87,960
9	10.50%	$914.74	$229,306	$1,105.40	$98,972
10	11.50%	$990.29	$256,505	$1,168.19	$110,274
11	12.50%	$1,067.26	$284,213	$1,232.52	$121,854

(a) Total Interest

Less than $6,000 of the principal has been paid off

5 years (60 months)

	A	B	C	D
1	Amortization Schedule			
2				
3	Principal		$100,000	
4	Annual Interest		7.50%	
5	Term (in years)		30	
6	Monthly Payment		$699.21	
7				
8	Month	Toward Interest	Toward Principal	Balance
9				$100,000.00
10	1	$625.00	$74.21	$99,925.79
11	2	$624.54	$74.68	$99,851.11
12	3	$624.07	$75.15	$99,775.96
13	4	$623.60	$75.61	$99,700.35
14	5	$623.13	$76.09	$99,624.26
15	6	$622.65	$76.56	$99,547.70
...	...	...	...	...
65	56	$594.67	$104.55	$95,042.20
66	57	$594.01	$105.20	$94,937.00
67	58	$593.36	$105.86	$94,831.14
68	59	$592.69	$106.52	$94,724.62
69	60	$592.03	$107.19	$94,617.44

(b) Amortization Schedule

FIGURE 3.5 15- vs 30-Year Mortgage

If, like most people, you move before you pay off the mortgage, you will discover that almost all of the early payments in the 30-year loan go to interest rather than principal. The amortization schedule in Figure 3.5b shows that if you were to move at the end of five years (60 months), less than $6,000 (of the $44,952 you paid during those five years) goes toward the principal. (A 15-year mortgage, however, would pay off almost $22,000 during the same five-year period. The latter number is not shown, but can be displayed by changing the term of the mortgage in cell C5.)

Our objective is not to convince you of the merits of one loan over another, but to show you how useful a worksheet can be in the decision-making process. If you do eventually buy a home, and you select a 15-year mortgage, think of us.

Relative versus Absolute Addresses

Figure 3.6 displays the cell formulas for the mortgage analysis. All of the formulas are based on the amount borrowed and the starting interest, in cells C1 and C2, respectively. You can vary either or both of these parameters, and the worksheet will automatically recalculate the monthly payments.

The similarity in the formulas from one row to the next implies that the copy operation will be essential to the development of the worksheet. You must, however, remember the distinction between a ***relative*** and an ***absolute reference***—that is, a cell reference that changes during a copy operation (relative) versus one that does not (absolute). Consider the PMT function as it appears in cell B6:

=PMT(A6/12,30*12,−$C$1)

- The amount of the loan, −$C$1, is an absolute reference that remains constant
- Number of periods (30 years*12 months/year)
- The interest rate, A6/12, is a relative reference that changes

The entry A6/12 (which is the first argument in the formula in cell B6) is interpreted to mean "divide the contents of the cell one column to the left by 12." Thus, when the PMT function in cell B6 is copied to cell B7, it (the copied formula) is adjusted to maintain this relationship and will contain the entry A7/12. The Copy command does not duplicate a relative address exactly, but adjusts it from row to row (or column to column) to maintain the relative relationship. The cell reference for the amount of the loan should not change when the formula is copied, and hence it is specified as an absolute address.

Relative reference (adjusts during copy operation)

Absolute reference (doesn't adjust during copy operation)

	A	B	C	D
1	Amount Borrowed		$100,000	
2	Starting Interest		7.50%	
3				
4	Monthly Payment			
5	Interest	30 Years	15 Years	Difference
6	=C2	=PMT(A6/12,30*12,-$C$1)	=PMT(A6/12,15*12,-$C$1)	=C6-B6
7	=A6+0.01	=PMT(A7/12,30*12,-$C$1)	=PMT(A7/12,15*12,-$C$1)	=C7-B7
8	=A7+0.01	=PMT(A8/12,30*12,-$C$1)	=PMT(A8/12,15*12,-$C$1)	=C8-B8
9	=A8+0.01	=PMT(A9/12,30*12,-$C$1)	=PMT(A9/12,15*12,-$C$1)	=C9-B9
10	=A9+0.01	=PMT(A10/12,30*12,-$C$1)	=PMT(A10/12,15*12,-$C$1)	=C10-B10
11	=A10+0.01	=PMT(A11/12,30*12,-$C$1)	=PMT(A11/12,15*12,-$C$1)	=C11-B11

FIGURE 3.6 Cell Formulas

ISOLATE ASSUMPTIONS

The formulas in a worksheet should be based on cell references rather than specific values—for example, C1 or $C$1 rather than $100,000. The cells containing these values should be clearly labeled and set apart from the rest of the worksheet. You can then vary the inputs (assumptions) to the worksheet and immediately see the effect. The chance for error is also minimized because you are changing the contents of a single cell, rather than changing multiple formulas.

You already know enough about Excel to develop the worksheet for the mortgage analysis. Excel is so powerful, however, and offers so many shortcuts, that we would be remiss not to show you alternative techniques. This section introduces the fill handle as a shortcut for copying cells, and pointing as a more accurate way to enter cell formulas.

The Fill Handle

The ***fill handle*** is a tiny black square that appears in the lower-right corner of the selected cells—it is the fastest way to copy a cell (or range of cells) to an *adjacent* cell (or range of cells). The process is quite easy, and you get to practice in the exercise (see Figure 3.8b) that follows shortly. In essence, you:

- Select the cell or cells to be copied.
- Point to the fill handle for the selected cell(s), which changes the mouse pointer to a thin crosshair.
- Click and drag the fill handle over the destination range. A border appears to outline the destination range.
- Release the mouse to complete the copy operation.

Pointing

A cell address is entered into a formula by typing the reference explicitly (as we have done throughout the text) or by pointing. If you type the address, it is all too easy to make a mistake, such as typing A40 when you really mean A41. ***Pointing*** is more accurate, since you use the mouse or arrow keys to select the cell directly as you build the formula. The process is much easier than it sounds, and you get to practice in the hands-on exercise (see Figure 3.8d). In essence, you:

- Select (click) the cell to contain the formula.
- Type an equal sign to begin entering the formula. The status bar indicates that you are in the ***Enter mode,*** which means that the formula bar is active and the formula can be entered.
- Click the cell you want to reference in the formula (or use the arrow keys to move to the cell). A moving border appears around the cell, and the cell reference is displayed in both the cell and formula bar. The status bar indicates the ***Point mode.***
- Type any arithmetic operator to place the cell reference in the formula and return to the Enter mode.
- Continue pointing to additional cells and entering arithmetic operators until you complete the formula. Press the enter key to complete the formula.

As with everything else, the more you practice, the easier it is. The hands-on exercises will give you ample opportunity to practice everything you have learned.

Functions

The functions in Excel are grouped into categories, as shown in the Paste Function dialog box in Figure 3.7a. Select the function category you want, then choose the desired function from within that category. Click OK to display the ***Formula Palette*** in Figure 3.7b, in which you specify the arguments for the function.

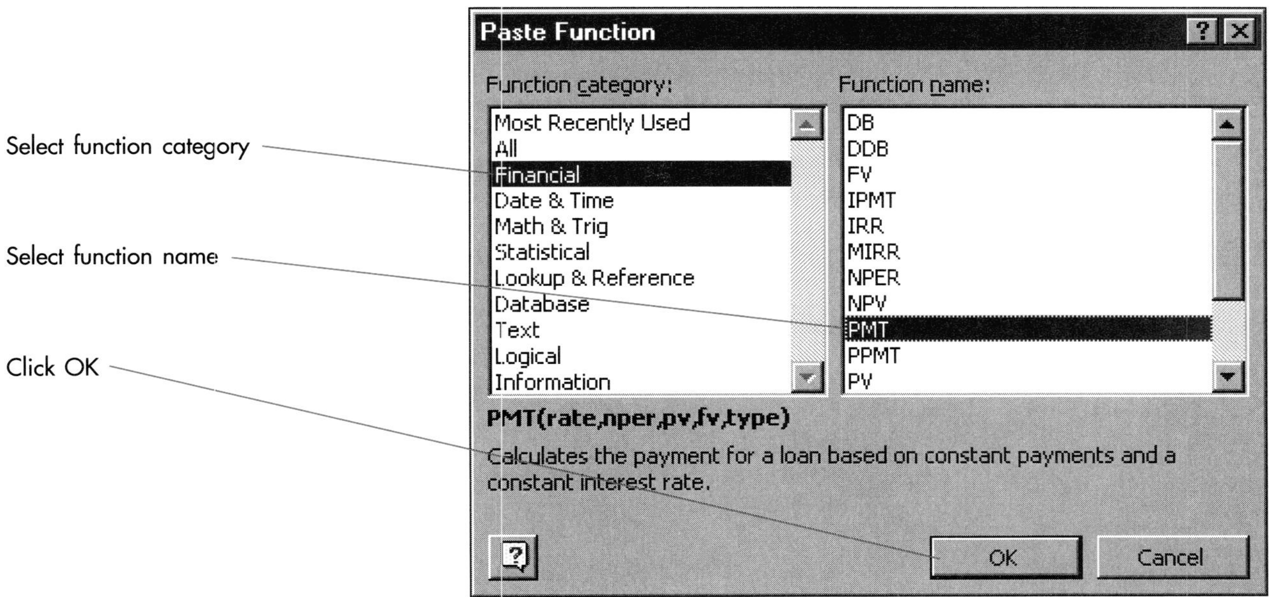

(a) Paste Function Dialog Box

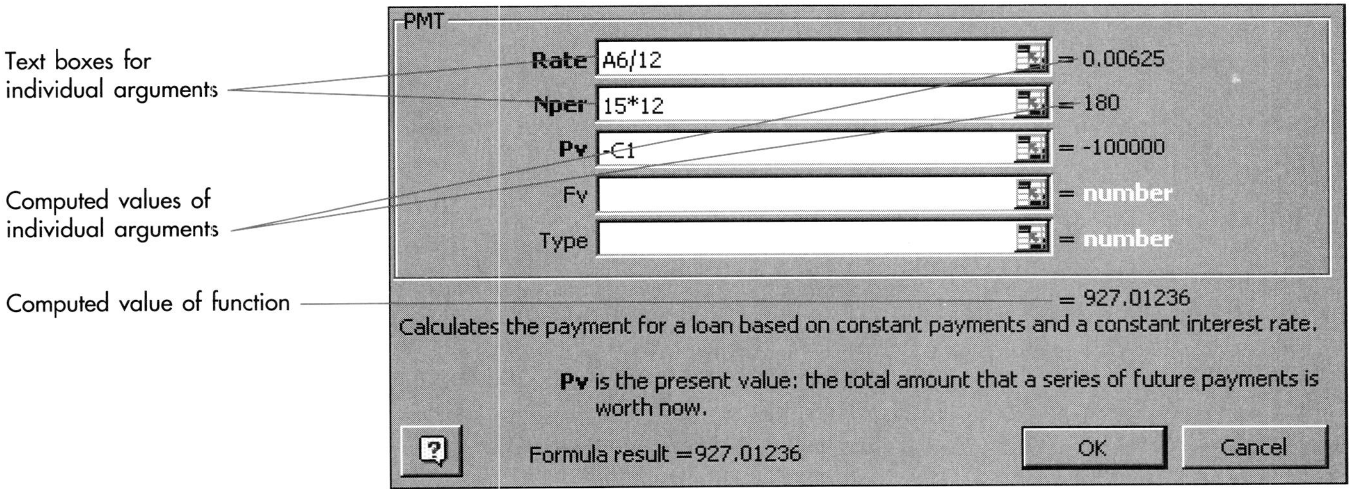

(b) Formula Palette

FIGURE 3.7 The Paste Function

The Formula Palette displays a text box for each argument, a description of each argument (as the text box is selected), and an indication of whether or not the argument is required. (Only the first three arguments are required in the PMT function.) Enter the value, cell reference, or formula for each argument by clicking in the text box and typing the entry, or by clicking the appropriate cell(s) in the worksheet.

Excel displays the calculated value for each argument immediately to the right of the argument. It also shows the computed value for the function as a whole at the bottom of the dialog box. All you need to do is click the OK button to insert the function into the worksheet.

HANDS-ON EXERCISE 2

Mortgage Analysis

Objective: To develop the worksheet for the mortgage analysis; to use pointing to enter a formula and drag-and-drop to copy a formula. Use Figure 3.8 as a guide in the exercise.

STEP 1: Enter the Descriptive Labels and Initial Conditions

- Start Excel. Click in **cell A1.** Type **Amount Borrowed.** Do not be concerned that the text is longer than the cell width, as cell B1 is empty and thus the text will be displayed in its entirety. Press the **enter key** or **down arrow** to complete the entry and move to cell A2.
- Type **Starting Interest** in cell A2. Click in **cell A4.** Type **Monthly Payment.** Enter the remaining labels in cells A5 through D5 as shown in Figure 3.8a. Do not worry about formatting at this time as all formatting will be done at the end of the exercise.
- Click in **cell C1.** Type **$100,000** (include the dollar sign and comma). Press the **enter key** or **down arrow** to complete the entry and move to cell C2. Type **7.5%** (include the percent sign). Press **enter.**
- Save the workbook as **Variable Rate Mortgage** in the **Exploring Excel folder.**

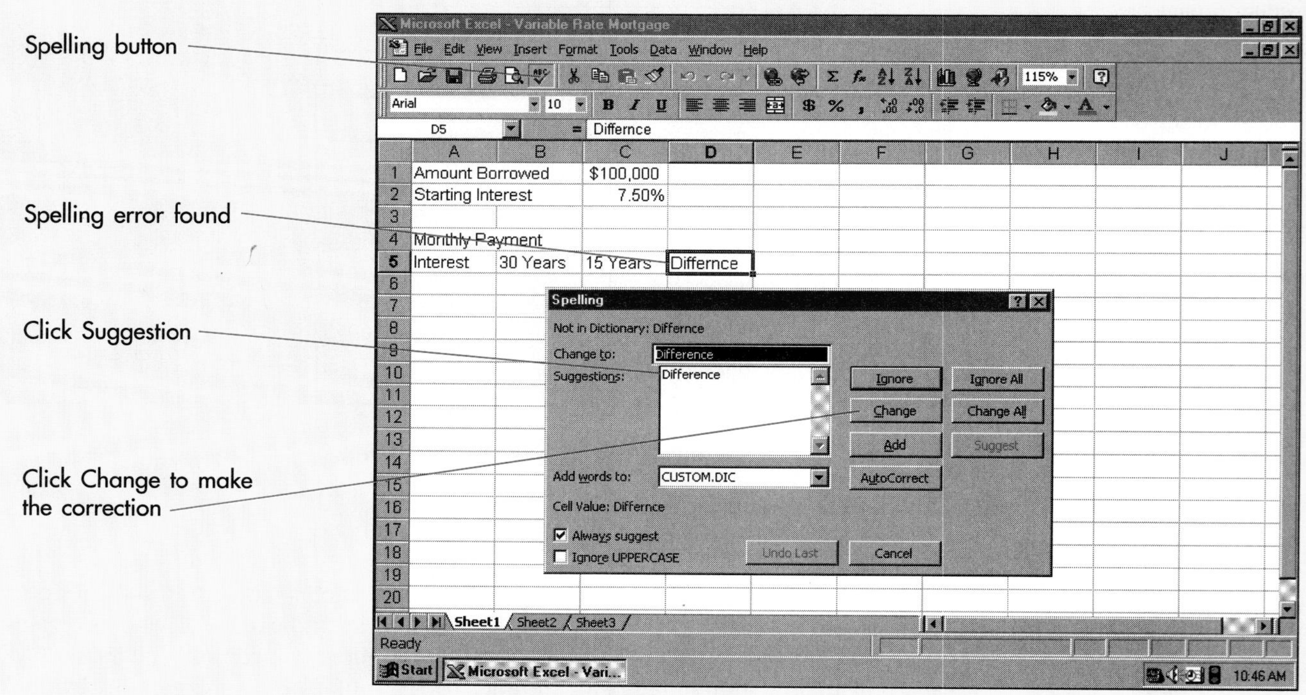

(a) Enter the Descriptive Labels and Spell Check (steps 1 & 2)

FIGURE 3.8 Hands-on Exercise 2

TIPS FROM THE OFFICE ASSISTANT

The Office Assistant indicates it has a suggestion by displaying a lightbulb. Just click the bulb to display the tip, then click the Back or Next buttons as appropriate to view additional tips. The Assistant will not, however, repeat a tip from an earlier session unless you reset it at the start of a new session. This is especially important in a laboratory situation where you are sharing a computer with many students. To reset the tips, click the Assistant to display a balloon asking what you want to do, click the Options button in the balloon, click Options, then click the button to Reset My Tips.

STEP 2: The Spell Check

- Click in **cell A1** to begin the spell check at the beginning of the worksheet.
- Click the **Spelling button** on the Standard toolbar to initiate the spell check as shown in Figure 3.8a. Make corrections, as necessary, just as you would in Microsoft Word.
- Save the workbook.

THE SPELL CHECK

Anyone familiar with a word processor takes the spell check for granted, but did you know the same capability exists within Excel? Click the Spelling button on the Standard toolbar to initiate the spell check, then implement corrections just as you do in Microsoft Word. All of the applications in Microsoft Office share the same custom dictionary, so that any words you add to the custom dictionary in one application are automatically recognized in the other applications.

STEP 3: The Fill Handle

- Click in **cell A6.** Type **=C2** to reference the starting interest rate in cell C2.
- Click in **cell A7.** Type the formula **=A6+.01** to compute the interest rate in this cell, which is one percent more than the interest rate in row 6. Press **enter.**
- Click in **cell A7.** Point to the **fill handle** in the lower corner of cell A7. The mouse pointer changes to a thin crosshair.
- Drag the **fill handle** over cells **A8** through **A11.** A border appears, indicating the destination range as in Figure 3.8b. Release the mouse to complete the copy operation. The formula and associated percentage format in cell A7 have been copied to cells A8 through A11.
- Click in **cell C2.** Type **5%.** The entries in cells A6 through A11 change automatically. Click the **Undo button** on the Standard toolbar to return to the 7.5% interest rate.
- Save the workbook.

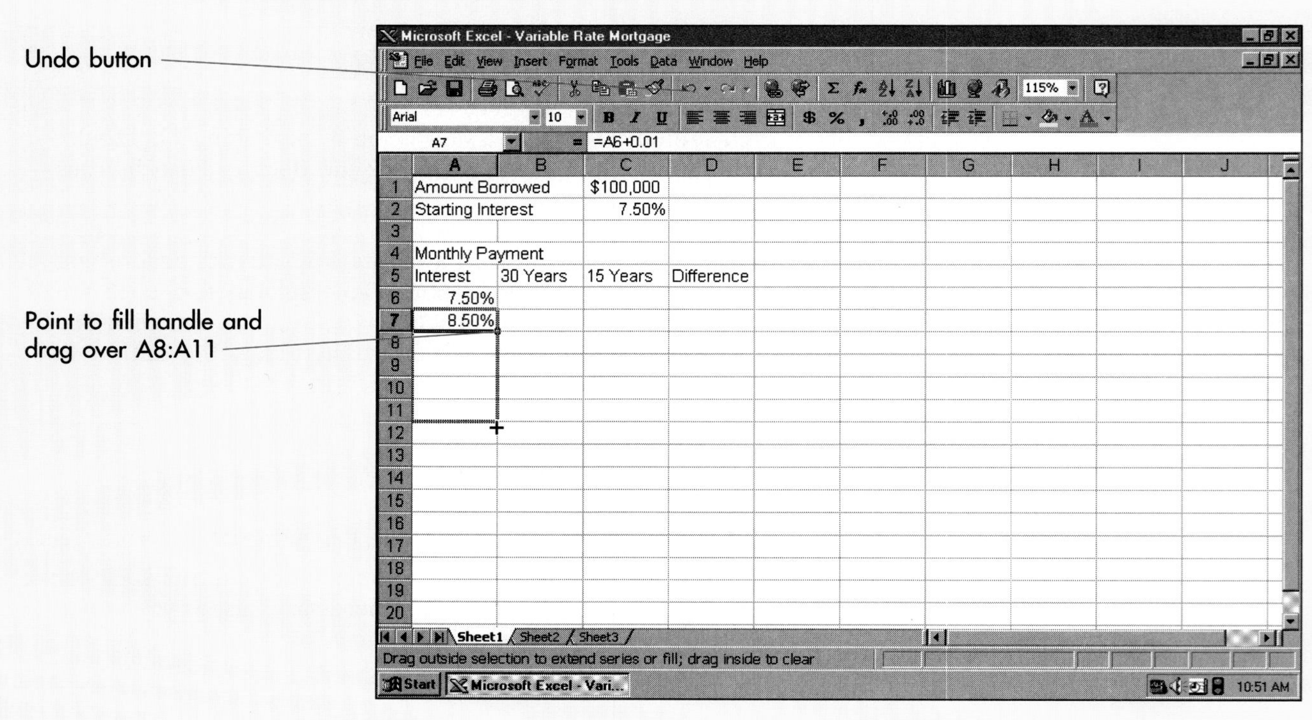

(b) The Fill Handle (step 3)

FIGURE 3.8 Hands-on Exercise 2 (continued)

STEP 4: Determine the 30-Year Payments

- Click in **cell B6.** Type the formula **=PMT(A6/12,30*12,−$C$1).** Press the **enter key.** Click in cell B6, which should display $699.21 as shown in Figure 3.8c.
- Click in **cell B6.** Point to the **fill handle** in the bottom-right corner of cell B6. The mouse pointer changes to a thin crosshair. Drag the **fill handle** over cells **B7** through **B11.** A border appears to indicate the destination range. Release the mouse to complete the copy operation.
- The PMT function in cell B6 has been copied to cells B7 through B11. (You may see a series of pound signs in cell B11, meaning that the column is too narrow to display the computed results in the selected format. Increase the column width.)
- Save the workbook.

THE OPTIMAL (AUTOFIT) COLUMN WIDTH

The appearance of pound signs within a cell indicates that the cell width (column width) is insufficient to display the computed results in the selected format. Double click the right border of the column heading to change the column width to accommodate the widest entry in that column. For example, to increase the width of column B, double click the border between the column headings for columns B and C.

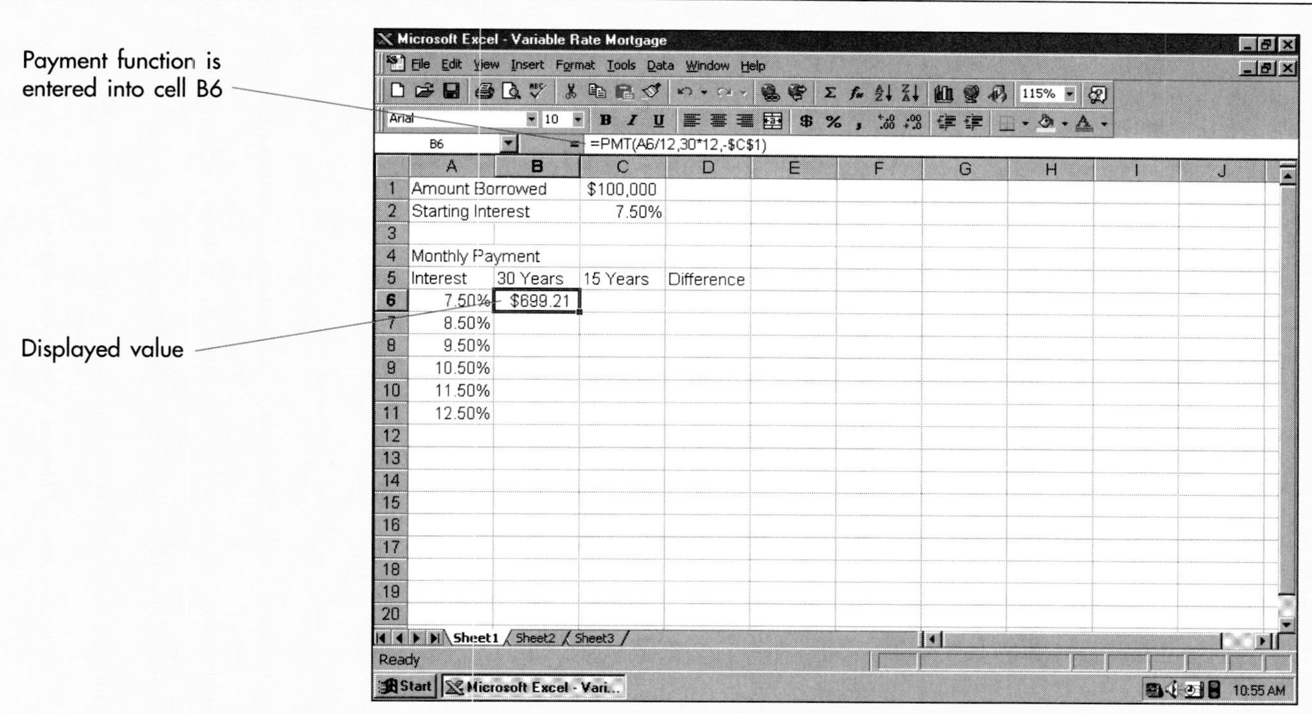

(c) Determine the 30-Year Payments (step 4)

FIGURE 3.8 Hands-on Exercise 2 (continued)

STEP 5: The Formula Palette

➤ Click in **cell C6.** Pull down the **Insert menu** and click **Function** (or click the **Paste Function button** on the Standard toolbar) to display the Paste Function dialog box.

➤ Click **Financial** in the Function Category list box. Click **PMT** in the Function Name list box. Click **OK.** Click and drag the Formula Palette so that you can see the underlying cells as shown in Figure 3.8d.

➤ Click the text box for **rate.** Type **A6/12.** The Formula Palette displays the computed value of .00625.

➤ Click the text box for the number of periods **(Nper).** Type **15*12,** corresponding to 15 years and 12 months per year.

➤ Click the text box for the present value **(Pv).** Type **−$C$1.** Be sure to include the minus sign in front of the absolute reference.

THE FORMULA PALETTE AND FUNCTION BOX

Click the equal sign on the Formula Bar to display the Formula Palette and Function Box, then click the down arrow on the Function Box to display the list of most recently used functions. Select (click) the desired function to display the Formula Palette in which you enter the necessary arguments.

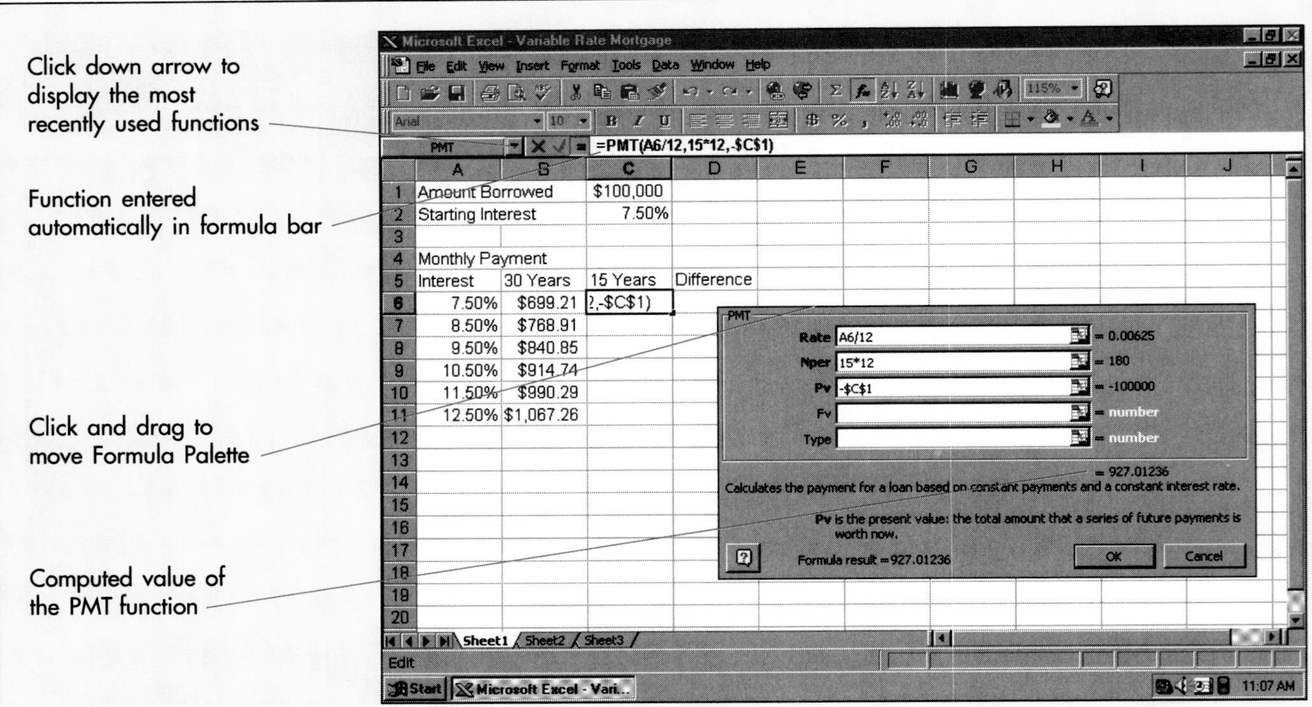

(d) The Formula Palette (step 5)

FIGURE 3.8 Hands-on Exercise 2 (continued)

- Check that the computed values on your monitor match those in Figure 3.8d. Make corrections as necessary. Click **OK** to insert the function into the worksheet. Cell C6 should display $927.01.

STEP 6: Copy the 15-Year Payments

- Check that cell C6 is still selected. Point to the **fill handle** in the lower-right corner of cell C6. The mouse pointer changes to a thin crosshair.
- Drag the **fill handle** to copy the PMT function to cells **C7** through **C11.** Adjust the width of these cells so that you can see the displayed values.
- Cell C11 should display $1,232.52 if you have done this step correctly. Save the workbook.

MORE ABOUT THE FILL HANDLE

Use the fill handle as a shortcut for the Edit Clear command. To clear the contents of a cell, drag the fill handle to the top of the cell (the cell will be shaded in gray) and release the mouse. To clear the contents *and* the format, press and hold the Ctrl key as you drag the fill handle to the top of the cell. You can apply the same technique to a cell range by selecting the range, then dragging the fill handle to the top (or left) of the range.

STEP 7: Compute the Monthly Difference (Pointing)

➤ Click in **cell D6.** Type = to begin the formula. Press the **left arrow key** (or click in **cell C6**), which produces the moving border around the entry in cell C6. The status bar indicates the point mode as shown in Figure 3.8e.

➤ Press the **minus sign,** then press the **left arrow key** twice (or click in **cell B6**).

➤ Press **enter** to complete the formula. Cell D6 should display $227.80.

➤ Use the **fill handle** to copy the contents of cell D6 to cells **D7** through **D11.** If you have done the step correctly, cell D11 will display $165.26.

➤ Save the workbook.

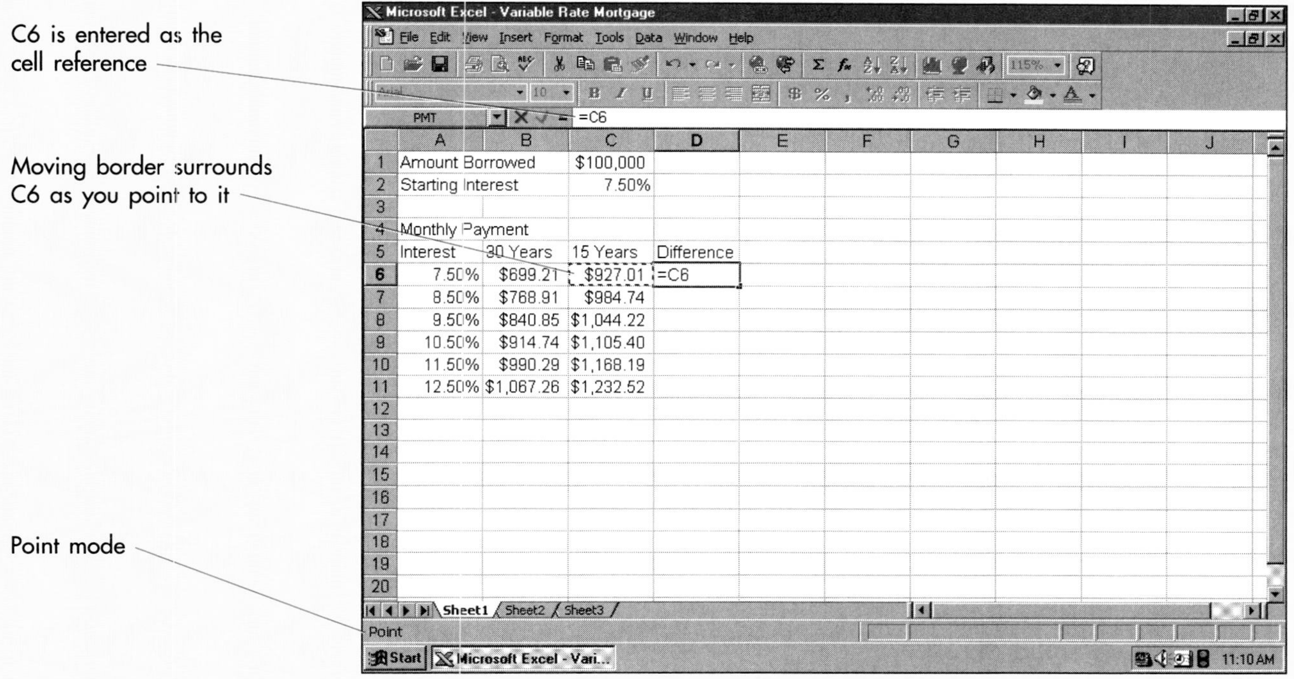

(e) Pointing (step 7)

FIGURE 3.8 Hands-on Exercise 2 (continued)

STEP 8: The Finishing Touches

➤ Type **Financial consultant:** in cell A13. Enter **your name** in cell C13 as shown in Figure 3.8f.

➤ Add formatting as necessary, using Figure 3.8f as a guide:

- Click **cell A4.** Drag the mouse over cells **A4** through **D4.** Click the **Merge and Center button** on the Formatting toolbar to center the entry over four columns.
- Center the column headings in row 5. Add boldface and/or italics to the text and/or numbers as you see fit.

➤ Save the workbook.

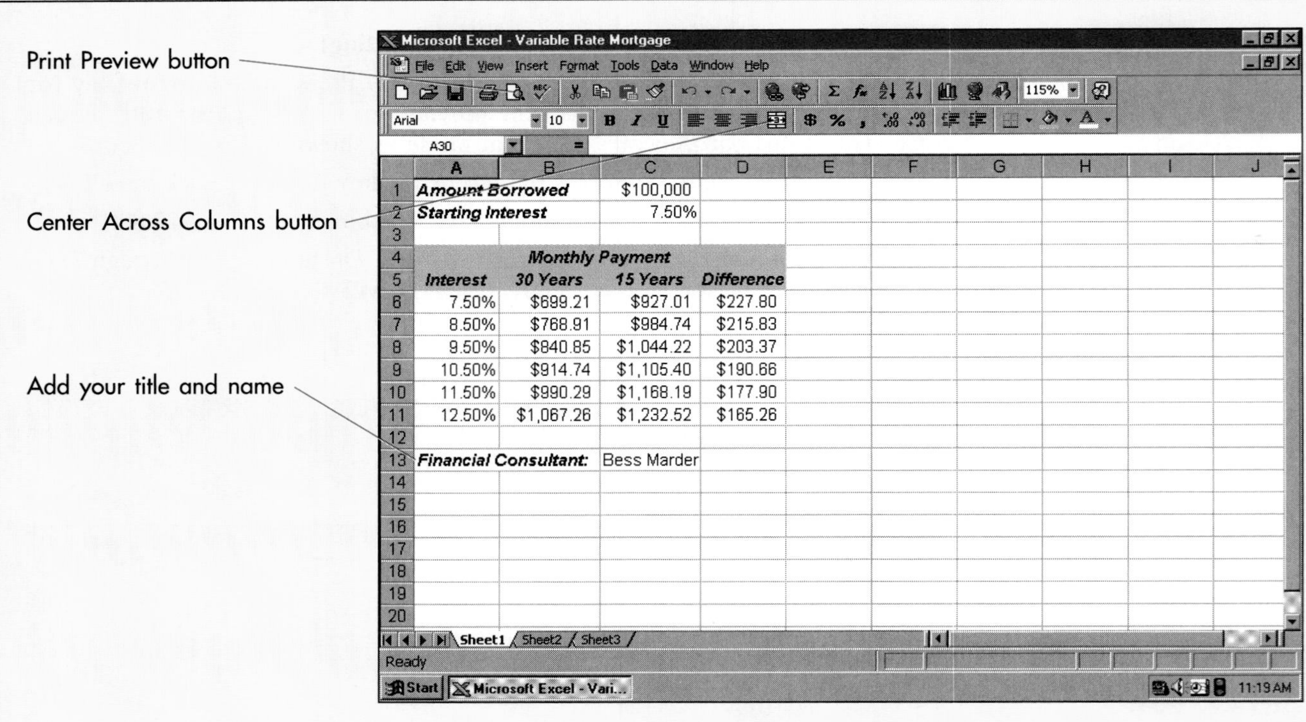

(f) Finishing Touches (step 8)

FIGURE 3.8 Hands-on Exercise 2 (continued)

STEP 9: Print the Worksheet

- Pull down the **File menu** and click **Print Preview** (or click the **Print Preview button** on the Standard toolbar).
- Click the **Setup command button** to display the Page Setup dialog box.
  - Click the **Margins tab.** Check the box to center the worksheet Horizontally.
  - Click the **Sheet tab.** Check the boxes to include Row and Column Headings and Gridlines.
  - Click **OK** to exit the Page Setup dialog box.
- Click the **Print command button** to display the Print dialog box, then click **OK** to print the worksheet.
- Press **Ctrl+`** to display the cell formulas. (The left quotation mark is on the same key as the ~.) Widen the cells as necessary to see the complete cell formulas.
- Click the **Print button** on the Standard toolbar to print the cell formulas.
- Close the workbook. Click **No** when asked whether you want to save the changes, or else you will save the workbook with the settings to print the cell formulas rather than the displayed values.
- Exit Excel if you do not want to continue with the next exercise at this time.

CREATE A CUSTOM VIEW

You can save the various column widths and other settings used to print the cell formulas by creating a custom view(s). Format the spreadsheet to print the displayed values, then pull down the View menu and click Custom Views to display the Custom Views dialog box. Click the button to add a view, enter the name (e.g., displayed values), and click OK. Press Ctrl+` to display the cell formulas, adjust the column widths as necessary, then pull down the View menu a second time to create a second custom view (e.g., cell formulas). You can switch to either view at any time by selecting the Custom Views command and selecting the appropriate view.

THE GRADE BOOK REVISITED

Financial functions are only one of several categories of functions that are included in Excel. Our next example presents an expanded version of the professor's grade book. It introduces several new functions and shows how those functions can aid in the professor's determination of a student's grade. The worksheet shown in Figure 3.9 illustrates several additional features. Consider:

Statistical functions: The AVERAGE, MAX, and MIN functions are used to compute the statistics on each test for the class as a whole. The range on each test is computed by subtracting the minimum value from the maximum value.

	A	B	C	D	E	F	G	H	I	J
1	Professor's Grade Book									
2										
3	Name	Student ID	Test 1	Test 2	Test 3	Test 4	Test Average	Homework	Semester Average	Grade
4	Adams, John	011-12-2333	80	71	70	84	77.8	Poor	77.8	C
5	Barber, Maryann	444-55-6666	96	98	97	90	94.2	OK	97.2	A
6	Boone, Dan	777-88-9999	78	81	70	78	77.0	OK	80.0	B
7	Borow, Jeff	123-45-6789	65	65	65	60	63.0	OK	66.0	D
8	Brown, James	999-99-9999	92	95	79	80	85.2	OK	88.2	B
9	Carson, Kit	888-88-8888	90	90	90	70	82.0	OK	85.0	B
10	Coulter, Sara	100-00-0000	60	50	40	79	61.6	OK	64.6	D
11	Fegin, Richard	222-22-2222	75	70	65	95	80.0	OK	83.0	B
12	Ford, Judd	200-00-0000	90	90	80	90	88.0	Poor	88.0	B
13	Glassman, Kris	444-44-4444	82	78	62	77	75.2	OK	78.2	C
14	Goodman, Neil	555-55-5555	92	88	65	78	80.2	OK	83.2	B
15	Milgrom, Marion	666-66-6666	94	92	86	84	88.0	OK	91.0	A
16	Moldof, Adam	300-00-0000	92	78	65	84	80.6	OK	83.6	B
17	Smith, Adam	777-77-7777	60	50	65	80	67.0	Poor	67.0	D
18										
19	Average		81.9	78.3	71.4	80.6	HW Bonus:	3	Grading Criteria	
20	Highest Grade		96	98	97	95			(No Curve)	
21	Lowest Grade		60	50	40	60			0	F
22	Range		36	48	57	35			60	D
23									70	C
24	Exam Weights		20%	20%	20%	40%			80	B
25									90	A

Statistical functions — IF function — Table Lookup function

FIGURE 3.9 The Expanded Grade Book

IF function: The IF function conditionally adds a homework bonus of three points to the semester average, prior to determining the letter grade. The bonus is awarded to those students whose homework is "OK." Students whose homework is not "OK" do not receive the bonus.

VLOOKUP function: The expanded grade book converts a student's semester average to a letter grade, in accordance with the table shown in the lower-right portion of the worksheet. A student with an average of 60 to 69 will receive a D, 70 to 79 a C, and so on. Any student with an average less than 60 receives an F.

Scenario Manager: The table for grading criteria indicates that grades (in this worksheet) are determined without a curve. The professor also has the capability to enter an alternative set of criteria (scenario) in which he or she assigns grades based on a curve.

Statistical Functions

The ***MAX, MIN,*** and ***AVERAGE*** functions return the highest, lowest, and average values, respectively, from an argument list. The list may include individual cell references, ranges, numeric values, functions, or mathematical expressions (formulas). The ***statistical functions*** are illustrated in the worksheet of Figure 3.10.

The first example, =AVERAGE(A1:A3), computes the average for cells A1 through A3 by adding the values in the indicated range (70, 80, and 90), then dividing the result by three, to obtain an average of 80. Additional arguments in the form of values and/or cell addresses can be specified within the parentheses; for example, the function =AVERAGE(A1:A3,200), computes the average of cells A1, A2, and A3, and the number 200.

Cells that are empty or cells that contain text values are *not* included in the computation. Thus, since cell A4 is empty, the function =AVERAGE(A1:A4)

Function	Value
=AVERAGE(A1:A3)	80
=AVERAGE(A1:A3,200)	110
=AVERAGE(A1:A4)	80
=AVERAGE(A1:A3,A5)	80
=MAX(A1:A3)	90
=MAX(A1:A3,200)	200
=MAX(A1:A4)	90
=MAX(A1:A3,A5)	90
=MIN(A1:A3)	70
=MIN(A1:A3,200)	70
=MIN(A1:A4)	70
=MIN(A1:A3,A5)	70
=COUNT(A1:A3)	3
=COUNT(A1:A3,200)	4
=COUNT(A1:A4)	3
=COUNT(A1:A3,A5)	3
=COUNTA(A1:A3)	3
=COUNTA(A1:A3,200)	4
=COUNTA(A1:A4)	3
=COUNTA(A1:A3,A5)	4

Empty and/or text values are not included in the computation

Empty and/or text values are not included in the computation (COUNT)

Empty cells are not included in the computation (COUNTA)

Text values are included in the computation (COUNTA)

Illustrative functions

	A
1	70
2	80
3	90
4	
5	Study hard

Empty cell

Text value

The spreadsheet

FIGURE 3.10 Statistical Functions with a Text Entry

also returns an average of 80 (240/3). In similar fashion, the function =AVERAGE(A1:A3,A5) includes only three values in its computation (cells A1, A2, and A3), because the text entry in cell A5 is excluded. The results of the MIN and MAX functions are obtained in a comparable way, as indicated in Figure 3.10. As with the AVERAGE function, empty cells and text entries are not included in the computation.

The COUNT and COUNTA functions each tally the number of entries in the argument list and are subtly different. The ***COUNT function*** returns the number of cells containing a numeric entry, including formulas that evaluate to numeric results. The ***COUNTA function*** includes cells with text as well as numeric values. In Figure 3.10, the functions =COUNT(A1:A3) and =COUNTA(A1:A3) both return a value of 3 as do the two functions =COUNT(A1:A4) and =COUNTA(A1:A4). (Cell A4 is empty and is excluded from the latter computations.) The function =COUNT(A1:A3,A5) also returns a value of 3 because it does not include the text entry in cell A5. However, the function =COUNTA(A1:A3,A5) returns a value of 4 because it includes the text entry in cell A5.

Arithmetic Expressions versus Functions

Many worksheet calculations, such as an average or a sum, can be performed in two ways. You can enter a formula such as =(A1+A2+A3)/3, or you can use the equivalent function =AVERAGE(A1:A3). *The use of functions is generally preferable* as shown in Figure 3.11.

The two worksheets in Figure 3.11a may appear equivalent, but the SUM function is superior to the arithmetic expression. This is true despite the fact that the entries in cell A5 of both worksheets return a value of 100.

Consider what happens if a new row is inserted between existing rows 2 and 3, with the entry in the new cell equal to 25. The ***SUM function*** adjusts automatically to include the new value (returning a sum of 125) because the SUM function was defined originally for the cell range *A1 through A4.* The new row is inserted within these cells, moving the entry in cell A4 to cell A5, and changing the range to include cell A5.

No such accommodation is made in the arithmetic expression, which was defined to include four *specific* cells rather than a range of cells. The addition of the new row modifies the cell references (since the values in cells A3 and A4 have been moved to cells A4 and A5), and does not include the new row in the adjusted expression.

Similar reasoning holds for deleting a row. Figure 3.11c deletes row two from the *original* worksheets, which moves the entry in cell A4 to cell A3. The SUM function adjusts automatically to =SUM(A1:A3) and returns the value 80. The formula, however, returns an error (to indicate an illegal cell reference) because it is still attempting to add the entries in four cells, one of which no longer exists. In summary, a function expands and contracts to adjust for insertions or deletions, and should be used wherever possible.

#REF!—ILLEGAL CELL REFERENCE

The #REF! error occurs when you refer to a cell that is not valid. The error is displayed whenever Excel is unable to evaluate a formula because of an illegal cell reference. The most common cause of the error is deleting the row, column, or cell that contained the original cell reference.

Function

	A
1	10
2	20
3	30
4	40
5	=SUM(A1:A4)

Formula

	A
1	10
2	20
3	30
4	40
5	=A1+A2+A3+A4

(a) Spreadsheets as Initially Entered

Cell references adjust to follow moved entries

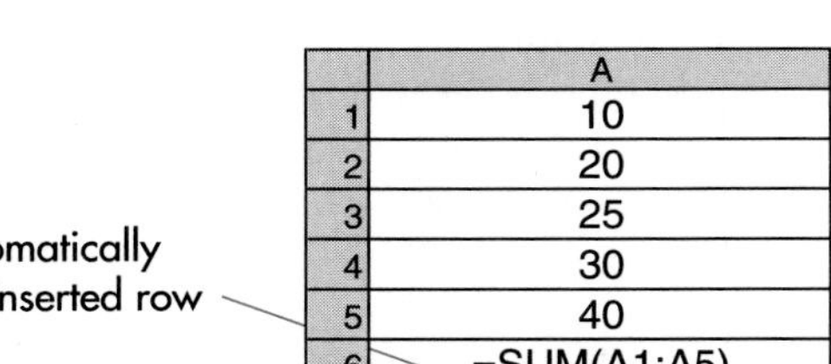

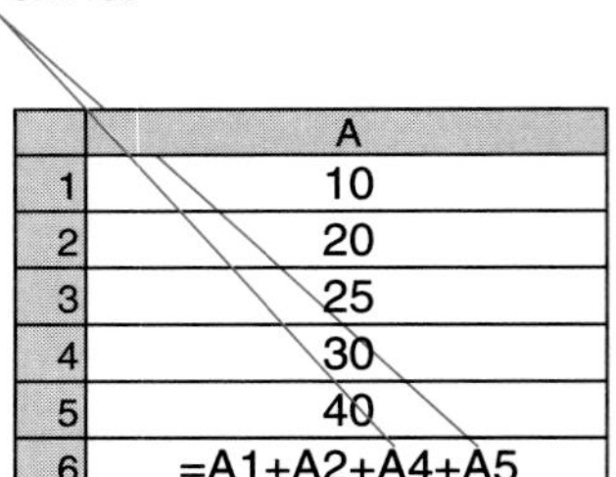

6 =SUM(A1:A5)

A
1 10
2 20
3 25
4 30
5 40
6 =A1+A2+A4+A5

(b) Spreadsheets after the Addition of a New Row

Range is automatically adjusted for deleted row

	A
1	10
2	30
3	40
4	=SUM(A1:A3)

#REF! indicates that a referenced cell has been deleted

	A
1	10
2	30
3	40
4	=A1+#REF!+A2+A3

(c) Spreadsheets after the Deletion of a Row

FIGURE 3.11 Arithmetic Expressions vs. Functions

IF Function

The ***IF function*** enables decision making to be implemented within a worksheet—for example, a conditional bonus for students whose homework is satisfactory. Students with inferior homework do not get this bonus.

The IF function has three arguments: a condition that is evaluated as true or false, the value to be returned if the condition is true, and the value to be returned if the condition is false. Consider:

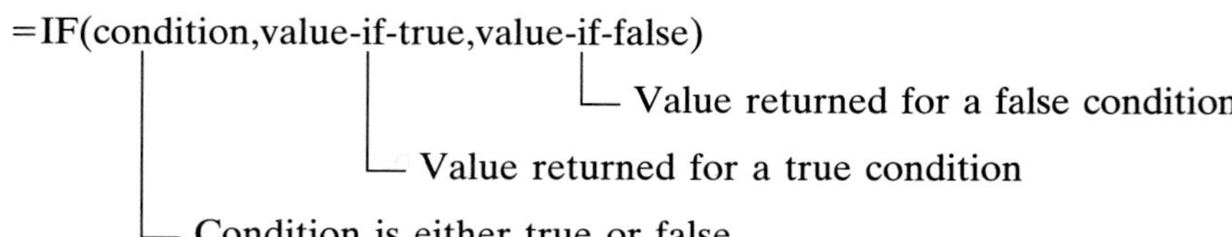

=IF(condition,value-if-true,value-if-false)

The IF function returns either the second or third argument, depending on the result of the condition; that is, if the condition is true, the function returns the second argument, whereas if the condition is false, the function returns the third argument.

The condition uses one of the six ***relational operators*** in Figure 3.12a to perform ***logical tests.*** The IF function is illustrated in the worksheet in Figure 3.12b, which is used to create the examples in Figure 3.12c. In every instance the condition is evaluated, then the second or third argument is returned, depending on whether the condition is true or false. The arguments may be numeric (1000 or 2000), a cell reference to display the contents of the specific cell (B1 or B2), a formula (=B1+10 or =B1−10), a function (MAX(B1:B2) or MIN(B1:B2)), or a text entry enclosed in quotation marks ("Go" or "Hold").

Operator	Description
=	Equal to
<>	Not equal to
<	Less than
>	Greater than
<=	Less than or equal to
>=	Greater than or equal to

(a) Relational Operators

	A	B	C
1	10	15	April
2	10	30	May

(b) The Spreadsheet

IF Function	Evaluation	Result
=IF(A1=A2,1000,2000)	10 is equal to 10: TRUE	1000
=IF(A1<>A2,1000,2000)	10 is not equal to 10: FALSE	2000
=IF(A1<>A2,B1,B2)	10 is not equal to 10:FALSE	30
=IF(A1<B2,MAX(B1:B2),MIN(B1:B2)	10 is less than 30: TRUE	30
=IF(A1<A2,B1+10,B1-10)	10 is less than 10:FALSE	5
=IF(A1=A2,C1,C2)	10 is equal to 10: TRUE	April
=IF(SUM(A1:A2)>20,"Go","Hold")	10+10 is greater than 20:FALSE	Hold

(c) Examples

FIGURE 3.12 The IF Function

The IF function is used in the grade book of Figure 3.9 to award a bonus for homework. Students whose homework is "OK" receive the bonus, whereas other students do not. The IF function to implement this logic for the first student is entered in cell H4 as follows:

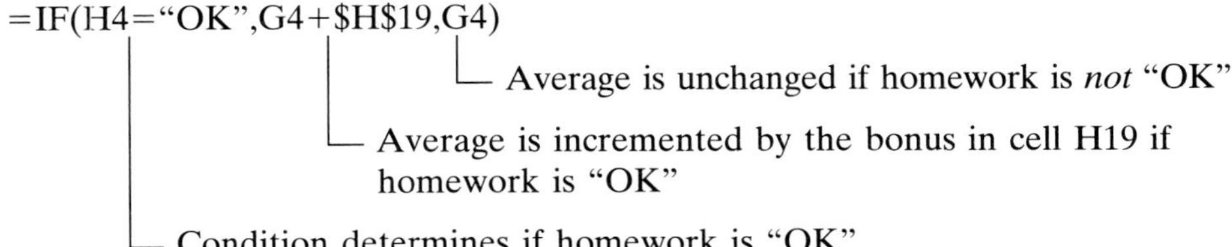
=IF(H4="OK",G4+$H$19,G4)
Average is unchanged if homework is *not* "OK"
Average is incremented by the bonus in cell H19 if homework is "OK"
Condition determines if homework is "OK"

The IF function compares the value in cell H4 (the homework grade) to the literal "OK." If the condition is true (the homework is "OK"), the bonus in cell H19 is added to the student's test average in cell G4. If, however, the condition is false (the homework is not "OK"), the average is unchanged.

The bonus is specified as a cell address rather than a specific value so that the number of bonus points can be easily changed; that is, the professor can make a single change to the worksheet by increasing (decreasing) the bonus in cell H19 and see immediately the effect on every student without having to edit or retype any other formula. An absolute (rather than a relative) reference is used to reference the homework bonus so that when the IF function is copied to the other rows in the column, the address will remain constant. A relative reference, however, was used for the student's homework and semester averages, in cells H4 and G4, because these addresses change from one student to the next.

VLOOKUP Function

Consider, for a moment, how the professor assigns letter grades to students at the end of the semester. He or she computes a test average for each student and conditionally awards the bonus for homework. The professor then determines a letter grade according to a predetermined scale; for example, 90 or above is an A, 80 to 89 is a B, and so on.

The ***VLOOKUP*** (vertical lookup) ***function*** duplicates this process within a worksheet, by assigning an entry to a cell based on a numeric value contained in another cell. In other words, just as the professor knows where on the grading scale a student's numerical average will fall, the VLOOKUP function determines where within a specified table (the grading criteria) a numeric value (a student's average) is found, and retrieves the corresponding entry (the letter grade).

The VLOOKUP function requires three arguments: the numeric value to look up, the range of cells containing the table in which the value is to be looked up, and the column-number within the table that contains the result. These concepts are illustrated in Figure 3.13, which was taken from the expanded grade book in Figure 3.9. The table in Figure 3.13 extends over two columns (I and J), and five rows (21 through 25); that is, the table is located in the range I21:J25. The ***breakpoints*** or matching values (the lowest numeric value for each grade) are contained in column I (the first column in the table) and are in ascending order. The corresponding letter grades are found in column J.

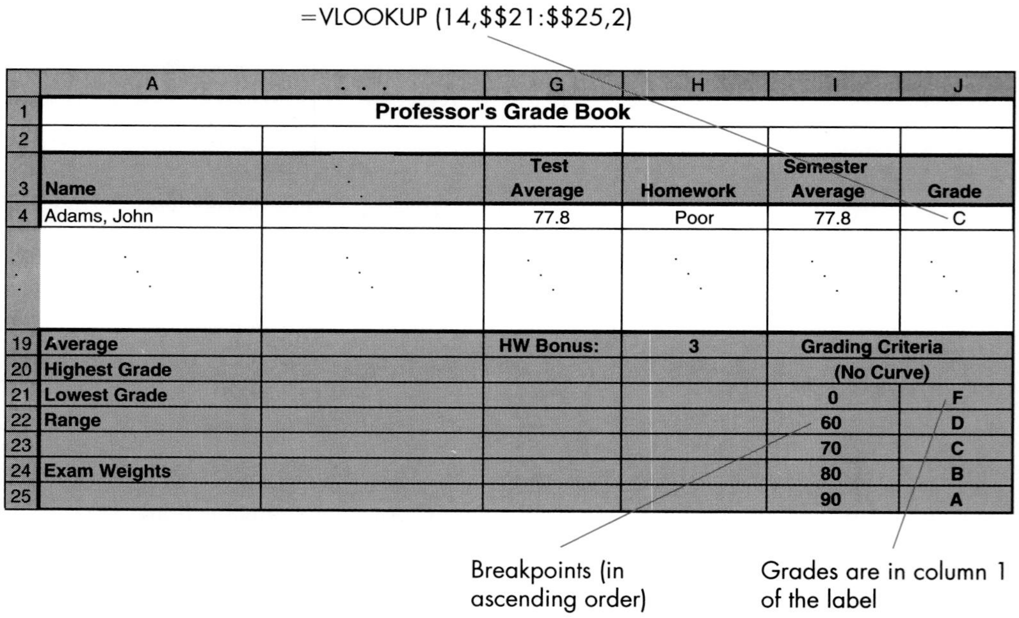

=VLOOKUP (14,$$21:$$25,2)

	A	. . .	G	H	I	J
1			Professor's Grade Book			
2						
3	Name		Test Average	Homework	Semester Average	Grade
4	Adams, John		77.8	Poor	77.8	C
. . .	. . .	. . .	. . .	. . .	. . .	. . .
19	Average		HW Bonus:	3	Grading Criteria	
20	Highest Grade				(No Curve)	
21	Lowest Grade				0	F
22	Range				60	D
23					70	C
24	Exam Weights				80	B
25					90	A

Breakpoints (in ascending order)

Grades are in column 1 of the label

FIGURE 3.13 Table Lookup Function

The VLOOKUP function in cell J4 determines the letter grade (for John Adams) based on the computed average in cell I4. Consider:

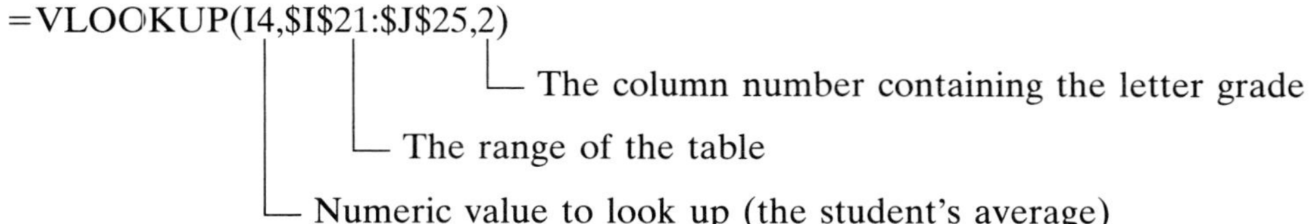

The first argument is the value to look up, which in this example is Adams's computed average, found in cell I4. A relative reference is used so that the address will adjust when the formula is copied to the other rows in the worksheet.

The second argument is the range of the table, found in cells I21 through J25, as explained earlier. Absolute references are specified so that the addresses will not change when the function is copied to determine the letter grades for the other students. The first column in the table (column I in this example) contains the breakpoints, which must be in ascending order.

The third argument indicates the column containing the value to be returned (the letter grades). To determine the letter grade for Adams (whose computed average is 77.8), the VLOOKUP function searches cells I21 through I25 for the largest value less than or equal to 77.8 (the computed average in cell I4). The lookup function finds the number 70 in cell I23. It then retrieves the corresponding letter grade from the second column in that row (cell J23). Adams, with an average of 77.8, is assigned a grade of C.

Scrolling

A large worksheet, such as the extended grade book, can seldom be seen on the monitor in its entirety; that is, only a portion of the worksheet is in view at any given time. The specific rows and columns that are displayed are determined by an operation called ***scrolling,*** which shows different parts of a worksheet at different times. Scrolling enables you to see any portion of the worksheet at the expense of not seeing another portion. The worksheet in Figure 3.14a, for example, displays column J containing the students' grades, but not columns A and B, which contain the students' names and social security numbers. In similar fashion, you can see rows 21 through 25 that display the grading criteria, but you cannot see the column headings, which identify the data in those columns.

Scrolling comes about automatically as the active cell changes and may take place in both horizontal and vertical directions. Clicking the right arrow on the horizontal scroll bar (or pressing the right arrow key when the active cell is already in the rightmost column of the screen) causes the entire screen to move one column to the right. In similar fashion, clicking the down arrow in the vertical scroll bar (or pressing the down arrow key when the active cell is in the bottom row of the screen) causes the entire screen to move down one row.

Freezing Panes

Scrolling brings distant portions of a large worksheet into view, but it also moves the descriptive headings for existing rows and/or columns off the screen. You can, however, retain these headings by freezing panes as shown in Figure 3.14b. The grades and grading criteria are visible as in the previous figure, but so too are the student names at the left of the worksheet and the column headings at the top.

Can't see columns A–B or rows 1–9

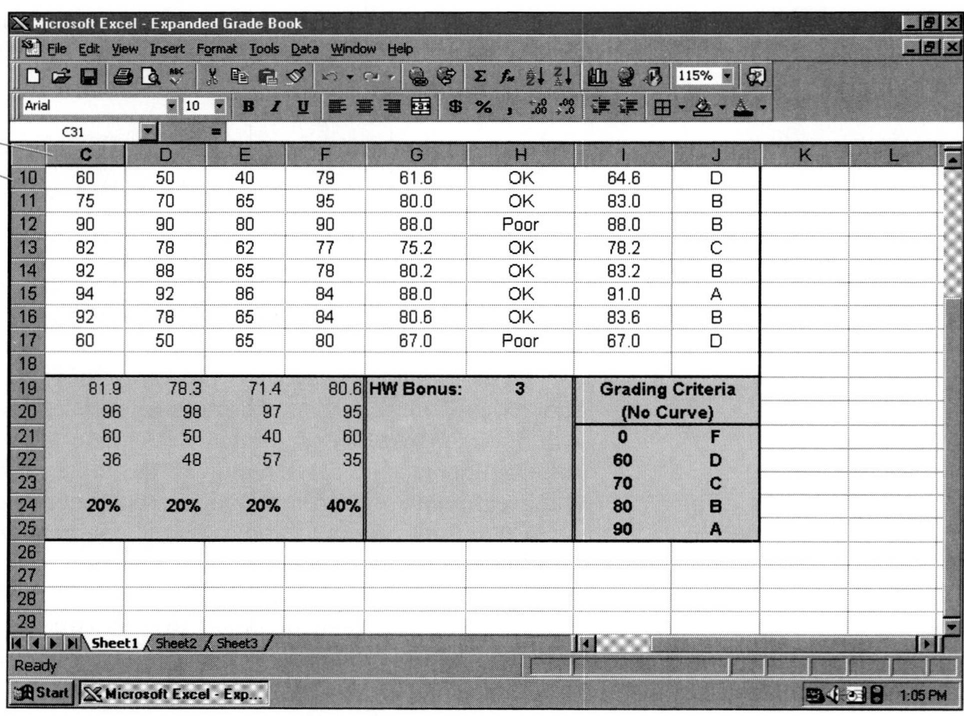

(a) Scrolling

Column A remains on the screen as B–D scroll off

Rows 1–3 remain on the screen as rows 4–9 scroll off

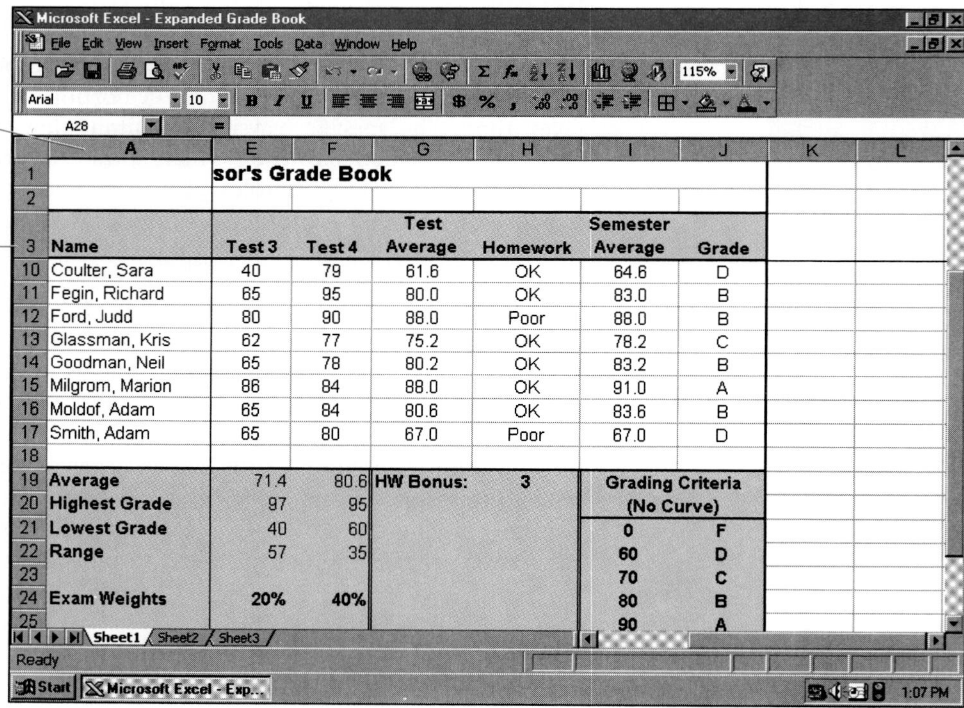

(b) Freezing Panes

FIGURE 3.14 Large Spreadsheets

Look closely at Figure 3.12b and you will see that columns B through D (social security number, test 1, and test 2) are missing, as are rows 4 through 9 (the first six students). You will also notice a horizontal line under row 3, and a vertical line after column A, to indicate that these rows and columns have been frozen. Scrolling still takes place as you move beyond the rightmost column or below the bottom row, but you will always see column A and rows 1, 2, and 3 displayed on the monitor.

The ***Freeze Panes command,*** in the Window menu, displays the desired rows or columns regardless of the scrolling in effect. It is especially helpful when viewing or entering data in a large worksheet. The rows and/or columns that are frozen are the ones above and to the left of the active cell when the command is issued. You may still access (and edit) cells in the frozen area by clicking the desired cell. The ***Unfreeze Panes command,*** also in the Window menu, returns to normal scrolling.

SCROLLING: THE MOUSE VERSUS THE KEYBOARD

You can use either the mouse or the keyboard to scroll within the worksheet, but there is one critical difference. Scrolling with the keyboard also changes the active cell. Scrolling with the mouse does not.

Scenario Manager

The ***Scenario Manager*** enables you to evaluate multiple sets of initial conditions and assumptions (scenarios). Each ***scenario*** represents a different set of what-if conditions that you want to consider in assessing the outcome of a spreadsheet model. You could, for example, look at optimistic, most likely, and pessimistic assumptions in a financial forecast. Our professor will use the Scenario Manager to evaluate his semester grades with and without a curve.

Figure 3.15 illustrates the use of the Scenario Manager in conjunction with the expanded grade book. Each scenario is stored under its own name, such as "Curve" and "No Curve" as shown in Figure 3.15a. Each scenario is comprised of a set of cells whose values vary from scenario to scenario, as well as the values for those cells. Figure 3.15b shows the scenario when no curve is in effect and contains the values for the homework bonus and the breakpoints for the grade distribution table. Figure 3.15c displays a different scenario in which the professor increases the homework bonus and introduces a curve in computing the grades for the class.

Once the individual scenarios have been defined, you can display the worksheet under any scenario by clicking the Show button in the Scenario Manager dialog box. The professor can consider the outcome (the grades assigned to individual students) under the different scenarios and arrive at the best possible decision (the grading criteria to use).

AutoFill

The ***AutoFill capability*** is a wonderful shortcut and the fastest way to enter certain series into adjacent cells. In essence, you enter the first value(s) of a series, then drag the fill handle to the adjacent cells that are to contain the remaining values in that series. Excel creates the series for you based on the initial value(s) you supply. If, for example, you wanted the months of the year to appear in 12 successive cells, you would enter January (or Jan) in the first cell, then drag the

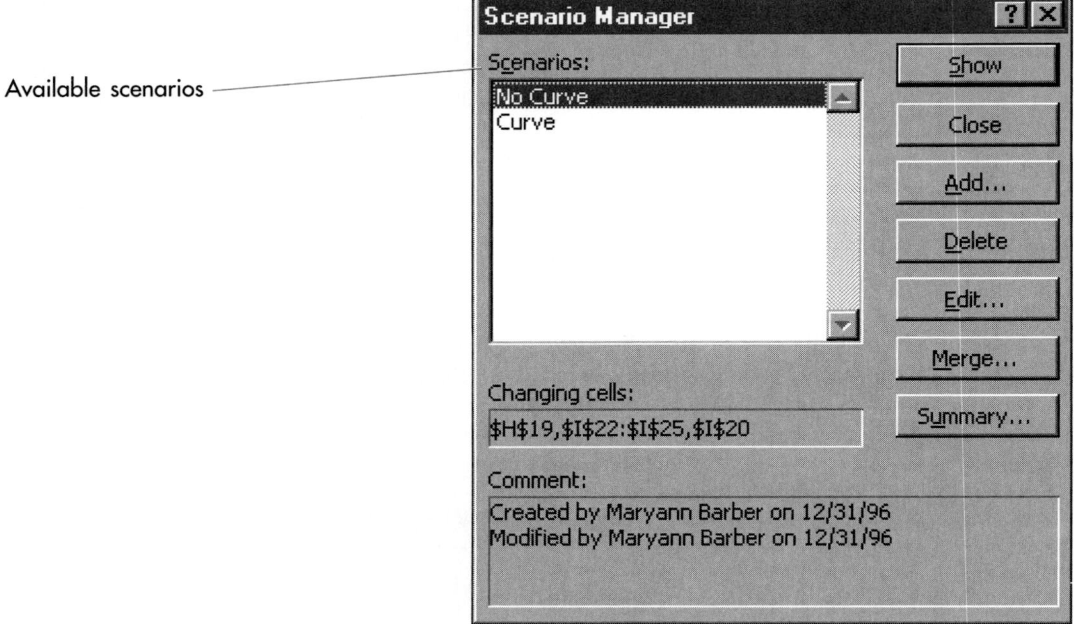

(a) Existing Scenarios

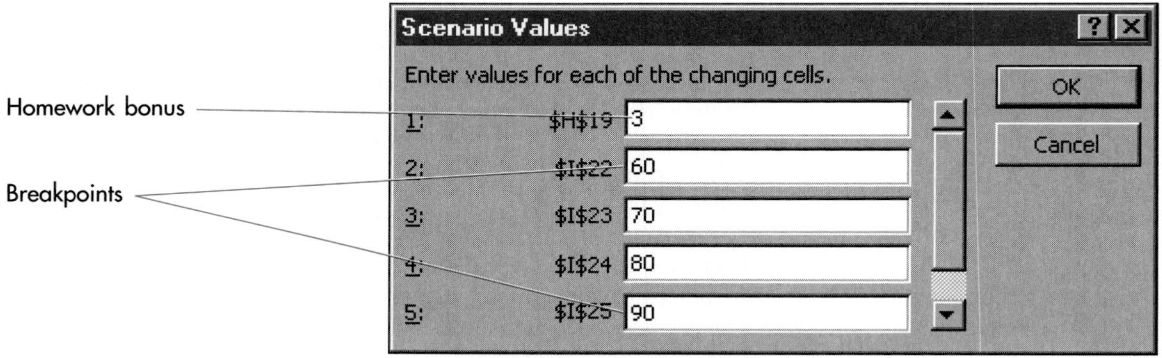

(b) Scenario Values (No Curve)

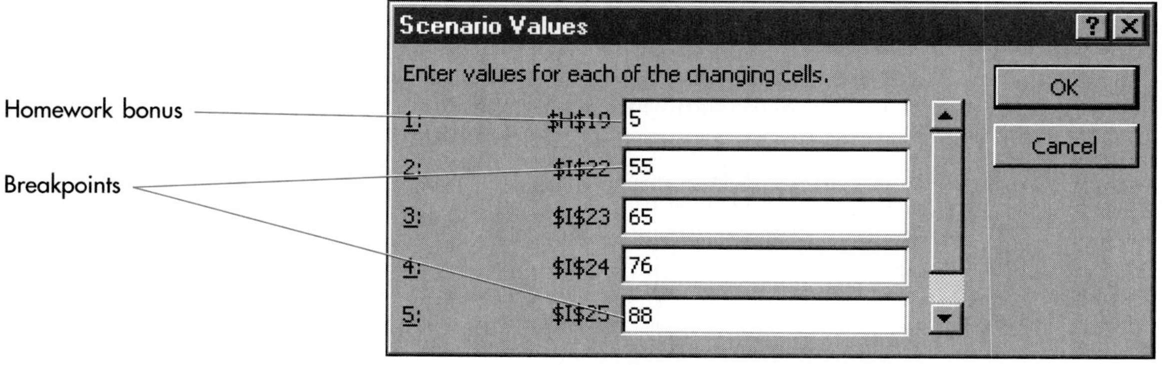

(c) Scenario Values (Curve)

FIGURE 3.15 Scenario Manager

fill handle over the next 11 cells in the direction you want to fill. Excel will enter the remaining months of the year in those cells.

Excel "guesses" at the type of series you want and fills the cells accordingly. You can type Monday (rather than January), and Excel will return the days of the week. You can enter a text and numeric combination, such as Quarter 1 or 1st Quarter, and Excel will extend the series appropriately. You can also create a numeric series by entering the first two numbers in that series; for example, to enter the years 1990 through 1999, type 1990 and 1991 in the first two cells, select both of these cells, and drag the fill handle in the appropriate direction over the destination range.

HANDS-ON EXERCISE 3

The Expanded Grade Book

Objective: To develop the expanded grade book; to use statistical (AVERAGE, MAX, and MIN) and logical (IF and VLOOKUP) functions; to demonstrate scrolling and the Freeze Panes command; to illustrate the AutoFill capability and the Scenario Manager. Use Figure 3.16 as a guide in the exercise.

STEP 1: Open the Extended Grade Book

- Pull down the **File menu** and click **Open** (or click the **Open button** on the Standard toolbar) to display the Open dialog box.
- Click the **drop-down arrow** on the Look In list box. Click the appropriate drive, drive C or drive A, depending on the location of your data. Double click the **Exploring Excel folder** to make it the active folder (the folder from which you will retrieve the workbook).
- Double click **Expanded Grade Book** to open the workbook.
- Pull down the **File menu** and save the workbook as **Finished Expanded Grade Book** so that you can always return to the original workbook if necessary.

SORTING THE STUDENT LIST

The students are listed in the gradebook in alphabetical order, but you can rearrange the list according to any other field, such as the test average. Click in the row containing the data for any student, click in the field on which you want to sort, then click the Ascending or Descending Sort button on the Standard toolbar. Click the Undo command if the result is different from what you intended.

STEP 2: The AutoFill Capability

- Click in **cell C3,** the cell containing the label Test 1. Point to the **fill handle** in the lower-right corner, as shown in Figure 3.16a. The mouse pointer changes to a thin crosshair.
- Click and drag the **fill handle** over cells **D3, E3,** and **F3** (a ScreenTip shows the projected result in cell F3), then release the mouse. Cells D3, E3, and F3 now contain the labels Test 2, Test 3, and Test 4, respectively.

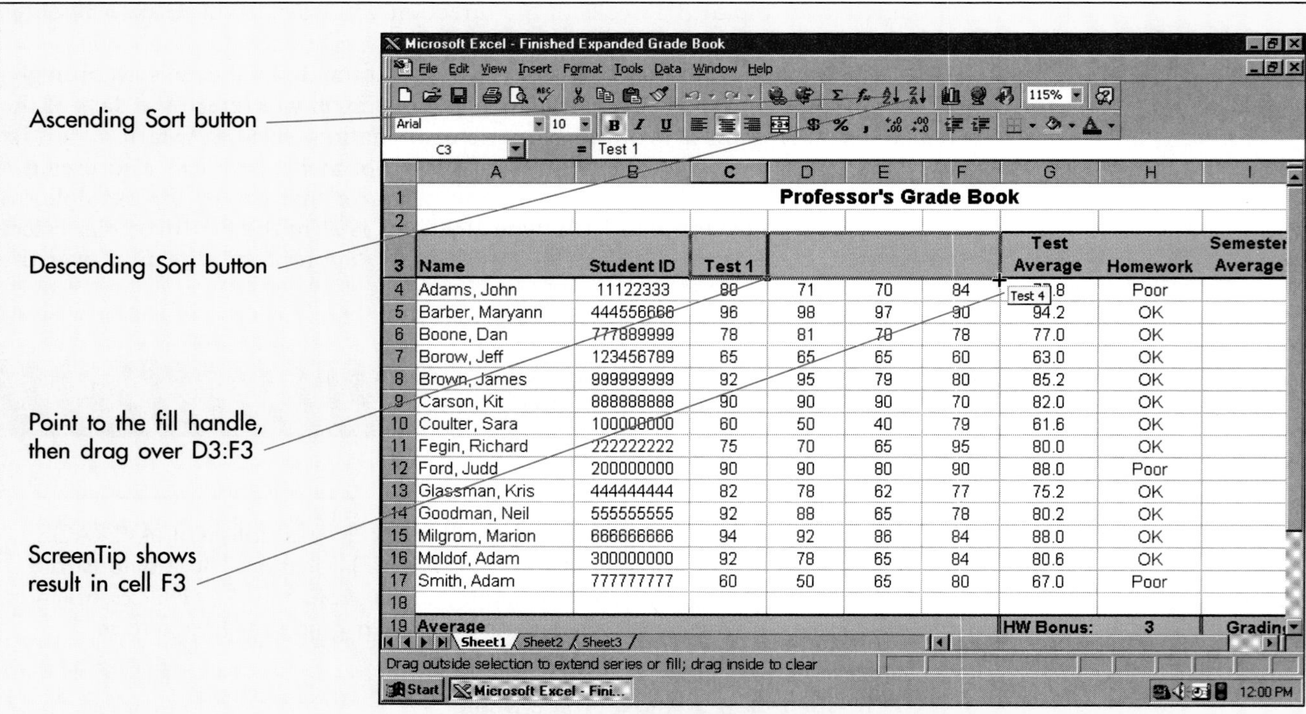

(a) The AutoFill Command (step 2)

FIGURE 3.16 Hands-on Exercise 3

CREATE A CUSTOM SERIES

A custom series is very helpful if you repeatedly enter the same lists of data. Pull down the Tools menu, click Options, then click the Custom Lists tab. Click New List in the Custom Lists box to position the insertion point in the List Entries box. Enter the items in the series (e.g., Tom, Dick, and Harry), using a comma or the enter key to separate one item from the next. Click the Add button. Click OK. The next time you type Tom, Dick, or Harry in a cell and drag the fill handle, you will see the series Tom, Dick, and Harry repeated through the entire range.

STEP 3: Format the Social Security Numbers

- Click and drag to select cells **B4** through **B17,** the cells containing the unformatted social security numbers.
- Point to the selected cells and click the **right mouse button** to display a shortcut menu. Click the **Format Cells command,** click the **Number tab,** then click **Special** in the Category list box.
- Click **Social Security Number** in the Type box, then click **OK** to accept the formatting and close the Format Cells dialog box. The social security numbers are displayed with hyphens.
- Save the workbook.

STEP 4: Scrolling and Freezing Panes

- Press **Ctrl+Home** to move to cell A1. Click the **right arrow** on the horizontal scroll bar until column A scrolls off the screen. Cell A1 is still the active cell, as can be seen in the Name box, because scrolling with the mouse does not change the active cell.
- Press **Ctrl+Home.** Press the **right arrow key** until column A scrolls off the screen. The active cell changes as you scroll with the keyboard.
- Press **Ctrl+Home** to return to cell A1. Click the **down arrow** on the vertical scroll bar (or press the **down arrow key** until row 1 scrolls off the screen). Note whether the active cell changes or not.
- Press **Ctrl+Home** again, then click in **cell B4.** Pull down the **Window menu.** Click **Freeze Panes** as shown in Figure 3.16b. You will see a line to the right

KEYBOARD SHORTCUTS: MOVING WITHIN A WORKSHEET

Press PgUp or PgDn to scroll an entire screen in the indicated direction. Press Ctrl+Home or Ctrl+End to move to the beginning and end of a worksheet—that is, to cell A1 and to the cell in the lower-right corner, respectively. If these keys do not work, it is because the transition navigation keys (i.e., Lotus 1-2-3 conventions) are in effect. Pull down the Tools menu, click Options, and click the Transition tab. Clear the check in the Transition Navigation Keys check box, then click OK.

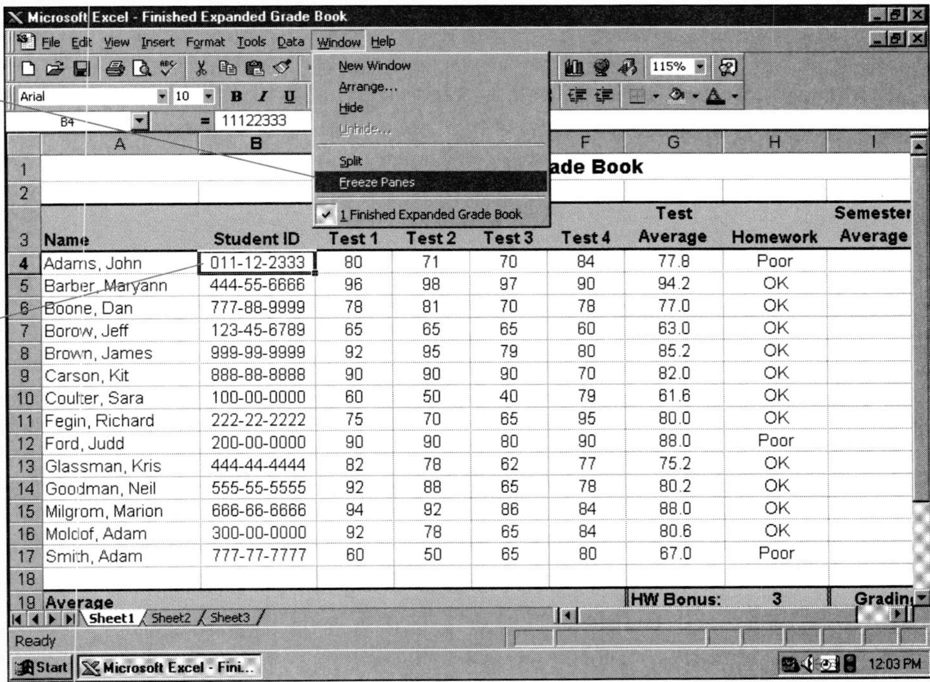

	A	B	C	D	E	F	G	H	I
3	Name	Student ID	Test 1	Test 2	Test 3	Test 4	Test Average	Homework	Semester Average
4	Adams, John	011-12-2333	80	71	70	84	77.8	Poor	
5	Barber, Maryann	444-55-6666	96	98	97	90	94.2	OK	
6	Boone, Dan	777-88-9999	78	81	70	78	77.0	OK	
7	Borow, Jeff	123-45-6789	65	65	65	60	63.0	OK	
8	Brown, James	999-99-9999	92	95	79	80	85.2	OK	
9	Carson, Kit	888-88-8888	90	90	90	70	82.0	OK	
10	Coulter, Sara	100-00-0000	60	50	40	79	61.6	OK	
11	Fegin, Richard	222-22-2222	75	70	65	95	80.0	OK	
12	Ford, Judd	200-00-0000	90	90	80	90	88.0	Poor	
13	Glassman, Kris	444-44-4444	82	78	62	77	75.2	OK	
14	Goodman, Neil	555-55-5555	92	88	65	78	80.2	OK	
15	Milgrom, Marion	666-66-6666	94	92	86	84	88.0	OK	
16	Moldof, Adam	300-00-0000	92	78	65	84	80.6	OK	
17	Smith, Adam	777-77-7777	60	50	65	80	67.0	Poor	
18									
19	Average						HW Bonus:	3	Gradin

(b) Freeze Panes Command (step 4)

FIGURE 3.16 Hands-on Exercise 3 (continued)

of column A and below row 3; that is, column A and rows 1 through 3 will always be visible regardless of scrolling.

- Click the **right arrow** on the horizontal scroll bar (or press the **right arrow key**) repeatedly until column J is visible. Note that column A is visible (frozen), but that one or more columns are not shown.
- Click the **down arrow** on the vertical scroll bar (or press the **down arrow key**) repeatedly until row 25 is visible. Note that rows one through three are visible (frozen), but that one or more rows are not shown.

STEP 5: The IF Function

- Scroll to the top of the worksheet, then scroll until Column I is visible on the screen. Click in **cell I4.**
- Click the **Paste Function button** on the Standard toolbar. Click **Logical** in the Function Category list box. Click **IF** in the Function Name list box, then click **OK** to display the Formula Palette in Figure 3.16c.
- Enter the arguments for the IF function as shown in the figure. You can enter the arguments directly, or you can use pointing as follows:
  - Click the **Logical_test** text box. Click **cell H4** in the worksheet. (You may need to click and drag the top border of the Formula Palette of the dialog box to move it out of the way.) Type =“**OK**” to complete the logical test.
  - Click the **Value_if_true** text box. Click **cell G4** in the worksheet, type a **plus sign,** click **cell H19** in the worksheet (scrolling if necessary), and finally press the **F4 key** (see boxed tip) to convert the reference to cell H19 to an absolute reference ($H$19).

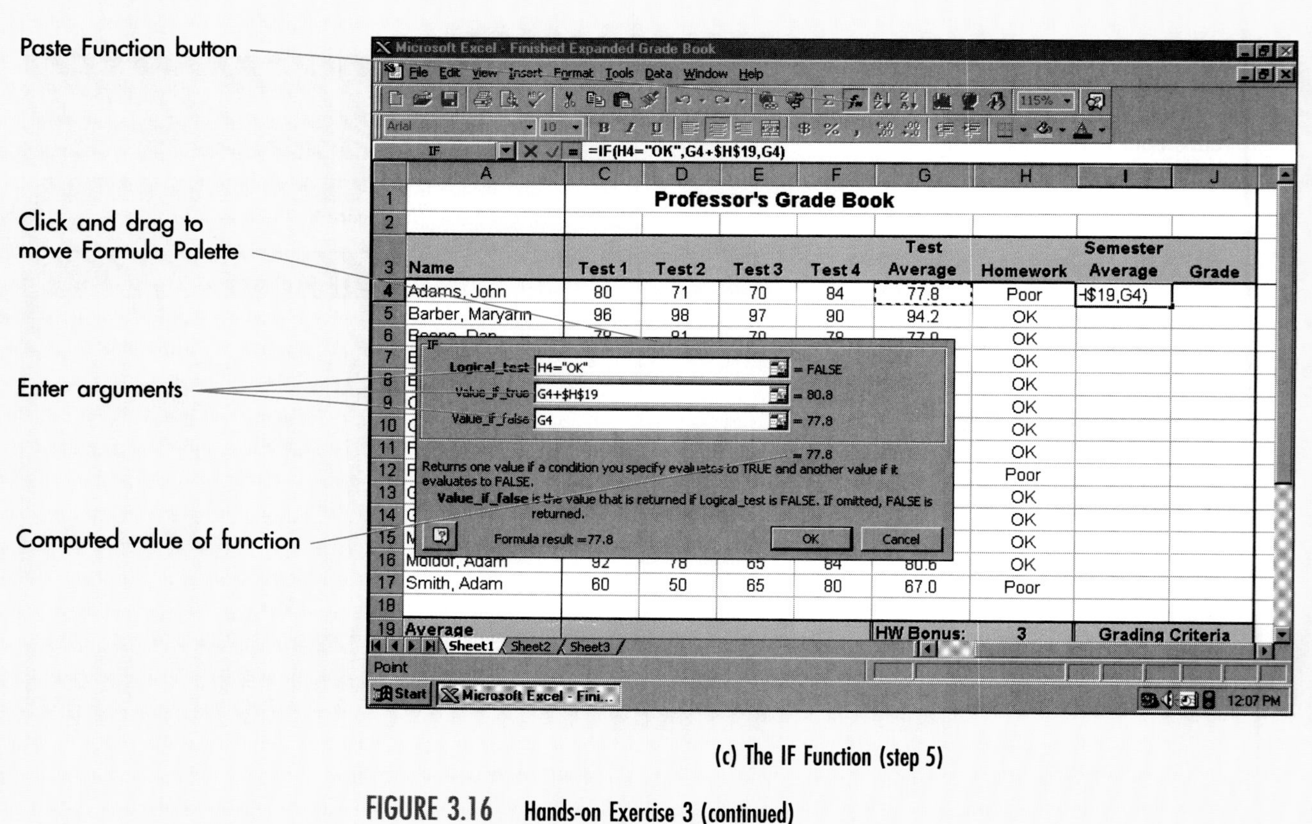

(c) The IF Function (step 5)

FIGURE 3.16 Hands-on Exercise 3 (continued)

- Click the **Value_if_false** text box. Click **cell G4** in the worksheet, scrolling if necessary.

➤ Check that the dialog box on your worksheet matches the one in Figure 3.16c. Make corrections as necessary. Click **OK** to insert the function into your worksheet.

➤ Save the workbook.

THE COLLAPSE DIALOG BUTTON

You can enter a cell reference in one of two ways. You can type it directly in the Formula Palette, or alternatively, you can click the cell in the worksheet. The Formula Palette typically hides the underlying cell, however, in which case you can click the Collapse Dialog button (which appears to the right of any parameter within the dialog box). This collapses (hides) the Formula Palette so that you can click the underlying cell, which is now visible. Click the Collapse Dialog button a second time to display the entire dialog box.

STEP 6: The VLOOKUP Function

➤ Click in **cell J4.**

➤ Click the **Paste Function button** on the Standard toolbar. Click **Lookup & Reference** in the Function Category list box. Scroll in the Function name list box until you can select **VLOOKUP.** Click **OK** to display the Formula Palette in Figure 3.16d.

➤ Enter the arguments for the VLOOKUP function as shown in the figure. You can enter the arguments directly, or you can use pointing as follows:

- Click the **Lookup_value** text box. Click **cell I4** in the worksheet.
- Click the **Table_array** text box. Click **cell I21** and drag to cell **J25** (scrolling if necessary). Press the **F4 key** to convert to an absolute reference.
- Click the **Col_index_num** text box. Type **2.**

➤ Check that the dialog box on your worksheet matches the one in Figure 3.16d. Make corrections as necessary. Click **OK** to insert the function into your worksheet.

➤ Save the workbook.

THE F4 KEY

The F4 key cycles through relative, absolute, and mixed addresses. Click on any reference within the formula bar; for example, click on A1 in the formula =A1+A2. Press the F4 key once, and it changes to an absolute reference. Press the F4 key a second time, and it becomes a mixed reference, A$1; press it again, and it is a different mixed reference, $A1. Press the F4 key a fourth time, and it returns to the original relative address, A1.

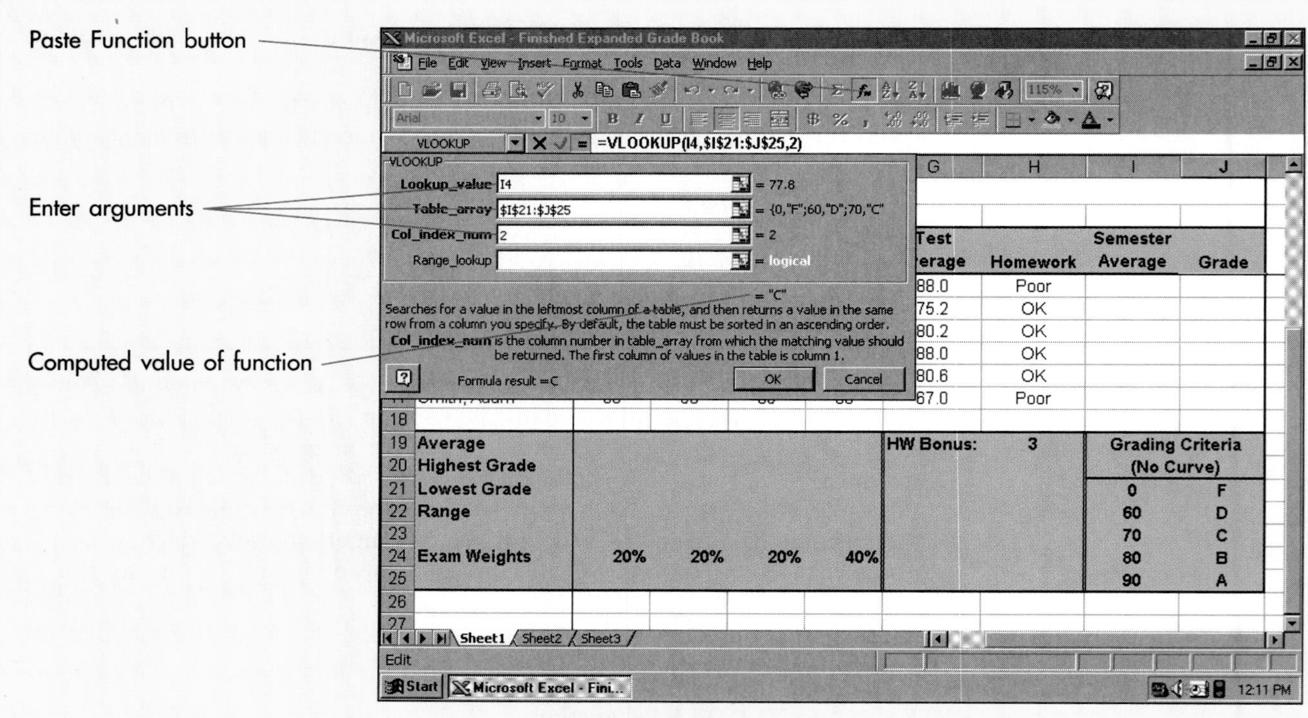

(d) The VLOOKUP Function (step 6)

FIGURE 3.16 Hands-on Exercise 3 (continued)

STEP 7: Copy the IF and VLOOKUP Functions (the Fill Handle)

- If necessary, scroll to the top of the worksheet. Select cells **I4** and **J4** as in Figure 3.16e.
- Point to the **fill handle** in the lower-right corner of the selected range. The mouse pointer changes to a thin crosshair.
- Drag the **fill handle** over cells **I5** through **J17.** A border appears, indicating the destination range as shown in Figure 3.16e. Release the mouse to complete the copy operation. If you have done everything correctly, Adam Smith should have a grade of D based on a semester average of 67. Format the semester averages in column I to one decimal place.
- Save the workbook.

STEP 8: Statistical Functions

- Scroll until you can click in **cell C19.** Type **=AVERAGE(C4:C17).** Press **enter.** Cell C19 should display 81.857. Format the average to one decimal place.
- Click in **cell C20.** Type **=MAX(C4:C17).** Press **enter.** Cell C20 should display a value of 96.
- Click in **cell C21.** Type **=MIN(C4:C17).** Press **enter.** Cell C21 should display a value of 60.
- Click in **cell C22.** Type **=C20-C21.** Press **enter.** Cell C22 should display 36.

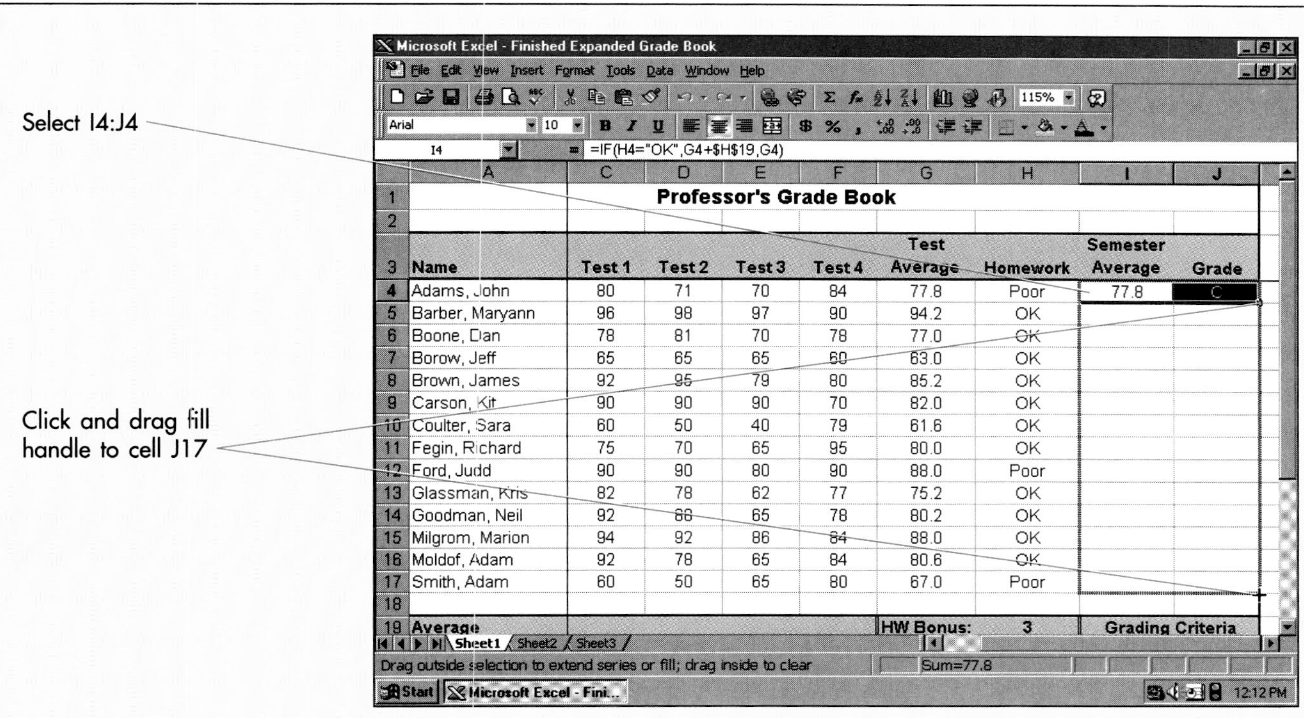

	A	C	D	E	F	G	H	I	J
1		Professor's Grade Book							
2									
3	Name	Test 1	Test 2	Test 3	Test 4	Test Average	Homework	Semester Average	Grade
4	Adams, John	80	71	70	84	77.8	Poor	77.8	C
5	Barber, Maryann	96	98	97	90	94.2	OK		
6	Boone, Dan	78	81	70	78	77.0	OK		
7	Borow, Jeff	65	65	65	60	63.0	OK		
8	Brown, James	92	95	79	80	85.2	OK		
9	Carson, Kit	90	90	90	70	82.0	OK		
10	Coulter, Sara	60	50	40	79	61.6	OK		
11	Fegin, Richard	75	70	65	95	80.0	OK		
12	Ford, Judd	90	90	80	90	88.0	Poor		
13	Glassman, Kris	82	78	62	77	75.2	OK		
14	Goodman, Neil	92	88	65	78	80.2	OK		
15	Milgrom, Marion	94	92	86	84	88.0	OK		
16	Moldof, Adam	92	78	65	84	80.6	OK		
17	Smith, Adam	60	50	65	80	67.0	Poor		
18									
19	Average					HW Bonus:	3	Grading Criteria	

(e) The Fill Handle (step 7)

FIGURE 3.16 Hands-on Exercise 3 (continued)

#NAME? AND OTHER ERRORS

Excel displays an error value when it is unable to calculate the formula in a cell. Misspelling a function name (e.g., using AVG instead of AVERAGE) results in #NAME?, which is perplexing at first, but easily corrected once you know the meaning of the error. All error values begin with a pound sign (#). Pull down the Help menu, click Contents & Index, click the Index tab, then enter # for a list of the error values. Click the desired error value, then click the Display button for an explanation.

STEP 9: Copy the Statistical Functions (Shortcut Menu)

- Select cells **C19** through **C22** as shown in Figure 3.16f. Click the **right mouse button** to display the shortcut menu shown in the figure. Click **Copy.** A moving border appears around the selected cells.
- Drag the mouse over cells **D19** through **F19.** Click the **Paste button** on the Standard toolbar to complete the copy operation, then press **Esc** to remove the moving border. If you have done everything correctly, cells F19, F20, F21, and F22 will display 80.6, 95, 60, and 35, respectively.
- Save the workbook.

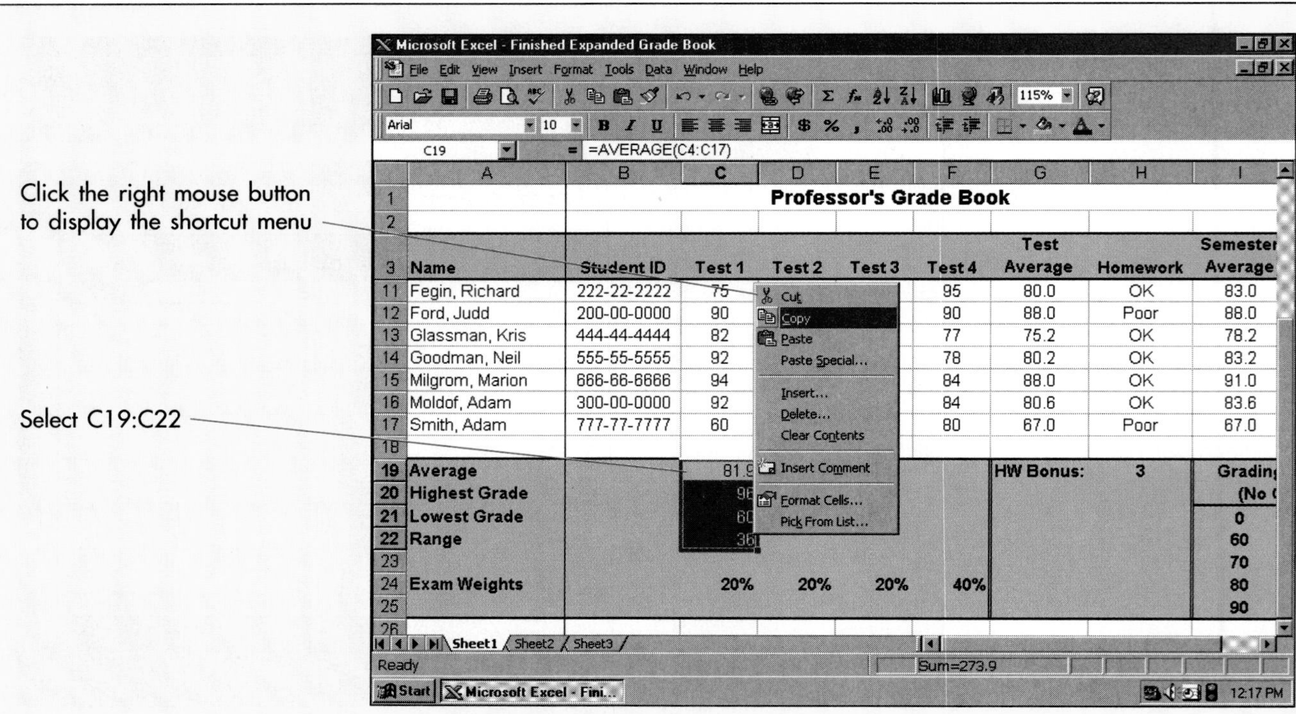

Click the right mouse button to display the shortcut menu
Select C19:C22

(f) Shortcut Menus (step 9)

FIGURE 3.16 Hands-on Exercise 3 (continued)

SEE THE WHOLE WORKSHEET

Press Ctrl+Home to move to the beginning of the worksheet. Press the F8 key to enter the extended selection mode (EXT will appear on the status bar), then press Ctrl+End to move to the end of the worksheet and simultaneously select the entire worksheet. Pull down the View menu, click Zoom, then click the Fit Selection option button. Click OK to close the dialog box. The magnification shrinks to display the entire worksheet on the screen; how well you can read the display depends on the size of your monitor and the size of the worksheet.

STEP 10: Create the No Curve Scenario

- Click in **cell H19.** Pull down the **Tools menu.** Click **Scenarios** to display the Scenario Manager dialog box. Click the **Add command button** to display the Add Scenario dialog box in Figure 3.16g.
- Type **No Curve** in the Scenario Name text box.
- Click in the **Changing Cells text box** to the right of H19. Cell H19 (the active cell) is already entered as the first cell in the scenario. Type a **comma,** then click and drag to select cells **I22** through **I25** (the cells containing the breakpoints for the grade distribution table). Scroll to these cells if necessary.
- Type another **comma,** then click in **cell I20.** The Add Scenarios dialog box should match the display in Figure 3.16g. Click **OK.**

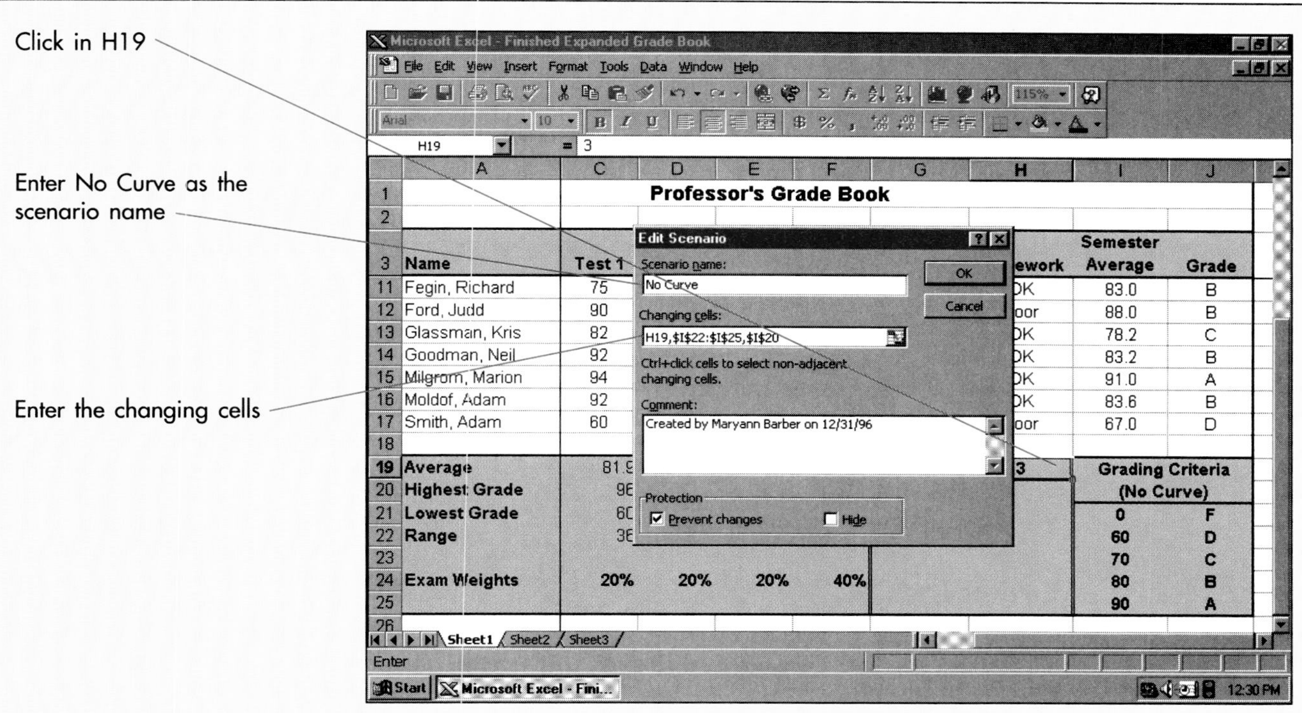

(g) Add a Scenario (step 10)

FIGURE 3.16 Hands-on Exercise 3 (continued)

- You should see the Scenario Values dialog box with the values of this scenario (No Curve) already entered. Only the first five cells are displayed, and you must scroll to see the others.
- Click **OK** to complete the No Curve scenario and close the Scenario Values dialog box.

STEP 11: Add the Curve Scenario

- The Scenario Manager dialog box should still be open. Click the **Add button** to add a second scenario and display the Add Scenario dialog box.
- Type **Curve** in the Scenario Name text box. The changing cells are already entered and match the changing cells in the No Curve scenario. Click **OK.**
- Enter **5** as the new value for cell H19 (the bonus for homework). Press the **Tab key** to move to the text box for the next cell. Enter 55, 65, 76, and 88 as the values for cells I22 through I25, respectively.
- Enter **(Curve)** as the value for cell I20. Click **OK** to complete the scenario and close the Scenario Values dialog box.

INCLUDE THE SCENARIO NAME

A scenario is composed of one or more changing cells whose values you want to consider in evaluating the outcome of a spreadsheet model. We find it useful to include an additional cell within the scenario that contains the name of the scenario itself, so that the scenario name appears within the worksheet when the worksheet is printed.

STEP 12: View the Scenarios

- The Scenario Manager dialog box should still be open as shown in Figure 3.16h. (If necessary, pull down the **Tools menu** and click the **Scenarios command** to reopen the Scenario Manager.) There should be two scenarios listed, No Curve and Curve, corresponding to the scenarios that were just created.
- Select the **Curve** scenario, then click the **Show button** to display the grade book under this scenario. Some, but not all, of the grades will change under the easier criteria. Ford, for example, goes from a B to an A.
- Select the **No Curve** scenario. Click the **Show button** to display the grades under the initial set of assumptions. Click the **Close button** and review the changes. Ford goes from an A back to a B.
- Show the grades under the **Curve** scenario a second time, then click the **Close button** to exit the Scenario Manager. Save the workbook.

THE SCENARIO MANAGER LIST BOX

The Scenario Manager List Box enables you to select a scenario directly from a toolbar. Point to any toolbar, click the right mouse button to display a shortcut menu, then click Customize to display the Customize dialog box. Click the Commands tab, click Utility in the Categories list box, then scroll until you can click and drag the Scenario list box to an empty space within a toolbar. Close the dialog box. Click the down arrow on the Scenario list box, which now appears on the toolbar, to choose from the scenarios that have been defined within the current workbook.

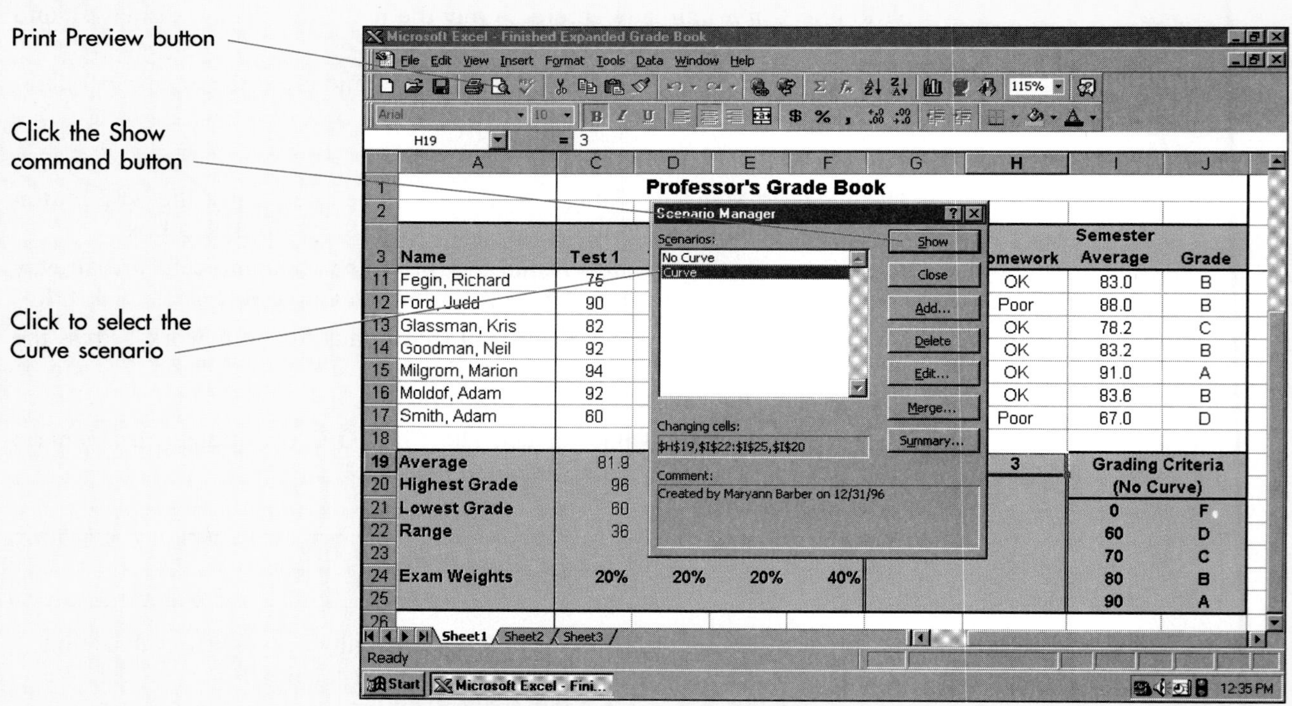

(h) View the Scenarios (step 12)

FIGURE 3.16 Hands-on Exercise 3 (continued)

STEP 13: Print the Worksheet

- Add your name and title (**Grading Assistant**) in cells G26 and G27. Save the workbook.
- Pull down the **File menu.** Click **Page Setup** to display the Page Setup dialog box:
  - Click the **Page tab.** Click the **Landscape option button.** Click the option button to **Fit to 1 page.**
  - Click the **Margins tab.** Check the box to center the worksheet Horizontally on the page.
  - Click the **Sheet tab.** Check the boxes for **Row and Column Headings** and for **Gridlines.**
- Click the **Print Preview button** to display the completed spreadsheet, which should match the screen in Figure 3.16i. Click the **Print command button** and click **OK** to print the workbook.
- Press **Ctrl+´** to show the cell formulas rather than the displayed values. Click the **Print Preview button** as previously, click the **Setup button** (within the Print Preview window), then make the necessary changes (see the boxed tip on page 122) to show the cell formulas.
- Print the worksheet a second time with the cell formulas. Exit Excel. Submit both printouts (the displayed values and the cell formulas) to your instructor.

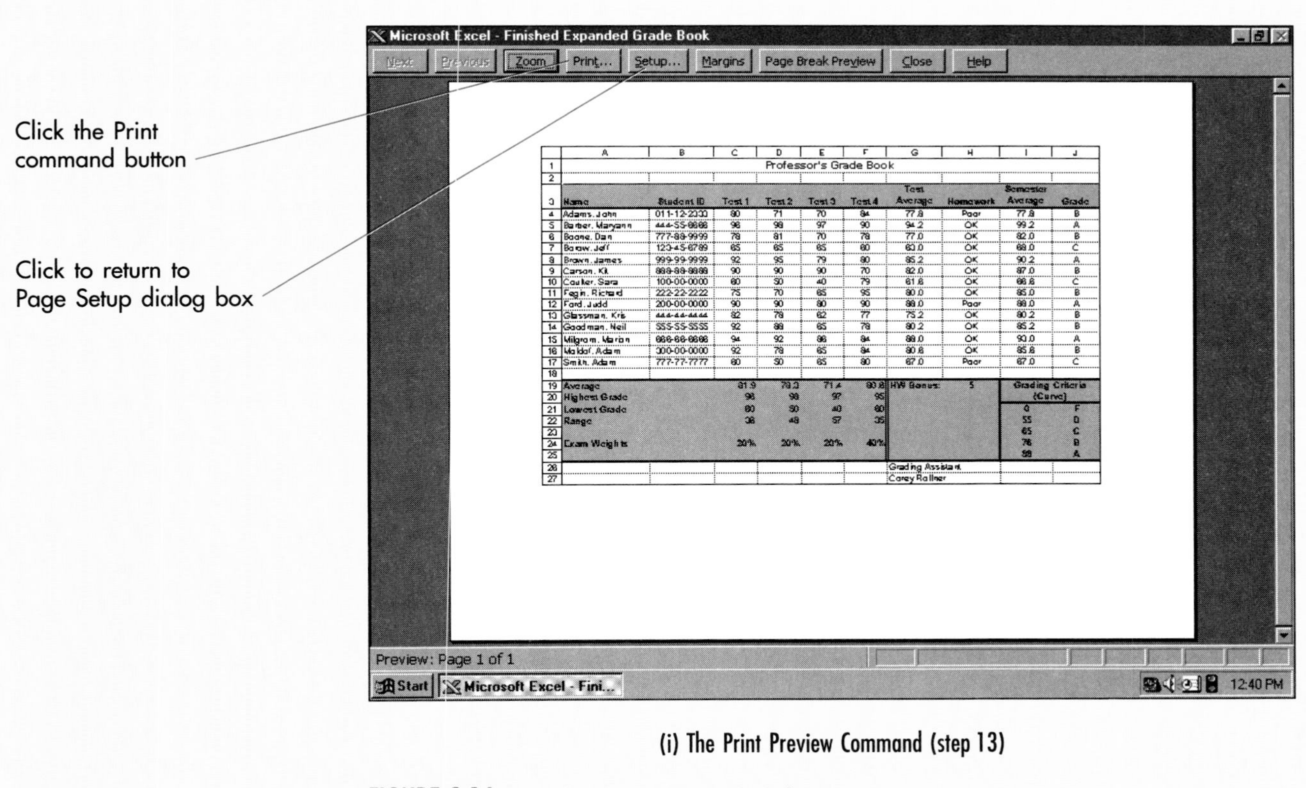

(i) The Print Preview Command (step 13)

FIGURE 3.16 Hands-on Exercise 3 (continued)

MAKE IT FIT

The Page Setup command offers several ways to make a large worksheet fit on one page. Click the Print Preview button on the Standard toolbar to view the worksheet prior to printing. Click the Margins command button to display (hide) sizing handles for the page margins and column widths, then drag any handle to adjust the margin or column width. You can also click the Setup command button from the Print Preview screen to display the Page Setup dialog box. Use the Page tab to change to landscape printing and/or to select the scaling option to Fit to 1 page.

SUMMARY

Excel contains several categories of built-in functions. The PMT function computes the periodic payment for a loan based on three arguments (the interest rate per period, the number of periods, and the amount of the loan). The PMT function was used in the analysis of a car loan and in the comparison of 15- and 30-year mortgages.

Statistical functions were also discussed. The AVERAGE, MAX, and MIN functions return the average, highest, and lowest values in the argument list. The COUNT function returns the number of cells with numeric entries. The COUNTA function displays the number of cells with numeric and/or text entries.

The IF and VLOOKUP functions implement decision making within a worksheet. The IF function has three arguments: a logical test, which is evaluated as true or false; a value if the test is true; and a value if the test is false. The VLOOKUP (table lookup) function also has three arguments: the numeric value to look up, the range of cells containing the table, and the column number within the table that contains the result.

The hands-on exercises introduced several techniques to make you more proficient. The fill handle is used to copy a cell or group of cells to a range of adjacent cells. Pointing is a more accurate way to enter a cell reference into a formula as it uses the mouse or arrow keys to select the cell as you build the formula. The AutoFill capability creates a series based on the initial value(s) you supply.

Scrolling enables you to view any portion of a large worksheet but moves the labels for existing rows and/or columns off the screen. The Freeze Panes command keeps the row and/or column headings on the screen while scrolling in a large worksheet.

A spreadsheet is first and foremost a tool for decision making, and thus Excel includes several commands to aid in that process. The Goal Seek command lets you enter the desired end result of a spreadsheet model (such as the monthly payment on a car loan) and determines the input (the price of the car) to produce that result. The Scenario Manager enables you to specify multiple sets of assumptions (scenarios), and see at a glance the results of any scenario.

The assumptions and initial conditions in a spreadsheet should be clearly labeled and set apart from the rest of the worksheet. This facilitates change and reduces the chance for error.

A worksheet should always be printed twice, once with displayed values and once with cell formulas. The Print Preview command displays a worksheet as it will appear when printed. The Page Setup command gives you complete control of the printed worksheet.

KEY WORDS AND CONCEPTS

=AVERAGE
=COUNT
=COUNTA
=IF
=MAX
=MIN
=PMT
=SUM
=VLOOKUP
Absolute reference
Arguments
Assumptions
AutoFill capability
Breakpoint
Custom series
Enter mode
Fill handle
Formula Palette
Freeze Panes command
Function
Goal Seek command
Logical test
Pointing
Point mode
Relational operator
Relative reference
Scenario
Scenario Manager
Scrolling
Spell check
Statistical functions
Template
Unfreeze Panes command

MULTIPLE CHOICE

1. Which of the following options may be used to print a large worksheet?
(a) Landscape orientation
(b) Scaling
(c) Reduced margins
(d) All of the above

2. If the results of a formula contain more characters than can be displayed according to the present format and cell width,
(a) The extra characters will be truncated under all circumstances
(b) All of the characters will be displayed if the cell to the right is empty
(c) A series of asterisks will be displayed
(d) A series of pound signs will be displayed

3. Which cell—A1, A2, or A3—will contain the amount of the loan, given the function =PMT(A1,A2,A3)?
(a) A1
(b) A2
(c) A3
(d) Impossible to determine

4. Which of the following will compute the average of the values in cells D2, D3, and D4?
(a) The function =AVERAGE(D2:D4)
(b) The function =AVERAGE(D2,D4)
(c) Both (a) and (b)
(d) Neither (a) nor (b)

5. The function =IF(A1>A2,A1+A2,A1*A2) returns
   (a) The product of cells A1 and A2 if cell A1 is greater than A2
   (b) The sum of cells A1 and A2 if cell A1 is less than A2
   (c) Both (a) and (b)
   (d) Neither (a) nor (b)
6. Which of the following is the preferred way to sum the values contained in cells A1 to A4?
   (a) =SUM(A1:A4)
   (b) =A1+A2+A3+A4
   (c) Either (a) or (b) is equally good
   (d) Neither (a) nor (b) is correct
7. Which of the following will return the highest and lowest arguments from a list of arguments?
   (a) HIGH/LOW
   (b) LARGEST/SMALLEST
   (c) MAX/MIN
   (d) All of the above
8. Which of the following is a *required* technique to develop the worksheet for the mortgage analysis?
   (a) Pointing
   (b) Copying with the fill handle
   (c) Both (a) and (b)
   (d) Neither (a) nor (b)
9. Given that cells B6, C6, and D6 contain the numbers 10, 20, and 30, respectively, what value will be returned by the function =IF(B6>10,C6*2,D6*3)?
   (a) 10
   (b) 40
   (c) 60
   (d) 90
10. Which of the following is not an input to the Goal Seek command?
    (a) The cell containing the end result
    (b) The desired value of the end result
    (c) The cell whose value will change to reach the end result
    (d) The value of the input cell that is required to reach the end result
11. Each scenario in the Scenario Manager:
    (a) Is stored in a separate worksheet
    (b) Contains the value of a single assumption or input condition
    (c) Both (a) and (b)
    (d) Neither (a) nor (b)
12. Which function will return the number of nonempty cells in the range A2 through A6, including in the result cells that contain text as well as numeric entries?
    (a) =COUNT(A2:A6)
    (b) =COUNTA(A2:A6)
    (c) =COUNT(A2,A6)
    (d) =COUNTA(A2,A6)

13. What happens if you select a range, then press the right (alternate) mouse button?
   (a) The range will be deselected
   (b) Nothing; that is, the button has no effect
   (c) The Edit and Format menus will be displayed in their entirety
   (d) A shortcut menu with commands from both the Edit and Format menus will be displayed

14. The worksheet displayed in the monitor shows columns A and B, skips columns D, E, and F, then displays columns G, H, I, J, and K. What is the most likely explanation for the missing columns?
   (a) The columns were previously deleted
   (b) The columns are empty and thus are automatically hidden from view
   (c) Either (a) or (b) is a satisfactory explanation
   (d) Neither (a) nor (b) is a likely reason

15. Given the function =VLOOKUP(C6,D12:F18,3)
   (a) The entries in cells D12 through D18 are in ascending order
   (b) The entries in cells D12 through D18 are in descending order
   (c) The entries in cells F12 through F18 are in ascending order
   (d) The entries in cells F12 through F18 are in descending order

ANSWERS

1. d	**6.** a	**11.** d
2. d	**7.** c	**12.** b
3. c	**8.** d	**13.** d
4. a	**9.** d	**14.** d
5. d	**10.** d	**15.** a

PRACTICE WITH EXCEL 97

1. Startup Airlines: The partially completed spreadsheet in Figure 3.17 is used by a new airline to calculate the fuel requirements and associated cost for its available flights. The airline has only two types of planes, B27s and DC-9s. The fuel needed for any given flight depends on the aircraft and number of flying hours; for example, a five-hour flight in a DC-9 can be expected to use 40,000 gallons. In addition, the plane must carry an additional 10% of the required fuel to maintain a holding pattern (4,000 gallons in this example) and an additional 20% as reserve (8,000 gallons in this example).

   Retrieve the partially completed *Chapter 3 Practice 1* from the data disk and save it as *Finished Chapter 3 Practice 1*. Compute the fuel necessary for the listed flights based on a fuel price of $1.00 per gallon. Your worksheet should be completely flexible and amenable to change; that is, the hourly fuel requirements, price per gallon, holding and reserve percentages are all subject to change at a moment's notice.

   After completing the cell formulas, format the spreadsheet as you see fit. Add your name somewhere in the worksheet, then print the completed worksheet and cell formulas, and submit the assignment to your instructor.

	A	B	C	D	E	F	G	H
1	Fuel Estimates							
2								
3	Plane	Flight	Flying Hours	Flying Fuel	Reserve Fuel	Holding Fuel	Total Fuel Needed	Estimated Fuel Cost
4	Boeing-727	MIA-JFK	2.75					
5	DC-9	MIA-ATL	1.25					
6	Boeing-727	MIA-IAH	2.25					
7	Boeing-727	MIA-LAX	5.5					
8	DC-9	MIA-MSY	1.5					
9		Totals						
10								
11	Fuel Facts:							
12	Gallons per hour: Boeing-727		10000			% of Flying Fuel required for:		
13	Gallons per hour: DC-9		8000			Reserve Fuel		0.2
14	Fuel cost per gallon		1			Holding Fuel		0.1

FIGURE 3.17 Spreadsheet for Practice Exercise 1

2. A partially completed version of the worksheet in Figure 3.18 can be found on the data disk as *Chapter 3 Practice 2.* To complete the spreadsheet, you need to understand the discount policy, which states that a discount is given if the total sale is equal to or greater than the discount threshold. (The amount of the discount is equal to the total sale multiplied by the discount percentage.) If the total sale is less than the discount threshold, no discount is given.

   Complete the worksheet in Figure 3.18, then create two additional scenarios for different selling strategies. In one scenario lower the discount threshold and discount percentage to $3000 and 12%, respectively. Increase these values in a second scenario to $10,000 and 20%. Add your name somewhere in the worksheet, then print all three scenarios (the two you created plus the original set of numbers) and submit the completed assignment.

	A	B	C	D	E	F	G	H	I
1	Hot Spot Software Distributors								
2	Miami, Florida								
3									
4	Customer Name	Program	Current Price	Units Sold	Total Sale	Amount of Discount	Discounted Total	Sales Tax	Amount Due
5	AAA Software Sales	Norton Utilities	$116.99	35	$4,094.65	$0.00	$4,094.65	$266.15	$4,360.80
6	CompuSoft, Inc.	Microsoft Office 97	$317.95	45	$14,307.75	$2,146.16	$12,161.59	$790.50	$12,952.09
7	Kings Bay Software	Adobe Photoshop	$159.55	15	$2,393.25	$0.00	$2,393.25	$155.56	$2,548.81
8	MicroSales, Inc	Quicken Deluxe	$59.99	30	$1,799.70	$0.00	$1,799.70	$116.98	$1,916.68
9	PC and Me Software	Microsoft Office 97	$317.95	17	$5,405.15	$810.77	$4,594.38	$298.63	$4,893.01
10	Personal Software Sales	Quicken Deluxe	$59.99	30	$1,799.70	$0.00	$1,799.70	$116.98	$1,916.68
11	Service Software	Adobe Photoshop	$159.99	35	$5,599.65	$839.95	$4,759.70	$309.38	$5,069.08
12	Software and More	Norton Utilities	$116.99	50	$5,849.50	$877.43	$4,972.08	$323.18	$5,295.26
13	Software To Go	Norton Utilities	$116.99	35	$4,094.65	$0.00	$4,094.65	$266.15	$4,360.80
14	Unique Software Sales	Microsoft Office 97	$317.95	50	$15,897.50	$2,384.63	$13,512.88	$878.34	$14,391.21
15									
16	Discount Threshold	$5,000.00					Number of customers		10
17	Discount Percentage	15.0%					Highest current price		$317.95
18	Sales Tax	6.5%					Fewest units sold		15
19							Average Discount		$705.89
20							Total Amount Due		$57,704.43

FIGURE 3.18 Spreadsheet for Practice Exercise 2

3. Object Linking and Embedding: Figure 3.19 extends the analysis of a car loan to include monthly expenditures for gas, insurance, and maintenance. It also includes an IF function in cell B13 that compares the total monthly cost to $500 (the maximum you can afford), and prints "Yes" or "No" depending on the answer. And finally, it uses the Insert Picture command to insert a picture of the car from the Microsoft Clip Gallery.

   Enter realistic terms for a car loan in today's economy. Add your name somewhere in the worksheet, insert a clip art object, then print the completed worksheet and submit it to your instructor.

	A	B
1	Price of car	$13,999
2	Manufacturer's rebate	$1,000
3	Down payment	$3,000
4	Amount to finance	$9,999
5	Interest rate	8%
6	Term (years)	4
7	Monthly payment	$244
8	Insurance	$100
9	Gas	$75
10	Maintenance	$50
11	Total	$469
12		
13	Can I afford it?	Yes
14		
15		
16		
17		
18		
19		
20		

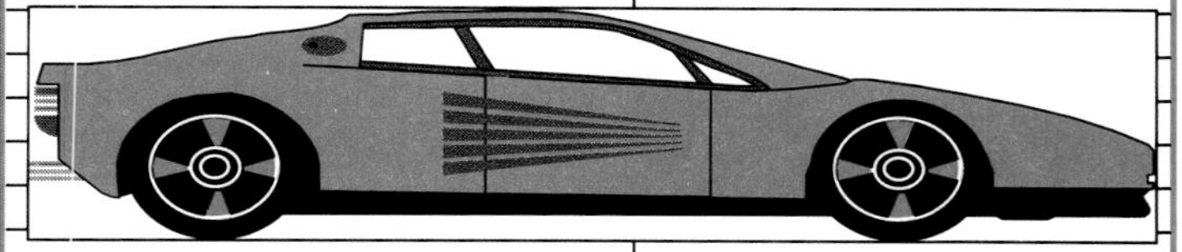

FIGURE 3.19 Spreadsheet for Practice Exercise 3

4. Scenario Summary: The report in Figure 3.20 illustrates the summary capability within Scenario Manager and is based on the completed financial forecast from Chapter 2. Return to the Finished Financial Forecast that you created in the third hands-on exercise, then add the Optimistic and Pessimistic scenarios as shown in Figure 3.20. The Scenario Summary is to appear as a separate worksheet in the Finished Financial Forecast workbook.

The changing cells in both scenarios are cells B18 and B19, which contain the first-year sales and selling price, and cells D18 and D19 containing the projected increase in these values. [Note, however, that the summary table uses descriptive names rather than cell references (e.g., FirstYearSales

Scenario Summary			
	Current Values:	Optmistic	Pessimistic
Changing Cells:			
FirstYearSales	$100,000	$150,000	$75,000
SellingPrice	$3.00	$4.50	$2.50
SalesIncrease	10.0%	15.0%	8.0%
PriceIncrease	5.0%	8.0%	5.0%
Result Cells:			
$B$15	$75,000	$375,000	$0
$C$15	$84,750	$473,475	-$1,275
$D$15	$94,710	$595,298	-$3,542
$E$15	$104,579	$745,818	-$7,126
$F$15	$113,936	$931,591	-$12,434

Notes: Current Values column represents values of changing cells at time Scenario Summary Report was created. Changing cells for each scenario are highlighted in gray.

FIGURE 3.20 Spreadsheet for Practice Exercise 4

instead of cell B18) because the Insert Name command was used to assign a descriptive name to the associated cell reference. This should be done prior to using the Scenario Manager. (Use online help to learn how to name a formula or reference.)]

The Scenario Summary is created by clicking the Summary command button within Scenario Manager, then choosing the Scenario Summary option button from the available report types. To create the summary, you will need to specify the result cells (cells B15 through F15 in the financial forecast) whose values will be displayed in the summary table shown in the figure.

Create one additional scenario (with any values you like) that identifies you by name, then print the scenario summary and submit it to your instructor.

5. The spreadsheet in Figure 3.21 illustrates the use of the PMT function to compute the amortization schedule on a loan. The spreadsheet was created in such a way, however, as to accommodate an optional extra payment every month, which is applied directly to the balance. Use the Goal Seek command to determine the amount of the extra payment so that the loan is paid off in 10 years rather than 15. Add your name to the worksheet, then print the completed spreadsheet (which pays off the loan in 10 years) and submit it to your instructor.

	A	B	C	D	E
1	**Amortization Schedule**				
2					
3	Principal				$100,000
4	Annual Interest				7.50%
5	Term (years)				15
6	Monthly payment				$927.01
7	Extra payment (optional)				$0
8					
9	Month	Toward Interest	Toward Principal	Extra Payment	Balance
10					$100,000
11	1	$625.00	$302.01	$0	$99,697.99
12	2	$623.11	$303.90	$0	$99,394.09
13	3	$621.21	$305.80	$0	$99,088.29
14	4	$619.30	$307.71	$0	$98,780.58
15	5	$617.38	$309.63	$0	$98,470.94
16	6	$615.44	$311.57	$0	$98,159.38
17	7	$613.50	$313.52	$0	$97,845.86
18	8	$611.54	$315.48	$0	$97,530.38
19	9	$609.56	$317.45	$0	$97,212.94
20	10	$607.58	$319.43	$0	$96,893.50
21	11	$605.58	$321.43	$0	$96,572.08
22	12	$603.58	$323.44	$0	$96,248.64
23	13	$601.55	$325.46	$0	$95,923.18
24	14	$599.52	$327.49	$0	$95,595.69
25	15	$597.47	$329.54	$0	$95,266.15

FIGURE 3.21 Spreadsheet for Practice Exercise 5

6. The compound document in Figure 3.22 contains a spreadsheet to compute a car payment together with a description and picture of the associated car. The latter two were taken from the Web site carpoint.msn.com. Choose any car you like, then go to the indicated Web site to obtain the retail price of that car so you can create the spreadsheet. In addition, download a picture and description of the car so that you can create a compound document similar to Figure 3.22. *Be sure to credit the source in your document.* Add your name to the completed document and submit it to your instructor.

The Camaro Coupe

The description and picture of the Camaro was taken from the Microsoft site, carpoint.msn.com. The spreadsheet calculations are mine. The calculations are based on the retail price of the 1997 fully loaded Z28 convertible. The monthly payment is well beyond my budget, but it never hurts to dream.

Price of car	$25,520
Manufacturer's rebate	$0
Down payment	$0
Amount to finance	$25,520
Interest rate	8%
Term (years)	4
Monthly payment	$623.02

"Chevrolet introduced the Camaro in 1967 as its entry into what came to be called the 'Pony Car' segment created by the Ford Mustang. Though it has always been available with options to suit a wide range of sports-coupe buyers, performance has been what the name Camaro brings to mind for most people. Camaros have been winning races almost from the time the car was introduced, and you can be sure if a race is going on somewhere in America, Camaros will be competing. Today's car, the fourth-generation model introduced in 1993, offers a high level of performance at a competitive price. While you'd expect the hot Z28 model to be a favorite of male buyers, sales of the base Camaro RS are evenly split between men and women. A very limited number of special 30th Anniversary Camaros will be available in 1997."

FIGURE 3.22 Document for Practice Exercise 6

7. Figure 3.23 contains another variation on the mortgage example in which we vary the principal and interest rate. The user inputs an initial principal (e.g., $200,000) and interest rate (e.g., 8%) and the amounts by which to vary those values ($10,000 and 1%, respectively). The spreadsheet then computes the monthly payment for different combinations of the interest and principal. Your assignment is to duplicate the spreadsheet in Figure 3.23.

   The trick to the assignment is to develop a formula with mixed references in cell B11 that can be copied to the remaining rows and columns. Your spreadsheet is to be completely flexible in that the user can input any assumption or initial condition in cells B4 through B8, then see the results in the body of the spreadsheet. Print the cell formulas and displayed values and submit both to your instructor as proof that you did this exercise. (See the case study on Data Tables as an alternate means of developing this spreadsheet.)

	A	B	C	D	E	F	G
1	**Mortgage Calculator**						
2	*Change any parameter in cells B4 through B8 and the table is recalculated automatically*						
3							
4	***Initial principal***	$200,000					
5	*Increment*	$10,000					
6	***Starting Interest***	6.00%					
7	*Increment*	1.00%					
8	***Term (years)***	15					
9							
10		**$200,000**	**$210,000**	**$220,000**	**$230,000**	**$240,000**	**$250,000**
11	**6.00%**	$1,687.71	$1,772.10	$1,856.49	$1,940.87	$2,025.26	$2,109.64
12	**7.00%**	$1,797.66	$1,887.54	$1,977.42	$2,067.31	$2,157.19	$2,247.07
13	**8.00%**	$1,911.30	$2,006.87	$2,102.43	$2,198.00	$2,293.57	$2,389.13
14	**9.00%**	$2,028.53	$2,129.96	$2,231.39	$2,332.81	$2,434.24	$2,535.67
15	**10.00%**	$2,149.21	$2,256.67	$2,364.13	$2,471.59	$2,579.05	$2,686.51
16	**11.00%**	$2,273.19	$2,386.85	$2,500.51	$2,614.17	$2,727.83	$2,841.49
17	**12.00%**	$2,400.34	$2,520.35	$2,640.37	$2,760.39	$2,880.40	$3,000.42
18	**13.00%**	$2,530.48	$2,657.01	$2,783.53	$2,910.06	$3,036.58	$3,163.11

FIGURE 3.23 Spreadsheet for Practice Exercise 7

CASE STUDIES

The Financial Consultant

A friend of yours is in the process of buying a home and has asked you to compare the payments and total interest on a 15- and a 30-year loan. You want to do as professional a job as possible and have decided to analyze the loans in Excel, then incorporate the results into a memo written in Microsoft Word. As of now, the principal is $150,000, but it is very likely that your friend will change his mind several times, and so you want to use the OLE capability within Windows to dynamically link the worksheet to the word processing document. Your memo should include a letterhead that takes advantage of the formatting capabilities within Word; a graphic logo would be a nice touch.

Compensation Analysis

A corporation typically uses several different measures of compensation in an effort to pay its employees fairly. Most organizations closely monitor an employee's salary history, keeping both the present and previous salary in order to compute various statistics, including:

- The percent salary increase, which is computed by taking the difference between the present and previous salary, and dividing by the previous salary.
- The months between increase, which is the elapsed time between the date the present salary took effect and the date of the previous salary. (Assume 30 days per month for ease of calculation.)
- The annualized rate of increase, which is the percent salary increase divided by the months between increase; for example, a 5% raise after 6 months is equivalent to an annualized increase of 10%; a 5% raise after two years is equivalent to an annual increase of 2.5%.

Use the data in the *Compensation Analysis* workbook on the data disk to compute salary statistics for the employees who have had a salary increase; employees who have not received an increase should have a suitable indication in the cell. Compute the average, minimum, and maximum value for each measure of compensation for those employees who have received an increase.

The Automobile Dealership

The purchase of a car usually entails extensive bargaining between the dealer and the consumer. The dealer has an asking price but typically settles for less. The commission paid to a salesperson depends on how close the selling price is to the asking price. Exotic Motors has the following compensation policy for its sales staff:

- A 3% commission on the actual selling price for cars sold at 95% or more of the asking price.
- A 2% commission on the actual selling price for cars sold at 90% or more (but less than 95%) of the asking price
- A 1% commission on the actual selling price for cars sold at less than 90% of the asking price. The dealer will not go below 85% of his asking price.

The dealer's asking price is based on the dealer's cost plus a 20% markup; for example, the asking price on a car that cost the dealer $20,000 would be $24,000. Develop a worksheet to be used by the dealer that shows his profit (the selling price minus the cost of the car minus the salesperson's commission) on every sale. The worksheet should be completely flexible and allow the dealer to vary the markup or commission percentages without having to edit or recopy any of the formulas. Use the data in the *Exotic Motors* workbook to test your worksheet.

The Lottery

Many states raise money through lotteries that advertise prizes of several million dollars. In reality, however, the actual value of the prize is considerably less than the advertised value, although the winners almost certainly do not care. One state, for example, recently offered a twenty million dollar prize that was to be distributed in twenty annual payments of one million dollars each. How much was the prize actually worth, assuming a long-term interest rate of seven percent?

A Penny a Day

What if you had a rich uncle who offered to pay you "a penny a day," then double your salary each day for the next month? It does not sound very generous, but you will be surprised at how quickly the amount grows. Create a simple worksheet that enables you to use the Scenario Manager to answer the following questions. On what day of the month (if any) will your uncle pay you more than one million dollars? How much money will your uncle pay you on the 31st day?

Data Tables

A data table is a tool that shows the effect of varying one or two variables in a formula. You could, for example, use a data table to show how changes in principal and/or interest affect the monthly payment on a loan. Data tables do not really represent a new capability, as you can achieve the same result by building a worksheet with the appropriate combination of relative, absolute, and/or mixed references. Use the Help command in Excel to learn about data tables, then construct a data table that is equivalent to the spreadsheet in Figure 3.23 in conjunction with practice exercise 7. Which technique do you prefer, mixed references or data tables? Why?

4

GRAPHS AND CHARTS: DELIVERING A MESSAGE

OBJECTIVES

After reading this chapter you will be able to:

1. Distinguish between the different types of charts, stating the advantages and disadvantages of each.
2. Distinguish between a chart embedded in a worksheet and one in a separate chart sheet; explain how many charts can be associated with the same worksheet.
3. Use the Chart Wizard to create and/or modify a chart.
4. Enhance a chart by using arrows and text.
5. Differentiate between data series specified in rows and data series specified in columns.
6. Describe how a chart can be statistically accurate yet totally misleading.
7. Create a compound document consisting of a word processing memo, a worksheet, and a chart.

OVERVIEW

Business has always known that the graphic representation of data is an attractive, easy-to-understand way to convey information. Indeed, business graphics has become one of the most exciting Windows applications, whereby charts (graphs) are easily created from a worksheet, with just a few simple keystrokes or mouse clicks.

The chapter begins by emphasizing the importance of determining the message to be conveyed by a chart. It describes the different types of charts available within Excel and how to choose among them. It explains how to create a chart using the Chart Wizard, how to embed a chart within a worksheet, and how to create a chart in a separate chart sheet. It also describes how to enhance a chart with arrows and additional text.

The second half of the chapter explains how one chart can plot multiple sets of data, and how several charts can be based on the same worksheet. It also describes how to create a compound document, in which a chart and its associated worksheet are dynamically linked to a memo created by a word processor. All told, we think you will find this to be one of the most enjoyable chapters in the text.

CHART TYPES

A ***chart*** is a graphic representation of data in a worksheet. The chart is based on descriptive entries called ***category labels,*** and on numeric values called ***data points.*** The data points are grouped into one or more ***data series*** that appear in row(s) or column(s) on the worksheet. In every chart there is exactly one data point, in each data series, for each value of the category label.

The worksheet in Figure 4.1 will be used throughout the chapter as the basis for the charts we will create. Your manager believes that the sales data can be understood more easily from charts than from the strict numerical presentation of a worksheet. You have been given the assignment of analyzing the data in the worksheet and are developing a series of charts to convey that information.

	A	B	C	D	E	F
1	Superior Software Sales					
2						
3		Miami	Denver	New York	Boston	Total
4	Word Processing	$50,000	$67,500	$9,500	$141,000	$268,000
5	Spreadsheets	$44,000	$18,000	$11,500	$105,000	$178,500
6	Database	$12,000	$7,500	$6,000	$30,000	$55,500
7	Total	$106,000	$93,000	$27,000	$276,000	$502,000

FIGURE 4.1 Superior Software

The sales data in the worksheet can be presented several ways—for example, by city, by product, or by a combination of the two. Ask yourself which type of chart is best suited to answer the following questions:

- What percentage of total revenue comes from each city? from each product?
- What is the dollar revenue produced by each city? by each product?
- What is the rank of each city with respect to sales?
- How much revenue does each product contribute in each city?

In every instance realize that a chart exists only to deliver a message, and that you cannot create an effective chart unless you are sure of what that message is. The next several pages discuss various types of business charts, each of which is best suited to a particular type of message.

KEEP IT SIMPLE

Keep it simple. This rule applies to both your message and the means of conveying that message. Excel makes it almost too easy to change fonts, styles, type sizes, and colors, but such changes will often detract from, rather than enhance, a chart. More is not necessarily better, and you do not have to use the features just because they are there. Remember that a chart must ultimately succeed on the basis of content, and content alone.

Pie Charts

A ***pie chart*** is the most effective way to display proportional relationships. It is the type of chart to select whenever words like *percentage* or *market share* appear in the message to be delivered. The pie, or complete circle, denotes the total amount. Each slice of the pie corresponds to its respective percentage of the total.

The pie chart in Figure 4.2a divides the pie representing total sales into four slices, one for each city. The size of each slice is proportional to the percentage of total sales in that city. The chart depicts a single data series, which appears in cells B7 through E7 on the associated worksheet. The data series has four data points corresponding to the total sales in each city.

To create the pie chart, Excel computes the total sales ($502,000 in our example), calculates the percentage contributed by each city, and draws each slice of the pie in proportion to its computed percentage. Boston's sales of $276,000 account for 55 percent of the total, and so this slice of the pie is allotted 55 percent of the area of the circle.

An ***exploded pie chart,*** as shown in Figure 4.2b, separates one or more slices of the pie for emphasis. Another way to achieve emphasis in a chart is to choose a title that reflects the message you are trying to deliver. The title in Figure 4.2a, for example, *Revenue by Geographic Area*, is neutral and leaves the reader to develop his or her own conclusion about the relative contribution of each area. By contrast, the title in Figure 4.2b, *New York Accounts for Only 5% of Revenue,* is more suggestive and emphasizes the problems in this office. Alternatively, the title could be changed to *Boston Exceeds 50% of Total Revenue* if the intent were to emphasize the contribution of Boston.

Three-dimensional pie charts may be created in exploded or nonexploded format as shown in Figures 4.2c and 4.2d, respectively. Excel also enables you to add arrows and text for emphasis.

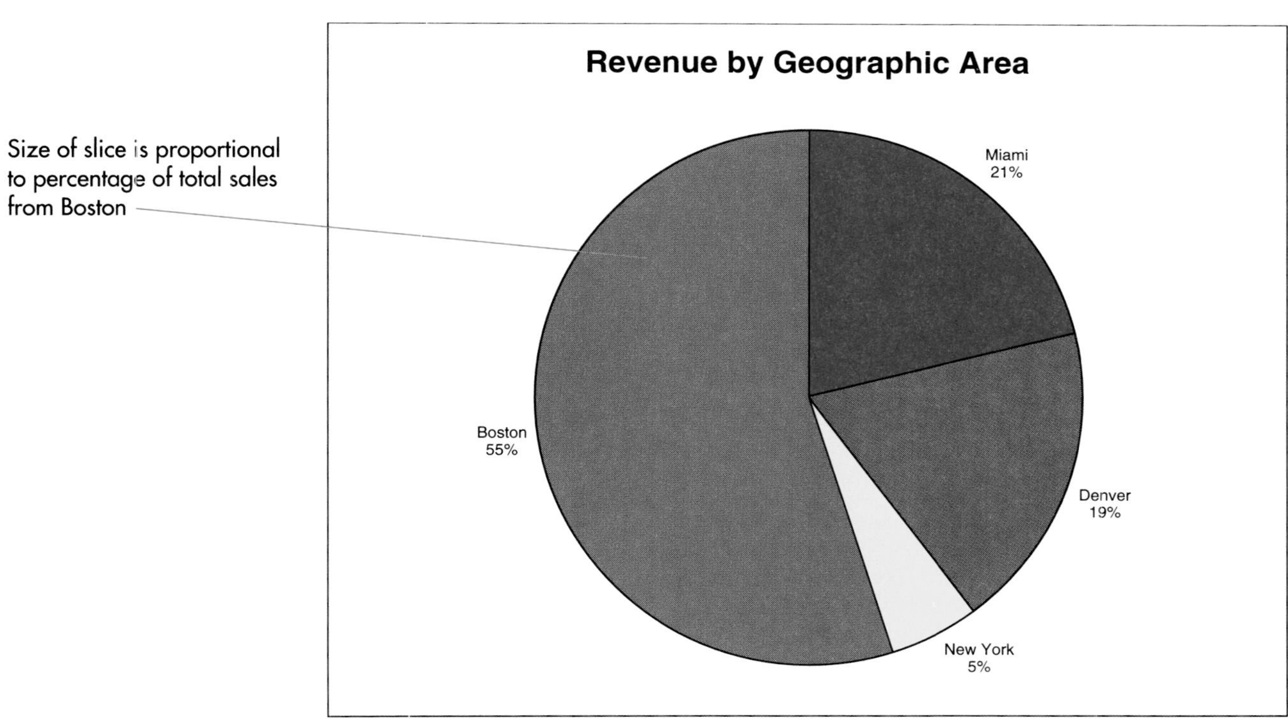

(a) Simple Pie Chart

FIGURE 4.2 Pie Charts

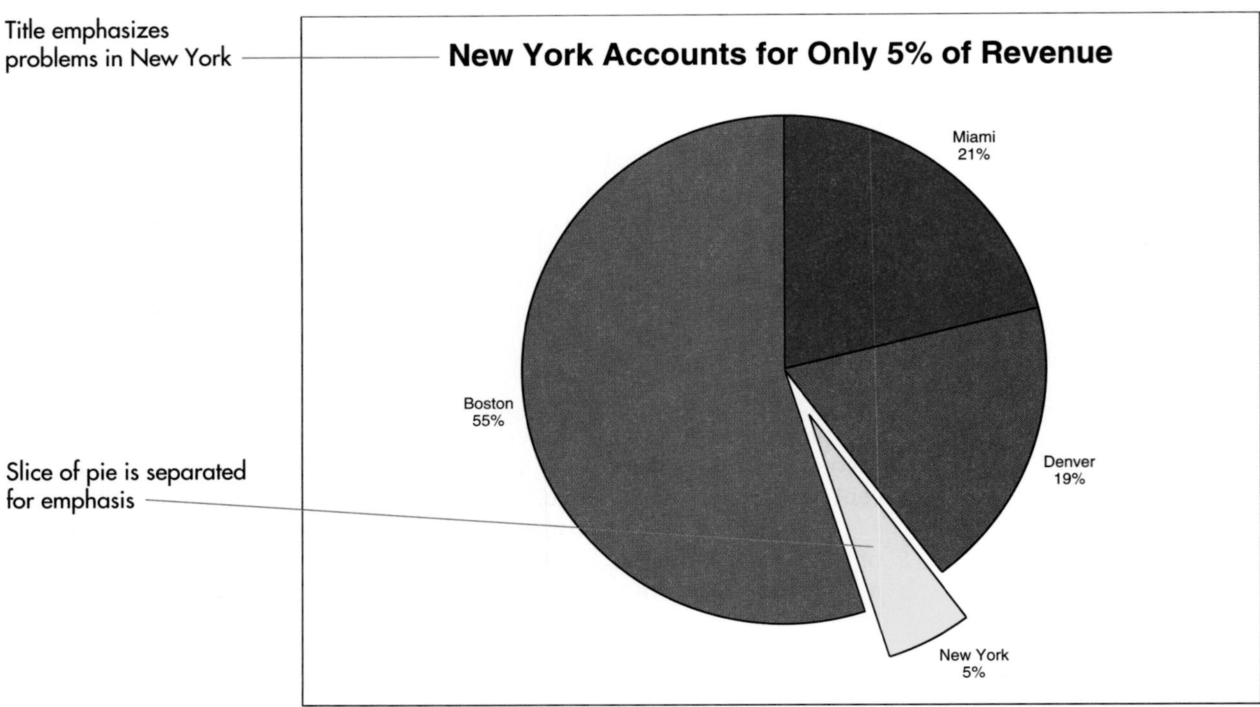

(b) Exploded Pie Chart

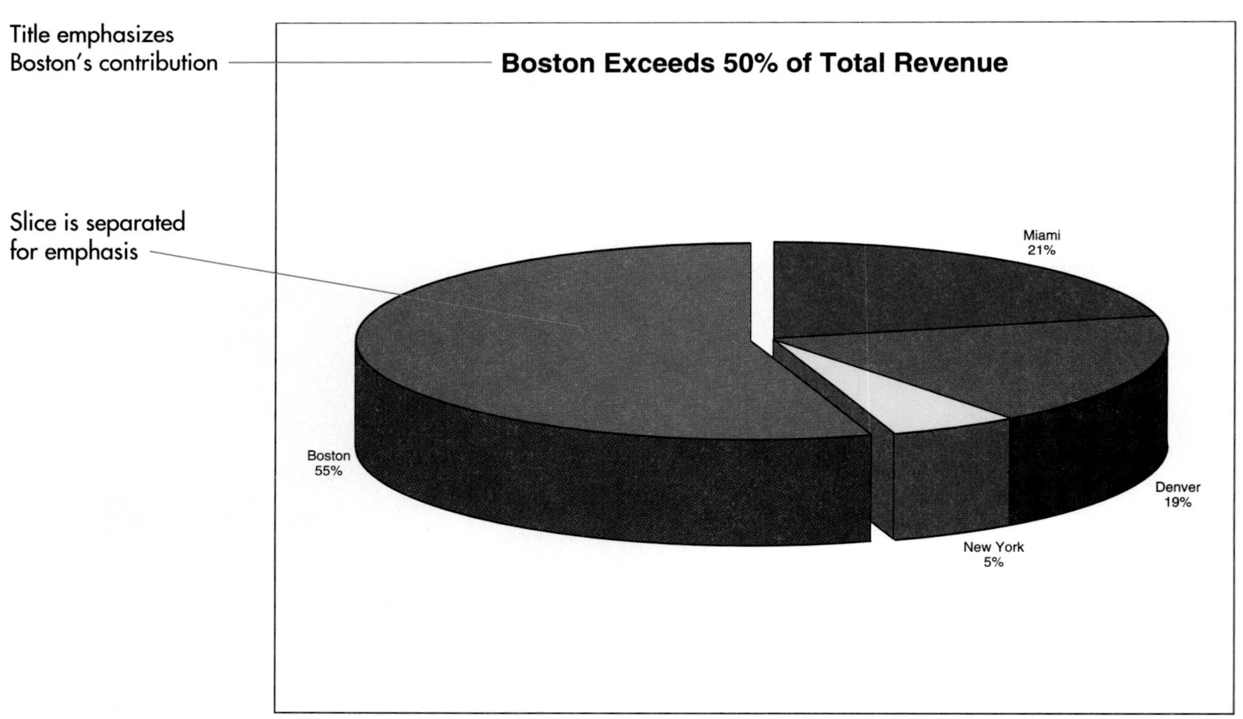

(c) Three-dimensional Pie Chart

FIGURE 4.2 Pie Charts (continued)

Arrows and text added for emphasis

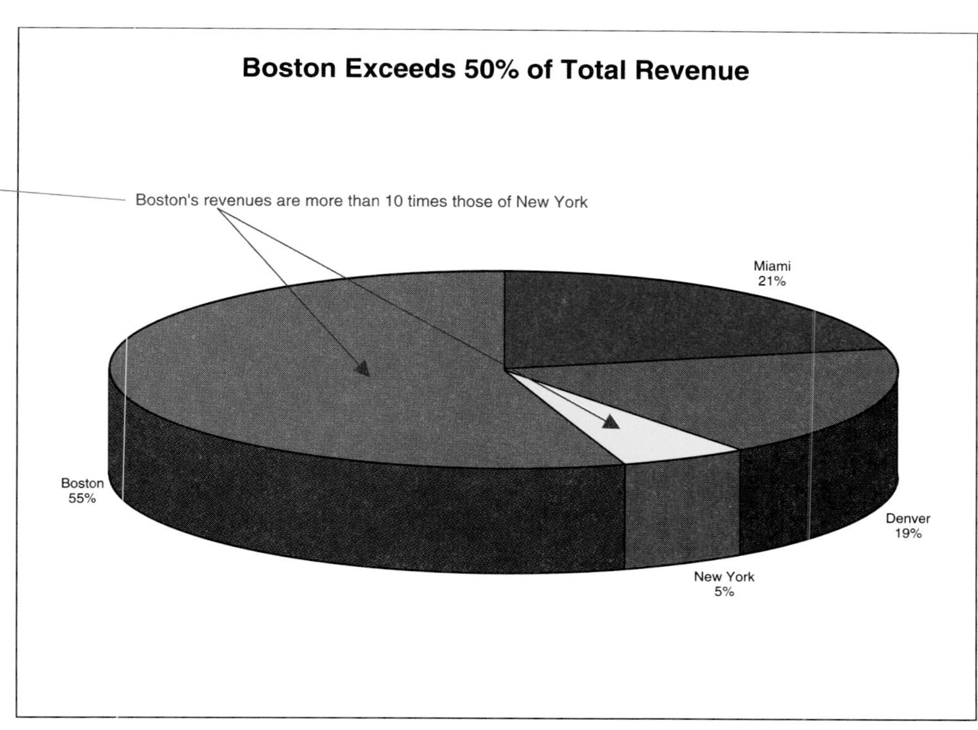

(d) Enhanced Pie Chart

FIGURE 4.2 Pie Charts (continued)

A pie chart is easiest to read when the number of slices is limited (i.e., not more than six or seven), and when small categories (percentages less than five) are grouped into a single category called "Other."

EXPLODED PIE CHARTS

Click and drag wedges out of a pie chart to convert an ordinary pie chart to an exploded pie chart. For best results pull the wedge out only slightly from the main body of the pie.

Column and Bar Charts

A ***column chart*** is used when there is a need to show actual numbers rather than percentages. The column chart in Figure 4.3a plots the same data series as the earlier pie chart, but displays it differently. The category labels (Miami, Denver, New York, and Boston) are shown along the ***X*** (horizontal) ***axis.*** The data points (monthly sales) are plotted along the ***Y*** (vertical) ***axis,*** with the height of each column reflecting the value of the data point.

A column chart can be given a horizontal orientation and converted to a ***bar chart*** as in Figure 4.3b. Some individuals prefer the bar chart over the corresponding column chart because the longer horizontal bars accentuate the difference between the items. Bar charts are also preferable when the descriptive labels are long to eliminate the crowding that can occur along the horizontal axis of a

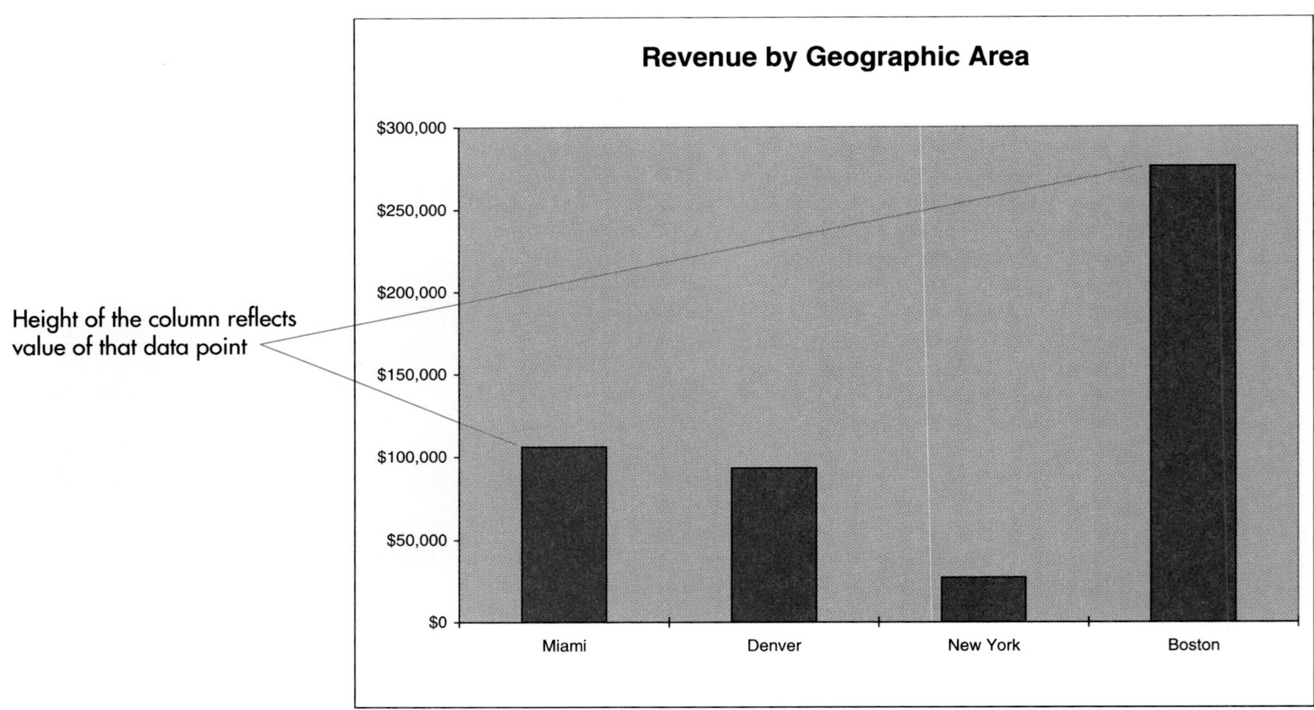

(a) Column Chart

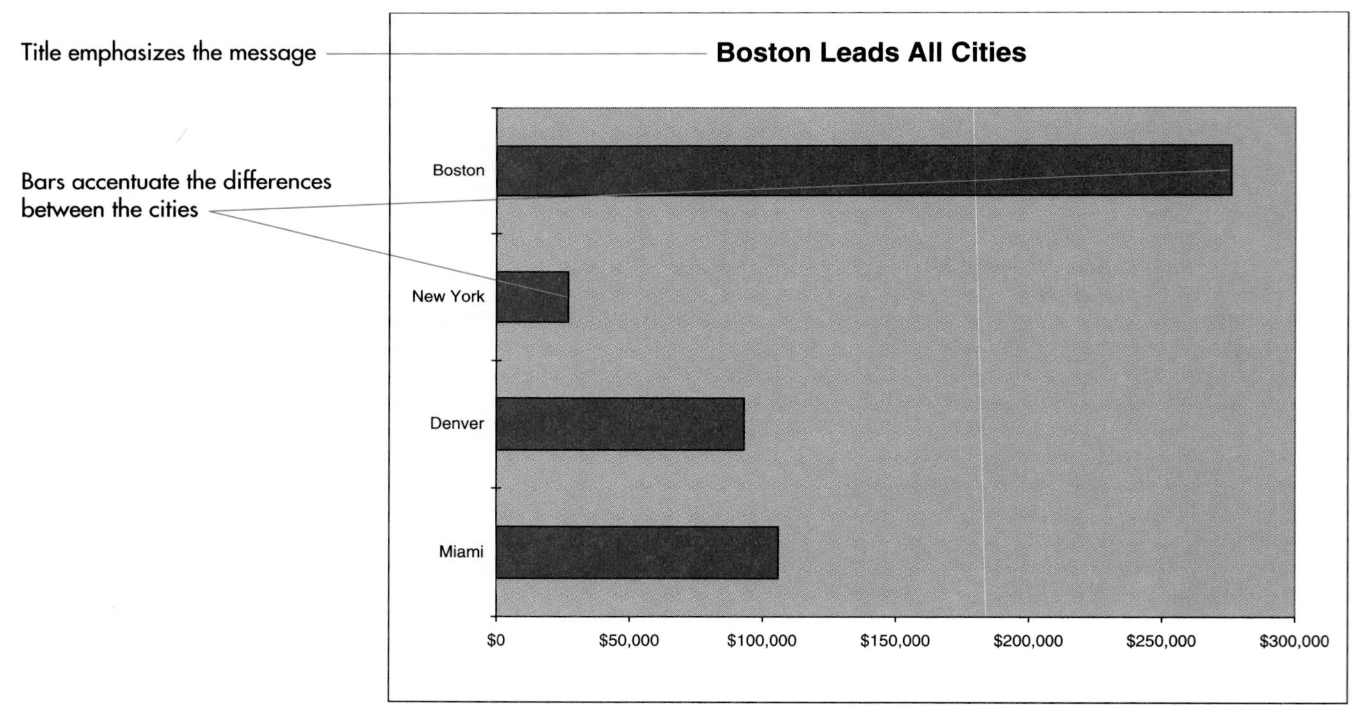

(b) Horizontal Bar Chart

FIGURE 4.3 Column/Bar Charts

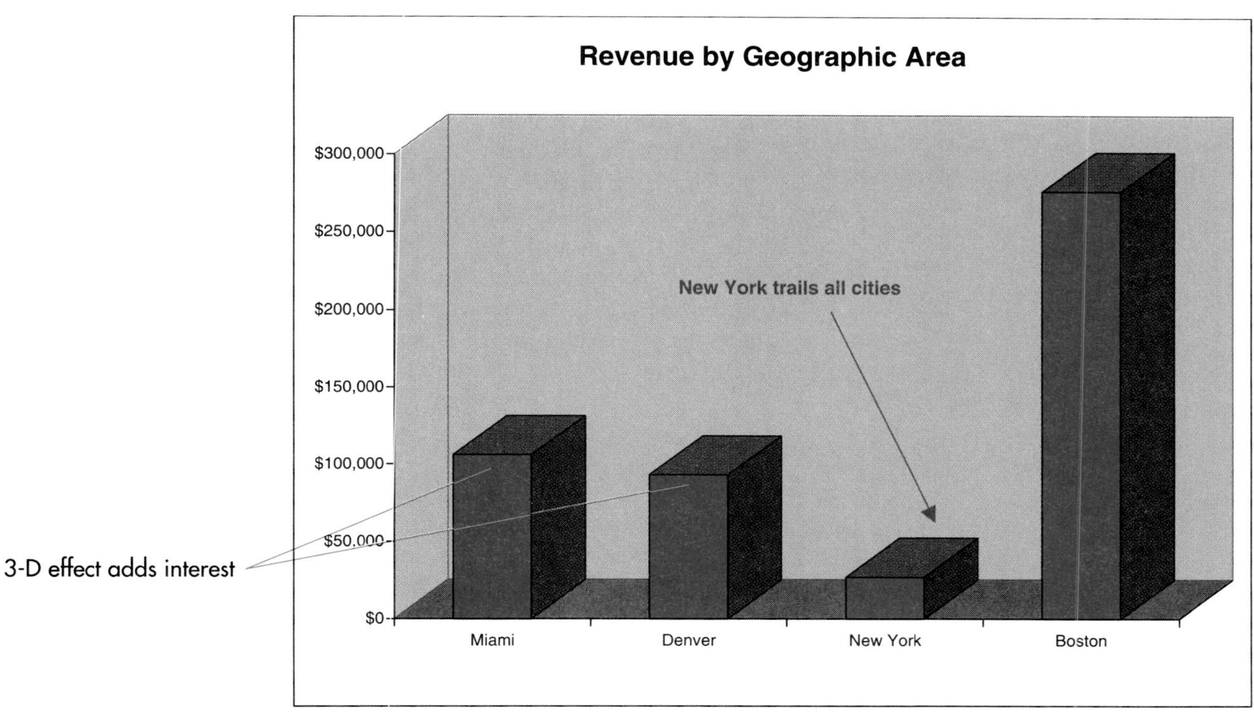

(c) Three-dimensional Column Chart

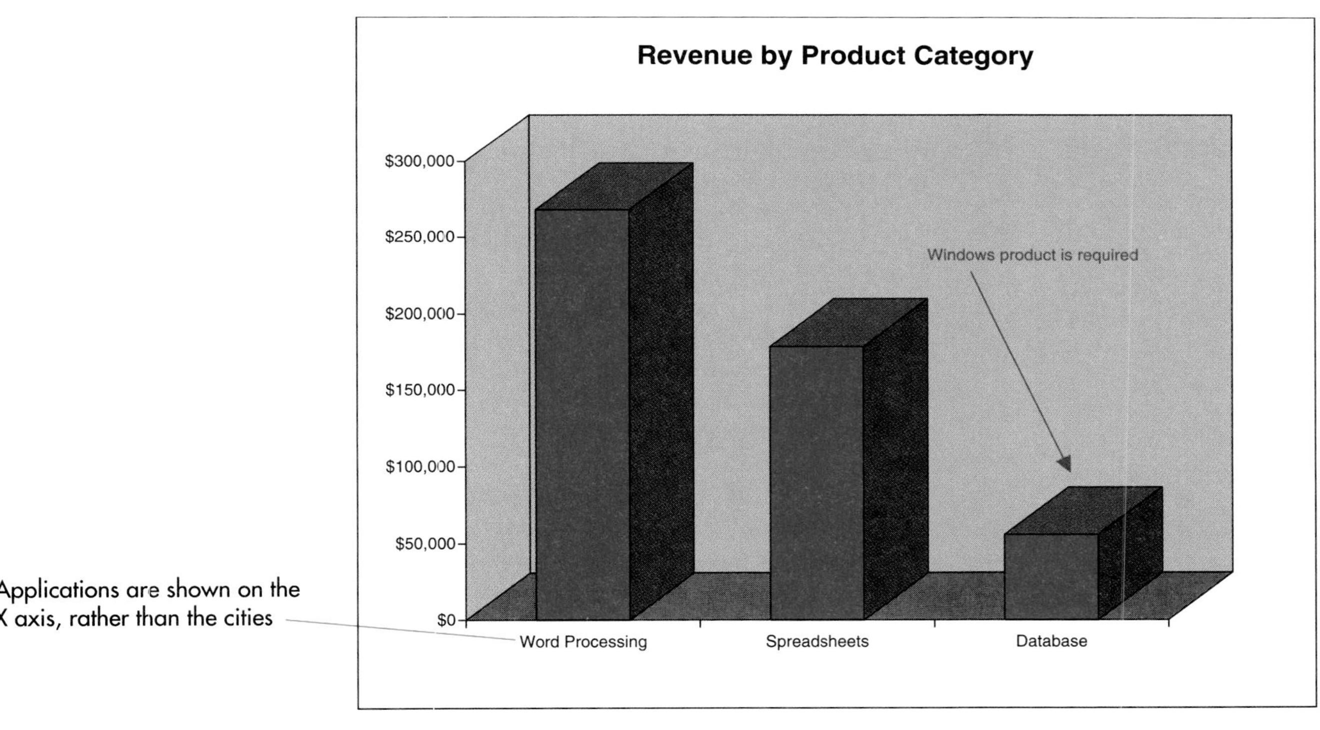

(d) Alternate Column Chart

FIGURE 4.3 Column/Bar Charts (continued)

column chart. As with the pie chart, a title can lead the reader and further emphasize the message, as with *Boston Leads All Cities* in Figure 4.3b.

A three-dimensional effect can produce added interest as shown in Figures 4.3c and 4.3d. Figure 4.3d plots a different set of numbers than we have seen so far (the sales for each product, rather than the sales for each city). The choice between the charts in Figures 4.3c and 4.3d depends on the message you want to convey—whether you want to emphasize the contribution of each city or each product. The title can be used to emphasize the message. Arrows and text can be added to either chart to enhance the message.

As with a pie chart, column and bar charts are easiest to read when the number of categories is relatively small (seven or fewer). Otherwise the columns (bars) are plotted so close together that labeling becomes impossible.

CREATING A CHART

There are two ways to create a chart in Excel. You can embed the chart in a worksheet, or you can create the chart in a separate ***chart sheet.*** Figure 4.4a displays an embedded column chart. Figure 4.4b shows a pie chart in its own chart sheet. Both techniques are valid. The choice between the two depends on your personal preference.

Regardless of where it is kept (embedded in a worksheet or in its own chart sheet), a chart is linked to the worksheet on which it is based. The charts in Figure 4.4 plot the same data series (the total sales for each city). Change any of these data points on the worksheet, and both charts will be updated automatically to reflect the new data.

Both charts are part of the same workbook (Software Sales) as indicated in the title bar of each figure. The tabs within the workbook have been renamed to indicate the contents of the associated sheet. Additional charts may be created and embedded in the worksheet and/or placed on their own chart sheets. And, as previously stated, if you change the worksheet, the chart (or charts) based upon it will also change.

Study the column chart in Figure 4.4a to see how it corresponds to the worksheet on which it is based. The descriptive names on the X axis are known as ***category labels*** and match the entries in cells B3 through E3. The quantitative values (data points) are plotted on the Y axis and match the total sales in cells B7 through E7. Even the numeric format matches; that is, the currency format used in the worksheet appears automatically on the scale of the Y axis.

The ***sizing handles*** on the embedded chart indicate it is currently selected and can be sized, moved, or deleted the same way as any other Windows object:

- To size the selected chart, point to a sizing handle (the mouse pointer changes to a double arrow), then drag the handle in the desired direction.
- To move the selected chart, point to the chart (the mouse pointer is a single arrow), then drag the chart to its new location.
- To copy the selected chart, click the Copy button to copy the chart to the clipboard, click in the workbook where you want the copied chart to go, then click the Paste button to paste the chart at that location.
- To delete the selected chart, press the Del key.

The same operations apply to any of the objects within the chart (e.g., its title), as will be discussed in the section on enhancing a chart. Note, too, that both figures contain a chart toolbar that enables you to modify a chart after it has been created.

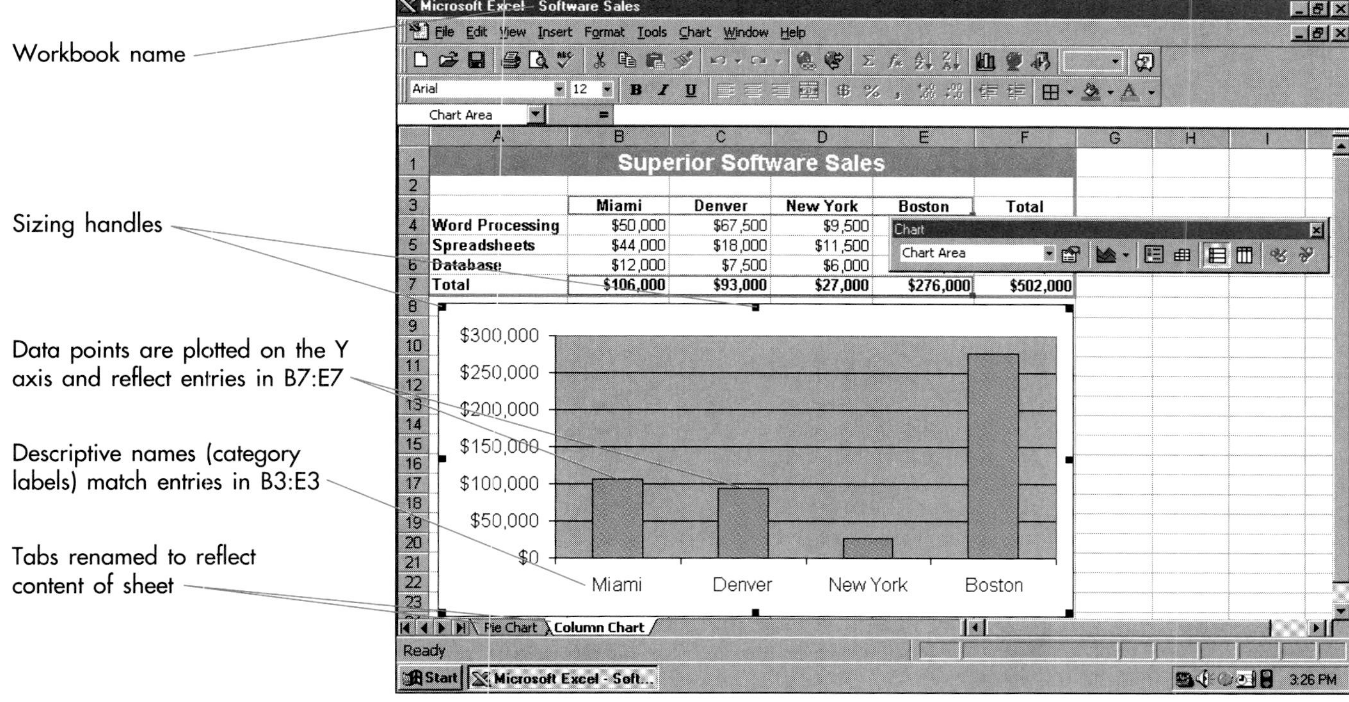

(a) Embedded Chart

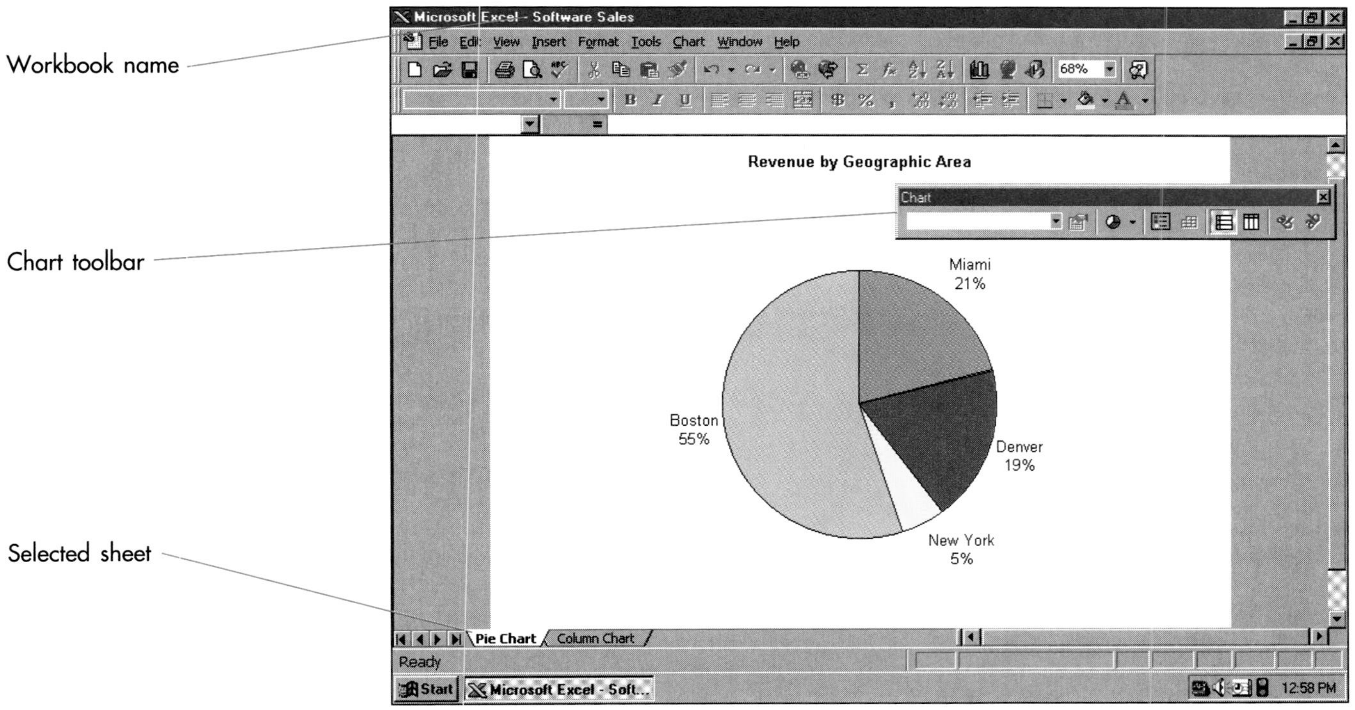

(b) Chart Sheet

FIGURE 4.4 Creating a Chart

The Chart Wizard

The ***Chart Wizard*** is the easiest way to create a chart. Just select the cells that contain the data as shown in Figure 4.5a, click the Chart Wizard button on the Standard toolbar, and let the wizard do the rest. The process is illustrated in Figure 4.5, which shows how the Wizard creates a column chart to plot total sales by geographic area (city).

The steps in Figure 4.5 appear automatically as you click the Next command button to move from one step to the next. You can retrace your steps at any time by pressing the Back command button, access the Office Assistant for help with the Chart Wizard, or abort the process with the Cancel command button.

Step 1 in the Chart Wizard (Figure 4.5b) asks you to choose one of the available chart types. Step 2 (Figure 4.5c) shows you a preview of the chart and enables you to confirm (and, if necessary, change) the data series specified earlier. (Only one data series is plotted in this example. Multiple data series are illustrated later in the chapter.) Step 3 (Figure 4.5d) asks you to complete the chart by entering its title and specifying additional options (such as the position of a legend and gridlines). And finally, step 4 (Figure 4.5e) has you choose whether the chart is to be created as an embedded chart (an object) within a specific worksheet, or whether it is to be created in its own chart sheet. The entire process takes but a few minutes.

Selected cells (B3:E3 and B7:E7)

	A	B	C	D	E	F
1	Superior Software Sales					
2						
3		Miami	Denver	New York	Boston	Total
4	Word Processing	$50,000	$67,500	$9,500	$141,000	$268,000
5	Spreadsheets	$44,000	$18,000	$11,500	$105,000	$178,500
6	Database	$12,000	$7,500	$6,000	$30,000	$55,500
7	Total	$106,000	$93,000	$27,000	$276,000	$502,000

(a) The Worksheet

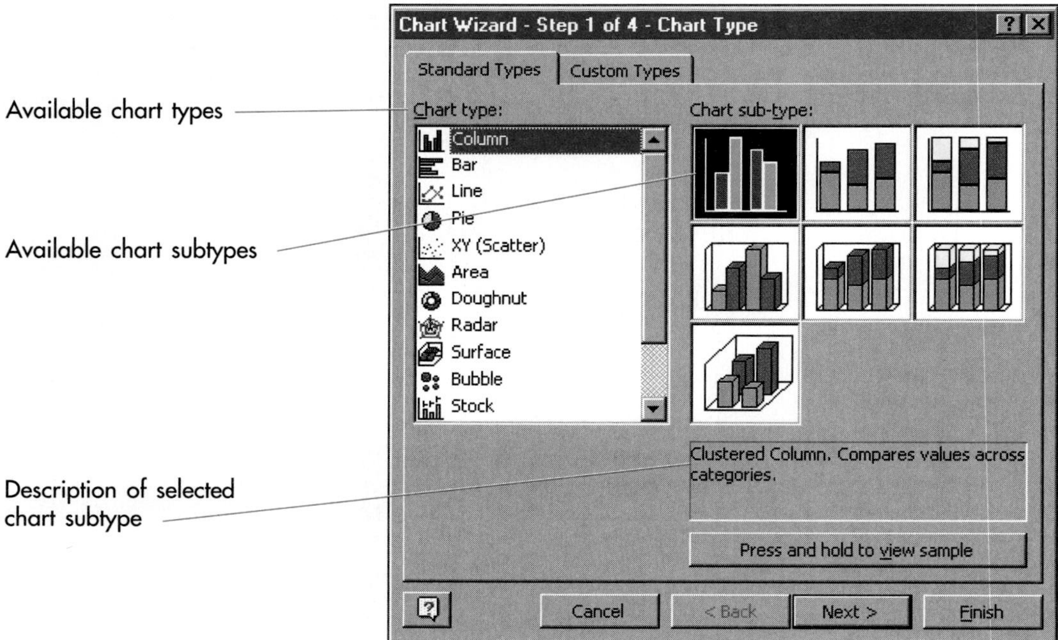

(b) Select the Chart Type (step 1)

FIGURE 4.5 The Chart Wizard

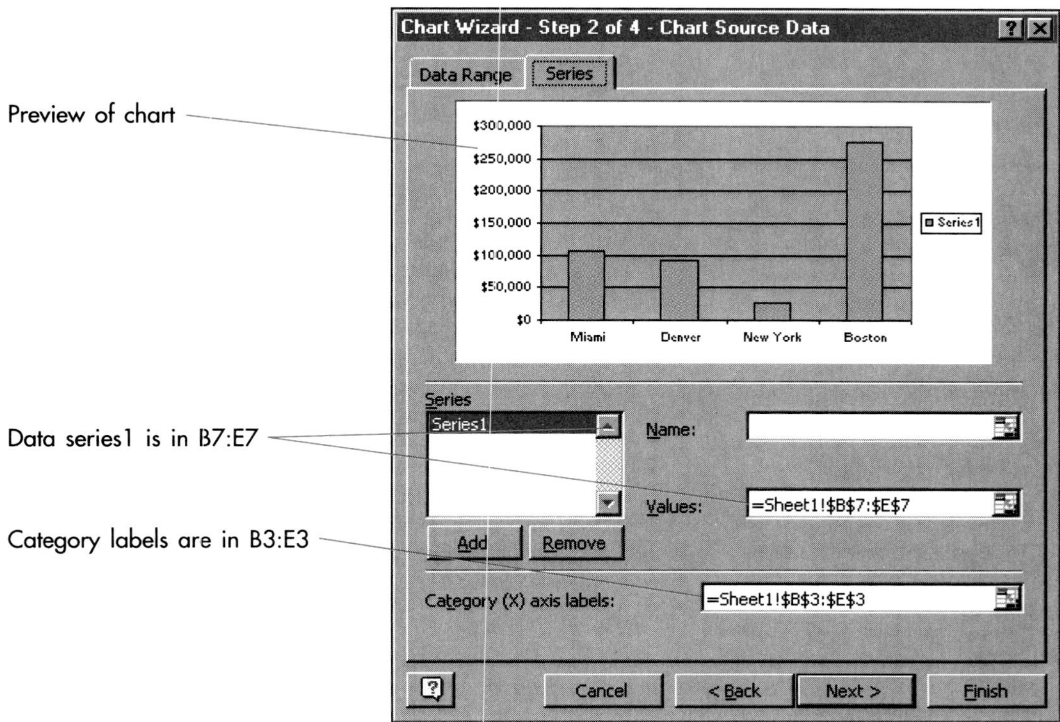

(c) Check the Data Series (step 2)

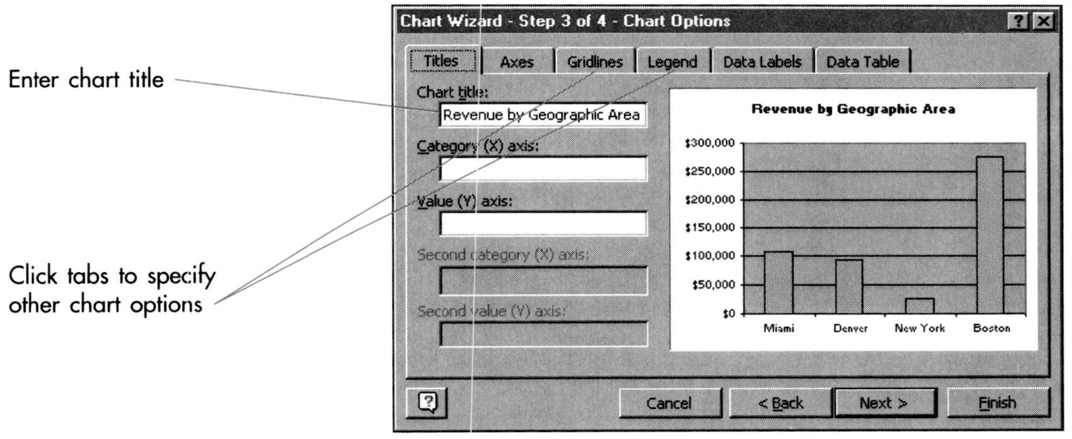

(d) Complete the Chart Options (step 3)

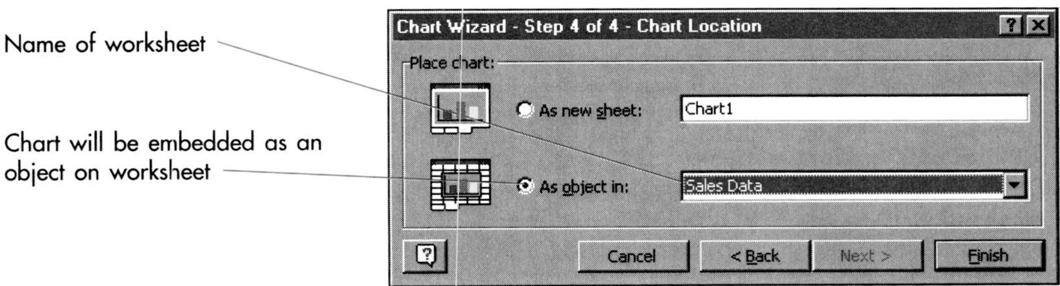

(e) Choose the Location (step 4)

FIGURE 4.5 The Chart Wizard (continued)

Enhancing a Chart

After a chart is created, it can be enhanced in several ways. You can change the chart type, add (or remove) a legend, and/or add (or remove) gridlines by executing the appropriate command from the Chart menu. You can change the font, size, color, and style of existing text anywhere in the chart, by selecting the text, then changing its format. You can also use the ***Drawing toolbar*** to add arrows and other objects to a chart for added emphasis.

Figure 4.6 shows an enhanced version of the column chart created earlier. The ***Chart toolbar*** is displayed automatically whenever any object of a chart is selected. Note, too, the drop-down list box on the Chart toolbar, which enables you to select the component(s) to modify. The Drawing toolbar appears at the bottom of the window and contains various tools to further enhance the chart (or any Office document). The use of both toolbars is explained further in the following hands-on exercise.

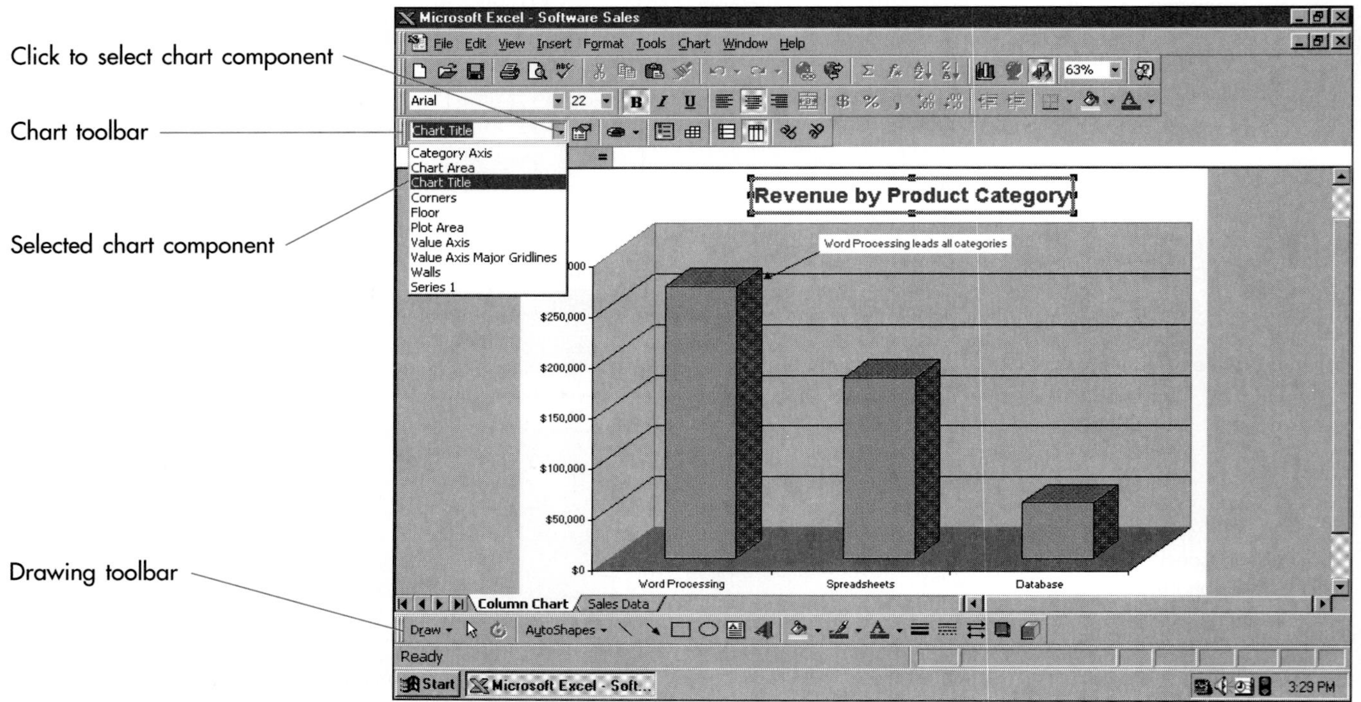

FIGURE 4.6 Enhancing a Chart

SET A TIME LIMIT

Excel enables you to customize virtually every aspect of every object within a chart. You can change the color, shape, or pattern of a data series or the font and style of text anywhere in the chart. It's fun to experiment, but the gain is often minimal. Set a time limit and stop when you reach the allocated time. The default settings are usually adequate to convey your message, and further experimentation is often counter productive.

HANDS-ON EXERCISE 1

The Chart Wizard

Objective: To create and modify a chart by using the Chart Wizard; to embed a chart within a worksheet; to enhance a chart to include arrows and text. Use Figure 4.7 as a guide in the exercise.

STEP 1: Start the Chart Wizard

- Start Excel. Open the **Software Sales** workbook in the **Exploring Excel** folder. Save the workbook as **Finished Software Sales.**
- Drag the mouse over cells **B3 through E3** to select the category labels (the names of the cities). Press and hold the **Ctrl key** as you drag the mouse over cells **B7 through E7** to select the data series (the cells containing the total sales for the individual cities).
- Check that cells B3 through E3 and B7 through E7 are selected. Click the **Chart Wizard button** on the Standard toolbar to start the wizard.
- You should see the dialog box for step 1 as shown in Figure 4.7a. The **Column** chart type and **Clustered column** subtype are selected by default. Click **Next** to continue.

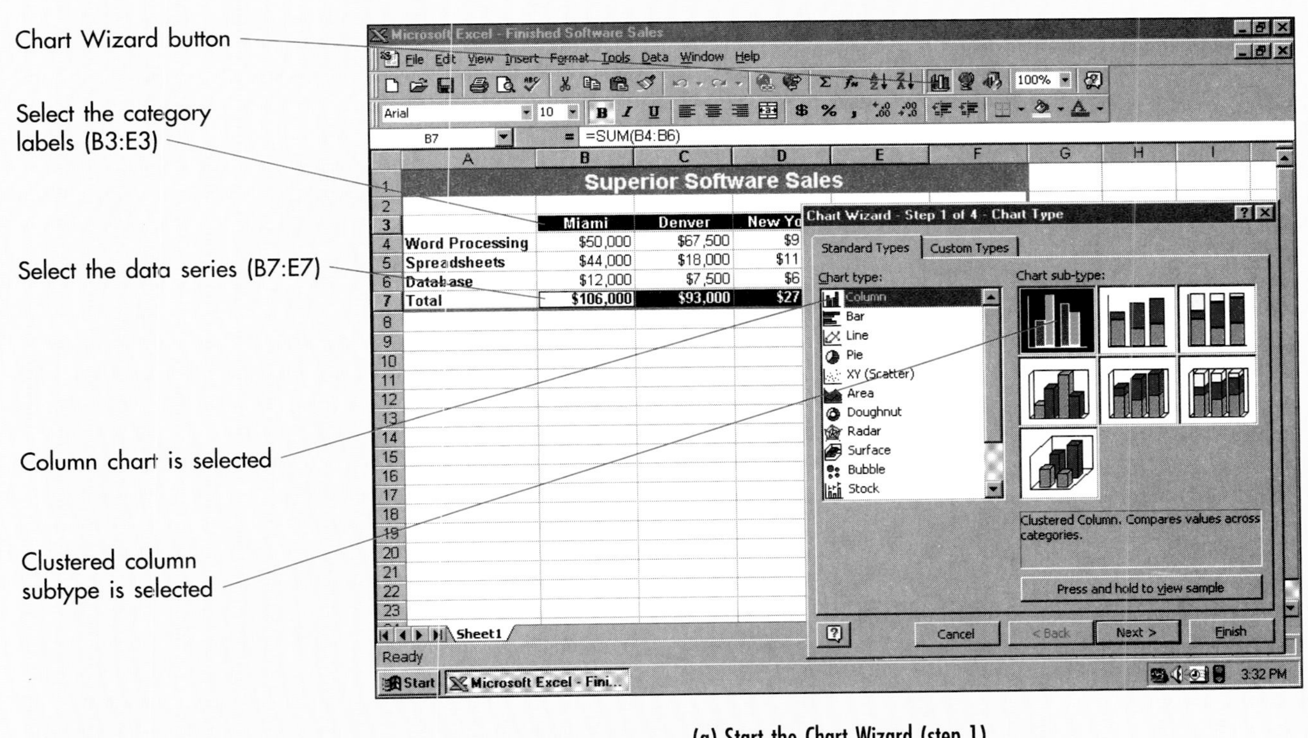

(a) Start the Chart Wizard (step 1)

FIGURE 4.7 Hands-on Exercise 1

STEP 2: Start the Chart Wizard (continued)

➤ You should see step 2 of the Chart Wizard. Click the **Series tab** in the dialog box so that your screen matches Figure 4.7b. Note that the values (the data being plotted) are in cells B7 through E7, and that the Category labels for the X axis are in cells B3 through E3. Click **Next** to continue.

➤ You should see step 3 of the Chart Wizard. If necessary, click the **Titles tab,** then click in the text box for the Chart title. Type **Revenue by Geographic Area.** Click the **Legend tab** and clear the box to show a legend. Click **Next.**

➤ You should see step 4 of the Chart Wizard. If necessary, click the option button to place the chart **As object** in Sheet1 (the name of the worksheet in which you are working). Click **Finish.**

RETRACE YOUR STEPS

The Chart Wizard guides you every step of the way, but what if you make a mistake or change your mind? Click the Back command button at any time to return to a previous screen in order to enter different information, then continue working with the wizard.

STEP 3: Move and Size the Chart

➤ You should see the completed chart as shown in Figure 4.7c. The sizing handles indicate that the chart is selected and will be affected by subsequent commands. The Chart toolbar is displayed automatically whenever a chart is selected.

➤ Move and/or size the chart just as you would any other Windows object:

- To move the chart, click the chart (background) area to select the chart (a ScreenTip, "Chart Area," is displayed), then click and drag (the mouse pointer changes to a four-sided arrow) to move the chart.
- To size the chart, drag a corner handle (the mouse pointer changes to a double arrow) to change the length and width of the chart simultaneously, keeping the chart in proportion as it is resized.

➤ Click outside the chart to deselect it. The sizing handles disappear and the Chart toolbar is no longer visible.

EMBEDDED CHARTS

An embedded chart is treated as an object that can be moved, sized, copied, or deleted just as any other Windows object. To move an embedded chart, click the background of the chart to select the chart, then drag it to a new location in the worksheet. To size the chart, select it, then drag any of the eight sizing handles in the desired direction. To delete the chart, select it, then press the Del key. To copy the chart, select it, click the Copy button on the Standard toolbar to copy the chart to the clipboard, click elsewhere in the workbook where you want the copied chart to go, then click the Paste button.

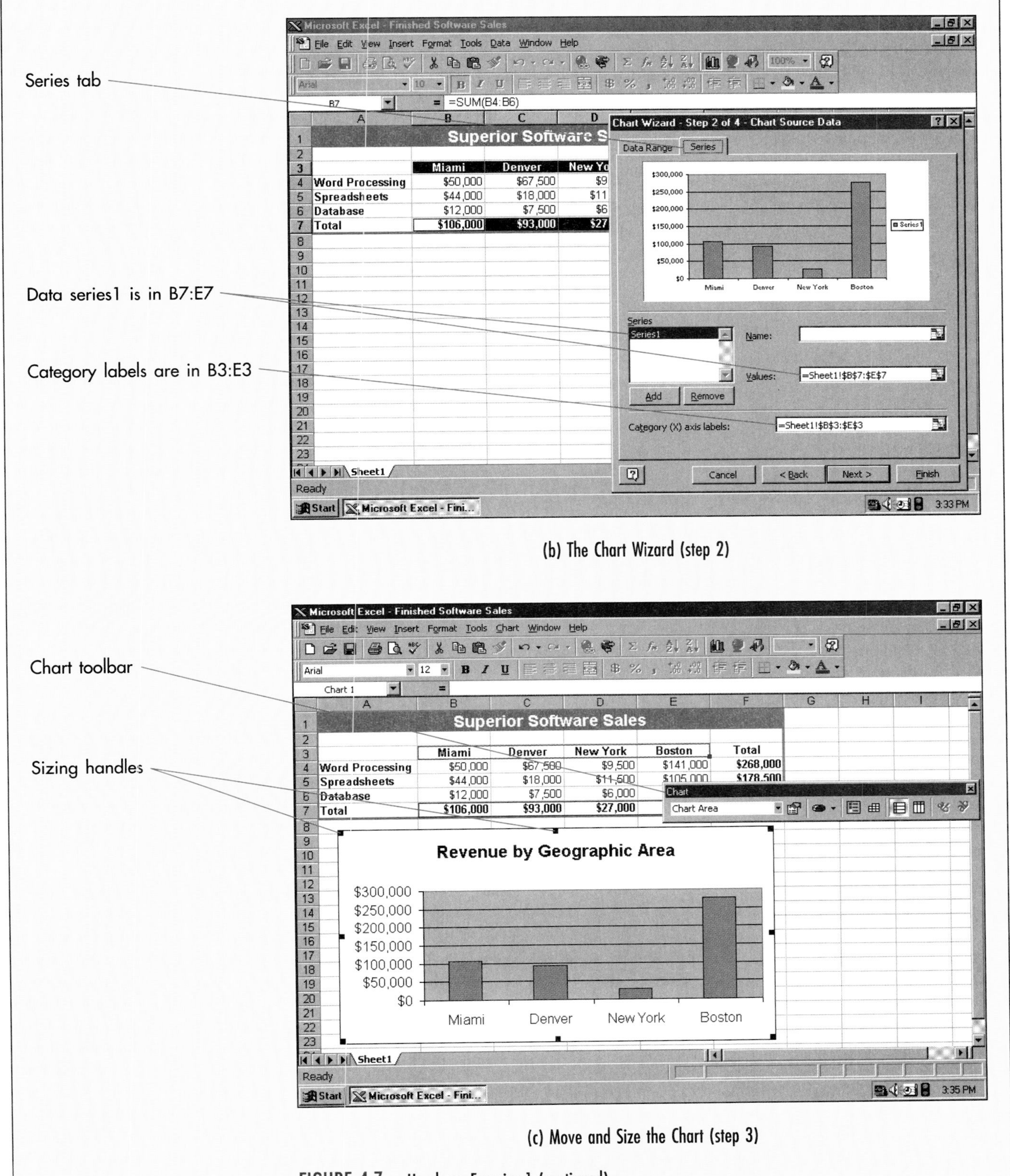

(b) The Chart Wizard (step 2)

(c) Move and Size the Chart (step 3)

FIGURE 4.7 Hands-on Exercise 1 (continued)

STEP 4: Change the Worksheet

- Any changes in a worksheet are automatically reflected in the associated chart. Click in cell **B4,** change the entry to **$400,000,** and press the **enter key.**
- The total sales for Miami in cell B7 change automatically to reflect the increased sales for word processing, as shown in Figure 4.7d. The column for Miami also changes in the chart and is now larger than the column for Boston.
- Click in cell **B3.** Change the entry to **Chicago.** Press **enter.** The category label on the X axis changes automatically.
- Click the **Undo button** to change the city back to Miami. Click the **Undo button** a second time to return to the initial value of $50,000. The worksheet and chart are restored to their earlier values.

CREATE AN ATTRACTIVE CHART BORDER

Dress up an embedded chart by changing its border. Point to the chart area (the white background area near the border), click the right mouse button to display a shortcut menu, then click Format Chart Area to display the Format Chart Area dialog box. If necessary, click the Patterns tab, click the option button for a Custom border, then check the boxes for a shadow and round corners. Click the drop-down arrows in the style, color, and weight list boxes to specify a different border style, thickness (weight), or color. Click OK to accept these settings.

STEP 5: Change the Chart Type

- Click the chart (background) area to select the chart, click the **drop-down arrow** on the Chart type button on the Chart toolbar, then click the **3-D Pie Chart icon.** The chart changes to a three-dimensional pie chart.
- Point to the chart area, click the **right mouse button** to display a shortcut menu, then click the **Chart Options command** to display the Chart Options dialog box shown in Figure 4.7e.
- Click the **Data Labels tab,** then click the option button to **Show label and percent.** Click **OK** to accept the settings and close the Chart Options dialog box.
- The pie chart changes to reflect the options you just specified, although the chart may not appear exactly as you would like. Accordingly, you can modify each component as necessary:
  - Select (click) the (gray) **Plot area.** Click and drag the sizing handles to increase the size of the plot area within the embedded chart.
  - Point to any of the labels, click the **right mouse button** to display a shortcut menu, and click **Format Data Labels** to display a dialog box. Click the **Font tab,** and select a smaller point size. It may also be necessary to click and drag the labels away from the plot area.
- Make other changes as necessary. Save the workbook.

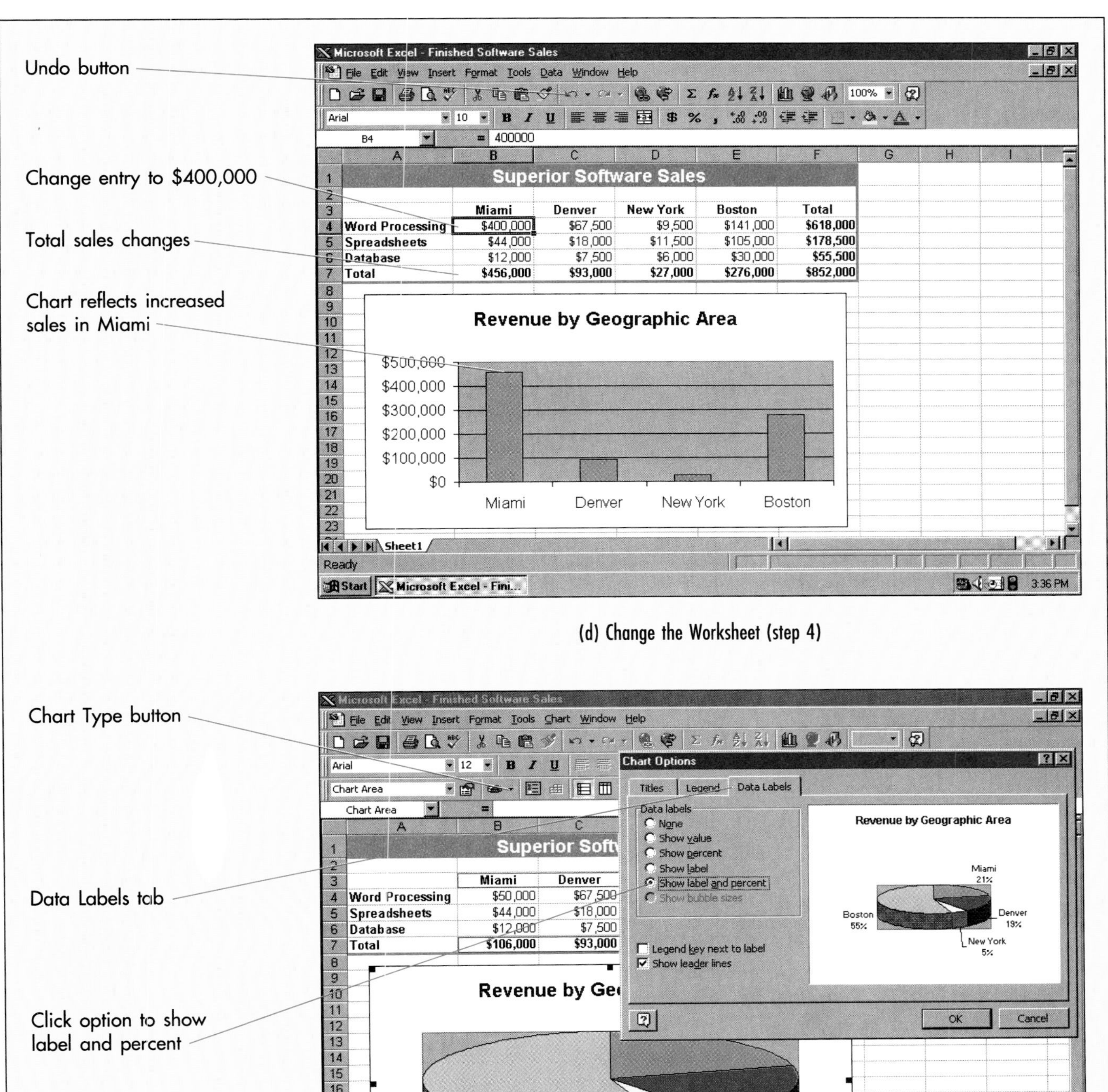

(d) Change the Worksheet (step 4)

(e) Change the Chart Type (step 5)

FIGURE 4.7 Hands-on Exercise 1 (continued)

ANATOMY OF A CHART

A chart is composed of multiple components (objects), each of which can be selected and changed separately. Point to any part of a chart to display a ScreenTip indicating the name of the component, then click the mouse to select that component and display the sizing handles. You can then click and drag the object within the chart and/or click the right mouse button to display a shortcut menu with commands pertaining to the selected object.

STEP 6: Create a Second Chart

- Click and drag to select cells **A4 through A6** in the worksheet. Press and hold the **Ctrl key** as you drag the mouse over cells **F4 through F6** to select the data series.
- Click the **Chart Wizard button** on the Standard toolbar to start the Chart Wizard and display the dialog box for step 1 as shown in Figure 4.7f. The Column Chart type is already selected. Click the **Clustered column with a 3-D visual effect subtype.** Click **Next.**
- Click the **Series tab** in the dialog box for step 2 to confirm that you selected the correct data points. The values for series1 should consist of cells F4 through F6. The Category labels for the X axis should be cells A4 through A6. Click **Next.**
- You should see step 3 of the Chart Wizard. Click the **Titles tab,** then click in the text box for the Chart title. Type **Revenue by Product Category.** Click the **Legend tab** and clear the box to show a legend. Click **Next.**
- You should see step 4 of the Chart Wizard. Select the option button to create the chart **As new sheet** (Chart1). Click **Finish.**
- The 3-D column chart has been created in the chart sheet labeled Chart1. Save the workbook.

SELECTING NONCONTIGUOUS RANGES

Any time you select a cell or cell range (a row or column, or a group of rows and columns) you automatically deselect the previous selection. You can, however, select noncontiguous (nonadjacent) ranges by selecting the first range in the normal fashion, then pressing and holding the Ctrl key as you select the additional range(s). This technique is very useful in conjunction with the Chart Wizard, or when the same command is to be applied to multiple ranges within a worksheet.

STEP 7: Enhance the Chart

- Point to any visible toolbar, click the **right mouse button** to display a shortcut menu listing the available toolbars, then click **Drawing** to display the Drawing toolbar. (Your toolbar may be in a different position from ours.)
- Click the **drop-down arrow** on the **AutoShapes button,** click **Callouts** to display the various styles of callouts, then click **Line Callout 2** (No Border) as shown in Figure 4.7g.

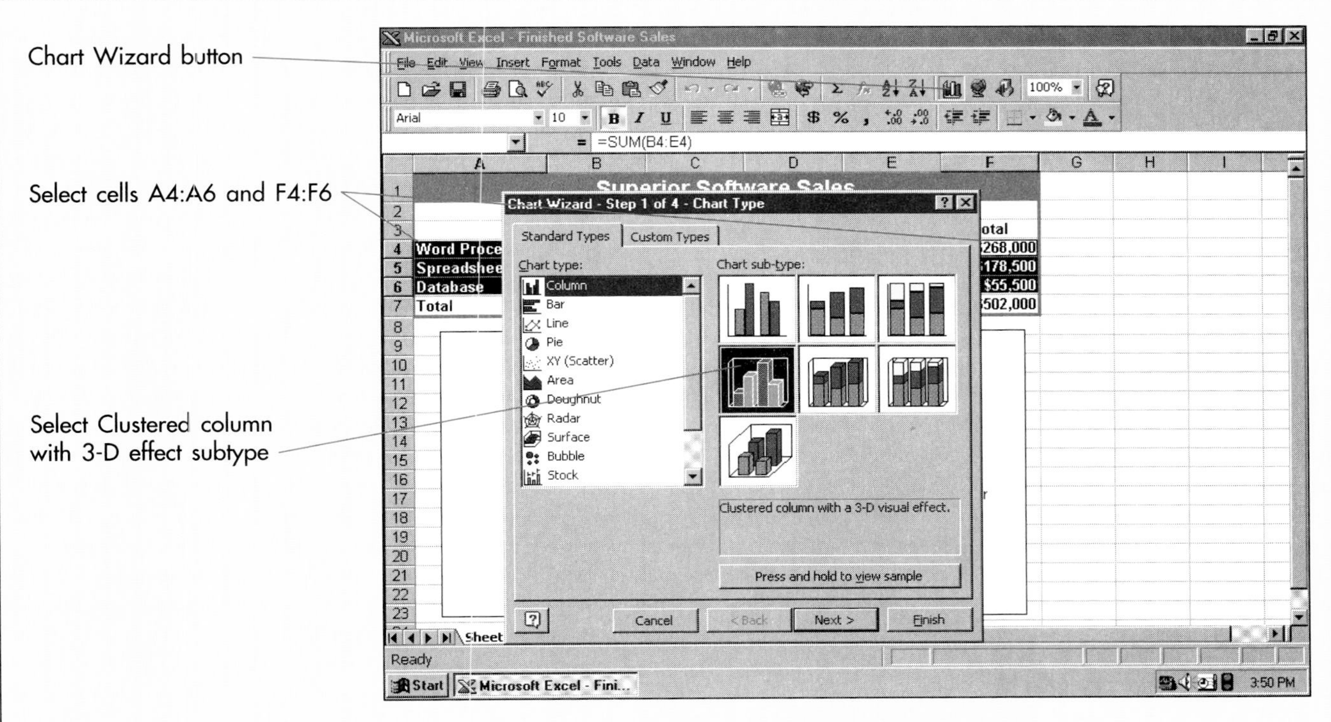

(f) Create the Second Chart (step 6)

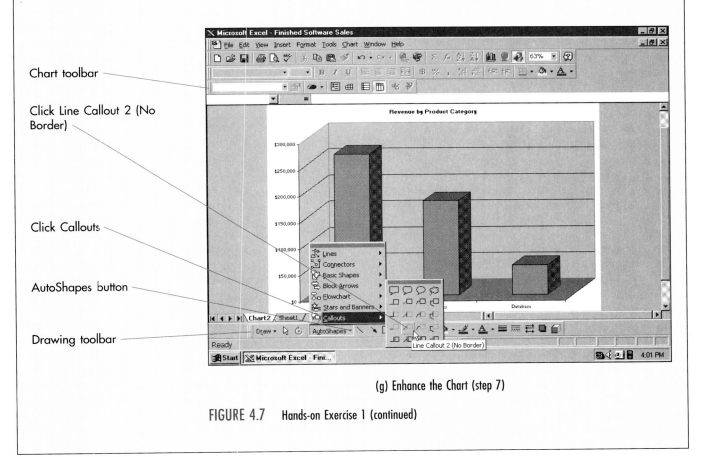

(g) Enhance the Chart (step 7)

FIGURE 4.7 Hands-on Exercise 1 (continued)

- The mouse pointer changes to a thin crosshair. Click the column representing the sales for word processing (the point in the chart where you want the callout to begin), then drag the mouse to create a line from the callout to the associated text. Release the mouse. Enter the text of the callout (e.g., Word Processing leads all categories). Size the text box as necessary, then click outside the text box.
- Click the title of the chart. You will see sizing handles around the title to indicate it has been selected.
- Click the **drop-down arrow** in the Font Size box on the Formatting toolbar. Click **18** to increase the size of the title.
- Use the **Text Box tool** on the Drawing toolbar to add your name somewhere in the chart so that your instructor will know the assignment is from you.

FLOATING TOOLBARS

Any toolbar can be docked along the edge of the application window or it can be displayed as a floating toolbar within the application window. To move a docked toolbar, drag the toolbar background. To move a floating toolbar, drag its title bar. To size a floating toolbar, drag any border in the direction you want to go. Double click the background of any toolbar to toggle between a floating toolbar and a docked (fixed) toolbar.

STEP 8: Format the Data Series

- Click any of the columns to select the data series. (All three columns will be selected. You can also click a column after the data series has been selected to select only that column and deselect the others.) Be sure that all three columns are selected.
- Point to any column and click the **right mouse button** to display a shortcut menu, then click **Format Data Series** to display the Format Data Series dialog box as shown in Figure 4.7h. Click the **Patterns tab,** select (click) a different color, then click **OK** to accept the change and close the dialog box.
- Save the workbook. Exit Excel if you do not want to continue with the next exercise at this time.

THE EXCEL WORKBOOK

An Excel workbook is the electronic equivalent of a three-ring binder. A workbook contains one or more worksheets and/or chart sheets, each of which is identified by a tab at the bottom of the document window. (Click the appropriate tab to go from one sheet to another.) The sheets in a workbook are typically related to one another. One worksheet, for example, may contain data for several charts, each of which appears on a separate chart sheet in the workbook. The advantage of a workbook is that all of its sheets are stored in a single file, which is accessed as a unit.

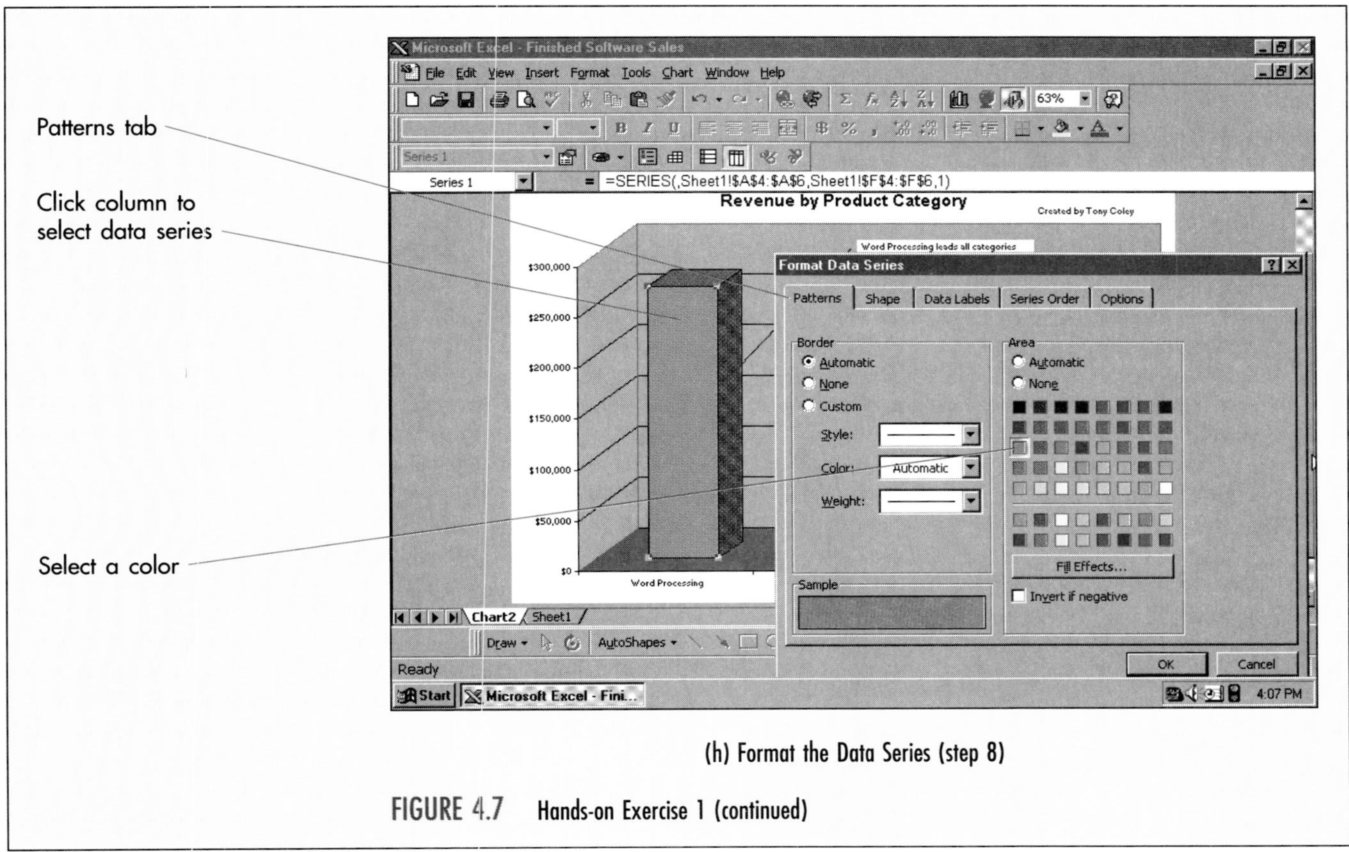

(h) Format the Data Series (step 8)

FIGURE 4.7 Hands-on Exercise 1 (continued)

MULTIPLE DATA SERIES

The charts presented so far displayed only a single data series—for example, the total sales by location or the total sales by product category. Although such charts are useful, it is often necessary to view ***multiple data series*** on the same chart.

Figure 4.8a displays the sales in each location according to product category. We see how the products compare within each city, and further, that word processing is the leading application in three of the four cities. Figure 4.8b plots the identical data but in ***stacked columns*** rather than side-by-side.

The choice between the two types of charts depends on your message. If, for example, you want your audience to see the individual sales in each product category, the side-by-side columns are more appropriate. If, on the other hand, you want to emphasize the total sales for each city, the stacked columns are preferable. Note, too, the different scale on the Y axis in the two charts. The side-by-side columns in Figure 4.8a show the sales of each product category and so the Y axis goes only to $160,000. The stacked columns in Figure 4.8b, however, reflect the total sales for each city and thus the scale goes to $300,000.

The biggest difference is that the stacked column explicitly totals the sales for each city while the side-by-side column does not. The advantage of the stacked column is that the city totals are clearly shown and can be easily compared, and further the relative contributions of each product category within each city are apparent. The disadvantage is that the segments within each column do not start at the same point, making it difficult to determine the actual sales for the individual product categories or to compare the product categories among cities.

Realize, too, that for a stacked column chart to make sense, its numbers must be additive. This is true in Figure 4.8b, where the stacked columns consist of three

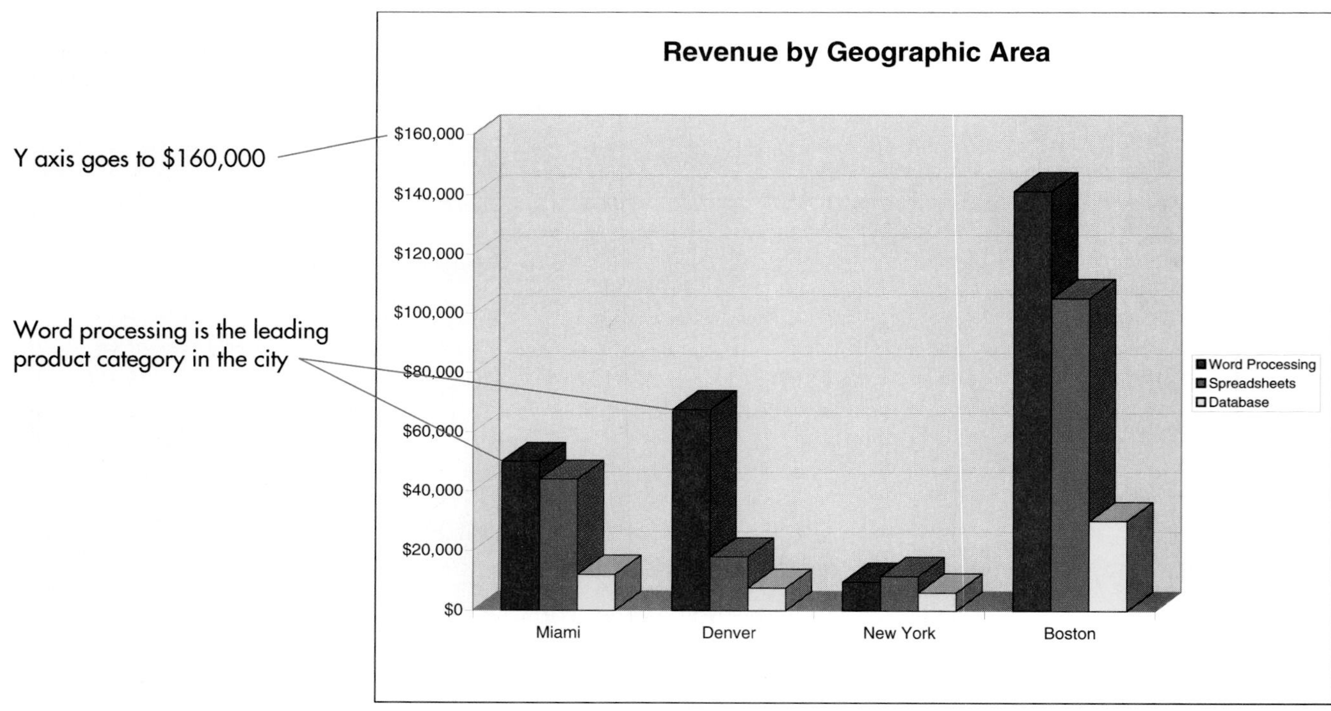

(a) Side-by-Side Column Chart

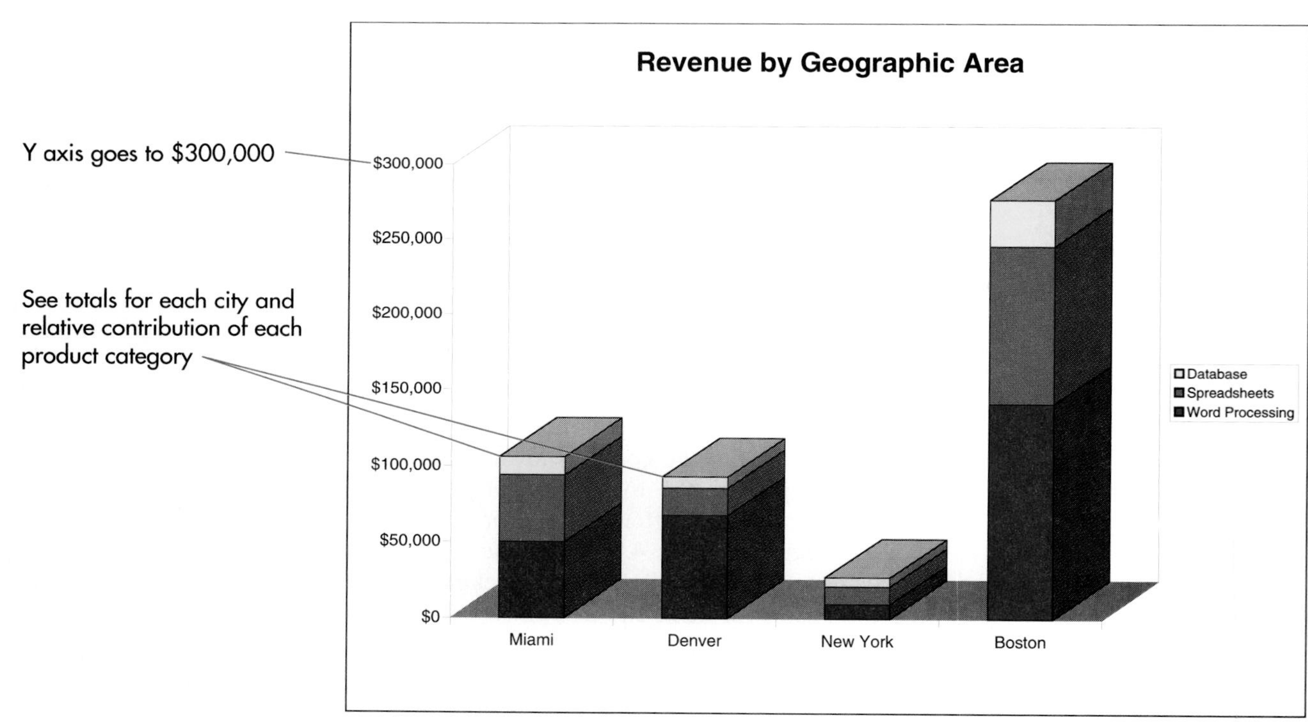

(b) Stacked Column Chart

FIGURE 4.8 Column Charts

components, each of which is measured in dollars, and which can be logically added together to produce a total. You shouldn't, however, automatically convert a side-by-side column chart to its stacked column equivalent. It would not make sense, for example, to convert a column chart that plots unit sales and dollar sales side-by-side, into a stacked column chart that adds the two, because units and dollars represent different physical concepts and are not additive.

Rows versus Columns

Figure 4.9 illustrates a critical concept associated with multiple data series—whether the data series are in rows or columns. Figure 4.9a displays the worksheet with multiple data series selected. (Column A and Row 3 are included in the selection to provide the category labels and legend.) Figure 4.9b contains the chart when the data series are in rows (B4:E4, B5:E5, and B6:E6). Figure 4.9c displays the chart based on data series in columns (B4:B6, C4:C6, D4:D6, and E4:E6).

Both charts plot a total of twelve data points (three product categories for each of four locations), but they group the data differently. Figure 4.9b displays the data by city; that is, the sales of three product categories are shown for each of four cities. Figure 4.9c is the reverse and groups the data by product category; this time the sales in the four cities are shown for each of the three product categories. The choice between the two depends on your message and whether you want to emphasize revenue by city or by product category. It sounds complicated, but it's not, and Excel will create either chart for you according to your specifications.

- If the data series are in rows (Figure 4.9b), the Wizard will:
  - Use the first row (cells B3 through E3) in the selected range for the category labels on the X axis
  - Use the first column (cells A4 through A6) for the legend text
- If the data series are in columns (Figure 4.9c), the Wizard will:
  - Use the first column (cells A4 through A6) in the selected range for the category labels on the X axis
  - Use the first row (cells B3 through E3) for the legend text

Stated another way, the data series in Figure 4.9b are in rows. Thus, there are three data series (B4:E4, B5:E5, and B6:E6), one for each product category. The first data series plots the word processing sales in Miami, Denver, New York, and Boston; the second series plots the spreadsheet sales for each city, and so on.

The data series in Figure 4.9c are in columns. This time there are four data series (B4:B6, C4:C6, D4:D6, and E4:E6), one for each city. The first series plots the Miami sales for word processing, spreadsheets, and database; the second series plots the Denver sales for each software category, and so on.

A3:E6 is selected

	A	B	C	D	E	F
1	Superior Software Sales					
2						
3		Miami	Denver	New York	Boston	Total
4	Word Processing	$50,000	$67,500	$9,500	$141,000	$268,000
5	Spreadsheets	$44,000	$18,000	$11,500	$105,000	$178,500
6	Database	$12,000	$7,500	$6,000	$30,000	$55,500
7	Total	$106,000	$93,000	$27,000	$276,000	$502,000

(a) The Worksheet

FIGURE 4.9 Multiple Data Series

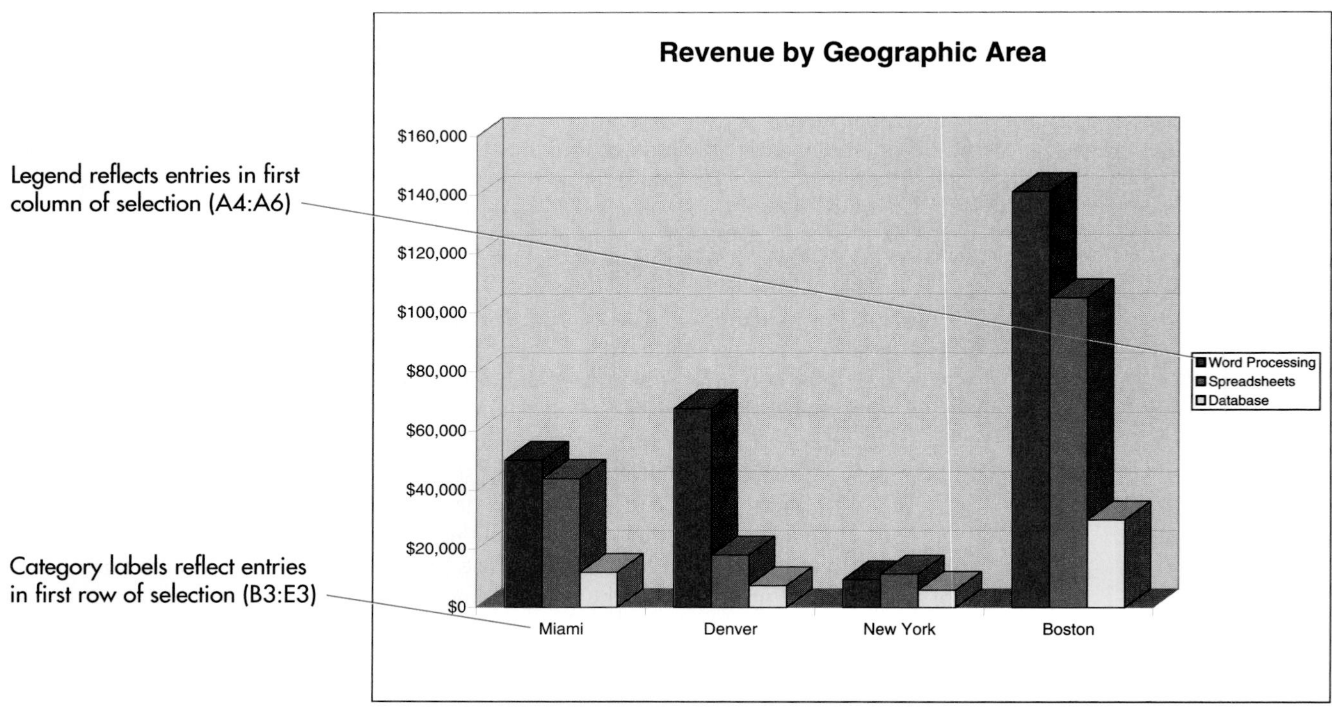

(b) Data in Rows

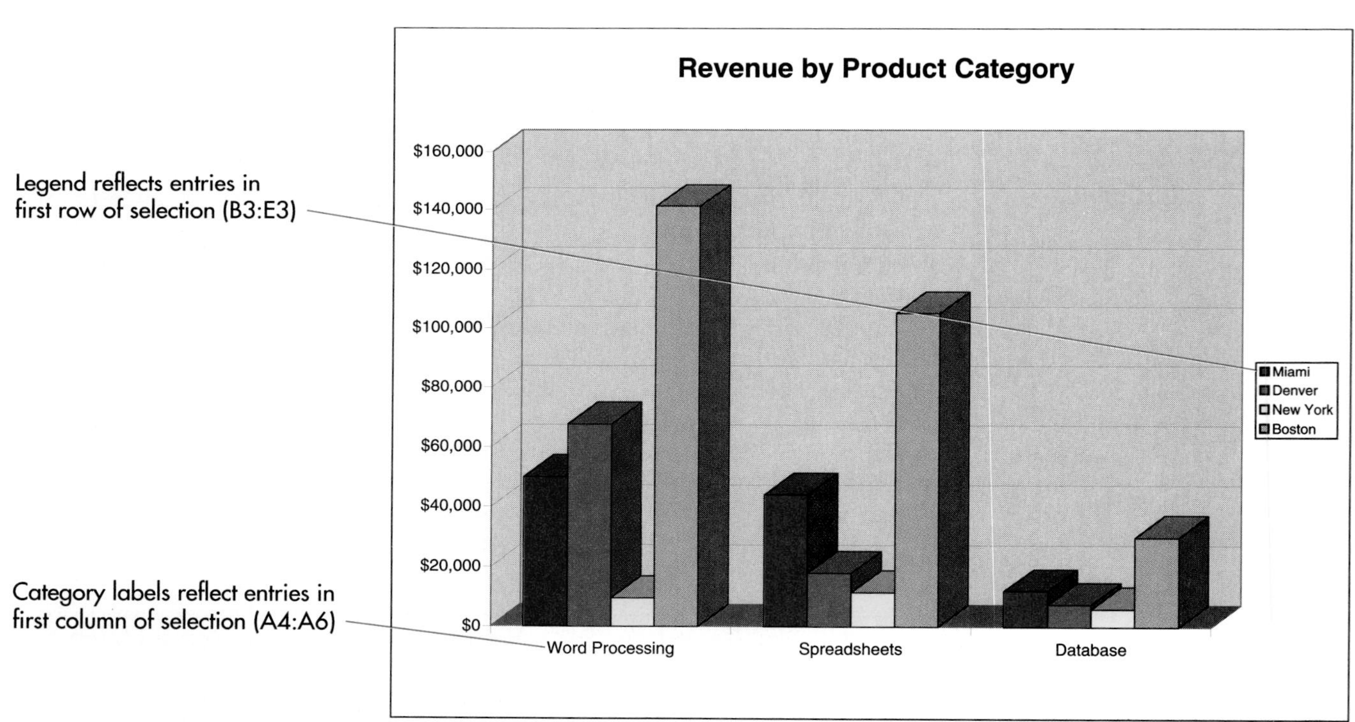

(c) Data in Columns

FIGURE 4.9 Multiple Data Series (continued)

HANDS-ON EXERCISE 2

Multiple Data Series

Objective: To plot multiple data series in the same chart; to differentiate between data series in rows and columns; to create and save multiple charts associated with the same worksheet. Use Figure 4.10 as a guide in the exercise.

STEP 1: Rename the Worksheets

- Open the **Finished Software Sales** workbook from the previous exercise as shown in Figure 4.10a. The workbook contains an embedded chart and a separate chart sheet.
- Point to the workbook tab labeled **Sheet1,** click the **right mouse button** to display a shortcut menu, then click the **Rename** command. The name of the worksheet (Sheet1) is selected. Type **Sales Data** to change the name of the worksheet to the more descriptive name. Press the **enter key.**
- Point to the tab labeled **Chart1** (which contains the three-dimensional column chart created in the previous exercise). Click the **right mouse button** to display a shortcut menu, click **Rename,** then enter **Column Chart** as the name of the chart sheet. Press the **enter key.**
- Save the workbook.

Click Rename

Point to Sheet1 tab and right click to display shortcut menu

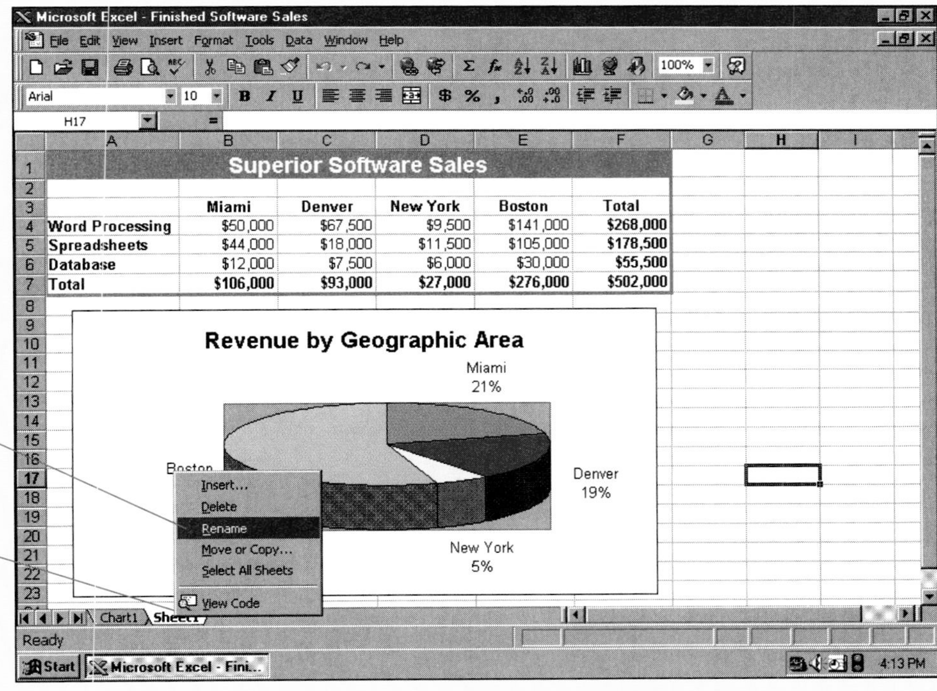

(a) Rename the Worksheet Tabs (step 1)

FIGURE 4.10 Hands-on Exercise 2

THE RIGHT MOUSE BUTTON

Point to a cell (or group of selected cells), a chart or worksheet tab, a toolbar, or chart (or a selected object on the chart), then click the right mouse button to display a shortcut menu. All shortcut menus are context-sensitive and display commands appropriate for the selected item. Right clicking a toolbar, for example, enables you to display (hide) additional toolbars. Right clicking a sheet tab enables you to rename, move, copy, or delete the sheet.

STEP 2: The Office Assistant

- Click the **Sales Data tab,** then click and drag to select cells **A3 through E6.** Click the **Chart Wizard button** on the Standard toolbar to start the wizard and display the dialog box shown in Figure 4.10b.
- If necessary, click the **Office Assistant button** in the Chart Wizard dialog box to display the Office Assistant and the initial help screen. Click the option button for **Help with this feature.**
- The display for the Assistant changes to offer help about the various chart types available. (It's up to you whether you want to explore the advice at this time. You can close the Assistant, or leave it open and drag the title bar out of the way.)
- Select **Column** as the chart type and **3-D visual effect Clustered column** as the subtype. Click **Next** to continue with the Chart Wizard.

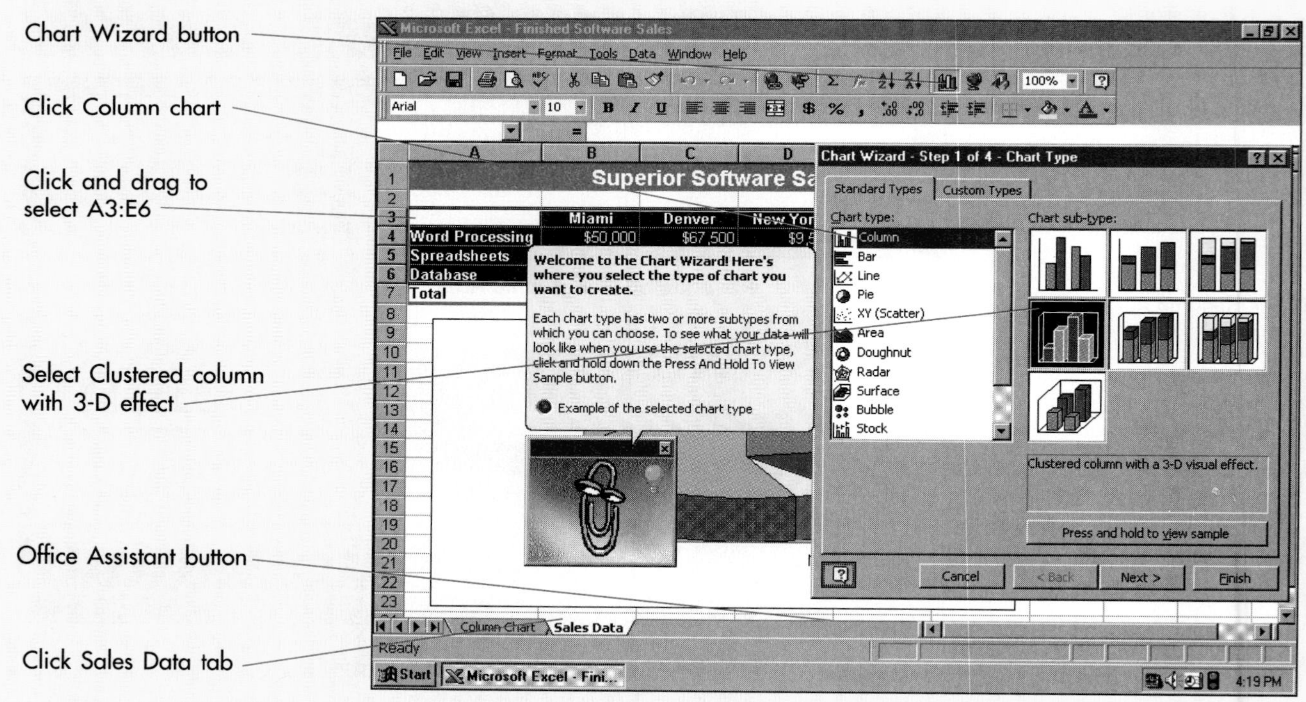

(b) The Office Assistant (step 2)

FIGURE 4.10 Hands-on Exercise 2 (continued)

THE OFFICE ASSISTANT

The Office Assistant button is common to all Office applications and is an invaluable source of online help. You can activate the Assistant at any time by clicking its button on the Standard toolbar or from within a specialized dialog box. You can ask the Assistant a specific question and/or you can have the Assistant monitor your work and suggest tips as appropriate. You can tell that the Assistant has a suggestion when you see a lightbulb on the Office Assistant button on the Standard toolbar.

STEP 3: View the Data Series

- You should see step 2 of the Chart Wizard as shown in Figure 4.10c. The help supplied by the Office Assistant changes automatically with the steps in the Chart Wizard.
- The data range should be specified as **Sales Data!$A$3:$E$6** as shown in Figure 4.10c. The option button for **Series in Rows** should be selected. To appreciate the concept of data series in rows (versus columns), click the **Series tab:**
  - The series list box shows three data series (Word Processing, Spreadsheets, and Database) corresponding to the legends for the chart.
  - The **Word Processing** series is selected by default. The legend in the sample chart shows that the data points in the series are plotted in blue. The values are taken from cells B4 through E4 in the Sales Data Worksheet.
  - Click **Spreadsheets** in the series list box. The legend shows that the series is plotted in red. The values are taken from cells B5 through E5 in the Sales Data worksheet.
  - Click **Database** in the series list box. The legend shows that the series is plotted in yellow. The values are taken from cells B6 through E6 in the Sales Data worksheet.

DEFAULT SELECTIONS

Excel makes a default determination as to whether the data is in rows or columns by assuming that you want fewer data series than categories. Thus, if the selected cells contain fewer rows than columns (or if the number of rows and columns are equal), it assumes the data series are in rows. If, on the other hand, there are fewer columns than rows, it will assume the data series are in columns.

STEP 4: Complete the Chart

- Click **Next** to continue creating the chart. You should see step 3 of the Chart Wizard. Click the **Titles tab.** Click the text box for Chart title. Type **Revenue by City.** Click **Next.**
- You should see step 4 of the Chart Wizard. Click the option button for **As new sheet.** Type **Revenue by City** in the associated text box to give the chart sheet a meaningful name. Click **Finish.**
- Excel creates the new chart in its own sheet named Revenue by City. Close the Assistant. Save the workbook.

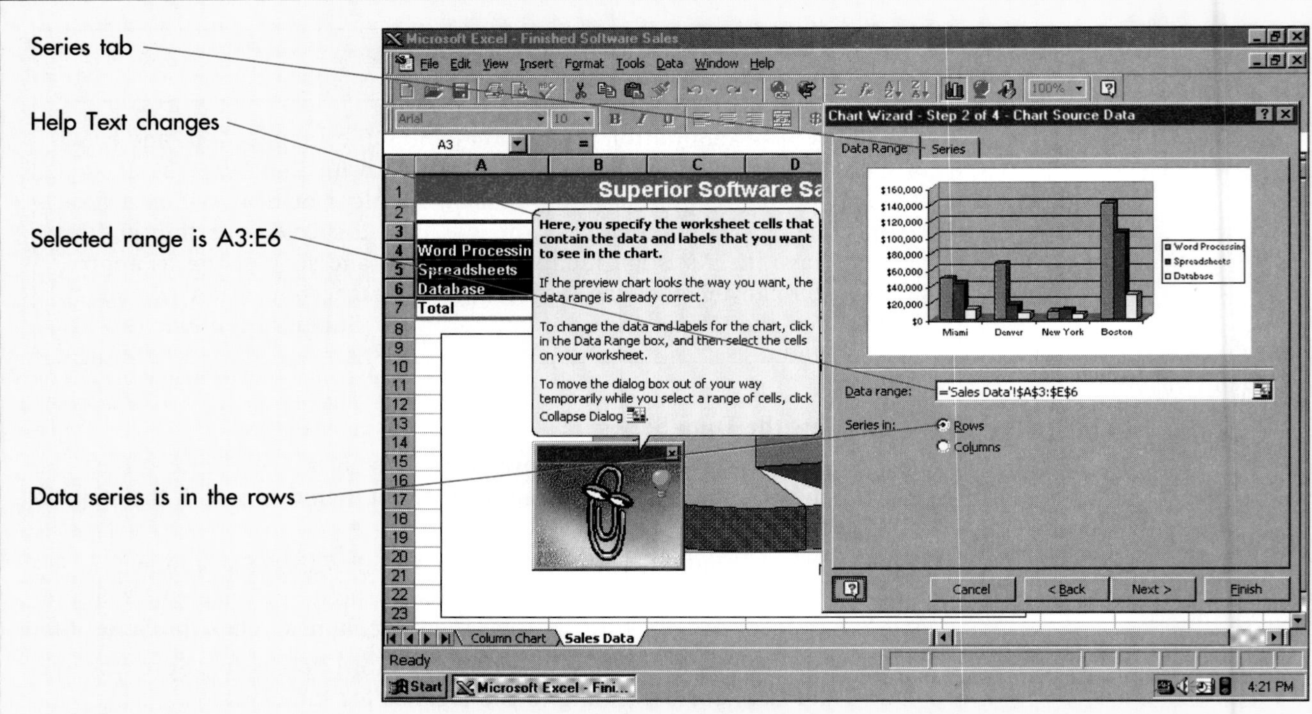

(c) View the Data Series (step 3)

FIGURE 4.10 Hands-on Exercise 2 (continued)

> **THE F11 KEY**
>
> The F11 key is the fastest way to create a chart in its own sheet. Select the data, including the legends and category labels, then press the F11 key to create the chart according to the default format built into the Excel column chart. After the chart has been created, you can use the menu bar, Chart toolbar, or shortcut menus to choose a different chart type and/or customize the formatting.

STEP 5: Copy the Chart Sheet

- Point to the tab named **Revenue by City.** Click the **right mouse button.** Click **Move or Copy** to display the dialog box in Figure 4.10d.
- Click **Sales Data** in the Before Sheet list box. Check the box to **Create a Copy.** Click **OK.**
- A duplicate worksheet called Revenue by City(2) is created and appears before (to the left of) the Sales Data worksheet.
- Rename the copied sheet **Revenue by Product.** Save the workbook.

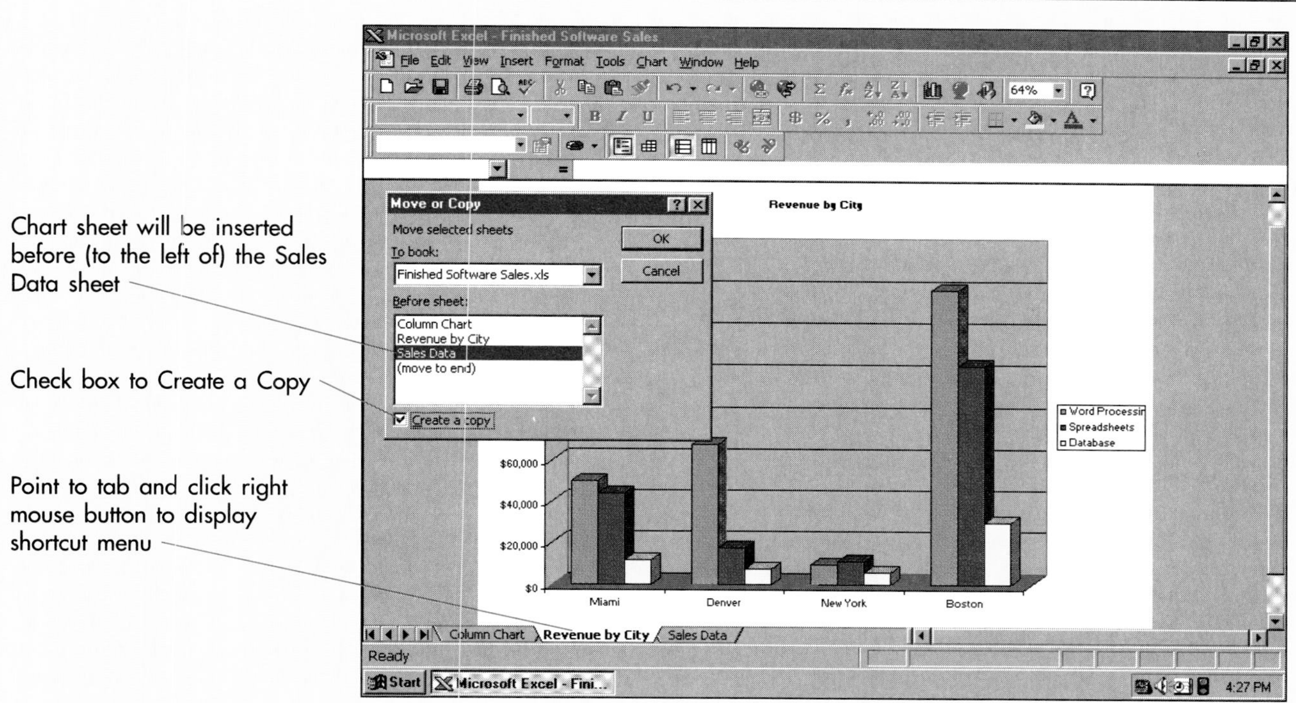

(d) Copy the Chart (step 5)

FIGURE 4.10 Hands-on Exercise 2 (continued)

MOVING AND COPYING A CHART SHEET

The fastest way to move or copy a chart sheet is to drag its tab. To move a sheet, point to its tab, then click and drag the tab to its new position. To copy a sheet, press and hold the Ctrl key as you drag the tab to the desired position for the second sheet. Rename the copied sheet (or any sheet for that matter) by pointing to its tab and clicking the right mouse button to produce a shortcut menu. Click Rename, then enter the new name.

STEP 6: Change the Source Data

- ➤ Click the **Revenue by Product tab** to make it the active sheet. Click anywhere in the title of the chart, drag the mouse over the word **City** to select the text, then type **Product Category** to replace the selected text. Click outside the title to deselect it.
- ➤ Pull down the **Chart menu.** Click **Source Data** (you will see the Sales Data worksheet), then click the **Columns option button** so that your screen matches Figure 4.10e. Click the **Series tab** and note the following:
  - The current chart (outside the dialog box) plots the data in rows. There are three data series (one series for each product). Each data series has four data points, one point for each city.

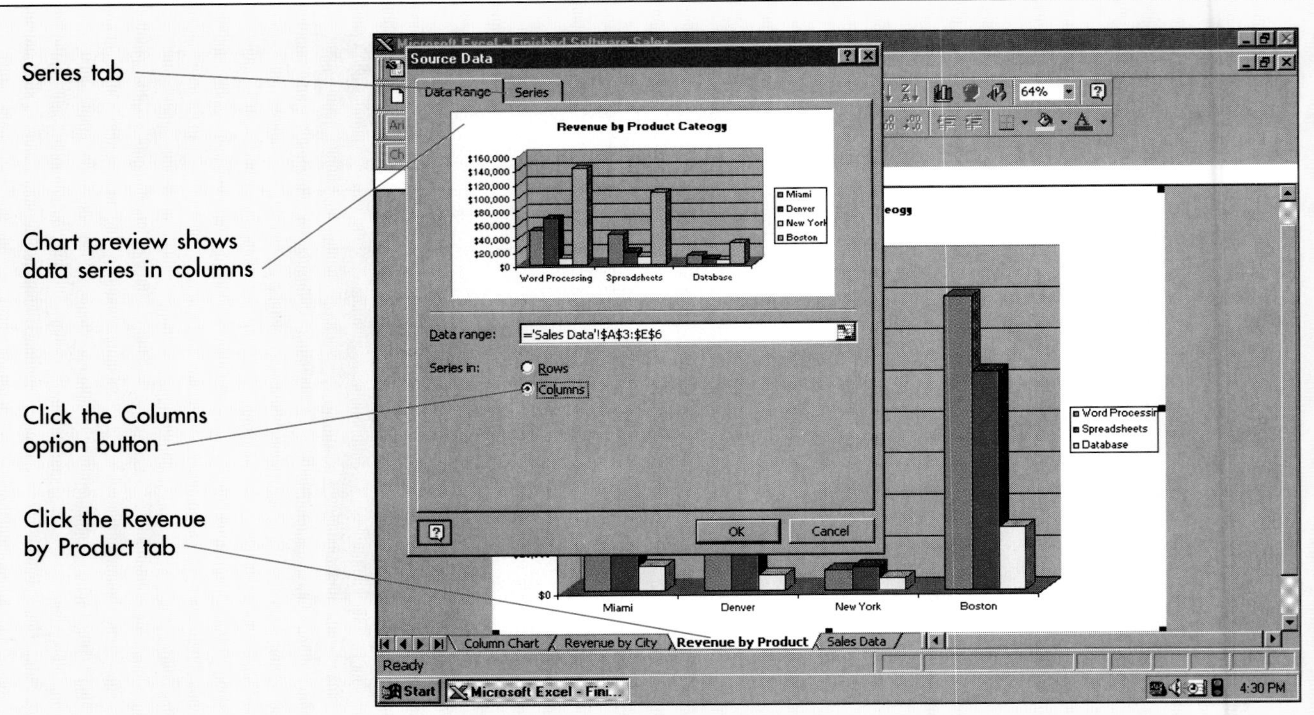

(e) Change the Source Data (step 6)

FIGURE 4.10 Hands-on Exercise 2 (continued)

- The new chart (shown in the dialog box) plots the data in columns. There are four data series (one series for each city as indicated in the Series list box). Each data series has three data points, one point for each product.

➤ Click **OK** to close the Source Data dialog box and plot the data in columns. Save the workbook.

THE HORIZONTAL SCROLL BAR

The horizontal scroll bar contains four scrolling buttons to scroll through the sheet tabs in a workbook. Click ◀ or ▶ to scroll one tab to the left or right. Click |◀ or ▶| to scroll to the first or last tab in the workbook. Once the desired tab is visible, click the tab to select it.

STEP 7: The Stacked Column Chart

➤ Point to the chart area, click the **right mouse button** to display a shortcut menu, then click the **Chart Type** command to display the Chart Type dialog box.

➤ Select the **3-D visual effect Stacked Column chart** (the middle entry in the second row). Click **OK.** The chart changes to a stacked column chart as shown in Figure 4.10f. Save the workbook.

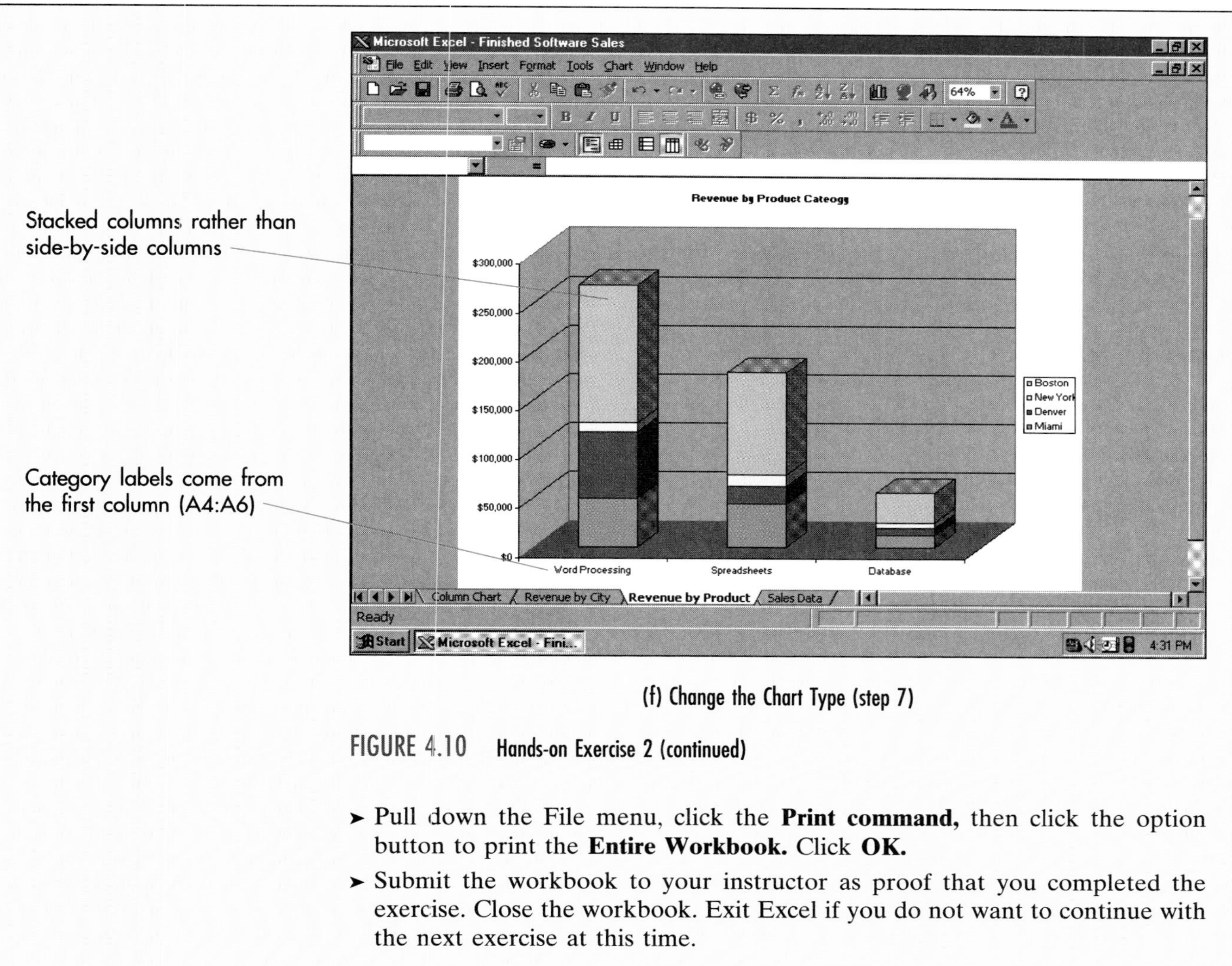

(f) Change the Chart Type (step 7)

FIGURE 4.10 Hands-on Exercise 2 (continued)

- Pull down the File menu, click the **Print command,** then click the option button to print the **Entire Workbook.** Click **OK.**
- Submit the workbook to your instructor as proof that you completed the exercise. Close the workbook. Exit Excel if you do not want to continue with the next exercise at this time.

OBJECT LINKING AND EMBEDDING

One of the primary advantages of the Windows environment is the ability to create a ***compound document*** that contains data ***(objects)*** from multiple applications. The memo in Figure 4.11 is an example of a compound document. The memo was created in Microsoft Word, and it contains objects (a worksheet and a chart) that were developed in Microsoft Excel. ***Object Linking and Embedding*** (***OLE,*** pronounced "oh-lay") is the means by which you create the compound document.

The essential difference between linking and embedding is whether the object is stored within the compound document ***(embedding)*** or in its own file ***(linking).*** An ***embedded object*** is stored in the compound document, which in turn becomes the only client for that object. A ***linked object*** is stored in its own file, and the compound document is one of many potential clients for that object. The compound document does not contain the linked object per se, but only a representation of the object as well as a pointer (link) to the file containing the object. The advantage of linking is that any document that is linked to the object is updated automatically if the object is changed.

The choice between linking and embedding depends on how the object will be used. Linking is preferable if the object is likely to change and the compound

Superior Software

Miami, Florida

To: Mr. White
Chairman, Superior Software

From: Heather Bond
Vice President, Marketing

Subject: May Sales Data

The May sales data clearly indicate that Boston is outperforming our other geographic areas. It is my feeling that Ms. Brown, the office supervisor, is directly responsible for its success and that she should be rewarded accordingly. In addition, we may want to think about transferring her to New York, as they are in desperate need of new ideas and direction. I will be awaiting your response after you have time to digest the information presented.

Superior Software Sales					
	Miami	**Denver**	**New York**	**Boston**	**Total**
Word Processing	$50,000	$67,500	$9,500	$141,000	**$268,000**
Spreadsheets	$44,000	$18,000	$11,500	$105,000	**$178,500**
Database	$12,000	$7,500	$6,000	$30,000	**$55,500**
Total	**$106,000**	**$93,000**	**$27,000**	**$276,000**	**$502,000**

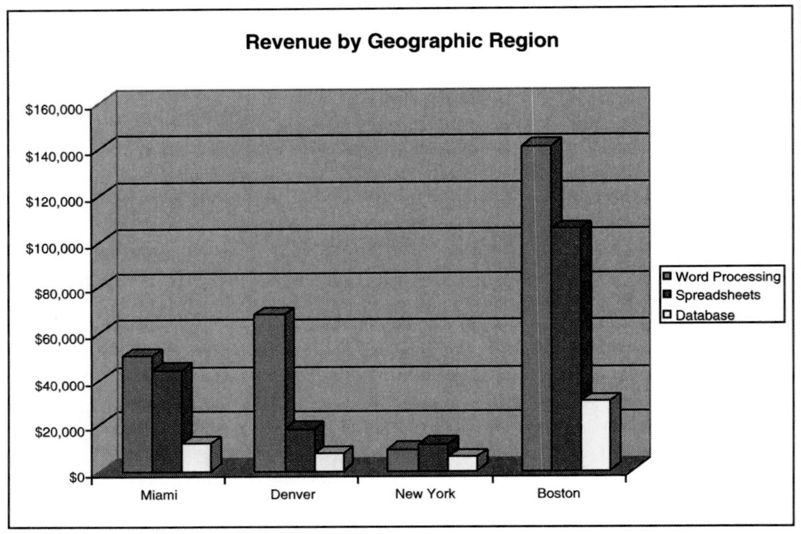

FIGURE 4.11 A Compound Document

document requires the latest version. Linking should also be used when the same object is placed in many documents, so that any change to the object has to be made in only one place. Embedding should be used if you need to take the object with you—for example, if you intend to edit the compound document on a different computer.

The following exercise uses linking to create a Word document containing an Excel worksheet and chart. As you do the exercise, both applications (Word and Excel) will be open, and it will be necessary to switch back and forth between the two. This in turn demonstrates the ***multitasking*** capability within Windows 95 and the use of the Windows 95 taskbar to switch between the open applications.

HANDS-ON EXERCISE 3

Object Linking and Embedding

Objective: To create a compound document consisting of a memo, worksheet, and chart. Use Figure 4.12 as a guide in the exercise.

STEP 1: Open the Software Memo

➤ Click the **Start button** on the taskbar to display the Start menu. Click (or point to) the **Programs menu,** then click **Microsoft Word** to start the program. Close the Office Assistant if it appears.

➤ Word is now active, and the taskbar contains a button for Microsoft Word. It may (or may not) contain a button for Microsoft Excel, depending on whether or not you closed Excel at the end of the previous exercise.

➤ If necessary, click the **Maximize button** in the application window so that Word takes the entire desktop as shown in Figure 4.12a. (The Open dialog box is not yet visible.) Click the **Maximize button** in the document window (if necessary) so that the document window is as large as possible.

➤ Pull down the **File menu** and click **Open** (or click the **Open button** on the Standard toolbar).

- Click the **drop-down arrow** in the Look In list box. Click the appropriate drive, drive C or drive A, depending on the location of your data.
- Double click the **Exploring Excel folder** (we placed the Word memo in the Exploring Excel folder) to open the folder. Double click the **Software Memo** to open the document.
- Save the document as **Finished Software Memo.**

➤ Pull down the **View menu.** Click **Page Layout** to change to the Page Layout view. Pull down the **View menu.** Click **Zoom.** Click **Page Width.**

OBJECT LINKING AND EMBEDDING

Object Linking and Embedding (OLE) enables you to create a compound document containing objects (data) from multiple Windows applications. The two techniques, linking and embedding, can be implemented in different ways. Although OLE is one of the major benefits of working in the Windows environment, it would be impossible to illustrate all of the techniques in a single exercise. Accordingly, we have created the icon at the left to help you identify the many examples of object linking and embedding that appear throughout the *Exploring Windows* series.

STEP 2: Copy the Worksheet

➤ Open (or return to) the **Finished Software Sales workbook** from the previous exercise.

- If you did not close Microsoft Excel at the end of the previous exercise, you will see its button on the taskbar. Click the **Microsoft Excel button** to return to or open the Finished Software Sales workbook.
- If you closed Microsoft Excel, click the **Start button** to start Excel, then open the Finished Software Sales workbook.

- ➤ The taskbar should now contain a button for both Microsoft Word and Microsoft Excel. Click either button to move back and forth between the open applications. End by clicking the Microsoft Excel button so that you see the Finished Software Sales workbook.
- ➤ Click the tab for **Sales Data.** Click and drag to select **A1** through **F7** to select the entire worksheet as shown in Figure 4.12b.
- ➤ Point to the selected area and click the **right mouse button** to display the shortcut menu. Click **Copy.** A moving border appears around the entire worksheet, indicating that it has been copied to the clipboard.

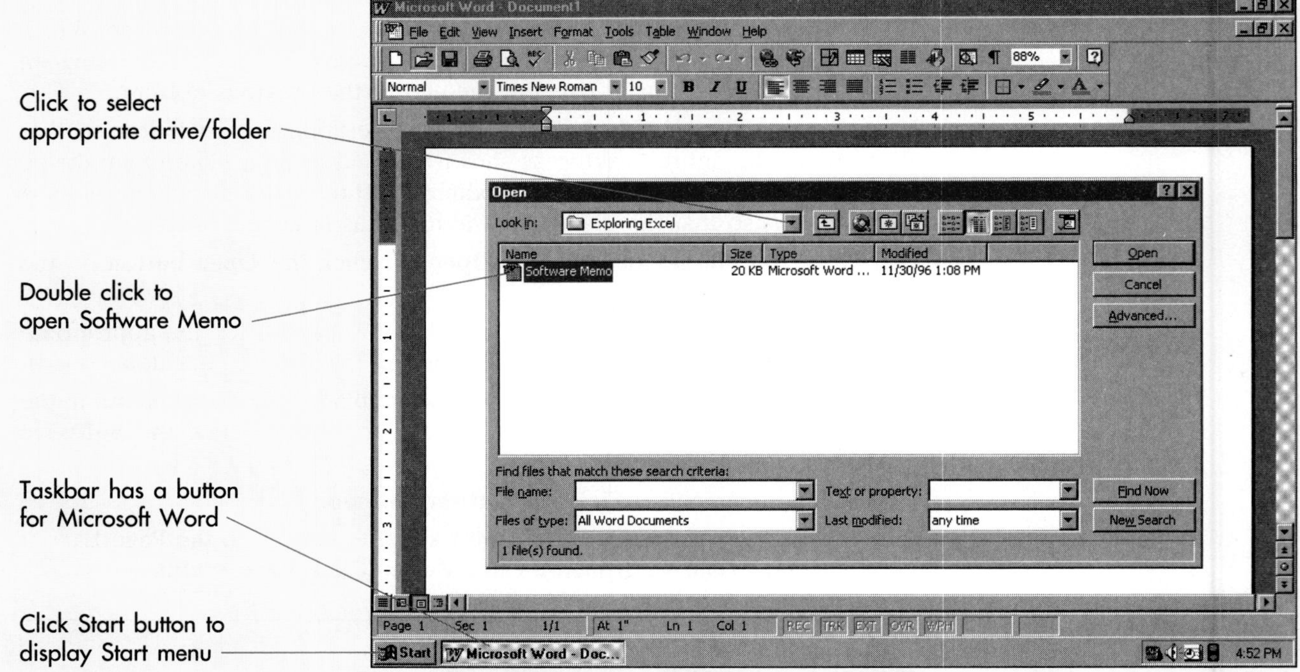
Click to select appropriate drive/folder
Double click to open Software Memo
Taskbar has a button for Microsoft Word
Click Start button to display Start menu

(a) Open the Software Sales Document (step 1)

FIGURE 4.12 Hands-on Exercise 3

THE WINDOWS 95 TASKBAR

Multitasking, the ability to run multiple applications at the same time, is one of the primary advantages of the Windows environment. Each button on the taskbar appears automatically when its application or folder is opened, and disappears upon closing. (The buttons are resized automatically according to the number of open windows.) The taskbar can be moved to the left or right edge of the desktop, or to the top of the desktop, by dragging a blank area of the taskbar to the desired position.

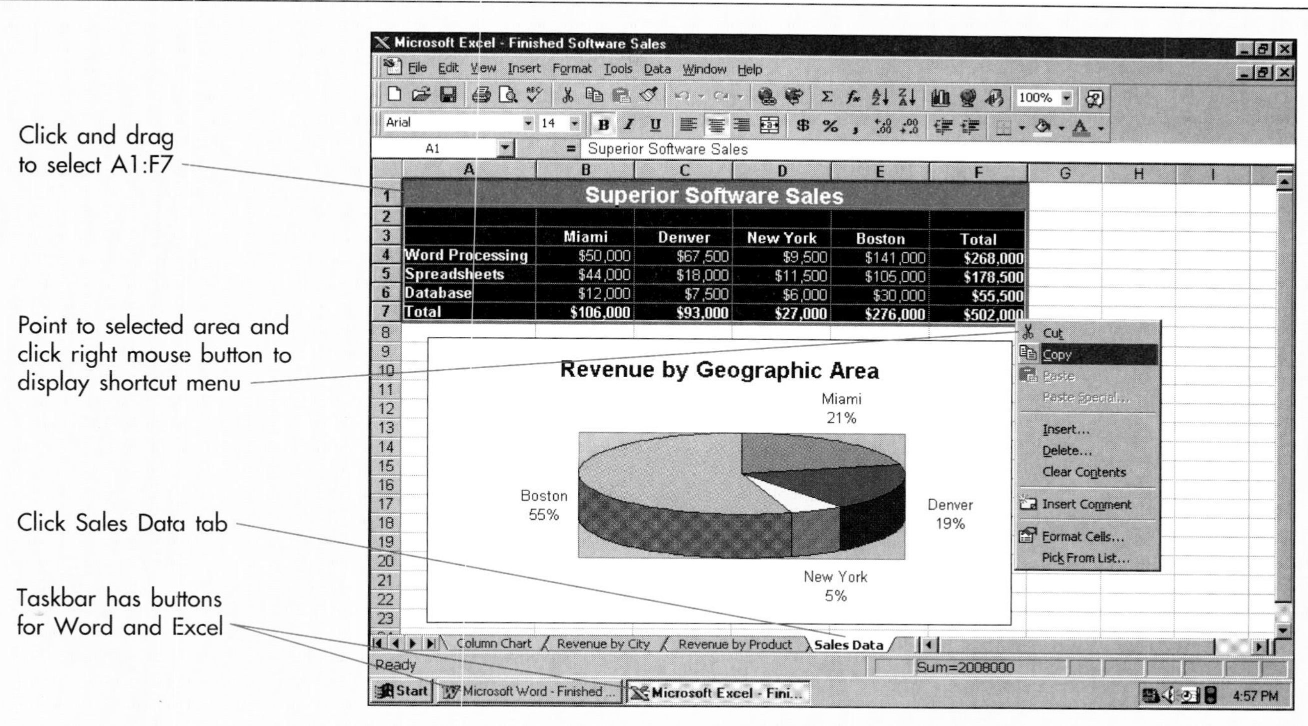

(b) Copy the Worksheet (step 2)

FIGURE 4.12 Hands-on Exercise 3 (continued)

STEP 3: Create the Link

- Click the **Microsoft Word button** on the taskbar to return to the memo as shown in Figure 4.12c. Press **Ctrl+End** to move to the end of the memo, which is where you will insert the Excel worksheet.
- Pull down the **Edit menu.** Click **Paste Special** to display the dialog box in Figure 4.12c.
- Click **Microsoft Excel Worksheet Object** in the As list. Click the **Paste Link option button.** Click **OK** to insert the worksheet into the document.
- Click and drag to center the worksheet between the margins. Save the memo.

THE COMMON USER INTERFACE

The common user interface provides a sense of familiarity from one Windows application to the next. Even if you have never used Microsoft Word, you will recognize many of the elements present in Excel. The applications share a common menu structure with consistent ways to execute commands from those menus. The Standard and Formatting toolbars are present in both applications. Many keyboard shortcuts are also common, such as Ctrl+Home and Ctrl+End to move to the beginning and end of a document.

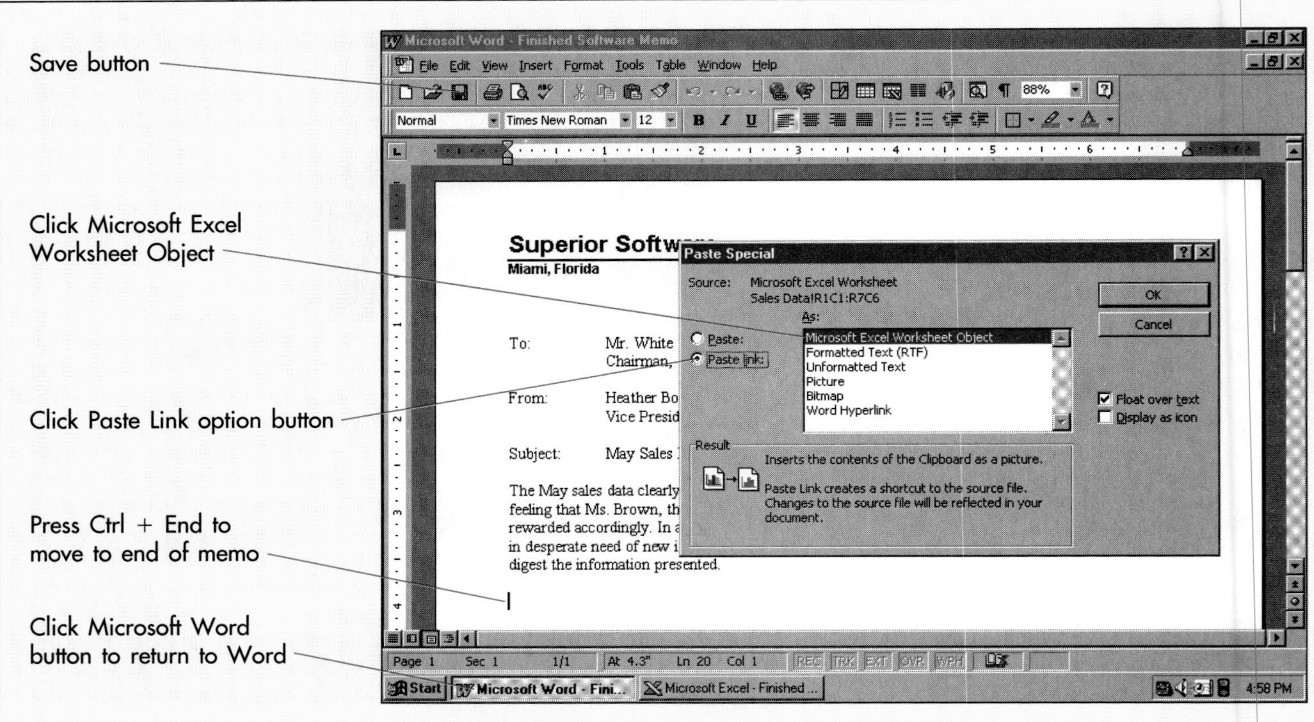

(c) Create the Link (step 3)

FIGURE 4.12 Hands-on Exercise 3 (continued)

STEP 4: Copy the Chart

- Click the **Microsoft Excel button** on the taskbar to return to the worksheet. Click outside the selected area (cells A1 through F7) to deselect the cells. Press **Esc** to remove the moving border.
- Click the **Revenue by City tab** to select the chart sheet. Point to the chart area, then click the left mouse button to select the chart. Be sure you have selected the entire chart and that you see the same sizing handles as in Figure 4.12d.
- Pull down the **Edit menu** and click **Copy** (or click the **Copy button** on the Standard toolbar). A moving border appears around the entire chart.

ALT+TAB STILL WORKS

Alt+Tab was a treasured shortcut in Windows 3.1 that enabled users to switch back and forth between open applications. The shortcut also works in Windows 95. Press and hold the Alt key while you press and release the Tab key repeatedly to cycle through the open applications, whose icons are displayed in a small rectangular window in the middle of the screen. Release the Alt key when you have selected the icon for the application you want.

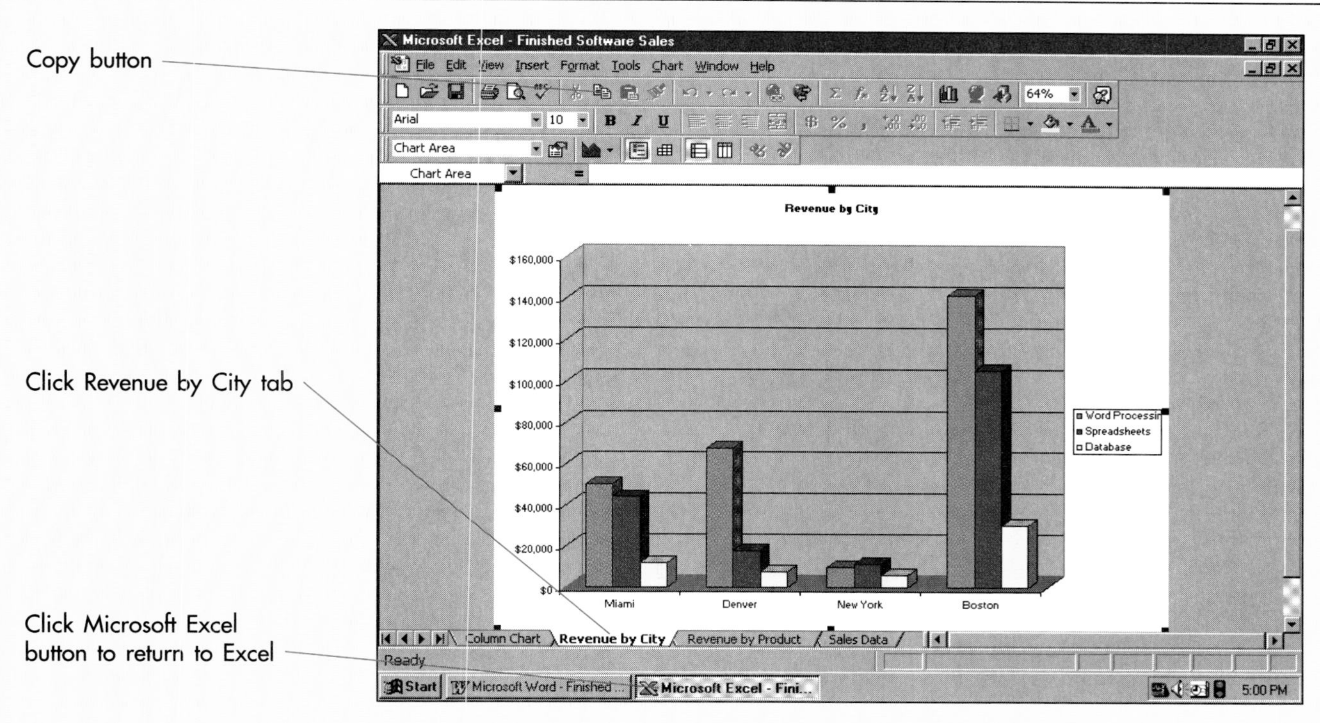

(d) Copy the Chart to the Clipboard (step 4)

FIGURE 4.12 Hands-on Exercise 3 (continued)

STEP 5: Add the Chart

- Click the **Microsoft Word button** on the taskbar to return to the memo. If necessary, press **Ctrl+End** to move to the end of the Word document. Press the **enter key** to add a blank line.
- Pull down the **Edit menu.** Click **Paste Special.** Click the **Paste Link** option button. If necessary, click **Microsoft Excel Chart Object.** Click **OK** to insert the chart into the document.
- Zoom to **Whole Page** to facilitate moving and sizing the chart. You need to reduce its size so that it fits on the same page as the memo. Thus, click on the chart to select it and display the sizing handles as shown in Figure 4.12e. Click and drag a corner sizing handle inward to make the chart smaller, then center it on the page.
- Zoom to **Page Width.** Look carefully at the worksheet and chart in the document. The sales for Word Processing in New York are currently $9,500, and the chart reflects this amount. Save the memo.
- Point to the **Microsoft Excel button** on the taskbar and click the **right mouse button** to display a shortcut menu. Click **Close** to close Excel. Click **Yes** if prompted whether to save the changes to the Finished Software Sales workbook.
- The Microsoft Excel button disappears from the taskbar, indicating that Excel has been closed. Word is now the only open application.

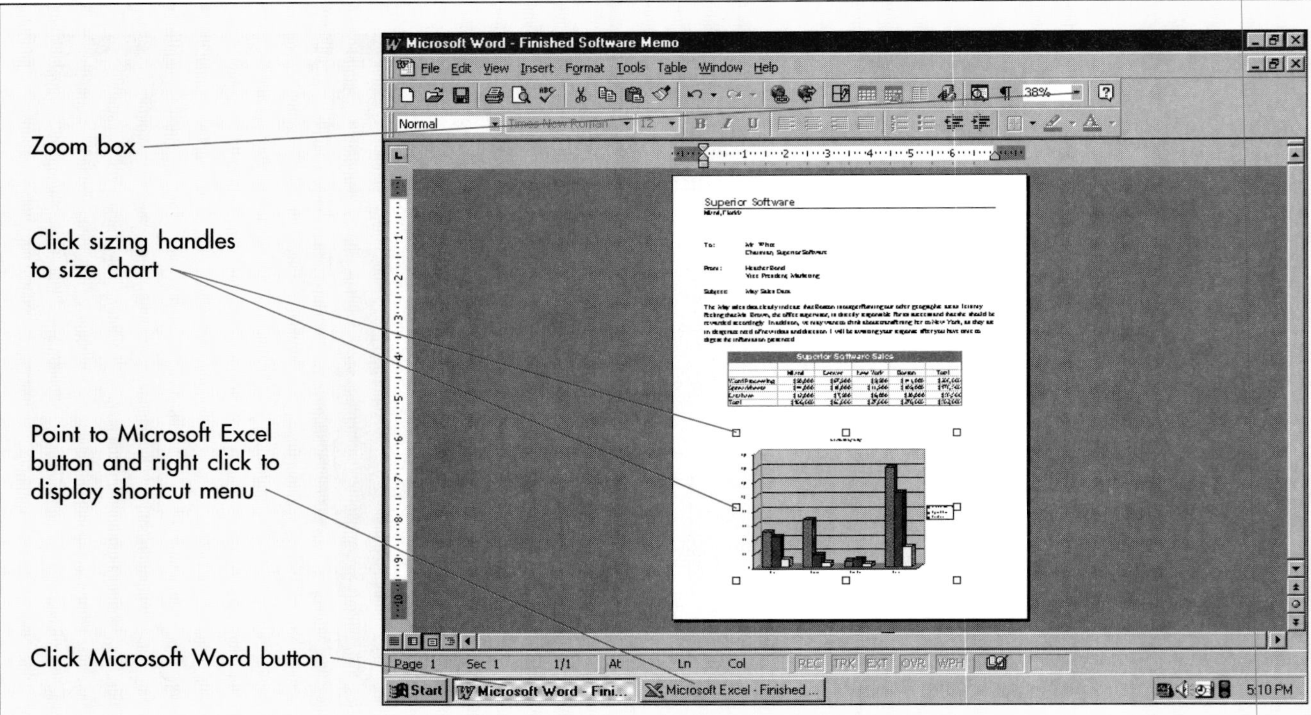

(e) Add the Chart (step 5)

FIGURE 4.12 Hands-on Exercise 3 (continued)

LINKING VERSUS EMBEDDING

A linked object maintains its connection to the source file. An embedded object does not. Thus, a linked object can be placed in any number of destination files, each of which maintains a pointer (link) to the same source file. Any change to the object in the source file is reflected automatically in every destination file containing that object.

STEP 6: Modify the Worksheet

- ➤ Click anywhere in the worksheet to select the worksheet and display the sizing handles as shown in Figure 4.12f.
- ➤ The status bar indicates that you can double click to edit the worksheet. Double click anywhere within the worksheet to reopen Excel in order to change the data.
- ➤ The system pauses as it loads Excel and reopens the Finished Software Sales workbook. If necessary, click the **Maximize button** to maximize the Excel window. Close the Office Assistant if it appears.
- ➤ If necessary, click the **Sales Data tab** within the workbook. Click in **cell D4.** Type **$200,000.** Press **enter.**
- ➤ Click the **|◄ button** to scroll to the first tab. Click the **Revenue by City tab** to select the chart sheet. The chart has been modified automatically and reflects the increased sales for New York.

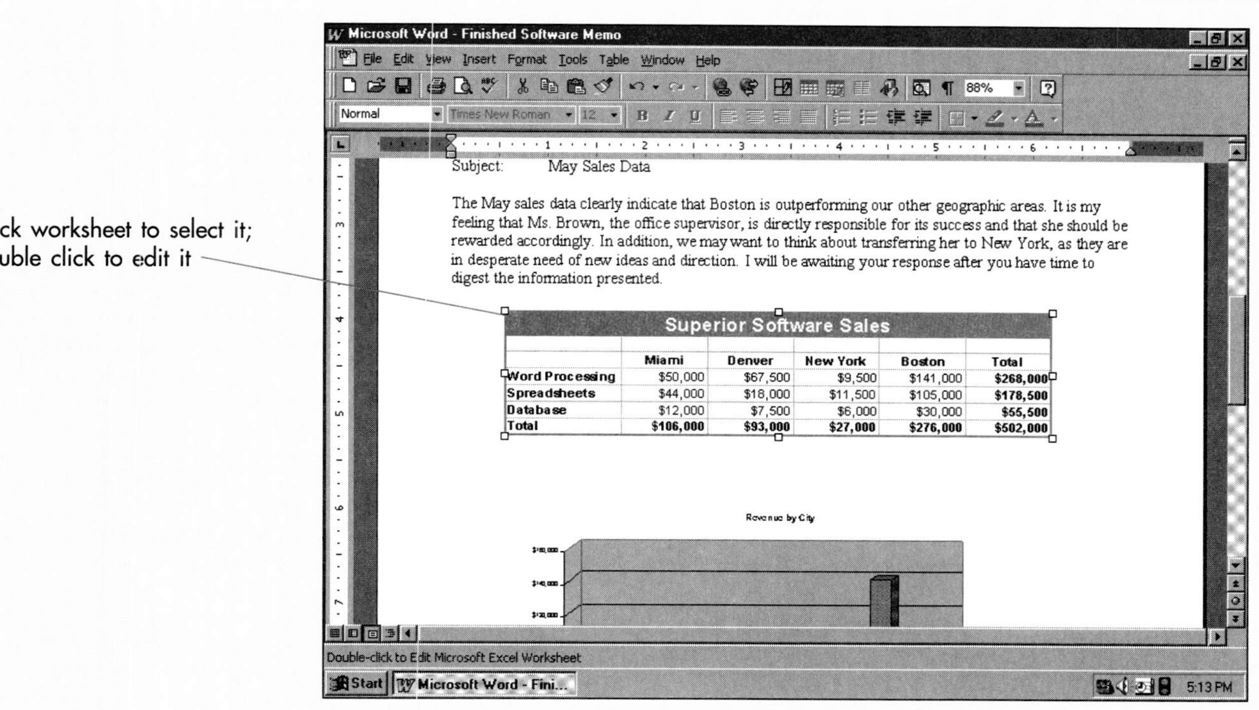

(f) Modify the Worksheet (step 6)

FIGURE 4.12 Hands-on Exercise 3 (continued)

STEP 7: Update the Links

- Click the **Microsoft Word button** on the taskbar to return to the Software memo. The links for the worksheet and chart should be updated automatically. If not:
  - Pull down the **Edit menu.** Click **Links to** display the Links dialog box in Figure 4.12g.
  - Select the link(s) to update. (You can press and hold the **Ctrl key** to select multiple links simultaneously.)
  - Click the **Update Now button** to update the selected links.
  - Close the Links dialog box.
- The worksheet and chart should both reflect $200,000 for word processing sales in New York. Save the Word document.

UPDATE LINKS BEFORE PRINTING

Word will automatically update any linked information prior to printing a document, provided the options are set properly. Pull down the Tools menu, click the Options command, click the Print tab, then check the Update links check box.

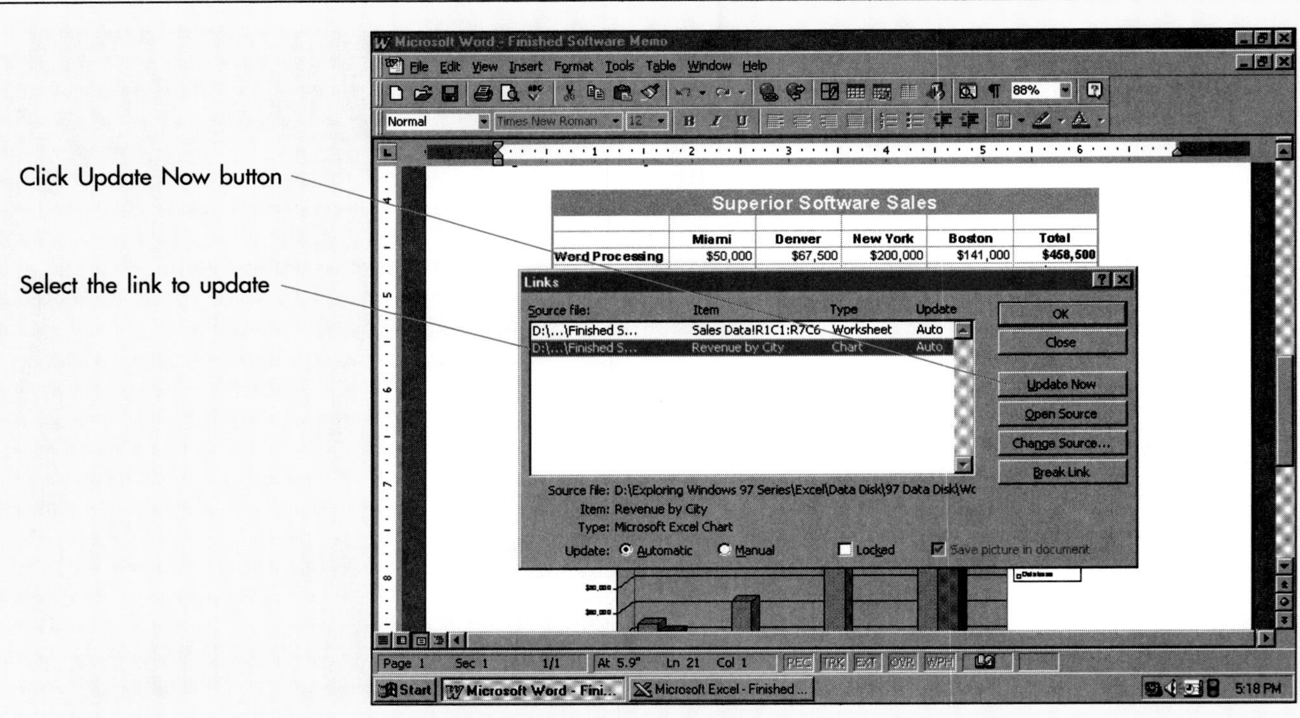

(g) Update the Links (step 7)

FIGURE 4.12 Hands-on Exercise 3 (continued)

STEP 8: The Finishing Touches

- Point to the chart, click the **right mouse button** to display a shortcut menu, then click the **Format Object command** to display the Format Object dialog box in Figure 4.12h.
- Click the **Colors and Lines Tab,** click the **drop-down arrow** in the Line Color box, then click **black** to display a line (border) around the worksheet. Click **OK.** Deselect the chart to see the border.
- Zoom to the **Whole Page** to view the completed document. Click and drag the worksheet and/or the chart within the memo to make any last minute changes. Save the memo a final time.
- Print the completed memo and submit it to your instructor. Exit Word. Exit Excel. Save the changes to the Finished Software Sales workbook.
- Congratulations on a job well done.

TO CLICK OR DOUBLE CLICK

Clicking an object selects the object and displays the sizing handles, which let you move and/or size the object or change its properties. Double clicking an object starts the application that created the object and enables you to change underlying data. Any changes to the object in the source file (e.g., the worksheet) are automatically reflected in the object in the destination file (e.g., the Word document) provided the two are properly linked to one another.

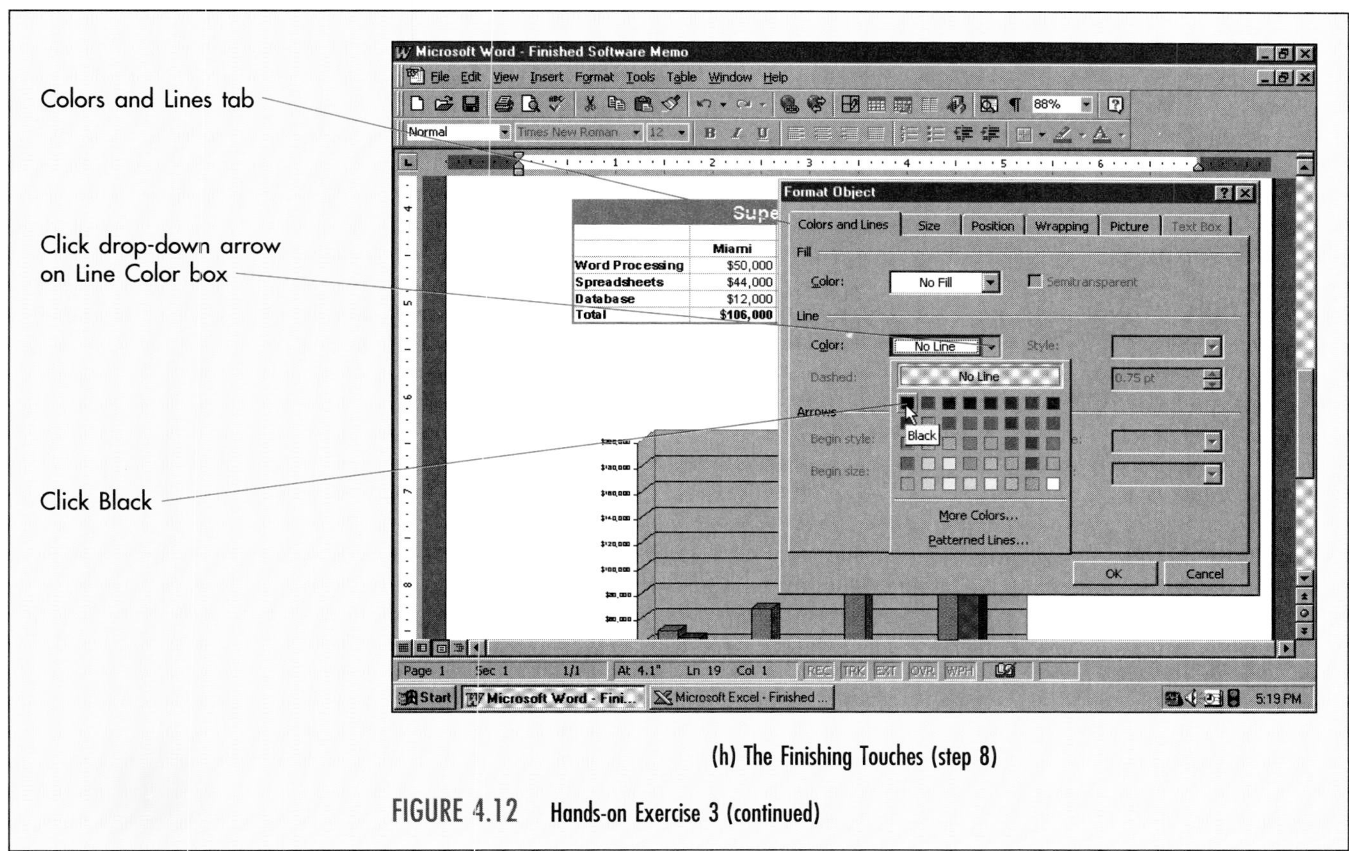

(h) The Finishing Touches (step 8)

FIGURE 4.12 Hands-on Exercise 3 (continued)

ADDITIONAL CHART TYPES

Excel offers a total of 14 standard ***chart types,*** each with several formats. The chart types are displayed in the Chart Wizard (see Figure 4.5b) and are listed here for convenience. The chart types are: Column, Bar, Line, Pie, XY (scatter), Area, Doughnut, Radar, Surface, Bubble, Stock, Cylinder, Cone, and Pyramid.

It is not possible to cover every type of chart, and so we concentrate on the most common. We have already presented the bar, column, and pie charts and continue with the line and combination charts. We use a different example, the worksheet in Figure 4.13a, which plots financial data for the National Widgets Corporation in Figures 4.13b and 4.13c. Both charts were created through the Chart Wizard, then modified as necessary using the techniques from the previous exercises.

	A	B	C	D	E	F
1	National Widgets Financial Data					
2						
3		*1992*	*1993*	*1994*	*1995*	*1996*
4	***Revenue***	$50,000,000	$60,000,000	$70,000,000	$80,000,000	$90,000,000
5	***Profit***	$10,000,000	$8,000,000	$6,000,000	$4,000,000	$2,000,000
6	***Stock Price***	$40	$35	$36	$31	$24

(a) The Worksheet

FIGURE 4.13 Additional Chart Types

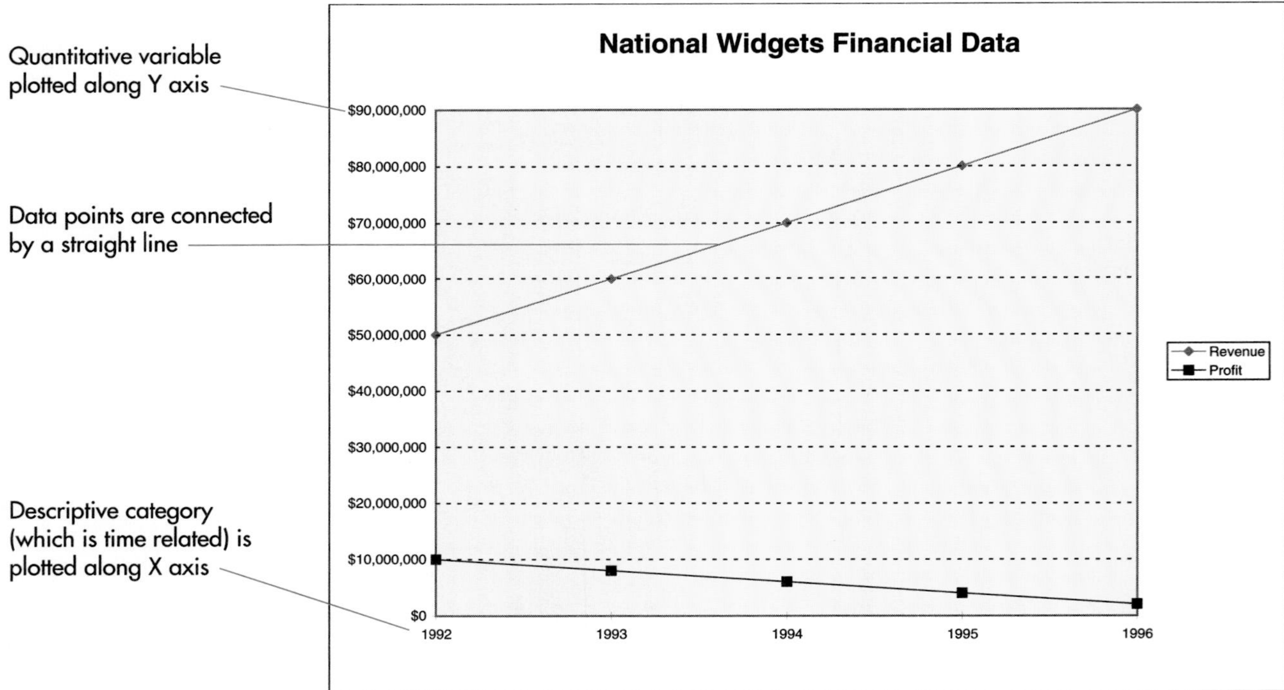

(b) Line Chart

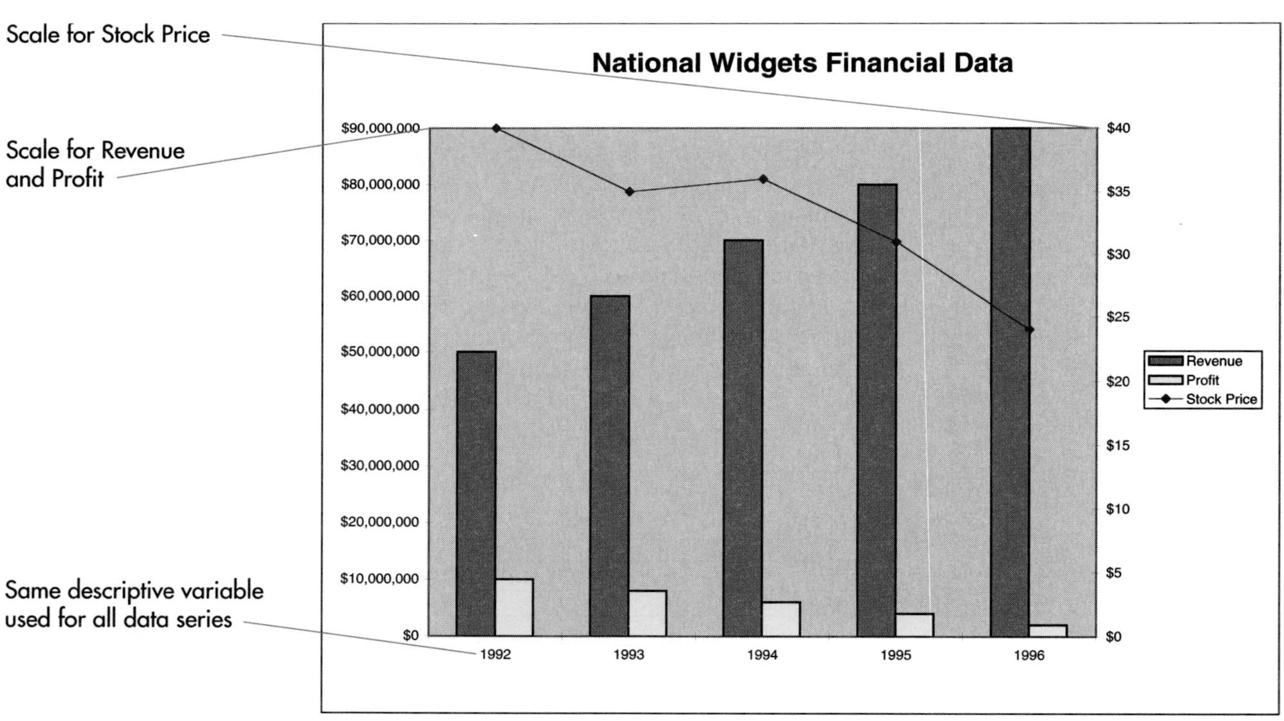

(c) Combination Chart

FIGURE 4.13 Additional Chart Types (continued)

Line Chart

A ***line chart*** is best to display time-related information, such as the five-year trend of revenue and profit in Figure 4.13b. A line chart plots one or more data series (e.g., revenue and profit) against a descriptive category (e.g., year). As with a column chart, the quantitative values are plotted along the vertical scale (Y axis) and the descriptive category along the horizontal scale (X axis).

Combination Chart

A ***combination chart*** uses two or more chart types to display different kinds of information or when different scales are required for multiple data series. The chart in Figure 4.13c plots revenue, profit, and stock price over the five-year period. The same scale can be used for revenue and profit (both are in millions of dollars), but an entirely different scale is needed for the stock price. Investors in National Widgets can see at a glance the true status of their company.

USE AND ABUSE OF CHARTS

The hands-on exercises in the chapter demonstrate how easily numbers in a worksheet can be converted to their graphic equivalent. *The numbers can, however, just as easily be converted into erroneous or misleading charts, a fact that is often overlooked.* Indeed, some individuals are so delighted just to obtain the charts, that they accept the data without question. Accordingly, we present two examples of statistically accurate yet entirely misleading graphical data, drawn from charts submitted by our students in response to homework assignments.

> Lying graphics cheapen the graphical art everywhere . . . When a chart on television lies, it lies millions of times over; when a *New York Times* chart lies, it lies 900,000 times over to a great many important and influential readers. The lies are told about the major issues of public policy—the government budget, medical care, prices, and fuel economy standards, for example. The lies are systematic and quite predictable, nearly always exaggerating the rate of recent change.
>
> **Edward Tufte**

Improper (Omitted) Labels

The difference between *unit sales* and *dollar sales* is a concept of great importance, yet one that is often missed. Consider, for example, the two pie charts in Figures 4.14a and 4.14b, both of which are intended to identify the leading salesperson, based on the underlying worksheet in Figure 4.14c. The charts yield two different answers, Jones and Smith, respectively, depending on which chart you use.

As you can see, the two charts reflect different percentages and would appear therefore to contradict each other. Both charts, however, are technically correct, as the percentages depend on whether they express unit sales or dollar sales. *Jones is the leader in terms of units, whereas Smith is the leader in terms of dollars.* The latter is generally more significant, and hence the measure that is probably most important to the reader. Neither chart, however, was properly labeled (there is no indication of whether units or dollars are plotted), which in turn may lead to erroneous conclusions on the part of the reader.

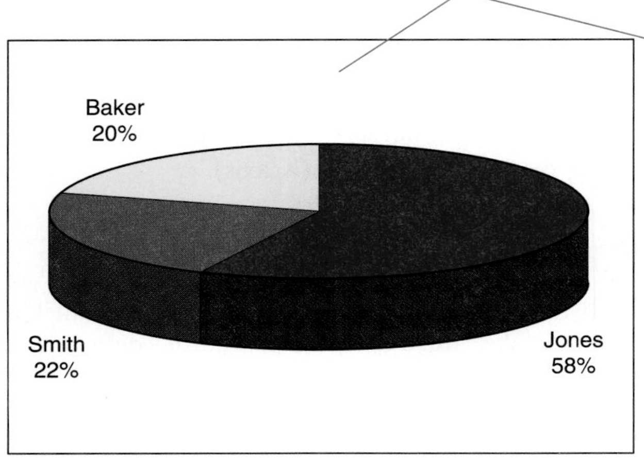

(a) Units

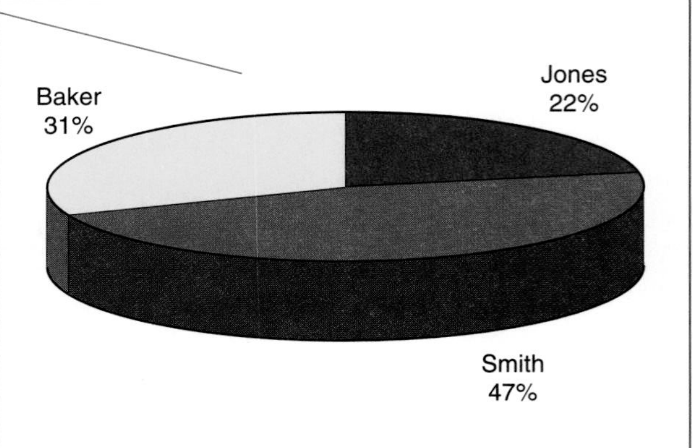

(b) Dollars

Sales Data - First Quarter							
		Jones		Smith		Baker	
	Price	Units	Dollars	Units	Dollars	Units	Dollars
Product 1	**$1**	200	$200	20	$20	30	$30
Product 2	**$5**	50	$250	30	$150	30	$150
Product 3	**$20**	5	$100	50	$1,000	30	$600
	Totals	255	$550	100	$1,170	90	$780

(c) Underlying Spreadsheet

FIGURE 4.14 Omitted Labels

Good practice demands that every chart have a title and that as much information be included on the chart as possible to help the reader interpret the data. Use titles for the X axis and Y axis if necessary. Add text boxes for additional explanation.

Adding Dissimilar Quantities

The conversion of a side-by-side column chart to a stacked column chart is a simple matter, requiring only a few mouse clicks. Because the procedure is so easy, however, it can be done without thought, and in situations where the stacked column chart is inappropriate.

Figures 4.15a and 4.15b display a side-by-side and a stacked column chart, respectively. One chart is appropriate and one chart is not. The side-by-side columns in Figure 4.15a indicate increasing sales in conjunction with decreasing profits. This is a realistic portrayal of the company, which is becoming less efficient because profits are decreasing as sales are increasing.

The stacked column chart in Figure 4.15b plots the identical numbers. It is deceptive, however, as it implies an optimistic trend whose stacked columns reflect a nonsensical addition. The problem is that although sales and profits are both measured in dollars, they should not be added together because the sum does not represent a meaningful concept.

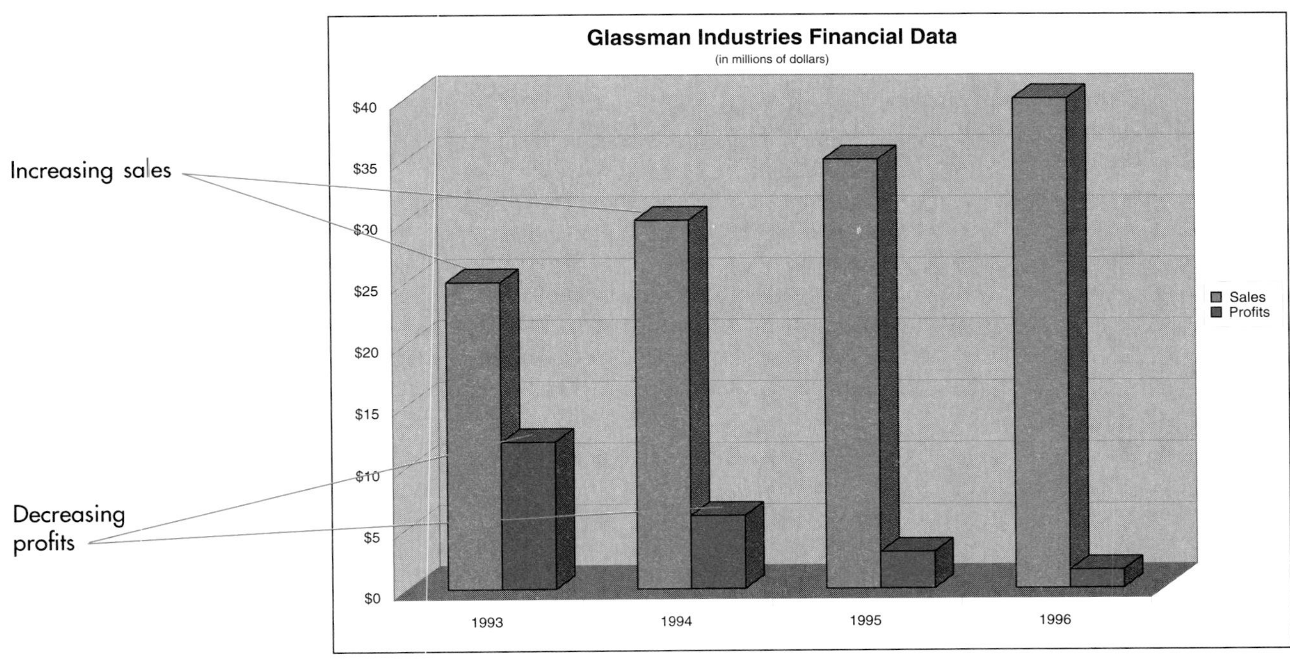

(a) Multiple Bar Chart

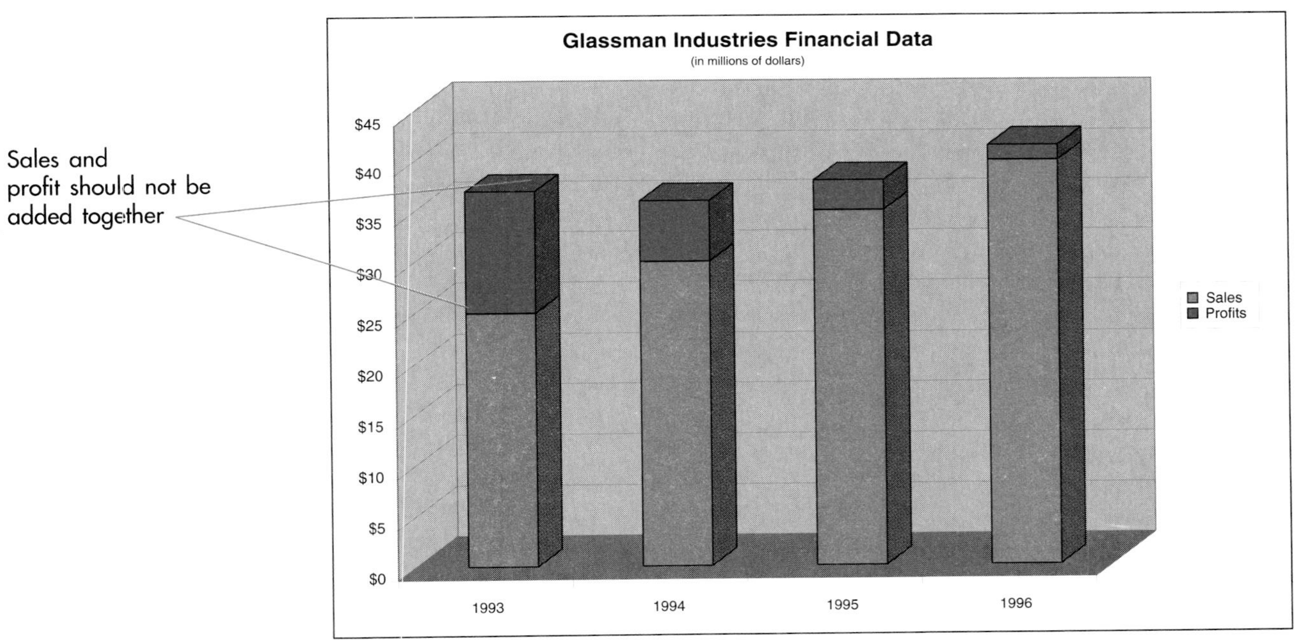

(b) Stacked Bar Chart

FIGURE 4.15 Adding Dissimilar Quantities

SUMMARY

A chart is a graphic representation of data in a worksheet. The type of chart chosen depends on the message to be conveyed. A pie chart is best for proportional relationships. A column or bar chart is used to show actual numbers rather than percentages. A line chart is preferable for time-related data. A combination chart uses two or more chart types when different scales are required for different data series.

The Chart Wizard is the easiest way to create a chart. Once created, a chart can be enhanced with arrows and text boxes found on the Drawing toolbar.

A chart may be embedded in a worksheet or created in a separate chart sheet. An embedded chart may be moved within a worksheet by selecting it and dragging it to its new location. An embedded chart may be sized by selecting it and dragging any of the sizing handles in the desired direction.

Multiple data series may be specified in either rows or columns. If the data is in rows, the first row is assumed to contain the category labels, and the first column is assumed to contain the legend. Conversely, if the data is in columns, the first column is assumed to contain the category labels, and the first row the legend. The Chart Wizard makes it easy to switch from rows to columns and vice versa.

Object Linking and Embedding enables the creation of a compound document containing data (objects) from multiple applications. The essential difference between linking and embedding is whether the object is stored within the compound document (embedding) or in its own file (linking). An embedded object is stored in the compound document, which in turn becomes the only user (client) of that object. A linked object is stored in its own file, and the compound document is one of many potential clients of that object.

It is important that charts are created accurately and that they do not mislead the reader. The difference between dollar sales and unit sales is an important concept, which should be clearly indicated. Stacked column charts should not add dissimilar quantities.

KEY WORDS AND CONCEPTS

Bar chart
Category label
Chart
Chart sheet
Chart toolbar
Chart type
Chart Wizard
Column chart
Combination chart
Common user interface
Compound document
Data point
Data series
Default chart
Docked toolbar
Drawing toolbar
Embedded chart
Embedded object
Embedding
Exploded pie chart
Floating toolbar
Legend
Line chart
Linked object
Linking
Multiple data series
Multitasking
Object
Object Linking and Embedding (OLE)
Pie chart
Sizing handles
Stacked columns
Taskbar
Three-dimensional column chart
Three-dimensional pie chart
X axis
Y axis

Multiple Choice

1. Which type of chart is best to portray proportion or market share?
   (a) Pie chart
   (b) Line
   (c) Column chart
   (d) Combination chart
2. Which of the following is a true statement about the Chart Wizard?
   (a) It is accessed via a button on the Standard toolbar
   (b) It enables you to choose the type of chart you want as well as specify the location for that chart
   (c) It enables you to retrace your steps via the Back command button
   (d) All of the above
3. Which of the following chart types is *not* suitable to display multiple data series?
   (a) Pie chart
   (b) Horizontal bar chart
   (c) Column chart
   (d) All of the above are equally suitable
4. Which of the following is best to display additive information from multiple data series?
   (a) A column chart with the data series stacked one on top of another
   (b) A column chart with the data series side by side
   (c) Both (a) and (b) are equally appropriate
   (d) Neither (a) nor (b) is appropriate
5. A workbook must contain:
   (a) A separate chart sheet for every worksheet
   (b) A separate worksheet for every chart sheet
   (c) Both (a) and (b)
   (d) Neither (a) nor (b)
6. Which of the following is true regarding an embedded chart?
   (a) It can be moved elsewhere within the worksheet
   (b) It can be made larger or smaller
   (c) Both (a) and (b)
   (d) Neither (a) nor (b)
7. Which of the following will produce a shortcut menu?
   (a) Pointing to a workbook tab and clicking the right mouse button
   (b) Pointing to an embedded chart and clicking the right mouse button
   (c) Pointing to a selected cell range and clicking the right mouse button
   (d) All of the above
8. Which of the following is done *prior* to invoking the Chart Wizard?
   (a) The data series are selected
   (b) The location of the embedded chart within the worksheet is specified
   (c) Both (a) and (b)
   (d) Neither (a) nor (b)

9. Which of the following will display sizing handles when selected?
   (a) An embedded chart
   (b) The title of a chart
   (c) A text box or arrow
   (d) All of the above

10. How do you switch between open applications?
    (a) Click the appropriate button on the taskbar
    (b) Use Alt+Tab to cycle through the applications
    (c) Both (a) and (b)
    (d) Neither (a) nor (b)

11. Which of the following is true regarding the compound document (the memo containing the worksheet and chart) that was created in the chapter?
    (a) The compound document contains more than one object
    (b) Excel is the server application and Word for Windows is the client application
    (c) Both (a) and (b)
    (d) Neither (a) nor (b)

12. In order to represent multiple data series on the same chart:
    (a) The data series must be in rows and the rows must be adjacent to one another on the worksheet
    (b) The data series must be in columns and the columns must be adjacent to one another on the worksheet
    (c) The data series may be in rows or columns so long as they are adjacent to one another
    (d) The data series may be in rows or columns with no requirement to be next to one another

13. If multiple data series are selected and rows are specified:
    (a) The first row will be used for the category (X axis) labels
    (b) The first column will be used for the legend
    (c) Both (a) and (b)
    (d) Neither (a) nor (b)

14. If multiple data series are selected and columns are specified:
    (a) The first column will be used for the category (X axis) labels
    (b) The first row will be used for the legend
    (c) Both (a) and (b)
    (d) Neither (a) nor (b)

15. Which of the following is true about the scale on the Y axis in a column chart that plots multiple data series side-by-side versus one that stacks the values one on top of another?
    (a) The scale for the stacked columns will contain larger values than if the columns are plotted side-by-side
    (b) The scale for the side-by-side columns will contain larger values than if the columns are stacked
    (c) The values on the scale will be the same regardless of whether the columns are stacked or side-by-side
    (d) The values on the scale will be different but it is not possible to tell which chart will contain the higher values

ANSWERS

1. a	**6.** c	**11.** c
2. d	**7.** d	**12.** d
3. a	**8.** a	**13.** c
4. a	**9.** d	**14.** c
5. d	**10.** c	**15.** a

PRACTICE WITH EXCEL 97

1. The worksheet in Figure 4.16 is to be used as the basis of several charts that analyze the sales data for the chain of four Michael Moldof clothing boutiques. The worksheet is found on the data disk in the *Chapter 4 Practice 1 Workbook.* Use the worksheet to develop the following charts:

a. A pie chart showing the percentage of total sales attributed to each store.

b. A column chart showing the total sales for each store.

c. A stacked column chart showing total sales for each store, broken down by clothing category.

d. A stacked column chart showing total dollars for each clothing category, broken down by store.

e. Create each chart in its own chart sheet. Rename the various chart sheets to reflect the charts they contain.

f. Title each chart appropriately and enhance each chart as you see fit.

g. Print the entire workbook (the worksheet and all four chart sheets).

h. Add a title page with your name and date, then submit the completed assignment to your instructor.

	A	B	C	D	E	F
1	Michael Moldof Men's Boutique					
2	January Sales					
3						
4		Store 1	Store 2	Store 3	Store 4	Total
5	*Slacks*	$25,000	$28,750	$21,500	$9,400	$84,650
6	*Shirts*	$43,000	$49,450	$36,900	$46,000	$175,350
7	*Underwear*	$18,000	$20,700	$15,500	$21,000	$75,200
8	*Accessories*	$7,000	$8,050	$8,000	$4,000	$27,050
9						
10	Total	$93,000	$106,950	$81,900	$80,400	$362,250

FIGURE 4.16 Spreadsheet for Practice Exercise 1

2. The worksheet in Figure 4.17 is to be used by the corporate marketing manager in a presentation in which she describes sales over the past four years. The manager has placed the worksheet on the data disk (in the *Chapter 4 Practice 2 Workbook*) and would like you, her student intern, to do all of the following:

a. Format the worksheet attractively so that it can be used as part of the presentation. Include your name somewhere in the worksheet.

	A	B	C	D	E	F
1	Unique Boutiques					
2	Sales for 1993-1996					
3						
4	Store	1993	1994	1995	1996	Totals
5	Miami	1500000	2750000	3000000	3250000	10500000
6	London	4300000	5500000	6700000	13000000	29500000
7	Paris	2200000	1800000	1400000	1000000	6400000
8	Rome	2000000	3000000	4000000	5000000	14000000
9	Totals	10000000	13050000	15100000	22250000	60400000

FIGURE 4.17 Spreadsheet for Practice Exercise 2

b. Create any chart(s) you think appropriate to emphasize the successful performance enjoyed by the London office.

c. Use the same data and chart type(s) as in part (a) but modify the title (and/or callouts) to emphasize the disappointing performance of the Paris office.

d. Print the worksheet together with all charts and submit them to your instructor. Be sure to title all charts appropriately and to use the text and arrow tools to add the required emphasis.

3. The worksheet in Figure 4.18 is to be used as the basis for several charts depicting information on hotel capacities. Each of the charts is to be created in its own chart sheet within the *Chapter 4 Practice 3 Workbook* on the data disk. We describe the message we want to convey, but it is up to you to determine the appropriate chart and associated data range(s). Accordingly, you are to create a chart that:

a. Compares the total capacity of the individual hotels to one another.

b. Shows the percent of total capacity for each hotel.

c. Compares the number of standard and deluxe rooms for all hotels, with the number of standard and deluxe rooms side-by-side for each hotel.

d. Compares the standard and deluxe room rates for all hotels, with the two different rates side-by-side for each hotel.

e. Add your name to the worksheet as the Hotel Manager, then print the complete workbook, which will consist of the original worksheet plus the four chart sheets you created.

	A	B	C	D	E	F
1	**Hotel Capacities and Room Rates**					
2						
3	***Hotel***	***No. of Standard Rooms***	***Standard Rate***	***No. of Deluxe Rooms***	***Deluxe Rate***	***Total Number of Rooms***
4	***Holiday Inn***	300	100	100	150	400
5	***Hyatt***	225	120	50	175	275
6	***Ramada Inn***	150	115	35	190	185
7	***Sheraton***	175	95	25	150	200
8	***Marriott***	325	100	100	175	425
9	***Hilton***	250	80	45	120	295
10	***Best Western***	150	75	25	125	175
11	***Days Inn***	100	50	15	100	115

FIGURE 4.18 Spreadsheet for Practice Exercise 3

4. A partially completed version of the worksheet in Figure 4.19 can be found on the data disk in the file *Chapter 4 Practice 4.* Open the workbook and make all necessary entries so that your worksheet matches the one in Figure 4.19. Next, create a memo to your instructor containing the worksheet and a chart that plots the sales data in columns to emphasize the contribution of each salesperson. Use any wording you think is appropriate for the memo. Print the completed memo, add your name, and submit it to your instructor as proof you did this exercise.

	A	B	C	D	E	F
1	Ralph Cordell Sporting Goods					
2	Quarterly Sales Report					
3						
4	**Salesperson**	**1st Qtr**	**2nd Qtr**	**3rd Qtr**	**4th Qtr**	**Total**
5	Powell	$50,000	$55,000	$62,500	$85,400	$252,900
6	Blaney	$34,000	$48,500	$62,000	$62,000	$206,500
7	Rego	$49,000	$44,000	$42,500	$41,000	$176,500
8	**Total**	$133,000	$147,500	$167,000	$188,400	$635,900

FIGURE 4.19 Worksheet for Practice Exercise 4

5. Object Linking and Embedding: The compound document in Figure 4.20 contains a memo and combination chart. (The worksheet is contained in the *Chapter 4 Practice 5 Workbook*. The text of the memo is in the *Chapter 4 Practice 5 Memo,* which exists as a Word document in the Exploring Excel folder on the data disk.) You are to complete the compound document and submit it to your instructor by completing the following steps:
   a. Create a letterhead for the memo containing your name, address, phone number, and any other information you deem appropriate.
   b. Create the combination chart that appears in the memo. Select the data for the Chart Wizard in the usual fashion. You must, however, specify the custom chart type (Line–Column on 2 Axis) as opposed to a standard line or column chart. (Click the Custom Types tab in step 1 of the Chart Wizard.)
   c. Link the chart to the memo.
   d. Print the compound document and submit it to your instructor.

6. Create the compound document in Figure 4.21 based on the partially completed worksheet in *Chapter 4 Practice 6.* You need to enter the text of the memo yourself, and in addition, create an interesting letterhead using Microsoft WordArt. You need not duplicate our letterhead exactly. This exercise gives you the opportunity to practice a variety of skills.

CASE STUDIES

University Enrollments

Your assistantship has placed you in the Provost's office, where you are to help create a presentation for the Board of Trustees. The Provost is expected to make recommendations to the Board regarding the expansion of some programs and the reduction of others. You are expected to help the Provost by developing a series of charts to illustrate enrollment trends. The Provost has created the *Student Enrollments workbook* on the data disk, which contains summary data.

Steven Stocks

Financial Investments • 100 Century Tower • New York, NY 10020

To: Carlos Rosell

From: Steven Stocks

Subject: Status Report on National Widgets

I have uncovered some information that I feel is important to the overall health of your investment portfolio. The graph below clearly shows that while revenues for National Widgets have steadily increased since 1992, profits have steadily decreased. In addition, the stock price is continuing to decline. Although at one time I felt that a turnaround was imminent, I am no longer so optimistic and am advising you to cut your losses and sell your National Widgets stock as soon as possible.

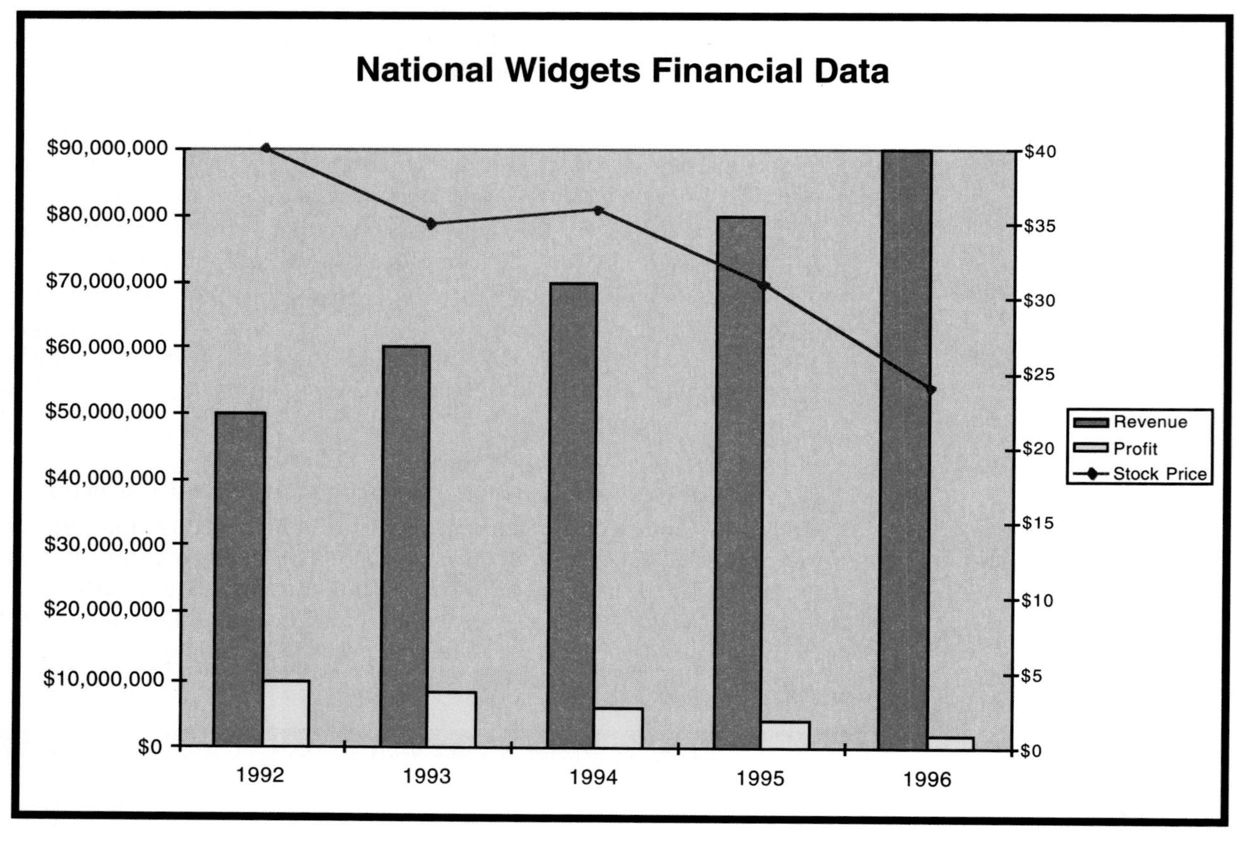

FIGURE 4.20 Compound Document for Practice Exercise 5

Office of Residential Living

University of Miami • P.O. Box 248904 • Coral Gables, FL 33124

January 10, 1998

Mr. Jeffrey Redmond, President
Dynamic Dining Services
4329 Palmetto Lane
Miami, FL 33157

Dear Jeff,

As per our conversation, occupancy is projected to be back up from last year. I have enclosed a spreadsheet and chart that show the total enrollment for the past four school years. Please realize, however, that the 1997-1998 figures are projections, as the Spring 1998 numbers are still incomplete. The final 1997-1998 numbers should be confirmed within the next two weeks. I hope that this helps with your planning. If you need further information, please contact me at the above address.

Dorm Occupancy

	94-95	95-96	96-97	97-98
Beatty	330	285	270	250
Broward	620	580	620	565
Graham	450	397	352	420
Rawlings	435	470	295	372
Tolbert	550	554	524	635
Totals	2385	2286	2061	2242

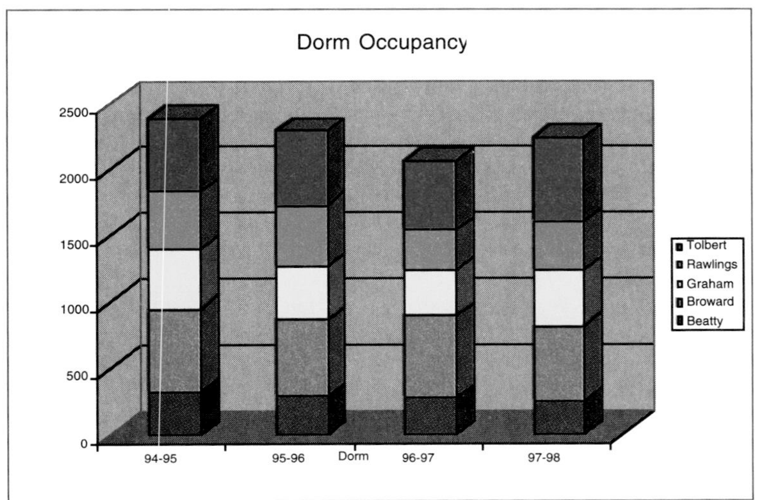

FIGURE 4.21 Compound Document for Practice Exercise 6

The Federal Budget

The National debt is staggering—in excess of $5 trillion, more than $1 trillion of which has been added under President Clinton. The per capita share is almost $20,000 for every man, woman, and child in the United States. The annual budget is approximately $1.5 trillion, with the deficit in the neighborhood of $150 billion. Medicare, defense, and interest on the debt itself are the largest expenditures and consume approximately 35%, 24%, and 14%, respectively. Personal income taxes and Social Security (including Medicare) taxes account for approximately 36% and 31% of the government's income.

Use the Internet to obtain exact figures for the current year, then create the appropriate charts to reflect the government's distribution of income and expenditures. Do some additional research and obtain data on the budget, the deficit, and the national debt for the years 1945, 1967, and 1980. The numbers may surprise you. For example, how does the interest expense for the current year compare to the total budget in 1967 (at the height of the Viet Nam War)? To the total budget in 1945 (at the end of World War II)?

The Annual Report

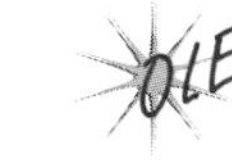

Corporate America spends a small fortune to produce its annual reports, which are readily available to the public at large. Choose any company and obtain a copy of its most recent annual report. Consolidate the information in the company's report to produce a two-page document of your own. Your report should include a description of the company's progress in the last year, a worksheet with any data you deem relevant, and at least two charts in support of the worksheet or written material. Use Microsoft Word in addition to the worksheet to present the information in an attractive manner.

Computer Mapping

Your boss has asked you to look into computer mapping in an effort to better analyze sales data for your organization. She suggested you use the online help facility to explore the Data Map feature within Excel, which enables you to create color-coded maps from columns of numerical data. You mentioned this assignment to a colleague who suggested that you open the *Mapstats workbook* that is installed with Excel to see the sample maps and demographic data included with Excel. You have two days to learn the potential for computer mapping. Your boss expects at least a three-page written report with real examples.

The Census Bureau

Use your favorite search engine to locate the home page of the United States Census Bureau, then download one or more series of population statistics of interest to you. Use the data to plot one or more charts that describe the population growth of the United States. There is an abundance of information available and you are free to choose any statistics you deem relevant.

A

APPENDIX A: TOOLBARS

OVERVIEW

Microsoft Excel has 20 predefined toolbars that provide access to commonly used commands. The toolbars are displayed in Figure A.1 and are listed here for convenience. They are the Standard, Formatting, Auditing, Chart, Circular Reference, Control Toolbox, Drawing, Exit Design Mode, External Data, Forms, Full Screen, Picture, Pivot Table, Reviewing, Shadow Settings, Stop Recording, Visual Basic, Web, WordArt, and 3-D Settings toolbars.

The Standard and Formatting toolbars are displayed by default and appear immediately below the menu bar. The other predefined toolbars are displayed (hidden) at the discretion of the user, and in some cases are displayed automatically when their corresponding features are in use (e.g., the Chart toolbar and the Pivot Table toolbar).

The buttons on the toolbars are intended to indicate their functions. Clicking the Printer button (the fourth button from the left on the Standard toolbar), for example, executes the Print command. If you are unsure of the purpose of any toolbar button, point to it, and a ScreenTip will appear that displays its name.

You can display multiple toolbars at one time, move them to new locations on the screen, customize their appearance.

- To display or hide a toolbar, pull down the View menu and click the Toolbars command. Select (deselect) the toolbar(s) that you want to display (hide). The selected toolbar(s) will be displayed in the same position as when last displayed. You may also point to any toolbar and click with the right mouse button to bring up a shortcut menu, after which you can select the toolbar to be displayed (hidden).
- To change the size of the buttons or suppress the display of the ScreenTips, pull down the View menu, click Toolbars, and click Customize to display the Customize dialog box. If necessary, click the Options tab, then select (deselect) the appropriate check box.

- Toolbars are either docked (along the edge of the window) or floating (in their own window). A toolbar moved to the edge of the window will dock along that edge. A toolbar moved anywhere else in the window will float in its own window. Docked toolbars are one tool wide (high), whereas floating toolbars can be resized by clicking and dragging a border or corner as you would with any window.
  - To move a docked toolbar, click anywhere in the gray background area and drag the toolbar to its new location. You can also click and drag the move handle (the pair of parallel lines) at the left of the toolbar.
  - To move a floating toolbar, drag its title bar to its new location.
- To customize one or more toolbars, display the toolbar(s) on the screen. Then pull down the View menu, click Toolbars, click Customize to display the Customize dialog box, then select the Toolbars tab. Alternatively, you can click on any toolbar with the right mouse button, select Customize from the shortcut menu, and then click the Toolbars tab.
  - To move a button, drag the button to its new location on that toolbar or any other displayed toolbar.
  - To copy a button, press the Ctrl key as you drag the button to its new location on that toolbar or any other displayed toolbar.
  - To delete a button, drag the button off the toolbar and release the mouse button.
  - To add a button, click the Commands tab in the Customize dialog box, select the category from the Categories list box that contains the button you want to add, then drag the button to the desired location on the toolbar. (To see a description of a tool's function before adding it to a toolbar, select the tool, then click the Description command button.)
  - To restore a predefined toolbar to its default appearance, pull down the View menu, click Toolbars, click Customize, click the Toolbars tab, select (highlight) the desired toolbar, and click the Reset command button.
- Buttons can also be moved, copied, or deleted without displaying the Customize dialog box.
  - To move a button, press the Alt key as you drag the button to the new location.
  - To copy a button, press the Alt and Ctrl keys as you drag the button to the new location.
  - To delete a button, press the Alt key as you drag the button off the toolbar.
- To create your own toolbar, pull down the View menu, click Toolbars, click Customize, click the Toolbars tab, then click the New command button. Alternatively, you can click on any toolbar with the right mouse button, select Customize from the shortcut menu, click the Toolbars tab, and then click the New command button.
  - Enter a name for the toolbar in the dialog box that follows. The name can be any length and can contain spaces.
  - The new toolbar will appear on the screen. Initially it will be big enough to hold only one button. Add, move, and delete buttons following the same procedures as outlined above. The toolbar will automatically size itself as new buttons are added and deleted.
  - To delete a custom toolbar, pull down the View menu, click Toolbars, click Customize, and click the Toolbars tab. *Verify that the custom toolbar to be deleted is the only one selected (highlighted).* Click the Delete command button. Click Yes to confirm the deletion. (Note that a predefined toolbar cannot be deleted.)

Standard Toolbar

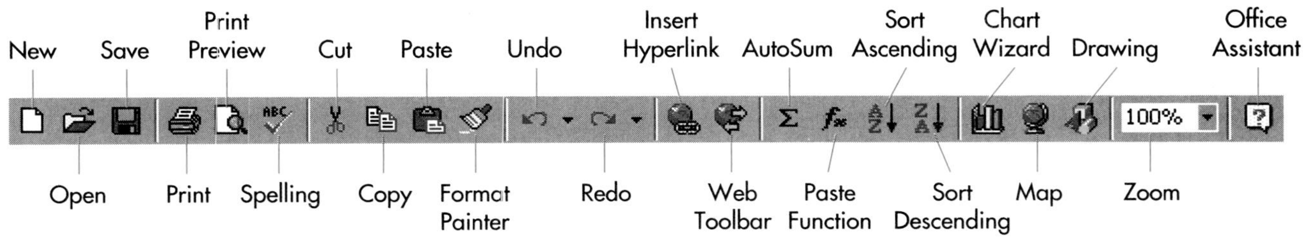

Formatting Toolbar

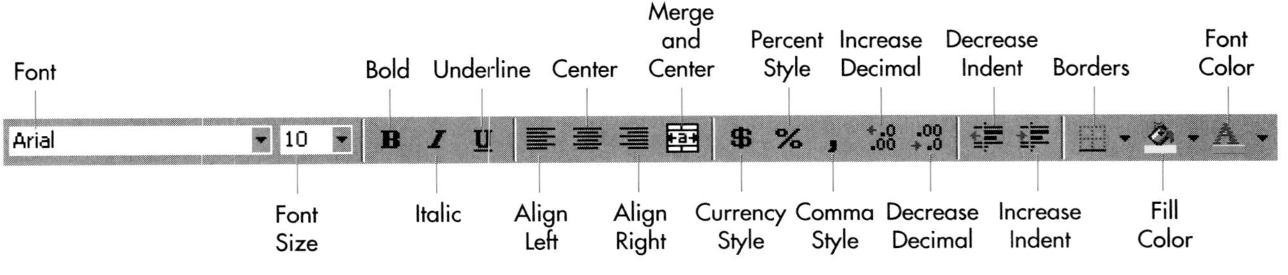

Auditing Toolbar

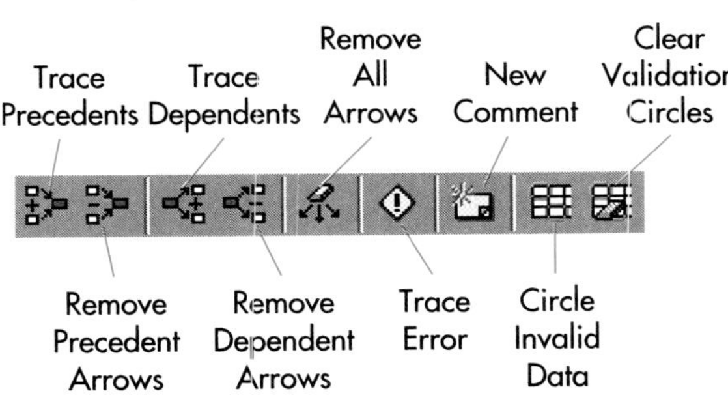

Chart Toolbar

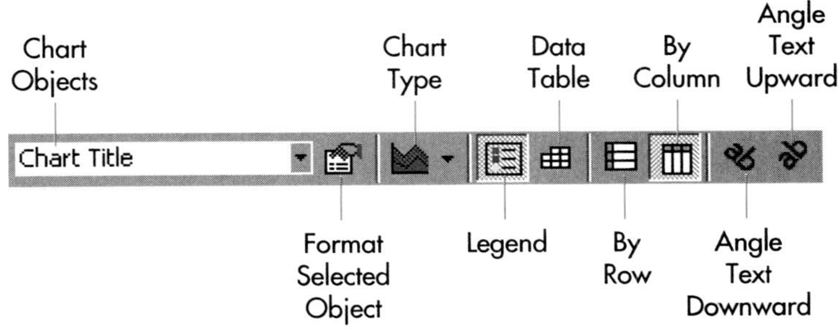

Circular Reference

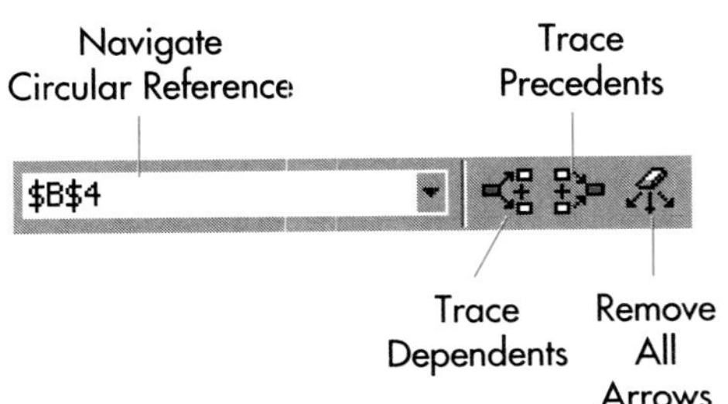

Control Toolbox Toolbar

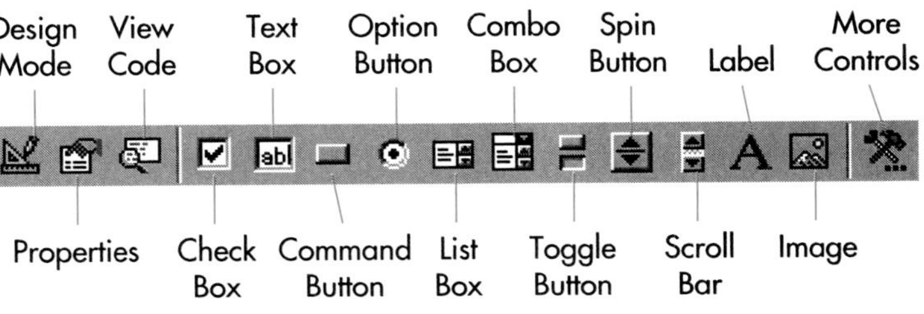

FIGURE A.1 Toolbars

Drawing Toolbar

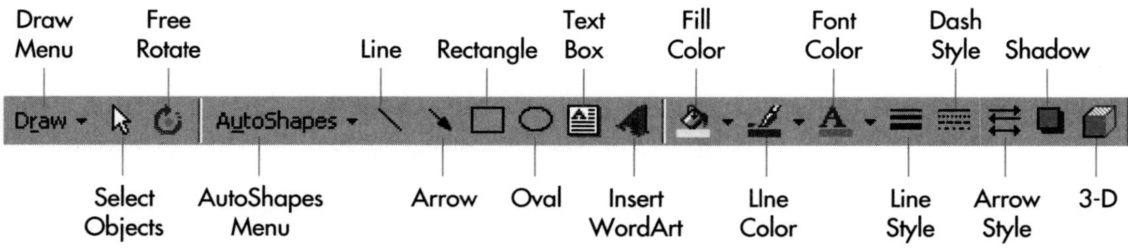

Exit Design Mode Toolbar

Design Mode

External Data Toolbar

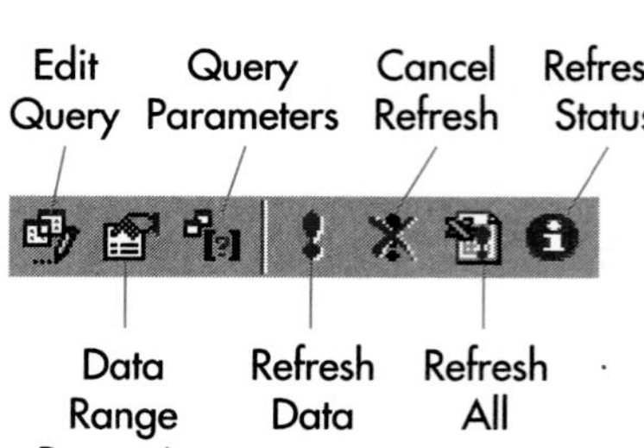

Forms Toolbar

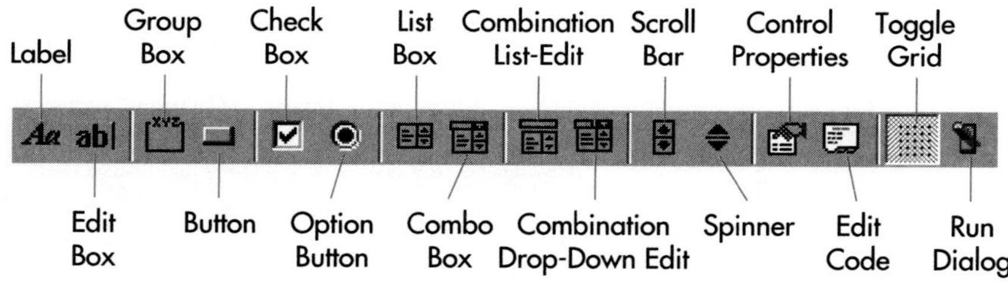

Full Screen Toolbar

Toggle Full-Screen View

Full Screen

Picture Toolbar

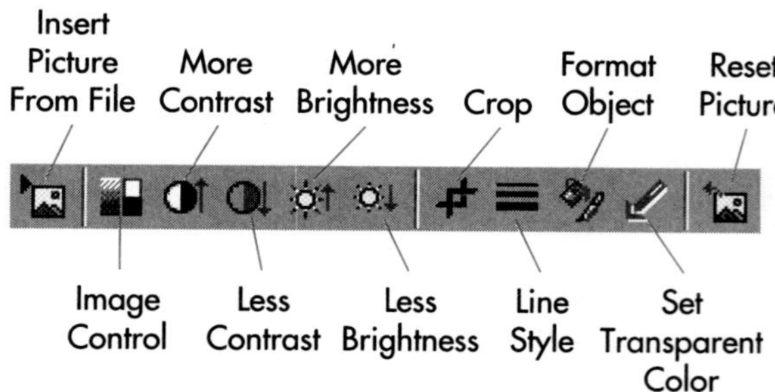

FIGURE A.1 Toolbars (continued)

Pivot Table Toolbar

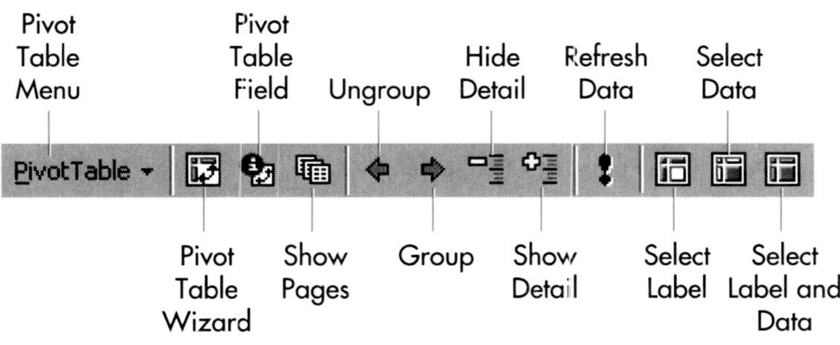

Shadow Settings Toolbar

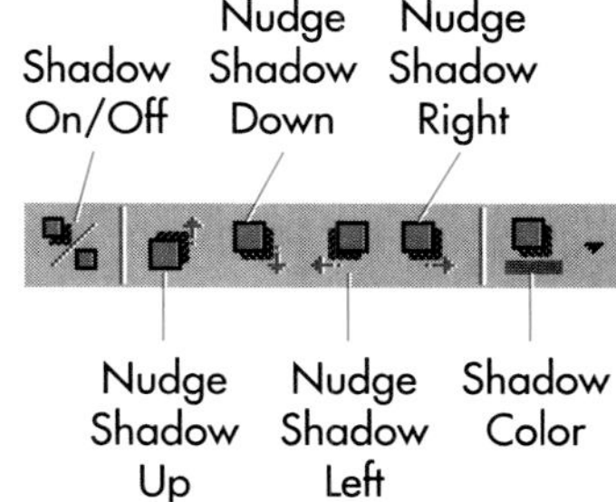

Reviewing Toolbar

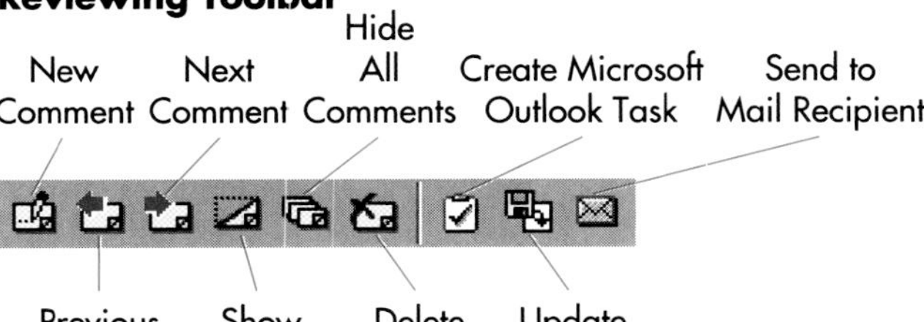

Stop Recording Toolbar

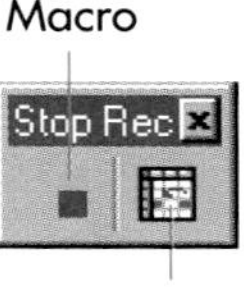

Visual Basic Toolbar

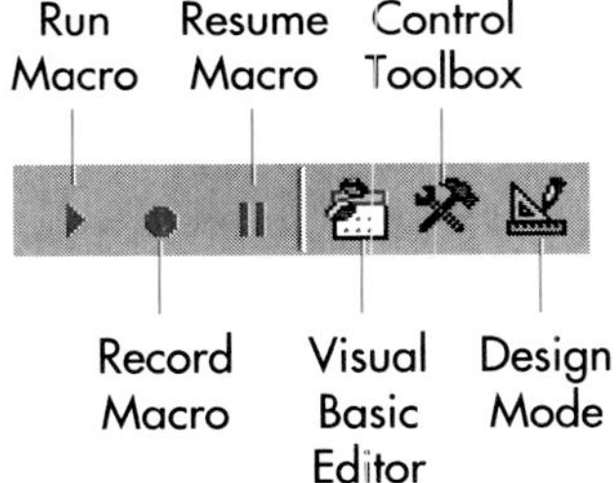

WordArt Toolbar

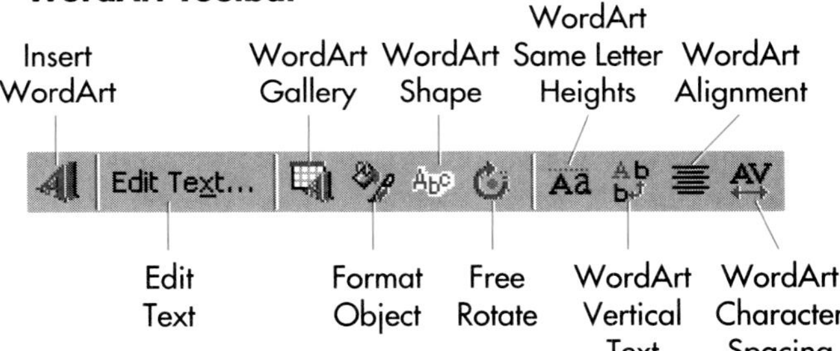

Web Toolbar

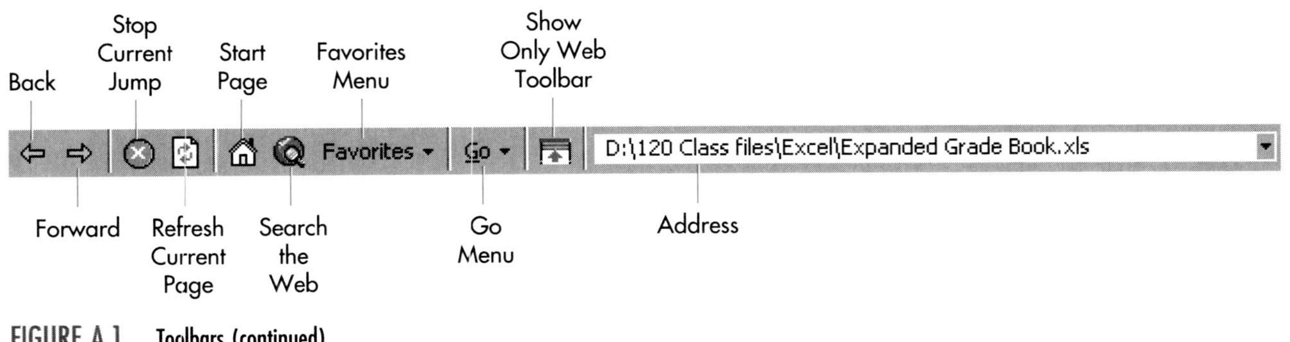

FIGURE A.1 Toolbars (continued)

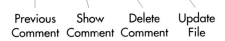

3-D Settings Toolbar

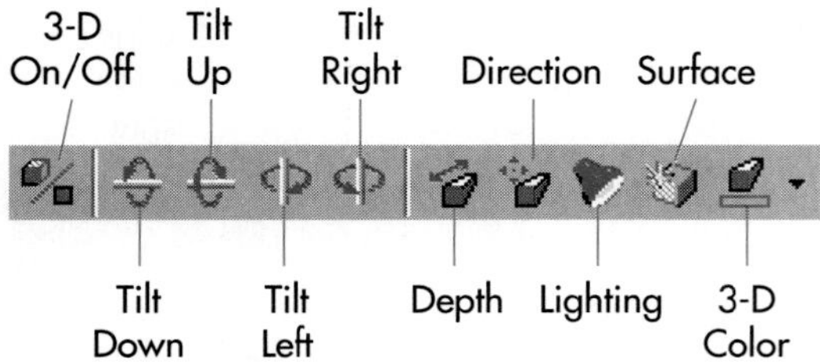

FIGURE A.1 Toolbars (continued)

7

INTRODUCTION TO MICROSOFT ACCESS: WHAT IS A DATABASE?

OBJECTIVES

After reading this chapter you will be able to:

1. Define the terms *field, record, table,* and *database.*
2. Start Microsoft Access; describe the Database window and the objects in an Access database.
3. Add, edit, and delete records within a table; use the Find command to locate a specific record.
4. Describe the record selector; explain when changes are saved to a table.
5. Explain the importance of data validation in table maintenance.
6. Describe a relational database; distinguish between a one-to-many and a many-to-many relationship.

OVERVIEW

All businesses and organizations maintain data of one kind or another. Companies store data about their employees. Schools and universities store data about their students and faculties. Magazines and newspapers store data about their subscribers. The list goes on and on, and while each of these examples refers to different types of data, they all operate under the same basic principles of database management.

This chapter provides a broad-based introduction to database management through the example of a college bookstore. We begin by showing how the mechanics of manual record keeping can be extended to a computerized system. We discuss the basic operations in maintaining data and stress the importance of data validation.

The chapter also introduces you to Microsoft Access, the fourth major application in the Microsoft Office Professional suite. We describe the objects within an Access database and show you how to add, edit, and delete records in an Access table. We also explain how the real power of Access is derived from a database with multiple tables that are related to one another.

The hands-on exercises in the chapter enable you to apply all of the material at the computer, and are indispensable to the learn-by-doing philosophy we follow throughout the text. As you do the exercises, you may recognize many commands from other Windows applications, all of which share a common user interface and consistent command structure.

CASE STUDY: THE COLLEGE BOOKSTORE

Imagine, if you will, that you are the manager of a college bookstore and that you maintain data for every book in the store. Accordingly, you have recorded the specifics of each book (the title, author, publisher, price, and so on) in a manila folder, and have stored the folders in one drawer of a file cabinet.

One of your major responsibilities is to order books at the beginning of each semester, which in turn requires you to contact the various publishers. You have found it convenient, therefore, to create a second set of folders with data about each publisher such as the publisher's phone number, address, discount policy, and so on. You also found it necessary to create a third set of folders with data about each order such as when the order was placed, the status of the order, which books were ordered, how many copies, and so on.

Normal business operations will require you to make repeated trips to the filing cabinet to maintain the accuracy of the data and keep it up to date. You will have to create a new folder whenever a new book is received, whenever you contract with a new publisher, or whenever you place a new order. Each of these folders must be placed in the proper drawer in the filing cabinet. In similar fashion, you will have to modify the data in an existing folder to reflect changes that occur, such as an increase in the price of a book, a change in a publisher's address, or an update in the status of an order. And, lastly, you will need to remove the folder of any book that is no longer carried by the bookstore, or of any publisher with whom you no longer have contact, or of any order that was canceled.

The preceding discussion describes the bookstore of 40 years ago—before the advent of computers and computerized databases. The bookstore manager of today needs the same information as his or her predecessor. Today's manager, however, has the information readily available, at the touch of a key or the click of a mouse, through the miracle of modern technology. The concepts are identical in both the manual and computerized systems.

You can think of the file cabinet, which contains the various sets of folders, as a ***database.*** Each set of folders in the file cabinet corresponds to a ***table*** within the database. In our example the bookstore database consists of three separate tables—for books, publishers, and orders. Each table, in turn, consists of multiple ***records,*** corresponding to the folders in the file cabinet. The Books table, for example, contains a record for every book title in the store. The Publishers table has a record for each publisher, just as the Orders table has a record for each order.

Each fact (or data element) that is stored within a record is called a ***field.*** In our example each book record consists of six fields—ISBN (a unique identifying number for the book), title, author, year of publication, price, and publisher. The table is constructed in such a way that every record has the same fields in the same order. In similar fashion, every record in the Publishers table will have the same fields for each publisher, just as every record in the Orders table has the same fields for each order. This terminology (field, record, table, and database) is extremely important and will be used throughout the text.

INTRODUCTION TO MICROSOFT ACCESS

Microsoft Access, the fourth major application in the Microsoft Office, is used to create and manage a database such as the one for the college bookstore. Consider now Figure 1.1, which shows how Microsoft Access appears on the desktop. Our discussion assumes a basic familiarity with Windows 95 and the user interface that is common to all Windows applications. You should recognize, therefore, that the desktop in Figure 1.1 has two open windows—an application window for Microsoft Access and a document (database) window for the database that is currently open.

Each window has its own title bar and Minimize, Maximize (or Restore), and Close buttons. The title bar in the application window contains the name of the application (Microsoft Access). The title bar in the document (database) window contains the name of the database that is currently open (Bookstore). The application window for Access has been maximized to take up the entire desktop, and hence the Restore button is visible. The database window has not been maximized.

A menu bar appears immediately below the application title bar. A toolbar (similar to those in other Office applications) appears below the menu bar and offers alternative ways to execute common commands. The Windows 95 taskbar appears at the bottom of the screen and shows the open applications.

The Database Window

The ***Database window*** displays the various objects in an Access database. There are six types of objects—tables, queries, forms, reports, macros, and modules. Every database must contain at least one table, and it may contain any or all (or

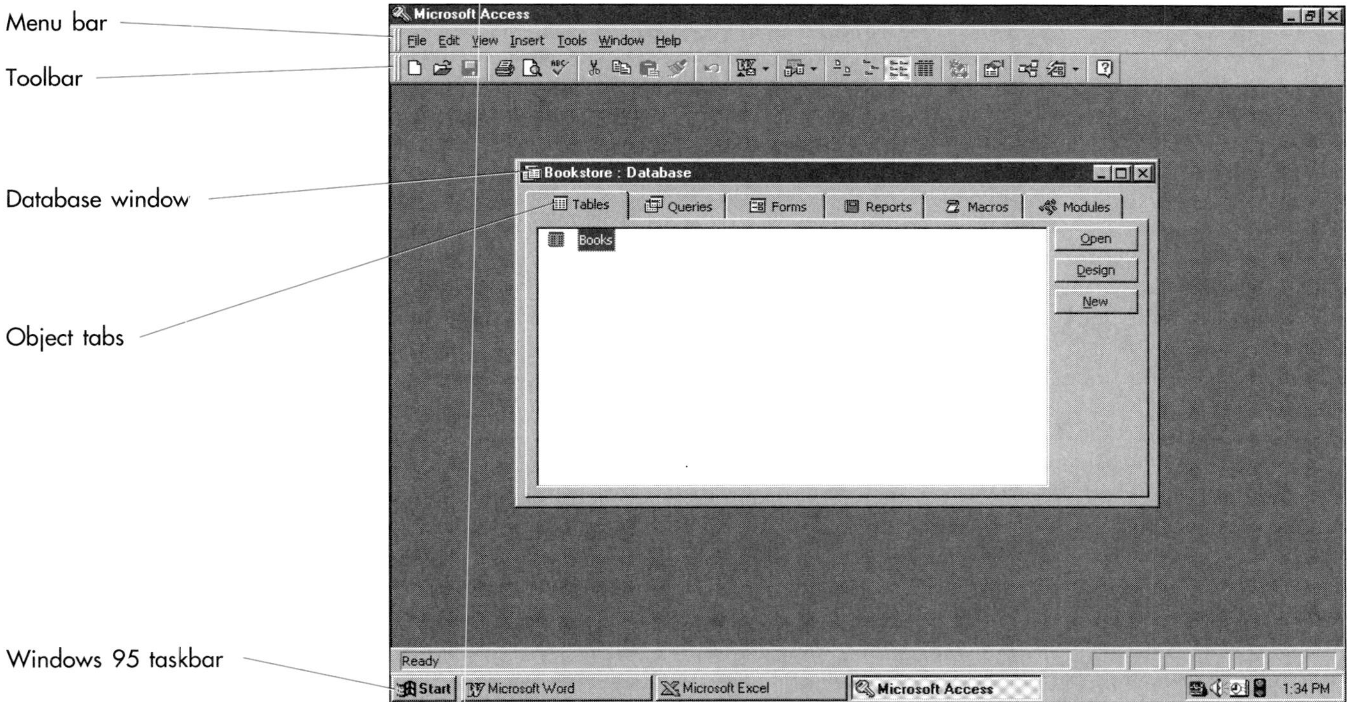

FIGURE 1.1 The Database Window

none) of the other objects. Each object type is accessed through the appropriate tab within the Database window. In this chapter we concentrate on tables, but we briefly describe the other types of objects as a preview of what you will learn as you read our book.

- A ***table*** stores data about an entity (a person, place, or thing) and is the basic element in any database. A table is made up of records, which in turn are made up of fields. It is columnar in appearance, with each record in a separate row of the table and each field in a separate column.
- A ***form*** provides a more convenient and attractive way to enter, display, and/or print the data in a table. Forms are discussed in Chapter 2.
- A ***query*** answers a question about the database. The most common type of query specifies a set of criteria, then searches the database to retrieve the records that satisfy the criteria. Queries are introduced in Chapter 3.
- A ***report*** presents the data in a table or query in attractive fashion on the printed page. Reports are described in Chapter 3.
- A ***macro*** is analogous to a computer program and consists of commands that are executed automatically one after the other. Macros are used to automate the performance of any repetitive task.
- A ***module*** provides a greater degree of automation through programming in Access Basic. Modules are beyond the scope of this text.

ONE FILE HOLDS ALL

All of the objects in an Access database (tables, forms, queries, reports, macros, and modules) are stored in a single file on disk. The database itself is opened through the Open command in the File menu or by clicking the Open button on the Database toolbar. The individual objects within a database are opened through the database window.

Tables

A table (or set of tables) is the heart of any database, as it contains the actual data. In Access a table is displayed in one of two views—the Design view or the Datasheet view. The ***Design view*** is used to define the table initially and to specify the fields it will contain. It is also used to modify the table definition if changes are subsequently necessary. The Design view is discussed in detail in Chapter 2. The ***Datasheet view***—the view you use to add, edit, or delete records—is the view on which we focus in this chapter.

Figure 1.2 shows the Datasheet view for the Books table in our bookstore. The first row in the table contains the ***field names.*** Each additional row contains a record (the data for a specific book). Each column represents a field (one fact about a book). Every record in the table contains the same fields in the same order: ISBN Number, Title, Author, Year, List Price, and Publisher.

The status bar at the bottom of Figure 1.2a indicates that there are five records in the table and that you are positioned on the first record. This is the record you are working on and is known as the ***current record.*** (You can work on only one record at a time.) There is a ***record selector symbol*** (either a triangle or a pencil) next to the current record to indicate its status.

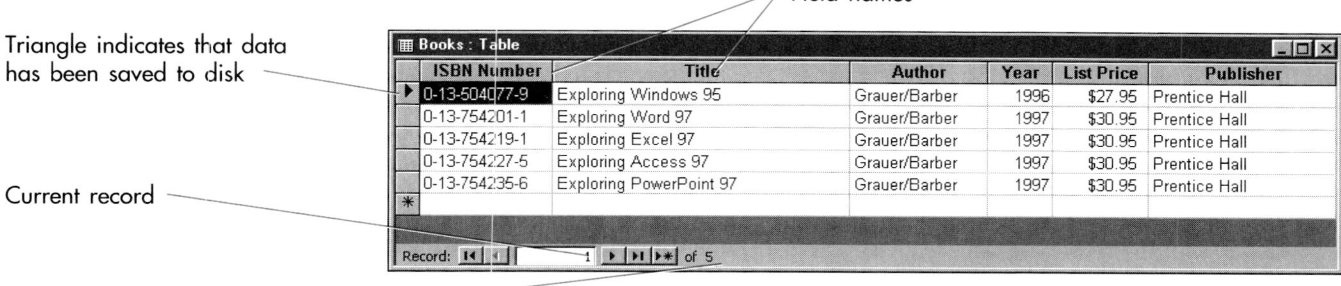

ISBN Number	Title	Author	Year	List Price	Publisher
0-13-504077-9	Exploring Windows 95	Grauer/Barber	1996	$27.95	Prentice Hall
0-13-754201-1	Exploring Word 97	Grauer/Barber	1997	$30.95	Prentice Hall
0-13-754219-1	Exploring Excel 97	Grauer/Barber	1997	$30.95	Prentice Hall
0-13-754227-5	Exploring Access 97	Grauer/Barber	1997	$30.95	Prentice Hall
0-13-754235-6	Exploring PowerPoint 97	Grauer/Barber	1997	$30.95	Prentice Hall

(a) All Data Has Been Saved

Pencil indicates that data has not yet been saved to disk

Asterisk represents the blank record at end of every table

Insertion point indicates that data is being entered

Books : Table

ISBN Number	Title	Author	Year	List Price	Publisher
0-13-504077-9	Exploring Windows 95	Grauer/Barber	1996	$27.95	Prentice Hall
0-13-754201-1	Exploring Word 97	Grauer/Barber	1997	$30.95	Prentice Hall
0-13-754219-1	Exploring Excel 97	Grauer/Barber	1997	$30.95	Prentice Hall
0-13-754227-5	Exploring Access 97	Grauer/Barber	1997	$30.95	Prentice Hall
0-13-754235-6	Exploring PowerPoint 97	Grauer/Barber	1997	$30.95	Prentice Hall
0-13-754243-7	Exploring Microsoft Office 97 Volume I	Grauer/Barber	1997	$45.00	Prentice

Record: 6 of 6

(b) During Data Entry

FIGURE 1.2 Tables

A ***triangle*** indicates that the record has been saved to disk. A ***pencil*** indicates that you are working on the record and that the changes have not yet been saved. As soon as you move to the next record, however, the pencil changes to a triangle to indicate that the record on which you were working has been saved. (Access, unlike other Office applications, automatically saves changes made to a record without your having to execute the Save command.) An ***asterisk*** appears next to the blank record at the end of every table.

Figure 1.2a shows the table as it would appear immediately after you opened it. The first field in the first record is selected (highlighted), and anything you type at this point will replace the selected data. (This is the same convention as in any other Windows application.) The triangle next to the current record (record 1) indicates that changes have not yet been made. An asterisk appears as the record selector symbol next to the blank record at the end of the table. The blank record is used to add a record to the table and is not counted in determining the number of records in the table.

Figure 1.2b shows the table as you are in the process of entering data for a new record at the end of the table. The current record is now record 6. The ***insertion point*** (a flashing vertical bar) appears at the point where text is being entered. The record selector for the current record is a pencil, indicating that the record has not yet been saved. The asterisk has moved to the blank record at the end of the table, which now contains one more record than the table in Figure 1.2a.

Note, too, that each table in a database must have a field (or combination of fields) known as the ***primary key,*** which is unique for every record in the table. The ISBN (International Standard Book Number) is the primary key in our example, and it ensures that each record in the Books table is different from every other record. (Other fields may also have a unique value for every record, but only one field is designated as the primary key.)

HANDS-ON EXERCISE 1

Introduction to Microsoft Access

Objective: To open an existing database; to add a record to a table within the database. Use Figure 1.3 as a guide in the exercise.

STEP 1: Welcome to Windows

- Turn on the computer and all of its peripherals. The floppy drive should be empty prior to starting your machine. This ensures that the system starts by reading from the hard disk, which contains the Windows files, as opposed to a floppy disk, which does not.
- Your system will take a minute or so to get started, after which you should see the desktop in Figure 1.3a. Do not be concerned if the appearance of your desktop is different from ours. If necessary, click the **Close button** to close the Welcome window.

TAKE THE WINDOWS 95 TOUR

Windows 95 greets you with a Welcome window that contains a command button to take you on a 10-minute tour. Click the command button and enjoy the show. If you do not see the Welcome window, click the Start button, click Run, type WELCOME in the Open text box, and press enter. Windows 97 was not available when we went to press, but we expect it to have a similar option.

(a) Welcome to Windows (step 1)

FIGURE 1.3 Hands-on Exercise 1

STEP 2: Obtain the Practice Files:

- ➤ We have created a series of practice files for you to use throughout the text. Your instructor will make these files available to you in a variety of ways:
  - You can download the files from our Web site if you have access to the Internet and World Wide Web (see boxed tip).
  - The files may be on a network drive, in which case you use the Windows Explorer to copy the files from the network to a floppy disk.
  - There may be an actual "data disk" that you are to check out from the lab in order to use the Copy Disk command to duplicate the disk.
- ➤ Check with your instructor for additional information.

DOWNLOAD THE PRACTICE FILES

You can download the practice files for any book in the *Exploring Windows* series from Bob Grauer's home page (www.bus.miami.edu/~rgrauer). Use any Web browser to get to Bob's page, then click the link to the *Exploring Windows* series where you choose the appropriate book and download the file. Be sure to read the associated "read me" file, which provides additional information about downloading the file.

STEP 3: Start Microsoft Access

- ➤ Click the **Start button** to display the Start menu. Click (or point to) the **Programs menu,** then click **Microsoft Access** to start the program. Close the Office Assistant if it appears. (The Office Assistant is described in the next hands-on exercise.)
- ➤ You should see the Microsoft Access dialog box with the option button to **Open an Existing Database** already selected. Click **More Files,** then click **OK** to display the Open dialog box in Figure 1.3b.
- ➤ Click the **Details button** to change to the Details view. Click and drag the vertical border between columns to increase (or decrease) the size of a column.
- ➤ Click the **drop-down arrow** on the Look In list box. Click the appropriate drive (drive C is recommended rather than drive A), depending on the location of your data. Double click the **Exploring Access folder.**
- ➤ Click the **down scroll arrow** until you can click the **Bookstore database.** Click the **Open command button** to open the database.

WORK ON DRIVE C

Even in a lab setting it is preferable to work on the local hard drive, as opposed to a floppy disk. The hard drive is much faster, which becomes especially important when working with the large file sizes associated with Access. Use the Windows Explorer to copy the database from the network drive to the local hard drive prior to the exercise, then work on drive C throughout the exercise. Once you have completed the exercise, use the Explorer a second time to copy the modified database to a floppy disk that you can take with you.

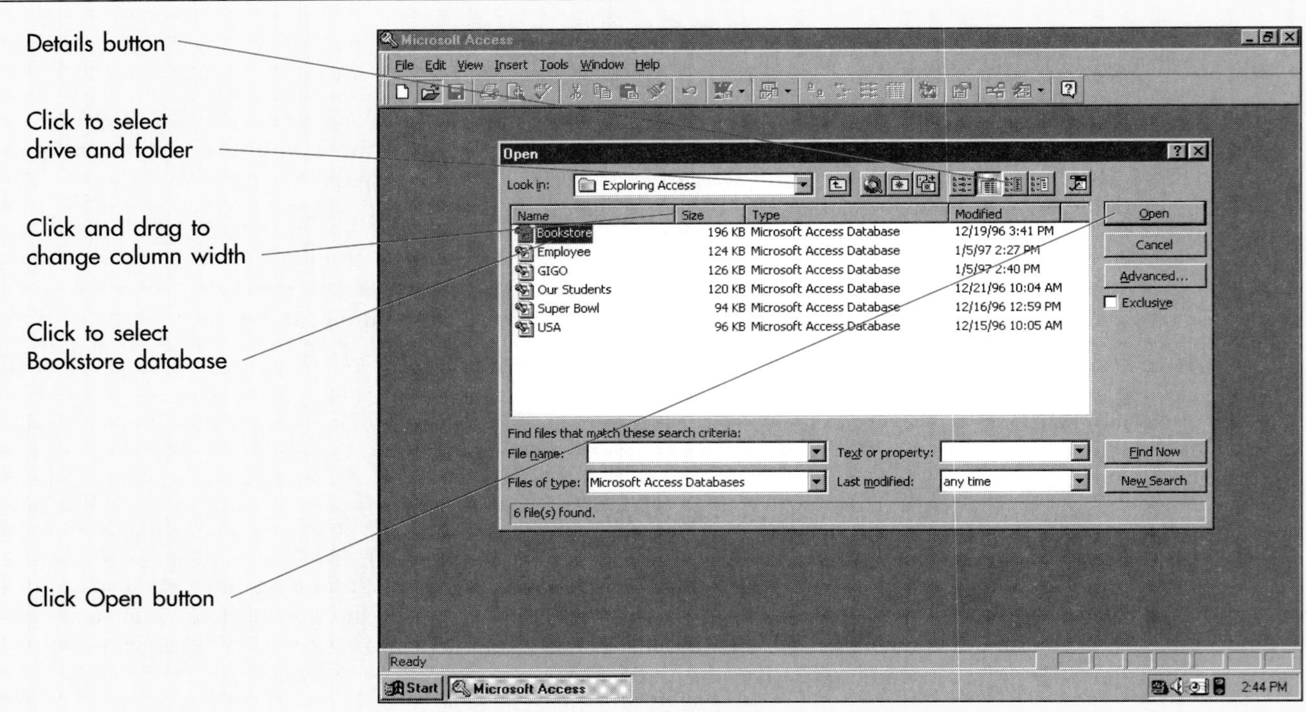

(b) Open an Existing Database (step 3)

FIGURE 1.3 Hands-on Exercise 1 (continued)

STEP 4: Open the Books Table

- You should see the database window for the Bookstore database with the **Tables tab** already selected. Double click the icon next to **Books** to open the table as shown in Figure 1.3c.
- Click the **Maximize button** so that the Books table fills the Access window and reduces the clutter on the screen.
- If necessary, click the **Maximize button** in the application window so that Access takes the entire desktop.

> **A SIMPLER DATABASE**
>
> The real power of Access is derived from a database with multiple tables that are related to one another. For the time being, however, we focus on a database with only one table so that you can learn the basics of Access. After you are comfortable working with a single table, we will show you how to work with multiple tables and how to relate them to one another.

STEP 5: Moving within a Table

- Click in any field in the first record. The status bar at the bottom of the Books Table indicates record 1 of 22.
- The triangle symbol in the record selector indicates that the record has not changed since it was last saved.

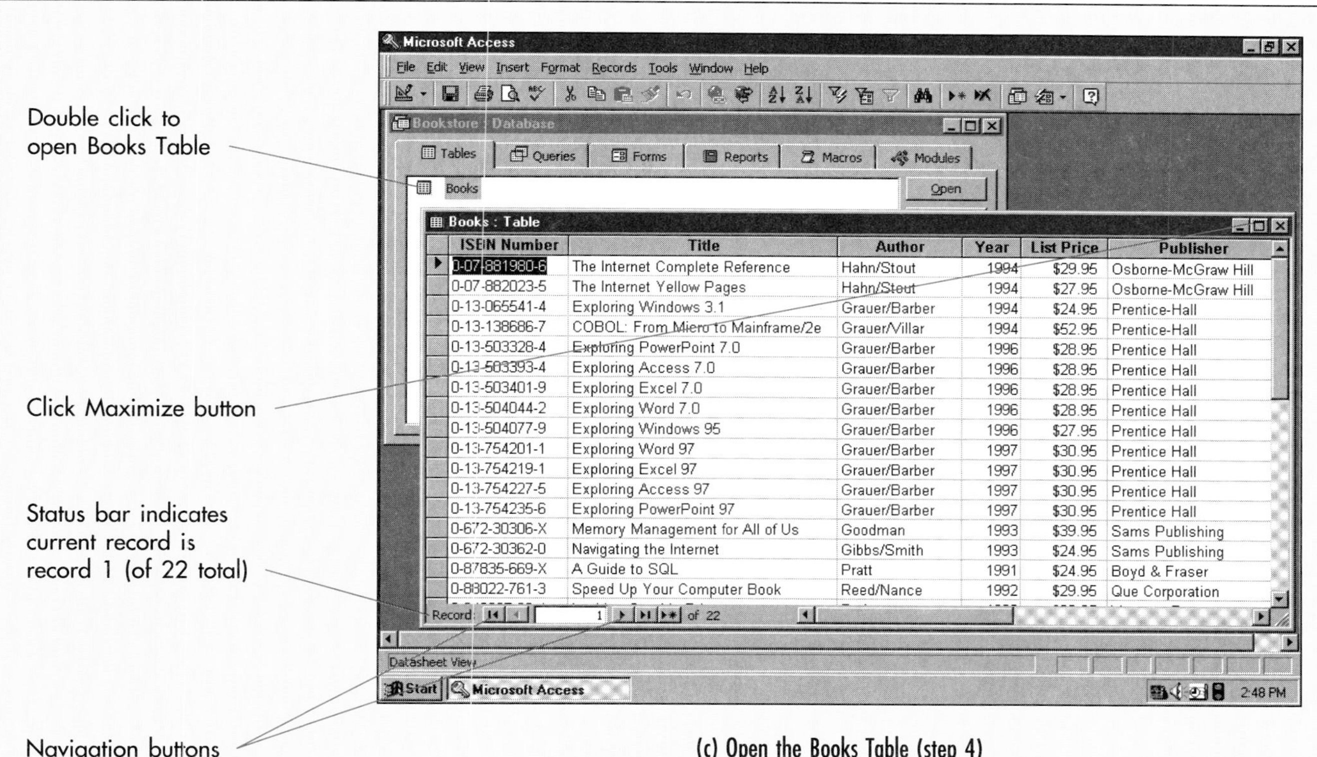

ISBN Number	Title	Author	Year	List Price	Publisher
0-07-881980-6	The Internet Complete Reference	Hahn/Stout	1994	$29.95	Osborne-McGraw Hill
0-07-882023-5	The Internet Yellow Pages	Hahn/Stout	1994	$27.95	Osborne-McGraw Hill
0-13-065541-4	Exploring Windows 3.1	Grauer/Barber	1994	$24.95	Prentice-Hall
0-13-138686-7	COBOL: From Micro to Mainframe/2e	Grauer/Villar	1994	$52.95	Prentice-Hall
0-13-503328-4	Exploring PowerPoint 7.0	Grauer/Barber	1996	$28.95	Prentice Hall
0-13-503393-4	Exploring Access 7.0	Grauer/Barber	1996	$28.95	Prentice Hall
0-13-503401-9	Exploring Excel 7.0	Grauer/Barber	1996	$28.95	Prentice Hall
0-13-504044-2	Exploring Word 7.0	Grauer/Barber	1996	$28.95	Prentice Hall
0-13-504077-9	Exploring Windows 95	Grauer/Barber	1996	$27.95	Prentice Hall
0-13-754201-1	Exploring Word 97	Grauer/Barber	1997	$30.95	Prentice Hall
0-13-754219-1	Exploring Excel 97	Grauer/Barber	1997	$30.95	Prentice Hall
0-13-754227-5	Exploring Access 97	Grauer/Barber	1997	$30.95	Prentice Hall
0-13-754235-6	Exploring PowerPoint 97	Grauer/Barber	1997	$30.95	Prentice Hall
0-672-30306-X	Memory Management for All of Us	Goodman	1993	$39.95	Sams Publishing
0-672-30362-0	Navigating the Internet	Gibbs/Smith	1993	$24.95	Sams Publishing
0-87835-669-X	A Guide to SQL	Pratt	1991	$24.95	Boyd & Fraser
0-88022-761-3	Speed Up Your Computer Book	Reed/Nance	1992	$29.95	Que Corporation

(c) Open the Books Table (step 4)

FIGURE 1.3 Hands-on Exercise 1 (continued)

➤ You can move from record to record (or field to field) using either the mouse or the arrow keys:

- Click in any field in the second record. The status bar indicates record 2 of 22.
- Press the **down arrow key** to move to the third record. The status bar indicates record 3 of 22.
- Press the **left and right arrow keys** to move from field to field within the third record.

➤ You can also use the navigation buttons above the status bar to move from one record to the next:

- Click |◄ to move to the first record in the table.
- Click ► to move forward in the table to the next record.
- Click ◄ to move back in the table to the previous record.

MOVING FROM FIELD TO FIELD

Press the Tab key, the right arrow key, or the enter key to move to the next field in the current record (or the first field in the next record if you are already in the last field of the current record). Press Shift+Tab or the left arrow key to return to the previous field in the current record (or the last field in the previous record if you are already in the first field of the current record).

- Click ►| to move to the last record in the table.
- Click ►* to move beyond the last record in order to insert a new record.

➤ Click |◄ to return to the first record in the table.

STEP 6: Add a Record

➤ Pull down the **Insert menu** and click **New Record** (or click the **New Record button** on the Table Datasheet toolbar). The record selector moves to the last record (now record 23). The insertion point is positioned in the first field (ISBN Number).

➤ Enter data for the new record as shown in Figure 1.3d. The record selector changes to a pencil as soon as you enter the first character in the new record.

➤ Press the **enter key** when you have entered the last field for the record. The new record is saved, and the record selector changes to a triangle and moves automatically to the next record.

New Record button

Record selector is a pencil as you enter data

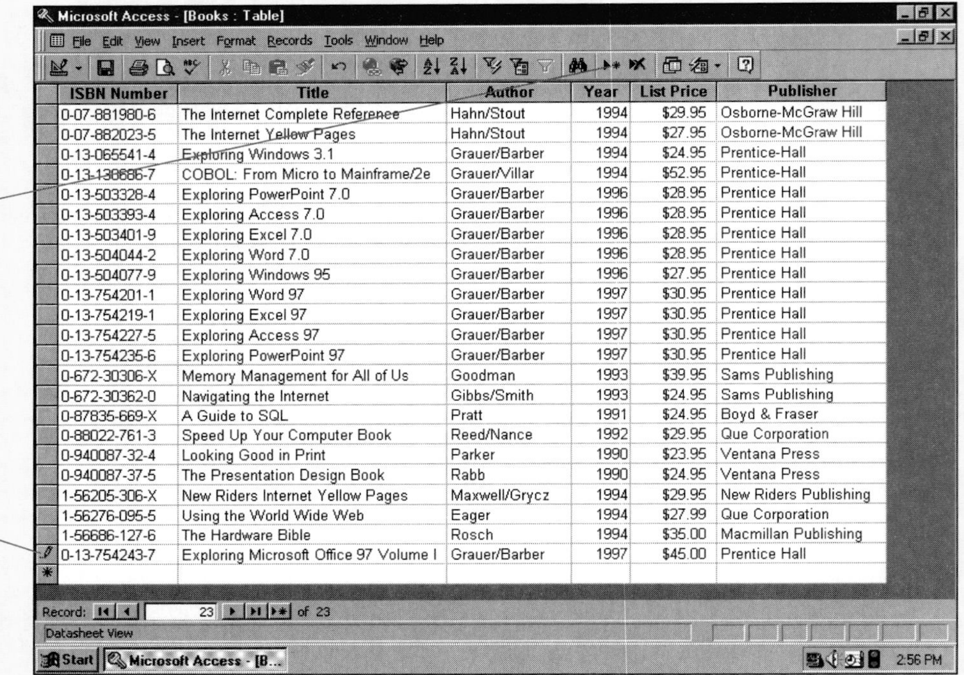

ISBN Number	Title	Author	Year	List Price	Publisher
0-07-881980-6	The Internet Complete Reference	Hahn/Stout	1994	$29.95	Osborne-McGraw Hill
0-07-882023-5	The Internet Yellow Pages	Hahn/Stout	1994	$27.95	Osborne-McGraw Hill
0-13-065541-4	Exploring Windows 3.1	Grauer/Barber	1994	$24.95	Prentice-Hall
0-13-138686-7	COBOL: From Micro to Mainframe/2e	Grauer/Villar	1994	$52.95	Prentice-Hall
0-13-503328-4	Exploring PowerPoint 7.0	Grauer/Barber	1996	$28.95	Prentice Hall
0-13-503393-4	Exploring Access 7.0	Grauer/Barber	1996	$28.95	Prentice Hall
0-13-503401-9	Exploring Excel 7.0	Grauer/Barber	1996	$28.95	Prentice Hall
0-13-504044-2	Exploring Word 7.0	Grauer/Barber	1996	$28.95	Prentice Hall
0-13-504077-9	Exploring Windows 95	Grauer/Barber	1996	$27.95	Prentice Hall
0-13-754201-1	Exploring Word 97	Grauer/Barber	1997	$30.95	Prentice Hall
0-13-754219-1	Exploring Excel 97	Grauer/Barber	1997	$30.95	Prentice Hall
0-13-754227-5	Exploring Access 97	Grauer/Barber	1997	$30.95	Prentice Hall
0-13-754235-6	Exploring PowerPoint 97	Grauer/Barber	1997	$30.95	Prentice Hall
0-672-30306-X	Memory Management for All of Us	Goodman	1993	$39.95	Sams Publishing
0-672-30362-0	Navigating the Internet	Gibbs/Smith	1993	$24.95	Sams Publishing
0-87835-669-X	A Guide to SQL	Pratt	1991	$24.95	Boyd & Fraser
0-88022-761-3	Speed Up Your Computer Book	Reed/Nance	1992	$29.95	Que Corporation
0-940087-32-4	Looking Good in Print	Parker	1990	$23.95	Ventana Press
0-940087-37-5	The Presentation Design Book	Rabb	1990	$24.95	Ventana Press
1-56205-306-X	New Riders Internet Yellow Pages	Maxwell/Grycz	1994	$29.95	New Riders Publishing
1-56276-095-5	Using the World Wide Web	Eager	1994	$27.99	Que Corporation
1-56686-127-6	The Hardware Bible	Rosch	1994	$35.00	Macmillan Publishing
0-13-754243-7	Exploring Microsoft Office 97 Volume I	Grauer/Barber	1997	$45.00	Prentice Hall

(d) Add a New Record (step 6)

FIGURE 1.3 Hands-on Exercise 1 (continued)

WHEN IS DATA SAVED?

There is one critical difference between Access and other Office applications such as Word for Windows or Microsoft Excel. *Access automatically saves any changes in the current record as soon as you move to the next record or when you close the table.* In other words, you do *not* have to execute the Save command explicitly to save the data in the table.

STEP 7: Add a Second Record

- The record selector is at the end of the table where you can add another record. Enter **0-13-271693-3** as the ISBN number for this record. Press the **Tab, enter,** or **right arrow key** to move to the Title field.
- Enter the title of this book as **Exploring teh Internet/2nd Edition** (deliberately misspelling the word "the"). Try to look at the monitor as you type to see the AutoCorrect feature (common to all Office applications) in action. Access will correct the misspelling and change *teh* to *the.*
- If you did not see the correction being made, press the **backspace key** several times to erase the last several characters in the title, then re-enter the title.
- Complete the entry for this book. Enter **Grauer/Marx** for the author. Enter **1997** for the year of publication. Enter **28.95** for the list price. Enter **Prentice Hall** for the publisher, then press **enter.**

CREATE YOUR OWN SHORTHAND

Use the AutoCorrect feature that is common to all Office applications to expand abbreviations such as "PH" for Prentice Hall. Pull down the Tools menu, click AutoCorrect, type the abbreviation in the Replace text box and the expanded entry in the With text box. Click the Add command button, then click OK to exit the dialog box and return to the document. The next time you type PH (in upper- or lowercase) as you enter a record, it will automatically be expanded to Prentice Hall.

STEP 8: Print the Table

- Pull down the **File menu.** Click **Page Setup** to display the Page Setup dialog box in Figure 1.3e.
- Click the **Page tab.** Click the **Landscape option button.** Click **OK** to accept the settings and close the dialog box.
- Click the **Print button** on the toolbar to print the table. Alternatively, you can pull down the **File menu,** click **Print** to display the Print dialog box, click the **All options button,** then click **OK.**

ABOUT MICROSOFT ACCESS

Pull down the Help menu and click About Microsoft Access to display the specific release number as well as other licensing information, including the product serial number. This help screen also contains two very useful command buttons, System Info and Tech Support. The first button displays information about the hardware installed on your system, including the amount of memory and available space on the hard drive. The Tech Support button provides telephone numbers for technical assistance.

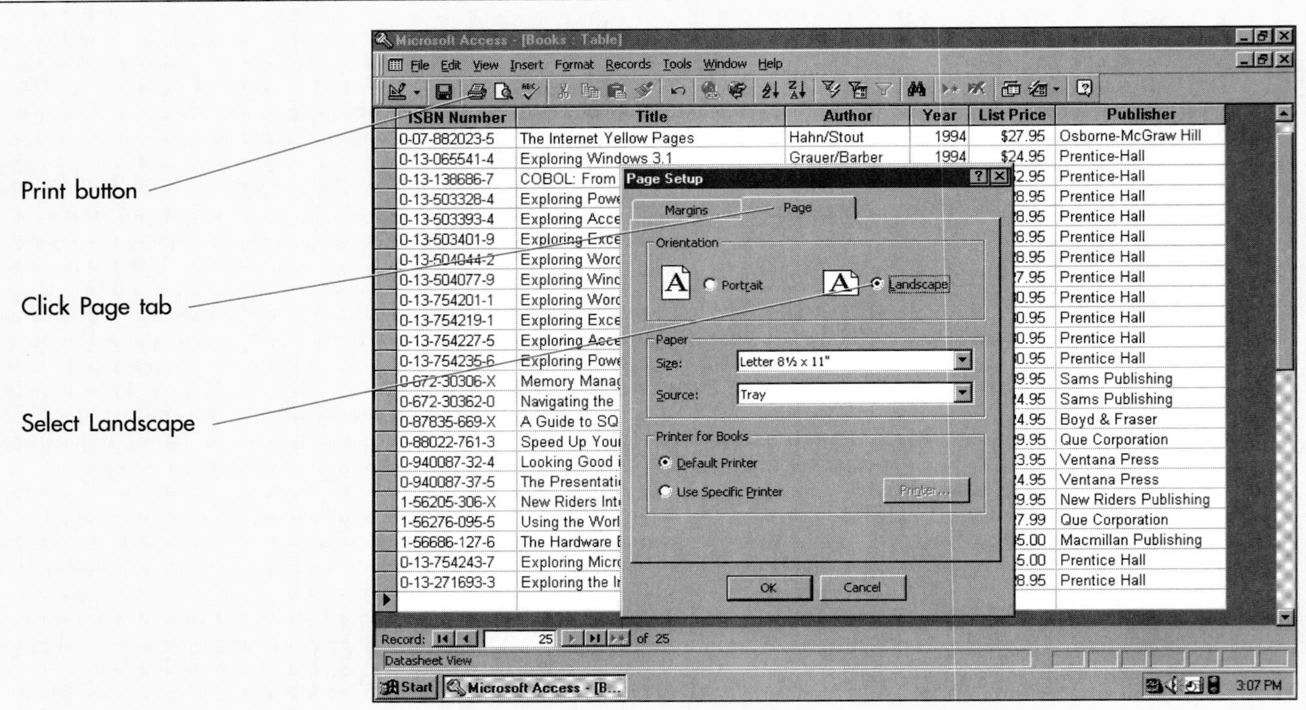

(e) Print the Table (step 8)

FIGURE 1.3 Hands-on Exercise 1 (continued)

STEP 9: Exit Access

➤ You need to close both the Books table and the Bookstore database:

- Pull down the **File menu** and click **Close** (or click the **Close button)** to close the Books table. Answer **Yes** if asked to save changes to the layout of the table.
- Pull down the **File menu** and click **Close** (or click the **Close button)** to close the Bookstore database.

➤ Pull down the **File menu** and click **Exit** to close Access if you do not want to continue with the next exercise at this time.

OUR FAVORITE BOOKSTORE

This exercise has taken you through our hypothetical bookstore database. It's more fun, however, to go to a real bookstore. Amazon Books (www.amazon.com), with a virtual inventory of more than one million titles, is one of our favorite sites on the Web. You can search by author, subject, or title, read reviews written by other Amazon visitors, or contribute your own review. It's not as cozy as your neighborhood bookstore, but you can order any title for mail-order delivery. And you never have to leave home.

The exercise just completed showed you how to open an existing table and add records to that table. You will also need to edit and/or delete existing records in order to maintain the data as changes occur. These operations require you to find the specific record and then make the change. You can search the table manually, or more easily through the Find and Replace commands.

Find and Replace Commands

The Find and Replace commands are similar in function to the corresponding commands in all other Office applications. The ***Find command*** in Microsoft Access enables you to locate a specific record(s) by searching a table for a particular value. You could, for example, search the Books table for the title of a book as in Figure 1.4a, then move to the appropriate field to change its price. The ***Replace command*** incorporates the Find command and allows you to locate and optionally replace (one or more occurrences of) one value with another. The Replace command in Figure 1.4b, for example, searches for *PH* in order to substitute *Prentice Hall.*

Searches can be made more efficient by making use of the various options. A case-sensitive search, for example, matches not only the specific characters, but also the use of upper- and lowercase letters. Thus, *PH* is different from *ph,* and a case-sensitive search on one will not identify the other. A case-insensitive search (where Match Case is *not* selected) will find both *PH* and *ph.* Any search may specify a match on whole fields to identify *Davis,* but not *Davison.* And finally, a

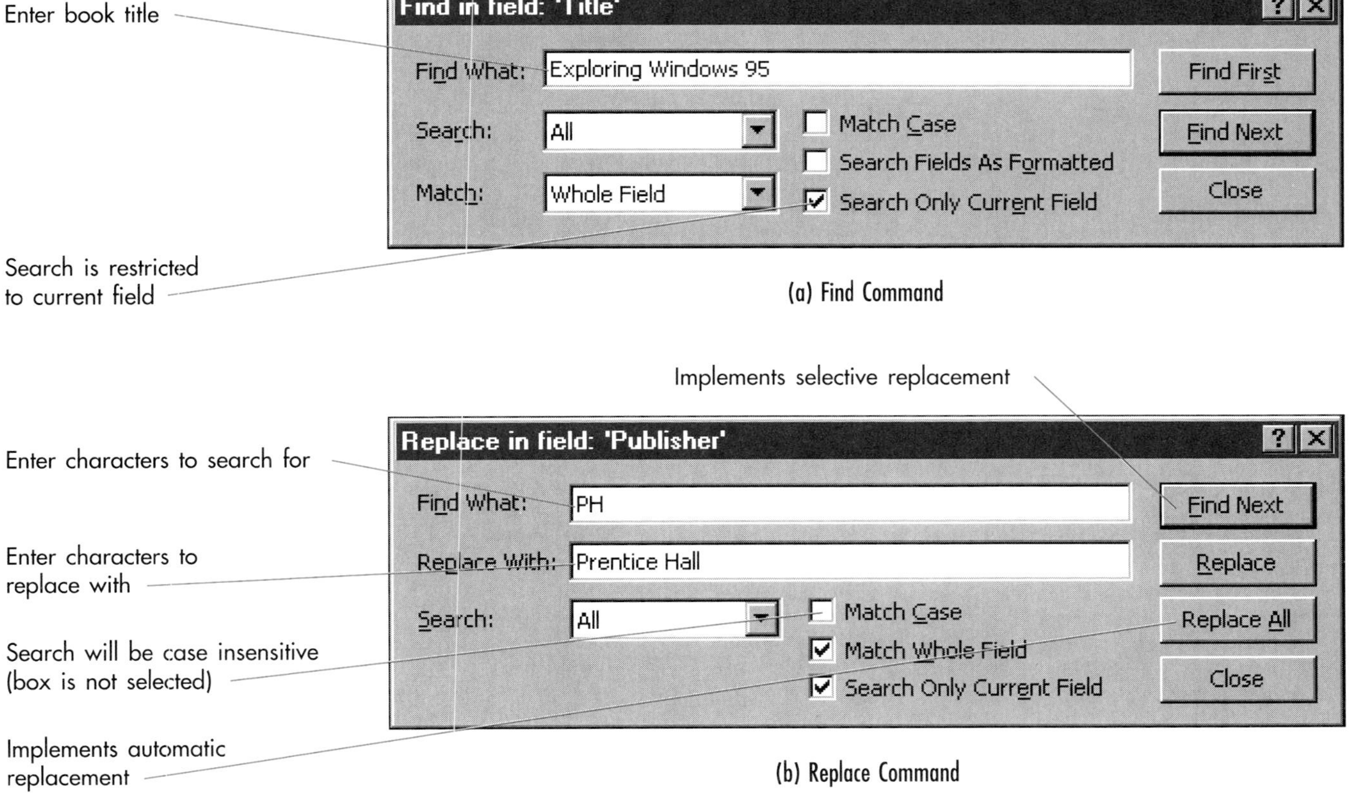

FIGURE 1.4 Find and Replace Commands

search can also be made more efficient by restricting it to the current field (e.g., Publisher), as opposed to searching every field.

The replacement can be either selective or automatic. Selective replacement lets you examine each successful match in context and decide whether to replace it. Automatic replacement makes the substitution without asking for confirmation (and is generally not recommended). Selective replacement is implemented by clicking the Find Next command button, then clicking (or not clicking) the Replace button to make (or not make) the substitution. Automatic replacement (through the entire table) is implemented by clicking the Replace All button.

Data Validation

It is unwise to simply add (edit or delete) a record without adequate checks on the validity of the data. Ask yourself, for example, whether a search for all books by Prentice Hall (without a hyphen) will also return all books by *Prentice-Hall* (with a hyphen). The answer is *no* because the publisher's name is spelled differently and a search for one will not locate the other. *You* know the publisher is the same in both instances, but the computer does not.

Data validation is a crucial part of any system. Good systems will anticipate errors you might make and reject those errors prior to accepting data. Access automatically implements certain types of data validation. It will not, for example, let you enter letters where a numeric value is expected (such as the Year and List Price fields in our example.) More sophisticated types of validation are implemented by the user when the table is created. You may decide, for example, to reject any record that omits the title or author. Data validation is described more completely in Chapter 2.

GARBAGE IN, GARBAGE OUT (GIGO)

A computer does exactly what you tell it to do, which is not necessarily what you want it to do. It is absolutely critical, therefore, that you validate the data that goes into a system, or else the associated information may not be correct. No system, no matter how sophisticated, can produce valid output from invalid input. In other words: ***garbage in, garbage out.***

FORMS, QUERIES, AND REPORTS

As previously indicated, an Access database can contain as many as six different types of objects. Thus far we have concentrated on tables, but now we extend the discussion to include forms, queries, and reports as illustrated in Figure 1.5.

Figure 1.5a contains the Books table as it exists after the first hands-on exercise. There are 24 records in the table and six fields for each record. The status bar indicates that you are currently positioned in the first record. You can enter new records in the table as was done in the previous exercise. You can also edit or delete an existing record, as will be illustrated in the next exercise.

Figure 1.5b displays a form that is based on the table of Figure 1.5a. A form provides a friendlier interface than does a table and is easier to understand and use. Note, for example, the command buttons in the form to add a new record, or to find and/or delete an existing record. The status bar at the bottom of the form indicates that you are on the first of 24 records, and is identical to the status bar for the table in Figure 1.5a.

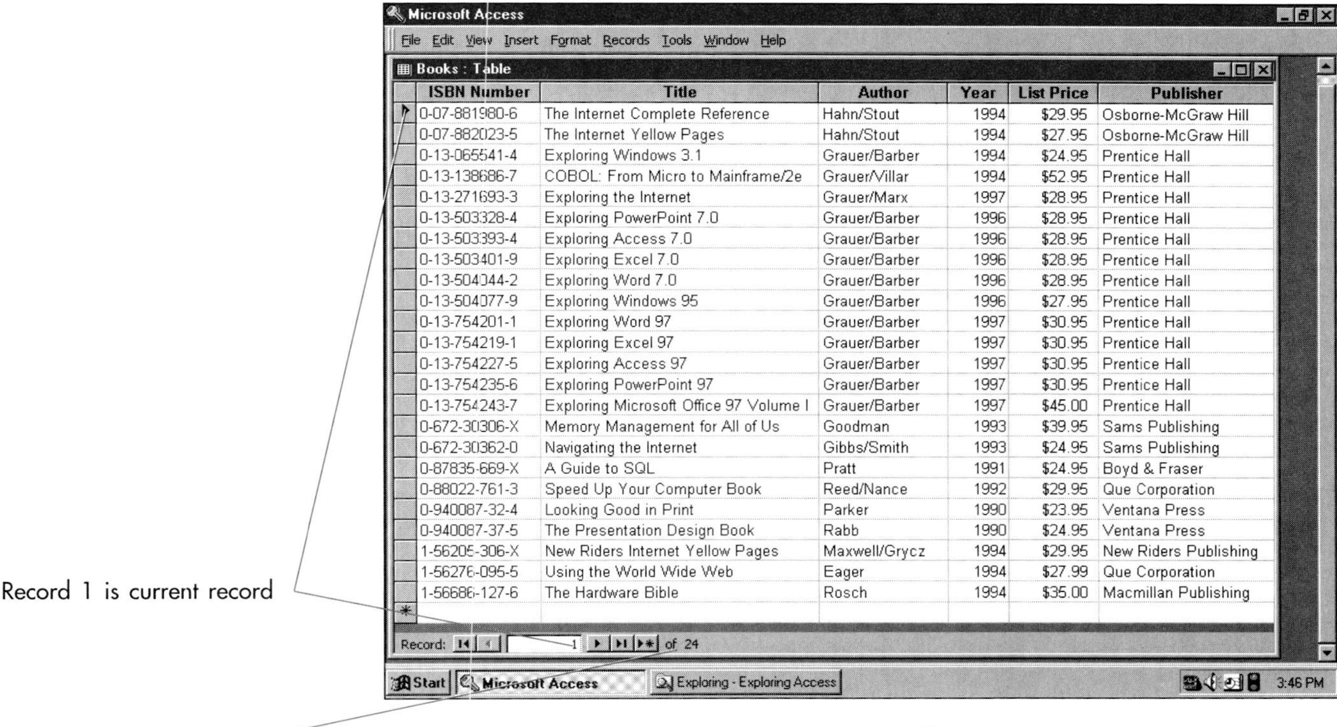

ISBN Number	Title	Author	Year	List Price	Publisher
0-07-881980-6	The Internet Complete Reference	Hahn/Stout	1994	$29.95	Osborne-McGraw Hill
0-07-882023-5	The Internet Yellow Pages	Hahn/Stout	1994	$27.95	Osborne-McGraw Hill
0-13-065541-4	Exploring Windows 3.1	Grauer/Barber	1994	$24.95	Prentice Hall
0-13-138686-7	COBOL: From Micro to Mainframe/2e	Grauer/Villar	1994	$52.95	Prentice Hall
0-13-271693-3	Exploring the Internet	Grauer/Marx	1997	$28.95	Prentice Hall
0-13-503328-4	Exploring PowerPoint 7.0	Grauer/Barber	1996	$28.95	Prentice Hall
0-13-503393-4	Exploring Access 7.0	Grauer/Barber	1996	$28.95	Prentice Hall
0-13-503401-9	Exploring Excel 7.0	Grauer/Barber	1996	$28.95	Prentice Hall
0-13-504044-2	Exploring Word 7.0	Grauer/Barber	1996	$28.95	Prentice Hall
0-13-504077-9	Exploring Windows 95	Grauer/Barber	1996	$27.95	Prentice Hall
0-13-754201-1	Exploring Word 97	Grauer/Barber	1997	$30.95	Prentice Hall
0-13-754219-1	Exploring Excel 97	Grauer/Barber	1997	$30.95	Prentice Hall
0-13-754227-5	Exploring Access 97	Grauer/Barber	1997	$30.95	Prentice Hall
0-13-754235-6	Exploring PowerPoint 97	Grauer/Barber	1997	$30.95	Prentice Hall
0-13-754243-7	Exploring Microsoft Office 97 Volume I	Grauer/Barber	1997	$45.00	Prentice Hall
0-672-30306-X	Memory Management for All of Us	Goodman	1993	$39.95	Sams Publishing
0-672-30362-0	Navigating the Internet	Gibbs/Smith	1993	$24.95	Sams Publishing
0-87835-669-X	A Guide to SQL	Pratt	1991	$24.95	Boyd & Fraser
0-88022-761-3	Speed Up Your Computer Book	Reed/Nance	1992	$29.95	Que Corporation
0-940087-32-4	Looking Good in Print	Parker	1990	$23.95	Ventana Press
0-940087-37-5	The Presentation Design Book	Rabb	1990	$24.95	Ventana Press
1-56205-306-X	New Riders Internet Yellow Pages	Maxwell/Grycz	1994	$29.95	New Riders Publishing
1-56276-095-5	Using the World Wide Web	Eager	1994	$27.99	Que Corporation
1-56686-127-6	The Hardware Bible	Rosch	1994	$35.00	Macmillan Publishing

(a) The Books Table

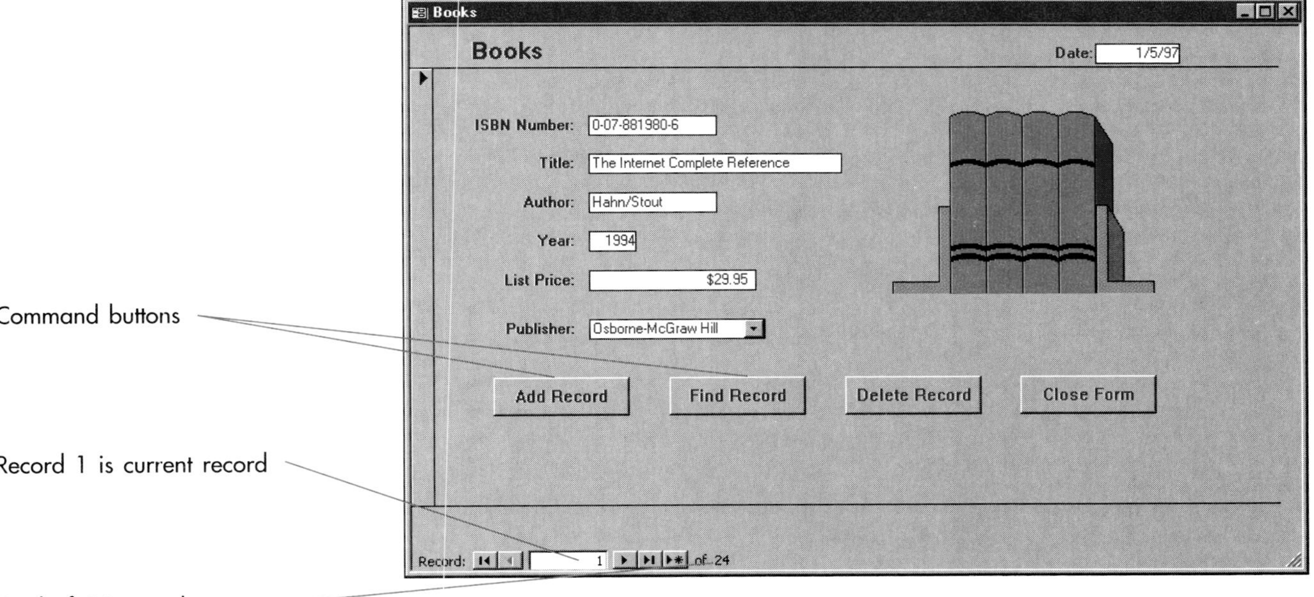

(b) The Books Form

FIGURE 1.5 The Objects in a Database

Figure 1.5c displays a query to list the books for a particular publisher (Prentice Hall in this example). A query consists of a question (e.g., enter the publisher name) and an answer (the records that satisfy the query). The results of the query are similar in appearance to the underlying table, except that the query contains selected records and/or selected fields for those records. The query may also list the records in a different sequence from that of the table.

Publisher : Select Query

Publisher	Author	Title	ISBN Number	Year	List Price
Prentice Hall	Grauer/Barber	Exploring Access 7.0	0-13-503393-4	1996	$28.95
Prentice Hall	Grauer/Barber	Exploring Access 97	0-13-754227-5	1997	$30.95
Prentice Hall	Grauer/Barber	Exploring Excel 7.0	0-13-503401-9	1996	$28.95
Prentice Hall	Grauer/Barber	Exploring Excel 97	0-13-754219-1	1997	$30.95
Prentice Hall	Grauer/Barber	Exploring Microsoft Office 97 Volume I	0-13-754243-7	1997	$45.00
Prentice Hall	Grauer/Barber	Exploring PowerPoint 7.0	0-13-503328-4	1996	$28.95
Prentice Hall	Grauer/Barber	Exploring PowerPoint 97	0-13-754235-6	1997	$30.95
Prentice Hall	Grauer/Barber	Exploring Windows 3.1	0-13-065541-4	1994	$24.95
Prentice Hall	Grauer/Barber	Exploring Windows 95	0-13-504077-9	1996	$27.95
Prentice Hall	Grauer/Barber	Exploring Word 7.0	0-13-504044-2	1996	$28.95
Prentice Hall	Grauer/Barber	Exploring Word 97	0-13-754201-1	1997	$30.95
Prentice Hall	Grauer/Marx	Exploring the Internet	0-13-271693-3	1997	$28.95
Prentice Hall	Grauer/Villar	COBOL: From Micro to Mainframe/2e	0-13-138686-7	1994	$52.95

Record: 1 of 13

Books are in sequence by author, and within the same author, by title

(c) The Publisher Query

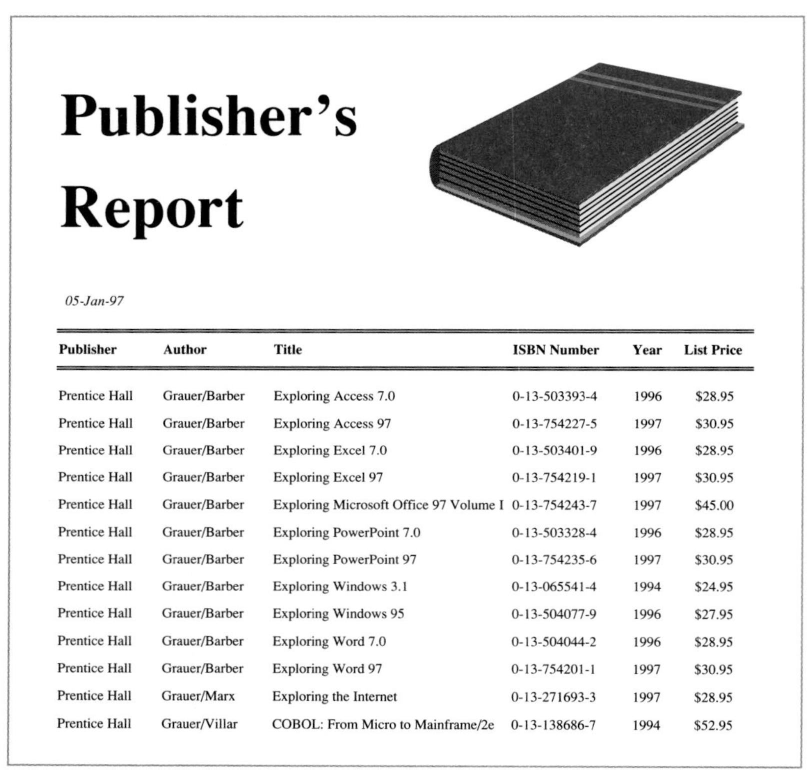

Publisher's Report

05-Jan-97

Publisher	Author	Title	ISBN Number	Year	List Price
Prentice Hall	Grauer/Barber	Exploring Access 7.0	0-13-503393-4	1996	$28.95
Prentice Hall	Grauer/Barber	Exploring Access 97	0-13-754227-5	1997	$30.95
Prentice Hall	Grauer/Barber	Exploring Excel 7.0	0-13-503401-9	1996	$28.95
Prentice Hall	Grauer/Barber	Exploring Excel 97	0-13-754219-1	1997	$30.95
Prentice Hall	Grauer/Barber	Exploring Microsoft Office 97 Volume I	0-13-754243-7	1997	$45.00
Prentice Hall	Grauer/Barber	Exploring PowerPoint 7.0	0-13-503328-4	1996	$28.95
Prentice Hall	Grauer/Barber	Exploring PowerPoint 97	0-13-754235-6	1997	$30.95
Prentice Hall	Grauer/Barber	Exploring Windows 3.1	0-13-065541-4	1994	$24.95
Prentice Hall	Grauer/Barber	Exploring Windows 95	0-13-504077-9	1996	$27.95
Prentice Hall	Grauer/Barber	Exploring Word 7.0	0-13-504044-2	1996	$28.95
Prentice Hall	Grauer/Barber	Exploring Word 97	0-13-754201-1	1997	$30.95
Prentice Hall	Grauer/Marx	Exploring the Internet	0-13-271693-3	1997	$28.95
Prentice Hall	Grauer/Villar	COBOL: From Micro to Mainframe/2e	0-13-138686-7	1994	$52.95

(d) The Publisher Report

FIGURE 1.5 The Objects in a Database (continued)

Figure 1.5d illustrates a report that includes only the books from Prentice Hall. A report provides presentation-quality output and is preferable to printing the results of a table or query. Note, too, that a report may be based on either a table or a query. You could, for example, base the report in Figure 1.5d on the Books table, in which case it would list every book in the table. Alternatively, the report could be based on a query, as in Figure 1.5d, and list only the books that satisfy the criteria within the query.

Later chapters discuss forms, queries, and reports in depth. The exercise that follows is intended only as a brief introduction to what can be accomplished in Access.

HANDS-ON EXERCISE 2

Maintaining the Database

Objective: To add, edit, and delete a record; to demonstrate data validation; to introduce forms, queries, and reports. Use Figure 1.6 as a guide in doing the exercise.

STEP 1: Open the Bookstore Database

- Start Access. The Bookstore database should appear within the list of recently opened databases as shown in Figure 1.6a.
- Select the **Bookstore database** (its drive and folder may be different from that in Figure 1.6a). Click **OK** to open the database.
- Close the Office Assistant if it appears.

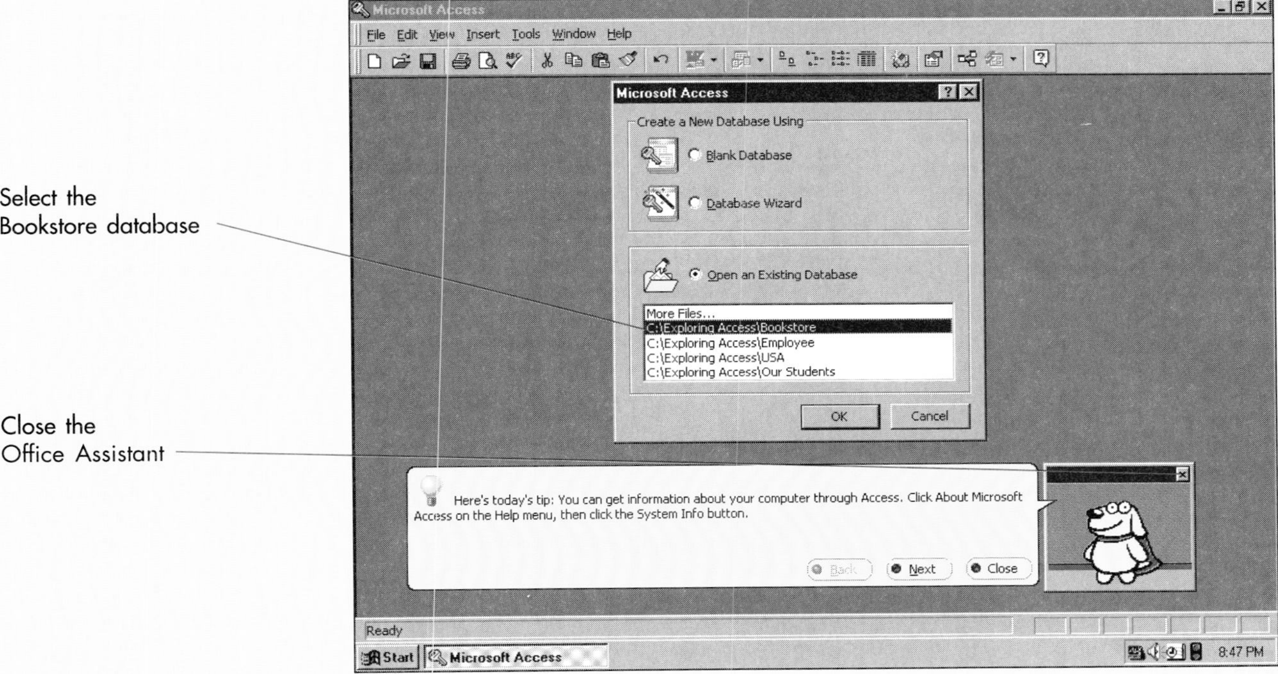

(a) Open the Bookstore Database (step 1)

FIGURE 1.6 Hands-on Exercise 2

CHOOSE YOUR OWN ASSISTANT

You can choose your own personal assistant from one of several available images. Click the Office Assistant button on any visible toolbar to display the Assistant, click the Options button to display the Office Assistant dialog box, click the Gallery tab, then click the Next button repeatedly to cycle through the available images. Click OK to select the character and close the dialog box. (The Office 97 CD is required for certain characters.)

STEP 2: The Find Command

- Click the **Tables tab** in the Database window. Double click the icon for the **Books table** to open the table from the previous exercise.
- You should see the Books table in Figure 1.6b. (The Find dialog box is not yet displayed).
- If necessary, click the **Maximize button** to maximize the Books table within the Access window.
- Exploring Office 95 and Exploring the Internet, the books you added in the previous exercise, appear in sequence according to the ISBN number because this field is the primary key for the Books table.
- Click in the **Title field** for the first record. Pull down the **Edit menu** and click **Find** (or click the **Find button** on the toolbar) to display the dialog box in Figure 1.6b. (You are still positioned in the first record.)
- Enter **Exploring Windows 95** in the Find What text box. Check that the other parameters for the Find command match the dialog box in Figure 1.6b. Be sure that **Search Only Current Field** is selected.
- Click the **Find First command button.** Access moves to record 10, the record containing the designated character string, and selects the Title field for that record. Click **Close** to close the Find dialog box.
- Press the **tab key** three times to move from the Title field to the List Price field. The current price ($27.95) is already selected. Type **28.95,** then press the **enter key** to change the price to $28.95.

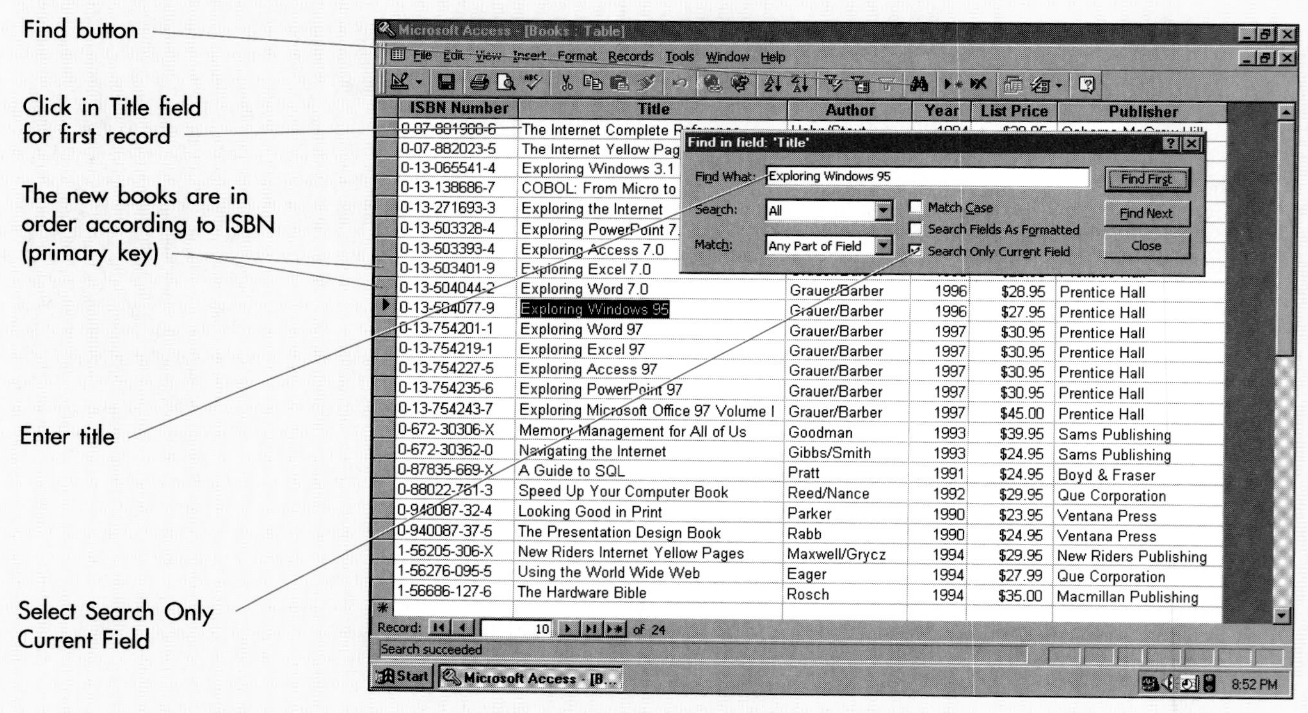

(b) The Find Command (step 2)

FIGURE 1.6 Hands-on Exercise 2 (continued)

EDITING A RECORD

The fastest way to replace the value in an existing field is to select the field, then type the new value. Access automatically selects the field for you when you use the keyboard (Tab, enter, or arrow keys) to move from one field to the next. Click the mouse within the field (to deselect the field) if you are replacing only one or two characters rather than the entire field.

STEP 3: The Undo Command

- Pull down the **Edit menu** and click **Undo Current Field/Record** (or click the **Undo button** on the toolbar). The price for Exploring Windows 95 returns to its previous value.
- Pull down the **Edit menu** a second time. The Undo command is dim (as is the Undo button on the toolbar), indicating that you can no longer undo any changes. Press **Esc.**
- Correct the List Price field a second time and move to the next record to save your change.

THE UNDO COMMAND

The Undo command is common to all Office applications, but is implemented differently from one application to the next. Microsoft Word, for example, enables you to undo the last 100 operations. Access, however, because it saves changes automatically as soon as you move to the next record, enables you to undo only the most recent command.

STEP 4: The Delete Command

- Click any field in the record for **A Guide to SQL.** (You can also use the **Find command** to search for the title and move directly to its record.)
- Pull down the **Edit menu.** Click **Select Record** to highlight the entire record.
- Press the **Del key** to delete the record. You will see a dialog box as shown in Figure 1.6c, indicating that you are about to delete a record and asking you to confirm the deletion. Click **Yes.**
- Pull down the **Edit menu.** The Undo command is dim, indicating that you cannot undelete a record. Press **Esc** to continue working.

THE RECORD SELECTOR

Click the record selector (the box immediately to the left of the first field in a record) to select the record without having to use a pull-down menu. Click and drag the mouse over the record selector for multiple rows to select several sequential records at the same time.

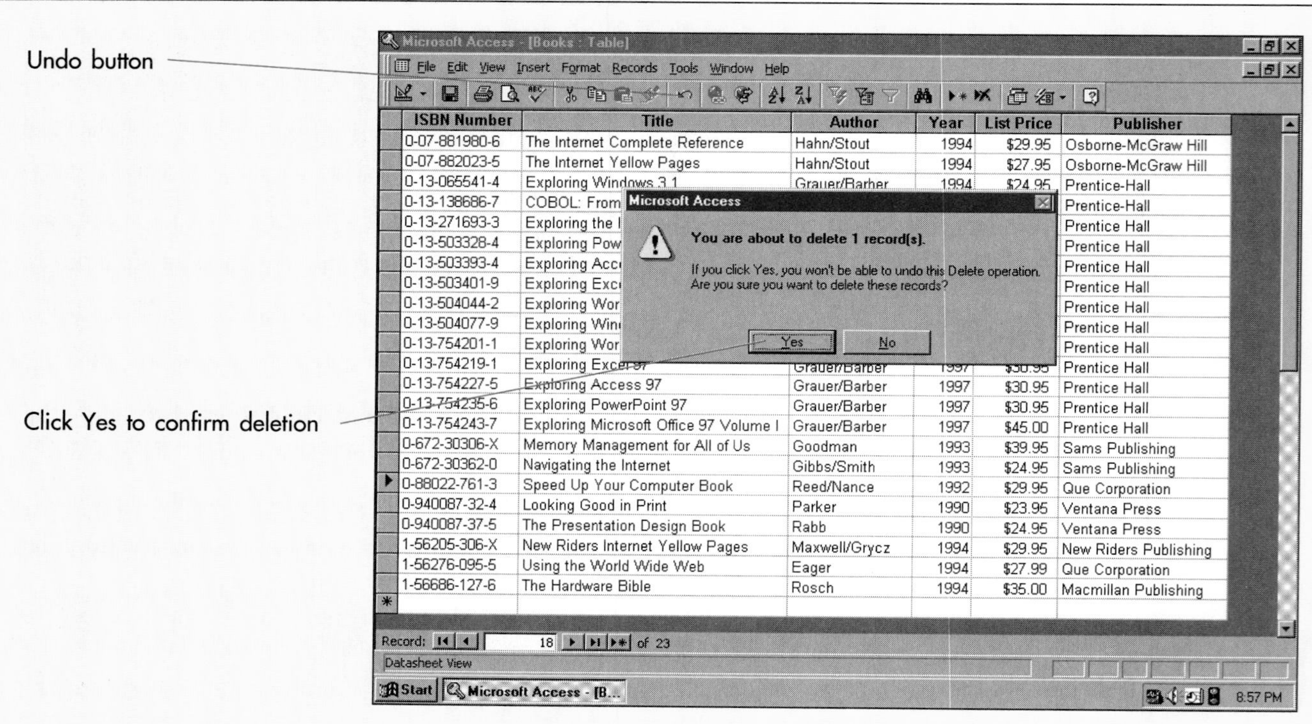

(c) The Delete Command (step 4)

FIGURE 1.6 Hands-on Exercise 2 (continued)

STEP 5: Data Validation

- Click the **New Record button** on the toolbar. The record selector moves to the last record (record 24).
- Add data as shown in Figure 1.6d, being sure to enter an invalid price **(XXX)** in the List Price field. Press the **Tab key** to move to the next field.
- Access displays the dialog box in Figure 1.6d, indicating that the value you entered (XXX) is inappropriate for the List Price field; in other words, you cannot enter letters when Access is expecting a numeric entry.
- Click the **OK command button** to close the dialog box and return to the table. Drag the mouse to select XXX, then enter the correct price of **$39.95.**
- Press the **Tab key** to move to the Publisher field. Type **IDG Books Worldwide.** Press the **Tab key, right arrow key,** or **enter key** to complete the record.
- Click the **Close button** to close the Books table.

STEP 6: Open the Books Form

- Click the **Forms tab** in the Database window. Double click the **Books form** to open the form as shown in Figure 1.6e, then (if necessary) maximize the form so that it takes the entire window.
- Click the **Add Record command button** to move to a new record. The status bar shows record 25 of 25.
- Click in the text box for **ISBN number,** then use the **Tab key** to move from field to field as you enter data for the book as shown in Figure 1.6e.
- Click the **drop-down arrow** on the Publisher's list box to display the available publishers and to select the appropriate one. The use of a list box ensures that you cannot misspell a publisher's name.

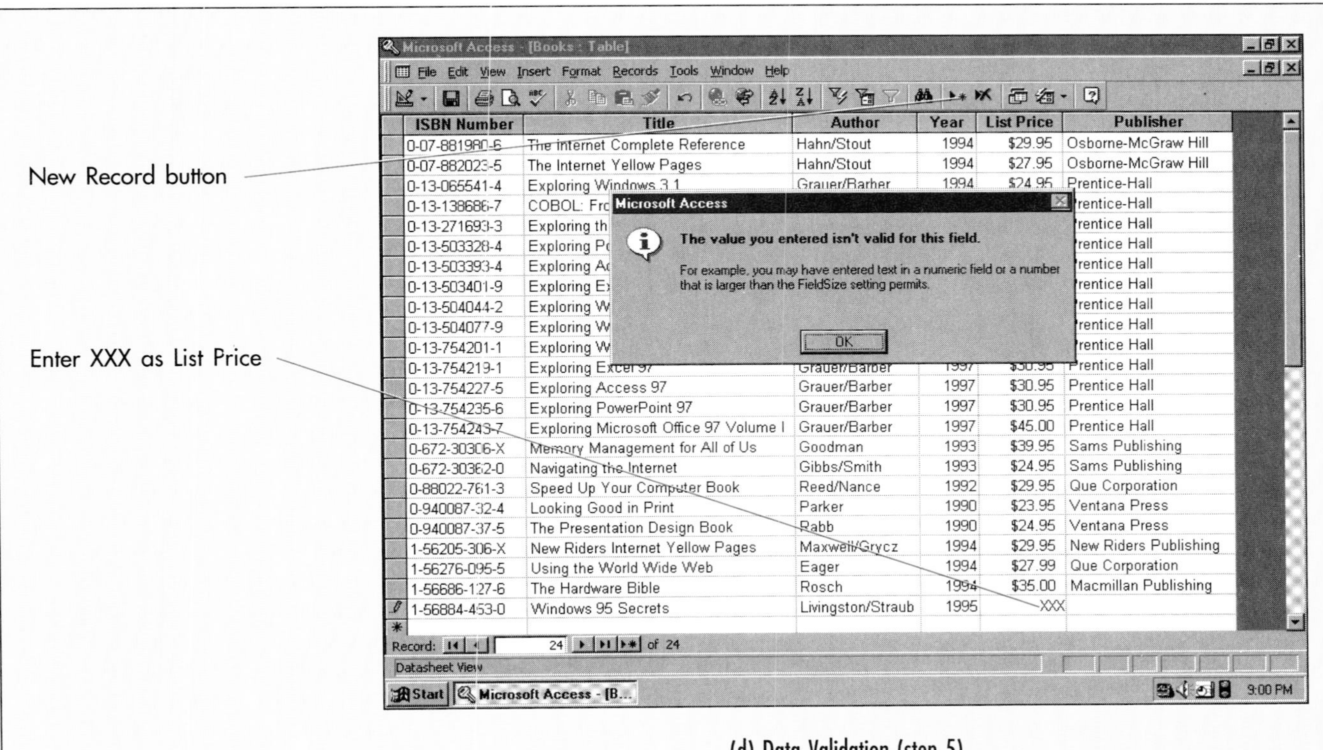

(d) Data Validation (step 5)

Click in text box for ISBN number and enter data

Click drop-down arrow to display Publisher names

Click to add a new record

Current record is 25 of 25

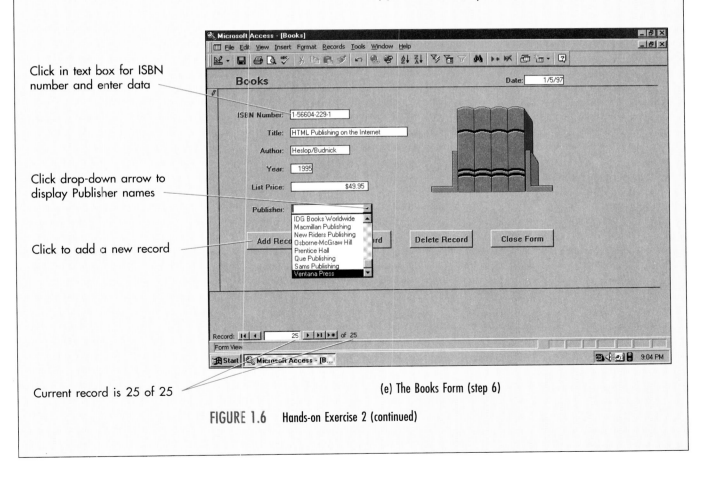

(e) The Books Form (step 6)

FIGURE 1.6 Hands-on Exercise 2 (continued)

STEP 7: The Replace Command

- Pull down the **View menu.** Click **Datasheet** to switch from the Form view to the Datasheet view to display the table on which the form is based.
- Press **Ctrl+Home** to move to the first record in the Books table, then click in the **Publisher field** for that record. Pull down the **Edit menu.** Click **Replace** to display the dialog box in Figure 1.6f.
- Enter the parameters as they appear in Figure 1.6f, then click the **Find Next button** to move to the first occurrence of Prentice-Hall.
- Click **Replace** to make the substitution in this record and move to the next occurrence.
- Click **Replace** to make the second (and last) substitution, then close the dialog box when Access no longer finds the search string.
- Click the **Close button** to close the table.

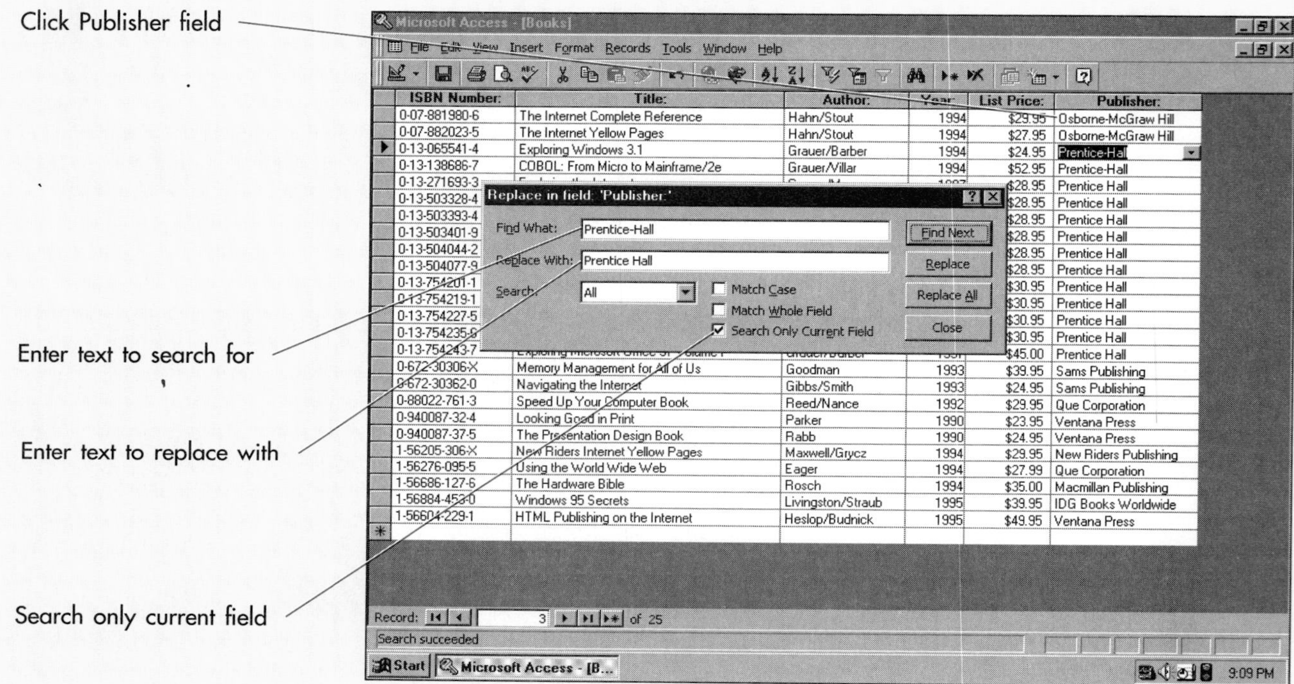

(f) The Replace Command (step 7)

FIGURE 1.6 Hands-on Exercise 2 (continued)

THE COMMON USER INTERFACE

Ctrl+Home and Ctrl+End are keyboard shortcuts that apply universally to virtually every Windows application and move to the beginning and end of a document, respectively. Microsoft Access is no exception. Press Ctrl+Home to move to the first field in the first record of a table. Press Ctrl+End to move to the last field in the last record. Press Home and End to move to the first and last fields in the current record, respectively. Other common shortcuts you may find useful are Ctrl+X, Ctrl+C, and Ctrl+V to cut, copy, and paste, respectively.

STEP 8: Run a Query

- Click the **Queries tab** in the Database window. Double click the **Publisher query** to run the query.
- You will see the Enter Parameter Value dialog box in Figure 1.6g. Type **Prentice Hall,** then press **enter** to see the results of the query, which should contain 13 books by Prentice Hall. (If you do not see all of the books, it is probably because you failed to replace Prentice-Hall with Prentice Hall in step 7.)
- Click the **Close button** to close the query, which returns you to the Database window.

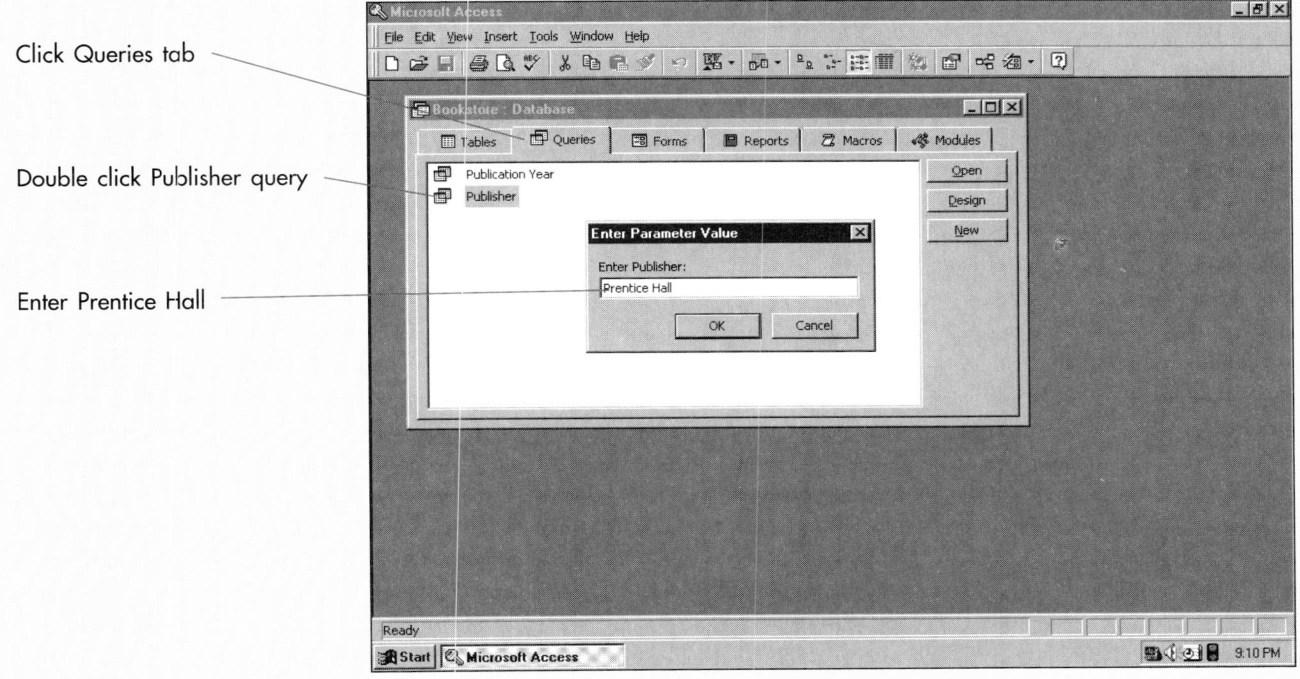

(g) Run a Query (step 8)

FIGURE 1.6 Hands-on Exercise 2 (continued)

STEP 9: Print a Report

- Click the **Reports tab** in the Database window to display the available reports.
- Double click the icon for the **Publisher report.** Type **Prentice Hall** (or the name of any other publisher) in the Parameter dialog box. Press **enter** to create the report.
- If necessary, click the **Maximize button** in the Report Window so that the report takes the entire screen as shown in Figure 1.6h.
- Click the **arrow** on the Zoom box on the Report toolbar, then click **Fit** to display the whole page. Note that all of the books in the report are published by Prentice Hall, which is consistent with the parameter you entered earlier.
- Click the **Print button** on the Report toolbar.
- Click the **Close Window button** to close the Report window.

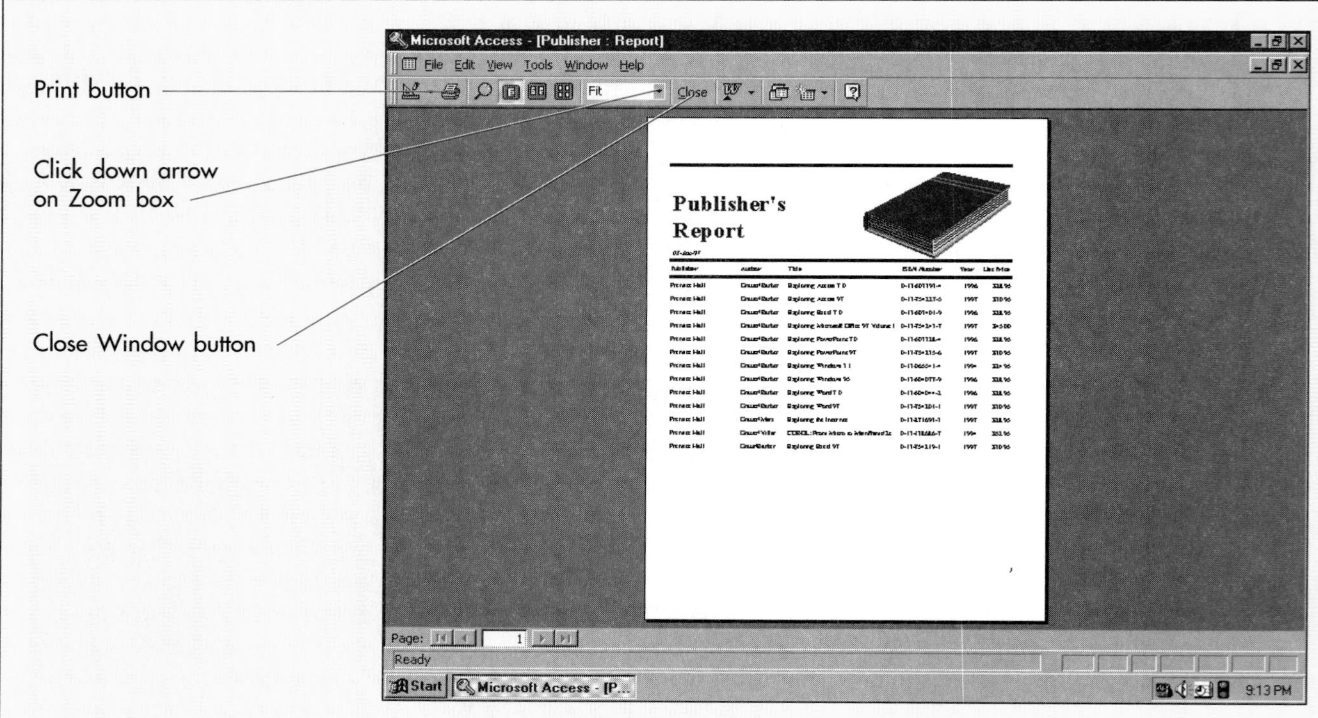

(h) Run a Report (step 9)

FIGURE 1.6 Hands-on Exercise 2 (continued)

TIP OF THE DAY

You can set the Office Assistant to greet you with a "Tip of the Day" whenever you start Access. If the Office Assistant is not visible, click the Office Assistant button on the Standard toolbar to start the Assistant, then click the options button to display the Office Assistant dialog box. Check the Show the Tip of the Day at startup box, then click OK. The next time you start Access, the Assistant will greet you with a tip of the day.

STEP 10: The Office Assistant

- Click the **Office Assistant button** on the Standard toolbar to display the Office Assistant. (You may see a different character than the one we have selected.)
- Enter your question, for example, **What is a table** as shown in Figure 1.6i, then click the **Search button** to look for the answer.
- The size of the dialog box expands as the Assistant suggests several topics that may be appropriate to answer your question.
- Click the topic **Tables: What they are and how they work** to display a help screen that reviews (and extends) much of the material in this chapter.
- There are three help screens in this topic, each of which contains several graphic elements. You go from one screen to the next by clicking the number (1, 2, or 3) at the upper left of the Help Window.

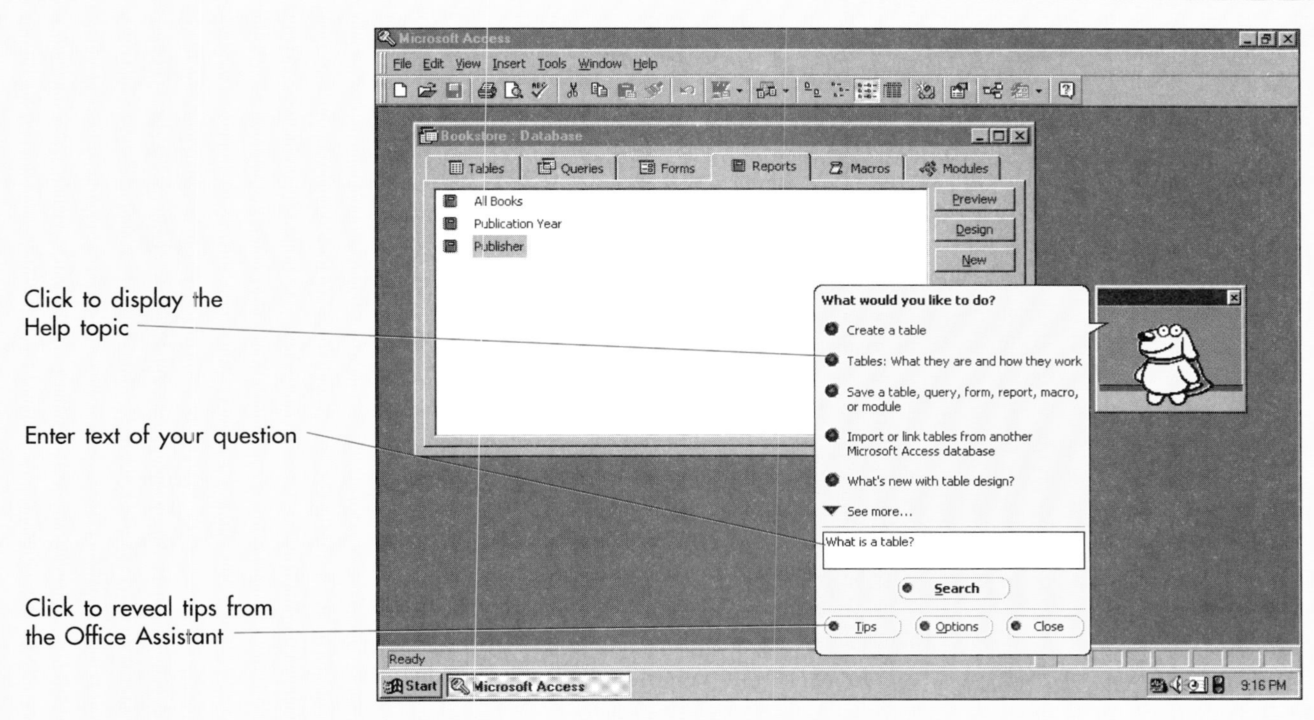

(i) The Office Assistant (step 10)

FIGURE 1.6 Hands-on Exercise 2 (continued)

- These help screens also contain a series of screen tips (indicated by a red border). Point to any tip (the mouse pointer changes to a hand), then click to display additional information.
- Continue to read the help screen(s), then close the Help Window.

ADVICE FROM THE OFFICE ASSISTANT

The Office Assistant indicates it has a suggestion by displaying a lightbulb. Click the lightbulb to display the tip, then click the Back or Next buttons as appropriate to view additional tips. The Assistant will not, however, repeat a tip from an earlier session unless you reset it at the start of a new session. To reset the tips, click the Assistant to display a balloon asking what you want to do, click the Options button in the balloon, click the Options tab, then click the button to Reset My Tips.

STEP 11: Exit Access

- Pull down the **File menu.** Click **Exit** to close the Bookstore database and also exit from Access.
- Remember to use the Windows Explorer to copy the Bookstore database from drive C to a floppy disk that you will keep as backup.

LOOKING AHEAD: A RELATIONAL DATABASE

The database we have been using is a simple database in that it contains only one table. The real power of Access, however, is derived from multiple tables and the relationships between those tables. This type of database is known as a ***relational database.***

This section extends the Bookstore example by including the additional tables for Publishers and Orders. We will ask you to look at the data in those tables in order to answer questions about the database. You will need to consider several tables at the same time, but that is precisely what Access does. Once you see how the tables are related to one another, you will be well on your way to designing your own applications.

Pretend again that you are the manager of the bookstore and think about how you would actually use the database. You want information about the individual books, but you also need information about the publishers of those books. At the very least you need the publishers' addresses and phone numbers so that you can order the books. And once you order the books, you need to be able to track the orders, to know when each order was placed, which books were ordered, and how many of each. These requirements give rise to a database with several additional tables as shown in Figure 1.7.

The Books table in Figure 1.7a is similar to the table in the hands-on exercise, with one modification. This is the substitution of a (shorter) PublisherID field instead of the publisher's name. The Books table contains only fields that pertain to a specific book, such as the book's ISBN, Title, Author, Year (of publication), List Price, and PublisherID. The Publishers table has fields that pertain to the publisher: PublisherID, Publisher Name, Address, City, State, Zipcode, and Phone. The PublisherID appears in both tables, enabling us to obtain the publisher's address and phone number for a particular book. Consider:

Query: What are the address and telephone number for the publisher of the book *Exploring Windows 95?*

Answer: *Exploring Windows 95* is published by Prentice Hall, which is located at 1 Lake Street, Upper Saddle River, NJ 07458. The telephone number is (800) 526-0485.

To determine the answer, Access would search the Books table for *Exploring Windows 95* to obtain the PublisherID (P4 in this example). It would then search the Publishers table for the publisher with this PublisherID and obtain the address and phone number from that record. The relationship between the publishers and books is an example of a ***one-to-many relationship.*** One publisher can have many books, but a book can have only one publisher.

Query: Which books are published by Ventana Press?

Answer: Three books—*Looking Good in Print, The Presentation Design Book,* and *HTML Publishing on the Internet*—are published by Ventana Press.

To answer this query, Access would begin in the Publishers table and search for Ventana Press to determine the PublisherID. It would then select all records in the Books table with a PublisherID of P6. It's easy once you recognize the relationship between the tables.

The Bookstore database in Figure 1.7 has a second one-to-many relationship between publishers and orders. One publisher can receive many orders, but a given order goes to only one publisher. Use this relationship to answer the following queries:

ISBN	Title	Author	Year	List Price	PublisherID
0-07-881980-6	The Internet Complete Reference	Hahn/Stout	1994	$29.95	P3
0-07-882023-5	The Internet Yellow Pages	Hahn/Stout	1994	$27.95	P3
0-13-065541-4	Exploring Windows 3.1	Grauer/Barber	1994	$24.95	P4
0-13-138686-7	COBOL: From Micro to Mainframe/2e	Grauer/Villar	1994	$52.95	P4
0-13-503328-4	Exploring PowerPoint 7.0	Grauer/Barber	1996	$28.85	P4
0-13-503393-4	Exploring Access 7.0	Grauer/Barber	1996	$28.85	P4
0-13-503401-9	Exploring Excel 7.0	Grauer/Barber	1996	$28.85	P4
0-13-504044-2	Exploring Word 7.0	Grauer/Barber	1996	$28.85	P4
0-13-504051-5	Exploring the Internet	Marks	1996	$28.85	P4
0-13-504069-8	Exploring Office 95	Grauer/Barber	1996	$34.95	P4
0-13-504077-9	Exploring Windows 95	Grauer/Barber	1996	$28.95	P4
0-672-30306-X	Memory Management for All of Us	Goodman	1993	$39.95	P8
0-672-30362-0	Navigating the Internet	Gibbs/Smith	1993	$24.95	P8
0-88022-761-3	Speed Up Your Computer Book	Reed/Nance	1992	$29.95	P5
0-940087-32-4	Looking Good in Print	Parker	1990	$23.95	P6
0-940087-37-5	The Presentation Design Book	Rabb	1990	$24.95	P6
1-56205-306-X	New Riders Internet Yellow Pages	Maxwell/Grycx	1994	$29.95	P7
1-56276-095-5	Using the World Wide Web	Eager	1994	$27.99	P5
1-56604-229-1	HTML Publishing on the Internet	Heslop/Budnick	1995	$49.95	P6
1-56686-127-6	The Hardware Bible	Rosch	1994	$35.00	P2
1-56884-453-0	Windows 95 Secrets	Livingston/Straub	1995	$39.95	P1

(a) Books Table

PublisherID	Publisher Name	Address	City	State	Zipcode	Phone
P1	IDG Books Worldwide	919 E. Hillsdale Blvd.	Foster City	CA	94404	(800)762-2974
P2	Macmillan Publishing	201 West 103 Street	Indianapolis	IN	46290	(317)871-6724
P3	Osborne-McGraw Hill	2600 Tenth Street	Berkeley	CA	94710	(800)338-3987
P4	Prentice Hall	1 Lake Street	Upper Saddle River	NJ	07458	(800)526-0485
P5	Que Corporation	201 West 103 Street	Indianapolis	IN	46290	(317)581-3500
P6	Ventana Press	P.O. Box 2468	Chapel Hill	NC	27515	(800)743-5369
P7	New Riders Publishing	201 West 103 Street	Indianapolis	IN	46290	(317)581-3500
P8	Sams Publishing	11711 N. College Ave.	Carmel	IN	46032	(800)526-0465

(b) Publishers Table

OrderID	Date	PublisherID
O1	1/12/96	P4
O2	3/15/96	P5
O3	11/15/95	P4
O4	2/3/96	P3
O5	1/15/96	P2
O6	12/16/95	P1
O7	3/30/96	P4
O8	11/11/95	P6
O9	12/15/95	P8
O10	2/2/96	P6

(c) Orders Table

OrderID	ISBN	Quantity
O1	0-13-504077-9	200
O1	0-13-503393-4	200
O2	1-56276-095-5	35
O3	0-13-503393-4	450
O3	0-13-503401-9	450
O3	0-13-504044-2	450
O4	0-07-881980-6	50
O4	0-07-882023-5	75
O5	1-56686-127-6	25
O6	1-56884-453-0	30
O7	0-13-503328-4	60
O7	0-13-503401-9	60
O7	0-13-504044-2	60
O7	0-13-504069-8	350
O8	0-940087-32-4	75
O8	1-56604-229-1	125
O9	0-672-30362-0	150
O10	1-56604-229-1	50

(d) Order Details Table

FIGURE 1.7 The Bookstore Database

Query: What is the publisher and address associated with order number O4?
Answer: Osborne-McGraw Hill at 2600 Tenth Street, Berkeley, CA 94710.

To determine the publisher's address, Access first has to identify the publisher. Thus it would search the Orders table (Figure 1.7c) for the specific order (order number O4 in this example) to obtain the corresponding PublisherID (P3). It would then search the Publishers table for the matching PublisherID and return the publisher's name and address.

You probably have no trouble recognizing the need for the Books, Publishers, and Orders tables in Figure 1.7. You may be confused, however, by the presence of the Order Details table, which is made necessary by the ***many-to-many relationship*** between orders and books. One order can specify several books; at the same time, one book can appear in many orders. Consider:

Query: Which books were included in order number O7?
Answer: *Exploring PowerPoint 7.0, Exploring Excel 7.0, Exploring Word 7.0,* and *Exploring Office 95.*

To answer the query, Access would search the Order Details table for all records with an Order ID of O7. Access would then take the ISBN number found in each of these records and search the Books table for the records with matching ISBN numbers. Can you answer the next query, which is also based on the many-to-many relationship between books and orders?

Query: How many copies of *Exploring Access 7.0* were ordered?
Answer: A total of 650 copies.

This time, Access searches the Books table to obtain the ISBN number for *Exploring Access 7.0,* then searches the Order Details table for all records with this ISBN number (0-13-503393-4). It finds two such records (associated with orders 1 and 3), then it adds these quantities (200 and 450) to obtain the total number of copies that were ordered.

We trust that you were able to answer our queries by intuitively relating the tables to one another. Eventually, you will learn how to do this automatically in Access, but you must first gain a solid understanding of how to work with one table at a time. This is the focus of Chapters 2 and 3.

THE INTERNATIONAL STANDARD BOOK NUMBER

The International Standard Book Number (ISBN) is an internationally recognized number that uniquely identifies a book. The first part of the ISBN indicates the publisher; for example, every book published by Prentice Hall begins with 0-13. The founder of Prentice Hall was very superstitious and the selection of the number 13 was not an accident. Prentice Hall was founded in 1913, its first office was on 13th Street in New York City, and its first phone number ended in 1300. The original name of the company included a hyphen. "Prentice-Hall" (including the hyphen) is thirteen characters.

SUMMARY

A database consists of multiple tables that are related to each other. Each table in the database is composed of records, and each record is in turn composed of fields. Every record in a given table has the same fields in the same order.

An Access database has six types of objects—tables, forms, queries, reports, macros, and modules. The database window displays these objects and enables you to open an existing object or create a new object.

A table is displayed in one of two views—the Design view or the Datasheet view. The Design view is used to define the table initially and to specify the fields it will contain. The Datasheet view is the view you use to add, edit, or delete records.

A record selector symbol is displayed next to the current record and signifies the status of that record. A triangle indicates that the record has been saved. A pencil indicates that the record has not been saved and that you are in the process of entering (or changing) the data. An asterisk appears next to the blank record present at the end of every table, where you add a new record to the table.

Access automatically saves any changes in the current record as soon as you move to the next record or when you close the table. The Undo Current Record command cancels (undoes) the changes to the previously saved record.

No system, no matter how sophisticated, can produce valid output from invalid input. Data validation is thus a critical part of any system. Access automatically imposes certain types of data validation during data entry. Additional checks can be implemented by the user.

A relational database contains multiple tables and enables you to extract information from multiple tables at the same time. The tables in the database are connected to one another through a one-to-many or many-to-many relationship.

The Office Assistant is new to Office 97 and is activated by clicking the Office Assistant button on the Standard toolbar, by pulling down the Help menu and requesting Word help, or by pressing the F1 function key. The Assistant enables you to ask a question in English, then it returns a series of topics that attempt to answer your question.

KEY WORDS AND CONCEPTS

Asterisk (record selector) symbol
AutoCorrect
Current record
Data validation
Database
Database window
Datasheet view
Design view
Field
Field name
Find command
Form
GIGO (garbage in, garbage out)
Insertion point
Macro
Many-to-many relationship
Microsoft Access
Module
One-to-many relationship
Pencil (record selector) symbol
Primary key
Query
Record
Record selector symbol
Relational database
Replace command
Report
Table
Triangle (record selector) symbol
Undo command

Multiple Choice

1. Which sequence represents the hierarchy of terms, from smallest to largest?
   (a) Database, table, record, field
   (b) Field, record, table, database
   (c) Record, field, table, database
   (d) Field, record, database, table

2. Which of the following is true regarding movement within a record (assuming you are not in the first or last field of that record)?
   (a) Press Tab or the right arrow key to move to the next field
   (b) Press Shift+Tab or the left arrow key to return to the previous field
   (c) Both (a) and (b)
   (d) Neither (a) nor (b)

3. You're performing routine maintenance on a table within an Access database. When should you execute the Save command?
   (a) Immediately after you add, edit, or delete a record
   (b) Periodically during a session—for example, after every fifth change
   (c) Once at the end of a session
   (d) None of the above since Access automatically saves the changes as they are made

4. Which of the following objects are contained within an Access database?
   (a) Tables and forms
   (b) Queries and reports
   (c) Macros and modules
   (d) All of the above

5. Which of the following is true about the objects in an Access database?
   (a) Every database must contain at least one object of every type
   (b) A database may contain at most one object of each type
   (c) Both (a) and (b)
   (d) Neither (a) nor (b)

6. Which of the following is true of an Access database?
   (a) Every record in a table has the same fields as every other record in that table
   (b) Every table contains the same number of records as every other table
   (c) Both (a) and (b)
   (d) Neither (a) nor (b)

7. Which of the following is a *false* statement about the Open Database command?
   (a) It can be executed from the File menu
   (b) It can be executed by clicking the Open button on the Database toolbar
   (c) It loads a database from disk into memory
   (d) It opens the selected table from the Database window

8. Which of the following is true regarding the record selector symbol?
   (a) A pencil indicates that the current record has already been saved
   (b) A triangle indicates that the current record has not changed
   (c) An asterisk indicates the first record in the table
   (d) All of the above

9. Which view is used to add, edit, and delete records in a table?
   (a) The Design view
   (b) The Datasheet view
   (c) Either (a) or (b)
   (d) Neither (a) nor (b)

10. Which of the following is true with respect to a table within an Access database?
   (a) Ctrl+End moves to the last field in the last record of a table
   (b) Ctrl+Home moves to the first field in the first record of a table
   (c) Both (a) and (b)
   (d) Neither (a) nor (b)

11. What does GIGO stand for?
   (a) Gee, I Goofed, OK
   (b) Grand Illusions, Go On
   (c) Global Indexing, Global Order
   (d) Garbage In, Garbage Out

12. The find and replace values in a Replace command must be:
   (a) The same length
   (b) The same case
   (c) Both (a) and (b)
   (d) Neither (a) nor (b)

13. An Access table containing 10 records, and 10 fields per record, requires two pages for printing. What, if anything, can be done to print the table on one page?
   (a) Print in Landscape rather than Portrait mode
   (b) Decrease the left and right margins
   (c) Both (a) and (b)
   (d) Neither (a) nor (b)

14. Which of the following best describes the relationship between publishers and books as implemented in the Bookstore database within the chapter?
   (a) One to one
   (b) One to many
   (c) Many to many
   (d) Impossible to determine

15. Which of the following best describes the relationship between books and orders as implemented in the Bookstore database within the chapter?
   (a) One to one
   (b) One to many
   (c) Many to many
   (d) Impossible to determine

ANSWERS

1. b	**6.** a	**11.** d
2. c	**7.** d	**12.** d
3. d	**8.** b	**13.** c
4. d	**9.** b	**14.** b
5. d	**10.** c	**15.** c

PRACTICE WITH ACCESS 97

1. Do the two hands-on exercises in the chapter, then modify the Bookstore database to accommodate the following:

a. Add the book *Welcome to CompuServe* (ISBN: 1-55828-353-6), written by Banks, published in 1994 by MIS Press, and selling for $24.95.

b. Change the price of *Memory Management for All of Us* to $29.95.

c. Delete *The Presentation Design Book.*

d. Print the *All Books Report* after these changes have been made.

2. The table in Figure 1.8 exists within the Employee database on the data disk. Open the table and do the following:

a. Add a new record for yourself. You have been hired as a trainee earning $25,000 in Boston.

b. Delete the record for Kelly Marder.

c. Change Pamela Milgrom's salary to $59,500.

d. Use the Replace command to change all occurrences of "Manager" to "Supervisor".

e. Print the table after making the changes in parts a through d.

f. Print the Employee Census Report after making the changes in parts a through d.

g. Create a cover page (in Microsoft Word), then submit the output from parts e and f to your instructor.

Employees : Table

SocialSecurityNumber	LastName	FirstName	Location	Title	Salary	Sex
000-01-0000	Milgrom	Pamela	Boston	Manager	$57,500.00	F
000-02-2222	Adams	Jennifer	Atlanta	Trainee	$19,500.00	F
111-12-1111	Johnson	James	Chicago	Account Rep	$47,500.00	M
123-45-6789	Coulter	Tracey	Atlanta	Manager	$100,000.00	F
222-23-2222	Marlin	Billy	Miami	Manager	$125,000.00	M
222-52-5555	James	Mary	Chicago	Account Rep	$42,500.00	F
333-34-3333	Manin	Ann	Boston	Account Rep	$49,500.00	F
333-43-4444	Smith	Frank	Atlanta	Account Rep	$65,000.00	M
333-66-1234	Brown	Marietta	Atlanta	Trainee	$18,500.00	F
444-45-4444	Frank	Vernon	Miami	Manager	$75,000.00	M
555-22-3333	Rubin	Patricia	Boston	Account Rep	$45,000.00	F
555-56-5555	Charles	Kenneth	Boston	Account Rep	$40,000.00	M
776-67-6666	Adamson	David	Chicago	Manager	$52,000.00	M
777-78-7777	Marder	Kelly	Chicago	Account Rep	$38,500.00	F

Record: 1 of 14

FIGURE 1.8 Screen for Practice Exercise 2

3. Figure 1.9 displays a table from the United States (USA) database that is one of our practice files. The database contains statistical data about all 50 states and enables you to produce various reports such as the 10 largest states in terms of population.
   a. Open the USA database, then open the USstates table. Click anywhere in the Population field, then click the Sort Descending button to list the states in descending order. Click and drag to select the first ten records so that you have selected the ten most populous states.
   b. Pull down the File menu, click the Print command, then click the option button to print the selected records. Be sure to print in Landscape mode so that all of the data fits on one page. (Use the Page Setup command in the File menu prior to printing.)
   c. Repeat the procedure in steps a and b, but this time print the ten states with the largest area.
   d. Repeat the procedure once again to print the first thirteen states admitted to the Union. (You have to sort in ascending rather than descending sequence.)
   e. Submit all three pages together with a title page (created in Microsoft Word) to your instructor.

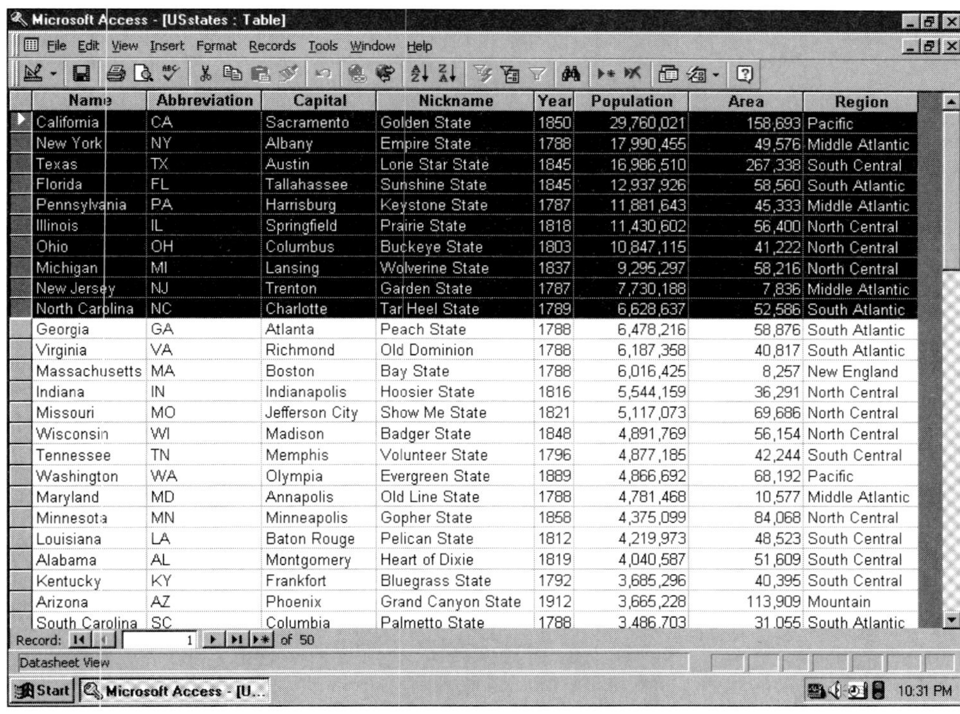

Name	Abbreviation	Capital	Nickname	Year	Population	Area	Region
California	CA	Sacramento	Golden State	1850	29,760,021	158,693	Pacific
New York	NY	Albany	Empire State	1788	17,990,455	49,576	Middle Atlantic
Texas	TX	Austin	Lone Star State	1845	16,986,510	267,338	South Central
Florida	FL	Tallahassee	Sunshine State	1845	12,937,926	58,560	South Atlantic
Pennsylvania	PA	Harrisburg	Keystone State	1787	11,881,643	45,333	Middle Atlantic
Illinois	IL	Springfield	Prairie State	1818	11,430,602	56,400	North Central
Ohio	OH	Columbus	Buckeye State	1803	10,847,115	41,222	North Central
Michigan	MI	Lansing	Wolverine State	1837	9,295,297	58,216	North Central
New Jersey	NJ	Trenton	Garden State	1787	7,730,188	7,836	Middle Atlantic
North Carolina	NC	Charlotte	Tar Heel State	1789	6,628,637	52,586	South Atlantic
Georgia	GA	Atlanta	Peach State	1788	6,478,216	58,876	South Atlantic
Virginia	VA	Richmond	Old Dominion	1788	6,187,358	40,817	South Atlantic
Massachusetts	MA	Boston	Bay State	1788	6,016,425	8,257	New England
Indiana	IN	Indianapolis	Hoosier State	1816	5,544,159	36,291	North Central
Missouri	MO	Jefferson City	Show Me State	1821	5,117,073	69,686	North Central
Wisconsin	WI	Madison	Badger State	1848	4,891,769	56,154	North Central
Tennessee	TN	Memphis	Volunteer State	1796	4,877,185	42,244	South Central
Washington	WA	Olympia	Evergreen State	1889	4,866,692	68,192	Pacific
Maryland	MD	Annapolis	Old Line State	1788	4,781,468	10,577	Middle Atlantic
Minnesota	MN	Minneapolis	Gopher State	1858	4,375,099	84,068	North Central
Louisiana	LA	Baton Rouge	Pelican State	1812	4,219,973	48,523	South Central
Alabama	AL	Montgomery	Heart of Dixie	1819	4,040,587	51,609	South Central
Kentucky	KY	Frankfort	Bluegrass State	1792	3,685,296	40,395	South Central
Arizona	AZ	Phoenix	Grand Canyon State	1912	3,665,228	113,909	Mountain
South Carolina	SC	Columbia	Palmetto State	1788	3,486,703	31,055	South Atlantic

FIGURE 1.9 Screen for Practice Exercise 3

4. Filtering and Sorting: A filter is a set of criteria that is applied to a table in order to display a subset of that table. Access has four types of filters, the easiest of which, Filter by Selection, is illustrated in Figure 1.10.
   a. Open the Super Bowl database on the data disk and display the table in Figure 1.10. Our data stops with the 1996 Super Bowl and is no longer current. Thus, the first thing you need to do is update our table.

b. Pull down the View menu, click Toolbars, then toggle the Web toolbar on. Enter the address of the NFL home page (www.nfl.com) in the Address bar, then click the link to the Super Bowl. Follow the links that will allow you to determine the teams and score of any game(s) not included in our table.

c. Click the New Record button and enter the additional data in the table. The additional data will be entered at the end of the table, and hence you need to sort the data after it is entered. Click anywhere in the Year field, then click the Descending Sort button to display the most recent Super Bowl first.

d. Select the winner in any year (e.g., NFC in 1996 as shown in Figure 1.10). Click the Filter by Selection button to display only those records (i.e., the years in which the NFC won the game). Print these records.

e. Click the Remove Filter button. Select any year in which the AFC won, then click the Filter by Selection button to display the years in which the AFC won. Print these records. Remove the filter.

f. Create one additional filter (e.g., the years in which your team won the big game). Print these records as well.

g. Create a cover sheet, then submit all three reports to your instructor.

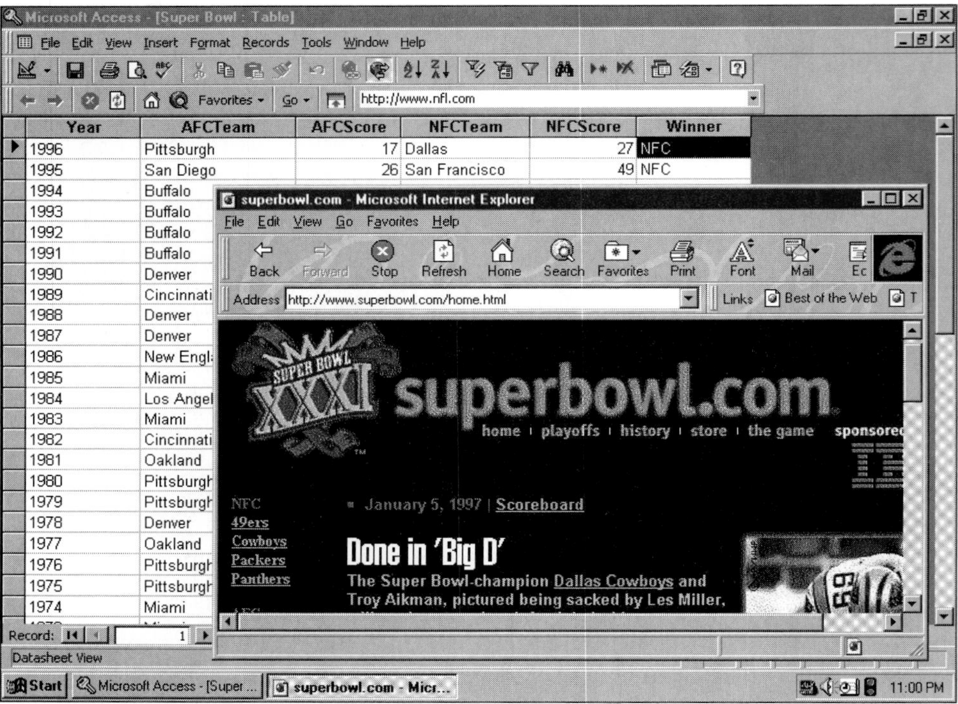

FIGURE 1.10 Screen for Practice Exercise 4

5. This problem is different from the other exercises in that it does not require you to work with a specific database. Instead, we ask you to use the Help facility to review the conceptual information in the chapter.

a. Start the Office Assistant and ask the question, "What is a database?" Select the topic, "Databases: What they are and how they work", to display the screen in Figure 1.11

b. Click the numbers in the upper left corner to read the additional help pages as shown on the screen of Figure 1.11. This will review (and extend) the information about a relational database that was presented at the end of the chapter. The help topic contains a total of seven screens, all of which present helpful information.

c. Was this a useful review? Did you learn anything new that was not covered directly in the chapter? Bring your comments to the next class to discuss your impression with your instructor and classmates.

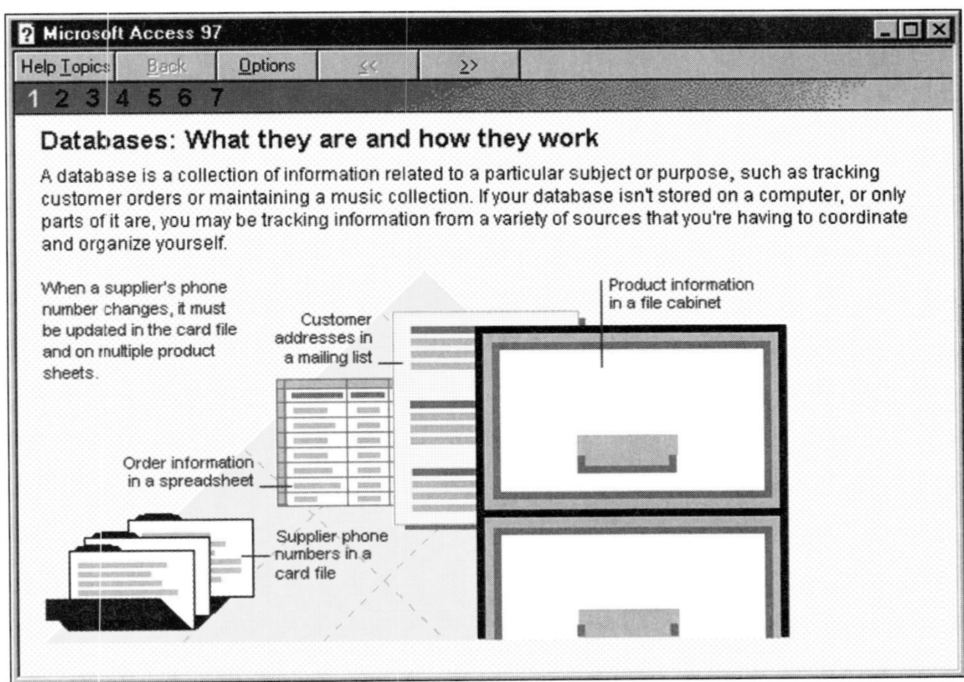

FIGURE 1.11 Screen for Practice Exercise 5

CASE STUDIES

Planning for Disaster

This case has nothing to do with databases per se, but it is perhaps the most important case of all, as it deals with the question of backup. Do you have a backup strategy? Do you even know what a backup strategy is? Now is a good time to learn because sooner or later you will wish you had one. There will come a time when you will accidentally erase a file, be unable to read from a floppy disk, or worse yet, suffer a hardware failure in which you are unable to access the hard drive. The problem always seems to occur the night before an assignment is due. The ultimate disaster is the disappearance of your computer, by theft or natural disaster (e.g., Hurricane Andrew, the floods in the Midwest, or the Los Angeles earthquake). Describe in 250 or fewer words the backup strategy you plan to implement in conjunction with your work in this class.

The Common User Interface

One of the most significant benefits of the Windows environment is the common user interface, which provides a sense of familiarity when you go from one application to another—for example, when you go from Excel to Access. How many similarities can you find between these two applications? Which menus are common to both? Which keyboard shortcuts? Which formatting conventions? Which toolbar icons? Which shortcut menus?

Garbage In, Garbage Out

Your excellent work in this class has earned you an internship in the registrar's office. Your predecessor has created a student database that appears to work well, but in reality has several problems in that many of its reports do not produce the expected information. One problem came to light in conjunction with a report listing business majors: the report contained far fewer majors than were expected. Open the GIGO database on the data disk and see if you can find and correct the problem.

The Database Consultant

The university's bookstore manager has asked your instructor for help in improving the existing database. The manager needs to know which books are used in which courses. One course may require several books, and the same book is often used in many courses. A book may be required in one course and merely recommended in a different course. The manager also needs to be able to contact the faculty coordinator in charge of each course. Which additional table(s) should be added to the database in Figure 1.7 on page 27 to provide this information? Which fields should be present in those tables?

Microsoft Online

Help for Microsoft Access is available from a variety of sources. You can consult the Office Assistant or you can pull down the Help menu to display the Help Contents and Index. Both techniques were illustrated in the chapter. In addition, you can go to the Microsoft Web site to obtain more recent, and often more detailed, information. You will find the answer to the most frequently asked questions and you can access the same knowledge base used by Microsoft support engineers. Experiment with various sources of help, then submit a summary of your findings to your instructor. Try to differentiate between the various techniques and suggest the most appropriate use for each.

2

TABLES AND FORMS: DESIGN, PROPERTIES, VIEWS, AND WIZARDS

OBJECTIVES

After reading this chapter you will be able to:

1. Describe in general terms how to design a table; discuss three guidelines you can use in the design process.
2. Describe the data types and properties available within Access and the purpose of each; set the primary key for a table.
3. Use the Table Wizard to create a table; add and delete fields in an existing table.
4. Discuss the importance of data validation and how it is implemented in Access.
5. Use the Form Wizard to create one of several predefined forms.
6. Distinguish between a bound control, an unbound control, and a calculated control; explain how each type of control is entered on a form.
7. Modify an existing form to include a combo box, command buttons, and color.
8. Switch between the Form view, Design view, and Datasheet view; use a form to add, edit, and delete records in a table.

OVERVIEW

This chapter introduces a new case study, that of a student database, which we use to present the basic principles of table and form design. Tables and forms are used to input data into a system from which information can be produced. The value of that information depends entirely on the quality of the underlying data, which must be both complete and accurate. We begin, therefore, with a conceptual discussion emphasizing the importance of proper design and develop essential guidelines that are used throughout the book.

After the design has been developed, we turn our attention to implementing that design in Access. We show you how to create a table using the Table Wizard, then show you how to refine its design by changing the properties of various fields within the table. We also stress the importance of data validation during data entry.

The second half of the chapter introduces forms as a more convenient way to enter and display data. We introduce the Form Wizard to create a basic form, then show you how to modify that form to include command buttons, a list box, a check box, and an option group.

As always, the hands-on exercises in the chapter enable you to apply the conceptual material at the computer. This chapter contains three exercises, after which you will be well on your way toward creating a useful database in Access.

CASE STUDY: A STUDENT DATABASE

As a student you are well aware that your school maintains all types of data about you. They have your social security number. They have your name and address and phone number. They know whether or not you are receiving financial aid. They know your major and the number of credits you have completed.

Think for a moment about the information your school requires, then write down all of the data needed to produce that information. This is the key to the design process. You must visualize the output the end user will require to determine the input to produce that output. Think of the specific fields you will need. Try to characterize each field according to the type of data it contains (such as text, numbers, or dates) as well as its size (length).

Our solution is shown in Figure 2.1, which may or may not correspond to what you have written down. The order of the fields within the table is not significant. Neither are the specific field names. What is important is that the table contain all necessary fields so that the system can perform as intended.

Field Name	Type
SSN	Text
FirstName	Text
LastName	Text
Address	Text
City	Text
State	Text
PostalCode	Text
PhoneNumber	Text
Major	Text
BirthDate	Date/Time
FinancialAid	Yes/No
Gender	Text
Credits	Number
QualityPoints	Number

FIGURE 2.1 The Students Table

Figure 2.1 may seem obvious upon presentation, but it does reflect the results of a careful design process based on three essential guidelines:

1. Include all of the necessary data
2. Store data in its smallest parts
3. Do not use calculated fields

Each guideline is discussed in turn. As you proceed through the text, you will be exposed to many applications that help you develop the experience necessary to design your own systems.

Include the Necessary Data

How do you determine the necessary data? The best way is to create a rough draft of the reports you will need, then design the table so that it contains the fields necessary to create those reports. In other words, ask yourself what information will be expected from the system, then determine the data required to produce that information.

Consider, for example, the type of information that can and cannot be produced from the table in Figure 2.1:

- You can contact a student by mail or by telephone. You cannot, however, contact the student's parents if the student lives on campus or has an address different from his or her parents.
- You can calculate a student's grade point average (GPA) by dividing the quality points by the number of credits. You cannot produce a transcript listing the courses a student has taken.
- You can calculate a student's age from his or her date of birth. You cannot determine how long the student has been at the university because the date of admission is not in the table.

Whether or not these omissions are important depends on the objectives of the system. Suffice it to say that you must design a table carefully, so that you are not disappointed when it is implemented. *You must be absolutely certain that the data entered into a system is sufficient to provide all necessary information;* otherwise the system is almost guaranteed to fail.

DESIGN FOR THE NEXT 100 YEARS

Your system will not last 100 years, but it is prudent to design as though it will. It is a fundamental law of information technology that systems evolve continually and that information requirements will change. Try to anticipate the future needs of the system, then build in the flexibility to satisfy those demands. Include the necessary data at the outset and be sure that the field sizes are large enough to accommodate future expansion.

Store Data in Its Smallest Parts

Figure 2.1 divides a student's name into two fields (first name and last name) to reference each field individually. You might think it easier to use a single field consisting of both the first and last name, but that approach is inadequate. Consider, for example, the following list in which the student's name is stored as a single field:

Allison Foster
Brit Reback
Carrie Graber
Danielle Ferrarro

The first problem in this approach is one of flexibility, in that you cannot separate a student's first name from her last name. You could not, for example, create a salutation of the form "Dear Allison" or "Dear Ms. Foster" because the first and last name are not accessible individually.

A second difficulty is that the list of students cannot be put into alphabetical order because the last name begins in the middle of the field. Indeed, whether you realize it or not, the names in the list are already in alphabetical order (according to the design criteria of a single field) because sorting always begins with the leftmost position in a field. Thus the "A" in Allison comes before the "B" in Brit, and so on. The proper way to sort a file is on the last name, which can be done only if the last name is stored as a separate field.

CITY, STATE, AND ZIP CODE: ONE FIELD OR THREE?

The city, state, and zip code should always be stored as separate fields. Any type of mass mailing requires you to sort on zip code to take advantage of bulk mail. Other applications may require you to select records from a particular state or zip code, which can be done only if the data is stored as separate fields. The guideline is simple—store data in its smallest parts.

Avoid Calculated Fields

A ***calculated field*** is a field whose value is derived from a formula or function that references an existing field or combination of fields. Calculated fields should not be stored in a table because they are subject to change, waste space, and are otherwise redundant.

The Grade Point Average (GPA) is an example of a calculated field as it is computed by dividing the number of quality points by the number of credits. It is both unnecessary and undesirable to store GPA in the Students table, because the table contains the fields on which the GPA is based. In other words, Access is able to calculate the GPA from these fields whenever it is needed, which is much more efficient than doing it manually. Imagine, for example, having to manually recalculate the GPA for 10,000 students each semester.

BIRTHDATE VERSUS AGE

A person's age and date of birth provide equivalent information, as one is calculated from the other. It might seem easier, therefore, to store the age rather than the birth date, and thus avoid the calculation. That would be a mistake because age changes continually (and would need to be updated continually), whereas the date of birth remains constant. Similar reasoning applies to an employee's length of service versus date of hire.

There are two ways to create a table. The easier way is to use the ***Table Wizard,*** an interactive coach that lets you choose from several predefined tables. The Table Wizard asks you questions about the fields you want to include in your table, then creates the table for you. Alternatively, you can create a table yourself by defining every field in the table. Regardless of how a table is created, you can modify it to include a new field or to delete an existing field.

Every field has a ***field name*** to identify the data that is entered into the field. The field name should be descriptive of the data and can be up to 64 characters in length, including letters, numbers, and spaces. We do not, however, use spaces in our field names, but use uppercase letters to distinguish the first letter of a new word. This is consistent with the default names provided by Access in its predefined tables.

Every field also has a ***data type*** that determines the type of data that can be entered and the operations that can be performed on that data. Access recognizes nine data types: Number, Text, Memo, Date/Time, Currency, Yes/No, OLE Object, AutoNumber, and Hyperlink.

- A ***Number field*** contains a value that can be used in a calculation such as the number of quality points or credits a student has earned. The contents of a number field are restricted to numbers, a decimal point, and a plus or minus sign.
- A ***Text field*** stores alphanumeric data such as a student's name or address. It can contain alphabetic characters, numbers, and/or special characters (e.g., an apostrophe in O'Malley). Fields that contain only numbers but are not used in a calculation (e.g., social security number, telephone number, or zip code) should be designated as text fields for efficiency purposes. A text field can hold up to 255 characters.
- A ***Memo field*** can be up to 64,000 characters long. Memo fields are used to hold descriptive data (several sentences or paragraphs).
- A ***Date/Time field*** holds formatted dates or times (e.g., mm/dd/yy) and allows the values to be used in date or time arithmetic.
- A ***Currency field*** can be used in a calculation and is used for fields that contain monetary values.
- A ***Yes/No field*** (also known as a Boolean or Logical field) assumes one of two values such as Yes or No, or True or False.
- An ***OLE field*** contains an object created by another application. OLE objects include pictures, sounds, or graphics.
- An ***AutoNumber field*** is a special data type that causes Access to assign the next consecutive number each time you add a record. The value of an AutoNumber field is unique for each record in the file, and thus AutoNumber fields are frequently used as the primary key.
- A ***Hyperlink field*** stores a Web address (URL). All Office 97 documents are Web-enabled so that you can click a hyperlink within an Access database and display the associated Web page, provided that you have access to the Internet.

Primary Key

The ***primary key*** is a field (or combination of fields) that uniquely identifies a record. There can be only one primary key per table and, by definition, every record in the table must have a different value for the primary key.

A person's name is not used as the primary key because names are not unique. A social security number, on the other hand, is unique and is a frequent choice for the primary key as in the Students table in this chapter. The primary key emerges naturally in many applications such as a part number in an inventory system, or the ISBN in the Books table of Chapter 1. If there is no apparent primary key, a new field can be created with the AutoNumber field type.

Views

A table has two views—the Datasheet view and the Design view. The Datasheet view is the view you used in Chapter 1 to add, edit, and delete records. The Design view is the view you will use in this chapter to create (and modify) a table.

Figure 2.2a shows the Datasheet view corresponding to the table in Figure 2.1. (Not all of the fields are visible.) The ***Datasheet view*** displays the record selector symbol for the current record (a pencil or a triangle). It also displays an asterisk in the record selector column next to the blank record at the end of the table.

Figure 2.2b shows the Design view of the same table. The ***Design view*** displays the field names in the table, the data type of each field, and the properties of the selected field. The Design view also displays a key indicator next to the field (or combination of fields) designated as the primary key.

Students : Table

SSN	First Name	Last Name	Address	City	State	Postal Code	Phone Number
111-11-1111	Ronnie	Adili	3543 Queen Avenue	Minneapolis	MN	55476-9899	(612) 445-7654
222-22-2222	Christopher	Gibson	9807 S.W. 152 Street	Miami	FL	33157-2332	(305) 235-4563
333-33-3333	Nickolas	Korba	85 Bayshore Drive	San Francisc	CA	94114-5533	(415) 664-0900
444-44-4444	Wendy	Solomon	426 Savona Avenue	Coral Gables	FL	33124-9066	(305) 666-4532
555-55-5555	Eileen	Faulkner	8122 N.W. 76 Street	Ft. Lauderda	FL	33312-5540	(305) 489-8876
666-66-6666	Kevin	DiGiacomo	234 Rivo Alto	Miami Beach	FL	33139-4432	(305) 531-7652
777-77-7777	Cedric	Joseph	544 Best Street	Atlanta	GA	30316-4442	(404) 667-8955

Record: 1 of 7

Current record

Blank record

(a) Datasheet View

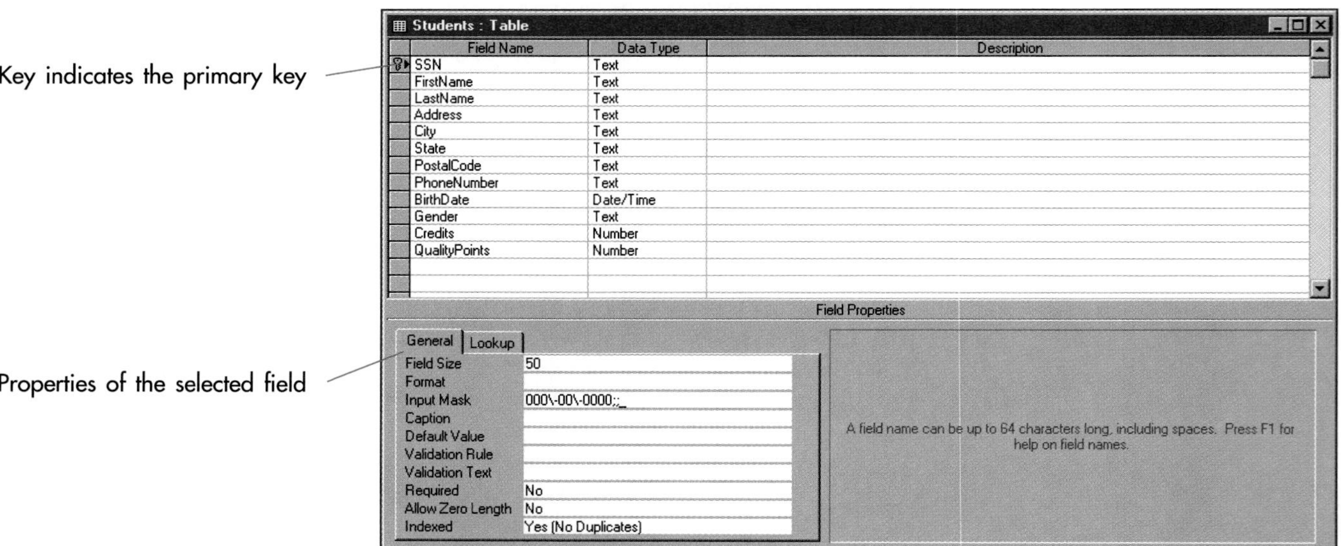
Students : Table

Field Name	Data Type	Description
SSN	Text	
FirstName	Text	
LastName	Text	
Address	Text	
City	Text	
State	Text	
PostalCode	Text	
PhoneNumber	Text	
BirthDate	Date/Time	
Gender	Text	
Credits	Number	
QualityPoints	Number	

Field Properties

General | Lookup

Field Size	50
Format	
Input Mask	000\-00\-0000;;_
Caption	
Default Value	
Validation Rule	
Validation Text	
Required	No
Allow Zero Length	No
Indexed	Yes (No Duplicates)

A field name can be up to 64 characters long, including spaces. Press F1 for help on field names.

(b) Design View

FIGURE 2.2 The Views of a Table

Properties

A ***property*** is a characteristic or attribute of an object that determines how the object looks and behaves. Every Access object (tables, forms, queries, and reports) has a set of properties that determine the behavior of that object. The properties for an object are displayed and/or changed in a ***property sheet,*** which is described in more detail later in the chapter.

Each field has its own set of properties that determine how the data in the field are stored and displayed. The properties are set to default values according to the data type, but can be modified as necessary. The properties are displayed in the Design view and described briefly below:

- The ***Field Size property*** adjusts the size of a text field or limits the allowable value in a number field. Microsoft Access uses only the amount of space it needs even if the field size allows a greater number.
- The ***Format property*** changes the way a field is displayed or printed, but does not affect the stored value.
- The ***Input Mask property*** facilitates data entry by displaying characters, such as hyphens in a social security number or slashes in a date. It also imposes data validation by ensuring that the data entered by the user fits within the mask.
- The ***Caption property*** specifies a label other than the field name for forms and reports.
- The ***Default Value property*** automatically assigns a designated (default) value for the field in each record that is added to the table.
- The ***Validation Rule property*** rejects any record where the data does not conform to the specified rules for data entry.
- The ***Validation Text property*** specifies the error message that is displayed when the validation rule is violated.
- The ***Required property*** rejects any record that does not have a value entered for this field.
- The ***Allow Zero Length property*** allows text or memo strings of zero length.
- The ***Indexed property*** increases the efficiency of a search on the designated field. (The primary key in a table is always indexed.)

The following exercise has you create a table using the Table Wizard and then modify the table by including additional fields. It also has you change the properties for various fields within the table.

CHANGE THE DEFAULT FOLDER

The default folder is the folder Access uses to retrieve (and save) a database unless it is otherwise instructed. To change the default folder, pull down the Tools menu, click Options, then click the General tab in the Options dialog box. Enter the name of the default database folder (e.g., C:\Exploring Access), then click OK to accept the settings and close the Options dialog box. The next time you access the File menu the default folder will reflect the change.

HANDS-ON EXERCISE 1

Creating a Table

Objective: To use the Table Wizard to create a table; to add and delete fields in an existing table; to change the primary key of an existing table; to establish an input mask and validation rule for fields within a table; to switch between the Design and Datasheet views of a table. Use Figure 2.3 as a guide.

STEP 1: Create a New Database

- ➤ Click the **Start button** to display the Start menu. Click (or point to) the **Programs menu,** then click **Microsoft Access** to start the program.
- ➤ You should see the Microsoft Access dialog box. Click the option button to create a new database using a **Blank Database.** Click **OK.** You should see the File New Database dialog box shown in Figure 2.3a.
- ➤ Click the **Details button** to change to the Details view. Click and drag the vertical border between columns to change the size of a column.
- ➤ Click the **drop-down arrow** on the Save In list box. Click the appropriate drive (e.g., drive C), depending on the location of your data. Double click the **Exploring Access folder** to make it the active folder.
- ➤ Click in the **File Name text box** and drag to select **db1.** Type **My First Database** as the name of the database you will create. Click the **Create button.**

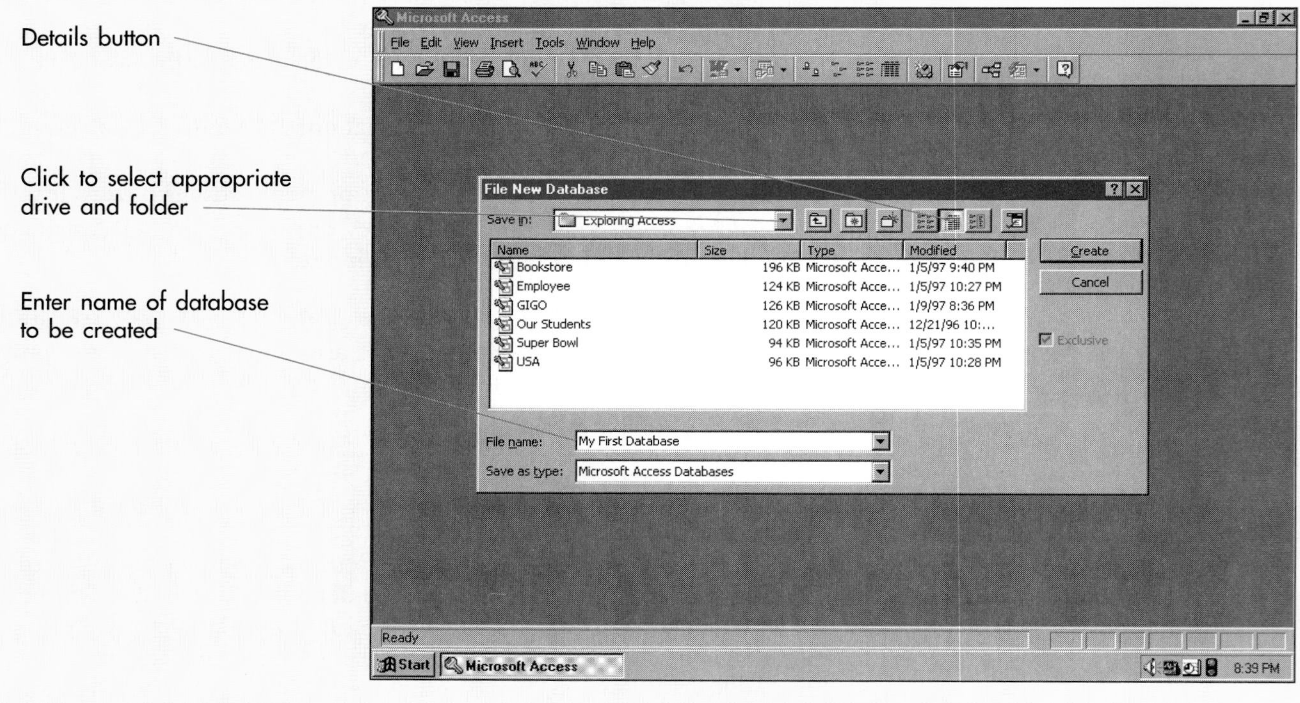

(a) Create a New Database (step 1)

FIGURE 2.3 Hands-on Exercise 1

STEP 2: Create the Table

- The Database window for My First Database should appear on your monitor. The **Tables tab** is selected by default.
- Click and drag an edge or border of the Database window to change its size to match that in Figure 2.3b. Click and drag the title bar of the Database window to change its position on the desktop.
- Click the **New command button** to display the New Table dialog box shown in Figure 2.3b. Click (select) **Table Wizard** in the New Table dialog box, then click **OK** to start the Table Wizard.

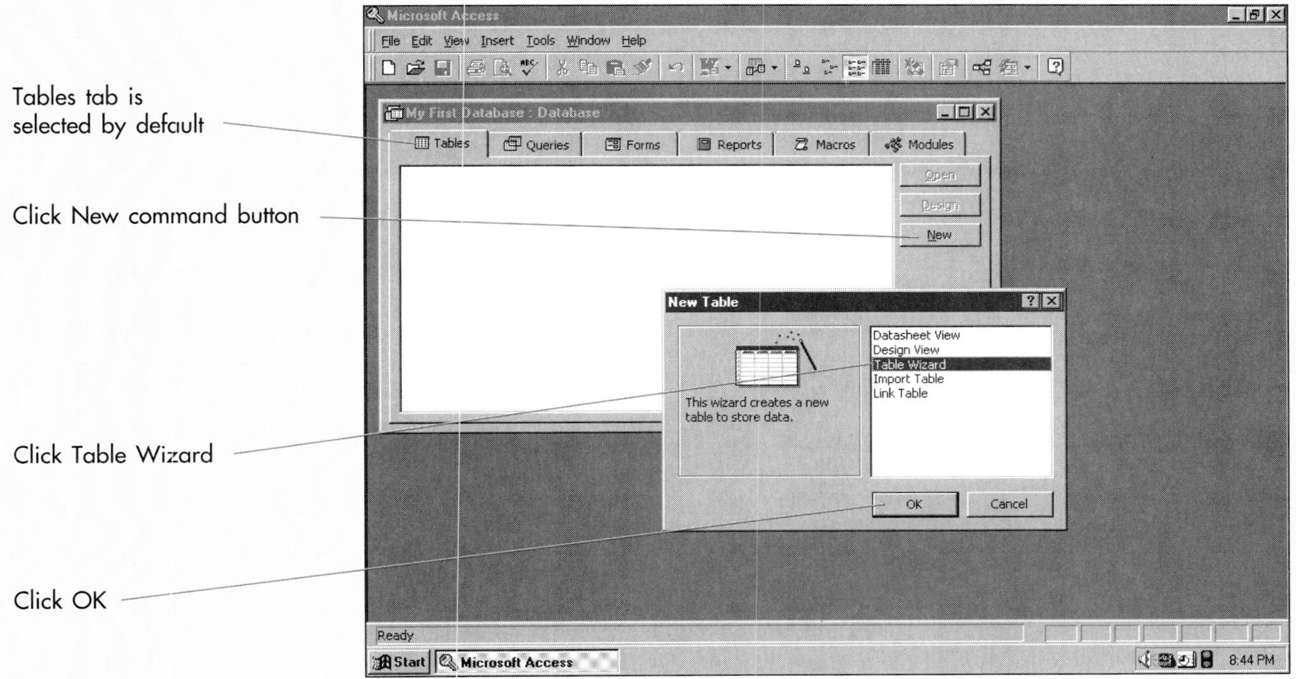

(b) The Table Wizard (step 2)

FIGURE 2.3 Hands-on Exercise 1 (continued)

STEP 3: The Table Wizard

- If necessary, click the **Business option button.** Click the **down arrow** on the **Sample Tables list box** to scroll through the available business tables. Click (select) **Students** within the list of sample tables. The tables are *not* in alphabetical order, and the Students table is found near the very bottom of the list.
- The **StudentID field** is already selected in the Sample Fields list box. Click the > **button** to enter this field in the list of fields for the new table as shown in Figure 2.3c.
- Enter the additional fields for the new table by selecting the field and clicking the > **button** (or by double clicking the field). The fields to enter are: **FirstName, LastName, Address, City,** and **StateOrProvince** as shown in the figure.

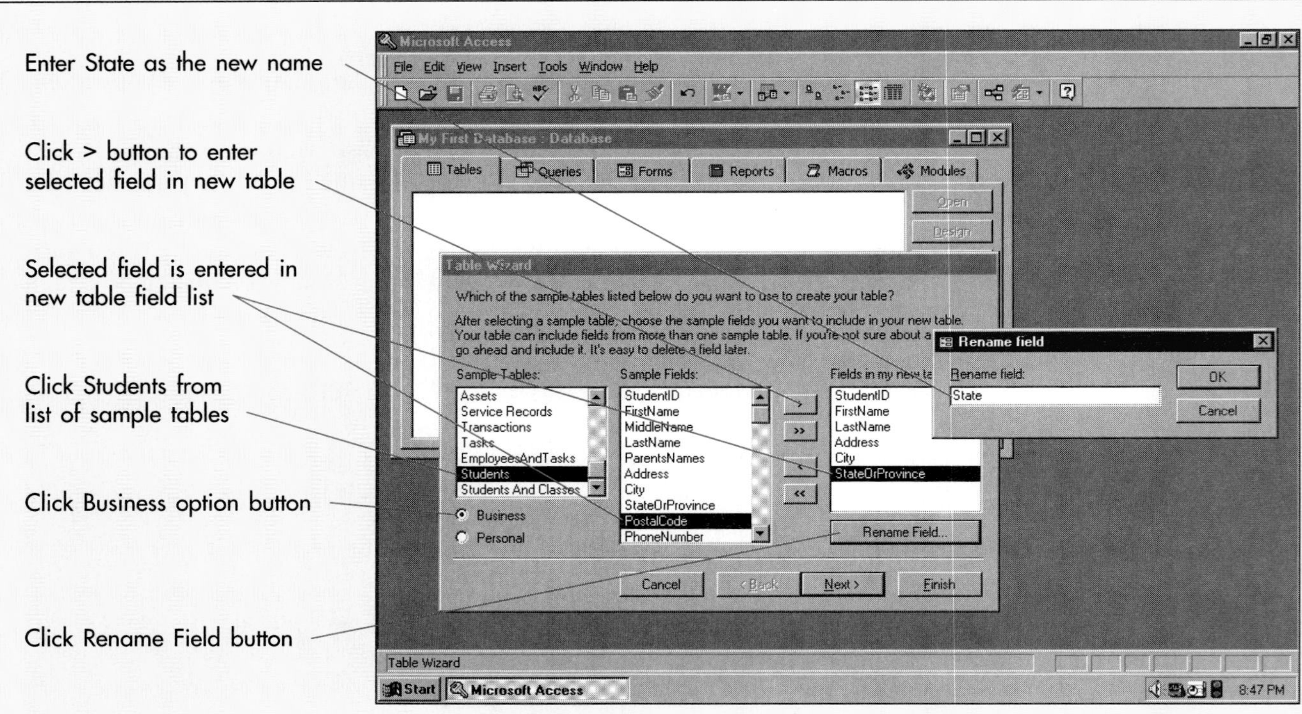

(c) The Table Wizard (step 3)

FIGURE 2.3 Hands-on Exercise 1 (continued)

➤ Click the **Rename Field command button** after adding the StateOrProvince field to display the Rename Field dialog box. Enter **State** to shorten the name of this field. Click **OK.**

➤ Add **PostalCode** and **PhoneNumber** as the last two fields in the table. Click the **Next command button** when you have entered all the fields.

WIZARDS AND BUTTONS

Many Wizards present you with two open list boxes and expect you to copy some or all fields from the list box on the left to the list box on the right. The > and >> buttons work from left to right. The < and << buttons work in the opposite direction. The > button copies the selected field from the list box on the left to the box on the right. The >> button copies all of the fields. The < button removes the selected field from the list box on the right. The << removes all of the fields.

STEP 4: The Table Wizard (continued)

➤ The next screen in the Table Wizard asks you to name the table and determine the primary key.

- Accept the Wizard's suggestion of **Students** as the name of the table.
- Make sure that the option button **Yes, set a primary key for me** is selected.
- Click the **Next command button** to accept both of these options.

- ➤ The final screen in the Table Wizard asks what you want to do next.
  - Click the option button to **Modify the table design.**
  - Click the **Finish command button.** The Students table should appear on your monitor.
- ➤ Pull down the **File menu** and click **Save** (or click the **Save button** on the Table Design toolbar) to save the table.

STEP 5: Add the Additional Fields

- ➤ Click the **Maximize button** to give yourself more room to work. Click the cell immediately below the last field in the table (PhoneNumber). Type **BirthDate** as shown in Figure 2.3d.
- ➤ Press the **Tab key** to move to the Data Type column. Click the **down arrow** on the drop-down list box. Click **Date/Time** as the data type for the BirthDate field.
- ➤ Add the remaining fields with the indicated data types to the Students table:
  - Add **Gender** as a Text field.
  - Add **Credits** as a Number field.
  - Add **QualityPoints** as a Number field. (There is no space in the field name.)
- ➤ Save the table.

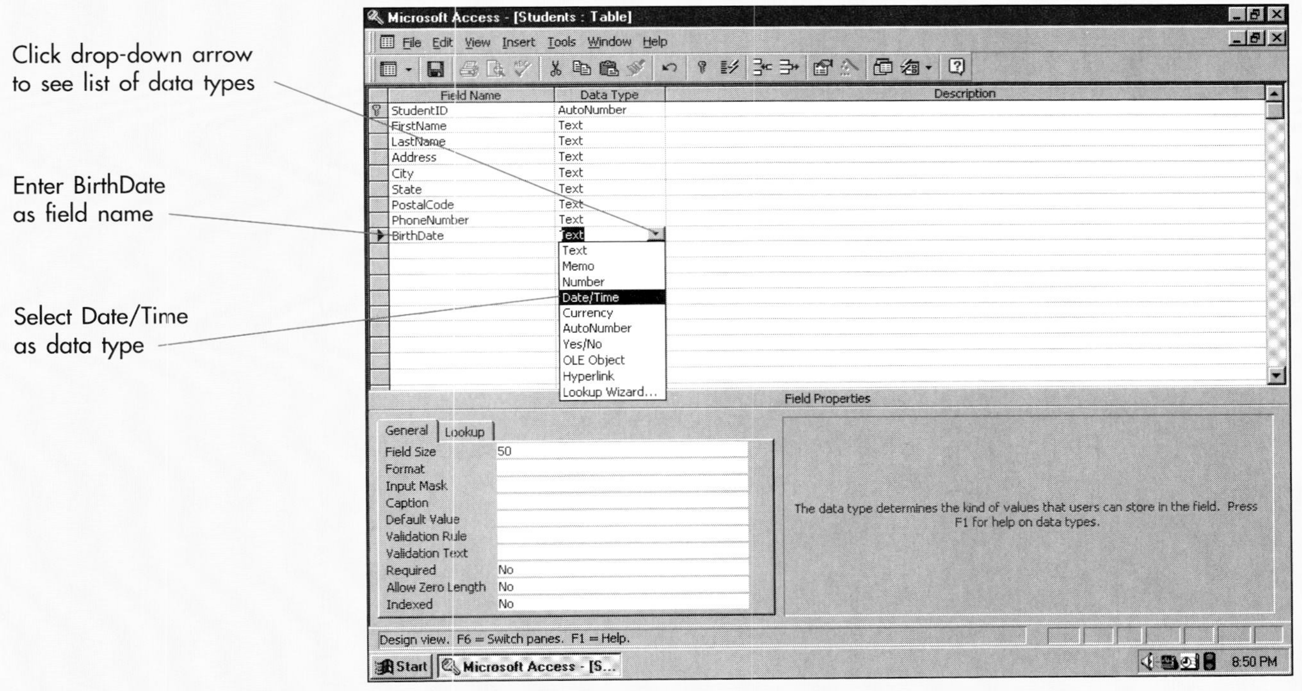

(d) Add the Additional Fields (step 5)

FIGURE 2.3 Hands-on Exercise 1 (continued)

CHOOSING A DATA TYPE

The fastest way to specify the data type is to type the first letter—T for Text, D for Date, N for Number, and Y for Yes/No. Text is the default data type and is entered automatically.

STEP 6: Change the Primary Key

- Point to the first row of the table and click the **right mouse button** to display the shortcut menu in Figure 2.3e. Click **Insert Rows.**
- Click the **Field Name column** in the newly inserted row. Type **SSN** (for social security number) as the name of the new field. Press **enter.** The data type will be set to Text by default.
- Click the **Required box** in the Properties area. Click the drop-down arrow and select **Yes.**
- Click in the Field Name column for **SSN,** then click the **Primary Key button** on the Table Design toolbar to change the primary key to social security number. The primary key symbol has moved from the StudentID field to SSN.
- Point to the **StudentID field** in the second row. Click the **right mouse button** to display the shortcut menu. Click **Delete Rows** to remove this field from the table definition.
- Save the table.

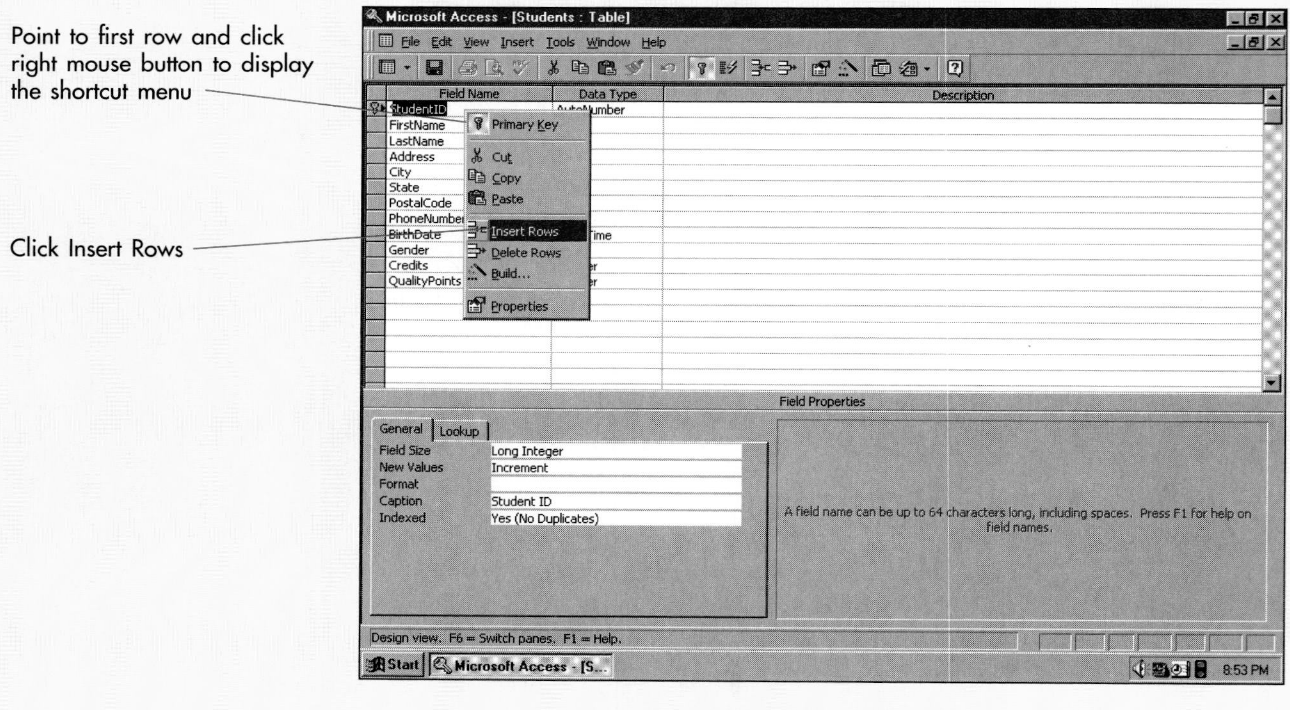

(e) Change the Primary Key (step 6)

FIGURE 2.3 Hands-on Exercise 1 (continued)

INSERTING OR DELETING FIELDS

To insert or delete a field, point to an existing field, then click the right mouse button to display a shortcut menu. Click Insert Row or Delete Row to add or remove a field as appropriate. To insert (or delete) multiple fields, point to the field selector to the left of the field name, click and drag the mouse over multiple rows to extend the selection, then click the right mouse button to display a shortcut menu.

STEP 7: Add an Input Mask

- Click the field selector column for **SSN.** Click the **Input Mask box** in the Properties area. (The box is currently empty.)
- Click the **Build button** to display the Input Mask Wizard. Click **Social Security Number** in the Input Mask Wizard dialog box as shown in Figure 2.3f.
- Click the **Try It** text box and enter a social security number to see how the mask works. If necessary, press the **left arrow key** until you are at the beginning of the text box, then enter a social security number (digits only). Click the **Finish command button** to accept the input mask.
- Click the field selector column for **BirthDate,** then follow the steps detailed above to add an input mask. (Choose the **Short Date** format.) Click **Yes** if asked whether to save the table.
- Save the table.

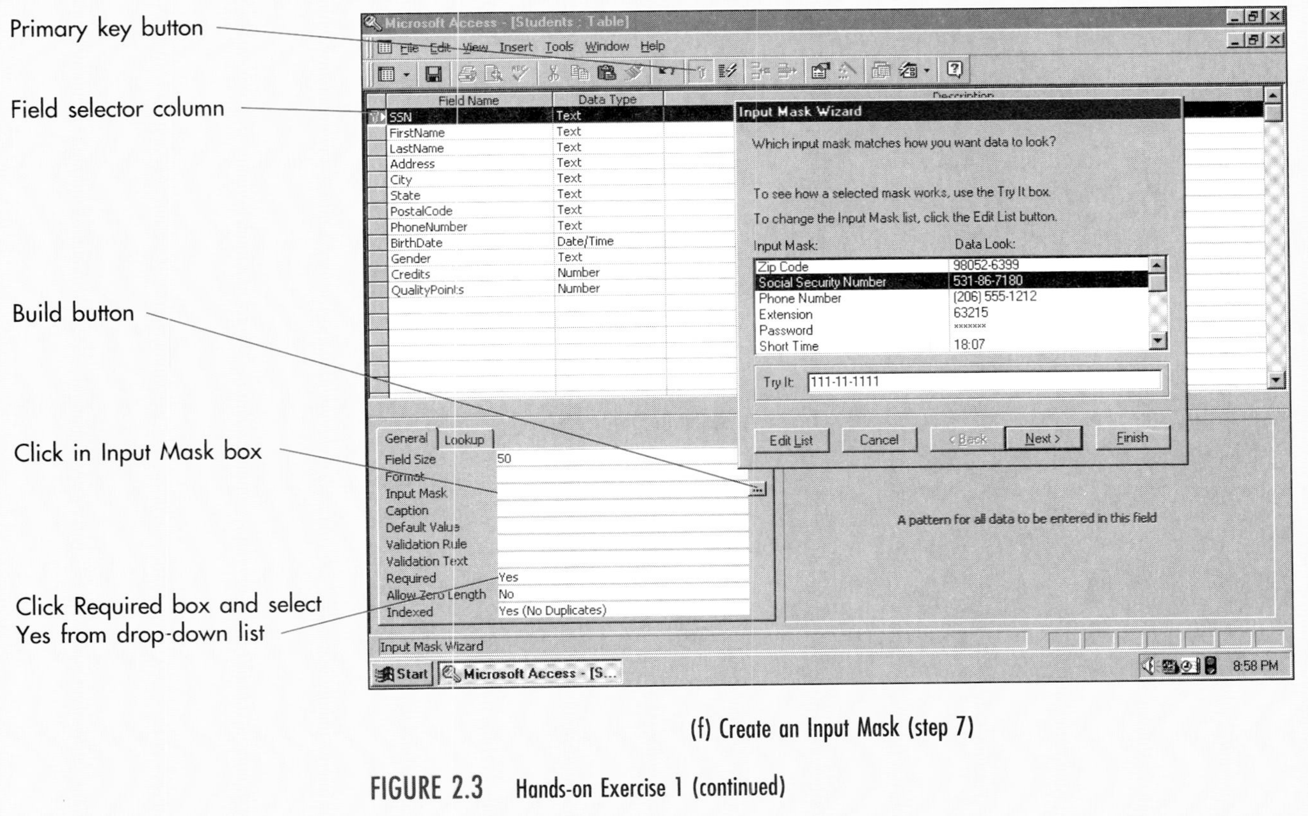

(f) Create an Input Mask (step 7)

FIGURE 2.3 Hands-on Exercise 1 (continued)

STEP 8: Change the Field Properties

➤ Click the field selector column for the **FirstName** field:

- Click the **Field Size box** in the Properties area and change the field size to **25.** (You can press the F6 key to toggle between the field name and the Properties area.)
- Click the **Required box** in the Properties area. Click the **drop-down arrow** and select **Yes.**

➤ Click the field selector column for the **LastName** field:

- Click the **Field Size box** in the Properties area. Change the field size to **25.**
- Click the **Required box** in the Properties area. Click the **drop-down arrow** and select **Yes.**

➤ Click the field selector column for the **State** field.

- Click the **Field Size box** in the Properties area and change the field size to **2,** corresponding to the accepted abbreviation for a state.
- Click the **Format box** in the Properties area. Type a **> sign** to convert the data to uppercase.

➤ Click the field selector column for the **Credits** field:

- Click the **Field Size box** in the Properties area, click the **drop-down arrow** to display the available field sizes, then click **Integer.**
- Click the **Default Value box** in the Properties area. Delete the **0.**

➤ Click the field selector column for the **QualityPoints** field:

- Click the **Field Size box** in the Properties area, click the **drop-down arrow** to display the available field sizes, then click **Integer.**
- Click the **Default Value box** in the Properties area. Delete the **0.**

➤ Save the table.

THE FIELD SIZE PROPERTY

The field size property for a Text or Number field determines the maximum number of characters that can be stored in that field. The property should be set to the smallest possible setting because smaller data sizes are processed more efficiently. A text field can hold from 0 to 255 characters (50 is the default). Number fields (which do not contain a decimal value) can be set to Byte, Integer, or Long Integer field sizes, which hold values up to 255, or 32,767, or 2,147,483,647, respectively. The Single or Double sizes are required if the field is to contain a decimal value, as they specify the precision with which a value will be stored. (See online Help for details.)

STEP 9: Add a Validation Rule

➤ Click the field selector column for the **Gender** field. Click the **Field Size box** and change the field size to **1** as shown in Figure 2.3g.

➤ Click the **Format box** in the Properties area. Type a **> sign** to convert the data entered to uppercase.

- Click the **Validation Rule box.** Type **"M" or "F"** to accept only these values on data entry.
- Click the **Validation Text box.** Type **You must specify M or F.**
- Save the table.

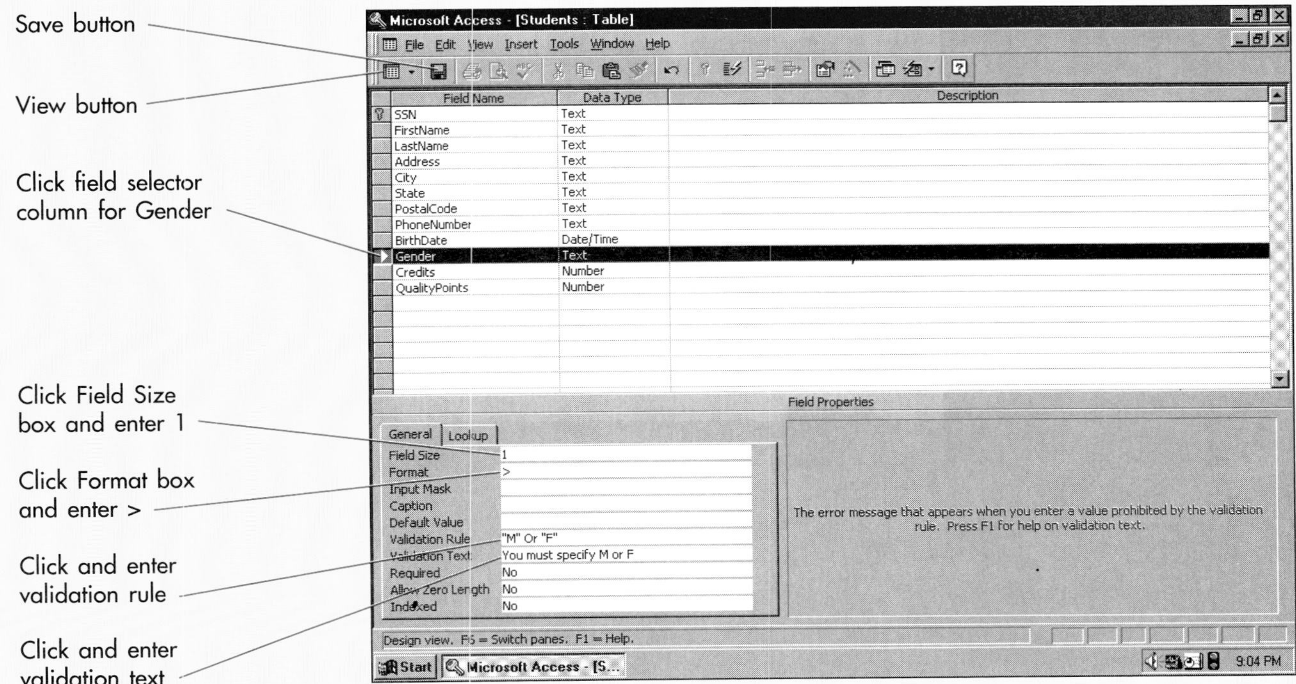

(g) Add a Validation Rule (step 9)

FIGURE 2.3 Hands-on Exercise 1 (continued)

STEP 10: The Datasheet View

- Pull down the **View menu** and click **Datasheet View** (or click the **View button** on the toolbar) to change to the Datasheet view as shown in Figure 2.3h.
- The insertion point (a flashing vertical line indicating the position where data will be entered) is automatically set to the first field of the first record.
- Type **111111111** to enter the social security number for the first record. (The mask will appear as soon as you enter the first digit.)
- Press the **Tab key,** the **right arrow key,** or the **enter key** to move to the FirstName field. Enter the data for Ronnie Adili as shown in Figure 2.3h. Make up data for the fields you cannot see.
- Scrolling takes place automatically as you move within the record.

CHANGE THE FIELD WIDTH

Drag the border between field names to change the displayed width of a field. Double click the right boundary of a field name to change the width to accommodate the widest entry in that field.

Print button

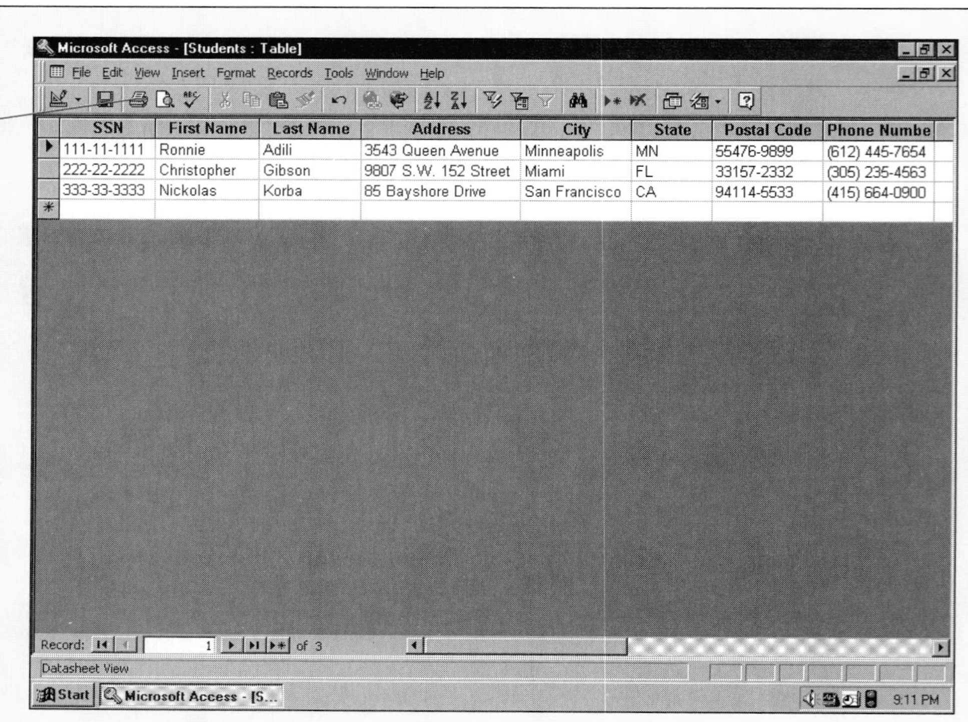

(h) Datasheet View (steps 10 & 11)

FIGURE 2.3 Hands-on Exercise 1 (continued)

STEP 11: Enter Additional Data

➤ Enter data for the two additional students shown in the figure, but enter deliberately invalid data to experiment with the validation capabilities built into Access. Here are some of the errors you may encounter:

- The message, *The value you entered isn't valid for this field,* implies that the data type is wrong—for example, alphabetic characters in a numeric field such as Credits.
- The message, *You must specify M or F,* means you entered a letter other than "M" or "F" in the Gender field (or you didn't enter a value at all).
- The message, *The changes you requested to the table were not successful because they would create duplicate values in the index, primary key, or relationship,* indicates that the value of the primary key is not unique.
- The message, *The field 'Students.LastName' can't contain a Null value,* implies that you left a required field blank.
- If you encounter a data validation error, press **Esc** (or click **OK**), then reenter the data.

STEP 12: Print the Students Table

➤ Pull down the **File menu** and click **Print** (or click the **Print button**). Click the **All option button** to print the entire table. Click **OK.** Do not be concerned if the table prints on multiple pages. (You can, however, use the Page Setup command to change the way the data are printed.)

➤ Pull down the **File menu** and click **Close** to close the Students table. Click **Yes** if asked to save the changes to the table.

- Pull down the **File menu** and click the **Close** command to close the database and remain in Access.
- Pull down the **File menu** a second time and click **Exit** if you do not want to continue with the next exercise at this time.

THE PAGE SETUP COMMAND

The Page Setup command controls the margins and orientation of the printed page and may enable you to keep all fields for a single record on the same page. Pull down the File menu, click Page Setup, click the Margins tab, then decrease the left and right margins (to .5 inch each) to increase the amount of data that is printed on one line. Be sure to check the box to Print Headings so that the field names appear with the table. Click the Page tab, then click the Landscape option button to change the orientation, which further increases the amount of data printed on one line. Click OK to exit the Page Setup dialog box.

FORMS

A ***form*** provides an easy way to enter and display the data stored in a table. You type data into a form, such as the one in Figure 2.4, and Access stores the data in the corresponding (underlying) table in the database. One advantage of using a form (as opposed to entering records in the Datasheet view) is that you can see all of the fields in a single record without scrolling. A second advantage is that a form can be designed to resemble a paper form, and thus provide a sense of familiarity for the individuals who actually enter the data.

A form has different views, as does a table. The ***Form view*** in Figure 2.4a displays the completed form and is used to enter or modify the data in the underlying table. The ***Design view*** in Figure 2.4b is used to create or modify the form.

Controls

All forms consist of ***controls*** (objects) that accept and display data, perform a specific action, or add descriptive information. There are three types of controls—bound, unbound, and calculated. A ***bound control*** (such as the text boxes in Figure 2.4a) has a data source (a field in the underlying table) and is used to enter or modify the data in that table. An ***unbound control*** has no data source. Unbound controls are used to display titles, labels, lines, graphics, or pictures. Note, too, that every bound control (***text box***) in Figure 2.4a is associated with an unbound control (***label***). The bound control for social security number, for example, is preceded by a label (immediately to the left of the control) that indicates to the user the value that is to be entered.

A ***calculated control*** has as its data source an expression rather than a field. An ***expression*** is a combination of operators (e.g., +, −, *, and /), field names, constants, and/or functions. A student's Grade Point Average (GPA in Figure 2.4a) is an example of a calculated control, since it is computed by dividing the number of quality points by the number of credits.

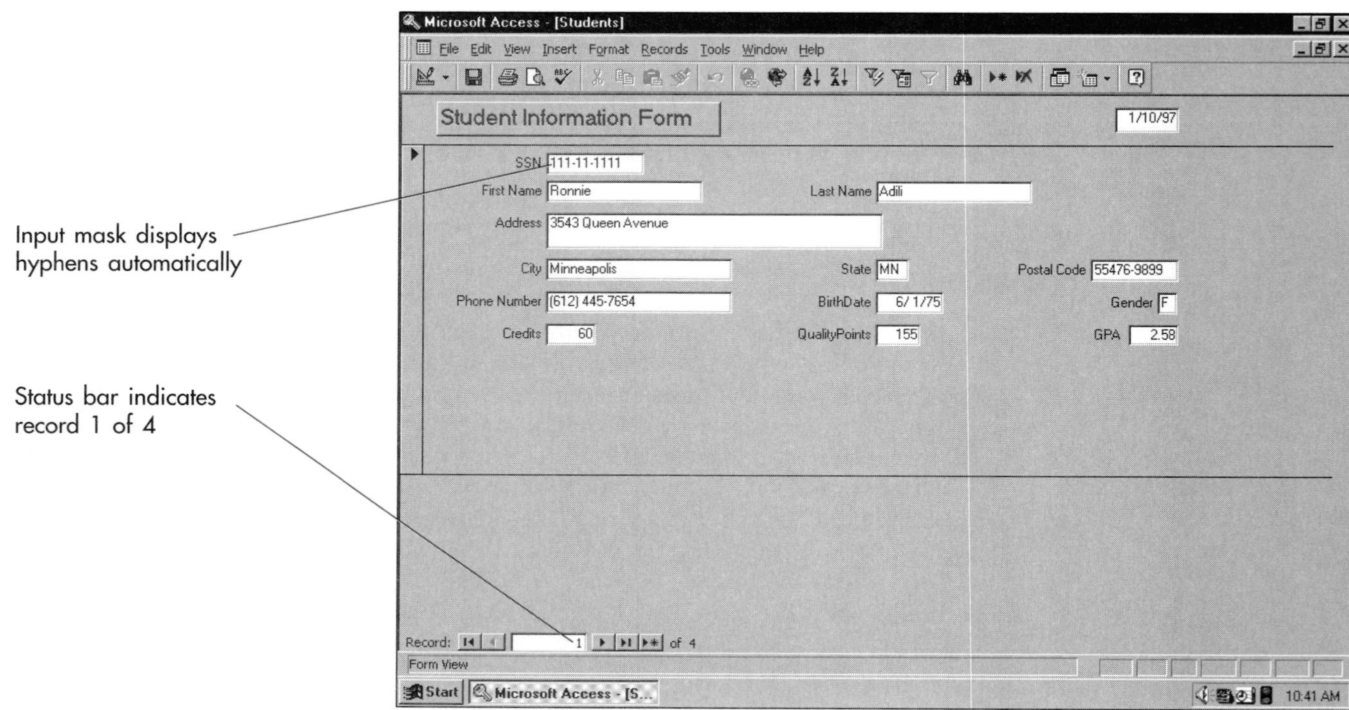

(a) Form View

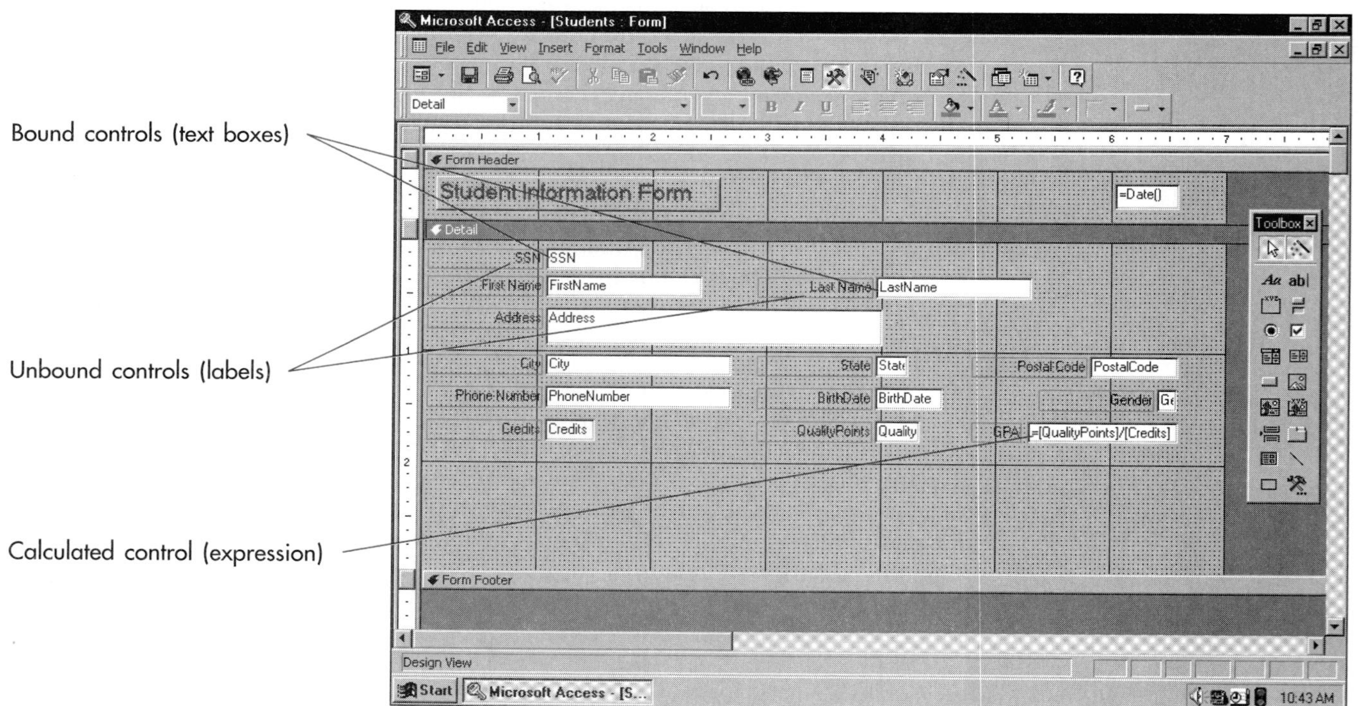

(b) Design View

FIGURE 2.4 Forms

ANATOMY OF A FORM

A form is divided into one or more sections. Virtually every form has a detail section to display or enter the records in the underlying table. You can, however, increase the effectiveness or visual appeal of a form by adding a header and/or footer. Either section may contain descriptive information about the form such as a title, instructions for using the form, or a graphic or logo.

Properties

As previously stated, a ***property*** is a characteristic or attribute of an object that determines how the object looks and behaves. Each control in a form has its own set of properties, just as every field in a table has its own set of properties. The properties for a control are displayed in a ***property sheet,*** as shown in Figure 2.5.

Figure 2.5a displays the property sheet for the Form Header Label. There are 32 different properties (note the vertical scroll bar) that control every aspect of the label's appearance. The properties are determined automatically as the object is created; that is, as you move and size the label on the form, the properties related to its size and position (Left, Top, Width, and Height in Figure 2.5a) are established for you.

Other actions, such as various formatting commands, set the properties that determine the font name and size (MS Sans Serif and 14 point in Figure 2.5a). You can change the appearance of an object in two ways—by executing a command to change the object on the form, which in turn changes the property sheet, *or* by changing the property within the property sheet, which in turn changes the object's appearance on the form.

Figure 2.5b displays the property sheet for the bound SSN control. The name of the control is SSN. The source for the control is the SSN field in the Students table. Thus, various properties of the SSN control, such as the input mask, are inherited from the SSN field in the underlying table. Note, too, that the list of properties in Figure 2.5b, which reflects a bound control, is different from the list of properties in Figure 2.5a for an unbound control. Some properties, however (such as left, top, width, and height, which determine the size and position of an object), are present for every control and determine its location on the form.

The Form Wizard

The easiest way to create a form is with the ***Form Wizard.*** The Form Wizard asks a series of questions, then builds a form according to your answers. You can use the form as is, or you can customize it to better suit your needs.

Figure 2.6 displays the New Form dialog box from which you call the Form Wizard. The Form Wizard, in turn, requires that you specify the table or query on which the form will be based. (Queries are discussed in Chapter 3.) The form in this example will be based on the Students table created in the previous exercise. Once you specify the underlying table, you select one or more fields from that table as shown in Figure 2.6b. Each field that is selected is entered automatically on the form as a bound control. The Form Wizard asks you to select a layout (e.g., Columnar in Figure 2.6c) and a style (e.g., Colorful 1 in Figure 2.6d). The Form Wizard then has all of the information it needs, and creates the form for you. You can enter data immediately, or you can modify the form in the Form Design view.

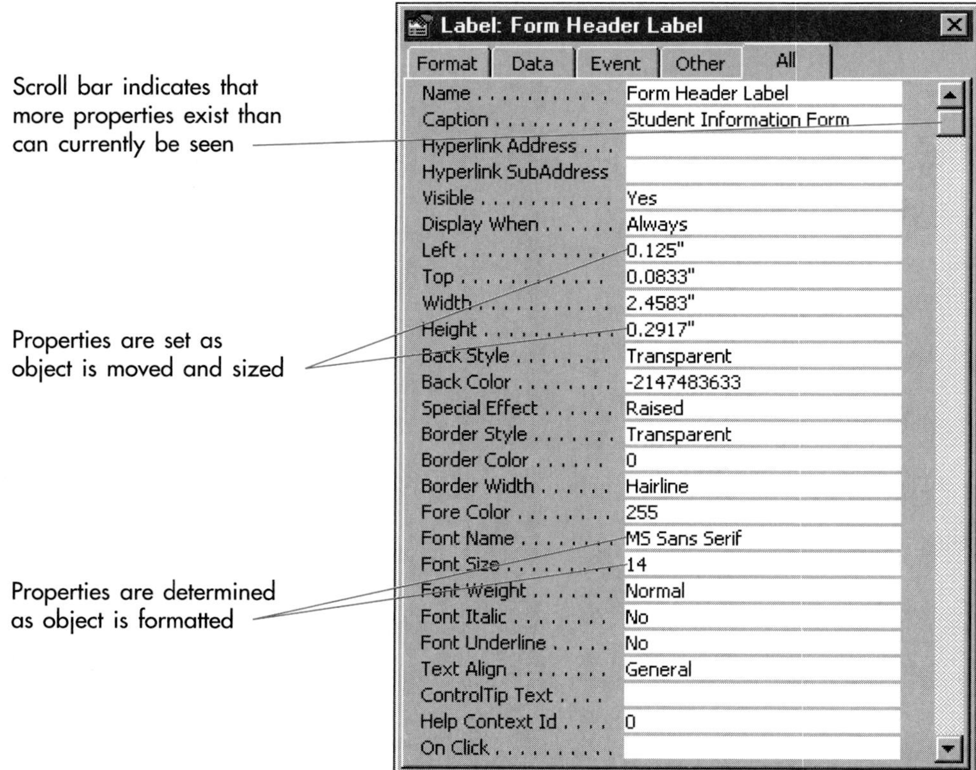

(a) Form Header Label (unbound control)

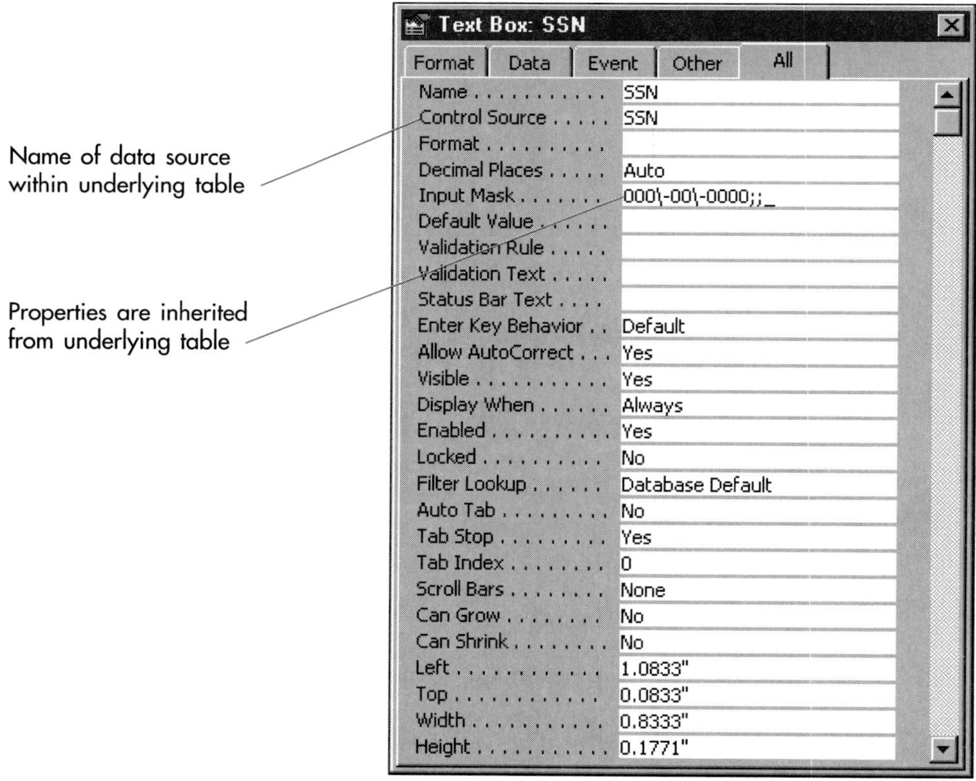

(b) SSN Text Box (bound control)

FIGURE 2.5 Property Sheets

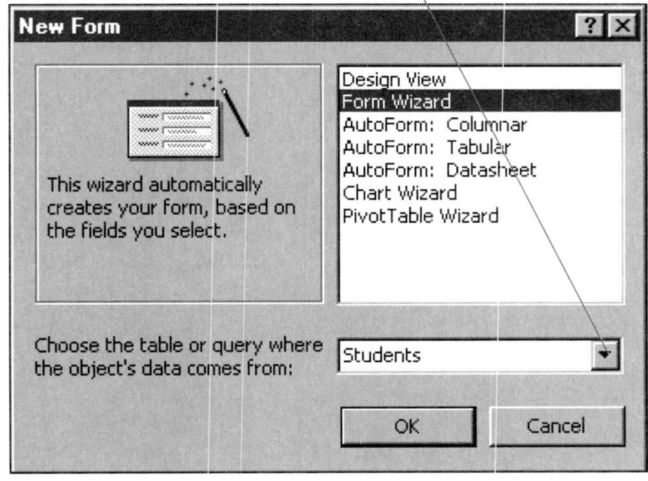

(a) Specify the Underlying Table

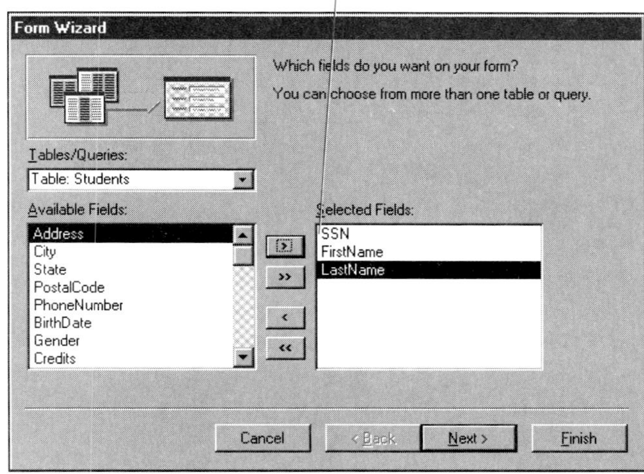

(b) Select the Fields

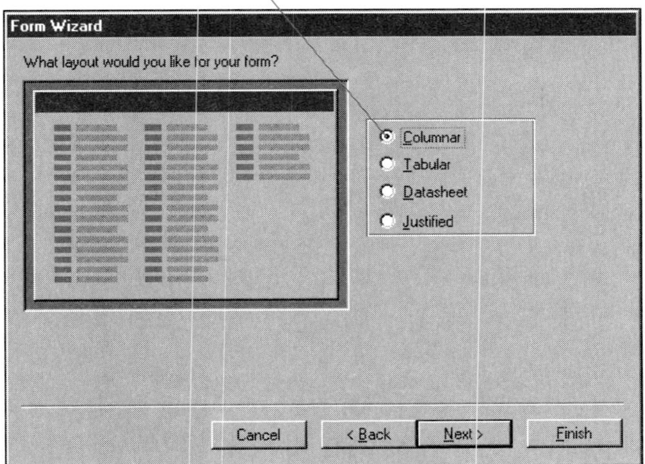

(c) Choose the Layout

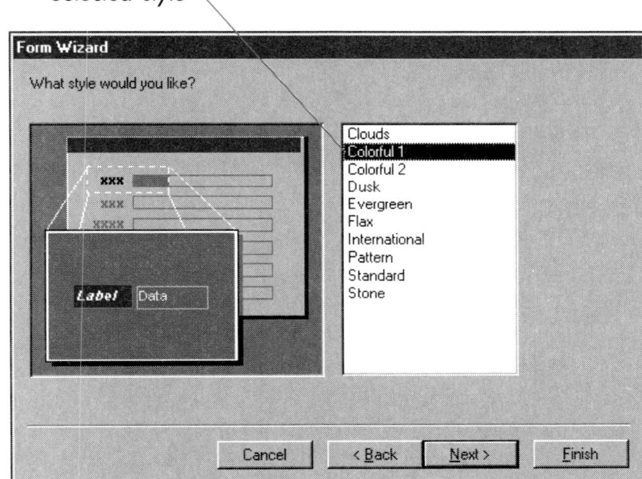

(d) Choose the Style

FIGURE 2.6 The Form Wizard

Modifying a Form

The Form Wizard provides an excellent starting point, but you typically need to customize the form by adding other controls (e.g., the calculated control for GPA) and/or by modifying the controls that were created by the Wizard. Each control is treated as an object, and moved or sized like any other Windows object. In essence, you select the control, then click and drag to resize the control or position it elsewhere on the form. You can also change the properties of the control through buttons on the various toolbars or by displaying the property sheet for the control and changing the appropriate property. Consider:

- *To select a bound control and its associated label (an unbound control),* click either the control or the label. If you click the control, the control has sizing handles and a move handle, but the label has only a move handle. If you click the label, the opposite occurs; that is, the label will have both sizing handles and a move handle, but the control will have only a move handle.

- *To size a control,* click the control to select the control and display the sizing handles, then drag the sizing handles in the appropriate direction. Drag the handles on the top or bottom to size the box vertically. Drag the handles on the left or right side to size the box horizontally. Drag the handles in the corner to size both horizontally and vertically.
- *To move a control and its label,* click and drag the border of either object. To move either the control or its label, click and drag the move handle (a tiny square in the upper left corner) of the appropriate object.
- *To change the properties of a control,* point to the control, click the right mouse button to display a shortcut menu, then click Properties to display the property sheet. Click the text box for the desired property, make the necessary change, then close the property sheet.
- *To select multiple controls,* press and hold the Shift key as you click each successive control. The advantage of selecting multiple controls is that you can modify the selected controls at the same time rather than working with them individually.

HANDS-ON EXERCISE 2

Creating a Form

Objective: To use the Form Wizard to create a form; to move and size controls within a form; to use the completed form to enter data into the associated table. Use Figure 2.7 as a guide in the exercise.

STEP 1: Open the Existing Database

- Start Access as you did in the previous exercise. Select (click) **My First Database** from the list of recently opened databases, then click **OK.** (Click the **Open Database button** on the Database toolbar if you do not see My First Database.)
- Click the **Forms tab** in the Database window. Click the **New command button** to display the New Form dialog box as shown in Figure 2.7a.
- Click **Form Wizard** in the list box. Click the **drop-down arrow** to display the available tables and queries in the database on which the form can be based.
- Click **Students** to select the Students table from the previous exercise. Click **OK** to start the Form Wizard.

THE MOST RECENTLY OPENED FILE LIST

The easiest way to open a recently used database is to select it from the Microsoft Access dialog box that appears when Access is first started. Check to see if your database appears on the list of the four most recently opened databases, and if so, simply double click the database to open it. The list of the most recently opened databases can also be found at the bottom of the File menu.

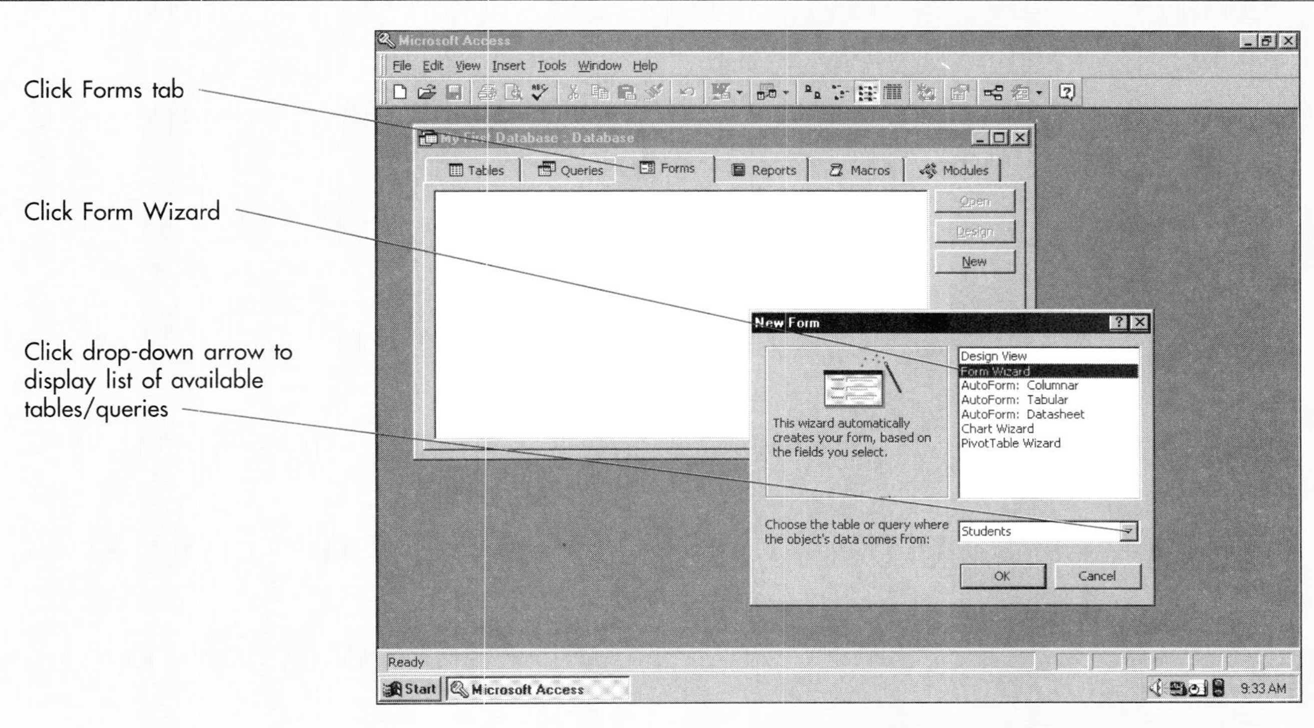

(a) Create a Form (step 1)

FIGURE 2.7 Hands-on Exercise 2

STEP 2: The Form Wizard

- You should see the dialog box in Figure 2.7b, which displays all of the fields in the Students table. Click the **>> button** to enter all of the fields in the table on the form. Click the **Next command button.**
- The **Columnar layout** is already selected. Click the **Next command button.**
- Click **Standard** as the style for your form. Click the **Next command button.**
- The Form Wizard asks you for the title of the form and what you want to do next.
  - The Form Wizard suggests **Students** as the title of the form. Keep this entry.
  - Click the option button to **Modify the form's design.**
- Click the **Finish command button** to display the form in Design view.

FLOATING TOOLBARS

A toolbar is typically docked (fixed) along the edge of the application window, but it can be displayed as a floating toolbar within the application window. To move a docked toolbar, drag the toolbar background. To move a floating toolbar, drag its title bar. To size a floating toolbar, drag any border in the direction you want to go. Double click the background of any toolbar to toggle between a floating toolbar and a docked (fixed) toolbar.

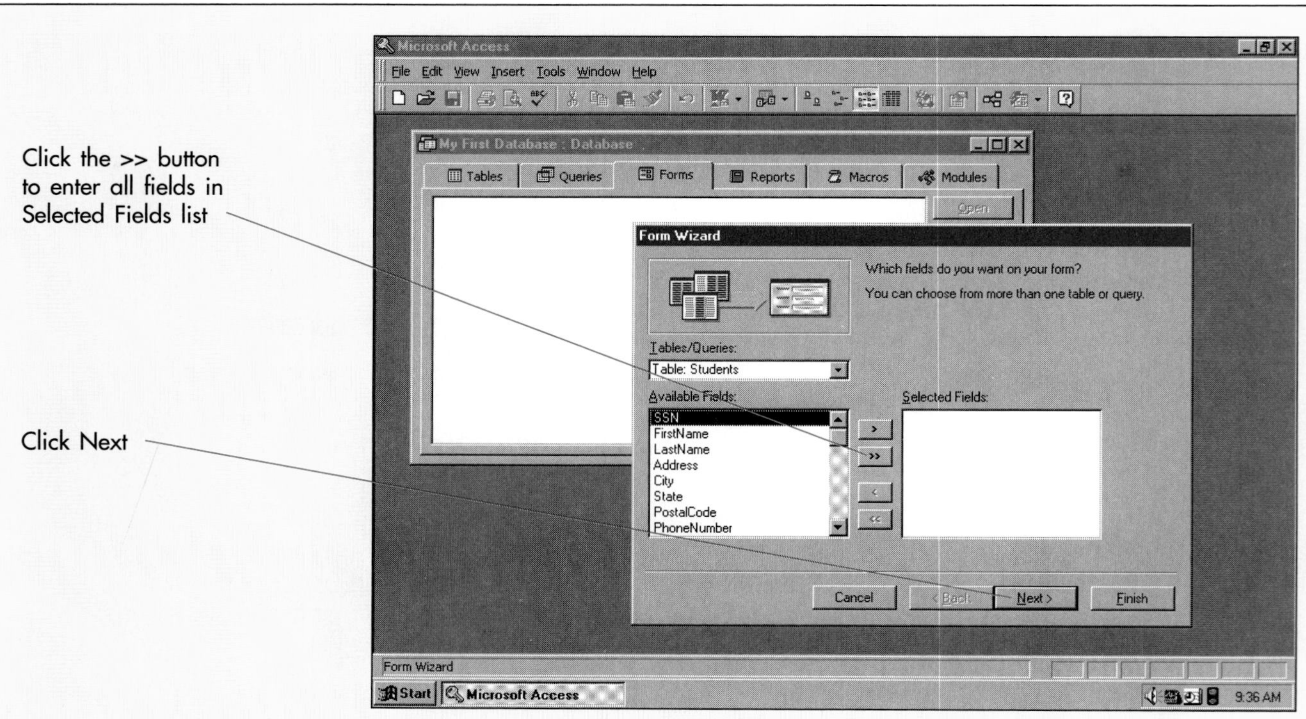

(b) The Form Wizard (step 2)

FIGURE 2.7 Hands-on Exercise 2 (continued)

STEP 3: Move the Controls

- If necessary, click the **Maximize button** so that the form takes the entire screen as shown in Figure 2.7c. The Form Wizard has arranged the controls in columnar format, but you need to rearrange the controls.
- Click the **LastName control** to select the control and display the sizing handles. (Be sure to select the text box and *not* the attached label.) Click and drag the **border** of the control (the pointer changes to a hand) so that the LastName control is on the same line as the FirstName control. Use the grid to space and align the controls.
- Click and drag the **Address control** under the FirstName control (to take the space previously occupied by the last name).
- Click and drag the **border** of the form to **7 inches** so that the City, State, and PostalCode controls will fit on the same line. (Click and drag the title bar of the Toolbox toolbar to move the toolbar out of the way.)
- Click and drag the **State control** so that it is next to the City control, then click and drag the **PostalCode control** so that it is on the same line as the other two. Press and hold the **Shift key** as you click the **City, State,** and **PostalCode controls** to select all three, then click and drag the selected controls under the Address control.
- Place the controls for **PhoneNumber, BirthDate,** and **Gender** on the same line.
- Place the controls for **Credits** and **QualityPoints** on the same line.
- Pull down the **File menu** and click **Save** (or click the **Save button**) to save the form.

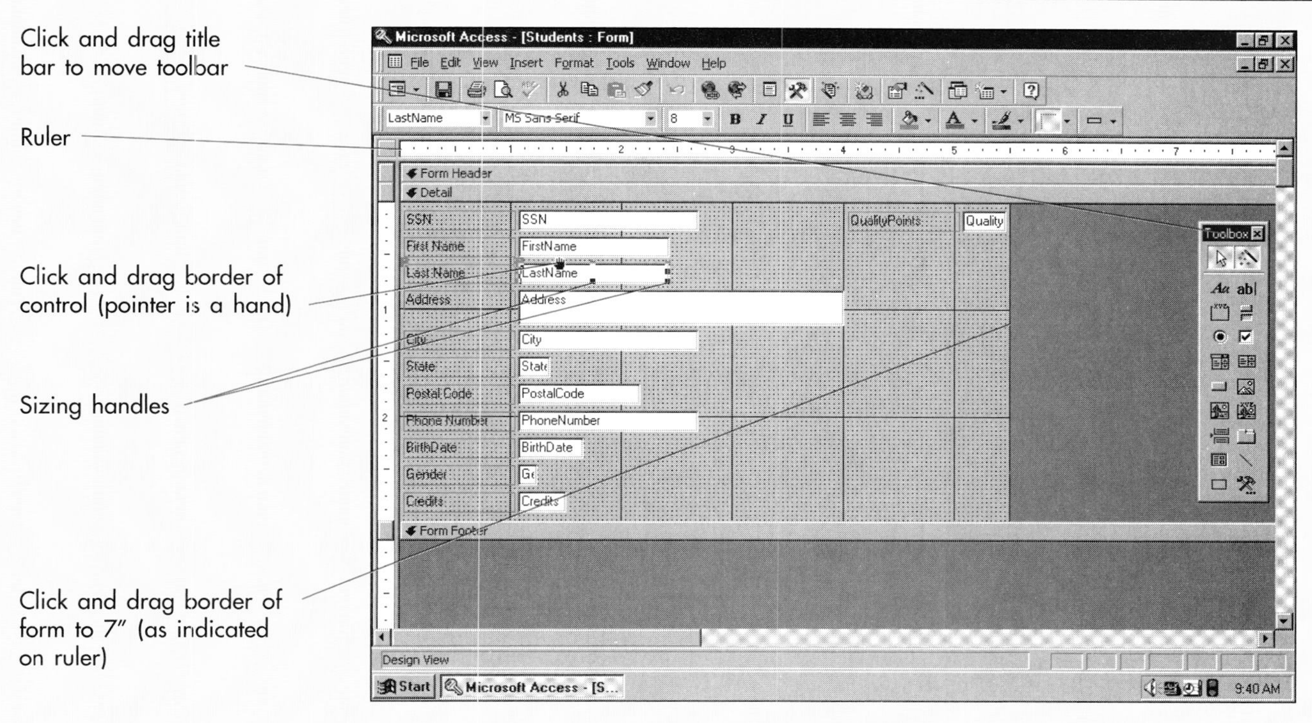

(c) Move the Controls (step 3)

FIGURE 2.7 Hands-on Exercise 2 (continued)

THE UNDO COMMAND

The Undo command is invaluable at any time, and is especially useful when moving and sizing controls. Pull down the Edit menu and click Undo (or click the Undo button on the toolbar) immediately to reverse the effects of the last command.

STEP 4: Add a Calculated Control (GPA)

- Click the **Text Box tool** in the toolbox as shown in Figure 2.7d. The mouse pointer changes to a tiny crosshair with a text box attached.
- Click and drag in the form where you want the text box (the GPA control) to go. Release the mouse. You will see an Unbound control and an attached label containing a field number (e.g., Text24) as shown in Figure 2.7d.
- Click in the **text box** of the control. The word Unbound will disappear, and you can enter an expression:
  - Enter =**[QualityPoints]/[Credits]** to calculate a student's GPA. Do not be concerned if you cannot see the entire entry as scrolling will take place as necessary.
  - You must enter the field names *exactly* as they were defined in the table; that is, do *not* include a space between Quality and Points.
- Select the attached label (Text24), then click and drag to select the text in the attached label. Type **GPA** as the label for this control. Size the text box

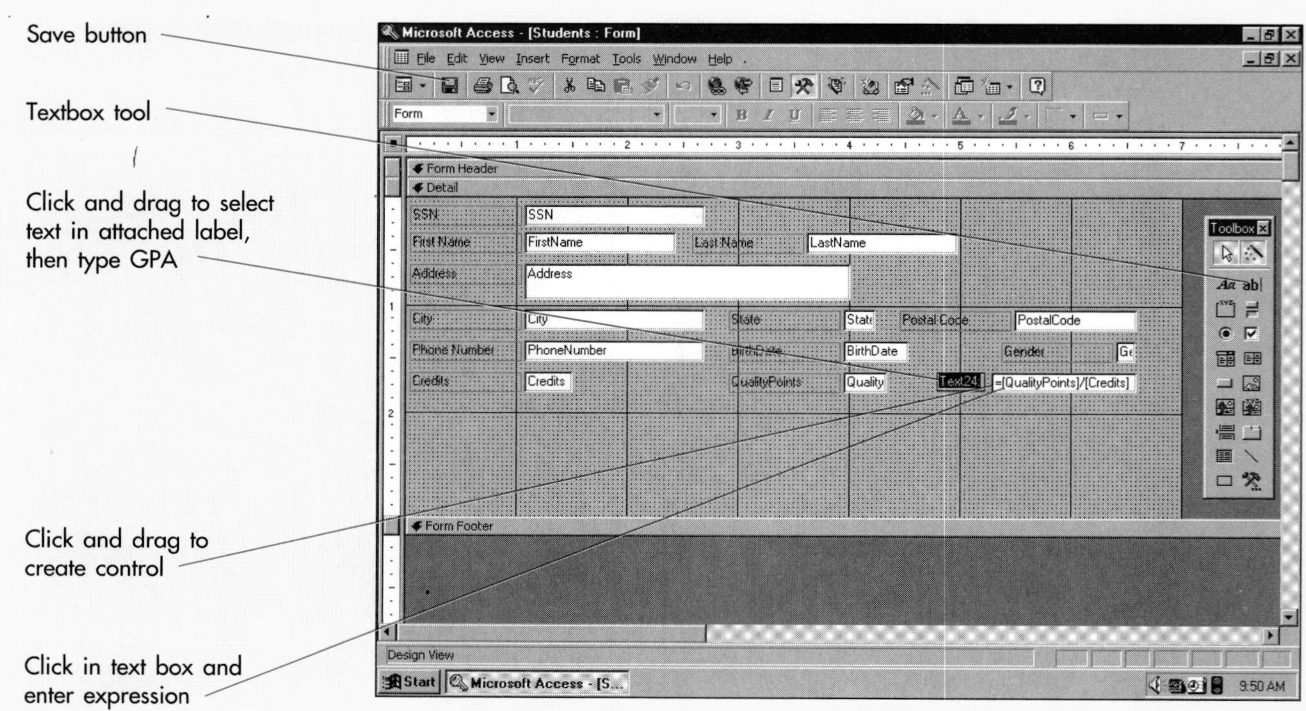

(d) Add a Calculated Control (step 4)

FIGURE 2.7 Hands-on Exercise 2 (continued)

appropriately for GPA. Click the **move handle** on the label so that you can move the label closer to the text box.

➤ Click the **Save button.**

SIZING OR MOVING A CONTROL AND ITS LABEL

A bound control is created with an attached label. Select (click) the control, and the control has sizing handles and a move handle, but the label has only a move handle. Select the label (instead of the control), and the opposite occurs; the control has only a move handle, but the label will have both sizing handles and a move handle. To move a control and its label, click and drag the border of either object. To move either the control or its label, click and drag the move handle (a tiny square in the upper left corner) of the appropriate object.

STEP 5: Modify the Property Sheet

➤ Point to the GPA control and click the **right mouse button** to display a shortcut menu. Click **Properties** to display the Properties dialog box.

➤ If necessary, click the **All tab** as shown in Figure 2.7e. The Control Source text box contains the entry =[QualityPoints]/[Credits] from the preceding step.

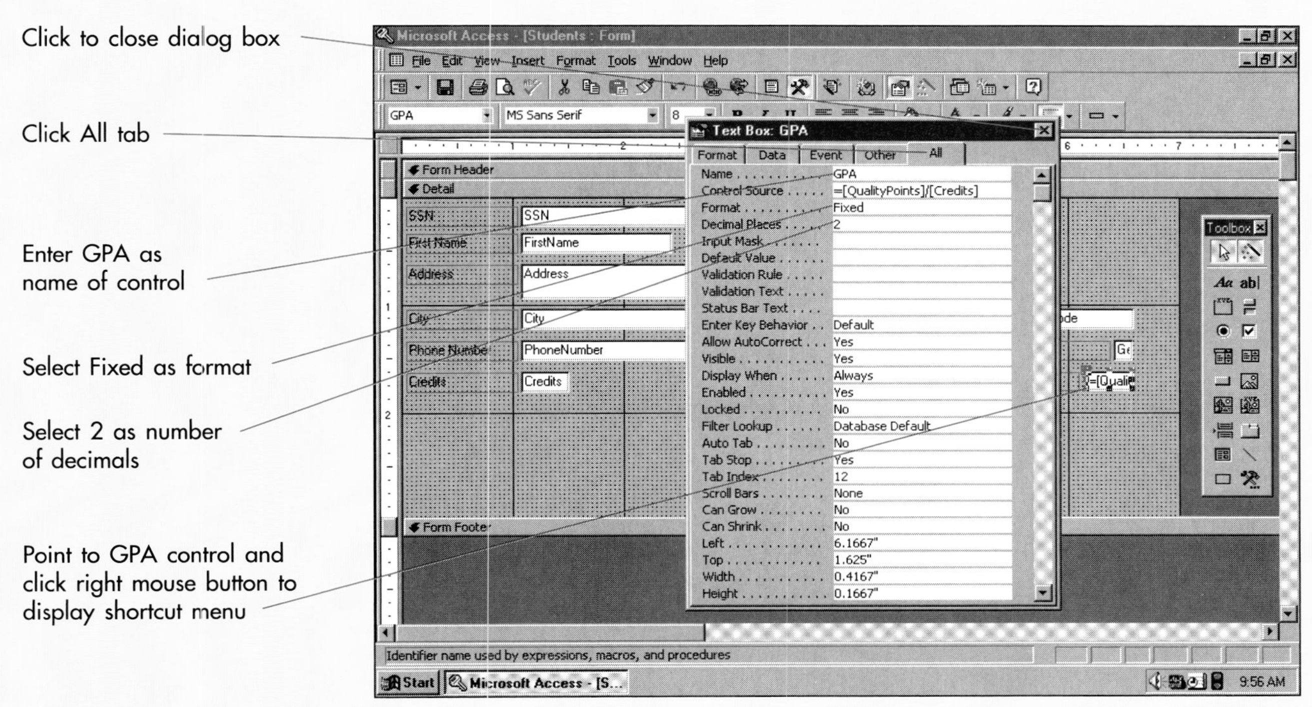
Click to close dialog box
Click All tab
Enter GPA as name of control
Select Fixed as format
Select 2 as number of decimals
Point to GPA control and click right mouse button to display shortcut menu

(e) Modify the Property Sheet (step 5)

FIGURE 2.7 Hands-on Exercise 2 (continued)

- Click the **Name text box.** Replace the original name (e.g., Text24) with **GPA.**
- Click the **Format box.** Click the **drop-down arrow,** then scroll until you can select **Fixed.**
- Click the box for the **Decimal places.** Click the **drop-down arrow** and select **2** as the number of decimal places.
- Close the Properties dialog box to accept these settings and return to the form.

USE THE PROPERTY SHEET

You can change the appearance or behavior of a control in two ways—by changing the actual control on the form itself or by changing the underlying property sheet. Anything you do to the control automatically changes the associated property, and conversely, any change to the property sheet is reflected in the appearance or behavior of the control. In general, you can obtain greater precision through the property sheet, but we find ourselves continually switching back and forth between the two techniques.

STEP 6: Align the Controls

- Press and hold the **Shift key** as you click the label for each control on the form. This enables you to select multiple controls at the same time in order to apply uniform formatting to the selected controls.
- All labels should be selected as shown in Figure 2.7f. Click the **Align Right button** on the Formatting toolbar to move the labels to the right so that each label is closer to its associated control.
- Click anywhere on the form to deselect the controls, then fine-tune the form as necessary to make it more attractive. We moved LastName to align it with State. We also made the SSN and PostalCode controls smaller.

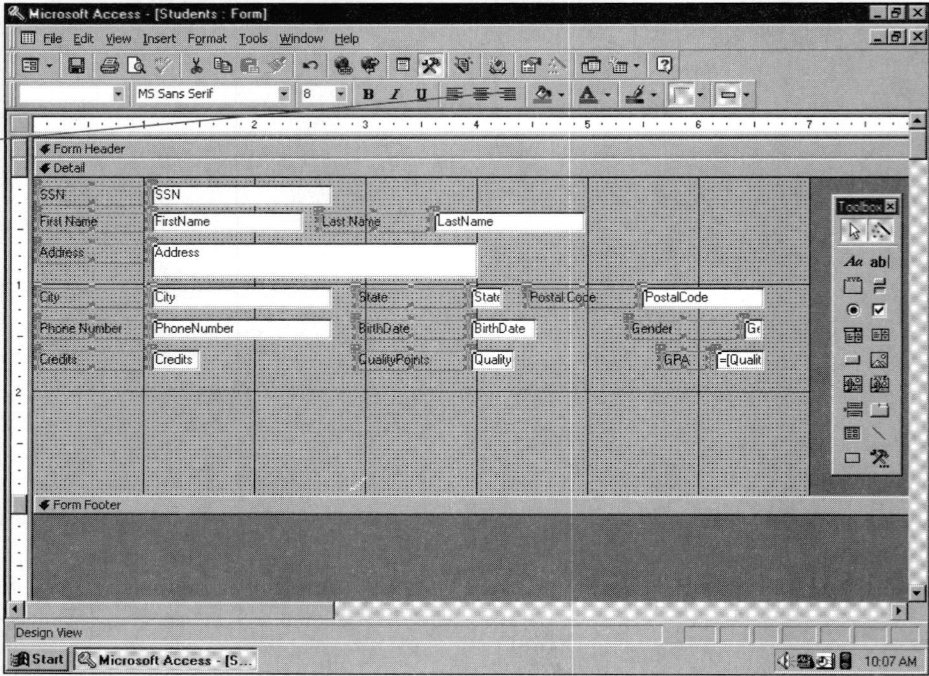

(f) Align the Controls (step 6)

FIGURE 2.7 Hands-on Exercise 2 (continued)

ALIGN THE CONTROLS

To align controls in a straight line (horizontally or vertically), press and hold the Shift key and click the labels of the controls to be aligned. Pull down the Format menu, click Align, then select the edge to align (Left, Right, Top, and Bottom). Click the Undo command if you are not satisfied with the result.

STEP 7: Create the Form Header

- Click and drag the line separating the border of the Form Header and Detail to provide space for a header as shown in Figure 2.7g.
- Click the **Label tool** on the Toolbox toolbar (the mouse pointer changes to a cross hair combined with the letter A). Click and drag the mouse pointer to create a label within the header. The insertion point (a flashing vertical line) is automatically positioned within the label.
- Type **Student Information Form.** Do not be concerned about the size or alignment of the text at this time. Click outside the label when you have completed the entry, then click the control to select it.

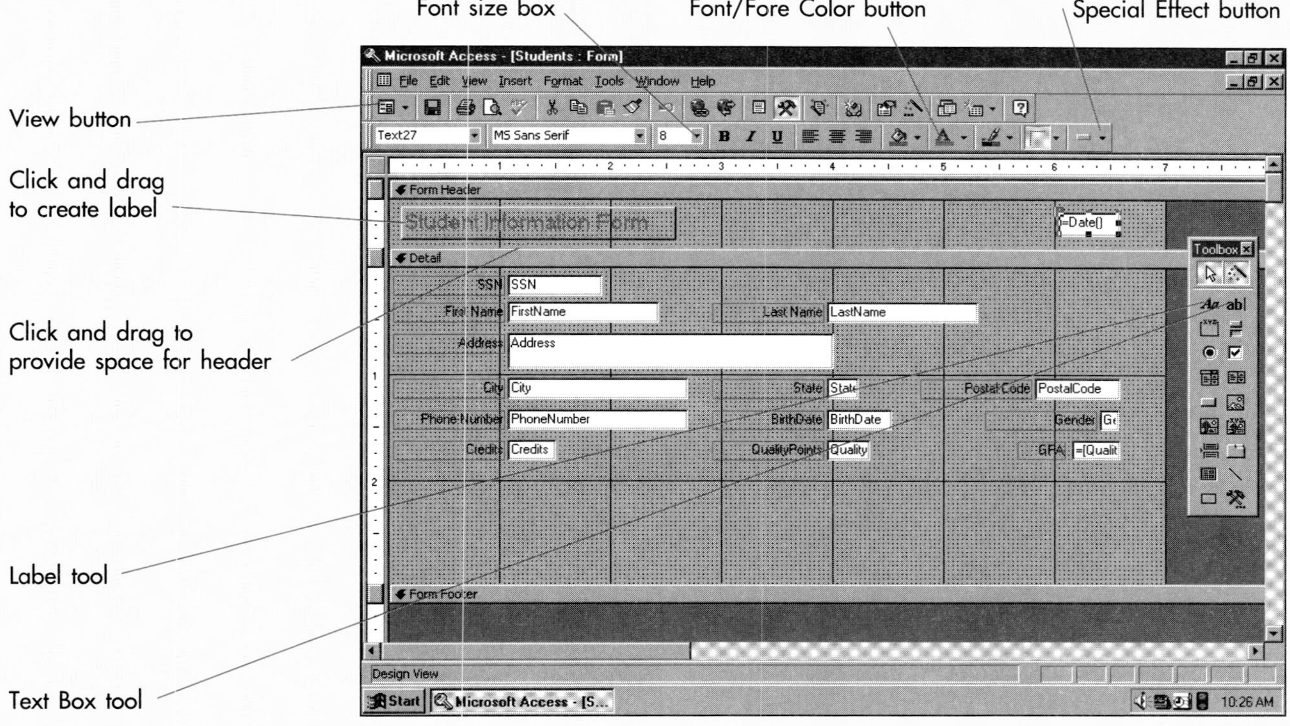

(g) Create the Header (steps 7 & 8)

FIGURE 2.7 Hands-on Exercise 2 (continued)

THE FORMATTING TOOLBAR

The Formatting toolbar contains many of the same buttons that are found on the Formatting toolbars of the other Office applications. These include buttons for boldface, italics, and underlining, as well as left, center, and right alignment. You will find drop-down list boxes to change the font or point size. The Formatting toolbar also contains drop-down palettes to change the foreground or background color, the border color and width, and the special effect.

- ➤ Click the **drop-down arrow** on the **Font Size list box** on the Formatting toolbar. Click **14.** The size of the text changes to the larger point size.
- ➤ Click the **drop-down arrow** next to the **Special Effect button** on the Formatting toolbar to display the available effects. Click the **Raised button** to highlight the label.
- ➤ Click the **drop-down arrow** next to the **Font/Fore Color button** on the Formatting toolbar. Click **Red.**
- ➤ Click outside the label to deselect it. Click the **Save button** to save the form.

STEP 8: Add the Date

- ➤ Click the **Textbox tool** on the Toolbox toolbar. The mouse pointer changes to a tiny crosshair with a text box attached. Click and drag in the form where you want the text box for the date, then release the mouse.
- ➤ You will see an Unbound control and an attached label containing a number (e.g., Text27). Click in the text box, and the word Unbound will disappear. Type **=Date().** Click the attached label. Press the **Del key** to delete the label.

STEP 9: The Form View

- ➤ Click the **Form view button** to switch to the Form view. You will see the first record in the table that was created in the previous exercise.
- ➤ Click the **New Record button** to move to the end of the table to enter a new record as shown in Figure 2.7h. Enter data for yourself:
  - The record selector symbol changes to a pencil as you begin to enter data.
  - Press the **Tab key** to move from one field to the next within the form. All properties (masks and data validation) have been inherited from the Students table created in the first exercise.

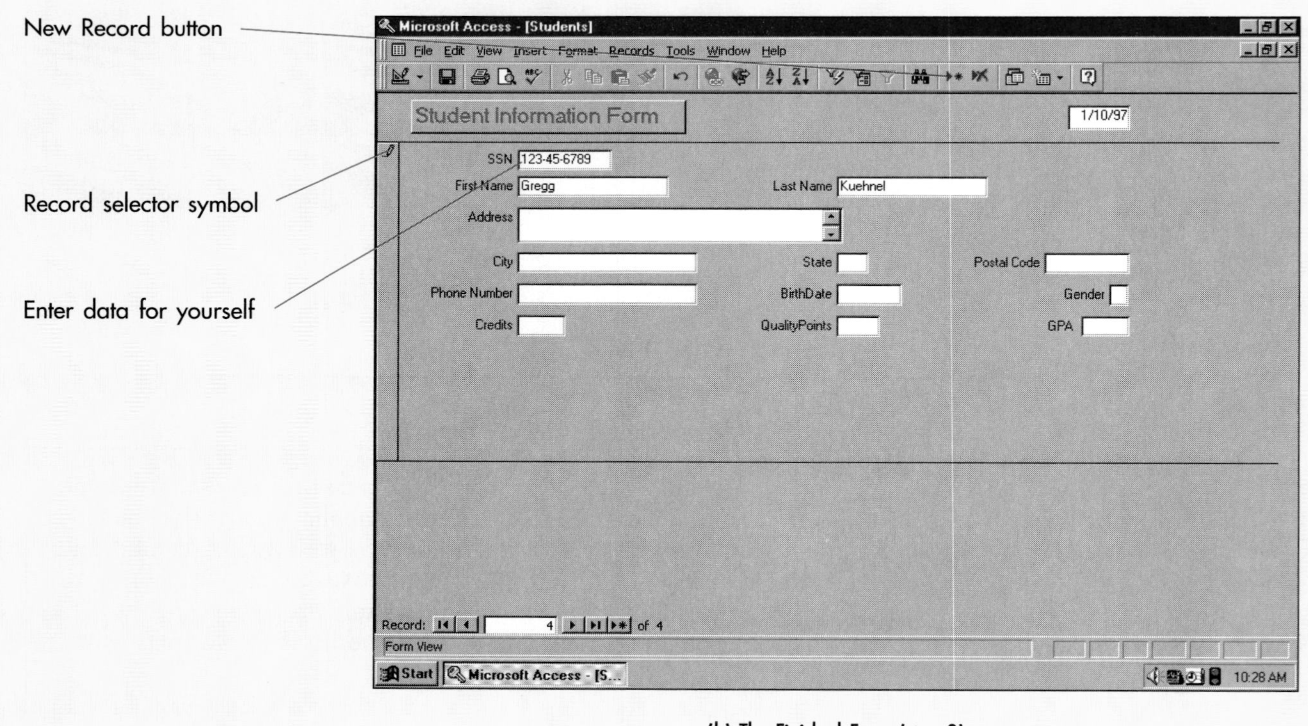

(h) The Finished Form (step 9)

FIGURE 2.7 Hands-on Exercise 2 (continued)

➤ Pull down the **File menu** and click **Close** to close the form. Click **Yes** if asked to save the changes to the form.

➤ Pull down the **File menu** and click **Close** to close the database and remain in Access. Pull down the **File menu** a second time and click **Exit** if you do not want to continue with the next exercise at this time.

ERROR MESSAGES—#NAME? OR #ERROR?

The most common reason for either message is that the control source references a field that no longer exists, or a field whose name is misspelled. Go to the Design view, right click the control, click the Properties command, then click the All tab within the Properties dialog box. Look at the Control Source property and check the spelling of every field. Be sure there are brackets around each field in a calculated control; for example =[QualityPoints]/[Credits].

A MORE SOPHISTICATED FORM

The Form Wizard provides an excellent starting point but stops short of creating the form you really want. The exercise just completed showed you how to add controls to a form that were not in the underlying table, such as the calculated control for the GPA. The exercise also showed how to move and size existing controls to create a more attractive and functional form.

Consider now Figure 2.8, which further improves on the form from the previous exercise. Three additional controls have been added—for major, financial

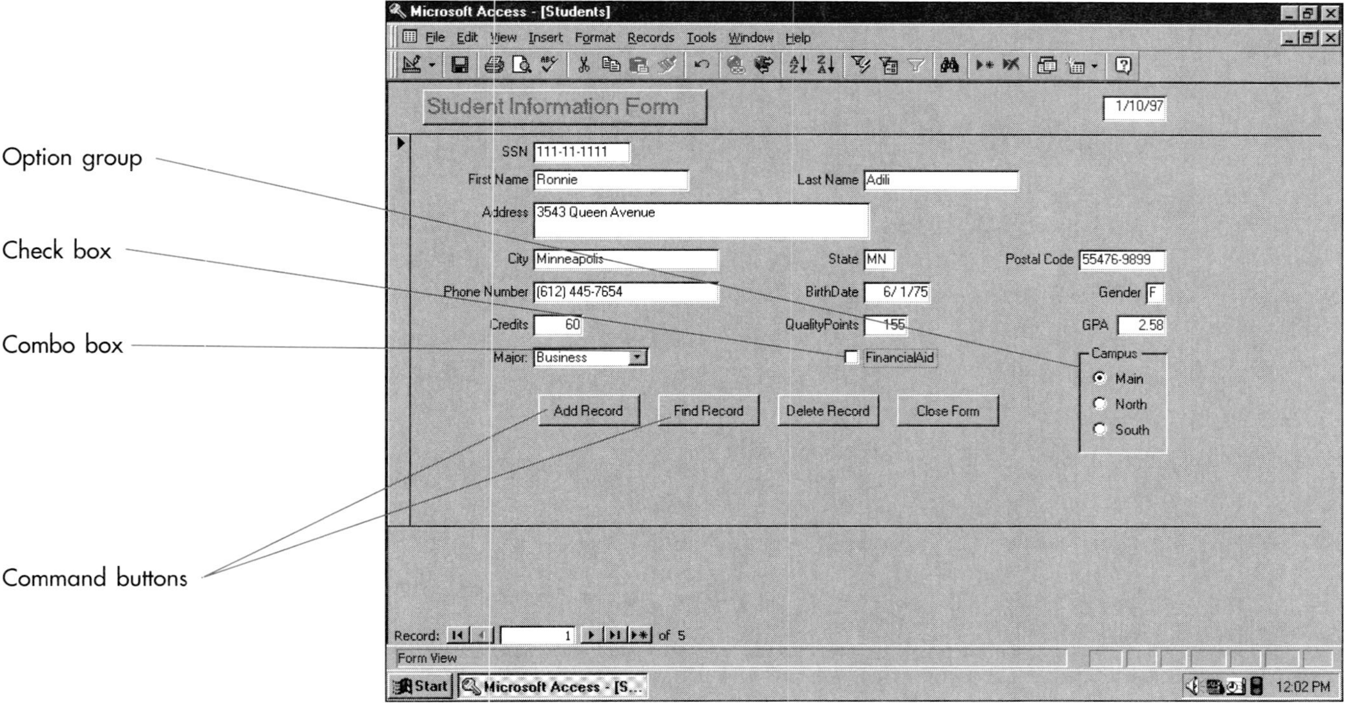

FIGURE 2.8 An Improved Form

aid, and campus—to illustrate other ways to enter data than through a text box. The student's major is selected from a ***drop-down list box.*** The indication of financial aid (a Yes/No field) is entered through a ***check box.*** The student's campus is selected from an ***option group,*** in which you choose one of three mutually exclusive options.

Command buttons have also been added to the bottom of the form to facilitate the way in which the user carries out certain procedures. To add a record, for example, the user simply clicks the Add Record command button, as opposed to having to click the New Record button on the Database toolbar or having to pull down the Insert menu. The next exercise has you retrieve the form you created in Hands-on Exercise 2 in order to add these enhancements.

HANDS-ON EXERCISE 3

A More Sophisticated Form

Objective: To add fields to an existing table; to use the Lookup Wizard to create a combo box; to add controls to an existing form to demonstrate inheritance; to add command buttons to a form. Use Figure 2.9 as a guide in the exercise.

STEP 1: Modify the Table

- Open **My First Database** that we have been using throughout the chapter. If necessary, click the **Tables tab** in the Database window. The **Students table** is already selected since that is the only table in the database.
- Click the **Design command button** to open the table in Design view as shown in Figure 2.9a. (The FinancialAid, Campus, and Major fields have not yet been added.) Maximize the window.
- Click the **Field Name box** under QualityPoints. Enter **FinancialAid** as the name of the new field. Press the **enter (Tab,** or **right arrow) key** to move to the Data Type column. Type **Y** (the first letter in a Yes/No field) to specify the data type.
- Click the **Field Name box** on the next row. Type **Campus.** (There is no need to specify the Data Type since Text is the default.)
- Press the **down arrow key** to move to the Field Name box on the next row. Enter **Major.** Press the **enter (Tab,** or **right arrow) key** to move to the Data Type column. Click the **drop-down arrow** to display the list of data types as shown in Figure 2.9a. Click **Lookup Wizard.**

STEP 2: The Lookup Wizard

- The first screen in the Lookup Wizard asks how you want to look up the data. Click the option button that indicates **I will type in the values that I want.** Click **Next.**
- You should see the dialog box in Figure 2.9b. The number of columns is already entered as one. Click the **text box** to enter the first major. Type **Business.** Press **Tab** or the **down arrow key** (do *not* press the enter key) to enter the next major.
- Complete the entries shown in Figure 2.9b. Click **Next.** The Wizard asks for a label to identify the column. (Major is already entered.) Click **Finish** to exit the Wizard and return to the Design View.
- Click the **Save button** to save the table. Close the table.

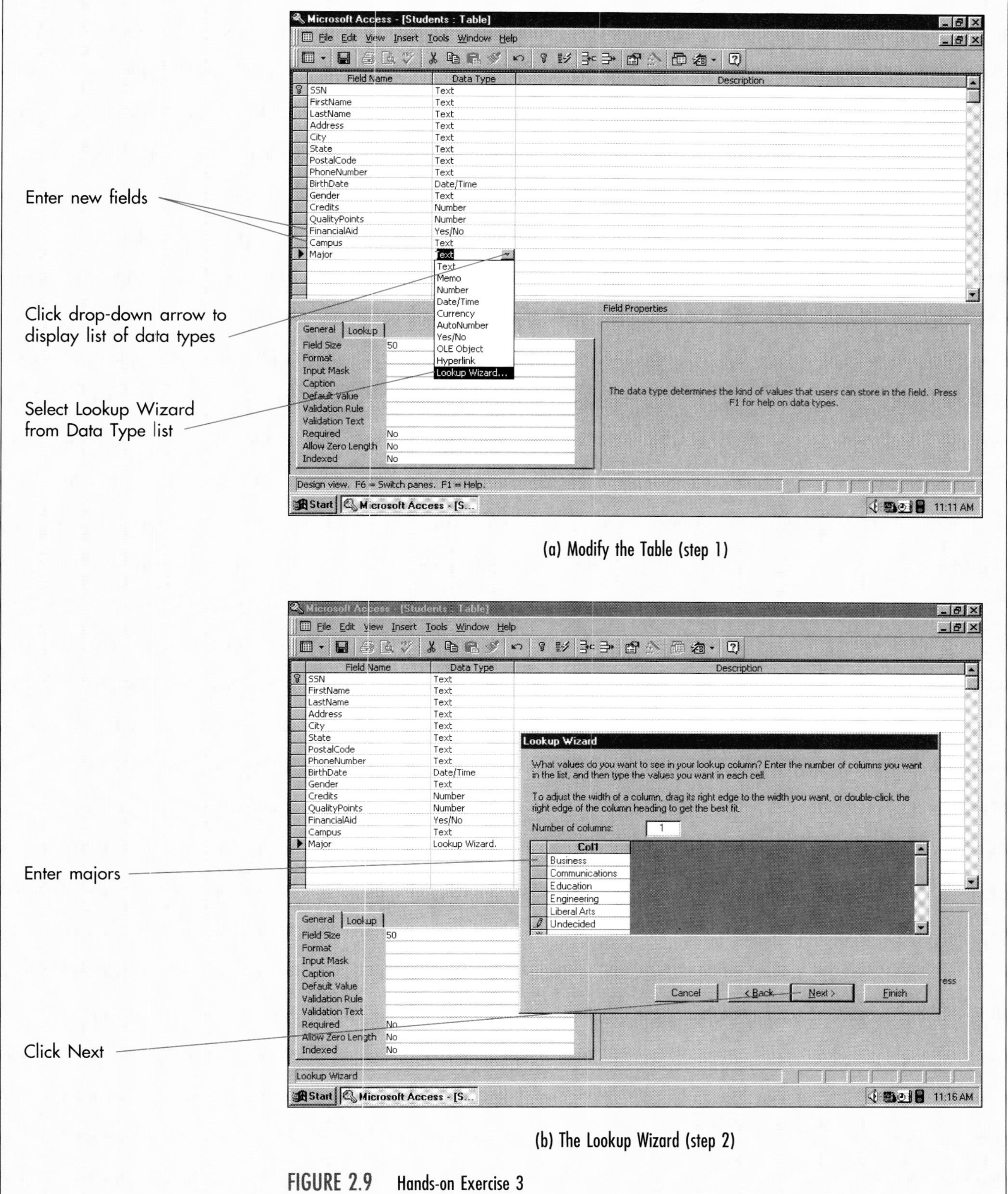

(a) Modify the Table (step 1)

(b) The Lookup Wizard (step 2)

FIGURE 2.9 Hands-on Exercise 3

STEP 3: Add the New Controls

- Click the **Forms tab** in the Database window. The Students form is already highlighted since there is only one form in the database.
- Click the **Design command button** to open the form from the previous exercise. If necessary, click the **Maximize button** so that the form takes the entire window.
- Pull down the **View menu.** Click **Field List** to display the field list for the table on which the form is based. You can move and size the field list just like any other Windows object.
  - Click and drag the **title bar** of the field list to the position in Figure 2.9c.
  - Click and drag a **corner** or **border** of the field list so that you can see all of the fields at the same time.
- Fields can be added to the form from the field list in any order. Click and drag the **Major field** from the field list to the form. The Major control is created as a combo box because of the list in the underlying table.
- Click and drag the **FinancialAid field** from the list to the form. The FinancialAid control is created as a check box because FinancialAid is a Yes/No field in the underlying table.
- Save the form.

INHERITANCE

A bound control inherits the same properties as the associated field in the underlying table. A check box, for example, appears automatically next to any bound control that was defined as a Yes/No field. In similar fashion, a drop-down list will appear next to any bound control that was defined through the Lookup Wizard. Changing the property setting of a field *after* the form has been created will *not* change the property of the associated control. And finally, changing the property setting of a control does *not* change the property setting of the field because the control inherits the properties of the field rather than the other way around.

STEP 4: Create an Option Group

- Click the **Option Group button** on the Toolbox toolbar. The mouse pointer changes to a tiny crosshair attached to an option button when you point anywhere in the form. Click and drag in the form where you want the option group to go, then release the mouse.
- You should see the Option Group Wizard as shown in Figure 2.9d. Enter **Main** as the label for the first option, then press the **Tab key** to move to the next line. Type **North** and press **Tab** to move to the next line. Enter **South** as the third and last option. Click **Next.**
- The option button to select Main (the first label that was entered) as the default is selected. Click **Next.**
- Main, North, and South will be assigned the values 1, 2, and 3, respectively. (Numeric entries are required for an option group.) Click **Next.**
- Click the **drop-down arrow** to select the field in which to store the value of the option group, then scroll until you can select **Campus.** Click **Next.**

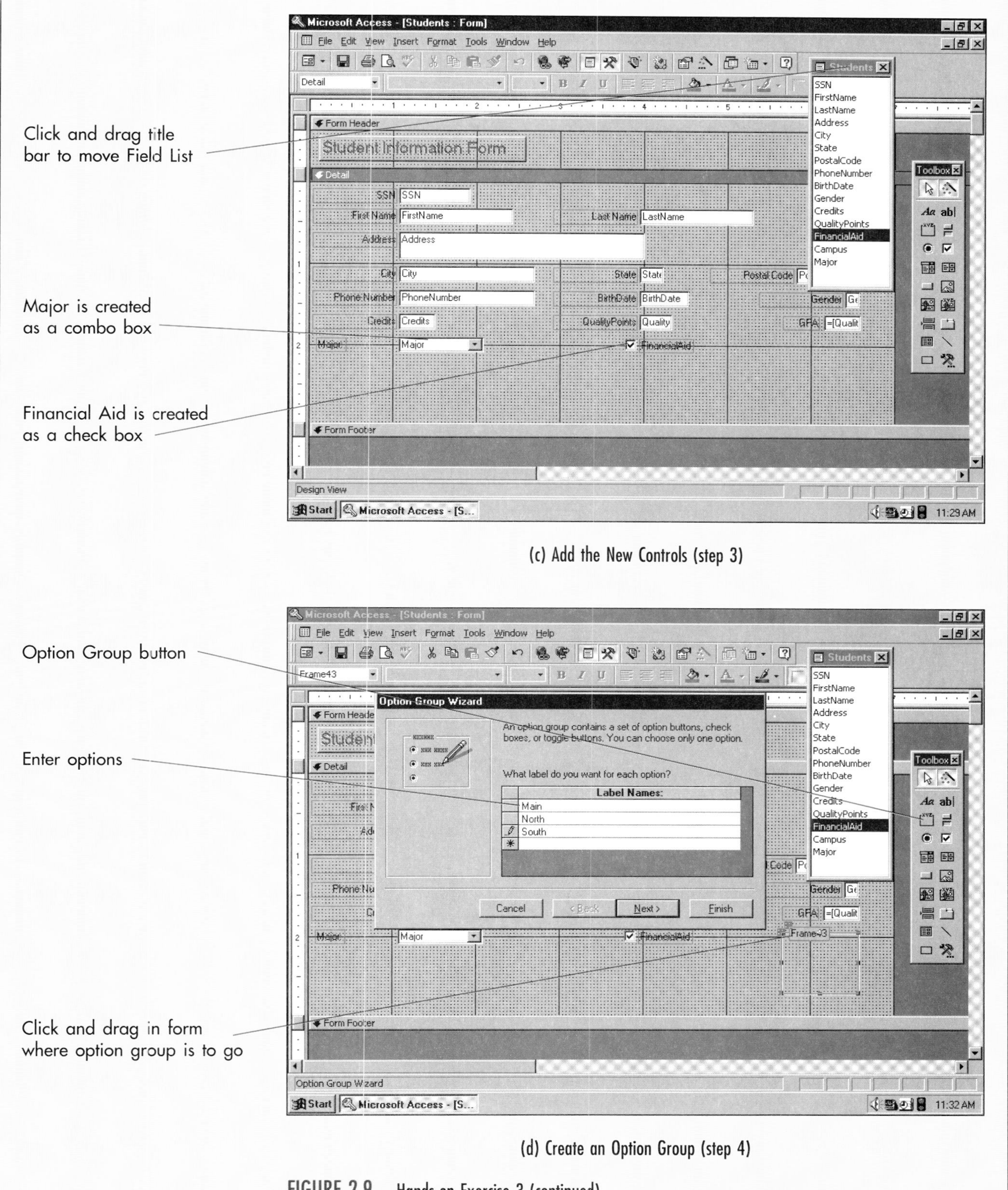

(c) Add the New Controls (step 3)

(d) Create an Option Group (step 4)

FIGURE 2.9 Hands-on Exercise 3 (continued)

- Make sure the Option button is selected as the type of control.
- Click the option button for the **Sunken style** to match the other controls on the form. Click **Next.**
- Enter **Campus** as the caption for the group. Click the **Finish command button** to create the option group on the form. Click and drag the option group to position it on the form under the GPA control.
- Point to the border of the option group on the form, click the **right mouse button** to display a shortcut menu, and click **Properties.** Click the **All tab.** Change the name to **Campus.** Close the dialog box. Save the form.

MISSING TOOLBARS

The Form Design, Formatting, and Toolbox toolbars appear by default in the Form Design view, but any (or all) of these toolbars may be hidden at the discretion of the user. Point to any visible toolbar, click the right mouse button to display a shortcut menu, then check the name of any toolbar you want to display. You can also click the Toolbox button on the Form Design toolbar to display (hide) the Toolbox toolbar.

STEP 5: Add a Command Button

- Click the **Command Button tool.** The mouse pointer changes to a tiny crosshair attached to a command button when you point anywhere in the form.
- Click and drag in the form where you want the button to go, then release the mouse. This draws a button and simultaneously opens the Command Button Wizard as shown in Figure 2.9e. (The number in your button may be different from ours.)
- Click **Record Operations** in the Categories list box. Choose **Add New Record** as the operation. Click **Next.**
- Click the **Text option button** in the next screen. Click **Next.**
- Type **Add Record** as the name of the button, then click the **Finish command button.** The completed command button should appear on your form. Save the form.

STEP 6: Create the Additional Command Buttons

- Click the **Command Button tool.** Click and drag on the form where you want the second button to go.
- Click **Record Navigation** in the Categories list box. Choose **Find Record** as the operation. Click the **Next command button.**
- Click the **Text option button.** Click the **Next command button.**
- Type **Find Record** as the name of the button, then click the **Finish command button.** The completed command button should appear on the form.
- Repeat these steps to add the command buttons to delete a record (Record Operations) and close the form (Form Operations).
- Save the form.

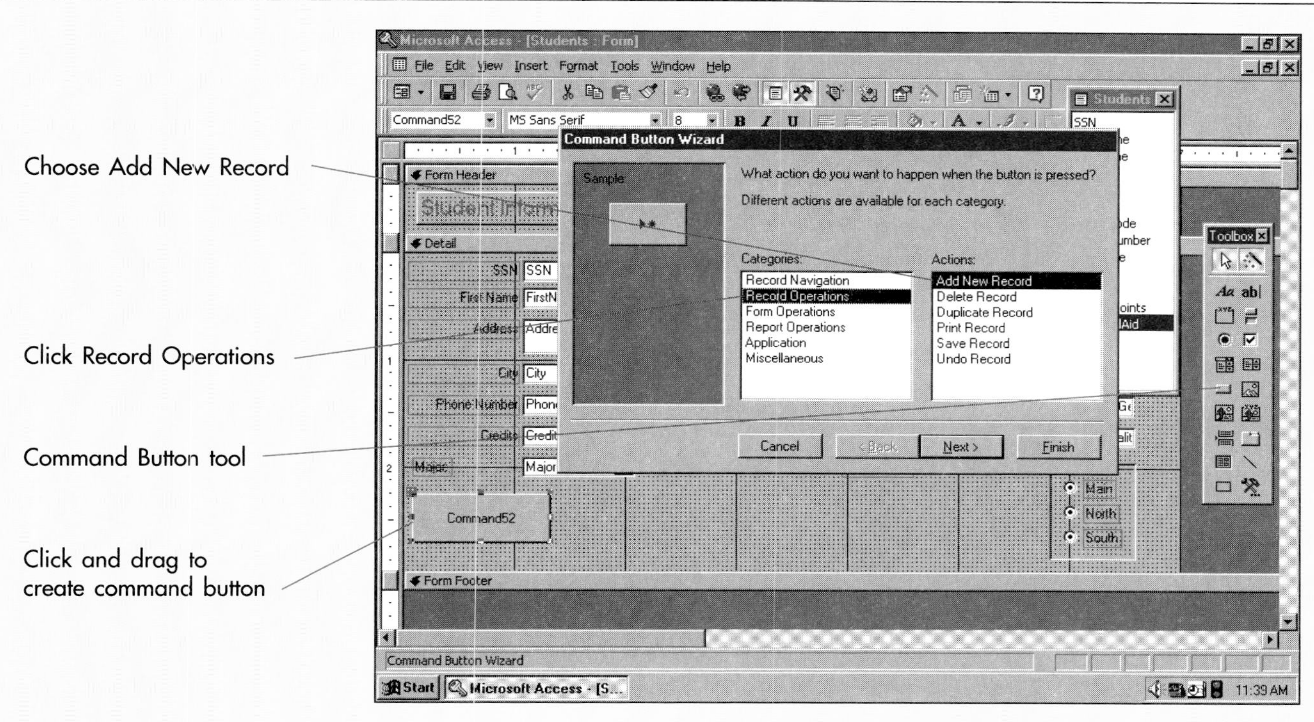

(e) Add a Command Button (step 5)

FIGURE 2.9 Hands-on Exercise 3 (continued)

STEP 7: Align the Command Buttons

- Select the four command buttons by pressing and holding the **Shift key** as you click each button. Release the Shift key when all buttons are selected.
- Pull down the **Format menu.** Click **Size** to display the cascade menu shown in Figure 2.9f. Click **to Widest** to set a uniform width.
- Pull down the **Format menu** a second time, click **Size,** then click **to Tallest** to set a uniform height.
- Pull down the **Format menu** again, click **Horizontal Spacing,** then click **Make Equal** so that each button is equidistant from the other buttons.
- Pull down the **Format menu** a final time, click **Align,** then click **Bottom** to complete the alignment. Drag the buttons to the center of the form.

MULTIPLE CONTROLS AND PROPERTIES

Press and hold the Shift key as you click one control after another to select multiple controls. To view or change the properties for the selected controls, click the right mouse button to display a shortcut menu, then click Properties to display a property sheet. If the value of a property is the same for all selected controls, that value will appear in the property sheet; otherwise the box for that property will be blank. Changing a property when multiple controls are selected changes the property for all selected controls.

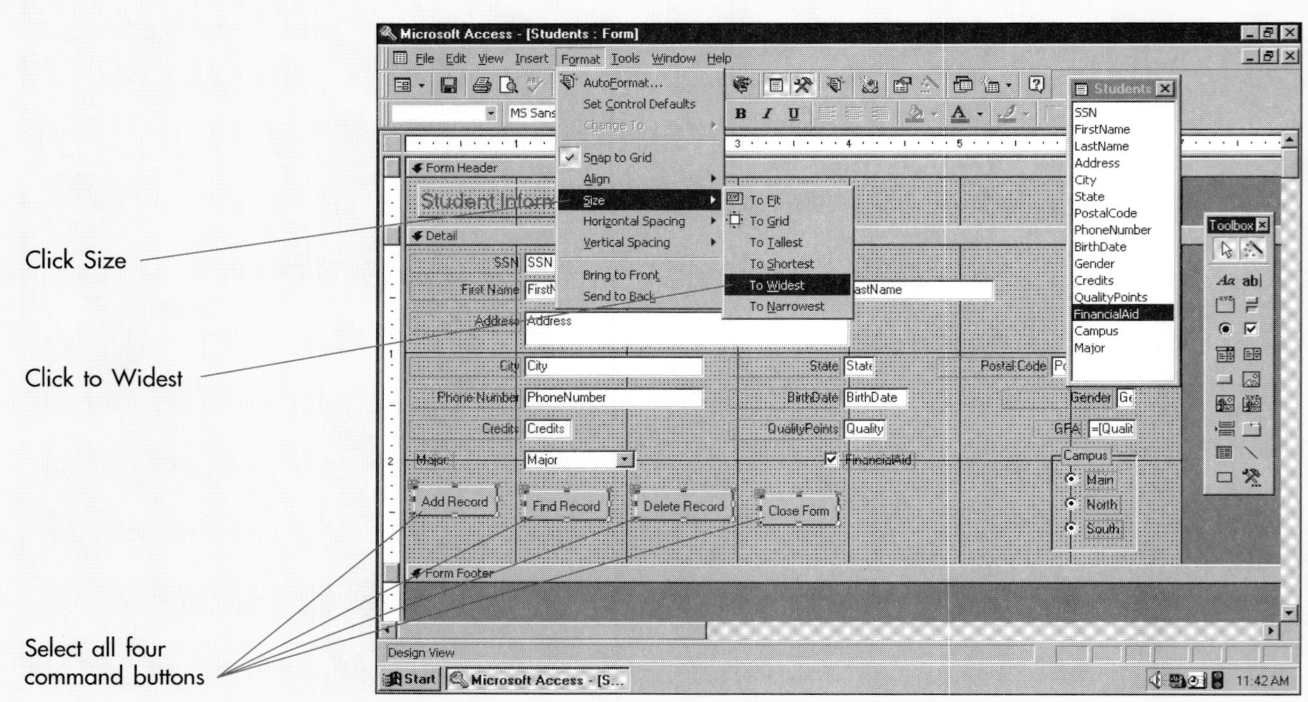

(f) Align the Buttons (step 7)

FIGURE 2.9 Hands-on Exercise 3 (continued)

STEP 8: Reset the Tab Order

- Click anywhere in the Detail section. Pull down the **View menu.** Click **Tab Order** to display the Tab Order dialog box in Figure 2.9g.
- Click the **AutoOrder command button** so that the tab key will move to fields in left-to-right, top-to-bottom order as you enter data in the form. Click **OK** to close the Tab Order dialog box.
- Check the form one more time in order to make any last-minute changes.
- Save the form.

CHANGE THE TAB ORDER

The Tab key provides a shortcut in the finished form to move from one field to the next; that is, you press Tab to move forward to the next field and Shift+Tab to return to the previous field. The order in which fields are selected corresponds to the sequence in which the controls were entered onto the form, and need not correspond to the physical appearance of the actual form. To restore a left-to-right, top-to-bottom sequence, pull down the View menu, click Tab Order, then select AutoOrder. Alternatively, you can specify a custom sequence by clicking the selector for the various controls within the Tab Order dialog box, then moving the row up or down within the list.

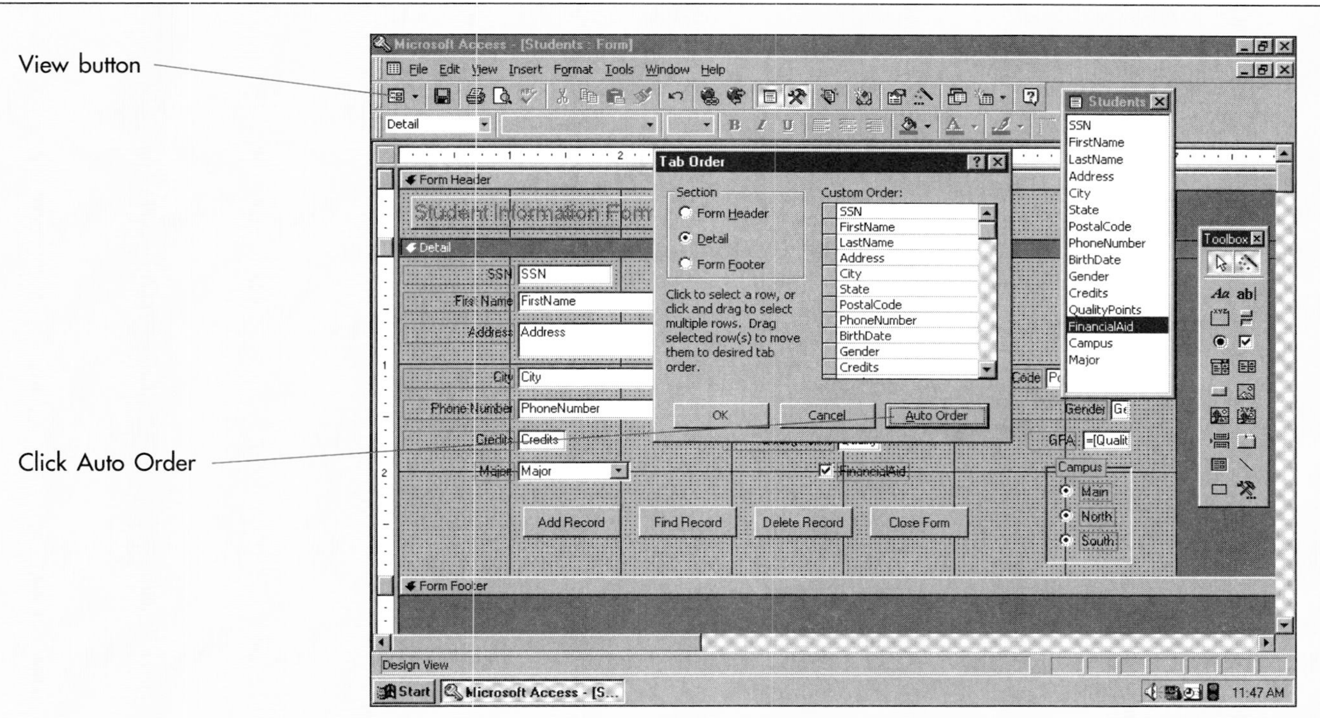

(g) Modify the Tab Order (step 8)

FIGURE 2.9 Hands-on Exercise 3 (continued)

STEP 9: The Page Setup Command

- Point to any blank area in the Detail section of the form. Click the **right mouse button** to display a shortcut menu, then click **Properties** to display the Properties dialog box for the Detail section. Click the **All tab.**
- Click the text box for **Height.** Enter **3.5** to change the height of the Detail section to three and one-half inches. Close the Properties dialog box.
- If necessary, click and drag the **right border** of the form so that all controls are fully visible. Do *not* exceed a width of 7 inches for the entire form.
- Pull down the **File menu.** Click **Page Setup** to display the Page Setup dialog box. If necessary, click the **Margins tab.**
- Change the left and right margins to **.75** inch. Click **OK** to accept the settings and close the Page Setup dialog box.

CHECK YOUR NUMBERS

The width of the form, plus the left and right margins, cannot exceed the width of the printed page. Thus increasing the width of a form may require a corresponding decrease in the left and right margins or a change to landscape (rather than portrait) orientation. Pull down the File menu and choose the Page Setup command to modify the dimensions of the form prior to printing.

STEP 10: The Completed Form

- Click the **View button** to switch to the Form view and display the first record in the table.
- Complete the record by adding appropriate data (choose any values you like) for the Major, FinancialAid, and Campus fields that were added to the form in this exercise.
- Click the **Add Record command button** to create a new record. Click the text box for **Social Security Number.** Add the record shown in Figure 2.9h. The record selector changes to a pencil as soon as you begin to enter data to indicate the record has not been saved.
- Press the **Tab key** or the **enter key** to move from field to field within the record. Click the **arrow** on the drop-down list box to display the list of majors, then click the desired major. Complete all of the information in the form.
- Click the **selection area** (the thin vertical column to the left of the form) to select only the current record. The record selector changes from a pencil to an arrow. The selection area is shaded to indicate that the record has been selected.
- Pull down the **File menu.** Click **Print** to display the Print dialog box. Click the option button to **print Selected Records**—that is, to print only the one record. Click **OK.**

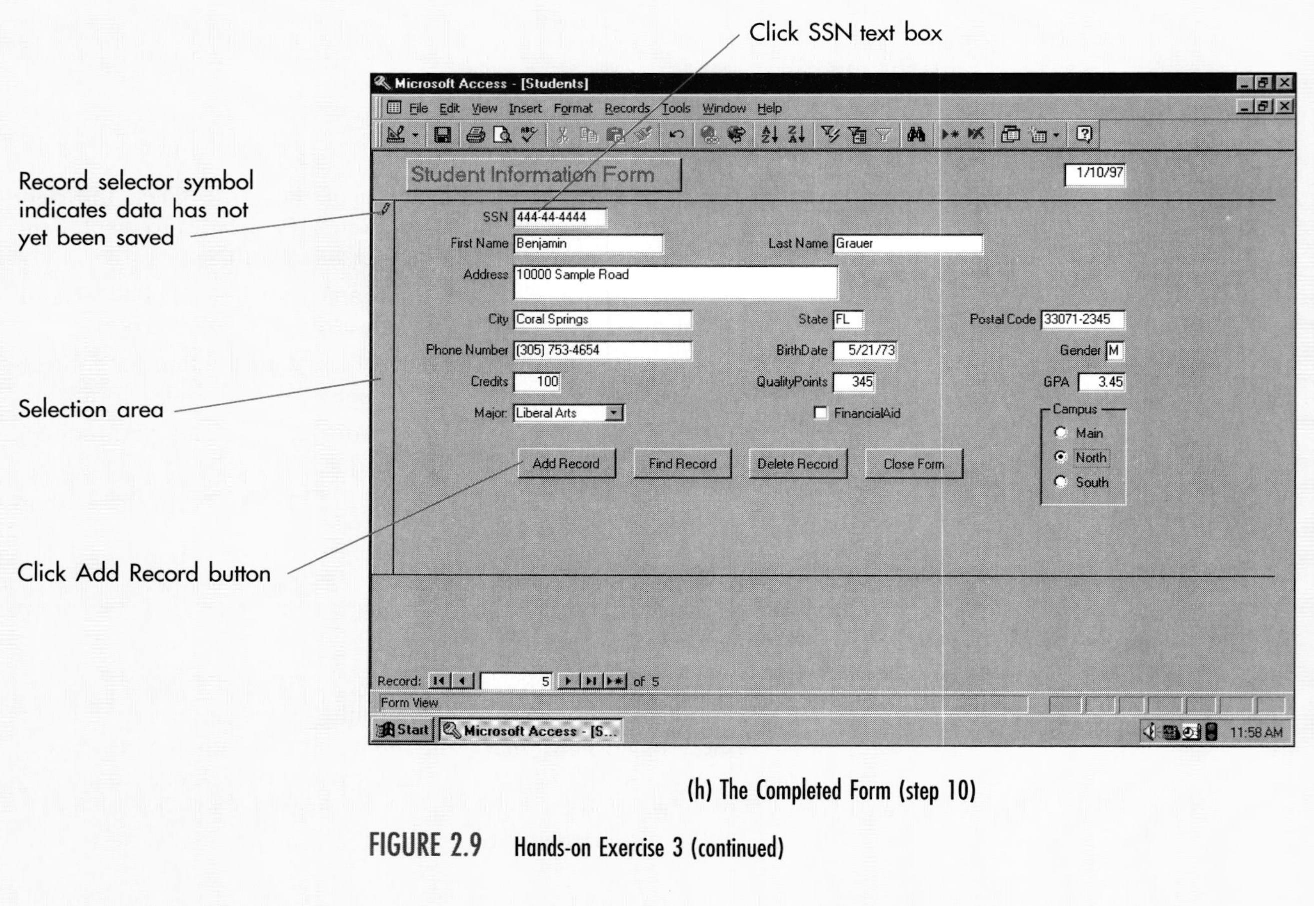

(h) The Completed Form (step 10)

FIGURE 2.9 Hands-on Exercise 3 (continued)

➤ Examine your printed output to be sure that the form fits on a single page. It if doesn't, you need to adjust the margins of the form itself and/or change the margins using the Page Setup command in the File menu, then print the form a second time.

KEYBOARD SHORTCUTS

Press Tab to move from one field to the next in a finished form. Press Shift+Tab to return to the previous field. Type the first letter of an item's name to select the first item in a drop-down list beginning with that letter; for example, type "B" to select the first item in Major beginning with that letter. Type the first two letters quickly—for example, Bu—and you will go directly to Business. Press the space bar to toggle a check box on and off. Press the down arrow key to move from one option to the next within an option group.

STEP 11: Exit Access

➤ Click the **Close Form command button** when you have completed the record. Click **Yes** if you see a message asking to save changes to the form.

➤ Pull down the **File menu.** Click **Exit** to leave Access. Congratulations on a job well done.

SUMMARY

The information produced by a system depends entirely on the underlying data. The design of the database is of critical importance and must be done correctly. Three guidelines were suggested. These are to include the necessary data, to store data in its smallest parts, and to avoid the use of calculated fields in a table.

The Table Wizard is the easiest way to create a table. It lets you choose from a series of business or personal tables, asks you questions about the fields you want, then creates the table for you.

A table has two views—the Design view and the Datasheet view. The Design view is used to create the table and display the fields within the table, as well as the data type and properties of each field. The Datasheet view is used after the table has been created to add, edit, and delete records.

A form provides a user-friendly way to enter and display data, in that it can be made to resemble a paper form. The Form Wizard is the easiest way to create a form. The Design view enables you to modify an existing form.

A form consists of objects called controls. A bound control has a data source such as a field in the underlying table. An unbound control has no data source. A calculated control contains an expression. Controls are selected, moved, and sized the same way as any other Windows object.

A property is a characteristic or attribute of an object that determines how the object looks and behaves. Every Access object (e.g., tables, fields, forms, and controls) has a set of properties that determine the behavior of that object. The properties for an object are displayed in a property sheet.

KEY WORDS AND CONCEPTS

Allow Zero Length property
AutoNumber field
AutoOrder
Bound control
Calculated control
Calculated field
Caption property
Check box
Combo box
Command button
Control
Currency field
Data type
Datasheet view
Date/Time field
Default Value property
Design view
Drop-down list box
Expression
Field name
Field Size property
Form
Form view
Form Wizard
Format property
Hyperlink field
Indexed property
Inheritance
Input Mask property
Label
Lookup Wizard
Memo field
Number field
OLE field
Option group
Page Setup
Primary key
Print Preview
Property
Property sheet
Required property
Selection area
Tab Order
Table Wizard
Text box
Text field
Toolbox toolbar
Unbound control
Validation Rule property
Validation Text property
Yes/No field

MULTIPLE CHOICE

1. Which of the following is true?
   (a) The Table Wizard must be used to create a table
   (b) The Form Wizard must be used to create a form
   (c) Both (a) and (b)
   (d) Neither (a) nor (b)
2. Which of the following is implemented automatically by Access?
   (a) Rejection of a record with a duplicate value of the primary key
   (b) Rejection of numbers in a text field
   (c) Both (a) and (b)
   (d) Neither (a) nor (b)
3. Social security number, phone number, and zip code should be designated as:
   (a) Number fields
   (b) Text fields
   (c) Yes/No fields
   (d) Any of the above depending on the application
4. Which of the following is true of the primary key?
   (a) Its values must be unique
   (b) It must be defined as a text field
   (c) It must be the first field in a table
   (d) It can never be changed

5. Social security number rather than name is used as a primary key because:
   (a) The social security number is numeric, whereas the name is not
   (b) The social security number is unique, whereas the name is not
   (c) The social security number is a shorter field
   (d) All of the above

6. Which of the following is true regarding buttons within the Form Wizard?
   (a) The > button copies a selected field from a table onto a form
   (b) The < button removes a selected field from a form
   (c) Both (a) and (b)
   (d) Neither (a) nor (b)

7. Which of the following was *not* a suggested guideline for designing a table?
   (a) Include all necessary data
   (b) Store data in its smallest parts
   (c) Avoid calculated fields
   (d) Designate at least two primary keys

8. Which of the following are valid parameters for use with a form?
   (a) Portrait orientation, a width of 6 inches, left and right margins of 1¼ inch
   (b) Landscape orientation, a width of 9 inches, left and right margins of 1 inch
   (c) Both (a) and (b)
   (d) Neither (a) nor (b)

9. Which view is used to add, edit, or delete records in a table?
   (a) The Datasheet view
   (b) The Form view
   (c) Both (a) and (b)
   (d) Neither (a) nor (b)

10. Which of the following is true?
   (a) Any field added to a table after a form has been created is automatically added to the form as a bound control
   (b) Any calculated control that appears in a form is automatically inserted into the underlying table
   (c) Every bound and unbound control in a form has an underlying property sheet
   (d) All of the above

11. In which view will you see the record selector symbols of a pencil and a triangle?
   (a) Only the Datasheet view
   (b) Only the Form view
   (c) The Datasheet view and the Form view
   (d) The Form view, the Design view, and the Datasheet view

12. To move a control (in the Design view), you select the control, then:
   (a) Point to a border (the pointer changes to an arrow) and click and drag the border to the new position
   (b) Point to a border (the pointer changes to a hand) and click and drag the border to the new position

(c) Point to a sizing handle (the pointer changes to an arrow) and click and drag the sizing handle to the new position
(d) Point to a sizing handle (the pointer changes to a hand) and click and drag the sizing handle to the new position

13. Which fields are commonly defined with an input mask?
(a) Social security number and phone number
(b) First name, middle name, and last name
(c) City, state, and zip code
(d) All of the above

14. Which data type appears as a check box in a form?
(a) Text field
(b) Number field
(c) Yes/No field
(d) All of the above

15. Which properties would you use to limit a user's response to two characters, and automatically convert the response to uppercase?
(a) Field Size and Format
(b) Input Mask, Validation Rule, and Default Value
(c) Input Mask and Required
(d) Field Size, Validation Rule, Validation Text, and Required

ANSWERS

1. d	**6.** c	**11.** c
2. a	**7.** d	**12.** b
3. b	**8.** c	**13.** a
4. a	**9.** c	**14.** c
5. b	**10.** c	**15.** a

PRACTICE WITH ACCESS 97

1. Modify the Student form created in the hands-on exercises to match the form in Figure 2.10. (The form contains three additional controls that must be added to the Students table.)

a. Add the DateAdmitted and EmailAddress as a date and a text field, respectively, in the Students table. Add a Yes/No field to indicate whether or not the student is an International student.
b. Add controls for the additional fields as shown in Figure 2.10.
c. Modify the State field in the underlying Students table to use the Lookup Wizard, and set CA, FL, NJ, and NY as the values for the list box. (These are the most common states in the Student population.) The control in the form will not, however, inherit the list box because it was added to the table after the form was created. Hence you have to delete the existing control in the form, display the field list, then click and drag the State field from the field list to the form.

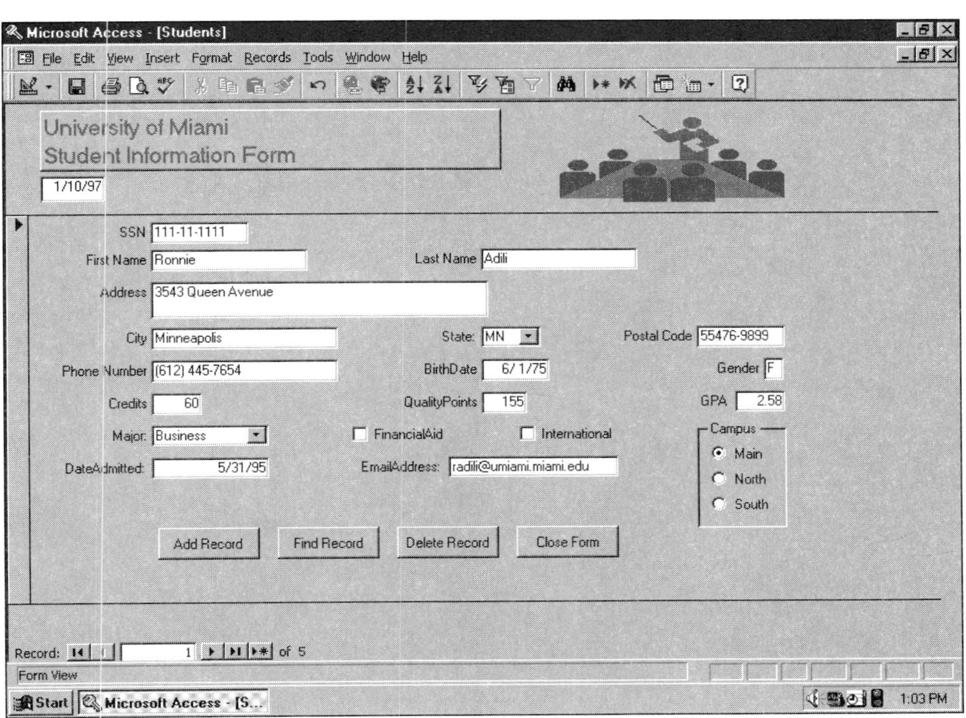

FIGURE 2.10 Screen for Practice Exercises 1 and 2

d. Resize the control in the Form Header so that *University of Miami Student Information Form* takes two lines. Press Ctrl+Enter to force a line break within the control. Resize the Form Header.
e. Change the tab order to reflect the new fields in the form.
f. Add a graphic as described in problem 2.

2. This exercise is a continuation of problem 1 and describes how to insert a graphic created by another application onto an Access form. (The faster your machine, the more you will enjoy the exercise.)
a. Open the Students form in My First Database in the Design view. Move the date in the header under the label.
b. Click the Unbound Object Frame tool on the toolbox. (If you are unsure as to which tool to click, just point to the tool to display the name of the tool.)
c. Click and drag in the Form Header to size the frame, then release the mouse to display an Insert Object dialog box.
d. Click the Create New option button. Select the Microsoft Clip Gallery as the object type. Click OK.
e. Click the Clip Art tab in the Microsoft Clip Gallery dialog box. Choose the category and picture you want from within the Clip Gallery. Click the Insert button to insert the picture into the Access form and simultaneously close the Clip Gallery dialog box. Do *not* be concerned if only a portion of the picture appears on the form.
f. Right click the newly inserted object to display a shortcut menu, then click Properties to display the Properties dialog box. Select (click) the Size Mode property and select Stretch from the associated list. Change the Back Style property to Transparent, the Special Effect property to Flat, and the Border Style property to Transparent. Close the Properties dialog box.

g. You should see the entire clip art image, although it may be distorted because the size and shape of the frame you inserted in steps (b) and (c) do not match the image you selected. Click and drag the sizing handles on the frame to size the object so that its proportions are correct. Click anywhere in the middle of the frame (the mouse pointer changes to a hand) to move the frame elsewhere in the form.

h. If you want to display a different object, double click the clip art image to return to the Clip Gallery in order to select another object.

3. Open the Employee database in the Exploring Access folder to create a form similar to the one in Figure 2.11. (This is the same database that was referenced in problem 2 in Chapter 1.)

a. The form was created using the Form Wizard and Colorful1 style. The various controls were then moved and sized to match the arrangement in the figure.

b. The label in the Form Header, date of execution, and command buttons were added after the form was created, using the techniques in the third hands-on exercise.

c. To add lines to the form, click the Line tool in the toolbox, then click and drag on the form to draw the line. To draw a straight line, press and hold the Shift key as you draw the line.

d. You need not match our form exactly, and we encourage you to experiment with a different design.

e. Add a record for yourself (if you have not already done so in Chapter 1), then print the form containing your data. Submit the printed form to your instructor as proof you did this exercise.

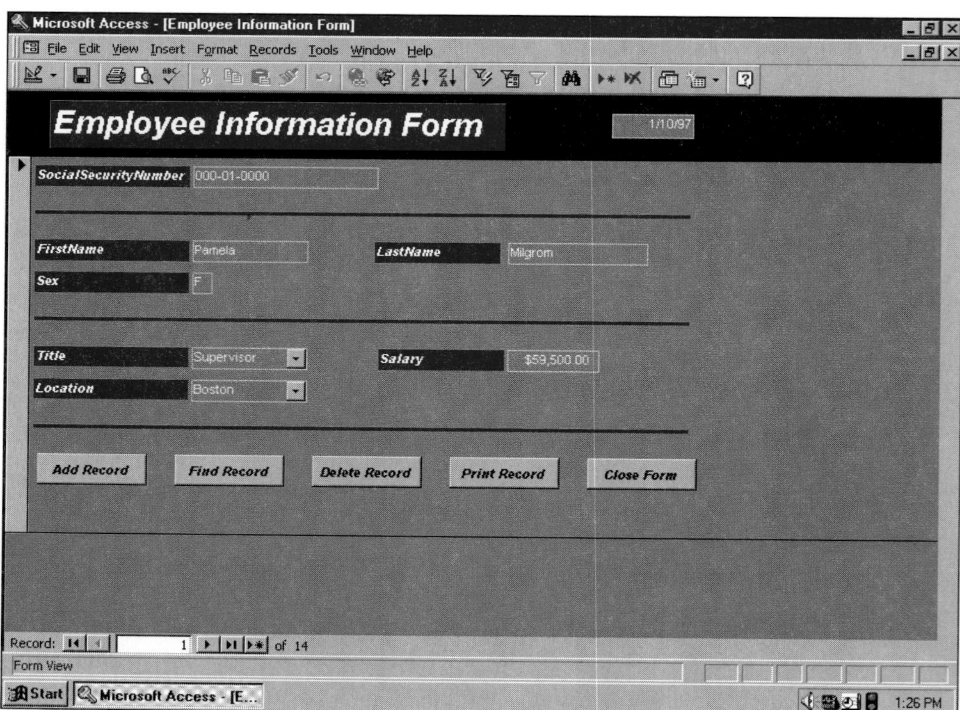

FIGURE 2.11 Screen for Practice Exercise 3

4. Open the USA database found in the Exploring Access folder to create a form similar to the one in Figure 2.12.
   a. The form was created using the Form Wizard and Standard style. The controls were moved and sized to match the arrangement in the figure.
   b. Population density is a calculated control and is computed by dividing the population by the area. Format the density to two decimal places.
   c. You need not match our form exactly, and we encourage you to experiment with different designs.
   d. The Find command can be used after the form has been created to search through the table and answer questions about the United States. The dialog box in Figure 2.12, for example, will identify the Empire State.
   e. Add the graphic, following the steps in the second exercise.
   f. Print the form of your favorite state and submit it to your instructor. Be sure to choose the option to print only the selected record.

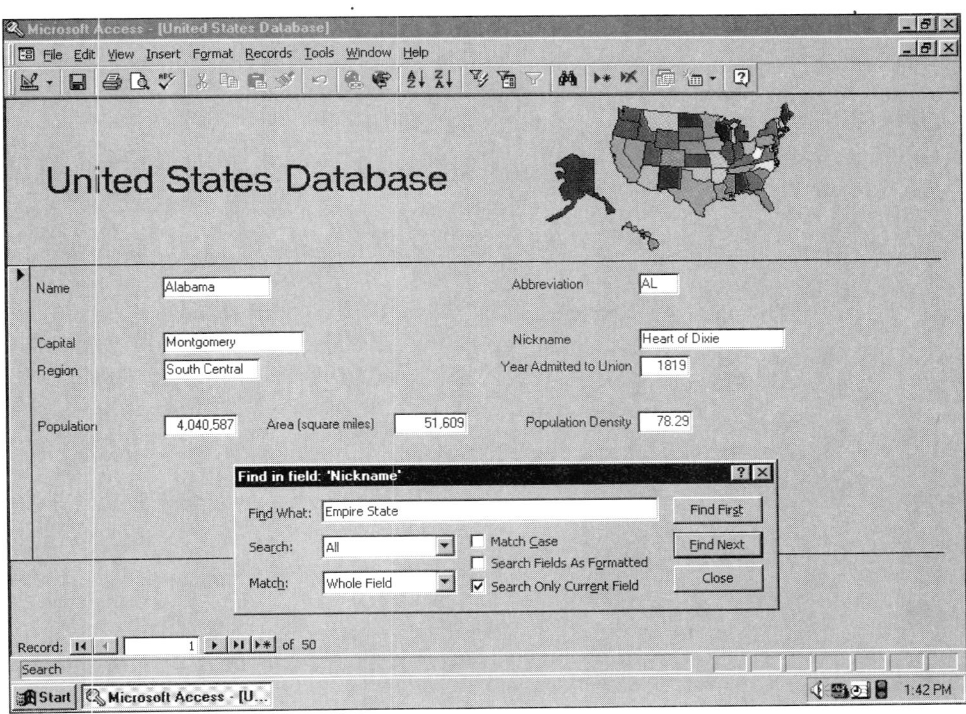

FIGURE 2.12 Screen for Practice Exercise 4

5. Figure 2.13 displays the Design view of a form to maintain an address book of friends and acquaintances. The picture is an added touch and well worth the effort, but it requires you to obtain pictures of your friends in machine-readable form. Each picture is stored initially in its own file (in GIF or JPEG format). The form and underlying table build upon the information in the chapter and should adhere to the following guidelines:
   a. Create an Address Book database containing a table and associated form, using Figure 2.13 as a guide. You can add or delete fields as appropriate with the exception of the FriendID field, which is designated as the primary key. The FriendID should be defined as an AutoNumber field whose value is created automatically each time a record is added to the table.

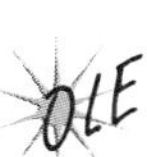

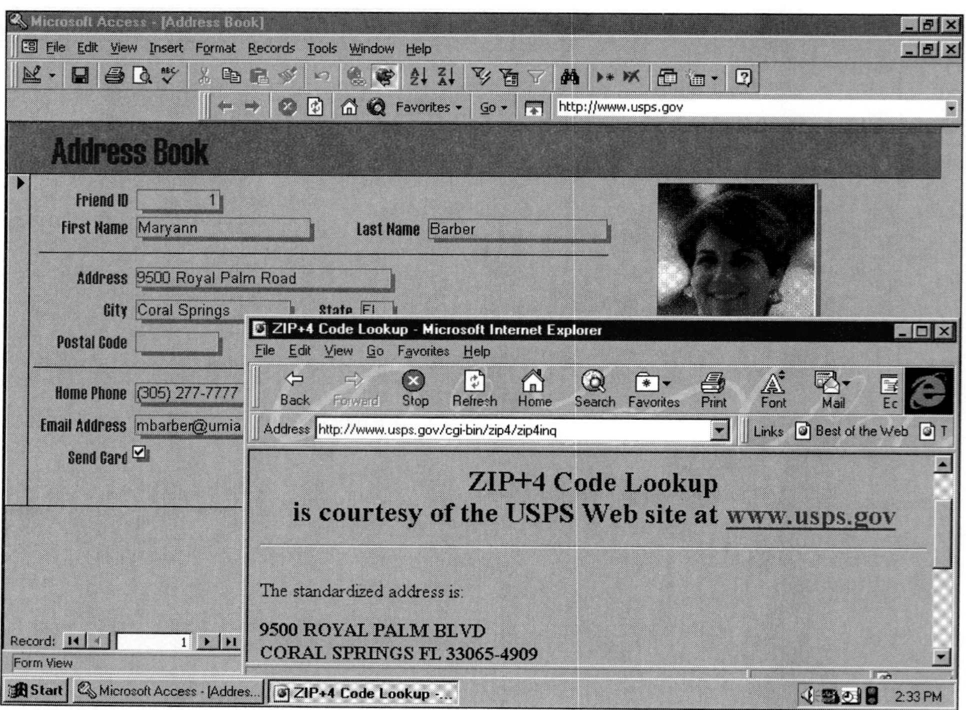

FIGURE 2.13 Screen for Practice Exercise 5

b. Define the postal code as a nine-digit zip code. You can obtain the additional four digits from the U.S. Postal Service as shown in Figure 2.13. Pull down the View menu, click Toolbars, then toggle the Web toolbar on. Enter the address of the Postal Service (www.usps.gov), then click the appropriate link to obtain the complete zip code.

c. Include a logical field (e.g., SendCard) in the underlying table. This will enable you to create a report of those people who are to receive a birthday card (or season's greetings card) once the data have been entered.

d. Include an OLE field in the table, regardless of whether or not you actually have a picture, and be sure to leave space in the form for the picture. Those records that have an associated picture will display the picture in the form; those records that do not have a picture will display a blank space. To insert a picture into the database, open the table, click in the OLE field, pull down the Insert menu, and click the Object command. Click the Create from File option button, click the Browse button in the associated dialog box, then select the appropriate file name and location.

e. Enter data for yourself in the completed form, then print the associated form to submit to your instructor as proof you did this exercise.

6. The potential of Access is limited only by your imagination. Figure 2.14, for example, shows a (partially completed) table to hold statistics for players in the National Basketball Association. The decision on which fields to include is up to you; e.g., you can include statistics for the player's career and/or the current year. We suggest, however, the inclusion of a memo field to add descriptive notes (e.g., career highlights) about each player. You can also include an optional picture field provided you can obtain the player's picture. Design the table, create the associated form, then go the home page of the NBA to obtain statistics for your favorite player. Print the completed form for your player as proof you did this exercise.

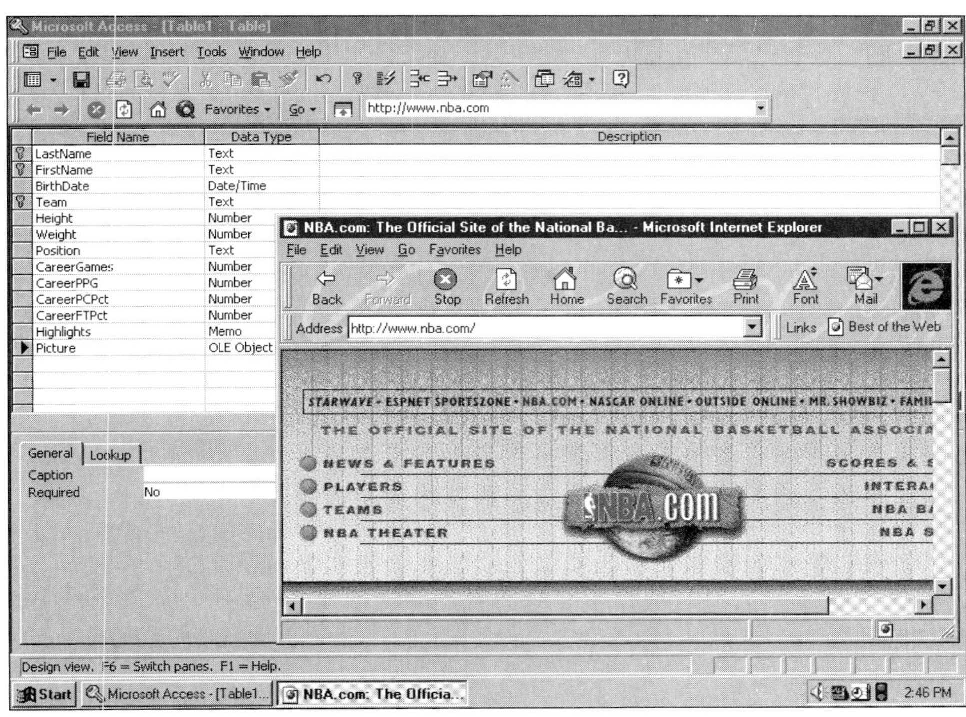

FIGURE 2.14 Screen for Practice Exercise 6

CASE STUDIES

Personnel Management

You have been hired as the Personnel Director for a medium-sized firm (500 employees) and are expected to implement a system to track employee compensation. You want to be able to calculate the age of every employee as well as the length of service. You want to know each employee's most recent performance evaluation. You want to be able to calculate the amount of the most recent salary increase, both in dollars and as a percentage of the previous salary. You also want to know how long the employee had to wait for that increase—that is, how much time elapsed between the present and previous salary. Design a table capable of providing this information.

The Stockbroker

A good friend has come to you for help. He is a new stockbroker whose firm provides computer support for existing clients, but does nothing in the way of data management for prospective clients. Your friend wants to use a PC to track the clients he is pursuing. He wants to know when he last contacted a person, how the contact was made (by phone or through the mail), and how interested the person was. He also wants to store the investment goals of each prospect, such as growth or income, and whether a person is interested in stocks, bonds, and/or a retirement account. And finally, he wants to record the amount of money the person has to invest. Design a table suitable for the information requirements.

Metro Zoo

Your job as Director of Special Programs at the Metro Zoo has put you in charge of this year's fund-raising effort. You have decided to run an "Adopt an Animal" campaign and are looking for contributions on three levels: $25 for a reptile, $50 for a bird, and $100 for a mammal. Adopting "parents" will receive a personalized adoption certificate, a picture of their animal, and educational information about the zoo. You already have a great mailing list—the guest book that is maintained at the zoo entrance. Your main job is to computerize that information and to store additional information about contributions that are received. Design a table that will be suitable for this project.

Form Design

Collect several examples of such real forms as a magazine subscription, auto registration, or employment application. Choose the form you like best and implement the design in Access. Start by creating the underlying table (with some degree of validation), then use the Form Wizard to create the form. How closely does the form you create resemble the paper form with which you began?

File Compression

Photographs add significantly to the value of a database, but they also add to its size. Accordingly, you might want to consider acquisition of a file compression program to facilitate copying large documents to a floppy disk in order to transport your documents to and from school, home, or work. You can download an evaluation copy of the popular WinZip program at www.winzip.com. Investigate the subject of file compression, then submit a summary of your findings to your instructor.

Copyright Infringement

It's fun to download images from the Web for inclusion into a database, but is it legal? Copyright protection (infringement) is one of the most pressing legal issues on the Web. Search the Web for sites that provide information on current copyright law. One excellent site is the copyright page at the Institute for Learning Technologies at www.ilt.columbia.edu/projects/copyright. Another excellent reference is the page at www.benedict.com. Research these and other sites, then summarize your findings in a short note to your instructor.

The Digital Camera

The art of photography is undergoing profound changes with the introduction of the digital camera. The images are stored on disk rather than traditional film and are available instantly. Search the Internet for the latest information on digital cameras and report back to the class with the results of your research. Perhaps one of your classmates has access to a digital camera, in which case you can take pictures of the class for inclusion in an Access database.

3

INFORMATION FROM THE DATABASE: REPORTS AND QUERIES

OBJECTIVES

After reading this chapter you will be able to:

1. Describe the various types of reports available through the Report Wizard.
2. Describe the various views in the Report Window and the purpose of each.
3. Describe the similarities between forms and reports with respect to bound, unbound, and calculated controls.
4. List the sections that may be present in a report and explain the purpose of each.
5. Differentiate between a query and a table; explain how the objects in an Access database (tables, forms, queries, and reports) interact with one another.
6. Use the design grid to create and modify a select query.
7. Explain the use of multiple criteria rows within the design grid to implement AND and OR conditions in a query.
8. Describe the various views in the Query window and the purpose of each.

OVERVIEW

Data and information are not synonymous. Data refers to a fact or facts about a specific record, such as a student's name, major, quality points, or number of completed credits. Information can be defined as data that has been rearranged into a more useful format. The individual fields within a student record are considered data. A list of students on the Dean's List, however, is information that has been produced from the data about the individual students.

Chapters 1 and 2 described how to enter and maintain data through the use of tables and forms. This chapter shows how to convert the data to information through queries and reports. Queries enable you to ask questions about the database. Reports provide presentation quality output and display detail as well as summary information about the records in a database.

As you read the chapter, you will see that the objects in an Access database (tables, forms, reports and queries) have many similar characteristics. We use these similarities to build on what you have learned in previous chapters. You already know, for example, that the controls in a form inherit their properties from the corresponding fields in a table. The same concept applies to the controls in a report. And since you know how to move and size controls within a form, you also know how to move and size the controls in a report. As you read the chapter, look for these and other similarities to apply your existing knowledge to the new material.

REPORTS

A ***report*** is a printed document that displays information from a database. Figure 3.1 shows several sample reports, each of which will be created in this chapter. The reports were created with the Report Wizard and are based on the Students table that was presented in Chapter 2. (The table has been expanded to 24 records.) As you view each report, ask yourself how the data in the table was rearranged to produce the information in the report.

The ***columnar (vertical) report*** in Figure 3.1a is the simplest type of report. It lists every field for every record in a single column (one record per page) and typically runs for many pages. The records in this report are displayed in the same sequence (by social security number) as the records in the table on which the report is based.

The ***tabular report*** in Figure 3.1b displays fields in a row rather than in a column. Each record in the underlying table is printed in its own row. Unlike the previous report, only selected fields are displayed, so the tabular report is more concise than the columnar report of Figure 3.1a. Note, too, that the records in the report are listed in alphabetical order rather than by social security number.

The report in Figure 3.1c is also a tabular report, but it is very different from the report in Figure 3.1b. The report in Figure 3.1c lists only a selected set of students (those students with a GPA of 3.50 or higher), as opposed to the earlier reports, which listed every student. The students are listed in descending order according to their GPA.

The report in Figure 3.1d displays the students in groups, according to their major, then computes the average GPA for each group. The report also contains summary information (not visible in Figure 3.1d) for the report as a whole, which computes the average GPA for all students.

DATA VERSUS INFORMATION

Data and information are not synonymous although the terms are often interchanged. Data is the raw material and consists of the table (or tables) that compose a database. Information is the finished product. Data is converted to information by selecting records, performing calculations on those records, and/or changing the sequence in which the records are displayed. Decisions in an organization are made on the basis of information rather than raw data.

Student Roster

SSN	111-11-1111
FirstName	Jared
LastName	Berlin
Address	900 Main Highway
City	Charleston
State	SC
PostalCode	29410-0560
PhoneNumber	(803) 223-7868
BirthDate	1/15/72
Gender	M
Credits	100
QualityPoints	250
FinancialAid	Yes
Campus	1
Major	Engineering

Saturday, January 11, 1997 Page 1 of 24

(a) Columnar Report

Student Master List

Last Name	First Name	Phone Number	Major
Adili	Ronnie	(612) 445-7654	Business
Berlin	Jared	(803) 223-7868	Engineering
Camejo	Oscar	(716) 433-3321	Liberal Arts
Coe	Bradley	(415) 235-6543	Undecided
Cornell	Ryan	(404) 755-4490	Undecided
DiGiacomo	Kevin	(305) 531-7652	Business
Faulkner	Eileen	(305) 489-8876	Communications
Frazier	Steven	(410) 995-8755	Undecided
Gibson	Christopher	(305) 235-4563	Business
Heltzer	Peter	(305) 753-4533	Engineering
Huerta	Carlos	(212) 344-5654	Undecided
Joseph	Cedric	(404) 667-8955	Communications
Korba	Nickolas	(415) 664-0900	Education
Ortiz	Frances	(303) 575-3211	Communications
Parulis	Christa	(410) 877-6565	Liberal Arts
Price	Lori	(310) 961-2323	Communications
Ramsay	Robert	(212) 223-9889	Business
Slater	Erica	(312) 545-6978	Communications
Solomon	Wendy	(305) 666-4532	Engineering
Watson	Ana	(305) 595-7877	Liberal Arts
Watson	Ana	(305) 561-2334	Business
Weissman	Kimberly	(904) 388-8605	Liberal Arts
Zacco	Michelle	(617) 884-3434	Undecided
Zimmerman	Kimberly	(713) 225-3434	Education

Saturday, January 11, 1997 Page 1 of 1

(b) Tabular Report

Dean's List

First Name	Last Name	Major	CreditsQuality	Points	GPA
Peter	Heltzer	Engineering	25	100	4.00
Cedric	Joseph	Communications	45	170	3.78
Erica	Slater	Communications	105	390	3.71
Kevin	DiGiacomo	Business	105	375	3.57
Wendy	Solomon	Engineering	50	175	3.50

Saturday, January 11, 1997 Page 1 of 1

(c) Dean's List

GPA by Major

Major	Last Name	First Name	GPA
Business			
	Adili	Ronnie	2.58
	Cornell	Ryan	1.78
	DiGiacomo	Kevin	3.57
	Gibson	Christopher	1.71
	Ramsay	Robert	3.24
	Watson	Ana	2.50
		Average GPA for Major	2.56
Communications			
	Faulkner	Eileen	2.67
	Joseph	Cedric	3.78
	Ortiz	Frances	2.14
	Price	Lori	1.75
	Slater	Erica	3.71
		Average GPA for Major	2.81
Education			
	Korba	Nickolas	1.66
	Zimmerman	Kimberly	3.29
		Average GPA for Major	2.48
Engineering			
	Berlin	Jared	2.50
	Heltzer	Peter	4.00
	Solomon	Wendy	3.50
		Average GPA for Major	3.33
Liberal Arts			
	Camejo	Oscar	2.80
	Parulis	Christa	1.80
	Watson	Ana	2.79
	Weissman	Kimberly	2.63
		Average GPA for Major	2.51

Saturday, January 11, 1997 Page 1 of 2

(d) Summary Report

FIGURE 3.1 Report Types

Anatomy of a Report

All reports are based on an underlying table or query within the database. (Queries are discussed later in the chapter, beginning on page 102.) A report, however, displays the data or information in a more attractive fashion because it contains various headings and/or other decorative items that are not present in either a table or a query.

The easiest way to learn about reports is to compare a printed report with its underlying design. Consider, for example, Figure 3.2a, which displays the tabular report, and Figure 3.2b, which shows the underlying design. The latter shows how a report is divided into sections, which appear at designated places when the report is printed. There are seven types of sections, but a report need not contain all seven.

The ***report header*** appears once, at the beginning of a report. It typically contains information describing the report, such as its title and the date the report was printed. (The report header appears above the page header on the first page of the report.) The ***report footer*** appears once at the end of the report, above the page footer on the last page of the report, and displays summary information for the report as a whole.

The ***page header*** appears at the top of every page in a report and can be used to display page numbers, column headings, and other descriptive information. The ***page footer*** appears at the bottom of every page and may contain page numbers (when they are not in the page header) or other descriptive information.

A ***group header*** appears at the beginning of a group of records to identify the group. A ***group footer*** appears after the last record in a group and contains summary information about the group. Group headers and footers are used only when the records in a report are sorted (grouped) according to a common value in a specific field. These sections do not appear in the report of Figure 3.2, but were shown earlier in the report of Figure 3.1d.

The ***detail section*** appears in the main body of a report and is printed once for every record in the underlying table (or query). It displays one or more fields for each record in columnar or tabular fashion, according to the design of the report.

The Report Wizard

The ***Report Wizard*** is the easiest way to create a report, just as the Form Wizard is the easiest way to create a form. The Report Wizard asks you questions about the report you want, then builds the report for you. You can accept the report as is, or you can customize it to better suit your needs.

Figure 3.3a displays the New Report dialog box, from which you can select the Report Wizard. The Report Wizard, in turn, requires you to specify the table or query on which the report will be based. The report in this example will be based on an expanded version of the Students table that was created in Chapter 2.

After you specify the underlying table, you select one or more fields from that table, as shown in Figure 3.3b. The Report Wizard then asks you to select a layout (e.g., Tabular in Figure 3.3c.) and a style (e.g., Soft Gray in Figure 3.3d). This is all the information the Report Wizard requires, and it proceeds to create the report for you. The controls on the report correspond to the fields you selected and are displayed in accordance with the specified layout.

Apply What You Know

The Report Wizard provides an excellent starting point, but typically does not create the report exactly as you would like it to be. Accordingly, you can modify a

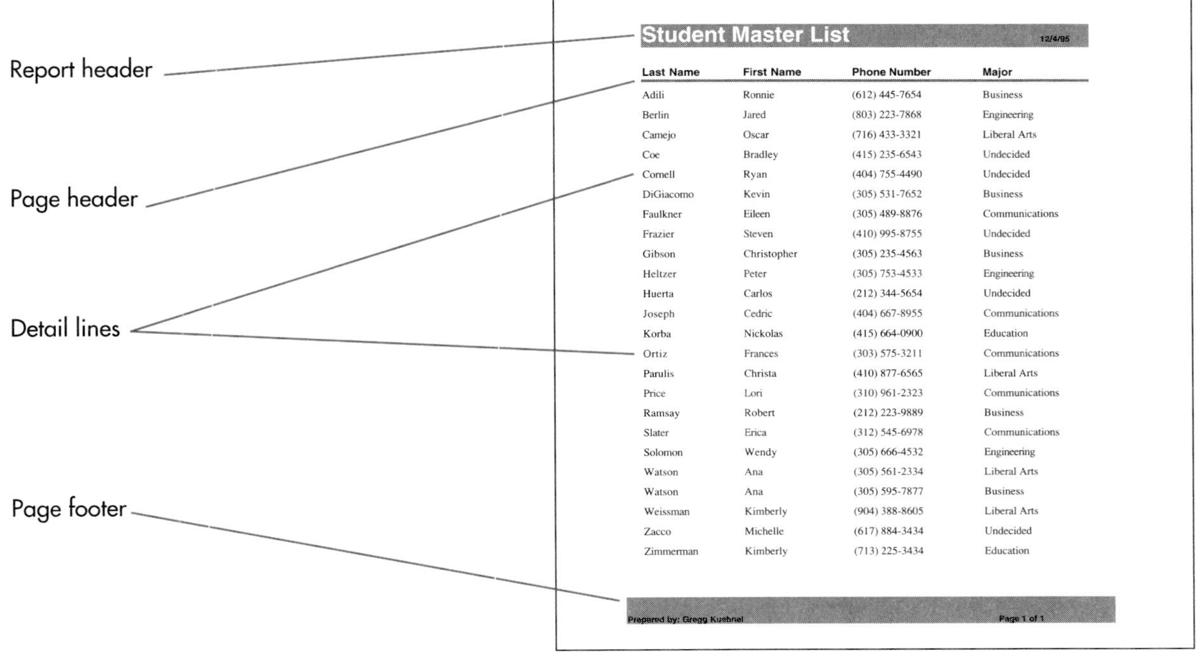

Student Master List 12/4/95

Last Name	First Name	Phone Number	Major
Adili	Ronnie	(612) 445-7654	Business
Berlin	Jared	(803) 223-7868	Engineering
Camejo	Oscar	(716) 433-3321	Liberal Arts
Coe	Bradley	(415) 235-6543	Undecided
Cornell	Ryan	(404) 755-4490	Undecided
DiGiacomo	Kevin	(305) 531-7652	Business
Faulkner	Eileen	(305) 489-8876	Communications
Frazier	Steven	(410) 995-8755	Undecided
Gibson	Christopher	(305) 235-4563	Business
Heltzer	Peter	(305) 753-4533	Engineering
Huerta	Carlos	(212) 344-5654	Undecided
Joseph	Cedric	(404) 667-8955	Communications
Korba	Nickolas	(415) 664-0900	Education
Ortiz	Frances	(303) 575-3211	Communications
Parulis	Christa	(410) 877-6565	Liberal Arts
Price	Lori	(310) 961-2323	Communications
Ramsay	Robert	(212) 223-9889	Business
Slater	Erica	(312) 545-6978	Communications
Solomon	Wendy	(305) 666-4532	Engineering
Watson	Ana	(305) 561-2334	Liberal Arts
Watson	Ana	(305) 595-7877	Business
Weissman	Kimberly	(904) 388-8605	Liberal Arts
Zacco	Michelle	(617) 884-3434	Undecided
Zimmerman	Kimberly	(713) 225-3434	Education

Prepared by: Gregg Kuehnel Page 1 of 1

(a) The Printed Report

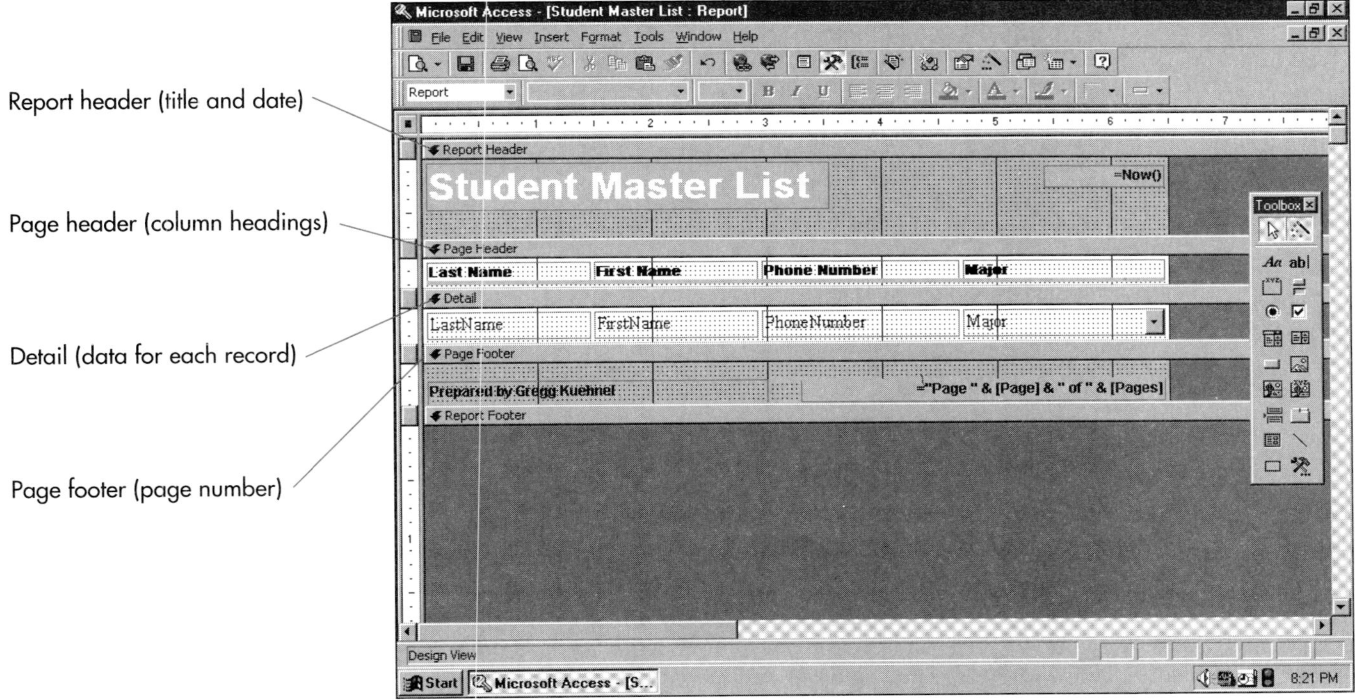

(b) Design View

FIGURE 3.2 Anatomy of a Report

Select the underlying table/query

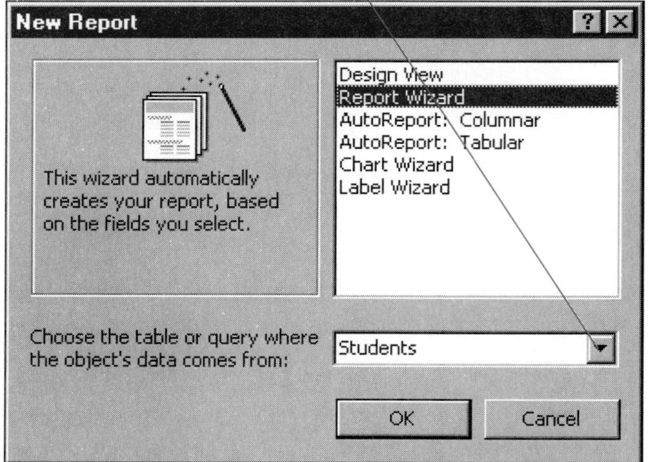

(a) Select the Underlying Table

Selected fields for report

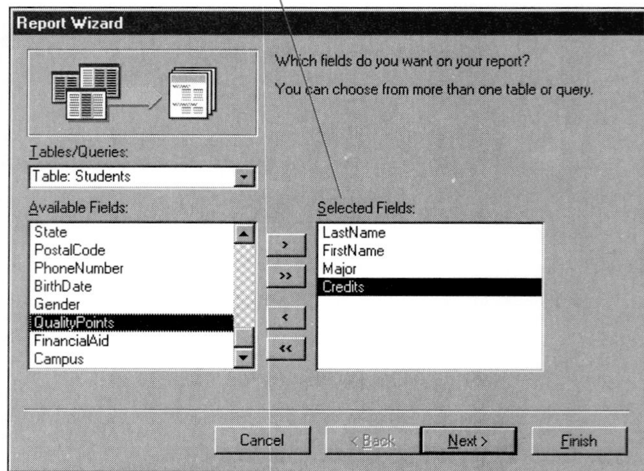

(b) Select the Fields

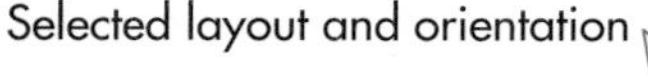

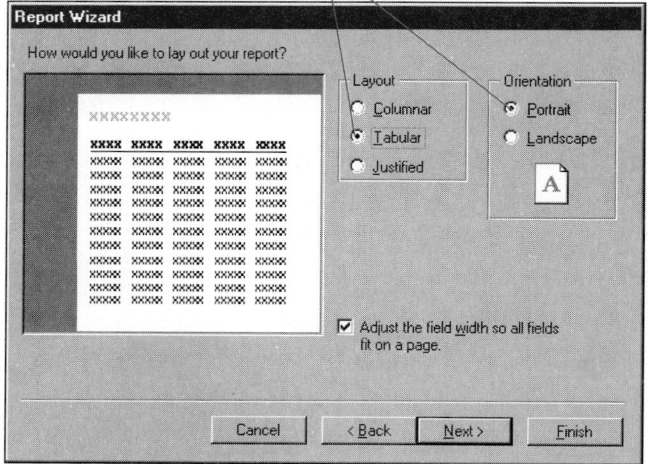

(c) Choose the Layout

Selected style

Report Wizard

What style would you like?

Bold
Casual
Compact
Corporate
Formal
Soft Gray

Title

Label from Detail

Control from Detail

Cancel < Back Next > Finish

(d) Choose the Style

FIGURE 3.3 The Report Wizard

report created by the Report Wizard, just as you can modify a form created by the Form Wizard. The techniques are the same, and you should look for similarities between forms and reports so that you can apply what you already know. Knowledge of one is helpful in understanding the other.

Controls appear in a report just as they do in a form, and the same definitions apply. A ***bound control*** has as its data source a field in the underlying table. An ***unbound control*** has no data source and is used to display titles, labels, lines, rectangles, and graphics. A ***calculated control*** has as its data source an expression rather than a field. A student's Grade Point Average is an example of a calculated control since it is computed by dividing the number of quality points by the number of credits. The means for selecting, sizing, moving, aligning, and deleting controls are the same, regardless of whether you are working on a form or a report. Thus:

- To select a control, click anywhere on the control. To select multiple controls, press and hold the Shift key as you click each successive control.
- To size a control, click the control to select it, then drag the sizing handles. Drag the handles on the top or bottom to size the box vertically. Drag the handles on the left or right side to size the box horizontally. Drag the handles in the corner to size both horizontally and vertically.
- To move a control, point to any border, but not to a sizing handle (the mouse pointer changes to a hand), then click the mouse and drag the control to its new position.
- To change the properties of a control, point to the control, click the right mouse button to display a shortcut menu, then click Properties to display the property sheet. Click the text box for the desired property, make the necessary change, then close the property sheet.

INHERITANCE

A bound control inherits the same property settings as the associated field in the underlying table. Changing the property setting for a field after the report has been created does *not,* however, change the property of the corresponding control in the report. In similar fashion, changing the property setting of a control in a report does *not* change the property setting of the field in the underlying table.

HANDS-ON EXERCISE 1

The Report Wizard

Objective: To use the Report Wizard to create a new report; to modify an existing report by adding, deleting, and/or modifying its controls. Use Figure 3.4 as a guide in the exercise.

STEP 1: Open the Our Students Database

- ➤ Start Access. You should see the Microsoft Access dialog box with the option button to **Open an Existing Database** already selected.
- ➤ Double click the **More Files** selection to display the Open dialog box. Click the **drop-down arrow** on the Look In list box, click the drive containing the **Exploring Access folder,** then open that folder.

THE OUR STUDENTS DATABASE

The Our Students database has the identical design as the database you created in Chapter 2. We have, however, expanded the Students table so that it contains 24 records. The larger table enables you to create more meaningful reports and to obtain the same results as we do in the hands-on exercise.

- Click the **down scroll arrow,** if necessary, and select the **Our Students** database. Click the **Open command button** to open the database.
- Click the **Reports tab** in the database window, then click the **New command button** to display the New Report dialog box in Figure 3.4a. Select the **Report Wizard** as the means of creating the report.
- Click the **drop-down arrow** to display the tables and queries in the database in order to select the one on which the report will be based. Click **Students** (the only table in the database). Click **OK** to start the Report Wizard.

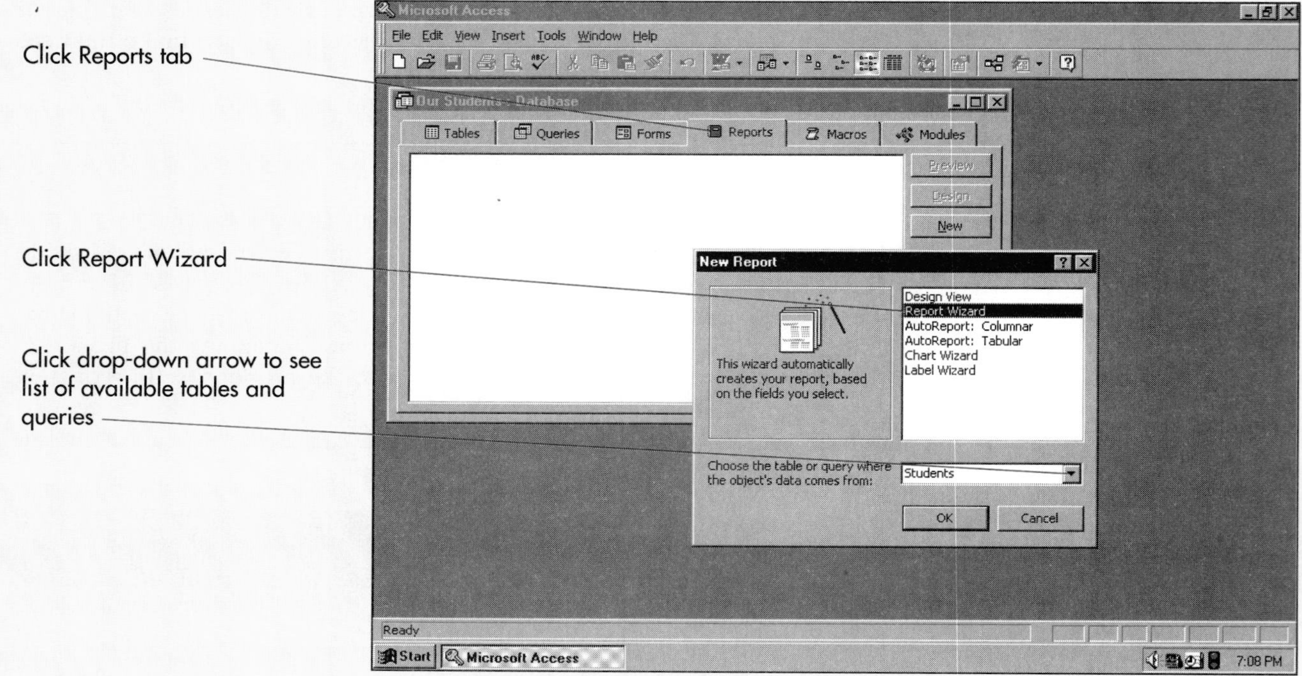

(a) Create a Report (step 1)

FIGURE 3.4 Hands-on Exercise 1

STEP 2: The Report Wizard

- You should see the dialog box in Figure 3.4b, which displays all of the fields in the Students table. Click the **LastName field** in the Available Fields list box, then click the **> button** to enter this field in the Selected Fields list, as shown in Figure 3.4b.
- Enter the remaining fields (FirstName, PhoneNumber, and Major) one at a time, by selecting the field name, then clicking the **> button.** Click the **Next command button** when you have entered all fields.

WHAT THE REPORT WIZARD DOESN'T TELL YOU

The fastest way to select a field is by double clicking; that is, double click a field in the Available Fields list box, and it is automatically moved to the Selected Fields list for inclusion in the report. The process also works in reverse; that is, you can double click a field in the Selected Fields list to remove it from the report.

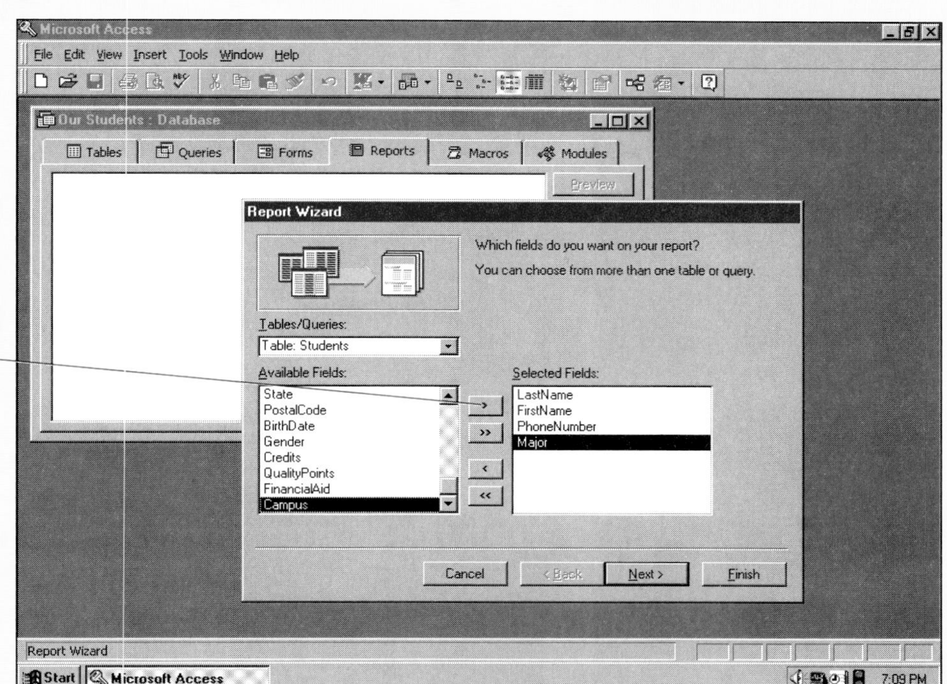

(b) The Report Wizard

FIGURE 3.4 Hands-on Exercise 1 (continued)

STEP 3: The Report Wizard (continued)

- The Report Wizard displays several additional screens asking about the report you want to create. The first screen asks whether you want to choose any grouping levels. Click **Next** without specifying a grouping level.
- The next screen asks whether you want to sort the records. Click the **drop-down arrow** to display the available fields, then select **LastName.** Click **Next.**
- The **Tabular layout** is selected, as is **Portrait orientation.** Be sure the box is checked to **Adjust field width so all fields fit on a page.** Click **Next.**
- Choose **Soft Gray** as the style. Click **Next.**
- Enter **Student Master List** as the title for your report. The option button to **Preview the Report** is already selected. Click the **Finish command button** to exit the Report Wizard and view the report.

AUTOMATIC SAVING

The Report Wizard automatically saves a report under the name you supply for the title of the report. To verify that a report has been saved, change to the Database window by pulling down the Window menu or by clicking the Database Window button that appears on every toolbar. Once you are in the Database window, click the Reports tab to see the list of existing reports. Note, however, that any subsequent changes must be saved explicitly by clicking the Save button in the Report Design view, or by clicking Yes in response to the warning prompt should you attempt to close the report without saving the changes.

STEP 4: Preview the Report

- ➤ Click the **Maximize button** so the report takes the entire window as shown in Figure 3.4c. Note the report header at the beginning of the report, the page header (column headings) at the top of the page, and the page footer at the bottom of the page.
- ➤ Click the **drop-down arrow** on the Zoom Control box so that you can view the report at **75%.** Click the **scroll arrows** on the vertical scroll bar to view the names of additional students.
- ➤ Click the **Close button** to close the Print Preview window and change to the Report Design view.

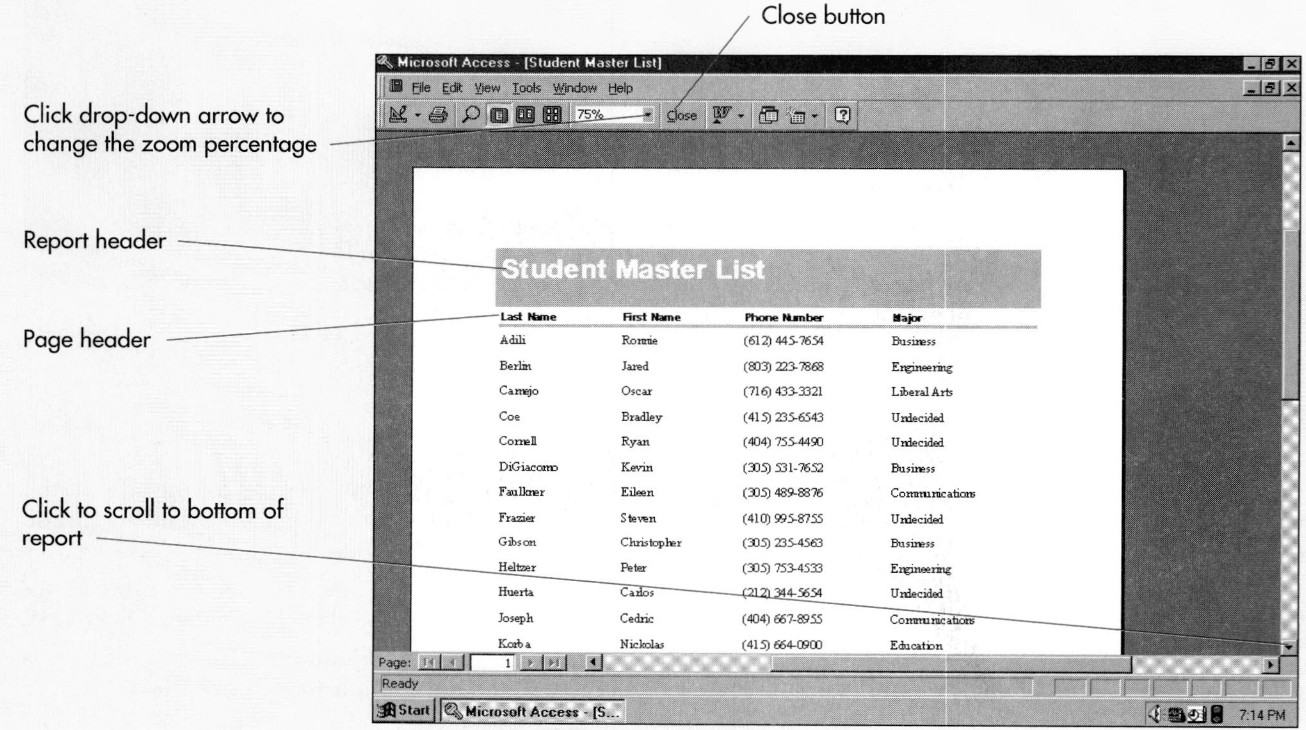

(c) The Initial Report (step 4)

FIGURE 3.4 Hands-on Exercise 1 (continued)

THE PRINT PREVIEW WINDOW

The Print Preview window enables you to preview a report in various ways. Click the One Page, Two Page, or Multiple Page buttons for different views of a report. Use the Zoom button to toggle between the full page and zoom (magnified) views, or use the Zoom Control box to choose a specific magnification. The Navigation buttons at the bottom of the Print Preview window enable you to preview a specific page, while the vertical scroll bar at the right side of the window lets you scroll within a page.

STEP 5: Modify an Existing Control

- Click and drag the control containing the **Now function** from the report footer to the report header as shown in Figure 3.4d. Size the control as necessary, then check that the control is still selected and click the **Align Right button** on the Formatting toolbar.
- Point to the control, then click the **right mouse button** to display a shortcut menu and click **Properties** to display the Properties sheet.
- Click the **Format tab** in the Properties sheet, click the **Format property,** then click the **drop-down arrow** to display the available formats. Click **Short Date,** then close the Properties sheet.
- Pull down the **File menu** and click **Save** (or click the **Save button**) to save the modified design

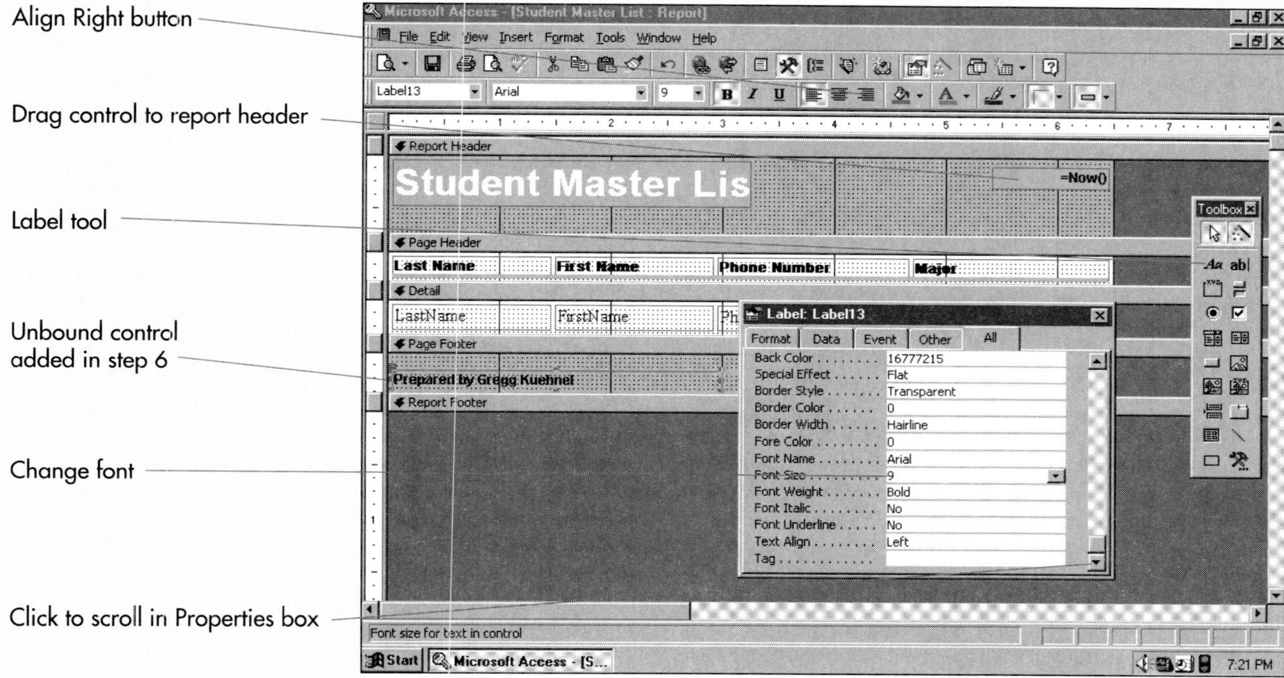

(d) Modify the Report (steps 5 & 6)

FIGURE 3.4 Hands-on Exercise 1 (continued)

ACCESS FUNCTIONS

Access contains many built-in functions, each of which returns a specific value or the result of a calculation. The Now function, for example, returns the current date and time. The Page and Pages functions return the specific page number and total number of pages, respectively. The Report Wizard automatically adds these functions at appropriate places in a report. You can also add these (or other) functions explicitly, by creating a text box, then replacing the default unbound control by an equal sign, followed by the function name (and associated arguments if any)—for example, =Now( ) to insert the current date and time.

STEP 6: Add an Unbound Control

- Click the **Label tool** on the Toolbox toolbar, then click and drag in the report footer where you want the label to go and release the mouse. You should see a flashing insertion point inside the label control. (If you see the word *Unbound* instead of the insertion point, it means you selected the Text box tool rather than the Label tool; delete the text box and begin again.)
- Type **Prepared by** followed by your name as shown in Figure 3.4d. Press **enter** to complete the entry and also select the control. Point to the control, click the **right mouse button** to display the shortcut menu, then click **Properties** to display the Properties dialog box.
- Click the **down arrow** on the scroll bar, then scroll until you see the Font Size property. Click in the **Font Size box,** click the **drop-down arrow,** then scroll until you can change the font size to **9.** Close the Property sheet.

MISSING TOOLBARS

The Report Design, Formatting, and Toolbox toolbars appear by default in the Report Design view, but any (or all) of these toolbars may be hidden at the discretion of the user. If any of these toolbars do not appear, point to any visible toolbar, click the right mouse button to display a shortcut menu, then click the name of the toolbar you want to display. You can also click the Toolbox button on the Report Design toolbar to display (hide) the Toolbox toolbar.

STEP 7: Change the Sort Order

- Pull down the **View menu.** Click **Sorting and Grouping** to display the Sorting and Grouping dialog box. The students are currently sorted by last name.
- Click the **drop-down arrow** in the Field Expression box. Click **Major.** (The ascending sequence is selected automatically.)
- Click on the next line in the Field Expression box, click the **drop-down arrow** to display the available fields, then click **LastName** to sort the students alphabetically within major as shown in Figure 3.4e.
- Close the Sorting and Grouping dialog box. Save the report.

STEP 8: View the Modified Report

- Click the **Print Preview button** to preview the finished report. If necessary, click the **Zoom button** on the Print Preview toolbar so that the display on your monitor matches Figure 3.4f. The report has changed so that:
  - The date appears in the report header (as opposed to the report footer). The format of the date has changed to a numbered month, and the day of the week has been eliminated.
  - The students are listed by major and, within each major, alphabetically according to last name.
  - Your name appears in the Report Footer. Click the **down arrow** on the vertical scroll bar to move to the bottom of the page to see your name.
- Click the **Print button** to print the report and submit it to your instructor. Click the **Close button** to exit the Print Preview window.
- Click the **Close button** in the Report Design window. Click **Yes** if asked whether to save the changes to the Student Master List report.

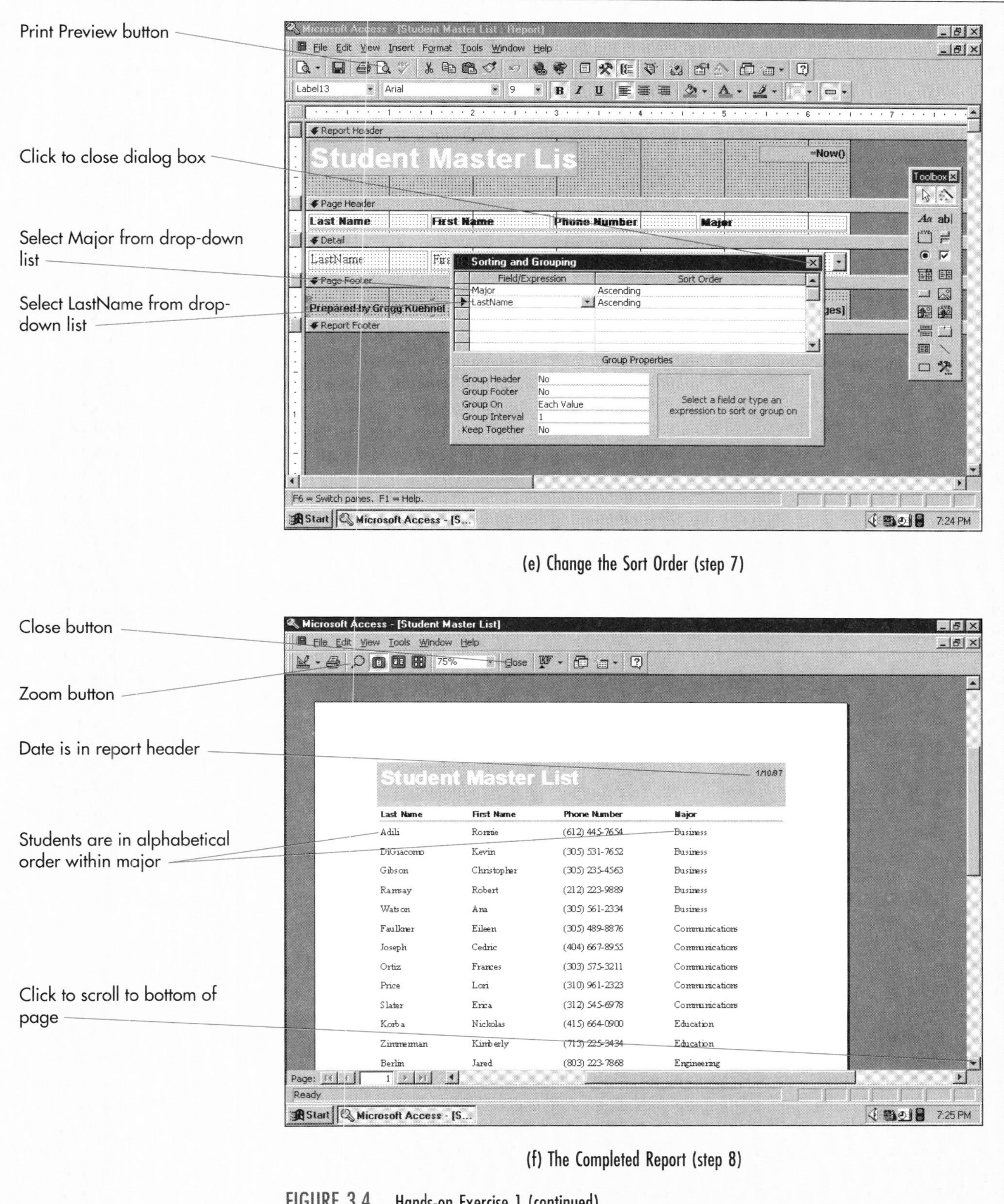

(e) Change the Sort Order (step 7)

(f) The Completed Report (step 8)

FIGURE 3.4 Hands-on Exercise 1 (continued)

STEP 9: Report Properties

- The Database window for the Our Students database should be displayed on the screen as shown in Figure 3.4g. Click the **Restore button** to restore the window to its earlier size.
- The **Reports tab** is already selected. Point to the **Student Master List** (the only report in the database), click the **right mouse button** to display a shortcut menu, then click **Properties** to display the Properties dialog box as shown in Figure 3.4g.
- Click the **Description text box,** then enter the description shown in the figure. Click **OK** to close the Properties dialog box.
- Close the database. Exit Access if you do not wish to continue with the next exercise at this time.

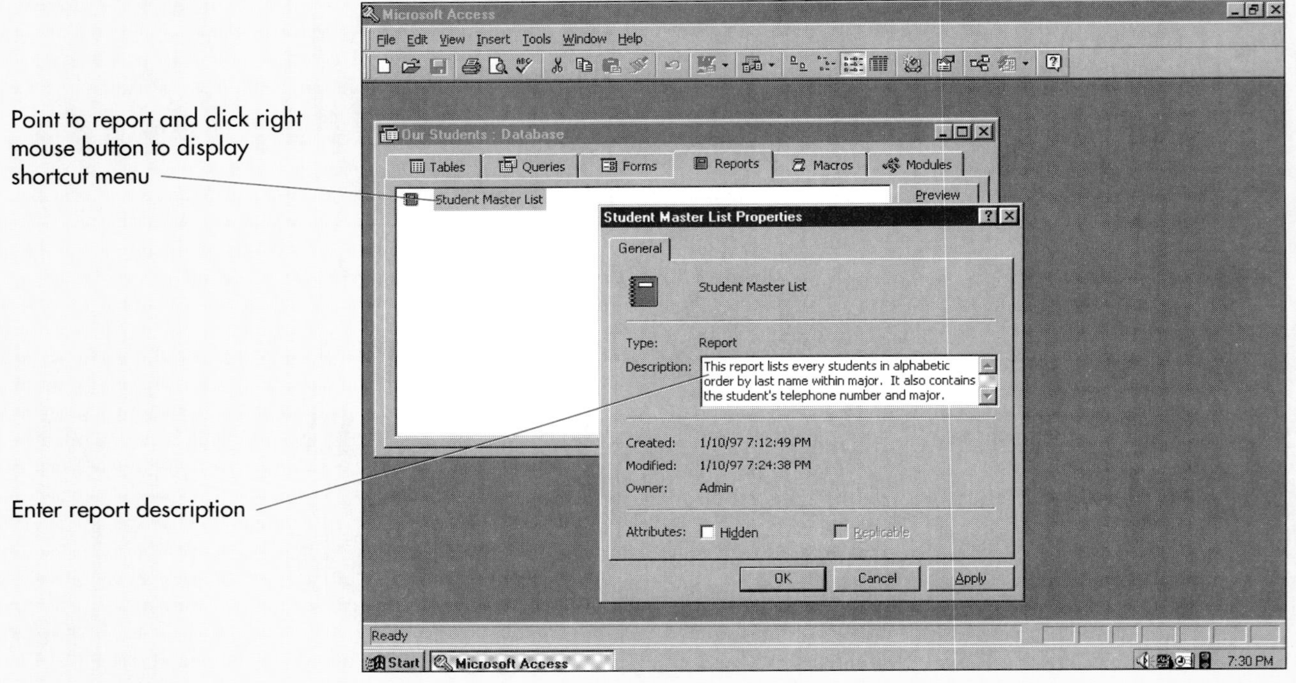

(g) Report Properties

FIGURE 3.4 Hands-on Exercise 1 (continued)

DESCRIBE YOUR OBJECTS

A working database will contain many different objects of the same type, making it all too easy to forget the purpose of the individual objects. It is important, therefore, to use meaningful names for the objects themselves, and further to take advantage of the Description property to enter additional information about the object. Once a description has been created, you can right click any object in the Database window, then click the Properties command from the shortcut menu to display the Properties dialog box with the description of the object.

The report you just created displayed every student in the underlying table. What if, however, we wanted to see just the students who are majoring in Business? Or the students who are receiving financial aid? Or the students who are majoring in Business *and* receiving financial aid? The ability to ask questions such as these, and to see the answers to those questions, is provided through a query. Queries represent the real power of a database.

A ***query*** lets you see the data you want in the sequence that you want it. It lets you select specific records from a table (or from several tables) and show some or all of the fields for the selected records. It also lets you perform calculations to display data that is not explicitly stored in the underlying table(s), such as a student's GPA.

A query represents a question and an answer. The question is developed by using a graphical tool known as the ***design grid.*** The answer is displayed in a ***dynaset,*** which contains the records that satisfy the criteria specified in the query.

A dynaset looks and acts like a table, but it isn't a table; it is a *dyna*mic sub*set* of a table that selects and sorts records as specified in the query. A dynaset is similar to a table in appearance and, like a table, it enables you to enter a new record or modify or delete an existing record. Any changes made in the dynaset are automatically reflected in the underlying table.

Figure 3.5a displays the Students table we have been using throughout the chapter. (We omit some of the fields for ease of illustration.) Figure 3.5b contains the design grid used to select students whose major is "Undecided" and further, to list those students in alphabetical order. (The design grid is explained in the next section.) Figure 3.5c displays the answer to the query in the form of a dynaset.

The table in Figure 3.5a contains 24 records. The dynaset in Figure 3.5c has only five records, corresponding to the students who are undecided about their major. The table in Figure 3.5a has 15 fields for each record (some of the fields are hidden). The dynaset in Figure 3.5c has only four fields. The records in the table are in social security number order (the primary key), whereas the records in the dynaset are in alphabetical order by last name.

The query in Figure 3.5 is an example of a ***select query,*** which is the most common type of query. A select query searches the underlying table (Figure 3.5a in the example) to retrieve the data that satisfies the query. The data is displayed in a dynaset (Figure 3.5c), which you can modify to update the data in the underlying table(s). The specifications for selecting records and determining which fields will be displayed for the selected records, as well as the sequence of the selected records, are established within the design grid of Figure 3.5b.

The design grid consists of columns and rows. Each field in the query has its own column and contains multiple rows. The ***Field row*** displays the field name. The ***Sort row*** enables you to sort in ***ascending*** or ***descending sequence.*** The ***Show row*** controls whether or not the field will be displayed in the dynaset. The ***Criteria row(s)*** determine the records that will be selected, such as students with an undecided major.

REPORTS, QUERIES, AND TABLES

Every report is based on either a table or a query. The design of the report may be the same with respect to the fields that are included, but the actual reports will be very different. A report based on a table contains every record in the table and is in sequence by the primary key. A report based on a query contains only the records that satisfy the criteria in the query in the specified sequence.

Records in table are in order by SSN

Students : Table

SSN	First Name	Last Name	Major	BirthDate	Gender	Credits	QualityPoints
111-11-1111	Jared	Berlin	Engineering	1/15/72	M	100	250
111-22-3333	Christopher	Gibson	Business	3/12/73	M	35	60
112-12-1212	Peter	Heltzer	Engineering	3/8/73	M	25	100
222-22-2222	Cedric	Joseph	Communications	4/12/74	M	45	170
223-34-2323	Kimberly	Zimmerman	Education	4/18/70	F	120	395
233-33-4444	Robert	Ramsay	Business	5/1/74	M	50	162
333-22-1111	Steven	Frazier	Undecided	9/9/68	M	35	45
333-33-3333	Kimberly	Weissman	Liberal Arts	11/11/74	F	63	166
334-44-4444	Christa	Parulis	Liberal Arts	7/15/72	F	50	90
444-44-4444	Oscar	Camejo	Liberal Arts	3/10/75	M	100	280
445-55-4444	Ronnie	Adili	Business	6/1/75	F	60	155
446-66-7777	Ana	Watson	Business	4/18/75	F	30	75
555-55-5555	Ana	Watson	Liberal Arts	8/1/75	F	70	195
556-66-7777	Frances	Ortiz	Communications	2/3/74	F	28	60
666-33-1111	Bradley	Coe	Undecided	8/22/71	M	52	143
666-66-6666	Nickolas	Korba	Education	11/11/71	M	100	166
666-77-7766	Erica	Slater	Communications	5/1/72	F	105	390
777-77-7777	Wendy	Solomon	Engineering	1/31/75	F	50	175
777-88-8888	Ryan	Cornell	Undecided	9/30/74	M	45	80
888-77-7777	Lori	Price	Communications	7/1/72	F	24	42
888-88-8888	Michelle	Zacco	Undecided	10/24/75	F	21	68
888-99-9999	Eileen	Faulkner	Communications	9/12/75	F	30	80
999-11-1111	Kevin	DiGiacomo	Business	5/31/72	M	105	375
999-99-9999	Carlos	Huerta	Undecided	6/18/75	M	15	40

Record: 1 of 24

(a) Students Table

Students will be listed in alphabetical order by LastName

Only those students with an Undecided major will be included

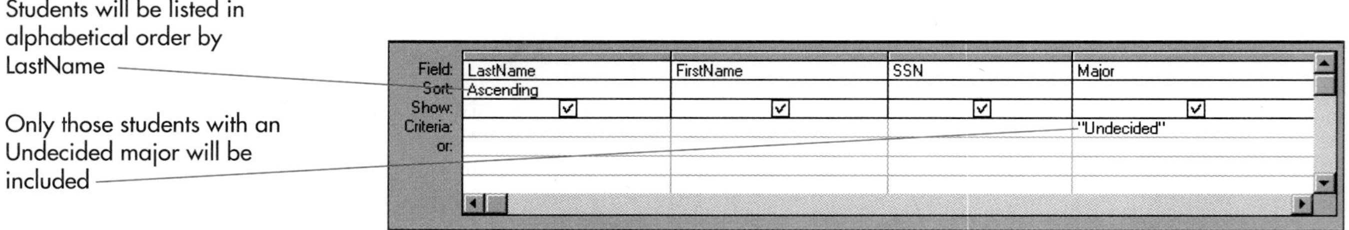

(b) Design Grid

Records in dynaset are in alphabetical order by LastName

Only Undecided majors will be included

Query1 : Select Query

Last Name	First Name	SSN	Major
Coe	Bradley	666-33-1111	Undecided
Cornell	Ryan	777-88-8888	Undecided
Frazier	Steven	333-22-1111	Undecided
Huerta	Carlos	999-99-9999	Undecided
Zacco	Michelle	888-88-8888	Undecided

Record: 1 of 5

(c) Dynaset

FIGURE 3.5 Queries

Query Window

The ***Query window*** has three views. The ***Design view*** is displayed by default and is used to create (or modify) a select query. The ***Datasheet view*** displays the resulting dynaset. The ***SQL view*** enables you to use SQL (Structured Query Language) statements to modify the query and is beyond the scope of the present

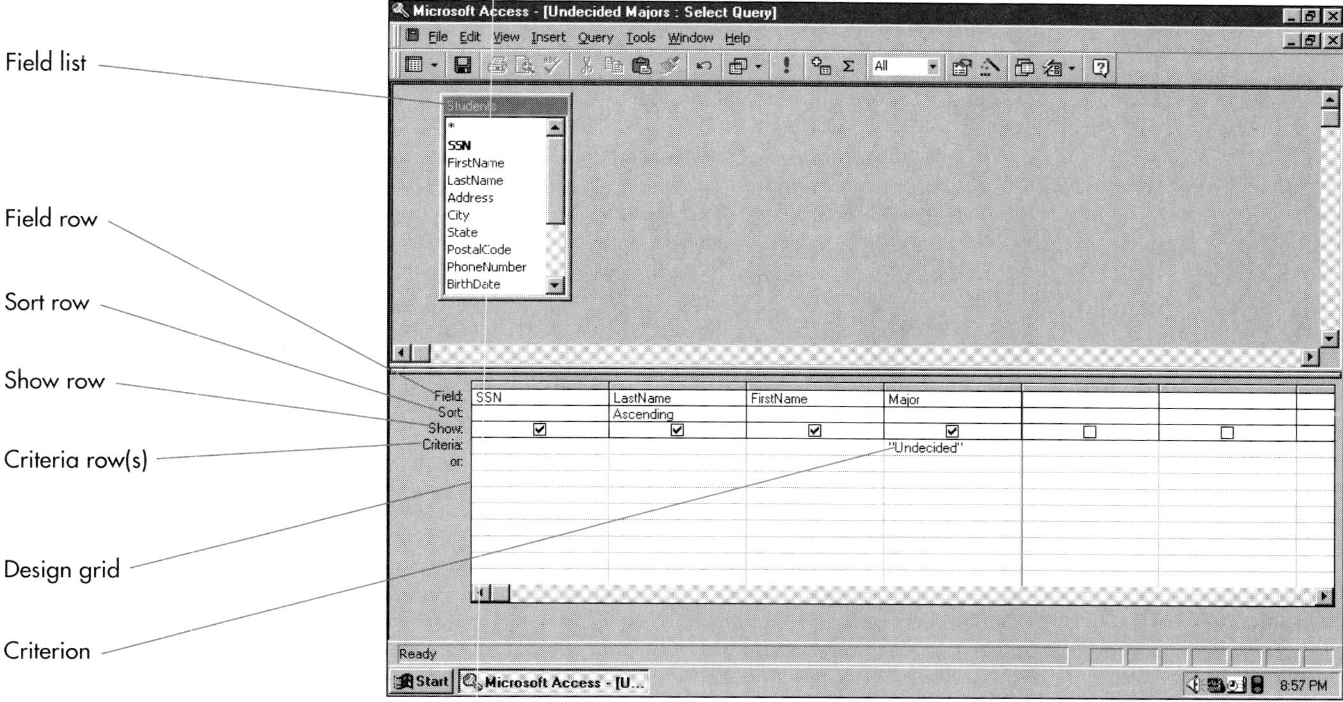

FIGURE 3.6 Query Design View

discussion. The Query Design toolbar contains the buttons to display all three views.

A select query is created in the Design view as shown in Figure 3.6a. The upper portion of the Design view window contains the field list for the table(s) on which the query is based (the Students table in this example). The lower portion of the window displays the design grid, which is where the specifications for the select query are entered. A field is added to the design grid by dragging it from the field list.

The data type of a field determines the way in which the criteria are specified for that field. The criterion for a text field is enclosed in quotation marks. The criteria for number, currency, and counter fields are shown as digits with or without a decimal point. (Commas and dollar signs are not allowed.) Dates are enclosed in pound signs and are entered in the mm/dd/yy format. The criterion for a Yes/No field is entered as Yes (or True) or No (or False).

CONVERSION TO STANDARD FORMAT

Access accepts values for text and date fields in the design grid in multiple formats. The value for a text field can be entered with or without quotation marks (Undecided or "Undecided"). A date can be entered with or without pound signs (1/1/97 or #1/1/97#). Access converts your entries to standard format as soon as you move to the next cell in the design grid. Thus, text entries are always shown in quotation marks, and dates are enclosed in pound signs.

Selection Criteria

To specify selection criteria in the design grid, enter a value or expression in the Criteria row of the appropriate column. Figure 3.7 contains several examples of simple criteria and provides a basic introduction to select queries.

The criterion in Figure 3.7a selects the students majoring in Business. The criteria for text fields are case-insensitive. Thus, *"Business"* is the same as *"business"* or *"BUSINESS"*.

Values entered in multiple columns of the same Criteria row implement an ***AND condition*** in which the selected records must meet *all* of the specified criteria. The criteria in Figure 3.7b select students who are majoring in Business *and* who are from the state of Florida. The criteria in Figure 3.7c select Communications majors who are receiving financial aid.

Values entered in different Criteria rows are connected by an ***OR condition*** in which the selected records may satisfy *any* of the indicated criteria. The criteria in Figure 3.7d select students who are majoring in Business *or* who are from Florida or both.

Field:	LastName	State	Major	BirthDate	FinancialAid	Credits
Sort:						
Show:	☑	☑	☑	☑	☑	☑
Criteria:			"Business"			
or:						

(a) Business Majors

Field:	LastName	State	Major	BirthDate	FinancialAid	Credits
Sort:						
Show:	☑	☑	☑	☑	☑	☑
Criteria:		"FL"	"Business"			
or:						

(b) Business Majors from Florida

Field:	LastName	State	Major	BirthDate	FinancialAid	Credits
Sort:						
Show:	☑	☑	☑	☑	☑	☑
Criteria:			"Communications"		Yes	
or:						

(c) Communications Majors Receiving Financial Aid

Field:	LastName	State	Major	BirthDate	FinancialAid	Credits
Sort:						
Show:	☑	☑	☑	☑	☑	☑
Criteria:		"FL"				
or:			"Business"			

(d) Business Majors or Students from Florida

FIGURE 3.7 Criteria

Relational operators (>, <, >=, <=, =, and <>) are used with date or number fields to return records within a designated range. The criteria in Figure 3.7e select Engineering majors with fewer than 60 credits. The criteria in Figure 3.7f select Communications majors who were born on or after April 1, 1974.

Field:	LastName	State	Major	BirthDate	FinancialAid	Credits
Sort:						
Show:	☑	☑	☑	☑	☑	☑
Criteria:			"Engineering"			<60
or:						

(e) Engineering Majors with Fewer than 60 Credits

Field:	LastName	State	Major	BirthDate	FinancialAid	Credits
Sort:						
Show:	☑	☑	☑	☑	☑	☑
Criteria:			"Communications"	>=#4/1/74#		
or:						

(f) Communications Majors Born on or after April 1, 1974

Field:	LastName	State	Major	BirthDate	FinancialAid	Credits
Sort:						
Show:	☑	☑	☑	☑	☑	☑
Criteria:			"Engineering"			<60
or:			Communications	>=#4/1/74#		

(g) Engineering Majors with Fewer than 60 Credits or Communications Majors Born on or after April 1, 1974

Field:	LastName	State	Major	BirthDate	FinancialAid	Credits
Sort:						
Show:	☑	☑	☑	☑	☑	☑
Criteria:						Between 60 and 90
or:						

(h) Students with between 60 and 90 Credits

Field:	LastName	State	Major	BirthDate	FinancialAid	Credits
Sort:						
Show:	☑	☑	☑	☑	☑	☑
Criteria:			Not "Liberal Arts"			
or:						

(i) Students with Majors Other Than Liberal Arts

FIGURE 3.7 Criteria (continued)

Criteria can grow more complex by combining multiple AND and OR conditions. The criteria in Figure 3.7g select Engineering majors with fewer than 60 credits *or* Communications majors who were born on or after April 1, 1974.

Other functions enable you to impose still other criteria. The ***Between function*** selects records that fall within a range of values. The criterion in Figure 3.7h selects students who have between 60 and 90 credits. The ***NOT function*** selects records that do not contain the designated value. The criterion in Figure 3.7i selects students with majors other than Liberal Arts.

WILD CARDS

Select queries recognize the question mark and asterisk wild cards that enable you to search for a pattern within a text field. A question mark stands for a single character in the same position as the question mark; thus H?ll will return Hall, Hill, and Hull. An asterisk stands for any number of characters in the same position as the asterisk; for example, S*nd will return Sand, Stand, and Strand.

HANDS-ON EXERCISE 2

Creating a Select Query

Objective: To create a select query using the design grid; to show how changing values in a dynaset changes the values in the underlying table; to create a report based on a query. Use Figure 3.8 as a guide in the exercise.

STEP 1: Open the Existing Database

- Start Access as you did in the previous exercise. Our Students (the database you used in the previous exercise) should appear within the list of recently opened databases.
- Select (click) **Our Students,** then click **OK** (or simply double click the name of the database) to open the database and display the database window.
- Click the **Queries tab** in the database window. Click the **New command button** to display the New Query dialog box as shown in Figure 3.8a.
- **Design View** is already selected as the means of creating a query. Click **OK** to begin creating the query.

THE SIMPLE QUERY WIZARD

The Simple Query Wizard is exactly what its name implies—simple. It lets you select fields from an underlying table, but it does not let you enter values or a sort sequence. We prefer, therefore, to bypass the Wizard and to create the query entirely from the Query Design window.

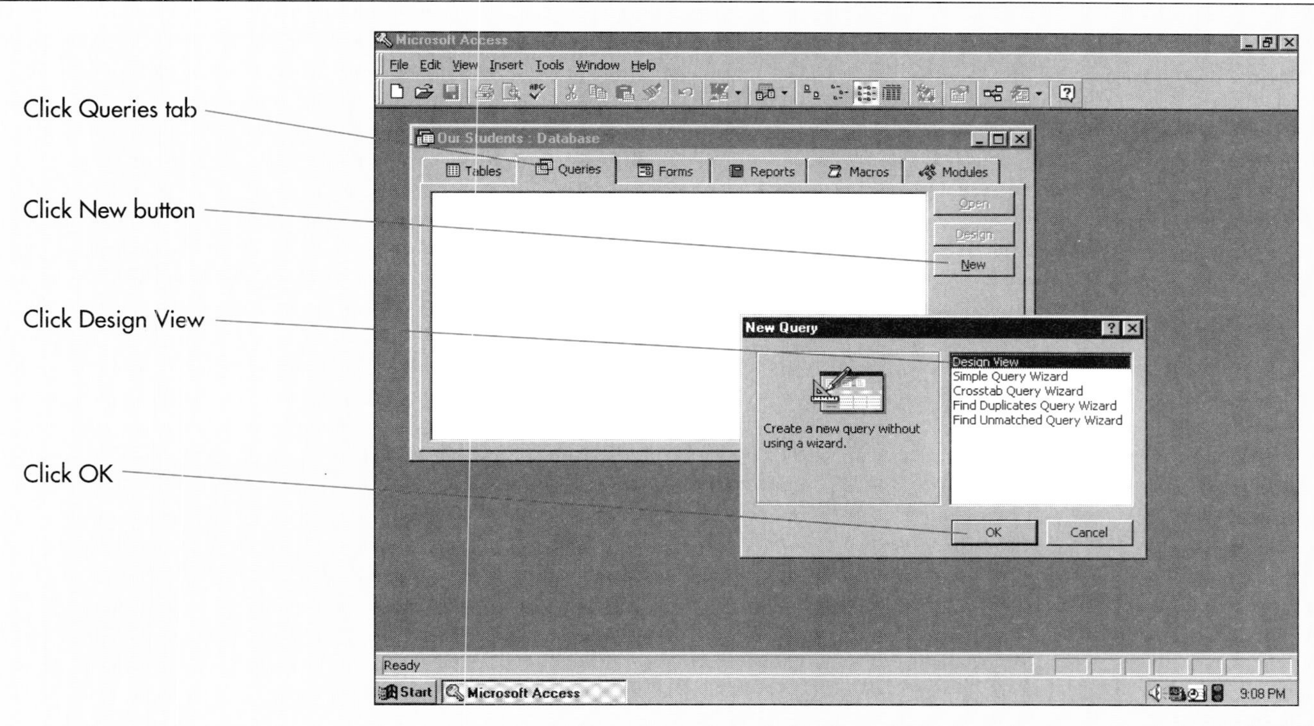

(a) Open the Our Students Database (step 1)

FIGURE 3.8 Hands-on Exercise 2

STEP 2: Add the Students Table

- The Show Table dialog box appears as shown in Figure 3.8b, with the **Tables tab** already selected.
- Click the **Add button** to add the Students table to the query. (You can also double click the Students table.)
- The field list should appear within the Query Design window. Click **Close** to close the Show Table dialog box.
- Click the **Maximize button** so that the Query Design window takes up the entire screen.

CUSTOMIZE THE QUERY WINDOW

The Query window displays the field list and design grid in its upper and lower halves, respectively. To increase (decrease) the size of either portion of the window, drag the line dividing the upper and lower sections. Drag the title bar to move a field list. You can also size a field list by dragging a border just as you would size any other window. Press the F6 key to toggle between the upper and lower halves of the Design window.

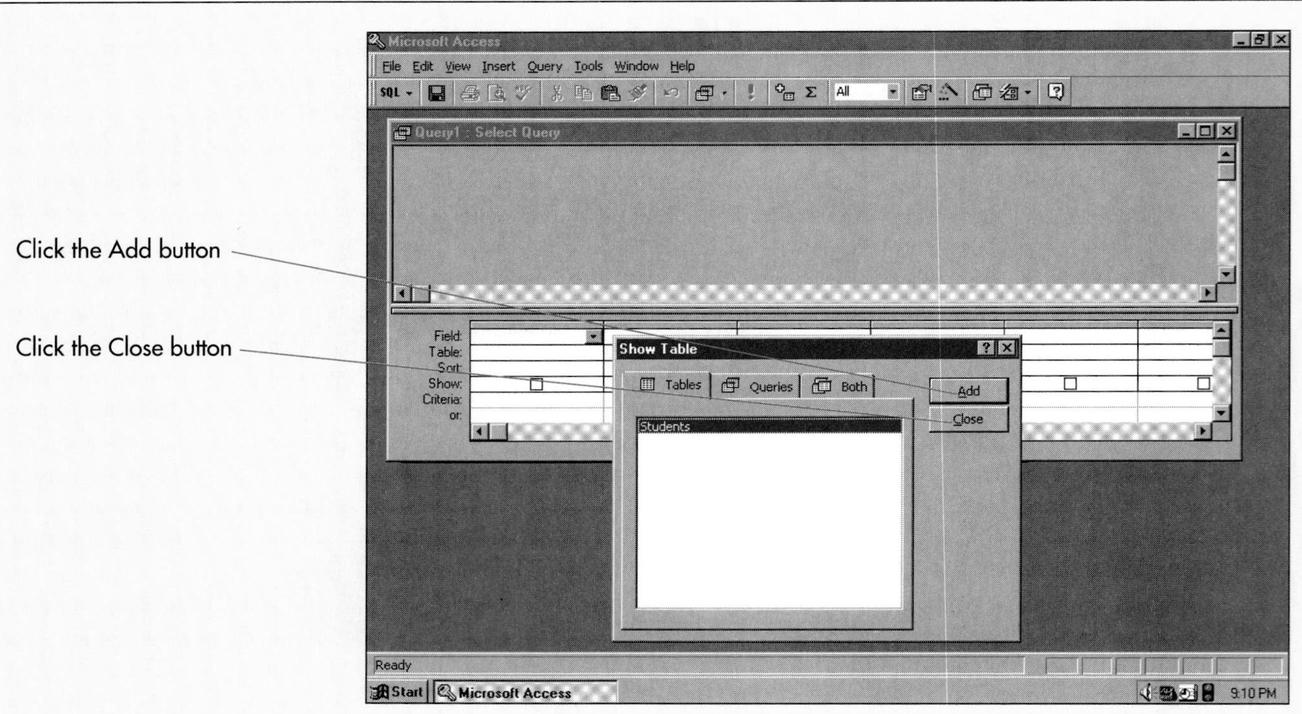

(b) Add the Students Table (step 2)

FIGURE 3.8 Hands-on Exercise 2 (continued)

STEP 3: Create the Query

➤ Click and drag the **LastName field** from the Students field list to the Field row in the first column of the QBE grid as shown in Figure 3.8c.

➤ Click and drag the **FirstName, PhoneNumber, Major,** and **Credits fields** (in that order) in similar fashion, dragging each field to the next available column in the Field row.

➤ A check appears in the Show row under each field name to indicate that the field will be displayed in the dynaset. (The show box functions as a toggle switch; thus, you can click the box to clear the check and hide the field in the dynaset. Click the box a second time to display the check and show the field.)

ADDING AND DELETING FIELDS

The fastest way to add a field to the design grid is to double click the field name in the field list. To add more than one field at a time, press and hold the Ctrl key as you click the fields within the field list, then drag the group to a cell in the Field row. To delete a field, click the column selector above the field name to select the column, then press the Del key.

STEP 4: Specify the Criteria

➤ Click the **Criteria row** for Major. Type **Undecided.**

➤ Click the **Sort row** under the LastName field, click the **drop-down arrow,** then select **Ascending** as the sort sequence.

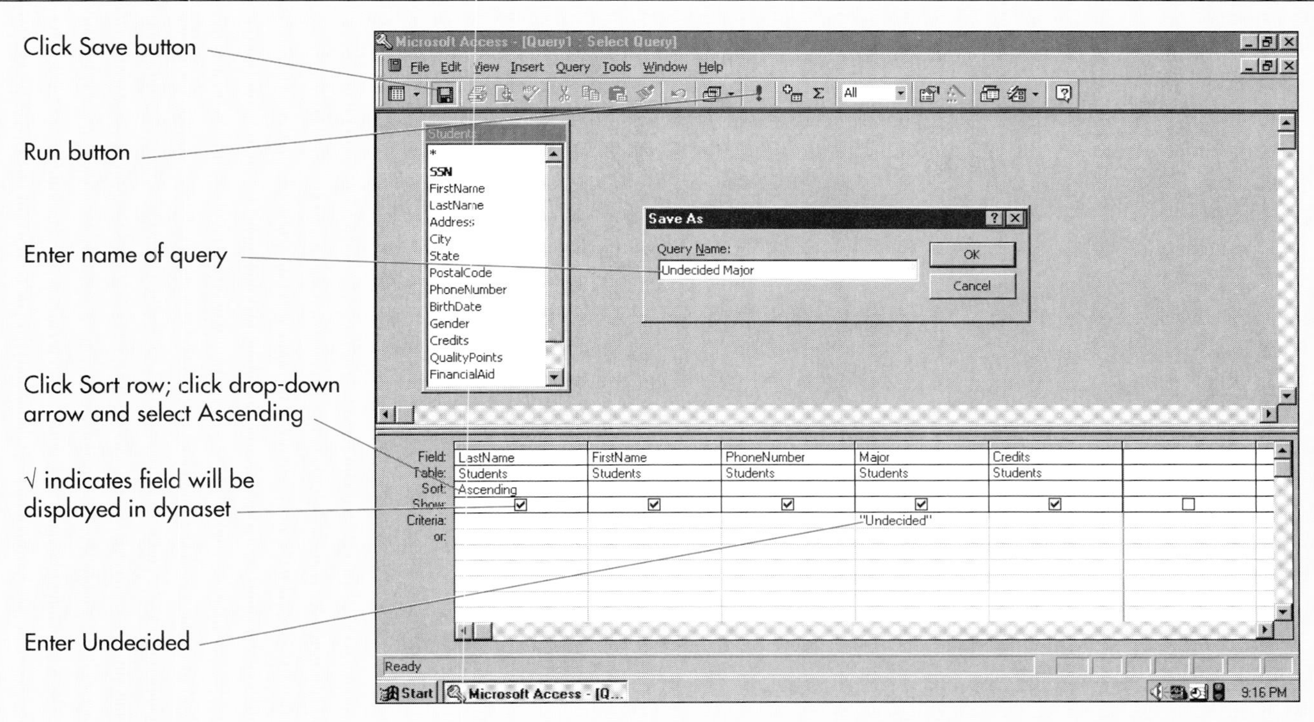

(c) Create the Query (steps 3 & 4)

FIGURE 3.8 Hands-on Exercise 2 (continued)

- Pull down the **File menu** and click **Save** (or click the **Save button**) to display the dialog box in Figure 3.8c.
- Type **Undecided Major** as the query name. Click **OK.**

FLEXIBLE CRITERIA

Access offers a great deal of flexibility in the way you enter the criteria for a text field. Quotation marks and/or an equal sign are optional. Thus "Undecided", Undecided, =Undecided, or ="Undecided" are all valid, and you may choose any of these formats. Access will convert your entry to standard format ("Undecided" in this example) after you have moved to the next cell.

STEP 5: Run the Query

- Pull down the **Query menu** and click **Run** (or click the **Run button**) to run the query and change to the Datasheet view.
- You should see the five records in the dynaset of Figure 3.8d. Change Ryan Cornell's major to Business by clicking in the **Major field,** clicking the **drop-down arrow,** then choosing **Business** from the drop-down list.
- Click the **View button** to change the query.

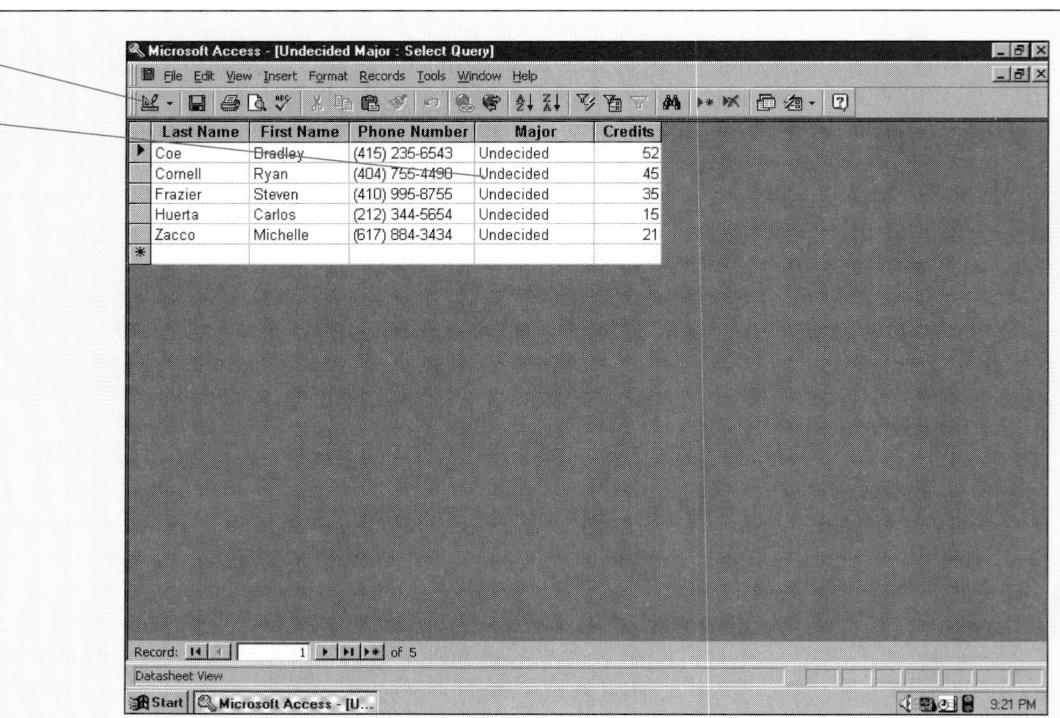

(d) Run the Query (step 5)

FIGURE 3.8 Hands-on Exercise 2 (continued)

STEP 6: Modify the Query

- Click the **Show check box** in the Major field to remove the check as shown in Figure 3.8e.
- Click the **Criteria row** under credits. Type >**30** to select only the Undecided majors with more than 30 credits.
- Click the **Save button** to save the revised query. Click the **Run button** to run the revised query. This time there are only two records (Bradley Coe and Steven Frazier) in the dynaset, and the major is no longer displayed.
  - Ryan Cornell does not appear because he has changed his major.
  - Carlos Huerta and Michelle Zacco do not appear because they do not have more than 30 credits.

STEP 7: Create a Report

- Pull down the **Window menu** and click **1 Our Students: Database** (or click the **Database window button** on the toolbar). You will see the Database window in Figure 3.8f.
- Click the **Reports tab,** then click the **New button** to create a report based on the query you just created. Select **Report Wizard** as the means of creating the report.
- Select **Undecided Major** from the drop-down list as shown in Figure 3.8f. Click **OK** to begin the Report Wizard.
- You should see the Report Wizard dialog box, which displays all of the visible fields (Major has been hidden) in the Undecided Major query. Click the >> **button** to select all of the fields from the query for the report. Click **Next.**

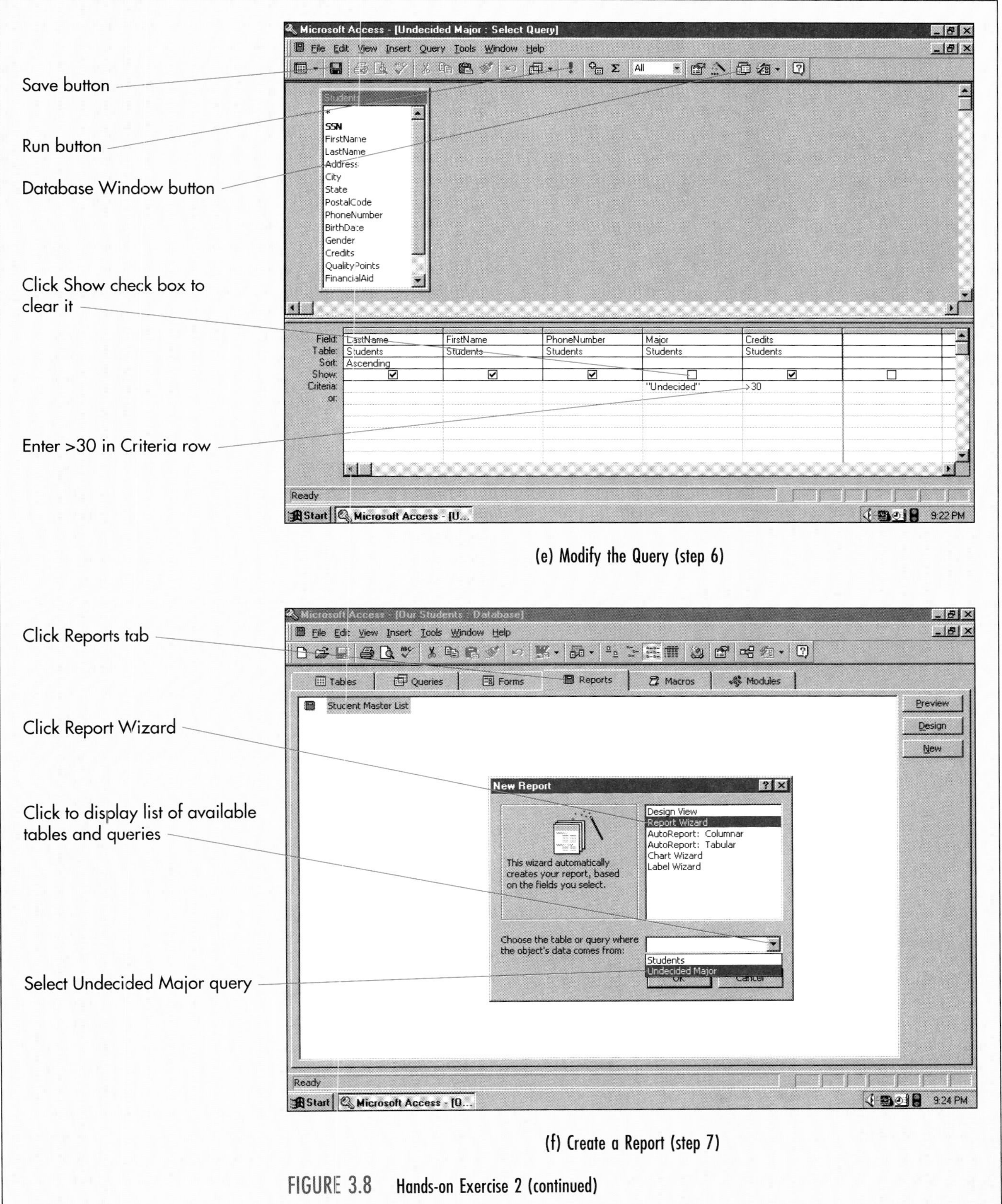

(e) Modify the Query (step 6)

(f) Create a Report (step 7)

FIGURE 3.8 Hands-on Exercise 2 (continued)

- ➤ You do not want to choose additional grouping levels. Click **Next** to move to the next screen.
- ➤ There is no need to specify a sort sequence. Click **Next.**
- ➤ The **Tabular layout** is selected, as is **Portrait orientation.** Be sure the box is checked to **Adjust field width so all fields fit on a page.** Click **Next.**
- ➤ Choose **Soft Gray** as the style. Click **Next.**
- ➤ If necessary, enter **Undecided Major** as the title for your report. The option button to **Preview the Report** is already selected. Click the **Finish command button** to exit the Report Wizard and view the report.

THE BACK BUTTON

The Back button is present on every screen within the Report Wizard and enables you to recover from mistakes or simply to change your mind about how you want the report to look. Click the Back button at any time to return to the previous screen, then click it again if you want to return to the screen before that, and continue, if necessary, all the way back to the beginning.

STEP 8: View the Report

- ➤ If necessary, click the **Maximize button** to see the completed report as shown in Figure 3.8g. Click the **Zoom button** to see the full page.

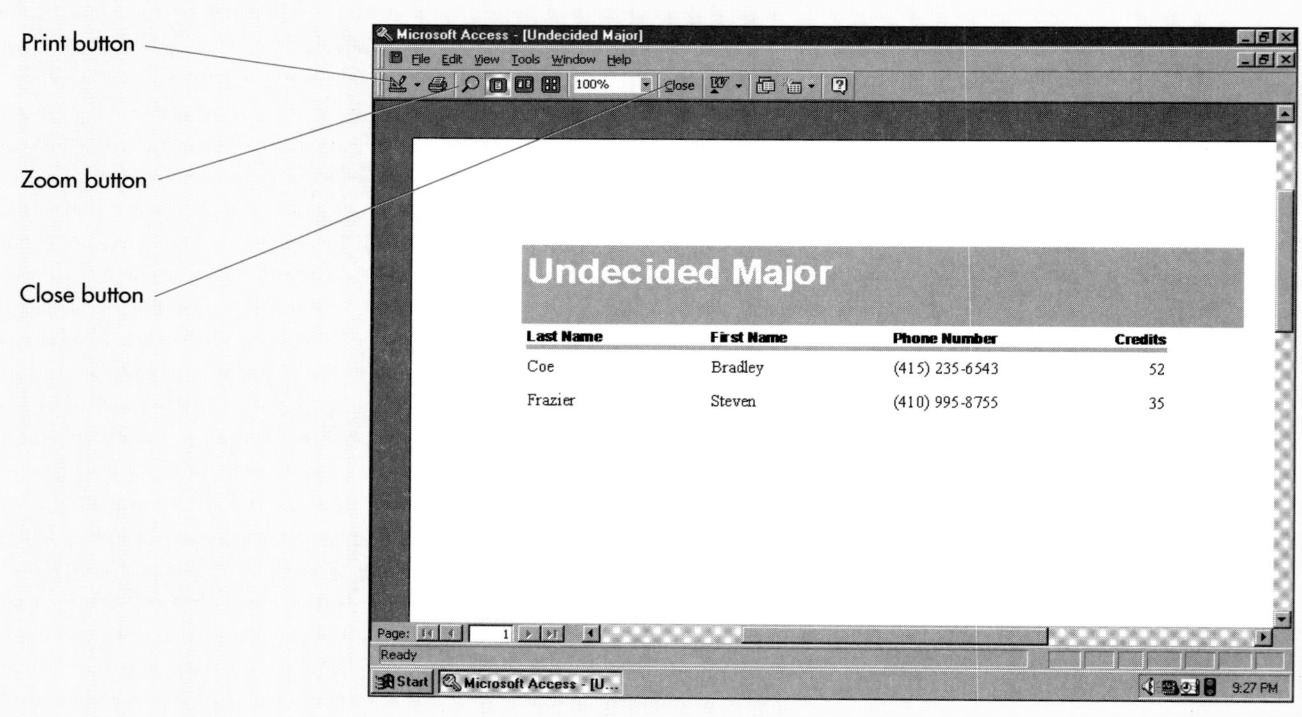

(g) The Completed Report (step 8)

FIGURE 3.8 Hands-on Exercise 2 (continued)

- ➤ Click the **Print button** to print the report and submit it to your instructor. Click the **Close button** to exit the Print Preview window.
- ➤ Click the **Close button** in the Report Design window.
- ➤ If necessary, click the **Database Window button** on the toolbar to return to the Database window. Click the **Maximize button**:
  - Click the **Queries tab** to display the names of the queries in the Our Students database. You should see the *Undecided Major* query created in this exercise.
  - Click the **Reports tab.** You should see two reports: *Student Master List* (created in the previous exercise) and *Undecided Major* (created in this exercise).
  - Click the **Forms tab.** You should see the *Students* form corresponding to the form you created in Chapter 2.
  - Click the **Tables tab.** You should see the *Students* table, which is the basis of all other objects in the database.
- ➤ Close the **Our Students database** and exit Access if you do not wish to continue with the next exercise. Click **Yes** if asked to save changes to any of the objects in the database.

DATABASE PROPERTIES

The tabs within the Database window display the objects within a database, but show only one type of object at a time. You can, for example, see all of the reports or all of the queries, but you cannot see the reports and queries at the same time. There is another way. Pull down the File menu, click Database Properties, then click the Contents tab to display the contents (objects) in the database. You cannot, however, use the Database Properties dialog box to open those objects.

GROUPING RECORDS

The records in a report are often grouped according to the value of a specific field. The report in Figure 3.9a, for example, groups students according to their major, sorts them alphabetically according to last name within each major, then calculates the average GPA for all students in each major. A group header appears before each group of students to identify the group and display the major. A group footer appears at the end of each group and displays the average GPA for students in that major

Figure 3.9b displays the Design view of the report in Figure 3.9a, which determines the appearance of the printed report. Look carefully at the design to relate each section to the corresponding portion of the printed report:

- The report header contains the title of the report and appears once, at the beginning of the printed report.
- The page header contains the column headings that appear at the top of each page. The column headings are labels (or unbound controls) and are formatted in bold.

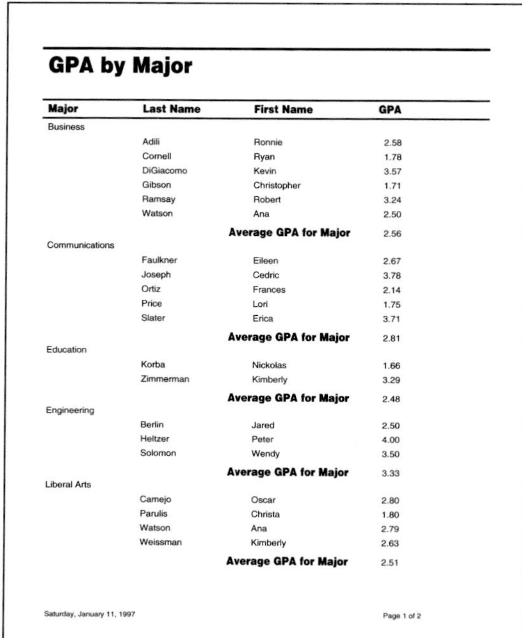

GPA by Major

Major	Last Name	First Name	GPA
Business			
	Adili	Ronnie	2.58
	Cornell	Ryan	1.78
	DiGiacomo	Kevin	3.57
	Gibson	Christopher	1.71
	Ramsay	Robert	3.24
	Watson	Ana	2.50
		Average GPA for Major	2.56
Communications			
	Faulkner	Eileen	2.67
	Joseph	Cedric	3.78
	Ortiz	Frances	2.14
	Price	Lori	1.75
	Slater	Erica	3.71
		Average GPA for Major	2.81
Education			
	Korba	Nickolas	1.66
	Zimmerman	Kimberly	3.29
		Average GPA for Major	2.48
Engineering			
	Berlin	Jared	2.50
	Heltzer	Peter	4.00
	Solomon	Wendy	3.50
		Average GPA for Major	3.33
Liberal Arts			
	Camejo	Oscar	2.80
	Parulis	Christa	1.80
	Watson	Ana	2.79
	Weissman	Kimberly	2.63
		Average GPA for Major	2.51

Saturday, January 11, 1997 Page 1 of 2

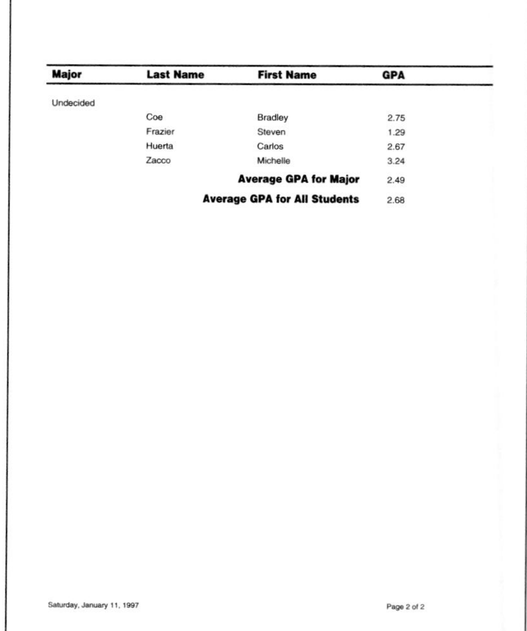

Major	Last Name	First Name	GPA
Undecided			
	Coe	Bradley	2.75
	Frazier	Steven	1.29
	Huerta	Carlos	2.67
	Zacco	Michelle	3.24
		Average GPA for Major	2.49
		Average GPA for All Students	2.68

Saturday, January 11, 1997 Page 2 of 2

(a) The Printed Columnar Report

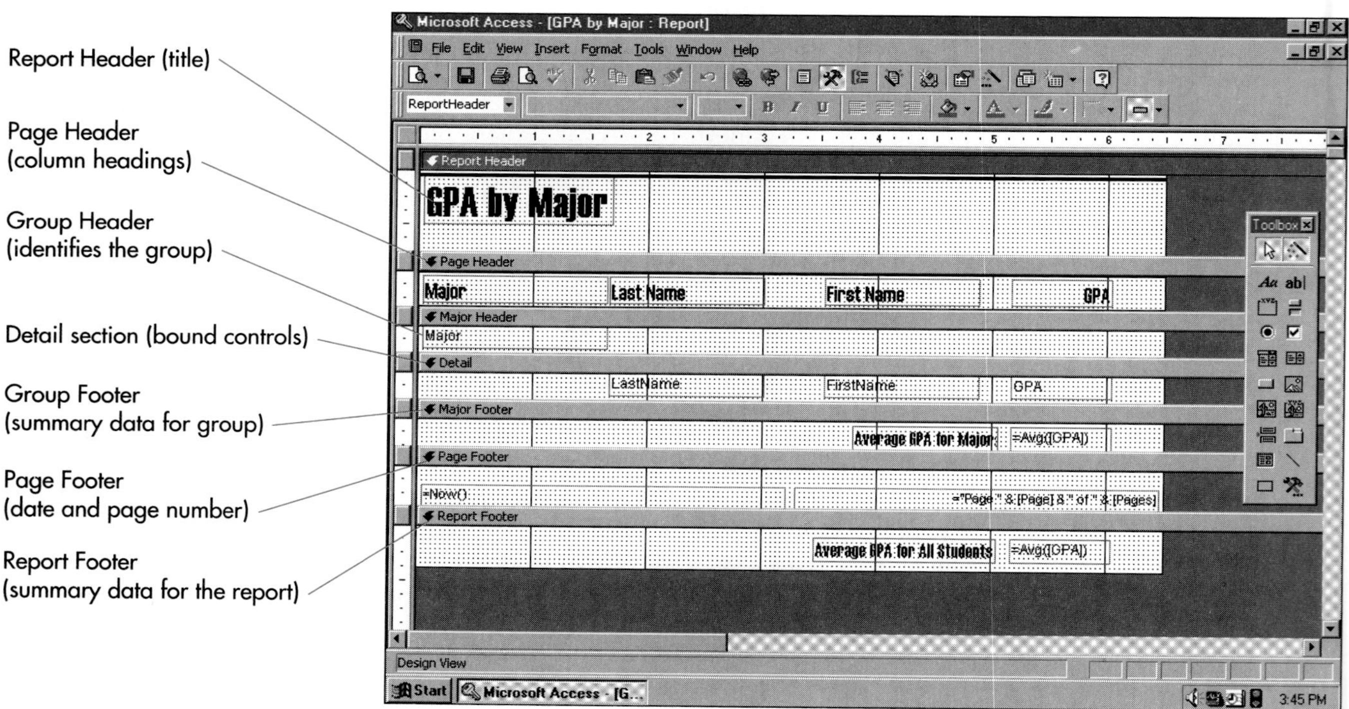

(b) Design View

FIGURE 3.9 Summary Reports

- The group header consists of a single bound control that displays the value of the major field prior to each group of detail records.
- The detail section consists of bound controls that appear directly under the corresponding heading in the page header. The detail section is printed once for each record in each group.

- The group footer appears after each group of detail records. It consists of an unbound control (Average GPA for Major:) followed by a calculated control that computes the average GPA for each group of students.
- The page footer appears at the bottom of each page and contains the date, page number, and total number of pages in the report.
- The report footer appears at the end of the report. It consists of an unbound control (Average GPA for All Students:) followed by a calculated control that computes the average GPA for all students.

Grouping records within a report enables you to perform calculations on each group of records as was done in the group footer of Figure 3.9. The calculations in our example made use of the ***Avg function,*** but other types of calculations are possible:

- The ***Sum function*** computes the total of a specific field for all records in the group.
- The ***Min function*** determines the minimum value for all records in the group.
- The ***Max function*** determines the maximum value for all records in the group.
- The ***Count function*** counts the number of records in the group.

The following exercise has you create the report in Figure 3.9. The report is based on a query containing a calculated control, GPA, which is computed by dividing the QualityPoints field by the Credits field. The Report Wizard is used to design the basic report, but additional modifications are necessary to create the group header and group footer.

HANDS-ON EXERCISE 3

Grouping Records

Objective: To create a query containing a calculated control, then create a report based on that query; to use the Sorting and Grouping command to add a group header and group footer to a report. Use Figure 3.10 as a guide.

STEP 1: Create the Query

- Start Access and open the **Our Students database** from the previous exercise.
- Click the **Queries tab** in the database window, then click the **New command button** to display the New Query dialog box. **Design View** is already selected as the means of creating a query. Click **OK** to begin creating the query.
- The Show Table dialog box appears; the **Tables tab** is already selected, as is the **Students table.**
- Click the **Add button** to add the table to the query (the field list should appear within the Query window). Click **Close** to close the Show Table dialog box.
- Click the **Maximize button** so that the window takes up the entire screen as shown in Figure 3.10a. Drag the border between the upper and lower portions of the window to give yourself more room in the upper portion. Make the field list larger, to display more fields at one time.
- Scroll (if necessary) within the field list, then click and drag the **Major field** from the field list to the query. Click and drag the **LastName, FirstName, QualityPoints,** and **Credits fields** (in that order) in similar fashion.

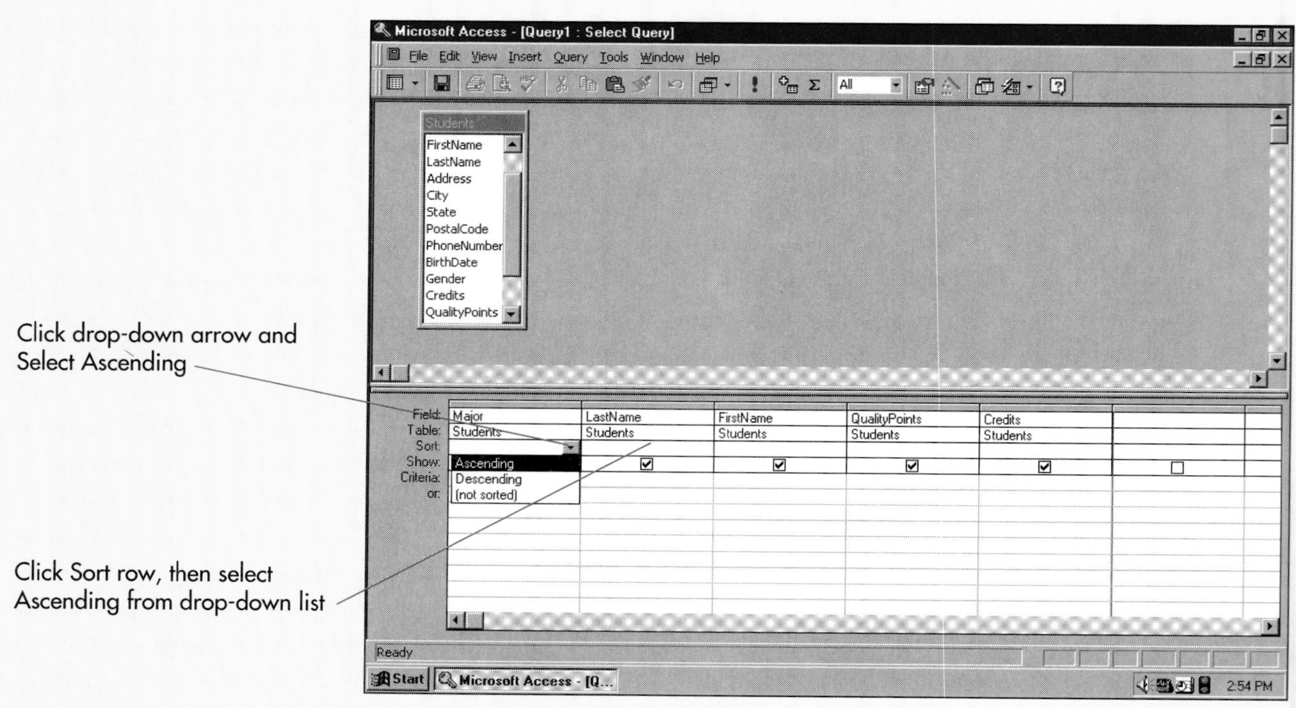

(a) Create the Query (step 1)

FIGURE 3.10 Hands-on Exercise 3

- Click the **Sort row** for the Major field. Click the **down arrow** to open the drop-down list box. Click **Ascending.**
- Click the **Sort row** for the LastName field. Click the **down arrow** to open the drop-down list box. Click **Ascending.**

> **SORTING ON MULTIPLE FIELDS**
>
> You can sort a query on more than one field, but you must be certain that the fields are in the proper order within the design grid. Access sorts from left to right (the leftmost field is the primary sort key), so the fields must be arranged in the desired sort sequence. To move a field within the design grid, click the column selector above the field name to select the column, then drag the column to its new position.

STEP 2: Add a Calculated Control

- Click in the first blank column in the Field row. Enter the expression **=[QualityPoints]/[Credits].** Do not be concerned if you cannot see the entire expression.
- Press **enter.** Access has substituted Expr1: for the equal sign you typed initially. Drag the **column selector boundary** so that the entire expression is vis-

ible as in Figure 3.10b. (You may have to make some of the columns narrower to see all of the fields in the design grid.)

➤ Pull down the **File menu** and click **Save** (or click the **Save button**) to display the dialog box in Figure 3.10b. Enter **GPA By Major** for the Query Name. Click **OK.**

USE DESCRIPTIVE NAMES

An Access database contains multiple objects—tables, forms, queries, and reports. It is important, therefore, that the name assigned to each object be descriptive of its function so that you can select the proper object from the Database window. The name of an object can contain up to 64 characters and can include any combination of letters, numbers, and spaces. (Names may not, however, include leading spaces, a period, an exclamation mark, or brackets ([ ]).

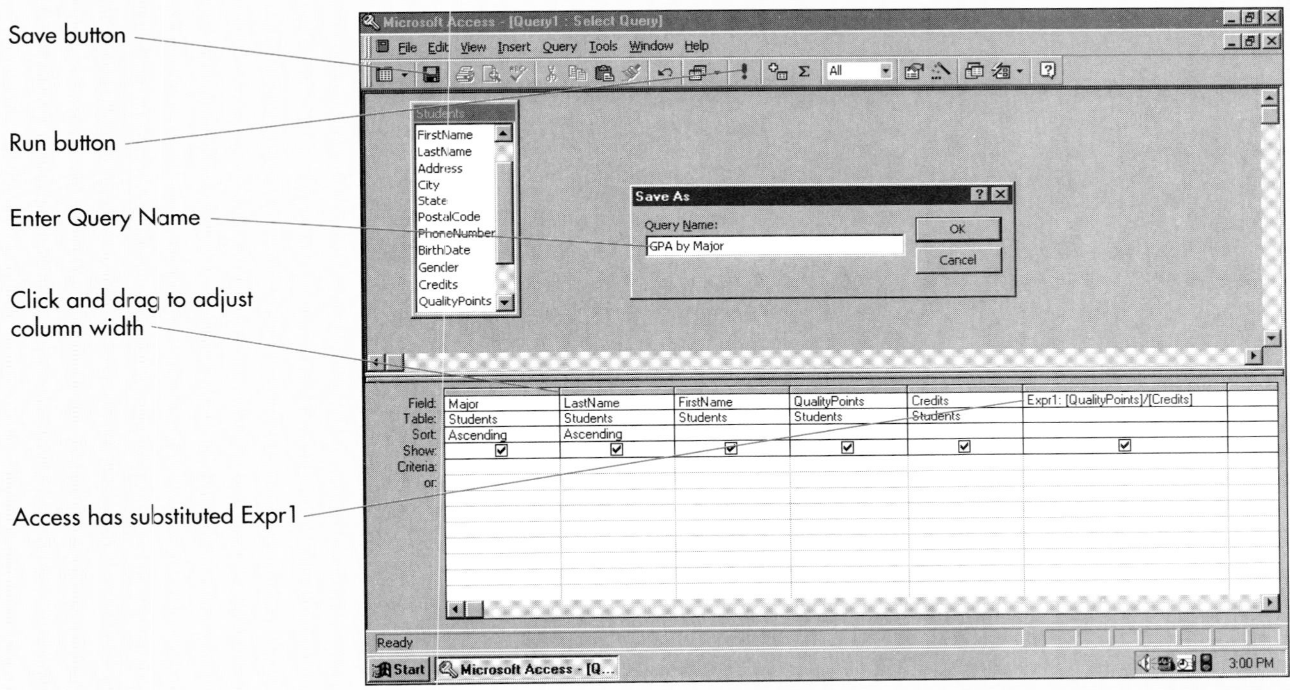

(b) Add a Calculated Control (step 2)

FIGURE 3.10 Hands-on Exercise 3 (continued)

STEP 3: Run the Query

➤ Pull down the **Query menu** and click **Run** (or click the **Run button** on the Query Design toolbar). You will see the dynaset in Figure 3.10c:

- Students are listed by major and alphabetically by last name within major.
- The GPA is calculated to several places (you may not even see the number to the left of the decimal) and appears in the Expr1 field.

➤ Click the **View button** in order to modify the query.

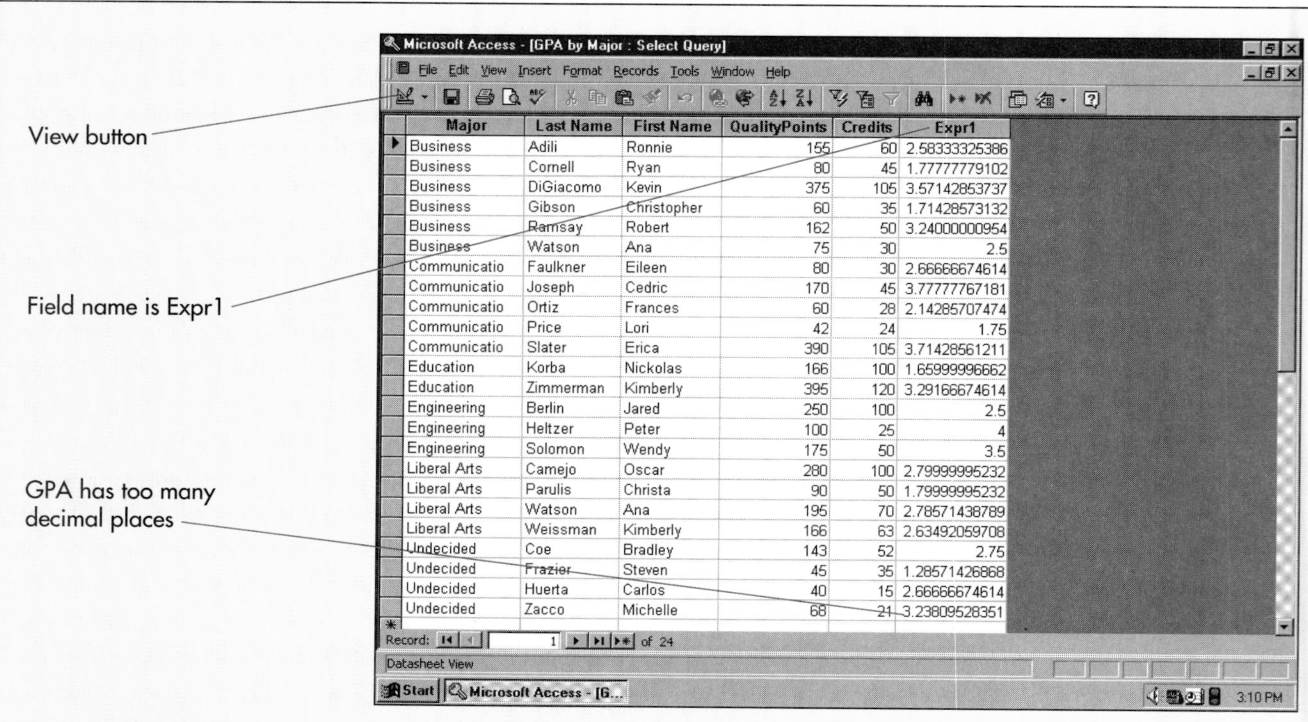

Major	Last Name	First Name	QualityPoints	Credits	Expr1
Business	Adili	Ronnie	155	60	2.58333325386
Business	Cornell	Ryan	80	45	1.77777779102
Business	DiGiacomo	Kevin	375	105	3.57142853737
Business	Gibson	Christopher	60	35	1.71428573132
Business	Ramsay	Robert	162	50	3.24000000954
Business	Watson	Ana	75	30	2.5
Communicatio	Faulkner	Eileen	80	30	2.66666674614
Communicatio	Joseph	Cedric	170	45	3.77777767181
Communicatio	Ortiz	Frances	60	28	2.14285707474
Communicatio	Price	Lori	42	24	1.75
Communicatio	Slater	Erica	390	105	3.71428561211
Education	Korba	Nickolas	166	100	1.65999996662
Education	Zimmerman	Kimberly	395	120	3.29166674614
Engineering	Berlin	Jared	250	100	2.5
Engineering	Heltzer	Peter	100	25	4
Engineering	Solomon	Wendy	175	50	3.5
Liberal Arts	Camejo	Oscar	280	100	2.79999995232
Liberal Arts	Parulis	Christa	90	50	1.79999995232
Liberal Arts	Watson	Ana	195	70	2.78571438789
Liberal Arts	Weissman	Kimberly	166	63	2.63492059708
Undecided	Coe	Bradley	143	52	2.75
Undecided	Frazier	Steven	45	35	1.28571426868
Undecided	Huerta	Carlos	40	15	2.66666674614
Undecided	Zacco	Michelle	68	21	3.23809528351

(c) Run the Query (step 3)

FIGURE 3.10 Hands-on Exercise 3 (continued)

ADJUST THE COLUMN WIDTH

Point to the right edge of the column you want to resize, then drag the mouse in the direction you want to go; drag to the right to make the column wider or to the left to make it narrower. Alternatively, you can double click the column selector line (right edge) to fit the longest entry in that column. Adjusting the column width in the Design view does not affect the column width in the Datasheet view, but you can use the same technique in both views.

STEP 4: Modify the Query

- Click and drag to select **Expr1** in the Field row for the calculated field. (Do not select the colon). Type **GPA** to substitute a more meaningful field name.
- Point to the column and click the **right mouse button** to display a shortcut menu. Click **Properties** to display the Field Properties dialog box in Figure 3.10d. Click the **General tab** if necessary:
  - Click the **Description text box.** Enter **GPA** as shown in Figure 3.10d.
  - Click the **Format text box.** Click the **drop-down arrow** to display the available formats. Click **Fixed.**
  - Close the Field Properties dialog box.
- Click the **Save button** to save the modified query.

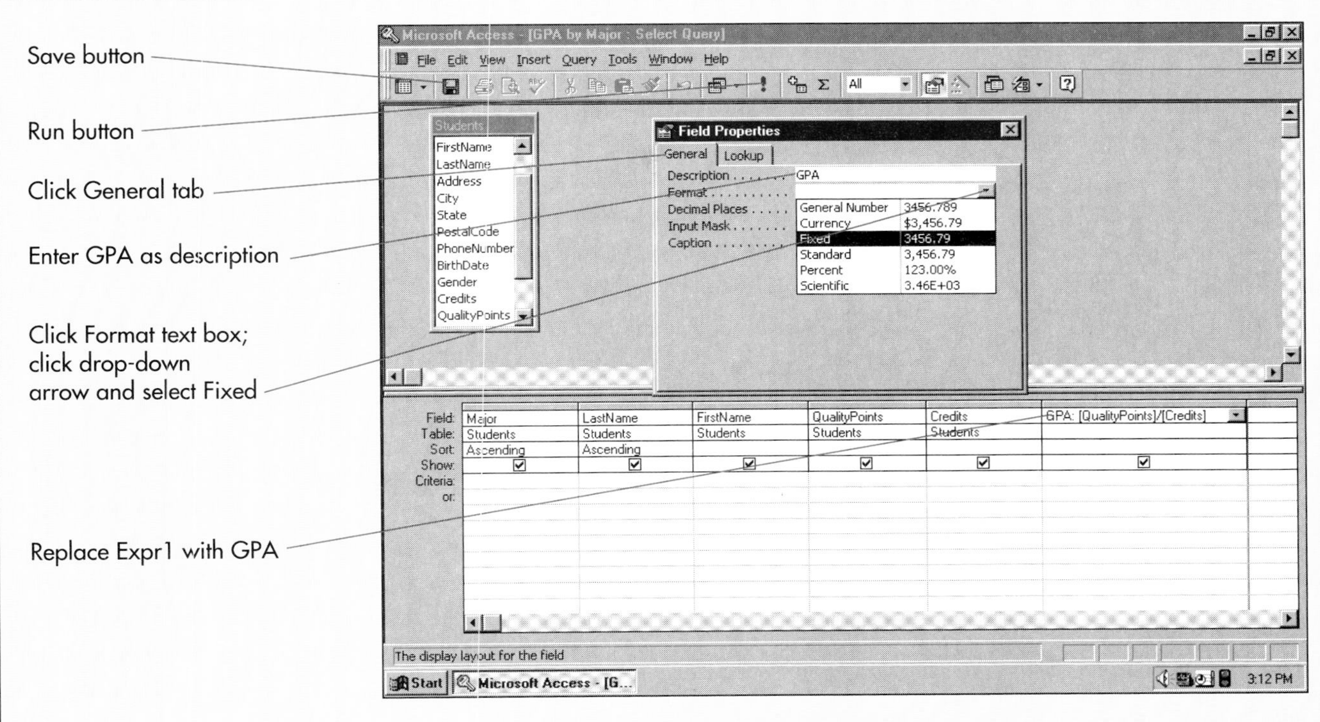

(d) Modify the Query (step 4)

FIGURE 3.10 Hands-on Exercise 3 (continued)

THE TOP VALUES PROPERTY

Can you create a query that lists only the five students with the highest or lowest GPA? It's easy, if you know about the Top Values property. First, sort the query according to the desired sequence—for example, students in descending order by GPA to see the students with the highest GPA. (Remove all other sort keys within the query.) Point anywhere in the gray area in the upper portion of the Query window, click the right mouse button to display a shortcut menu, then click Properties to display the Query Properties sheet. Click the Top Values box and enter the desired number of students (e.g., 5 for five students, or 5% for the top five percent). When you run the query you will see only the top five students. (You can see the bottom five instead if you specify ascending rather than descending as the sort sequence.)

STEP 5: Rerun the Query

➤ Click the **Run button** to run the modified query. You will see a new dynaset corresponding to the modified query as shown in Figure 3.10e. Resize the column widths (as necessary) within the dynaset.

- Students are still listed by major and alphabetically within major.
- The GPA is calculated to two decimal places and appears under the GPA field.

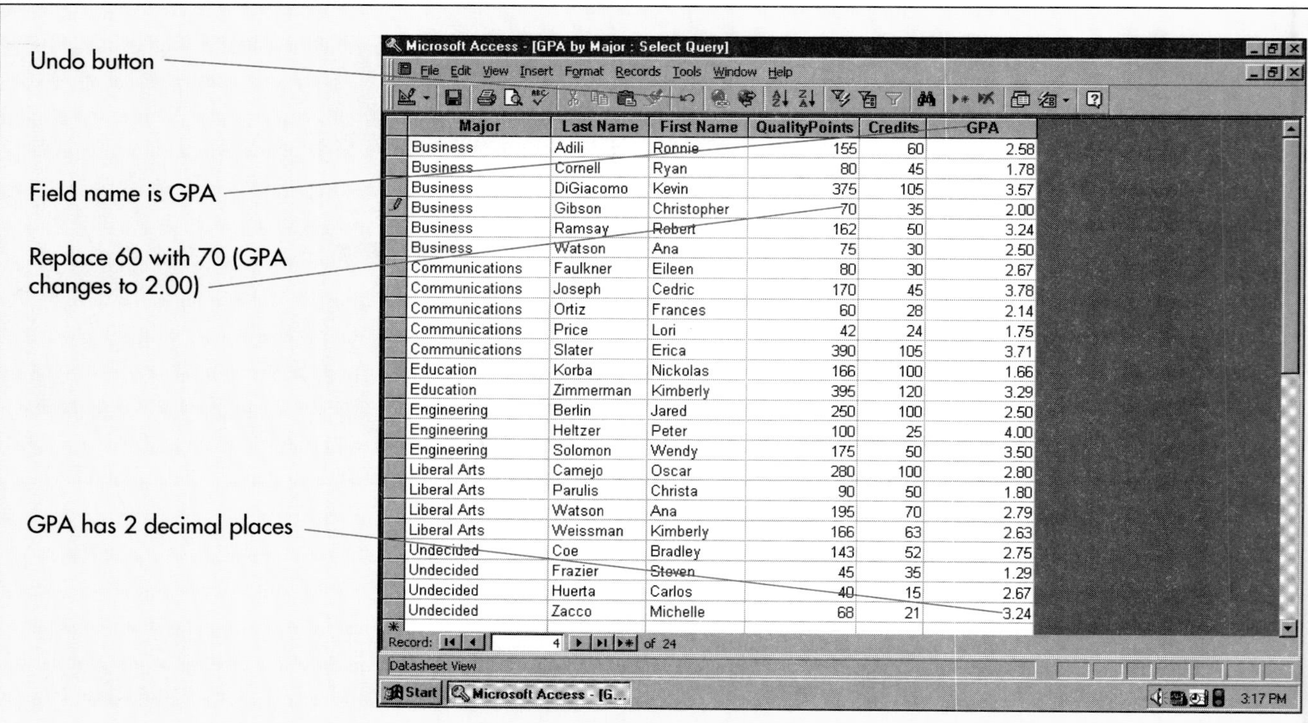

Major	Last Name	First Name	QualityPoints	Credits	GPA
Business	Adili	Ronnie	155	60	2.58
Business	Cornell	Ryan	80	45	1.78
Business	DiGiacomo	Kevin	375	105	3.57
Business	Gibson	Christopher	70	35	2.00
Business	Ramsay	Robert	162	50	3.24
Business	Watson	Ana	75	30	2.50
Communications	Faulkner	Eileen	80	30	2.67
Communications	Joseph	Cedric	170	45	3.78
Communications	Ortiz	Frances	60	28	2.14
Communications	Price	Lori	42	24	1.75
Communications	Slater	Erica	390	105	3.71
Education	Korba	Nickolas	166	100	1.66
Education	Zimmerman	Kimberly	395	120	3.29
Engineering	Berlin	Jared	250	100	2.50
Engineering	Heltzer	Peter	100	25	4.00
Engineering	Solomon	Wendy	175	50	3.50
Liberal Arts	Camejo	Oscar	280	100	2.80
Liberal Arts	Parulis	Christa	90	50	1.80
Liberal Arts	Watson	Ana	195	70	2.79
Liberal Arts	Weissman	Kimberly	166	63	2.63
Undecided	Coe	Bradley	143	52	2.75
Undecided	Frazier	Steven	45	35	1.29
Undecided	Huerta	Carlos	40	15	2.67
Undecided	Zacco	Michelle	68	21	3.24

(e) Rerun the Query (step 5)

FIGURE 3.10 Hands-on Exercise 3 (continued)

- Click the **QualityPoints field** for Christopher Gibson. Replace 60 with **70.** Press **enter.** The GPA changes automatically to 2.
- Pull down the **Edit menu** and click **Undo Current Field/Record** (or click the **Undo button** on the Query toolbar). The GPA returns to its previous value.
- Tab to the **GPA field** for Christopher Gibson. Type **2.** Access will beep and prevent you from changing the GPA because it is a calculated field as indicated on the status bar.
- Click the **Close button** to close the query and return to the Database window. Click **Yes** if asked whether to save the changes.

THE DYNASET

A query represents a question and an answer. The question is developed by using the design grid in the Query Design view. The answer is displayed in a dynaset that contains the records that satisfy the criteria specified in the query. A dynaset looks and acts like a table but it isn't a table; it is a dynamic subset of a table that selects and sorts records as specified in the query. A dynaset is like a table in that you can enter a new record or modify or delete an existing record. It is dynamic because the changes made to the dynaset are automatically reflected in the underlying table.

STEP 6: The Report Wizard

➤ You should see the Database window. Click the **Reports tab,** then click the **New button** to create a report based on the query you just created. Select **Report Wizard** as the means of creating the report.

➤ Select **GPA By Major** from the drop-down list at the bottom of the dialog box. Click **OK** to begin the Report Wizard. You should see the Report Wizard dialog box, which displays all of the fields in the GPA by Major query.

- Click the **Major field** in the Available fields list box. Click the **> button.**
- Add the **LastName, FirstName,** and **GPA fields** one at a time.
- Do not include the QualityPoints or Credits fields. Click **Next.**

➤ You should see the screen asking whether you want to group the fields. Click (select) the **Major field,** then click the **> button** to display the screen in Figure 3.10f. The Major field appears above the other fields to indicate that the records will be grouped according to the value of the Major field. Click **Next.**

➤ The next screen asks you to specify the order for the detail records. Click the **drop-down arrow** on the list box for the first field. Click **LastName** to sort the records alphabetically by last name within each major. Click **Next.**

➤ The **Stepped Option button** is already selected for the report layout, as is **Portrait orientation.** Be sure the box is checked to **Adjust field width so all fields fit on a page.** Click **Next.**

➤ Choose **Compact** as the style. Click **Next.**

➤ **GPA By Major** (which corresponds to the name of the underlying query) is already entered as the name of the report. Click the Option button to **Modify the report's design.** Click **Finish** to exit the Report Wizard.

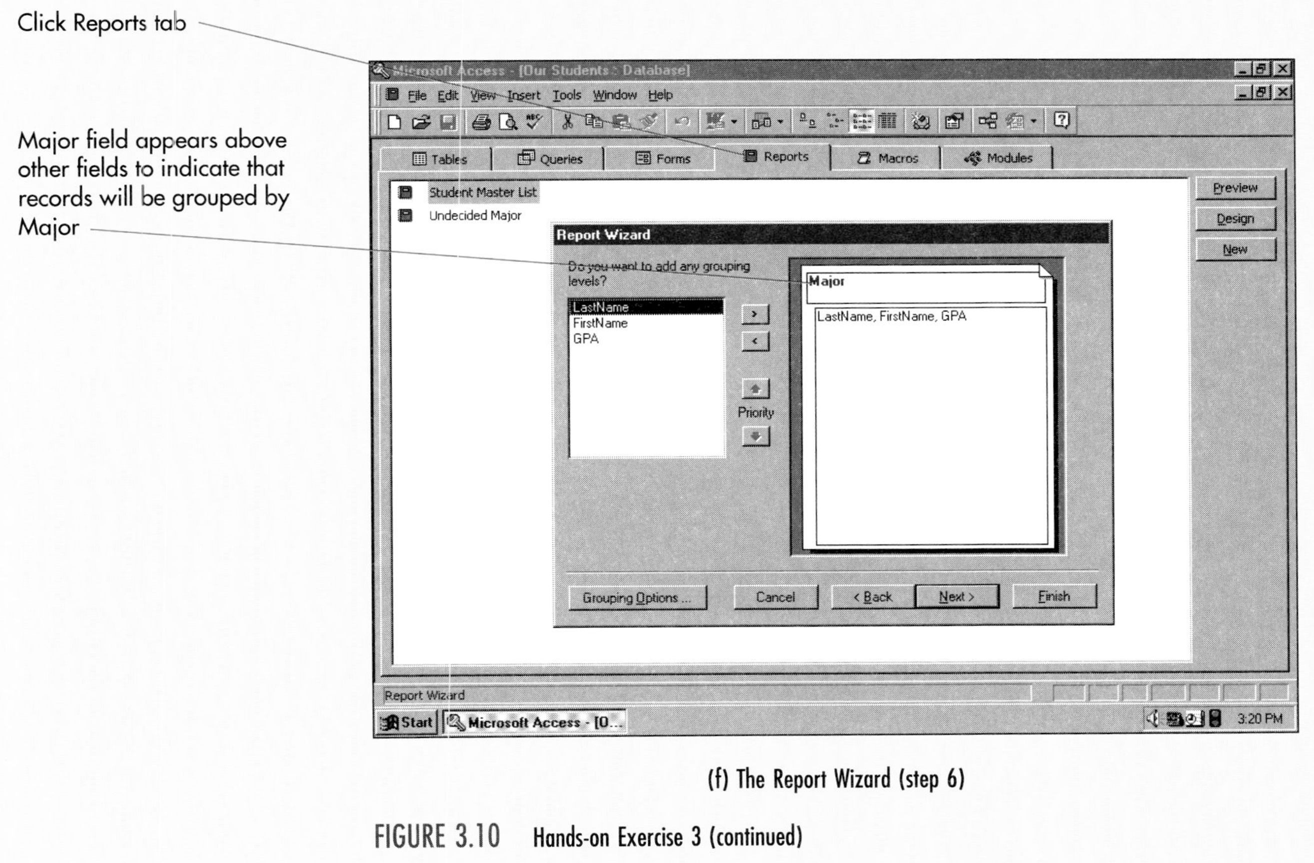

(f) The Report Wizard (step 6)

FIGURE 3.10 Hands-on Exercise 3 (continued)

STEP 7: Sorting and Grouping

- ➤ You should see the Report Design view as shown in Figure 3.10g. (The Sorting and Grouping dialog box is not yet visible.)
- ➤ Maximize the Report window (if necessary) so that you have more room in which to work.
- ➤ Move, size, and align the column headings and bound controls as shown in Figure 3.10g. We made GPA (label and bound control) smaller. We also moved FirstName (label and bound control) to the right.
- ➤ Pull down the **View menu.** Click **Sorting and Grouping** to display the Sorting and Grouping dialog box.

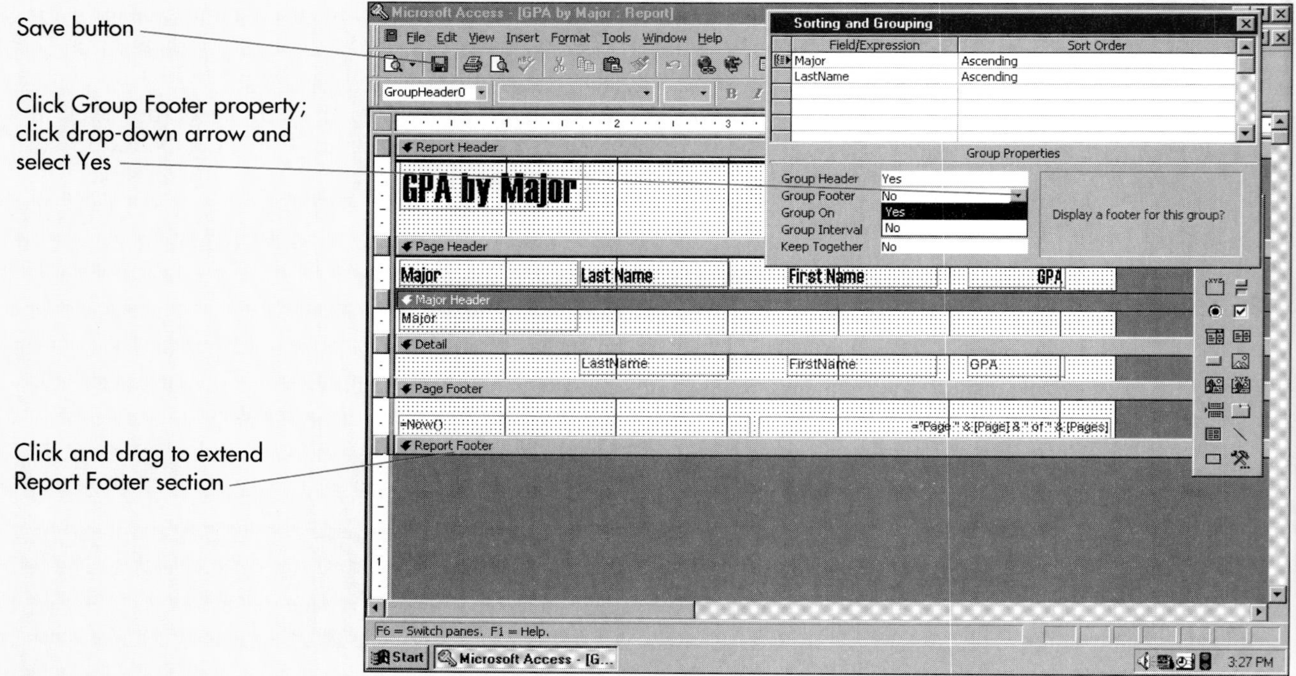

(g) Sorting and Grouping (step 7)

FIGURE 3.10 Hands-on Exercise 3 (continued)

SELECTING MULTIPLE CONTROLS

Select (click) a column heading in the page header, then press and hold the Shift key as you select the corresponding bound control in the Detail section. This selects both the column heading and the bound control and enables you to move and size the objects in conjunction with one another. Continue to work with both objects selected as you apply formatting through various buttons on the Formatting toolbar, or change properties through the property sheet. Click anywhere on the report to deselect the objects when you are finished.

➤ The **Major field** should already be selected. Click the **Group Footer** property, click the **drop-down arrow,** then click **Yes** to create a group footer for the Major field.

➤ Close the dialog box. The Major footer has been added to the report. Click the Save button to save the modified report.

STEP 8: Create the Group Footer

➤ Click the **Text Box button** on the Toolbox toolbar. The mouse pointer changes to a tiny crosshair with a text box attached.

➤ Click and drag in the group footer where you want the text box (which will contain the average GPA) to go. Release the mouse. You will see an Unbound control and an attached label containing a field number (e.g., Text 14).

➤ Click in the **text box** of the control (Unbound will disappear). Enter **=Avg(GPA)** to calculate the average of the GPA for all students in this group as shown in Figure 3.10h.

➤ Click in the attached unbound control, click and drag to select the text (Text14), then type **Average GPA for Major** as the label for this control. Size, move, and align the label as shown in the figure. (See the boxed tip on sizing or moving a control and its label.)

➤ Point to the **Average GPA control,** click the **right mouse button** to display a shortcut menu, then click **Properties** to display the Properties dialog box. If necessary, click the **All tab,** then scroll to the top of the list to view and/or modify the existing properties:

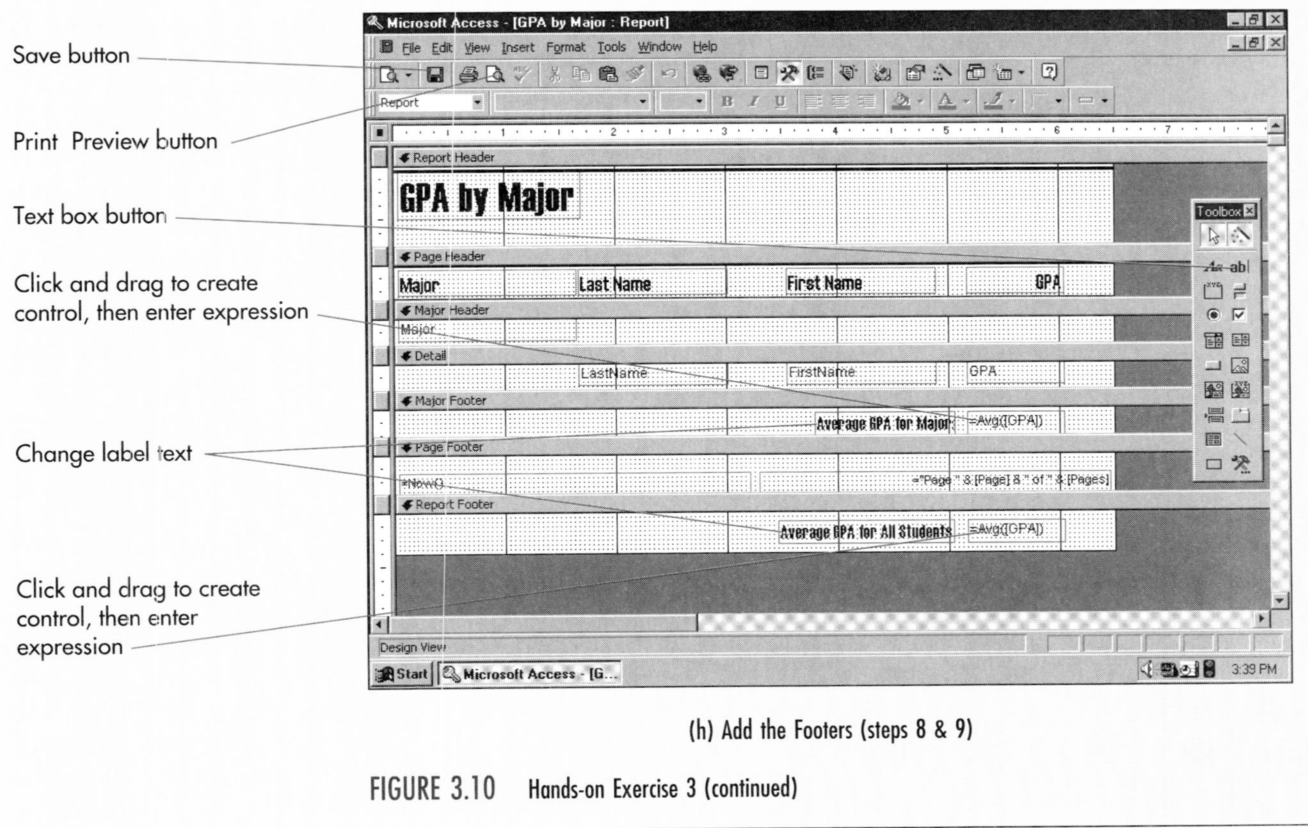

(h) Add the Footers (steps 8 & 9)

FIGURE 3.10 Hands-on Exercise 3 (continued)

- The Control Source text box contains the entry =Avg([GPA]) from the preceding step.
- Click the **Name text box.** Replace the original name (e.g., Text14) with **Average GPA for Major.**
- Click the **Format box.** Click the **drop-down arrow** and select **Fixed.**
- Click the box for the **Decimal places.** Click the **drop-down arrow** and select (click) **2.**
- Close the Properties dialog box to accept these settings and return to the report.

➤ Click the **Save button** on the toolbar.

SIZING OR MOVING A BOUND CONTROL AND ITS LABEL

A bound control is created with an attached label. Select (click) the control, and the control has sizing handles and a move handle, but the label has only a move handle. Select the label (instead of the control), and the opposite occurs: the control has only a move handle, but the label will have both sizing handles and a move handle. To move a control and its label, click and drag the border of either object. To move either the control or its label (but not both), click and drag the move handle (a tiny square in the upper left corner) of the appropriate object. (Use the Undo command if the result is not what you expect; then try again.)

STEP 9: Create the Report Footer

➤ The report footer is created in similar fashion to the group footer. Click and drag the bottom of the report footer to extend the size of the footer as shown in Figure 3.10h.

➤ Click the **Text Box button** on the Toolbox toolbar, then click and drag in the report footer where you want the text box to go. Release the mouse. You will see an Unbound control and an attached label containing a field number (e.g., Text16).

➤ Click in the **text box** of the control (Unbound will disappear). Enter **=Avg(GPA)** to calculate the average of the grade point averages for all students in the report.

➤ Click in the attached label, click and drag to select the text (Text16), then type **Average GPA for All Students** as the label for this control. Move, size, and align the label appropriately.

➤ Size the text box, then format the control:

- Point to the control, click the **right mouse button** to display a shortcut menu, then click **Properties** to display the Properties dialog box. Change the properties to **Fixed Format** with **2 decimal places.** Change the name to **Average GPA for All Students.**
- Close the Properties dialog box to accept these settings and return to the report.

➤ Click the **Save button** on the toolbar.

SECTION PROPERTIES

Each section in a report has properties that control its appearance and behavior. Point to the section header, click the right mouse button to display a shortcut menu, then click Properties to display the property sheet and set the properties. You can hide the section by changing the Visible property to No. You can also change the Special Effect property to Raised or Sunken.

STEP 10: View the Report

- Click the **Print Preview button** to view the completed report as shown in Figure 3.10i. The status bar shows you are on page 1 of the report.
- Click the **Zoom button** to see the entire page. Click the **Zoom button** a second time to return to the higher magnification, which lets you read the report.
- Click the **Navigation button** to move to the next page (page 2). Click the **Navigation button** to return to page 1.
- Be sure that you are satisfied with the appearance of the report and that all controls align properly with their associated labels. If necessary, return to the Design view to modify the report.
- Pull down the **File menu** and click **Print** (or click the **Print button**) to display the Print dialog box. The **All option button** is already selected under Print Range. Click **OK** to print the report.

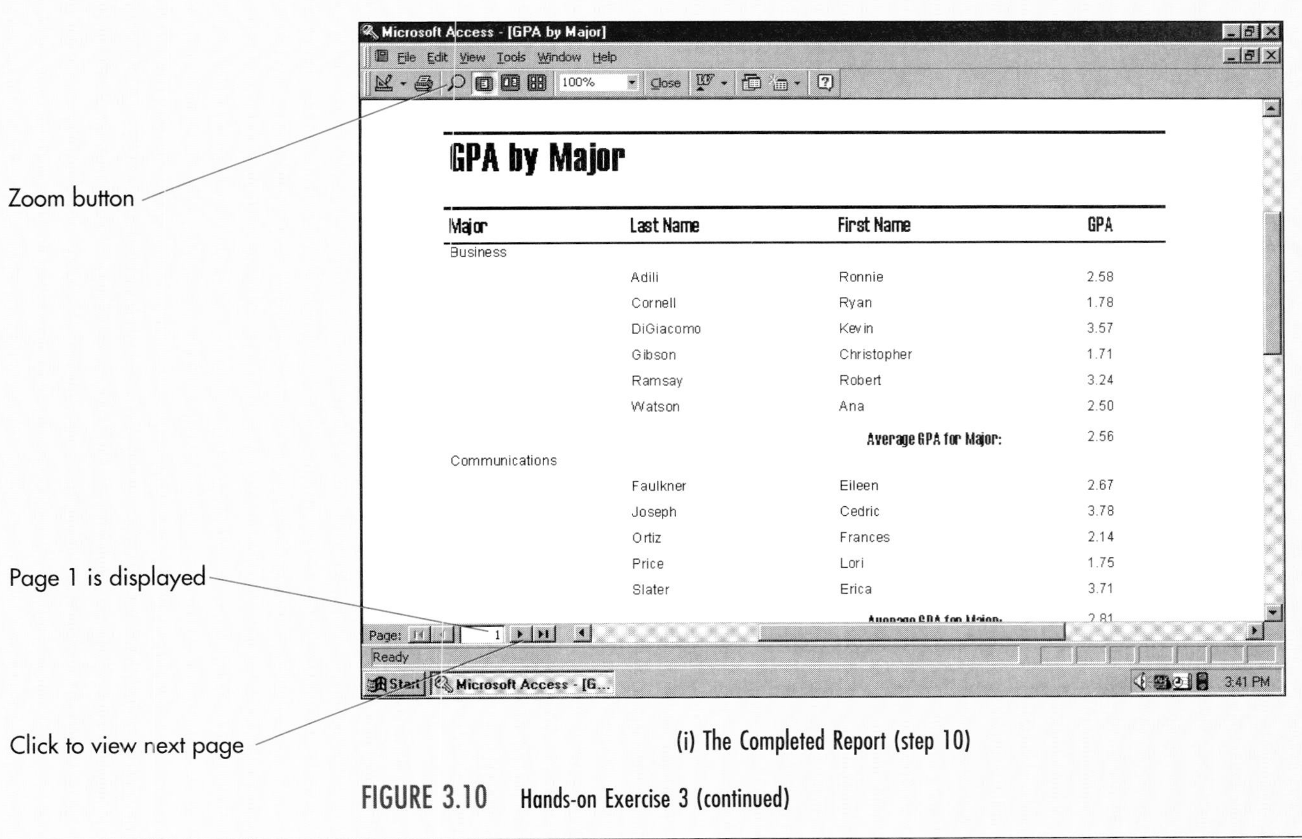

(i) The Completed Report (step 10)

FIGURE 3.10 Hands-on Exercise 3 (continued)

THE BORDER PROPERTY

The Border property enables you to display a border around any type of control. Point to the control (in the Design view), click the right mouse button to display a shortcut menu, then click Properties to display the Properties dialog box. Select the Format tab, click the Border Style property, then choose the type of border you want (e.g., solid to display a border or transparent to suppress a border). Use the Border Color and Border Width properties to change the appearance of the border.

STEP 11: Exit Access

- ➤ Pull down the **File menu** and click **Close** to close the GPA by Major report. Click **Yes** if asked to save design changes to the report.
- ➤ Close the **Our Students database** and exit Access.

COMPACTING A DATABASE

The size of an Access database is quite large even if the database contains only a limited number of records. It is not surprising to see simple databases, such as the Our Students database in this chapter, grow to 500KB or more. You can, however, reduce the storage requirements by compacting the database, a practice we highly recommend. See the case study at the end of the chapter.

SUMMARY

Data and information are not synonymous. Data refers to a fact or facts about a specific record. Information is data that has been rearranged into a more useful format. Data may be viewed as the raw material, whereas information is the finished product.

A report is a printed document that displays information from the database. Reports are created through the Report Wizard, then modified as necessary in the Design view. A report is divided into sections. The report header (footer) occurs at the beginning (end) of the report. The page header (footer) appears at the top (bottom) of each page. The detail section is found in the main body of the report and is printed once for each record in the report.

Each section is comprised of objects known as controls. A bound control has a data source such as a field in the underlying table. An unbound control has no data source. A calculated control contains an expression. Controls are selected, moved, and sized the same way as any other Windows object.

Every report is based on either a table or a query. A report based on a table contains every record in that table. A report based on a query contains only the records satisfying the criteria in the query.

A query enables you to select records from a table (or from several tables), display the selected records in any order, and perform calculations on fields within the query. A select query is the most common type of query and is created using the design grid. A select query displays its output in a dynaset that can be used to update the data in the underlying table(s).

The records in a report are often grouped according to the value of a specific field within the record. A group header appears before each group to identify the group. A group footer appears at the end of each group and can be used to display the summary information about the group.

All objects (tables, forms, queries, and reports) in an Access database are named according to the same rules. The name can contain up to 64 characters (letters or numbers) and can include spaces. A form and/or a report can have the same name as the table or query on which it is based to emphasize the relationship between the two.

KEY WORDS AND CONCEPTS

AND condition
Ascending sequence
Avg function
Between function
Bound control
Calculated control
Columnar report
Compacting
Count function
Criteria row
Database Properties
Datasheet view
Descending sequence
Design grid
Design view
Detail section
Dynaset
Field row
Group footer
Group header
Inheritance
Label tool
Max function
Min function
NOT function
Now function
OR condition
Page footer
Page header
Print Preview
Query
Query window
Relational operators
Report
Report footer
Report header
Report Wizard
Select query
Show row
Sort row
Sorting and Grouping
Sum function
Tabular report
Text box tool
Top Values property
Unbound control
Wild card

MULTIPLE CHOICE

1. Which of the following is a reason for basing a report on a query rather than a table?
   (a) To limit the report to selected records
   (b) To include a calculated field in the report
   (c) Both (a) and (b)
   (d) Neither (a) nor (b)
2. An Access database may contain:
   (a) One or more tables
   (b) One or more queries
   (c) One or more reports
   (d) All of the above

3. Which of the following is true regarding the names of objects within an Access database?
   (a) A form or report may have the same name as the underlying table
   (b) A form or report may have the same name as the underlying query
   (c) Both (a) and (b)
   (d) Neither (a) nor (b)

4. The dynaset created by a query may contain:
   (a) A subset of records from the associated table but must contain all of the fields for the selected records
   (b) A subset of fields from the associated table but must contain all of the records
   (c) Both (a) and (b)
   (d) Neither (a) nor (b)

5. Which toolbar contains a button to display the properties of a selected object?
   (a) The Query Design toolbar
   (b) The Report Design toolbar
   (c) Both (a) and (b)
   (d) Neither (a) nor (b)

6. Which of the following does *not* have both a Design view and a Datasheet view?
   (a) Tables
   (b) Forms
   (c) Queries
   (d) Reports

7. Which of the following is true regarding the wild card character within Access?
   (a) A question mark stands for a single character in the same position as the question mark
   (b) An asterisk stands for any number of characters in the same position as the asterisk
   (c) Both (a) and (b)
   (d) Neither (a) nor (b)

8. Which of the following will print at the top of every page?
   (a) Report header
   (b) Group header
   (c) Both (a) and (b)
   (d) Neither (a) nor (b)

9. A query, based on the Our Students database within the chapter, contains two fields from the Student table (QualityPoints and Credits) as well as a calculated field (GPA). Which of the following is true?
   (a) Changing the value of Credits or QualityPoints in the query's dynaset automatically changes these values in the underlying table
   (b) Changing the value of GPA automatically changes its value in the underlying table
   (c) Both (a) and (b)
   (d) Neither (a) nor (b)

10. Which of the following must be present in every report?
    (a) A report header and a report footer
    (b) A page header and a page footer
    (c) Both (a) and (b)
    (d) Neither (a) nor (b)

11. Which of the following may be included in a report as well as in a form?
    (a) Bound control
    (b) Unbound control
    (c) Calculated control
    (d) All of the above

12. The navigation buttons ► and ◄ will:
    (a) Move to the next or previous record in a table
    (b) Move to the next or previous page in a report
    (c) Both (a) and (b)
    (d) Neither (a) nor (b)

13. Assume that you created a query based on an Employee table, and that the query contains fields for Location and Title. Assume further that there is a single criteria row and that New York and Manager have been entered under the Location and Title fields, respectively. The dynaset will contain:
    (a) All employees in New York
    (b) All managers
    (c) Only the managers in New York
    (d) All employees in New York and all managers

14. You have decided to modify the query from the previous question to include a second criteria row. The Location and Title fields are still in the query, but this time New York and Manager appear in *different* criteria rows. The dynaset will contain:
    (a) All employees in New York
    (b) All managers
    (c) Only the managers in New York
    (d) All employees in New York and all managers

15. Which of the following is true about a query that lists employees by city and alphabetically within city?
    (a) The design grid should specify a descending sort on both city and employee name
    (b) The City field should appear to the left of the employee name in the design grid
    (c) Both (a) and (b)
    (d) Neither (a) nor (b)

ANSWERS

1. c	**6.** d	**11.** d
2. d	**7.** c	**12.** c
3. c	**8.** d	**13.** c
4. d	**9.** a	**14.** d
5. d	**10.** d	**15.** b

PRACTICE WITH MICROSOFT ACCESS 97

1. Use the Our Students database as the basis for the following queries and reports:
   a. Create a select query for students on the Dean's List (GPA >= 3.50). Include the student's name, major, quality points, credits, and GPA. List the students alphabetically.
   b. Use the Report Wizard to prepare a tabular report based on the query in part a. Include your name in the report header as the academic advisor.
   c. Create a select query for students on academic probation (GPA < 2.00). Include the same fields as the query in part a. List the students in alphabetical order.
   d. Use the Report Wizard to prepare a tabular report similar to the report in part b.
   e. Print both reports and submit them to your instructor as proof that you did this exercise.

2. Use the Employee database in the Exploring Access folder to create the reports listed below. (This is the same database that was used earlier in Chapters 1 and 2.)
   a. A report containing all employees in sequence by location and alphabetically within location. Show the employee's last name, first name, location, title, and salary. Include summary statistics to display the total salaries in each location as well as for the company as a whole.
   b. A report containing all employees in sequence by title and alphabetically within title. Show the employee's last name, first name, location, title, and salary. Include summary statistics to show the average salary for each title as well as the average salary in the company.
   c. Add your name to the report header in the report so that your instructor will know the reports came from you. Print both reports and submit them to your instructor.

3. Use the United States database in the Exploring Access folder to create the report shown in Figure 3.11. (This is the same database that was used in Chapters 1 and 2.) The report lists states by geographic region, and alphabetically within region. It includes a calculated field, Population Density, which is computed by dividing a state's population by its area. Summary statistics are also required as shown in the report.

   Note that the report header contains a map of the United States that was taken from the Microsoft Clip Gallery. The instructions for inserting an object can be found on page 81 in conjunction with an earlier problem. Be sure to include your name in the report footer so that your instructor will know that the report comes from you.

4. Use the Bookstore database in the Exploring Access folder to create the report shown in Figure 3.12. (This is the same database that was used in the hands-on exercises in Chapter 1.)

   The report header in Figure 3.12 contains a graphic object that was taken from the Microsoft Clip Gallery. You are not required to use this specific image, but you are required to insert a graphic. The instructions for inserting an object can be found on page 81 in conjunction with an earlier problem. Be sure to include your name in the report header so that your instructor will know that the report comes from you.

United States By Region

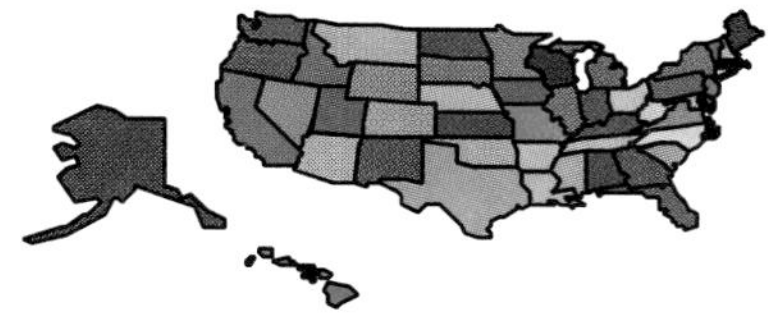

Region	Name	Capital	Population	Area	Population Density
Middle Atlantic					
	Delaware	Dover	666,168	2,057	323.85
	Maryland	Annapolis	4,781,468	10,577	452.06
	New Jersey	Trenton	7,730,188	7,836	986.50
	New York	Albany	17,990,455	49,576	362.89
	Pennsylvania	Harrisburg	11,881,643	45,333	262.10
		Total for Region:	43,049,922	115,379	
		Average for Region:	8,609,984.40	23,075.80	477.48
Mountain					
	Arizona	Phoenix	3,665,228	113,909	32.18
	Colorado	Denver	3,294,394	104,247	31.60
	Idaho	Boise	1,006,749	83,557	12.05
	Montana	Helena	799,065	147,138	5.43
	Nevada	Carson City	1,201,833	110,540	10.87
	New Mexico	Santa Fe	1,515,069	121,666	12.45
	Utah	Salt Lake City	1,722,850	84,916	20.29
	Wyoming	Cheyenne	453,588	97,914	4.63
		Total for Region:	13,658,776	863,887	
		Average for Region:	1,707,347.00	107,985.88	16.19
New England					
	Connecticut	Hartford	3,287,116	5,009	656.24
	Maine	Augusta	1,227,928	33,215	36.97
	Massachusetts	Boston	6,016,425	8,257	728.65
	New	Concord	1,109,252	9,304	119.22
	Rhode Island	Providence	1,003,464	1,214	826.58
	Vermont	Montpellier	562,758	9,609	58.57
		Total for Region:	13,206,943	66,608	
		Average for Region:	2,201,157.17	11,101.33	404.37

Saturday, January 11, 1997 — Page 1 of 3

FIGURE 3.11 Screen for Practice Exercise 3

University of Miami Book Store

Publisher	ISBN Number	Author	Title	List Price
IDG Books Worldwide				
	1-56884-453-0	Livingston/Straub	Windows 95 Secrets	$39.95
			Number of Books:	1
			Average List Price:	$39.95
Macmillan Publishing				
	1-56686-127-6	Rosch	The Hardware Bible	$35.00
			Number of Books:	1
			Average List Price:	$35.00
MIS Press				
	1-55828-353-6	Banks	Welcome to CompuServe	$24.95
			Number of Books:	1
			Average List Price:	$24.95
New Riders Publishing				
	1-56205-306-X	Maxwell/Grycz	New Riders Internet Yellow Pages	$29.95
			Number of Books:	1
			Average List Price:	$29.95
Osborne-McGraw Hill				
	0-07-882023-5	Hahn/Stout	The Internet Yellow Pages	$27.95
	0-07-881980-6	Hahn/Stout	The Internet Complete Reference	$29.95
			Number of Books:	2
			Average List Price:	$28.95
Prentice Hall				
	0-13-754235-6	Grauer/Barber	Exploring PowerPoint 97	$30.95
	0-13-065541-4	Grauer/Barber	Exploring Windows 3.1	$24.95

Saturday, January 11, 1997 Page 1 of 2

FIGURE 3.12 Screen for Practice Exercise 4

Super Bowl

http://www.nfl.com

Year	AFC Team	AFC Score	NFC Team	NFC Score
1997	New England	21	Green Bay	35
1996	Pittsburgh	17	Dallas	27
1995	San Diego	26	San Francisco	49
1994	Buffalo	13	Dallas	30
1993	Buffalo	17	Dallas	52
1992	Buffalo	24	Washington	37
1991	Buffalo	19	Giants	20
1990	Denver	10	San Francisco	55
1989	Cincinnati	16	San Francisco	20
1988	Denver	10	Washington	42
1987	Denver	20	Giants	39
1986	New England	10	Chicago	46
1985	Miami	16	San Francisco	38
1984	Los Angeles	38	Washington	9
1983	Miami	17	Washington	27
1982	Cincinnati	21	San Francisco	26
1981	Oakland	27	Philadelphia	10
1980	Pittsburgh	31	Los Angeles	19
1979	Pittsburgh	35	Dallas	31
1978	Denver	10	Dallas	27
1977	Oakland	32	Minnesota	14
1976	Pittsburgh	21	Dallas	17
1975	Pittsburgh	16	Minnesota	6
1974	Miami	24	Minnesota	7
1973	Miami	14	Washington	7
1972	Miami	3	Dallas	24
1971	Baltimore	16	Dallas	13

Saturday, January 11, 1997 — Page 1 of 2

FIGURE 3.13 Screen for Practice Exercise 5

5. Use the Super Bowl database in the Exploring Access folder to create the report in Figure 3.13, which lists the participants and scores in every game played to date. It also displays the Super Bowl logo, which we downloaded from the home page of the NFL (www.nfl.com). Be sure to include your name in the report footer so that your instructor will know that the report comes from you. (See the Super Bowl case study for suggestions on additional reports or queries that you can create from this database.)

6. There are many sources of help for Access as well as every Office application. You can use the regular Help facility or you can go to the Microsoft web site to obtain the latest information. Start Access, pull down the Help menu, click Microsoft on the Web, then click online support to go to the home page for Microsoft Access. Explore the various options that are available, then write a short summary of your findings and submit it to your instructor as proof you did this exercise. Figure 3.14 displays the feature articles that were available when this book went to press and provides an indication of what you can expect to find.

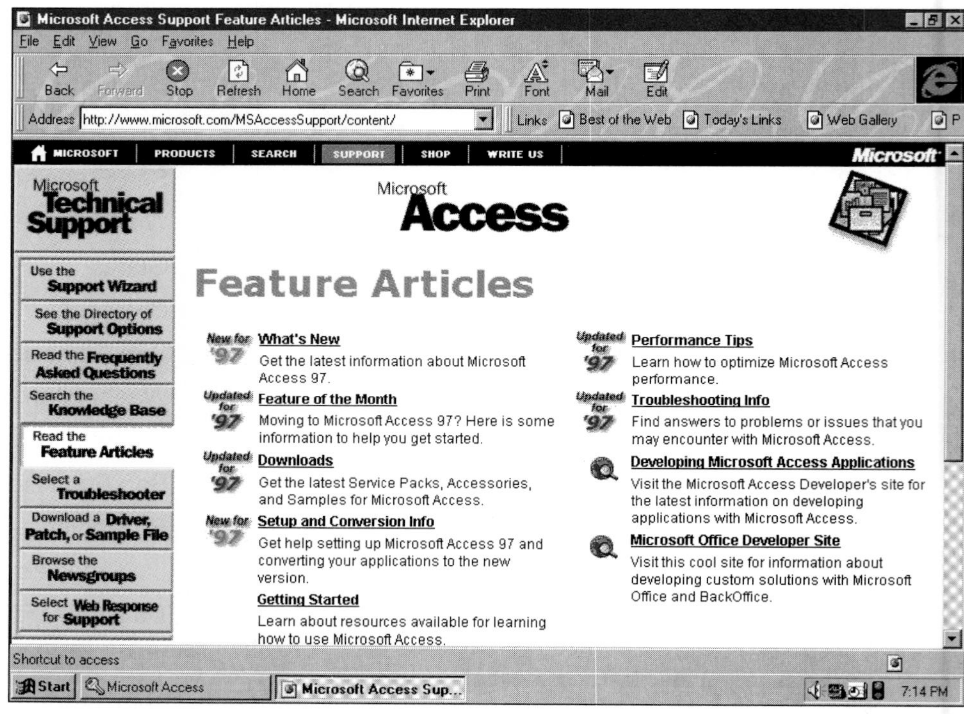

FIGURE 3.14 Screen for Practice Exercise 6

CASE STUDIES

The Fortune 500

Research the Fortune 500 (or a similar list) to obtain the gross revenue and net income for the present and previous year for the 20 largest corporations. Create an Access database to hold a table for this data and an associated form to enter the data. Validate your data carefully, then produce at least three reports based on the data. An alternative to entering the data manually is to use your favorite search engine to locate the home page of *Fortune* magazine. Once there, you will find a link to the *Fortune 500,* from where you can download an Excel workbook with current information. You then have to copy that information into an Access table. (Use online Help to find out how.)

The United States of America

What is the total population of the United States? What is its area? Can you name the 13 original states or the last five states admitted to the Union? Do you know the 10 states with the highest population or the five largest states in terms of area? Which states have the highest population density (people per square mile)?

The answers to these and other questions can be obtained from the United States database that is available on the data disk. The key to the assignment is to use the Top Values property within a query that limits the number of records returned in the dynaset. Use the database to create several reports that you think will be of interest to the class.

The Super Bowl (continued)

How many times has the NFC won the Super Bowl? When was the last time the AFC won? What was the largest margin of victory? What was the closest game? What is the most points scored by two teams in one game? How many times have the Miami Dolphins appeared? How many times did they win? Use the data in the Super Bowl database to create a trivia sheet on the Super Bowl, then incorporate your analysis into a letter addressed to NBC Sports. Convince them you are a super fan and that you merit two tickets to next year's game. Go to the home page of the National Football League (www.nfl.com) to obtain score(s) from the most recent game(s) to update our table if necessary.

Mail Merge

A mail merge takes the tedium out of sending form letters, as it creates the same letter many times, changing the name, address, and other information as appropriate from letter to letter. The form letter is created in a word processor (e.g., Microsoft Word), but the data file may be taken from an Access table or query. Use the Our Students database as the basis for two different form letters sent to two different groups of students. The first letter is to congratulate students on the Dean's list (GPA of 3.50 or higher). The second letter is a warning to students on academic probation (GPA of less than 2.00).

Compacting versus Compressing

An Access database becomes fragmented, and thus unnecessarily large, as objects (e.g., reports and forms) are modified or deleted. It is important, therefore, to periodically compact a database to reduce its size (enabling you to back it up on a floppy disk). Choose a database with multiple objects; e.g., the Our Students database used in this chapter. Use the Windows Explorer to record the file size of the database as it presently exists. Start Access, open the database, pull down the Tools menu and select Database Utilities to compact the database, then record the size of the database after compacting. You can also compress a compacted database (using a standard Windows utility such as WinZip) to further reduce the requirement for disk storage. Summarize your findings in a short report to your instructor. Try compacting and compressing at least two different databases to better appreciate these techniques.

A

APPENDIX A: TOOLBARS

OVERVIEW

Microsoft Access has 20 predefined toolbars that provide access to commonly used commands. Twelve of the toolbars are tied to a specific view and are displayed automatically when you work in that view. These twelve toolbars are shown in Figure A.1 and are listed here for convenience: the Database, Relationships, Table Design, Table Datasheet, Query Design, Query Datasheet, Form Design, Form View, Report Design, Print Preview, Macro Design, and Visual Basic toolbars.

The remaining eight toolbars are shown in Figure A.2. The Toolbox and Formatting (Form/Report Design) toolbars are displayed by default in both the Form Design and Report Design views. The Formatting (Datasheet) toolbar is displayed by default in both the Table Datasheet and Query Datasheet views. The Web toolbar can be displayed (hidden) in any view at the discretion of the user. The Utility 1 and Utility 2 toolbars are used to create custom toolbars that can be used with any database, and are initially blank. The Filter/Sort toolbars and the Source Control Code toolbars are displayed at the discretion of the user.

The buttons on the toolbars are intended to indicate their functions. Clicking the Print button, for example (the fourth button from the left on the Database toolbar), executes the Print command. If you are unsure of the purpose of any toolbar button, point to it, and a ScreenTip will appear that displays its name.

You can display multiple toolbars at one time, move them to new locations on the screen, customize their appearance, or suppress their display.

- To display or hide a toolbar, pull down the View menu and click the Toolbars command. The toolbars appropriate to that view will be listed in the submenu, and can be toggled on (off) by clicking the appropriate name. Other toolbars, not tied to that view, can be displayed (hidden) by pulling down the View menu, clicking the Toolbars command, clicking the Customize command, clicking the Toolbars tab, and then clicking the check box next to the desired toolbar to turn the display on (off). The selected toolbar(s) will be displayed in the same position as when last displayed. You may also point to any toolbar and click with the right mouse button to bring up a shortcut menu. You may then either toggle on (off) a listed toolbar or click the Customize command to display (hide) any of the toolbars, as described above.

- To change the size of the buttons, suppress the display of the ScreenTips, or display the associated shortcut key with the ScreenTips (if available), pull down the View menu, click Toolbars, and click Customize to display the Customize dialog box. If necessary, click the Options tab, then select (deselect) the appropriate check box. Alternatively, you can right click on any toolbar, click the Customize command from the context-sensitive menu, then select (deselect) the appropriate check box from within the Options tab in the Customize dialog box.
- Toolbars are either docked (along the edge of the window) or floating (in their own window). A toolbar moved to the edge of the window will dock along that edge. A toolbar moved anywhere else in the window will float in its own window. Docked toolbars are one tool wide (high), whereas floating toolbars can be resized by clicking and dragging a border or corner as you would with any window.
  - To move a docked toolbar, click anywhere in the gray background area and drag the toolbar to its new location. You can also click and drag the move handle (the pair of parallel lines) at the left of the toolbar.
  - To move a floating toolbar, drag its title bar to its new location.
- To customize one or more toolbars, display the toolbar(s) on the screen. Then pull down the View menu, click Toolbars, click Customize to display the Customize dialog box, then select the Toolbars tab. Alternatively, you can click on any toolbar with the right mouse button, select Customize from the shortcut menu, and then click the Toolbars tab.
  - To move a button, drag the button to its new location on that toolbar or any other displayed toolbar.
  - To copy a button, press the Ctrl key as you drag the button to its new location on that toolbar or any other displayed toolbar.
  - To delete a button, drag the button off the toolbar and release the mouse button.
  - To add a button, click the Commands tab in the Customize dialog box, select the category from the Categories list box that contains the button you want to add, then drag the button to the desired location on the toolbar. (To see a description of a tool's function before adding it to a toolbar, select the tool, then click the Description command button.)
  - To restore a predefined toolbar to its default appearance, pull down the View menu, click Toolbars, click Customize, click the Toolbars tab, select (highlight) the desired toolbar, and click the Reset command button.
- Buttons can also be moved, copied, or deleted without displaying the Customize dialog box.
  - To move a button, press the Alt key as you drag the button to the new location.
  - To copy a button, press the Alt and Ctrl keys as you drag the button to the new location.
  - To delete a button, press the Alt key as you drag the button off the toolbar.
- To create a new toolbar that can be displayed with any database, pull down the View menu, click Toolbars, click Customize, click the Toolbars tab, and

then select the Utility 1 or Utility 2 toolbar, which is initially one tool wide and empty. (Alternatively, you can click any toolbar with the right mouse button and select Customize from the shortcut menu.) Add, move, and delete tools following the same procedure as outlined above. The toolbar will automatically resize itself as new tools are added and deleted.

- To create a toolbar that can be displayed only in the database in which it was created, pull down the View menu, click Toolbars, click Customize, click the Toolbars tab, then click the New command button. Alternatively, you can click on any toolbar with the right mouse button, select Customize from the shortcut menu, click the Toolbars tab, and then click the New command button.
  - Enter a name for the toolbar in the dialog box that follows. The name can be any length and can contain spaces.
  - The new toolbar will appear on the screen. Initially it will be big enough to hold only one button. Add, move, and delete buttons following the same procedures as outlined above. The toolbar will automatically size itself as new buttons are added and deleted.
  - To delete a custom toolbar, pull down the View menu, click Toolbars, click Customize, and click the Toolbars tab. *Verify that the custom toolbar to be deleted is the only one selected (highlighted).* Click the Delete command button. Click Yes to confirm the deletion. (Note that a predefined toolbar cannot be deleted.)

Database Toolbar

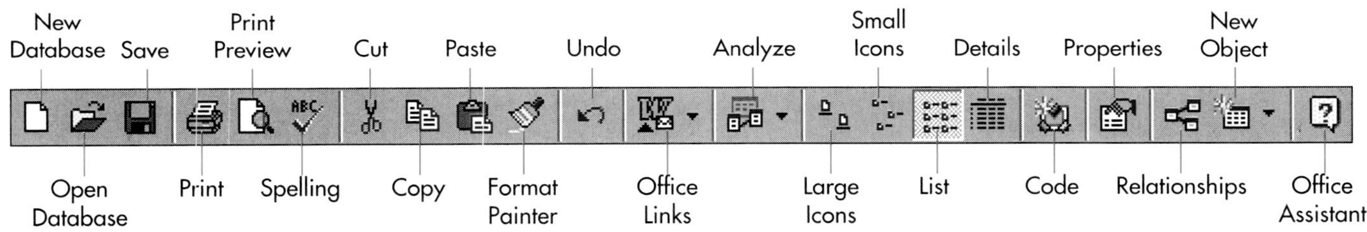

Relationships Toolbar

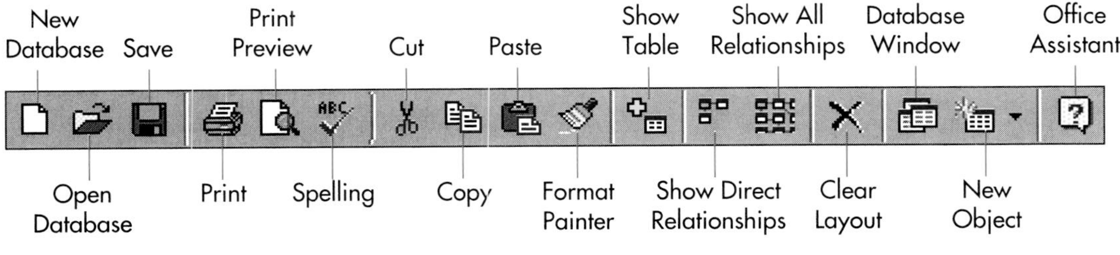

Table Design Toolbar

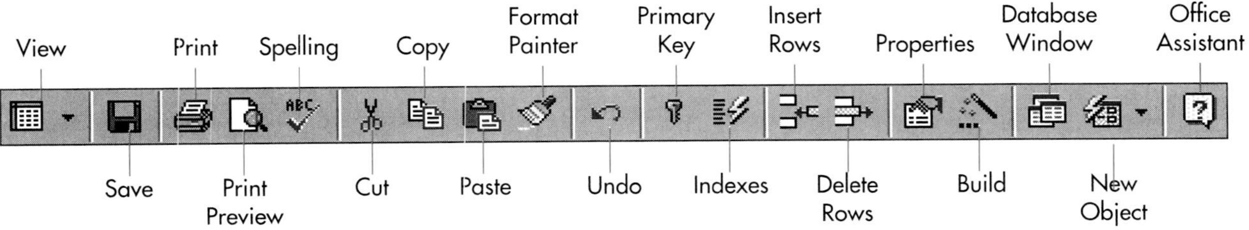

FIGURE A.1 Access Toolbars Tied to Specific Views

Table Datasheet Toolbar

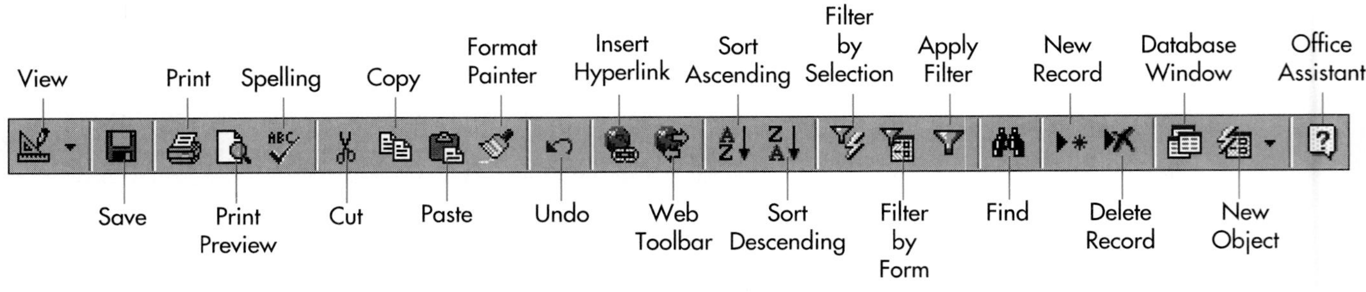

Query Design Toolbar

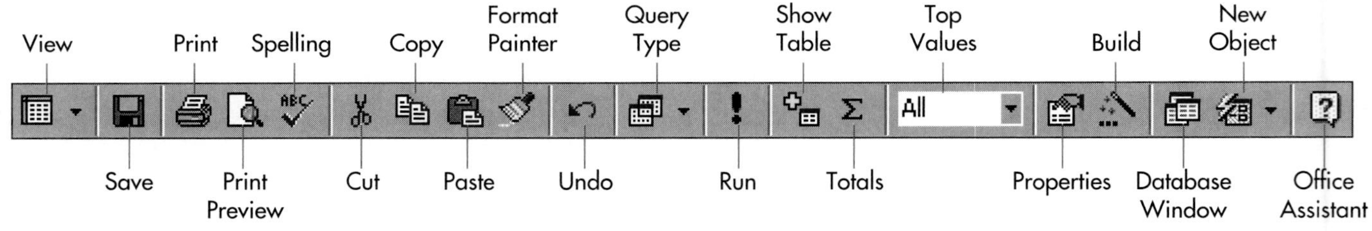

Query Datasheet Toolbar

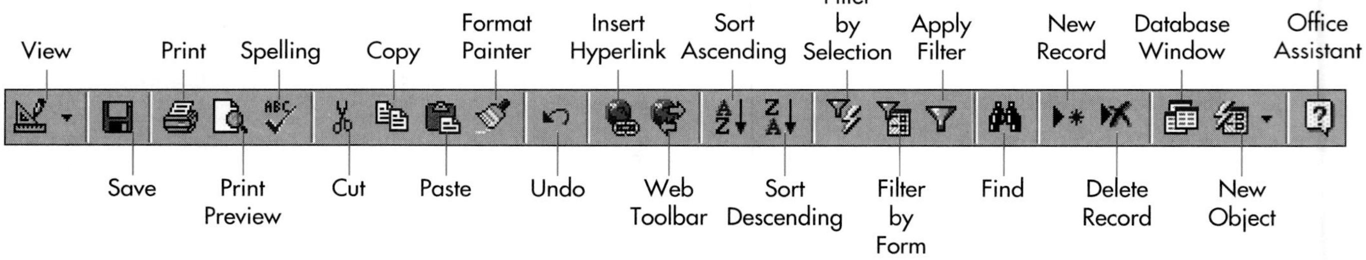

Form Design Toolbar

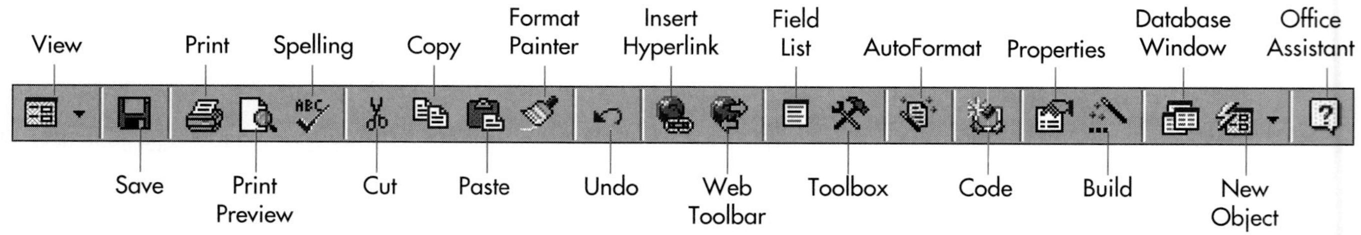

FIGURE A.1 Access Toolbars Tied to Specific Views (continued)

Form View Toolbar

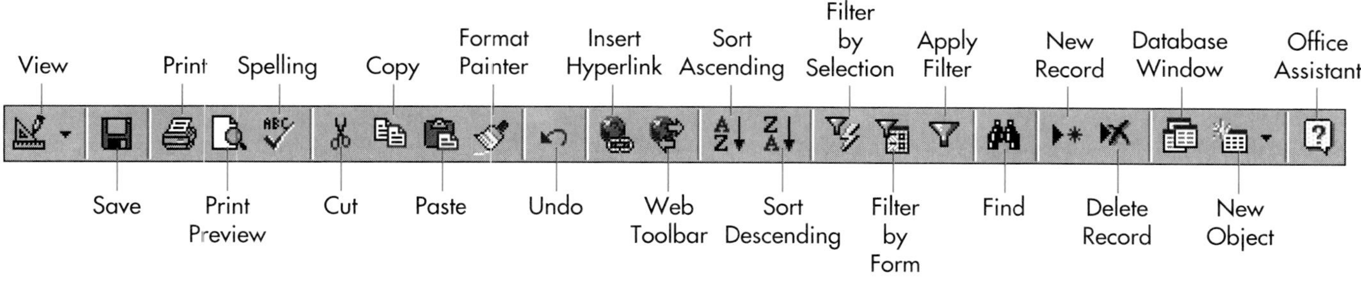

Report Design Toolbar

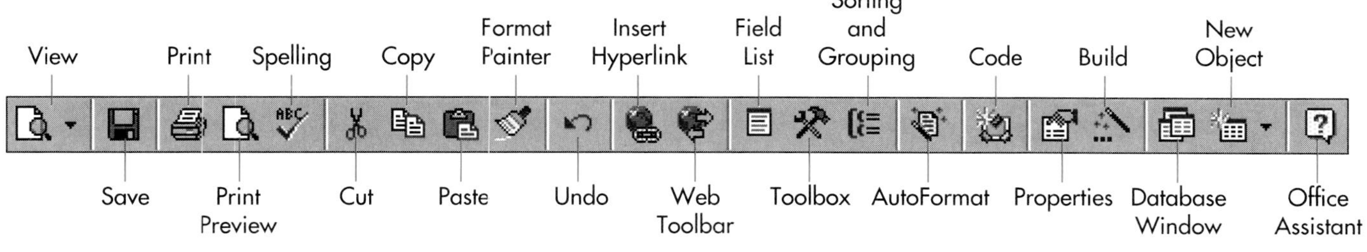

Print Preview Toolbar

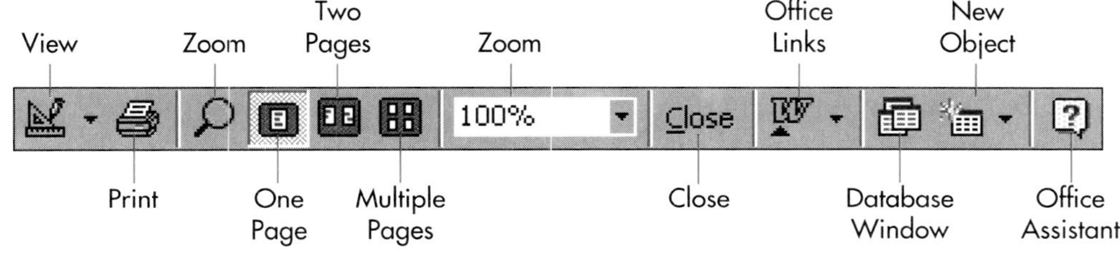

Macro Design Toolbar

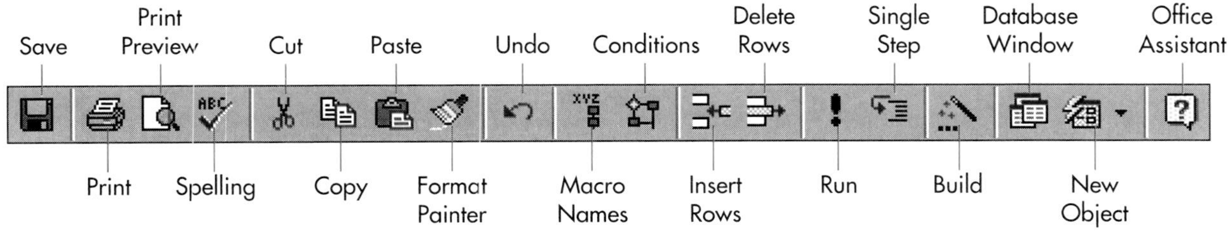

Visual Basic Toolbar

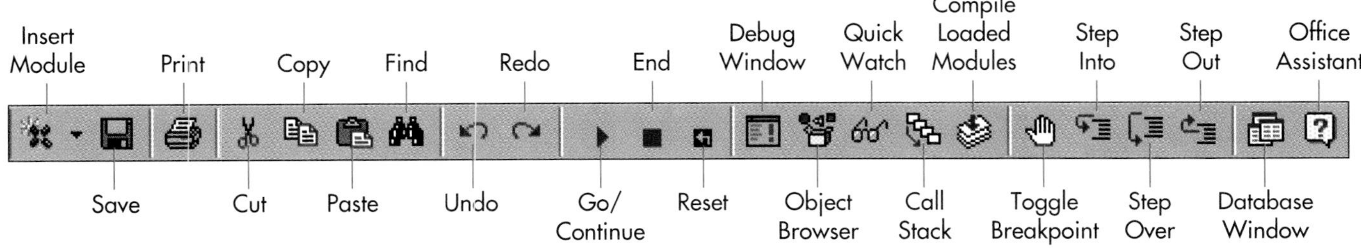

FIGURE A.1 Access Toolbars Tied to Specific Views (continued)

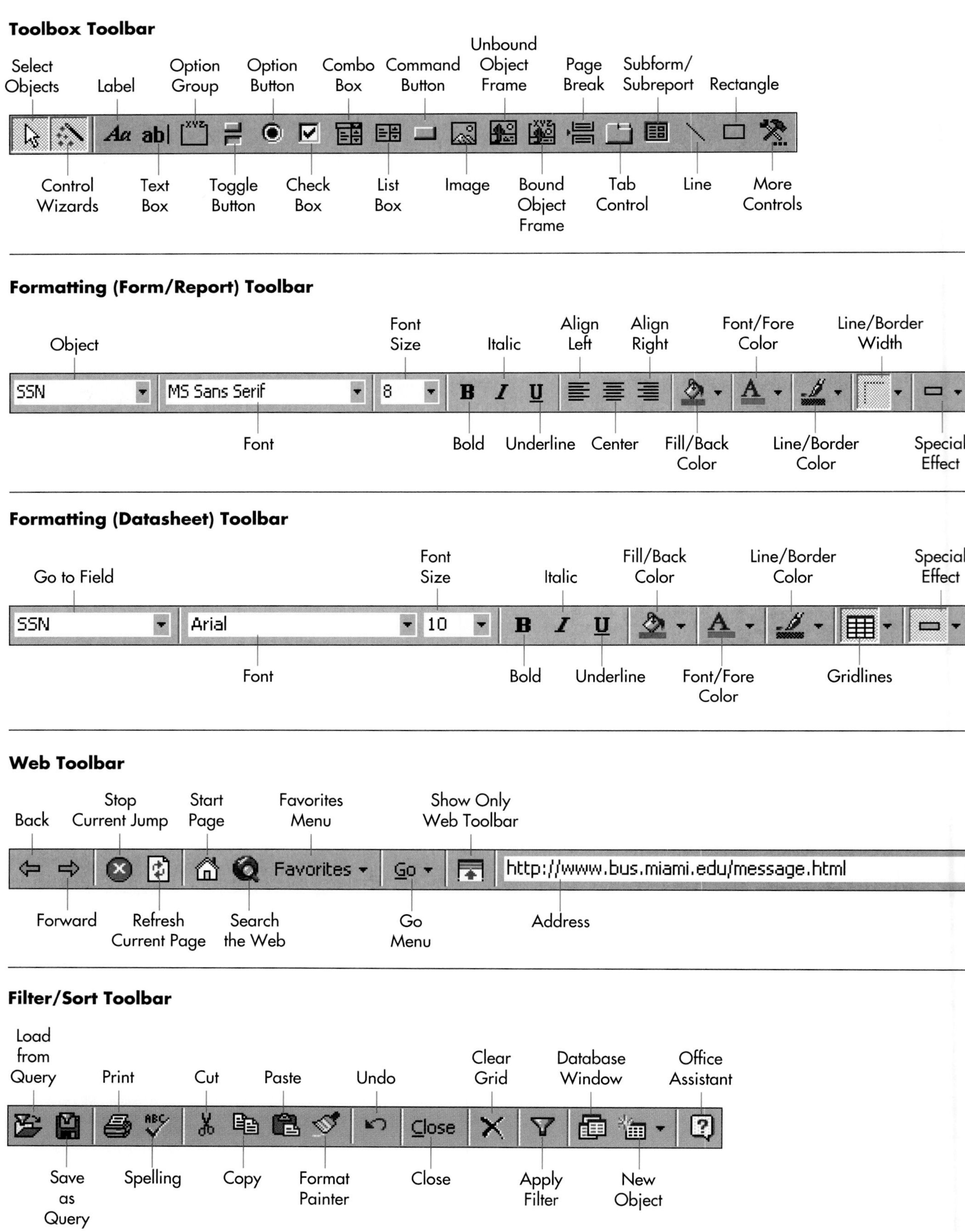

FIGURE A.2 Other Access Toolbars

Source Control Code Toolbar

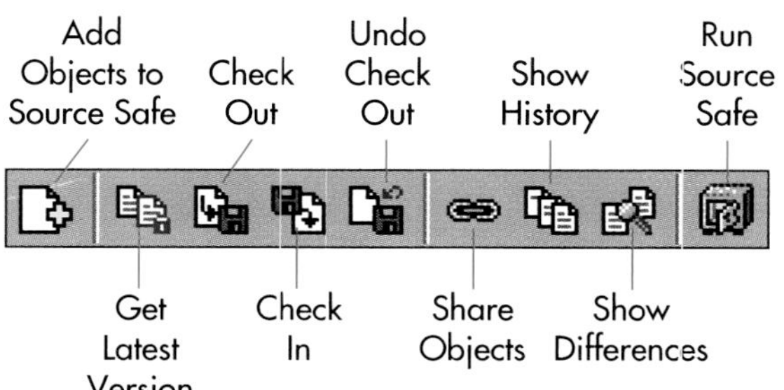

Utility 1 Toolbar

Utility 2 Toolbar

FIGURE A.2 Other Access Toolbars (continued)

7

INTRODUCTION TO POWERPOINT: PRESENTATIONS MADE EASY

OBJECTIVES

After reading this chapter you will be able to:

1. Describe the common user interface; give several examples of how PowerPoint follows the same conventions as other Microsoft applications.
2. Start PowerPoint; open, modify, and view an existing presentation.
3. Describe the various ways to print a presentation.
4. List the views in PowerPoint; describe the unique features of each view.
5. Use the Outline view to add slides to, and/or delete slides from, an existing presentation and/or to modify the text on an existing slide.
6. Add clip art to an existing slide.
7. Use the Rehearse Timings feature to time a presentation.
8. Describe the Meeting Minder, Slide Navigator, and Pen; explain how these tools are used to enhance a presentation.

OVERVIEW

This chapter introduces you to PowerPoint, one of the four major applications in the Professional version of Microsoft Office (Microsoft Word, Microsoft Excel, and Microsoft Access are the other three). In essence, PowerPoint helps you to create a professional presentation without relying on others. It enables you to deliver a presentation on the computer (or via 35-mm slides or overhead transparencies) and to print that presentation in a variety of formats.

PowerPoint is easy to learn because it is a Windows application and follows all of the conventions associated with the common user interface. Thus, if you already use one Windows application, it is that much easier to learn PowerPoint because you can apply much of what you know. It's even easier if you use Microsoft Word, Excel, or Access, since there are over 100 commands that are common to the Microsoft Office.

The chapter begins by showing you an actual PowerPoint presentation so that you can better appreciate what you will be able to do. We describe the five PowerPoint views and the unique capabilities of each view. We show you how to add slides to, and delete slides from, an existing presentation, how to modify the text of a presentation; and how to add clip art. (We will show you how to create your own presentation in Chapter 2.) We also provide three hands-on exercises, in which you apply the conceptual material at the computer. The exercises are essential to the learn-by-doing philosophy we follow throughout the text, and it is through the exercises that you will truly master the material.

One final point, before we begin, is that while PowerPoint can help you create attractive presentations, the content and delivery are still up to you. It is important that you express yourself clearly and that you deliver the presentation effectively. The chapter ends with several suggestions to help you in this regard.

A POWERPOINT PRESENTATION

A PowerPoint presentation consists of a series of slides such as those shown in Figure 1.1. Each slide contains different elements, including text, clip art, photographs and/or a chart. Nevertheless, the presentation has a consistent look from slide to slide with respect to its overall design and color scheme.

You might think that creating a presentation such as Figure 1.1 is difficult, but it isn't. It is remarkably easy, and that is the beauty of PowerPoint. In essence, PowerPoint allows you to concentrate on the *content* of a presentation without worrying about its *appearance.* You supply the text and supporting elements and leave the formatting to PowerPoint.

In addition to helping you create the presentation, PowerPoint provides a variety of ways to deliver it. You can show the presentation on a computer using animated transition effects as you move from one slide to the next. You can include sound in the presentation, provided your system has a sound card and speakers. You can also automate the presentation and distribute it on a disk for display at a convention booth or kiosk. If you cannot show the presentation on a computer, you can convert it to 35-mm slides or overhead transparencies.

PowerPoint gives you the ability to print the presentation in various ways to distribute to your audience. You can print one slide per page, or you can print miniature versions of each slide and can choose between two, three, or six slides per page. You can prepare speaker notes for yourself, consisting of a picture of each slide together with notes for its delivery. You can also print the entire presentation in outline form. Giving the audience a copy of the presentation (in any format) enables them to follow it more closely, and to take it home when the session is over.

POLISH YOUR DELIVERY

The speaker is still the most important part of any presentation, and a poor delivery will kill even the best presentation. Look at the audience as you speak to open communication and gain credibility. Don't read from a prepared script. Speak clearly and try to vary your delivery. Pause to emphasize key points and be sure the person in the last row can hear you.

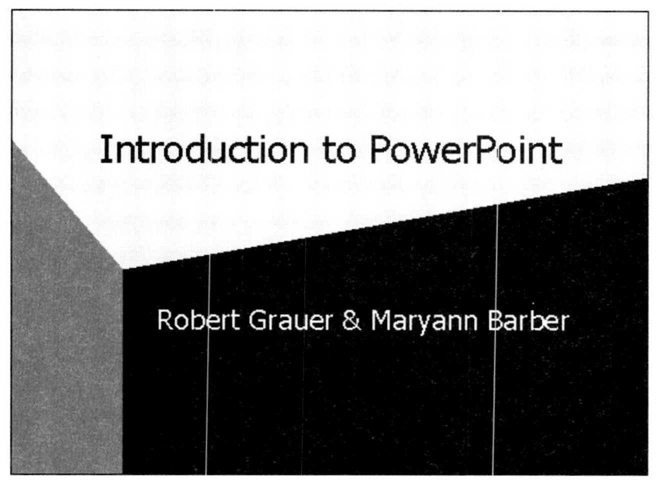

(a) Title Slide

(b) Bullet Slide

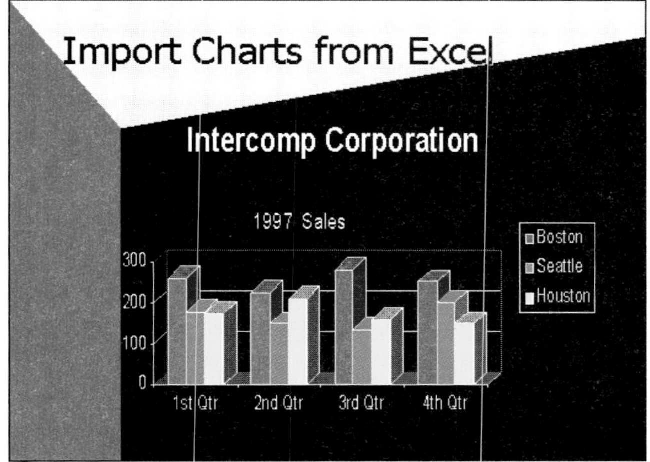

(c) Charts

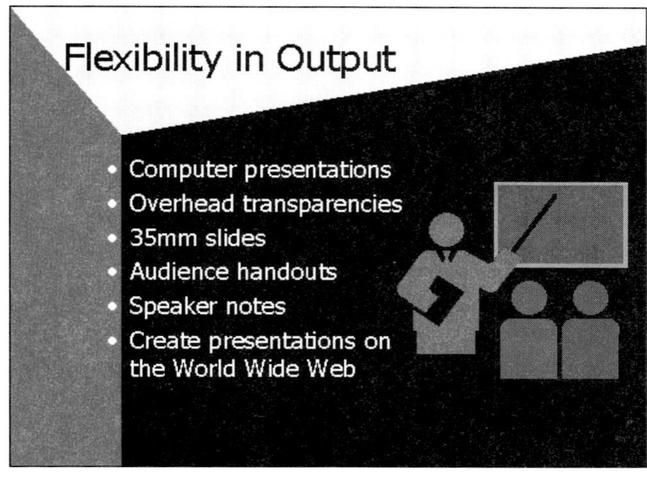

(d) Clip Art

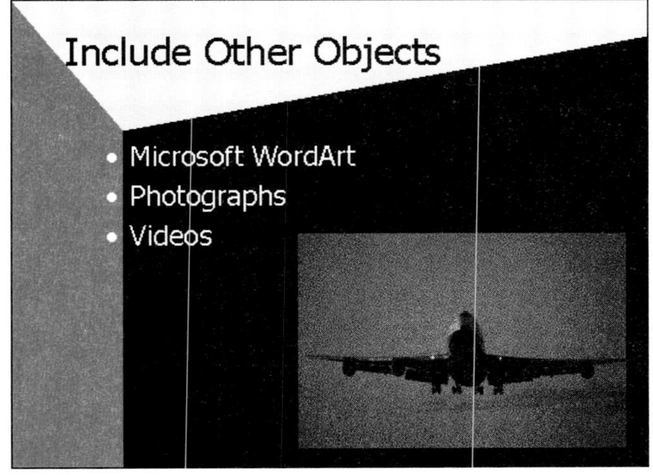

(e) Photographs

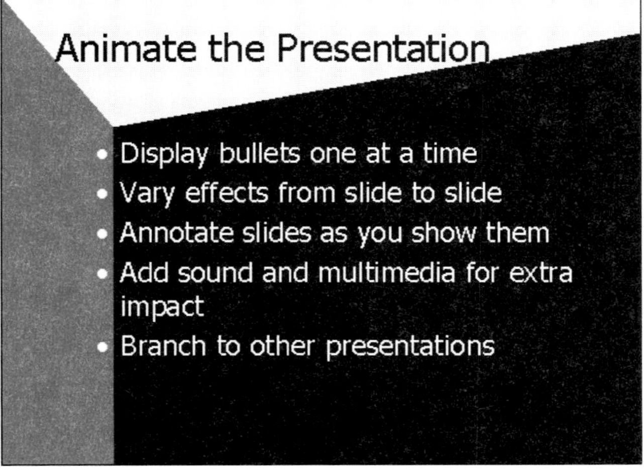

(f) Animation

FIGURE 1.1 A PowerPoint Presentation

The desktop in Figure 1.2 should look somewhat familiar, even if you have never used PowerPoint, because PowerPoint shares the common user interface that is present in every Windows application. You should recognize, therefore, the two open windows in Figure 1.2—the application window for PowerPoint and the document window for the current presentation.

Each window has its own Minimize, Maximize (or Restore), and Close buttons. Both windows have been maximized, and thus the title bars have been merged into a single title bar that appears at the top of the application window. The title bar indicates the application (Microsoft PowerPoint) as well as the name of the presentation (Introduction to PowerPoint) on which you are working.

A ***menu bar*** appears immediately below the title bar. The Standard and Formatting toolbars appear below the menu bar. ***Scroll bars*** appears at the right and bottom of the document window. The Windows 95 taskbar appears at the bottom of the screen and shows the open applications—Microsoft PowerPoint, Word, and Excel. The taskbar enables you to switch from one application to the next by clicking the appropriate button.

The ***status bar*** at the bottom of the application window displays information about what you are seeing and doing as you work on a presentation. It indicates the slide you are working on (e.g., Slide 1 in Figure 1.2), or it provides information about a command you have selected.

The ***view buttons*** are located to the left of the horizontal scroll bar, immediately above the Drawing toolbar, and are used to switch between the five different views of a presentation. (The Slide view is displayed in Figure 1.2.) Each view offers a different way of looking at a presentation and has unique capabilities. PowerPoint views are discussed later in the chapter.

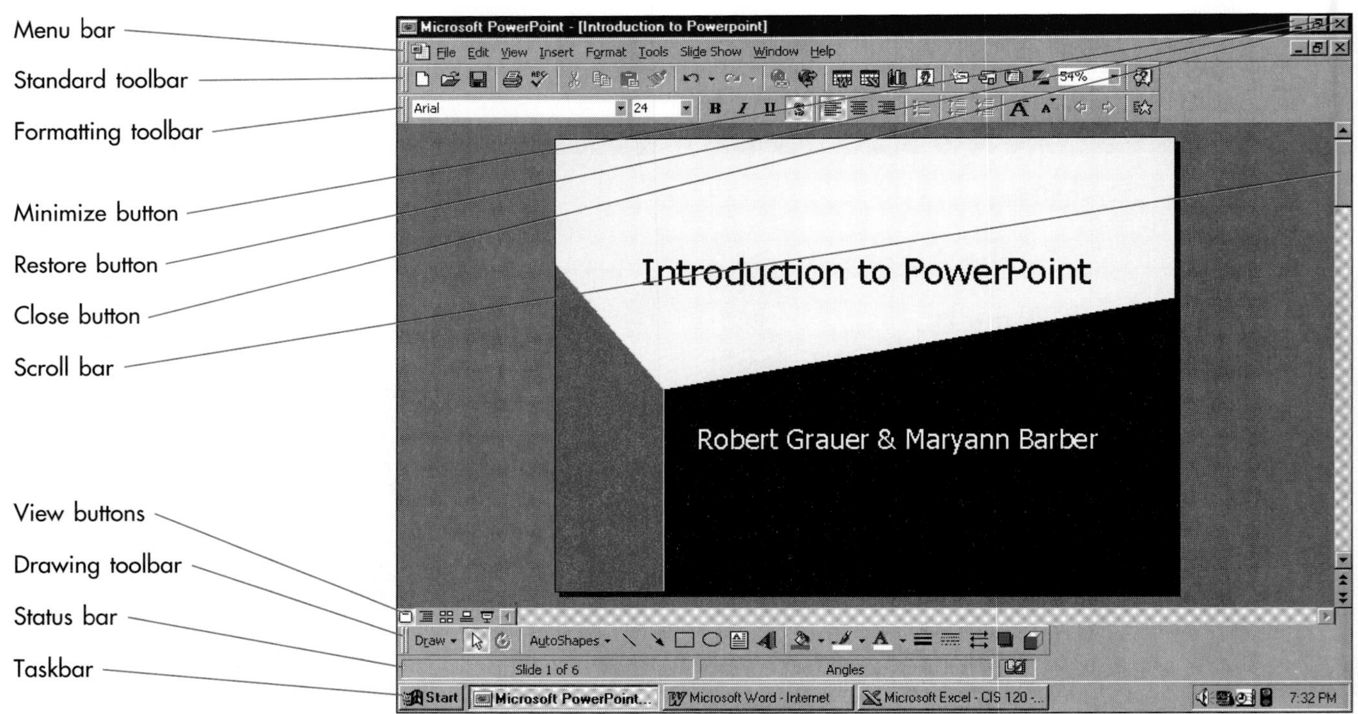

FIGURE 1.2 The PowerPoint Window

Toolbars

The Standard and Formatting toolbars are similar to those in Word and Excel, and you may recognize several buttons from those applications. The ***Standard toolbar*** appears immediately below the menu bar and contains buttons for the most basic commands in PowerPoint—for example, opening, saving, and printing a presentation. The ***Formatting toolbar,*** under the Standard toolbar, provides access to formatting operations such as boldface, italics, and underlining. The ***Drawing toolbar*** appears at the bottom of the window and contains various tools with which to modify the slide.

As with all other Microsoft applications, you can point to any button on any toolbar and PowerPoint will display the name of the button, which indicates its function. You can also gain an overall appreciation for the toolbars by considering the buttons in groups, as shown in Figure 1.3.

Remember, too, that while PowerPoint is designed for a mouse, it provides keyboard equivalents for almost every command. You may at first wonder why there are so many different ways to do the same thing, but you will come to recognize the many options as part of PowerPoint's charm. The most appropriate technique depends on personal preference, as well as the specific situation.

If, for example, your hands are already on the keyboard, it is faster to use the keyboard equivalent. Other times, your hand will be on the mouse and that will be the fastest way. It is not necessary to memorize anything, nor should you even try; just be flexible and willing to experiment. The more you do, the easier it will be!

The File Menu

The ***File menu*** is a critically important menu in virtually every Windows application. It contains the ***Save command*** to save a presentation to disk and the ***Open command*** to retrieve (open) the presentation at a later time. The File menu also contains the ***Print command*** to print a presentation, the ***Close command*** to close the current presentation but continue working in PowerPoint, and the ***Exit command*** to quit PowerPoint altogether.

The Save command copies the presentation that is currently being edited (i.e., the presentation in memory) to disk. The Save dialog box appears the first time a presentation is saved so that you can specify the file name and other required information. All subsequent executions of the Save command save the presentation under the assigned name, replacing the previously saved version with the new version.

The file name (e.g., *My First Presentation* in Figure 1.4a) can be up to 255 characters in length and may contain both spaces and commas. The Save dialog box also requires the drive (and folder) in which the file is to be saved, as well as the file type, which determines the application the file is associated with. (Long-time DOS users will remember the three-character extension at the end of a file name, such as PPT to indicate a PowerPoint presentation. The extension is generally hidden in Windows 95, according to options set through the View menu in My Computer or the Windows Explorer.

The Open command brings a copy of a previously saved presentation into memory, enabling you to show, edit, and/or print the presentation. The Open command displays the Open dialog box in which you specify the file to retrieve. You indicate the drive (and the folder) that contains the file, as well as the type of file you want to retrieve. PowerPoint will then list all files of that type on the designated drive (and folder), enabling you to open the file you want.

Starts a new document, opens an existing document, or saves the document to disk

Prints the document or checks the spelling in the document

Cuts or copies the selection to the clipboard; pastes the clipboard contents; copies the format of the selected text

Undoes or redoes a previously executed command

Inserts a hyperlink or displays the Web toolbar

Inserts a Microsoft Word table, a Microsoft Excel worksheet, a graph, or a clip art image

61%

Inserts a new slide, applies a new slide layout, applies a design template, changes the display to black and white, or changes the zoom percentage

Starts the Office Assistant

(a) Standard Toolbar

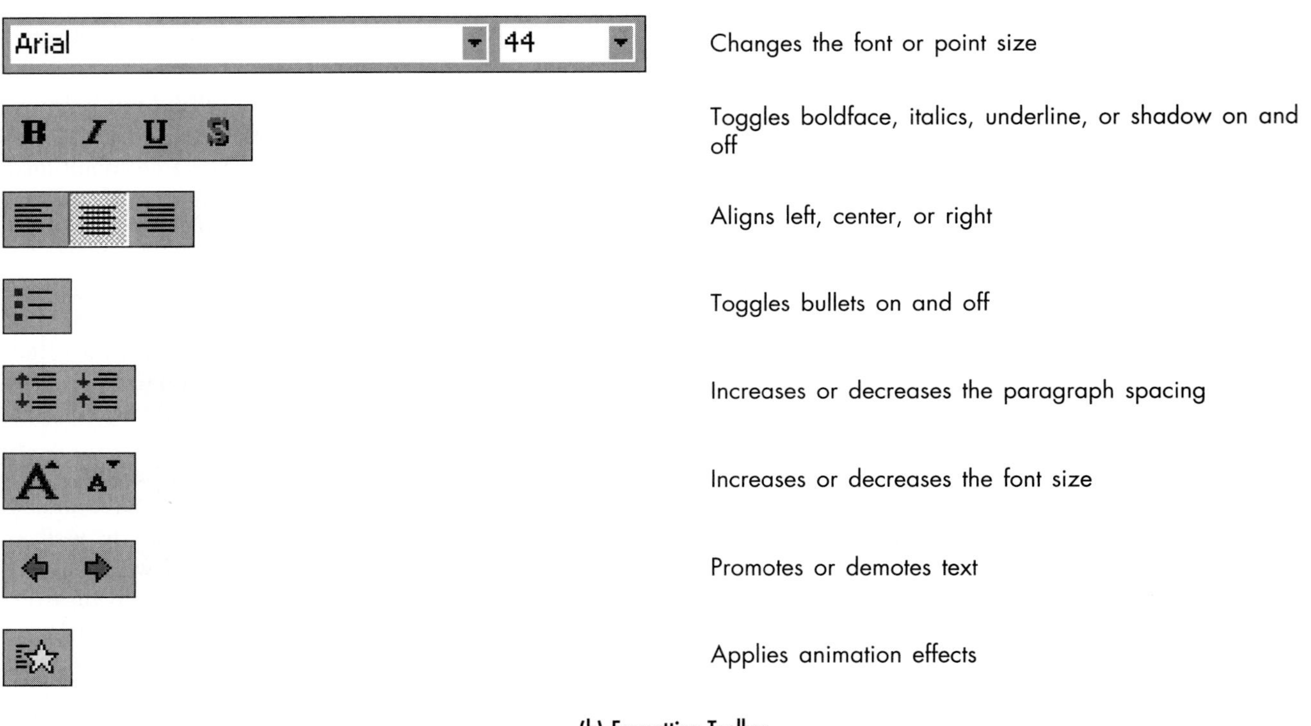

(b) Formatting Toolbar

FIGURE 1.3 Toolbars

The Save and Open commands work in conjunction with one another. The Save dialog box in Figure 1.4a, for example, saves the file *My First Presentation* onto the disk in the Exploring PowerPoint folder. The Open dialog box in Figure 1.4b brings that file back into memory so that you can work with the file, after which you can save the revised file for use at a later time.

The ***Save As*** command saves a presentation under a different name, and is useful when you want to retain a copy of the original presentation prior to making changes. The original presentation is kept on disk under its original name. A copy of the presentation is saved under a new name and remains in memory. All subsequent editing is done on the new presentation.

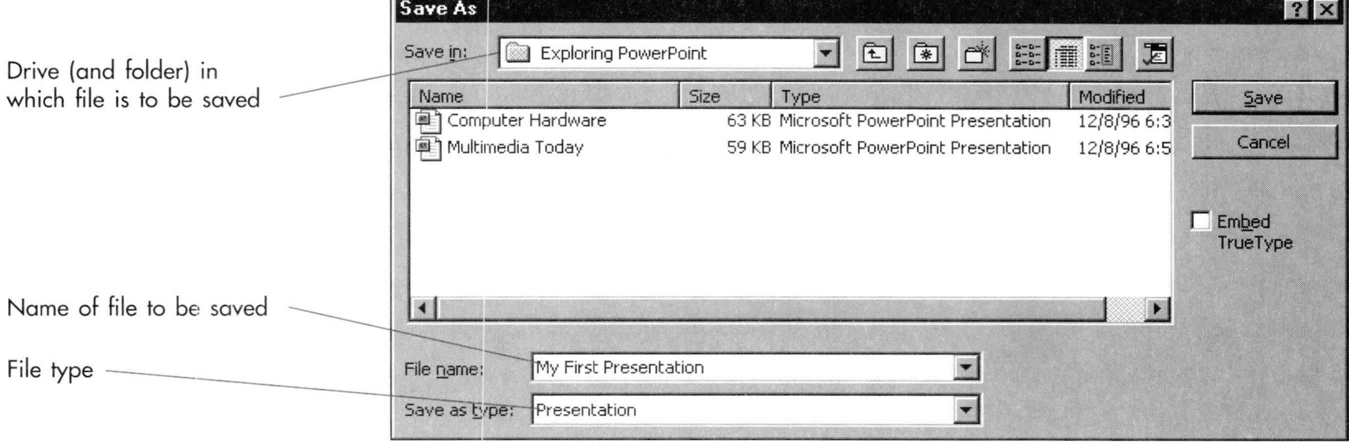

(a) File Save Dialog Box

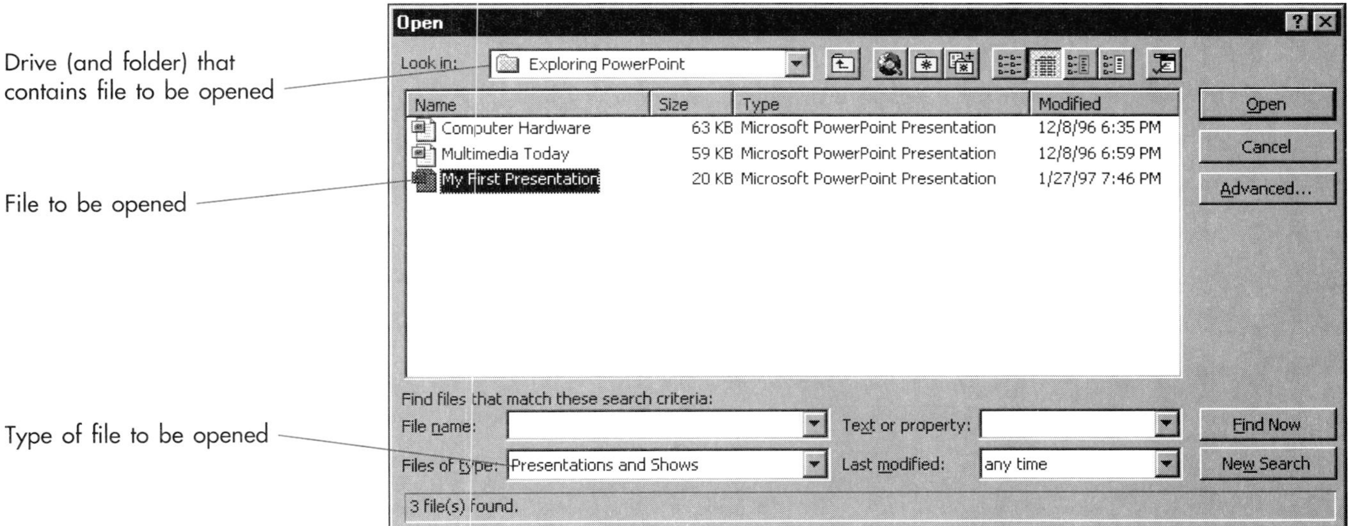

(b) File Open Dialog Box

FIGURE 1.4 The Save and Open Commands

LEARNING BY DOING

We believe strongly in learning by doing, and thus there comes a point where you must sit down at the computer if the discussion is to have real meaning. The exercise introduces you to the practice files or data disk that is available from your instructor and/or our Web site. The data disk contains the presentations referenced in the hands-on exercises throughout the text and enables you to build on the presentations we supply.

The following exercise has you open the presentation that was shown earlier in Figure 1.1. The exercise has you change the title slide to include your name, then directs you to view the presentation on the computer and to print the corresponding audience handouts. It's fun, it's easy, and it will give you a better appreciation for PowerPoint.

HANDS-ON EXERCISE 1

Introduction to PowerPoint

Objective: To start PowerPoint, open an existing presentation, and modify the text on an existing slide. To show an existing presentation and print handouts of its slides. Use Figure 1.5 as a guide in the exercise.

STEP 1: Welcome to Windows

- Turn on the computer and all of its peripherals. The floppy drive should be empty prior to starting your machine. This ensures that the system starts by reading from the hard disk, which contains the Windows files, as opposed to a floppy disk, which does not.
- Your system will take a minute or so to get started, after which you should see the desktop in Figure 1.5a. Do not be concerned if the appearance of your desktop is different from ours.
- You may see additional objects on the desktop in Windows 95 and/or the active desktop content in Windows 97. It doesn't matter which operating system you are using because Office 97 runs equally well under both Windows 95 and Windows 97 (as well as Windows NT).
- You may see a Welcome to Windows 95/Windows 97 dialog box with command buttons to take a tour of the operating system. If so, click the appropriate button(s) or close the dialog box.

TAKE THE WINDOWS 95 TOUR

Windows 95 may greet you with a Welcome window that contains a command button to take you on a 10-minute tour. Click the command button and enjoy the show. If you do not see the Welcome window when you start Windows 95, click the Start button, click Run, type WELCOME in the Open text box, and press enter. Windows 97 was not available when we went to press, but we expect it to have a similar option.

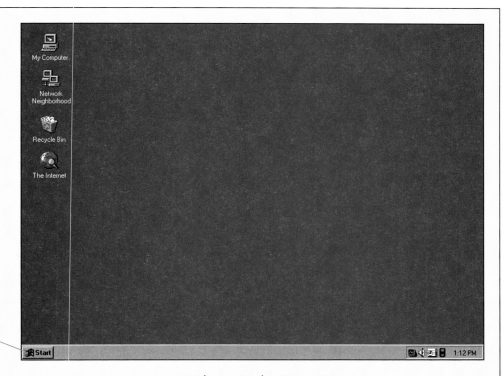

Click the Start button

(a) Welcome to Windows 95 (step 1)

FIGURE 1.5 Hands-on Exercise 1

STEP 2: Obtain the Practice Files

➤ We have created a series of practice files for you to use throughout the text. Your instructor will make these files available to you in a variety of ways:

- You can download the files from our Web site if you have access to the Internet and World Wide Web (see boxed tip).
- The files may be on a network drive, in which case you use the Windows Explorer to copy the files from the network to a floppy disk.
- There may be an actual "data disk" that you are to check out from the lab in order to use the Copy Disk command to duplicate the disk

➤ Check with your instructor for additional information.

DOWNLOAD THE PRACTICE FILES

You can download the practice files for any book in the *Exploring Windows* series from Bob Grauer's home page (www.bus.miami.edu/~rgrauer). Use any Web browser to get to Bob's page, then click the link to the *Exploring Windows* series where you choose the appropriate book and download the file. Be sure to read the associated "read me" file, which provides additional information about downloading the file.

STEP 3: Start PowerPoint

- Click the **Start button** to display the Start menu. Slide the mouse pointer over the various menu options and notice that each time you point to a submenu, its items are displayed; i.e., you can point rather than click a submenu.
- Point to (or click) the **Programs menu,** then click **Microsoft PowerPoint** to start the program and display the screen in Figure 1.2b. Close the Office Assistant if it appears.
- Click the **option button** to **Open an Existing Presentation,** the click **OK.** (If you do not see the PowerPoint dialog box, pull down the **File menu** and click **Open,** or click the **Open button** on the Standard toolbar.)

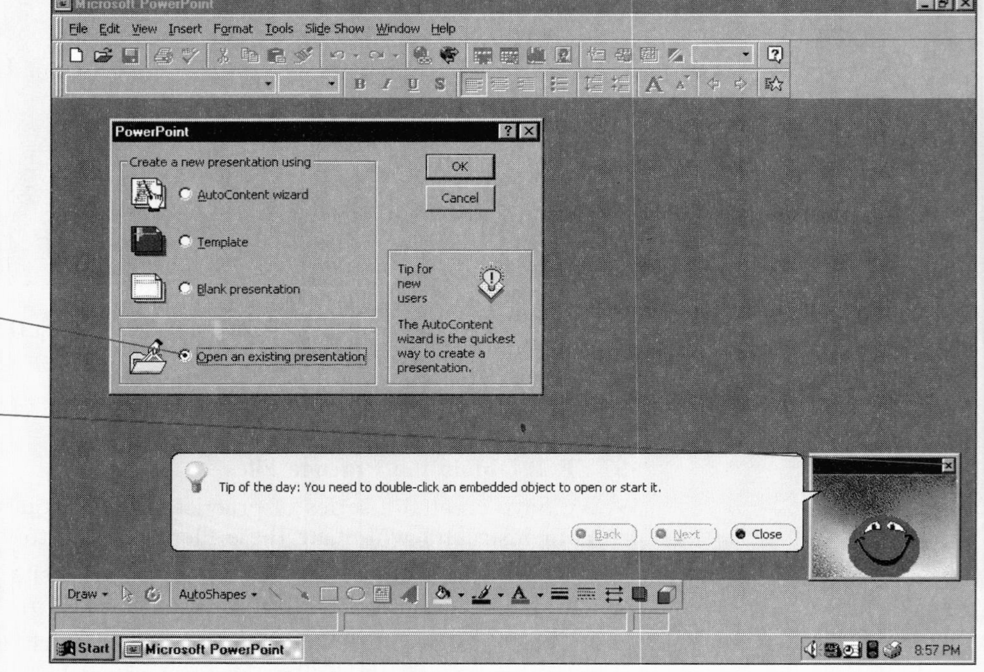

(b) Start PowerPoint (step 3)

FIGURE 1.5 Hands-on Exercise 1 (continued)

CHOOSE YOUR OWN ASSISTANT

You can choose your own personal assistant from one of several available images. Click the Office Assistant button on the Standard toolbar to display the Assistant, click the options button to display the Office Assistant dialog box, click the Gallery tab, then click the Next button repeatedly to cycle through the available images. Click OK to select the image and close the dialog box.

STEP 4: Open a Presentation

- You should see an Open dialog box similar to the one in Figure 1.5c. Click the **Details button** to change to the Details view. If necessary, click and drag the vertical border between columns to increase (or decrease) the size of a column.
- Click the **drop-down arrow** on the Look In list box. Click the appropriate drive, drive C or drive A, depending on the location of your data. Double click the **Exploring PowerPoint folder** to make it the active folder (the folder from which you will retrieve and into which you will save the presentation).
- Click **Introduction to PowerPoint** to select the presentation. Click the **Open button** to open the presentation and begin the exercise.

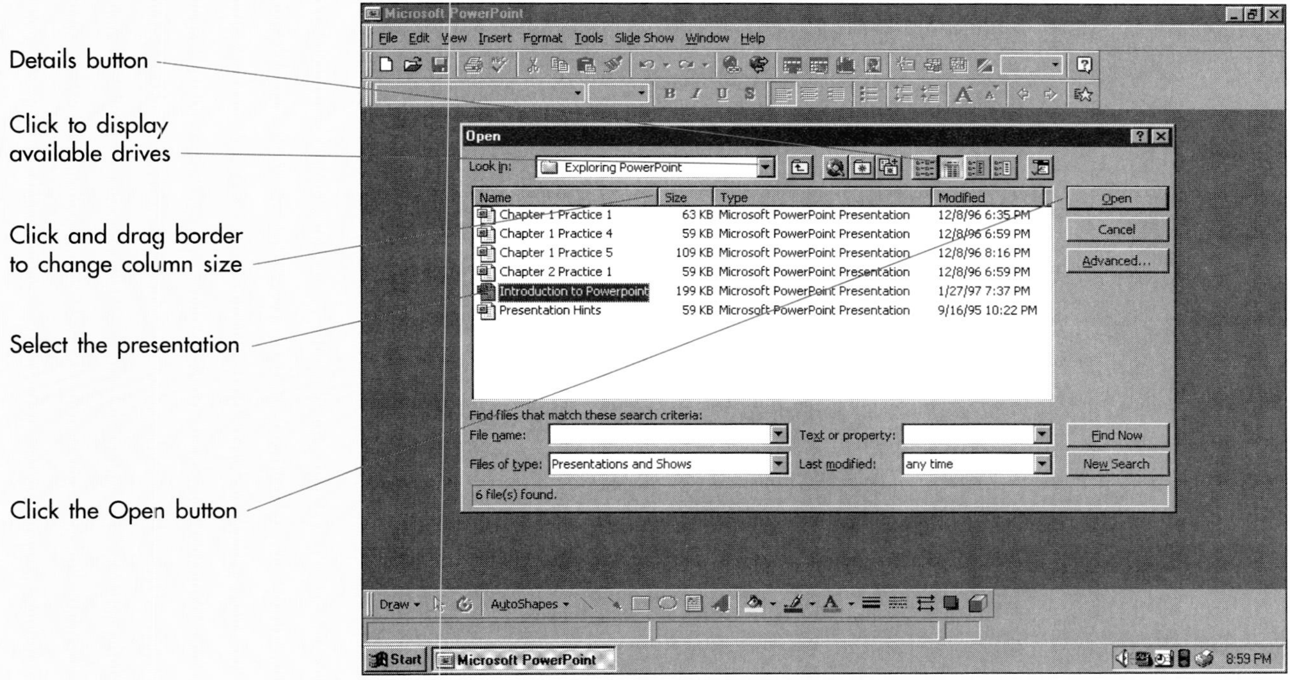

(c) Open an Existing Presentation (step 4)

FIGURE 1.5 Hands-on Exercise 1 (continued)

A VERY USEFUL TOOLBAR

The Open and Save dialog boxes display similar toolbars with several common buttons. Click the Details button to switch to the Details view and see the date and time the file was last modified, as well as its size. Click the List button to display an icon for each file, enabling you to see many more files at the same time than in the Details view. The Properties button displays information about the presentation, including the author's name and number of revisions.

STEP 5: The Save As Command

- If necessary, click the **Maximize button** in the application window so that PowerPoint takes the entire desktop. Click the **Maximize button** in the document window (if necessary) so that the document window is as large as possible.
- Pull down the **File menu.** Click **Save As** to display the dialog box shown in Figure 1.5d. Enter **Finished Introduction** as the name of the new presentation. (A file name may contain up to 255 characters; blanks are permitted.)
- Click the **Save button.** Press the **Esc key** or click the **Close button** if you see a Properties dialog box.

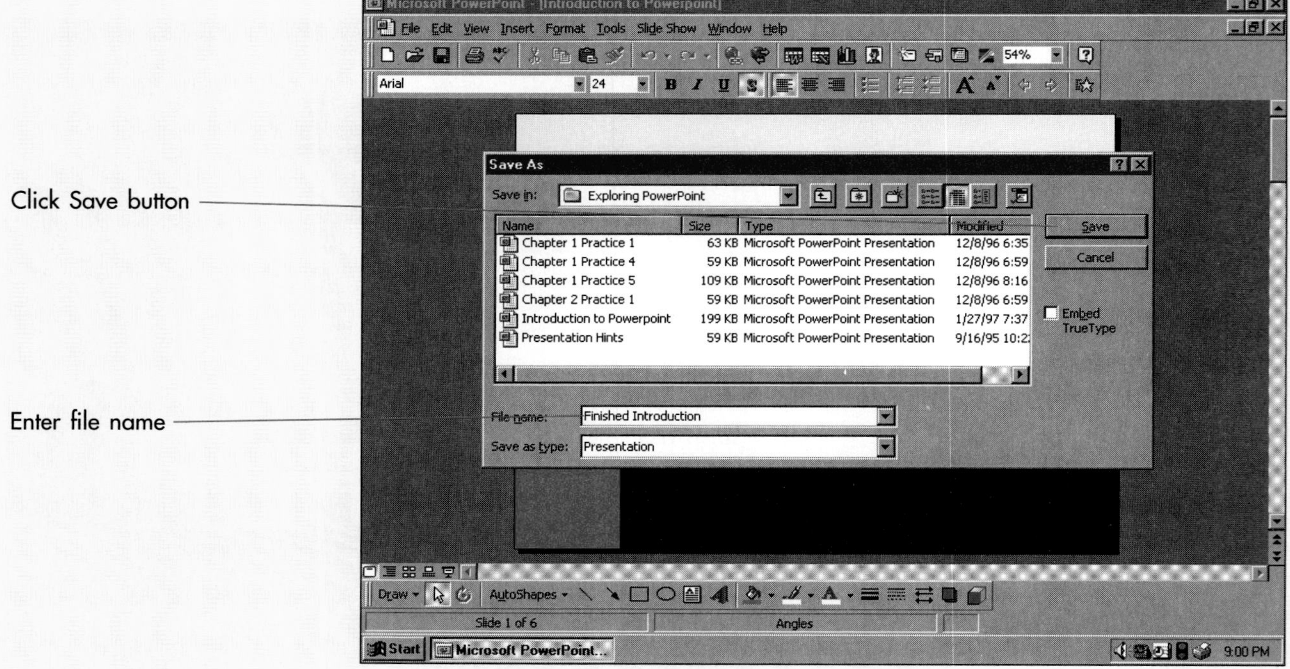

(d) The Save As Command (step 5)

FIGURE 1.5 Hands-on Exercise 1 (continued)

DIFFERENT FILE TYPES

The file format for PowerPoint 97 is incompatible with the format for PowerPoint 95. The newer release (PowerPoint 97) can open a presentation created in its predecessor (PowerPoint 95), but the reverse is not possible; that is, you cannot open a presentation created in PowerPoint 97 in PowerPoint 95. You can, however, use the Save As command in PowerPoint 97 to specify the PowerPoint 95 file type, enabling you to create a presentation in the new release and read it in the old (although you will lose any formatting unique to PowerPoint 97).

- There are now two identical copies of the file on disk: "Introduction to PowerPoint," which is the original presentation that we supplied, and "Finished Introduction," which you just created. The title bar shows the latter name, as it is the presentation currently in memory.

STEP 6: Modify a Slide

- Press and hold the left mouse button as you drag the mouse over the presenters' names (Robert Grauer and Maryann Barber). Release the mouse.
- The names should be highlighted (selected) as shown in Figure 1.5e. The selected text is the text that will be affected by the next command.
- Type your name, which automatically replaces the selected text. Click outside the placeholder to deselect it.

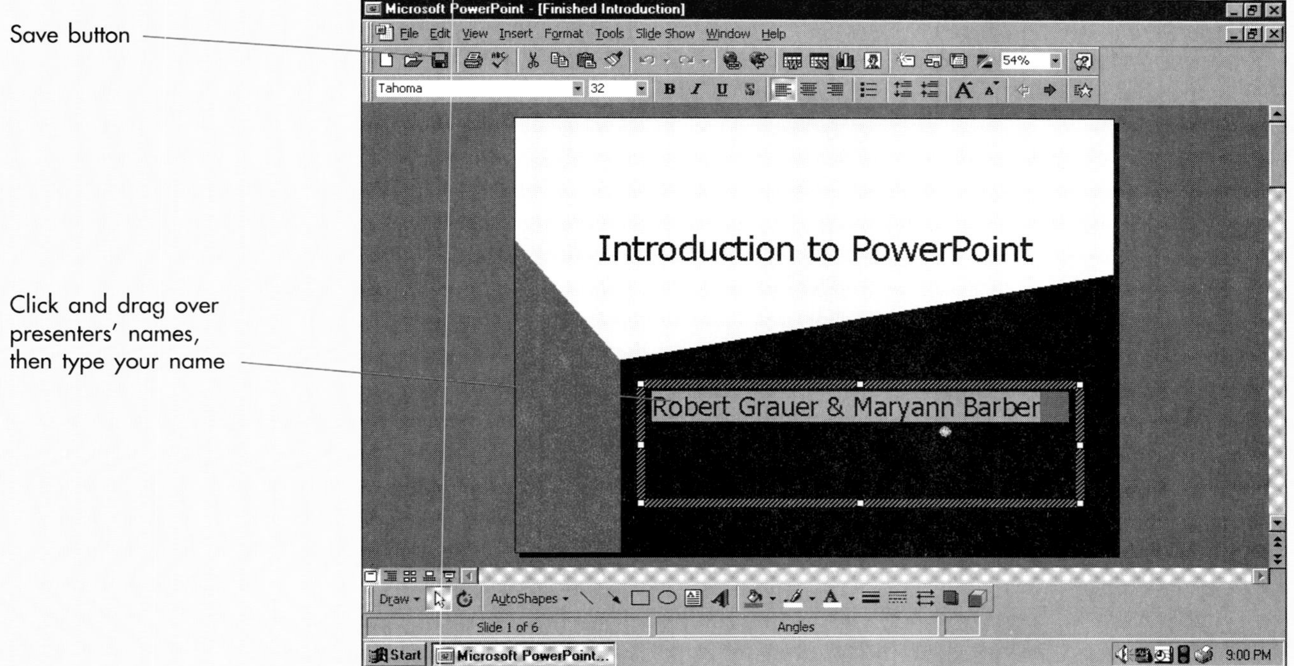

(e) Modify a Slide (step 6)

FIGURE 1.5 Hands-on Exercise 1 (continued)

THE AUTOMATIC SPELL CHECK

A red wavy line under a word indicates that the word is misspelled, or in the case of a proper name, that the word is spelled correctly but is not in the dictionary. In either event, point to the underlined word and click the right mouse button to display a shortcut menu. Select the appropriate spelling from the list of suggestions, ignore it, or add the word to the supplementary dictionary. To enable (disable) the automatic spell check, pull down the Tools menu, click the Options command, click the Spelling tab, then check (clear) the option to check spelling as you type.

STEP 7: The Office Assistant

- Click the **Office Assistant button** on the Standard toolbar to display the Office Assistant. (You may see a different character than the one we have selected.)
- Enter your question—for example, **How do I show a presentation?**—as shown in Figure 1.5f, then click the **Search button** to look for the answer.
- The size of the balloon expands as the Assistant suggests several topics that may be appropriate to answer your question.
- Select the topic, **Start a slide show**, which in turn displays a help screen with detailed information. Read the help screen, then close the Help Window.
- Close the Office Assistant.

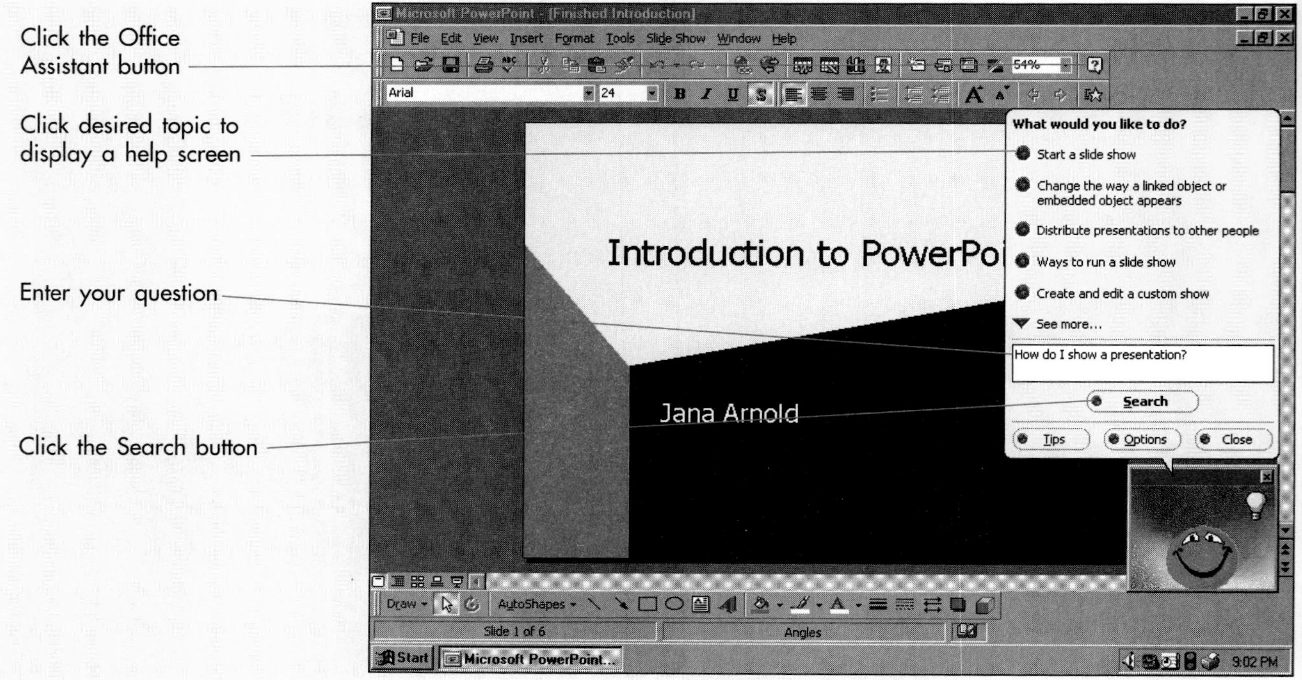

(f) The Office Assistant (step 7)

FIGURE 1.5 Hands-on Exercise 1 (continued)

TIP OF THE DAY

You can set the Office Assistant to greet you with a "Tip of the Day" whenever you start PowerPoint. If the Office Assistant is not visible, click the Office Assistant button on the Standard toolbar to start the Assistant, then click the Options button to display the Office Assistant dialog box. Click the Options tab, check the Show the Tip of the Day at startup box, then click OK. The next time you start PowerPoint, you will be greeted by the Assistant who will offer you a tip of the day.

STEP 8: Show the Presentation

- Pull down the **View menu** and click **Slide Show.**
- The presentation will begin with the first slide as shown in Figure 1.5g. You should see your name on the slide because of the modification you made in the previous step.
- Click the mouse to move to the second slide, which comes into the presentation from the left side of your monitor. (This is one of several transition effects available to add interest to a presentation.) Click the mouse again to move to the next (third) slide, which also comes in from the top of the screen.
- Continue to view the show until you come to the end of the presentation:
  - You can press the **Esc key** at any time to cancel the show and return to the PowerPoint window.
  - The last slide (Animate the Presentation) utilizes a build effect, which requires you to continue to click the mouse as you display each bullet.
- Click the left mouse button a final time to return to the regular PowerPoint window.

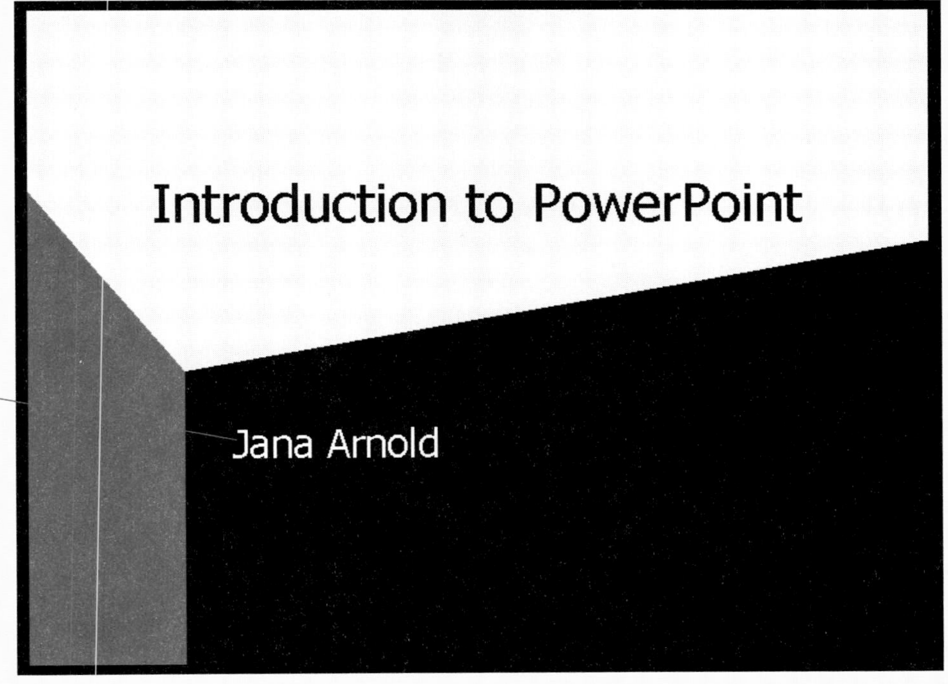

(g) Print the Presentation (step 8)

FIGURE 1.5 Hands-on Exercise 1 (continued)

STEP 9: Print the Presentation

- Pull down the **File menu.** Click **Print** to display the Print dialog box in Figure 1.5h.
  - Click the **down arrow** in the **Print What** drop-down list box.

- Scroll to, then click **Handouts (6 slides per page)** as shown in Figure 1.5h.
- Check the box to **Frame Slides.**
- Check that the **All option button** is selected under Print range.

➤ Click the **OK command button** to print the handouts for the presentation.

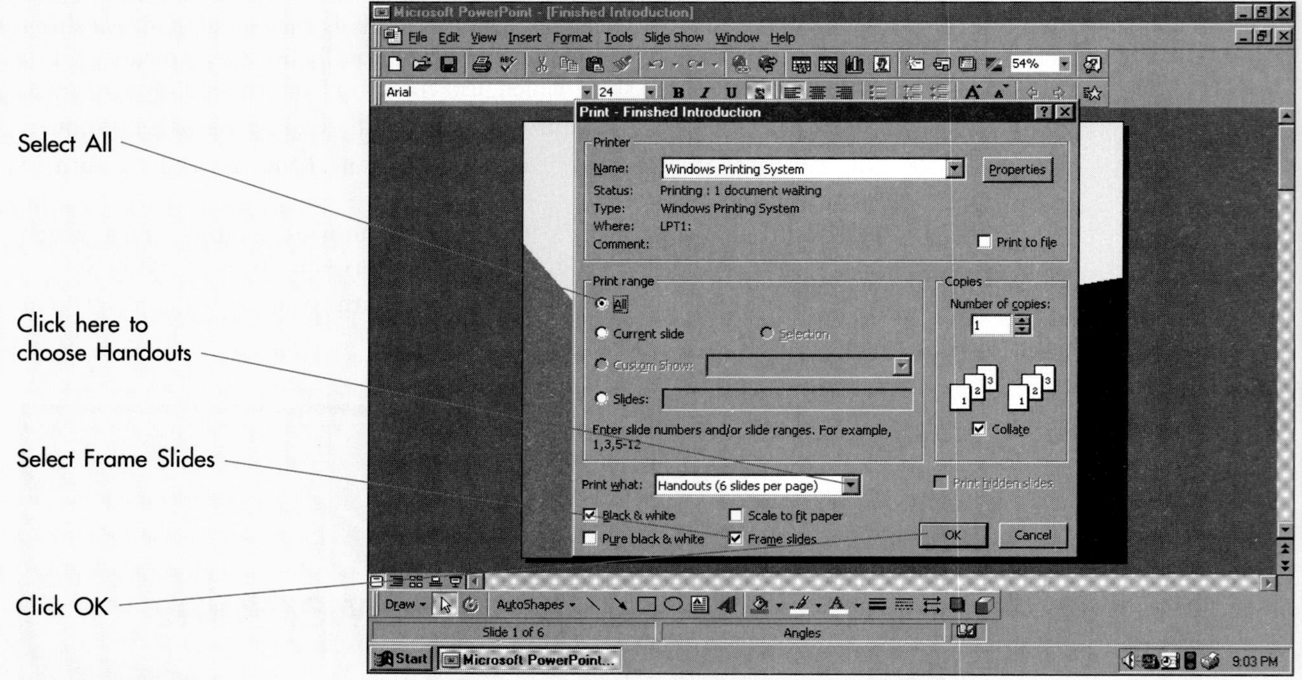

(h) Print the Presentation (step 9)

FIGURE 1.5 Hands-on Exercise 1 (continued)

THE COMMON USER INTERFACE

One of the most significant benefits of the Windows environment is the common user interface, which provides a sense of familiarity when you begin to learn a new application. In other words, once you know one Windows application, it will be that much easier for you to learn PowerPoint, because all applications work basically the same way. The benefits are magnified if you use other applications in Microsoft Office. Indeed, if you use either Word or Excel, you already know more than 100 commands in PowerPoint.

STEP 10: Exit PowerPoint

➤ Pull down the **File menu.** Click **Close** to close the presentation but remain in PowerPoint. Click **Yes** if asked whether to save the changes.

➤ Pull down the **File menu.** Click **Exit** to exit PowerPoint if you do not want to continue with the next exercise at this time.

FIVE DIFFERENT VIEWS

PowerPoint offers five different views in which to create, modify, and show a presentation. Figure 1.6 shows the five views for the introductory presentation from the first exercise. Each view represents a different way of looking at the presentation, and each view has unique capabilities. Some views display only a single slide, whereas others show multiple slides, making it easy to organize the presentation. You can switch back and forth between the views by clicking the appropriate view button at the bottom of the presentation window.

The ***Slide view*** in Figure 1.6a displays one slide at a time and enables all operations for that slide. You can enter, delete, or format text. You can draw or add objects such as a graph, clip art, or an organization chart. The ***Drawing Toolbar*** is displayed by default in this view.

The ***Slide Sorter view*** in Figure 1.6b displays multiple slides on the screen (each slide is in miniature) and lets you see the overall flow of the presentation. You can change the order of a presentation by clicking and dragging a slide from one position to another. You can delete a slide by clicking the slide and pressing the Del key. You can also set transition and/or animation effects on each slide to add interest to the presentation. The Slide Sorter view has its own toolbar, which is discussed in Chapter 2 in conjunction with creating animation effects.

The ***Outline view*** in Figure 1.6c shows the presentation in outline form. You can see all of the text on every slide, but you cannot see the graphic elements that may be present on the individual slides. You can, however, open a ***slide miniature*** to see the current slide within the Outline view.) The Outline view is the fastest way to enter or edit text, in that you type directly into the outline. You can copy and/or move text from one slide to another. You can also rearrange the order of the slides within the presentation. The Outline view has its own toolbar and is discussed more fully in Chapter 2.

The ***Notes Page view*** in Figure 1.6d lets you create speaker's notes for some or all of the slides in a presentation. These notes do not appear when you show the presentation, but can be printed prior to the presentation to help you remember what you want to say about each slide.

The ***Slide Show view*** displays the slides one at a time as an electronic presentation on the computer. The show may be presented manually, where you click the mouse to move from one slide to the next. The presentation can also be shown automatically, where each slide stays on the screen for a predetermined amount of time, after which the next slide appears automatically. Either way, the slide show may contain transition effects from one slide to the next as was demonstrated in the first hands-on exercise.

The easiest way to switch from one view to another is by clicking the appropriate view button. The buttons are displayed in the lower-left part of the screen (above the status bar) in all views except the Slide Show view.

POWERPOINT VIEWS

PowerPoint has five different views of a presentation, each with unique capabilities. Anything you do in one view is automatically reflected in the other views. If, for example, you rearrange the slides in the Slide Sorter view, the new arrangement is reflected in the Outline view. In similar fashion, if you add or format text in the Outline view, the changes are also made in the Slide view.

Drawing toolbar

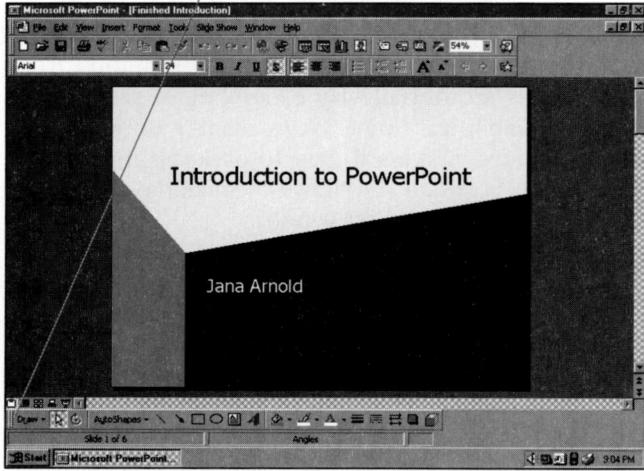

(a) Slide View

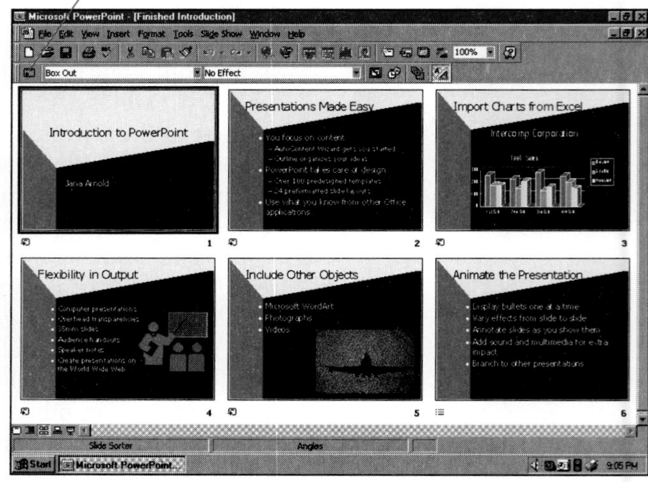

(b) Slide Sorter View

Outline toolbar

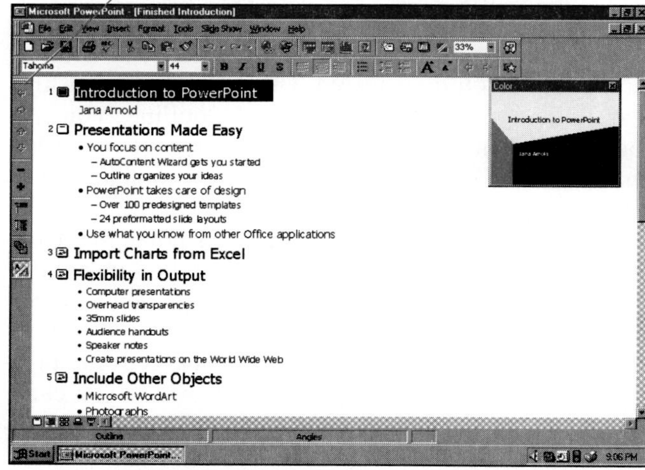

(c) Outline View

Enter notes for speaker

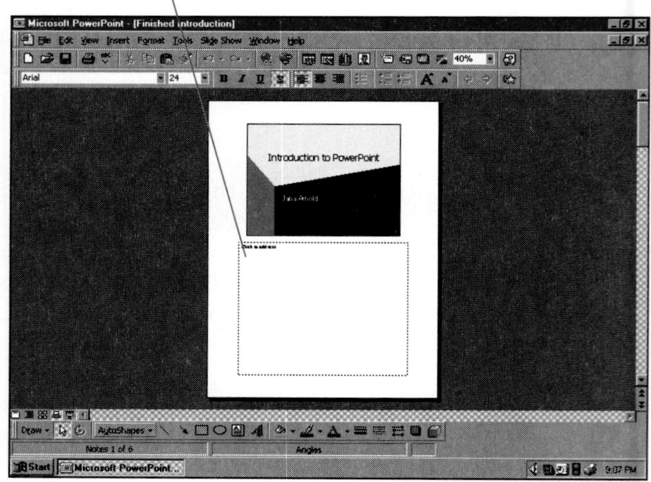

(d) Notes Page View

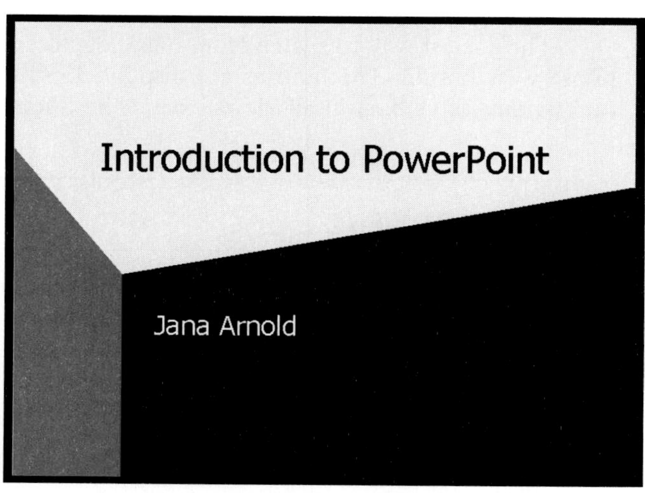

(e) Slide Show View

FIGURE 1.6 PowerPoint Views

Slides are added to a presentation by using one of 24 predefined slide formats known as ***AutoLayouts.*** Pull down the Insert menu and click the ***New Slide command*** to display the dialog box in Figure 1.7a, then choose the type of slide you want. (The slide will be added to the presentation immediately after the current slide.)

Figure 1.7a depicts the addition of a bulleted slide with ***clip art.*** The user chooses the desired layout, then clicks the OK command button to switch to the slide view in Figure 1.7b. The AutoLayout contains ***placeholders*** for the various

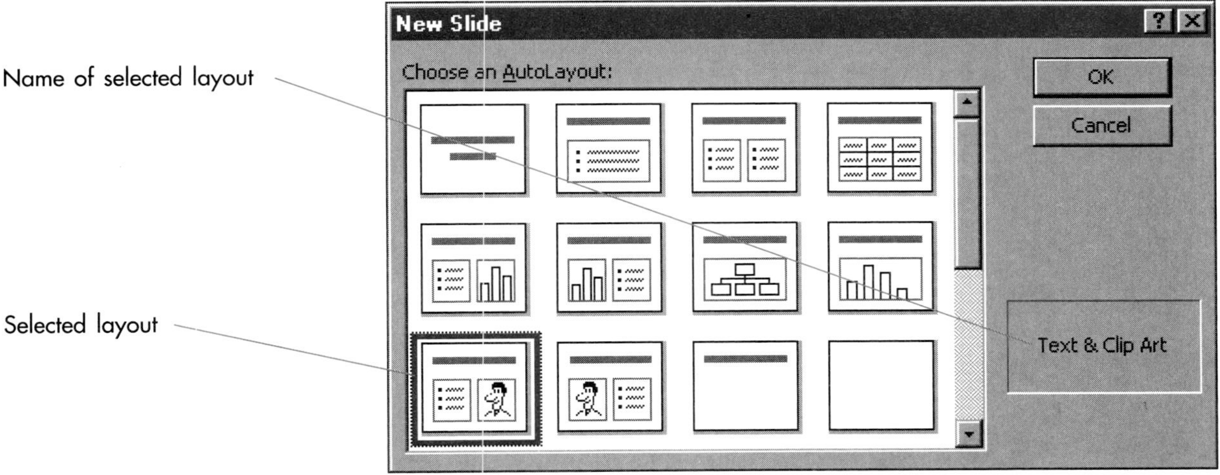

(a) AutoLayout

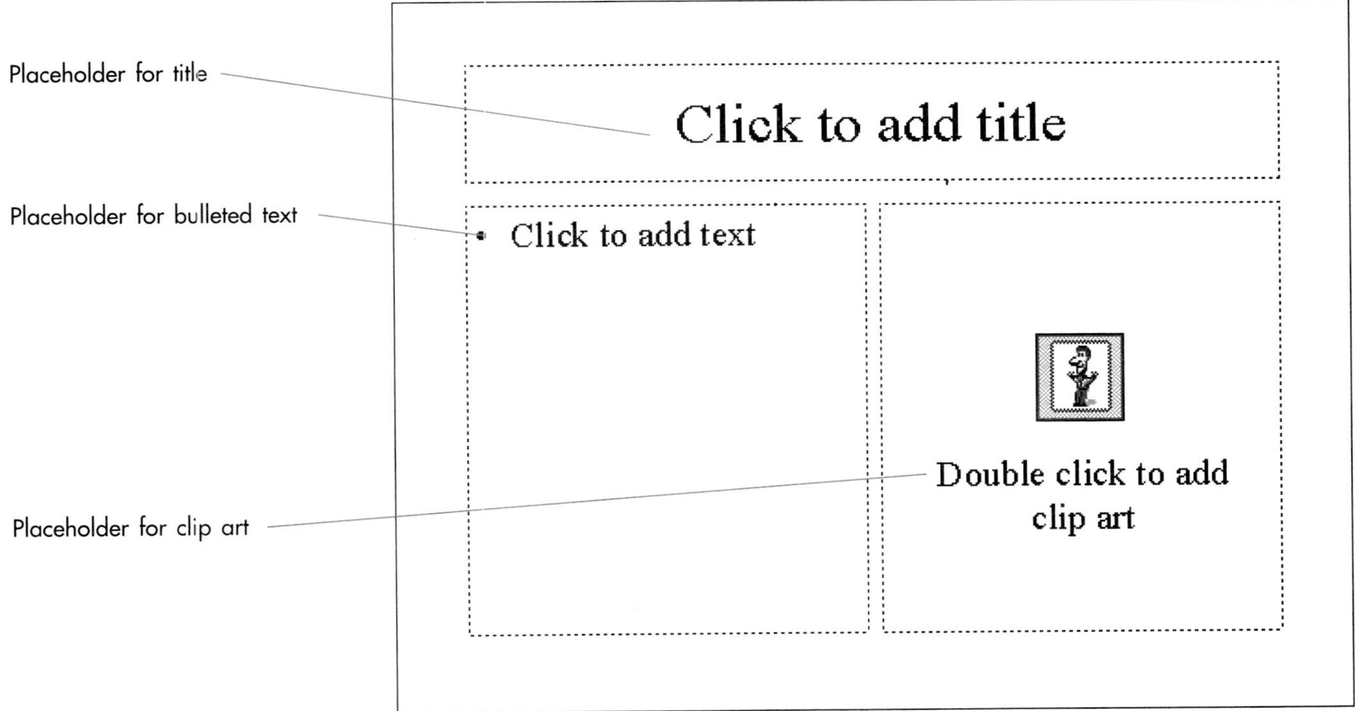

(b) Placeholders

FIGURE 1.7 Adding a Slide

objects on the slide to position them properly. There are three placeholders in Figure 1.7b—one for the title, one for the bulleted text, and one for the clip art. Just follow the directions on the slide by clicking the appropriate placeholder to add the title or text, or double clicking to add the clip art. It's that easy, as you will see in the exercise that follows shortly.

You can delete a slide from any view except the Slide Show view. To delete a slide from the Slide or Notes Page view, select the slide by making it the current slide, pull down the Edit menu, and choose the Delete Slide command. To delete a slide from the Slide Sorter or Outline view, select the slide, then press the Del key.

HANDS-ON EXERCISE 2

PowerPoint Views

Objective: To switch between the different views while modifying a presentation; to use the Microsoft Clip Gallery and add clip art to a slide; to add a slide to an existing presentation. Use Figure 1.8 as a guide in the exercise.

STEP 1: Add a New Slide

- ➤ Start PowerPoint. Follow the instructions from step 4 in the previous exercise to open the **Finished Introduction** presentation.
- ➤ Pull down the **Insert menu** and click **New slide** (or click the **New Slide button** on the Standard toolbar). You will see the New Slide dialog box in Figure 1.8a.

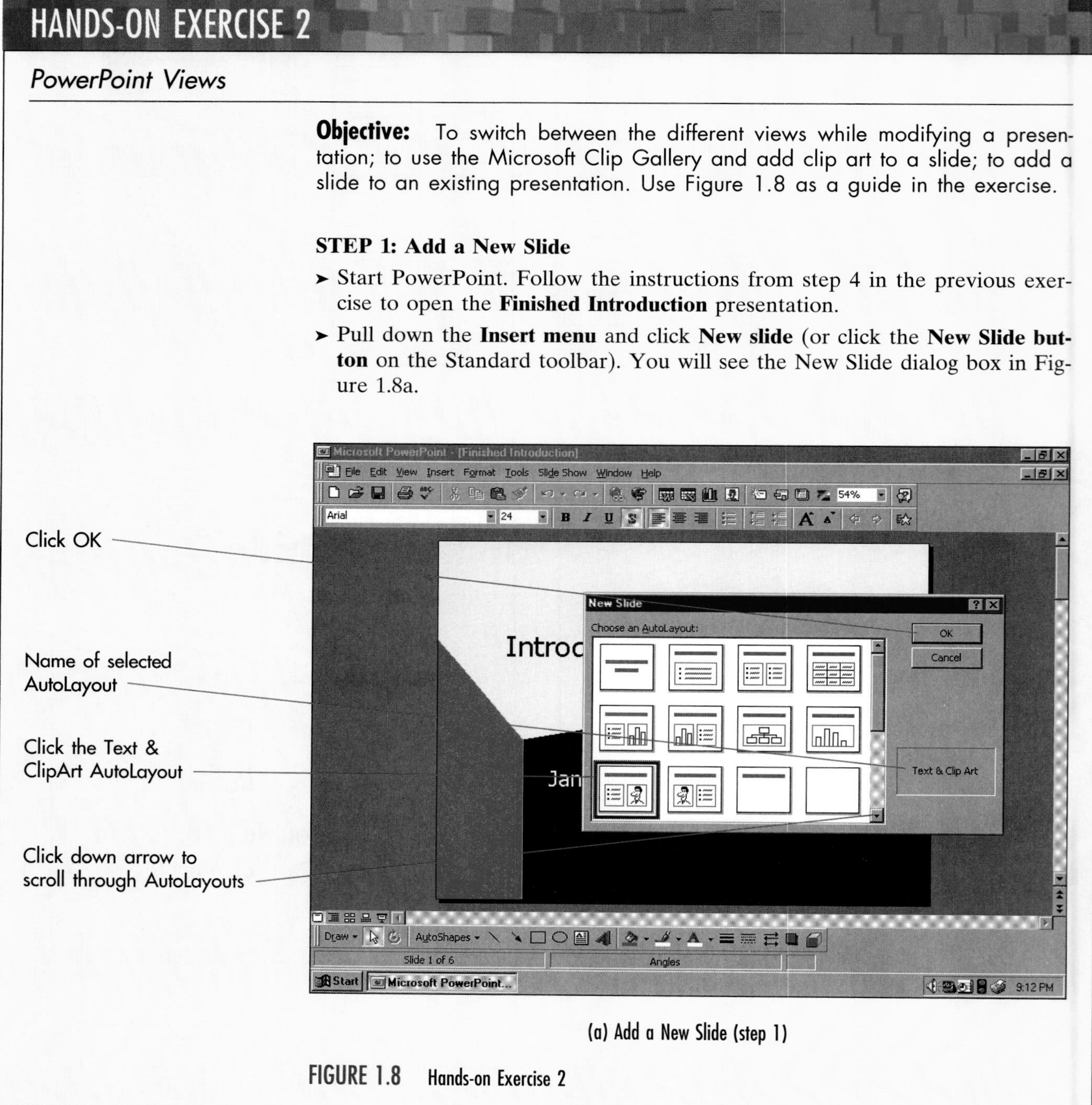

(a) Add a New Slide (step 1)

FIGURE 1.8 Hands-on Exercise 2

- Click the **down arrow** on the vertical scroll bar to scroll through AutoLayouts within PowerPoint.
- Select (click) the **Text & Clip Art layout** as shown in the figure. (The name of the selected layout appears in the lower-right corner of the dialog box.) Click the **OK command button.**

THE MOST RECENTLY OPENED FILE LIST

The easiest way to open a recently used presentation is to select the presentation directly from the File menu. Pull down the File menu, but instead of clicking the Open command, check to see if the presentation appears on the list of the most recently opened presentations located at the bottom of the menu. If so, you can click the presentation name rather than having to make the appropriate selections through the Open dialog box.

STEP 2: Click Here

- Click the **placeholder** where it says **Click to add title** in Figure 1.8b. Type **The Microsoft Clip Gallery** as the title of the slide.
- Click the **placeholder** where it indicates **Click to add text.** Type **Choose from many different categories** as the first bullet. Press **enter** to move to the next bullet.

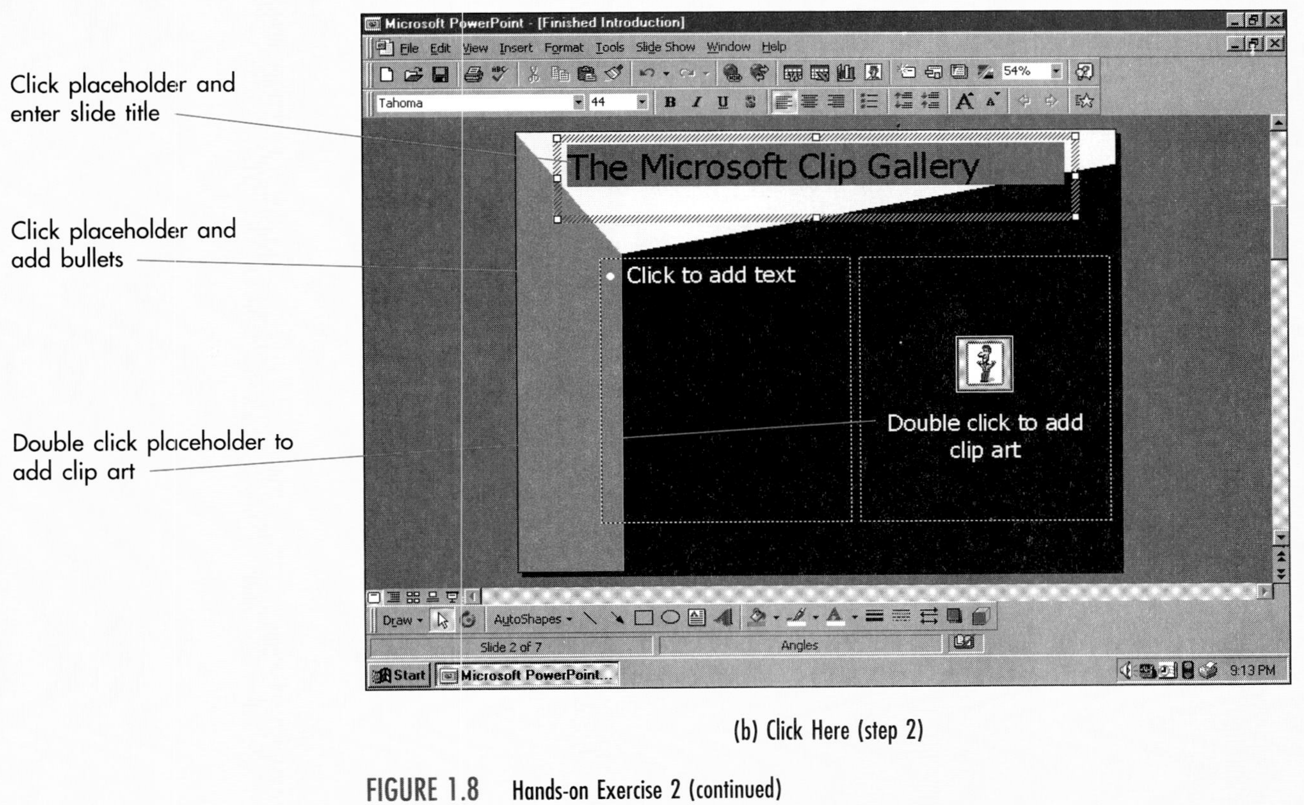

(b) Click Here (step 2)

FIGURE 1.8 Hands-on Exercise 2 (continued)

- Press **Tab** to indent the next bullet one level. Type **Cartoons.** Press **enter** to move to the next bullet.
- You do *not* have to press the Tab key because PowerPoint automatically aligns each succeeding bullet under the previous bullet. Type **Maps.** Press **enter** to move to the next bullet.
- Type **People.** Press **enter** to move to the next bullet.

➤ Press **Shift+Tab** to move the new bullet one level to the left. Enter **ValuPack on CD contains more than 3,000 images** as the final bullet. Do *not* press the enter key or else you will create another bullet.

BULLETS AND THE TAB (SHIFT+TAB) KEY

Bullets are entered one after another simply by typing the text of a bullet and pressing the enter key. A new bullet appears automatically under the previous bullet. Press the Tab key to indent the new bullet or press Shift+Tab to move the bullet back one level to the left.

STEP 3: Add Clip Art

➤ Double click the **placeholder** for the **clip art.** You will see the Clip Gallery dialog box shown in Figure 1.8c (although you may not see all of the categories listed in the figure).

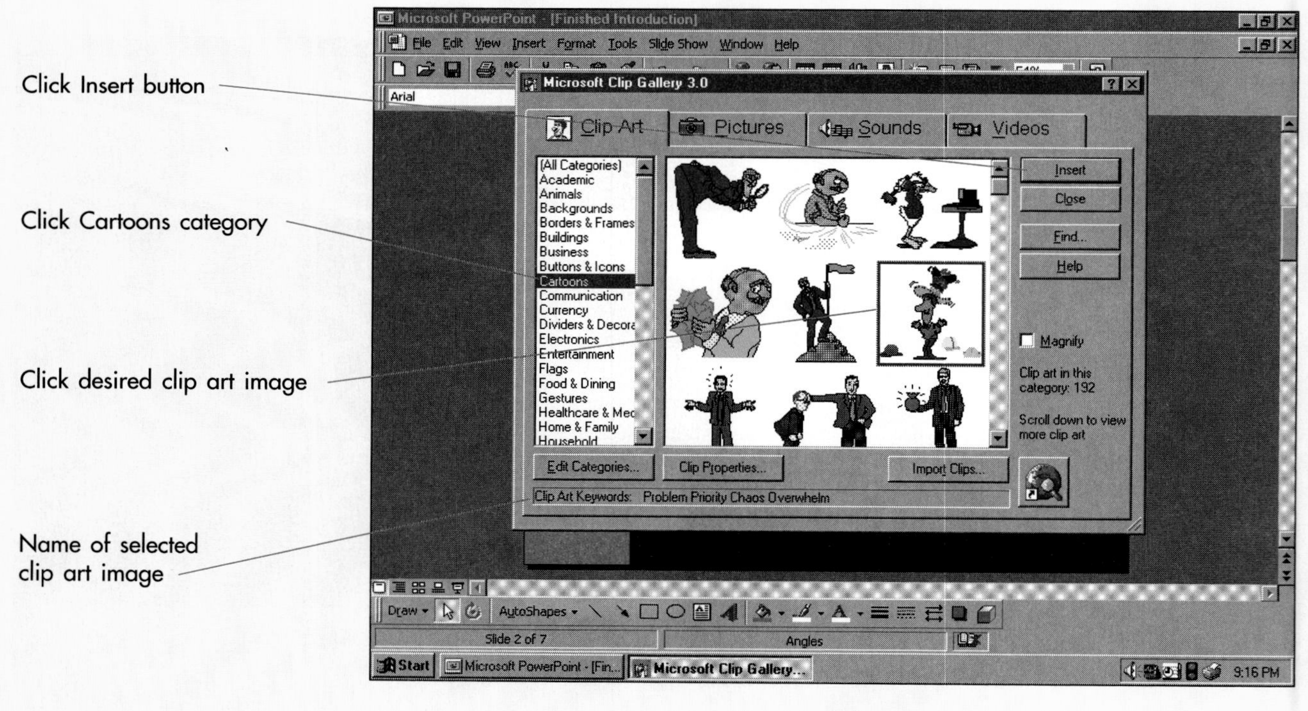

(c) The ClipArt Gallery (step 3)

FIGURE 1.8 Hands-on Exercise 2 (continued)

- ➤ Click the **ClickArt tab.** Click the **Cartoons** ategory. If necessary, click the **down arrow** on the scroll bar to scroll through the available cartoons until you see the image you want.
- ➤ Select (click) the **Problem Priority** cartoon as shown in Figure 1.8c. Click the **Insert button** to insert the clip art onto the slide.

ADDITIONAL CLIP ART

The Microsoft Clip Gallery contains over 100MB of data consisting of more than 3,000 clip art images, 144 photographs, 28 sounds, and 20 video clips. Only a fraction of these are installed with Microsoft Office, but you can access the additional objects from the Office CD at any time. You can also install some or all of the objects on your hard disk, provided you have sufficient space. Start the Windows Explorer, then open the ClipArt folder on the Office CD. Double click the Setup icon to start the Setup Wizard, then follow the on-screen instructions to install the additional components you want.

STEP 4: Select-Then-Do

- ➤ You should see the completed slide in Figure 1.8d. Click and drag to select the number 3,000.
  - Click the **Bold button** on the Formatting toolbar to boldface the selected text.

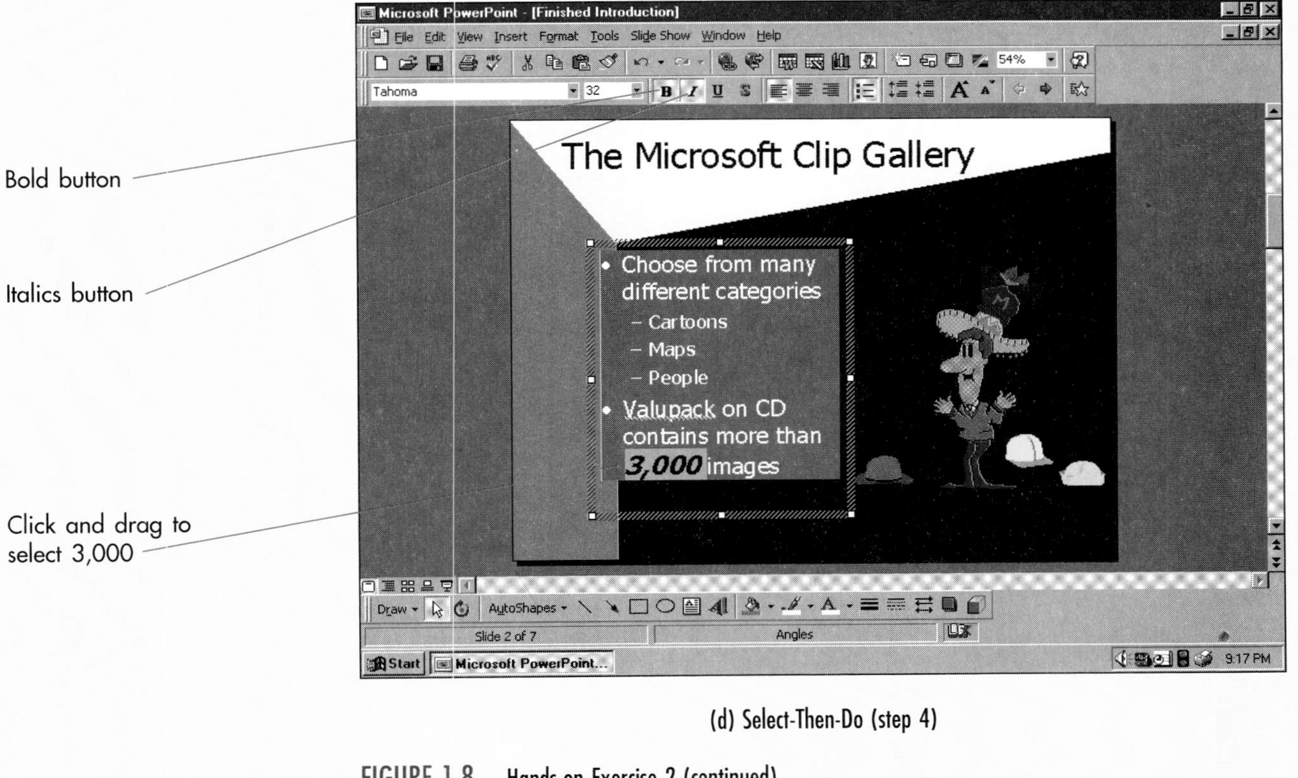

(d) Select-Then-Do (step 4)

FIGURE 1.8 Hands-on Exercise 2 (continued)

- Click the **Italic button** on the Formatting toolbar to italicize the selected text.
- Click the **Increase font size button** on the Formatting toolbar to increase the size of the selected text.

➤ Click outside the text area to deselect the text to see the results. Save the presentation.

SELECT-THEN-DO

All editing and formatting operations take place within the context of select-then-do; that is, you select a block of text, then you execute the command to operate on that text. Selected text is affected by any subsequent operation; for example, clicking the Boldface or Italic button changes the selected text to boldface or italics, respectively. In similar fashion, pressing the Del key deletes the selected text. And finally, the fastest way to replace existing text is to select the text, then type a new entry while the text is still selected. Selected text remains highlighted until you click elsewhere on the slide.

STEP 5: The Slide Sorter View

➤ Pull down the **View menu** and click **Slide Sorter** (or click the **Slide Sorter View button** on the status bar). This changes to the Slide Sorter view in Figure 1.8e.

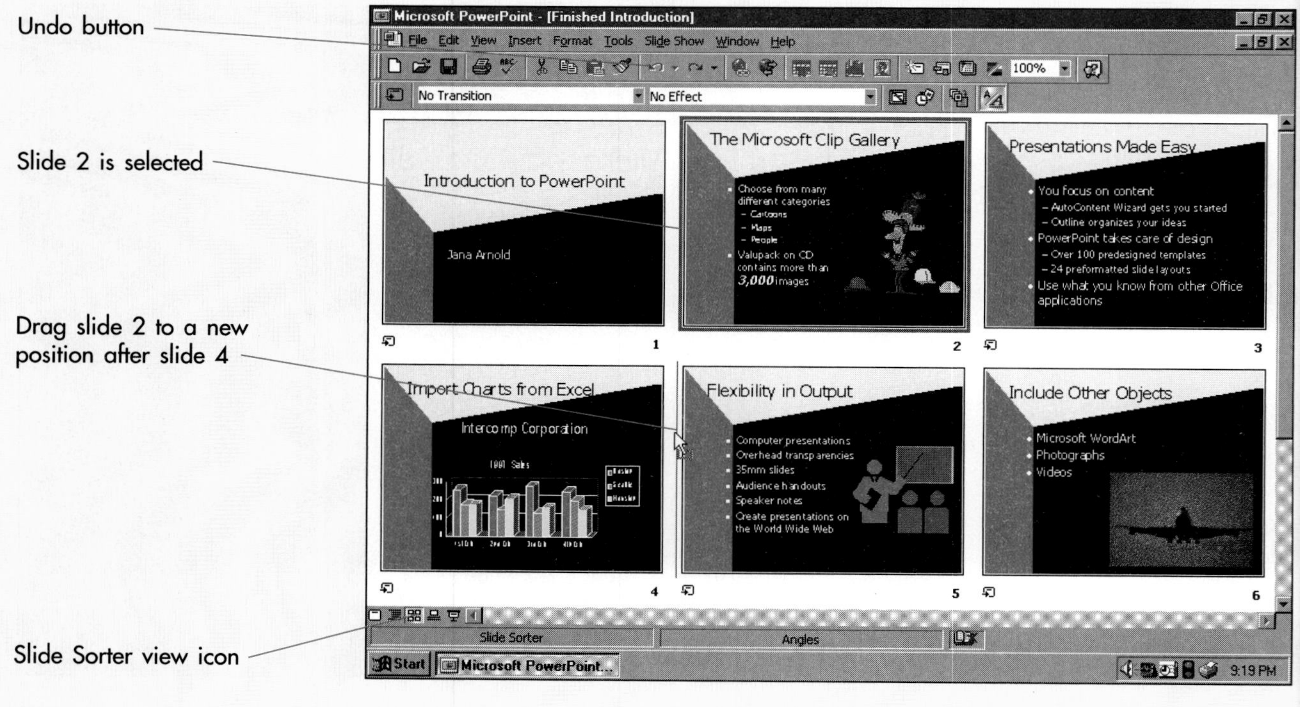

(e) Slide Sorter View (step 5)

FIGURE 1.8 Hands-on Exercise 2 (continued)

- ➤ Slide 2 (the slide you just created) is already selected as indicated by the heavy border around the slide.
- ➤ Click and drag slide 2 and move it after slide 4. (A vertical line appears in the presentation as you drag the slide to indicate where it will be placed.)
- ➤ Release the mouse. The existing slides are automatically renumbered to reflect the new sequence.
- ➤ Pull down the **Edit menu** and click **Undo Drag and Drop** (or click the **Undo button** on the Standard toolbar). The slide containing the clip art goes back to its original position.
- ➤ Click and drag slide 2 and move it after slide 4.
- ➤ Save the presentation.

MULTIPLE-LEVEL UNDO

The Undo command reverses (undoes) the most recent command. The command is executed from the Edit menu or more easily by clicking the Undo button on the Standard toolbar. Each click of the Undo button reverses one command; that is, click the Undo button and you reverse the last command. Click the Undo button a second time and you reverse the previous command. The Redo command works in reverse and undoes the most recent Undo command (i.e., it redoes the command you just undid). The maximum number of Undo commands (the default is 20) is set through the Tools menu. Pull down the Tools menu, click Options, click the Edit tab, then enter the desired number.

STEP 6: The Outline View

- ➤ Click the **Outline View button** on the status bar to change to the Outline view in Figure 1.8f. Press **Ctrl+End** to move to the end of the outline. Press **enter.** Press **Shift+Tab** to begin a new slide:
  - Type **Five Different Views** (the title of the slide). Press **enter.**
  - Press the **Tab key** to indent one level. Type **Slide view** as shown in Figure 1.8f. Press **enter** to move to the next bullet.
  - Type **Outline view.** Press **enter.**
  - Type **Slide Sorter view.** Press **enter.**

SLIDE MINIATURES

The Outline view displays the text of the presentation, but not the graphic elements. You can, however, open a slide miniature window to display these elements from within the Outline view. The slide miniature is shown by default but can be toggled on and off by pulling down the View menu and checking (clearing) the Slide Miniature command.

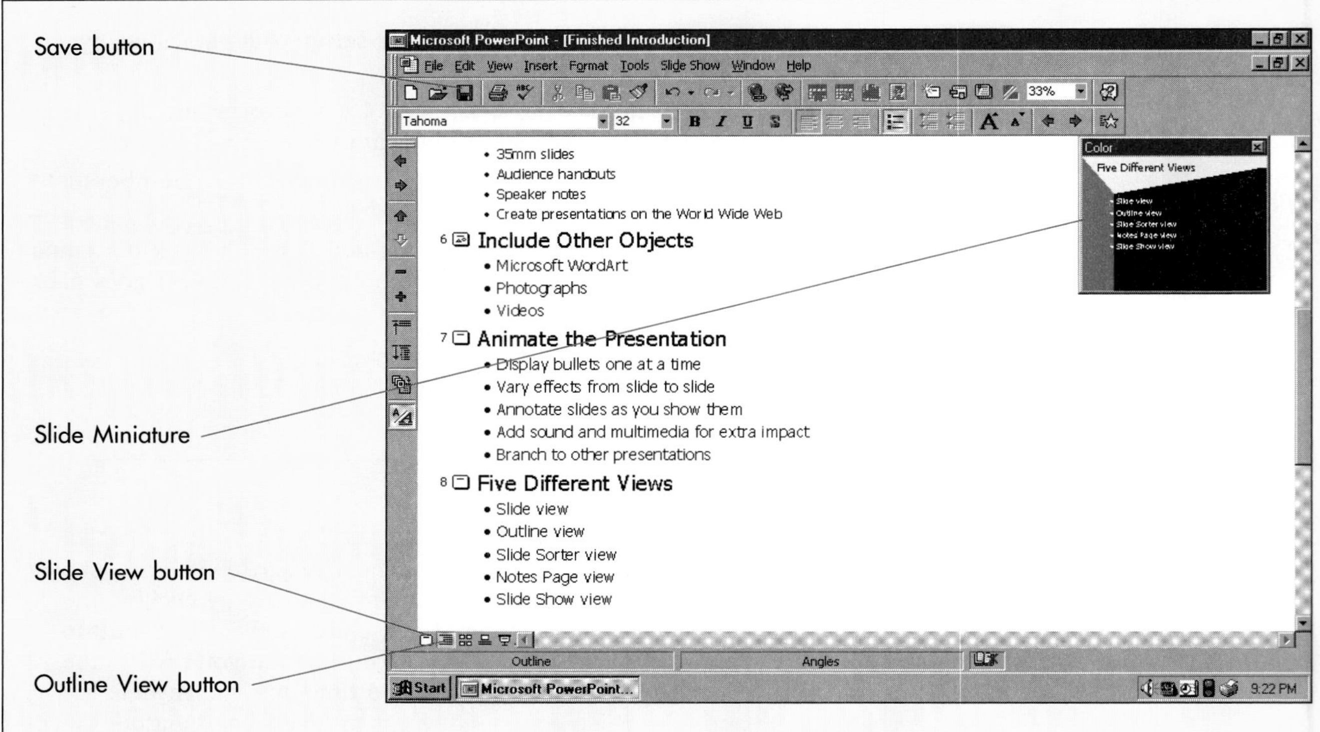

(f) Outline View (step 6)

FIGURE 1.8 Hands-on Exercise 2 (continued)

- Type **Notes Page view.** Press **enter.**
- Type **Slide Show view.**

➤ The slide is complete. Click the **Save button** on the Standard toolbar to save the presentation.

STEP 7: The Slide View

➤ Click the **Slide View button** to change to the Slide view as shown in Figure 1.8g. You should see the Slide view of the slide created in the previous step.

➤ Click the **Previous Slide button** on the vertical scroll bar (or press the **PgUp key**) to move to the previous slide (slide 7) in the presentation.

➤ Click the **Next Slide button** on the vertical scroll bar (or press the **PgDn key**) to move to the next slide (slide 8).

THE SLIDE ELEVATOR

PowerPoint uses the scroll box (common to all Windows applications) in the vertical scroll bar as an elevator to move up and down within the presentation. Click and drag the elevator to go to a specific slide; as you drag, you will see a ScreenTip indicating the slide you are about to display. Release the mouse when you see the number (title) of the slide you want.

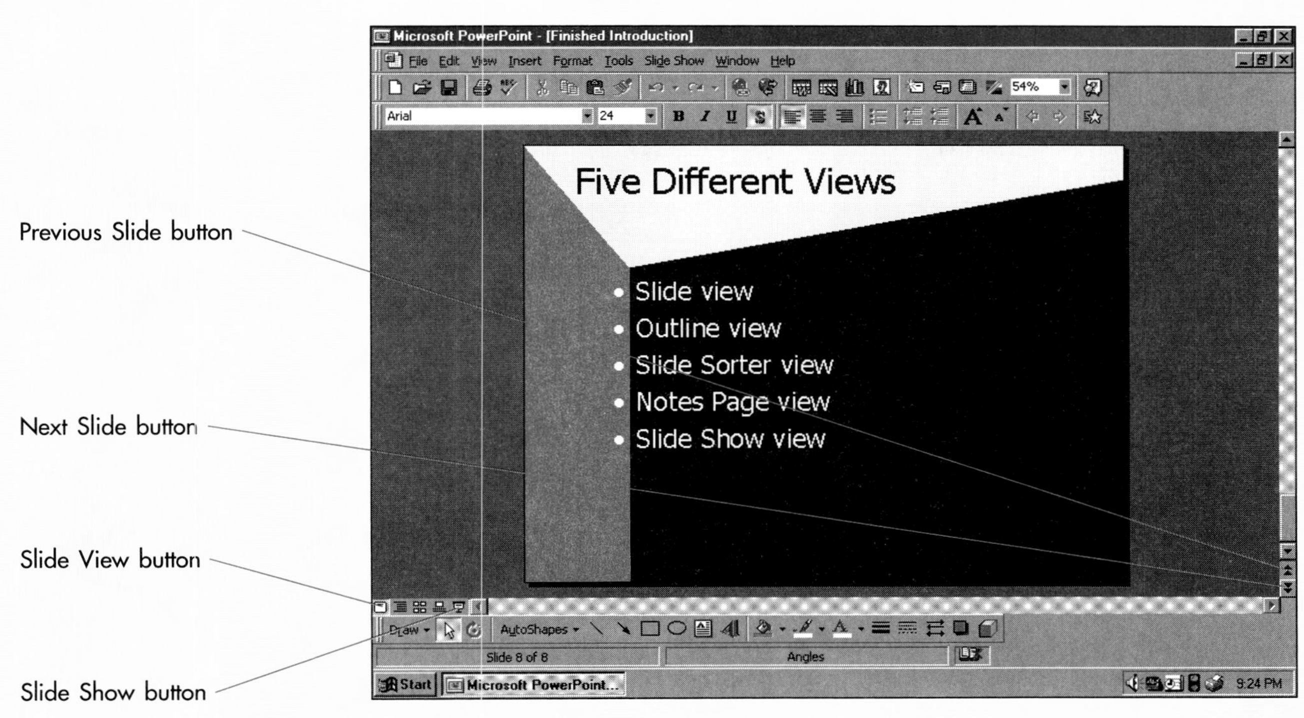

(g) Slide View (step 7)

FIGURE 1.8 Hands-on Exercise 2 (continued)

STEP 8: The Slide Show View

➤ Press **Ctrl+Home** to move to the beginning of the presentation. Click the **Slide Show button** to view the presentation as follows:

- Click the **left mouse button** (or press the **PgDn key**) to move forward in the presentation. Continue to click the left mouse button to move from one slide to the next.
- Click the **right mouse button** and click **Previous** from the shortcut menu (or press the **PgUp key**) to move backward in the presentation.
- Press the **Esc key** at any time to quit the presentation and return to the Slide view.

TRANSITIONS AND ANIMATIONS

Transitions add interest and variety to a presentation by changing the way in which you progress from one slide to the next. Slides may move onto the screen from the left or right, be uncovered by horizontal or vertical blinds, fade, dissolve, etc. Animations may also be applied to individual bullets to display the bullets one at a time with a variety of special effects (e.g., a letter at a time accompanied by the sound of a typewriter.) Transitions and animations are further described in Chapter 2.

STEP 9: The Notes Page View

- Press **Ctrl+Home** to move to the beginning of the presentation. Click the **Notes Page View button** to change to this view, as shown in Figure 1.8h. (If necessary, click the **down arrow** on the Zoom Control box to change to **100%** magnification so that you will be able to see what you are typing.)
- Click in the **notes placeholder,** then enter the text in Figure 1.8h. (The information is for the presenter rather than the audience.) Click outside the placeholder to deselect it. Save the presentation.
- Pull down the **File menu.** Click **Print** to display the Print dialog box.
- Click the **down arrow** in the **Print What** drop-down list box. Scroll so that you can click **Notes Page.** Click the **Current Slide option button** to print just this slide. Click **OK.**
- Close the presentation. Exit PowerPoint if you do not want to continue with the next exercise.

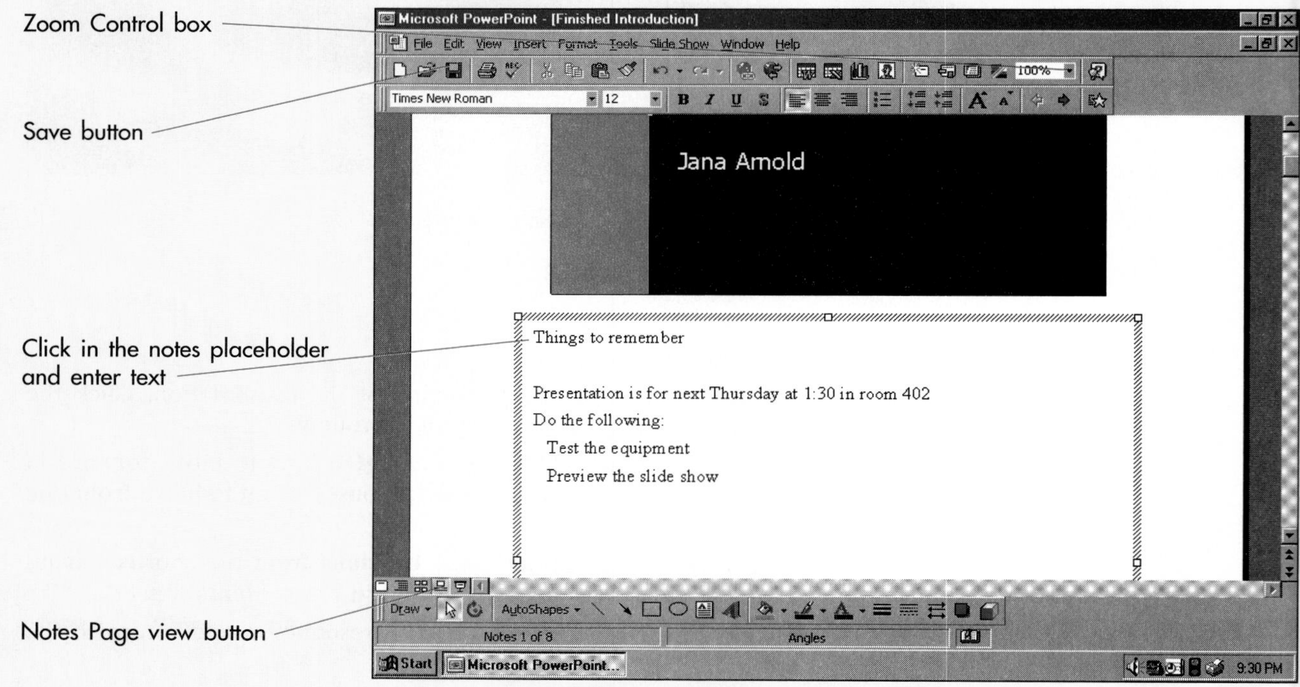

(h) Notes Page View (step 9)

FIGURE 1.8 Hands-on Exercise 2 (continued)

ADD SPEAKER NOTES IN ANY VIEW

You do not have to be in the Notes Page view in order to add notes to a slide. Go to any view (other than Notes Page), pull down the View menu, click Speaker Notes to display the Speaker Notes dialog box, add your note, then close the dialog box. Change to the Notes Page view and your note will appear. The advantage of the Speaker Notes dialog box is that you can continue to develop your presentation without having to leave a slide to add a note.

PowerPoint can help you create an attractive presentation, but it is up to you to deliver the presentation effectively. Accordingly, PowerPoint provides a series of Slide Show tools to help you accomplish this goal. The tools can be accessed from any slide during the slide show by clicking the right mouse button to display a shortcut menu. The tools are discussed briefly in conjunction with the presentation in Figure 1.9, then illustrated in detail in a hands-on exercise.

Rehearse Timings

The Slide Show view in Figure 1.9a displays a presentation consisting of five slides. It is similar to the Slide Show view shown earlier in the chapter, but with one significant difference. Look carefully under the slides and you will see a number preceded by a colon (e.g., :30 under slide 1) corresponding to the amount of time the presenter intends to devote to the slide. The timings were entered through the ***Rehearse Timings*** feature that enables you to time your presentation. This feature is extremely valuable because it provides a sense of timing as you practice your presentation. (The Rehearse Timings feature can also be used to automate a presentation so that each slide will be shown for the set time, after which the next slide will appear automatically.)

PRACTICE MAKES PERFECT

You have worked hard to gain the opportunity to present your ideas. Be prepared! You cannot bluff your way through a presentation. Practice aloud several times, preferably under the same conditions as the actual presentation. Everyone is nervous, but the more you practice, the more confident you will be.

Action Items

Questions arise during any presentation, suggestions are given, and action items are developed. The ***Meeting Minder*** enables you to keep track of these items as they occur and to summarize them at the end of the presentation. The slide in Figure 1.9b, for example, is not part of the original presentation (it does not appear in the Slide Sorter view) but is created *during* the presentation, as explained in the hands-on exercise.

Note, too, the annotation that has been added to the Action Items slide. The mouse pointer has changed from an arrow to a pencil, changing the effect of the mouse to an annotation tool. This enables you to click anywhere on the slide in order to ***annotate the slide*** as shown in Figure 1.9b.

ARRIVE EARLY

You need time to gather your thoughts and set up the presentation. Start PowerPoint and open the presentation prior to beginning. Be sure you have your notes. Check that water is available for you during the presentation. Try to relax. Greet the audience as they come in.

Time allotted to slide with Rehearse Timings feature

Icon indicates a hidden slide

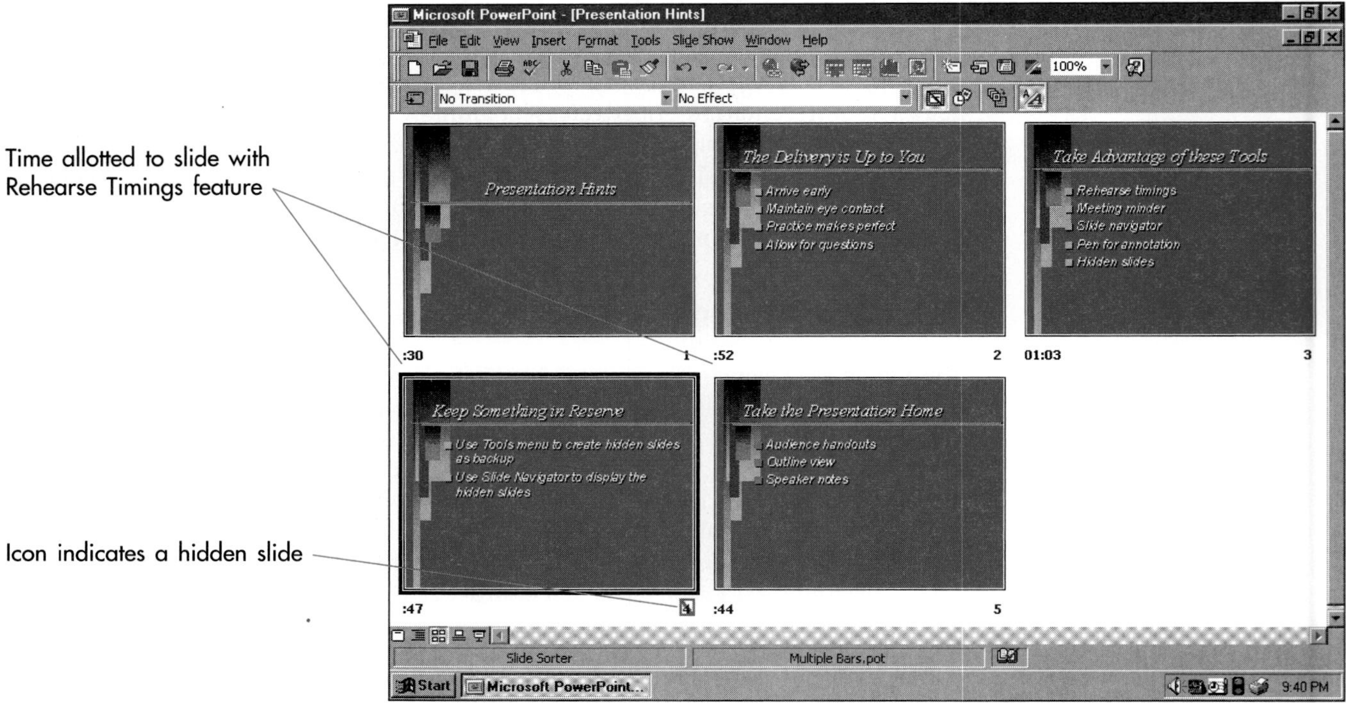

(a) Timings and Hidden Slides

Action Items slide created during presentation through Meeting Minder

Annotation added to slide

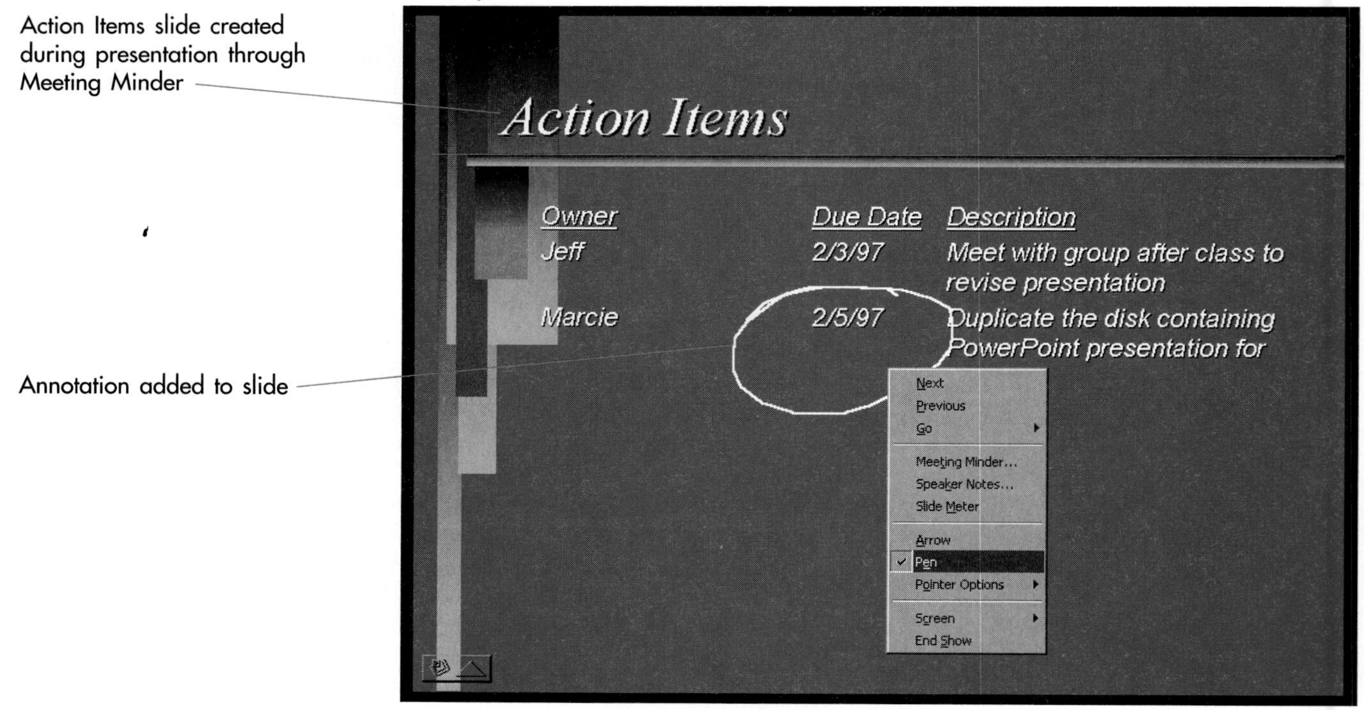

(b) Action Items and Annotation

FIGURE 1.9 Slide Show

Hidden Slides

The icon under slide number 4 in Figure 1.9a indicates that it is a ***hidden slide.*** The slide is contained within the presentation, but the presenter has elected not to display the slide in the slide show. This is a common practice among experienced speakers who anticipate probing questions that may arise during the presentation. The presenter prefers not to address the topic initially and elects to hide the slide. The presenter can, however, access the slide during the show (through the ***Slide Navigator***) should it become necessary.

> **BE FLEXIBLE**
>
> Every presentation begins with its slides in a specific order. Each audience is different, however, and you may find it necessary to change the order, to jump to a later slide, or to return to an earlier slide. You may also find it necessary to display a hidden slide, a slide that you kept in reserve should a specific question arise. Be flexible and use the Slide Navigator to respond appropriately to questions from the audience.

HANDS-ON EXERCISE 3

Slide Show Tools

Objective: To use the Rehearse Timings feature to time a presentation; to hide a slide, then use the Slide Navigator to display that slide on demand; to use the Meeting Minder to create a list of action items during a presentation; and to annotate a slide for emphasis. Use Figure 1.10 as a guide in the exercise.

STEP 1: Open the Existing Presentation

- Start PowerPoint. Open **Presentation Hints** in the **Exploring PowerPoint folder** as shown in Figure 1.10a. Click where indicated to add your name to the title slide.
- Pull down the **File menu,** click the **Save As command** to display the Save As dialog box, then save the presentation as **Finished Presentation Hints.** (Press the **Esc key** or click the **Close button** if you see a Properties dialog box after saving the file.)

> **CHANGE THE DEFAULT FOLDER**
>
> The default folder is the folder where PowerPoint retrieves (saves) presentations unless it is otherwise instructed. To change the default folder, pull down the Tools menu, click Options, click the Advanced tab, then enter the name of the default folder (for example, C:\Exploring PowerPoint) in the Default File Location text box. Click OK. The next time you execute the Open command, PowerPoint looks in this folder.

Click to add your name to the slide

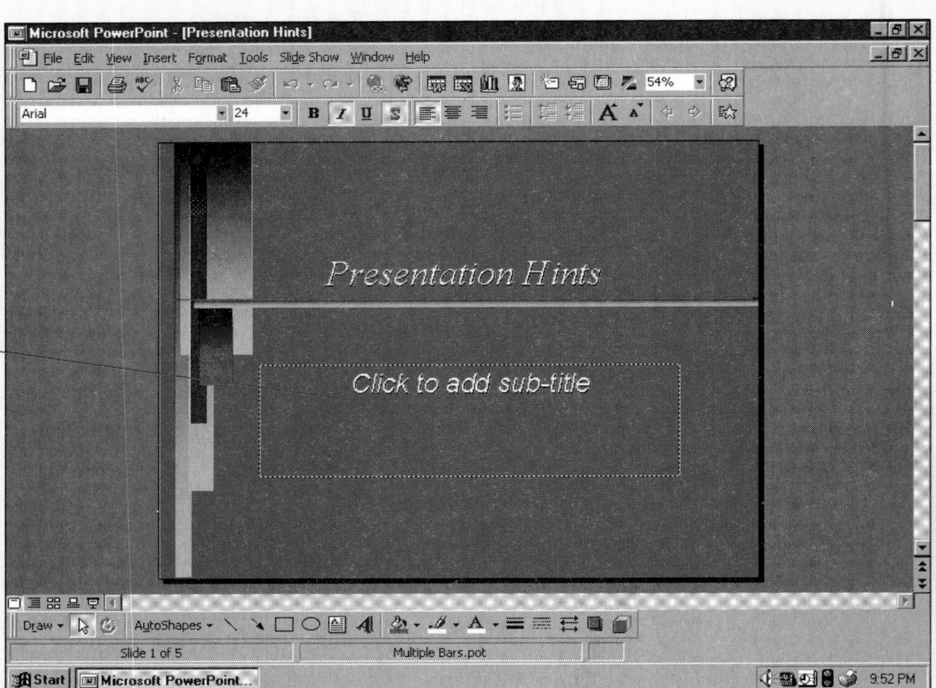

(a) Open the Presentation (step 1)

FIGURE 1.10 Hands-on Exercise 3

STEP 2: Hide a Slide

- Click the **Slide Sorter View button** (or pull down the **View menu** and click **Slide Sorter**).
- If necessary, click the **down arrow** on the Zoom Control box to zoom to 100%. The slides are larger and easier to read as shown in Figure 1.10b.
- Point to slide 4 (Keep Something in Reserve), then click the **right mouse button** to select the slide and simultaneously display a shortcut menu.
- Click **Hide Slide** as shown in Figure 1.10b. The menu closes and a hidden slide icon is displayed under slide 4. The slide remains in the presentation, but it will *not* be displayed during the slide show.
- The Hide Slide command functions as a toggle switch. Click the command once and the slide is hidden. Click the command a second time and the slide is no longer hidden.
- Save the presentation. Click on the first slide, then lick the **Slide Show button** to move quickly through the presentation.
- You will not see the slide titled Keep Something in Reserve because it has been hidden. (You can still access this slide through the Slide Navigator as described in step 5.)

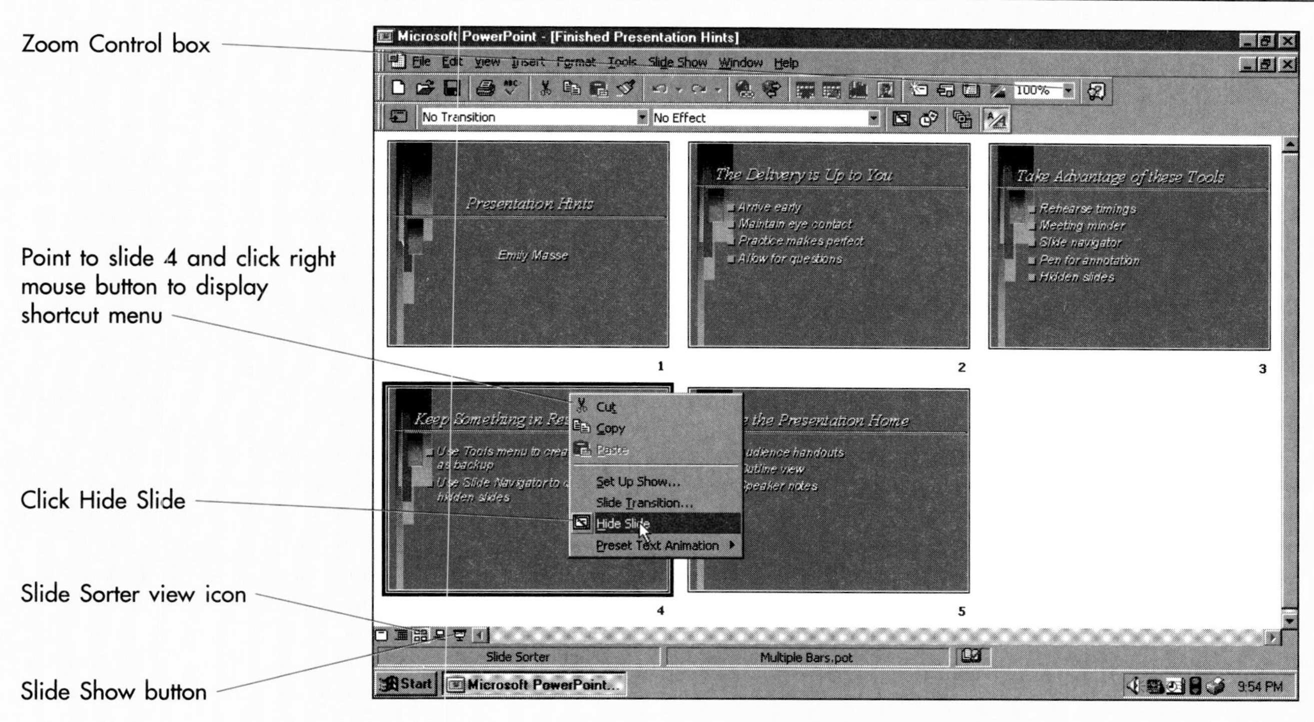

(b) Hide a Slide (step 2)

FIGURE 1.10 Hands-on Exercise 3 (continued)

> **MOVING WITHIN THE PRESENTATION**
>
> Ctrl+Home and Ctrl+End are universal Windows shortcuts that move to the beginning or end of a document. Not only do the techniques work in PowerPoint, but they work in four of the five views (the Slide Show view is the exception). The shortcuts are quite valuable as you develop a presentation because you often need to move to the first or last slide.

STEP 3: Rehearse the Presentation

➤ Press **Ctrl+Home** to return to the first slide. Pull down the **Slide Show menu** and click **Rehearse Timings.**

➤ The first slide appears in the Slide Show view, and the Rehearsal dialog box is displayed in the lower-right corner of the screen. Speak as though you were presenting the slide, then click the mouse to register the elapsed time for that slide and move to the next slide.

➤ The second slide in the presentation should appear as shown in Figure 1.10c. Speak as though you were presenting the slide and note the times that appear in the dialog box. The cumulative time appears on the left (1 minute and 6 seconds). The time for this specific slide (39 seconds) is shown at the right.

- Click the **Repeat button** to redo the timing for the slide.
- Click the **Pause button** to (temporarily) stop the clock. Click the **Pause button** a second time to resume the clock.
- Click the **Next Slide button** to record the timing and move to the next slide.

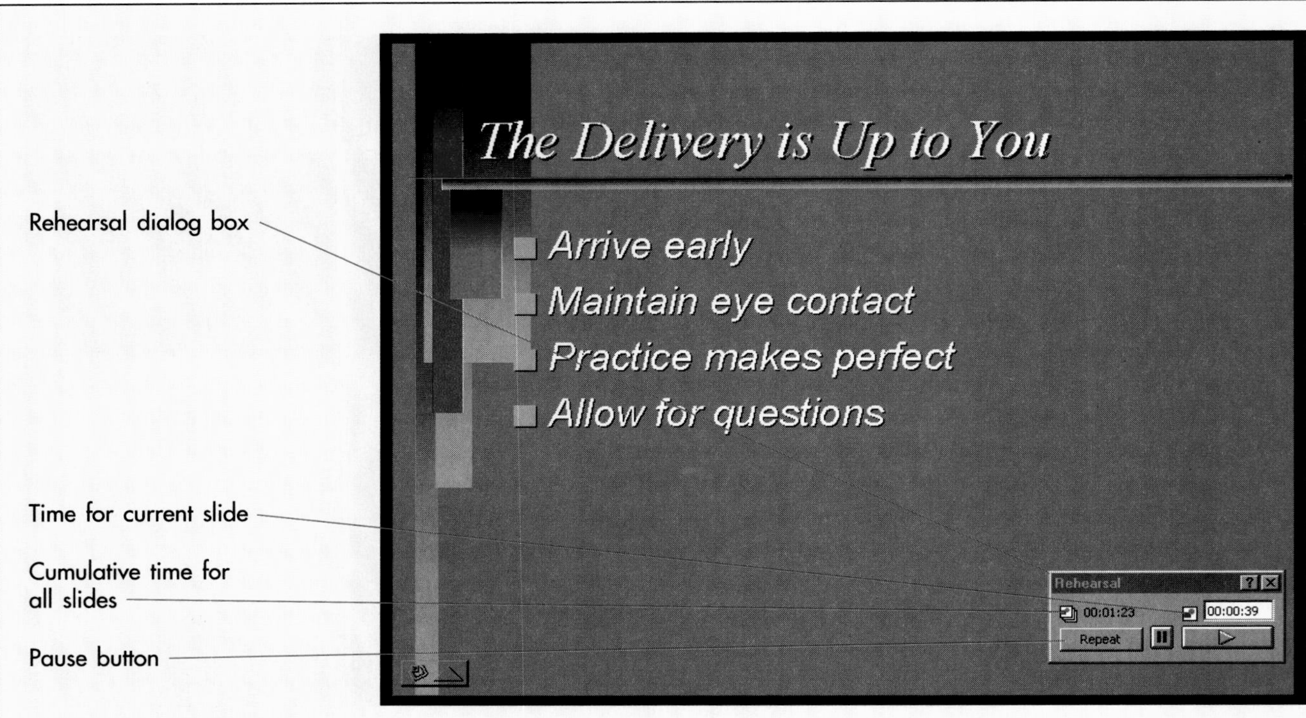

(c) Rehearse Timings (step 3)

FIGURE 1.10 Hands-on Exercise 3 (continued)

- Continue rehearsing the show until you reach the end of the presentation.
- You should see a dialog box at the end of the presentation that indicates the total time of the slide show. Click **Yes** when asked whether you want to record the new timings. Click **Yes** when asked whether you want to review the timings in the Slide Sorter view.
- PowerPoint returns to the Slide Sorter view and records the timings under each slide (except for the hidden slide). Note, too, the hidden icon under the fourth slide.

STEP 4: The Meeting Minder

- Click the **first slide** (or press **Ctrl+Home**) to move to the beginning of the presentation. Click the **Slide Show button** to show the presentation.
- You should see the title slide as shown in Figure 1.10d. Point anywhere on the slide and click the **right mouse button** to display a shortcut menu.
- Click **Meeting Minder** to display the Meeting Minder dialog box, then click the **Action Items tab** as shown in Figure 1.10d.
- Enter the first action item in Figure 1.10d. Press the **Tab key** to move to the Assigned To box to enter a person's name. Enter a Due Date, then click the **Add button** to complete the task. Enter a second action item of your own choosing. Click **OK** to close the dialog box.
- Click the mouse to move from one slide to the next (you can enter an action item from any slide) until you reach the end of the presentation (the slide titled Action Items). A new slide has been created containing the action items you just supplied. Leave this slide on the screen.

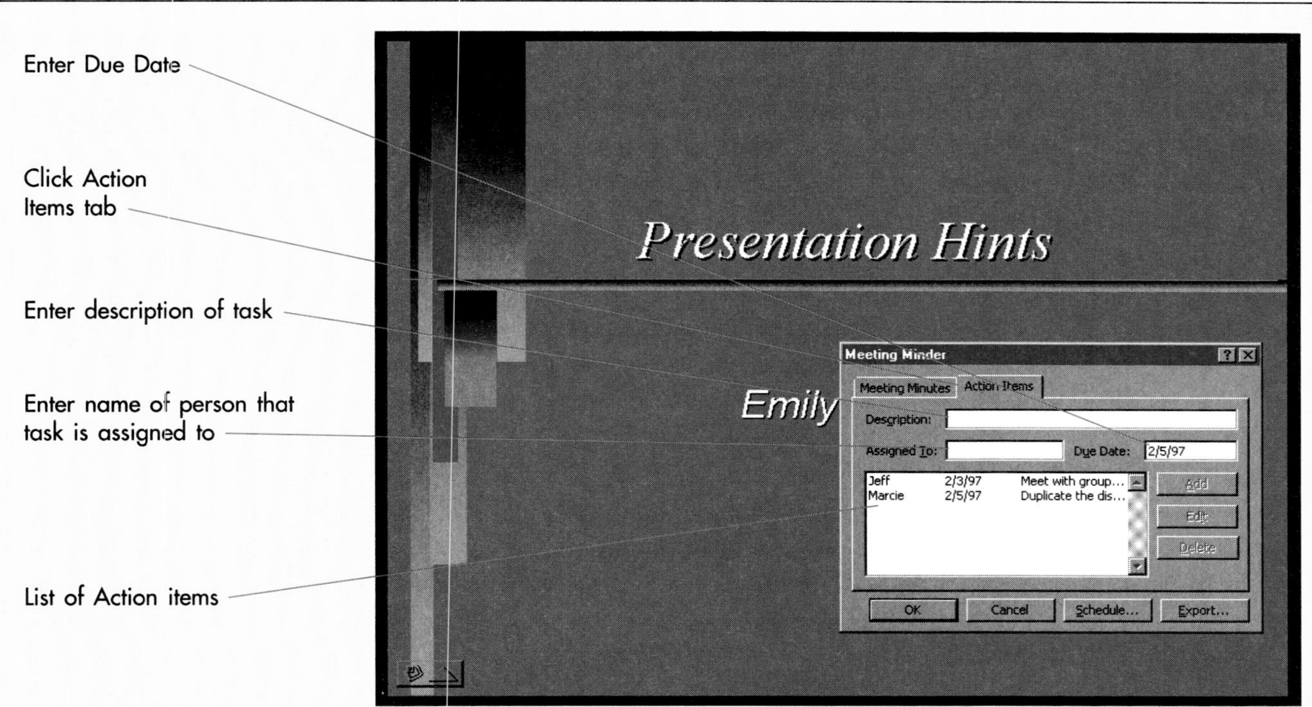

(d) Meeting Minder (step 4)

FIGURE 1.10 Hands-on Exercise 3 (continued)

> **QUESTIONS AND ANSWERS (Q & A)**
>
> Indicate at the beginning of your talk whether you will take questions during the presentation or collectively at the end. Announce the length of time that will be allocated to questions. Rephrase all questions so the audience can hear, then use the Slide Navigator to return to the appropriate slide in order to answer the question. Rephrase hostile questions in a neutral way and try to disarm the challenger by paying a compliment. If you don't know the answer, say so.

STEP 5: The Slide Navigator

- You should be positioned on the last slide (Action Items). Click the **right mouse button** to display a shortcut menu, click **Go,** then click **Slide Navigator** to display the Slide Navigator dialog box as shown in Figure 1.10e.
- The titles of all slides (including the hidden slide) are displayed in the Slide Navigator dialog box. The number of the hidden slide, however, is enclosed in parentheses to indicate it is a hidden slide.
- Select (click) the **hidden slide,** then click the **Go To button** to display this slide.

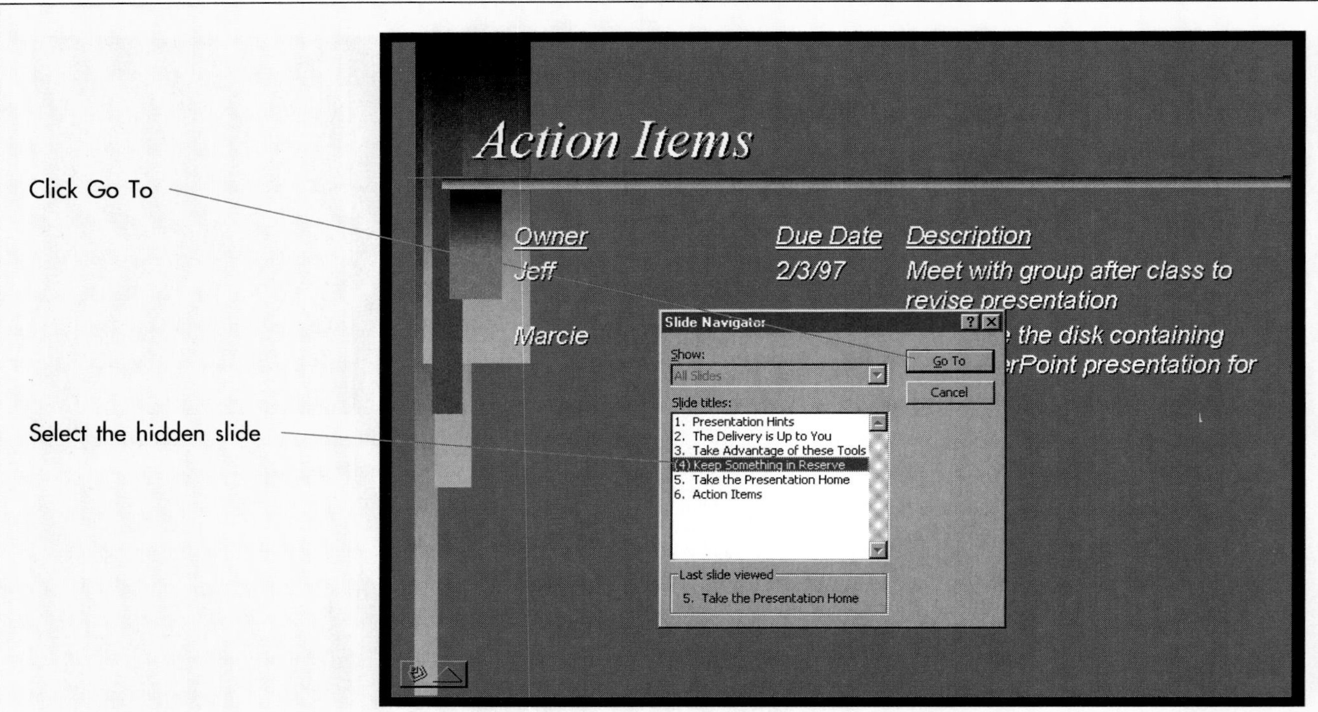

(e) Slide Navigator (step 5)

FIGURE 1.10 Hands-on Exercise 3 (continued)

BACK UP IMPORTANT FILES

We cannot overemphasize the importance of adequate backup. Hard disks die, files are accidentally deleted or lost, and viruses may infect a system. It takes only a few minutes to copy your data files to a floppy disk, so do it now. You will thank us when (not if) you lose an important file and wish you had another copy.

STEP 6: Annotate a Slide

- You should see the slide in Figure 1.10f. Click the **right mouse button** to display the shortcut menu containing the Slide Show tools. Click **Pen.** The mouse pointer changes from an arrow to a pencil.
- Click and drag on the slide to annotate the slide as shown in Figure 1.10f. The annotation is temporary and will be visible only as long as you display the slide.
- Press **N** (or the **PgDn key**) to move to the next slide, then press **P** (or the **PgUp key**) to return to the previous slide. The annotation is gone.
- Click the **right mouse button,** point to (or click) **Pointer Options,** point to (or click) **Pen Color,** then choose (click) a different color. The mouse pointer automatically changes to the pen, and you can annotate the slide in the new color.

Draw annotation with Pen

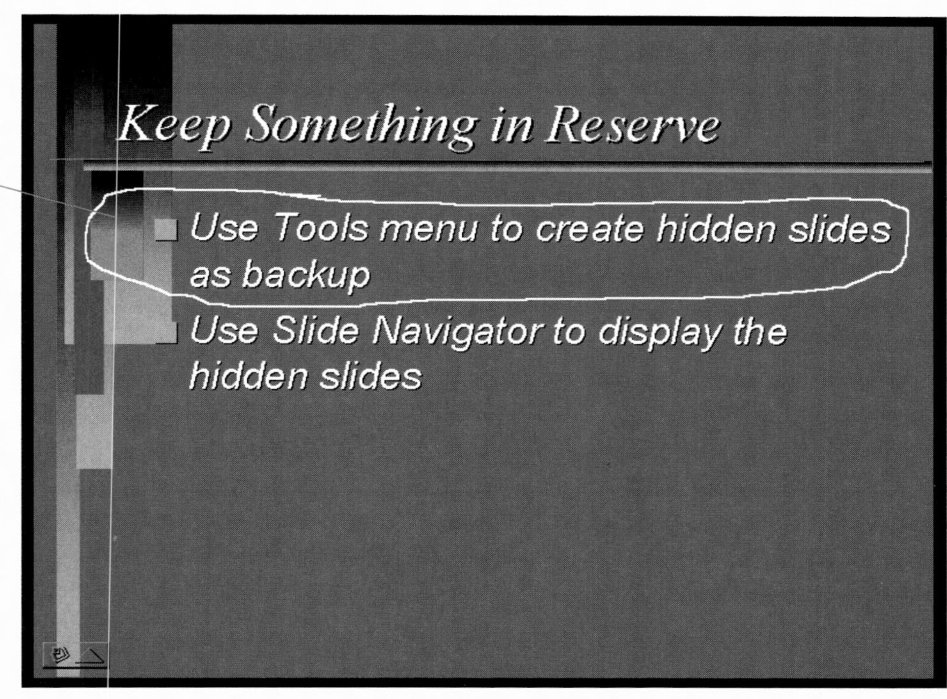

(f) Annotate a Slide (step 6)

FIGURE 1.10 Hands-on Exercise 3 (continued)

> **THE PEN AND THE ARROW**
>
> The shortcut menu can be used to toggle the mouse pointer between the Pen and the arrow, but we find various other shortcuts easier. For example, press Ctrl+P or Ctrl+A at any time to change to the pencil or an arrow, respectively. You can also press the Esc key to return the mouse to a pointer after using it as a Pen. And finally, you can use the keyboard to move to a different slide, which automatically resets the mouse to the pointer.

STEP 7: End the Show

- Click the **right mouse button** to display the shortcut menu, then click **End Show** to end the presentation.
- Pull down the **File menu.** Click **Print** to produce the Print dialog box. Click the **arrow** in the **Print What** drop-down list box. Click **Handouts (6 slides per page).** Check the boxes for **Frame Slides** and **Print Hidden Slides.**
- Check that the **All option button** is selected under Print Range. You will print every slide in the presentation, including the hidden slide and the slide containing the action items. Click **OK.**
- Pull down the **File menu** and click **Exit** to leave PowerPoint. Click **Yes** when asked whether to save the changes to the presentation.

SUMMARY

A PowerPoint presentation consists of a series of slides with a consistent design and color scheme. A PowerPoint presentation may be delivered on a computer, via overhead transparencies or 35-mm slides, and/or printed in a variety of formats.

The PowerPoint window contains the basic elements of any Windows application. The benefits of the common user interface are magnified further if you are familiar with other applications in the Microsoft Office such as Word or Excel. PowerPoint is designed for a mouse, but it provides keyboard equivalents for almost every command. Toolbars provide still another way to execute the most frequent operations.

PowerPoint has five different views, each with unique capabilities. The Slide view displays one slide at a time and enables all operations on that slide. The Slide Sorter view displays multiple slides on one screen (each slide is in miniature) and lets you see the overall flow of the presentation. The Outline view shows the presentation text in outline form and is the fastest way to enter or edit text. The Notes Page view enables you to create speaker's notes for use in giving the presentation. The Slide Show view displays the slides one at a time with transition and animation effects for added interest.

Slides are added to a presentation using one of 24 predefined slide formats known as AutoLayouts. Each AutoLayout contains placeholders for the different objects on the slide. A slide may be deleted from a presentation in any view except the Slide Show view.

PowerPoint includes several slide show tools to help you enliven a presentation. The Rehearse Timings feature enables you to time and/or automate a presentation. The Slide Navigator enables you to branch directly to any slide, including hidden slides. The Pen lets you annotate a slide for added emphasis. The Meeting Minder enables you to create a list of action items.

Although PowerPoint helps to create attractive presentations, you are still the most important element in delivering the presentation. The chapter ended with several hints on how to rehearse and present presentations effectively.

KEY WORDS AND CONCEPTS

Action items
Animation effects
Annotating a slide
AutoLayout
Clip art
Close command
Drawing toolbar
Elevator
Exit command
File menu
Formatting toolbar
Hidden slide
Meeting Minder
Menu bar
New Slide command
Notes Page view
Open command
Outline view
Pen
Placeholders
Print Command
Redo command
Rehearse Timings
Save command
ScreenTip
Slide miniature
Slide Navigator
Slide Show view
Slide Sorter view
Slide view
Standard toolbar
Status bar
Transition effects
Undo command
View buttons

MULTIPLE CHOICE

1. How do you save changes to a PowerPoint presentation?
   (a) Pull down the File menu and click the Save command
   (b) Click the Save button on the Standard toolbar
   (c) Both (a) and (b)
   (d) Neither (a) nor (b)

2. Which toolbars are displayed by default in all views?
   (a) The Standard toolbar
   (b) The Formatting toolbar
   (c) Both (a) and (b)
   (d) Neither (a) nor (b)

3. Which view displays multiple slides on a single screen?
   (a) Outline view
   (b) Slide Sorter view
   (c) Both (a) and (b)
   (d) Neither (a) nor (b)

4. Which view displays multiple slides and also shows the graphical elements in each slide?
   (a) Outline view (with slide miniature displayed)
   (b) Slide Sorter view
   (c) Both (a) and (b)
   (d) Neither (a) nor (b)

5. Which view lets you delete a slide?
   (a) Outline view
   (b) Slide Sorter view
   (c) Both (a) and (b)
   (d) Neither (a) nor (b)

6. Which of the following can be printed in support of a PowerPoint presentation?
   (a) Audience handouts
   (b) Speaker's notes
   (c) An outline
   (d) All of the above

7. Which menu contains the Undo command?
   (a) File menu
   (b) Edit menu
   (c) Tools menu
   (d) Format menu

8. Ctrl+Home and Ctrl+End are keyboard shortcuts that move to the beginning or end of the presentation in the:
   (a) Outline view
   (b) Slide Sorter view
   (c) Slide view
   (d) All of the above

9. The predefined slide formats in PowerPoint are known as:
   (a) Views
   (b) AutoLayouts
   (c) Audience handouts
   (d) Speaker notes
10. Which menu contains the command to print a presentation?
   (a) The Tools menu
   (b) The File menu
   (c) The View menu
   (d) The Edit menu
11. The Open command:
   (a) Brings a presentation from disk into memory
   (b) Brings a presentation from disk into memory, then erases the presentation on disk
   (c) Stores the presentation in memory on disk
   (d) Stores the presentation in memory on disk, then erases the presentation from memory
12. The Save command:
   (a) Brings a presentation from disk into memory
   (b) Brings a presentation from disk into memory, then erases the presentation on disk
   (c) Stores the presentation in memory on disk
   (d) Stores the presentation in memory on disk, then erases the presentation from memory
13. Which of the following is true about hidden slides?
   (a) Hidden slides are invisible in every view
   (b) Hidden slides cannot be accessed during a slide show
   (c) Both (a) and (b)
   (d) Neither (a) nor (b)
14. Which view displays timings for individual slides after the timings have been established by rehearsing the presentation?
   (a) Slide view
   (b) Outline view
   (c) Slide Sorter view
   (d) All of the above
15. Which of the following is true about annotating a slide?
   (a) The annotations are permanent and cannot be erased
   (b) The annotations are entered by using the pen during the slide show
   (c) Both (a) and (b)
   (d) Neither (a) nor (b)

ANSWERS

1. c	**6.** d	**11.** a
2. c	**7.** b	**12.** c
3. c	**8.** d	**13.** d
4. c	**9.** b	**14.** c
5. c	**10.** b	**15.** b

Practice with Microsoft PowerPoint 97

1. Figure 1.11 displays the Outline view of a presentation that was created by one of our students in a successful job search.
   a. Open the *Chapter 1 Pratice 1* presentation in the set of practice files (it is found in the Exploring PowerPoint folder), then modify the presentation to reflect your personal data.
   b. Print the title slide as a cover page for your assignment.
   c. Print the revised audience handouts (six per page) and submit them to your instructor.

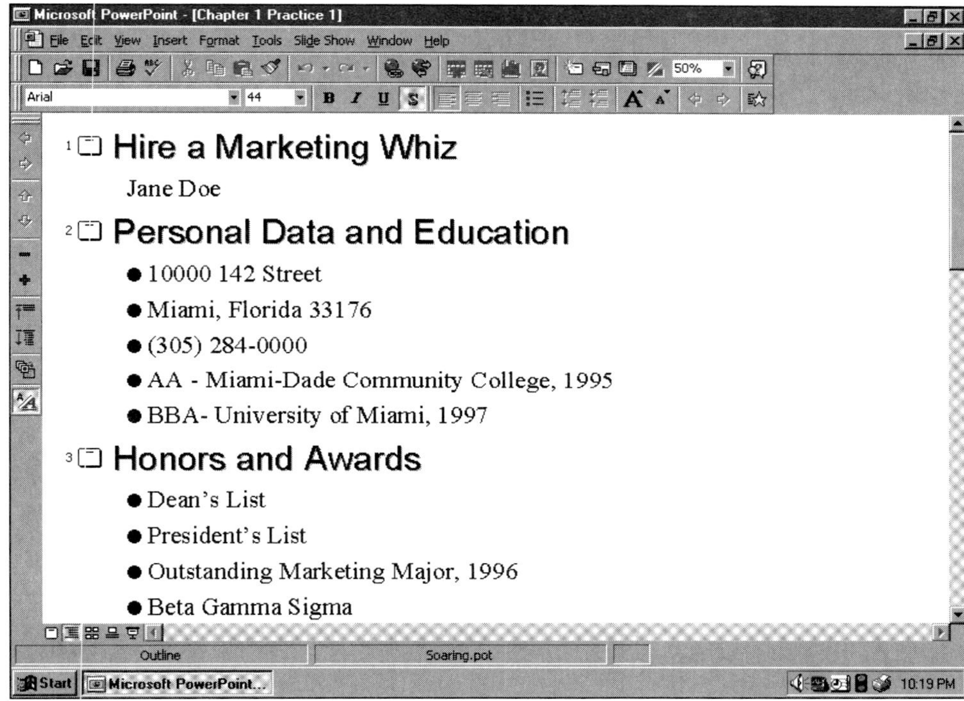

FIGURE 1.11 Screen for Practice Exercise 1

2. Ready-made presentations: The most difficult part of a presentation is getting started. PowerPoint anticipates the problem and provides general outlines on a variety of topics as shown in Figure 1.12.
   a. Pull down the File menu, click New, click the Presentations tab (if necessary), then click the Details button so that your screen matches Figure 1.12.
   b. Select Recommending a Strategy (Standard) as shown in Figure 1.12. Click OK to open the presentation.
   c. Change to the Outline view so that you can see the text of the overall presentation, which is general in nature and intended for any type of strategy. Modify the presentation to develop a strategy for doing well in this class.
   d. Add your name to the title page.
   e. Print the presentation in miniature and submit it to your instructor.

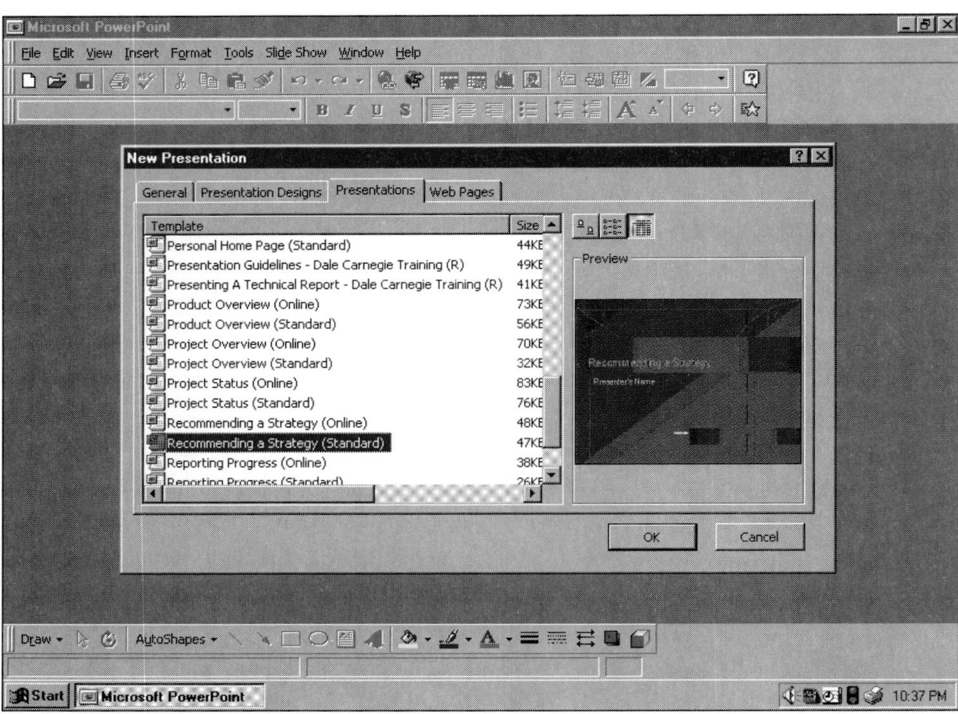

FIGURE 1.12 Screen for Practice Exercise 2

3. The Send To command enables you to import a presentation into a Word document as shown in Figure 1.13. The command combines audience handouts with speaker notes to display several slides on one page with notes for each. It also gives you the option to link the slides to the Word document, so that if a slide changes, the Word document is updated automatically. (The document is not, however, updated to reflect the insertion or deletion of slides.)

   a. Do Hands-on Exercises 1 and 2 as described in the hands-on exercises in the chapter, then retrieve the Finished Introduction presentation as the basis of this problem.

   b. Click the Black and White view button on the Standard toolbar. Pull down the File menu, click the Send To command, then click Microsoft Word.

   c. Click the option button for the type of document you want (e.g., Notes Next to Slide so that you will create Figure 1.13 at the end of this exercise).

   d. Click the option button to Paste Link the slides to a Word document, then click OK. PowerPoint will create a document similar to the one in Figure 1.13. Be patient, for this step takes time, especially on a non-Pentium machine.

   e. Change to the Page Layout view in Word and zoom to Two Pages. Click in the cell next to each slide (the Word document is a table) and enter an appropriate comment.

   f. Save and print the document just as you would any other document in Microsoft Word.

   g. Submit the finished document to your instructor as proof that you did this exercise.

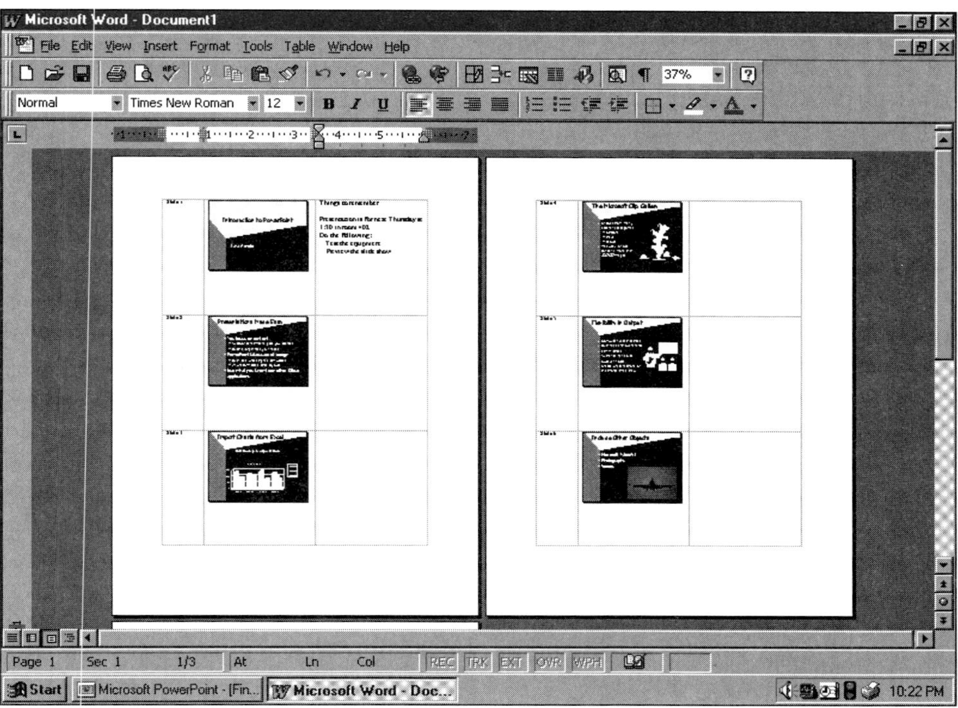

FIGURE 1.13 Screen for Practice Exercise 3

4. A partially completed version of the presentation in Figure 1.14 can be found in the file *Chapter 1 Practice 4.* Open the presentation, then make the following changes:

   a. Add your name and e-mail address on the title page.

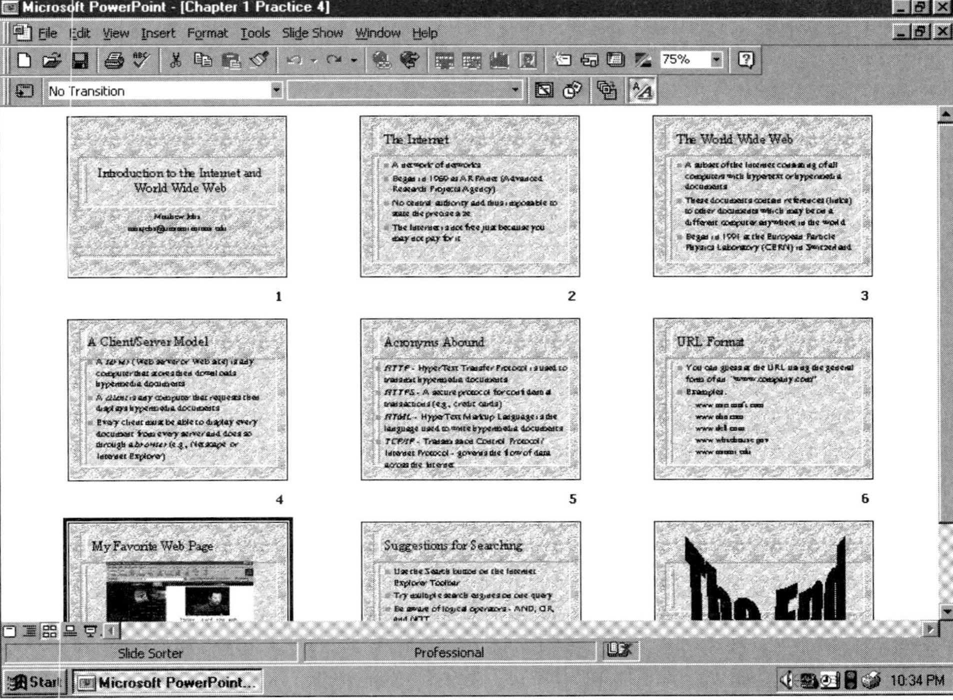

FIGURE 1.14 Screen for Practice Exercise 4

b. Boldface and italicize the terms, *server, client,* and *browser* on slide 4. Boldface and italicize the acronyms, *HTTP, HTTPS, HTML,* and *TCP/IP* on slide 5.

c. Use Internet Explorer to go to your favorite Web page. Press the Print Screen key to capture the screen image of that page and copy it to the clipboard, then use the Windows 95 taskbar to switch to PowerPoint. Select the seventh slide, then click the Paste button on the Standard toolbar to paste the screen into the PowerPoint presentation. Size the image as appropriate.

d. Double click the WordArt image on the last slide to open the WordArt application. Change the words *Thank You* to *The End.* Change the style of the WordArt in any other way you see fit.

e. Print the slide miniatures six per page and submit them to your instructor as proof you did this exercise.

5. This problem is more difficult than the previous exercises as it asks you to create a presentation similar to the one in Figure 1.15. We have started the presentation for you in and have created the file *Chapter 1 Practice 5.* This presentation consists of three slides—a title slide and two slides containing an object and text.

a. Go to the White House Web site (www.whitehouse.com). Click the link to White House History & Tours, then click the link to the Presidents of the USA and select your favorite president(s). Point to the picture of the president, click the right mouse button to display a shortcut menu, then save the picture on your PC.

b. Use the Windows 95 taskbar to switch to PowerPoint, then double click the placeholder on slide two to add an object. Indicate that you are inserting the object from a file, click the Browse button, then select the file containing the president's picture.

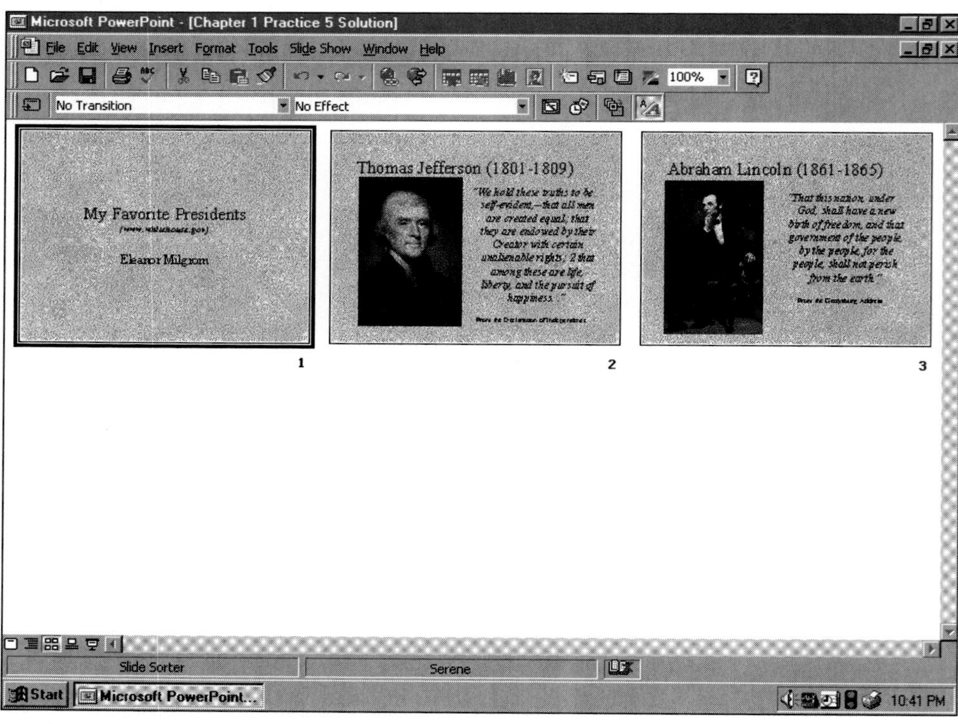

FIGURE 1.15 Screen for Practice Exercise 5

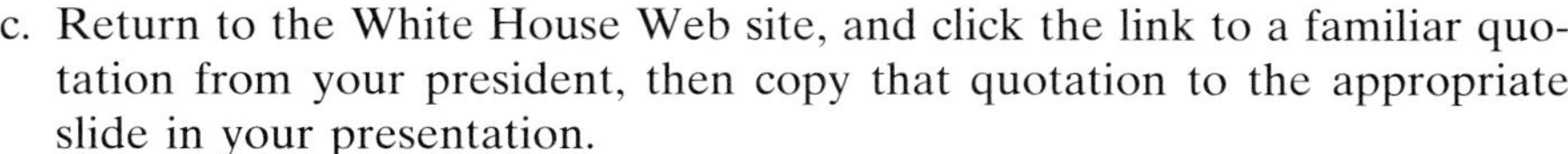

c. Return to the White House Web site, and click the link to a familiar quotation from your president, then copy that quotation to the appropriate slide in your presentation.
d. Create an appropriate title for this slide consisting of the president's name and years in office. Be sure to cite the source of the picture on this slide.
e. Repeat these steps for a second president.
f. Create a title slide for the presentation with your name somewhere on the slide. Print all three slides and submit them to your instructor as proof you did this exercise.

6. This exercise builds on the previous problem as it has you download pictures from the Internet for use in a presentation. Search the Web to select three landmarks, download the picture of each, then create a short presentation consisting of a title slide plus three additional slides similar to the one in Figure 1.16. This chapter did not tell you how to create a new presentation, but it's very straightforward as described below.
   a. Start PowerPoint. If necessary, select the option button to create a blank presentation, then click OK to display the New Slide dialog box.
   b. Choose the Title layout for your first slide. Enter the title of the presentation, *Landmarks Around the World,* and your name.
   c. Click the new slide button to add a slide containing text and an object, then follow the instructions from the previous exercise.
   d. Be sure to include an appropriate reference to the Web page where you obtained each picture.
   e. Print the completed presentation for your instructor as proof you did this exercise.

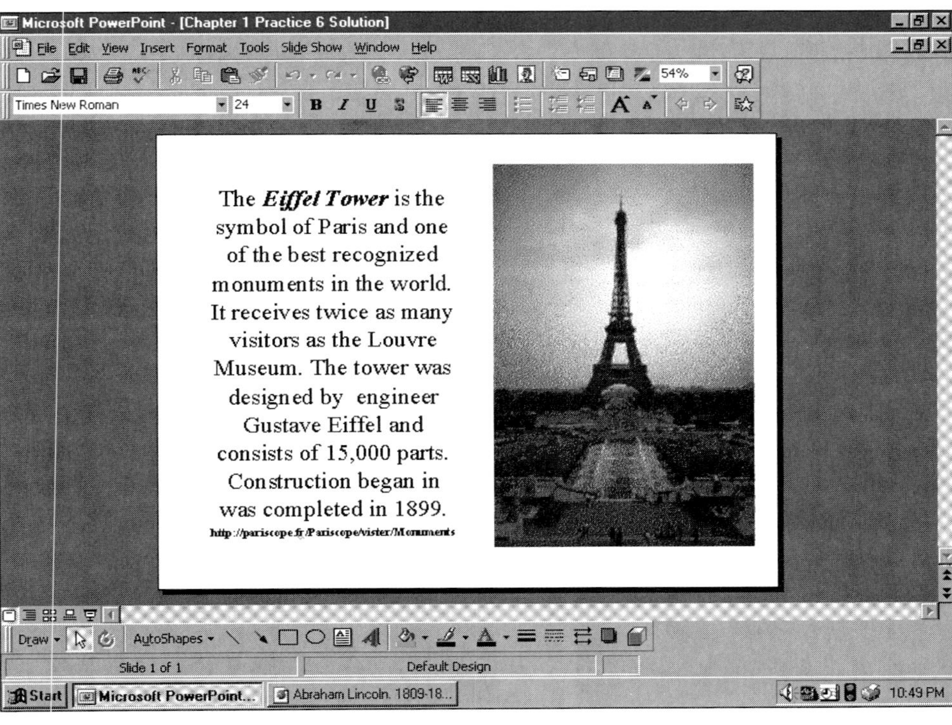

FIGURE 1.16 Screen for Practice Exercise 6

7. The subject of a PowerPoint presentation is limited only by your imagination. Use any Internet search engine to locate information about your favorite singer or recording group, then download information about that person or group to create a presentation of four to six slides. Follow the instructions in the previous problems with respect to creating a new presentation and incorporating a picture from the Web. (Be sure to include the reference to the appropriate Web page.)

   Figure 1.17 displays one of the slides in our presentation about LeAnn Rimes. Print your presentation in miniature (six slides per page) and submit it to your instructor as proof you did this exercise.

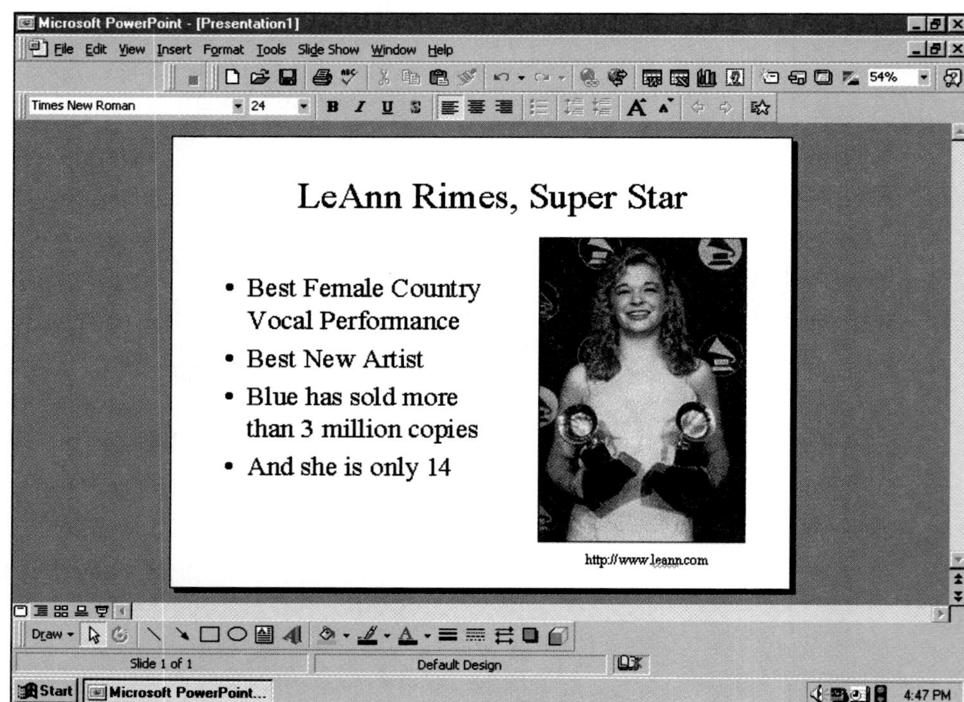

FIGURE 1.17 Screen for Practice Exercise 7

Case Studies

Planning for Disaster

This case has nothing to do with presentations per se, but it is perhaps the most important case of all, as it deals with the question of backup. Do you have a backup strategy? Do you even know what a backup strategy is? This is a good time to learn, because sooner or later you will need to recover a file. The problem always seems to occur the night before an assignment is due. You accidentally erased a file, are unable to read from a floppy disk, or worse yet, suffer a hardware failure in which you are unable to access the hard drive. The ultimate disaster is the disappearance of your computer, by theft or natural disaster (e.g.,

Hurricane Andrew, the floods in the Midwest, or the Los Angeles earthquake). Describe in 250 or fewer words the backup strategy you plan to implement in conjunction with your work in this class.

Slides To Go

You have created the perfect presentation and are scheduled to deliver it next week. The presentation looks great on your PC, but you have to deliver the presentation without the aid of a computer. How do you create 35-mm slides or overhead transparencies as an alternative to the slide show? It's much easier than you think as PowerPoint provides access to the Genigraphics Corporation through the Send command on the File menu. Use the Genigraphics Wizard to determine what can be done, then call the company (an 800 number is provided) to determine the exact costs for a 20-slide presentation. Summarize your findings in a one-page report to your instructor.

Clip Art

Clip art—you see it all the time, but where do you get it, and how much does it cost? A limited number of images are installed automatically with PowerPoint, but you will quickly grow tired of this selection. Additional clip art is available on the ValuPack, and we recommend that you install this clip art to your hard drive (assuming you have the space). Scan the computer magazines and find at least two sources for additional clip art. Return to class with specific information on price and the nature of the clip art. You might also research the availability of photographs, as opposed to clip art.

Microsoft Online

Help for Microsoft PowerPoint is available from a variety of sources. You can consult the Office Assistant or you can pull down the Help menu to display the Help Contents and Index. Both techniques were illustrated in the chapter. In addition, you can go to the Microsoft Web site to obtain more recent, and often more detailed, information. You will find answers to the most frequently asked questions and you can access the same Knowledge Base used by Microsoft support engineers. Experiment with various sources of help, then submit a summary of your findings to your instructor. Try to differentiate between the various techniques and suggest the most appropriate use for each.

The ValuPack and PowerPoint Central

The CD version of Microsoft Office contains a ValuPack folder that contains additional resources for PowerPoint. You will find extra clip art, videos, sound clips, graphic effects, templates, and tips for creating a presentation. You can access the ValuPack folder through the PowerPoint Central command on the Tools menu which opens a presentation describing these resources. Go through the presentation, then write a short summary for your instructor describing what is available.

2

CREATING A PRESENTATION: CONTENT, FORMATTING, AND ANIMATION

OBJECTIVES

After reading this chapter you will be able to:

1. Use the Outline view to create and edit a presentation; display and hide text within the Outline view.
2. Check the spelling in a presentation.
3. Apply a design template to a presentation.
4. Add transition effects to the slides in a presentation; apply animation effects to the bullets and graphical objects in a specific slide.
5. Modify the template of an existing presentation by changing its color scheme and/or background shading.
6. Explain the role of masters in formatting a presentation; modify the slide master to include a company name.
7. Explain how the AutoContent Wizard facilitates the creation of a presentation.

OVERVIEW

There are in essence two independent steps to creating a PowerPoint presentation. You must develop the content, and you must format the presentation. PowerPoint lets you do the steps in either order, but we suggest you start with the content. Both steps are iterative in nature, and you are likely to go back and forth many times before you are finished.

We begin the chapter by showing you how to enter the text of a presentation in the Outline view. We show you how to move and copy text within a slide (or from one slide to another) and how to rearrange the order of the slides within the presentation. We describe how the AutoContent Wizard facilitates the creation of a presentation. We also illustrate the use of the Spell Check and AutoCorrect features that are common to all Office applications.

The chapter also shows you how to format a presentation using one of many professionally designed templates that are supplied with PowerPoint. The templates control every aspect of a presentation, from the formatting of the text to the color scheme of the slides. We describe how to change the template and/or how to vary a color scheme. We show you how to add transition and animation effects to individual slides to enhance a presentation as it is given on a computer. The chapter also shows you how to fine-tune a presentation by changing the slide master to include a corporate logo (or other text) on every slide.

CRYSTALLIZE YOUR MESSAGE

Every presentation exists to deliver a message, whether it's to sell a product, present an idea, or provide instruction. Decide on the message you want to deliver, then write the text for the presentation. Edit the text to be sure it is consistent with your objective. Then, and only then, should you think about formatting, but always keep the message foremost in your mind.

CREATING A PRESENTATION

The text of a presentation can be developed in the Slide view or the Outline view or a combination of the two. You can begin in the Outline view, switch to the Slide view to see how a particular slide will look, return to the Outline view to enter the text for additional slides, and so on. We prefer the Outline view because it displays the text for many slides at once. It also enables you to change the order of slides and to move and copy text from one slide to another.

The Outline View

Figure 2.1 displays the outline of the presentation we will develop in this chapter. The outline shows the title of each slide, followed by the text on that slide. (Graphic elements such as clip art and charts are not visible in the Outline.) Each slide is numbered, and the numbers adjust automatically for the insertion or deletion of slides as you edit the presentation.

A ***slide icon*** appears between the number and title of the slide. The icon is subtly different, depending on the slide layout. In Figure 2.1, for example, the same icon appears next to slides 1 through 6 and indicates the slides contain only text. A different icon appears next to slide 7 and indicates the presence of a graphic element, such as clip art.

Each slide begins with a title, followed by bulleted items, which are indented one to five levels corresponding to the importance of the item. The main points appear on level one. Subsidiary items are indented below the main point to which they apply. Any item can be ***promoted*** to a higher level or ***demoted*** to a lower level, either before or after the text is entered.

Consider, for example, slide 4 in Figure 2.1a. The title of the slide, *Develop the Content*, appears immediately after the slide number and icon. The first bullet, *Use the Outline view,* is indented one level under the title, and it in turn has two subsidiary bullets. The next main bullet, *Review the flow of ideas,* is moved back to level one, and it, too, has two subsidiary bullets.

The outline is (to us) the ideal way to create and edit the presentation. The ***insertion point*** marks the place where new text is entered; this is established by

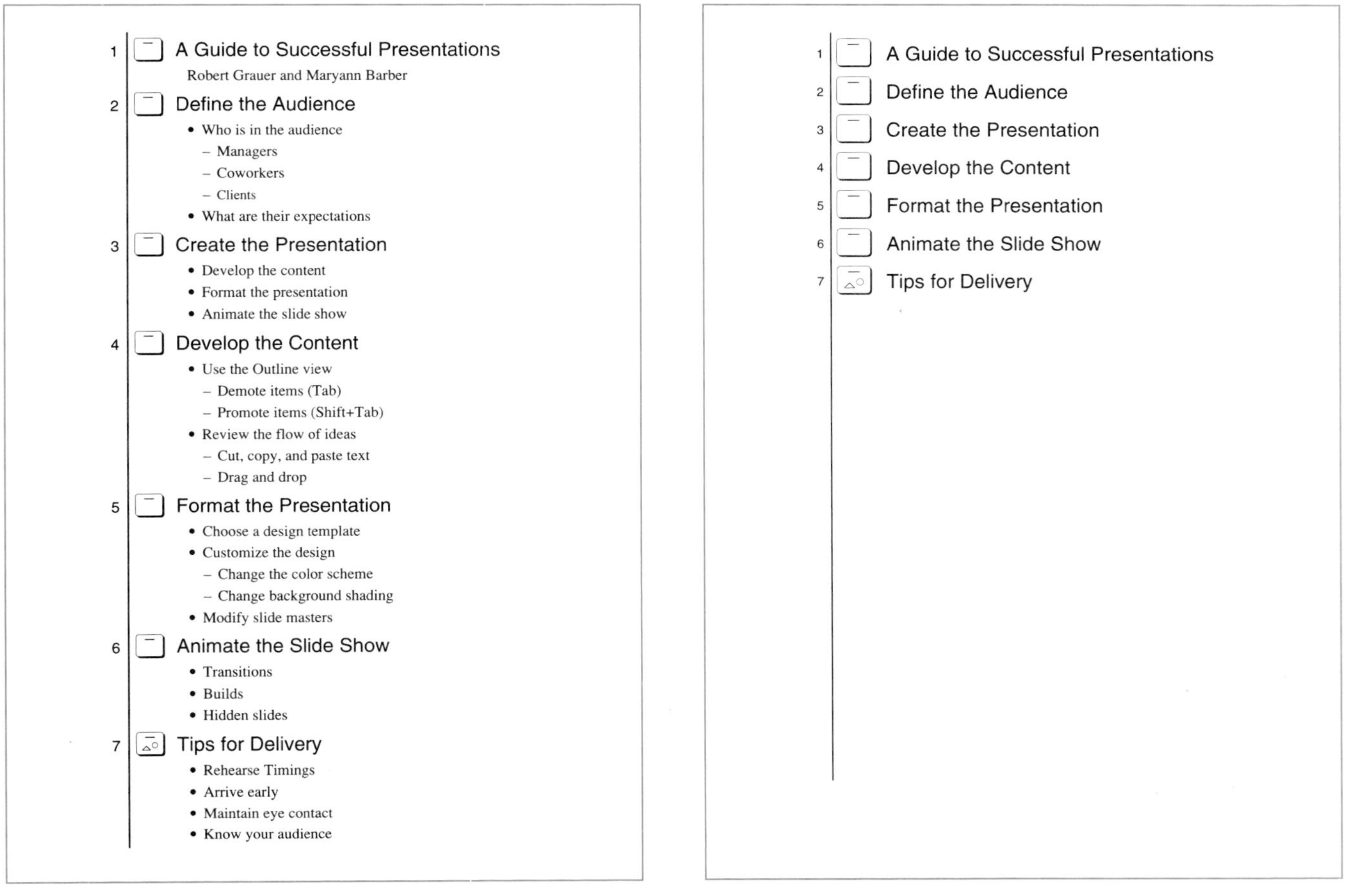

1 A Guide to Successful Presentations
Robert Grauer and Maryann Barber

2 Define the Audience
- Who is in the audience
  - Managers
  - Coworkers
  - Clients
- What are their expectations

3 Create the Presentation
- Develop the content
- Format the presentation
- Animate the slide show

4 Develop the Content
- Use the Outline view
  - Demote items (Tab)
  - Promote items (Shift+Tab)
- Review the flow of ideas
  - Cut, copy, and paste text
  - Drag and drop

5 Format the Presentation
- Choose a design template
- Customize the design
  - Change the color scheme
  - Change background shading
- Modify slide masters

6 Animate the Slide Show
- Transitions
- Builds
- Hidden slides

7 Tips for Delivery
- Rehearse Timings
- Arrive early
- Maintain eye contact
- Know your audience

(a) The Expanded Outline

1 A Guide to Successful Presentations
2 Define the Audience
3 Create the Presentation
4 Develop the Content
5 Format the Presentation
6 Animate the Slide Show
7 Tips for Delivery

(b) The Collapsed Outline

FIGURE 2.1 The Outline View

clicking anywhere in the outline. (The insertion point is automatically placed at the title of the first slide in a new presentation.) To enter text, click in the outline to establish the insertion point, then start typing. Press enter after typing the title of a slide or after entering the text of a bulleted item, which starts a new slide or bullet, respectively. The new item may then be promoted (by pressing **Shift+Tab**) or demoted (by pressing **Tab**) as necessary.

Editing is accomplished through the same techniques used in other Windows applications. For example, you can use the Cut, Copy, and Paste commands in the Edit menu (or the corresponding buttons on the Standard toolbar) to move and copy selected text, or you can simply drag and drop text from one place to another.

Figure 2.1b displays a collapsed view of the outline, which displays only the title of each slide. The advantage to this view is that you can see more slides on the screen at the same time, making it easier to move slides within the presentation. The slides are expanded or collapsed by using the appropriate tool on the Outline toolbar as described in a hands-on exercise. (The ***Outline toolbar*** appears automatically when you switch to the Outline view. As with the Standard and Formatting toolbars in Chapter 1, a ScreenTip will appear when you point to a button to describe its function.)

Text is formatted by using the select-then-do approach common to Word and Excel; that is, you select the text, then you execute the appropriate command or click the appropriate button. The selected text remains highlighted and is affected by all subsequent commands until you click elsewhere in the outline.

TEMPLATES

PowerPoint enables you to concentrate on the content of a presentation without concern for its appearance. You focus on what you are going to say, and trust in PowerPoint to format the presentation attractively. The formatting is implemented automatically by selecting one of the many templates that are supplied with PowerPoint.

A ***template*** is a design specification that controls every element in a presentation. It specifies the color scheme for the slides and the arrangement of the different elements (placeholders) on each slide. It determines the formatting of the text, the fonts that are used, and the size and placement of the bulleted text.

Figure 2.2 displays the title slide of a presentation in four different templates. Just choose the template you like, and PowerPoint formats the entire presentation according to that template. And don't be afraid to change your mind. You can use the Format menu at any time to select a different template and change the look of your presentation.

(a) Double Lines

(b) Sparkle

(c) Coins

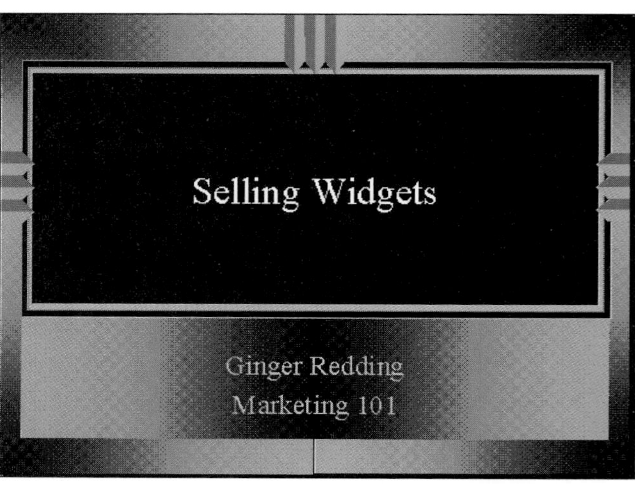

(d) Bevel

FIGURE 2.2 Templates

HANDS-ON EXERCISE 1

Creating a Presentation

Objective: To create a presentation by entering text in the Outline view; to check a presentation for spelling errors; and to apply a design template to a presentation. Use Figure 2.3 as a guide in the exercise.

STEP 1: Create a New Presentation

- ➤ Start PowerPoint. Close the Office Assistant if it appears. (You can reopen the Assistant at any time by clicking its button on the Standard toolbar.)
- ➤ Click the **option button** to create a new presentation using a **Blank Presentation**. Click **OK**.
- ➤ You should see the **New Slide** dialog box in Figure 2.3a with the AutoLayout for the title slide already selected. Click **OK** to create a title slide and simultaneously close the New Slide dialog box.
- ➤ If necessary, click the **Maximize buttons** in both the application and document windows so that PowerPoint takes the entire desktop and the current presentation is as large as possible. Both Maximize buttons will be replaced with Restore buttons as shown in Figure 2.3a.

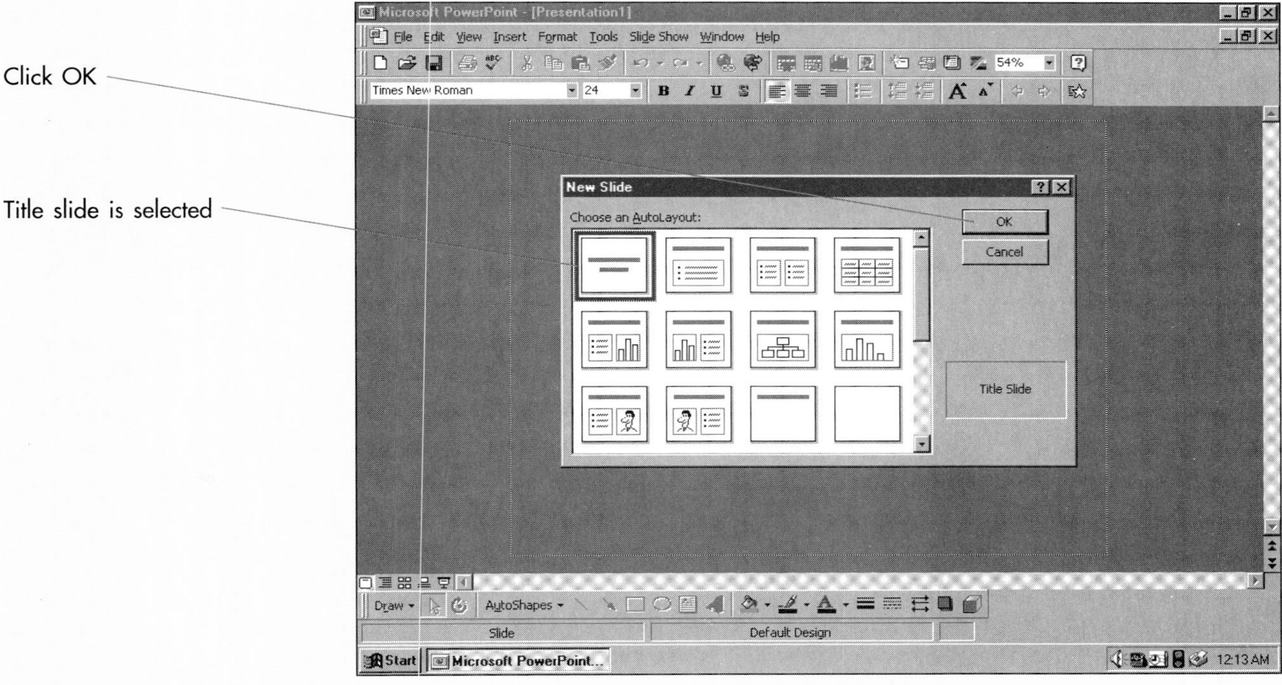

(a) Start PowerPoint (step 1)

FIGURE 2.3 Hands-on Exercise 1

CONTENT, CONTENT, AND CONTENT

It is much more important to focus on the content of the presentation than to worry about how it will look. Start with the AutoContent Wizard (described later in the chapter) or with a blank presentation in the Outline view. Save the formatting for last. Otherwise you will spend too much time changing templates and too little time developing the text.

STEP 2: Create the Title Slide

➤ Click anywhere in the box containing **Click to add title**, then type the title, **A Guide to Successful Presentations** as shown in Figure 2.3b. The title will automatically wrap to a second line.

➤ Click anywhere in the box containing **Click to add sub-title** and enter your name. Click outside the sub-title placeholder when you have entered your name.

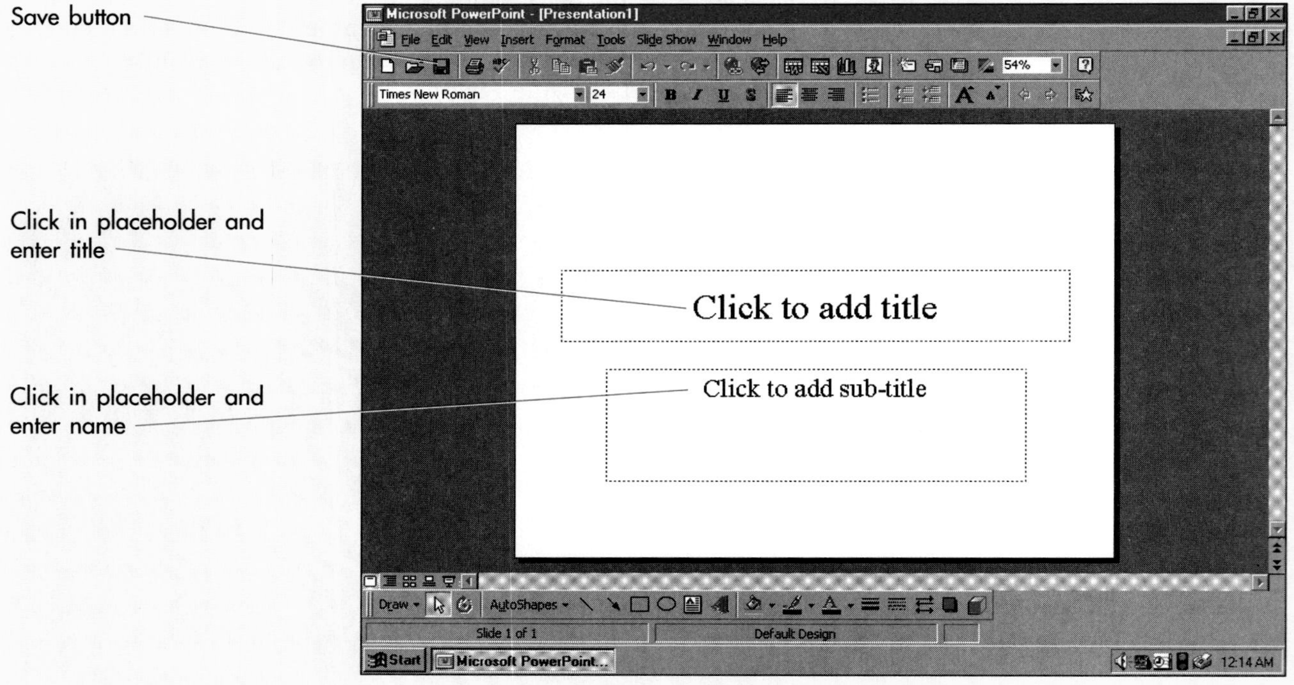

(b) Create the Title Slide (step 2)

FIGURE 2.3 Hands-on Exercise 1 (continued)

THE DEFAULT PRESENTATION

PowerPoint supplies a default presentation containing the specifications for color (a plain white background with black text), formatting, and AutoLayouts. The default presentation is selected automatically when you work on a blank presentation, and it remains in effect until you choose a different template.

STEP 3: Save the Presentation

- Pull down the **File menu** and click **Save** (or click the **Save button** on the Standard toolbar). You should see the Save dialog box in Figure 2.3c. If necessary, click the **Details button**.
- To save the file:
  - Click the **drop-down arrow** on the Save In list box.
  - Click the appropriate drive, drive C or drive A, depending on whether or not you installed the data disk on your hard drive.
  - Double click the **Exploring PowerPoint folder,** to make it the active folder (the folder in which you will save the document).
  - Enter **My First Presentation** as the name of the presentation.
  - Click **Save** or press the **enter key.** Click **Cancel** or press the **Esc key** if you see the Properties dialog box. The title bar changes to reflect the name of the presentation.

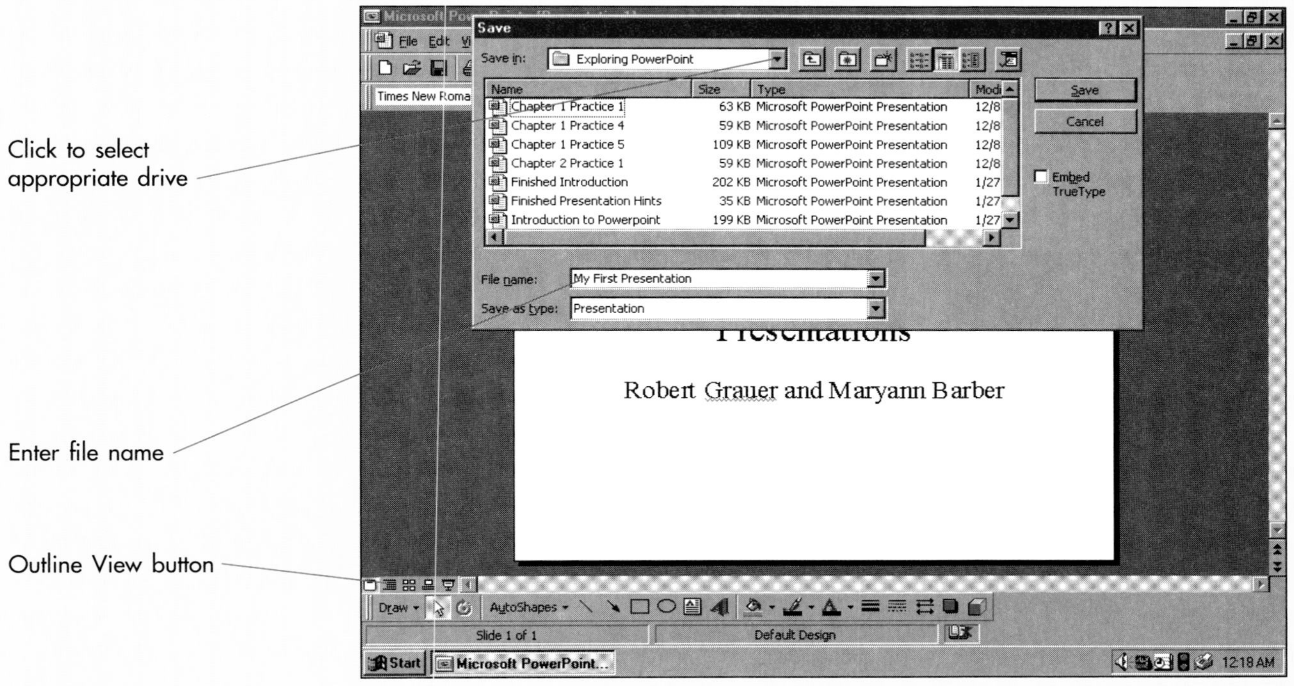

(c) The Save Command (step 3)

FIGURE 2.3 Hands-on Exercise 1 (continued)

STEP 4: Create the Presentation

- Click the **Outline view button** above the status bar to change to the Outline view. Your presentation at this point contains only the title slide.
- Pull down the **View menu** and (if necessary) toggle **Slide miniature** on.
- Click the **New Slide button** on the **Standard toolbar**. Select the **Bulleted List** AutoLayout. Click OK. The icon for slide 2 will appear in the outline. Type **Define the Audience** as the title of the slide and press **enter.**
- Press the **Tab key** (or click the **Demote button** on the Outline toolbar) to enter the first bullet. Type **Who is in the audience** and press **enter.**

➤ Press the **Tab key** (or click the **Demote button** on the Outline toolbar) to enter the second-level bullets.

- Type **Managers.** Press **enter.**
- Type **Coworkers.** Press **enter.**
- Type **Clients.** Press **enter.**

➤ Press **Shift+Tab** (or click the **Promote button** on the Outline toolbar) to return to the first-level bullets.

- Type **What are their expectations.** Press **enter.**

➤ Press **Shift+Tab** to enter the title of the third slide. Type **Tips for Delivery.** Add the remaining text for this slide and for slide 4 as shown in Figure 2.3d.

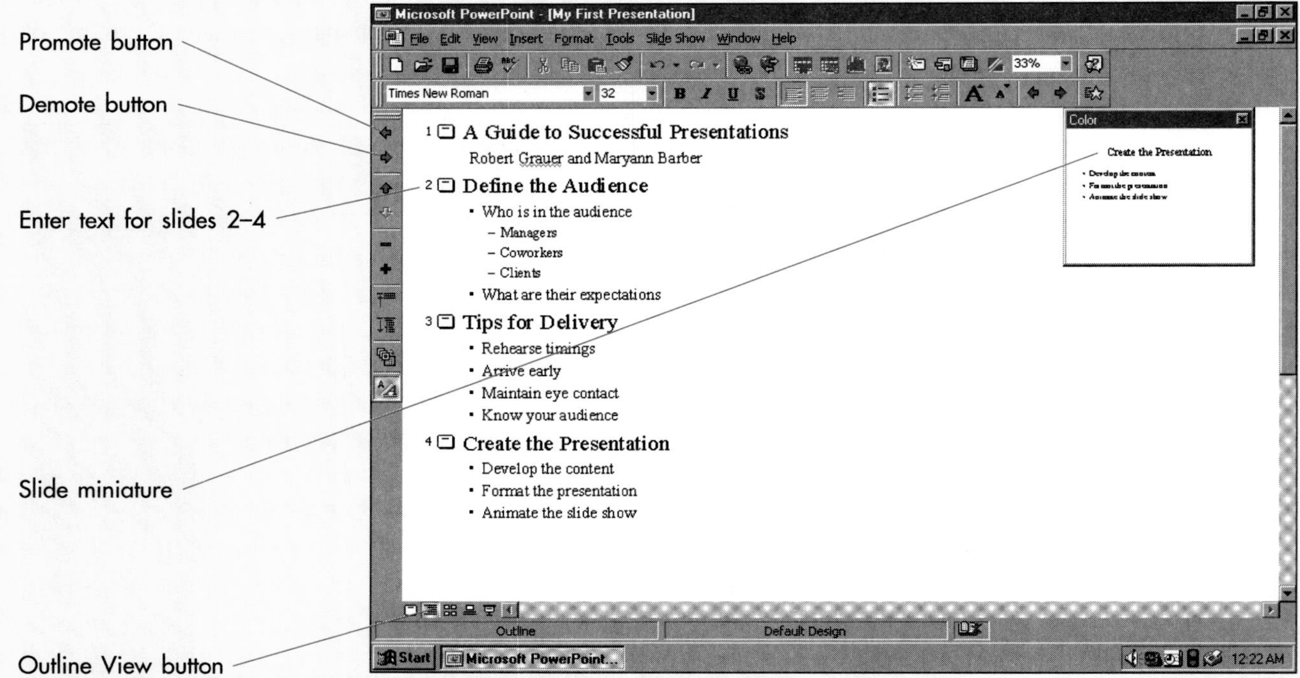

(d) Create the Presentation (step 4)

FIGURE 2.3 Hands-on Exercise 1 (continued)

JUST KEEP TYPING

The easiest way to enter the text for a presentation is in the Outline view. Just type an item, then press enter to move to the next item. You will be automatically positioned at the next item on the same level, where you can type the next entry. Continue to enter text in this manner. Press the Tab key as necessary to demote an item (move it to the next lower level). Press Shift+Tab to promote an item (move it to the next higher level).

STEP 5: The Spell Check

- Enter the title of the fifth slide as **Develop teh Content** (deliberately misspelling the word "the"). Try to look at the monitor as you type to see the AutoCorrect feature (common to all Office applications) in action. PowerPoint will correct the misspelling and change *teh* to *the*.
- If you did not see the correction being made, click the arrow next to the Undo button on the Standard toolbar and undo the last several actions. Click the arrow next to the Redo button and redo the corrections in order to see the error and subsequent auto correction.
- Enter the text of the remaining slides as shown in Figure 2.3e. Do *not* press enter after entering the last bullet on the last slide or else you will add a blank bullet.
- Click the **Spelling button** on the Standard toolbar to check the presentation for spelling:
  - The result of the Spell Check will depend on how accurately you entered the text of the presentation. We deliberately misspelled the word "Transitions" in the last slide.
  - Continue to check the document for spelling errors. Click **OK** when PowerPoint indicates it has checked the entire presentation.
- Click the **Save button** on the Standard toolbar to save the presentation.

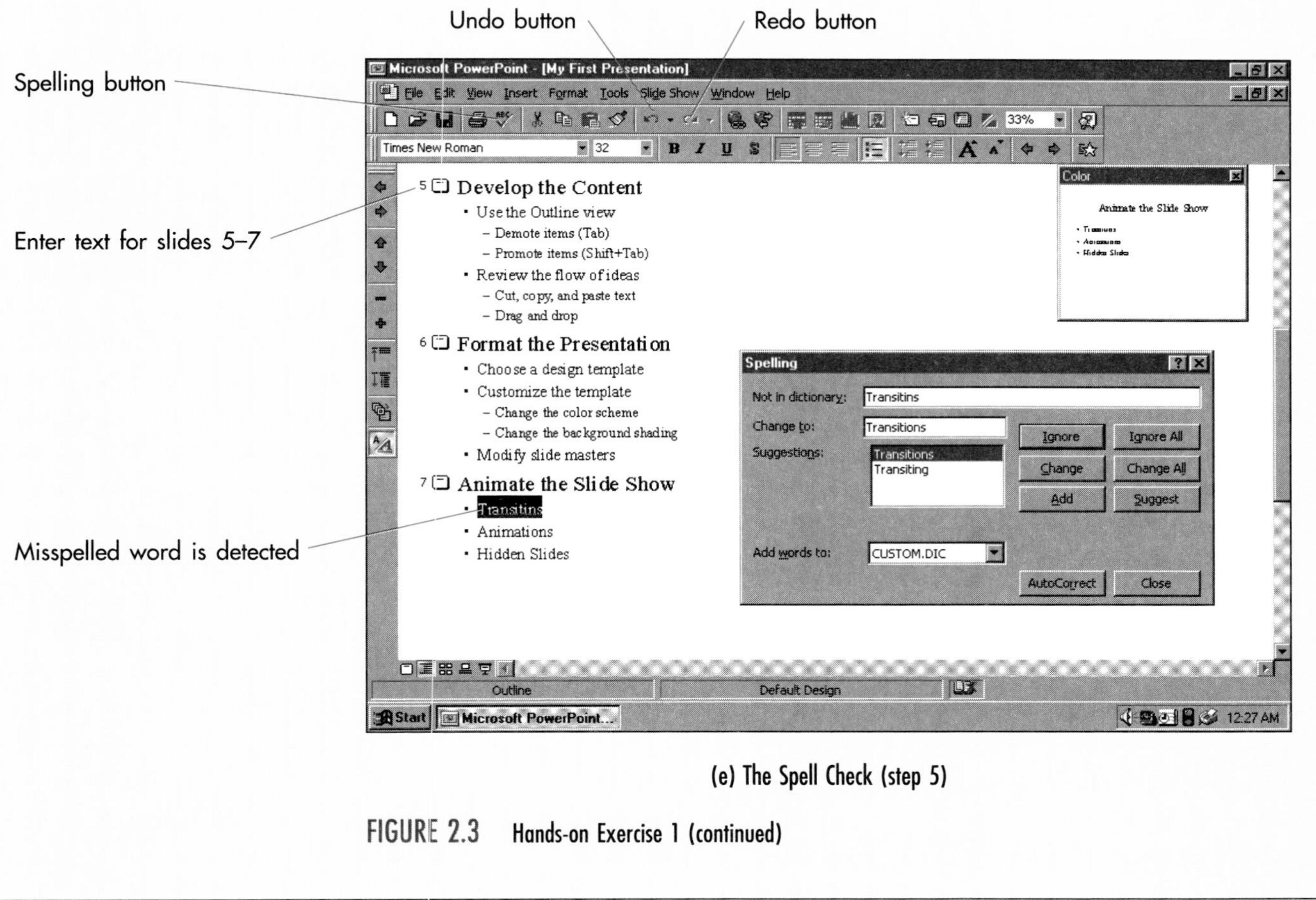

(e) The Spell Check (step 5)

FIGURE 2.3 Hands-on Exercise 1 (continued)

CREATE YOUR OWN SHORTHAND

Use the AutoCorrect feature, which is common to all Office applications, to expand abbreviations such as "usa" for United States of America. Pull down the Tools menu, click AutoCorrect, then type the abbreviation in the Replace text box and the expanded entry in the With text box. Click the Add command button, then click OK to exit the dialog box and return to the document. The next time you type usa in a presentation, it will automatically be expanded to United States of America.

STEP 6: Drag and Drop

- Press **Ctrl+Home** to move to the beginning of the presentation. Click the **Collapse All button** on the Outline toolbar to collapse the outline as shown in Figure 2.3f.
- Click the **icon** for **slide 3** (Tips for Delivery). The slide is selected and its title is highlighted. Point to the **slide icon** (the mouse pointer changes to a four-headed arrow), then click and drag to move the slide to the end of the presentation. Release the mouse.
- All of the slides have been renumbered. The slide titled Tips for Delivery has been moved to the end of the presentation and appears as slide 7. Click the **Expand All button** to display the contents of each slide. Click anywhere in the presentation to deselect the last slide.
- Click the **Save button** on the Standard toolbar to save the presentation.

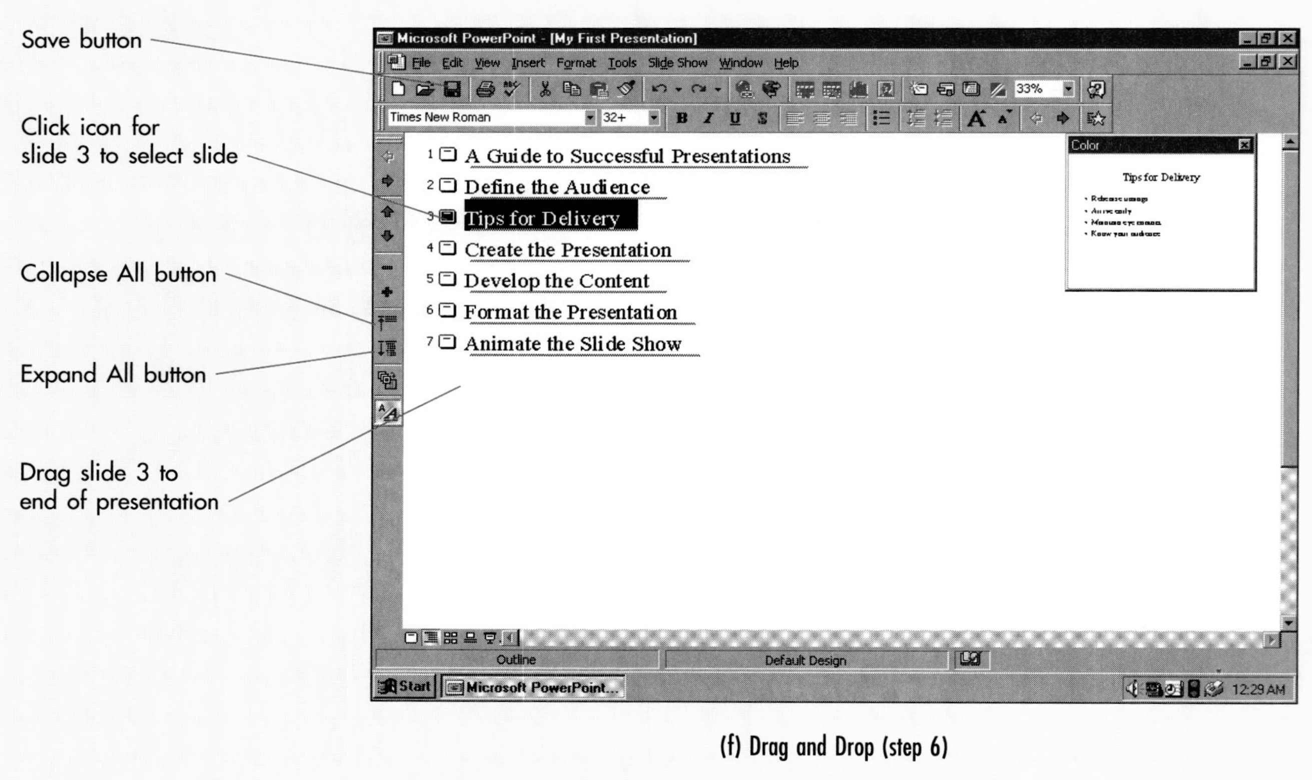

(f) Drag and Drop (step 6)

FIGURE 2.3 Hands-on Exercise 1 (continued)

> **SELECTING SLIDES IN THE OUTLINE VIEW**
>
> Click the slide icon or the slide number next to the slide title to select the slide. PowerPoint will select the entire slide (including its title, text, and any other objects that are not visible in the Outline view). Click the first slide, then press and hold the Shift key as you click the ending slide to select a group of sequential slides. Press Ctrl+A to select the entire outline. You can use these techniques to select multiple slides regardless of whether the outline is collapsed or expanded. The selected slides can be copied, moved, or deleted as a unit.

STEP 7: Choose a Design Template

➤ Pull down the **Format menu** and click **Apply Design** (or click the **Apply Design button** on the Standard toolbar) to display the dialog box in Figure 2.3g:

- The **Presentation Designs folder** should appear automatically in the List box. If it doesn't, change to this folder, which is contained within the Templates folder within the Microsoft Office Folder, which in turn is in the Programs Folder on drive c.
- **Presentation Templates** should be selected in the Files of Type list box. If it isn't, click the **drop-down arrow** to change to this file type.
- The **Preview view** should be selected. If it isn't, click the **Preview button** so that you can preview the selected template.
- Scroll through the available designs to select (click) the **Fireball template** as shown in Figure 2.3g. Click **Apply** to close the dialog box.

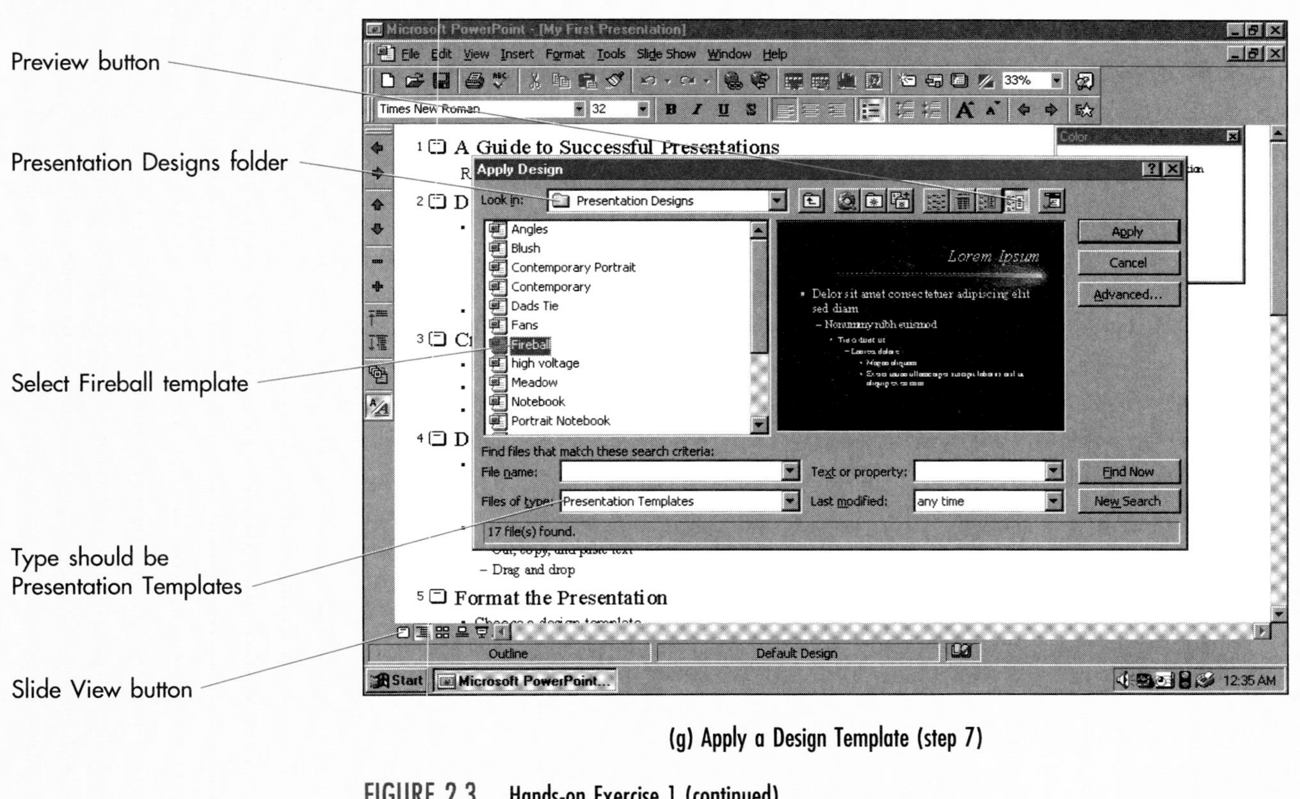

(g) Apply a Design Template (step 7)

FIGURE 2.3 Hands-on Exercise 1 (continued)

➤ You are still in the Outline view. The slide miniature, if open, will show the selected template. You can also click the **Slide View button** to change to the Slide view to see that the template has been applied. Save the presentation.

STEP 8: View the Presentation

➤ Press **Ctrl+Home** to move to the beginning of the presentation. Click the **Slide Show button** on the status bar to view the presentation as shown in Figure 2.3h.

- To move to the next slide: Click the **left mouse button,** type the letter **N,** or press the **PgDn key.**
- To move to the previous slide: Type the letter **P,** or press the **PgUp key.**

➤ Continue to move from one slide to the next until you come to the end of the presentation and are returned to the Slide view.

➤ Exit PowerPoint if you do not want to continue with the next exercise.

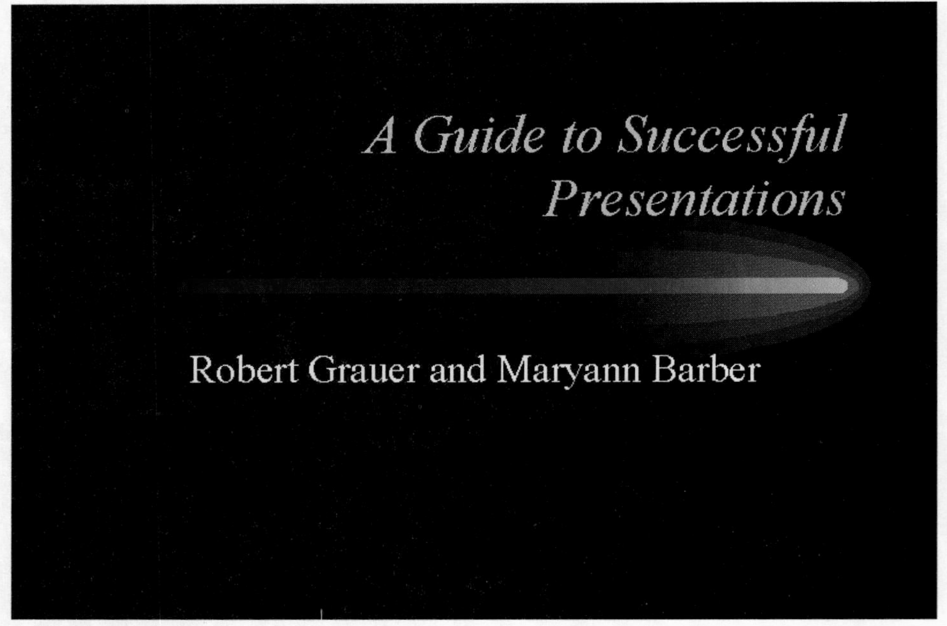

(h) View the Presentation (step 8)

FIGURE 2.3 Hands-on Exercise 1 (continued)

TIPS FROM THE OFFICE ASSISTANT

The Office Assistant indicates it has a suggestion by displaying a lightbulb. Click the lightbulb to display the tip, then click the Back or Next buttons as appropriate to view additional tips. The Assistant will not, however, repeat a tip from an earlier session unless you reset it at the start of a new session. This is especially important in a laboratory situation where you are sharing a computer with many students. To reset the tips, click the Assistant to display a balloon asking what you want to do, click the Options button, click the Options tab, then click the button to Reset My Tips.

CREATING A SLIDE SHOW

You develop the content of a presentation, then you format it attractively using a PowerPoint template. The most important step is yet to come—the delivery of the presentation to an audience, which is best accomplished through a computerized slide show (as opposed to using overhead transparencies or 35-mm slides). The computer becomes the equivalent of a slide projector, and the presentation is called a slide show.

PowerPoint can help you add interest to the slide show in two ways, transitions and animation effects. ***Transitions*** control the way in which one slide moves off the screen and the next slide appears. ***Animation effects*** vary the way in which objects on a slide appear during the presentation.

Transitions are created through the Slide Transition command in the Slide Show menu, which displays the dialog box in Figure 2.4a. The drop-down list box enables you to choose the transition effect. Slides may move on to the screen from the left or right, be uncovered by horizontal or vertical blinds, fade, dissolve, and so on. The dialog box also enables you to set the speed of the transition and/or to preview the effect.

Animation enables the bulleted items to appear one at a time with each successive mouse click. The effect is created through the Custom Animation command in the Slide Show menu, which displays the dialog box of Figure 2.4b. Each bullet can appear with its own transition effect. You can make the bullets appear one word or one letter at a time. You can specify that the bullets appear in reverse order (i.e., the bottom bullet first), and you can dim each bullet as the next one appears. You can even add sound and make the bullets appear in conjunction with a round of applause.

Transitions and animation effects can also be created from the Slide Sorter toolbar as shown in Figure 2.4c. As with the other toolbars, a ScreenTip is displayed when you point to a button on the toolbar.

ANIMATE THE OTHER OBJECTS

An animation effect can be applied to any object on a slide although it is used most frequently with bulleted text. You can create a special effect by animating another object, such as a piece of clip art or a chart. Point to the object, click the right mouse button to display a shortcut menu, then click the Custom Animations command to display a dialog box in which you choose the desired effect(s).

AUTOLAYOUTS

Every slide in a presentation is created according to one of 24 predefined slide formats known as AutoLayouts. The AutoLayout determines the objects that will appear on a slide (e.g., text, clip art, a chart, or other object) and specifies the placement for those objects. (Any text entered through the Outline view is automatically formatted according to the Bulleted List AutoLayout.)

What if, however, you want to add a graphic element, such as clip art (or a chart) to a bulleted slide that was created initially from the Outline view? The easiest way to do this is to change to the Slide view, then change the AutoLayout of the slide from a Bulleted List to one containing text and clip art (or text and a chart). This procedure is illustrated in steps 1 and 2 of the next hands-on exercise.

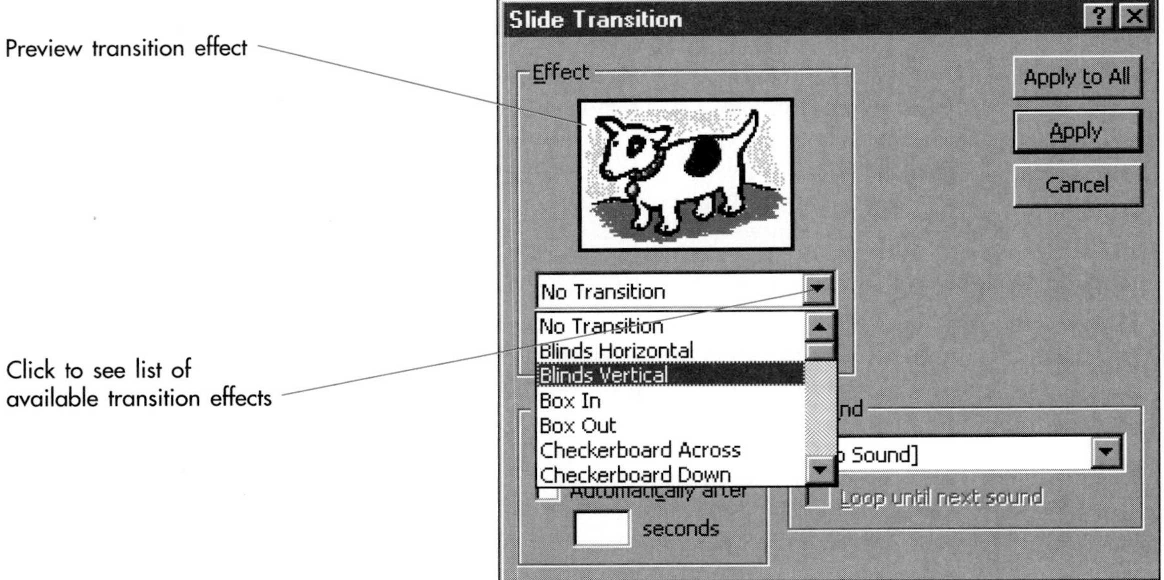

(a) Transitions

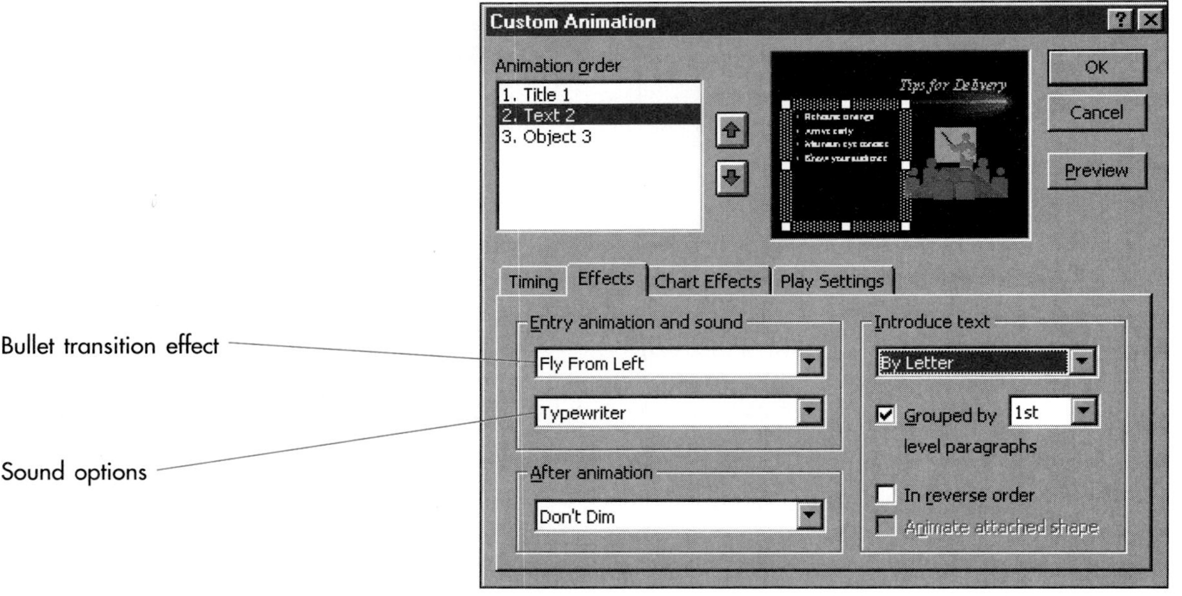

(b) Animation Effects

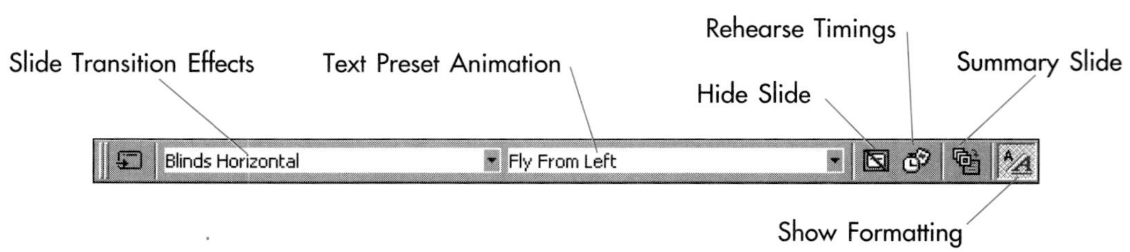

(c) Slide Sorter Toolbar

FIGURE 2.4 Transitions and Animation Effects

HANDS-ON EXERCISE 2

Animating the Presentation

Objective: To change the layout of an existing slide; to establish transition and animation effects. Use Figure 2.5 as a guide in the exercise.

STEP 1: Change the AutoLayout

- Start PowerPoint and open **My First Presentation** from the previous exercise. If necessary, switch to the **Slide view.** Press **Ctrl+End** to move to the last slide as shown in Figure 2.5a, which is currently a bulleted list.
- Pull down the **Format menu** and click **Slide Layout** (or click the **Slide Layout button** on the Standard toolbar).
- Choose the **Text and Clip Art layout** as shown in Figure 2.5a. Click the **Apply command button** to change the slide layout.

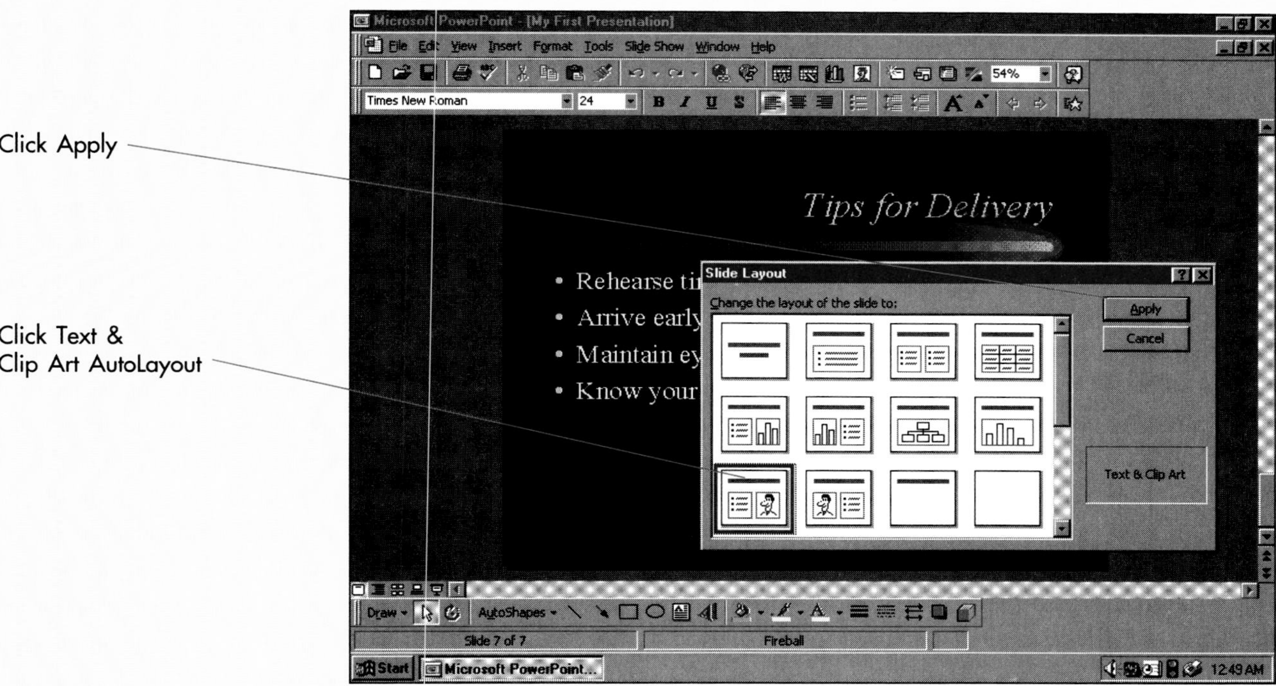

(a) Change the AutoLayout (step 1)

FIGURE 2.5 Hands-on Exercise 2

THE DOCUMENTS SUBMENU

One of the fastest ways to get to a recently used document, regardless of the application, is through the Windows 95 Start menu, which includes a Documents submenu containing the last 15 documents that were opened. Click the Start button, click (or point to) the Documents submenu, then click the document you wish to open (e.g., My First Presentation) if it appears on the submenu.

STEP 2: Add the Clip Art

- Double click the **placeholder** on the slide to add clip art. You will see the Microsoft Clip Gallery dialog box as shown in Figure 2.5b (although you may not see all of the categories listed in the figure).
- Click the **Clip Art tab.** Select the **Academic category**. Click the **down arrow** to scroll through the available images until you can select the image in Figure 2.5b. Click **Insert** to add the clip art to the slide.
- Save the presentation.

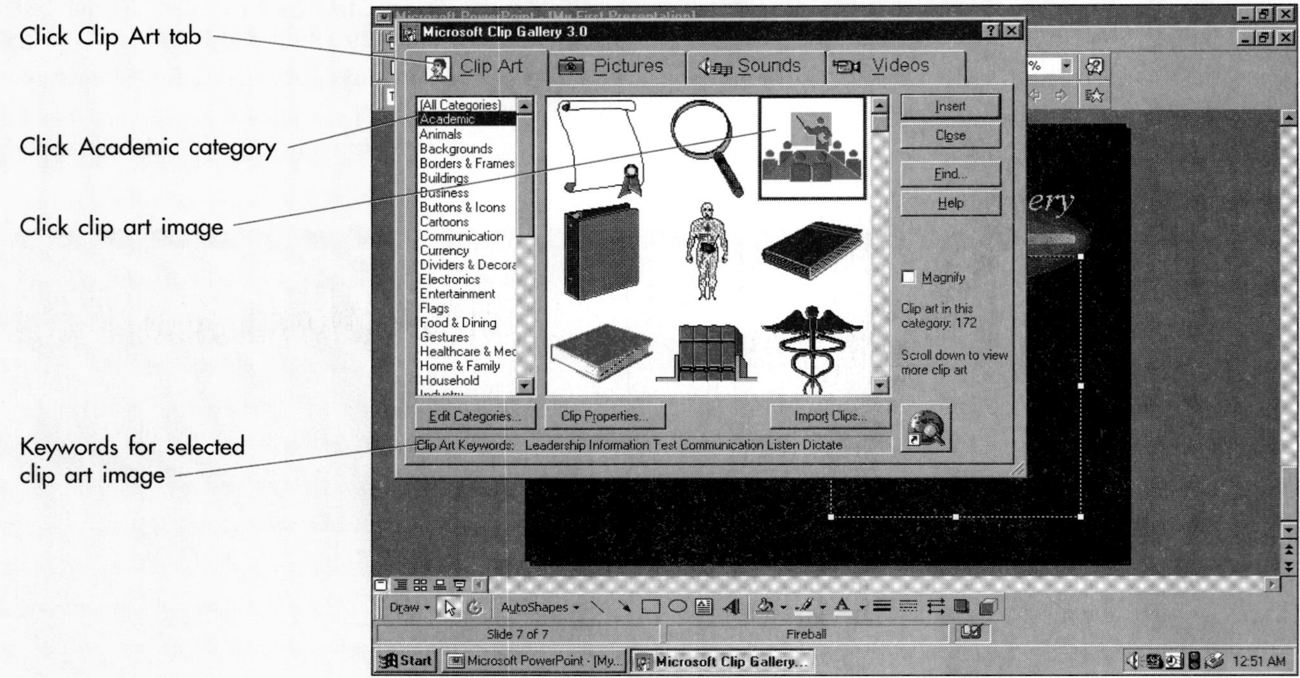

(b) Add the Clip Art (step 2)

FIGURE 2.5 Hands-on Exercise 2 (continued)

FIND THE RIGHT CLIP ART

The Find button within the Clip Gallery enables you to search for specific images. Open the Clip Gallery, then click the Find button to display the Find Clip dialog box. Click in the Keyword text box, then enter a key word (e.g., communication) that describes the clip art you want. Click the Find Now button, and the Clip Gallery will search for images that match the description. Be sure to have the Office CD-ROM available, or install the additional clip art to your hard drive.

STEP 3: Add Transition Effects

- Click the **Slide Sorter View button** to change to the Slide Sorter view as shown in Figure 2.5c. The number of slides you see at one time depends on the resolution of your monitor and the zoom percentage.
- Press **Ctrl+Home** to select the first slide. Pull down the **Slide Show menu,** then click **Slide Transition** to display the dialog box in Figure 2.5c. Click the **down arrow** on the Effect list box, then click the **Blinds Vertical** effect. You will see the effect displayed on the sample slide (dog) in the effect preview area. If you miss the effect, click the **dog** (or the **key**) to repeat the effect.
- Click **Apply** to accept the transition and close the dialog box. A slide icon appears under slide 1, indicating a transition effect.
- Point to slide 2, click the **right mouse button** to display a shortcut menu, then click the **Slide Transition command.** Choose **Checkerboard Across.** Click the **Slow option button.** Click **Apply** to close the dialog box.

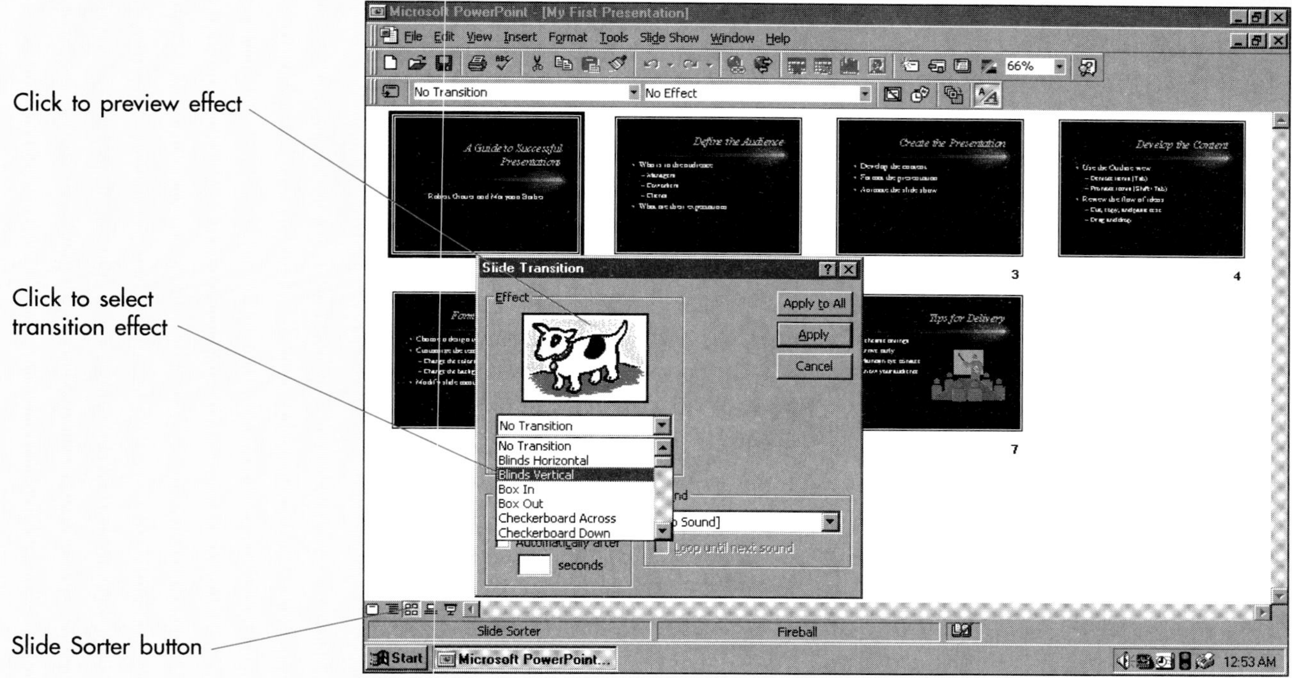

(c) Add Transition Effects (step 3)

FIGURE 2.5 Hands-on Exercise 2 (continued)

CHANGE THE MAGNIFICATION

Click the down arrow on the Zoom Control box to change the display magnification, which in turn controls the size of individual slides. The higher the magnification, the easier it is to read the text of an individual slide, but the fewer slides you see at one time. Conversely, changing to a smaller magnification decreases the size of the individual slides, but enables you to see more of the presentation.

STEP 4: Create a Summary Slide

- Pull down the **Edit menu** and press **Select All** to select every slide in the presentation. (Alternatively, you can also press and hold the **Shift key** as you click each slide in succession.)
- Click the **Summary Slide button** on the Slide Sorter toolbar to create a summary slide containing a bullet with the title of each selected slide. The new slide appears at the beginning of the presentation as shown in Figure 2.5d.
- Click and drag the **Summary slide** to the end of the presentation. (As you drag the slide, the mouse pointer changes to include the outline of a miniature slide and a vertical line appears to indicate the new position of the slide.)
- Release the mouse. The Summary slide has been moved to the end of the presentation and the slides are renumbered automatically.
- Save the presentation.

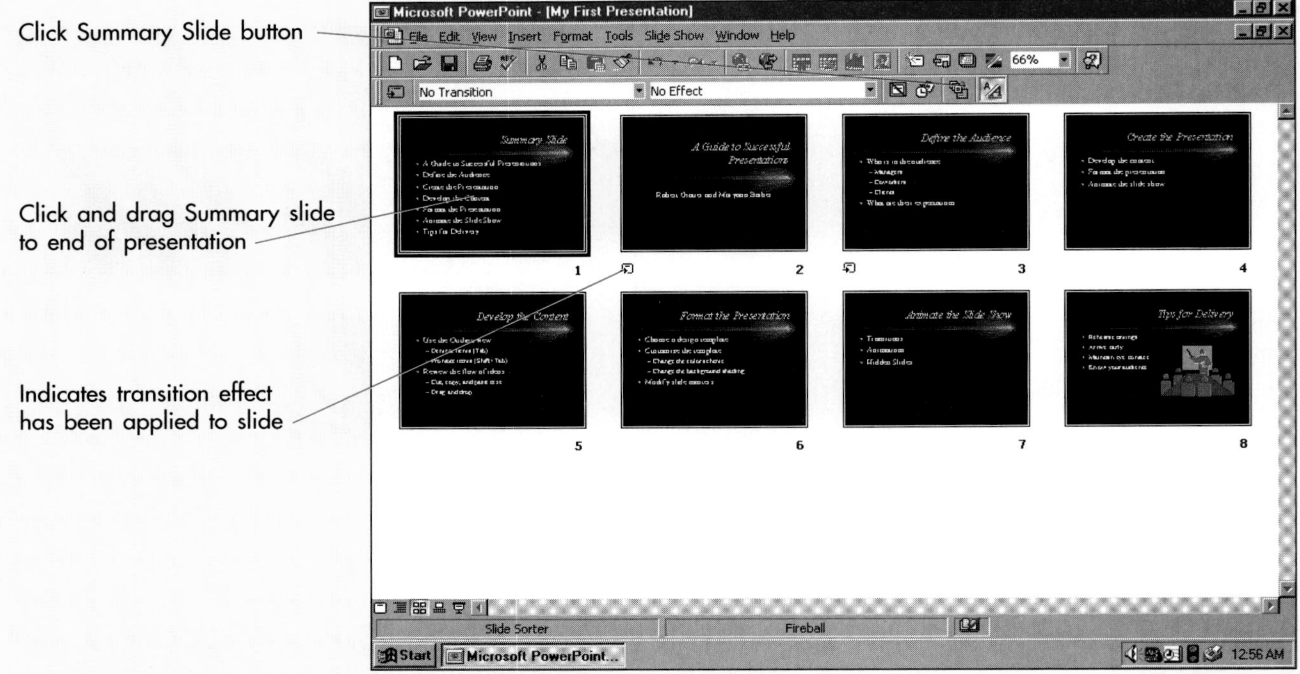

(d) Create a Summary Slide (step 4)

FIGURE 2.5 Hands-on Exercise 2 (continued)

> **SELECTING MULTIPLE SLIDES**
>
> You can apply the same transition or animation effect to multiple slides with a single command. Change to the Slide Sorter view, then select the slides by pressing and holding the Shift key as you click the slides. Use the Slide Show menu or the Slide Sorter toolbar to choose the desired transition or animation effect when all the slides have been selected. Click anywhere in the Slide Sorter view to deselect the slides and continue working.

STEP 5: Create the Animation Effects

- Double click the Summary slide to select the slide and simultaneously change to the Slide view. Click anywhere within the title to select the title.
- Pull down the **Slide Show menu**, click **Preset Animation** to display a cascade menu, then click **Typewriter** to display the title with this effect during the slide show.
- Click anywhere within the bulleted text to select the bulleted text (and deselect the title). Pull down the **Slide Show menu** and select **Custom Animation** to display the dialog box in Figure 2.5e.
- Click the **Effects tab.** Click the first **drop-down arrow** under Entry animation and sound to display the entry transitions. Click **Fly From Left**.
- Click the **drop-down arrow** to show the Introduce Text effects and select **All at Once.** Click the **drop-down arrow** for sound effects, then scroll until you can select **Screeching Brakes**.
- Check that the title appears first within the animation order. If not, select the title, then click the up arrow to move it ahead of the text. Click **OK** to close the dialog box. Click outside the placeholder to deselect it.
- Pull down the **Slide Show menu** a second time. Click **Animation Preview** to display the slide miniature window to see (and hear) the animation effect. Close the miniature window. Save the presentation.

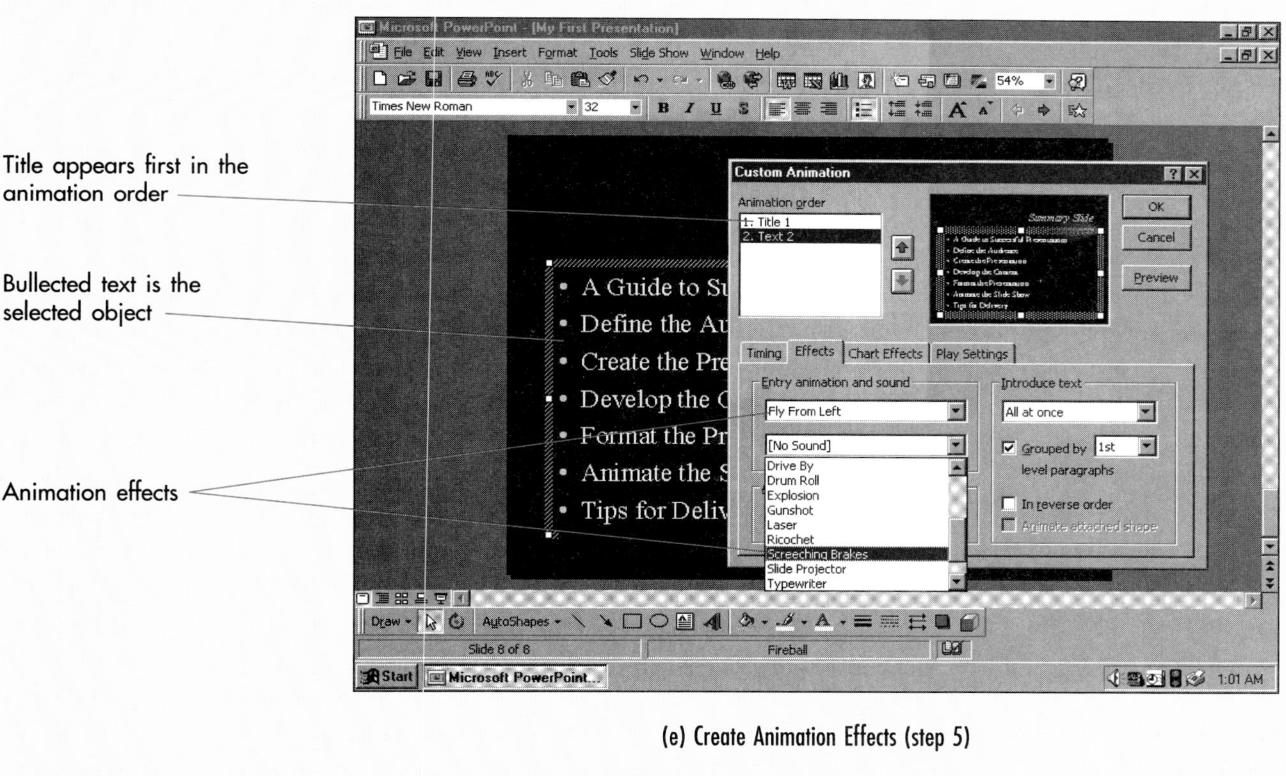

(e) Create Animation Effects (step 5)

FIGURE 2.5 Hands-on Exercise 2 (continued)

STEP 6: Show the Presentation

- Press **Ctrl+Home** to return to the first slide, then click the **Slide Show button** to view the presentation. You should see the opening slide in Figure 2.5f.
- Click the **left mouse button** to move to the next slide (or to the next bullet on the current slide when animation is in effect).
- Click the **right mouse button** to display the shortcut menu and return to the previous slide (or to the previous bullet on the current slide when a build is in effect).
- Continue to view the presentation until you come to the end. Click the left mouse button a final time to return to the regular PowerPoint window.
- Exit PowerPoint if you do not want to continue with the next exercise.

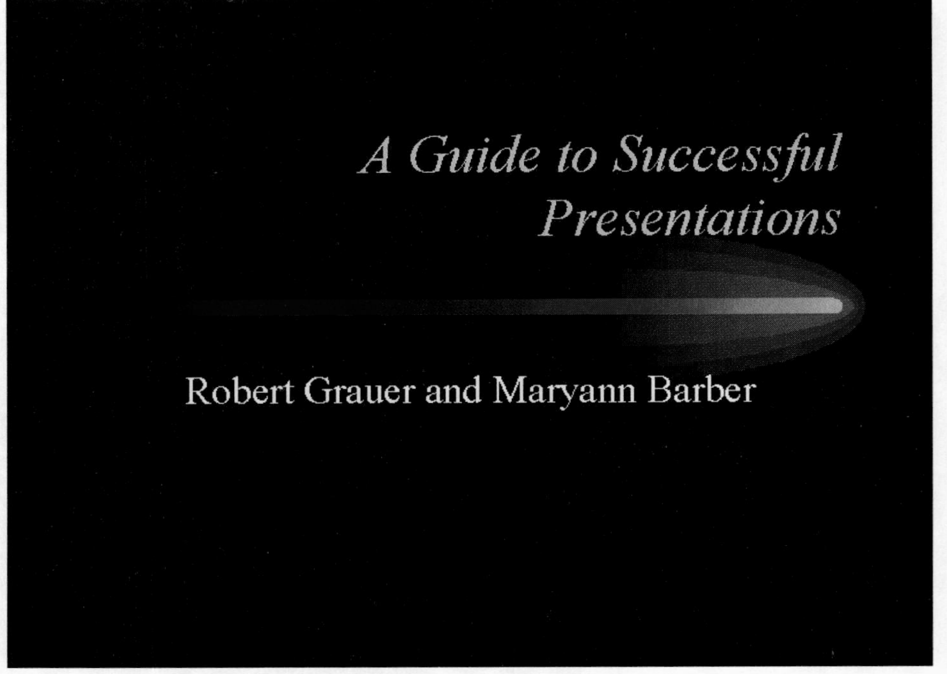

(f) Show the Presentation

FIGURE 2.5 Hands-on Exercise 2 (continued)

THE MEETING MINDER

The Meeting Minder enables you to keep track of action items as they occur during a presentation and to summarize them at the end of the presentation. Click the right mouse button at any time to display a shortcut menu, click Meeting Minder, then click the Action Items tab in the Meeting Minder dialog box. Enter the description assigned to Due Date for each item, click OK to close the dialog box, then continue through the slide show. An Action Items slide will appear at the end of the presentation with the items you added during the show.

One of the hardest things about creating a presentation is getting started. You have a general idea of what you want to say, but the words do not come easily to you. The AutoContent Wizard offers a potential solution. It asks you a series of questions, then it uses your answers to suggest a presentation. The presentation is not complete, but it does provide an excellent beginning.

The AutoContent Wizard is accessed through the New command in the File menu and is illustrated in Figure 2.6. The Wizard prompts you for the type of presentation in Figure 2.6a, for output options in Figure 2.6b, and for additional information in Figure 2.6c. The Wizard then has all the information it needs and proceeds to create a presentation for you. It even chooses a design template as illustrated by the title slide in Figure 2.6d. The template contains a color scheme and custom formatting to give your presentation a certain "look." You can change the design at any time to give your presentation a completely different look while retaining its content.

The real benefit of the Wizard, however, is the outline shown in Figure 2.6e, which corresponds to the topic you selected earlier (Marketing Plan). The outline is very general, as it must be, but it provides the essential topics to include in your presentation. You work with the outline provided by the AutoContent Wizard just as you would with any other outline. You can type over existing text, add or delete slides, move slides around, promote or demote items, and so on. In short, you don't use the AutoContent outline exactly as it is presented; instead you use the outline as a starting point, then modify it to fit the needs of your presentation.

The presentation created by the AutoWizard is based on one of several presentations that are provided with PowerPoint. You can use the Wizard as just described, or you can bypass the Wizard entirely and select the outline directly from the New command in the File menu. Either way you wind up with a professional presentation with respect to design and content. Naturally, you have to modify the content to fit your needs, but you have jump-started the creative process. You simply open the presentation, then you modify the existing text as necessary, while retaining the formatting in the selected template.

Figure 2.7 displays the title slides of several sample presentations that are included with PowerPoint. The presentations vary considerably in content and design. There is a presentation for a creativity session in Figure 2.7a, a business plan in Figure 2.7b, and even a presentation to communicate bad news in Figure 2.7c. The presentation in Figure 2.7d is one of several developed by the Dale Carnegie Foundation and is designed to thank a speaker. The presentations in Figure 2.7e and 2.7f are for an employee orientation and a Who's Who corporate list. Animation and branching are also built into several of the presentations. Look carefully at the Business Plan in Figure 2.7b, which contains a series of buttons that link directly to other slides in the presentation.

CHOOSE AN APPROPRIATE DESIGN

A design should enhance a presentation without calling attention to itself. It should be consistent with your message, and as authoritative or informal as the situation demands. Choosing the right template requires common sense and good taste. What works in one instance will not necessarily work in another. You would not, for example, use the same template to proclaim a year-end bonus as you would to announce a fourth-quarter loss and impending layoffs.

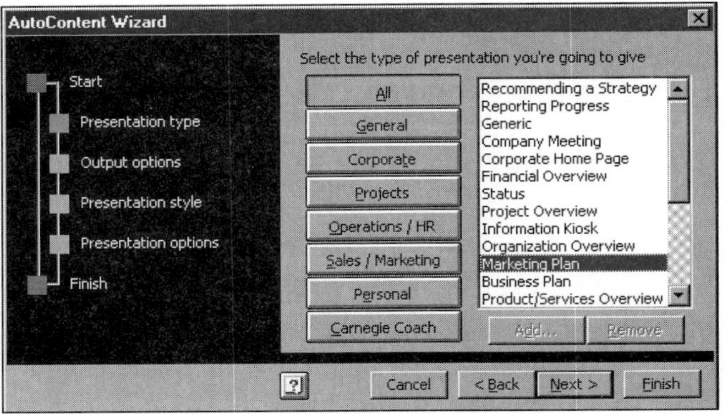

(a) Presentation Type

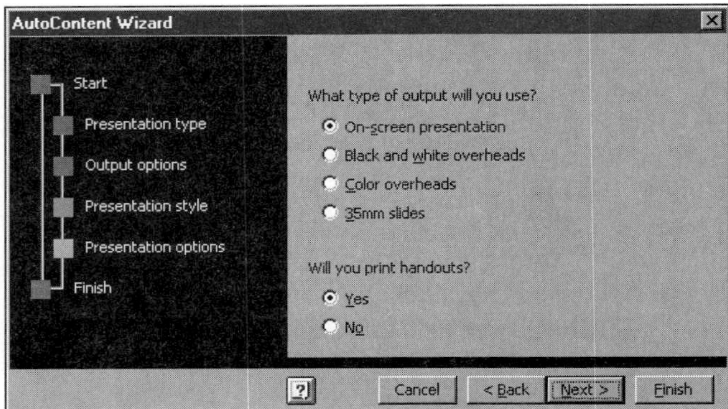

(b) Presentation Style

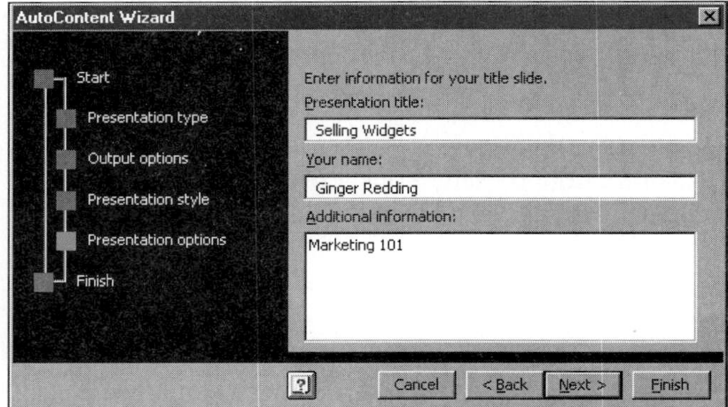

(c) Presentation Options

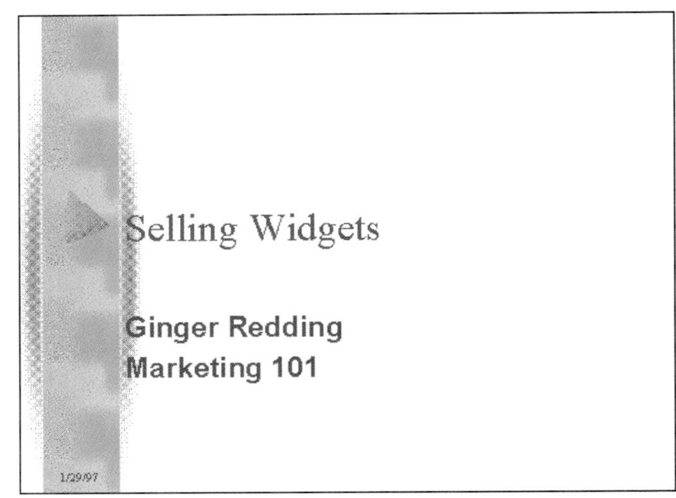

(d) Title Slide and Selected Template

1 Selling Widgets
- Ginger Redding
- Marketing 101

2 Market Summary
- Market Past, Present, & Future
  - Review changes in market share, leadership, players, market shifts, costs, pricing, competition

3 Product Definition
- Describe product/service being marketed

4 Competition
- The competitive landscape
  - Provide an overview of product competitors, their strengths and weaknesses
  - Position each competitor's product against new product

5 Positioning
- Positioning of product or service
  - Statement that distinctly defines the product in its market and against its competition over time
- Consumer promise
  - Statement summarizing the benefit of the product or service to the consumer

6 Communication Strategies
- Messaging by audience
- Target consumer demographics

(e) Suggested Outline (additional slides not shown)

FIGURE 2.6 The AutoContent Wizard

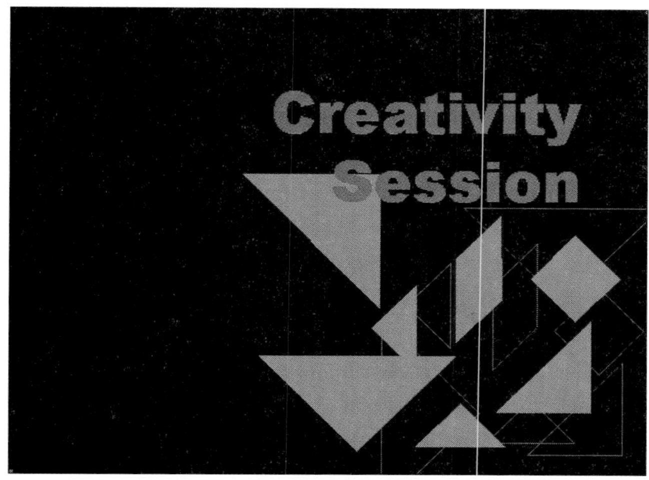

(a) Creativity Session

(b) Business Plan

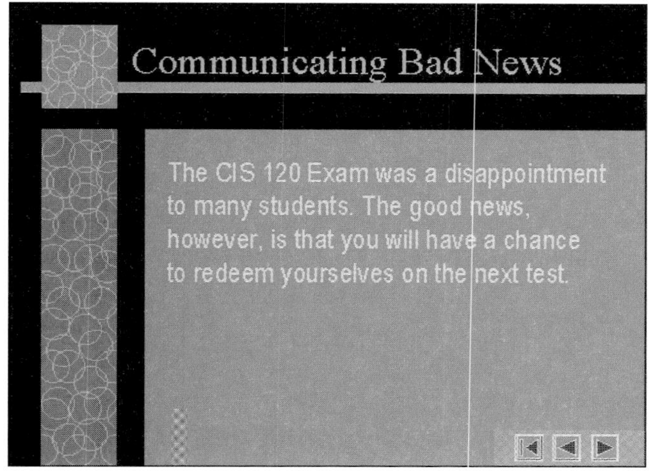

(c) Communicating Bad News

(d) Thanking a Speaker

(e) Employee Orientation

(f) Who's Who

FIGURE 2.7 Suggested Presentations

A template is a design specification that controls every aspect of a presentation. It specifies the background design, the formatting of the text, the fonts and colors that are used, and the design, size, and placement of the bullets. You can change the look of a presentation at any time by applying a different template. Changing from one template to another changes the appearance of the presentation in every way, while maintaining the content.

What if, however, you want to make subtle changes to the template? In other words, you are content with the overall design, but you want to change one or more of its elements. You don't want a radical change, but you want to fine-tune the presentation by modifying its color scheme and/or background shading. Or perhaps you want to add a consistent element to every slide, such as a corporate name or logo.

The Color Scheme

A ***color scheme*** is a set of eight balanced colors that is associated with a template. It consists of a background color, a color for the title of each slide, a color for lines and text, and five additional colors to provide accents to different elements, such as shadows and fill colors. Each template has a default color scheme, which is applied when the template is selected. Each template also has a set of alternate color schemes from which to choose.

Figure 2.8a displays the title slide of a presentation. The Fans template is selected and the default color scheme is in effect. Figure 2.8b displays the Color Scheme dialog box (which is accessed through the Format menu) with the suggested color schemes for this template. To choose one of the other color schemes, select the color scheme, then click the Apply All command button to apply the new color scheme to the entire presentation.

You have additional flexibility in that you can change any of the individual colors within a color scheme. Select the desired color scheme, click the Custom tab, select the color you wish to change (e.g., the color of the Title Text), then click the Change Color command button as shown in Figure 2.8c. Figure 2.8d displays the title slide after the color scheme has been changed to green, then further customized by changing the color of the title text to bright yellow.

SLIDES VERSUS TRANSPARENCIES

Choose the color scheme in conjunction with the means of delivery. Light backgrounds work best for overhead transparencies, whereas dark backgrounds are preferable for computer presentations and 35-mm slides. This suggestion is presented in the Color Scheme dialog box itself (as can be seen in Figure 2.8b). We urge you to look for similar tips as you use other PowerPoint features.

The Background Shading

The ***Background command*** in the Format menu changes the background color and/or shading of a slide, enabling you to truly fine-tune a presentation. Figure 2.9a displays the title slide of a presentation using the Soaring template. This design incorporates background shading that goes from blue to black as you go from left to right on the slide. The shading is built into the template according to the Shaded Fill dialog box in Figure 2.9b.

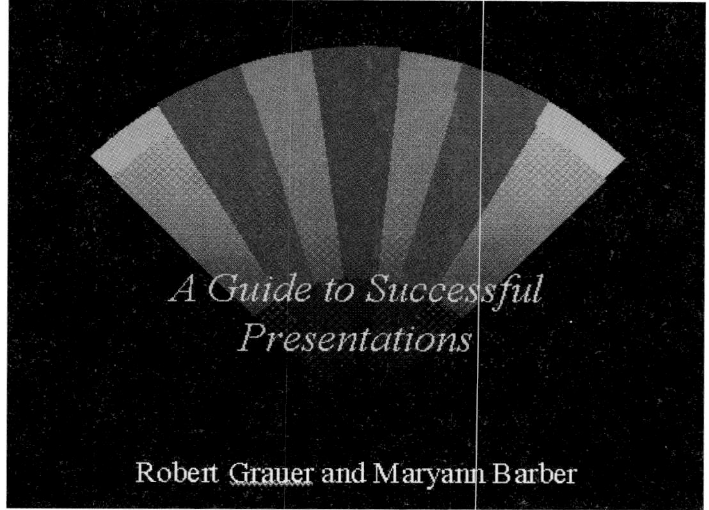

(a) Original Slide

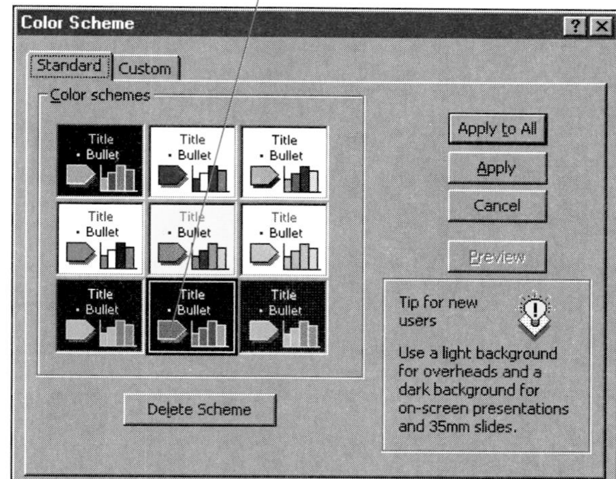

(b) Standard Color Schemes

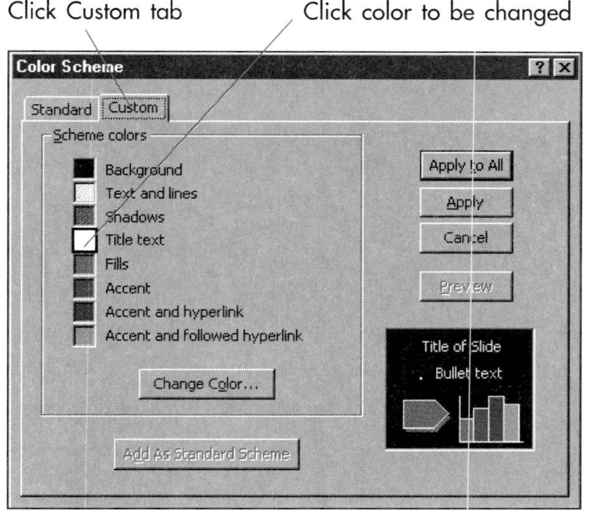

(c) Custom Colors

(d) Modified Slide

FIGURE 2.8 Changing the Color Scheme

Figure 2.9c changes the parameters within the Fill Effects dialog box to use a single color (blue) and a horizontal shading pattern. Again, you have additional flexibility in that you can change the variation in color by dragging the scroll box from dark to light or vice versa. You can also choose from one of four variations of horizontal shading. The modified title slide is shown in Figure 2.9d.

PowerPoint Masters

One of the best ways to customize a presentation is to add a unifying element to each slide, such as a corporate name or logo. You could add the element to every slide, but that would be unnecessarily tedious. It is much easier to use the View menu to add the element to the ***slide master,*** which defines the formatting and other elements that appear on the individual slides. Any change to the slide master is automatically reflected in every slide (except for the title slide).

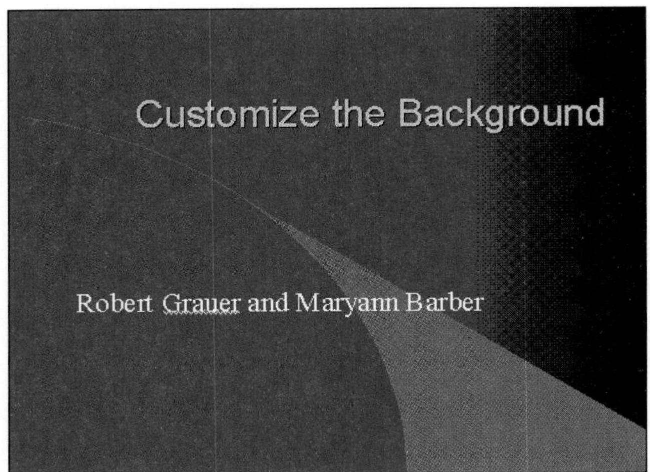

(a) Original Slide

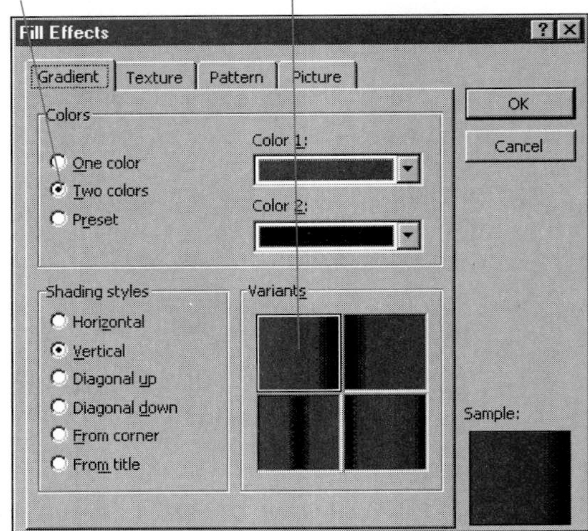

(b) Default Background

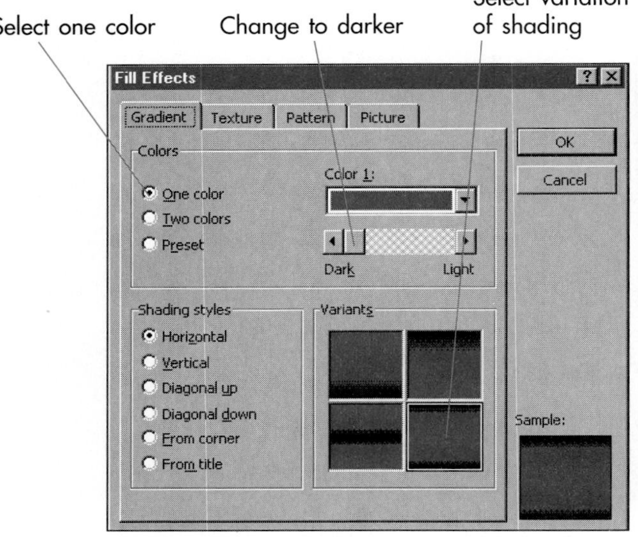

(c) Modified Background

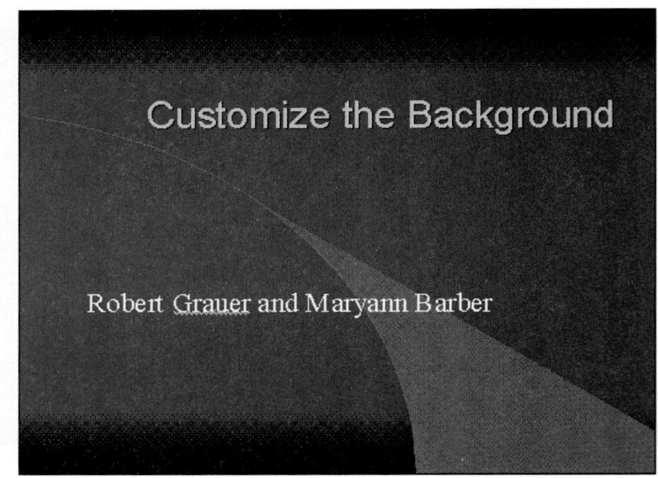

(d) Modified Slide

FIGURE 2.9 Customize the Background

Consider, for example, the slide master shown in Figure 2.10, which contains a placeholder for the title of the slide and a second placeholder for the bulleted text. The slide master also contains additional placeholders at the bottom of the slide for the date, footer, and slide number. Change the position and/or content of any of these elements on the master slide, and the corresponding element will be changed throughout the presentation. Thus, you could add the name of the organization in the footer area of the master slide, and have it appear on every slide in the presentation. In similar fashion, any change to the font, bullets, font color, point size, or alignment within a placeholder would also carry through to all of the individual slides.

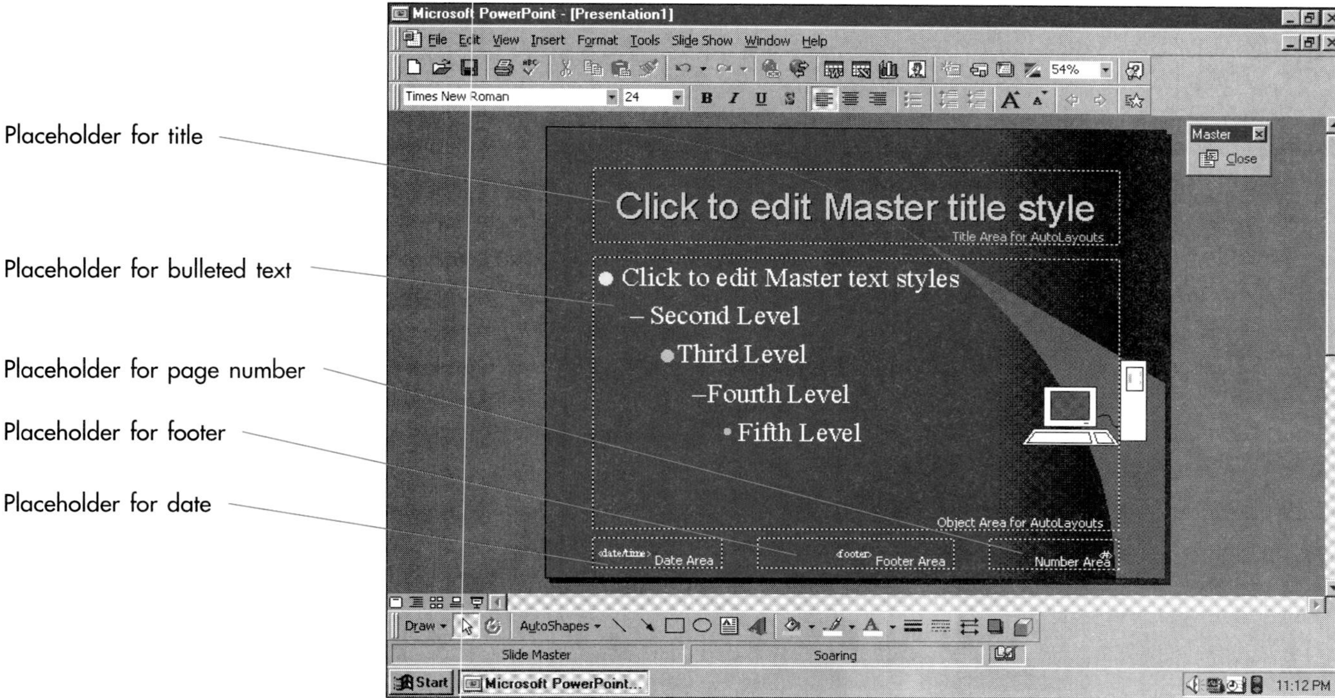

FIGURE 2.10 The Slide Master

The slide master is modified by using commands from the appropriate menu or toolbar. The easiest way to place a logo on the slide master (such as the small computer in Figure 2.10) is to click the Insert Clip Art button on the Standard toolbar. This in turn displays the Microsoft Clip Gallery dialog box, in which you select the desired clip art. Once the clip art has been added to the slide master, you can click and drag its sizing handles to move and size the clip art like any other Windows object. Every slide in the presentation will contain the clip art image that was added to the slide master.

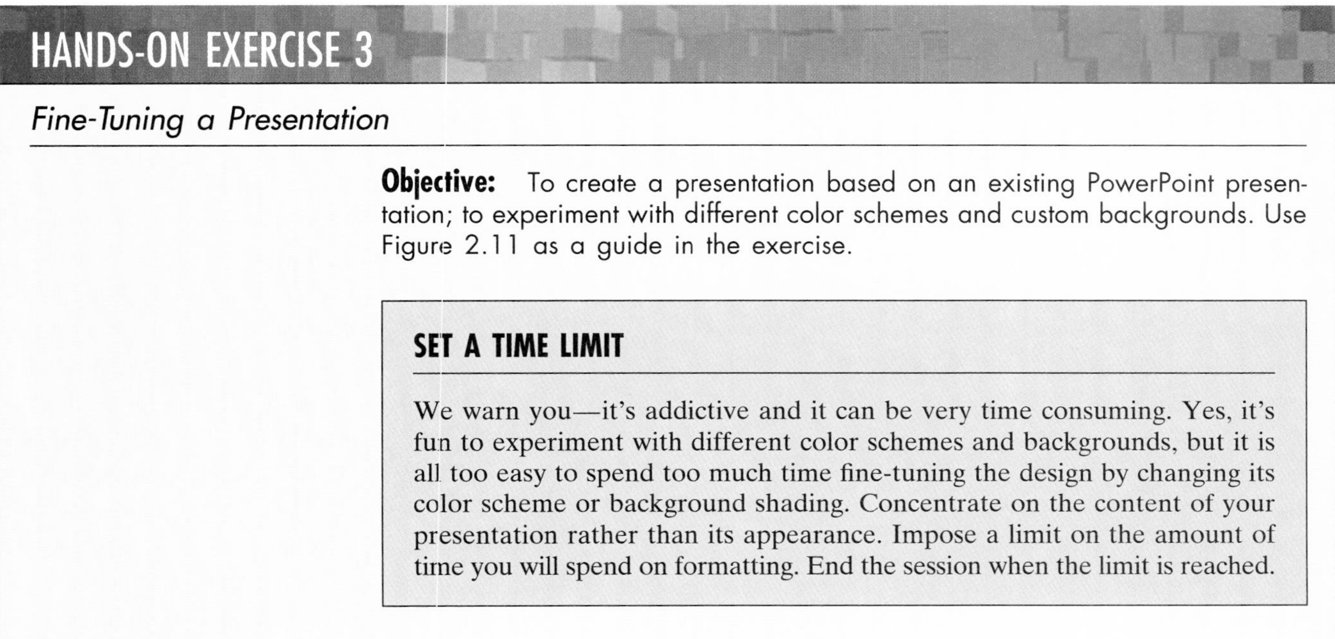

HANDS-ON EXERCISE 3

Fine-Tuning a Presentation

Objective: To create a presentation based on an existing PowerPoint presentation; to experiment with different color schemes and custom backgrounds. Use Figure 2.11 as a guide in the exercise.

SET A TIME LIMIT

We warn you—it's addictive and it can be very time consuming. Yes, it's fun to experiment with different color schemes and backgrounds, but it is all too easy to spend too much time fine-tuning the design by changing its color scheme or background shading. Concentrate on the content of your presentation rather than its appearance. Impose a limit on the amount of time you will spend on formatting. End the session when the limit is reached.

STEP 1: Open an Existing Presentation

- Start PowerPoint. Pull down the **File menu**, click **New** to display the New Presentations dialog box, then click the **Presentations tab.**
- Click the **Details button** so that you can see the title of each presentation more clearly. Scroll until you can select the **Reporting Progress (Standard)** presentation as shown in Figure 2.11a.
- Click **OK** to open the presentation. Save the presentation as **Reporting Progress.**

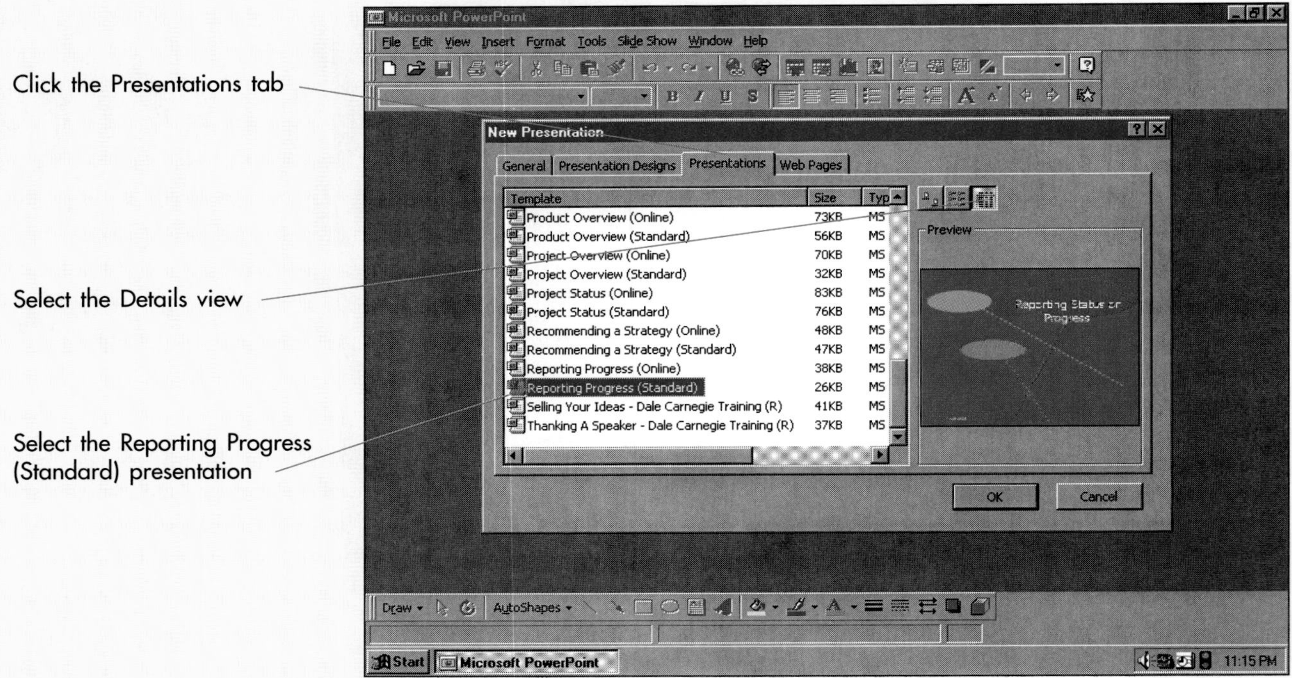

(a) Open the Presentation (step 1)

FIGURE 2.11 Hands-on Exercise 3

EXTRA PRESENTATIONS

The standard PowerPoint installation contains 38 suggested presentations on a variety of subjects. The variety is not as great as you might expect since many of the presentations come in both a standard and an online (Web) version, effectively halving the selection. Twenty-six additional presentations (on 13 topics) are available in the ValuPack folder on the CD-ROM. (Select the ValuPack folder, select the Template folder, then open the Presentation folder.) Ask your instructor for information about these additional presentations.

STEP 2: Modify the Outline

- Change to the **Outline view.** If necessary, pull down the **View menu** and toggle the **Slide Miniature** on as shown in Figure 2.11b.
- Change the entry on the title slide to **Reporting Progress.** Press the **enter key** at the end of the title to move to a new line. Press **Tab** to indent one level. Enter the names of your group (e.g., Tom, Dick, and Harry).
- Scroll through the nine slides, which are included in the default presentation. The outline is very general, as it must be, but it provides the essential topics to report the progress for your study group. Change the text as appropriate.
- Save the presentation.

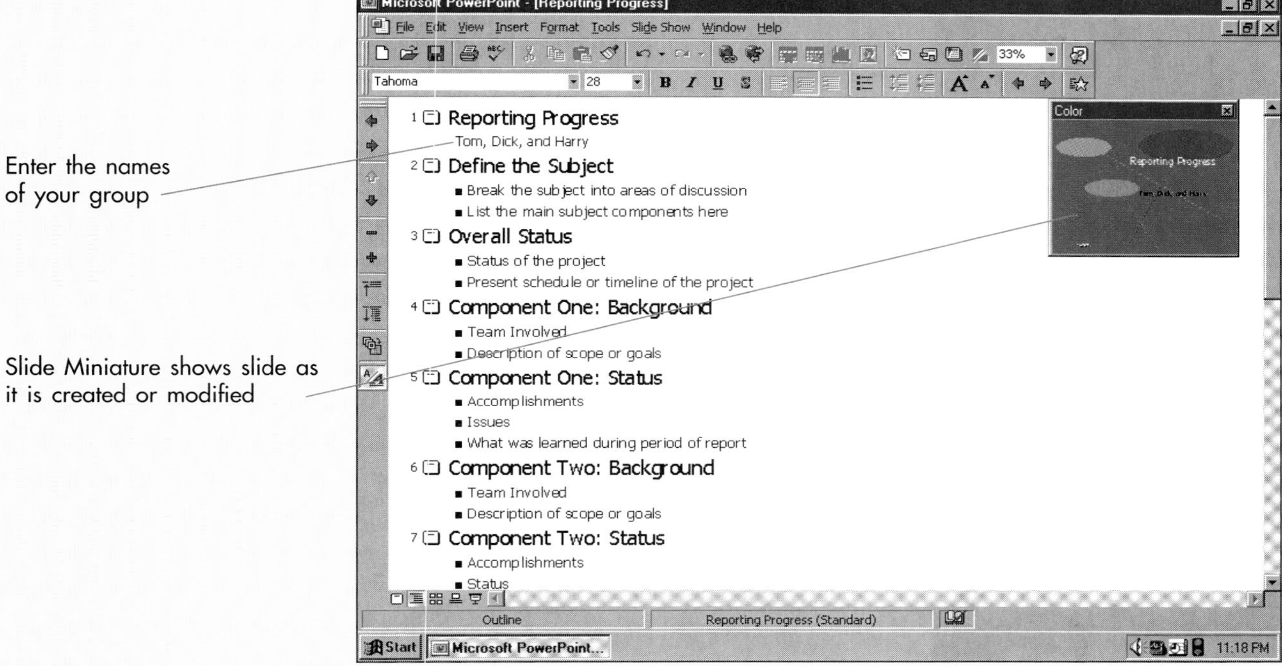

(b) Modify the Outline (step 2)

FIGURE 2.11 Hands-on Exercise 3 (continued)

> **ADDING CLIP ART**
>
> The easiest way to add clip art to a bulleted list is to change to the Slide view, then change the AutoLayout of the slide. Click the Slide Layout button on the Standard toolbar, choose the AutoLayout with Text and Clip Art, and click the Apply command button. Double click the clip art placeholder on the slide, then select the desired image from the Microsoft Clip Gallery.

STEP 3: Change the Slide Master

- Pull down the **View menu,** click **Master,** then click **Slide Master** to display the slide master as shown in Figure 2.11c. (The Header and Footer dialog box is not yet visible.)
- Click the **dashed lines** surrounding the number area at the bottom right of the slide to select this element. Press the **Del key** to delete this element.
- Click the **dashed lines** surrounding the footer area at the bottom left of the slide, then click and drag the footer to the right side of the slide as shown in Figure 2.11c.
- Pull down the **View menu.** Click **Header and Footer** to display the Header and Footer dialog box:
  - The **Date and Time** check box is selected. Click the option button to **Update Automatically.**
  - Select the **Footer** check box, then enter the name of your school as shown in Figure 2.11c.
  - Check the box to suppress the display on the title slide.
  - Click the **Apply to All command button** to accept these settings and close the dialog box.
- Click the **Slide view button** on the status bar, then press the **PgDn key** once or twice to move from slide to slide. You should see today's date and the name of your school at the bottom of each slide except for the title slide. (Press **Ctrl+Home** to view the title slide.)
- Save the presentation.

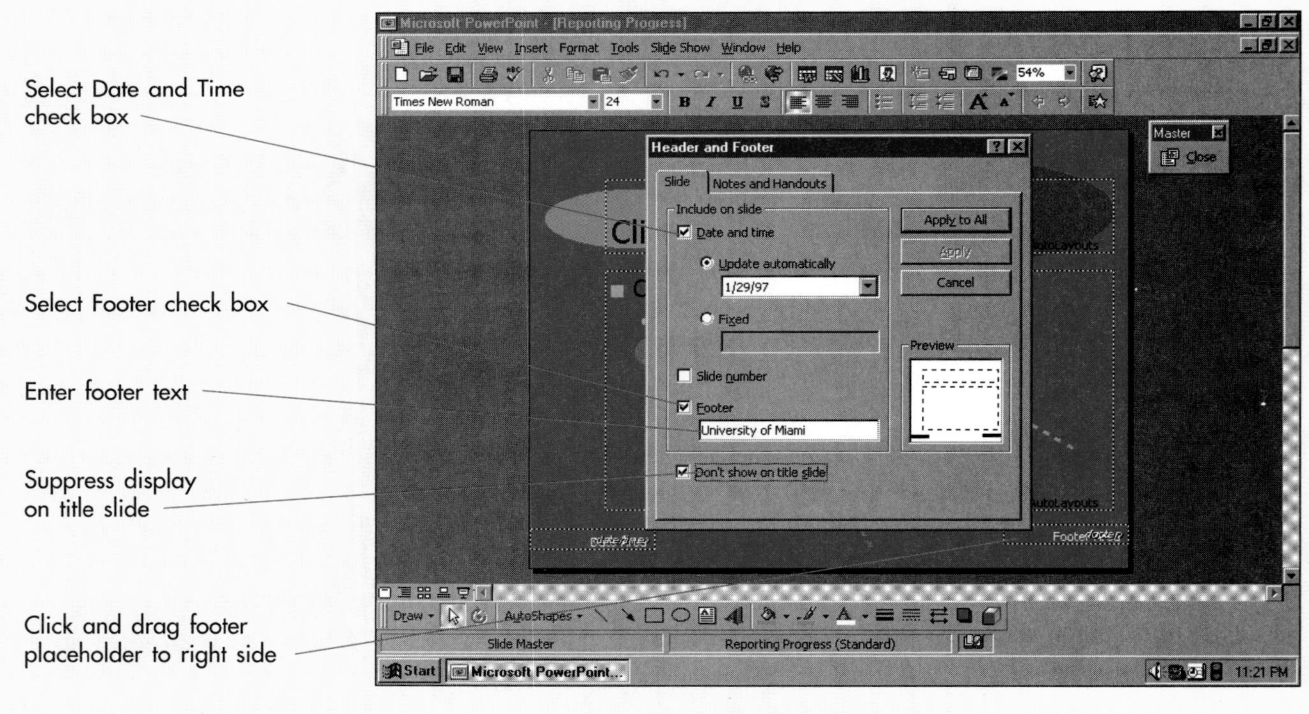

(c) Modify the Slide Master (step 3)

FIGURE 2.11 Hands-on Exercise 3 (continued)

THE VIEW BUTTONS AND THE SHIFT KEY

The Slide View button provides the fastest way to change to the slide master. Select any slide other than the title slide, then press and hold the Shift key as you click the Slide View button above the status bar to display the slide master. You can also press and hold the Shift key as you click the Slide Sorter or Outline View button to customize the Handout master.

STEP 4: Change the Color Scheme

- Change to the **Slide Sorter view.** You should see a footer (containing the name of your school) on every slide except the title slide, as shown in Figure 2.11d.
- Pull down the **Format menu.** Click **Slide Color Scheme** to display the Color Scheme dialog box. Select a different color scheme (e.g., blue), then click the **Apply to All button** to change the color scheme of every slide.

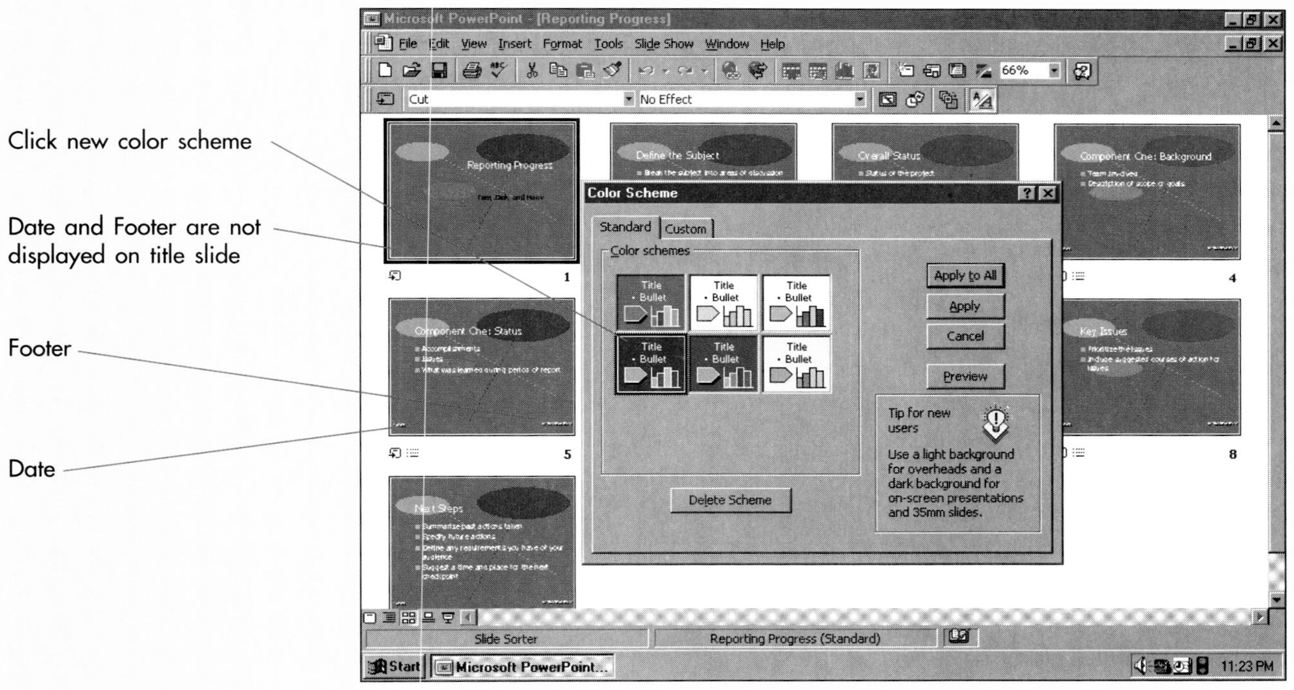

(d) Change the Color Scheme (step 4)

FIGURE 2.11 Hands-on Exercise 3 (continued)

STEP 5: Customize the Background

- Pull down the **Format menu.** Click **Background** to display the Background dialog box in Figure 2.11e.
- Click the **drop-down arrow** to display the various types of backgrounds, then click **Fill Effects** to display the Fill Effects dialog box in Figure 2.11e.

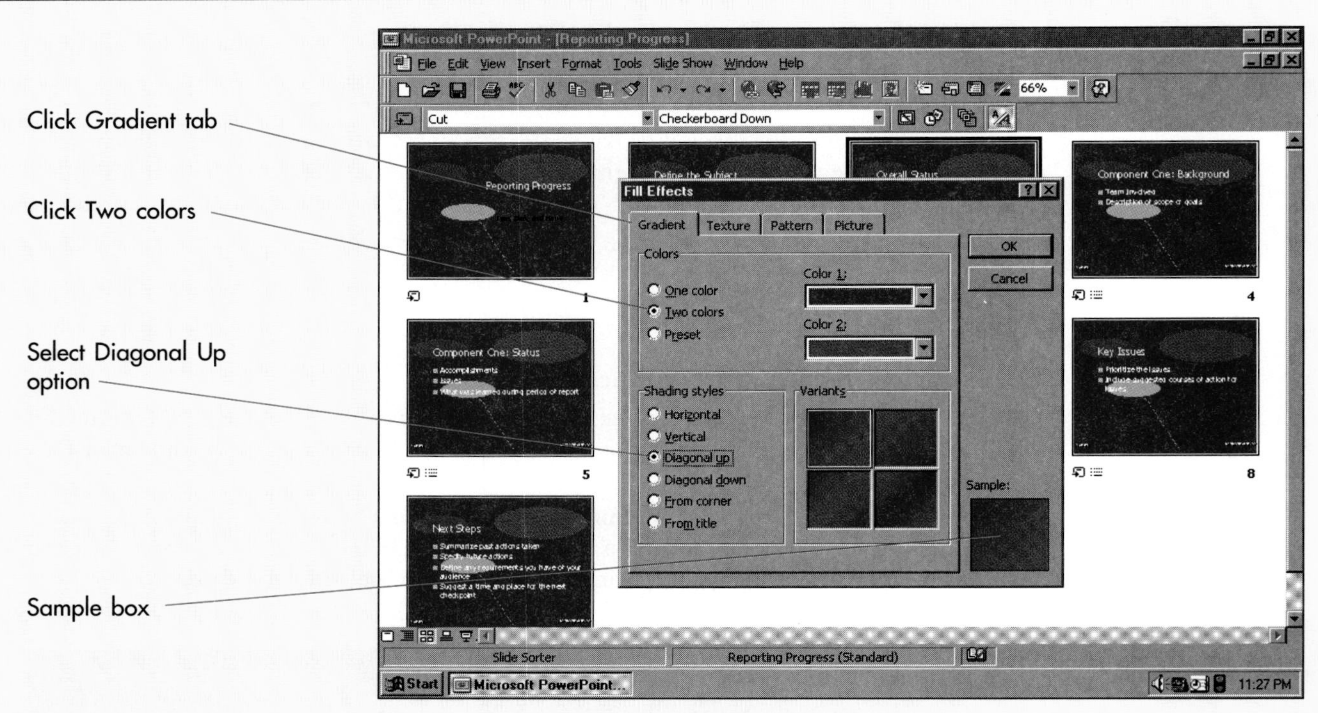

(e) Customize the Background (step 5)

FIGURE 2.11 Hands-on Exercise 3 (continued)

- If necessary, click the **Gradient tab.** Click the option button for **Two colors.** Click the **Diagonal Up option button** as the Shading Style. Click OK.
- You can see the effect of these changes in the Sample box. Experiment with additional changes, then click **OK** to accept the changes and close the Shaded Fill dialog box.
- Click **Apply to All** to apply the changes to all slides and close the Custom Background dialog box. Use the **Undo command** to return to the initial design if you are disappointed with your modification.

MULTIPLE-LEVEL UNDO COMMAND

The Undo command reverses (undoes) the most recent command. The command is executed from the Edit menu or more easily by clicking the Undo button on the Standard toolbar. Each click of the Undo button reverses one command; that is, click the Undo button and you reverse the last command. Click the Undo button a second time and you reverse the previous command. The Redo button works in reverse and undoes the most recent Undo command (i.e., it redoes the command you just undid). The maximum number of Undo commands (the default is 20) is set through the Tools menu. Pull down the Tools menu, click Options, click the Advanced tab, then enter the desired number.

STEP 6: Print the Audience Handouts

- Pull down the **File menu.** Click **Print** to display the Print dialog box in Figure 2.11f. Set the print options to match those in the figure:
  - Click the **All option button** as the print range.
  - Click the **down arrow** on the Print What list box to select **Handouts (6 slides per page).**
  - Check the boxes to **Frame Slides** and print in Black and White.
  - Click **OK**.
- Submit the audience handouts to your instructor as proof that you did the exercise. Save the presentation.
- Exit PowerPoint. Congratulations on a job well done.

PRINT THE OUTLINE

You can print the outline of a presentation and distribute it to the audience in the form of a handout. This enables the audience to follow the presentation as it is delivered and gives them an ideal vehicle on which to take notes. Pull down the File menu, click Print, then choose Outline view from the Print What list box. Be sure you know the expected size of the audience so that you will have an adequate number of handouts.

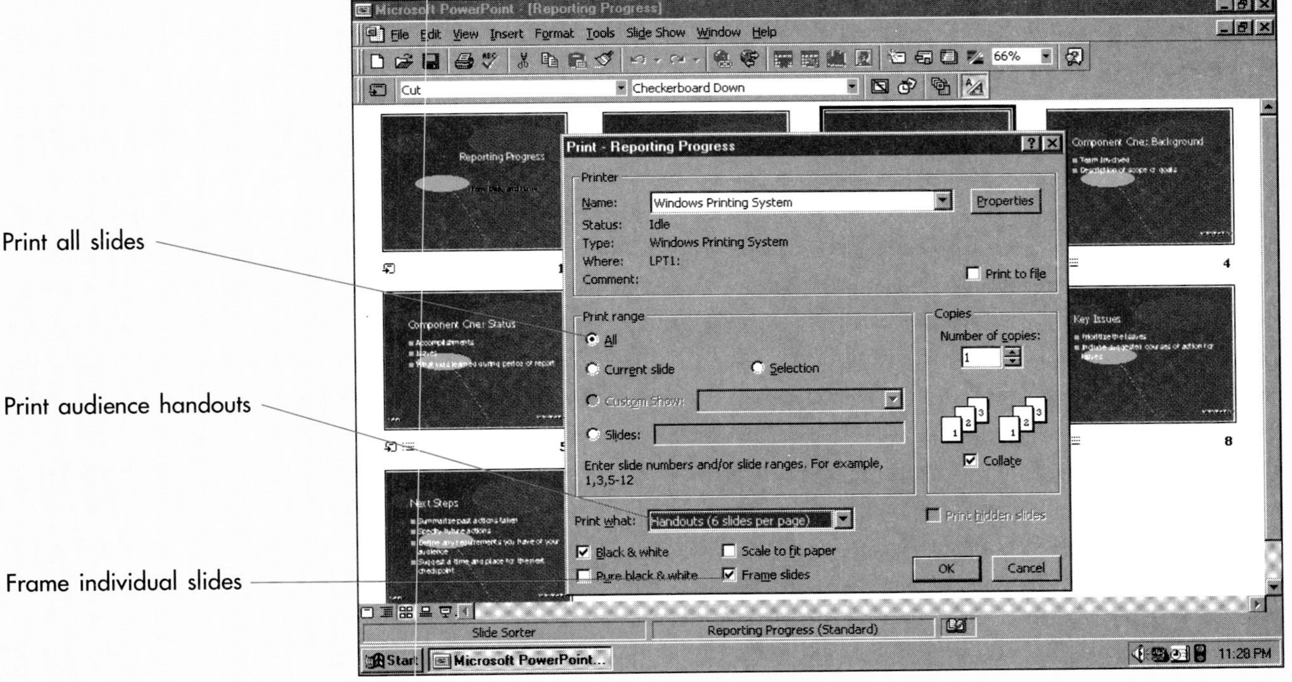

(f) Prepare the Audience Handouts (step 6)

FIGURE 2.11 Hands-on Exercise 3 (continued)

SUMMARY

There are in essence two independent steps to creating a PowerPoint presentation. You must develop the content, and you must format the presentation. Both steps are iterative in nature, and you are likely to go back and forth many times before you are finished.

The text of a presentation can be developed from the Slide view or the Outline view or a combination of the two. The Outline view is easier because it displays the contents of many slides at once, enabling you to see the overall flow of your ideas. You can change the order of the slides and/or move text from one slide to another as necessary. Text can be entered continually in the outline, then promoted or demoted so that it appears on the proper level in the slide.

A template is a design specification that controls every aspect of a presentation. It specifies the formatting of the text, the fonts and colors that are used, and the design, size, and placement of the bullets.

Transitions and animation effects can be added to a presentation for additional interest. Transitions control the way in which one slide moves off the screen and the next slide appears. Animation effects are used to display the individual elements on a single slide.

The design of a presentation can be customized by modifying its color scheme or background shading. The slide master enables you to add a unifying element to every slide, such as a corporate name or logo.

The AutoContent Wizard facilitates the creation of a new presentation. The Wizard asks a series of questions, then it uses your answers to suggest a presentation based on one of several general presentations included within PowerPoint. The end result of the Wizard is an outline based on the topic you selected. The outline is very general, as it must be, but it provides the essential topics to include in your presentation. It is the best way we know to jump-start the creation process.

KEY WORDS AND CONCEPTS

Animation effect	Demote	Slide master
AutoContent Wizard	Insertion point	Slide Sorter toolbar
AutoCorrect	Outline toolbar	Summary slide
Background command	Promote	Template
Color scheme	Slide icon	Transition

MULTIPLE CHOICE

1. Which view displays multiple slides while letting you change the text in a slide?
   (a) Outline view
   (b) Slide Sorter view
   (c) Both (a) and (b)
   (d) Neither (a) nor (b)

2. Where will the insertion point be after you complete the text for a bullet in the Outline view and press the enter key?
   (a) On the next bullet at the same level of indentation
   (b) On the next bullet at a higher level of indentation
   (c) On the next bullet at a lower level of indentation
   (d) Impossible to determine

3. Which of the following is true?
   (a) Shift+Tab promotes an item to the next higher level
   (b) Tab demotes an item to the next lower level
   (c) Both (a) and (b)
   (d) Neither (a) nor (b)

4. Which of the following is true about the Outline view?
   (a) The position of a slide may be changed by dragging its icon
   (b) All slides display the identical icon regardless of content
   (c) Both (a) and (b)
   (d) Neither (a) nor (b)

5. What advantage, if any, is there to collapsing the Outline view so that only the slide titles are visible?
   (a) More slides are displayed at one time, making it easier to rearrange the slides in the presentation
   (b) Transition and animation effects can be added
   (c) Graphic objects become visible
   (d) All of the above

6. Which of the following is true regarding transition and animation effects?
   (a) Every slide must have the same transition effect
   (b) Every bullet must have the same animation effect
   (c) Both (a) and (b)
   (d) Neither (a) nor (b)

7. The AutoContent Wizard provides suggested presentations for:
   (a) Communicating bad news
   (b) Selling a product, service, or idea
   (c) Both (a) and (b)
   (d) Neither (a) nor (b)

8. Which of the following is true?
   (a) Slides can be added to a presentation after a template has been chosen
   (b) The template can be changed after all of the slides have been created
   (c) Both (a) and (b)
   (d) Neither (a) nor (b)

9. What is the easiest way to add a corporate name to every slide (except the title slide) in the presentation?
   (a) Add the information to the handout master
   (b) Add the information to the slide master
   (c) Both (a) and (b)
   (d) Neither (a) nor (b)

10. Which of the following can be changed after a slide has been created?
    (a) Its layout and transition effect
    (b) Its position within the presentation
    (c) Both (a) and (b)
    (d) Neither (a) nor (b)

11. Which view enables you to select multiple slides?
    (a) Outline view
    (b) Slide sorter view
    (c) Both (a) and (b)
    (d) Neither (a) nor (b)

12. Which applications in Microsoft Office support the AutoCorrect feature?
    (a) PowerPoint
    (b) Word
    (c) Excel
    (d) All of the above

13. How do you move to the next slide during a slide show?
    (a) Click the left mouse button
    (b) Type the letter N
    (c) Press the PgDn key
    (d) All of the above

14. Which of the following is the best way to create a Summary slide?
    (a) Pull down the Insert menu and click the Summary Slide command
    (b) Pull down the Slide Show menu and click the Summary Slide command
    (c) Insert a new slide, then manually type the headings of all existing slides onto the new slide
    (d) Select all slides in the Slide Sorter view, then click the Summary Slide button on the Slide Sorter toolbar

15. Which of the following can be changed without changing the template?
    (a) The color scheme and background shading
    (b) The slide master
    (c) Both (a) and (b)
    (d) Neither (a) nor (b)

ANSWERS

1. a	**6.** d	**11.** c
2. a	**7.** c	**12.** d
3. c	**8.** c	**13.** d
4. a	**9.** b	**14.** d
5. a	**10.** c	**15.** c

PRACTICE WITH MICROSOFT POWERPOINT 97

1. Figure 2.12 displays the title slide of a presentation that can be found in the Exploring PowerPoint folder on the data disk. Much of the presentation has been created for you, but there are several finishing touches that need to be made:
   a. Open the existing presentation titled *Chapter 2 Practice 1,* then save it as *Chapter 2 Practice 1 Solution* so that you can return to the original presentation if necessary.
   b. Replace our name with your name on the title slide.
   c. Move the slide on Modems after the one on Multimedia Requirements.
   d. Delete the slide on The PC, Then and Now.
   e. Add a slide at the end of the presentation on software that should be considered in addition to Windows 95 and the Microsoft Office.
   f. Change the layout of slide 7 to a Two-column Text slide. Modify the text as necessary for the new layout.
   g. Select a different design template.
   h. Print the completed presentation in both outline and handout form. Submit both to your instructor.

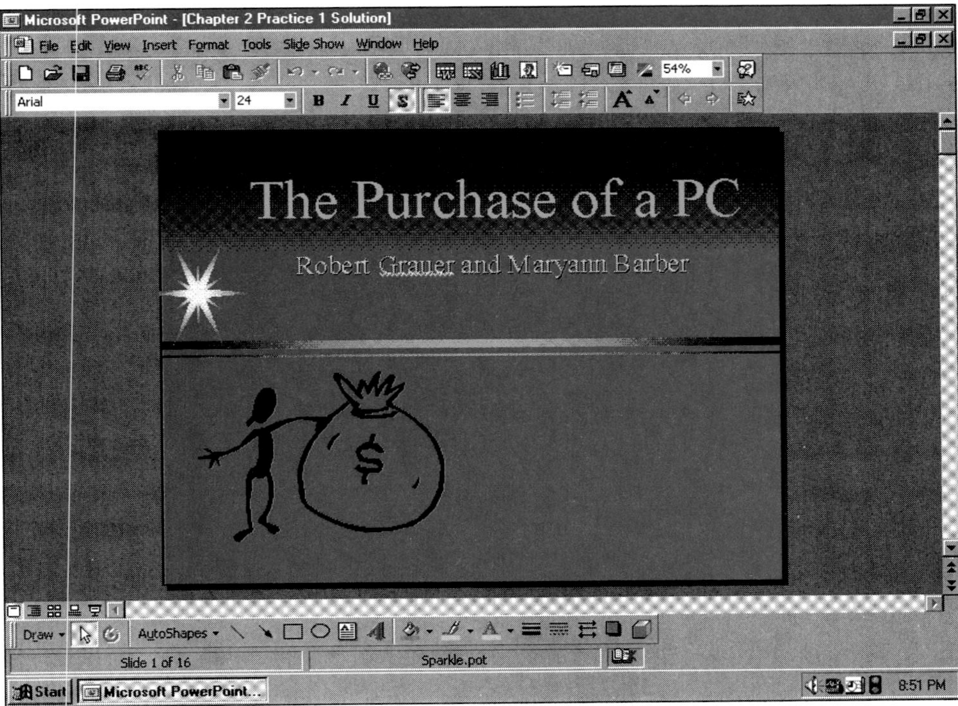

FIGURE 2.12 Screen for Practice Exercise 1

2. Figure 2.13 displays a very general outline for a presentation. The outline can be accessed through the AutoContent Wizard or directly through the File New command.

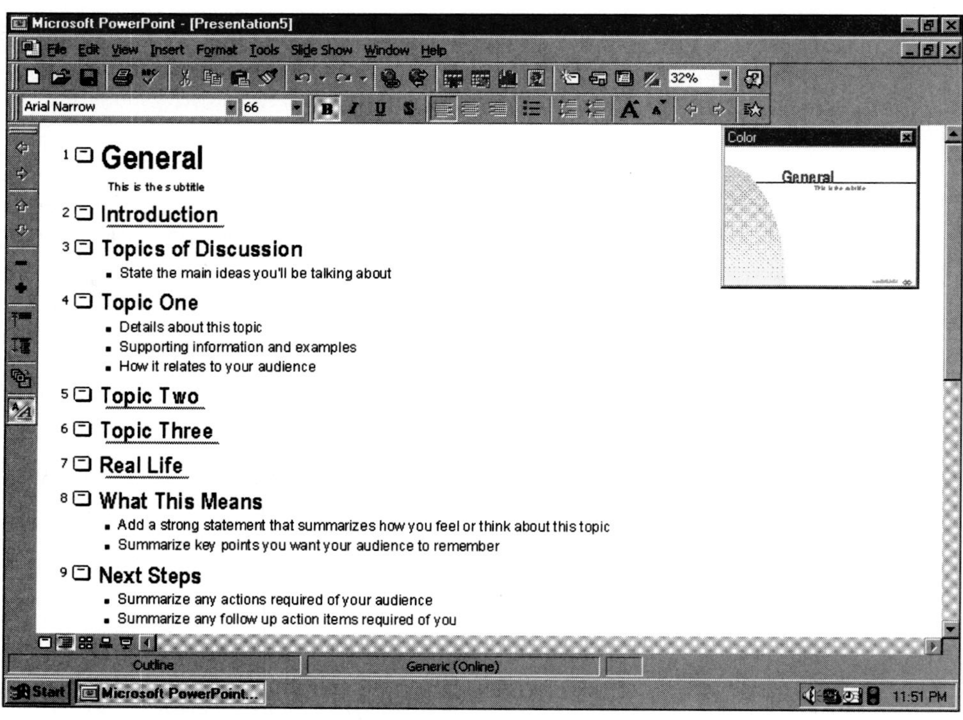

FIGURE 2.13 Screen for Practice Exercise 2

a. Pull down the File menu, click New to display the New Presentation dialog box, click the Presentations tab, then double click the Generic (standard) presentation.
b. Change to the Outline view to display the presentation in Figure 2.13. (Some slides have been collapsed in our outline as can be seen by the underlined slide titles.)
c. Choose any topic you like, then prepare a presentation on that topic using the outline provided. You need not follow the outline exactly, but it should provide a good beginning. The completed presentation should contain from six to ten slides.
d. Apply a new (different) design template to the completed presentation.
e. Print the completed presentation in both outline and miniature slide form. Submit both handouts to your instructor.

3. Figure 2.14 displays the Slide Sorter view of a presentation to sell an idea or product. The template is available in the ValuPack folder on the CD-ROM. (The complete path is ValuPack\Template\Present. Change the file type to Presentation Templates, then select the Sell_S template.) Assume that you have been appointed the Director of Marketing for a national corporation, then modify the presentation as follows:

a. Change the title slide to reflect the product you wish to sell.
b. Modify the remaining slides to reflect your sales strategy. You can change the slide layout and content.
c. Use the Header and Footer command in the View menu to print today's date on every slide except the title slide.
d. Modify the Slide master to include uniform clip art in the lower right corner of each slide (except the title slide).

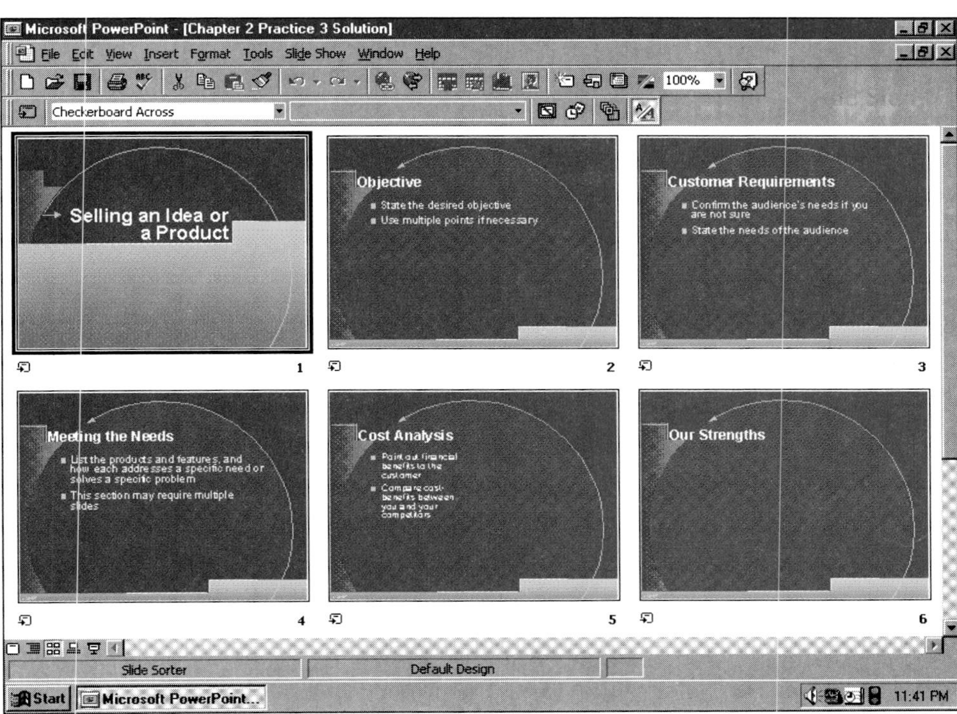

FIGURE 2.14 Screen for Practice Exercise 3

e. View the slide show of the completed presentation. Slide transitions are built into the presentation as can be seen by viewing the transition icon under each slide.

f. Print the completed presentation in slide miniature form and submit the printout to your instructor.

4. The potential uses of PowerPoint are limited only by your imagination. Figure 2.15, for example, displays an award certificate that was created using the drawing tools within Microsoft Office. The template is found in the Certificate Online presentation in the ValuPack folder on the CD-ROM.

a. Modify the existing template to award yourself for your efforts in this class.

b. Use the existing slide as the basis for three additional awards for real people in any category. Experiment with the various animation effects. It's best if you have a sound card so you can hear the sound of applause as the certificate is displayed.

c. Print the completed presentation and submit it to your instructor.

5. The presentation in Figure 2.16 is one of several provided by Dale Carnegie & Associates. Use the AutoContent Wizard to select the Presentation Guidelines presentation. (Alternatively, you can pull down the File menu, click New to display the New Presentation dialog box, click the Presentations tab, then double click Presentation Guidelines from the list of available presentations.)

a. Go to the first slide in the presentation, then switch to the Slide Show view and view the entire presentation.

b. Print the presentation in Outline view or Slide Miniatures (six slides per page) and keep it as a guide. This is a valuable reference, which you can use the next time you have to deliver a presentation.

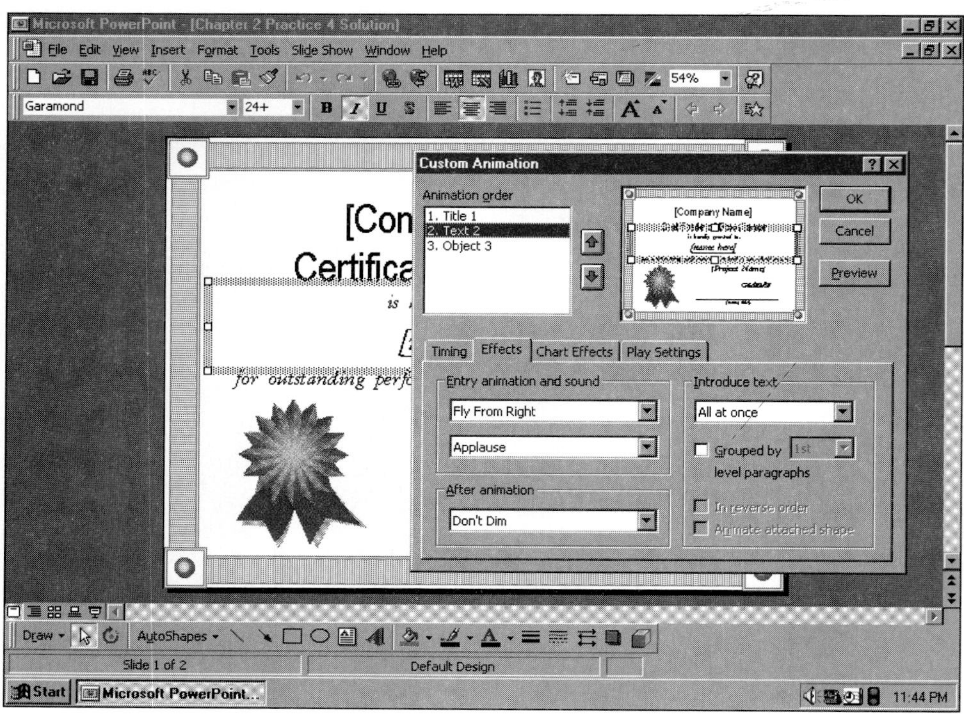

FIGURE 2.15 Screen for Practice Exercise 4

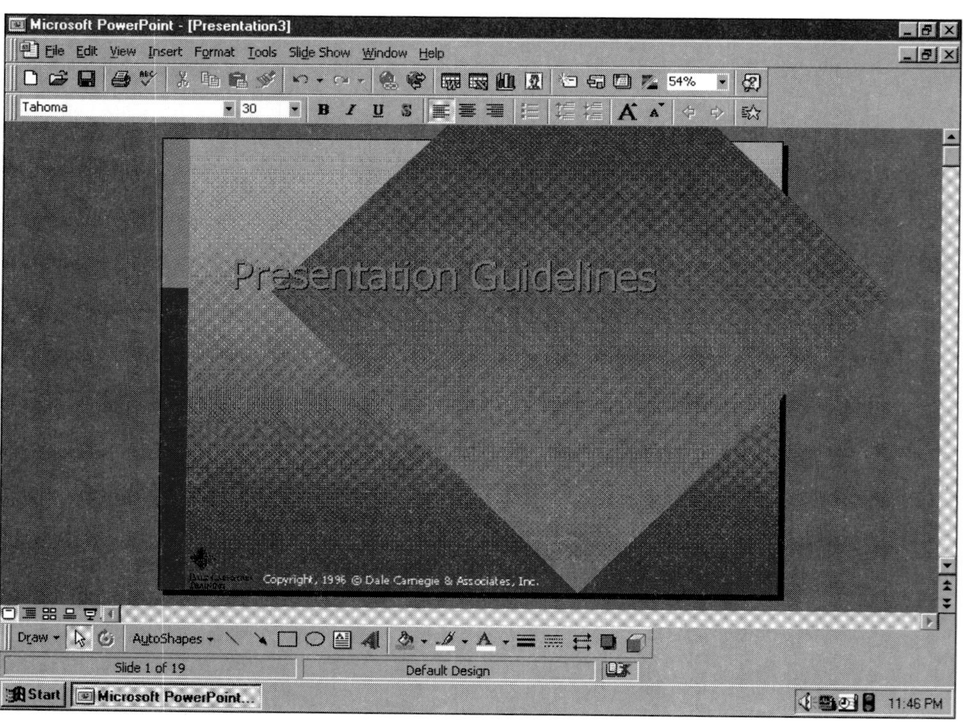

FIGURE 2.16 Screen for Practice Exercise 5

6. Figure 2.17 displays the Outline view of a presentation for a Creativity Session. (The template is available in the ValuPack folder on the CD-ROM. The complete path is ValuPack\Template\Present. Change the file type to Presentation Templates, then select the Brain_S template.) Ask your

instructor to divide the class into groups of three or four students each. Each group is given the assignment of creating a presentation to attract publicity for a political issue of interest to you and your classmates. Your group has a meeting scheduled for next Monday, at which point you are to decide on the issue and an associated strategy. Modify the text of the Creativity Session to facilitate the upcoming meeting.

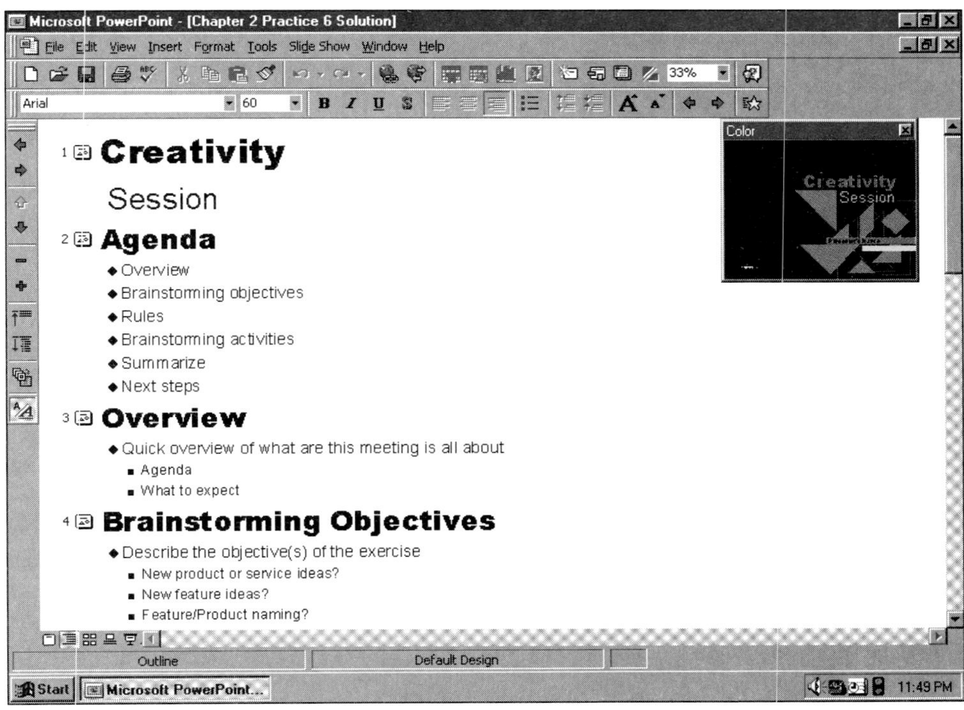

FIGURE 2.17 Screen for Practice Exercise 6

CASE STUDIES

Be Creative

One interesting way of exploring the potential of presentation graphics is to imagine how it might have been used by historical figures had it been available. Choose any historical figure or current personality and create at least a six-slide presentation. You could, for example, show how Columbus might have used PowerPoint to request funding from Queen Isabella, or how Elvis Presley might have pleaded for his first recording contract. The content of your presentation should be reasonable, but you don't have to spend an inordinate amount of time on research. Just be creative and use your imagination. Use clip art as appropriate, but don't overdo it. Place your name on the title slide as technical adviser.

The Annual Report

Corporate America spends a small fortune to produce its annual reports, which are readily available to the public. Choose any company and obtain a copy of its most recent annual report. Use your imagination on how best to obtain the data.

You might try a stockbroker, the 800 directory, or even the Internet. Use the information in the annual report as the basis for a PowerPoint presentation. PowerPoint is one step ahead of you and offers a suggested financial report through the AutoContent Wizard.

Director of Marketing

Congratulations on your appointment as Director of Marketing. The company that hired you has 50 sales representatives across the United States. Laptop computers have just been ordered for the entire sales staff and will be delivered at next week's annual sales meeting. Your job is to prepare a PowerPoint presentation that can be used by the sales staff in future sales calls. It's short notice, but it is a critical assignment. Use the Selling a Product template provided by the AutoContent Wizard as the basis for your presentation.

Take It on the Road

Your presentation looks great on the desktop, but you have to deliver it to an audience of 50, too many people to crowd around your machine. Fortunately, however, you have a notebook computer and a generous budget. What equipment do you need to show the presentation from your notebook computer? How much will the equipment cost to buy? Can you rent the equipment instead, and if so, from whom?

An Ad for Travel

The Clip Gallery includes the maps and flags of many foreign countries as well as maps of all 50 states and pictures of many landmarks. It's an excellent beginning, but why limit yourself as you can obtain additional resources on the Web. Design a six-slide presentation for a place you want to visit, in the United States or abroad. Print the miniatures of your presentation six slides to a page. Collect the assignments, then ask your instructor to hold a contest to select the most appealing document. It's fun, it's easy, and it's educational. Bon voyage!

File Compression

Photographs add significantly to the appearance of a presentation, but they also add to its size. Accordingly, you might want to consider acquiring a file compression program to facilitate copying large files to a floppy disk in order to transport your presentations to and from school, home, or work. You can download an evaluation copy of the popular WinZip program at www.winzip.com. Investigate the subject of file compression, then submit a summary of your findings to your instructor.

Copyright Infringement

It's fun to download images from the Web for inclusion in a presentation, but is it legal? Copyright protection (infringement) is one of the most pressing legal issues on the Web. Search the Web for sites that provide information on current copyright law. One excellent site is the copyright page at the Institute for Learning Technologies at www.ilt.columbia.edu/projects/copyright. Another excellent reference is the page at www.benedict.com. Research these and other sites, then summarize your findings in a short note to your instructor.

A

APPENDIX A: TOOLBARS

OVERVIEW

Microsoft PowerPoint has fourteen predefined toolbars that provide access to commonly used commands. The toolbars are displayed in Figure A.1 and are listed here for convenience. They are: the Standard, Formatting, Animation Effects, Common Tasks, Control Toolbox, Drawing, Picture, Reviewing, Shadow Settings, Stop Recording, Visual Basic, Web, WordArt, and 3-D Settings toolbars. The Standard and Formatting toolbars are displayed by default and appear immediately below the menu bar. The other predefined toolbars are displayed (hidden) at the discretion of the user.

The buttons on the toolbars indicate their functions. Clicking the Printer button, for example (the fourth button from the left on the Standard toolbar), executes the Print command. If you are unsure of the purpose of any toolbar button, point to it, and a ScreenTip will appear that displays its name.

You can display multiple toolbars at one time, move them to a new location, customize their appearance, or suppress their display.

- To display or hide a toolbar, pull down the View menu and click the Toolbars command. Select (deselect) the toolbar(s) that you want to display (hide). The selected toolbar(s) will be displayed in the same position as when last displayed. You may also point to any toolbar and click with the right mouse button to bring up a shortcut menu that lets you select the toolbar to be displayed (hidden). In either case, if you do not see the desired toolbar listed, click the Customize command to display the list of all available toolbars. Click the check box for the desired toolbar(s) and then click Close.
- To change the size of the buttons, suppress the display of the ScreenTips, or display the associated shortcut key (if available) with the ScreenTips, pull down the View menu, click Toolbars, and click Customize to display the Customize dialog box. If necessary, click the Options tab, then select (deselect) the appropriate check box.

- Toolbars are either docked (along the edge of the window) or floating (in their own window). A toolbar moved to the edge of the window will dock along that edge. A toolbar moved anywhere else in the window will float in its own window. Docked toolbars are one tool wide (high), whereas floating toolbars can be resized by clicking and dragging a border or corner as you would with any window.
  - To move a docked toolbar, click anywhere in the gray background area and drag the toolbar to its new location. You can also click and drag the move handle (the pair of parallel lines) at the left of the toolbar.
  - To move a floating toolbar, drag its title bar to its new location.
- To customize one or more toolbars, display the toolbar(s) on the screen. Then pull down the View menu, click Toolbars, click Customize to display the Customize dialog box, and select the Toolbars tab. Alternatively, you can click on any toolbar with the right mouse button, select Customize from the shortcut menu, and then click the Toolbars tab.
  - To move a button, drag the button to its new location on that toolbar or any other displayed toolbar.
  - To copy a button, press the Ctrl key as you drag the button to its new location on that toolbar or any other displayed toolbar.
  - To delete a button, drag the button off the toolbar and release the mouse button.
  - To add a button, click the Commands tab in the Customize dialog box, select the category from the Categories list box that contains the button you want to add, then drag the button to the desired location on the toolbar. (To see a description of a tool's function before adding it to a toolbar, select the tool, then click the Description command button.)
  - To restore a predefined toolbar to its default appearance, pull down the View menu, click Toolbars, click Customize, click the Toolbars tab, select (highlight) the desired toolbar, and click the Reset command button.
- Buttons can also be moved, copied, or deleted without displaying the Customize dialog box.
  - To move a button, press the Alt key as you drag the button to the new location.
  - To copy a button, press the Alt and Ctrl keys as you drag the button to the new location.
  - To delete a button, press the Alt key as you drag the button off the toolbar.
- To create your own toolbar, pull down the View menu, click Toolbars, click Customize, click the Toolbars tab, then click the New command button. Alternatively, you can click on any toolbar with the right mouse button, select Customize from the shortcut menu, click the Toolbars tab, and then click the New command button.
  - Enter a name for the toolbar in the dialog box that follows. The name can be any length and can contain spaces.
  - The new toolbar will appear on the screen. Initially it will be big enough to hold only one button. Add, move, and delete buttons following the same procedures as outlined above. The toolbar will automatically size itself as new buttons are added and deleted.
  - To delete a custom toolbar, pull down the View menu, click Toolbars, click Customize, and click the Toolbars tab. *Verify that the custom toolbar to be deleted is the only one selected (highlighted).* Click the Delete command button. Click Yes to confirm the deletion. (Note that a predefined toolbar cannot be deleted.)

Standard Toolbar

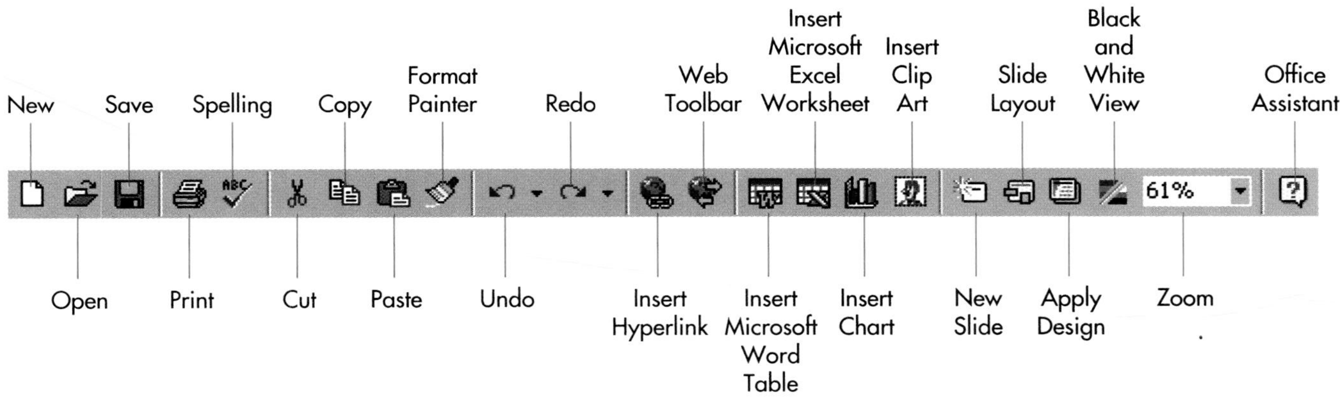

Formatting Toolbar

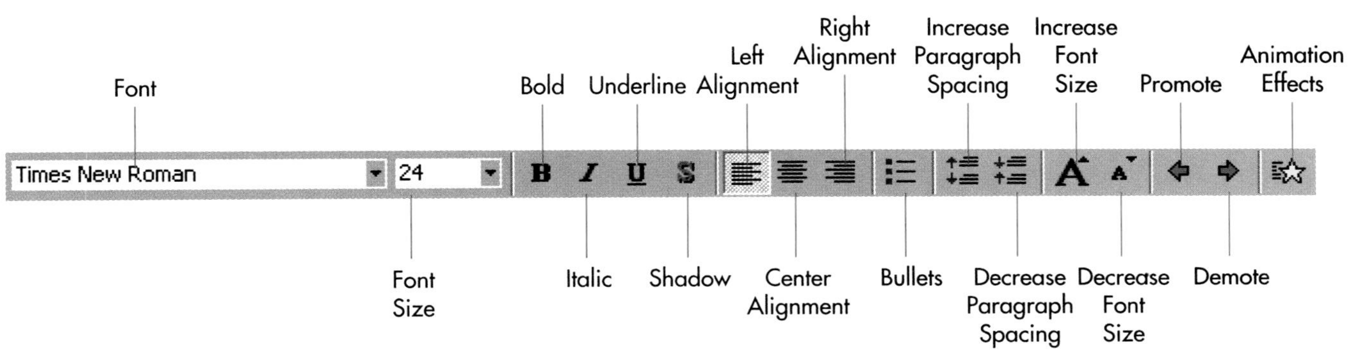

Animation Effects Toolbar

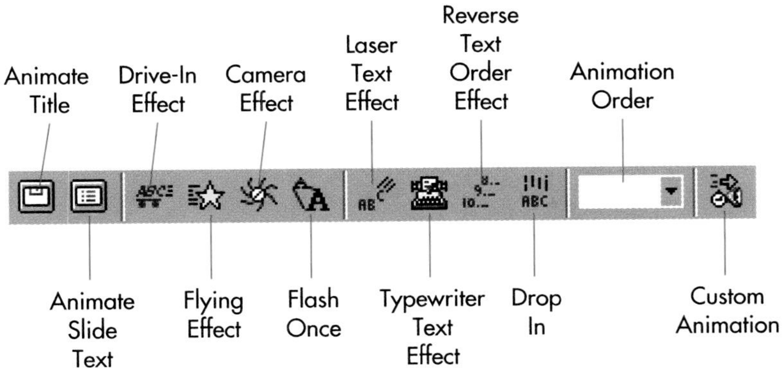

FIGURE A.1 Toolbars

Common Tasks Toolbar

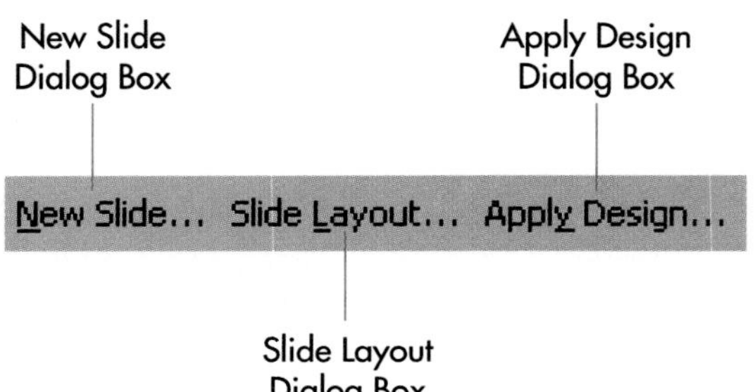

Control Toolbox Toolbar

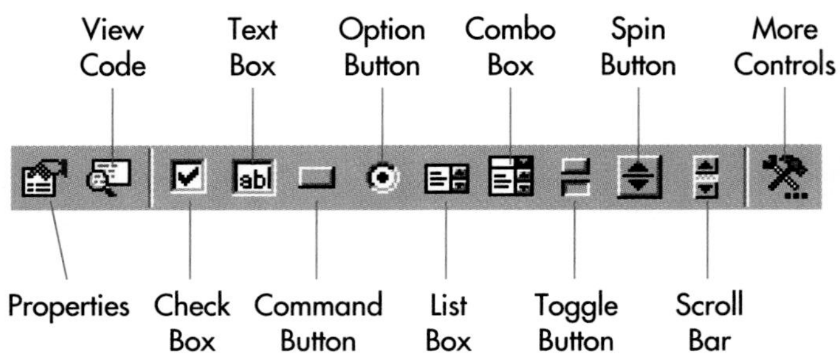

Drawing Toolbar

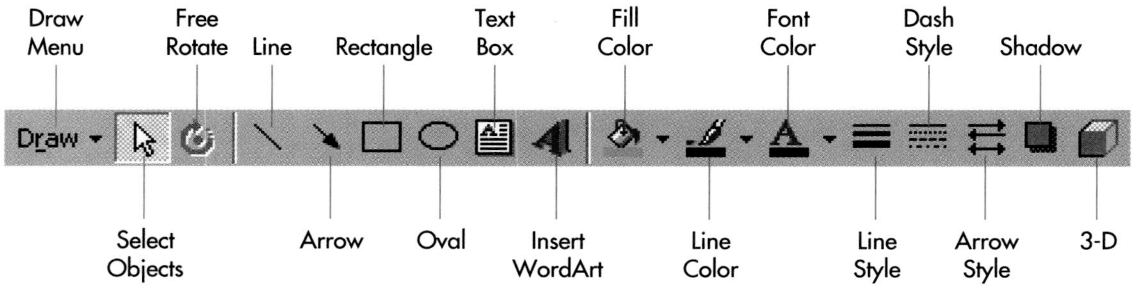

Picture Toolbar

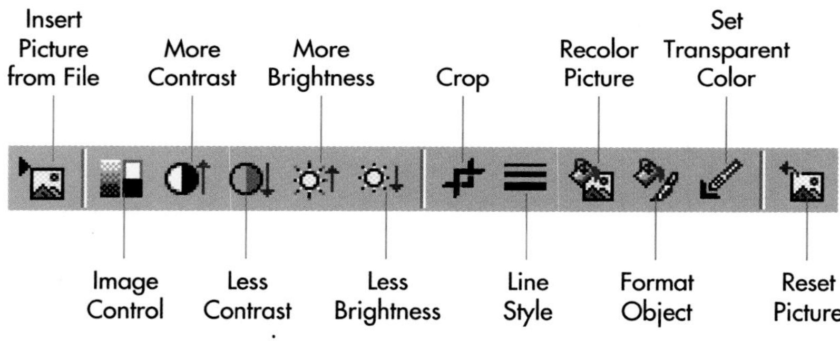

Reviewing Toolbar

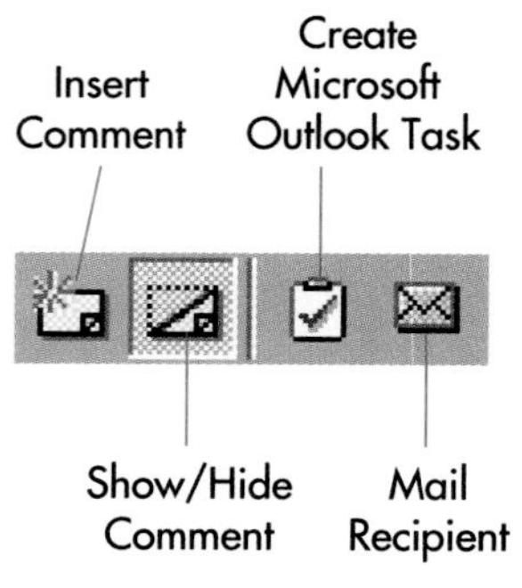

Shadow Settings Toolbar

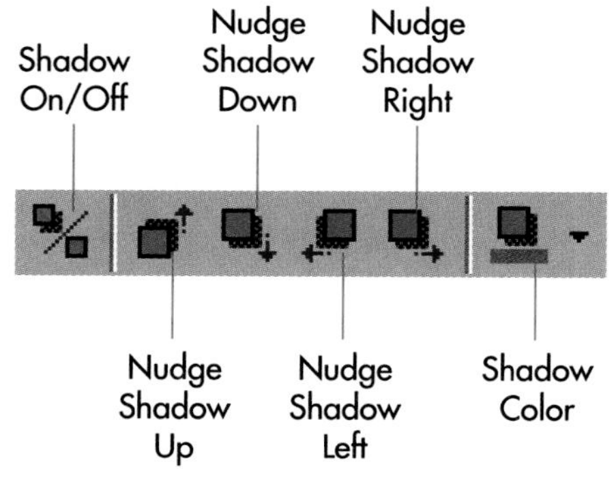

FIGURE A.1 Toolbars (continued)

Stop Recording Toolbar

Visual Basic Toolbar

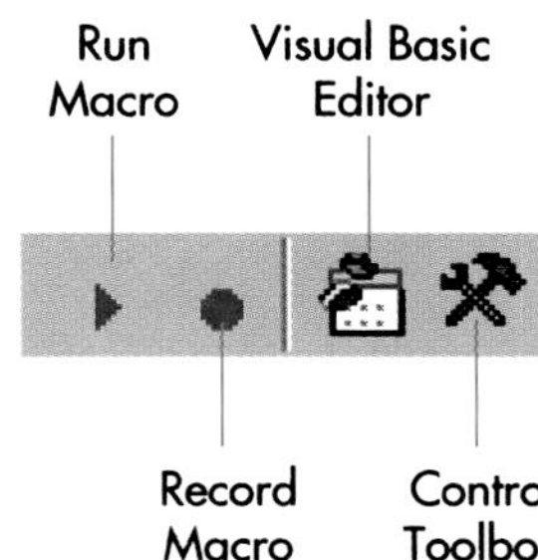

Web Toolbar

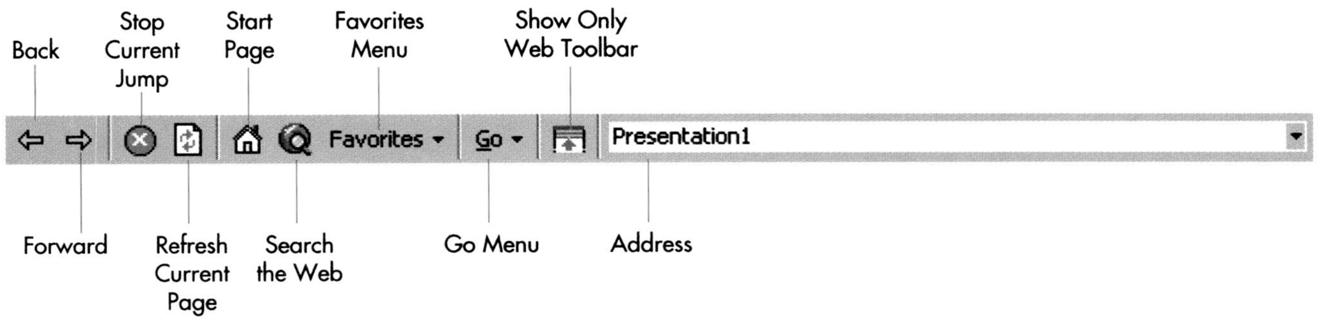

WordArt Toolbar

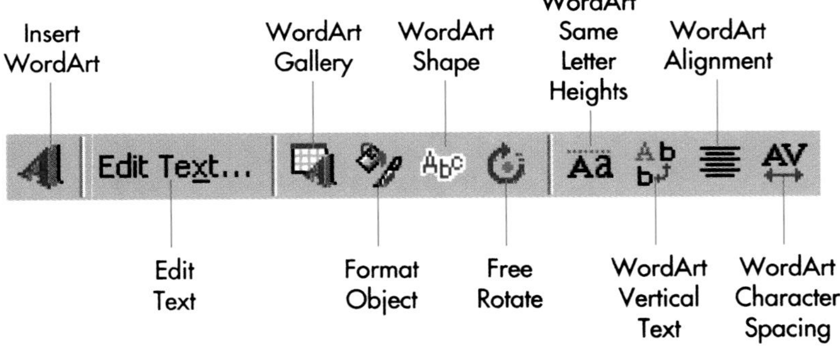

3-D Settings Toolbar

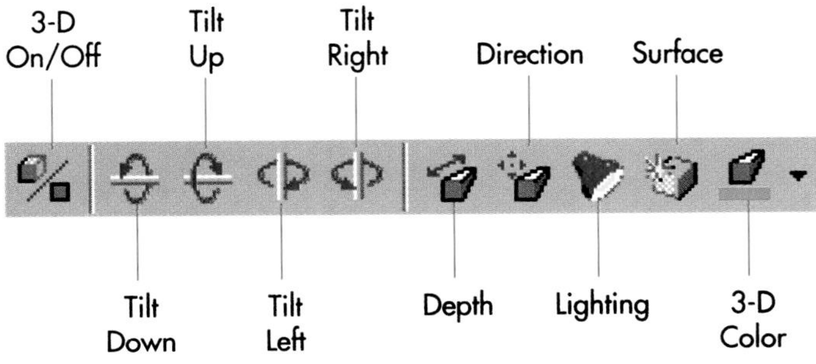

FIGURE A.1 Toolbars (continued)

7

WELCOME TO CYBERSPACE: THE INTERNET AND WORLD WIDE WEB

OBJECTIVES

After reading this chapter you will be able to:

1. Describe the Internet and its history; explain how to access the Internet in your campus computing environment.
2. Describe the World Wide Web in the context of hypertext and hypermedia; distinguish between a Web server and a Web client.
3. Distinguish between the HyperText Transfer Protocol (HTTP) and HyperText Markup Language (HTML).
4. Use Internet Explorer to access the World Wide Web; describe several similarities between Internet Explorer and other Windows applications.
5. Define a URL and give several specific examples; describe how to specify a Web address in Internet Explorer.
6. Describe the various buttons on the Internet Explorer toolbar.
7. Explain how to save the address of a favorite Web site and return to it later.

OVERVIEW

The Internet. You see the word on the cover of half the magazines on the newsstand. The media make continual reference to the Information Highway. Movie ads provide Internet addresses so you can download and view movie clips. Your friends at other colleges want to know your Internet e-mail address. But what exactly is the Internet, and how do you use it? Is the World Wide Web part of the Internet, or is it a separate entity? This chapter will answer these and other questions as you begin your journey through ***cyberspace,*** the term used to describe the invisible realm of the Internet.

We begin with a brief history of the Internet and World Wide Web. We describe how Web documents are accessed and created, and define basic terms such as HTTP (HyperText Transfer Protocol) and HTML (HyperText Markup Language). We also introduce Internet Explorer, the Web browser that is included in Office 97.

The World Wide Web cannot be appreciated, however, until you visit it yourself. As always, learning is best accomplished by doing, and so we include two hands-on exercises and provide our own guided tour so that you can experience first-hand what the excitement is all about.

THE INTERNET

The ***Internet*** is a network of networks that connects computers across the country and around the world. It grew out of a U.S. Department of Defense (DOD) experimental project begun in 1969 to test the feasibility of a wide area (long distance) computer network over which scientists and military personnel could share messages and data. The country was in the midst of the Cold War and the military imposed the additional requirement that the network be able to function with partial outages in times of national emergency (e.g., a nuclear disaster), when one or more computers in the network might be down.

The proposed solution was to create a network with no central authority. Each ***node*** (computer attached to the network) would be equal to all other nodes, with the ability to originate, pass, and receive messages. The path that a particular message took in getting to its destination would be insignificant. Only the final result was important, as the message would be passed from node to node until it arrived at its destination.

The experiment was (to say the least) enormously successful. Known originally as the ***ARPAnet (Advanced Research Projects Agency Network),*** the original network of four computers has grown exponentially to include millions of computers at virtually every major university and government agency, and an ever increasing number of private corporations and international sites. To say that the Internet is large is a gross understatement, but by its very nature, it's impossible to determine just how large it really is. How many networks there are, and how many users are connected to those networks, is of no importance as long as you yourself have access.

The Internet is a network of networks, but if that were all it were, there would hardly be so much commotion. It's what you can do on the Internet, coupled with the ease of access, that makes the Internet so exciting. In essence, the Internet provides two basic capabilities, information retrieval and worldwide communication, functions that are already provided by libraries and print media, the postal system and the telephone, television, and other types of long-distance media. The difference, however, is that the Internet is interactive in nature, and more important, it is both global and immediate.

TCP/IP

Data is transmitted from one computer to another across the Internet through a series of protocols known collectively as TCP/IP (Transmission Control Protocol/Internet Protocol). You can progress quite nicely through our text without knowing anything more about TCP/IP. We do, however, provide Appendix A in case you are curious about the internal workings of the Internet.

The Internet enables you to request a document from virtually anywhere in the world, and to begin to receive that document almost instantly. No other medium lets you do that. Television, for example, has the capability to send information globally and in real-time (while events are unfolding), but it is not interactive in that you cannot request a specific program. Federal Express promises overnight delivery, but that is hardly immediate. The stacks in your university library provide access to the information that is physically in that library, but that is not global access. Indeed, the Internet, and in particular the World Wide Web, is truly unique.

THE WORLD WIDE WEB

The original language of the Internet was uninviting and difficult to use. The potential was exciting, but you had to use a variety of esoteric programs (e.g., Telnet, FTP, Archie, and Gopher) to locate and download data. The programs were based on the Unix operating system and you had to know the precise syntax of each program. There was no common user interface to speed learning. And, even if you were able to find what you wanted, everything was communicated in plain text, as graphics and sound were not available. All of this changed in 1991 with the introduction of the World Wide Web.

The ***World Wide Web*** (***WWW*** or simply, the Web) can be thought of as a very large subset of the Internet, consisting of hypertext and/or hypermedia documents. A ***hypertext document*** is a document that contains a link (reference) to another hypertext document that may be on the same computer, or even on a different computer, with the latter located anywhere in the world. ***Hypermedia*** is similar in concept, except that it provides links to graphic, sound, and video files in addition to text files.

Either type of document enables you to move effortlessly from one document (or computer) to another. And therein lies the fascination of the Web, in that you simply click on link after link to move effortlessly from one document to the next. You can start your journey at your professor's home page in New York, for example, which may link to a document in the Library of Congress, which in turn may take you to a different document, and so on. So, off you go to Washington, D.C., and from there to a reference across the country or perhaps around the world.

Any computer that both stores a hypermedia document somewhere on the Web and makes that document available to other computers is known as a ***server*** (or ***Web server***). Any computer that is connected to the Web, and requests a document from a server, is known as a ***client.*** In other words, you work on a client computer (e.g., a node on a local area network or your PC at home) and by clicking a link in a hypermedia document, you are requesting information from a Web server.

HyperText Transfer Protocol (http)

In order for the Web to work, every client (be it a PC or a Mac) must be able to display every document from every server. This is accomplished by imposing a set of standards known as a ***protocol*** to govern the way data is transmitted across the Web. Thus, data travels from client to server and back through a protocol known as the ***HyperText Transfer Protocol*** (or http for short). In addition, in order to access the documents that are transmitted through this protocol, you need a special type of program known as a ***browser.*** Indeed, a browser is aptly named because it enables you to inspect the Web in a leisurely and casual way (the dictionary definition of the word *browse*). ***Internet Explorer*** is the browser included in Microsoft Office 97. (Other browsers are available, most notably the Netscape Navigator from the Netscape Corporation.)

Consider, for example, the hypermedia document in Figure 1.1 as it would appear in Internet Explorer. In order to display Figure 1.1 on your computer, you need to be connected to the Internet and you need to know the address of the document you are looking for, in this case, www.vtourist.com/vt. (Yes, it helps to know the addresses of interesting Web pages, and we suggest several sites to explore in Appendix B.) We describe the structure of Internet addresses in detail later in the chapter, but for the time being it is sufficient to realize that every server, and every document on every server, has a unique address. Note, too, that the *http* precedes the address to indicate that the document is being transferred according to the hypertext protocol we discussed earlier.

The first document you see at a Web site is its ***home page*** and that is where your journey begins. The document in Figure 1.1 is the home page of the Virtual Tourist and it is one of our favorite sites on the Web. Not only does it demonstrate the concept of hypertext, but it elegantly shows the global nature of the World Wide Web. Once you arrive at a home page, you can click any link that interests you.

Consider, for example, our path through Figure 1.1. We began by clicking on the image of North America in Figure 1.1a, which in turn displayed the document in Figure 1.1b. Note how the address of this document is different from the document in Figure 1.1a. Indeed, that is what the Web is all about as you move effortlessly from one document to another. Next we clicked on the image of the United States to display the map in Figure 1.1c. We clicked the state of California to display the list of cities in Figure 1.1d. We chose Los Angeles, which in turn displayed the list of attractions in Figure 1.1e, where we chose the Southwest Museum. This brought us to our "final" destination in Figure 1.1f, where we arrive at the home page for this fabulous museum.

As you review our trip, notice that a link may be embedded within a graphic as in the maps of Figures 1.1a, 1.1b, and 1.1c, or it may appear as underlined text as in Figures 1.1d and 1.1e. The latter appear in one of two colors, blue or green, depending on whether or not the link has been previously selected. Any link in blue (the majority of links in Figure 1.1d) indicates that the document has not yet been viewed. Links in green, however (e.g., Los Angeles in Figure 1.1d), imply that the associated document has been retrieved earlier in the session (or in a previous session).

Think for a moment of what we have just accomplished. We began with a map of the world. From there we went to North America, then to the United States, to California, to Los Angeles, and finally to a specific attraction. There is no beginning (other than the starting point or home page) and no end. You simply read a hypermedia document in any way that makes sense to you, jumping to explore whatever topic you want to see next. All of this is accomplished with a graphical browser such as Internet Explorer and a connection between your computer and the Internet.

Internet Explorer is easy to use because it shares the common user interface and consistent command structure present in every Windows application. Look, for example, at any of the screens in Figure 1.1 and you will see several familiar elements. These include the title bar, minimize, maximize (or restore), and close buttons. Commands are executed from pull-down menus or from command buttons that appear on a toolbar under the menu bar. A vertical and/or horizontal scroll bar appears if the entire document is not visible at one time. The title bar displays the name of the document you are currently viewing.

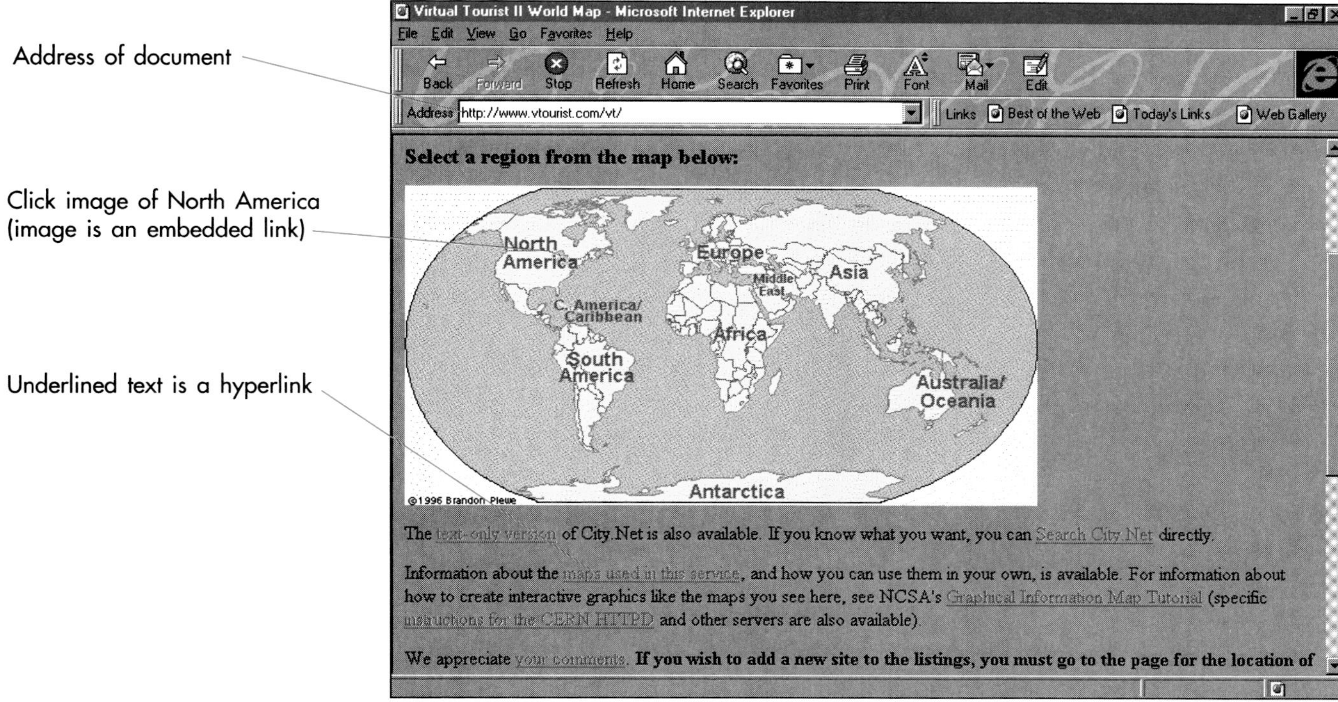

(a) World Map

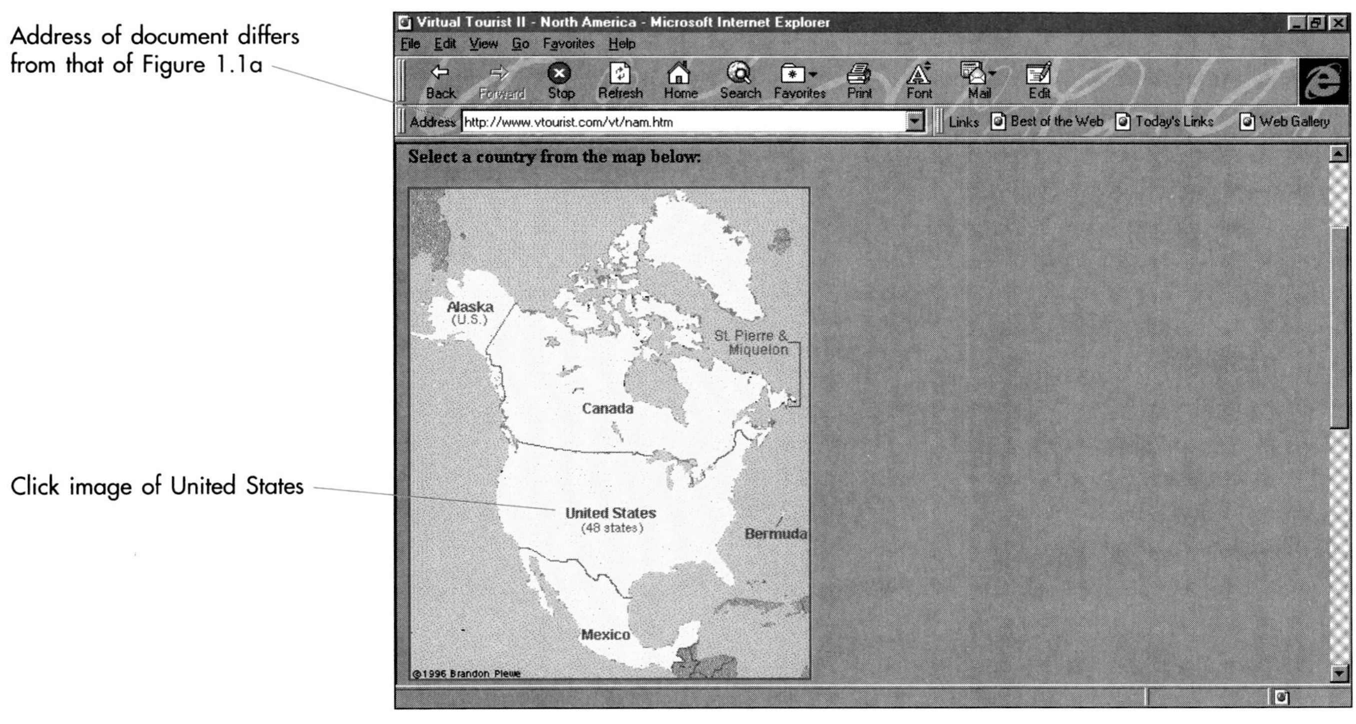

(b) North America

FIGURE 1.1 Hyperlinks (The Virtual Tourist)

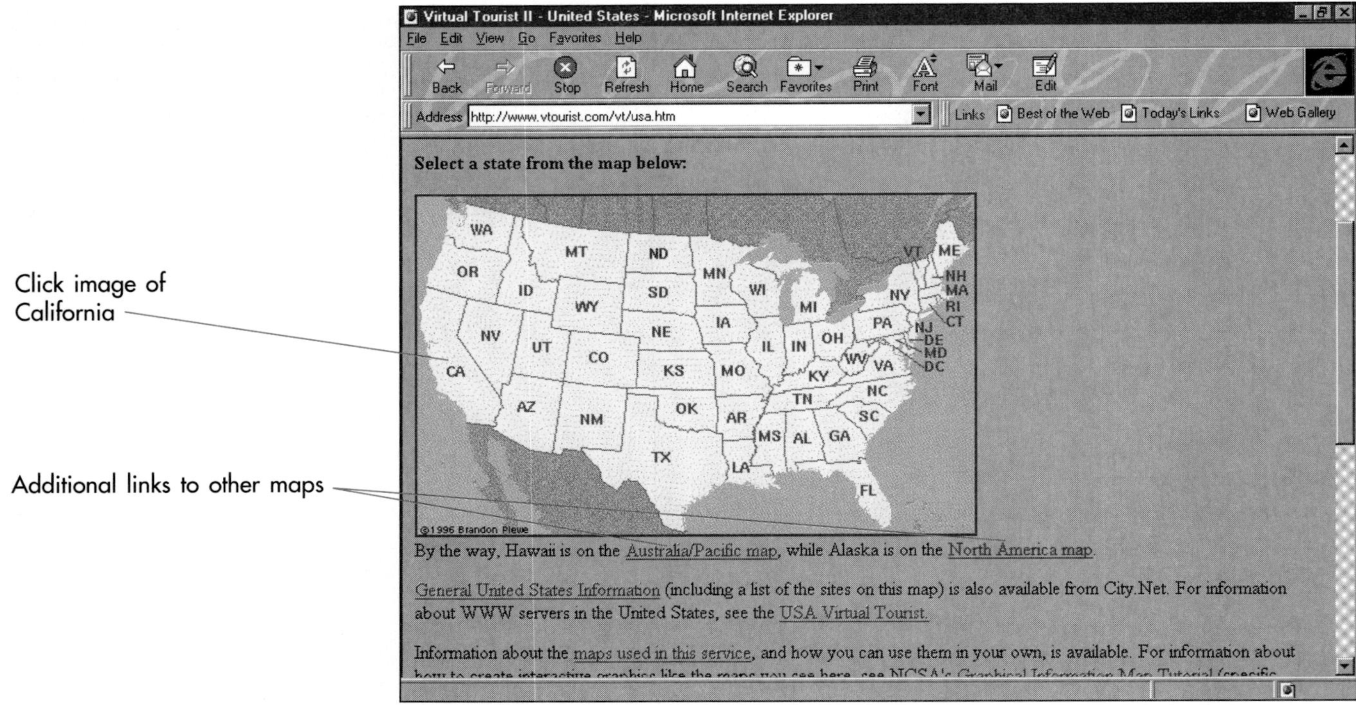

(c) United States

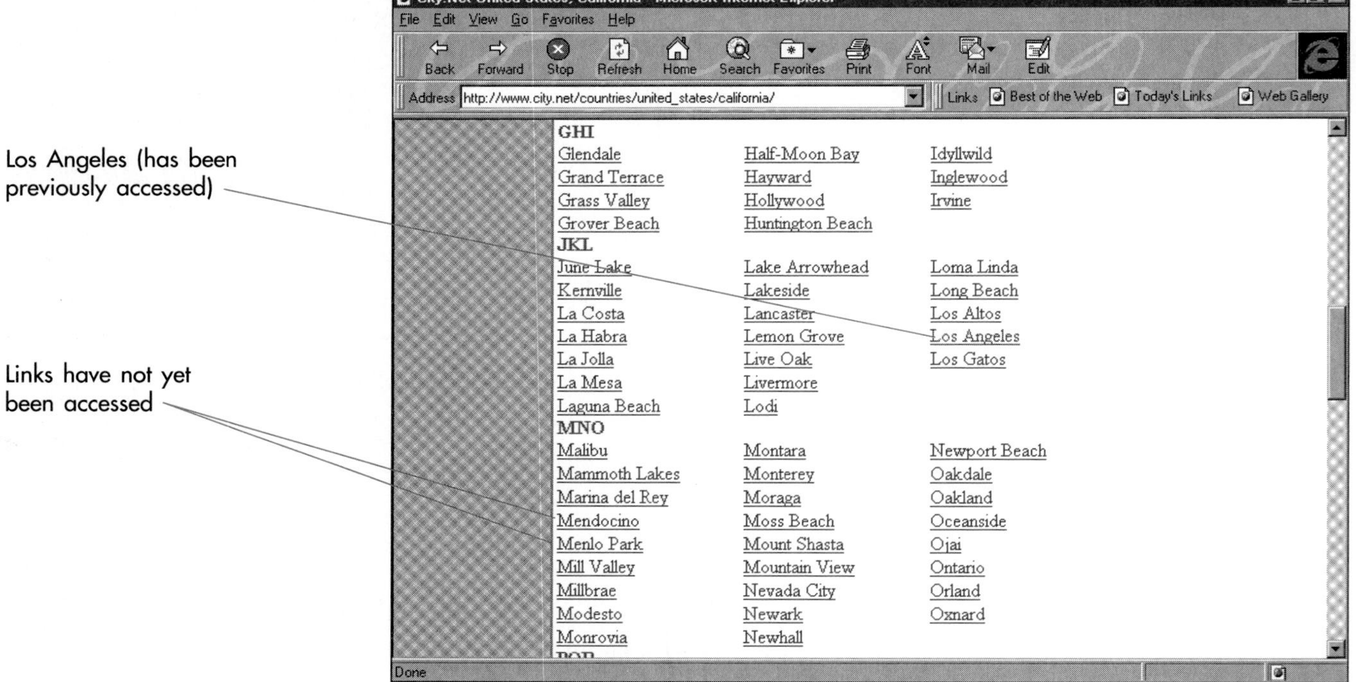

(d) Cities in California

FIGURE 1.1 Hyperlinks (The Virtual Tourist) (continued)

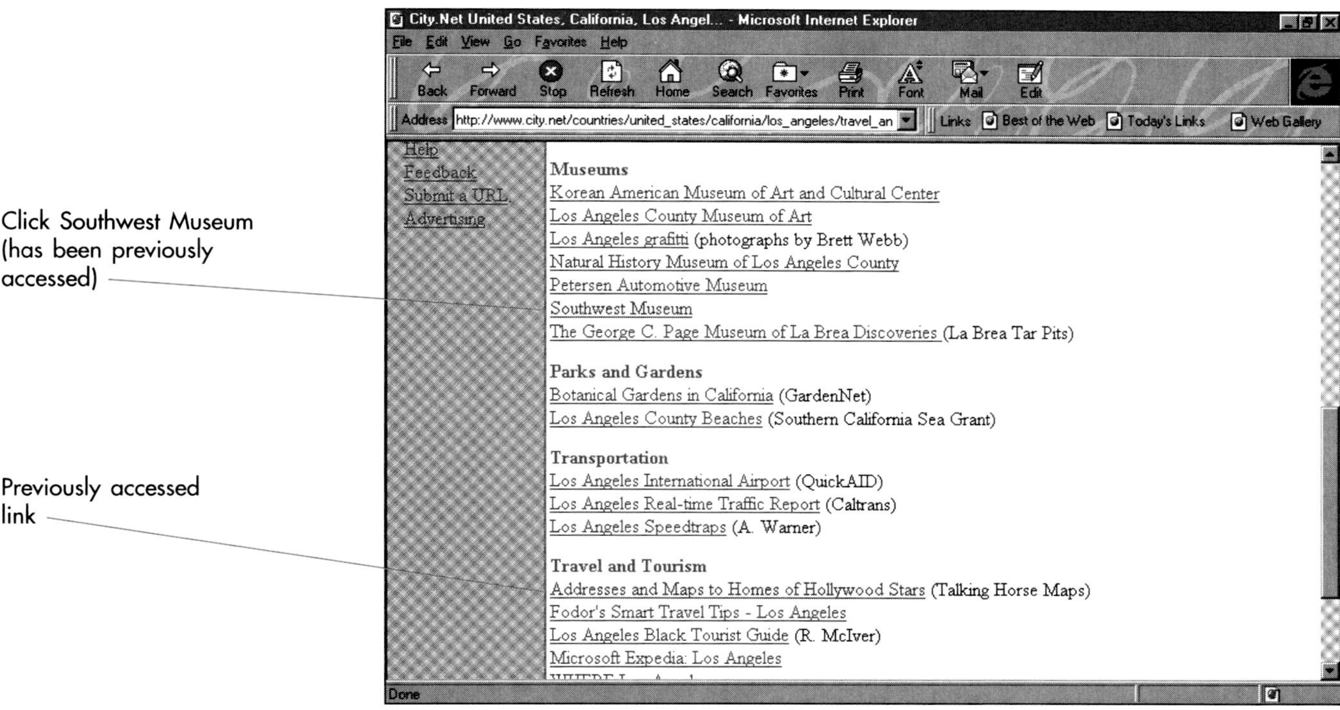

(e) Attractions in Los Angeles

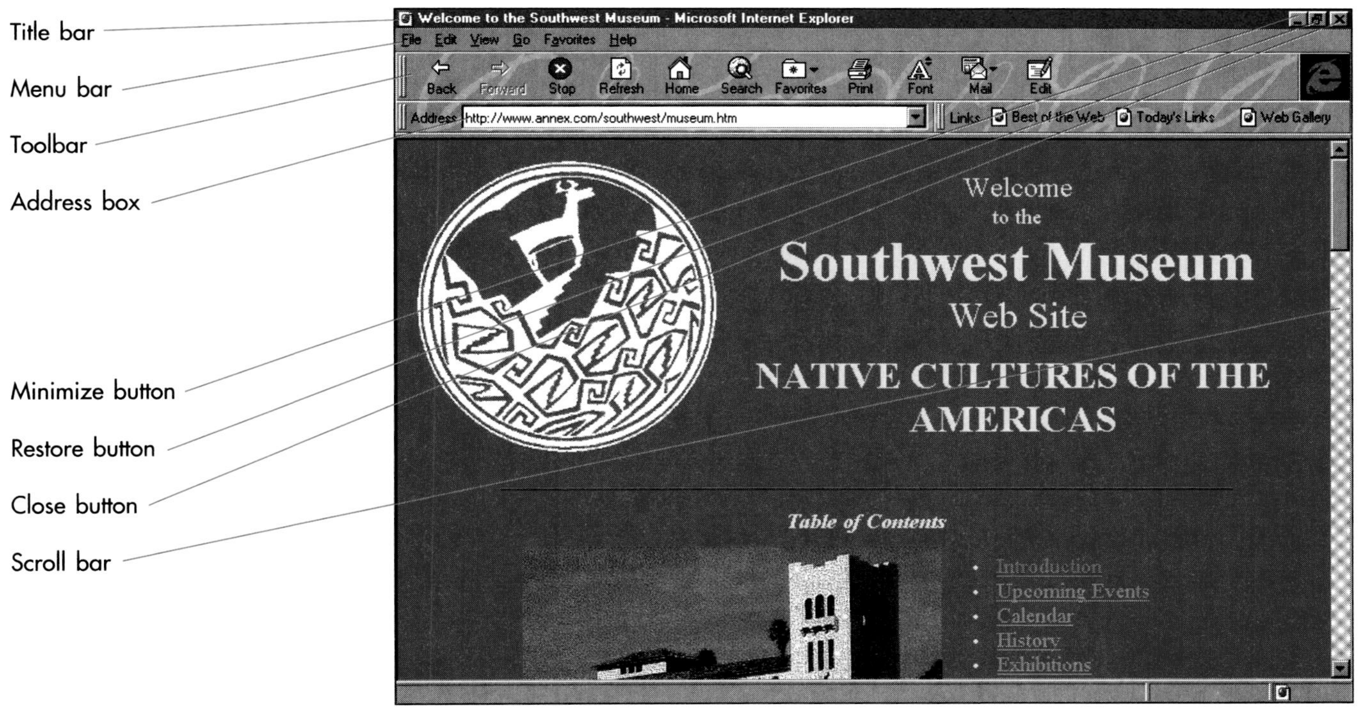

(f) The Southwest Museum

FIGURE 1.1 Hyperlinks (The Virtual Tourist) (continued)

SEARCH ENGINES—A LOOK AHEAD

There are two very general ways to navigate through the Web. You can start by entering the address of a specific site such as the Virtual Tourist, then once you arrive at the site, you can go leisurely from link to link. Browsing in this manner is interesting and enjoyable, but it is not efficient. Hence, when searching for specific information, you need a special tool called a search engine, with which you conduct a keyword search of the Web, much as you search a card catalog or online database in the library. Search engines are discussed in Chapter 2.

The Uniform Resource Locator (URL)

The location (or address) of the document appears in the ***Address box*** and is known as a ***Uniform Resource Locator (URL)*** or more simply as a Web address. The URL is the primary means of navigating the Web, as it indicates the address of the Web server (computer) from which you have requested a document. Change the URL (e.g., by clicking a link or by entering a new address in the Address box) and you jump to a different document, and possibly a different server.

A URL consists of several parts: the method of access, the Internet address of the Web server, an (optional) path in the directory structure on the Web server to a document, and the document name. Every time you click a link within a document, you are effectively entering a new address. Note, for example, how the contents of the Address box change within Figure 1.1 as you access the various Virtual Tourist pages. Consider, for example, the address in Figure 1.1c:

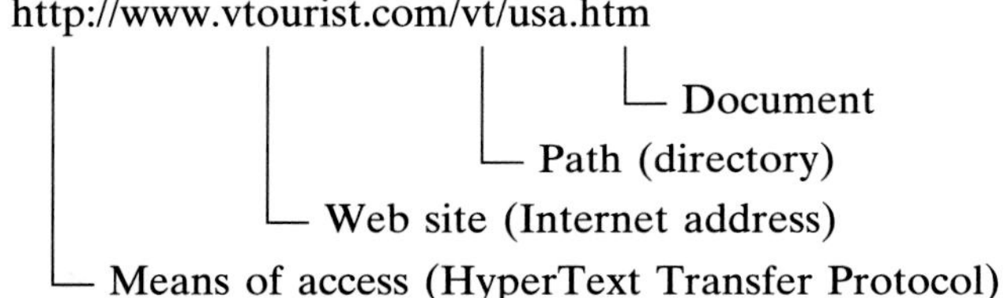

The components in the address can be read from right to left. In other words, the preceding address references the document usa.htm in the vt directory (folder) on the Web server www.vtourist.com according to the http protocol.

To go to a particular site, enter its address through the ***Open command*** in the File menu, or type the address directly in the Address box, press the enter key, and off you go. Once you arrive at a site, click the ***hyperlinks*** (underlined items) that interest you, which will take you to other documents at that site or at a different site. The resources on the Web are connected in such a way that you need not be concerned with where (on which computer) a document is located.

HTML OR HTM

All hypertext and hypermedia documents are written in HTML (HyperText Markup Language) and display the extension html at the end of the document name in the Web address. You will, however, see an extension of htm (rather than html) when a document is stored on a server that does not support long file names. Unix-based systems, which constitute the majority of Web servers, support long file names and so html is the more common extension.

CONNECTING TO THE INTERNET

There are two basic ways to connect to the Internet—from a local area network (LAN), or by dialing in. It's much easier if you connect from a LAN since the installation and setup has been done for you and all you have to do is follow the instructions provided by your professor. If you intend to dial in, however, you need to make additional arrangements.

To connect from home, for example, you need a ***modem*** and an account with an ***Internet Service Provider (ISP),*** a company or information service that enables you to access the Internet. A modem is the interface between your computer and the telephone system. Given the proper software and telephone number, your modem can access the ISP's computer, which in turn lets you access the Internet. The faster your modem, the faster the data will pass back and forth, and it is well worth your investment to purchase the fastest modem available.

The Internet provider will charge you a monthly fee in return for which you gain access to its computer, which maintains a continuous Internet connection. Your fee may entitle you to a set number of hours per month (after which you pay an additional fee) or it may give you unlimited access. The terms vary widely and you are well advised to shop around for the best possible deal. Be sure you are given a local access number (i.e., that you are not making a long distance call) or else your telephone bill will be outrageous. Check that the facilities of your provider are adequate and that you can obtain access whenever you want. Nothing is more frustrating than to receive continual busy signals.

DISABLE CALL WAITING

Your friend may understand if you excuse yourself in the middle of a conversation to answer another incoming call. A computer, however, is not so tolerant and will often break the current connection if another call comes in. Accordingly, check the settings of your communications program to disable call waiting prior to connecting to the Internet (typically by entering *70, in front of the access number). Your friends may complain of a busy signal, but you will be able to work without interruption.

LEARNING BY DOING

The Web cannot be appreciated until you experience it for yourself and so we come to our first hands-on exercise, which takes you to the Web site of the national newspaper, *USA Today.* You are accustomed to reading a newspaper in conventional fashion, perhaps with a morning cup of coffee. Now you can read that paper (and countless others) in an entirely different way. We suggest a specific starting point (the home page of *USA Today*) and a progression through that document. You can, however, start with any other home page, and choose any links you want. Going from one document to the next is what the World Wide Web is all about.

Remember, too, that the World Wide Web is a "living document" that changes continually, so don't be surprised if you cannot duplicate the hands-on exercise exactly. The information on the *USA Today* page varies from day to day, and thus the documents we display may no longer be there when you do the exercise. It doesn't matter, because you want current information, not "yesterday's headlines." Note, too, that the Web is quite busy during the middle of the day and hence you may be unable to connect to a given site because there are too many other visitors already at the site. Be patient and try again, or try another site.

HANDS-ON EXERCISE 1

Introduction to the World Wide Web

Objective: To access the Internet and World Wide Web and to practice basic commands in Internet Explorer (or another browser). Use Figure 1.2 as a guide in the exercise.

FIND OUT WHAT'S AVAILABLE

Your school or university may provide dial-in access to its Internet server, which enables you to access the Web at no charge from your home. Such a connection may be text-based rather than graphics-based; i.e., you can access the Internet, but you cannot use a graphics browser such as Internet Explorer. Alternatively, you may be able to dial in and use Internet Explorer from home, although this usually requires a more complicated setup on your PC than does text-based access. Ask your instructor, lab assistant, or system administrator for precise instructions on what is available.

STEP 1: Start Internet Explorer

- The way in which you start Internet Explorer depends on how you access the Internet. Your instructor will provide the instructions at school, whereas at home it is up to you:
  - In general, click the **Start button,** click (or point to) the **Programs command,** then click **Internet Explorer.** Alternatively, you can double click the **Internet icon** on the desktop.
  - If you do this exercise from school, most academic computing centers configure Internet Explorer to display the college or university home page as shown in Figure 1.2a.
  - If you do the exercise at home, Internet Explorer displays the Microsoft home page by default.
- The home page you see initially will be different from ours — it doesn't matter as long as you are able to start Internet Explorer (or whichever browser your are using).
- If necessary, click the **maximize button** so that Internet Explorer takes the entire desktop. Enter the address of the site you want to visit:
  - Pull down the **File** menu and click the **Open command** to display the Open dialog box in Figure 1.2a. Enter the address of the Web site you want to explore; in this case, **www.usatoday.com** (you don't have to enter http:// as it is assumed). Click **OK.**
  - *Or,* click in the **Address box** below the toolbar, which automatically selects the current address. Enter the address of the site you want to visit, **www.usatoday.com** (the http:// is assumed). Press **enter.**

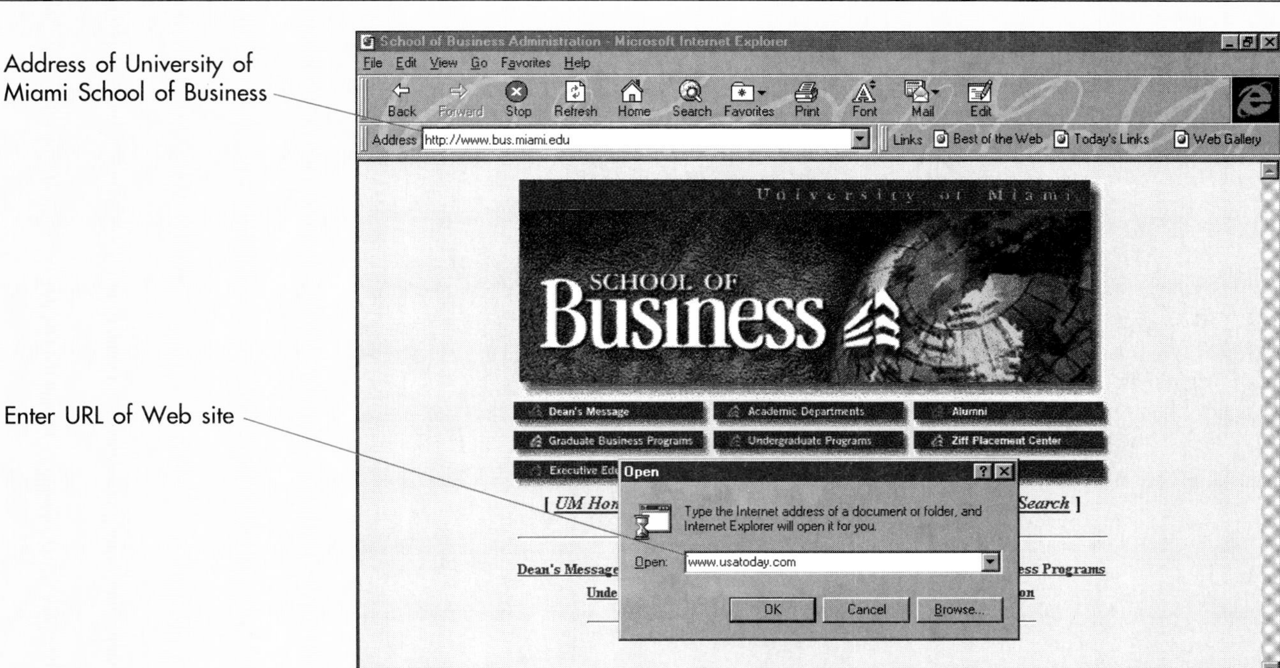

(a) Start Internet Explorer (step 1)

FIGURE 1.2 Hands-on Exercise 1

UNABLE TO LOCATE SERVER OR SERVER NOT RESPONDING

Two things have to occur in order for Internet Explorer to display the requested document—it must locate the server on which the document is stored, and it must be able to connect to that computer. The error message "Unable to Locate Server" will appear if you enter the address incorrectly. Click in the Address box and re-enter the address, being sure to enter it correctly. You may also see the message "Server Down or Not Responding," which implies that Internet Explorer located the server but was unable to connect because the site is busy. This means that too many visitors are already there and you need to try again later in the day.

STEP 2: USA Today

- You should see the home page of *USA Today,* as shown in Figure 1.2b, although the content will surely be different. Note how the address you entered in the previous step appears in the Address box on the Internet Explorer toolbar.
- If you are unable to get to the *USA Today* site, pull down the **File menu,** click **Open,** and re-enter the address shown in the Address box in Figure 1.2b. Press **Enter.**
- If you are still unable to get to the site, it may be down, or there may be too many visitors already at the site:

(b) USA Today (step 2)

FIGURE 1.2 Hands-on Exercise 1 (continued)

- If necessary click and drag the **parallel lines** (||) that appear to the right of the Address box so that the links on the right side of the toolbar are visible.
- Click **Today's Links** (shown to the right of the Address box) and select a different site to explore. Click any link that interests you, which in turn will take you to another Web document.

> **IT'S CASE-SENSITIVE**
>
> Many Web servers are based on the Unix operating system, which (unlike MS-DOS) is case-sensitive. It is important, therefore, that you enter an address correctly, in upper- or lowercase, or else the browser may not find the document. Most addresses are written exclusively in lowercase, although you will find exceptions.

STEP 3: Read the News

➤ This step assumes that you were able to connect to the *USA Today* site. Click the link to **Top News** to displays today's news. Scroll down the page to view the available links.

- You should see a new page similar to Figure 1.2c that displays the news story you selected, and that in turn has additional links.
- If necessary, click the link to **Full Story** to read the full article, then click the **Back button** to return to the original page. The link to the document you just selected has changed color (e.g., from blue to green on our page) to indicate that you have viewed the associated page.
- Continue to browse through the newspaper to view the day's events. Note how the address changes each time you go to a different page, and further how the color of various links changes to reflect pages that have been visited.

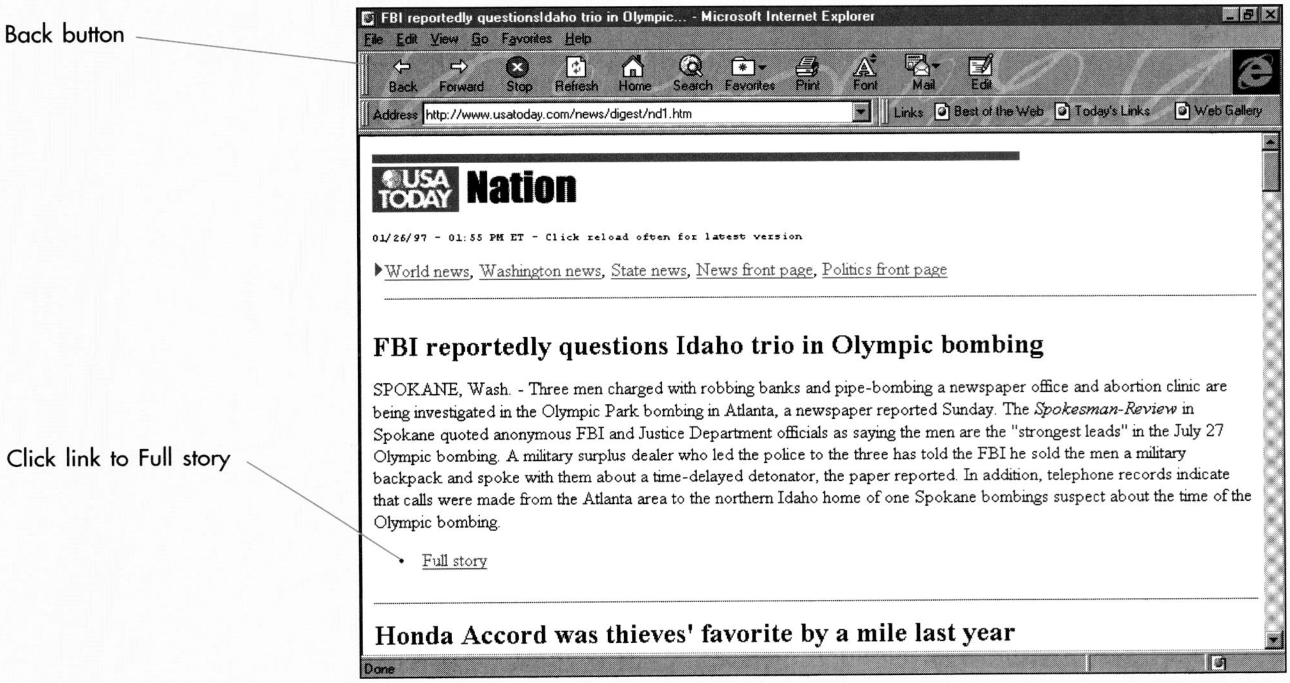

Back button

Click link to Full story

FBI reportedly questionsIdaho trio in Olympic... - Microsoft Internet Explorer

File Edit View Go Favorites Help

Back Forward Stop Refresh Home Search Favorites Print Font Mail Edit

Address http://www.usatoday.com/news/digest/nd1.htm

Links Best of the Web Today's Links Web Gallery

USA TODAY **Nation**

01/26/97 - 01:55 PM ET - Click reload often for latest version

World news, Washington news, State news, News front page, Politics front page

FBI reportedly questions Idaho trio in Olympic bombing

SPOKANE, Wash. - Three men charged with robbing banks and pipe-bombing a newspaper office and abortion clinic are being investigated in the Olympic Park bombing in Atlanta, a newspaper reported Sunday. The *Spokesman-Review* in Spokane quoted anonymous FBI and Justice Department officials as saying the men are the "strongest leads" in the July 27 Olympic bombing. A military surplus dealer who led the police to the three has told the FBI he sold the men a military backpack and spoke with them about a time-delayed detonator, the paper reported. In addition, telephone records indicate that calls were made from the Atlanta area to the northern Idaho home of one Spokane bombings suspect about the time of the Olympic bombing.

- Full story

Honda Accord was thieves' favorite by a mile last year

Done

(c) Read the News (step 3)

FIGURE 1.2 Hands-on Exercise 1 (continued)

CUSTOMIZE THE TOOLBAR

The elements you see in the Explorer window may differ from ours because of the options in effect. Our toolbar, for example, displays the standard buttons; text labels for those buttons; the Address bar, which contains the Address box; the Links, which contains five predefined links; and a background bitmap. To display (hide) any of these elements, pull down the View menu, click Options, click the General tab, then check (clear) the associated text box. To display (hide) the toolbar itself, pull down the View menu and toggle the elements on (off) as desired.

STEP 4: Print a Web Page

- Return to the *USA Today* home page. You can click the **Back button** repeatedly until you are back to the desired page, or alternatively, you can pull down the **Go menu** and select the desired page directly from the list of pages that were visited this session.
- Pull down the **File menu** and click the **Print command** (or click the **Print button** on the toolbar) to display the Print box as shown in Figure 1.2d.
- Click the **All option button** to print all of the pages, then click the **OK button** to print the document and submit it to your instructor as proof you did this exercise.

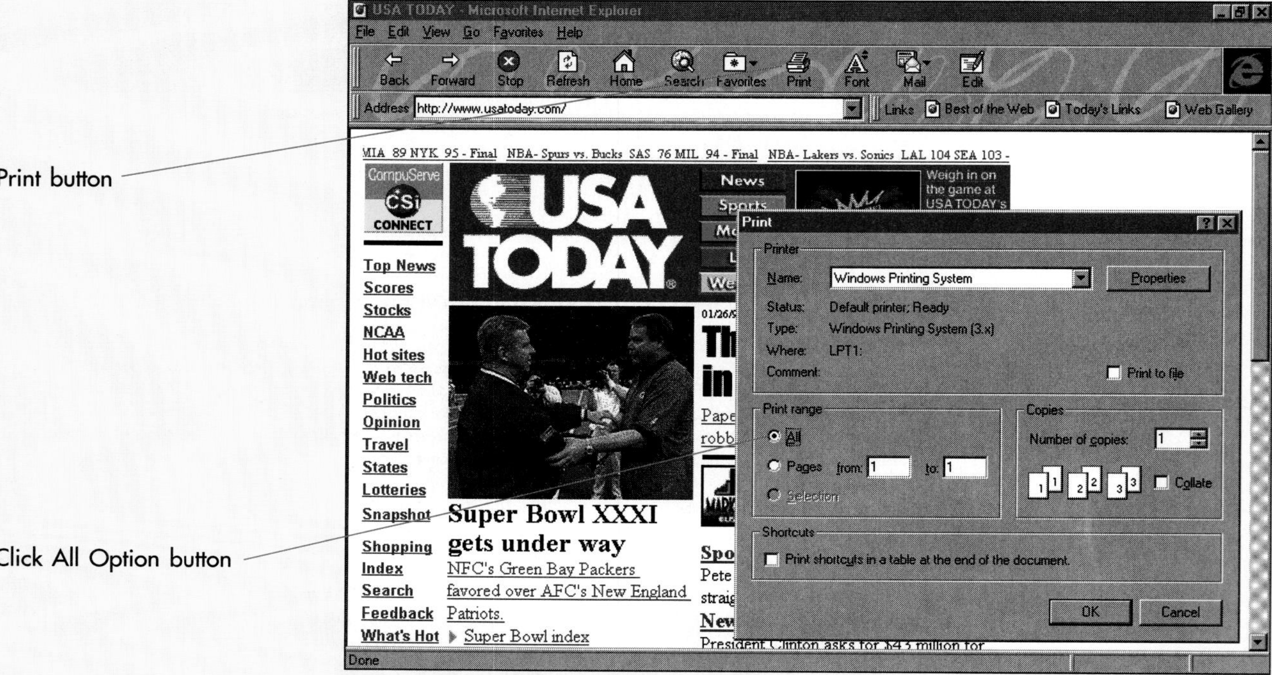

(d) Print a Page (step 4)

FIGURE 1.2 Hands-on Exercise 1 (continued)

THE GO MENU VERSUS THE HISTORY FOLDER

The Go menu displays the last five pages you visited this session and is emptied at the end of every session. The History folder (which is accessed from the Go menu) shows the complete list of all pages you have viewed in previous sessions. The pages in the History folder can be retained for as long as you want (the default is 20 days). Pull down the View menu, click the Options command, then click the Navigation tab. Click the up/down arrow in the History list box to change the number of days, then click OK to accept the setting and close the Options dialog box.

STEP 5: View the Source Code

- Pull down the **View menu** and click **Source** to display the underlying HTML for the page you are viewing. You will see a document similar to that in Figure 1.2e. Maximize the window.
- You need not understand the syntax of the HTML document. Indeed, that is the beauty of Internet Explorer as it interprets the HTML statements for you. Click the **Close button** to close the source document and return to the HTML view.

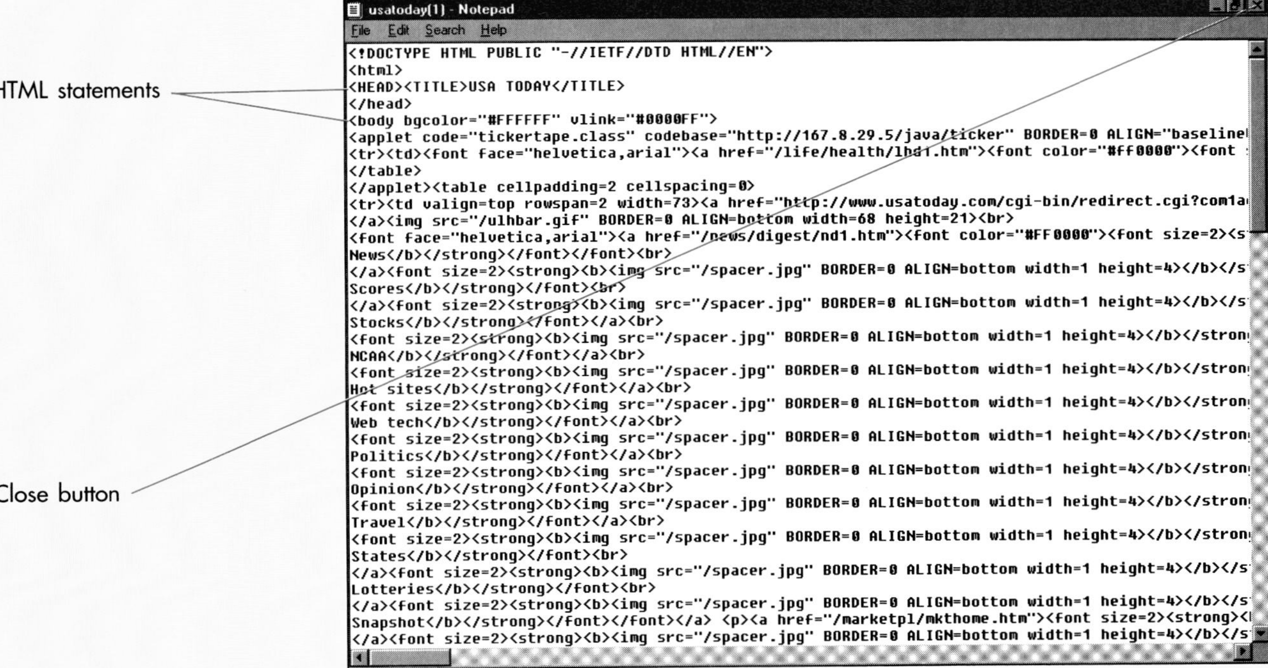


```
<!DOCTYPE HTML PUBLIC "-//IETF//DTD HTML//EN">
<html>
<HEAD><TITLE>USA TODAY</TITLE>
</head>
<body bgcolor="#FFFFFF" vlink="#0000FF">
<applet code="tickertape.class" codebase="http://167.8.29.5/java/ticker" BORDER=0 ALIGN="baseline
<tr><td><font face="helvetica,arial"><a href="/life/health/lhd1.htm"><font color="#ff0000"><font
</table>
</applet><table cellpadding=2 cellspacing=0>
<tr><td valign=top rowspan=2 width=73><a href="http://www.usatoday.com/cgi-bin/redirect.cgi?com1a
</a><img src="/ulhbar.gif" BORDER=0 ALIGN=bottom width=68 height=21><br>
<font face="helvetica,arial"><a href="/news/digest/nd1.htm"><font color="#FF0000"><font size=2><s
News</b></strong></font></font><br>
</a><font size=2><strong><b><img src="/spacer.jpg" BORDER=0 ALIGN=bottom width=1 height=4></b></s
Scores</b></strong></font><br>
</a><font size=2><strong><b><img src="/spacer.jpg" BORDER=0 ALIGN=bottom width=1 height=4></b></s
Stocks</b></strong></font></a><br>
<font size=2><strong><b><img src="/spacer.jpg" BORDER=0 ALIGN=bottom width=1 height=4></b></stron
NCAA</b></strong></font></a><br>
<font size=2><strong><b><img src="/spacer.jpg" BORDER=0 ALIGN=bottom width=1 height=4></b></stron
Hot sites</b></strong></font></a><br>
<font size=2><strong><b><img src="/spacer.jpg" BORDER=0 ALIGN=bottom width=1 height=4></b></stron
Web tech</b></strong></font></a><br>
<font size=2><strong><b><img src="/spacer.jpg" BORDER=0 ALIGN=bottom width=1 height=4></b></stron
Politics</b></strong></font></a><br>
<font size=2><strong><b><img src="/spacer.jpg" BORDER=0 ALIGN=bottom width=1 height=4></b></stron
Opinion</b></strong></font></a><br>
<font size=2><strong><b><img src="/spacer.jpg" BORDER=0 ALIGN=bottom width=1 height=4></b></stron
Travel</b></strong></font></a><br>
<font size=2><strong><b><img src="/spacer.jpg" BORDER=0 ALIGN=bottom width=1 height=4></b></stron
States</b></strong></font><br>
</a><font size=2><strong><b><img src="/spacer.jpg" BORDER=0 ALIGN=bottom width=1 height=4></b></s
Lotteries</b></strong></font><br>
</a><font size=2><strong><b><img src="/spacer.jpg" BORDER=0 ALIGN=bottom width=1 height=4></b></s
Snapshot</b></strong></font></font></a> <p><a href="/marketpl/mkthome.htm"><font size=2><strong><
</a><font size=2><strong><b><img src="/spacer.jpg" BORDER=0 ALIGN=bottom width=1 height=4></b></s
```

(e) View the Source Code (step 5)

FIGURE 1.2 Hands-on Exercise 1 (continued)

WHAT IS HTML?

All hypertext documents are written in HyperText Markup Language (HTML), a special language that indicates to Internet Explorer (and other browsers) how to display a document. You will want to learn more about HTML, especially if your college or university enables you to create and maintain your own home page on its Web server.

STEP 6: Surf the Net

- You've done what we have asked and have enjoyed a taste of the World Wide Web. Now it's time to explore on your own by going to new and different sites. Accordingly:

- Click the **Best of the Web** or **Today's Links buttons** to explore the current sites suggested by Internet Explorer. We don't know what you will find, but you can expect something interesting. Figure 1.2f, for example, displays one of the sites suggested by Internet Explorer on the day we went surfing, *or*
- Choose a specific site that you have heard about (or see Appendix B for suggestions) and enter the address for that site using the File Open command.

➤ Click the hyperlinks that interest you and off you go. Happy surfing!

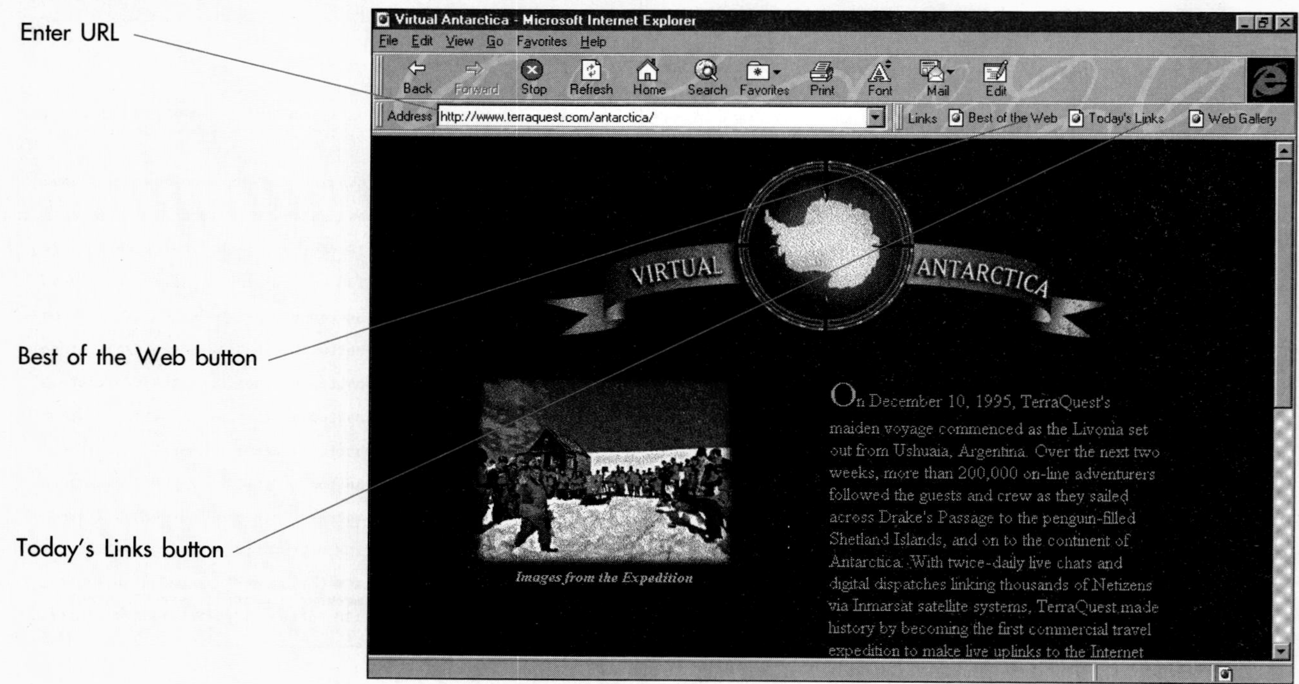

(f) Surf the Net (step 6)

FIGURE 1.2 Hands-on Exercise 1 (continued)

GUESS THE URL

You can often guess the address of a site according to a consistent addressing scheme; e.g., www.company.com. The address of the Lycos and Yahoo search engines (www.lycos.com and www.yahoo.com) both follow this pattern. So do the home pages of many companies; e.g., www.netscape.com and www.microsoft.com for Netscape and Microsoft, respectively. And if you are in the mood for sports, try www.nfl.com or www.nba.com to go to the home pages of the National Football League or National Basketball Association.

We trust that you enjoyed the hands-on exercise and that you completed it without difficulty. Our objective was to get you up and running as quickly as possible so that you could experience the Web and appreciate its potential. Internet Explorer is straightforward and easy to use because it is a Windows-based program that follows the common user interface. The next several pages examine Internet Explorer in more detail to help you use the program effectively.

Figure 1.3a displays the home page of Microsoft Corporation as it appears with the default settings of Internet Explorer. Figure 1.3b displays a different view of the same page (the address is the same in both figures) in order to illustrate additional features within Internet Explorer. The most obvious difference between the two is the display (omission) of the graphics, which enhance the appearance of a page but increase the time it takes to download the page and display it on your PC. The presence or absence of the graphics is controlled through the ***Options command*** in the View menu, one of several pull-down menus within Internet Explorer.

The ***menu bar*** provides access to all commands within Internet Explorer. Some menus (e.g., File, Edit, and Help) are common to most Windows applications, whereas others (e.g., Go and Favorites) are unique to Explorer. The ***Favorites menu*** is especially important as it enables you to store the addresses of your favorite pages in order to quickly return to those pages at a later date.

The ***Help menu*** functions in Internet Explorer just as it does in all other Microsoft applications and presents a tabbed dialog box with Contents and Index tabs. The Help menu also provides a link to online support, which takes you to the Microsoft Web site with more recent information. Help is illustrated in detail in the hands-on exercise that follows shortly.

The ***toolbar*** offers an alternate way to execute the most common commands. The toolbar in Figure 1.3a displays both text and graphic icons. The toolbar in Figure 1.3b, however, displays only the graphic icons and thus provides additional space within the Internet Explorer window to view the actual document. The appearance of the toolbar is controlled through the Options command in the View menu.

The ***Address box*** displays the address of the page you are currently viewing (http://www.microsoft.com in both Figures 1.3a and 1.3b), and its contents change automatically whenever you click a hyperlink to a different page. You can also click in the Address box to enter an address manually, after which you press the enter key to move to that page.

The ***Internet Explorer icon*** in the upper right corner is more than just a corporate logo. The icon is animated with a spinning globe when Internet Explorer is in the process of retrieving a page, and motionless after the document has been retrieved. You can also click the icon at any time to display the Microsoft home page.

Links (short for hyperlinks) and ***hotspots*** provide connections to other documents. A link appears as underlined text in either black or grey. Any link in black (e.g., IT Executive in Figure 1.3a) has not yet been selected, whereas links appearing in grey (e.g., Microsoft Office 97 is Here, in Figure 1.3b) indicate that the associated page has been previously retrieved. Hotspots are similar in concept, except that they are embedded within a graphic (e.g., Support in Figure 1.3a) as opposed to appearing as underlined text. (The mouse pointer changes to a hand when pointing to a link or hotspot.)

The ***status bar*** at the bottom of the window displays information about the current operation. If, for example, Explorer is in the process of retrieving a document, the status bar will show the progress of the file transfer; e.g., "Done" in Figure 1.3a. Alternatively, the status bar will display the underlying address whenever you are pointing to a link or hotspot.

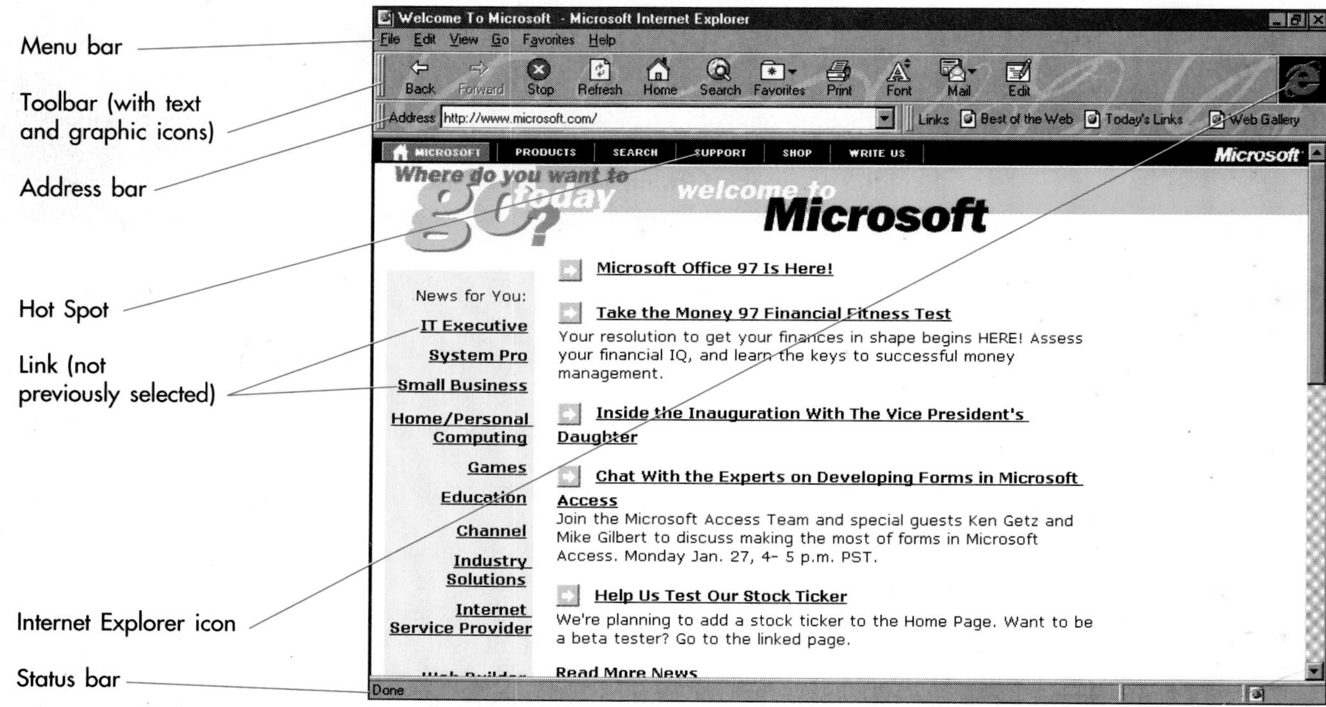

(a) Default Options

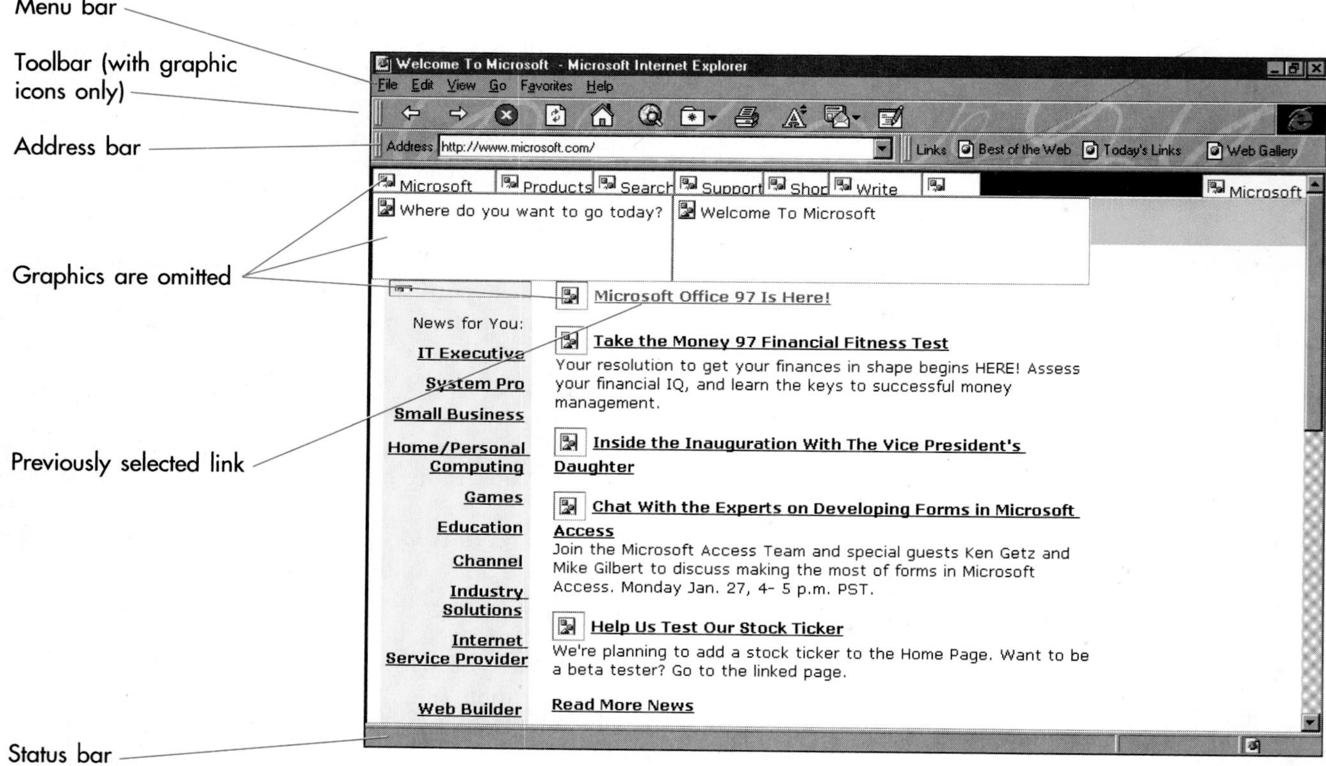

(b) Custom Options

FIGURE 1.3 Internet Explorer

www.nflhome.com and www.fi...com, respectively. ESPN (the television network) also maintains a site at espnet.sportszone.com. Choose any of these sites, or find your own, then summarize your findings in a one-page note to your instructor.

4. The Census Bureau: What is the current population of the United States? You can find the answer to this and many other questions at the official Web site of the U.S. Census Bureau as shown in Figure 1.8. Go to this site, answer our question, then explore the site to see what additional information is available. Summarize your findings in a brief note to your instructor.

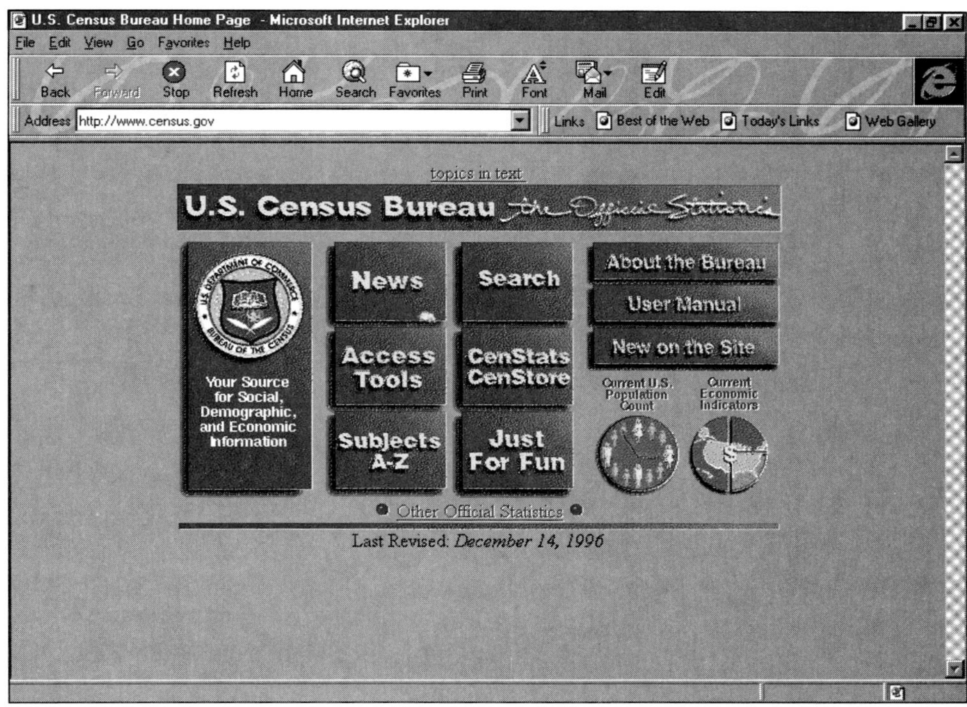

FIGURE 1.8 Screen for Practice Exercise 4

5. The Top 100: There are so many excellent sites on the Web that it is impossible to track them all. One site we visit frequently is that of *PC Magazine,* which provides a link to its list of the top 100 sites as shown in Figure 1.9. Another excellent list of suggested sites is found by clicking the Best of the Web link on the Internet Explorer toolbar. Visit at least three sites suggested by the magazine or Internet Explorer, then summarize your findings in a brief note to your instructor. Set a time limit for this assignment because surfing can become quite addictive.

6. Buying a PC: There are many sites on the Web that provide advice on how to purchase a PC. Go to Bob Grauer's home page (www.bus.miami.edu/~rgrauer), then click the link to Buying a Computer to display the page in Figure 1.10. Give yourself a budget of $2,000, choose two vendors, then determine the best configuration for your money. What additional options would you choose if your budget were $2,500 rather than $2,000? Print the results and submit them to your instructor as proof you did this exercise. You may also want to print our list of suggested tips and keep it as a reference in the event you are really in the market for a computer.

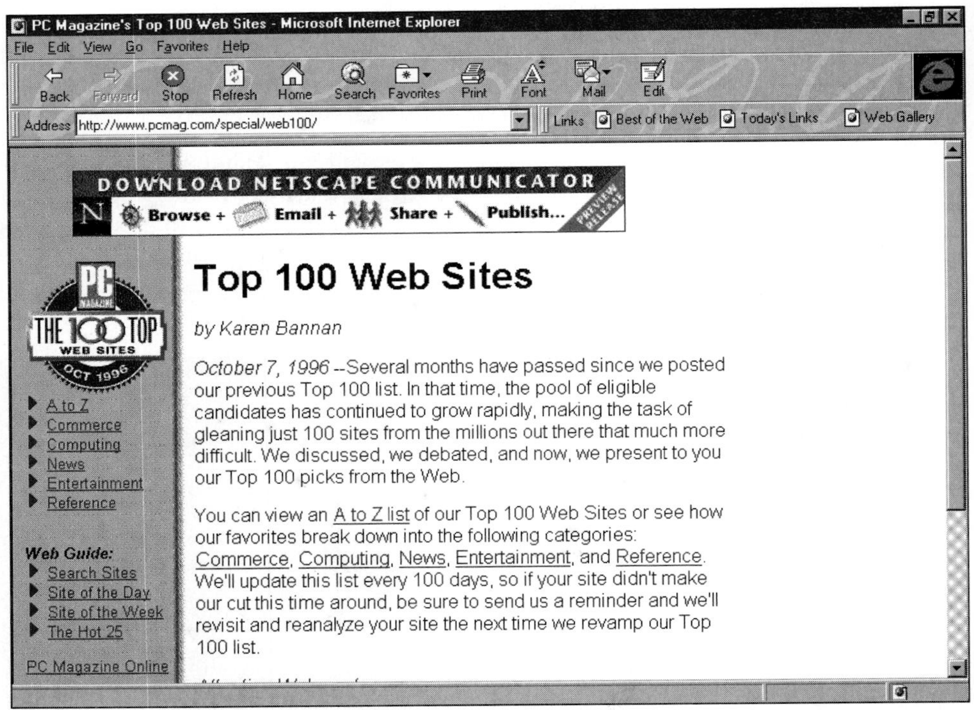

FIGURE 1.9 Screen for Practice Exercise 5

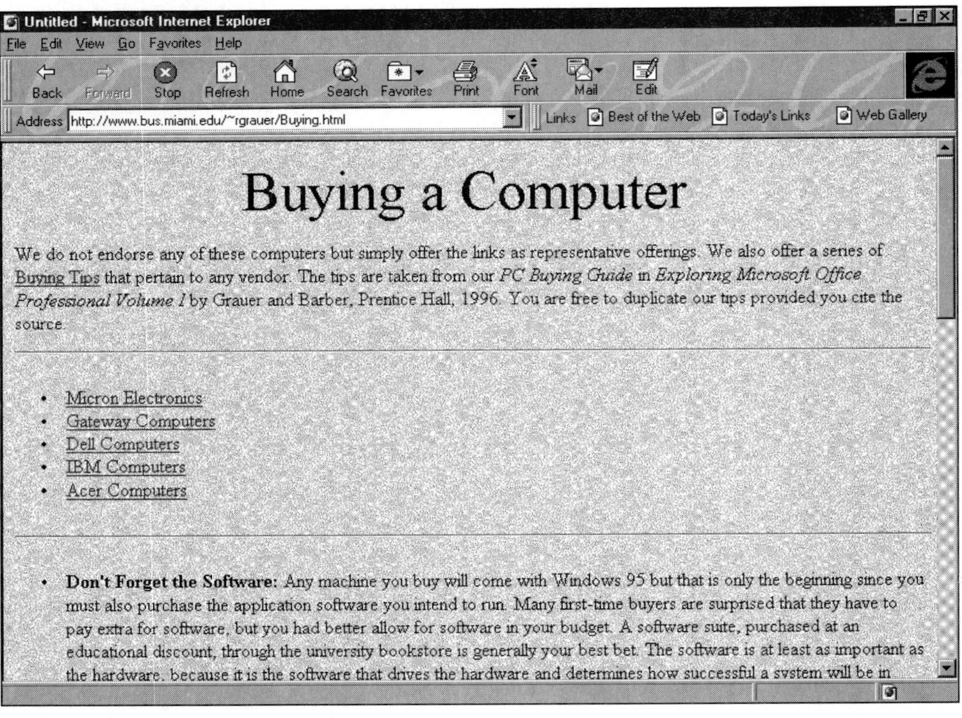

FIGURE 1.10 Screen for Practice Exercise 6

Access to the Internet

The easiest way to access the Internet is from a local area network on campus. But which students are given access, and what if anything do you have to do to open an account? Does the university provide an e-mail account? If so, what is your username and password? What is your e-mail address? Does your e-mail account expire at the end of the semester, or does it continue throughout your stay at the university? And finally, do you have dial-in access to your campus network? If so, can you use a graphical browser such as Internet Explorer from home? You don't have to put the answers to these questions in writing; you do, however, have to determine what resources are available to you in order to do the exercises in our text. Check with your instructor, then go to the Help desk for additional information.

It's the URL, Not the Browser

Our text focuses on Internet Explorer, but many other browsers are available. Choose a different browser such as the Netscape Navigator and use it to display several pages that were referenced in this chapter. What difference (if any) do you see in a given page when it is viewed in Netscape rather than Internet Explorer? Which browser is better from a developer's point of view? From a user's point of view?

The Concept of Cache

The concept of cache was referenced briefly in the second hands-on exercise, but the topic merits additional study if you are to use Internet Explorer efficiently. Use the Help menu or Knowledge Base to study the topic, then write a short summary of that information and submit it to your instructor. Be sure you address the following issues: What is a cache and how does it improve performance? What is the difference between a cache in memory versus one on disk? What is the default size of each, and how can you change these parameters? When, if ever, would you want to retrieve a page from the Internet if it is already in cache?

Is a Picture Worth a Thousand Words?

Much has been made of the World Wide Web and its ability to retrieve and display documents with embedded graphics. Go back through this chapter and cover the illustrations and screens with a piece of paper, reading just the text. What value do graphics add to these documents? Do graphics ever detract from a document? Summarize your findings in a brief report to your instructor in which you describe how to download documents with and without the graphics.

Our Favorite Bookstore

Amazon Books (www.amazon.com) is one of our favorite sites on the Web. The site is a perfect illustration of how a small company with an innovative idea can compete on an equal footing with large corporations. Amazon Books does not maintain a physical inventory, as does your local bookstore, but it provides access to more than one million titles. You order from Amazon, and Amazon in turn orders the book from the publisher for you at a discount. You can search by author, subject, or title, read reviews written by other Amazon visitors, or contribute your own review. Go to the site, find a book that you are interested in, then compare Amazon's price with that of your local bookstore.

Security on the Web

You can purchase almost anything on the Web (e.g., a book from Amazon Books as in the previous case study). How you pay for the item is another issue. Is it safe to transmit your credit card number over the Internet? What protection, if any, does the vendor provide to maintain the privacy of your credit card? How is the https protocol different from the http protocol that we have referenced throughout the chapter? What is the Secure Sockets layer? The answers to these questions are important, especially if you intend to actually buy an item over the Internet.

2

SEARCH ENGINES: FINDING INFORMATION ON THE WEB

OBJECTIVES

After reading this chapter you will be able to:

1. Use the Search button within Internet Explorer to access a search engine; describe how to access a search engine directly through its URL.
2. List three different search engines; explain why it is often necessary to use multiple search engines with a single query.
3. Distinguish between the Boolean operations And, Or, and Not; explain why it is important to qualify a search.
4. Explain why searching the Web is often a process of trial and error; discuss several techniques you can use to improve your chance for success.
5. Describe how to find a friend's e-mail address, given that you know the school or university he or she attends.
6. Describe the structure of a URL address; explain the nature of a "URL not found" error message.
7. Explain the use of the Find command within a Web document; describe how to access this command.
8. Download a graphic from the Web, then incorporate that graphic into a word processing document.

OVERVIEW

The Internet contains a wealth of information that is readily available. That's the good news. The bad news is that the Internet contains so much information that it is often difficult to find what you are looking for. Browsing, while interesting and enjoyable, is not a very efficient way to locate specific information. This chapter introduces the concept of a search engine, a program that systematically searches the Web for documents on a specific topic.

The chapter begins with an explanation of how search engines work and why they are essential. You will learn that multiple search engines are available, each of which is based on a different database of Web documents and each of which uses a different search algorithm. You will be encouraged, therefore, to use multiple engines when conducting research in order to find the greatest number of matching documents.

On the other hand, the Web contains literally millions of documents, and hence your initial search often yields many documents (hits) that may be only marginally relevant to your query. Accordingly, the second half of the chapter shows you how to qualify a search so that it is more likely to retrieve the documents you really want. We also give you an opportunity to apply this information as we guide you through two hands-on exercises at the computer.

AVOID TRAFFIC JAMS

Rush hour traffic is always tedious, whether you are on the city streets or the Information Superhighway. Sometimes it can't be helped in that you have to go to work at a certain time or use the computer lab when it's open. Try, however, to avoid the peak hours during the middle of the day when traffic on the Web is busiest and response is very slow. Go to the lab early in the morning or late at night. Not only will you (almost certainly) be guaranteed a computer, but you will avoid rush hour on the Internet as well.

SEARCH ENGINES

The same techniques apply to effective research, regardless of whether it is done in the library or on the World Wide Web (although the Web has made the task much easier). If, for example, you were using the library to do research for a term paper, you wouldn't do very well by randomly strolling through the stacks from floor to floor until you found what you wanted. It's equally inefficient to just browse through the Web, going from one link to another until you stumble onto a relevant document.

It's obvious that you would do much better in both cases to conduct a ***key word search,*** in which you look for documents on a specific topic. In yesterday's library you would look up the topic in the card catalog; in today's library you would use an online database; and on the Web you would use a ***search engine,*** the Web's equivalent of the library's card catalog or database.

A search engine is a program that systematically searches the Web for documents on a specific topic. You enter a ***query*** (a key word or phrase) into a ***search form*** and the search engine scans its database to see which documents (if any) are related to the key words you requested. The search engine will list the titles of the documents it finds, together with a hyperlink to each document. Some search engines also display an abstract of each document to help you determine its relevance to your query.

Many search engines are available, each of which uses its own database of Web documents. Each database stores information about each document it contains, typically the document's URL (i.e., its Web address) and selected information from the document. Some databases store only the document's title, others contain the first few lines of text, and still others contain every word in the document. Each engine uses its own version of a special program known as a ***spider*** to automatically search the Web on a periodic basis, looking for new pages to add to its database.

Some search engines are better than others, but there is no consensus on the "best" engine. In any event, a search engine is only as good as its database and the algorithm it uses to search that database for relevant documents. The larger the database, the greater the number of ***hits*** (documents matching your query) that are returned.

A large number of hits, however, does not necessarily guarantee a successful search, because you also need to be concerned with the relevance of those hits. In other words, just because a document contains a key word or phrase does not mean the document is useful to you. If, for example, you were searching for information about the University of Miami, you would probably not be interested in the home page of a student who attended the university. Accordingly, many engines rank the relevance of the documents they return according to the frequency with which the key words appear in the document.

Figure 2.1 displays the results from four search engines, each of which is looking for Web documents containing the key words *University of Miami.* The results vary widely according to the search engine, because every engine uses a different database as well as a different search algorithm. In other words, the same query produces different results with different engines, and it is important, therefore, to use multiple engines for the most complete results.

Note, too, that virtually all of the examples in Figure 2.1 return an excessive number of documents, most of which are not relevant to the query. Thus, another guideline for effective searching is to limit the scope of a search so that it returns fewer, albeit more relevant, documents. (We tell you how later in the chapter.) Despite the number of irrelevant documents, however, think of what was accomplished in a matter of seconds (depending on traffic and the speed of your connection). You were looking for information on a specific university, you searched through millions of documents, and you found several promising documents to examine.

Note, too, the diversity of titles that are visible in Figure 2.1. None of the documents reference the precise page for which you are searching (the University of Miami home page). Several documents, however, display links to various organizations at the University, which in turn will take you to its home page (e.g. University of Miami Department of Student Organizations in Figure 2.1a.). Other documents (e.g., those in Figure 2.1b) take you to a completely different university, Miami University in Ohio, as opposed to the University of Miami in Florida. Still other documents (those in Figure 2.1c or 2.1d) may take you to the home page of a specific student at either school. Suffice it to say that searching is often a matter of trial and error, but that it becomes easier with practice. You're ready for our next exercise.

CHECK OUT YOUR SCHOOL

The following exercise has you look for the e-mail address of one of the authors. In so doing, you will search for the University of Miami home page on the Web (the author's place of employment), then explore the UM site until you come to the e-mail directory. The UM site is typical of many other universities in that it provides links to a wealth of campus information. Hence, you can also use the exercise as a guide to learn more about your own college or university.

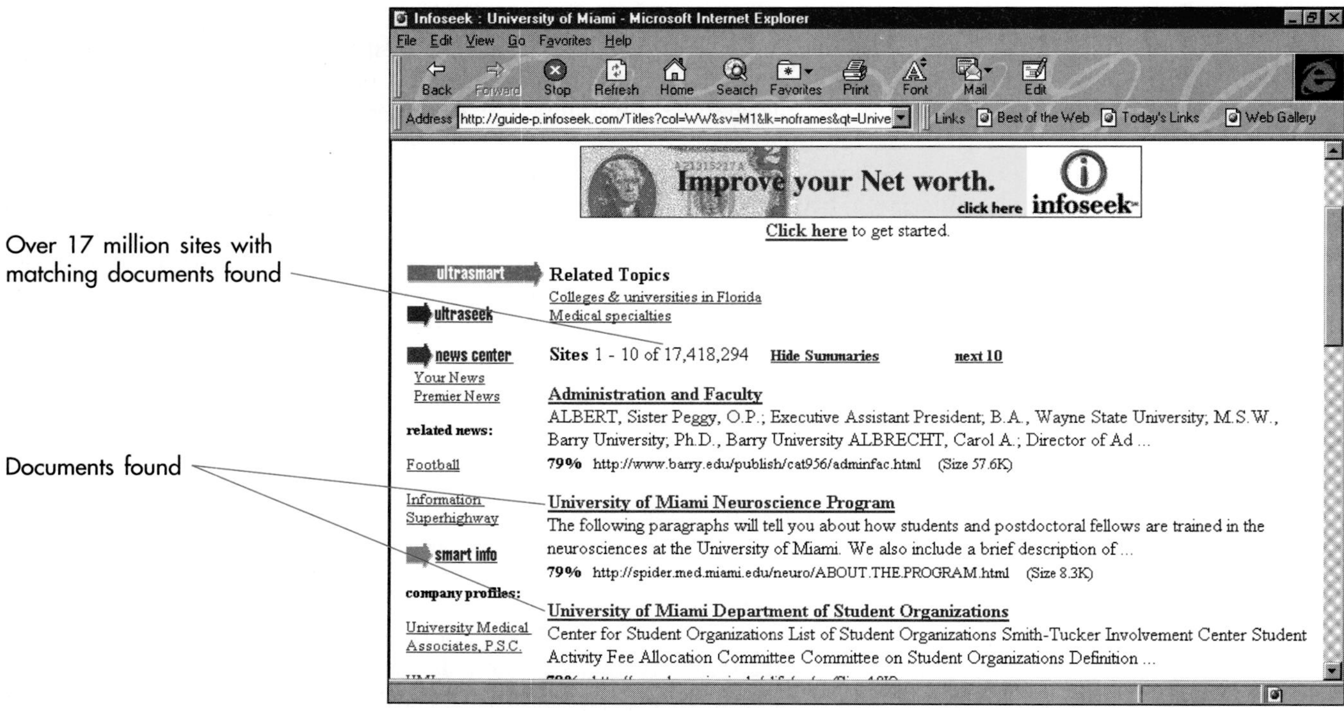

(a) Infoseek

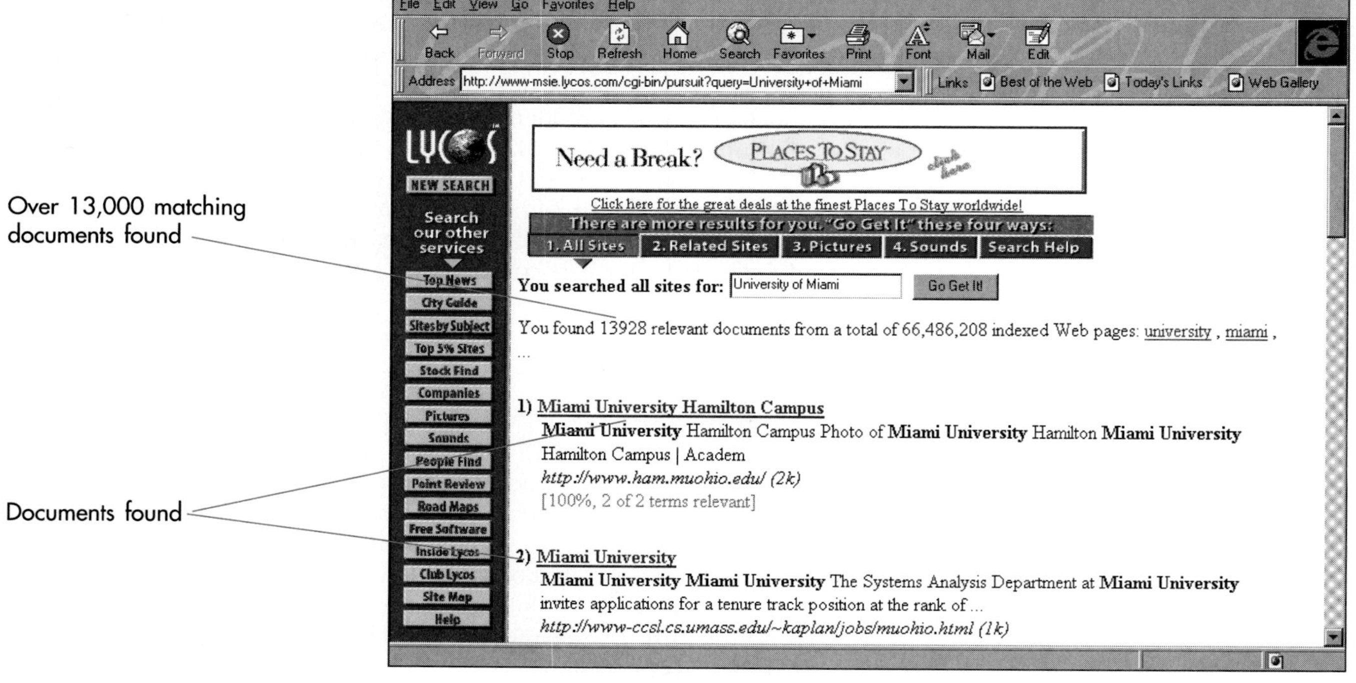

(b) Lycos

FIGURE 2.1 Search Engines

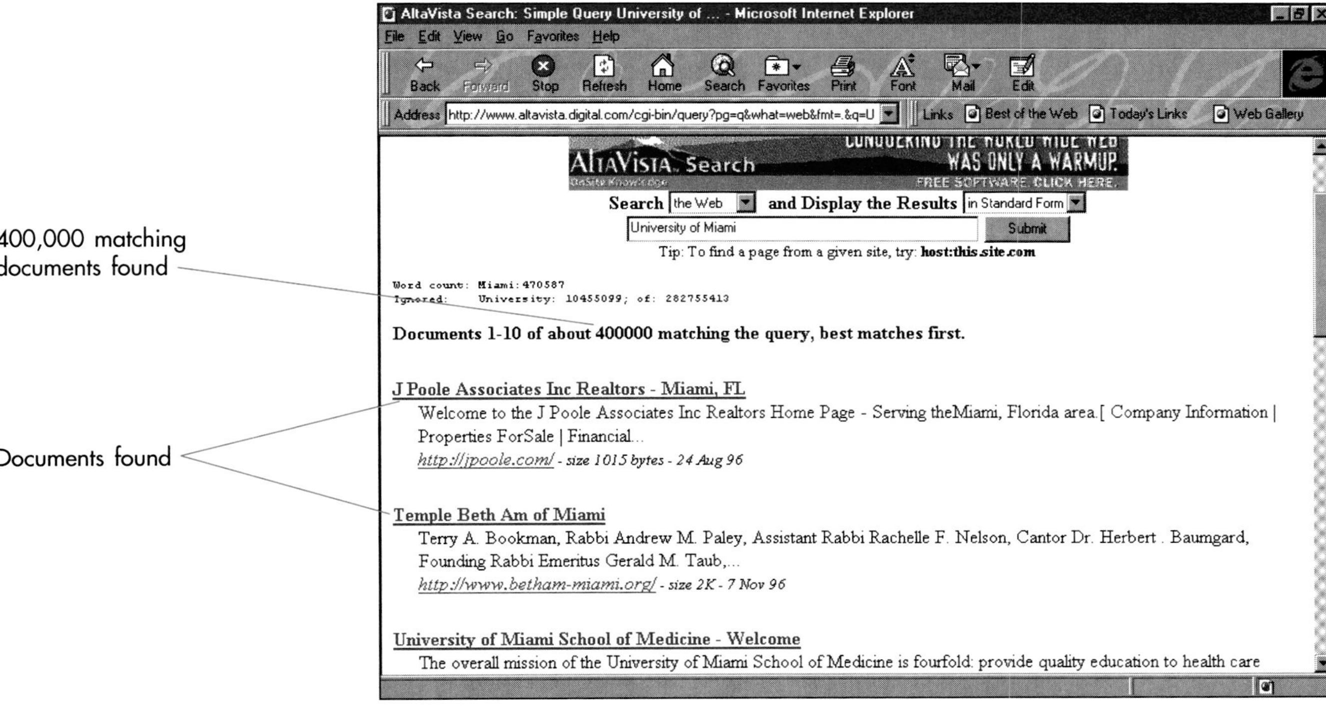

(c) AltaVista

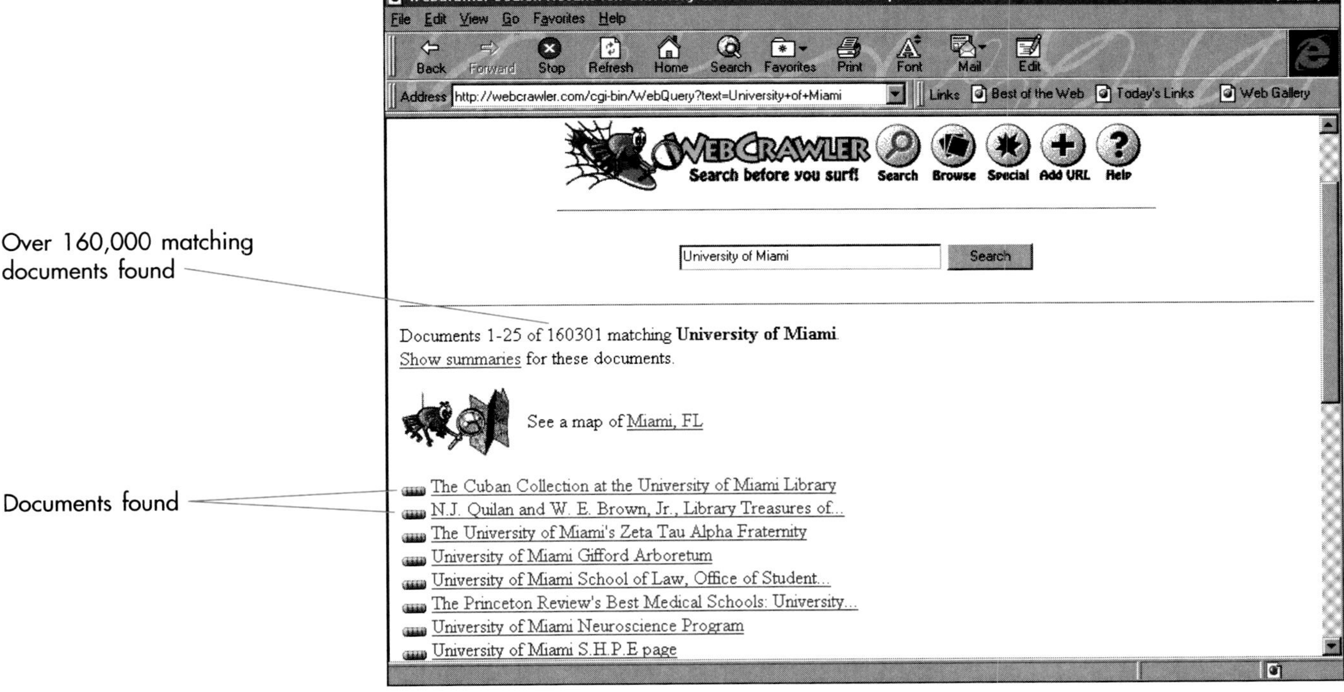

(d) WebCrawler

FIGURE 2.1 Search Engines (continued)

HANDS-ON EXERCISE 1

Searching the Web

Objective: To find the e-mail address of a friend; to use a Web search engine to go to the home page of your friend's college or university, then browse the Web site until you find the e-mail address. Use Figure 2.2 as a guide in the exercise.

STEP 1: Choose a Search Engine

- Start Internet Explorer as you did in Chapter 1. Click the **Search button** to display a screen similar to Figure 2.2a.
- You can use any of the listed search engines. You may find it interesting to compare the results of a given query with different engines.
- We chose the Yahoo engine. If necessary, click the **Yahoo option button** so that your results will be similar to ours.
- Click in the text box and enter **University of Miami,** then click the **Search button.** Click **Yes** if you see a security alert asking whether you want to continue.

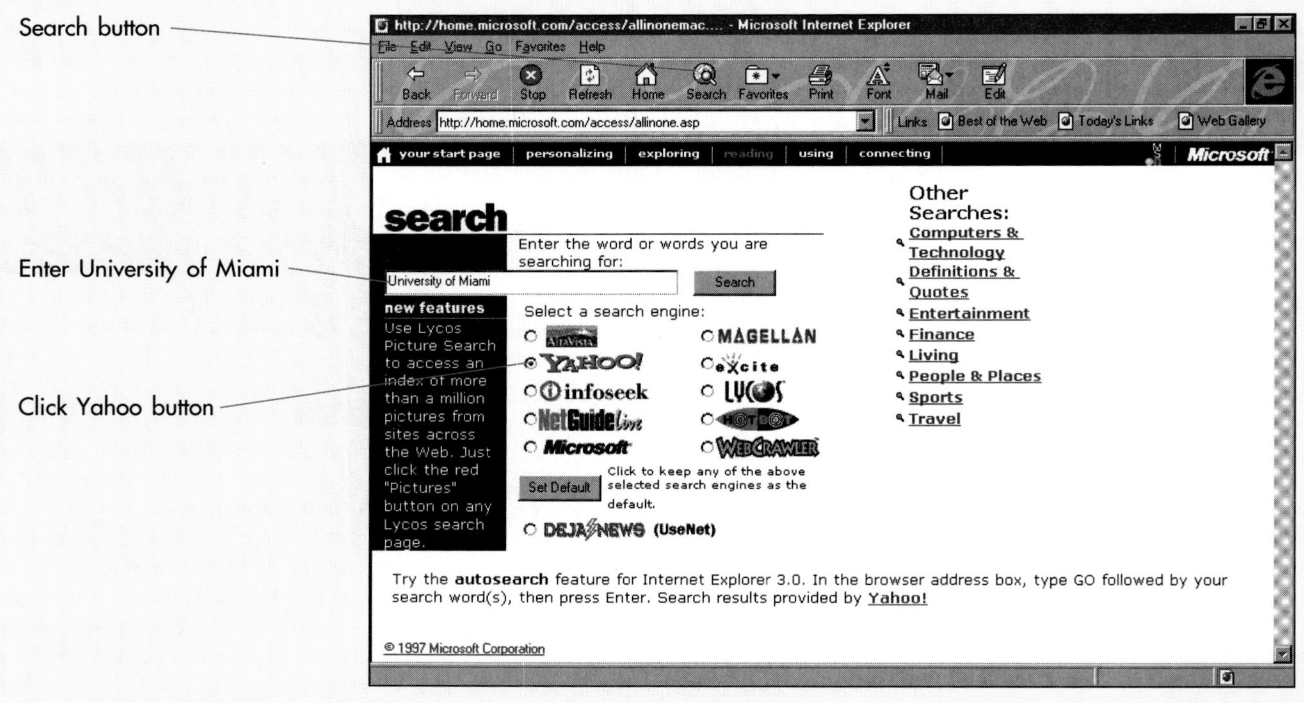

(a) Choose a Search Engine (step 1)

FIGURE 2.2 Hands-on Exercise 1

INTERNET SEARCH TOOLS

The Internet Explorer Search button displays a screen with access to a variety of interesting sites and references. You can, for example, use the People and Places category to find an 800 telephone number, an area code, a zip code given a street address, or an e-mail address. Scroll further down the page and you will find a variety of links in different categories. See practice exercise 2 at the end of the chapter.

STEP 2: Yahoo Results

➤ You should see a document similar to Figure 2.2b, although the number of hits will most likely differ from ours. Yahoo displays both Categories (groups of sites) as well as specific sites. There is no right or wrong way to go through the list. You may have to scroll down the page to see the links we reference.

- Click the first matching category, **University of Miami,** which indicates it includes information about the Coral Gables campus. This will take you to another Yahoo page showing the documents within the University of Miami category. From there, you can click a link to the University of Miami, *or*
- Scroll down the page until you can click the University of Miami link (under Reference: Libraries.University.Libraries). This will take you to the home page of the Otto G. Richter Library, which in turn contains a link to the University's home page, *or*

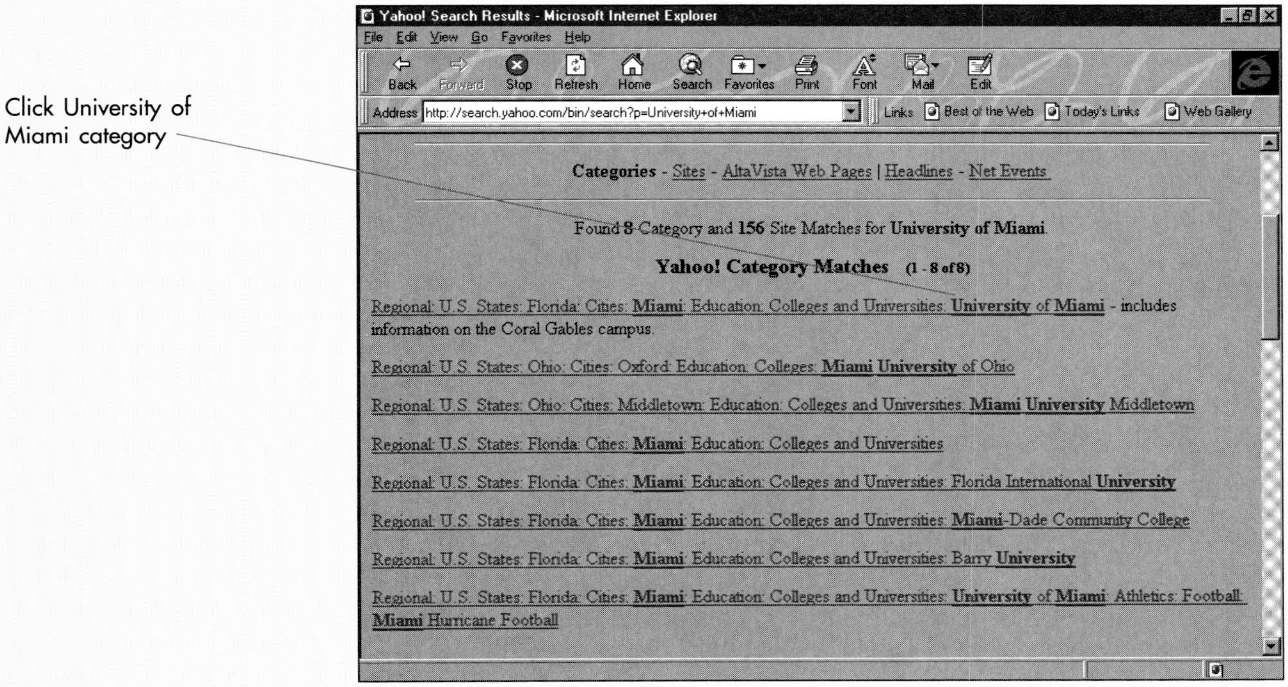

(b) Yahoo Results (step 2)

FIGURE 2.2 Hands-on Exercise 1 (continued)

- Select the Next 20 Site matches. Scroll further down the page until you can click the link to the University of Miami School of Business Administration, which also has a link back to the University's home page.

➤ There are many ways to get to the University of Miami Home page (www.miami.edu). It doesn't matter which page you choose as long as you find what you are looking for.

ABOUT YAHOO—CATEGORIES VERSUS DOCUMENTS

Yahoo (www.yahoo.com) is one of the oldest and best known search tools on the Web and returns categories as well as specific documents. A category (e.g., Florida Cities in the Regional U.S. States category or Colleges in the Education category) is simply a list of sites organized by topic. Click the Florida Cities category, for example, and you are taken to other cities in Florida, which in turn take you to other categories, which lead eventually to specific documents. You can browse leisurely through the listed categories, which often suggest related sites that you might not have considered initially. Either way, Yahoo is a site you want to visit.

STEP 3: The University of Miami Home Page

➤ You should see the University of Miami home page as shown in Figure 2.2c. (The appearance of the page may have changed since we did the exercise.)

➤ Every home page is different, but most well-designed sites provide access to some type of internal search engine to search the site, rather than the Internet as a whole.

➤ If necessary, click the **down arrow** on the vertical scroll bar to display the links at the bottom of the page. Click the link to **Search** the Miami Web pages.

➤ You should see a page to search the UM Web. Click the link to **Search the University of Miami e-mail directory.**

FAVORITES

The ability to save an address (and return to a specific site) is crucial and is accomplished through the Favorites menu. To save the address of a specific page, pull down the Favorites menu, click the Add to Favorites command to display the dialog box in which you can accept the default name for the page or substitute your own, then click OK to close the dialog box. The next time you want to return to a favorite site, pull down the Favorites menu, select (click) the desired site from the list of favorites, and you're there.

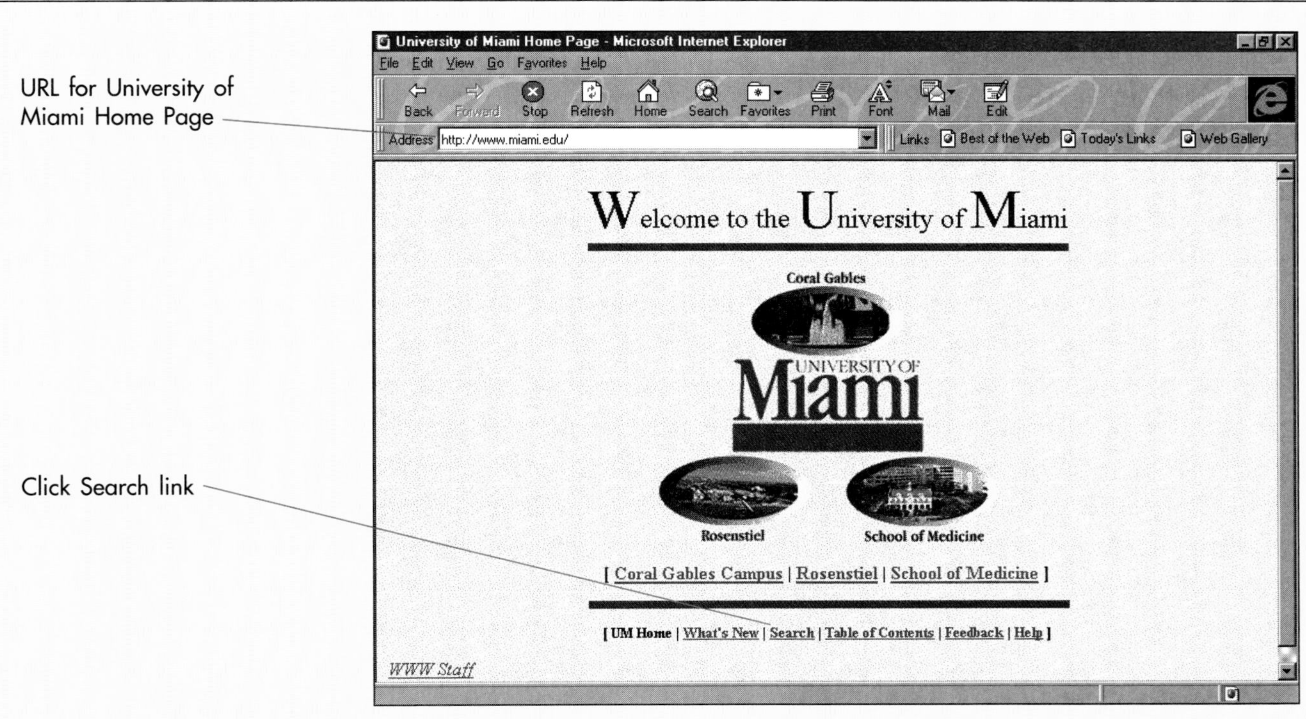

(c) University of Miami Home Page (step 3)

FIGURE 2.2 Hands-on Exercise 1 (continued)

STEP 4: Search the E-mail Directory

- You should see the e-mail search form in Figure 2.2d. Click in the **Name text box,** enter **Grauer** (the person you are looking for), then click the **Begin Search button.**
- Click **Yes** if you see the Security Information dialog box and are asked whether you want to continue.
- You will see a screen displaying the results of the query, which shows all Grauers at the University of Miami. Click on **Grauer, Robert** (in Computer Information Systems).
- You will see a second screen showing Bob's e-mail address, which concludes your search.

FINDING PEOPLE ON THE INTERNET

The exercise you just completed had you search for an individual's e-mail address starting from that person's school or organization. You can also find an e-mail address through various directories similar in concept to a traditional telephone directory, provided the person you are searching for is listed. One favorite directory is www.four11.com, which is illustrated in practice exercise 1 at the end of the chapter.

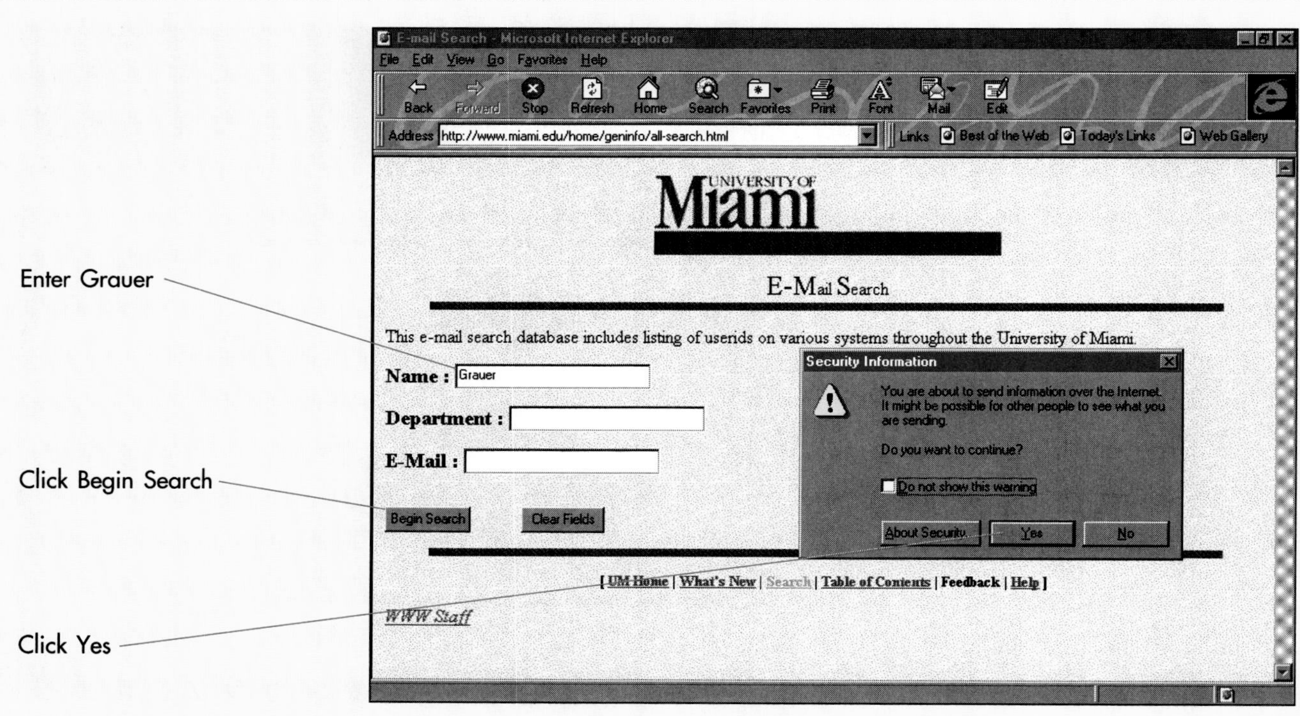

(d) E-mail Search Form (step 4)

FIGURE 2.2 Hands-on Exercise 1 (continued)

STEP 5: Look Around

- Pull down the **Go menu** and click **University of Miami Home Page** (or click the **Back button** until you are returned to the University's home page).
- Click the **Table of Contents link** to display the screen in Figure 2.3e. Click the **Quick Index** link at the bottom of the screen to display a second screen with a more comprehensive set of categories.
- We welcome you to visit our school, or visit your own. You will probably find services and organizations you didn't know existed.
- Print one or two relevant documents to prove to your instructor that you have completed this exercise.

SECURITY ON THE NET

Information travels freely across the Internet until it arrives at its destination. Each computer along the way has access to that information, which is potentially dangerous if the information is confidential (e.g., your credit card number). Accordingly, Internet Explorer will typically display a message (according to the security options set through the Options command in the View menu) indicating that the transmission is insecure and asking whether you want to continue. Be careful how you answer, especially if the data is confidential.

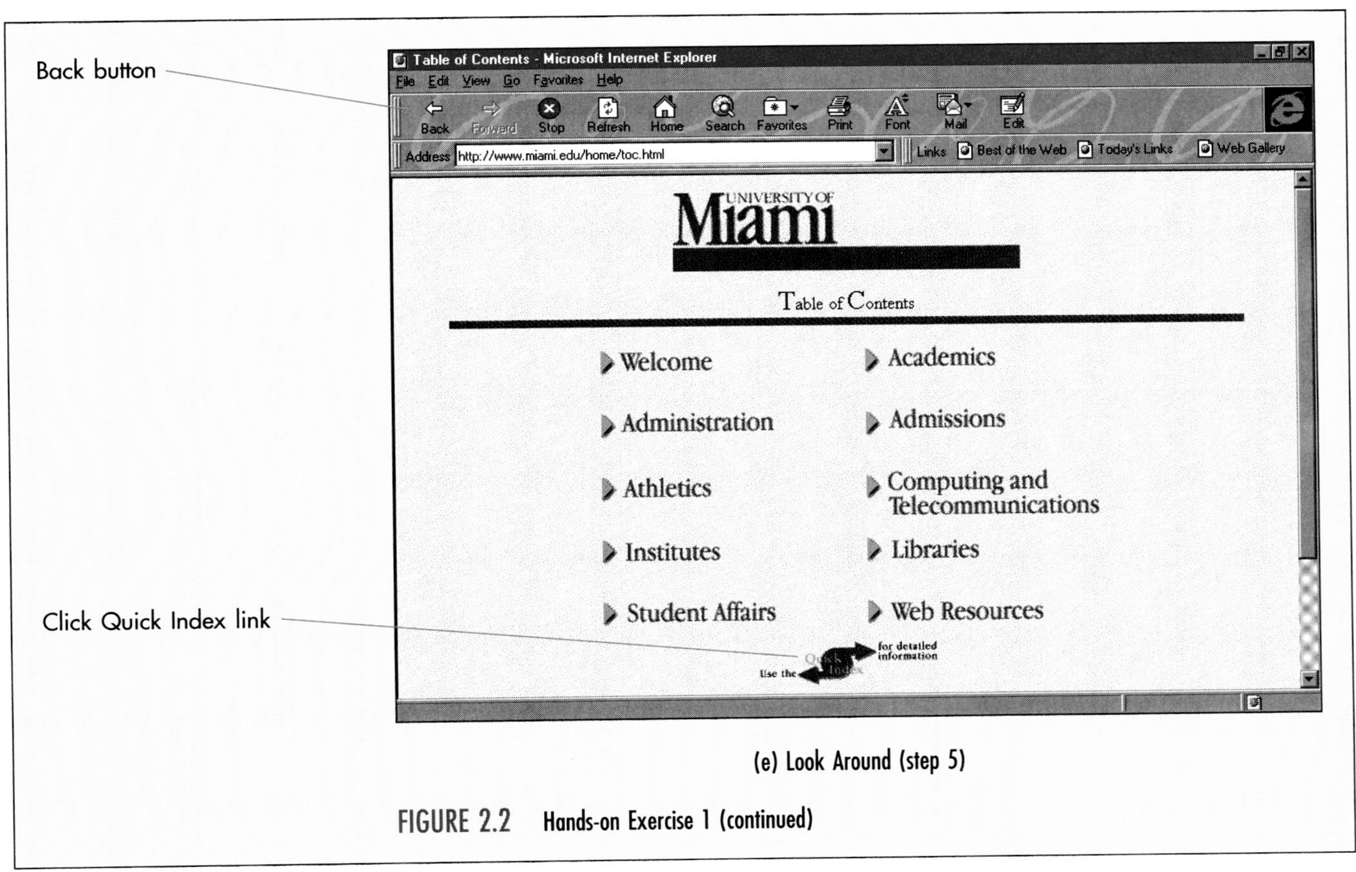

(e) Look Around (step 5)

FIGURE 2.2 Hands-on Exercise 1 (continued)

FINER POINTS OF SEARCHING

We trust that you completed the hands-on exercise without difficulty and that you have a better appreciation for the research potential of the World Wide Web. Searching for information is a trial-and-error process in which there is no guaranteed method for success. The Web may or may not contain the documents you need, and even if it does, there is no assurance that you will be able to find it. Nevertheless, we have been successful more often than not, and patience and common sense will usually prevail. The next several pages discuss various techniques that you can try as you search the Web.

Use Multiple Engines

As we have already indicated, there is no single best engine and you are well advised to try different engines on the same query. Each engine is based on a different database and uses a different search algorithm, so that the same query will return different results.

The easiest way to access a search engine is through a built-in link to a page of common search engines (such as provided by the Search button in Internet Explorer). Alternatively, you can enter the URL of the search engine into the Address box, which in turn takes you to the home page of the search engine. This often provides a more complete page in which to enter your search parameters than does the common search page. Table 2.1 contains a list of the URLs of some of the best search engines available at time of publication.

TABLE 2.1 Web Search Engines

Site	URL
AltaVista	www.altavista.digital.com
InfoSeek	www.infoseek.com
Lycos	www.lycos.com
OpenText	www.opentext.com
WebCrawler	Webcrawler.com
Yahoo	www.yahoo.com

Once you arrive at a particular engine, you will generally see a link to a ***search form*** into which you enter the parameters of the search (i.e., the key words you are looking for) and the relationship between those words (e.g., whether a document has to contain every key word or only one of many key words). In addition, and depending on the search engine, you may also be able to vary the way in which the results of the search are displayed; for example, how many documents are displayed at one time, and how much information is to be displayed for each document. And finally, there is usually a link to a help screen that illustrates the precise syntax for that engine as well as hints for making a search more efficient.

Search Rules and Techniques

Any given query can return hundreds of documents, so it is essential to structure queries in such a way as to return only the most relevant hits. In general, the more specific your query, the better. Thus, a search on *movies* would be unnecessarily broad if your real interest was *science fiction movies.* For example, using the Web Crawler search engine, our search on *movies* yielded 4,783 documents. A search on *science fiction movies,* however, resulted in 391 documents, a more manageable number. In similar fashion, the *movie* search in Lycos yielded 28,253 hits, while *science fiction movies* returned 4 hits. This example also illustrates the earlier point about trying multiple engines for best results.

All queries are, in essence, combinations of the logical ***(Boolean) operators,*** And, Or, and Not. The ***And*** operator requires that every key word must be present. Searching for *President* and *Clinton,* for example, will return documents about Mr. Clinton's presidency. The ***Or*** operator, however, requires that only one of the terms be present, so that searching for *President* or *Clinton* will return documents about presidents (any president) or Clinton (any Clinton). Some search engines also enable you to use ***Not.*** Searching for *Bill* and *Clinton,* but specifying not *President,* will return documents about other aspects of Mr. Clinton's life or other Bill Clintons. (The way in which you specify the Boolean operators depends on the search engine and is described in its online help.)

Figure 2.3 illustrates the use of the Yahoo search engine to look for information about Leonardo da Vinci. Figure 2.3a depicts the Yahoo search form in which we enter the parameters of the search. Note that the option to match on all words is selected (the Boolean And operation) as opposed to finding at least one word (the Boolean Or operation). In other words, the search engine will return those documents that contain references to both *Leonardo* and *da Vinci.*

This very specific query returns a limited number of documents in Figure 2.3b, one of which (Web Museum: Leonardo da Vinci) contained what we were looking for, as shown in Figures 2.3c and 2.3d. We were lucky because sometimes an overly specific search will not return any documents at all. There is no right or wrong approach and, as indicated earlier, it is often a matter of trial and error.

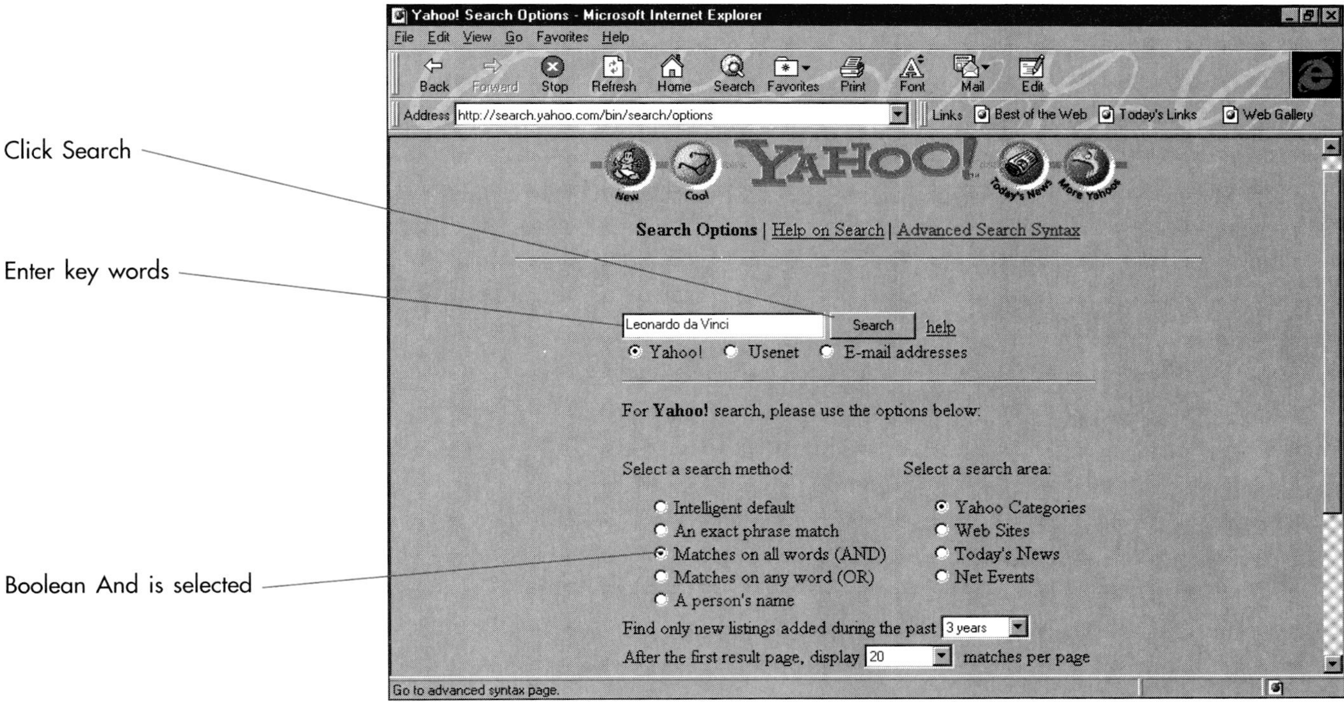

(a) Yahoo Search Form

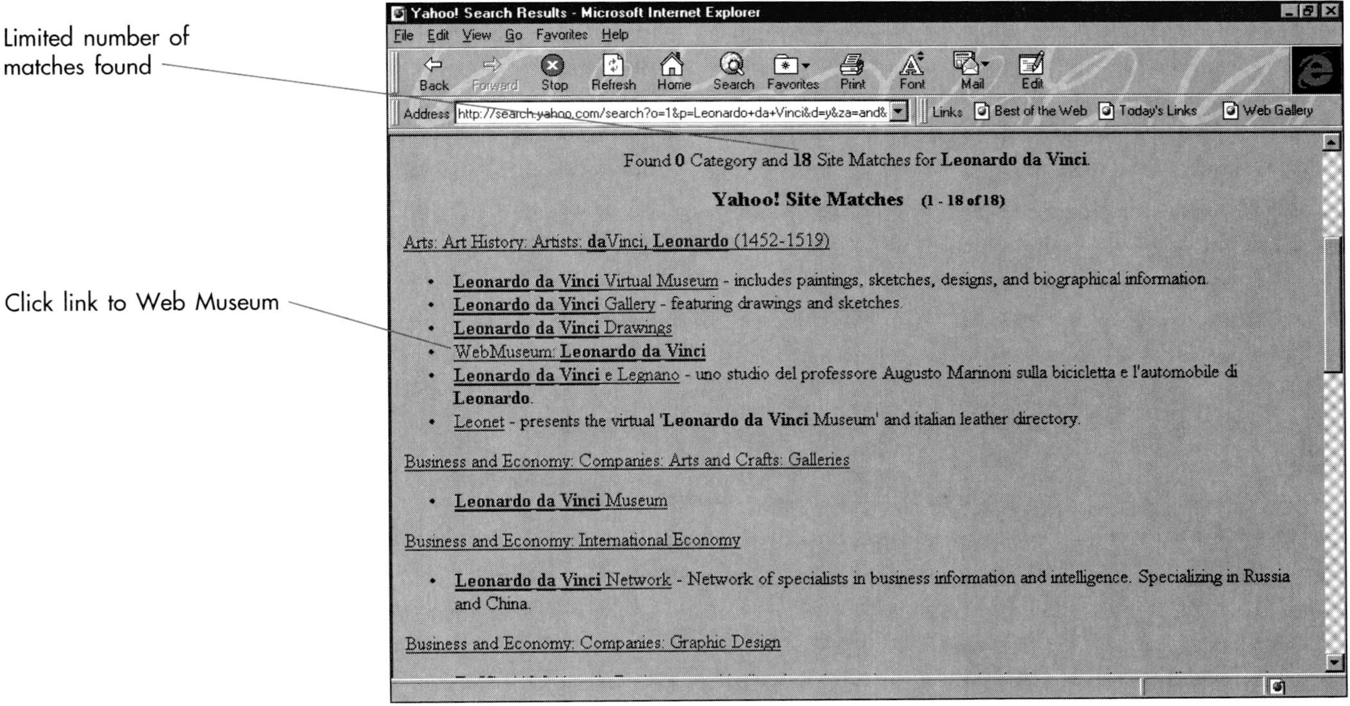

(b) Search Results

FIGURE 2.3 Conducting a Search

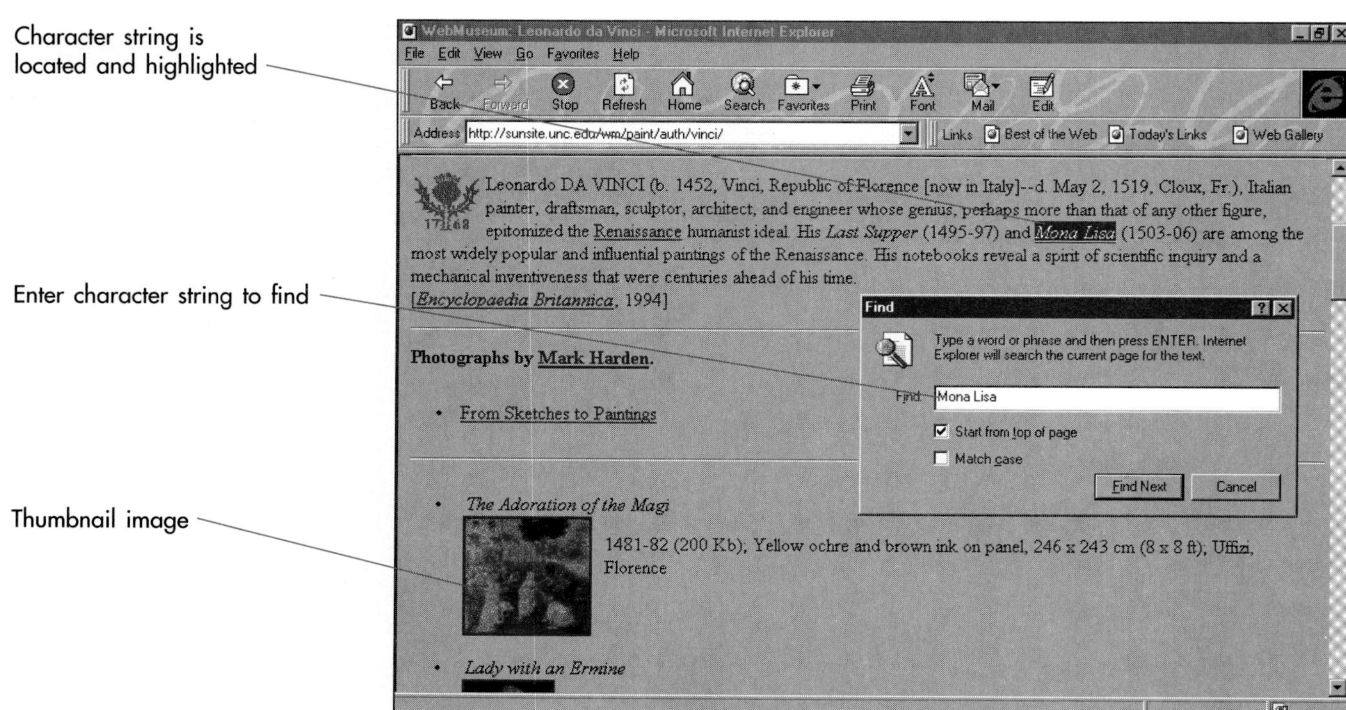

(c) The Find Command

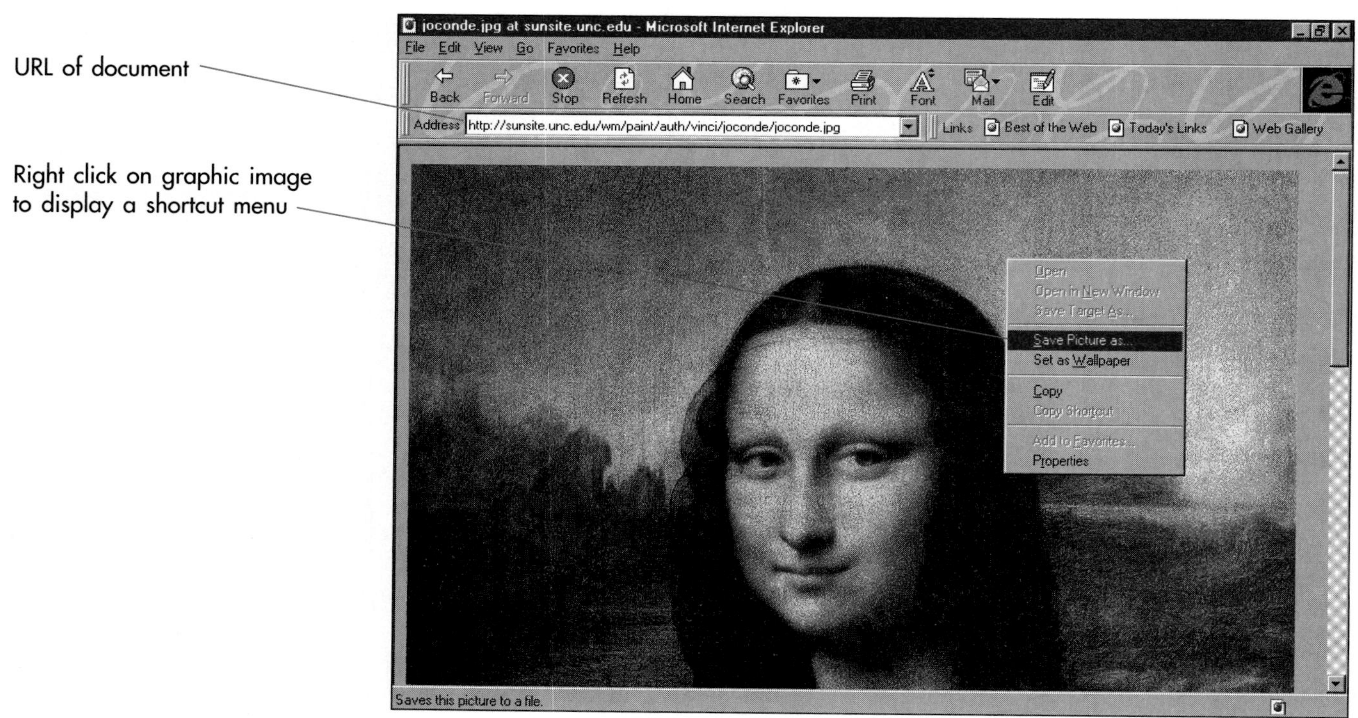

(d) The Save Picture As Command

FIGURE 2.3 Conducting a Search (continued)

The Find and Save Commands

The screens in Figures 2.3c and 2.3d illustrate two additional commands that are useful in the search process. The ***Find command*** (located in the Edit menu, as it is in many Windows applications) lets you search for a specific character string within a document. The document in Figure 2.3c describes da Vinci's life, and the Find command represents the fastest way to locate a reference to the Mona Lisa. Alternatively, you could scroll through the document manually until you came to what you were looking for.

Note, too, the ***thumbnail image*** (graphic icon or small version of a larger image) in Figure 2.3c, which appears in the document rather than the actual drawing. This is a nice touch used by many Web authors who want to include a large graphic, but who are considerate enough not to force the visitor to wait for the image each time the page is loaded. Thus, they include a thumbnail image that a visitor can click to bring up the entire graphic. (Viewing the image in this way requires that the user have the appropriate software, or ***viewer,*** configured on his or her system to view the image. Alternatively, the image may be embedded as an inline image, which is always displayed, but at the cost of increased time to download the document.)

Figure 2.3d displays the shortcut menu that appears when you right click the Mona Lisa (or any graphic image) within an HTML document. The ***Save Picture as command*** enables you to download the image onto your hard drive in order to include it in a document of your own (perhaps the cover page for your paper on Leonardo da Vinci).

Explore the URL

In searching the Web, there is no substitute for common sense and imagination on the part of the researcher. You will find, for example, that a server (Web site) often contains additional documents that may be relevant to your search if only you take the time to look. Consider, for example, the URL of the document in Figures 2.3c and 2.3d:

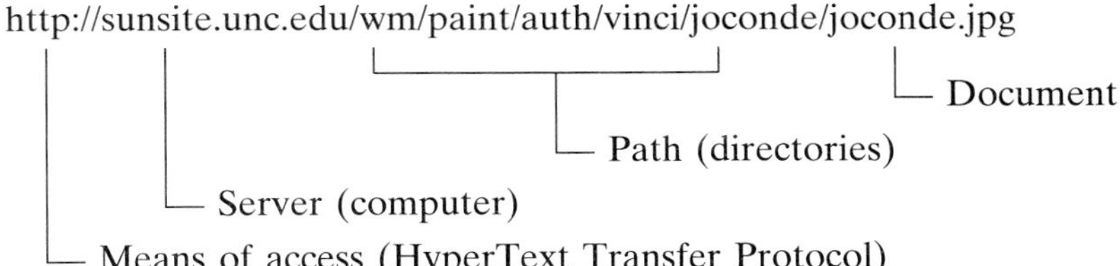

As you know from Chapter 1, the URL consists of several components: the means of access (typically http), the server (computer on which the document is located), the path on that computer (if any) to travel to the document, and finally the document itself. In other words, we found a specific server (whose address is sunsite.unc.edu) that contained a picture of the Mona Lisa. It's logical to think that the same computer may contain other pictures or information in which we would be interested.

On a hunch (born out of experience) we backed up one level at a time within the path for the Mona Lisa, until we came to the document shown in Figure 2.4. This proved to be a bonanza as it placed us in the Web museum, from where we had access to all types of art by a host of other artists.

Aside from being a wonderful way to browse, it may also be a boon to your research, because you are often searching for a concept rather than a specific term. You might, for example, be interested in Renaissance artists in general, rather than just da Vinci, and you have just discovered an invaluable resource.

URL of document (backed up one level at a time from URL in Figure 2.3d until reached this page)

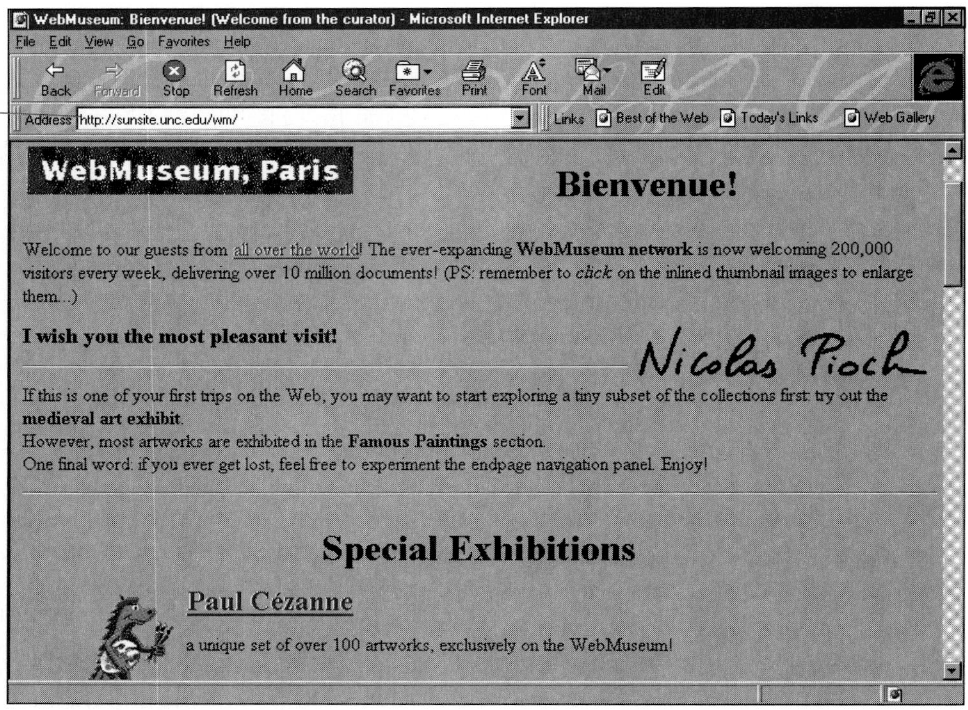

FIGURE 2.4 The Web Museum

DOCUMENT (OR OBJECT) NOT FOUND

Don't despair if you see this common error, which means that Internet Explorer found the server (i.e., the Web site), but not the document (or object). If you entered the URL yourself, check that you entered it correctly. Alternatively, if the message appears after clicking a hyperlink, it means that the document no longer exists, perhaps because it was moved somewhere else. Try modifying the URL by deleting the document name, and then, if necessary, by cutting back one level at a time in the path. Eventually you will come to a directory (or at worst the server) at which point you may be able to click a different set of links to arrive at a relevant document.

LEARNING BY DOING

Enough theory. It's time to practice. You've just left your American History class in which you were assigned a paper on Eleanor Roosevelt. You were going to go to the library, but you thought you would give the Web a chance. There is no guarantee that you will find what you are looking for, and indeed, there are several ways to search for the information.

We start with the Lycos search engine and obtain one set of documents. You could just as easily choose a different engine (or enter a different query using the same engine) and obtain an entirely different set of documents. Eventually, however, most engines and/or most queries will converge on a similar set of documents.

Our research also uncovers a picture of Mrs. Roosevelt, which you can download for inclusion in your report. The exercise also demonstrates the ***Insert Picture command*** in Microsoft Word, which can be used to create a title page that includes the picture. This is not part of Internet Explorer per se, but we think you will find the information very helpful. You can use a similar technique to download graphic images for inclusion in a PowerPoint presentation as well.

HANDS-ON EXERCISE 2

Finer Points of Searching

Objective: To illustrate the finer points of searching through search forms and Boolean operations; to download a graphic image and include it in a Word document. Use Figure 2.5 as a guide in the exercise.

STEP 1: The Lycos Search Engine

- Start Internet Explorer. Click in the Address box and enter **www.lycos.com,** which is the URL of the Lycos search engine. (The http:// is entered automatically by Internet Explorer, which assumes you are using this protocol.)
- Click the link for **Custom Search** (which appears to the right of the Go Get It button). You should see a Lycos search form similar to Figure 2.5a:
  - Enter **Eleanor Roosevelt** in the appropriate text box.
  - Click the **drop-down arrows** next to the Search Options and Display Options list boxes, then change options as necessary so that your selections match those in the figure.

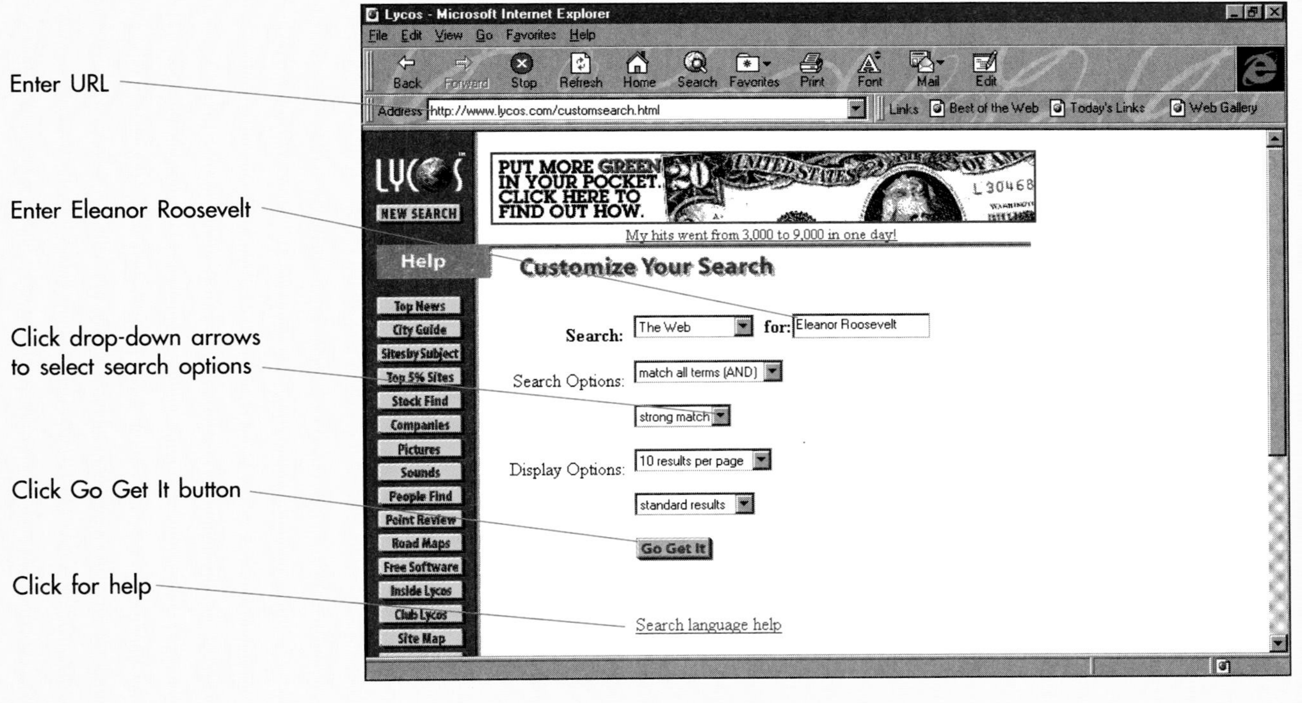

(a) Lycos Search Engine (step 1)

FIGURE 2.5 Hands-on Exercise 2

➤ Click the **Go Get It button** to initiate the search and display the relevant documents. Click **Yes** if you see a security alert asking whether you want to continue.

SEARCH LANGUAGE HELP

Each search engine has a different syntax and a different set of guidelines for efficient use, the details of which are accessed by clicking on Search Language Help (or a similar link). The Lycos engine, for example, suggests a "loose match" when you are searching initially in order to return the largest number of documents, although the hits will be less relevant than with a more restrictive search. Specifying a "strict match" will force Lycos to be more selective, which will return fewer documents, but each of those documents should be highly relevant. There is no "right technique"; just experiment and use what works for you.

STEP 2: Search Results

➤ Lycos indicates the progress of the search by displaying various messages on the status bar at the bottom of the window. The status bar will be clear when the search is complete.

➤ The results of your search may differ from ours because the Web has changed since we conducted our search, but you should see several documents similar to those in Figure 2.5b.

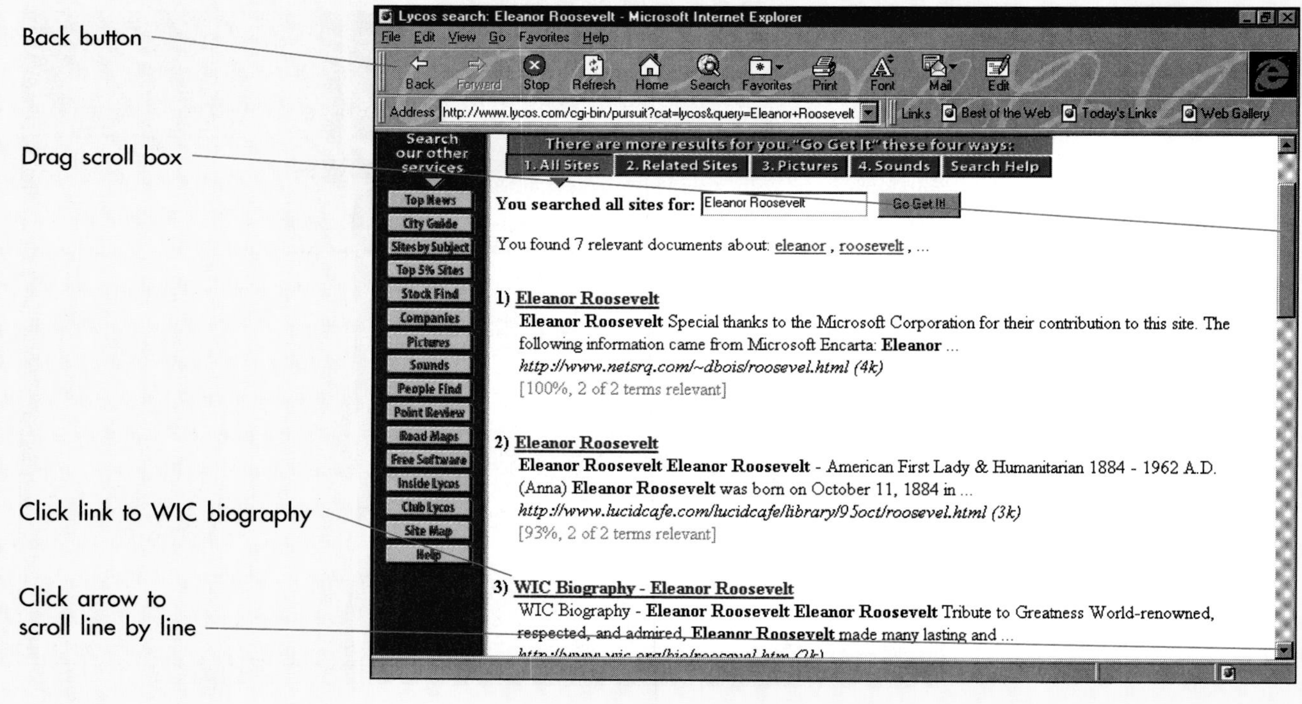

(b) Search Results (step 2)

FIGURE 2.5 Hands-on Exercise 2 (continued)

- Review the list of documents that were returned by the search. You can scroll through the list in various ways:
  - Click the down (up) arrow to scroll through the list of documents one line at a time.
  - Drag the scroll box within the vertical scroll bar to scroll more quickly.
  - Press **Ctrl+Home** or **Ctrl+End** to move to the beginning or end of the displayed list, respectively.
- Click the link to any document that interests you. Click the **Back button** to return to the list of documents.

THE AUTOSEARCH FEATURE

The fastest way to initiate a search is to click in the Address box, enter the key word *go* followed by the topic you are searching for (e.g., go Eleanor Roosevelt), then press the enter key. Internet Explorer automatically invokes the Yahoo search engine (imposing the Boolean And operation) and returns the relevant documents.

STEP 3: Print the Document

- Select the third document (e.g., WIC biography—Eleanor Roosevelt) to display the document in Figure 2.5c. It doesn't matter if you display a different document.

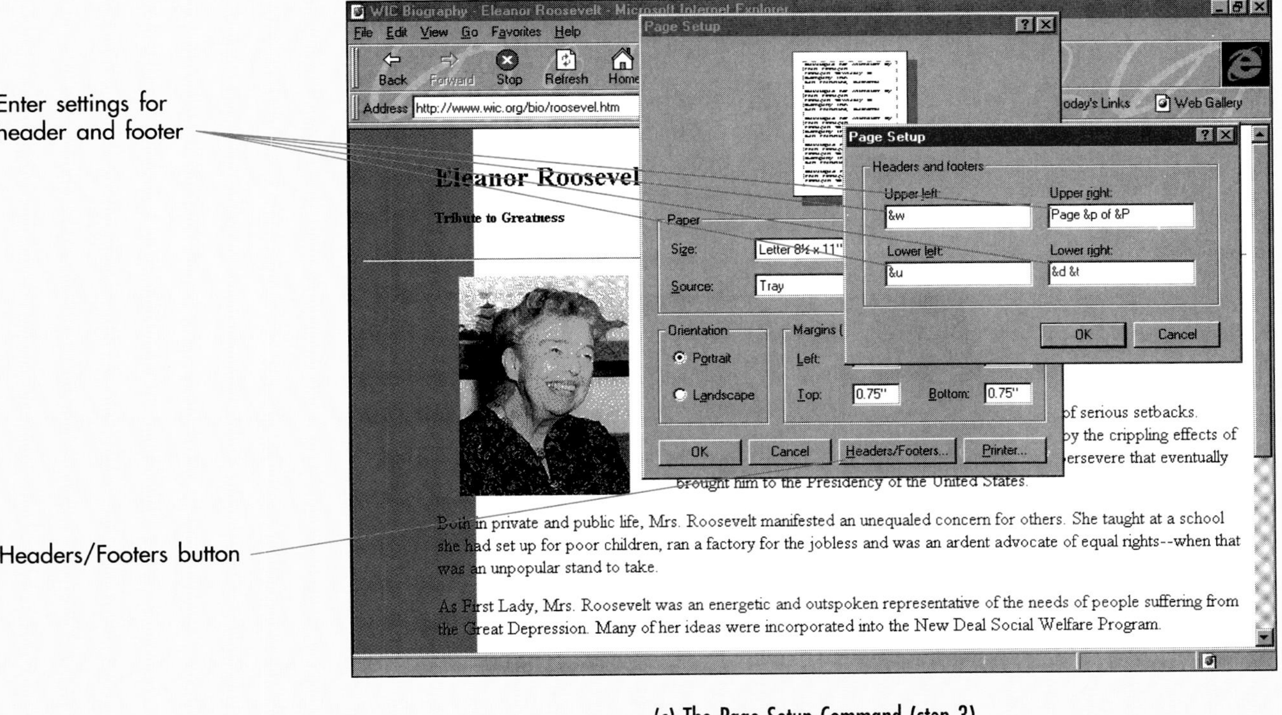

(c) The Page Setup Command (step 3)

FIGURE 2.5 Hands-on Exercise 2 (continued)

- Pull down the **File menu** and click **Page Setup** to display the Page Setup dialog box as shown in Figure 2.5c.
- Click the **Headers/Footers button** to display a second Page Setup dialog box. If necessary, change the settings on your screen so that they match our settings as shown below:
  - Upper left: &w (prints the title of the Web page)
  - Upper right: Page &p of &P (the current page and the total number of pages)
  - Bottom left: &u (the URL address of the page)
  - Bottom right: &d &t (the date and time)
- Click **OK** to accept the new settings and close the dialog box, then click **OK** a second time to close the initial Page Setup dialog box.
- Click the **Print button** on the toolbar to display the Print dialog box, then click **OK** to print the page. The dialog box closes and you are returned to the document.

CHANGE THE FONT SIZE

Internet Explorer enables you to view and print a page in one of five font settings (smallest, small, medium, large, and largest). Click the Font button on the toolbar to cycle through the various settings, or alternatively, pull down the View menu, click Fonts, then click the desired font size. The setting pertains to both the displayed page as well as the printed page.

STEP 4: The Save Command

- Point to the picture of Mrs. Roosevelt, click the **right mouse button** to display a shortcut menu, then click the **Save Picture as** command to display the Save As dialog box in Figure 2.5d.
- Click the **drop-down arrow** in the Save in list box to specify the drive and folder in which you want to save the graphic (e.g., the My Documents folder on drive C).
- The file name and file type are entered automatically by Internet Explorer. (You may change the name, but don't change the file type.) Click the **Save button** to download the image.

BROWSE WITH THE KEYBOARD

The mouse is the usual way of navigating through a Web page, but you can use the keyboard as well. Press Tab (Shift+Tab) to move to the next (previous) link or hotspot, then press enter to activate the link. You can also use Ctrl+D to add the current page to your list of favorites. Unlike the Add to Favorite command, however, Ctrl+D does not display the Add to Favorites dialog box; that is, the only way you can confirm that the favorite has been added is to view the Favorites menu.

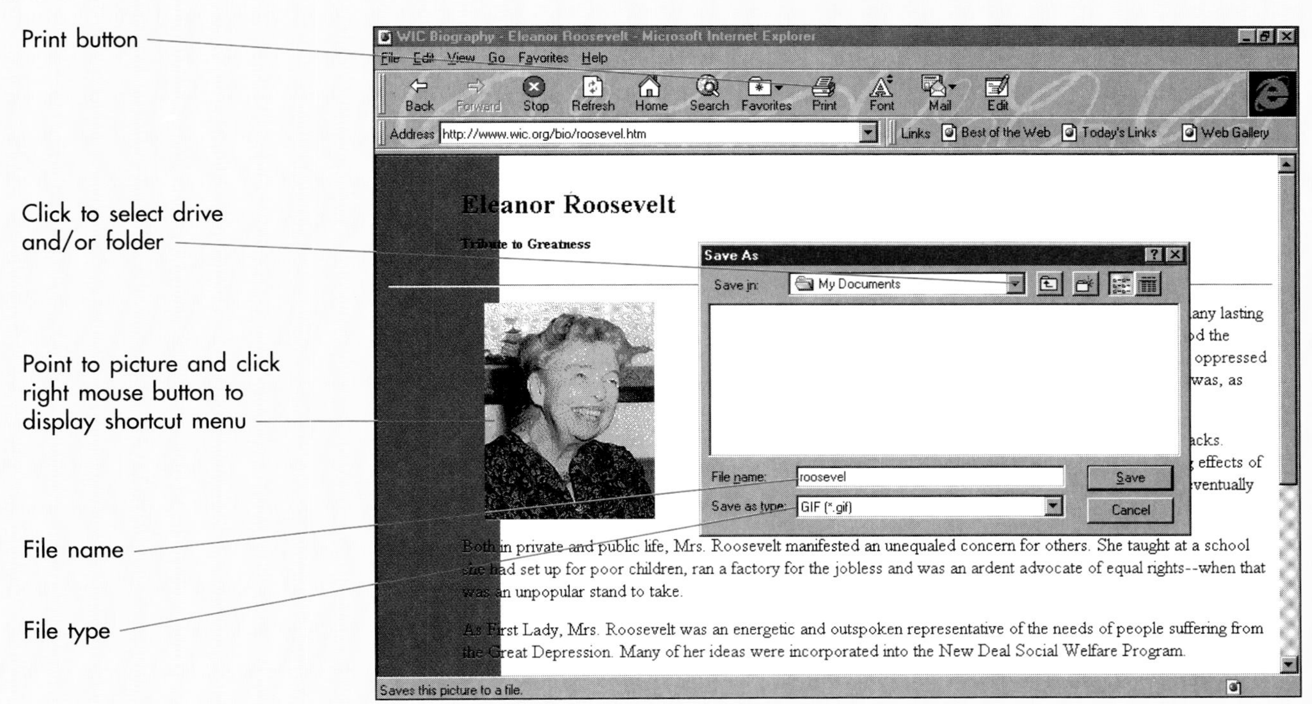

(d) The Save Command (step 4)

FIGURE 2.5 Hands-on Exercise 2 (continued)

STEP 5: The Insert Picture Command

- You have saved the picture and are ready to include it in a document. Information on the Web is protected by copyright, although you are generally allowed to use images for noncommercial purposes such as a term paper. Remember to credit your source via a footnote as described in step 7.
- Start Microsoft Word, and if necessary maximize the application window. The taskbar should contain buttons for Microsoft Word and Internet Explorer since both applications are open.
- Our instructions are for Word 97 and will vary slightly in earlier versions of the program. If necessary, click the **New button** on the Standard toolbar to start a new document.
- Enter the title for your paper in an appropriate font and point size as shown in Figure 2.5e. (The Insert Picture dialog box is not yet visible.)
- Type your name under the title and press the **enter key.** Enter any additional information required by your instructor, such as the name of the course and the semester. Press the **enter key** two or three times.
- Pull down the **Insert menu,** click **Picture,** then click **From File** to display the Insert Picture dialog box. Select the drive and folder in which you saved the picture (e.g., My Documents on drive C).
- Select (click) the picture (e.g., Roosevel), then click **Insert,** and the picture is inserted into the Word document. Do not worry about its size or position at this time.
- Save the document as Eleanor Roosevelt.

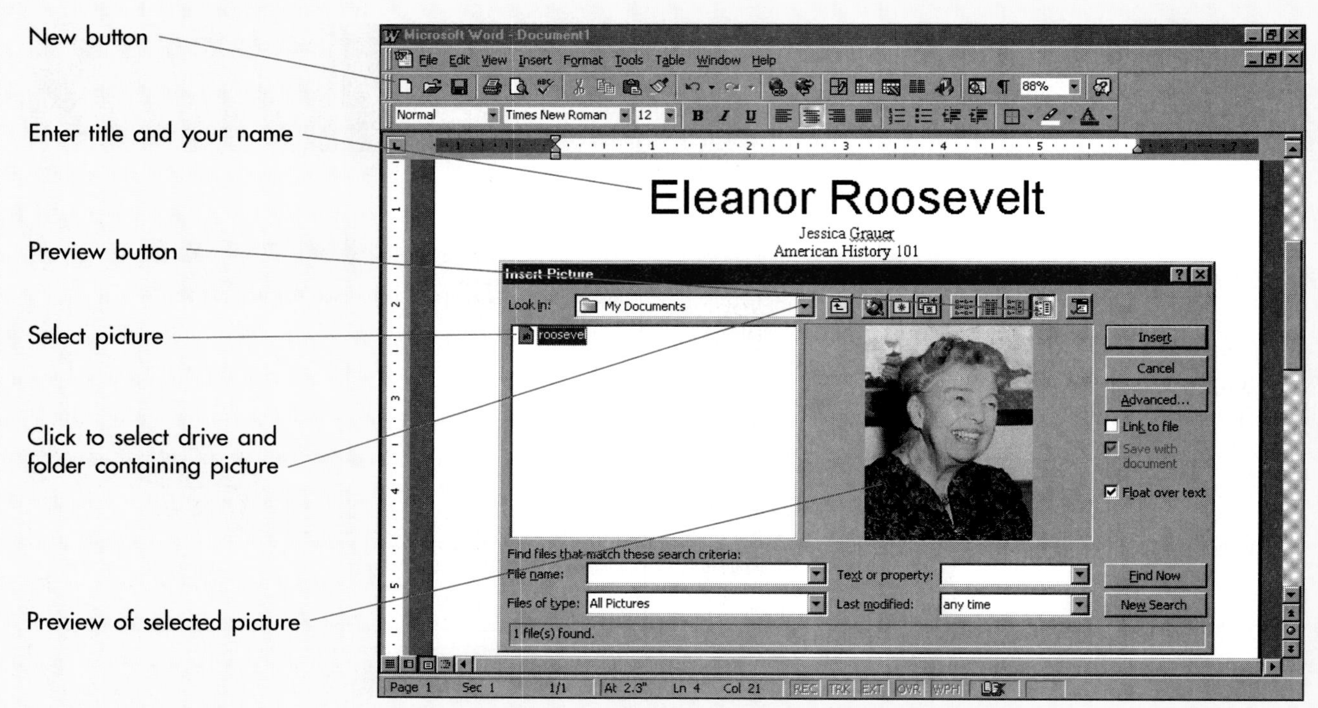

(e) Insert Picture Command (step 5)

FIGURE 2.5 Hands-on Exercise 2 (continued)

SEARCH FOR A CONCEPT

You can extend the reach of a search engine by thinking in terms of a concept rather than a key word; for example, search on *Franklin Roosevelt* or *first ladies* to find additional documents on Mrs. Roosevelt. In similar fashion, you might try searching on *Renaissance painting* to gain background information for a paper on Leonardo da Vinci or Michelangelo. See practice exercise 3 at the end of the chapter.

STEP 6: Move and Size the Picture

- If necessary, pull down the **View menu** and click **Page Layout,** then click the **drop-down arrow** on the zoom box to zoom to **Whole Page.** Click on the picture of Mrs. Roosevelt to display the sizing handles as shown in Figure 2.5f.
  - To size the picture, drag a corner handle (the mouse pointer changes to a double arrow) to change the length and width of the picture simultaneously; this keeps the graphic in proportion as it sizes it.
  - To move the picture, point to any part of the picture except a sizing handle (the mouse pointer changes to a four-sided arrow), then click and drag the picture elsewhere in the document.
- Save the document. Check that the picture is still selected. Click the **Line Style button** on the Picture toolbar to display a drop-down list of line styles. Click the **1 pt line** to place a one-point border around the picture.

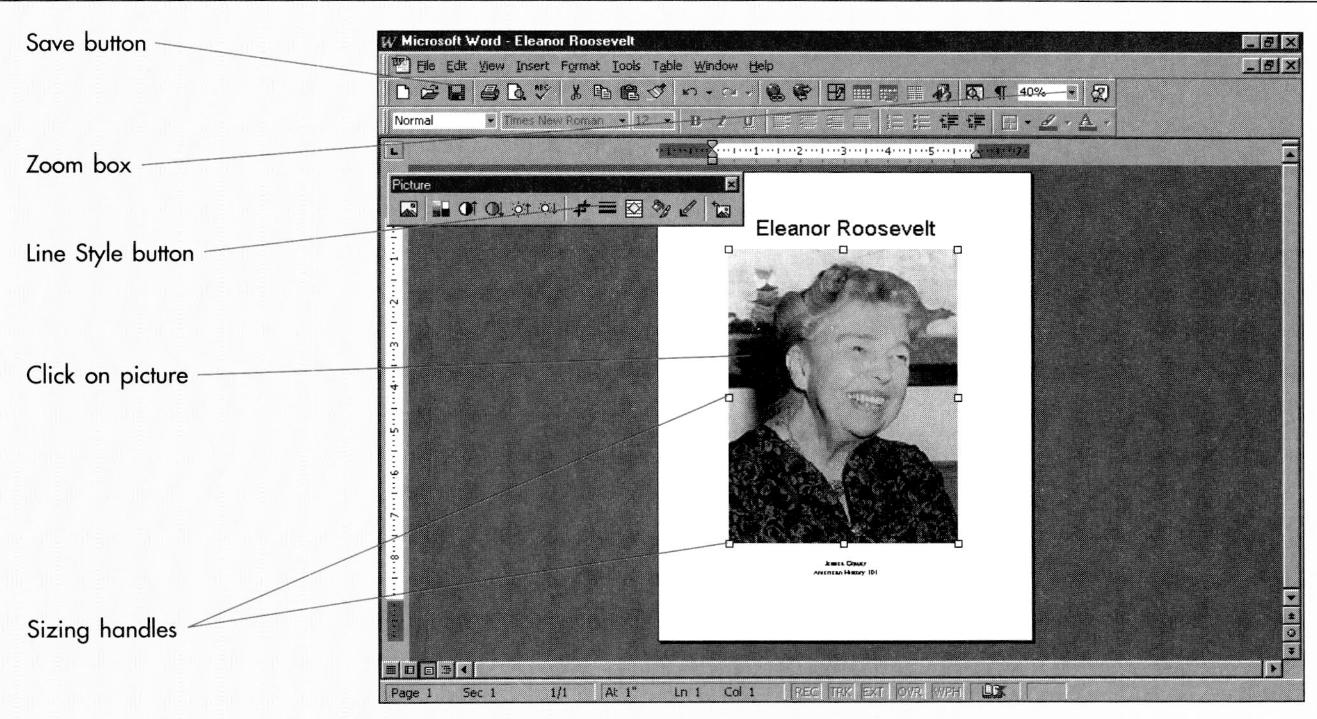

(f) Move and Size the Picture (step 6)

FIGURE 2.5 Hands-on Exercise 2 (continued)

> **CROPPING A PICTURE**
>
> Select (click) a picture and Word 97 automatically displays the Picture toolbar, which enables you to modify a picture in subtle ways. The Crop tool is one of the most useful as it enables you to eliminate (crop) part of a picture. Select the picture to display the Picture toolbar and display the sizing handles. Click the Crop tool (the ScreenTip will display the name of the tool), then click and drag a sizing handle to crop the part of the picture you want to eliminate.

STEP 7: Insert a Footnote

- Click after the word *Roosevelt* (the point at which you will insert the footnote) in the title of the document. The picture of Mrs. Roosevelt is deselected and the sizing handles disappear.
- Pull down the **Insert menu.** Click **Footnote** to display the Footnote and Endnote dialog box in Figure 2.5g.
- Check that the option buttons for **Footnote** and **AutoNumber** are selected, then click **OK.**
- Word inserts a new footnote and simultaneously positions you at the bottom of the page to add the actual note. Zoom to **Page Width.**

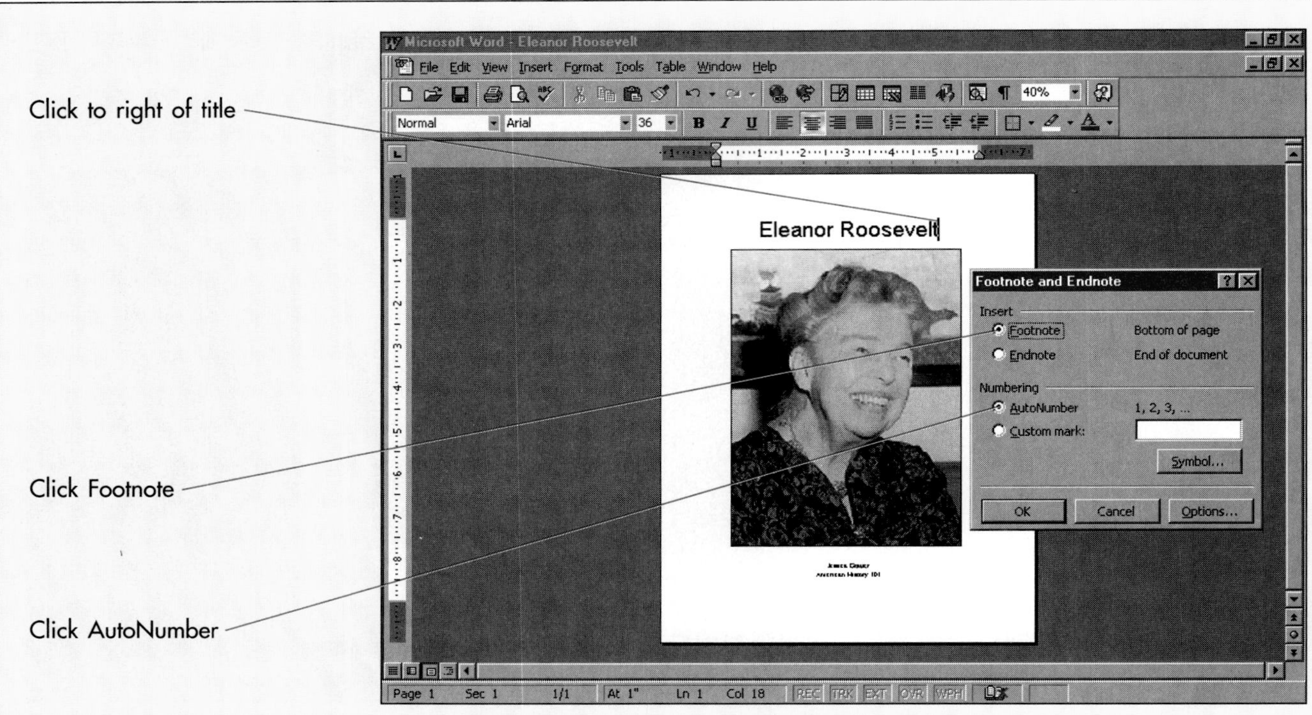

(g) Insert a Footnote (step 7)

FIGURE 2.5 Hands-on Exercise 2 (continued)

- Enter the address of the Web page from where you obtained the picture, www.wic.org/bio/roosevel.htm, with an appropriate reference.
- Save the document.

IT'S WEB-ENABLED

Word 97 will, by default, convert any Internet path (e.g., any text beginning with http:// or www) to a hyperlink, enabling you to click the link within Word. If the automatic formatting does not occur, pull down the Tools menu, click AutoCorrect, then click the AutoFormat as you Type tab. Check the box in the Replace as you type area for Internet and Network paths. Click OK. The next time you enter a Web or e-mail address, it will be converted automatically to a hyperlink.

STEP 8: Use Multiple Engines

- It is always worthwhile to make one last pass at the Web for additional material. Click the **Internet Explorer button** on the Windows taskbar to return to Internet Explorer.
- Click the **Search button** on the Internet Explorer toolbar to display a page with links to multiple search engines. Click the option button for a different engine, e.g., **AltaVista.** Enter **Eleanor Roosevelt** in the text box, then click the **Search command button** to initiate the search.

- ➤ The results of our search are shown in Figure 2.5h, but you will most likely see a different set of documents from ours.
- ➤ Browse through these documents for a few minutes, then refine the search as necessary.
- ➤ Review the information you have collected in preparation for the term paper (which you don't really have to write).
- ➤ Congratulations on a job well done. Research was never this easy.
- ➤ Exit Internet Explorer.

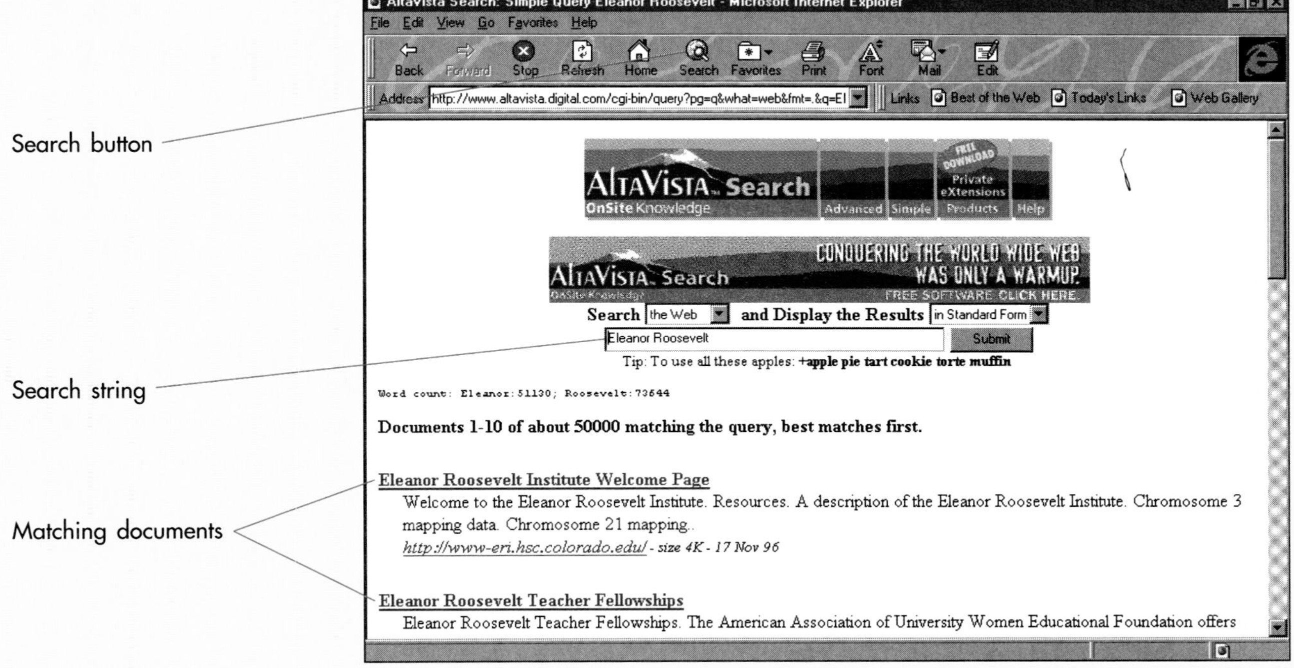

(h) Use Multiple Engines (step 8)

FIGURE 2.5 Hands-on Exercise 2 (continued)

THE SEARCH BUTTON

The Search button on Internet Explorer not only provides links to every major search engine, but it also contains links to several specialized searches. Click the link to Definitions and Quotes, for example, and you will find links to Bartlett's Quotations, Webster's Dictionary, the original Roget's Thesaurus, and Shakespeare online. The other specialized searches provide equally interesting pages. See practice exercise 2 at the end of the chapter.

SUMMARY

Search engines provide an efficient way to look for information on the World Wide Web. You enter a query consisting of key words you are searching for, and the search engine responds with a number of "hits," or Web documents that meet the search criteria. Searching is, however, a trial-and-error process with no guarantee of success. It is important, therefore, to try different engines with the same query, and further, to continually refine a query during the course of a search.

Any given query (request to a search engine) can return hundreds of documents, so it is essential to structure queries in such a way as to return only the most relevant hits. All queries are, in essence, combinations of the logical operations And, Or, and Not. In general, the more specific your query, the better.

Many search engines are available, each of which uses a different database. Each database stores information about its collection of Web documents (running into the millions) and consists of the document's URL (i.e., its Web address) and information (key words) about what is contained in each document. Each engine uses its own version of a special program known as a spider to automatically search the Web for new pages to add to its database.

Images can be downloaded from the Web and saved onto a local drive for subsequent inclusion in a document. The Insert Picture command inserts a graphic image into a Word document.

KEY WORDS AND CONCEPTS

AltaVista
And
Boolean operator
Favorite
Category
Find command
Hit
InfoSeek
Insert Picture command
Key word search
Lycos
Not
Or
Query
Save Picture as command
Search engine
Search form
Spider
Thumbnail image
Uniform Resource Locator (URL)
Web Crawler
Yahoo

MULTIPLE CHOICE

1. Which of the following is a true statement regarding search engines?
   (a) Different search engines can return different results for the same query
   (b) The same search engine can return different results for the same query at different times (e.g., a month apart)
   (c) Both (a) and (b)
   (d) Neither (a) nor (b)

2. Which of the following is a *false* statement about search engines?
   (a) Different engines are likely to give different results for the same query
   (b) The Search button provides shortcuts to several different search engines
   (c) All the documents that match a query are always displayed on one screen
   (d) You can access a search engine by entering its URL in the Address box

3. Which of the following is a *false* statement about search engines?
(a) Every search engine has a unique syntax
(b) Every search engine uses a unique database
(c) Every search engine permits the use of the And, Or, and Not operations
(d) Every search engine can be accessed through its URL

4. Which of the following is *not* a search engine?
(a) Internet Explorer
(b) Lycos
(c) InfoSeek
(d) Web Crawler

5. Which of the following is considered the best search engine, and thus the only engine you need to use?
(a) Yahoo
(b) Lycos
(c) Excite
(d) There is no agreement on the best search engine

6. Yahoo, Lycos, Web Crawler, and InfoSeek are examples of:
(a) URL addresses
(b) Boolean operations
(c) Web browsers
(d) Search engines

7. Which of the following operations should you use between the key words *American* and *Revolution* to implement the most restrictive search?
(a) And
(b) Or
(c) Not
(d) And, Or, or Not, depending on the search engine

8. Which of the following operations should you use between the key words *American* and *Revolution* to implement the least restrictive search?
(a) And
(b) Or
(c) Not
(d) And, Or, or Not, depending on the search engine

9. Which of the following will return the largest number of documents regardless of the search engine in use?
(a) *Yankees* and *Baseball*
(b) *Yankees* or *Baseball*
(c) *Yankees* not *Baseball*
(d) Impossible to determine

10. A spider is a program that:
(a) Displays HTML documents that are downloaded from the Web
(b) Automatically crawls through the Web searching for new pages to add to the database of a search engine
(c) Searches the Web for specific documents according to the entries in a search form
(d) Protects a computer against infection from viruses

11. Which part of the URL http://www.microsoft.com/ie/iedl.htm identifies the Internet address of the Web site (server)?
    (a) http://
    (b) www.microsoft.com
    (c) ie
    (d) iedl.htm

12. Which part of the URL http://www.microsoft.com/ie/iedl.htm identifies the actual Web document?
    (a) http://
    (b) www.microsoft.com
    (c) ie
    (d) iedl.htm

13. A thumbnail image is used:
    (a) As a graphic placeholder in a Web document to prevent the graphic from being downloaded initially
    (b) As a placeholder for text within an HTML document to indicate the contents of a Web page in the output of a search engine query
    (c) In a home page to indicate the author's interests
    (d) As a favorite whenever a page contains a graphic image

14. You enter the URL www.lyco.com, accidentally misspelling *lycos.* Which of the following errors is most likely to occur?
    (a) Unable to locate server
    (b) Server is down or nonresponsive
    (c) Unable to locate object on the designated server
    (d) Internet protocol not specified

15. What is the purpose of the Find command within the Edit menu?
    (a) It provides access to a list of common search engines
    (b) It initiates a search on the Web for all documents containing a designated set of key words
    (c) It enables a search within a document for a specific character string
    (d) All of the above

ANSWERS

1. c	**6.** d	**11.** b
2. c	**7.** a	**12.** d
3. c	**8.** b	**13.** a
4. a	**9.** b	**14.** a
5. d	**10.** b	**15.** c

PRACTICE WITH THE WORLD WIDE WEB

1. One way to search for a friend's e-mail address is to start with the home page of his or her school or university, as was done in the first hands-on exercise. Alternatively, you can use one of several search tools similar to the one in Figure 2.6.

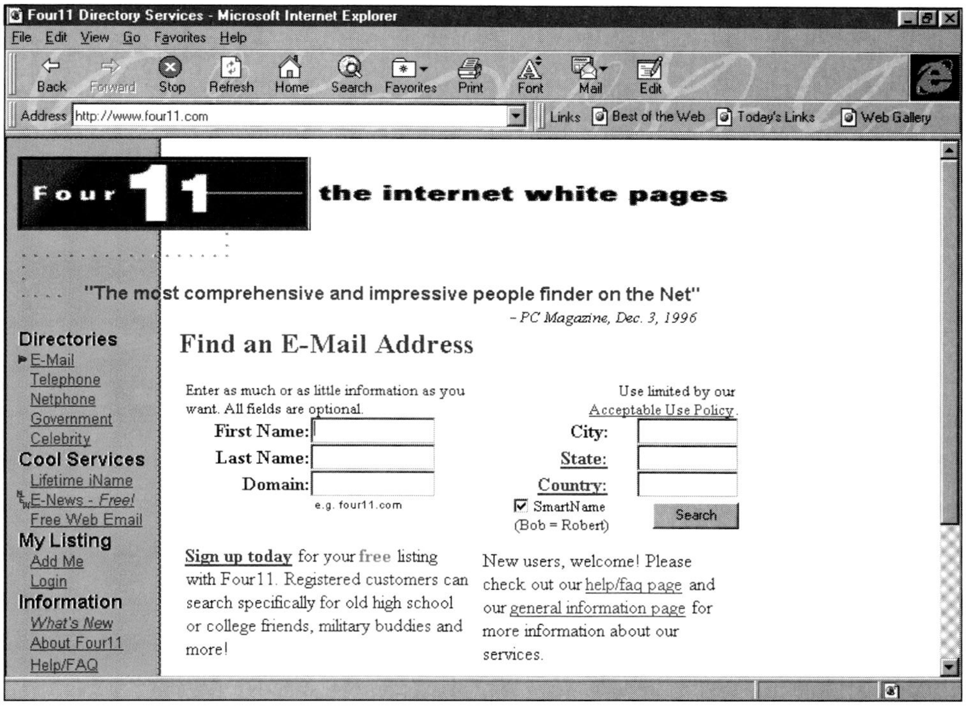

FIGURE 2.6 Screen for Practice Exercise 1

a. How do you display the document in Figure 2.6?
b. What is the advantage of searching for an e-mail address using a tool such as the one in Figure 2.6 as opposed to the technique illustrated in the first hands-on exercise? What is the disadvantage?
c. How do you add your name to the directory listing in Figure 2.6?
d. What information, in addition to the e-mail directory, is available via the document in Figure 2.6?

2. Information at Your Fingertips: The Search button on the Internet Explorer toolbar takes you to an all-in-one reference page as shown in Figure 2.7. The page contains links to every major search engine as well as additional links to other searches. The latter are extremely helpful and provide links to various Web pages that enable you to answer the following:
a. What is the toll-free number for Federal Express?
b. What is the zip code for 580 Fifth Avenue in New York City?
c. What is today's price of Microsoft stock?
d. What is the value of $1 in British pounds?
e. What does PCMCIA (associated with laptop computers) stand for?
f. When is Barbra Streisand's birthday?
g. Use any of the suggested links to return two additional facts that you think are interesting or useful.

3. Searching on a Concept: We were pleased with the results of our search on Eleanor Roosevelt using the Lycos engine. Lots of other information is available, however, especially if you search on a related concept. Choose any engine you like and search on *First Ladies* to see if you can find the color photograph in Figure 2.8. Download the graphic image, then print a one-page note to your instructor containing the photograph and describing how you found the picture.

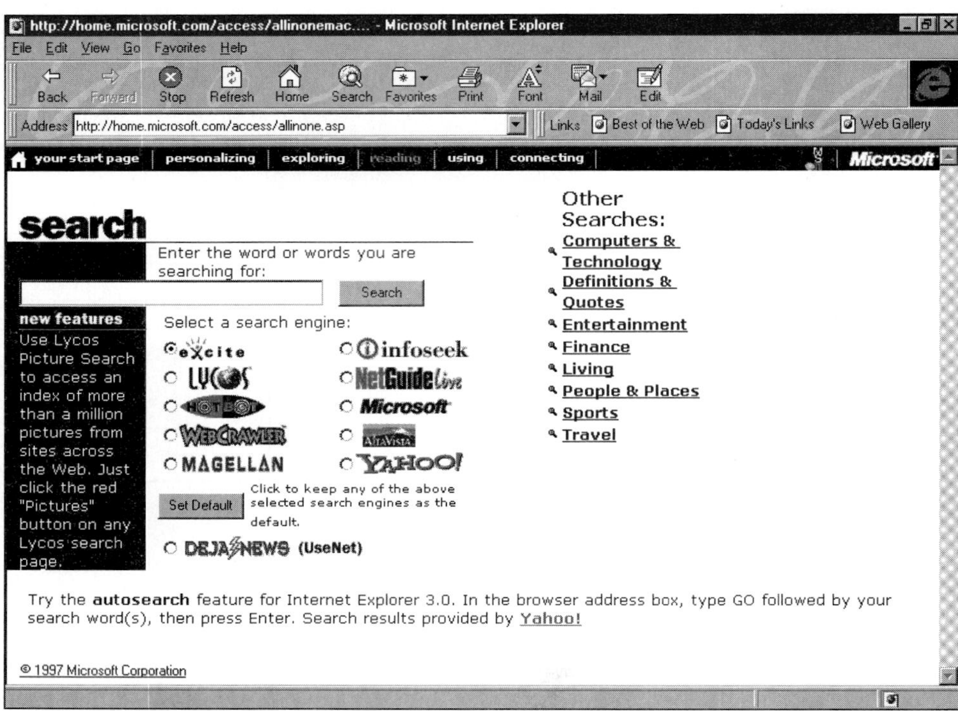

FIGURE 2.7 Screen for Practice Exercise 2

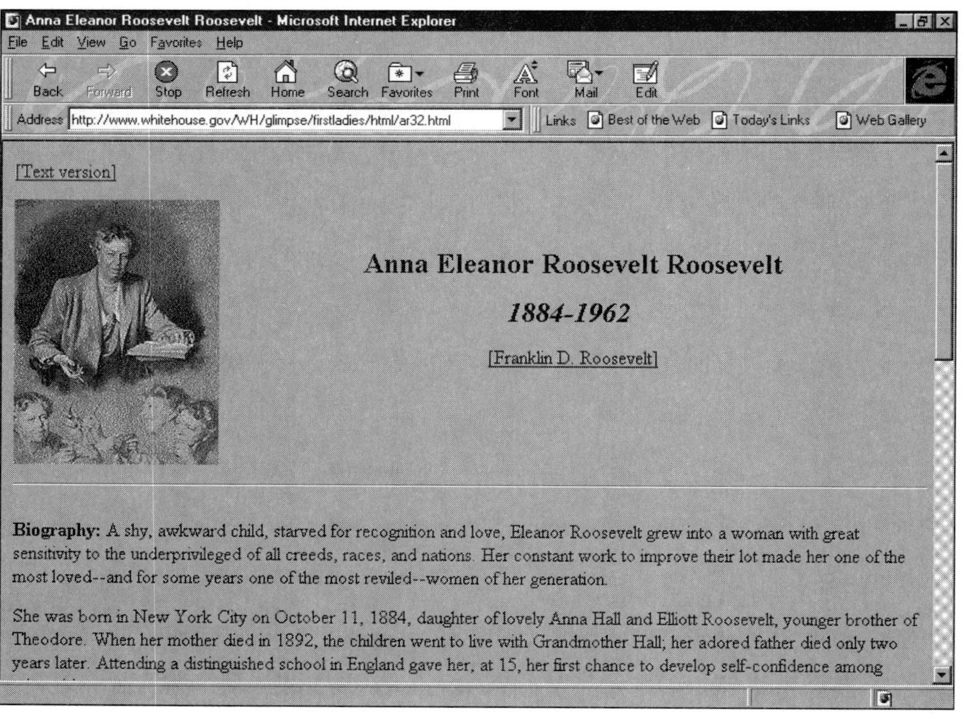

FIGURE 2.8 Screen for Practice Exercise 3

4. The iCOMP index was developed by Intel to compare the speed of various microprocessors to one another. We want you to search the Web and find a chart showing values in the current iCOMP index. (The chart you find need not be the same as the one in Figure 2.9.) Once you find the chart, download the graphic and incorporate it into a memo to your instructor. Add a paragraph or two describing the purpose of the index as shown in Figure 2.9.

A Comparison of Microcomputers

John Doe, CIS 120

(http://pentium.intel.com/procs/perf/icomp/index.htm)

The capability of a PC depends on the microprocessor on which it is based. Intel microprocessors are currently in their sixth generation, with each generation giving rise to increasingly powerful personal computers. All generations are upward compatible; that is, software written for one generation will automatically run on the next. This upward compatibility is crucial because it protects your investment in software when you upgrade to a faster computer.

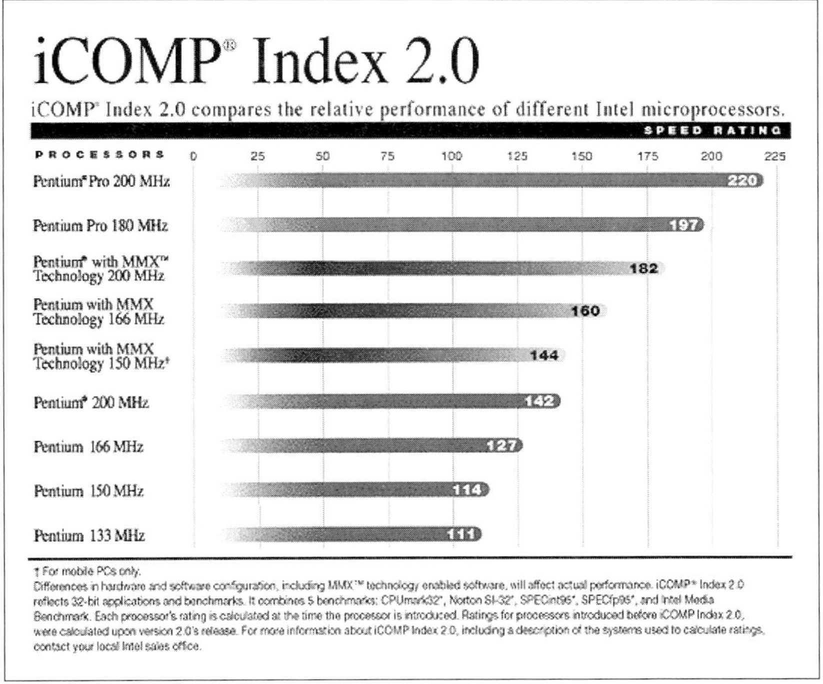

Each generation has multiple microprocessors that are differentiated by *clock speed*, an indication of how fast instructions are executed. Clock speed is measured in *megahertz* (MHz). The higher the clock speed, the faster the machine. Thus, all Pentiums are not created equal, because they operate at different clock speeds. The *Intel CPU Performance Index* (see chart) was created to compare the performance of one microprocessor to another. The index consists of a single number to indicate the relative performance of the microprocessor; the higher the number, the faster the processor.

FIGURE 2.9 Document for Practice Exercise 4

5. Shakespeare Online: Sooner or later you will take an English course in which you need to reference one or more works of William Shakespeare. There are many sites on the Web that you may consider, but the site in Figure 2.10 is our favorite. (We have erased the URL or else this problem would be too easy.) See if you can search the Web to identify the Shakespearean character who said, "*This above all, to thine ownself be true.*" From which play was the quotation taken? What other well-known advice appears within the same speech?

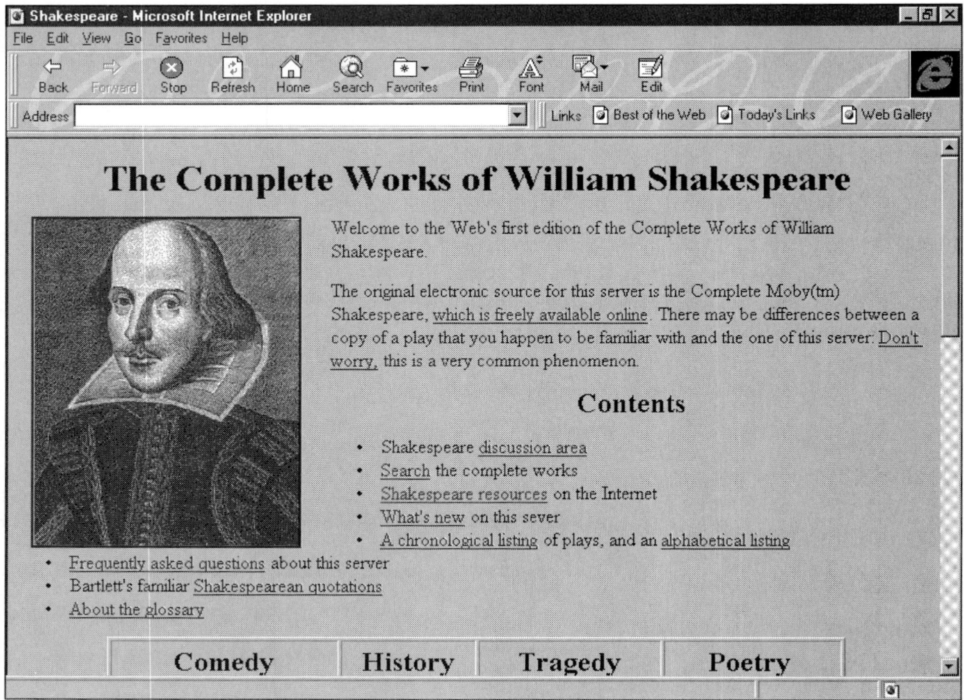

FIGURE 2.10 Screen for Practice Exercise 5

6. Music and Sound on the Web: Use your favorite search engine to look for sites that enable you to listen to live broadcasts and/or recorded music. Search on the keyword *RealAudio,* which is the name of the technology that enables you to play a sound file as it is downloaded, even over a 14.4bps modem. The RealAudio page will in turn take you to the Timecast site in Figure 2.11. Go to two or more sites on the Web and listen to what is available. Summarize your results in a brief report to your isntructor.

7. This loosely structured exercise asks you to experiment with various search engines and search parameters. Select any topic in which you are interested, choose a search engine, construct an initial query, then record the number of hits the engine returns. Choose a different engine, enter the identical query, and record the number of hits you get with that engine. Select the more promising result, then submit a new query that limits your search through inclusion of additional key words or other logical operators. Summarize the results in a one- or two-page Word document that you will submit to your instructor. The document should contain all the information you recorded manually in the preceding steps.

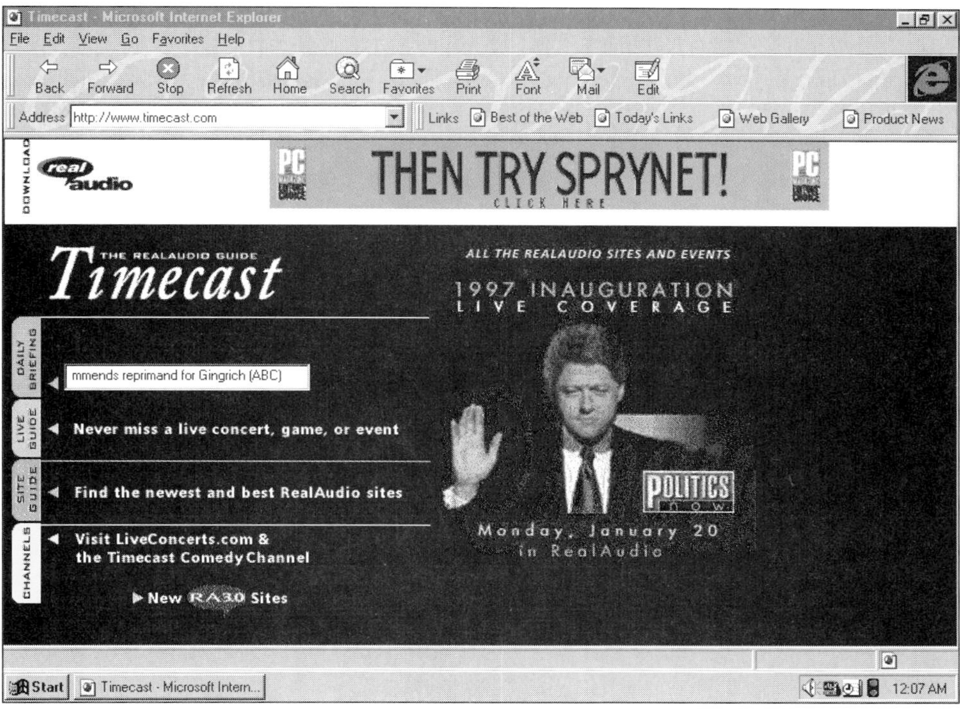

FIGURE 2.11 Screen for Practice Exercise 6

CASE STUDIES

File Compression

Photographs add significantly to the appearance of a document, but they also add to its size. Accordingly, you might want to consider acquiring a file compression program to facilitate copying large documents to a floppy disk in order to transport your documents to and from school, home, or work. You can download an evaluation copy of the popular WinZip program at *www.winzip.com.* Investigate the subject of file compression, then submit a summary of your findings to your instructor.

Copyright Infringement

It's fun to download images from the Web for inclusion in a document, but is it legal? Copyright protection and infringement is one of the most pressing legal issues on the Web. Search the Web for sites that provide information on current copyright law. One excellent site is the copyright page at the Institute for Learning Technologies at *www.ilt.columbia.edu/projects/copyright.* Another excellent reference is the page at *www.benedict.com.* Research these and other sites, then summarize your findings in a short note to your instructor.

Frequently Asked Questions (FAQs)

The Internet and the World Wide Web can be very intimidating to the newcomer. However, it doesn't have to be for long. All the information you need to understand the Web is on the Web! General information about popular subjects is often kept in files titled Frequently Asked Questions (FAQs). Compose a search to find out more about the World Wide Web; something like WWW FAQS should work. Follow the hyperlinks until you feel comfortable with the terms you're reading. Set up favorites to return to any interesting sites. Summarize your results in a one-page memo to your instructor.

What's Playing at the Movies?

There's lots of information on the Web about movies past and present. Can you tell us which film won the Oscar for best picture last year? Which actor and actress won the Oscar in the same year? Can you find a review of a current movie? Can you tell us where that movie is playing in your neighborhood and what time it starts? All of this information is on the Web. It's up to you to find it!

The Annual Report

America's public corporations spend a small fortune creating annual reports to report on the status of a company to its shareholders. You can write to a corporation and request a traditional printed report, or you can go online to view the report on the Web if it is available. Choose any public corporation, search the Web for its home page, then see if you can find the annual report. Another way to search for the same information is to structure a query to look for the words *annual report.* Summarize what you find in a one-page report to your instructor.

Going Abroad

Congratulations! You have just won a scholarship to spend your junior year abroad. You need a passport, and you need it quickly. Search the Web to learn how to apply for a passport. You should be able to find a site that enables you to download an actual passport application with specific instructions on where to apply; i.e., an address in the city in which you live or attend school. What additional software, if any, do you need to print the application?

Tax Time

April 15 is just around the corner and you have yet to file your income tax. Search the Web to download the necessary tax forms to file your federal income tax. What other information regarding your income taxes is available from this site? What additional software, if any, do you need to print the form on your PC? Extend your search to the necessary forms for state income taxes if you live in a state that has an income tax.

A

APPENDIX A: HOW THE INTERNET WORKS: THE BASICS OF TCP/IP

OVERVIEW

Data is transmitted across the Internet through a series of protocols known collectively as ***TCP/IP (Transmission Control Protocol/Internet Protocol).*** A ***protocol*** is an agreed-upon set of conventions that define the rules of communication. You follow a protocol in class; for example, you raise your hand and wait to be acknowledged by your professor. In similar fashion, the sending and receiving computers on the Internet follow the TCP/IP protocol to ensure that data is transmitted correctly.

The postal system provides a good analogy of how (but certainly not how fast) TCP/IP is implemented.[1] When you mail a regular letter, you drop it into a mailbox, where it is picked up along with a lot of other letters and delivered to the local post office. The letters are sorted and sent on their way to a larger post office, where the letters are sorted again, until eventually each letter reaches the post office closest to its destination, where it is delivered to the addressee by the local mail carrier. If, for example, you sent a letter from Coral Springs, Florida, to Upper Saddle River, New Jersey, the letter would not travel directly from Coral Springs to Upper Saddle River. Instead, the Postal Service would forward the letter from one substation to the next, making a new decision at each substation as to the best (most efficient) route; for example, from Coral Springs, to Miami, to Newark, and finally, to Upper Saddle River.

Each postal substation considers all of the routes it has available to the next substation and makes the best possible decision according to the prevailing conditions. This means that the next time you mail a letter from Coral Springs to Upper Saddle River, the letter may travel a completely different path. If the mail truck from Coral Springs to Miami had already left or was full to capacity, the letter could be routed through Fort Lauderdale to New York City, and then to Upper Saddle

[1]See Ed Krol, *The Whole Internet,* O'Reilly and Associates, Inc., Sebastopol, CA, 1992, pp. 24, 26.

River. The actual route taken by the letter is not important. All that matters is that the letter arrives at its destination.

The Internet works the same way, as data travels across the Internet through several levels of networks until it gets to its destination. E-mail messages arrive at the local post office (the mail server) from a remote PC connected by modem, or from a node on a local area network. The messages then leave the local post office and pass through a special-purpose computer known as a ***router,*** that ensures each message is sent to its correct destination.

A message may pass through several networks to get to its destination. Each network has its own router that determines how best to move the message closer to its destination, taking into account the traffic on the network. A message passes from one network to the next, until it arrives at the destination network, from where it can be sent to the recipient, who has a mailbox on that network. The process is depicted graphically in Figure A.1.

THE WINDOWS 95 TRACERT COMMAND

The TCP/IP protocol may sound like science fiction, but it works, and you can see it in action if you know how to look. Click the Start button in Windows 95, click the Programs command, then click the MS-DOS prompt to open a DOS window. Enter the command ***TRACERT*** followed by the name of a server—for example, TRACERT WWW.MICROSOFT.COM to connect to the Microsoft server. You will see the actual path traveled, together with the minimum, average, and maximum time for each hop. Type Exit at the C prompt to close the DOS window, then log off from your Internet provider.

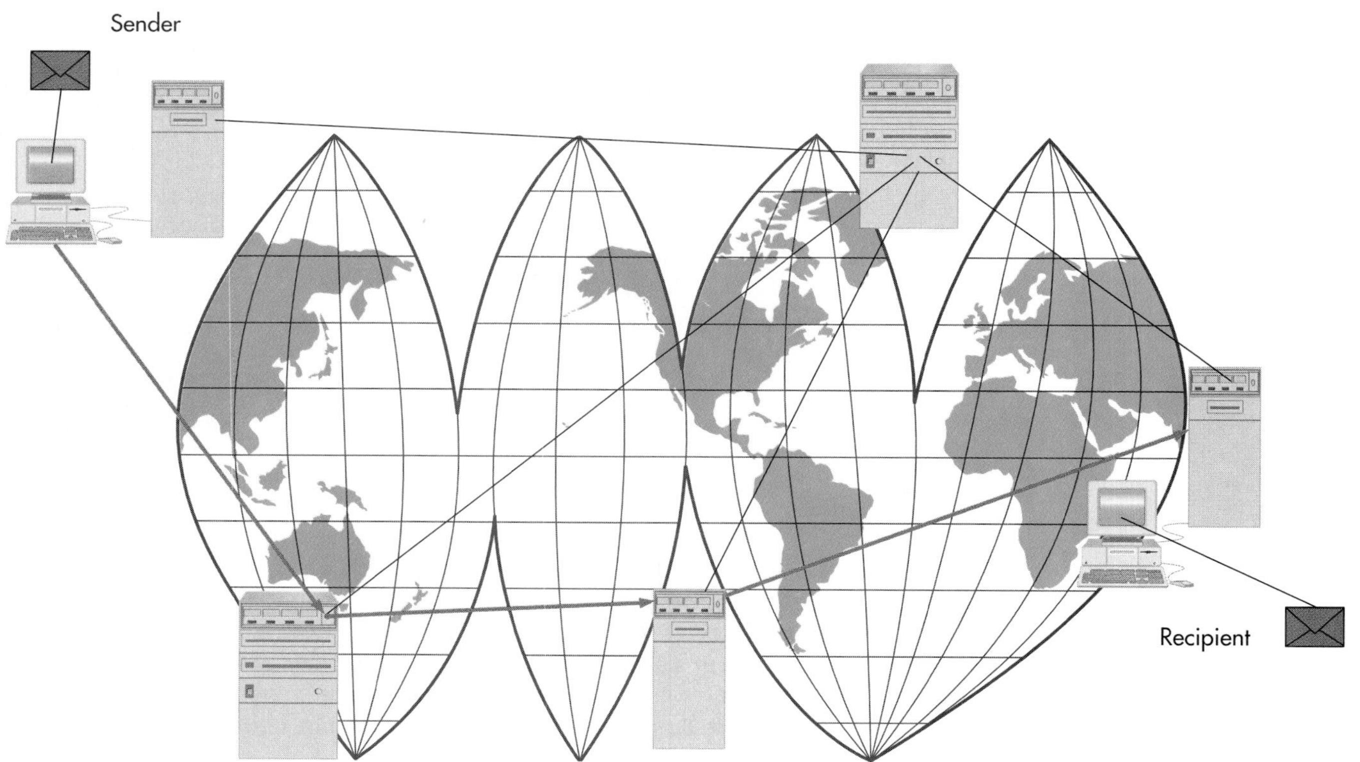

FIGURE A.1 A Message Travels the Internet

The TCP/IP protocol is more complex than what we have indicated, and it applies to all types of data, not just e-mail. To continue with the post office analogy, let's assume that you are sending a book, rather than a letter, and that the Post Office (for whatever reason) does not accept large packages. One alternative would be to rip the pages out of the book, mail each page individually by placing it into its own envelope, then trust that all of the envelopes arrive at the destination and finally, that the person on the other end would be able to reassemble the individual pages. That may sound awkward, but it is a truer picture of how the Internet works.

Data (whether it is an e-mail message or a Web page) is sent across the Internet in ***packets,*** with each packet limited in size. The rules for creating, addressing, and sending the packets are specified by TCP/IP, which is actually two separate protocols. The TCP portion divides the file that you want to send into packets, then numbers each packet so that the message can be reconstructed at the other end. The IP portion sends each packet on its way by specifying the addresses of the sending and receiving computers so that the routers will be able to do their job.

The TCP/IP protocol may seem unnecessarily complicated, but it is actually very clever. Dividing large files into smaller pieces ensures that no single file monopolizes the network. A second advantage has to do with ensuring that the data arrives correctly. Static or noise on a telephone line is merely annoying to people having a conversation, but devastating when a file (especially a computer program) is transmitted and a byte or two is lost or corrupted. The larger the file being sent, the greater the chance that noise will be introduced and that the file will be corrupted. Sending the data in smaller pieces (packets), and verifying that the packets were received correctly, helps ensure the integrity of the data. If one packet is received incorrectly, the entire file does not have to be sent again, only the corrupted packet.

A university or corporation can justify the high cost of a permanent TCP/IP connection to the Internet. This type of connection is very expensive and is reasonable only when multiple users on a LAN (Local Area Network) need to access the Internet simultaneously. A standalone PC, however (e.g., a home computer), will access the Internet through a dial-up connection via a modem. This provides a temporary connection known as a ***SLIP*** (Single Line Internet Protocol) or ***PPP*** (Point to Point Protocol) ***connection,*** but it enables full access to the Internet as long as you maintain the telephone connection.

WHAT IS ISDN?

ISDN (Integrated Services Digital Network) is a high-speed digital telephone service that speeds the transfer of data over the Internet for a dial-up connection. ISDN operates at speeds up to 128K bytes per second, or more than four times faster than a 28.8 modem. The disadvantage is cost. ISDN is expensive to install, and its monthly fee is more expensive than a standard telephone line. You also need specialized equipment and an Internet provider that supports ISDN connectivity. The march of technology assures us, however, that ISDN will become increasingly common and cost effective as time goes on.

Internet Architecture Layers

The Internet is built in layers that revolve around the TCP/IP protocol, as shown in Figure A.2. At the sending computer, the ***application layer*** creates the message and passes it to the ***transport layer,*** where the message is divided into packets. The packets are addressed at the ***Internet layer,*** then sent across the Internet using the ***network access layer,*** which traverses the various networks through which the data passes to get to its destination. The process is reversed at the receiving computer. The Internet layer receives the individual packets from the network access layer, then passes the packets to the transport layer, where they are reassembled in sequence and sent to the application layer to display the message.

Each computer on the Internet, whether dialing in or attached via a local area network, must have the necessary software (called TCP/IP drivers or stacks) to accomplish the task of the four layers. (The software is built into Windows 95.) Each computer also requires a unique ***IP address*** that identifies the computer as a node on the Internet. If you are connected to the Internet via a LAN, your workstation has a permanent IP address, which remains constant. A dial-up SLIP or PPP connection, however, provides you with only a temporary address, which changes from session to session.

The IP address is analogous to the street address on a letter. It is composed of four numbers, each less than 256, each separated by a period; for example, 192.25.13.01. (Fortunately, however, you can use a mnemonic address rather than the numeric IP address, as will be explained shortly.) Each site on the Internet must apply for a specific block of IP addresses from its Internet provider. Each PC, Mac, router, server, and other device on the network is then assigned an IP address by the network administrator, just as someone in your town has designated a number for every house or building on your street.

Let's consider the example shown in Figure A.2, in which Bob, at the University of Miami, composes and sends an e-mail message to Gretchen at Saint

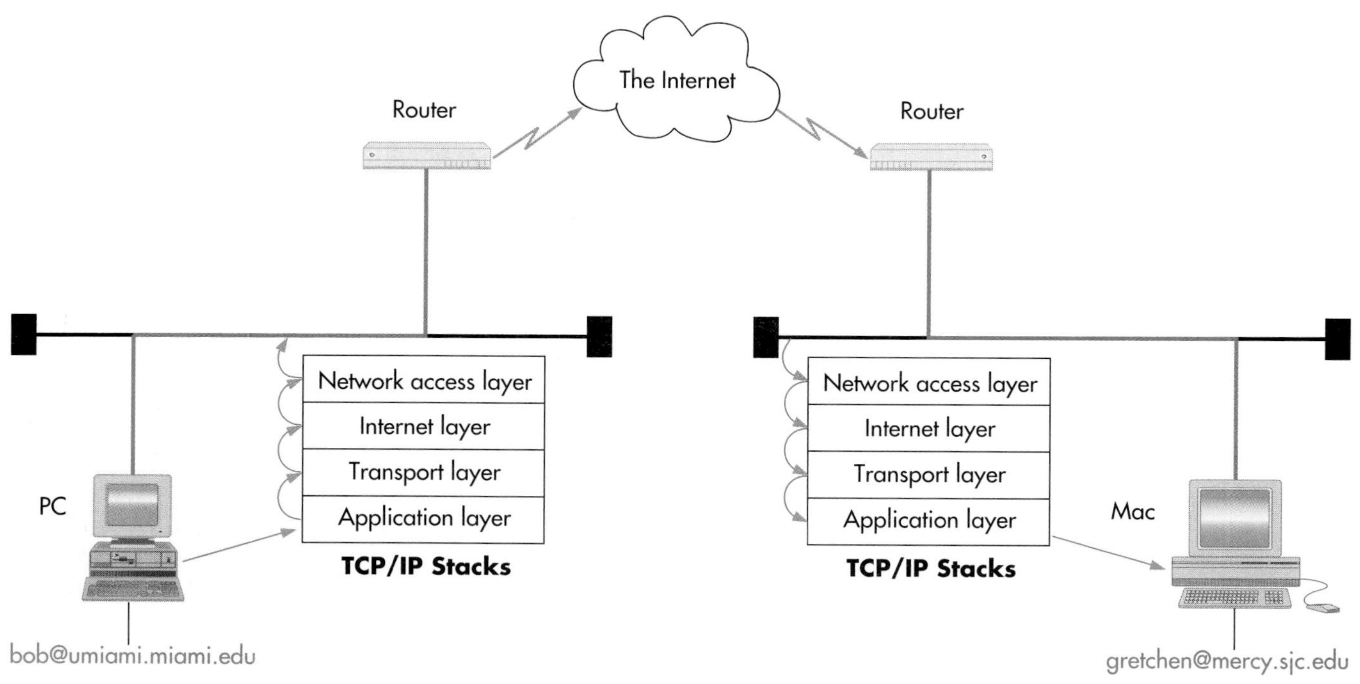

FIGURE A.2 The Internet Architecture

Joseph College. The application layer (Bob's e-mail program) creates the message and passes it to the transport layer, which divides the message into packets. The transport layer also records how many bytes are in each packet so that it can verify that the data was transmitted successfully. The transport layer then passes the packets to the Internet layer, where they are addressed and sent to the network access layer.

The network access layer, in turn, sends the individual packets out through the router onto the Internet. From there they are passed to another router, which examines the destination address and passes each packet on to another router. Each router contains a routing table, which determines where (to which network router) to send the packet next, based on the IP address of the message. This process continues until the destination router is reached and the TCP/IP software on the receiving computer delivers the message.

The Internet layer on the receiving end passes the individual packets to the transport layer, which sends an acknowledgment to the transport layer of the sending computer. The latter verifies that the data have been sent correctly, and automatically resends any erroneous packets. The transport layer on the receiving end then reassembles the packets, and delivers them to the application layer, which signals the arrival of Bob's message on Gretchen's computer. All of this happens in a matter of seconds, in a network that spans the globe.

The protocols that govern each layer are hardware independent, enabling the sender and recipient to use different types of computers, yet receive the messages without problems. In our diagram we show Bob working on a Windows 95 PC and Gretchen on a Mac. In addition, the networks themselves may be different—that is, use different types of wiring—in which case the Internet layer will change the size of the packets to that required for the specific network.

Think of the post office analogy. Some mail routes are handled by mail truck, others on foot. If the mail carrier is on a walking route, he or she must remove the mail from the plastic mail tub and place it in the mail shoulder bag. Not all of the mail will fit, so some pieces will wait for the carrier to return and load up for the second round. In a similar way, some Internet messages must be broken into different-sized packets for different parts of the physical network. The information about the type of protocols used is contained in the header information attached to the packets.

Fortunately, most, if not all of these functions are transparent to the user. You simply send an e-mail message, download a data file or program from a remote computer, or request a Web page, and off it goes, aided by the various software protocols installed on your system.

The Domain Name System

A numeric IP address is easily processed by a computer, but not so easily by a person. What's easier to remember, the IP address 123.201.85.244, or its mnemonic equivalent, www.myschool.edu? The ***Domain Name System (DNS)*** provides the mnemonic equivalent of a numeric IP address, and further, ensures that every site on the Internet has a unique address.

The DNS divides the Internet into a series of component networks called ***domains*** that enable e-mail (and other files) to be sent across the entire Internet. Each site attached to the Internet belongs to one of these domains. Universities, for example, belong to the EDU domain. Government agencies are in the GOV domain. Commercial organizations (companies) are in the COM domain. Large domains are in turn divided into smaller domains, with each domain responsible for maintaining unique addresses in the next lower-level domain, or subdomain. Table A.1 lists the six major Internet domains.

TABLE A.1 Internet Domains

Domain	Description	Example Subdomain
edu	Educational institutions	Your college or university
gov	Federal, state, and local government entities	NASA, the CIA, the U.S. Senate, the Library of Congress, the National Archives
mil	Military organizations	U.S. Navy
com	Commercial entities	Microsoft, Prentice Hall, Prodigy
net	Network service providers	The National Science Foundation's Internet Network Information Center
org	Nonprofit organizations	The Internet Town Hall

The mnemonic names you enter, either explicitly or implicitly, must be continually translated to the numeric addresses used by the TCP/IP protocol. This takes place automatically and is completely transparent to you. The host computer to which you are connected looks up the numeric IP address corresponding to the mnemonic DNS address by querying the nearest ***domain root server,*** one of several special computers on the Internet, which keeps information about IP addresses in its domain. This is similar to your going to the post office to look up a zip code for a letter you wish to send. You can keep the zip code handy in case you want to send a letter to that address again. In a similar fashion, the Internet host can keep a numeric IP address in memory, so it will not have to look it up again the next time a message is sent to that Internet address.

SUMMARY

Data is transmitted across the Internet through a series of protocols known collectively as TCP/IP (Transmission Control Protocol/Internet Protocol). The data are transmitted in packets, with each packet limited in size. The path that a particular message takes in getting to its destination is not important. All that matters is that the data arrives at its destination.

The Internet is built in layers that revolve around the TCP/IP protocol. The application layer at the sending computer creates a message and passes it to the transport layer where the message is divided into packets. The packets are addressed at the Internet layer, then sent across the Internet using the network access layer, which interacts with the various networks through which the data must travel to get to its destination. The process is reversed at the receiving computer.

Each computer connected to the Internet, whether dialing in or attached on a local area network (LAN), must have the software necessary to accomplish the task of the four layers. TCP/IP protocol drivers, or stacks as they are called, must be installed on each computer. Each computer must also have an IP address, a unique Internet address that identifies the computer as a node on the Internet. The IP address is composed of four numbers, each less than 256, each separated by a period—for example, 192.25.13.01.

The Domain Name System (DNS) provides the mnemonic equivalent of the numeric IP address and ensures that every site on the Internet has a unique address. The DNS divides the Internet into a series of component networks called domains. Large domains are in turn divided into smaller domains, with each domain responsible for maintaining unique addresses in the next lower-level domain, or subdomain.

B

APPENDIX B: HOT WEB SITES

This appendix lists approximately 100 Web sites in various categories for you to explore. By its very nature, however, the Web is changing daily and it is impossible for any printed list to be completely current. It is helpful, therefore, to suggest ways to explore the Web in addition to going to a specific site.

One very useful technique is to guess the address of a site according to a consistent addressing scheme, e.g, www.company.com. The address of both Netscape (www.netscape.com) and Microsoft (www.microsoft.com) follow this pattern. So do the home pages of many search engines; for example, www.lycos.com or www.yahoo.com will get you to the home page of the Lycos and Yahoo engines, respectively. Some magazines also follow the pattern, e.g., www.businessweek.com. as do various corporations such as www.ibm.com or www.dell.com.

It helps to look for lists of sites; www.nba.com and www.nfl.com take you to the home pages of the National Basketball Association and National Football League, respectively, which provide links to every team. Other lists of sites are not as obvious, but are equally valuable; for example, www.pathfinder.com takes you to the home page of Time Warner Communications, which provides links to multiple magazines including *Time, Fortune, Sports Illustrated, Money,* and *People.* The home page of Ziff-Davis publications (www.zdnet.com) directs you to computer publications, many of which have their own list of "hot" sites.

THE EXPLORING WINDOWS HOME PAGE

The *Exploring Windows* series has its own home page at www.prenhall.com/grauer. This site contains links to the data disks (or practice files) for the various books in the series and enables you to download those files to your PC. It also contains the links to our home pages at the University of Miami. Instructors may register their home pages and/or view the home pages of other instructors who are using our text.

Government, Political, and Nonprofit Organization Sites

Site Name	URL	Description
Concord Coalition	**ttp://sunsite.unc.edu/concord**	Learn more about the deficit—what you don't know could hurt you.
Electronic Frontier Foundation	**http://www2.eff.org/**	A nonprofit civil liberties organization working to protect privacy, free expression, and access to public resources
EPA	**http://www.epa.gov**	A searchable guide to the Environmental Protection Agency
FBI	**http://www.fbi.gov**	Contains the FBI's 10 most-wanted list and other law enforcement information
Federal Information Exchange	**http://www.fie.com/www/us_gov.htm**	List of U.S. government WWW servers with links to hundreds of other government sites
FedWorld	**http://www.fedworld.gov**	Searchable links to 120 government agencies
IRS	**http://www.irs.ustreas.gov**	Thousands of tax forms, advice, and information to help you file your taxes
Legislative Gopher	**gopher://gopher.legislate.com**	Contains text of all Congressional legislation since 1993
Library of Congress	**http://lcweb.loc.gov**	Start with the the American History Project, and browse for hours—a fantastic site.
NASA	**http://www.nasa.gov**	Find out about the latest space-shuttle launch and other vital NASA information.
National Park Service	**http://www.nps.gov/nps/**	A list of more than 350 sites in the National Park System
Right Side of Web	**http://www.rtside.com/rtsside**	Find out more about Newt Gingrich's Contract with America, Whitewater, and other conservative hot topics.
Small Business Administration	**http://www.sbaonline.sba.gov**	Thinking of starting a business? Here's the place to start.
Social Security Administration	**http://www.ssa.gov**	Everything you need to know about the Social Security Administration
Space Shuttle Site	**http://liftoff.msfc.nasa.gov**	Daily schedule of mission events, including video and virtual reality clips
U.S. Census	**http://www.census.gov**	Contains a wealth of demographic information about the United States
U.S. Congress	**http://thomas.loc.gov**	Searchable information from the last two congressional sessions
U.S. Geological Service	**http://edcwww.cr.usgs.gov**	The USGS declassified satellite photos—find your home or college from 50,000 feet.
U.S. House of Representatives	**http://www.house.gov**	Send a message to wired House members.

Government, Political, and Nonprofit Organization Sites (continued)

Site Name	URL	Description
U.S. Patent and Trademark Office	**http://www.uspto.gov**	Check here to see if someone already has a patent on your invention.
White House	**http://www.whitehouse.gov**	Obtain the text of the president's speeches, or tour the White House.

Fun, Education, Entertainment, Shopping, and Sports

Site Name	URL	Description
100 Hot Sites	**http://www.100hot.com/**	A constantly changing list of fun sites to explore.
America's Cup	**http://www.ac2000.org/**	Follow the progress of the race to win the cup back from the Kiwis.
Bob Grauer's Home Page	**http://www.bus.miami.edu/~rgrauer**	Bob's home page at the University of Miami
Branch Mall	**http://branch.com**	Shop without leaving your home.
ERIC Clearinghouse for Social Studies	**http://www.indiana.edu/~ssdc/eric-chess.html**	Education majors: Find out more about social studies here.
Games Domain	**http://www.gamesdomain.com/**	Contains links to computer and on-line games
Hang Gliders' Home Page	**http://cougar.stanford.edu:7878/HGMPSHomePage.html**	Lots of interesting links related to hang gliding and aviation
Homeopathy Home Page	**http://www.dungeon.com/home/cam/homeo.html**	Find out about treating many ailments without a prescription. The alternative to mainstream medicine.
Hostel's Europe Pages	**http://www.tardis.ed.ac.uk/~og/hostels.html**	How to find good hostels (and stay away from the bad ones) in Europe
Interactive Frog Dissection	**http://teach.virginia.edu/go/frog**	Biology without the formaldehyde
Interactive Geometry	**http://www.geom.umn.edu/apps/gallery.html**	Math on the Net
International Tutors	**http://www.iamot.org/it/**	Help is available from around the world in a wide variety of academic disciplines.
Internet Movie Database	**http://www.yahoo.com/Entertainment/Movies_and_Films/**	Searchable guide to all the movies there ever were. Provides links to filmography on actors.
Internet Plaza	**http://plaza.xor.com/**	Some vendors here let you browse; others let you place on-line orders.
Internet Shopkeeper	**http://shops.net/cgi-bin**	Another great place to shop
Internet Shopping Network	**http://www.internet.net**	Shop for computers and peripherals here.
Jason Project	**http://seawifs.gsfc.nasa.gov/scripts/JASON.html**	Descriptions of various scientific expeditions; provides fascinating information about everything from volcanoes to Mayan ruins.

Fun, Education, Entertainment, Shopping (continued)

Site Name	URL	Description
Keirsey Temperament Sorter	**http://www.sunsite.unc.edu/jembin/mb.pl**	Find out your personality type, based on the Meyers-Briggs Personality Type Indicator test.
Lego Home Page	**http://www.lego.com/**	Provides news on what's up in Legoland
Medical Matrix	**http://www.kumc.edu**	Links to online medical resources
National Basketball Association	**http://www.nba.com**	The home page for the NBA, with links to individual teams
National Football League	**http://www.nfl.com**	The home page for the NFL, with links to individual teams
The Movie Link	**http://web8.movielink.com**	A link to all sorts of movie information, including local show times
MTV Online	**http://www.mtv.com**	Your favorite channel does it on the Net.
National Organization for Women	**http://now.org/**	Women's rights are still an issue. Check out this page to see why.
Purdue Weather Server	**http://thunder.atms.purdue.edu/**	Get up-to-the-minute weather forecasts.
Roulette	**http://www.uroulette.com**	Click the URouLette link, and who knows where on the Web you will end up; random links to cyberspace.
Tennis Server	**http://www.tennisserver.com/Tennis.html**	Tennis anyone?
Ultimate Band List	**http://american.recordings.com**	Alphabetical listing of bands.
Ultimate TV List	**http://tvnet.com**	Everything you want to know about TV
Virtual Tourist	**http://www.vtourist.com/vt/**	An online map with links around the world
Warner Bros. Records	**http://www.wbr.com/**	Information on Warner Bros. artists
Women on the Net	**http://www.cybergrrl.com**	Links to many online resources for women, including information about domestic violence
WWW of Sports	**http://www.tns.lcs.mit.edu/cgi-bin/sports**	Sports home page, with links to many other sports sites

Internet Information/Web News

Site Name	URL	Description
Georgia Institute of Technology	**http://www.cc.gatech.edu/gvu/gvutop.html**	Links to Georgia Tech's graphics lab and survey of Web users
Global Network Navigator	**http://www.gnn.com/index.html**	Best of the Net, the Whole Internet Catalog, with lots of information about the Net, and a catalog of resource books
Online World Resources Handbook	**http://login.eunet.no/~presno**	Guide to using Web resources and downloading software

Internet Information/Web News (continued)

Site Name	URL	Description
Publicly Accessible Mailing Lists	**http://www.NeoSoft.com:80/internet/paml/bysubj.html**	Alphabetical list of mailing lists on lots of interesting topics
The Scout Report	**http://rs.internic.net/scout_report-index.html**	A weekly update on what's new and interesting on the Net; you can also subscribe to receive via e-mail.
University of North Carolina/Sun Microsystems, Inc.	**http://sunsite.unc.edu/**	An award-winning site with lots of information about the Internet
Virus FAQ	**ftp://rtfm.mit.edu//pub/usenet-by-hierarchy/comp/virus**	Learn about viruses and how you can protect yourself.
World Wide Web Consortium	**http://www.w3.org**	The point-of-origin of the World Wide Web

Software Sites

Site Name	URL	Description
Cybersource	**http://www.software.net**	The Internet software store
Internet Phone	**http://www.vocaltec.com**	Download software to send voice over the Internet.
MIRC Client	**ftp://cs-ftp.bu.edu/pub/irc/clients/pc/windows/mirc/**	Download MIRC client and start chatting.
RealAudio	**http://www.realaudio.com**	Audio over the Internet; uses compression methods to reduce audio files to 8% of original size.
Sun Microsystems, Inc.	**http://java.sun.com**	Check out Java software for the Web.
VMPEG Software	**ftp://ftp.netcom.com/pub/cf/cfogg/vmpeg/**	Download video software so you can see motion pictures from the Internet on your PC (vmpeg17.exe or latest version).
Web Wizard	**http://www.halcyon.com/artamedia/webwizard/**	HTML kit allows you to easily create your home page.

Online News, Newspapers, and Magazines

Site Name	URL	Description
ABC	**http://www.abc.com**	Home page of the ABC network.
Business Week	**http://www.businessweek.com/**	Home page of Business Week magazine
CBS	**http://www.cbs.com**	Home page of the CBS network
CNN	**http://www.cnn.com**	Home page of the CNN network
Fox	**http://www.fox.com**	Home page of the Fox network
NBC	**http://www.nbc.com**	Home page of the NBC network
New York Times	**http://www.nytimes.com**	"All the news that's fit to print"

Online News, Newspapers, and Magazines (continued)

Site Name	URL	Description
Pathfinder	**http://www.pathfinder.com**	Access to many magazines including *People, Money, Fortune,* and *Time*
PC Magazine	**http://www.pcmag.com**	Links to everything including PC magazine's current list of Web sites
Public Broadcasting Service	**http://www.cpb.org/**	Home Page of the Corporation for Public Broadcasting
San Jose Mercury News	**http://www.sjmercury.com**	The newspaper of Silicon Valley
Slate	**http://www.slate.com**	Microsoft's online magazine
USA Today	**http://www.usatoday.com**	Read today's paper online.
The Wall Street Journal	**http://www.wsj.com/**	Read today's paper online.
Washington Post	**http://www.newsservice.com**	Access to the *Los Angeles Times* and *Washington Post.*
Ziff-Davis Publishing	**http://www.zdnet.com**	Scroll down the page for links to many computer magazines.

Commercial Sites

Site Name	URL	Description
American Airlines	**http://www.americanair.com/**	You can now make reservations for ticketless travel at American's Web site.
AOL	**http://www.aol.com**	Subscribe to AOL here.
AT&T	**http://www.tollfree.att.net/dir800/**	AT&T 800 number directory
Dun & Bradstreet	**http://www.dbisna.com**	The D&B home page
Federal Reserve Bank of New York	**http://www.ny.frb.org/**	All sorts of banking and U.S. Treasury information
Fidelity Investments	**http://www.fid-inv.com**	Monitor your investment online.
Godiva On-line	**http://www.godiva.com/**	Chocolate anyone?
IBM	**http://www.ibm.com**	Find out about OS2 Warp and other IBM products.
InfoPost	**http://www.infopost.com**	The place to go if you want someone to create and maintain a home page for you
Intel	**http://www.intel.com**	Get a technology briefing and find out about Intel's PC plans.
Internet Yellow Pages	**http://www.yellow.com**	The Internet yellow pages
Microsoft	**http://www.microsoft.com/**	The best place to go for information about any Microsoft product
Netscape	**http://www.netscape.com**	Stay up to date with Netscape.

PREREQUISITES: ESSENTIALS OF WINDOWS 95

OBJECTIVES

After reading this appendix you will be able to:

1. Describe the objects on the Windows desktop; describe the programs available through the Start button.
2. Explain the function of the minimize, maximize, restore, and close buttons; move and size a window.
3. Discuss the function of a dialog box; describe the elements in a dialog box and the various ways in which information is supplied.
4. Use the Help menu to learn about features in Windows 95; format a floppy disk and implement a screen saver by following instructions from the Help menu.
5. Use the Internet Explorer to access the Internet and download the practice files for the *Exploring Windows* series.
6. Use Windows Explorer to locate a specific file or folder; describe the views available for Windows Explorer.
7. Describe how folders are used to organize a disk; create a new folder; copy and/or move a file from one folder to another.
8. Delete a file, then recover the deleted file from the Recycle Bin.

OVERVIEW

Windows 95 is a computer program (actually many programs) that controls the operation of your computer and its peripherals. ***Windows 97*** improves on Windows 95 to bring elements of the Internet to the desktop. Windows 97 was not available when we went to press, but we expect it to follow the same conventions as Windows 95. Thus, our introduction applies to both, as it emphasizes the common features of file management in support of Microsoft Office 97. (Microsoft Office runs equally well under Windows 95, Windows 97, or Windows NT.)

One of the most significant benefits of the Windows environment is the common user interface and consistent command structure that is imposed on every Windows application. Once you learn the basic concepts and techniques, you can apply that knowledge to every Windows application. This appendix teaches you those concepts so that you will be able to work productively in the Windows environment. It is written for you, the computer novice, and assumes no previous knowledge about a computer or about Windows. Our goal is to get you "up and running" as quickly as possible so that you can do the work you want to do.

We begin with an introduction to the Windows desktop, the graphical user interface that lets you work in intuitive fashion by pointing at icons and clicking the mouse. We identify the basic components of a window and describe how to execute commands and supply information through various elements in a dialog box. We introduce you to My Computer, an icon that is present on every Windows desktop, then show you how to use My Computer to access the various components of your system.

The appendix also shows you how to manage the hundreds (indeed, thousands) of files that are stored on the typical system. We show you how to create a new folder (the electronic equivalent of a manila folder in a filing cabinet) and how to move or copy a file from one folder to another. We show you how to rename a file, how to delete a file, and how to recover a deleted file from the Recycle Bin.

The appendix also contains four hands-on exercises, which enable you to apply the conceptual discussion in the text at the computer. The exercises are essential to the learn-by-doing philosophy we follow throughout the *Exploring Windows* series.

THE DESKTOP

Windows creates a working environment for your computer that parallels the working environment at home or in an office. You work at a desk. Windows operations take place on the ***desktop.***

There are physical objects on a desk such as folders, a dictionary, a calculator, or a phone. The computer equivalents of those objects appear as ***icons*** (pictorial symbols) on the desktop. Each object on a real desk has attributes (properties) such as size, weight, and color. In similar fashion, Windows assigns properties to every object on its desktop. And just as you can move the objects on a real desk, you can rearrange the objects on the Windows desktop.

Figure 1a displays the desktop when Windows is first installed on a new computer. This desktop has only a few objects and is similar to the desk in a new office, just after you move in. Figure 1b displays a different desktop, one with several open windows, and is similar to a desk during the middle of a working day. Do not be concerned if your Windows desktop is different from ours. Your real desk is arranged differently from those of your friends, and so your Windows desktop will also be different.

The simplicity of the desktop in Figure 1a helps you to focus on what is important. The ***Start button,*** as its name suggests, is where you begin. Click the Start button (mouse operations are described on page 9) and you see a menu that lets you start any program (e.g., Microsoft Word or Microsoft Excel) on your computer. The Start button also contains a ***Help command*** through which you can obtain information about every aspect of Windows.

Each icon on the desktop in Figure 1a provides access to an important function within Windows. ***My Computer*** enables you to browse the disk drives and optional CD-ROM drive that are attached to your computer. ***Network Neighborhood*** extends your view of the computer to include the accessible drives on the network to which your machine is attached, if indeed it is part of a network. (You

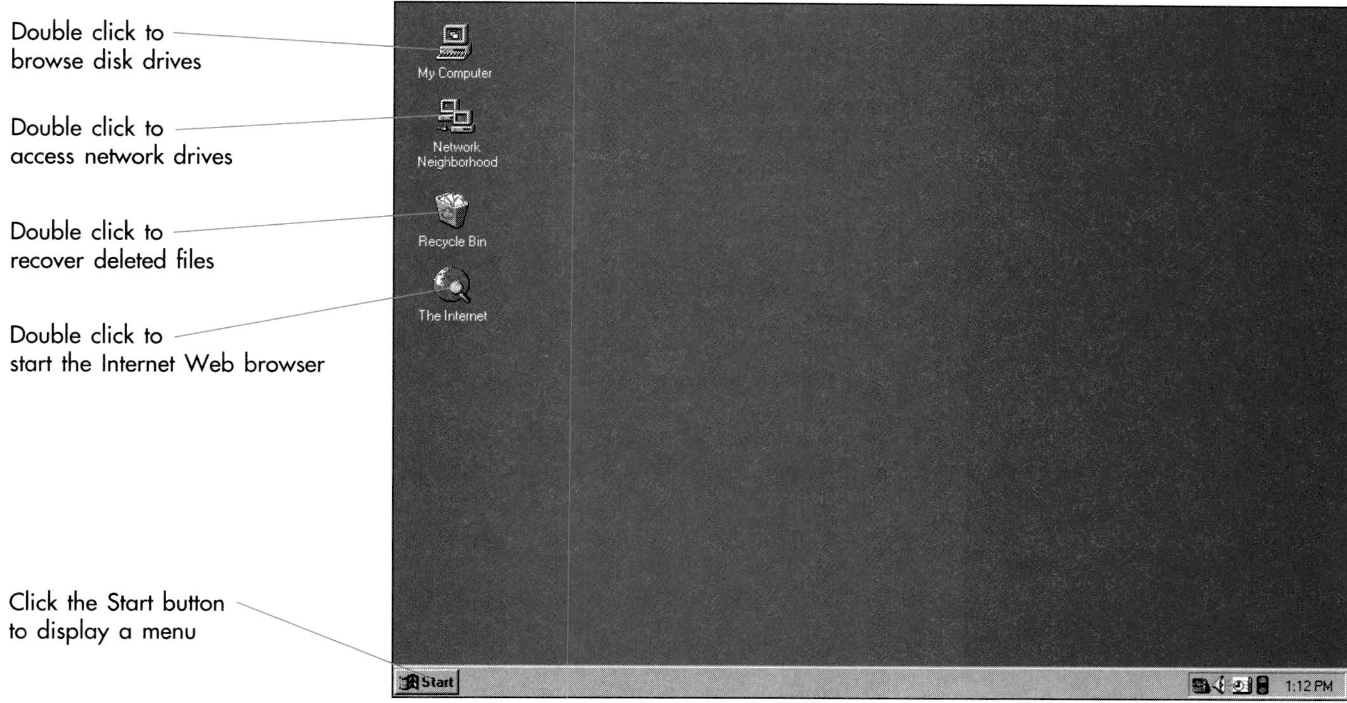

(a) New Desktop

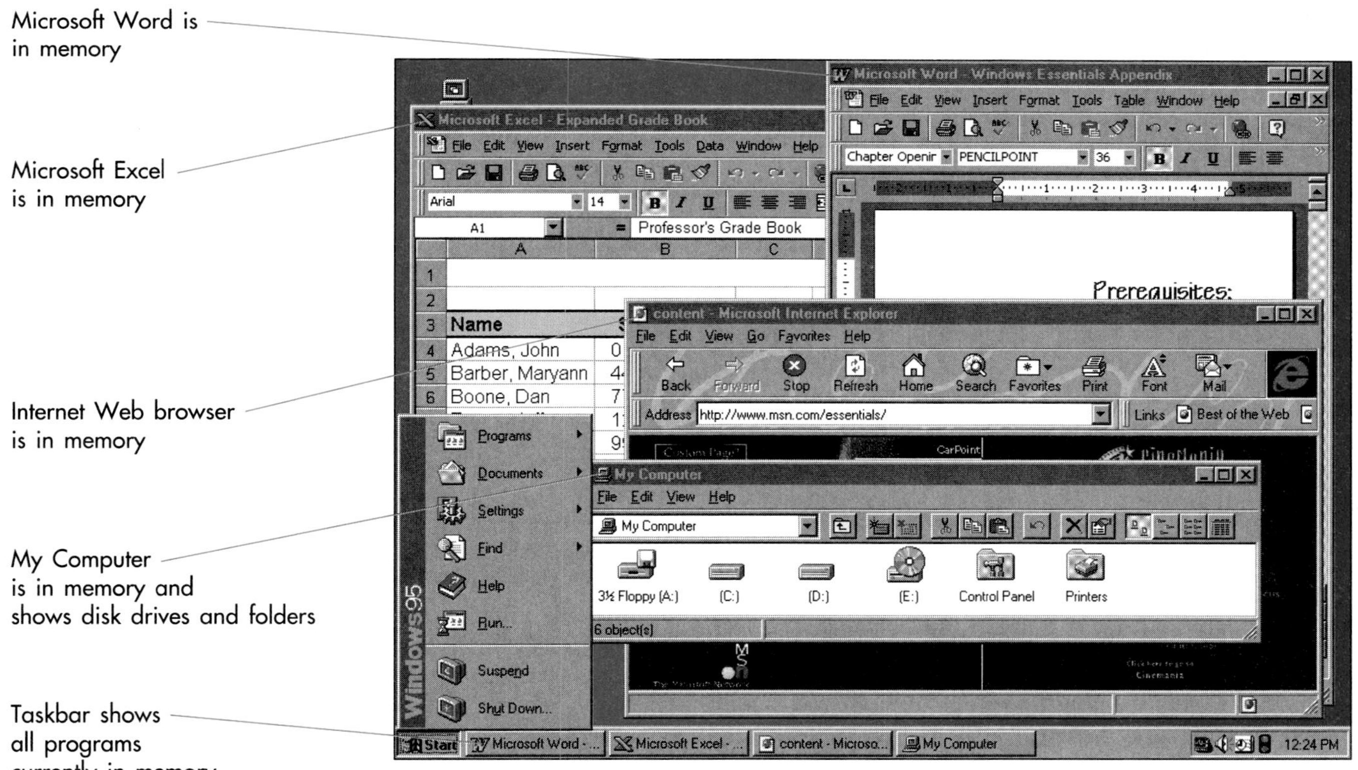

(b) A Working Desktop

FIGURE 1 The Windows Desktop

will not see this icon if you are not connected to a network.) The ***Recycle Bin,*** described later in the appendix, allows you to recover a file that was previously deleted. Double clicking the ***Internet icon*** starts the Web browser and initiates a connection to the Internet (assuming you have the necessary hardware).

Each icon on the desktop in Figure 1a opens into a window containing additional objects when you open (double click) the icon. Double click My Computer in Figure 1a, for example, and you see the objects contained in the My Computer window of Figure 2. The contents of the My Computer window depend on the hardware of the specific computer system. Our system, for example, has one floppy drive, two hard (fixed) disks, and a CD-ROM. The My Computer window also contains the Control Panel and Printer folders, which allow access to functions that control other elements in the environment on your computer. (A ***folder,*** called a directory under MS-DOS, may in turn contain other folders and/or individual files.)

The desktop in Figure 1b contains additional windows that display programs that are currently in use. Each window has a title bar that displays the name of the program and the associated document. You can work in any window as long as you want, then switch to a different window. ***Multitasking,*** the ability to run several programs at the same time, is one of the major benefits of the Windows environment. It lets you run a word processor in one window, a spreadsheet in a second window, surf the Internet in a third window, play a game in a fourth window, and so on.

The ***taskbar*** at the bottom of the desktop shows all of the programs that are currently active (open in memory). It contains a button for each open program and lets you switch back and forth between those programs by clicking the appropriate button. The taskbar in Figure 1a does not contain any buttons (other than the Start button) since there are no open applications. The taskbar in Figure 1b, however, contains four additional buttons, one for each open window.

ANATOMY OF A WINDOW

Figure 2 displays two views of the My Computer window and labels its essential elements. Every window has the same components as every other window, which include a title bar, a minimize button, a maximize or restore button, and a close button. Other elements that may be visible include a horizontal and/or vertical scroll bar, a menu bar, a status bar, and a toolbar. Every window also contains additional objects (icons) that pertain specifically to the programs or data associated with that window.

The ***title bar*** appears at the top of the window and displays the name of the window—for example, My Computer in both Figures 2a and 2b. The icon at the extreme left of the title bar provides access to a control menu that lets you select operations relevant to the window. The ***minimize button*** shrinks the window to a button on the taskbar. The ***maximize button*** enlarges the window so that it takes up the entire desktop. The ***restore button*** (not shown in Figure 2) appears instead of the maximize button after a window has been maximized, and restores the window to its previous size. The ***close button*** closes the window and removes it from the desktop.

The ***menu bar*** appears immediately below the title bar and provides access to pull-down menus (as discussed later in the appendix). A ***toolbar*** appears below the menu bar and lets you execute a command by clicking a button as opposed to pulling down a menu. The ***status bar*** at the bottom of the window displays information about the window as a whole or about a selected object within a window.

A ***vertical*** (or ***horizontal***) ***scroll bar*** appears at the right (or bottom) border of a window when its contents are not completely visible and provides access

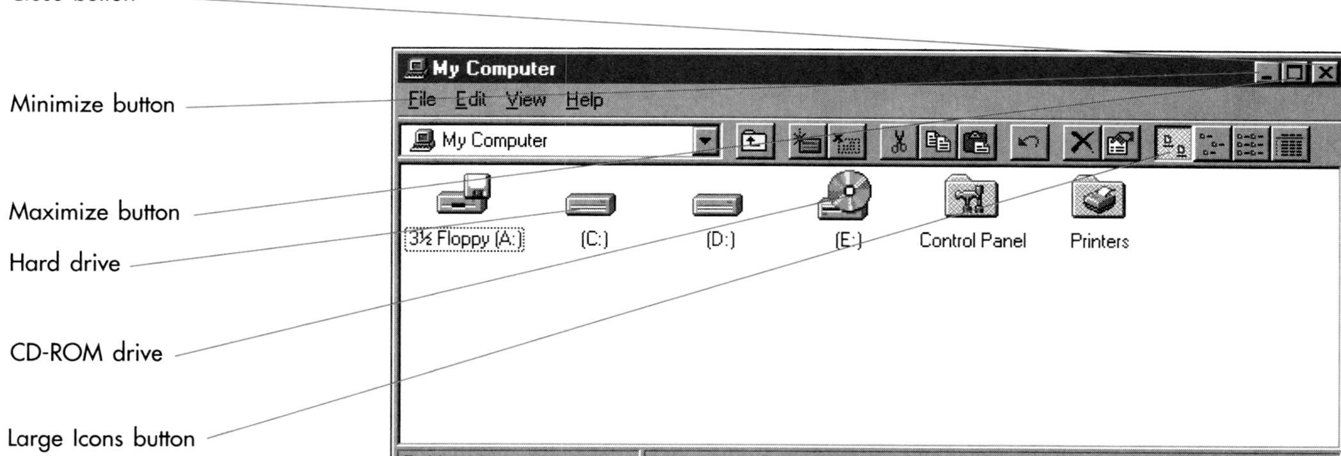

(a) Large Icons View

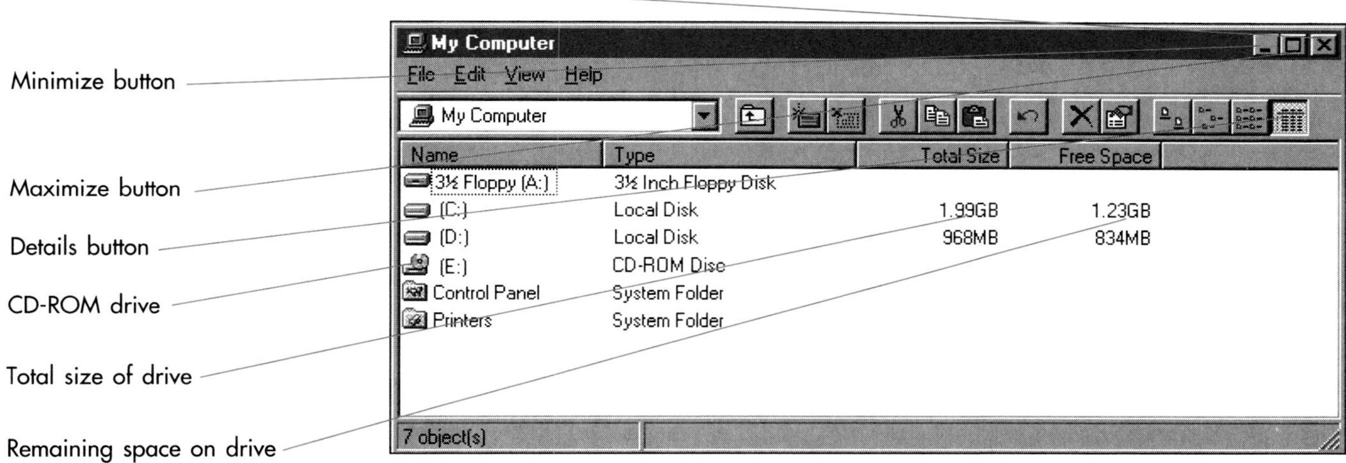

(b) Details View

FIGURE 2 Anatomy of a Window

to the unseen areas. Scroll bars do not appear in Figure 2 since all six objects in the window are visible.

The objects in any window can be displayed in four different views according to your preference or need. The choice between the views depends on your personal preference. You might, for example, choose the ***Large Icons view*** in Figure 2a if there are only a few objects in the window. The ***Details view*** in Figure 2b displays additional information about each object including the type of object, the total size of the disk, and the remaining space on the disk. You switch from one view to the next by choosing the appropriate command from the View menu or by clicking the corresponding button on the toolbar.

Moving and Sizing a Window

A window can be sized or moved on the desktop through appropriate actions with the mouse. To ***size a window,*** point to any border (the mouse pointer changes to a double arrow), then drag the border in the direction you want to go—inward to shrink the window or outward to enlarge it. You can also drag a corner (instead of a border) to change both dimensions at the same time. To ***move a window*** while retaining its current size, click and drag the title bar to a new position on the desktop.

Pull-down Menus

The menu bar provides access to ***pull-down menus*** that enable you to execute commands within an application (program). A pull-down menu is accessed by clicking the menu name or by pressing the Alt key plus the underlined letter in the menu name; for example, press Alt+V to pull down the View menu. Three pull-down menus associated with My Computer are shown in Figure 3.

The commands within a menu are executed by clicking the command or by typing the underlined letter (for example, C to execute the Close command in the File menu) once the menu has been pulled down. Alternatively, you can bypass the menu entirely if you know the equivalent keystrokes shown to the right of the command in the menu (e.g., Ctrl+X, Ctrl+C, or Ctrl+V to cut, copy, or paste as shown within the Edit menu).

A ***dimmed command*** (e.g., the Paste command in the Edit menu) means the command is not currently executable, and that some additional action has to be taken for the command to become available.

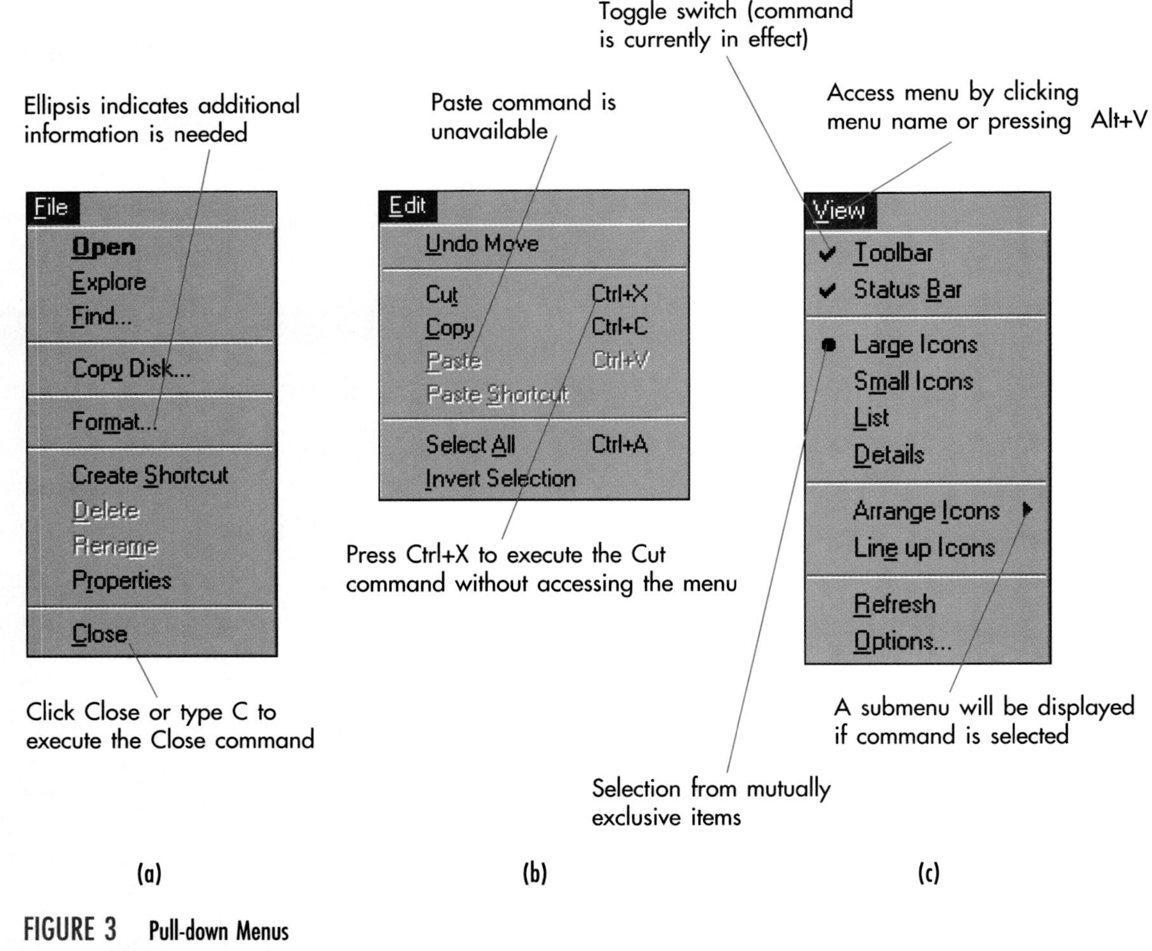

FIGURE 3 Pull-down Menus

An ***ellipsis*** (. . .) following a command indicates that additional information is required to execute the command; for example, selection of the Format command in the File menu requires the user to specify additional information about the formatting process. This information is entered into a dialog box (discussed in the next section), which appears immediately after the command has been selected.

A ***check*** next to a command indicates a toggle switch, whereby the command is either on or off. There is a check next to the Toolbar command in the View menu of Figure 3, which means the command is in effect (and thus the toolbar will be displayed). Click the Toolbar command and the check disappears, which suppresses the display of the toolbar. Click the command a second time and the check reappears, as does the toolbar in the associated window.

A ***bullet*** next to an item (e.g., Large Icons in Figure 3c) indicates a selection from a set of mutually exclusive choices. Click another option within the group (e.g., Small Icons) and the bullet will disappear from the previous selection (Large Icons) and appear next to the new selection (Small Icons).

An ***arrowhead*** after a command (e.g., the Arrange icons command in the View menu) indicates that a ***submenu*** (also known as a cascaded menu) will be displayed with additional menu options.

Dialog Boxes

A ***dialog box*** appears when additional information is needed to execute a command. The Format command, for example, requires information about which drive to format and the type of formatting desired.

Option (radio) buttons indicate mutually exclusive choices, one of which must be chosen—for example, one of three Format Type options in Figure 4a. Click a button to select an option, which automatically deselects the previously selected option.

Check boxes are used instead of option buttons if the choices are not mutually exclusive or if an option is not required. Multiple boxes can be checked as in Figure 4a, or no boxes may be checked as in Figure 4b. Individual options are selected (cleared) by clicking the appropriate check box.

A ***text box*** is used to enter descriptive information—for example, Bob's Disk in Figure 4a. A flashing vertical bar (an I-beam) appears within the text box when the text box is active, to mark the ***insertion point*** for the text you will enter.

A ***list box*** displays some or all of the available choices, any one of which is selected by clicking the desired item. A ***drop-down list box,*** such as the Capacity list box in Figure 4a, conserves space by showing only the current selection. Click the arrow of a drop-down list box to display the list of available options. An ***open list box,*** such as those in Figure 4b, displays multiple choices at one time. (A scroll bar appears within an open list box if some of the choices are not visible and provides access to the hidden choices.)

A ***tabbed dialog box*** provides multiple sets of options. The dialog box in Figure 4c, for example, has two tabs, each with its own set of options. Click either tab (the General tab is currently selected) to display the associated options.

The ***What's This button*** (a question mark at the right end of the title bar) provides help for any item in the dialog box. Click the button, then click the item in the dialog box for which you want additional information. The ***Close button*** (the X at the extreme right of the title bar) closes the dialog box.

All dialog boxes also contain one or more ***command buttons,*** the functions of which are generally apparent from the specific button's name. The Start button, in Figure 4a, for example, initiates the formatting process. The OK command button in Figure 4b accepts the settings and closes the dialog box. The Cancel button does just the opposite—it ignores (cancels) any changes made to the settings, then closes the dialog box without further action.

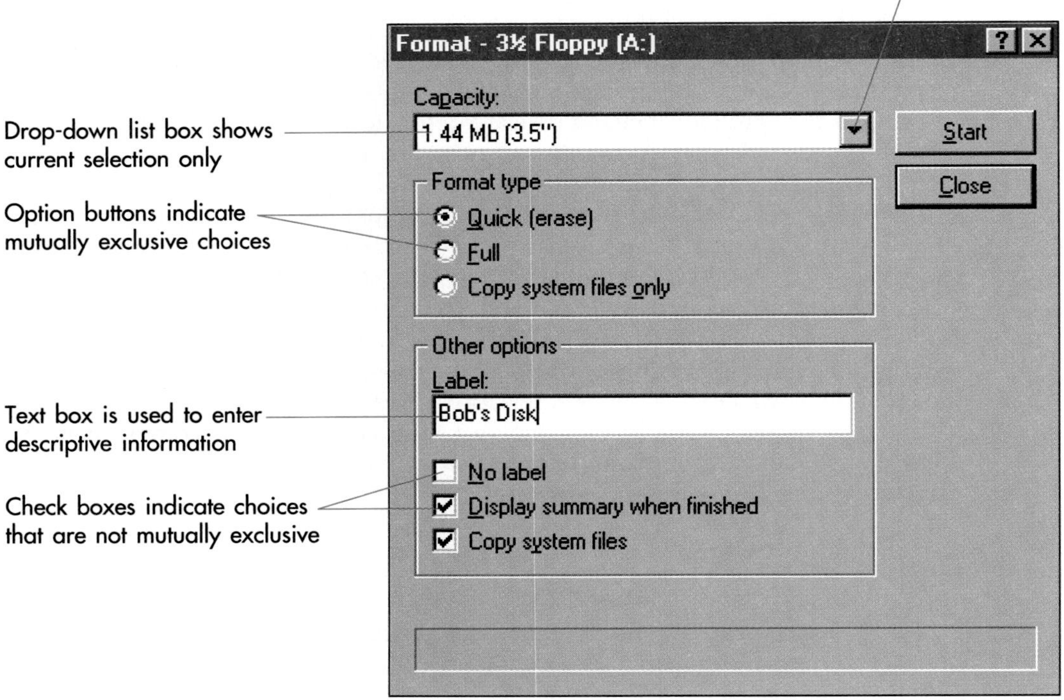

(a) Option Boxes and Check Boxes

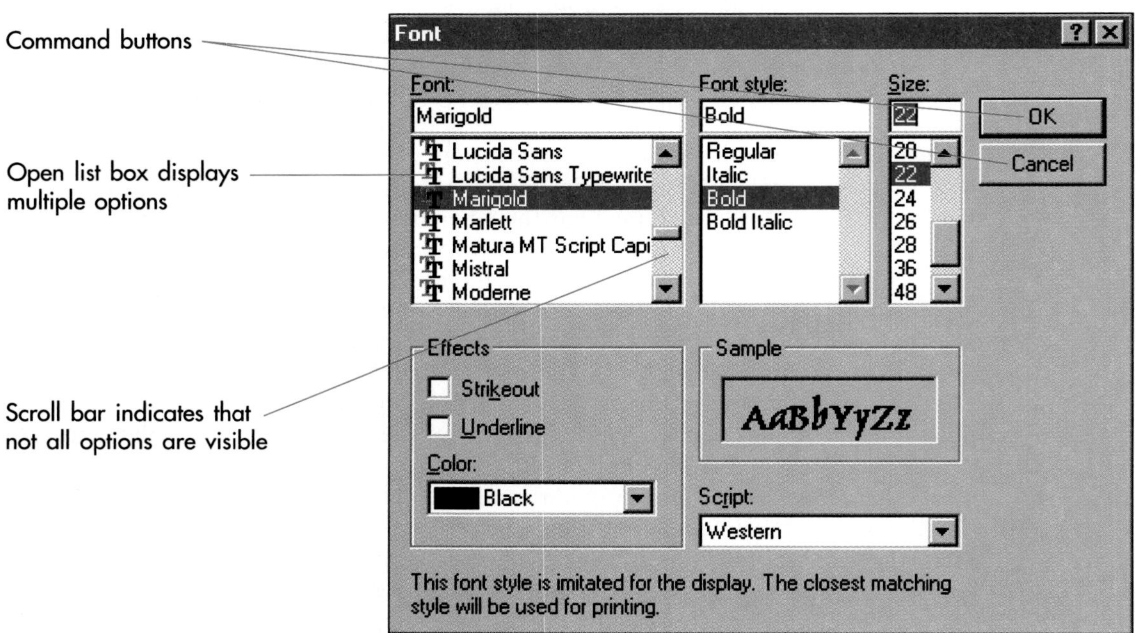

(b) List Boxes

FIGURE 4 Dialog Boxes

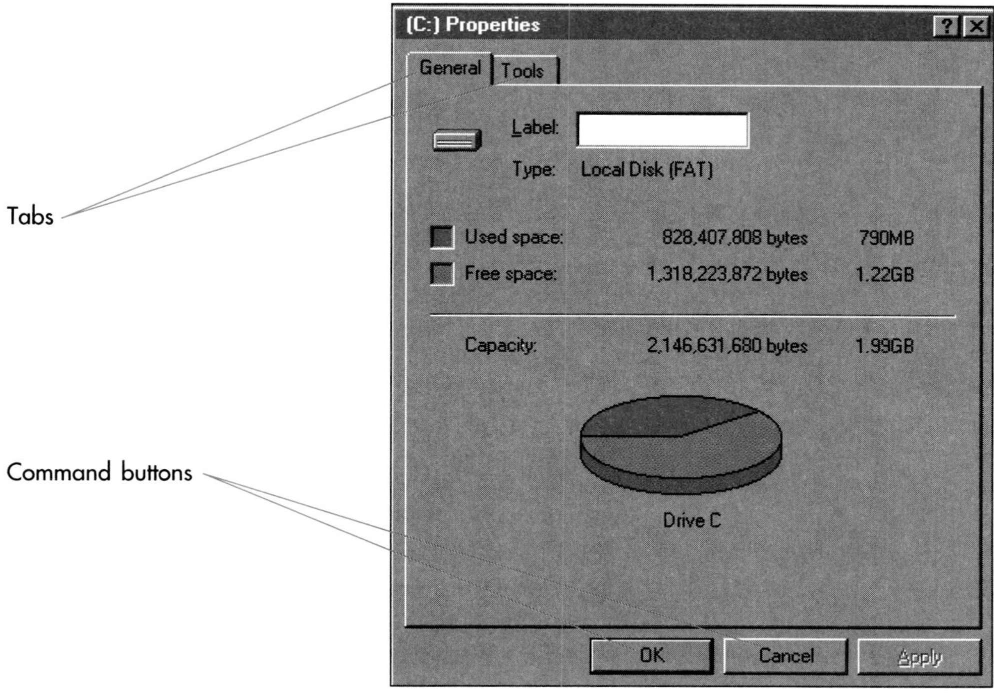

(c) Tabbed Dialog Box

FIGURE 4 Dialog Boxes (continued)

THE MOUSE

The mouse is indispensable to Windows and is referenced continually in the hands-on exercises throughout the text. There are four basic operations with which you must become familiar:

- To ***point*** to an object, move the mouse pointer over the object.
- To ***click*** an object, point to it, then press and release the left mouse button; to ***right click*** an object, point to the object, then press and release the right mouse button.
- To ***double click*** an object, point to it, then quickly click the left button twice in succession.
- To ***drag*** an object, move the pointer to the object, then press and hold the left button while you move the mouse to a new position.

The mouse is a pointing device—move the mouse on your desk and the ***mouse pointer,*** typically a small arrowhead, moves on the monitor. The mouse pointer assumes different shapes according to the location of the pointer or the nature of the current action. You will see a double arrow when you change the size of a window, an I-beam as you insert text, a hand to jump from one help topic to the next, or a circle with a line through it to indicate that an attempted action is invalid.

The mouse pointer will also change to an hourglass to indicate that Windows is processing your command, and that no further commands may be issued until the action is completed. The more powerful your computer, the less frequently the hourglass will appear, and conversely, the less powerful your system, the more you see the hourglass.

THE MICROSOFT INTELLIMOUSE

Microsoft has created a new mouse for Office 97. The mouse contains a wheel between the left and right buttons, allowing you to scroll through a document by rotating the wheel forward or back. You can also increase (or decrease) the magnification by holding the Ctrl key as you rotate the wheel on the mouse. Additional information is available from the IntelliPoint Online User's Guide. (Click the Start button, point to Programs, point to Microsoft Input Devices, and then point to Mouse.)

The Mouse Versus the Keyboard

Almost every command in Windows can be executed by using either the mouse or the keyboard. Most people start with the mouse but add keyboard shortcuts as they become more proficient. There is no right or wrong technique, just different techniques, and the one you choose depends entirely on personal preference in a specific situation. If, for example, your hands are already on the keyboard, it is faster to use the keyboard equivalent. Other times, your hand will be on the mouse and that will be the fastest way.

In the beginning, you may wonder why there are so many different ways to do the same thing, but you will eventually recognize the many options as part of Windows' charm. It is not necessary to memorize anything, nor should you even try; just be flexible and willing to experiment. The more you practice, the sooner all of this will become second nature to you.

THE HELP MENU

Windows has an extensive ***Help menu*** that contains information about virtually every topic in Windows. We believe that the best time to learn about Help is when you begin your study of Windows. Help is available at any time, and is accessed most easily by clicking the ***Help command*** on the Start menu, which displays the Help Topics dialog box in Figure 5.

The ***Contents tab*** in Figure 5a is similar to the table of contents in an ordinary book. The major topics are represented by books, each of which can be opened to display additional topics. These topics may be viewed and/or printed to access the indicated information.

The ***Index tab*** in Figure 5b is analogous to the index of an ordinary book. Type the first several letters of the topic you want to look up, click the topic when it appears in the window, then click the Display button to view the information. The Help screens are task-specific and provide easy-to-follow instructions.

The ***Find tab*** (not shown in Figure 5) contains a more extensive listing of entries than does the Index tab. It lets you enter a specific word (or Windows term), then it returns every Help screen that contains that word.

MICROSOFT ON THE WEB

The Microsoft Web site provides information beyond that found in the Help menu. Go to the Microsoft home page (www.microsoft.com), then click the Support tab where you choose the application. You will find articles about new features in the application, answers to frequently asked questions, as well as the knowledge base used by Microsoft support engineers.

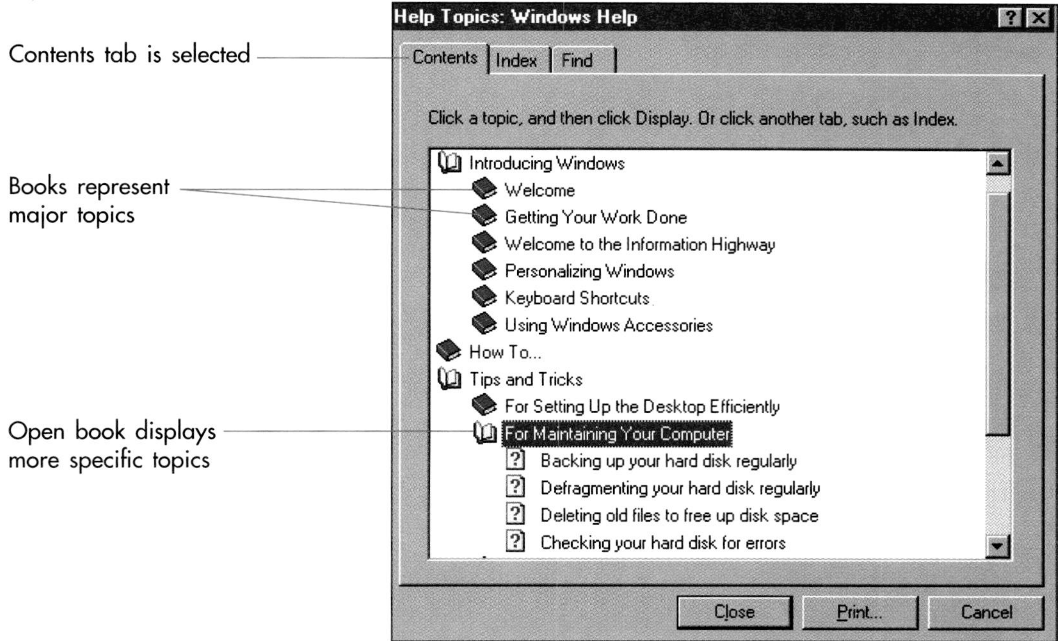

(a) Contents Tab

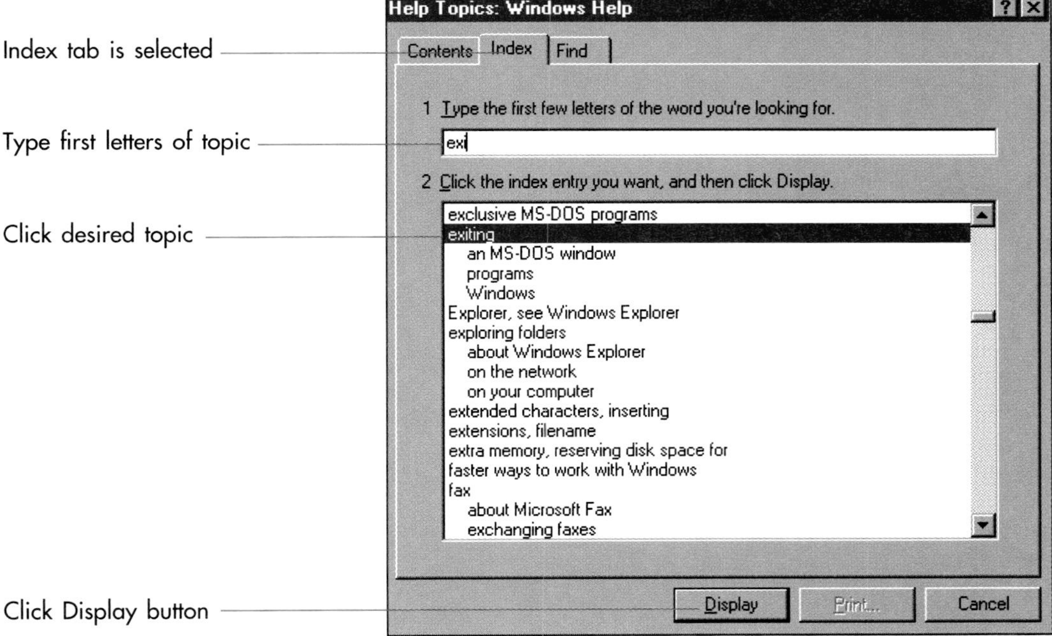

(b) Index Tab

FIGURE 5 The Help Command

FORMATTING A FLOPPY DISK

You will soon begin to work on the computer, which means that you will be using various applications to create different types of documents. Each document is saved in its own file and stored on disk, either on a hard disk (e.g., drive C) if you have your own computer, or on a floppy disk (drive A) if you are working in a computer lab at school.

Even if you have your own machine, however, you will want to copy files from the hard disk to a floppy disk for backup. Thus, you need to purchase a floppy disk(s), and further, you need to format the floppy disk so that it will be able to store the files you create. (You can purchase preformatted floppy disks, but it is very easy to format your own, and we provide instructions in the hands-on exercise that follows.) Be aware, however, that formatting erases any data that was previously on a disk, so be careful not to format a disk with important data (e.g., one containing today's homework assignment).

Formatting is accomplished through the ***Format command.*** The process is straightforward and has you enter all of the necessary information into a dialog box. One of the box's options is to copy system files onto the disk while formatting it. These files are necessary to start (boot) your computer, and if your hard disk were to fail, you would need a floppy disk with the system (and other) files in order to start the machine. (See Help for information on creating a ***boot disk*** containing the system files.) For ordinary purposes, however, you do not put the system files on a floppy disk because they take up space you could use to store data.

FORMAT AT THE PROPER CAPACITY

A floppy disk should be formatted at its rated capacity or else you may be unable to read the disk. There are two types of 3½-inch disks, double-density (720KB) and high-density (1.44MB). The easiest way to determine the type of disk you have is to look at the disk itself for the label DD or HD, for double- and high-density, respectively. You can also check the number of square holes in the disk; a double-density disk has one, whereas a high-density disk has two.

LEARNING BY DOING

Learning is best accomplished by doing, and so we come to the first of four hands-on exercises in this appendix. The exercises enable you to apply the concepts you have learned, then extend those concepts to further exploration on your own. The exercise welcomes you to Windows 95, shows you how to open, move, and size a window on the desktop, how to format a floppy disk, and how to use Help to install a screen saver.

A ***screen saver*** is a special program that protects your monitor by producing a constantly changing pattern after a designated period of inactivity. It is a delightful way to personalize your computer and an excellent illustration of how the Help menu can aid you in accomplishing a specific task. The answer to almost everything you need to know is found in one type of help or another. Start with the Help menu, then go to the Microsoft web site (www.microsoft.com) if you need additional information.

HANDS-ON EXERCISE 1

Welcome to Windows

Objective: To turn on the computer and start Windows; to use the Help facility; to open, move, and size a window; and to format a floppy disk. Use Figure 6 as a guide in the exercise.

STEP 1: Start the Computer

➤ The floppy drive should be empty prior to starting your machine. This ensures that the system starts by reading files from the hard disk (which contains the Windows files) as opposed to a floppy disk (which does not).

➤ The number and location of the on/off switches depend on the nature and manufacturer of the devices connected to the computer. The easiest possible setup is when all components of the system are plugged into a surge protector, in which case only a single switch has to be turned on. In any event, turn on the monitor, printer, and system unit.

➤ Your system will take a minute or so to get started after which you should see the desktop in Figure 6a. Do not be concerned if the appearance of your desktop is different from ours.

➤ You may see additional objects on the desktop in Windows 95 and/or the active desktop content in Windows 97.

Click the Start button to see a menu

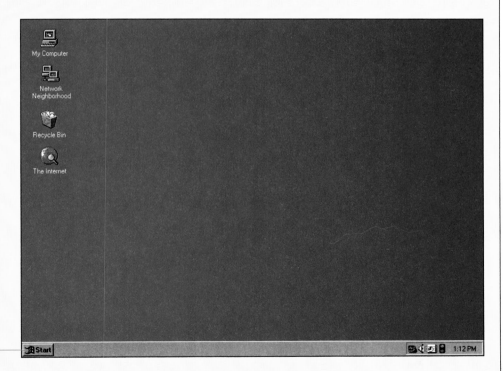

(a) Start the Computer (step 1)

FIGURE 6 Hands-on Exercise 1

STEP 2: Open My Computer

- Point to the **My Computer icon,** click the **right mouse button,** then click the **Open command** from the shortcut menu. (Alternatively, you can double click the icon to open it directly.)
- My Computer will open into a window as shown in Figure 6b. Do not be concerned if the contents of your window or its size and position on the desktop are different from ours.
- Pull down the **View menu** (point to the menu and click). Make or verify the following selections (you have to pull down the menu each time you choose a different command):
  - The **Toolbar command** should be checked. The Toolbar command functions as a toggle switch. Click the command and the toolbar is displayed; click the command a second time and the toolbar disappears.
  - The **Status bar command** should be checked. The status bar command also functions as a toggle switch.
  - **Large Icons** should be selected as the current view.
- Click the **Details button** on the toolbar to change to this view. Click the **Large Icons button** to return to this view.
- Pull down the **View menu** a final time. Click the **Arrange Icons command** and (if necessary) click the **AutoArrange command** so that a check appears.
- Click outside the menu (or press the **Esc key**) if the command is already checked.

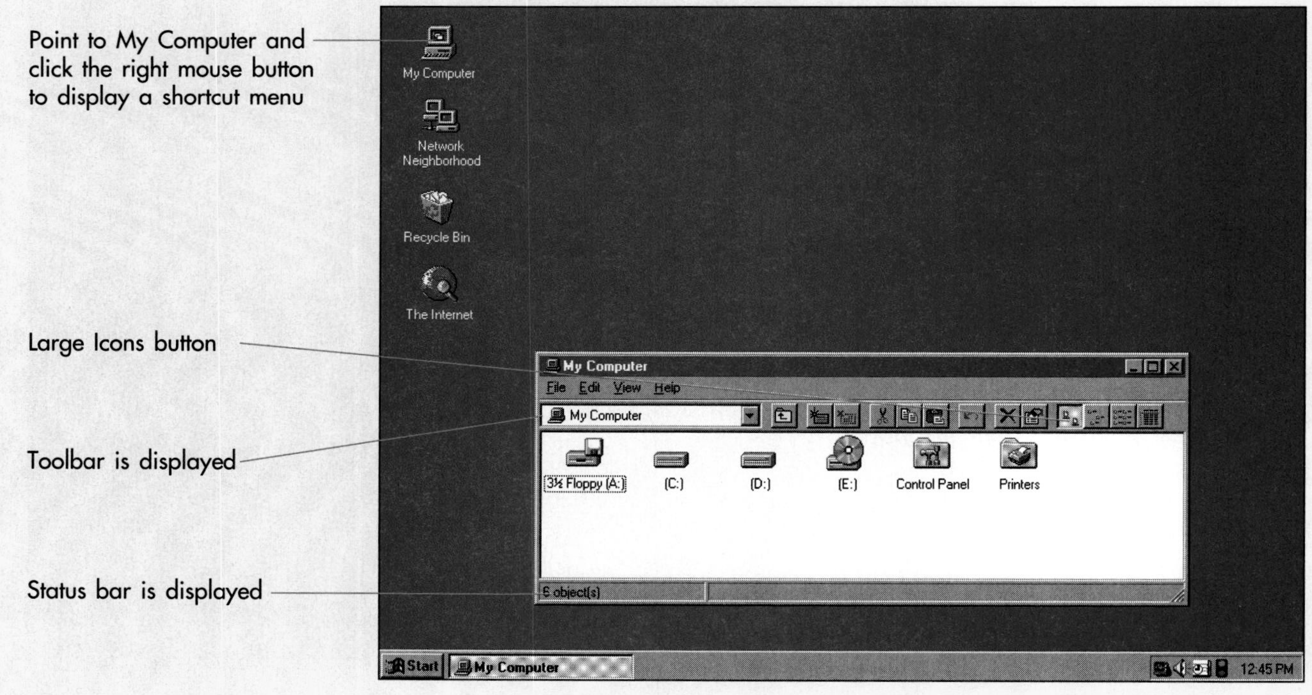

(b) My Computer (step 2)

FIGURE 6 Hands-on Exercise 1 (continued)

DESIGNATING THE DEVICES ON A SYSTEM

The first (usually only) floppy drive is always designated as drive A. (A second floppy drive, if it were present, would be drive B.) The first (often only) hard disk on a system is always drive C, whether or not there are one or two floppy drives. A system with one floppy drive and one hard disk (today's most common configuration) will contain icons for drive A and drive C. Additional hard drives (if any) and/or the CD-ROM are labeled from D on.

STEP 3: Move and Size a Window

- Click the **maximize button** so that the My Computer window expands to fill the entire screen.
- Click the **restore button** (which replaces the maximize button and is not shown in Figure 6c) to return the window to its previous size.
- Click the **minimize button** to shrink the My Computer window to a button on the taskbar. Click the My Computer button to reopen the window.
- Move and size the My Computer window on your desk to match the display in Figure 6c:

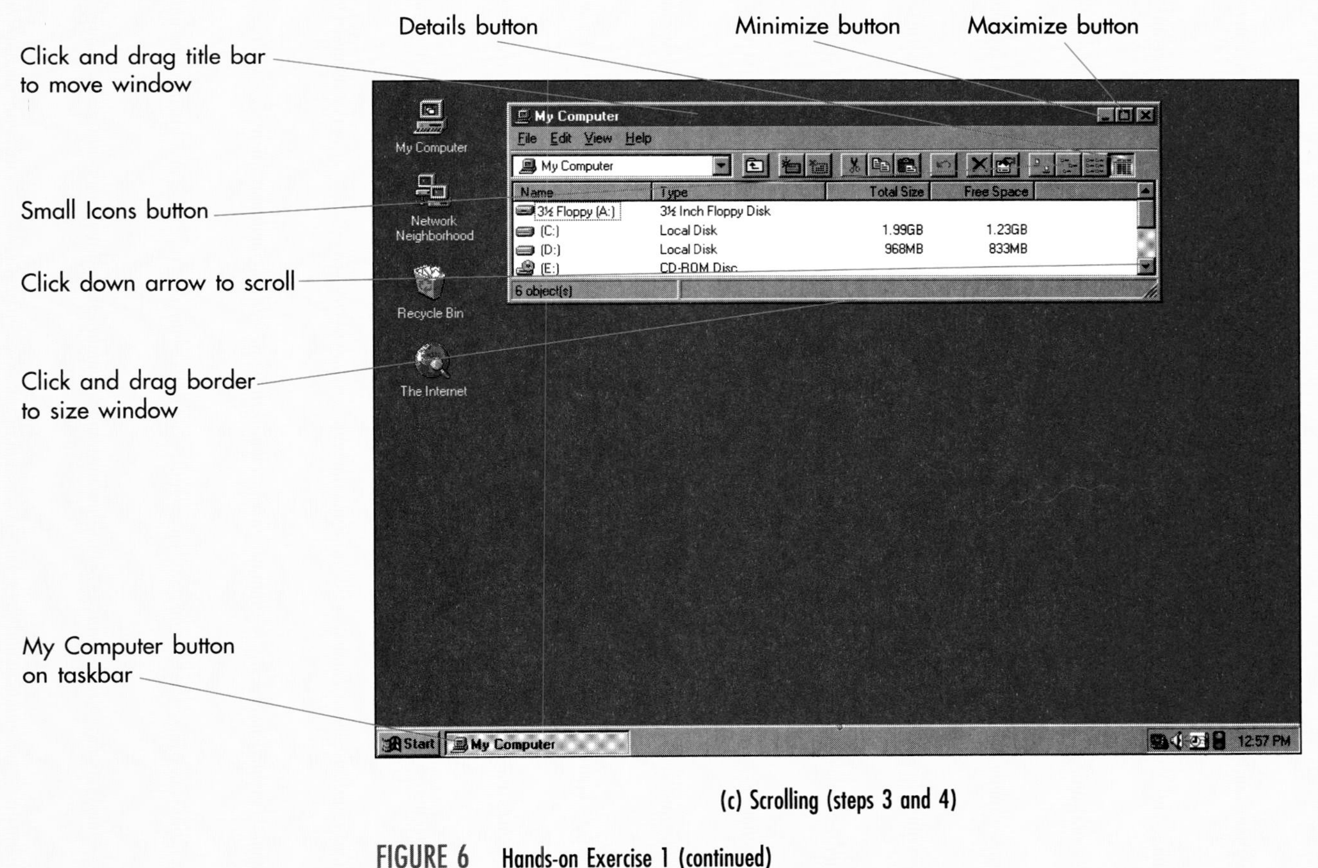

(c) Scrolling (steps 3 and 4)

FIGURE 6 Hands-on Exercise 1 (continued)

- To change the width or height of the window, click and drag a border (the mouse pointer changes to a double arrow) in the direction you want to go; drag the border inward to shrink the window or outward to enlarge it.
- To change the width and height at the same time, click and drag a corner rather than a border.
- To change the position of the window, click and drag the title bar.

➤ Click the **minimize button** to shrink the My Computer window to a button on the taskbar. My Computer is still open and remains active in memory.

➤ Click the **My Computer button** on the taskbar to reopen the window.

THE CONTROL PANEL

The Control Panel contains the utility programs (tools) used to change the hardware and/or software settings for the devices on your system (e.g., modem, monitor, mouse, and so on). Double click the Control Panel icon within My Computer to open the Control Panel window, then double click the icon of the device whose settings you want to modify. Additional information can be obtained through the Help facility.

STEP 4: Scrolling

➤ Pull down the **View menu** and click **Details** (or click the Details button on the toolbar). You are now in the Details view as shown in Figure 6c.

➤ If necessary, click and drag the bottom border of the window inward so that you see the vertical scroll bar in Figure 6c. The scroll bar indicates that the contents of the window are not completely visible.

➤ Click the **down arrow** on the scroll bar. The top line (for drive A) disappears from view and a new line containing the Control Panel comes into view.

➤ Click the **down arrow** a second time, which brings the Printers folder into view at the bottom of the window as the icon for drive C scrolls off the screen.

➤ Click the **Small icons** button on the toolbar. The scroll bar disappears because the contents of the window become completely visible.

➤ Click the **Details button** on the toolbar. The scroll bar returns because you can no longer see the complete contents. Move and/or size the window to your personal preference.

SCREENTIPS

Point to any button on the toolbar and Windows displays a ScreenTip containing the name of the button, which is indicative of its function. You can also point to other objects on the desktop to see similar ScreenTips. Point to the clock at the right end of the taskbar, for example, and you will see a ScreenTip with today's date. Point to the Start button and you will see a ScreenTip telling you to click here to begin.

STEP 5: Online Help

- Click the **Start button** on the taskbar, then click the **Help command** to display the Help Topics dialog box in Figure 6d.
- Click the **Index tab** as shown in Figure 6d. Type **For** (the first letters in formatting, the topic you are searching for). The Help system automatically displays the topics beginning with the letters you enter.
- Click **Disks** (under formatting) from the list of displayed topics, then click the **Display command button** (or double click the topic to avoid having to click the command button).
- The Help Topics dialog box is replaced by a Windows Help window with instructions on how to format a floppy disk.

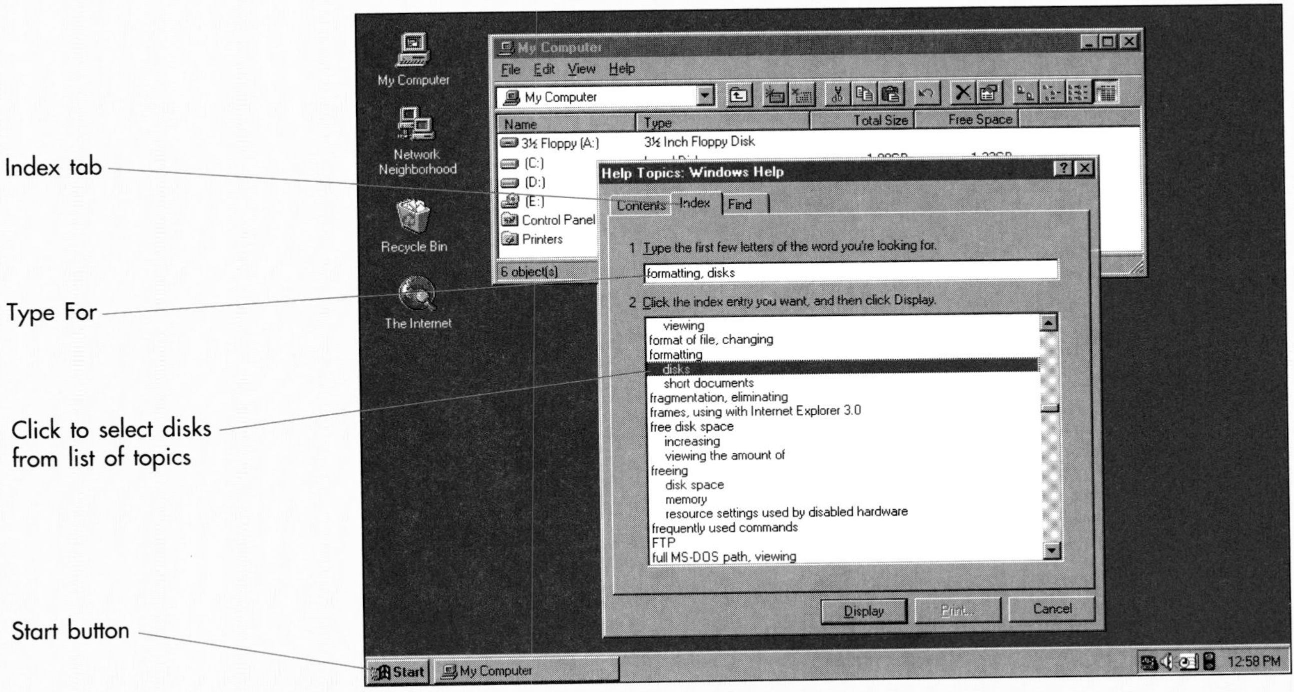

(d) The Help Command (step 5)

FIGURE 6 Hands-on Exercise 1 (continued)

PRINT THE HELP TOPIC

You can print the contents of any Help window by pointing anywhere within the window and clicking the right mouse button to display a shortcut menu. Click Print Topic, then click the OK command button in the resulting dialog box to print the topic.

STEP 6: Format a Floppy Disk

➤ Place a floppy disk in drive A. Remember, formatting erases everything on the disk, so be sure that you do not need anything on the disk you are about to format. Read the instructions in the Help window in Figure 6.3e, then follow our instructions, which provide more detail.

➤ Click the icon for **drive A.** Pull down the **File menu** and click **Format.** You will see the dialog box in Figure 6e.

- Set the **Capacity** to match the floppy disk you purchased (1.44MB for a high-density disk and 720KB for a double-density disk).
- Click the **Full option button** to choose a full format. This option is well worth the extra time as it ensures the integrity of your disk.
- Click the **Label text box** if it's empty or click and drag over the existing label if there is an entry. Enter a new label (containing up to 11 characters) such as **Bob's Disk** as shown in Figure 6e.
- Click the **Start command button** to begin the formatting operation. This will take about a minute and you can see the progress of the formatting process at the bottom of the dialog box.

➤ After the formatting process is complete, you will see an informational dialog box with the results of the formatting operation. Read the information, then click the **Close command button** to close the informational dialog box.

➤ Close the Format dialog box. Close the Help window.

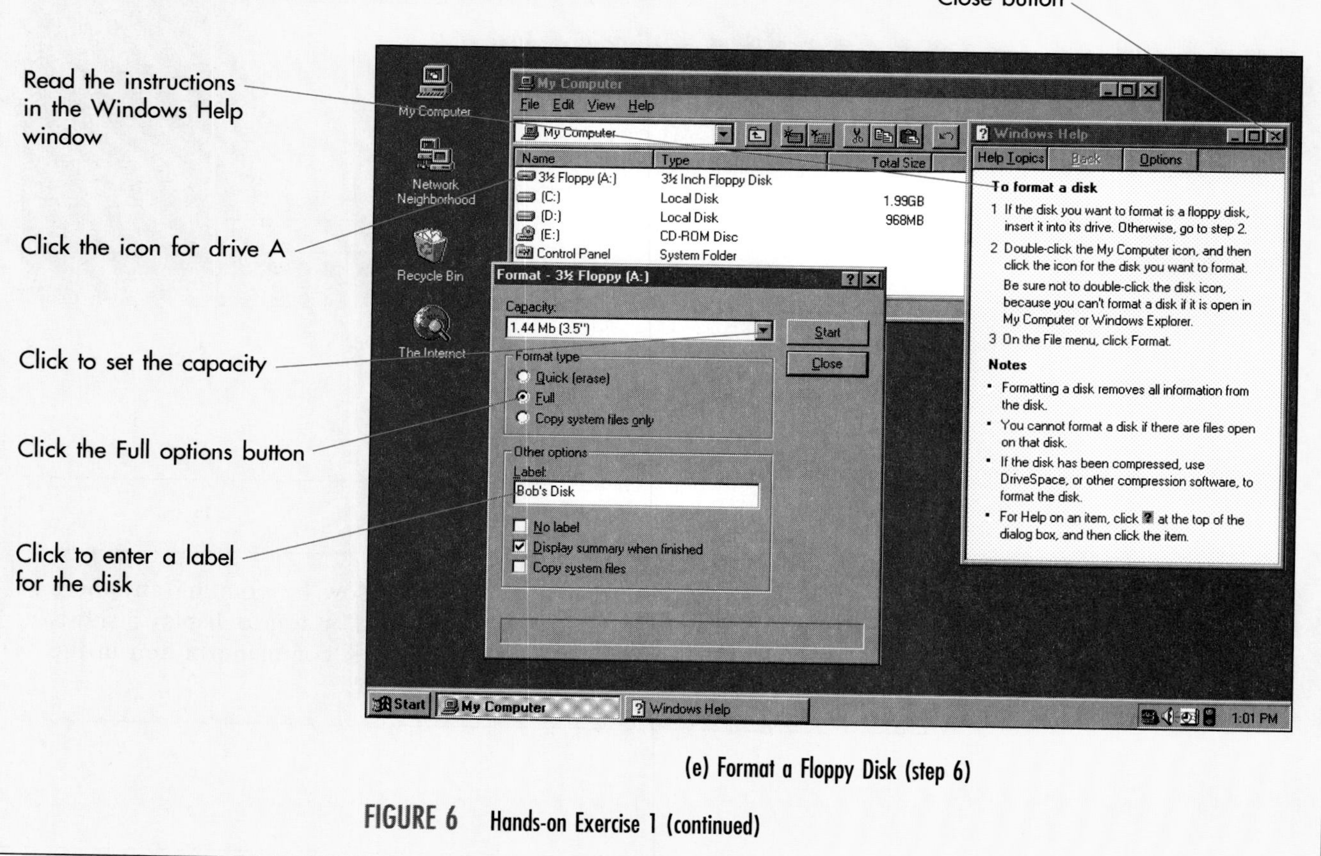

(e) Format a Floppy Disk (step 6)

FIGURE 6 Hands-on Exercise 1 (continued)

WHAT'S THIS?

The What's This button (a question mark) appears in the title bar of almost every dialog box. Click the question mark, then click the item you want information about (which then appears in a pop-up window). To print the contents of the pop-up window, click the right mouse button inside the window, and click Print Topic. Click outside the pop-up window to close the window and continue working.

STEP 7: Implement a Screen Saver

- If you are working in a lab environment, it is possible that your network administrator has disabled the ability to implement a screen saver, and that you will be unable to complete this step. If this is true at your site, skip the instructions below and go to step 8.
- Click the **Start button,** click the **Help command** to display the Help Topics dialog box, then click the **Index tab.** Type **Scr** (the first letters in *screen,* the topic you are searching for).
- Click **Screen Savers** from the list of displayed topics, then click the **Display button.** (You can also double click the topic to avoid having to click the command button.)
- You will see a second dialog box listing the available topics under Screen Savers. **Double click** the topic that begins **Protecting your screen.** You should see the Help window in Figure 6f. Click the **shortcut jump button** to display the Display Properties dialog box.
- Click the **drop-down arrow** in the Screen Saver box to display the available screen savers. Click one or more of the available screen savers until you come to one you like.
- Click the **OK command button** to accept the screen saver and exit the dialog box. Click the **Close button** to close the Windows Help window.

PROPERTIES EVERYWHERE

The fastest way to implement a screen saver (or to change the color or other properties of the desktop) is to display the Properties dialog box for the desktop. Point to the desktop, click the right mouse button to display a context-sensitive menu, then click Properties to open the Display Properties dialog box. Click the Screen Saver tab, make the appropriate selections, then click OK to accept the settings and close the dialog box.

STEP 8: Exit Windows

- Click the **Start button,** then click the **Shut Down command.** You will see a dialog box asking whether you're sure that you want to shut down the computer. (The option button to shut down the computer is already selected.)
- Click the **Yes command button,** then wait as Windows gets ready to shut down your system. Wait until you see another screen indicating that it is OK to turn off the computer.

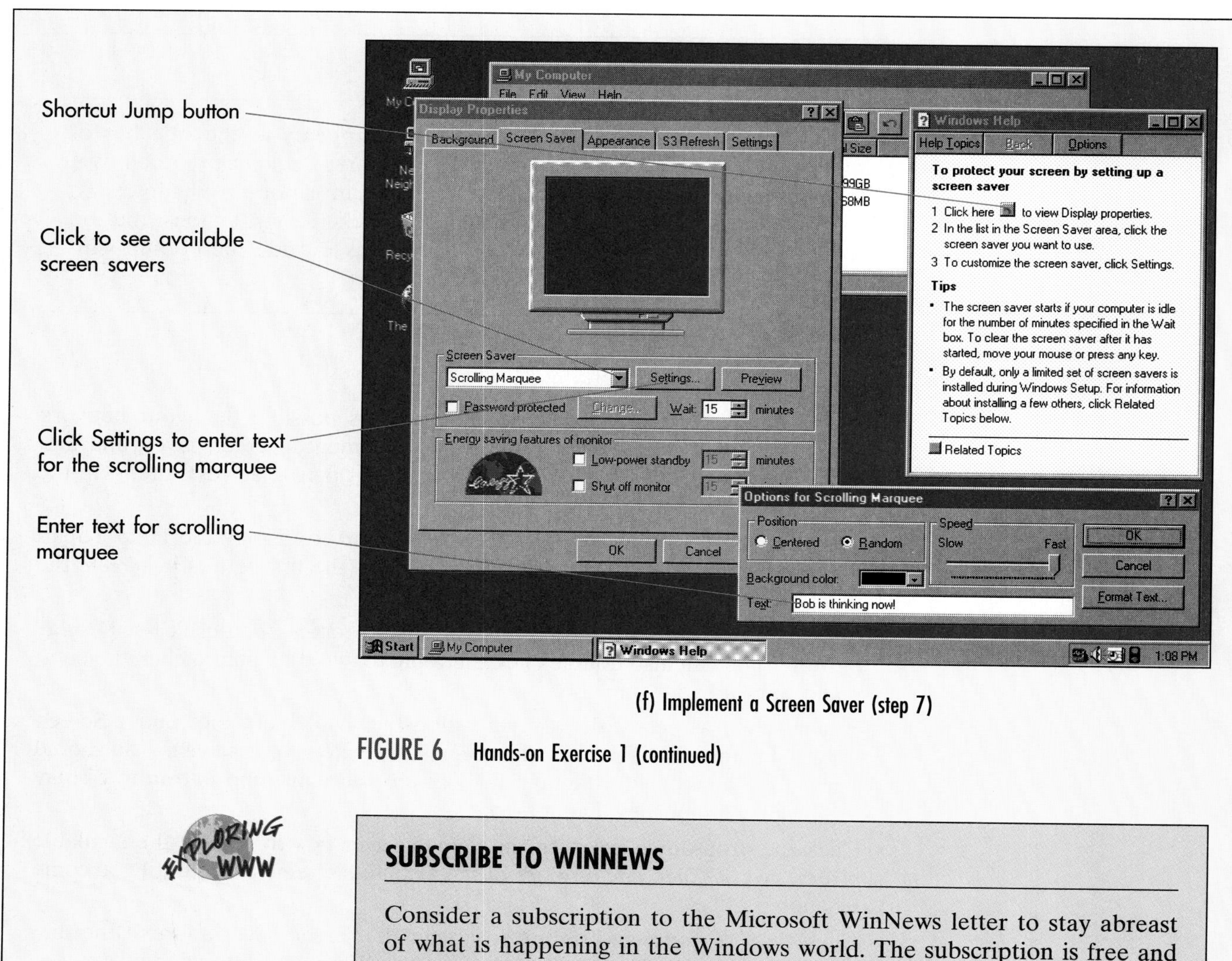

(f) Implement a Screen Saver (step 7)

FIGURE 6 Hands-on Exercise 1 (continued)

EXPLORING WWW

SUBSCRIBE TO WINNEWS

Consider a subscription to the Microsoft WinNews letter to stay abreast of what is happening in the Windows world. The subscription is free and the newsletter is delivered automatically to your e-mail address. To subscribe to the newsletter, send an e-mail message to enews99@microsoft.nwnet.com. The message should contain a single line with the text **Subscribe WinNews.**

FILES AND FOLDERS

The ultimate purpose of any computer system is to do useful work. This, in turn, requires the acquisition of various application software, such as Microsoft Office. Each document, spreadsheet, presentation, or database that you create is stored in a file on a disk, be it a hard disk or a floppy disk. It is important, therefore, that you understand the basics of file management so that you will be able to retrieve these files at a later time.

A ***file*** is data that has been given a name and stored on disk. There are, in general, two types of files, ***program files*** and ***data files.*** Microsoft Word and Microsoft Excel are program files. The documents and spreadsheets created by these programs are data files. A ***program file*** is executable because it contains instructions that tell the computer what to do. A ***data file*** is not executable and can be used only in conjunction with a specific program.

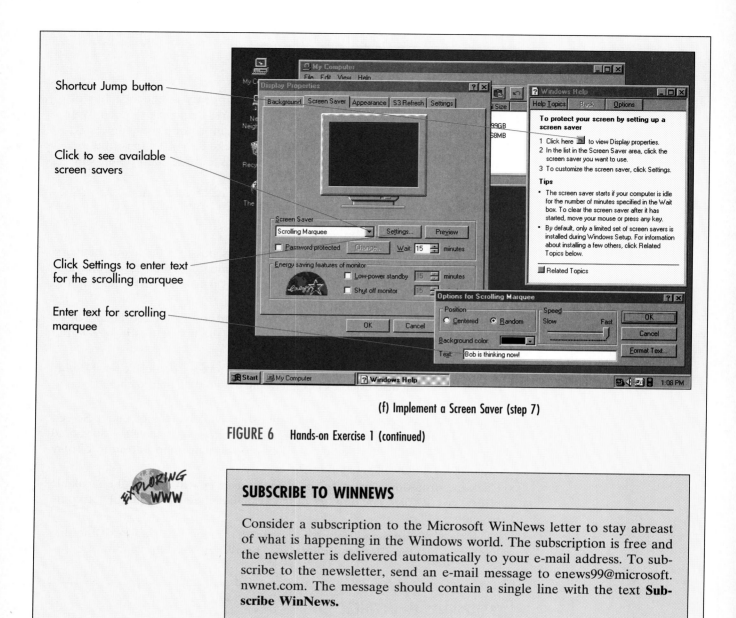

A file must have a name so that it can be identified. The file name can contain up to 255 characters and may include spaces and other punctuation. (This is very different from the rules that existed under MS-DOS, which limited file names to eight characters followed by an optional three-character extension.) Long file names permit descriptive entries such as *Term Paper for Western Civilization* (as opposed to a more cryptic *TPWCIV* that would be required under MS-DOS).

Files are stored in ***folders*** to better organize the hundreds (often thousands) of files on a hard disk. A Windows folder is similar in concept to a manila folder in a filing cabinet and contains one or more documents (files) that are somehow related to each other. An office worker stores his or her documents in manila folders. In Windows, you store your data files (documents) in electronic folders on disk.

Folders are the key to the Windows storage system. You can create any number of folders to hold your work just as you can place any number of manila folders into a filing cabinet. You can create one folder for your word processing documents and a different folder for your spreadsheets. Alternatively, you can create a folder to hold all of your work for a specific class, which may contain a combination of word processing documents and spreadsheets. The choice is entirely up to you and you can use any system that makes sense to you. Anything at all can go into a folder—program files, data files, even other folders.

Figure 7 displays two views of a folder containing six documents. The name of the folder (Homework) appears in the title bar next to the icon of an open folder. The minimize, maximize, and close buttons appear at the right of the title bar. A toolbar appears below the menu bar in each view.

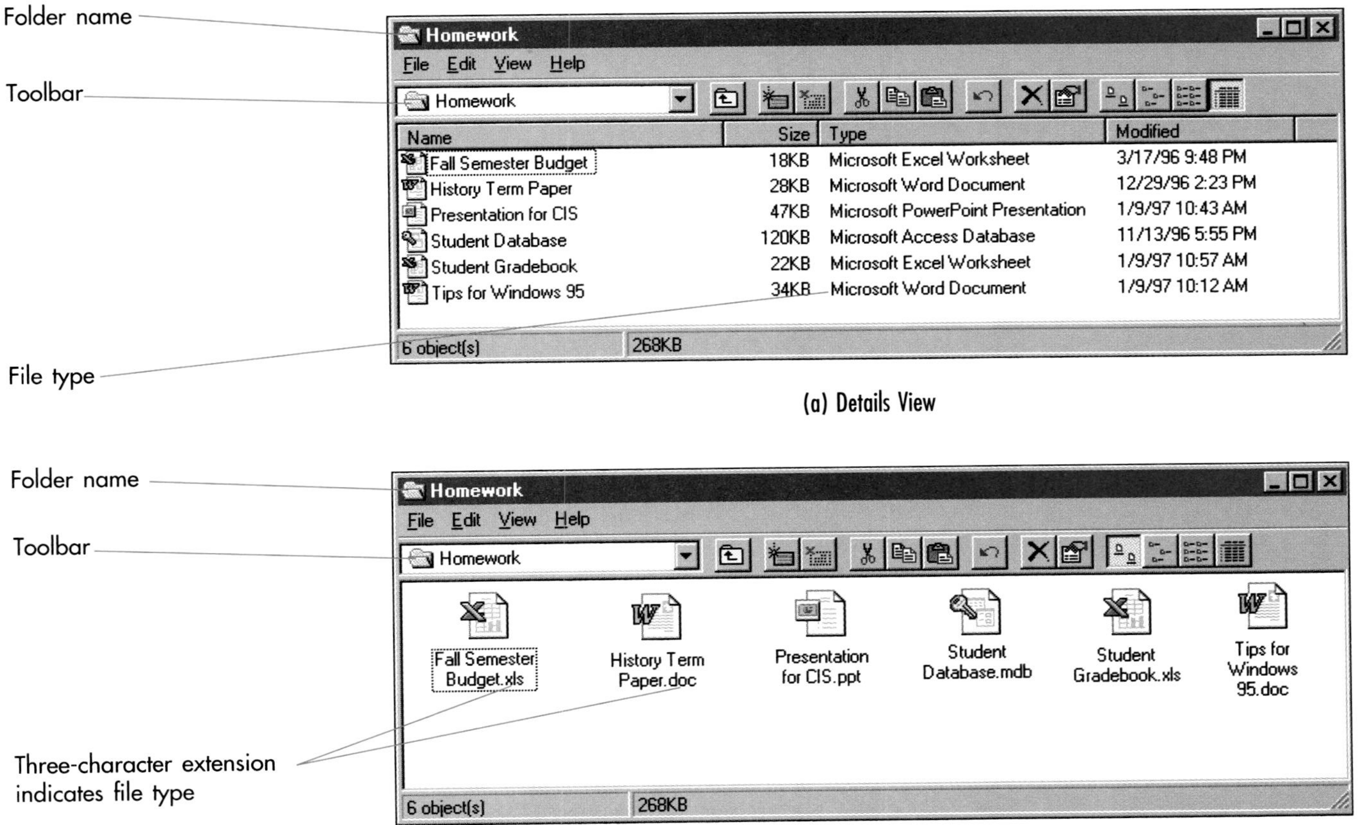

FIGURE 7 The Homework Folder

The Details view in Figure 7a displays a small icon representing the application that created the file. It also shows the name of each file in the folder (note the descriptive file name), the file size, the type of file, and the date and time the file was last modified. Figure 7b illustrates the Large Icons view, which displays only the file name and an icon representing the application that created the file. The choice between views depends on your personal preference. (A Small Icons view and List view are also available.)

File Type

Every data file has a specific ***file type*** that is determined by the application used to create the file. One way to recognize the file type is to examine the Type column in the Details view as shown in Figure 7a. The History Term Paper, for example, is a Microsoft Word document. The Student Gradebook is a Microsoft Excel worksheet.

You can also determine the file type (or associated application) from any view by examining the application icon displayed next to the file name. Look carefully at the icon next to the History Term Paper in Figure 7a, for example, and you will recognize the icon for Microsoft Word. The application icon is recognized more easily in the Large Icons view in Figure 7b.

Still another way to determine the file type is through a three-character extension, which is appended to the file name. (A period separates the filename from the extension.) Each application has a unique extension that is automatically assigned to the file name when the file is created. DOC and XLS, for example, are the extensions for Microsoft Word and Excel, respectively. The extension may be suppressed or displayed according to an option in the View menu of My Computer (or the Windows Explorer), but is best left suppressed in Windows 95/97.

My Computer

It is important to be able to locate a folder and/or its documents so that you can retrieve a document and go to work. Assume, for example, that you are looking for a term paper in American History that you began yesterday and saved in a folder called Homework. You know the folder is somewhere on drive C, but you are not quite sure where. You need to locate the folder in order to open the term paper and continue working. One way to accomplish this is through My Computer as shown in Figure 8.

You begin by double clicking the My Computer icon on the desktop to open the My Computer window and display the devices on your system. Next, you double click the icon for drive C since it contains the folder you are looking for. This opens a second window, which displays all of the folders on drive C. And finally, you double click the icon for the Homework folder to open a third window containing the documents in the Homework folder. Once in the Homework folder, you can double click the icon of an existing document, which starts the associated application and opens the document, enabling you to begin work.

The Exploring Windows Practice Files

There is only one way to master Windows 95 and that is to practice at the computer. One of the most important skills you need to acquire is that of file management; that is, you must be proficient in moving and copying files from one drive (or folder) to another. To do so requires that you have a series of files with which to work. Accordingly, we have created a set of practice files that we reference in the next several hands-on exercises. Your instructor will make these files available to you in a variety of ways:

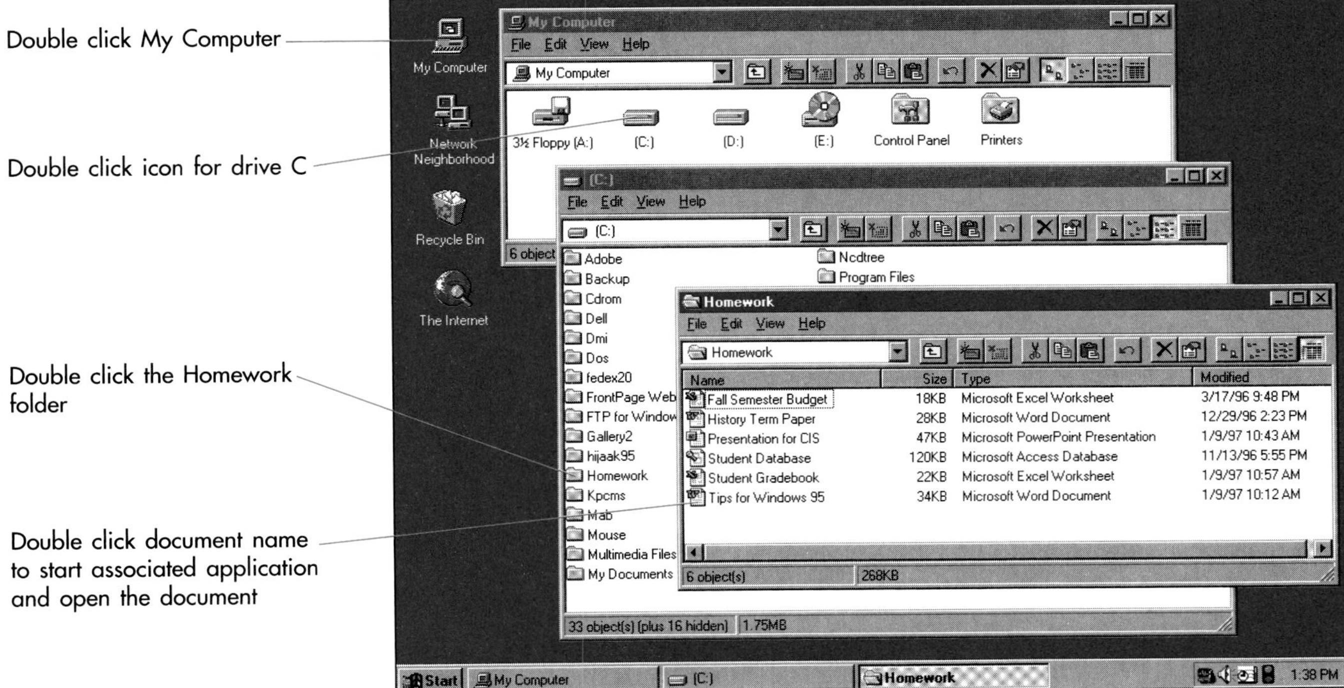

Double click My Computer
Double click icon for drive C
Double click the Homework folder
Double click document name to start associated application and open the document

FIGURE 8 Browsing My Computer

- The files can be downloaded from our Web site, as described in the next hands-on exercise. This assumes you have access to the Internet, and further, that you have a basic proficiency with a browser such as the ***Internet Explorer.***
- The files might be on a network drive, in which case you can use My Computer (or the Windows Explorer, which is discussed later in the chapter) to copy the files from the network drive to a floppy disk. The procedure to do this is described in hands-on exercise 3 later in the chapter.
- There may be an actual data disk in the computer lab. Go to the lab with a floppy disk, then use the Copy Disk command to duplicate the data disk to create a copy for yourself.

It doesn't matter how you obtain the practice files, only that you are able to do so. Indeed, you may try different techniques in order to gain additional practice with the Windows environment. All three methods will place the practice files on a floppy disk; hence you need the formatted floppy disk that was created in the first hands-on exercise. Note, too, the techniques described in the hands-on exercises apply to the practice files for any book in the *Exploring Windows* series.

EXPLORING WWW

THE EXPLORING WINDOWS SERIES

The text you are reading is one of several books in the *Exploring Windows* series, many of which reference a series of practice files for use with the hands-on exercises. One way to access these files is from the Prentice Hall Web site at www.prenhall.com/grauer. You can also go to Bob Grauer's home page (www.bus.miami.edu/~rgrauer) and click the *Exploring Windows* link. Bob's home page also provides links to the classes he is teaching at the University of Miami.

HANDS-ON EXERCISE 2

The Practice Files (via the World Wide Web)

Objective: To download the practice files from the *Exploring Windows* Web site. The exercise requires a formatted floppy disk and access to the Internet. Use Figure 9 as a guide in the exercise.

STEP 1: The *Exploring Windows* Series

- Start Internet Explorer. If you are working in class, your instructor will provide additional instructions. At home, however, it is incumbent on you to be able to know how to access the Internet.
- If necessary, click the **maximize button** so that the Internet Explorer takes the entire desktop. Enter the address of the site you want to visit as shown in Figure 9a.
  - Pull down the **File menu,** click the **Open command** to display the Open dialog box, and enter **www.prenhall.com/grauer** (the http:// is assumed). Click **OK.**
  - *Or,* click in the **Address box** below the toolbar, which automatically selects the current address (so that whatever you type replaces the current address). Enter the address of the site you want to visit, **www.prenhall.com/grauer** (the http:// is assumed). Press the **enter key.**
- You should see the *Exploring Windows* home page as shown in Figure 9a. Click the book **Exploring Office 97** to display the page for this series. Click the link to **Office 97.**

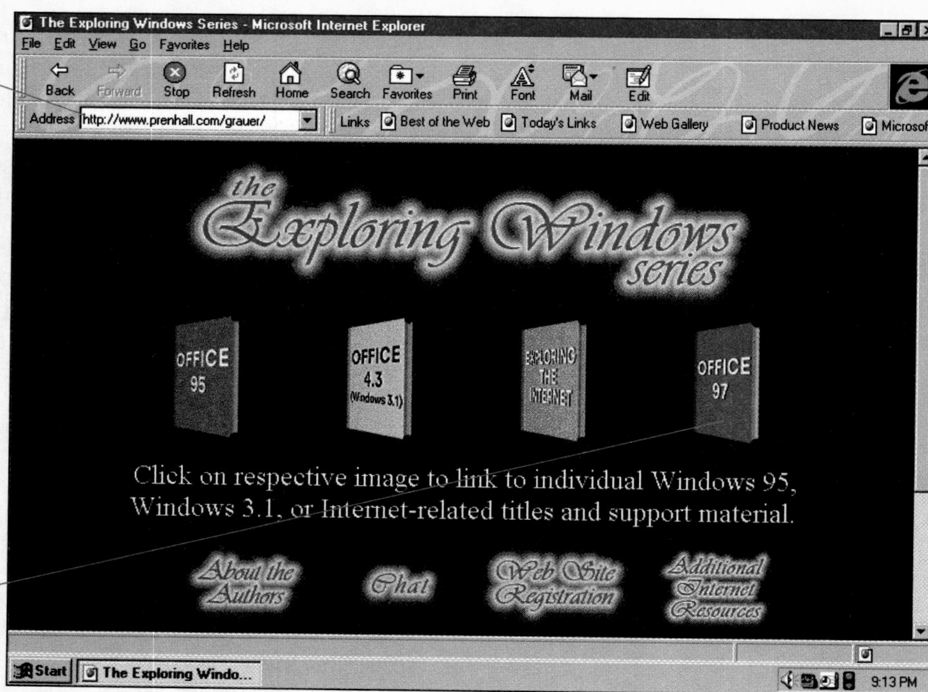

(a) The *Exploring Windows* series (step 1)

FIGURE 9 Hands-on Exercise 2

UNABLE TO LOCATE SERVER OR SERVER NOT RESPONDING

Two things must occur in order for Internet Explorer to display the requested document—it must locate the server on which the document is stored, and it must be able to connect to that computer. The error message "Unable to Locate Server" will appear if you enter the Web address incorrectly. Click the Address bar and re-enter the Web address, being sure to enter it correctly. You may also see the message "Server Down or Not Responding," which implies that Internet Explorer located the server but was unable to connect because the site is busy. This means that too many visitors are already there and you need to try again later in the day.

STEP 2: Download the Practice Files

- You should see a screen listing the various books for Office 97. Click the link to **Windows Prerequisites** to display the screen in Figure 9b. (The Save As dialog box is not yet visible.)
- Click **prerequisites.exe** (the file you will download to your PC). The File Download window opens, and after a few seconds, an Internet Explorer dialog box opens as well. The option button to **Save it to disk** is selected. Click **OK** to display the Save As dialog box in Figure 9b:
  - The **desktop** is selected as the destination in the Save in box. If this is not the case, click the **drop-down arrow** on the Save in box and select the desktop. Click **Save** to download the file.

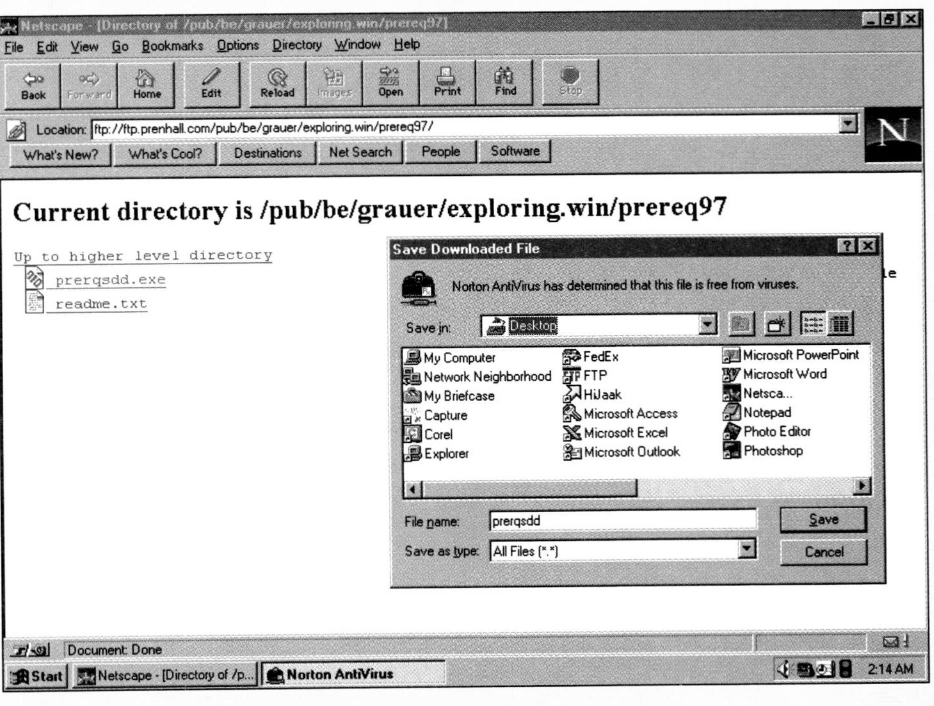

(b) Download the Practice Files (step 2)

FIGURE 9 Hands-on Exercise 2 (continued)

- If you are unable to save to the desktop because your network administrator has disabled this capability at your site, select drive A in the Save in box instead of the desktop (place a formatted floppy disk in drive A).

➤ The File Download window will reappear on your screen and show you the process of the downloading operation. Be patient, as this may take a few minutes. (The Exploring Prerequisites file is 52KB in size.) The File Download window will close automatically when downloading is complete.

➤ Minimize (do not close) Internet Explorer. The Internet Explorer window shrinks to a button on the taskbar, but the application remains open in memory. (We return to Internet Explorer in step 5.)

ABOUT INTERNET EXPLORER

Pull down the Help menu and click About Internet Explorer to see which version of the Internet Explorer you are using. Our exercises were done with Version 3.00, but you may have a later version if you installed the software after publication of our text. The command structure may vary slightly from one version to the next, but you should be able to complete the exercise without a problem, as long as you are running Version 3.00 or higher.

STEP 3: Install the Practice Files

➤ Double click the **Prerequisites icon** from the desktop or drive A, depending on where you downloaded the file.

- If you downloaded the file to the desktop, the Prerequisites icon should be visible on the desktop and you can simply double click the icon.
- If you downloaded the file to a floppy disk, double click the **My Computer icon** on the desktop to open the My Computer window, double click the icon for **drive A,** then double click the **Prerequisites icon.**

➤ You will see a dialog box thanking you for selecting the *Exploring Windows* series. Click **OK** when you have finished reading the dialog box to begin (or cancel) the installation.

FILE COMPRESSION

Software and other files are typically compressed to reduce the amount of storage space a file requires on disk and/or the time it takes to download the file. In essence, you download a compressed file from a Web site, then you uncompress the file on a local drive. Ideally a compressed file is created as a self-extracting (executable) file as opposed to a zip file, which requires a utility program outside Windows 95. Our files are executable. Thus, all you have to do is double click the executable file after it has been downloaded, and it will automatically install (uncompress) the practice files for you.

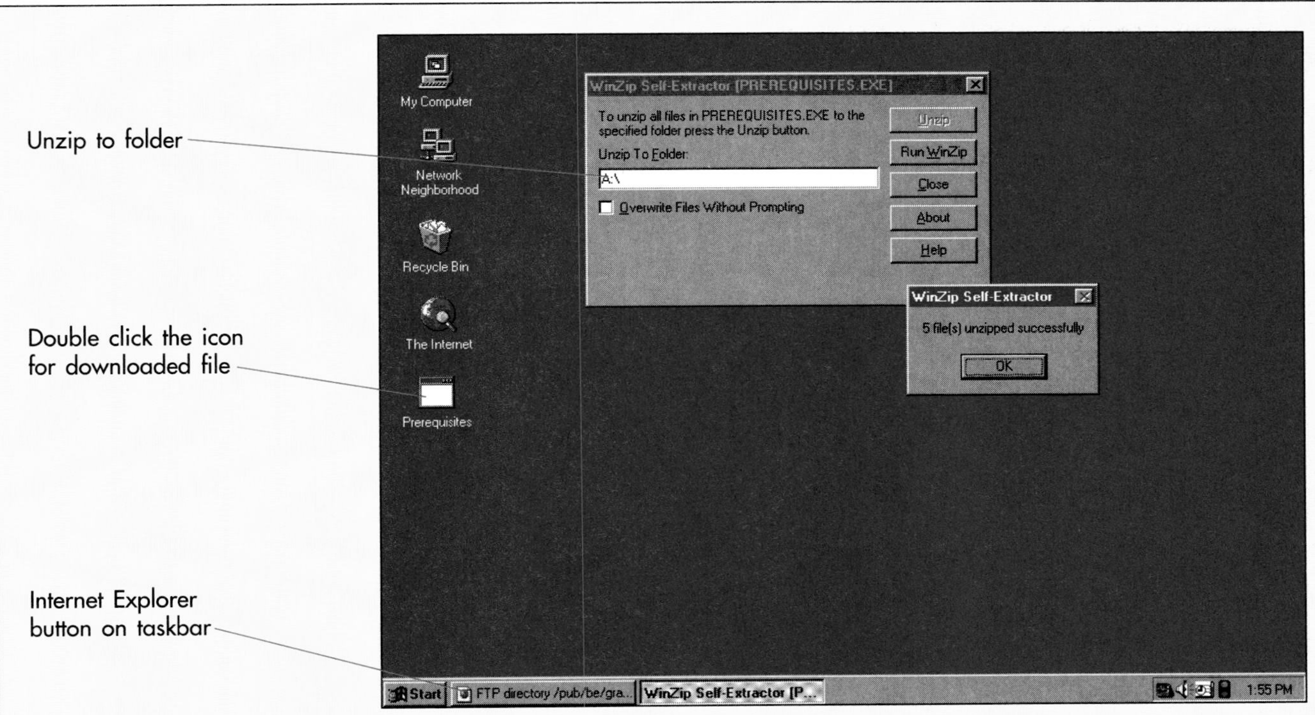

(c) Install the Practice Files (step 3)

FIGURE 9 Hands-on Exercise 2 (continued)

- If necessary, place a floppy disk in drive A, then verify that the Unzip to Folder text box is specified as A:\ (the floppy disk). If it is not, enter **A:** in the text box as shown in Figure 9c.
- Click the **Unzip button** to extract the practice files and copy them into the designated folder.
- Click **OK** after you see the message indicating that the files have been unzipped successfully. Close the WinZip dialog box.
- The practice files have been extracted and copied to drive A.

STEP 4: Open My Computer

- Double click **My Computer** to open the My Computer window in Figure 9d. If necessary, pull down the **View menu** to display the toolbar. Click the **Large Icons view.**
- Double click the icon for **drive A** to open a second window, which displays the contents of drive A. Use the **View menu** to display the toolbar, then change to the **Details view.**
- You should see five files, which are the practice files on the data disk. (There are three Word files, one Excel file, and one PowerPoint file.) These are the files that will be used in a hands-on exercise later in the chapter.
- Select (click) the **Prerequisites icon** on the desktop. Press the **Del key** to erase this file as it is no longer needed. Click **Yes** when asked whether to remove this file.
- Close the windows for drive A and My Computer as they are no longer needed in this exercise.

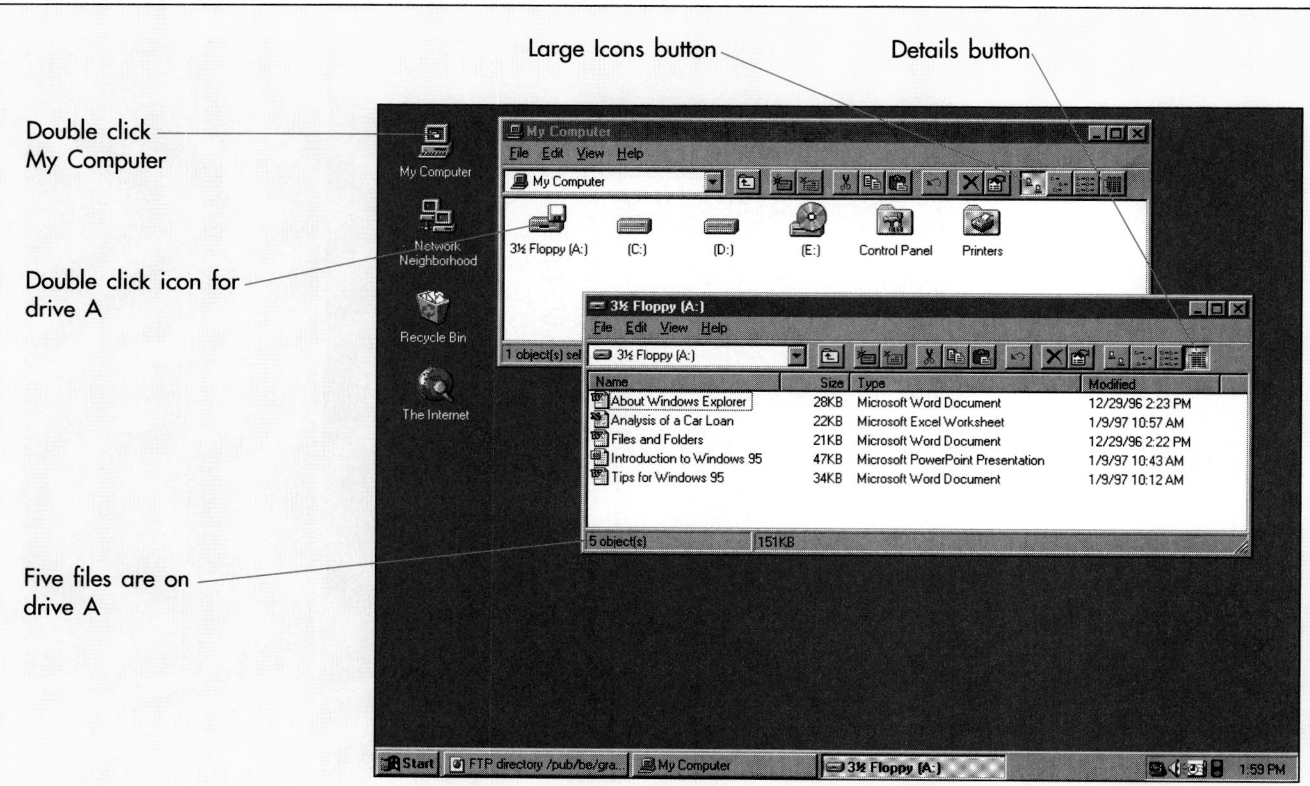

(d) Open My Computer (step 4)

FIGURE 9 Hands-on Exercise 2 (continued)

ONE WINDOW OR MANY

By default, My Computer opens a new window every time you open a new drive or folder. The multiple windows can clutter a desktop rather quickly, and hence you may prefer to change the display in the current window to the new drive or folder rather than open a new window. Pull down the View menu, click Options, click the Folder tab, then click the option button to browse folders using a single window.

STEP 5: Microsoft on the Web

- Click the **Internet Explorer button** on the taskbar to return to Internet Explorer. Click in the **Address box** below the toolbar. Enter **www.microsoft.com** Press the **enter key.**
- You should see Microsoft's home page. Click the link to **Products,** then scroll until you can click the link to **Windows 95** to display the page in Figure 9e.
- Your screen will be different from ours, as Microsoft is continually updating its information. Click any links that appeal to you to view additional information that is available from Microsoft via the Web.

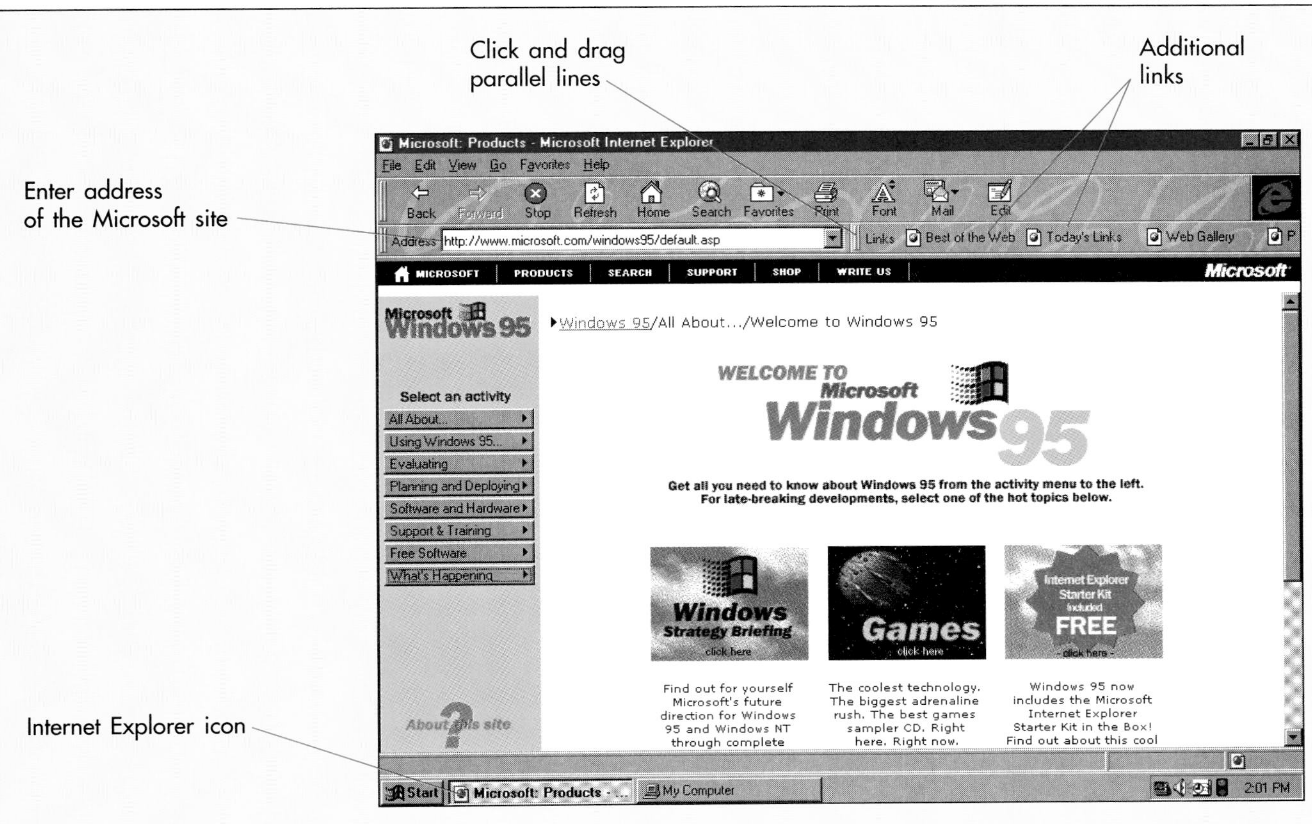

(e) Windows 95 Home Page (step 5)

FIGURE 9 Hands-on Exercise 2 (continued)

- You may also want to view additional sites suggested by Internet Explorer. If necessary, click and drag the parallel lines that appear to the right of the address box (the mouse pointer changes to a two-headed arrow) to display additional links.
- Click the **Best of the Web** or the **Today's Links button** to explore the current cool sites suggested by Internet Explorer.
- We don't know what you will find, but you can expect something interesting every day.
- Click the hyperlinks that interest you and off you go. Happy surfing!

SET A TIME LIMIT

We warn you that the Web is addictive, and that once you start surfing, it is difficult to stop. We suggest, therefore, that you set a time limit before you begin, and that you stick to it. Tomorrow is another day, with new places to explore.

One of the most important skills you need to acquire is the ability to locate a specific folder or file so that you can go to work. In essence you need to be able to copy, move, rename, and even delete the various files and folders on your system. There are two basic ways to accomplish these tasks. You can use My Computer to open successive windows until you come to the file or folder you are looking for. Alternatively, you can use the ***Windows Explorer*** to locate the object by navigating the hierarchical structure of your system. The difference between the two is shown in Figure 10.

Assume, for example, that you are taking five classes this semester, and that you are using the computer in each course. You've created a separate folder to hold the work for each class and have stored the contents of all five folders on a single floppy disk. Assume further that you need to retrieve your third English assignment so that you can modify it and submit the revised version.

You can use My Computer to browse the system as shown in Figure 10a. You would start by opening My Computer, double clicking the icon for drive A to open a second window, then double clicking the icon for the English folder to display its documents. The process is intuitive, but it can quickly lead to a desktop cluttered with open windows. And what if you next needed to work on a paper for Art History? That would require you to open the Art History folder, which produces yet another open window on the desktop.

The Windows Explorer in Figure 10b offers a more sophisticated way to browse the system, as it shows both the hierarchy of folders and the contents of the selected folder. The Explorer window is divided into two panes. The left pane contains a ***tree diagram*** of the entire system showing all drives and, optionally, the folders in each drive. One (and only one) object is always selected in the left pane, and its contents are displayed automatically in the right pane.

Look carefully at the tree diagram in Figure 10b and note that the English folder is currently selected. The icon for the selected folder is an open folder to differentiate it from the other folders, which are closed and are not currently selected. The right pane displays the contents of the selected folder (English in Figure 10b) and is seen to contain three documents, Assignments 1, 2, and 3. The right pane is displayed in the Details view, but could just as easily have been displayed in another view (e.g., Large or Small Icons) by clicking the appropriate button on the toolbar.

As indicated, only one folder can be selected (open) at a time in the left pane, and its contents are displayed in the right pane. To see the contents of a different folder (e.g., Accounting), you would click the Accounting folder, which automatically closes the English folder and opens the Accounting folder.

The tree diagram in the left pane displays the drives and their folders in hierarchical fashion. The desktop is always at the top of the hierarchy and contains My Computer, which in turn contains various drives, each of which contains folders, which in turn contain documents and/or additional folders. Each object may be expanded or collapsed by clicking the plus or minus sign, respectively.

Look again at the icon next to My Computer in Figure 10b and you see a minus sign, indicating that My Computer has been expanded to show the various drives on the system. There is also a minus sign next to the icon for drive A to indicate that it too has been expanded to show the folders on the disk. Note, however, the plus sign next to drives C and D, indicating that these parts of the tree are currently collapsed and thus their subordinates are not visible.

A folder may contain additional folders and thus individual folders may also be expanded or collapsed. The minus sign next to the Finance folder in Figure 10b, for example, shows that the folder has been expanded and contains two

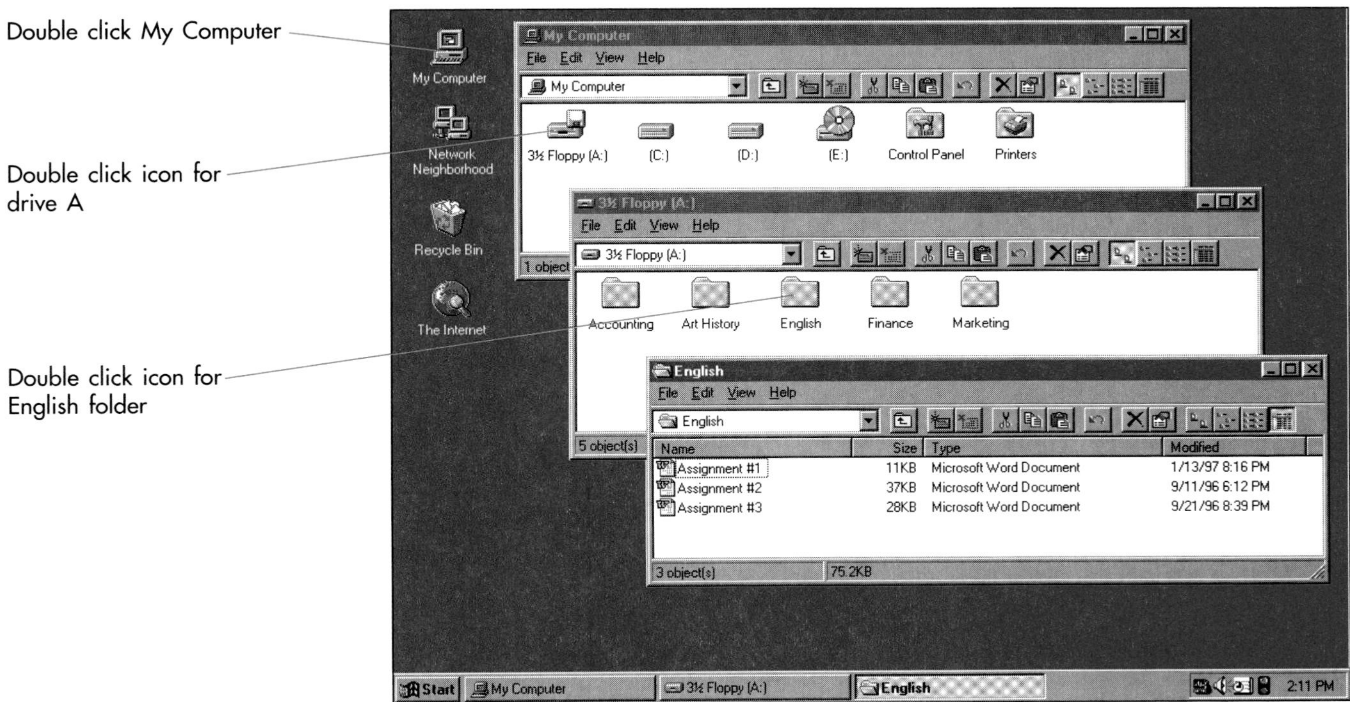

(a) My Computer

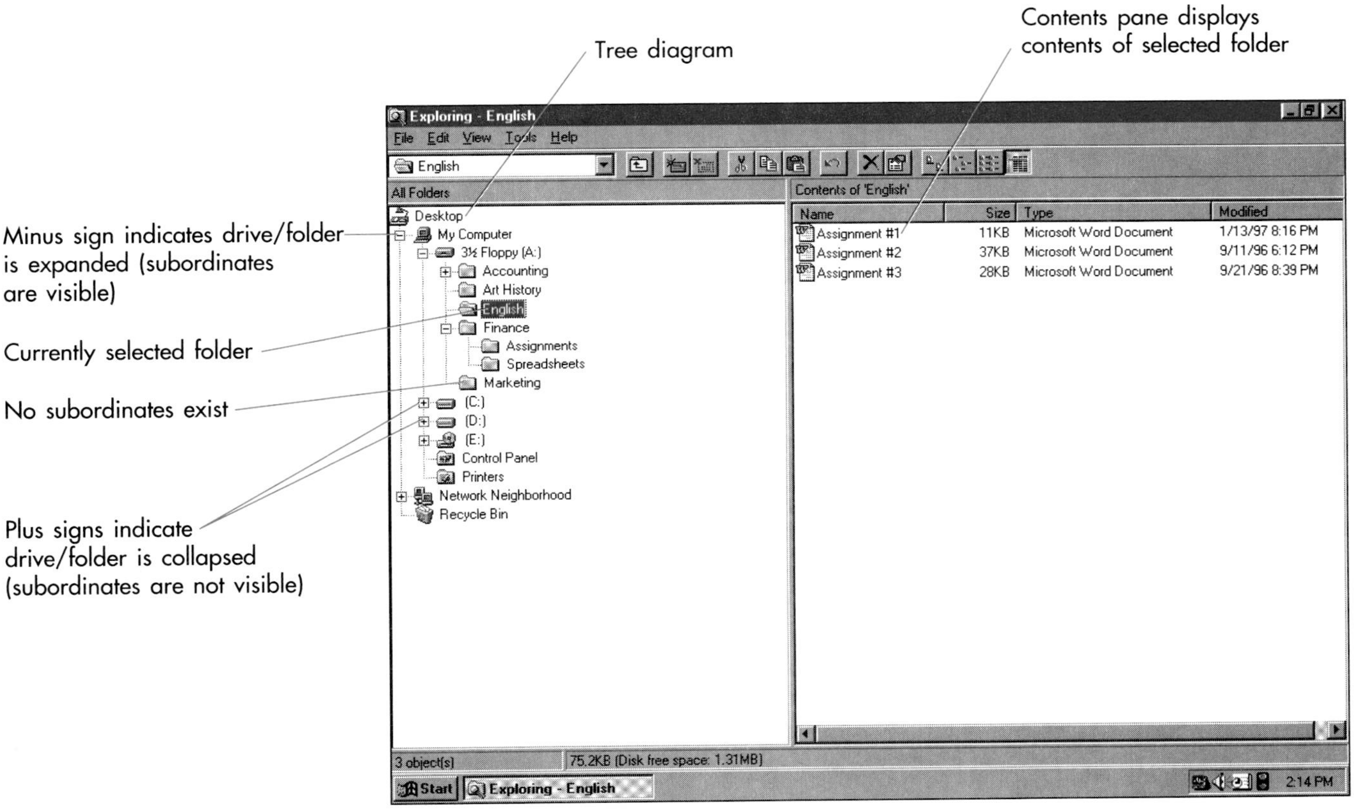

Tree diagram

Contents pane displays contents of selected folder

Minus sign indicates drive/folder is expanded (subordinates are visible)

Currently selected folder

No subordinates exist

Plus signs indicate drive/folder is collapsed (subordinates are not visible)

(b) Windows Explorer

FIGURE 10 Working with Files and Folders

additional folders, for Assignments and Spreadsheets, respectively. The plus sign next to the Accounting folder, however, indicates the opposite; that is, the folder is collapsed and its subordinate folders are not currently visible. A folder with neither a plus or minus sign, such as Art History or Marketing, does not contain additional folders and cannot be expanded or collapsed.

The advantage of the Windows Explorer over My Computer is the uncluttered screen and ease with which you switch from one folder to the next. If, for example, you wanted to see the contents of the Art History folder, all you would do would be to click its icon in the left pane, which automatically changes the display in the right pane to show the documents in Art History. The Explorer also makes it easy to move or copy a file from one folder or drive to another, as you will see in the hands-on exercise, which follows shortly.

ORGANIZE YOUR WORK

Organize your folders in ways that make sense to you, such as a separate folder for every class you are taking. You can also create folders within folders; for example, a correspondence folder may contain two folders of its own, one for business correspondence and one for personal letters. Use descriptive names for your folders so that you will remember their contents. (A name may contain up to 255 characters, including spaces.)

The Practice Files

As indicated, there are several ways to obtain the practice files associated with the various books in the *Exploring Windows* series. You can download the files from our Web site as described in the previous hands-on exercise. Alternatively, you can use the Windows Explorer to copy the files from a network drive (at school) to a floppy disk, as will be demonstrated in the following hands-on exercise.

The Windows Explorer is especially useful for moving or copying files from one folder or drive to another. You simply select (open) the folder that contains the file, use the scroll bar in the left pane (if necessary) so that the destination folder is visible, then click and drag the file(s) from the right pane to the destination folder. The Explorer is a powerful tool, but it takes practice to master.

EXPLORE THE PRACTICE FILES

The practice files are intended to teach you the basics of file management, but they are also interesting in and of themselves. The *Tips for Windows 95* document, for example, contains several tips that appeared throughout this appendix. The *Introduction to Windows 95* presentation summarizes much of the material in this appendix. *Analysis of a Car Loan* is an Excel workbook that computes a monthly car payment based on the cost of a car and the parameters of a loan. Double click any of these files from within the Windows Explorer to start the application and load the document.

HANDS-ON EXERCISE 3

The Practice Files (via a local area network)

Objective: To use the Windows Explorer to copy the practice files from a network drive to a floppy disk. The exercise requires a formatted floppy disk and access to a local area network. Use Figure 11 as a guide in the exercise.

STEP 1: Start the Windows Explorer

- Click the **Start Button,** click (or point to) the **Programs command,** then click **Windows Explorer** to start this program. Click the **maximize button** so that the Explorer takes the entire desktop as shown in Figure 11a. Do not be concerned if your screen is different from ours.
- Make or verify the following selections using the **View menu.** (You have to pull down the View menu each time you choose a different command.)
  - The **Toolbar command** should be checked.
  - The **Status bar command** should be checked.
  - The **Large Icons view** should be selected.
- Click (select) the **Desktop icon** in the left pane to display the contents of the desktop in the right pane.
- Our desktop contains only the icons for My Computer, Network Neighborhood, the Recycle Bin, and the Internet icon. Your desktop may have different icons, but your screen should otherwise match Figure 11a.

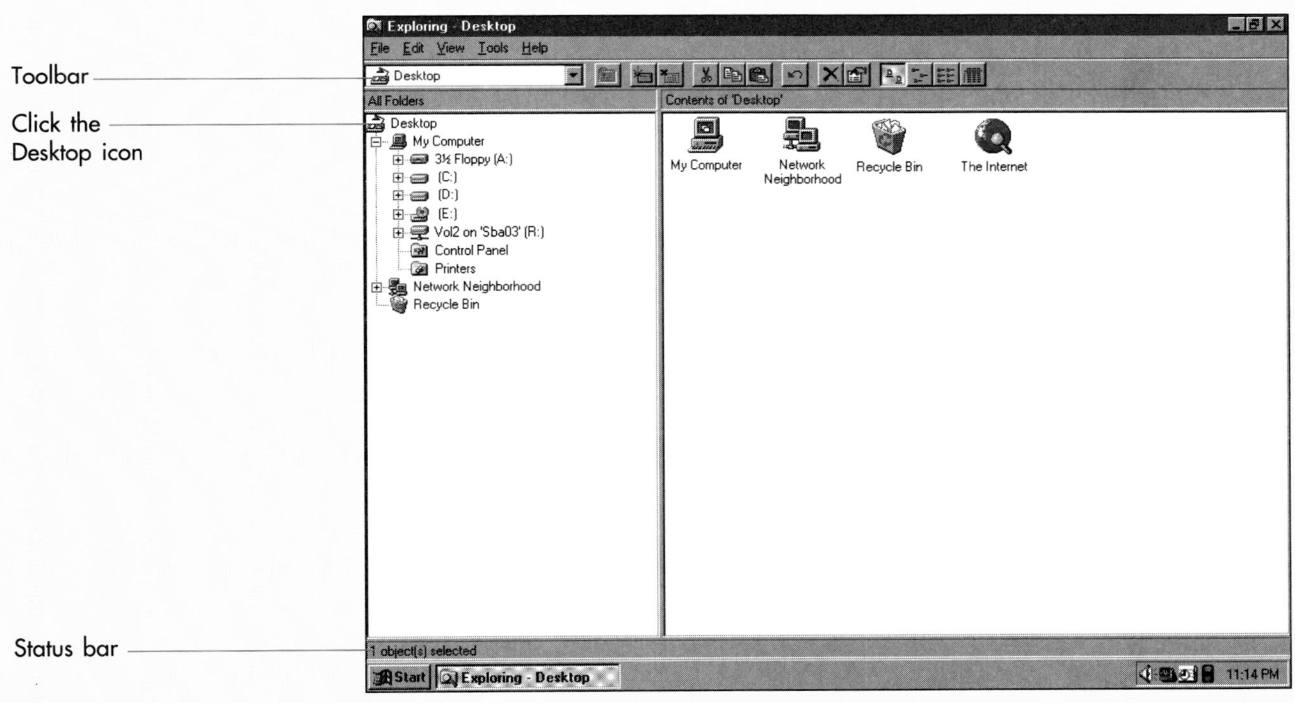

(a) Start the Windows Explorer (step 1)

FIGURE 11 Hands-on Exercise 3

FILE EXTENSIONS

Long-time DOS users remember a three-character extension at the end of a file name to indicate the file type—for example, DOC or XLS to indicate a Word document or Excel workbook, respectively. The extensions are displayed or hidden according to the option you establish through the View menu of the Windows Explorer. Pull down the View menu, click the Options command to display the Options dialog box, click the View tab, then check (or clear) the box to hide (or show) MS-DOS file extensions. Click OK to accept the setting and exit the dialog box. We prefer to hide the extensions.

STEP 2: Additional Practice

- The objective of this exercise is to obtain the practice files by copying files from a local area network (such as a computer lab at school) using the Windows Explorer. If you already downloaded the practice files from our Web site in the previous hands-on exercise, you can:
  - Use the practice files you already have and go to step 6 to continue with this exercise, *or*
  - Erase all of the files on your floppy disk (just reformat the disk), then proceed with steps 3 through 5 in this exercise.
- We suggest you continue with step 3 in order to practice with the Windows Explorer.

THE QUICK FORMAT COMMAND

The fastest way to erase the entire contents of a floppy disk is to use the Quick Format command. Start the Windows Explorer and select any drive except the floppy drive. (You cannot format a floppy disk in drive A when drive A is selected). Point to the icon for drive A in the left pane, click the right mouse button to display a shortcut menu, then click the Format command to display the Format dialog box. Click the option button for the Quick (erase) Format, then click the Start button to format the disk and erase its contents.

STEP 3: Collapse the Individual Drives

- Click the **minus** (or the plus) **sign** next to My Computer to collapse (or expand) My Computer and hide (display) the objects it contains.
- Toggle the signs back and forth a few times for practice. End with a minus sign next to the My Computer icon as shown in Figure 11b.
- Place a formatted floppy disk in drive A, then click the **plus sign** next to drive A. The plus sign disappears, as drive A does not have any folders.

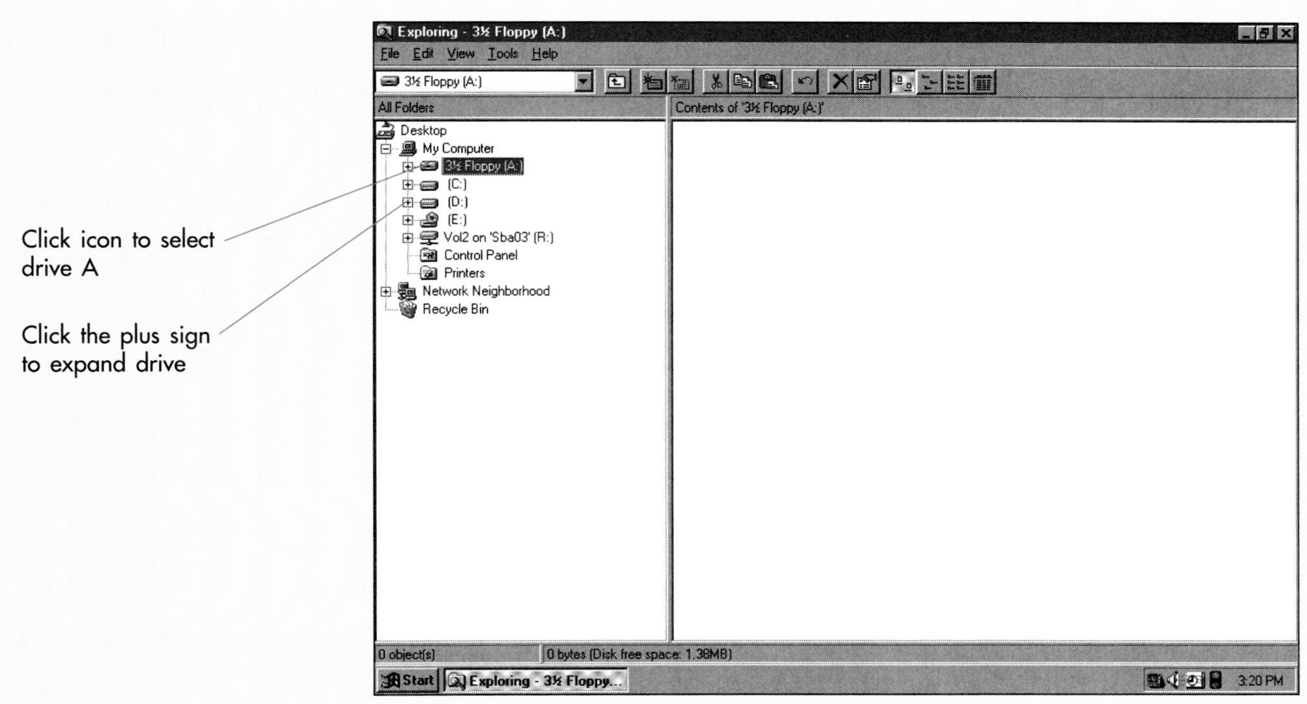

(b) Collapse the Individual Drives (step 3)

FIGURE 11 Hands-on Exercise 3 (continued)

- Click the **plus** (minus) **sign** next to the other drives to toggle back and forth between expanding (collapsing) the individual drives on your system.
- End this step with every drive collapsed; that is, there should be a **plus sign** next to every drive, as shown in Figure 11b.
- Click the drive icon next to drive A to select the drive and display its contents in the right pane. The disk does not contain any files, and hence the right pane is empty.

THE PLUS AND MINUS SIGN

Any drive, be it local or on the network, may be expanded or collapsed to display or hide its contents. A minus sign indicates that the drive has been expanded and that its folders are visible. A plus sign indicates the reverse; that is, the device is collapsed and its folders are not visible. Click either sign to toggle to the other. Clicking a plus sign, for example, expands the drive, then displays a minus sign next to the drive to indicate that the folders are visible. Clicking a minus sign has the reverse effect—it collapses the drive, hiding its folders.

STEP 4: Select the Network Drive

- Click the **plus sign** for the network drive, which contains the files you are to copy (e.g., drive R in Figure 11c). Select (click) the **Exploring Prerequisites**

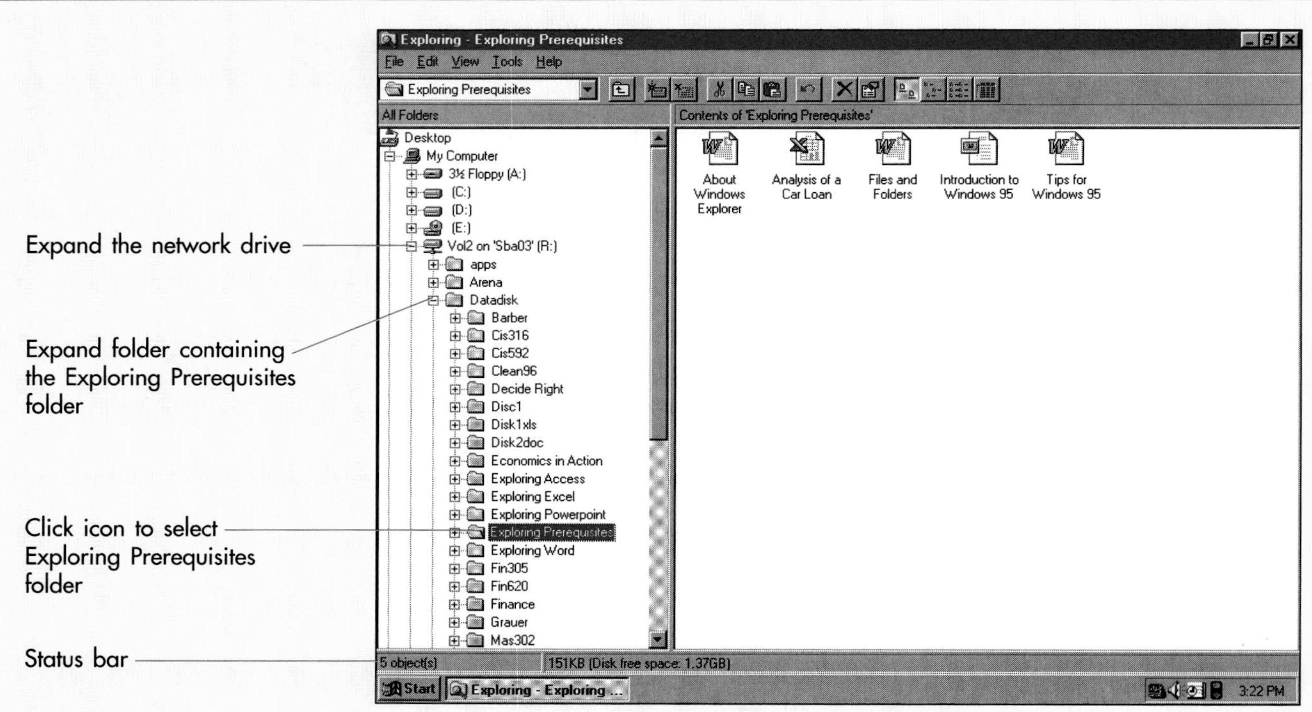

(c) Select the Exploring Prerequisites Folder (step 4)

FIGURE 11 Hands-on Exercise 3 (continued)

folder to select this folder. (You may need to expand other folders on the network drive as per instructions from your professor.) Note the following:

- The Exploring Prerequisites folder is highlighted in the left pane, its icon has changed to an open folder, and its contents are displayed in the right pane.
- The status bar indicates that the folder contains five objects and the total file size is 151KB.

➤ Click the icon next to any other folder to select the folder, which in turn deselects the Exploring Prerequisites folder. (Only one folder in the left pane can be selected at a time.) Reselect (click) the **Exploring Prerequisites folder** and its contents are again visible in the right pane.

➤ Pull down the **View menu** and select **Details** (or click the **Details button** on the toolbar) to change to the Details view. This enables you to see the file sizes of the individual files.

THE VIEW MENU

The objects in any window can be displayed in four different views—Large Icons, Small Icons, Details, and List—according to your preference or need. The choice of views depends on your personal preference. You can change from one view to another from the View menu, or by clicking the appropriate button on the toolbar. (Windows 97 provides access to a fifth view, the Web view, which displays the addresses of recently visited Web sites.)

STEP 5: Copy the Individual Files

- ➤ Select (click) the file **About Windows Explorer,** which highlights the file as shown in Figure 11d. The Exploring Prerequisites folder is no longer highlighted because a different object has been selected. The folder is still open, however, and its contents are displayed in the right pane.
- ➤ Click and drag the selected file in the right pane to the **drive A icon** in the left pane:
  - You will see the ⦸ symbol as you drag the file until you reach a suitable destination (e.g., until you point to the icon for drive A). The ⦸ symbol will change to a plus sign when the icon for drive A is highlighted, indicating that the file can be copied successfully.
  - Release the mouse to complete the copy operation. You will see a pop-up window, which indicates the progress of the copy operation. This may take several seconds, depending on the size of the file.
- ➤ Select (click) the file **Tips for Windows 95,** which automatically deselects the previously selected file (About Windows Explorer). Copy the selected file to drive A by dragging its icon from the right pane to the drive A icon in the left pane.
- ➤ Copy the three remaining files to drive A as well. (You can select multiple files at the same time by pressing and holding the **Ctrl key** as you click each file in turn. Point to any of the selected files, then click and drag the files as a group.)
- ➤ Select (click) drive **A** in the left pane, which in turn displays the contents of the floppy disk in the right pane. You should see the five files you have copied to drive A.

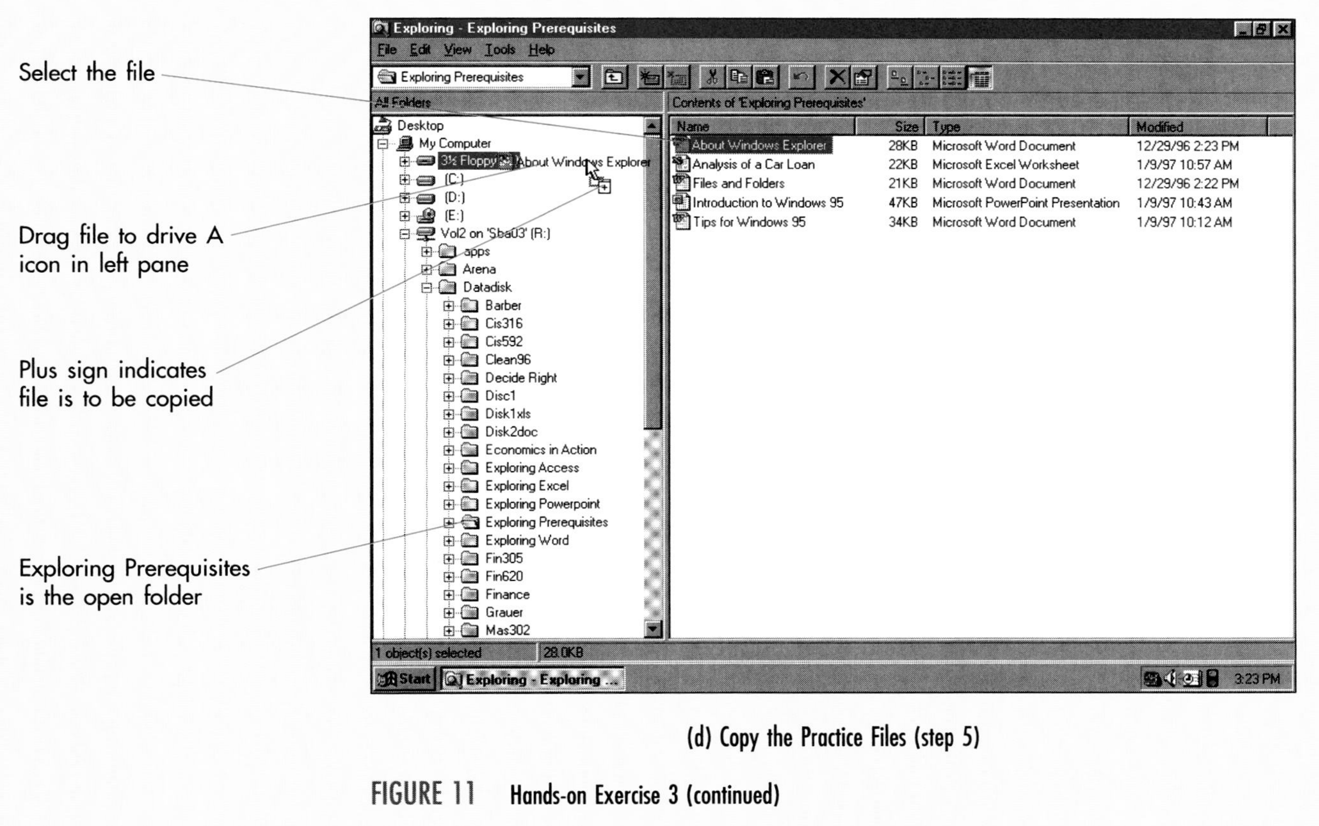

(d) Copy the Practice Files (step 5)

FIGURE 11 Hands-on Exercise 3 (continued)

SELECT MULTIPLE FILES

Selecting (clicking) one file automatically deselects the previously selected file. You can, however, select multiple files by pressing and holding the Ctrl key as you click each file in succession. You can also select multiple files that are adjacent to one another by using the Shift key; that is, click the icon of the first file, then press and hold the Shift key as you click the icon of the last file. You can also select every file in a folder through the Select All command in the Edit menu (or by clicking in the right pane and pressing Ctrl+A).

STEP 6: Check Your Work

➤ Prove to your instructor that you have done the exercise correctly by capturing the Exploring Windows screen, which appears on your monitor. The easiest way to do this is to use the Paint accessory as shown in Figure 11e. Accordingly:

- Press the **Print Screen key** to copy the current screen display to the clipboard (an area of memory that is available to every Windows application). Nothing appears to have happened, but the screen has in fact been copied to the clipboard.
- Click the **Start button,** click **Programs,** click **Accessories,** then click **Paint** to open the Paint accessory. If necessary, click the **maximize button** so that the Paint window takes the entire desktop.

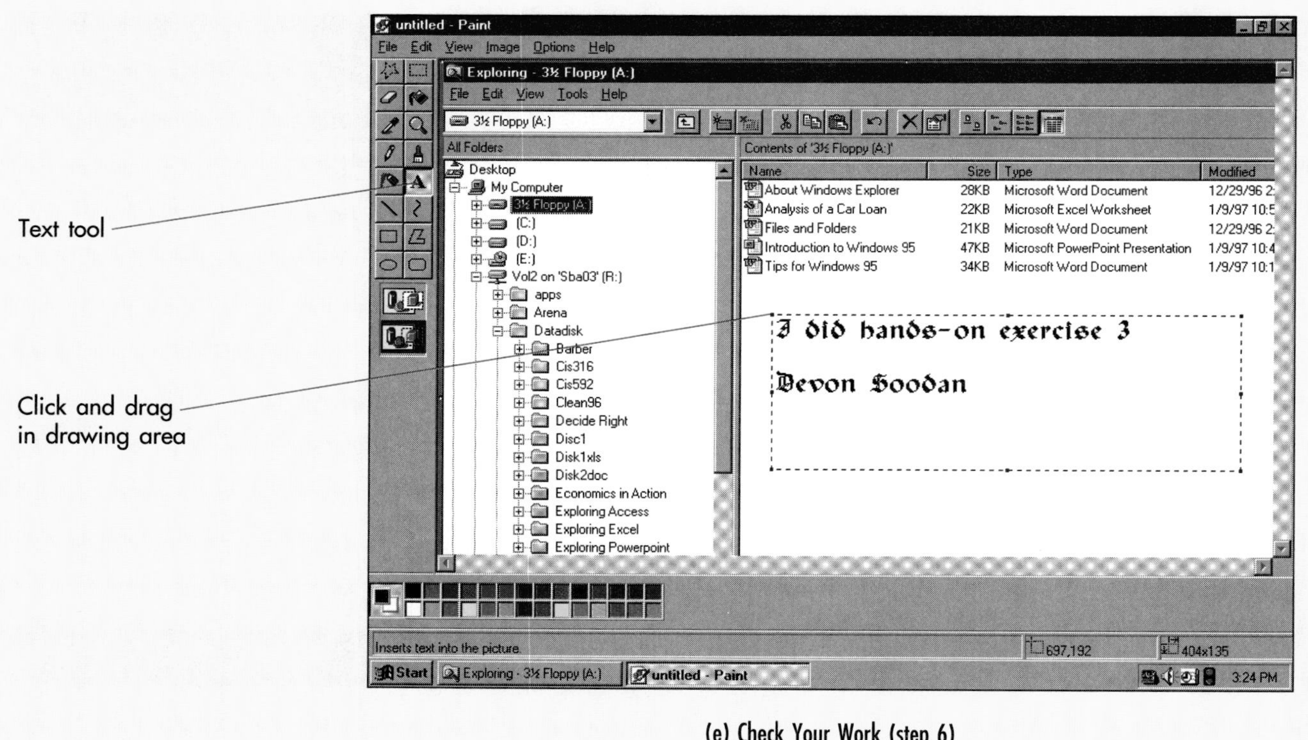

(e) Check Your Work (step 6)

FIGURE 11 Hands-on Exercise 3 (continued)

- Pull down the **Edit menu.** Click **Paste** to copy the screen from the clipboard to the drawing.
- Click the **text tool** (the capital A), then click and drag in the drawing area to create a dotted rectangle that will contain the message to your instructor. Type the text indicating that you did your homework. Click outside the rectangle to deselect it.
- Pull down the **File menu** and click the **Page Setup** command to display the Page Setup dialog box. Click the Landscape option button. Change the margins to one inch all around. Click **OK.**
- Pull down the **File menu** a second time. Click **Print.** Click **OK.** Click the **Close button** to exit Paint. Click **No** if asked to save the file.

➤ Close the Windows Explorer. Exit Windows if you do not want to continue with the next exercise at this time.

THE PAINT ACCESSORY

The Paint Accessory is included in Windows 95 and is an ideal way to create simple (or, depending on your ability, complex) drawings. There is also a sense of familiarity because the Paint accessory shares the common user interface of every Windows application, which includes a title bar, menu bar, minimize, restore, and close buttons, and vertical and horizontal scroll bars. You may also recognize a familiar command structure. The Print and Paste commands, for example, are found in the File and Edit menus, respectively, in Paint, as they are in every Windows application.

THE BASICS OF FILE MANAGEMENT

The exercise just completed had you copy the practice files from a drive on a local area network to your own floppy disk. As you grow to depend on the computer, you will create files of your own in various applications (e.g., Word or Excel). Learning how to manage those files is one of the most important skills you can acquire. This section describes the basic operations you will use.

Moving and Copying a File

Moving and copying a file from one location to another is the essence of file management. It is accomplished most easily by clicking and dragging the file icon from the source drive or folder, to the destination drive or folder, within the Windows Explorer. There is a subtlety, however, in that the result of dragging a file (whether the file is moved or copied) depends on whether the source and destination are on the same or different drives. Dragging a file from one folder to another folder on the same drive moves the file. Dragging a file to a folder on a different drive copies the file. (You can also click and drag a folder, in which case every file in that folder is moved or copied as per the rule for an individual file.)

This process is not as arbitrary as it may seem. Windows assumes that if you drag an object (a file or folder) to a different drive (e.g., from drive C to drive A), you want the object to appear in both places. Hence, the default action when you click and drag an object to a different drive is to copy the object. You can, however, override the default and move the object by pressing and holding the Shift key as you drag.

Windows also assumes that you do not want two copies of an object on the same drive as that would result in wasted disk space. Thus, the default action when you click and drag an object to a different folder on the same drive is to move the object. You can override the default and copy the object by pressing and holding the Ctrl key as you drag. It's not as complicated as it sounds, and you get a chance to practice in the hands-on exercise, which follows shortly.

Deleting Files

The ***Delete command*** deletes (removes) a file from a disk. The command can be executed in different ways, most easily by selecting a file, then pressing the Del key. Even after a file is deleted, however, you can usually get it back because it is not physically deleted from the hard disk, but moved instead to the Recycle Bin from where it can be recovered.

The ***Recycle Bin*** is a special folder that contains all files that were previously deleted from any hard disk on your system. Think of the Recycle Bin as similar to the wastebasket in your room. You throw out (delete) a report by tossing it into a wastebasket. The report is gone (deleted) from your desk, but you can still get it back by taking it out of the wastebasket as long as the basket wasn't emptied. The Recycle Bin works the same way. Files are not deleted from the hard disk per se, but are moved instead to the Recycle Bin from where they can be restored to their original location.

The Recycle Bin will eventually run out of space, in which case the files that have been in the Recycle Bin the longest are deleted to make room for additional files. Once a file is deleted from the Recycle Bin, however, it can no longer be recovered, as it has been physically deleted from the hard disk. Note, too, that the protection afforded by the Recycle Bin does not extend to files deleted from a floppy disk. Such files can be recovered, but only through utility programs outside of Windows 95.

Backup

It's not a question of whether it will happen, but when—hard disks die, files are lost, or viruses may infect a system. It has happened to us and it will happen to you, but you can prepare for the inevitable by creating adequate backup *before* the problem occurs. The essence of a backup strategy is to decide which files to back up, how often to do the backup, and where to keep the backup. Once you decide on a strategy, follow it, and follow it faithfully!

Our strategy is very simple—back up what you can't afford to lose, do so on a daily basis, and store the backup away from your computer. You need not copy every file, every day. Instead copy just the files that changed during the current session. Realize, too, that it is much more important to back up your data files than your program files. You can always reinstall the application from the original disks, or if necessary, go to the vendor for another copy of an application. You, however, are the only one who has a copy of the term paper that is due tomorrow. Forewarned is forearmed.

Write Protection

A floppy disk is normally ***write-enabled*** (the square hole is covered) so that you can change the contents of the disk. Thus, you can create (save) new files to a write-enabled disk and/or edit or delete existing files. Occasionally, however, you may want to ***write-protect*** a floppy disk (by sliding the tab to expose the square hole) so that its contents cannot be modified. This is typically done with a backup disk when you want to prevent the accidental deletion of a file or the threat of virus infection.

Our Last Exercise

As we have indicated throughout the appendix, the ability to move and copy files is of paramount importance. The only way to master these skills is through practice, and so we offer one last exercise in which you execute a variety of commands to reinforce the material.

The exercise begins with the floppy disk containing the five practice files in drive A. We ask you to create two folders on drive A (step 1) and to move the various files into these folders (step 2). Next, you copy a folder from drive A to drive C (step 3), modify one of the files in the folder on drive C (step 4), then copy the modified file back to drive A (step 5). We ask you to delete a file in step 6, then recover it from the Recycle Bin in step 7. There is a lot to do, so let's get started.

HANDS-ON EXERCISE 4

The Windows Explorer

Objective: To use the Windows Explorer to move, copy, and delete a file, then recover a deleted file from the Recycle Bin. Use Figure 12 as a guide in the exercise.

STEP 1: Create a New Folder

- ➤ Start the Windows Explorer and maximize its window. Place the floppy disk (from hands-on exercise 2 or 3) in drive A.
- ➤ Select (click) the icon for **drive A** in the left pane of the Explorer window. Drive A should contain the files shown in Figure 12a. It does not contain any folders.
- ➤ Point to a blank area anywhere in the **right pane,** then click the **right mouse button** to display a context-sensitive menu.
- ➤ Click (or point to) the **New command** in the menu, then click **Folder** to create a new Folder on drive A.
- ➤ The icon for a new folder will appear with the name of the folder (New Folder) highlighted. Type **Computing 101** to change the name of the folder. Press the **enter key.**
- ➤ Click the icon for **drive A** once again. Pull down the **File menu,** click (or point to) the **New command,** and click **Folder** as the type of object to create.
- ➤ Type **Other Files** to change the name of the folder. Press **enter.** The right pane should now contain five documents and two folders.
- ➤ Pull down the **View menu.** Click (or point to) the **Arrange icons command** to display a submenu, then click the **By Name command.** The folders are displayed in alphabetical order followed by the files in alphabetical order.

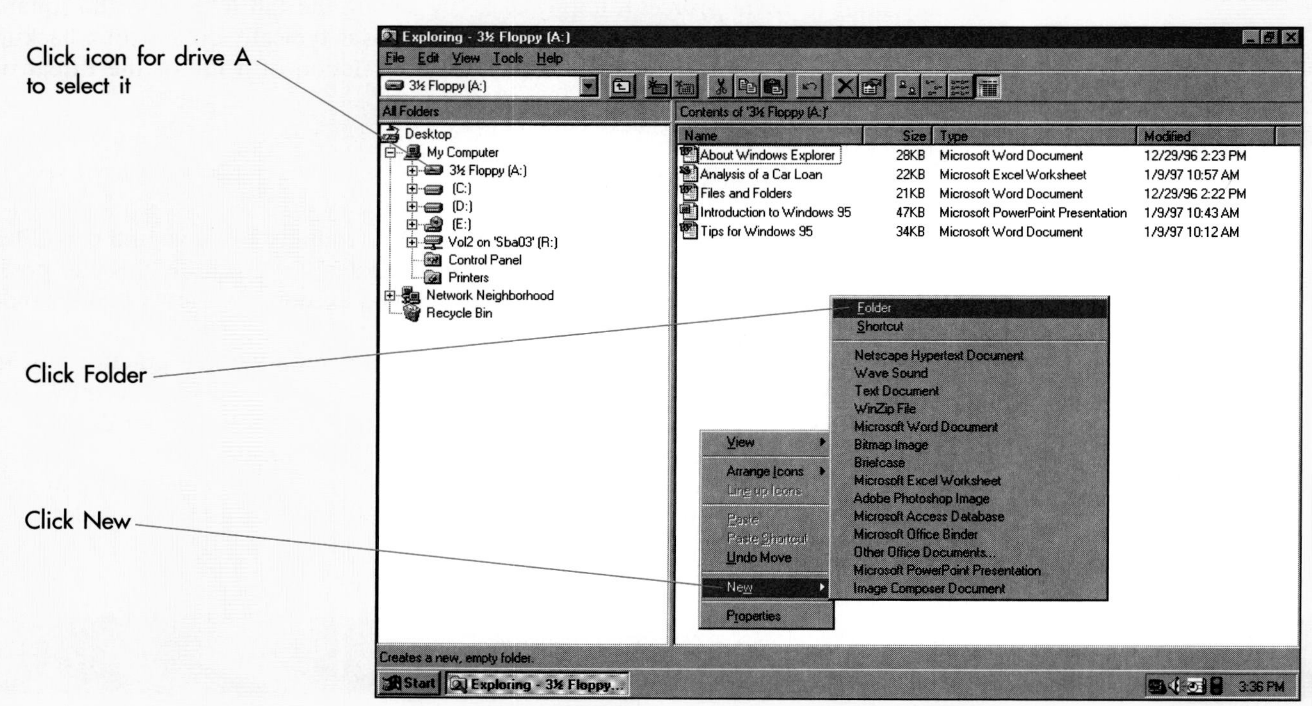

(a) Create a New Folder (step 1)

FIGURE 12 Hands-on Exercise 4

RENAME COMMAND

Point to a file or a folder, then click the right mouse button to display a menu with commands pertaining to the object. Click the Rename command. The name of the file or folder will be highlighted with the insertion point (a flashing vertical line) positioned at the end of the name. Enter a new name, to replace the selected name, or click anywhere within the name to change the insertion point and edit the name.

STEP 2: Move a File

- ➤ Click the **plus sign** next to drive A to expand the drive as shown in Figure 12b. Note the following:
  - Drive A is selected in the left pane. The right pane displays the contents of drive A (the selected object in the left pane). The folders are shown first and appear in alphabetical order. The file names are displayed after the folders and are also in alphabetical order.
  - There is a minus sign next to the icon for drive A in the left pane, indicating that its folders have been expanded. Thus, the folder names also appear under drive A in the left pane.
- ➤ Click and drag the icon for the file **About Windows Explorer** from the right pane to the **Computing 101 folder** in the left pane. This moves the file into that folder.

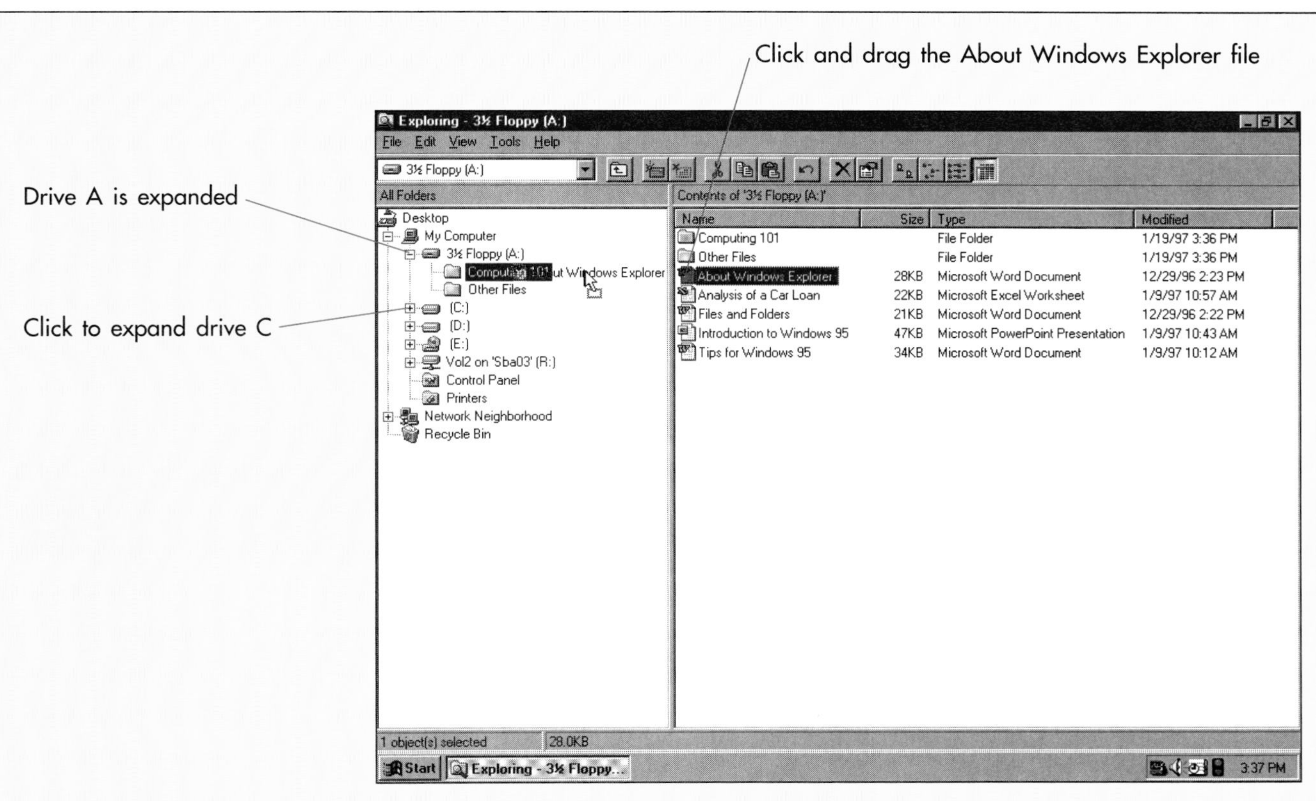

(b) Move the Files (step 2)

FIGURE 12 Hands-on Exercise 4 (continued)

- Click and drag the **Tips for Windows 95 icon** and the **Files and Folders icon** to the **Computing 101 folder** to move these files into the folder.
- Click the **Computing 101 icon** in the left pane to select the folder and display its contents in the right pane. You should see the three files that were just moved.
- Click the icon for **drive A** in the left pane, then click and drag the remaining files, **Analysis of a Car Loan** and **Introduction to Windows 95** to the **Other Files folder.**

USE THE RIGHT MOUSE BUTTON

The result of dragging a file with the left mouse button depends on whether the source and destination folders are on the same or different drives. Dragging a file to a folder on a different drive copies the file. Dragging the file to a folder on the same drive moves the file. If you find this hard to remember, and most people do, click and drag with the right mouse button to display a shortcut menu asking whether you want to copy or move the file. This simple tip can save you from making a careless (and potentially serious) error. Use it!

STEP 3: Copy a Folder

- If necessary, click the **plus sign** next to the icon for drive C to expand the drive and display its folders as shown in Figure 12c.
- Do *not* click the folder icon for drive C, as drive A is to remain selected. (You can expand or collapse an object without selecting it.)
- Point to the **Computing 101 folder** in either pane, click the **right mouse button** and drag the folder to the icon for **drive C** in the left pane, then release the mouse to display a shortcut menu. Click the **Copy Here** command.
- You should see the Copy files dialog box as the individual files within the folder are copied from drive A to drive C.

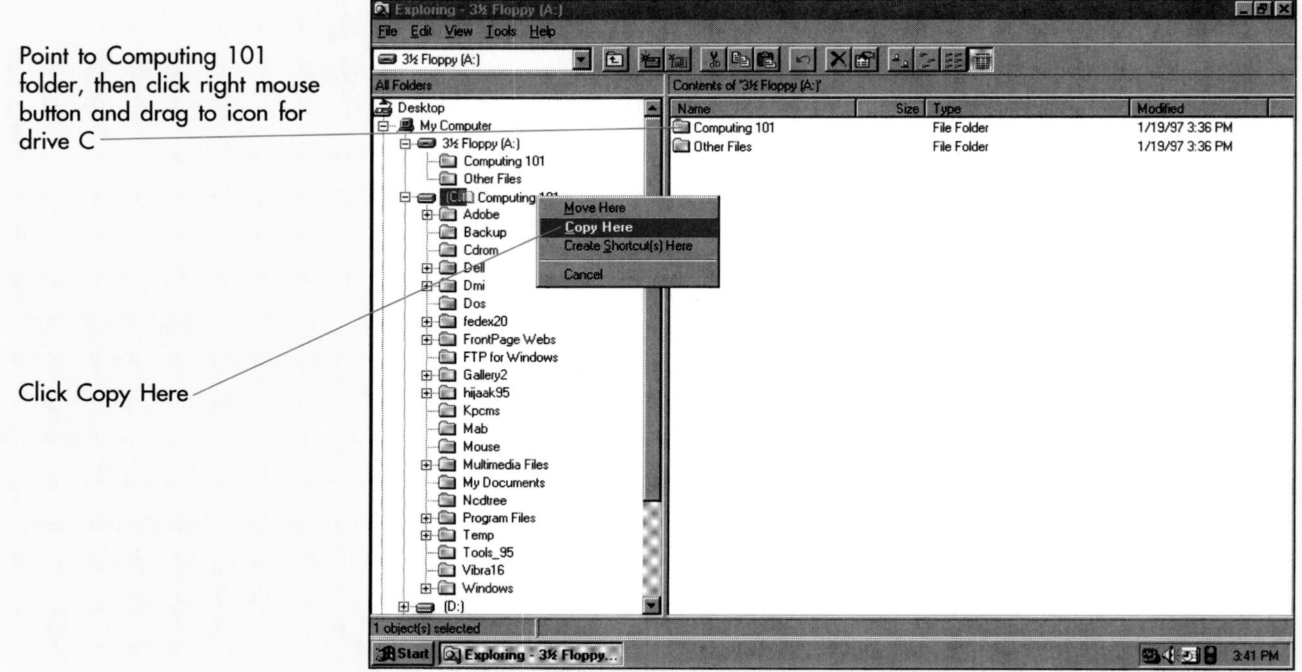

(c) Copy a Folder (step 3)

FIGURE 12 Hands-on Exercise 4 (continued)

> **CUSTOMIZE THE EXPLORER WINDOW**
>
> Increase (or decrease) the size of the left pane within the Explorer Window by dragging the vertical line separating the left and right panes in the appropriate direction. You can also drag the right border of the various column headings (Name, Size, Tip, and Modified) in the right pane to increase (or decrease) the width of the column in order to see more (or less) information in that column. Double click the right border of a column heading to automatically adjust the column width to accommodate the widest entry in that column.

- If you see the Confirm Folder Replace dialog box, it means that the previous student forgot to delete the Computing 101 folder when he or she did this exercise. Click the **Yes to All button** so that the files on your floppy disk will replace the previous versions on drive C.
- Please remember to **delete** the Computing 101 folder on drive C, as described in step 8 at the end of the exercise.

STEP 4: Modify a Document

- Click (select) the **Computing 101 folder** on drive C to open the folder as shown in Figure 12d. The contents of this folder are shown in the right pane.
- Double click the **About Windows Explorer** file to open the file and edit the document. Press **Ctrl+End** to move to the end of the document. Add the sentence shown in Figure 12d followed by your name. (See boxed tip on page 46 if you are unable to read the document.)
- Pull down the **File menu** and click **Save** to save the modified file (or click the **Save button** on the Standard toolbar). Pull down the **File menu** and click **Exit** to exit from Microsoft Word.
- The entire Windows Explorer window is again visible. Pull down the **View menu** and click **Refresh** (or press the **F5 key**) to update the contents of the right pane. The date and time associated with the About Windows Explorer file has been changed to indicate that the file has just been modified.

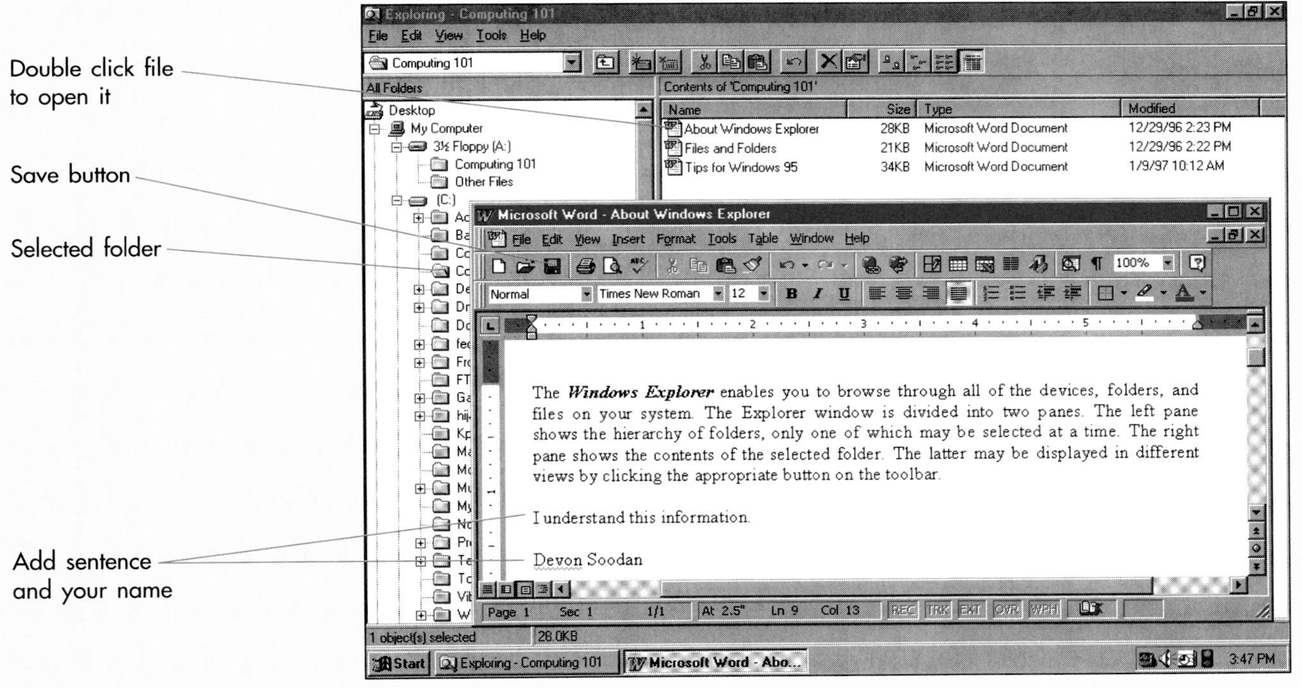

(d) Modify a Document (step 4)

FIGURE 12 Hands-on Exercise 4 (continued)

FILE FORMATS ARE INCOMPATIBLE

If you are unable to open the Word document in our exercise, it is because you are using Microsoft Word 7.0 (also known as Microsoft Word for Windows 95) rather than Word 97. The new release can read documents created in the earlier version, but the converse is not true—that is, Word 7.0 cannot read documents created by Word 97. (Our file was created in Word 97.) The incompatibility between Office 97 and its predecessor Office 95 is a potential problem for millions of users.

STEP 5: Copy (Back Up) a File

- Verify that the **Computing 101 folder** on drive C is the active folder as denoted by the open folder icon. Click and drag the icon for the **About Windows Explorer** file from the right pane to the **Computing 101 folder** on **drive A** in the left pane.
- You will see the message in Figure 12e, indicating that the folder (drive A) already contains a file called About Windows Explorer and asking whether you want to replace the existing file.
- Click **Yes** because you want to replace the previous version of the file on drive A with the updated version on drive C.
- You have just backed up the file; in other words, you have created a duplicate copy of a file on drive C on drive A. Thus, you can use the floppy disk to restore the file should anything happen to drive C.

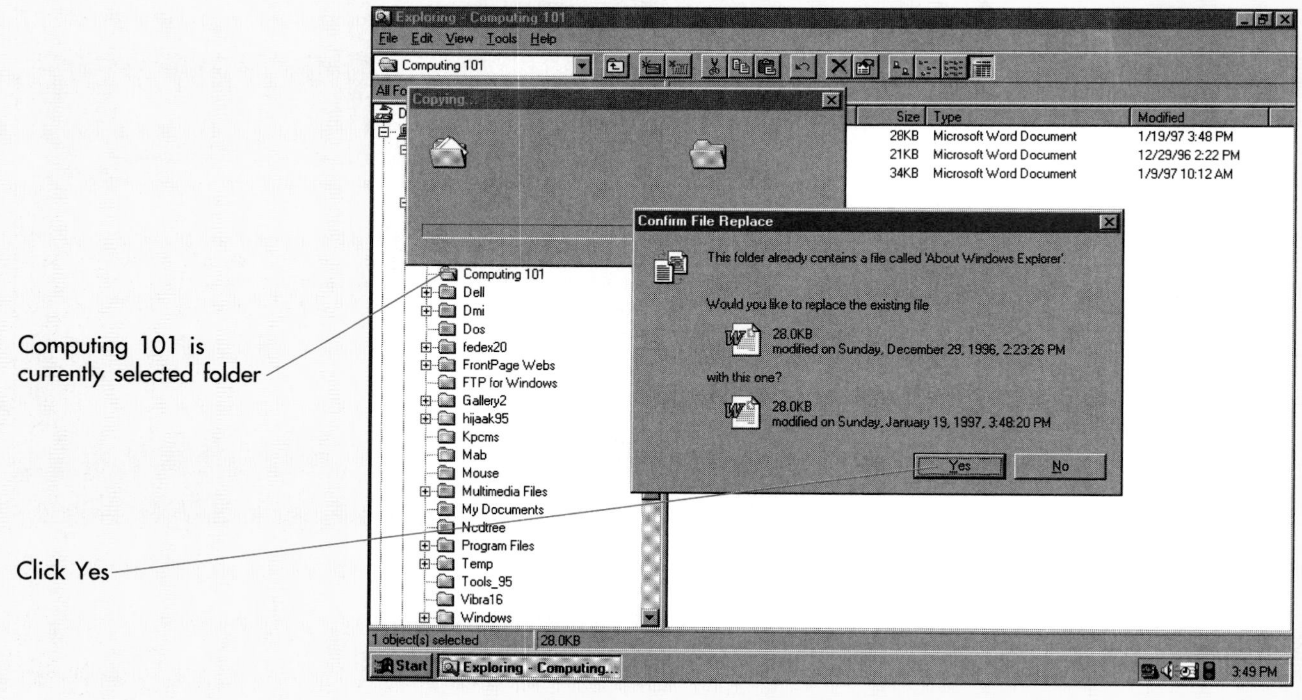

(e) Copy (Back Up) a File (step 5)

FIGURE 12 Hands-on Exercise 4 (continued)

COPYING FROM ONE FLOPPY DISK TO ANOTHER

You've learned how to copy a file from drive C to drive A, or from drive A to drive C, but how do you copy a file from one floppy disk to another? It's easy when you know how. Place the first floppy disk in drive A, select drive A in the left pane of the Explorer windows, then copy the file(s) from the right pane to a temporary folder on drive C in the left pane. Remove the first floppy disk, and replace it with the second. Press the F5 key to refresh the display in the right pane. Select the temporary folder on drive C in the left pane, then click and drag the file(s) from the left pane to the floppy disk in the right pane.

STEP 6: Delete a Folder

- Select (click) the **Computing 101 folder** on drive C in the left pane. Pull down the **File menu** and click **Delete** (or press the **Del key**).
- You will see the dialog box in Figure 12f asking whether you are sure you want to delete the folder (that is, send the folder and its contents to the Recycle Bin). Note the green recycle logo within the box, which implies that you will be able to restore the file.
- Click **Yes** to delete the folder. The folder disappears from drive C. Pull down the **Edit menu.** Click **Undo Delete.** The deletion is cancelled and the folder reappears in the left pane.

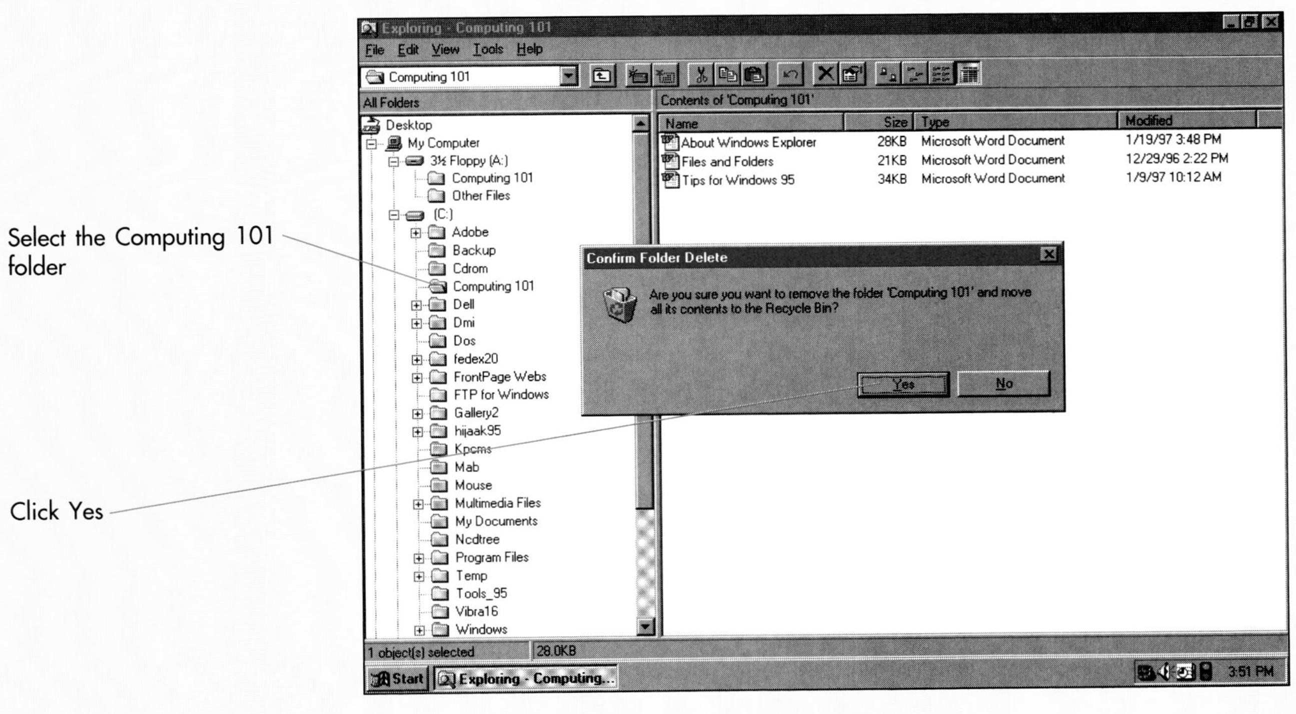

(f) Deleting a Folder (step 6)

FIGURE 12 Hands-on Exercise 4 (continued)

STEP 7: The Recycle Bin

- If necessary, select the **Computing 101 folder** on drive C in the left pane. Select (click) the **About Windows Explorer** file in the right pane. Press the **Del key,** then click **Yes** when asked whether to delete the file.
- Double click the **Recycle Bin icon** on the desktop if you can see its icon, *or* Double click the **Recycled icon** within the window for drive C. (You may have to scroll in order to see the icon.)
- The Recycle Bin contains all files that have been previously deleted from drive C, and hence you may see a different number of files than those displayed in Figure 12g.
- Point to the **About Windows Explorer** file, click the **right mouse button** to display the shortcut menu in Figure 12g, then click **Restore.** The file disappears from the Recycle Bin because it has been returned to the Computing 101 folder. Select the folder and verify the file is back.

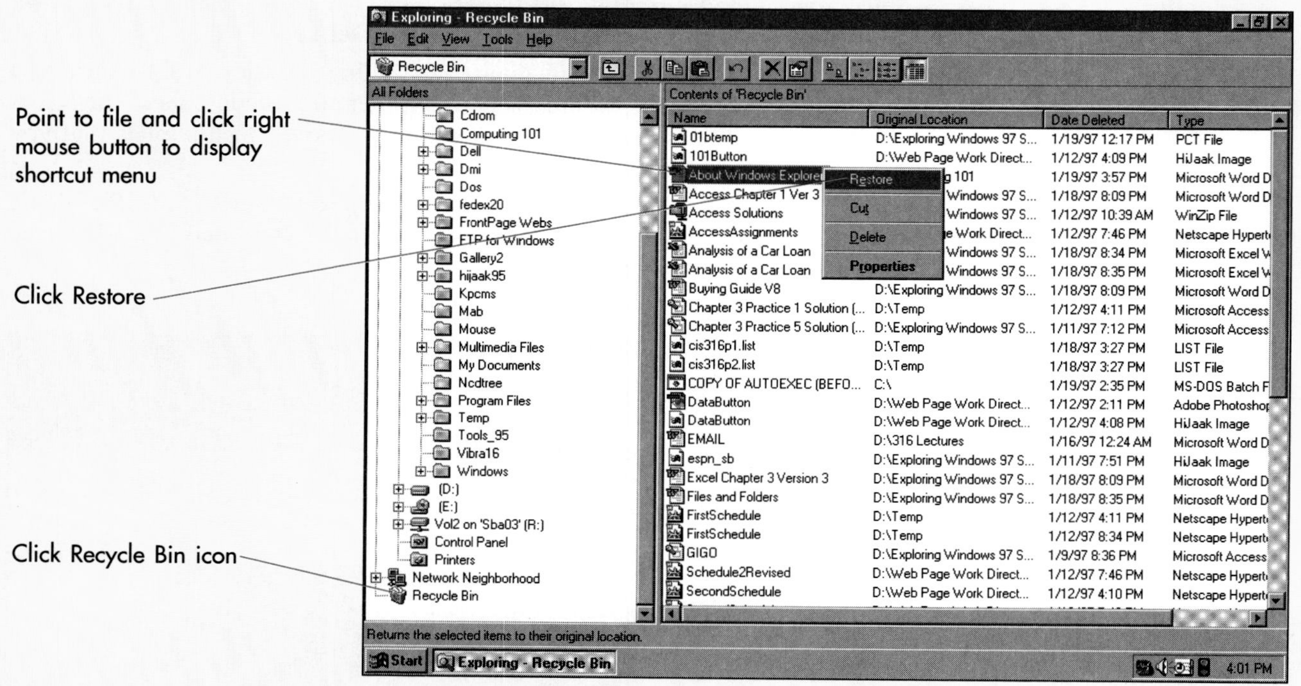

(g) Recover a File (step 7)

FIGURE 12 Hands-on Exercise 4 (continued)

STEP 8: Complete the Exercise

- Delete the **Computing 101 folder** on **drive C** as a courtesy to the next student.
- Click the **Computing 101 folder** on drive A in the left pane. Repeat the steps described on page 38 to capture the screen and prove to your instructor that you did the exercise.
- Exit Windows. Congratulations on a job well done. You have mastered the basics and are ready to begin working in Microsoft Office.

A PC BUYING GUIDE

OVERVIEW

Are you confused about all the ads for personal computers? You can buy from hundreds of companies, retail or through the mail, with no such thing as a standard configuration. The microprocessor can be one of many Pentium or Pentium Pro chips (or compatible chips from vendors other than Intel), each of which can be configured with any amount of memory. You can select a desktop, tower, mini-tower, or notebook-sized computer. You can choose from a variety of monitors in different sizes and can input data from different styles of keyboards, from a mouse, a trackball, or even a pen. Hard disks run up to several gigabytes. There are fax-modem cards, sound cards, video adapters, removable disk drives, CD-ROM and CD-recordable devices, and tape backup units.

The personal computer has, in effect, become a commodity where the consumer is able to select the individual elements in the configuration. And, like the purchase of any big-ticket item, you must understand what you are buying, so that the decision you make is right for you. This appendix will familiarize you with the components in a computer system so that you can select the machine best suited to your needs and budget. We also include a hands-on exercise that lets you visit the home pages of various vendors to obtain up-to-the-minute information.

DON'T FORGET THE SOFTWARE

Any machine you buy will come with Windows, but that is only the beginning since you must also purchase the application software you intend to run. Many first-time buyers are surprised that they have to pay extra for software, but you had better allow for software in your budget. The university bookstore is your best bet, as you can obtain a substantial educational discount.

The personal computer is a marvel of miniaturization and technology. We take it for granted, but the IBM PC, which jump-started the industry, is just a teenager. IBM announced the PC in 1981 and broke a longstanding corporate tradition by going to external sources for supporting hardware and software. ***Intel*** designed the ***microprocessor*** inside the PC. ***Microsoft*** developed the operating system.

In terms of today's capabilities, IBM's initial offering was hardly spectacular. A fully loaded system with two floppy disk drives (a hard disk was not available), monochrome monitor, and 80 cps (characters per second) dot matrix printer sold for $4,425. Software was practically nonexistent. It was a DOS (text-based) world, and Microsoft Office would not appear for almost 10 years. Yet the PC, with little software and limited hardware, was an instant success for two reasons. First, the IBM name, and its reputation for quality and service, meant that corporate America could order the machine and be assured that it would perform as promised.

Of equal, or even greater, significance was the PC's open design, which meant that independent vendors could offer supporting products to enhance performance. This was accomplished through ***expansion cards*** inside the PC that could hold additional circuit boards and thus add functionality to the basic PC. IBM made public the technical information to create these expansion cards (or adapters) so that other companies could build peripherals for the PC, thus enhancing its capabilities. Today you can purchase expansion cards that add sound, increase the number of colors, resolution, and speed of the monitor, or support peripheral devices such as CD-ROMs and removable disk drives that did not exist when the PC was introduced.

The open design of the PC was a mixed blessing for IBM, in that ***PC-compatibles,*** based on the same microprocessor and able to run the same software, began to appear as early as 1982 and offered superior performance for less money. Companies and individuals who were once willing to pay a premium for the IBM name began ordering the "same" machine from other vendors. IBM today has less than 10 percent of the market it was so instrumental in creating, as the personal computer has become a commodity. PC is now a generic term for any computer based on Intel-compatible microprocessors that is capable of running Microsoft Windows.

Figure 1 illustrates a typical Windows work station. We view the system from the front (Figure 1a), from the rear (Figure 1b), and from inside the system unit (Figure 1c). Your system will be different from ours, but you should be able to recognize the various components discussed in this appendix. Whether you choose a desktop, tower, or mini-tower for your system unit, or whether you purchase a laptop or notebook computer, you will have to decide on each component of your system.

BE KIND TO YOURSELF

Are you the type of person who will spend thousands on a new computer, only to set it up on your regular desk and sit on a $10 bridge chair? Don't. A conventional desk (or the dining room table) is 30 inches high, but the recommended typing height is 27 inches. The difference accounts for the stiff neck, tight shoulders, and aching backs reported by many people who sit at a computer over an extended period of time. Be kind to yourself and include in your budget a computer table with lots of room as well as a comfortable chair.

(a) Front View

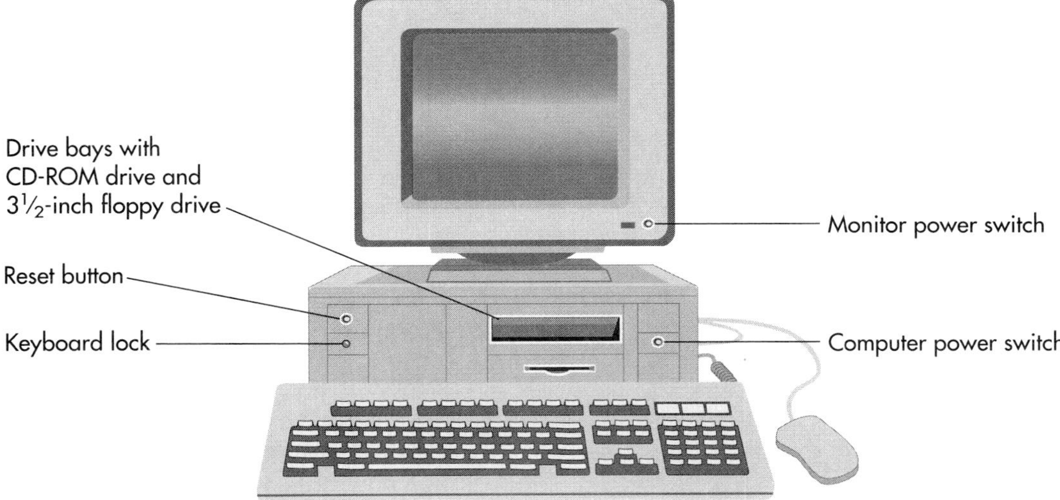

(b) Rear View

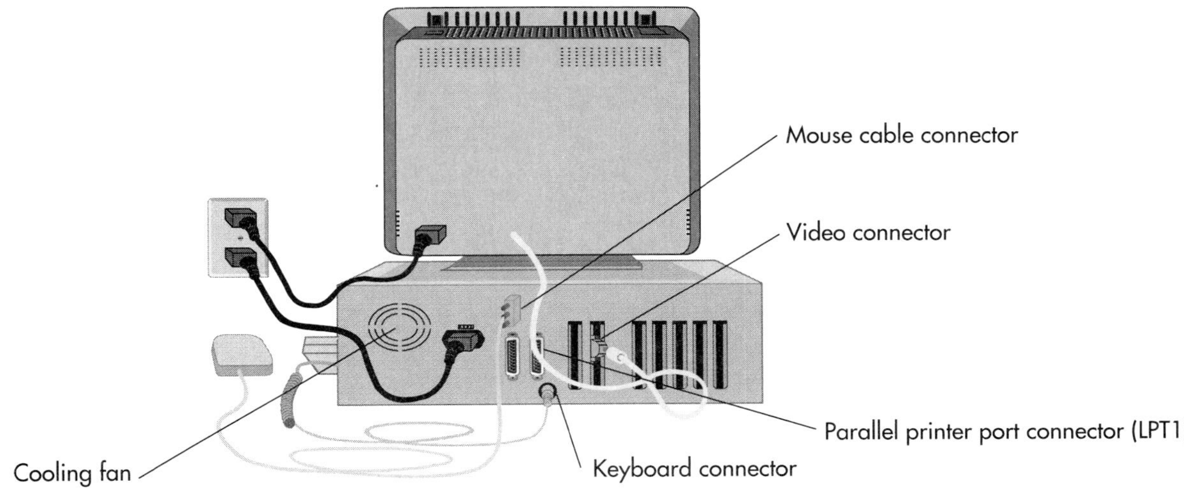

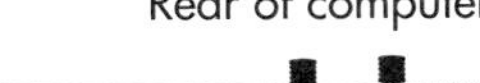

(c) Inside the Computer

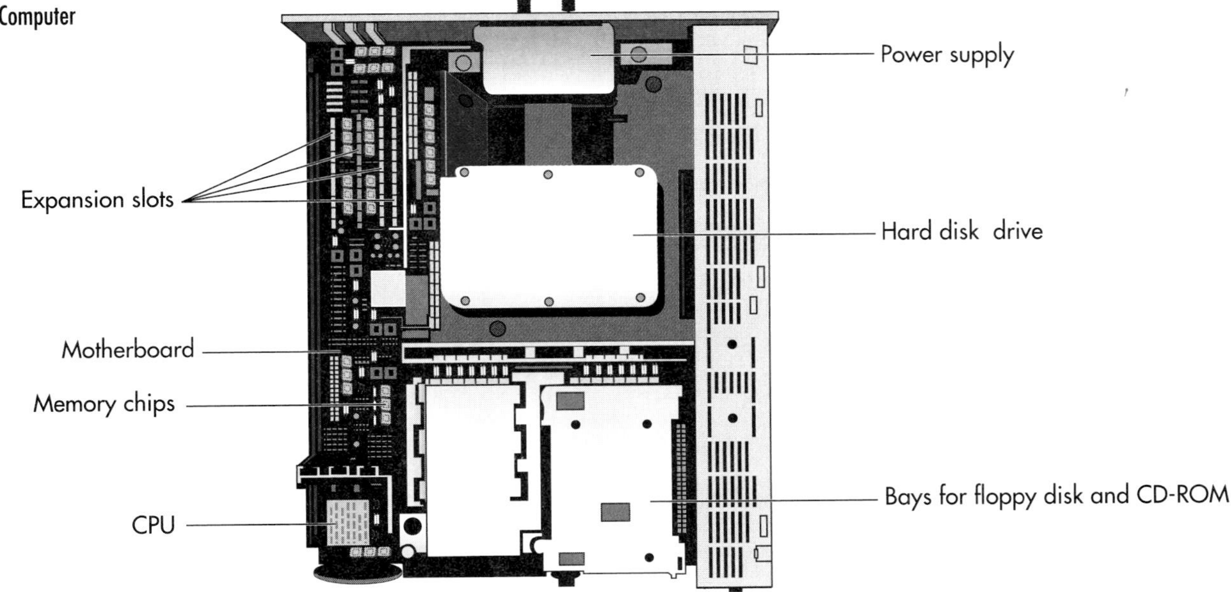

FIGURE 1 The Windows Workstation

The capability of a PC depends in large part on the microprocessor on which it is based. Intel (and Intel-compatible) microprocessors are currently in their sixth generation, with each generation giving rise to increasingly powerful personal computers. All generations are upward compatible; that is, software written for one generation will automatically run on the next. This upward compatibility is crucial because it protects your investment in software when you upgrade to a faster computer.

Today's purchase decision comes down to a fifth- or sixth-generation microprocessor, either a 586 (e.g., a Pentium Classic or Pentium with MMX technology) or a 686 (Pentium Pro), as the earlier generations are obsolete. Several companies besides Intel (e.g., AMD and Cyrix) manufacture similar chips. A Pentium or Pentium Pro, however, is available only from Intel, because the company has trademarked the Pentium name to differentiate its products from the competition.

Microprocessors are further differentiated by ***clock speed,*** an indication of how fast instructions are executed. The clock speed is measured in ***megahertz*** (MHz), and the higher the clock speed the faster the microprocessor (e.g., a Pentium running at 200MHz is faster than a Pentium running at 166MHz). To facilitate the comparison of one microprocessor to another, Intel has created the ***Intel CPU performance (iCOMP) index.*** The index consists of a single number to indicate the relative performance of a microprocessor; the higher the number, the faster the processor. Figure 2 displays the index values for selected Intel microprocessors (the index does not include Intel-compatible microprocessors manufactured by other vendors). This is the information to use when you are selecting a computer because you want to purchase the fastest machine you can afford.

Any comparison of one machine to another—for example, an IBM PC to one made by Dell or Gateway—must be based on the identical microprocessor, or else the comparison will not be valid. Realize, too, that machines based on different microprocessors should reflect a price differential. You would, for example, expect to pay more for a Pentium running at 200MHz than you would for one running at 100MHz.

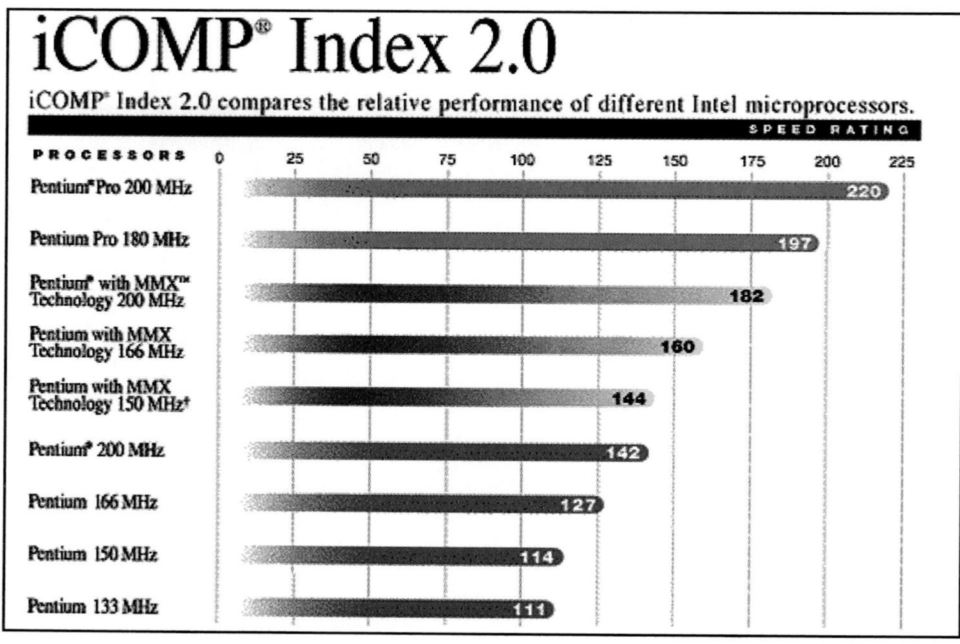

FIGURE 2 The iCOMP Index

THE ICOMP® INDEX (www.intel.com)

You can obtain the most current version of the iCOMP index, together with technical information about the index, by going to the Intel Web site. Intel is constantly redesigning its site, so we suggest you use its internal search engine to locate the index. Go to the Intel home page (www.intel.com), click the search command, and enter iCOMP index as the term you are searching for. Select the (first) document on the iCOMP index, scroll in the document until you find a list of figures, then select the first figure that displays the iCOMP ratings.

MEMORY

The microprocessor is the brain of the PC, but it needs instructions that tell it what to do, data on which to work, and a place to store the results of its calculations. All of this takes place in ***memory,*** a temporary storage area that holds data, instructions, and results, and passes everything back and forth to the CPU. The size of a system's memory is important because the larger the memory, the more sophisticated the programs are that the computer is capable of executing, and further, the more programs can remain in memory at the same time.

The ***memory*** of a computer (also known as ***r***andom ***a***ccess ***m***emory or ***RAM***) is made up of individual storage locations, each of which holds one ***byte,*** or one character. In the early days of the PC, memory was measured in ***kilobytes (KB).*** Today memory is measured in ***megabytes (MB).*** One KB and one MB are equal to approximately one thousand and one million characters, respectively. (In actuality 1KB equals 1024 bytes, or 2^{10} bytes, whereas 1MB is 1,048,576 bytes, or 2^{20} bytes.) Note, too, that memory is volatile, and that losing or shutting off the power erases everything in RAM. Accordingly, a permanent storage media, i.e., a disk drive, is also necessary and is discussed in the next section.

DON'T SKIMP ON MEMORY

The more memory a system has, the better its overall performance. Windows 95 and its associated applications are powerful, but they require adequate resources to run efficiently. 16MB of RAM is the minimum you should consider in today's environment, but you might also anticipate a future upgrade. Be sure the system you buy can accommodate additional memory easily and cheaply.

AUXILIARY STORAGE

A disk is a permanent storage device that retains its contents when the power is off. Disks fall into two categories—***floppy disks*** and ***hard disks.*** A hard disk is also known as a ***fixed disk*** because it remains permanently inside the system unit. The floppy disk gets its name because it is made of a flexible mylar plastic (although it is enclosed in a hard plastic case). The hard disk uses a series of rigid metal platters.

A hard (fixed) disk holds significantly more data than a floppy disk, and it accesses that data much faster. Hard disks are rated by capacity and access time.

Capacity is measured in ***gigabytes (GB)*** where 1GB is approximately one billion (2^{30} = 1,073,741,824) bytes. The ***access time*** is the time in milliseconds that a disk needs to locate and begin retrieving data. The shorter the access time, the faster the disk, and the more expensive.

The hard disk connects to the motherboard with one of two interfaces: EIDE (Enhanced Integrated Drive Electronics) or SCSI (Small Computer System Interface). We mention this only because you are likely to see these initials in any advertisement that you read. The EIDE technology is the cheaper and more common and more than adequate for the typical Windows user.

A floppy disk (and the corresponding drive) comes in two sizes, 3½ and 5¼ inches. The latter is obsolete and no longer a consideration. The capacity of a 3½-inch floppy disk is either 720KB or 1.44MB, depending on whether the disk is double-density or high-density. A ***high-density drive*** (the only kind you can buy today) can read either a double-density or high-density disk, whereas older ***double-density drives*** could read only double-density disks. We suggest that you use high-density disks exclusively.

MASS STORAGE: BUY MORE THAN YOU NEED

We purchased our first hard disk as an upgrade to the original PC in 1984. It was a "whopping" 10MB, and our main concern was that we would never fill it all. The storage requirements of application programs have increased significantly. Microsoft Office, for example, requires 150MB for a complete installation. A 2GB drive is the minimum you should consider in today's environment, but for an additional $100 (or less) you can add another gigabyte. It is money well spent.

VIDEO

The video system consists of the monitor and display adapter (video card). The ***resolution*** of a monitor is specified in ***pixels*** (the tiny dots or *pic*ture *el*ements that make up a picture) and is stated as the number of pixels across by the number down. ***VGA,*** for example, is 640 pixels across by 480 pixels down. ***Super VGA,*** another common resolution, is 800 pixels across by 600 pixels down. The higher the resolution, the greater the detail and the more information you can see.

Any image at a given resolution always contains the same number of pixels; for example, a Windows screen in Super VGA (800 × 600) contains 480,000 pixels regardless of the size of the monitor on which it is displayed. The advantage of the larger monitor is that the individual pixels are bigger and thus the image on the screen is easier to read. The advantage of the higher resolution is that more pixels are displayed and hence you see more on the screen at one time—for example, more columns in a spreadsheet or more pages in a word processing document. Table 1 lists the available resolutions and recommended monitor sizes.

The desired resolution and monitor size are selected in conjunction with one another, so that the image displayed on a screen can be easily read. It would be foolish, for example, to display a 1024 × 768 image on a 14-inch screen because the individual pixels would be too small and the display unreadable. Higher resolutions demand bigger monitors, which are significantly more expensive.

Another characteristic of which you should be aware is the ***dot pitch,*** or the distance between adjacent pixels. The smaller the dot pitch, the crisper the image; conversely, the larger the dot pitch, the more grainy the picture. We suggest you choose a monitor with a dot pitch of .28 or less. You may also hear a vendor cite

TABLE 1 Resolution and Monitor Size

Resolution	Number of Pixels	Minimum Screen Size
640 × 480 (VGA)	307,200	14 inches
800 × 600 (Super VGA)	480,000	15 inches
1024 × 768 (Extended VGA)	782,462	17 inches
1280 × 1024	1,310,720	20 inches

the ***vertical refresh rate,*** a number that specifies how frequently the screen is repainted from top to bottom. A rate that is too slow causes the screen to flicker because it is not being redrawn fast enough to fool the eye into seeing a constant pattern. A rate of 70Hz (70 cycles per second) is the minimum you should accept.

The ***video (display) adapter*** is a standard feature on today's PC and is either incorporated into the motherboard or added as a separate card in an expansion slot within the system unit. Either way, the video adapter accepts information from the CPU (central processing unit) and sends it to the monitor, which displays the image. For best performance, the video card should have its own processing capability in the form of an accelerator chip. This enables the CPU to perform other tasks while the image is displayed, thus improving the overall performance of the system. The video card should also have its own memory. A minimum of 1MB is suggested but 2MB is preferable. (The distinction between different types of video memory need not concern you at this time.)

THE LOCAL BUS

The ***bus*** is the circuitry on the motherboard that provides the path by which data travels from one component to another. (The motherboard, or system board, is the main board within the system unit that holds the microprocessor, memory, and adapter cards.) All peripheral devices including the hard disk, video display adapter, and printer transmit data along the same bus. As you might expect, the more data that is traveling within the system, the more crowded the bus, and like any highway, bottlenecks will occur if traffic moves too slowly.

Older PCs used a 16-bit bus that ran at 8MHz, regardless of the speed of the microprocessor. This type of bus was sufficient in the early days of the PC with low-speed devices and low data requirements, but it became grossly inadequate in the Windows environment with its high graphic requirements. The need to constantly refresh the screen, especially with displays that rendered 256 colors (or more), overwhelmed the bus and slowed the overall system.

Today's PC contains multiple local buses, each 32 bits wide and each connected to a specific device that no longer has to share the bus with the rest of the system. Think of the new buses as dedicated super highways where traffic goes directly from one place to another, with a higher speed limit (the speed of the microprocessor versus 8MHz), and with twice as many lanes (32 bits versus 16) as previously. Look for the letters PCI in a computer advertisement, which indicate the presence of a bus designed by Intel in conjunction with the Pentium or Pentium Pro processor.

PRINTERS

Printers vary greatly in terms of design, price, and capability. The ***dot matrix printer*** was the entry-level printer of choice for many years, but it has passed into obsolescence in favor of the inkjet printer. The dot matrix printer was inexpensive and versatile, but it had two major drawbacks—noise and a less-than-perfect print quality since each character was created with a pattern of dots.

The ***inkjet printer*** has become today's entry-level printer and it offers a significant improvement in both areas—it's quiet and its print quality rivals that of an entry-level laser printer. Best of all, it costs only a few hundred dollars, with color a very affordable option.

The ***laser printer*** is the top-of-the-line device and it offers speed and quality superior to that of an inkjet. The resolution of a laser printer is measured in dots per inch (dpi) and its speed is measured in pages per minute (ppm). Entry-level laser printers at 600 dpi and 8 ppm are available for approximately $600 in today's environment.

FAX/MODEM CARD

A ***modem*** connects your computer to the outside world, be it an information service such as America OnLine (AOL) or your friend two blocks away. All means of data communications process data in its most elementary form, as a series of electronic pulses represented numerically as ***bits*** (***bi***nary digi***ts***). Every message transmitted by a computer, be it words, numbers, or pictures, is broken down into a series of 1s and 0s, which are sent over the transmission medium. The telephone uses an analog signal whereas a computer uses a digital signal, and thus some type of conversion is necessary.

Modulation is the process of converting a digital signal to an analog one. Demodulation is the reverse process. A modem (derived from the combination of *mo*dulate and *dem*odulate) performs both functions. On the transmitting end, a modem converts binary signals (1s and 0s) produced by the computer to analog signals, which can be sent over the telephone system. On the receiving end, the modem converts the analog signal from the telephone back to a digital signal, which is forwarded to the computer or peripheral device.

The speed of a modem—that is, the maximum rate at which it can transmit or receive data—is measured in ***bits per second (bps).*** Today's standard is a 28,800 bps (or 28.8K) bps modem, but we suggest you opt for the faster 33,600 (33.6K) bps or the recently announced 57,600 (57.66K) bps modem, especially if you use the Internet and a graphic browser. A ***fax/modem card*** combines the functions of a modem and a fax machine into a single card (i.e., you get both functions for the price of one), and it has become a virtual standard.

CD-ROM

The ***CD-ROM,*** once an optional device but standard on today's PC, holds 650MB of data, making it the ideal medium for the mass distribution of data. CD-ROM stands for Compact Disk, Read Only Memory, meaning that you can read from the device but you cannot write to the device.

The performance of a CD-ROM is determined by two parameters, access time and transfer rate. ***Access time*** is the average time to find a specific item (the shorter, the better). ***Transfer rate*** is the amount of data that is read every second (the larger, the better). The first CD-ROM drives had access times of approximately 600 milliseconds (ms) and transfer rates of approximately 150KB per second. As with all technology, both parameters have improved significantly, giving rise to double speed (2×), quadruple speed (4×), and today's eight, 10, and even 12-speed (8×, 10×, and 12×) devices.

A new type of CD-ROM, known as ***DVD,*** is to appear in 1997. The new devices will have storage capacities from 4.5GB to 17GB, which is significantly more than the current capacity. ***CD-recordable devices,*** which enable you to write to the CD, are also starting to appear at affordable prices.

AUDIO

The standard PC comes with a simple speaker that is capable of little more than the beep, which you hear when you press the wrong key. True sound requires the installation of a sound card and the availability of speakers. A microphone is required if you want to record your own sound.

A ***sound card*** has two basic functions—to play a previously recorded sound and to record a new sound. Thus, every sound card contains (a minimum of) two chips. One chip converts the sound from a microphone to a digital form the PC can store on disk. The second chip works in reverse and translates a digital file into sound. More sophisticated (and more expensive) cards include voice recognition cards that enable you to talk to your computer and have it respond to your commands.

If you intend to run multimedia applications, look for a sound card that supports wave table synthesis (as opposed to older cards that used a technique known as FM synthesis). A wave table produces higher quality musical notes because it stores samples of actual instruments, then uses those samples to reproduce the music. And don't forget the speakers. No matter how good your sound card, you will be disappointed if you don't have a correspondingly good pair of speakers.

A GUIDE TO SMART SHOPPING

The purchase of a computer should be approached in much the same way as any other big-ticket item and requires similar research and planning. First and foremost, do not walk into a computer store without some idea of your hardware requirements—you will spend too much or buy the wrong system. Know the technical specifications in advance, in order to ask intelligent questions about the various brands and systems. Stick to your requirements and don't be swayed to purchasing a different item if the vendor is out of stock. You've waited this long to buy a computer and another week or two won't matter.

The purchase of a laptop (notebook) computer poses additional considerations beyond those of a desktop configuration—weight, size, battery life, keyboard, and screen. Is the computer light enough so that you won't leave it behind when you travel? Is the life of the battery sufficient to accomplish what you need to do? Can you type comfortably on the keyboard over long periods of time? Can you attach a mouse, or are you limited to a trackball? Is the screen easily read in different levels of light? Is the hard disk large enough to accommodate all of your applications and data? Is there a CD-ROM for multimedia or to facilitate the installation of additional applications? Does it have a modem so that you can communicate when you take the machine on the road? Be sure to see the machine and test it before you buy so that you won't be disappointed later.

LET YOUR FINGERS DO THE WALKING

A single issue of a computer magazine contains advertisements from many vendors, making it possible to comparison shop from multiple mail-order vendors from the convenience of home. Computer magazines are also a good source of the latest technical information, and thus a subscription to a magazine is a must for the serious user. Our three favorites (*PC Computing, PC Magazine,* and *Windows Magazine*) are found on most newsstands as well as the Internet.

The best place to start is often the ***university's computer center,*** which may allow a local vendor or manufacturer(s) to maintain a store on the premises. The university can use its buying power to secure a favorable price or educational discount, and the promise of additional business guarantees continuing service and support. In addition, people you know will purchase similar equipment, which means additional sources of help later on. Alternatively, you may consider a ***retail store*** (be it local or part of a national chain) or ***mail order.*** Either or both may be appropriate, and you may avail yourself of both sources, at different times and for different equipment.

Mail order will almost always offer better prices than a retail establishment, but price should not be the sole consideration. Local service and support are also important, especially if you are a nontechnical new user. A little research, however, and you can purchase through the mail with confidence, and save yourself money in the process. A good way to choose a vendor, mail order or retail, is to ask your friends where they purchased their systems, because a satisfied customer is always the best recommendation.

If you purchase by mail, confirm all orders in writing, stating exactly what you are expecting to receive and when. Include the specific brands and/or model numbers and the agreed-upon price, including shipping and handling, to have documentation in the event of a dispute. State that the seller is not to deviate from the terms in your letter without prior written agreement.

Look for a steady advertising history by the mail-order firm, searching back issues of the magazine to see if the company has been in business over time. Avoid companies that appear to be in financial difficulty—for example, a company that previously ran four-page, full-color ads and now runs a half-page, black-and-white advertisement. Check out service in advance by calling the toll-free technical support number to determine the level of service you can expect. You might also inquire about the cost of on-site service. If you buy locally, try to choose a vendor with an on-site facility.

Pay with a credit card that offers a buyer protection plan to extend the manufacturer's warranty (up to an additional year). The use of a credit card also gives you additional leverage if you are dissatisfied with an item. If you are purchasing by mail, make sure the charge is not entered until you receive the merchandise. Do not buy from anyone, retail store or mail order, that insists all sales are final, that offers a store credit in lieu of a refund, or that charges a restocking fee on returned items. Settle for nothing less than a no-strings attached, 30-day, money-back guarantee, and be sure the vendor guarantees in writing a rebate if the price goes down within 30 days.

DON'T BE FRUSTRATED WHEN PRICES DROP

The system you buy today will invariably cost less tomorrow, and further, tomorrow's machine will run circles around today's most powerful system. The IBM/XT, for example, sold for approximately $5,000 and was configured with an 8088 microprocessor, a 10MB hard disk, 128KB of RAM, and a monochrome monitor, but it was the best system you could buy in 1983. The point of this example is that you should enjoy the machine you buy today without concern for future technology. Indeed, if you wait until prices come down, you will never buy anything, because there will always be something better and cheaper.

Software bundling (the inclusion of "free" software with your purchase) may or may not be a good deal. Windows will be included with any system, but the vendor may also include applications or other software. Ask for credit on any items you don't want. (You probably will not get the credit, but it doesn't hurt to ask.) Conversely, bundled software may be a good deal if you need the software and don't already have it.

Our experience has been that the vast majority of dealers, both retail and mail order, are reputable; but as with any purchase, *caveat emptor*. Good luck and good shopping.

SHOPPING ON THE INTERNET

There are many ways to shop. We suggest you start with the purchase of a computer magazine to get an overview of current prices and capabilities from many vendors. You may also walk into a computer superstore and look at various systems to gain a better appreciation of their differences. Our favorite method, however, is to take advantage of the Internet and World Wide Web, to visit one or more vendors online.

The following exercise takes you to the home page of Dell Computer, but we do not in any way endorse one vendor over another. We selected Dell as the focus of our exercise because it consistently receives high ratings in the press, and further, because its site enables you to customize a configuration quite easily.

SHOPPING ON THE INTERNET (www.bus.miami.edu/~rgrauer)

The best place to obtain the latest information about current configurations and pricing is from vendor sites on the World Wide Web. You can guess the URL (e.g., www.company.com) or you can use your favorite search engine to find a specific site. You can also go to Bob's home page (www.bus.miami.edu/~rgrauer) and click the link to Buy a PC. Bob provides links to several vendors, as well as a list of tips on buying a computer.

HANDS-ON EXERCISE 1

Buying a Computer

Objective: To visit one or more computer vendors on the Web to configure a system. Use Figure 3 as a guide in the exercise.

STEP 1: Dell Computer

- Start Internet Explorer. Enter the Web address of the desired vendor, e.g., **www.dell.com,** to display the home page for Dell Computer, as shown in Figure 3a. (Do not be concerned if your page differs from ours, as Dell is continually updating its Web site.)
- Explore one or more of the links on the Dell home page to learn about the company and/or its various product lines. When you are ready to configure a system, scroll to the bottom of any page and click the link to **Buy a Dell (online store),** which appears in the left frame on the Dell home page.

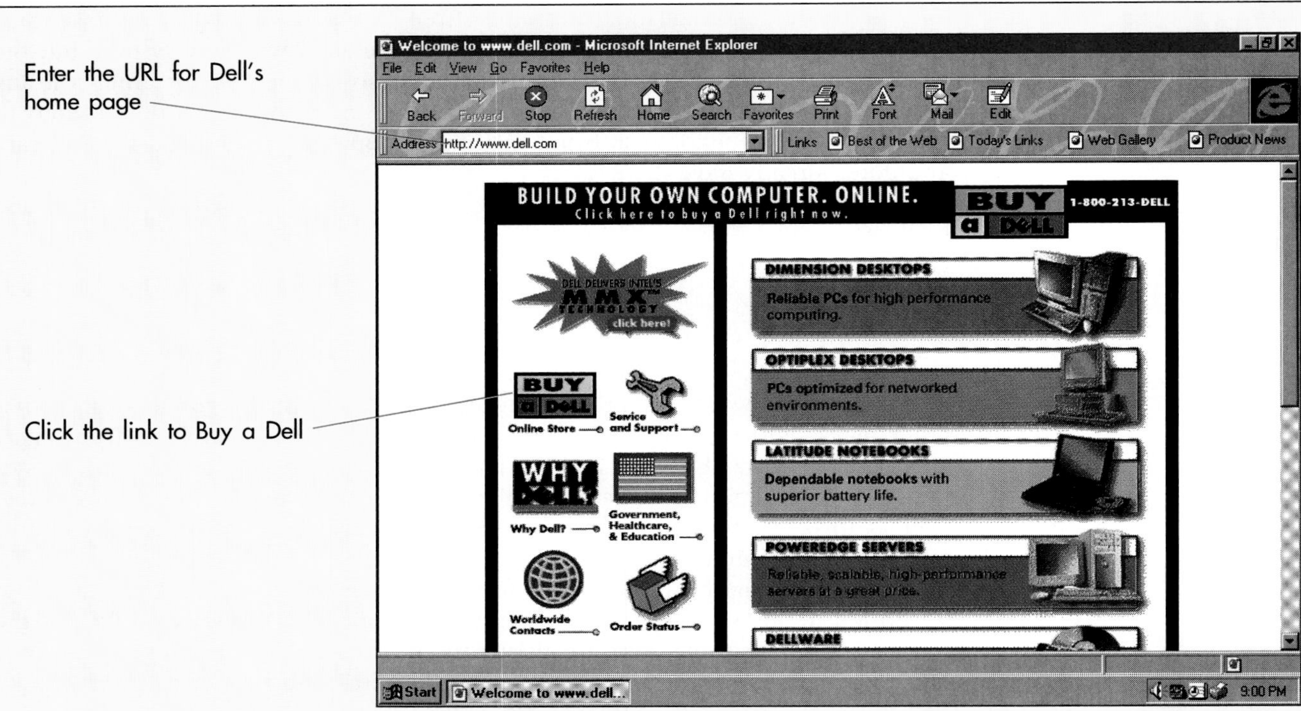

(a) Buy a Dell (step 1)

FIGURE 3 Hands-on Exercise 1

> ## GUESS THE URL
>
> You can often guess a vendor's Web address according to a consistent addressing scheme—www.company.com. The address of Dell Computer (www.dell.com) follows this pattern, as do Compaq (www.compaq.com), Micron (www.micron.com), and IBM (www.ibm.com). The home pages for the Lycos (www.lycos.com) and Yahoo (www.yahoo.com) search engines also follow this pattern. And if you are in the mood for sports, try www.nfl.com or www.nba.com to go to the home pages of the National Football League or National Basketball Association.

STEP 2: Configure the System

- You should see a page listing the various types of Dell computers. Click the link to **Dimension,** which presents entry-level systems. You should see a screen similar to Figure 3b.
- The configuration you see will probably be less expensive and/or more powerful than the one displayed in our figure, since technology is constantly improving.
- Our initial configuration is $1,769 and includes a 133MHz Pentium with 16MB of RAM and a 2.1GB hard disk.

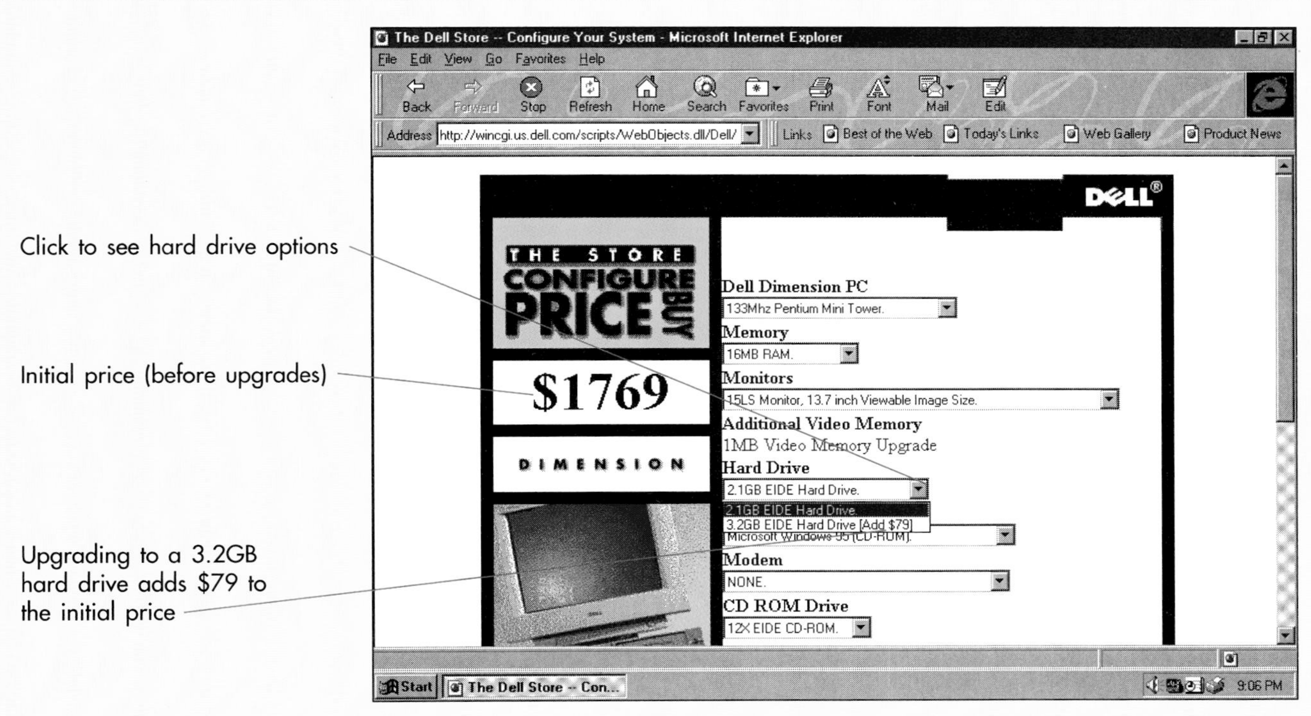

(b) Configure the System (step 2)

FIGURE 3 Hands-on Exercise 1 (continued)

- ➤ Click the **drop-down arrow** on the **Hard Drive** list box to see the incremental cost of upgrading to a larger drive (e.g., $79 to upgrade to a 3.2GB drive as shown in the figure).
- ➤ Select (click) the option for larger drive. Scroll to the bottom of the page and click **Recalc/More Choices** to see the cost of the upgraded configuration.
- ➤ Experiment with other options; for example, we added a sound card and speakers, but removed the network card. (You can also click the **Back button** on the Internet Explorer toolbar to return to the previous page to add a faster microprocessor or a different monitor.)
- ➤ Scroll to the bottom of the page when you are satisfied with your configuration. Click the **Shopping Cart** button.

30-DAY PRICE PROTECTION

A reputable vendor will provide a price protection policy that credits your account with any price reductions during the first 30 days you own your system. It is incumbent on you, however, to contact the vendor within the allotted time frame to request a refund. Don't forget to do so (and send us an e-mail message if we save you some money).

STEP 3: View Your Shopping Cart

➤ You should see a screen similar to Figure 3c, which summarizes your configuration and creates a shopping cart with the item(s) you select. Don't worry, you are under no obligation to buy.

- If this is not the configuration you want, click the **Back button** to return to the previous screen and reconfigure your system. Click the **Shopping Cart** to place the new system in your shopping cart.
- If necessary, click the **Remove from Cart button** to delete unwanted items from your cart.

➤ Click the **View Configuration link** to see the details of your system.

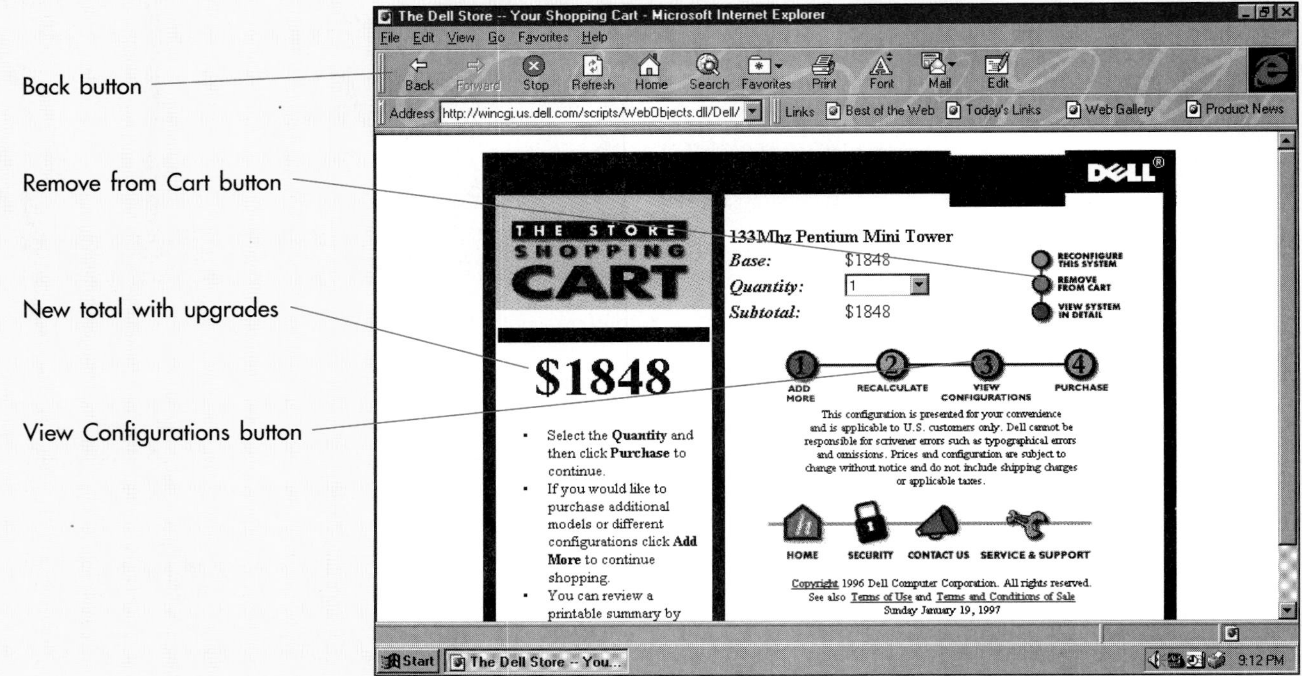

(c) View Your Shopping Cart (step 3)

FIGURE 3 Hands-on Exercise 1 (continued)

DOUBLE THE WARRANTY

Regardless of the vendor and regardless of how you make the purchase (e.g., via mail order or from a retail store), you can extend the warranty of any system (up to one additional year) by using a major credit card, provided it offers a "buyer's protection" policy. (Check with your credit card company to see whether it has this feature, and if it doesn't, consider getting a different credit card.) The extended warranty is free, and it goes into effect automatically when you charge your computer. It is applicable to any type of purchase except an automobile.

STEP 4: Print Your Order

- ➤ You should see a screen similar to Figure 3d, which displays the details of your order. (You have configured a system but have not placed an actual order and are under no obligation to buy.)
- ➤ Click the **Print button** on the Internet Explorer toolbar, then click **OK** to print this page and prove to your instructor that you did this exercise.
- ➤ Scroll to the bottom of the page to see the phone number for Dell Computer. You may want to call the company to inquire about additional options.

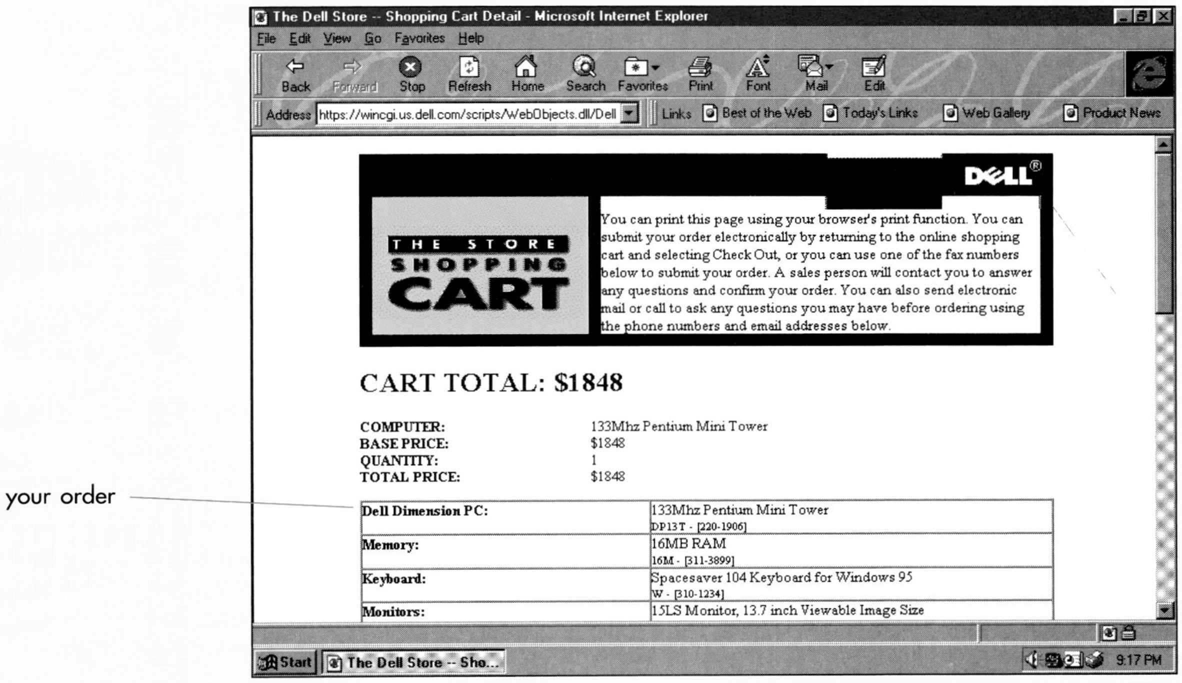

(d) View the Configuration (steps 3 and 4)

FIGURE 3 Hands-on Exercise 1 (continued)

ORDER BY PHONE

You are spending a lot of money for your system and we urge you to place the order by phone rather than via the Web. The salesperson will confirm the specifications of your system and may be able to suggest additional options that you overlooked. Our salesperson, for example, told us that Microsoft Office Professional would be bundled with our system for another $100. Indeed, if the vendor does not provide an 800 number on its Web site, you should consider another vendor.

STEP 5: Comparison Shopping

➤ You should always obtain competitive quotes for any product you buy. Remember, too, that price is not everything, and that above all, you should be confident that your vendor delivers a quality product:

- Choose another vendor and enter the URL in the location text box to go to that site. Use a Web search engine if you do not know the vendor's address.
- Go to Bob's home page (**www.bus.miami.edu/~rgrauer**) and click the link to **Buying a Computer,** which displays the page in Figure 3e.

➤ Obtain a comparable quote for your chosen configuration from the second vendor, then print that quote to submit to your instructor.

➤ Exit your Web browser. We hope you enjoyed your shopping expedition.

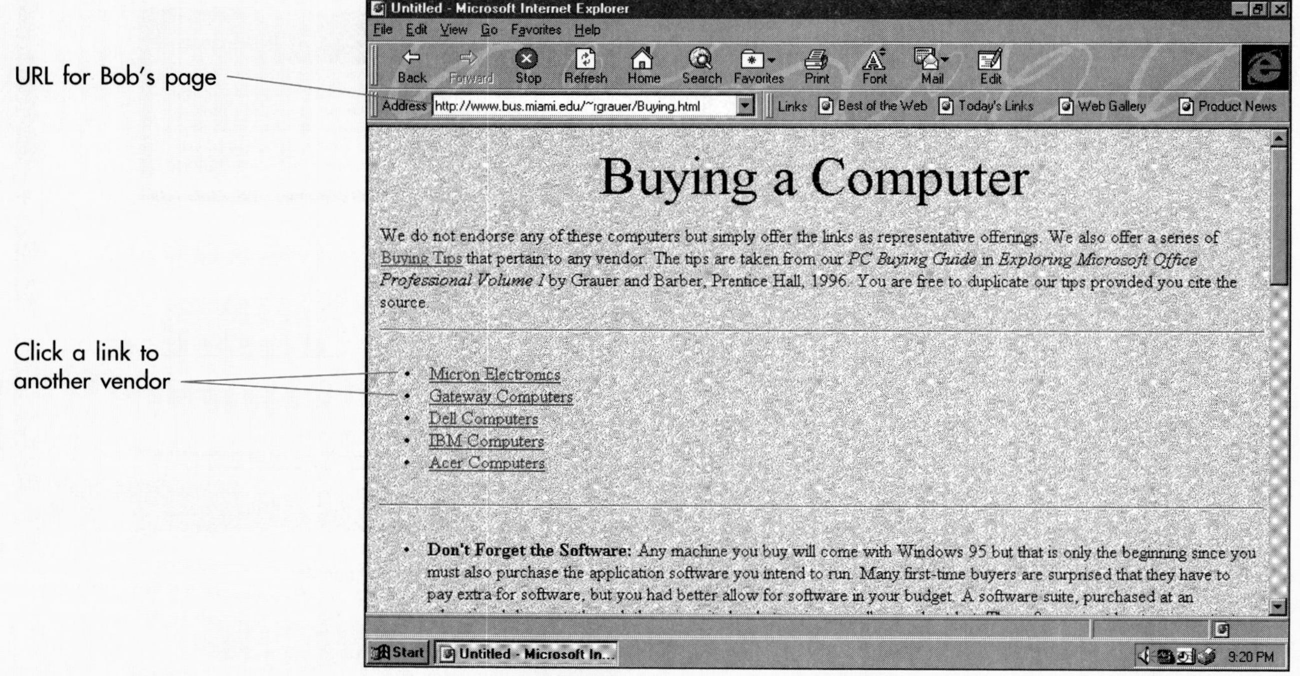

(e) Comparison Shopping (step 5)

FIGURE 3 Hands-on Exercise 1 (continued)

OUR RECOMMENDATION

As technology continues to advance, yesterday's top-of-the-line system has become today's entry-level computer. We recommend, therefore, that as of January 1997, you settle for nothing less than a Pentium 150MHz (with MMX technology), 16MB of RAM, a 2GB hard disk, 10X-speed CD-ROM with 16-bit sound card, a 15-inch monitor with .28 dot pitch, and a 33,600 bps modem. If your budget can stand it, go beyond this configuration to buy a faster CPU, a larger disk drive (3GB), and more RAM (32MB).

INDEX

A = Access
B = Buying Guide
E = Excel
IE = Internet Explorer
P = PowerPoint
PR = Windows Prerequisites
W = Word

D

E

F

G

H

I

K

L

Q

R

S

T

U

V

W

Y

Z